Victims in Criminal Procedure

Victims in Criminal Procedure

FOURTH EDITION

Douglas E. Beloof
PROFESSOR OF LAW
LEWIS & CLARK LAW SCHOOL

Paul G. Cassell
RONALD N. BOYCE PRESIDENTIAL PROFESSOR OF CRIMINAL LAW
S.J. QUINNEY COLLEGE OF LAW
UNIVERSITY OF UTAH

Meg Garvin
EXECUTIVE DIRECTOR
THE NATIONAL CRIME VICTIM LAW INSTITUTE
CLINICAL PROFESSOR OF LAW,
LEWIS & CLARK LAW SCHOOL

Steven J. Twist
ADJUNCT PROFESSOR, SANDRA DAY O'CONNOR COLLEGE OF LAW
ARIZONA STATE UNIVERSITY

CAROLINA ACADEMIC PRESS
Durham, North Carolina

LCCN: 2018949587
ISBN: 978-1-5310-0916-8
eISBN: 978-1-53100-917-5

Carolina Academic Press, LLC
700 Kent Street
Durham, North Carolina 27701
Telephone (919) 489-7486
Fax (919) 493-5668
www.cap-press.com

Printed in the United States of America

For the law students who would be crime victim lawyers.

— Douglas Beloof

To my wife, Trish.

— Paul Cassell

For Doug, Steve, and Paul for your mentorship.
For the team at the National Crime Victim Law Institute for fighting for victims each day to ensure the law advances and new cases can be added this book.
For Chris.

— Meg Garvin

With love to Mom and Dad, Shawn, Erik and J.P., Cassie and Caroline, Allison and Kristen, Carter, Mason, Cooper, Eliot, Steven, Leesy, Lily, and Henry, each of whom is surely evidence of God's grace in my life, and to the victims whose voices the nation still must hear.

— Steve Twist

Contents

Table of Cases

Secondary Authorities

Am. Jur. 2d, Arrest, Arrest by Private Person, vol. 5, § 56–58 (1995), 142–143

Ann Althouse, Thelma and Louise and the Law: Do Rape Shield Rules Matter? 25 Loy. L. Rev. 757 (1992), 363

David S. Ardia, Privacy and Court Records: Online Access and the Loss of Practical Obscurity, 2017 U. Ill. L. Rev. 1385 (2017), 308

Susan Bandes, A Reply to Paul Cassell: What We Know About Victim Impact Statements, 1999 Utah L. Rev. 545, 625

Susan Bandes, Empathy, Narrative, and Victim Impact Statements, 63 U. Chi. L. Rev. 361 (1996), 553, 691

Susan Bandes, Victim Standing, 1999 Utah L. Rev. 331, 32

Jayne W. Barnard, Allocution for Victims of Economic Crimes, 77 Notre Dame L. Rev. 39 (2001), 74, 717

Margaret Martin Barry, Protective Order Enforcement: Another Pirouette, 6 Hastings Women's L.J. (1995), 514

Douglas E. Beloof, Constitutional Implications of Victims as Participants, 88 Cornell L. Rev. 282 (2003), 617, 629

Douglas E. Beloof, Crime Victims' Rights: Critical Concepts for Animal Rights, 7 Animal L. Rev. 19 (2001), 48

Douglas E. Beloof, Enabling Rape Shield Procedures Under Crime Victims' State Constitutional Rights to Privacy, 38 Suffolk U. L. Rev. 291 (2005), 783

Douglas E. Beloof, The Third Model of Criminal Procedure: The Crime Control Model, 1999 Utah L. Rev. 289, 6, 29

Douglas E. Beloof, The Third Wave of Victims' Rights: Standing Remedy and Review, 2005 BYU L. Rev. 255, 36, 719, 727, 728, 754, 769, 773, 783, 789, 807

Douglas E. Beloof, Weighing Crime Victims' Interests in Judicially Crafted Criminal Procedure, 56 Cath. L. Rev. 1135 (2007), 192

Douglas E. Beloof & Paul Cassell, The Crime Victim's Right to Attend the Trial: The Reascendant National Consensus, 9 Lewis & Clark L. Rev. 481 (2005), 26, 545

Douglas E. Beloof & Joel Shapiro, Let the Truth Be Told: Proposed Hearsay Exceptions to Admit Domestic Violence Victims' Out of Court Statements as Substantive Evidence, 11 Colum. J. Gender & L. (2002), 494

Stephanos Bibas, The Machinery of Criminal Justice (2012), 28

Jennifer Bjorhus, Sexual Predator Flees Home After Fliers Go Up, The Oregonian, Sept. 20, 1997, 695

Paul Gustafson, Star-Tribune Newspaper of the Twin Cities, Mpls.-St. Paul, June 24, 1997

Cheryl Hanna, No Right to Choose: Mandated Victim Participation in Domestic Violence Prosecutions, 109 Harvard L. Rev. 1849 (1996), 493, 495

Hilary Hanson, Murderabilia Has Andy Kahan, Victim Advocate, Up in Arms, Huff. Post, Oct. 8, 2012, 676

Lynne Henderson, Whose Justice, Which Victims, 94 Mich L. Rev. 1596 (1996), 448

Lynn N. Henderson, The Wrongs of Victim's Rights, 37 Stanford L. Rev. 937 (1985), 288

Gabriel Hallevy, Therapeutic Victim-Offender Mediation Within the Criminal Justice Process—Sharpening the Evaluation of Personal Potential for Rehabilitation While Rights Wrongs Under the Alternative Dispute Resolution Philosophy, 16 Harv. Negot. L. Rev. 65 (2011), 467

Gail Heriot, An Essay on the Civil Criminal Distinction with Special Reference to Punitive Damages, 1 J. Contemp. Legal Issues 43 (1996), 18

Kathleen Howe, Comment, Is Free Speech Too High a Price to Pay for Crime? Overcoming the Constitutional Inconsistencies in Son of Sam Laws, 24 Loyola L.A. Entertain. L. Rev. 341 (2004), 675

Human Rights Watch, Mixed Results: U.S. Policy and International Standards on the Rights and Interests of Victims of Crime (2008), 5

Heidi M. Hurd & Michael S. Moore, Punishing Hatred and Prejudice, 56 Stan L. Rev. 1081 (2004), 100

Tom Jicha, The Risk of Forgiveness on 48 Hours, Mercy Raises Troubling Questions, Sun. Sentinel, Oct. 2, 1997, 627

Matti Joutsen, Listening to the Victim: The Victim's Role in European Criminal Systems, 34 Wayne L. Rev. 95 (1995), 580

Matthew Kaiser, Sit … Stay … Now Beg for Me: A Look at the Courthouse Dogs Program and the Legal Standard Pennsylvania Should Use to Determine Whether a Dog Can Accompany a Child on the Witness Stand, 60 Vill. L. Rev. 343 (2016), 560

Alice R. Kaminsky, The Victim's Son (1985), 625

Andrew A. Karmen, Who's Against Victims' Rights? The Nature of the Opposition to Pro-Victim Initiatives in Criminal Justice, 8 St. John's J. Legal Comment. 157 (1992), 32

Deborah P. Kelly, Victim's Perceptions of Criminal Justice, 11 Pepperdine L. Rev. 15 (1984), 26

Drew Kershen, Justice Denied in Oklahoma, N.Y. Times, Feb 28, 1996, 247

Marsha Kight, Forever Changed: Remembering Oklahoma City, April 19, 1995 (1998), 625

Gary Kinder, Victim: The Other Side of Murder (1980), 625

Jon Krakauer, Missoula: Rape and the Justice System in a College Town (2015), 123

Preface to the Fourth Edition

Joining us in this edition is Meg Garvin, Clinical Professor of Law and Director of the National Crime Victim Law Institute. As a result, the book has a new chapter concerning privacy, a needed improvement.

There are more legislated laws and case law than ever before as crime victim law matures in many jurisdictions. Where possible, we have chosen materials post-2000 to give an up-to-date experience to law students.

As victim interests and participation become legitimate, the conversation is changing from whether victims' rights are a good idea to how to blend the rights into existing procedures. In some states and the federal government, victims' enforceable rights have existed for quite some time. In other jurisdictions, such rights are new. These rights, coupled with other legal sources of victim participation are reshaping the experience of victims in the criminal process.

We are grateful for the contributions of courts, legislators and academics, which make this edition of the casebook the most robust yet.

Preface to the Third Edition

We are excited about the new, Third Edition of the casebook, which contains several significant changes. The Third Edition includes the federal Crime Victims' Rights Act. Many cases have resulted from this Act, which are bringing into sharper focus the role of victims' in the criminal justice process. As the Ninth Circuit stated in Kenna v. District Court, 435 F.3d 1011 (9th Cir. 2006): "The criminal justice system has long functioned on the assumption that crime victims should behave like good Victorian children — seen but not heard. The Crime Victims' Rights Act sought to change this by making victims independent participants in the criminal justice system."

We have also added new federal and state cases in lieu of narrative in many places. The new edition contains a separate chapter on domestic violence criminal procedures, as these are rather unique. Also included are excerpts from the Human Rights Watch Report, U.S. Policy and International Standards on the Rights and Interests of Crime Victims, which provides: "While there can be tensions between the legitimate interests of victims and defendants, a criminal justice system based on human rights standards can safeguard the rights of both while advancing justice and the rule of law."

We are also very grateful to the contribution of the many academics who have joined to the dialog concerning victim law in the years since the second edition, these efforts have made for a better edition. There now seems to be an increasing interest in the education of law students on crime victim issues. Victim law is truly coming of age.

Preface to the Second Edition

In the Preface to the First Edition I (then the sole author) wrote that "the role of the victim is expanding" and that the state of victim law education in the legal academy was "unfortunate" in that few academics or law students were educated or receiving education on the topic.

Professor Erin O'Hara of Vanderbilt has recently written: "Given that virtually all law professors were trained in criminal law classes that ignored victim involvement in the criminal justice process, it is perhaps not surprising that it is considered heretical to suggest that direct participation by victims might be warranted. Indirect participation by victims and even the attendance of victims at criminal proceedings are likewise viewed by many as problematic. In the legal academy, any other state of affairs threatens the very foundations of justice."

The marginalization of crime victim law by criminal procedure legal academics remains astonishing. By way of analogy, it would be as if civil procedure professors failed to teach the laws of intervention. In the real world, for prosecutors, defense counsel, victim lawyers, legislatures, judges, it is simply impossible to ignore the significance and expanding role of victims in criminal procedure. The academy is not meeting their educational needs.

I am joined in this Second Edition by two co-authors who are among the nation's foremost experts in the field, United States District Court Judge and Professor of Law at Utah — Paul Cassell, and Steve Twist, crime victim lawyer, adjunct Professor of Victim Law at Arizona State University and Counsel for many years in drafting and redrafting the proposed Victims' Amendment to the United States Constitution. I am grateful for their willingness to contribute. The Second Edition is much improved as a result.

Finally, I would like to acknowledge our publisher Carolina Academic Press and its Board of Advisors for perceiving that the topic Victims in Criminal Procedure is an important area of criminal procedure.

Professor Douglas Beloof

Preface to the First Edition

Criminal procedure cannot be truly understood without understanding the victim's role. This book is the product of a seminar I have taught for several years at Northwestern School of Law, Lewis and Clark College. The seminar has become so popular with the students that the seminar will soon become a criminal procedure class.

The book is divided up into procedural stages. This structure mimics conventional criminal procedure casebooks. Contrary to conventional criminal procedure casebooks, which have ignored or minimized the significance of the victim, this book consciously focuses on the victim's role in the criminal process. As a result, almost none of the material is found in conventional criminal procedure casebooks. I have taught the course both to students who had, and had not, taken other criminal procedure courses and no problems arose.

The role of the victim is expanding. In terms of legal evolution, this expansion is occurring quite rapidly. It probably represents the single greatest "revolution" in criminal procedure in twenty years. In most fields of law one would expect such a new and dynamic set of laws to have a prominent place in the education of law students. Yet, this has not proven to be true in the education of criminal procedure students. I have found that many legal academics, including those who teach criminal law and procedure, remain uniformed about the role of the victim. Most law students, including those who intend to practice criminal law and procedure, graduate from law schools having had no significant exposure to the law of victims in criminal procedure. This state of academic affairs is unfortunate.

I can be reached at beloof@lclark.edu.

Victims in Criminal Procedure

Chapter 1

An Introduction to the Victim's Role in the Criminal Process

A. Thinking about Victims in Criminal Procedure

The twenty-first century is witness to people's reaction to victimization. Black Lives Matter reacting to police shootings of African Americans; anti-human trafficking organizations; Dr. Larry Nassar, who sexually assaulted dozens of Team USA female gymnasts; Bernie Madoff, the Wall Street thief; and Stephen Paddock, the Las Vegas shooter, are just a few movements or names that immediately bring victims to mind.

This century is witnessing increased momentum toward inclusion of crime victims in criminal procedure. As just one example, efforts in the late 1900s had resulted in some enforceable state constitutional rights for victims. In the early 2000s, a robust new effort, Marsy's Law for All, is successfully supporting the enactment of enforceable victims' rights in state constitutions around the country.

Victims in criminal procedure is the greatest revolution in criminal procedure of your generation. This is because it re-introduces interests of the victim into consideration, an interest that was lost between roughly 1900 and the 1970s. Nevertheless, if your law school experience is a typical one, your focus has been directed exclusively to a two-party adversary legal process — the *State v. the Defendant*. And, in the analysis of this adversary process, you have paid almost exclusive attention to the authority of the state and rights of criminal defendants. By now you have probably taken a course in either criminal law or criminal procedure, where you explored subjects that are the standard fare of a law school curriculum: What is the appropriate criminal intent for homicide and other offenses? What is an unreasonable search and seizure under the Fourth Amendment? Crime victims' interests are curiously absent from the discussion. You may have wondered during these courses: "What about the victim's interests?"

This state and defendant duopoly in criminal procedure only existed from about 1900 to 1975. That roughly 75-year period saw the gradual exclusion of victims from criminal processes. In fact, the criminal procedure law was based, in part, on the idea that only the state is harmed by crime. Try explaining that to a non-lawyer, someone who has been sexually assaulted, their loved one murdered, or their retirement savings swindled. To be sure, the procedural rights of criminal defendants and the state are very important. As you will learn in this course, crime victims have legitimate interests in criminal cases as well. Every year, millions of Americans are victimized by violent and other serious crimes. These victims tend to be disproportionately drawn from the ranks of the poor, racial minorities, and residents of inner cities. These Americans look to the criminal justice system to respond appropriately to their victimization. Victims often run up against a system that pays virtually no attention to their concerns.

By 1975, the absence of crime victims was endemic to the system. The criminal justice system relied on victims only to report offenses and cooperate with authorities. Before the criminal apparatus swung into action, a victim (or, in a homicide case, a surviving family member) reported the crime. A victim became expendable after bringing the crime to the attention of the authorities. Police officers gather evidence and determine whether to present it to a government prosecutor. The prosecutor will then decide, in his discretion, whether the case has merit. If, in the prosecutor's judgment, the case is worth pursuing, the prosecutor files criminal charges in the name of "the state" or "the people." Once the prosecutor files charges, the court will appoint legal counsel for the criminal defendant. Defense counsel will then file various motions to protect the defendant's interests. The case would then proceed to resolution, typically by way of plea bargain reached solely by the prosecution and the defense attorney. If the case went to trial, the victim made a brief cameo appearance—as a witness, and dutifully answered questions posed by the prosecution and the defense. If a conviction resulted, the court would then determine the appropriate prison sentence.

Things were not always the way they were by 1975. At the birth of our nation, crime victims played a far more central role. Before our system of public prosecution became firmly entrenched, a system of private prosecution existed in which crime victims not only reported crimes, but often investigated and prosecuted them. Sentencing of criminals included orders of restitution and even damages paid directly to the victim. In short, crime victims were at the center of the system, not at its periphery.

This course examines how we are returning to a criminal justice system that is in the process of changing to be more inclusive of crime victims and their interests. Historically, victims were at the core of the process. Then they were removed from it, except as a witness, eventually even precluded from observing the trial. How are victims and their interests being reintegrated? This course focuses particularly on the criminal procedures that govern the ways in which serious criminal charges are investigated, charged, tried, and sentenced. In this course, you will consider:

- Who should society recognize as the "victim" of a crime?
- Should the safety and privacy of crime victims be protected?
- Should victims be able to investigate crimes and even file their own criminal charges?
- Should victims have the same procedural rights as we extend to criminal defendants, such as the right to counsel, to a speedy trial, and to discovery?
- Should victims have a voice at various points in the process, such as at bail hearings and during plea negotiations?

- Should victims be able to attend trials?
- Should victims be able to tell the sentencing judge about the impact of the crime and obtain restitution from the convicted defendant?
- How should victims' rights be enforced?

The answers to these questions are not simple. Few people would advocate, for example, a complete return to a system where crime victims had to shoulder the burden of investigating and prosecuting those who committed crimes against them. Moreover, you may find that your general legal ideology is of little assistance in reaching the right outcome. Are crime victims' rights a "liberal" agenda, supported for instance by the "women's rights" movement? Or a "conservative" agenda, supported for instance by "law and order" proponents? Or perhaps a little bit of both as evidenced by the "victim's rights movement"?

Consider this statement about victim's rights from Human Rights Watch, a prominent civil liberties organization:

Human Rights Watch, *Mixed Results: U.S. Policy and International Standards on the Rights and Interests of Victims of Crime*
(2008)

Many people have strong interests in the functioning of the criminal justice system: victims of crime, witnesses, those accused of committing crimes, and society at large, which requires the fair and effective administration of justice. In recent decades, both internationally and inside the United States, there has been a growing demand that greater attention be paid to the interests and rights of victims of crime as well as to ensuring their access to justice.

Unfortunately, the public debate on this topic too often casts the rights and interests of victims and defendants as a zero-sum game in which safeguards for defendants' rights — such as the presumption of innocence and the right to a fair trial — come at the expense of victims, and improvements in the treatment of victims impinge on defendants' rights. While there can be tensions between the legitimate interests of victims and defendants, a criminal justice system based on human rights standards can safeguard the rights of both while advancing justice and the rule of law.

While the precise answer to questions about the role of crime victims and their interests remains the subject of debate, it is fair to say that an increasingly dominant view has developed that the criminal justice system is improved with recognition of victims and their interests.

This chapter sets the stage for the detailed exploration of the victims' rights topics that follow. It begins by reviewing the often-forgotten history regarding private prosecutions by crime victims. Then it offers some tentative explanations about why our country moved away from a victim-driven system of criminal justice — including practical, historical, and cultural reasons. The chapter then considers whether sound reasons justify incorporating victims rights' into our criminal procedures—such as fairness to the victim, protecting the interests of society, and avoiding "secondary" victimization of the victim in the process itself. The chapter explores the general aims of this movement—which include ensuring that crime victims have the rights to be informed of, to be present at, and to be heard at important criminal justice proceedings. The movement, in short, seeks to create a third model of criminal procedure—one focusing not exclusively on prosecuting cases in the system or protecting the civil rights of criminal defendants, but also guaranteeing victims the right to participate in the process. In conclusion, the chapter briefly identifies the varied legal sources of victim participation in criminal procedure.

B. The Victim Participation Model

Reflecting the state's and defendant's interest, criminal procedure has been described with reference to two models: the crime control model and the due process model. The rise of victims as participants prompts a victim participation model.

Douglas Evan Beloof, *The Third Model of Criminal Process: The Victim Participation Model*
1999 Utah L. Rev. 289

Thirty of the states [in 1999] have chiseled victims' rights into their respective constitutions. The federal government and the rest of the states have statutory rights for victims. An amendment to the United States Constitution providing civil rights for crime victims has been proposed, passed out of the U.S. Senate Judiciary Committee, and is the topic of other presenters at this symposium. Make no mistake, the inclusion of the victim as a participant has shaken conventional assumptions about the criminal process to their foundation. In light of laws of victim participation, one core assumption that has occupied the field for many years is no longer true. This core assumption is that only two value systems compete with each other in the criminal process. Professor Packer labeled these two value systems the crime control model and the due process model. The crime control model has as its value the efficient suppression of crime. The due process model has as its value the primacy of the defendant and the related concept of limiting governmental power.

Thirty years ago, Professor Packer was basically accurate when he said:

> The kind of model we need is one that permits us to recognize explicitly the value choices that underlie the details of the criminal process. In a word what we need is a normative model or models. It will take more than one model, but it will not take more than two.

However, this last assertion of Packer's is no longer true; it now does take more than two models to recognize explicitly the value choices that underlie the details of the criminal process.

Professor Packer attempted to illuminate the values underlying our criminal process by articulating the crime control model and the due process model. These models have been modified by some and criticized by others. But, the models remain useful conceptual constellations above the sea of conflicts which underlie the criminal process. Taken together, the crime control model and the due process model have comprised a dominant two-model universe of values. The models were created by Packer to serve several functions. The models explicitly recognize "the value choices that underlie the details of the criminal process." This, in turn, provides a "convenient way to talk about the process" which operates between the "competing demands "of the two value systems. The models allow us to "detach ourselves from the . . . details" of the process so we can see how the entire system may be able to deal with the various tasks it is expected to accomplish. The models assist in understanding the process as dynamic, rather than static. And, the models may assist in revealing the relationship of criminal process to substantive criminal law.

Of course, Professor Packer did not anticipate laws of formal victim participation. So, it is not surprising that his two models do not include a conceptual framework in which victim participation can be adequately understood. Because victim participation does not rest primarily on the values underlying the two models, the two models alone do not and cannot facilitate an understanding of victim participation. Thus, it is time for a shift in a dominant paradigm of criminal procedure. The victim's formal participation does not harken the demise of either the crime control model or the due process model. To understand the operation of victim participation, a third model is needed as a complement to, but not as a replacement for, Packer's two models. I call this third model the victim participation model.

How the Values of the Three Models Differ

The Values Underlying the Crime Control Model

The primary value underlying the crime control model is the efficient suppression of crime. Efficiency is the capacity to process criminal offenders rapidly. Professor Packer provides an image of the crime control model:

> The image that comes to mind is an assembly line conveyor belt which moves an endless stream of cases, never stopping, carrying the cases to workers who stand at fixed stations and who perform on each case . . . the same small but essential operation that brings it one step closer being finished product, or, to exchange the metaphor for the reality, a closed file. The criminal process, in this model, is seen as a screening process in which each successive stage . . . involves a series of routinized operations whose success is gauged primarily by their tendency to pass the case along to a successful conclusion.

The Values Underlying the Due Process Model

Underlying the due process model is the value of the primary importance of the individual defendant and the related concept of limiting government power. Again, Professor Packer's image is helpful:

If the crime control model resembles an assembly line, the due process model looks very much like an obstacle course. Each of its successive stages is designed to present formidable impediments to carrying the accused any further along in the process . . . the aim of the process is as much to protect the factually innocent as it is to convict the factually guilty. It is a little like quality control in industrial technology. . . . The due process model resembles a factory that has had to devote a substantial part of its input to quality control. This necessarily cuts down on quantitative output.

Unlike the crime control model, in which the primary value is to effectively, swiftly and with finality suppress crime; the value of the primacy of the defendant seeks to assure reliability in determinations of guilt.

The Values of the Victim Participation Model

The mere existence of victim participation values which are external to the two-model concept is not sufficient justification for the creation of a new model. For a modern discussion to be worthwhile there needed to be a consensus in law that the values underlying the victim's role are genuine and significant. This consensus exists now. The consensus that victim participation values exist, are genuine and are significant is revealed in the laws that have created rights for victims of crime in all fifty states and the federal government.

The values underlying the victim participation model are expressly stated in the language of constitutional rights in many states and in federal, and state statutes. These values include: (1) fairness to the victim; (2) respect for the victim; and (3) dignity of the victim. Two or more of these three values appear in the vast majority of state constitutional victim rights provisions. Twenty states expressly set forth two or more of these values in their respective constitutional amendments. Seven other states have created constitutional civil rights for victims. These amendments implicitly recognize the value of the dignity of the victim. We have then a majority of thirty states recognizing the value of the dignity of a victim on a constitutional level. A separate group of eight states, have expressly set forth one or more of these values in statutory victim rights provisions. A federal statute expressly sets forth victim dignity as a value. Thus, we are presented with legitimization of the dignity of the victim which is further illuminated by the nature of particular rights granted. Generally, these rights are rights to notice, attendance and an opportunity to be heard. These rights resemble due process rights.

The justification for providing due process-like rights of participation to the victim is the harm to the victim. Crime victims are exposed to two kinds of harm. The first is primary harm which is the harm resulting from the crime itself. The other harm is secondary harm to the victim which comes from governmental processes and governmental actors within those processes. Together, primary and secondary harm provide the justification for victim participation in the criminal process. Primary harm operates as a justification for victim participation in the same way that harm to an individual, coupled with a legitimate theory of the liability of another, is a basis for standing in other legal contexts. Secondary harm provides justification most particularly for victim civil rights against government authority. The primacy of the individual victim—reflected in values of fairness, dignity and respect—is the value underlying the Victim Participation Model. The value of primacy of the victim derives from primary harm that is causally linked to the alleged criminal liability of another, taken together with the concept of minimizing secondary harm (governmental harm) to the victim.

I will borrow from Packer's use of a factory image to dramatize the function of the victim participation model. The image of the victim participation model is that of a victim following their own case down the assembly line. In the investigatory stage the victim consults with police and prosecutor. At formal proceedings the victim, when appropriate and in an appropriate manner, may speak and address the court. Victims are consulted by the prosecutor and the court before pretrial dispositions are finalized. Victims are consulted at sentencing and at release hearings. The consultant function of the victim is designed to ensure that the interest of the individual victim in the case is promoted. A core interest of the victim is that the truth be revealed. However, there is a significant limit to the victim consultant's role. The victim is a consultant about their case, but cannot control the critical decisions made in the factory by grand and petite juries, prosecutors or judges. At every critical stage in the factory, victims are consulted by government actors. This victim consultation may indirectly result in greater or lesser efficiency. Similarly, the consultation of the victim may indirectly support or challenge the primacy of the individual defendant. . . .

C. Historical Background in the United States

In America today, crime victims are often excluded from direct involvement with the machinery of the criminal justice process. Things have not always been this way. In fact, at the time our Constitution was drafted, victims were at the center of enforcing criminal laws.

William F. McDonald, *Towards a Bicentennial Revolution in Criminal Justice: The Return of the Victim*
13 Amer. Crim. L. Rev. 649 (1976)

II. The Role of the Victim in Colonial American Justice

The formal machinery of law enforcement in Colonial America was largely derived from the English, pre-urban past. This system functioned without a public prosecutor or an effective police force but, rather, was conducted by the private individuals victimized by crime, with the aid of officials who charged fees for their services.

Thus, during the 18th century, to obtain an arrest the victim of a crime called a watchman, if available, and afterwards applied to a justice of the peace for a warrant and a constable to help in making the arrest. The victim paid for the warrant and for the services of the constable. The burden of investigation also rested on the victim. He either performed his own detective work, usually with the aid of paid informers, or posted a reward for the successful prosecution of the offender. Except through the coroner's inquest, the state or town provided no help in identifying the unknown offender. Even after identification and arrest, the victim carried the burden of prosecution. He retained an attorney and paid to have the indictment written and the offender prosecuted.

Although revenge on the part of the victim surely was a motivating force behind these private prosecutions, so too was a system of restitution by the offender to the victim which was an accepted goal of the system. For many criminal offenses, the victim was awarded multiple damages. Where the offender was indigent, the victim was usually authorized to sell the defendant into service for a period corresponding to the amount of multiple damages. If the victim could not sell the convict within a reasonably short period of time, the offender would be released unless the victim compensated the government for the costs of keeping the defendant in jail.

Although this system of law enforcement was highly inadequate, it was preferred to the establishment of a professional prosecutor and police force for two important reasons. One was the fear of tyranny that colonists associated with a system of prosecutors and policemen paid by the government as was evidenced by the French experience. Second, the colonists followed the English approach of reducing costs by relying heavily on citizen initiative and funding the system only when necessary.

This system of private initiative underwent a radical change as the commercial revolution progressed throughout the colonies. In former times, law enforcement had relied greatly upon the ancient institution of the "hue and cry" whereby victims called upon their fellow townsmen to assist in pursuing criminals. However, this practice became unworkable as the growth of urban centers inhabited by increasingly mobile populations developed in response to commercial needs. As people lost communication and kinship with their neighbors, their sense of social responsibility diminished. In an effort to restore this lost sense of responsibility, laws were passed making communities responsible for the financial losses of victims caused by certain crimes. However, these laws proved increasingly unpopular and unsuccessful and were later replaced by a system of rewards to those who brought criminals to justice. By the middle of the 18th century, this system was firmly established as governments, insurance companies, businesses, and private individuals each offered rewards for specified convictions. This led eventually to a prosperous "information trade" in which common informers acting as free-lance policemen made handsome livings by convicting people of violations of numerous petty, usually regulatory, offenses. In addition, another species of private policeman known as "thief-takers" developed. These individuals made an occupation out of hunting and prosecuting the more dangerous law-violators, the professional criminals, who also brought the largest rewards.

Unfortunately, this system of law enforcement was unable to satisfy any of the affected interests in the community. Businessmen and property-owners were unable to prevent losses. Governments were frustrated in their desire to reduce crime and citizen complaints. Citizens were frequently unable to obtain redress for crimes committed against them. Finally, officers of the system were dissatisfied with their low status and pay. In this state, the colonial system that relied principally on private initiative was ready for reform.

III. The Decline of the Victim's Role in the Criminal Justice System

A. Beccaria and the Enlightenment

By the time of the American Revolution, the inadequacies and inequities of the existing criminal justice system had become apparent to many. Suggestions for reform were made and significant changes instituted during the 19th century. Gradually, reform of the police, prosecutorial and correctional systems occurred both in the colonies and in England. These changes followed closely the lines suggested by Enlightenment writers, particularly Cesare Beccaria, whose work, *Essay on Crimes and Punishment*, was the most influential of the time.

As a member of the Enlightenment, Beccaria sought to re-examine the proper role of the criminal justice system. He regarded society as being created by social contract and viewed the criminal justice system as a necessary expedient in obtaining protection against those members who sought to breach that contract. Applying the standard of the maximization of social good, Beccaria analyzed the system and took issue with many of the existing principles of criminal justice. . . .

Further, Beccaria took issue with the proposition that the primary purpose of the criminal justice system was to serve as an aid to private action in obtaining redress from the criminal. Since the system arose from a social contract, it should serve the interests of society, not the individual victim. Punishments inflicted by the system should primarily serve to deter the criminal, to repay his debt to society, or to deter others from committing similar acts. Punishments should not be imposed to redress private damages.

In making this argument, Beccaria distinguished the criminal from the civil suit. The society is damaged by crime and the criminal justice system should serve to prevent this social damage. Thus, the victim should not be allowed to control the decisions concerning prosecution and punishment. Take for example the case in which it would be beneficial to society to prosecute the criminal, but harmful to the victim, such as a sexual assault case where testimony by the victim might be psychologically damaging. To Beccaria, the only choice would be to prosecute because that course of action maximized social utility.

Overall, Beccaria's principles evidenced the start of the declining role of the victim in the criminal justice system. This new system required that the victim's roles as policeman, prosecutor, and punishment beneficiary be reduced to that of informant and witness only. These ideas strongly appealed to Americans who sought to emphasize the principles of rationality and utilitarianism, and had an enormous influence on the development of the American criminal justice system during the 19th century.

B. American Correctional Reform

This passing of the victim from his former place in corrections went unnoticed and uneventfully. It was not until the end of the 19th century that the victim's disappearance was noticed and some thought was given to restoring him to some role in the correctional process. One proposal was that instead of going to prison the defendant should work for the state, retaining for himself only enough to keep from starving. The balance would go into a fund for compensating the victim. If the offender were solvent, his property should be confiscated and restitution made therefrom by order of the court. Another proposal suggested that the convict should perform services for compensation for the state while in prison, and that the convict should remain in prison until restitution to the victim was completed.

These suggestions, however, met with little success. First, they were based on the assumption that prisoners would be able to earn a reasonable wage through prison labor. However, by the end of the 19th century, the emergence of the labor union movement in America and adverse publicity from a series of investigations into the prisons' abuses of prisoner labor helped foster strong opposition to these proposals. Later, the economic crises of the Great Depression prompted 33 states to quickly pass laws which forbade the sale of prison products on the open market. These laws severely limited most prison industry.

The second obstacle to the return of the victim through such compensation proposals was the fact that the honeymoon with the penitentiary was not over. While it had become clear by the 1850s that penitentiaries not only failed to reform inmates but had degenerated into places of corruption and cruelty, the solution advanced by the new generation of penologists was not to restore the victim's role in the system. Instead, they advocated modification of the great white elephants that had been erected. They urged early release for well-behaved prisoners, and the use of parole and separate institutions for young first offenders. But few of these proposals were enacted. Incarceration had become a value in its own right, and even if it did not rehabilitate it served a useful custodial function. By the end of the 19th century, the victim ceased to be a concern for the correctional authorities and the criminal justice system.

C. The Public Prosecutor

Another important change that occurred shortly after the Revolution that further displaced the victim from his former role in criminal justice was the emergence of the office of public prosecutor. The history of the development of this office in America is a puzzle. English common law made no provision for a public prosecutor such as our district attorney. All prosecutions were private prosecutions brought in the name of the king. The right and power to accuse, collect evidence, and manage prosecutions for the state rested with the individual citizen. The victim or whoever brought the prosecution retained his own counsel and had charge of the case as in a civil proceeding except that the Attorney General, as representative of the king, could refuse to allow it to go on. In addition to this system of private prosecutions there were prosecutions at the instance of the Crown brought by law officers of the Crown. But the powers of these officers were regarded at law as no different from those of a private prosecutor.

In Colonial America where the English common law was the law of the land, the system of private prosecutions was widely used; and no doubt it shared many of the same weaknesses as the English system. But, in America there also existed an office of public prosecutor. The office was first established by statute in Connecticut in 1704, whose example was soon followed by the other colonies. However, it was not until shortly after the Revolution that this office emerged as the predominant method of prosecution. [This point has been disputed by later historians who place the rise of the public prosecution at a later time.] During the 1780s the rebel government had brought numerous political prosecutions. These declined after 1790 but by then the government's interest in the outcome of many criminal cases continued for other reasons. With the imposition of hard labor instead of treble damages as the usual punishment for theft, the victim of theft no longer was the party of interest in theft prosecution. The government became the truly interested party. After 1805, when fines or imprisonment were the punishments in all cases, the government's interest was even greater.

The history of the role of the victim in the prosecution of criminal cases from 1810 to the present is difficult to trace. Unlike corrections and the police, the office of the public prosecutor has received only limited scholarly treatment. Thus, attention herein is focused upon the relationship between the victim and the public prosecutor during the 20th century.

Today [1976], in the opinion of many commentators, both victims and witnesses of crimes receive from public prosecutors what has been called the "administrative runaround." Both are required to make numerous trips to the courthouse to tell and retell their stories to a series of prosecutors responsible for different stages of the case, and often to sit for prolonged periods of time in dirty waiting rooms or corridors, frequently with the defendant nearby. Witness fees are generally inadequate to cover actual expenses, much less to compensate for the emotional stress. In many jurisdictions they are not paid at all.

Criticism has also been leveled at the legal profession for its pattern of neglect with regard to the interests of victims and witnesses. Victims and witnesses do not receive even a fraction of the protections and defenses that are accorded an accused. Typically, the interests of the victim and witnesses are subordinated to what are regarded as more important interests. A good example is the character cross-examination of a victim in rape cases. While the defendant has an interest in the introduction of relevant evidence on his behalf, the victim has important interests as well, such as freedom from intimidation, harassment, and further degradation, and the preservation of privacy. Yet, the legal profession seems remarkably willing to sacrifice such interests of the victim to those of the defendant in every instance.

Another area in which the victim gets little satisfaction from the public prosecutor is the matter of criminal fraud. This crime was not unknown at the time of the Revolution, but since then with the development of the modern marketplace the opportunity for such fraud has vastly increased. When the victim of such a crime seeks the public prosecutor's assistance, he is usually treated to a lecture on the difference between civil and criminal law. Thus, while the victim was the subject of a criminal law violation, he is encouraged only to hire a private attorney and file a civil suit. Generally, the prosecutor's position is that he lacks the resources to conduct such prosecutions; but even if he had them, the criminal prosecution would be conducted in the interests of society and no attempt would be made to recover the victim's losses. For example, if the prosecution showed chances of success, the defendant would probably be offered the opportunity to plead *nolo contendere*. This would supposedly serve the interests of the community by making conviction certain and reducing the costs of prosecution, but does a disservice to the interests of the victim who then would be unable to use the criminal conviction as *prima facie* evidence of guilt in a subsequent civil suit. Of course, in legal theory, the public prosecutor is not supposed to serve the particular interests of private individuals; nor, for that matter, is he to serve the public interest. Instead, he has the much greater burden of seeing that justice is done.

It is usually in these terms, for instance, that the practice of plea bargaining is justified. Although plea bargaining is the means by which most criminal convictions are obtained, it does not occur in an open hearing at which the victim could, if he wished, be present. Instead, it is usually conducted informally in hallways, private offices, and sometimes even by telephone. Not only is the victim seldom present but he is usually not consulted. Even worse, he is rarely informed of the outcome.

Therein lies the exquisite irony of modern law. The age-old struggle of civilization has been to persuade people not to take justice into their own hands but rather to let their vengeance and righteous indignation be wrought by the law. Western civilization had by the Middle Ages succeeded in substituting private prosecutions for blood feuds. The next step was to replace private prosecution with public prosecution, while asking the victim to forego whatever satisfaction he might derive from personally prosecuting his transgressor and settling for the more intangible satisfaction of knowing that justice would be done. Now, the modern criminal justice system operates in an age of computers and instant telecommunications, disposing of large numbers of cases without trial and without bothering to give the victim even the minimal satisfaction of knowing what happened to his case and why.

This ill-treatment afforded the victim of crime by the modern public prosecutor and the neglect to provide the victim with the information concerning the handling of his case reflects an historical and constricted understanding of his function. While the prosecutor is quick to state that his purpose is to maintain law and order in society, he sees his responsibility for doing this entirely in terms of punishing those who violate the law. However, while pursuing this ideal of impersonal justice, the system has neglected the continuing struggle of all societies to convince their members not to resort to personal vengeance to settle their grievances. Lawfulness in society is increased or diminished to the extent that this struggle is successful.

D. The Professional Police

The advent of professional police further diminished the victim's prominence in law enforcement. By the middle of the 18th century the inadequacies of a policing system composed of part-time, privately paid law enforcement officers and bounty-seeking private citizens led slowly to the development of government operated police forces.

Several factors combined to make the development of professional police inevitable. Traditional notions of community responsibility for mutual welfare had vanished in the impersonality of large urban concentrations. Citizens rarely aided peace officers in making arrests. Even monetary rewards had lost their power to motivate citizen cooperation, and toward the end of the 1820s payments of criminal fines to private informers had virtually ceased. Moreover, the traditional system had been singularly ineffective in preventing crime. The reformers touted the advantages of professional police who could uncover potential crime on their own initiative without being barred from action until some public disturbance or private complaint came to their attention.

Further, law enforcement financed by private fees had become not only inefficient but corrupt. Victims able to pay higher fees commanded disproportionate attention. The competitiveness of the fee system discouraged cooperation among lawmen in apprehending criminals. As victims were primarily interested in the return of their property, officers had little incentive to bring offenders to justice. Illicit arrangements between police and criminals were being made even in advance of the crime. Thus, a salaried police force responsible to the whole community became an increasingly attractive prospect.

A final development in the early 19th century enhanced the authority of the police to combat crime. Traditionally, both peace officers and private citizens could make arrests without warrants when a felony had been committed if there was reasonable suspicion that the arrestee was the guilty party. However, police and citizens alike were liable in a civil action for false arrest if they were mistaken that a crime in fact occurred. In 1827, a court decision established the power of police to make warrantless arrests on reasonable suspicion that a felony had been committed, insulating the police from false arrest suits if their reasonable suspicion proved unfounded. Police were thus able to pursue suspected criminal activity far more aggressively than before and private citizens were simultaneously encouraged to rely on the police to apprehend criminals.

Although the advent of the professional police curtailed the victim's direct role in law enforcement, he still retained a role in the detection and solution of crime. Successful police work depends greatly upon the victims' identification of their assailants. Moreover, victims generally initiate police responses to crime.

However, it is also understood that as many as two-thirds or more of all crimes committed are never reported to the police. This is attributed to victims' fears that the police would not want to be bothered with their cases, or would be unable to do anything about the crimes. Studies have found that victims are critical of the professional attitude of modern police and find them cold and impersonal. Further, victims are disturbed by the failure of police to offer advice on how to prevent the crime from reoccurring, or to inform them of the progress of their cases. Police are also criticized for confiscating property without explaining that it is needed for evidence or explaining the procedure for regaining the property after trial. Victims also resent repeating their stories to various officers.

In part these criticisms reflect the intractable fact that the police do approach crime, and victims, professionally. For the police, a particular crime is simply one crime among many; for the victim, his crime is a personal calamity. Perhaps the burden should fall more heavily on the police to offer victims some solicitude. To a greater extent, however, the criticisms reflect misunderstanding and misinformation among the public about police and legal procedures, and this is being addressed by a variety of new efforts to ease the victim's involuntary confrontation with the criminal law. . . .

In the contemporary American criminal justice system, the victim no longer controls the investigation and prosecution of crime. In many respects this evolution in law enforcement has benefitted the victim, who is no longer required to bear the risk of apprehending criminals, nor to expend his own funds and energy to bring offenders to justice. These responsibilities are entrusted to the particular expertise of police, prosecutors, and correctional officials, and society as a whole now bears the costs of enforcing the criminal law.

While the victim has been relieved of his responsibilities as law enforcer, the criminal justice system itself has become an institution designed to serve the entire society, and not the individual victim. It has been too easy to forget that the victim suffers peculiarly personal emotional and economic damage as a direct result of the crime, and that he is often bewildered by a complex prosecutorial system which he is powerless to control. The recent efforts to provide victims with personal support, and to clarify and expand their role in the prosecutorial process, reflects a growing awareness that a just and humane society cannot ignore the toll which crime exacts upon individual victims. The third century of American development will be enriched if these first tentative steps lead to a new accommodation for the victim within the criminal justice process.

D. Why Did the American Criminal Process Evolve by the 1970s to Exclude Victim Involvement?

As Professor MacDonald explained in the previous section, our criminal justice process has evolved from one in which crime victims were central players to one in which, until quite recently, victims were excluded. Why did the process evolve to exclude victims? Various explanations seem plausible.

1. Victim Exclusion as an Historical Misunderstanding

Abraham Goldstein, *Defining the Role of the Victim in Criminal Prosecution*

52 Mississippi L.J. 1 (1982)

The victim currently [1982] is denied a formal role-party status—at each of these [restitution] hearings. He has no right to present his views—the right of "allocution"— and he has no right to present evidence, to argue the issues, or to appeal. The victim's complaint may give rise to the prosecution and his testimony may be essential to sustain it, but he has no formal relation to the criminal case. The prosecutor alone is said to represent the public interest in criminal law. He has been endowed by the courts with a broad and virtually unreviewable discretion in these matters of charging and dismissal and restitution.

This "monopoly" of criminal prosecution by the district attorney is more the result of a misunderstanding of history than of explicit legislative direction. It traces to a time when the procedure for invoking criminal law was largely in private hands, as it is in England even today. When our system of public prosecution evolved, most statutes merely *authorized* the district attorney to prosecute all criminal cases in his county; they were silent as to whether the victim or anyone else could prosecute on his own. In a series of early opinions, however, the courts described the district attorney as exercising on the county level the powers of prosecution of the Attorney General of England whose actions could not be reviewed by the courts. From that historical analogy, the courts inferred that the district attorney's actions—particularly in deciding whether or not to initiate a prosecution were also not reviewable.

These opinions overlooked the fact that the English Attorney General was not a public prosecutor in our sense at all. Except for a limited class of cases, he did not initiate prosecutions. That was (and is) generally left to the victim and to the police as members of the public. He did have an unreviewable power in criminal cases— but only to enter a writ of *nolle prosequi*. That is, he could terminate prosecutions brought by private parties and the courts could not review his actions in doing so, and he could take over a private prosecution if he regarded it as in the public interest to do so. In short, the Attorney General of England exercised a *reviewing* authority over private prosecution, to ensure that criminal processes and criminal sanctions were not used for harassment or in a manner inconsistent with the public interest.

The American historical error confused the power to intervene and dismiss cases already initiated by private parties with the exclusive power to decide whether they should be initiated at all. It transformed the assertion of the public interest at a secondary review stage into a rationale for total control of the initial stage, the charge itself. In the United States, victims trying to prosecute or participate in criminal cases came to be regarded as pursuing private interests; only district attorneys, therefore, could be entrusted with the conduct of criminal prosecutions.

* * *

2. Victim Exclusion as a Practicality

The exclusion of the victim might also be explained as the practical result of a criminal system whose purpose is to punish wrongdoers.

Gail Heriot, *An Essay on the Civil Criminal Distinction with Special Reference to Punitive Damages*

1 J. Contemporary Legal Issues 43 (1996)

If one were to ask a person on the street about the basic structure of a criminal proceeding, the explanation given might go something like this: A criminal proceeding is a legal proceeding brought by the state against a defendant who is alleged to be a wrongdoer. If the allegation is proven, the defendant is punished for his wrongdoing.

If the same question were asked with regard to a civil proceeding, the reply might be that it is a legal proceeding brought by an injured person, called plaintiff, against a defendant who plaintiff alleges to have wrongfully caused his injury. If the allegation is proven, the defendant is ordered to compensate the plaintiff.

Let us accept this view of what is basic in the structure of criminal and civil cases. (We do have to start somewhere, and common understandings tend to be a more propitious starting point than most legal academics are willing to admit.) What is at the root of the distinction between civil and criminal proceedings? What accounts for their separate basic structure?

Fundamental Purposes and Extent to Which They Compel Basic Structure

Perhaps the most frequently identified single distinction is that the "purpose" of the civil law is compensation and the "purpose" of the criminal law is punishment. The civil law confronts a situation in which a loss has occurred and determines who shall bear it. It does not seek to punish—or at least so the argument runs. The criminal law, on the other hand, inflicts a loss that did not exist before, and it does so in order to effect a punishment.

Let us suppose for the moment that these are indeed in some sense the respective "purposes" of civil and of criminal law, rather than simply the tools used by them to achieve some deeper purpose or purposes. Surprisingly little concerning the basic structure of those great bodies of law follows as a matter of necessity from these purposes. Indeed, perhaps only two things result:

First, with regard to the civil law, the compensation purpose requires that there always be on hand an identifiable person who claims injury and is thus the potential recipient of compensation. No such person is necessary in order to carry out the criminal law's punishment purpose. Indeed, modern American criminal cases frequently involve activities that are considered essentially victimless (e.g., gambling and prostitution), or that are considered victimless on the facts of the particular case (e.g., reckless endangerment and attempt). In either case, the absence of a victim is no obstacle to punishment.

Second, with regard to the criminal law, the punishment goal requires that there must always be an identifiable person who allegedly should be punished. Such a person is not necessary to the goal of compensation in civil law. It is easy to imagine an institution that fulfills the purpose of compensation without obtaining that compensation from the person who caused the injury. Social insurance agencies and private insurers do it all the time.

That may be all: civil law needs an alleged victim; criminal law needs an alleged wrongdoer. The simple compensation/punishment distinction cannot account for the rest of the differences in the basic structure of the two bodies of law. These must be explained some other way.

Practicality and How It Compels Basic Structure

If conceptual necessity does not explain the whole of the basic structure of civil and criminal law, maybe practicalities can. For example, in the criminal law, it is not conceptually necessary to vest sole authority to initiate and direct the proceedings in the state. The purpose of punishment could be carried out without the state. Indeed, we know from the appeal of felony that there have been times in which the authority to bring proceedings to inflict punishment has been primarily vested in victims rather than in state.

Why victims? Relying upon victims to initiate and direct criminal proceedings may simply have been a practicality; it was probably less costly than establishing a prosecuting bureaucracy. Practicalities have a lot to do with the adoption of legal procedures.

Why did it change over time? Why did the state become the primary initiator of criminal prosecutions? For one thing, victims can be relied upon to initiate criminal actions only when they exist. For wrongdoing without specific identifiable victims, someone other than the victim must initiate the proceeding if that wrongdoing is going to be punished by the criminal law. The state is the only obvious party. Thus, once the decision is made to punish conspiracies, attempts and other conduct that does not necessarily lead to an identifiable victim, the state must be ready to step in.

That, of course, does not explain why the state would become the exclusive initiator of criminal proceedings as it has in American law or the near-exclusive initiator of criminal proceedings as it has in Great Britain. One explanation that is consistent with the punishment purpose is again a practical one rooted in social changes. The costs of initiating a prosecution have changed significantly as a consequence of urbanization. When private prosecutions were common, a higher proportion of crimes occurred in small towns and rural areas, simply because an overwhelmingly higher proportion of the population lived in such places. In such cases, victim, wrongdoer and witnesses were often personally acquainted. Little detective work was necessary or even possible. When the victim saw her husband's cousin setting her house afire, there was no need for police sketches, lineups, or other elaborate means to identify the perpetrator. A victim with even a weak taste for vengeance might be willing to undertake the costs necessary to initiate the prosecution.

As society became more urbanized, however, the likelihood that victim, wrongdoer and witnesses would be strangers increased significantly. Hence the need for serious detective work increased. Victims would thus be much more inclined to "chalk it up to experience" and refrain from prosecution. This is simply human nature. Why undertake the cost of prosecuting a criminal when the benefits of so doing will accrue to the community at large rather than the private prosecutor? It seems far more sensible for the victim to let these costs be borne by all who benefit.

After a while this was bound to increase the need for the state to act as prosecutor. At some point, these practical pressures created the basis for the development of the criminal legal proceeding that we are all familiar with: The state brings an action against a defendant-wrongdoer whose alleged wrongdoing may or may not have caused an actual harm to someone. If the state proves that the defendant wrongdoer should be punished, he is executed, imprisoned, fined or otherwise made to feel unpleasant. The victim, if any, is relegated to a supporting role. He may bring a civil action if he pleases, but he may not control the criminal proceeding. Indeed, the victim who is insistent upon a central role is viewed with suspicion. There is something vaguely distasteful about a victim who is too interested in punishing a wrongdoer.

Practical pressures probably also explain some of the basic structure of the civil law. For example, the civil law's putative compensatory purpose does not mandate that the victim be a "plaintiff" in the sense that he must be the person who initiates and in part directs the action. One could just as well imagine a legal proceeding concerned with compensation in which the state is the initiating party and the victim, although a necessary player, is simply a bystander.

Yet, the plaintiff is no bystander in the civil law and for good reason: Hundreds of years ago, it was probably less costly to rely upon victims to pursue their own remedy than it was to hire government officials and vest them with that authority. Indeed, this probably remains so today for most cases we would label "civil." Under such circumstances, one would expect the plaintiff-victim concept to evolve. Moreover, one would expect it to be stable. Unlike the prosecutor-victim in the criminal law, the plaintiff-victim in a civil case reaps the benefits of a successful case. She thus has no incentive to shirk.

3. Victim Exclusion as Fairness to the Defendant

Victims may have become excluded from the criminal justice system by virtue of a focus on defendants' interests. An argument for excluding victims from the process, other than as witnesses, rests on the understanding that the purpose of criminal trials is to determine the guilt or innocence of the criminal defendant. To reach a fair determination of guilt, public institutions detached from the crime should present the evidence. A criminal process constructed of public institutions (prosecutors, judges, and parole boards) and representatives of the community (jurors) is removed from the direct trauma of victimization. This distance arguably results in more neutral procedures and punishments and promotes a public perception of a fair procedure. Allowing a victim's participation could introduce the risk of vindictiveness and emotion and, thus, potential unfairness into the process.

To some extent, some actors in the criminal justice system may have reached a conclusion that fairness to defendants requires exclusion of victims. But even if the system has not consciously determined to exclude victims, exclusion may be a byproduct of increasing focus on defendants' rights. In the 1960s, defendants' rights developed considerably as the Warren Court expansively interpreted federal constitutional protections for criminal defendants. Even when the Supreme Court slowed this expansion, some state courts picked up the slack and interpreted state constitutions generously to protect defendants' interests. No comparable development has taken place for victims because victims' rights are not protected in the federal constitution and are absent (at least until recently) from state constitutions. This expansion and constitutionalization of defendants' rights left little room for victims and may have eliminated some of the informal accommodations to victims that were possible in earlier years. Indeed, some have argued that this is a strength.

4. Victim Exclusion as Truth Seeking

Stephen J. Schulhofer, *The Trouble with Trials; the Trouble with Us*
105 YALE L.J. 825 (1995)

. . . The purpose of the trial is to determine whether the defendant is factually and legally responsible for an offense. Indeed, the Supreme Court has sometimes implied that this truth-determining function should be virtually the *sole* task of the criminal trial. Presently, our society remains committed to a small number of devices that can sometimes interfere (mostly in modest ways) with the primary truth-seeking function of the trial. But we remain acutely aware of the costs of procedural rules that serve goals other than determining the truth, and we are rightly suspicious of efforts to burden our trial process by adding more rules of that sort. Any thoroughgoing effort to reshape the criminal trial to serve the victim, at the expense of truth seeking, would have dramatic and totally unacceptable costs. . . .

5. Victim Exclusion as a Cultural and Institutional Dynamic

Victim exclusion may also be the result of cultural and institutional dynamics. Crime victims tend to be disproportionately drawn from the ranks of the disempowered and disfavored. Moreover, actors at all of levels of the criminal justice system may tend to blame victims for the misfortune of being victimized. The facts can produce cultural and institutional dynamics that, at the very least, tend to lead the system to ignore the interests of victims.

The first problem is that crime victims tend to be those least able to cope with the victimization and assert their rights in the process. Victims are disproportionately the poor, the young, and people of color. The most recent victimizations surveys show that racial minorities—particularly African-Americans—are far more likely to be the victims of violent crime than are whites. Bureau of Justice Statistics, National Crime Victimization Survey, Criminal Victimization, 2003 (2004). For example, the national crime survey has repeatedly shown that blacks are victims of completed robbery at over four times the rate than whites. Given that victims frequently come from racial and socio-economic groups that tend to lack access to government machinery generally, it should come as no surprise that they are excluded in the criminal process.

A second barrier to appreciation of the "victim problem" is that people tend to believe that good is rewarded and evil punished. M. Lerner, *The Desire for Justice and Reactions to Victims,* in Altruism and Helping Behavior 207 (J. Macaullay & L. Berkowitz, eds. 1970). Furthermore, vestiges of puritanism (the strong survive and the wicked do not) and of social Darwinism (people who suffer misfortune are naturally inferior) continue to this day. *See* M. Bard & D. Sangrey, The Crime Victims Book (1979). This may produce a subconscious tendency to blame the victim and to focus on other interests ahead of victims'.

Third, the instinctive human reaction to the crime victim is one of avoidance: "It is not hard to turn away from victims, their pain is discomforting, their anger is sometimes embarrassing, their mutilations are upsetting." Statement of the Chairman, President's Task Force on Victims of Crime, Final Report (1982).

Fourth, people have been conditioned to think about and react to crime by focusing on the criminal's actions and how he will be treated in the justice system. *See* M. Bard & D. Sangrey, The Crime Victims Book (1979). For example, most media treatment of crime is devoted to exploits of criminals and consequent effort of police officers to catch them. *Id.*

Finally, bureaucratic pressures may also play a role: "From the perspective of a system that must handle a large number of cases with limited resources, victims are a nuisance." E. McCabe, *The Quality of Justice: Victims in the Criminal Justice System,* in Victimization of the Weak, (J. & G. Sheperd, eds. 1982).

6. Victim Exclusion as the Product of the Law School Curriculum?

Finally, it is worth thinking about whether law schools could do a better job of participating with students in a constructive dialog about crime victims and their interests.

Paul G. Cassell, *Barbarians at the Gates? A Reply to the Critics of the Victims' Rights Amendment*
1999 Utah L. Rev. 479

Many of the complaints [about victim's rights] rest on little more than an appeal to retain a legal tradition that excludes victims from participating in the process, to in some sense leave it up to the "professionals" — the judges, prosecutors, and defense attorneys — to do justice as they see fit. Such entreaties may sound attractive to members of the bar, who not only have vested interests in maintaining their monopolistic control over the criminal justice system, but also have grown up without any exposure to crime victims or their problems. The "legal culture" . . . is one that has not made room for crime victims. Law students learn to "think like lawyers" in classes such as criminal law and criminal procedure, where victims' interests receive no discussion. In the first year in criminal law, students learn in excruciating detail to focus on the state of mind of a criminal defendant, through intriguing questions about mens rea and the like. In the second year, students may take a course on criminal procedure, where defendants' and prosecutors' interests under the constitutional doctrine governing search and seizure, confessions, and right to counsel are the standard fare. Here, too, victims are absent. The most popular criminal procedure casebook, for example, spans some 877 pages; yet, victims' rights appear only in two paragraphs, made necessary because in California, a victims' rights initiative affected a defendant's right to exclude evidence. Finally, in their third year, students may take a clinical course in the criminal justice process, where they may be assigned to assist prosecutors or defense attorneys in actual criminal cases. Not only are they never assigned to represent crime victims, but in courtrooms they will see victims frequently absent, or participating only through prosecutors or the judicial apparatus, such as probation officers.

Given this socialization, it is no surprise to find that when those lawyers leave law school, they become part of a legal culture unsympathetic, if not overtly hostile, to the interests of crime victims. The legal insiders view with great suspicion demands from the outsiders — the barbarians, if you will — to be admitted into the process.

Erin Ann O'Hara, *Victim Participation in the Criminal Process*
8 Brook. J. Law & Policy 229–30 (2005)

Given that virtually all law professors were trained in criminal law classes that ignored victim involvement in the criminal justice process, it is perhaps not surprising that it is considered heretical to suggest that direct participation might be warranted.

7. Excluding Victims for Their Own Good

The notion behind the idea of excluding victims for their own good is that participation in the process itself exposes them to psychological trauma. An example of this view appears in Lynn Henderson, *The Wrongs of Victims' Rights*, 37 Stan. L. Rev. 937, 965-6 (1985): "A victim's contact with the criminal justice system may hinder him or her from coming to grips with death, meaning, responsibility, and isolation in innumerable ways. The criminal justice system provides a ready set of opportunities for blame and denial, proceeds on the basis of mistaken normative assumptions about victims, and emphasizes rationality — or the appearance of it."

E. Justifications for Including Victims in Criminal Procedures

Whatever the historical, cultural, or educational explanations for leaving victims outside of the criminal process, recent assessments have found several compelling justifications for bringing victims inside the process.

1. Fairness to the Victim

The overarching justification for victim participation in the process is that fundamental fairness demands it. Modern criminal procedure tends to view the *party* injured by crime as merely the state. Increasingly, however, both the public and the participants in the criminal justice process have recognized that this paradigm inadequately captures the full range of interests in the criminal process. Victimization frequently involves psychological and physical trauma. Sometimes the trauma is obvious, as in cases of violent crimes. In other cases, the trauma may be psychological yet pervasive, involving disruption of personal relationships or the loss of economic security. In short, whatever the legal understanding of the "parties" to a criminal action, in the realm of common sense victims are harmed by crimes — sometimes grievously so.

Given that victims are the persons harmed by the crime, a number of commentators have argued that their exclusion from the criminal justice process is unfair.

George P. Fletcher, With Justice for Some: Protecting Victims' Rights in Criminal Trials
(1995)

The theme that runs through all [my] proposals is that we develop a new conception of why we prosecute and punish criminals. The standard debate on this subject fluctuates between grandiose ambitions of social engineering and abstract propositions about punishing simply for the sake of justice and, as the philosopher Hegel put it, vindicating right over wrong. I have urged . . . a more realistic purpose of punishment. The primary task of the criminal trial is neither to change society nor to rectify a metaphysical imbalance in the moral order. The purpose of the trial is to stand by the victim. . . .

A just legal system must stand by its victims. We may neither deter future offenders, nor rehabilitate present inmates, nor achieve justice in the eyes of God. But by seeking to punish the guilty, we do not abandon the innocent who suffer. We do not become complicitous in the crimes against them. We seek justice not only for offenders but for all of us.

2. Protecting the Interests of Society

A credible argument can be made that a substantial part of the public's distrust of plea bargaining is that victims' interests and harm have not been valued in the public interest function of the plea bargain process. The legislated embodiment of public distrust is manifested in victims' rights of consultation with prosecutors, and laws that allow the victim to address the court at the sentencing hearing in all jurisdictions. Seen in this light, crime victims' rights push back against a restricted definition of "public interest" that had excluded individual victim harm and interests.

In some areas, protecting victims' interests might more effectively protect society's interests. In the modern era, the public prosecutor has been the sole representative of society. For example, in the context of plea bargaining, the prosecutor has traditionally decided what plea offer is in the best interests of society. Yet some debatable plea bargains have led to questions about whether a single representative of the government—the prosecutor—always act in society's best interests, and whether giving victims an oversight role in the plea process might lead to results more representative of the interests of society. As a result, in areas such as plea bargaining, victim participation can be justified as protecting society.

3. Avoiding Secondary Victimization

In addition to the death itself, victims cope with the violence of death, loss of intimacy, financial stresses and the destruction of the family structure, among other things. J. Lord, No Time for Goodbyes: Coping with Sorrow, Anger and Injustice after a Tragic Death (1987). For example, Professor Bard writes: "The violation . . . can hardly be called a positive experience, but it does represent an opportunity for change. One of two things will happen, either victims will become reordered or their experiences will promote further disorder with long term consequences." M. Bard & D. Sangrey, The Crime Victims Book, 47–48 (1979).

The victim may experience further disorder by the criminal justice system through "secondary victimization." "Victims' accounts of their encounters with the criminal justice system range from positive experiences resulting in feelings of satisfaction to tales of horror best described as a further victimization by the criminal justice system." E. McCabe, *The Quality of Justice: Victims in the Criminal Justice System*, in Victimization of the Weak 133 (J. Scherrer & G. Sheperd eds. 1982).

Dean Kilpatrick, Ph.D. in Psychology and Director of the Crime Victim's Research and Treatment Center at the Medical University of South Carolina, states that failure to give victims an opportunity for meaningful input at sentencing can increase secondary victimization. Kilpatrick, D., *Addressing the Needs of Traumatized Victims*, in National College of District Attorneys Course Materials, Victim Witness Training Program p. 2.

These secondary victimizations continue to occur despite the fact that "crime related trauma is a major contributing factor to the victim's failure to cooperate with the criminal justice system." *Id.* at 5.

4. Facilitating Truth Seeking

Douglas E. Beloof & Paul G. Cassell, *The Crime Victim's Right to Attend the Trial: The Reascendant National Consensus*

9 Lewis & Clark L. Rev. 481 (2005)

In considering victim sequestration and the truth-seeking process, it is important to understand that claims can be made in both directions. On balance, it appears that allowing victims to attend trials can actually facilitate the truth-seeking process more than harm it.

It is worth remembering that even in states without a victim's right to attend trial, victims still may be admitted where their presence is essential to the prosecution. Courts have long recognized that victims can be useful to prosecutors. Victims can assist the prosecution in many ways. In busy urban courtrooms, prosecutors often have to juggle dozens of cases at any one time, and likely will not have complete mastery of the facts at issue, even with the assistance of a case agent. A victim, on the other hand, has only one case to remember. Indeed, the events of that case may be seared into the mind of the victim. Apart from the defendant, *no one* knows more about the crime than the victim herself. The victim, therefore, may be useful—if not indispensable—in crafting appropriate direct and cross-examination questions. as the Justice Department has concluded: "the presence of victims in the courtroom can be a positive force in furthering the truth-finding process by alerting prosecutors to misrepresentations of the testimony of other witnesses." State prosecutors report similar experiences.

5. Preventing Victim Alienation

Deborah P. Kelly, Ph.D., *Victim's Perceptions of Criminal Justice*

11 Pepperdine L. Rev. 15 (1984)

* * *

Consider the judicial process from the victim's perspective: Victims are introduced to a system grounded on the legal fiction that victims are not the injured party. Victims soon learn they have no standing in court, no right to counsel, no control over the prosecution of their case and no voice in its disposition.

Abraham Goldstein, *Defining the Role of the Victim in Criminal Prosecution*

52 Miss. L. Rev. 515 (1982)

A. The Alienation of the Victim

A key assumption underlying the victims' movement is that the failure of victims to cooperate with the criminal justice system has reached epidemic proportions.

Recent statistical studies of victimization confirm what we have known for some time. Victims often do not report to the police the crimes that have been committed against them. And the more crime we have, the larger this "dark figure" of unreported crime becomes. Even when they report crimes, a remarkably large proportion of victims later refuse to testify, which leads prosecutors to dismiss or reduce charges. Conversely, victims often find police unwilling to investigate and prosecutors unwilling to charge. In short, each—authorities and victims—finds the other uncooperative, resulting in a reciprocal cycle of decline. Confidence in justice is eroded, enforcement efforts are impeded, and conviction rates, when measured against crimes actually committed, tumble downward.

This theme of alienation, which runs through the victims' movement, traces to a deeply held feeling that the victim has been so much separated from the crime against him that the crime is no longer "his." The sense of alienation probably began when the civil action for damages was split off from the criminal prosecution. A fine paid to the King became a substitute, at least in the criminal process, for compensation previously paid by the offender to the victim and his family. Alienation was accentuated when private prosecution—by victims or by any member of the public—was abandoned in the United States and the public prosecutor was given a monopoly of the criminal charge.

The victim has been left to play a distinctly secondary role. He reports crimes to public officials and leaves it to them to decide whether offenders should be prosecuted and punished. His injury becomes the occasion for a public cause of action, but he has no "standing" to compel prosecution of the crime against him, or to contest decisions to dismiss or reduce the charges or to accept plea bargains, or to challenge the sentence imposed on the offender who injured him, or to participate in hearings on restitution. He is, in a sense, represented by the district attorney, but if his interest in pressing the charge comes into conflict with the prosecutor's conception of the public interest, the latter will prevail. And what is seen to be in the public interest may consist of elements that have little or nothing to do with the victim's case—its strength or weakness—or the nature of the victim's injuries or his outrage against the defendant or even his fear that the crime may be repeated. It may turn on the utility of the defendant as a state witness in another case, or on correctional factors that make it seem preferable to abandon the victim's case rather than prosecute the offender on a serious charge or on any at all. It may turn on whether the particular offense has a high priority at the moment. Thefts and burglaries and consumer frauds may be low on the priority list, crimes of violence high. Spouse abuse may be a disfavored charge, assaults by the ghetto resident against another not worth bothering with. The decision to prosecute may not be made on qualitative grounds at all. The victim's interest may be subordinated to the more amorphous administrative objective of making the most of the prosecutor's limited resources, or keeping the court's dockets from being clogged, or keeping the prisons from overflowing.

It is easy to understand both the prosecutor's difficulties and the victim's frustrations. To the prosecutor, the victim is one among many competing interests. To the victim, the prosecutor is a bureaucrat who holds decisive power over his use of the criminal law—whether to give him emotional satisfaction or to deter the offender or to obtain financial reparation for his injuries. And the bureaucrat is often busy with things other than the victim's case—much more so today when the number of crimes and criminals is much greater than when public prosecution first supplanted the victim's right to prosecute on his own.

In any event, a collective memory has developed by now that makes the victim feel uninvolved in the crime against him, and that makes him regard criminal law as unresponsive to his concerns. He is told that he is not a "party" but a "mere witness." His complaints are often not investigated. The prosecutor need not tell him whether a charge has been filed or why it has been reduced from the offense complained of to a lesser one. Neither prosecutor, nor judge, need advise him of the terms of plea arrangements or sentences. And little or nothing need be done in the criminal case to facilitate his obtaining financial compensation for his injuries.

Though the victim may begin with the assumption that it is the wrong against him that is to be requited by the criminal law—that the prosecutor is his surrogate, proceeding in his place and on his behalf—he is too often persuaded by the "system" that the criminal prosecution is not really "his" business at all. It is little wonder that so many victims do not bring their complaints to the police or, if they do, that they become unwilling witnesses who are then responsible for the high rate of dismissals of prosecution.

6. Building a Moral Justice System

Stephanos Bibas, The Machinery of Criminal Justice
(Oxford Univ. Press 1st Ed. 2012)

The Victims' Rights Movement hopes to restore much of the focus that the machine [of criminal justice] has lost. It views criminal procedures not just as abstract rights or bargaining chips, but as important ways to heal and vindicate victims. And it restores a crucial focus on victims, who often get lost in lawyer dominated criminal procedure brought in the name of the state. . . .

Many scholars attack victim-impact statements at sentencing because they fear that victims will cloud justice with emotion and play on sentencers' biases. Others complain that giving victims the right to consult distorts prosecutors' neutral evaluation of justice. [Professor] Robert Mosteller even complains that victims' mere presence at trial may perhaps sway juries with emotional displays. Tellingly, he objects that emotion is illegitimate at jury trials, which misses the original point of jury trials as morality plays. These criticisms slight the role a victim deserves as the most interested party, the bearer of the grievance.

7. Including Victims So They May Chose to Participate or Not

Douglas E. Beloof, *The Third Model of Criminal Process: The Victim Participation Model*

1999 Utah L. Rev. 289

Because victims' rights allow the victim to decide about whether participation in the criminal process will be beneficial or harmful to them, it is paternalistic to [urge] exclu[sion] of all victims from the criminal process because some might be psychologically harmed by inclusion, particularly because victims are free to choose not to participate. This paternalistic view also focuses too narrowly within the broader issue of reduction or resolution of psychological trauma to the victim. The focus is too narrow because the view has no room for the idea that even if victims know they may be traumatized by the criminal process, they may yet choose to participate. If given a choice, victims who might be psychologically harmed by the criminal process do not necessarily prioritize the avoidance of psychological pain over participation. Crime victims may possess a sense of responsibility to see the truth revealed and an appropriate disposition achieved. This sense of responsibility may manifest itself by victim participation in the process, regardless of any psychological pain that results from the participation. Furthermore, for some victims the inability to choose to exercise this sense of responsibility may itself result in further trauma or in a delay of resolution of existing trauma.

8. Victim Dignity

O'Hear takes Professor Jerry Mashaw's scholarship on human dignity (as a basis for due process in administrative law) and applies it to crime victims' participation rights. Michael O'Hear, *Plea Bargaining and Victims: From Consultation to Guidelines*, 91 Marq. L. Rev. 323 (2007). This is a sensible approach given both the persuasive case Mashaw makes and the aptness of O'Hear's application to victim participation in criminal process. There is ample evidence in victims' rights laws to justify O'Hear's application of Mashaw's dignity theory. By 1999, 20 states expressly included the value of "dignity" in constitutional victims' rights. Other states have the same language in their respective statutes. The federal Crime Victims' Rights Act (CVRA) provides an express "right to be treated with fairness and with respect for the victim's dignity and privacy." The legislative history of the CVRA identifies the same type of concern for dignity that appears in Mashaw's scholarship: "Too often victims of crime experience a secondary victimization at the hands of the criminal justice system. This provision is intended to direct government agencies and employees . . . to treat victims of crime with the respect they deserve and to afford them due process."

Mary Margaret Giannini, *The Procreative Power of Dignity: Dignity's Evolution in the Victims' Rights Movement*

9 Drexel L. Rev. 43 (2016)

Dignity is a powerful term that permeates American legal jurisprudence. In the constitutional context, dignity has played a silent background role. As an unspoken value, it has generally served as a means for courts to interpret and give meaning to otherwise explicitly stated rights. By codifying dignity in state and federal legislation, the victims' rights movement has endowed dignity with more weight. Bringing dignity out of the shadows and into the explicit light of statutory and constitutional language, the victims' rights movement has elevated dignity from a background explanatory norm to a procreative power that enables courts and advocates to develop an extended body of rights for crime victims. By embracing dignity's spoken and procreative powers, the victims' rights movement has not only furthered its goal to eliminate the secondary victimization often suffered by crime victims in the criminal justice system, but has also expanded dignity's role within the law.

9. Victim Agency

Margaret Garvin, Douglas E. Beloof, *Crime Victim Agency: Independent Lawyers for Sexual Assault Victims*

13 Ohio St. J. Crim. L. 67 (2015)

Agency, broadly construed, is critically important for crime victims. Research reveals that for some victims who interact with the criminal justice system, participation is beneficial. It can allow them to experience improvement in depression and quality of life, provide a sense of safety and protection, and validate the harm done by the offender. For other victims, interaction with the criminal justice system leads to a harm beyond that of the original crime, a harm that is often referred to as "secondary victimization" and which is recognized to have significant negative impacts on victims. Specifically, re-victimization has been associated with posttraumatic stress disorder; physical, mental, and sexual distress; and negative impacts on self-esteem and trust in the legal system. Judith Herman summarized well the impacts of re-victimization when she noted, "if one set out intentionally to design a system for provoking symptoms of posttraumatic stress disorder, it might look very much like a court of law."

These negative impacts on individuals should be enough to concern policy makers about re-victimization; notably, however, the negative impacts of secondary victimization extend beyond the individual to substantially impair the functioning of the justice system. Disempowered victims may lose confidence in and respect for the system, may not report their victimization, or may disengage part way through the process. Disengagement of victims is significant. At the micro level, victims are important sources of information and the lack of their information can impair fair adjudication. On a grander scale, law and its processes are a constitutive rhetorical act, calling into being a common, collective identity and thereby marking the boundaries of community. When a swath of our community-i.e., sexual violence victims who are re-victimized by the process-are excluded and not interpolated into the common identity, the chance for meaningful progress in the fight against sexual violence is negligible.

A significant part of what accounts for the difference in experience is whether victims have the ability to meaningfully choose whether, when, how, and to what extent to meaningfully participate in the system and exercise their rights. In short, the difference in experience is explained by the existence-or lack of-agency.

10. Equality Inclusive of Victims

"Equality demands fairness not only between cases but also within cases. Victims and the public generally perceive great unfairness in a sentencing system with 'one side muted.'" Paul G. Cassell, *Barbarians at the Gates? A Reply to the Critics of the Victims' Rights Amendment*, 1999 UTAH L. REV. 479, 494–95 (citations omitted).

F. The Victims' Rights Movement

The victims' rights movement has developed from the belief that crime victims are not treated fairly in the criminal justice process. The victims' rights movement began as a collection of unlikely allies. First, mostly victims of violent crime, including victims from the civil rights movement concerned about police abuses. Second, the criminal justice arm of the women's movement, and finally the law and order movement. In terms of the last 20 years of the movement, it is fair to say that crime control advocates have significantly less influence today than they did early on because the victims' movement's focus is less on sentencing outcomes and more on due process rights for victims. Moreover, early advisers to laypersons seeking advice about victims' rights were often prosecutors. Today, there are lawyers and some law professors independent of the prosecutors who assist in drafting and litigating laws that include victims in the criminal process.

Not surprisingly, there has been resistance from some prosecutors and defense attorneys who are unfamiliar with how victims' rights work in practice or because they prefer the system without victims or because victims are seen to add more to the workload. Police may resist for similar reasons, or because it is not traditionally their job to provide victim support and information. On the other hand, there are many prosecutors and police who support victims' rights.

Note: Andrew A. Karmen, *Who's against Victims' Rights? The Nature of the Opposition to Pro-Victim Initiatives in Criminal Justice*

8 St. John's J. Legal Comment 157 (1992)

[I]t appears that most participants [in the victim's rights movement] would agree upon this basic critique:

(1) That criminal justice personnel—the police, prosecutors, defense attorneys, judges, probation officers, parole boards, corrections administrators—were systematically overlooking or neglecting the legitimate needs of crime victims until they began their campaign; (2) that there was a prevailing tendency on the part of the public as well as agency officials to unfairly blame victims for facilitating or even provoking crimes; (3) that explicit standards of fair treatment were required to protect the interests of complainants and prosecution witnesses, as well as injured parties whose cases were not solved; (4) that people who suffered injuries and losses inflicted by criminals ought to receive reimbursement from one source or another; and (5) that the best way to make sure that victims could pursue their personal goals and protect their own best interests was by granting them formal rights within the criminal justice system. . . .

Notes

1. The Human Rights Watch report excerpt at the beginning of the chapter assumes that victims' constitutional rights are civil liberties. There is a tension between civil libertarians with vested interests in pre-established civil liberties for criminal defendants and civil libertarians with an interest in enacting new civil rights for crime victims. As you study victims' rights, make up your own mind about how much or how little victims' rights infringe upon defendants' rights. For example, does a victim's right to speak at a plea proceeding take away rights or powers from the parties? From the judge?

2. Are "crime victims' rights" nothing more than prosecutors' rights? Consider the argument of Professor Susan Bandes, *Victim Standing*, 1999 Utah L. Rev. 331:

> Many of the important reforms sought by victims' rights advocates have been thwarted by the judicial construction of standing law and a host of related doctrines designed to insulate government, and particularly prosecutors, from any meaningful oversight or accountability. My thesis is that the sorts of victim initiatives that have been successful have been those, and only those, that advance the prosecution's own agenda, while preserving the prosecution's complete freedom from third party interference. To the extent victims seek their own standing to litigate or enforce interests that might diverge from the prosecution's, they have been unsuccessful—ending up instead mainly with unenforceable promises and the opportunity to assist (or some would say, be used by) the prosecution in attaining a harsh sentence.

3. What about victims' rights standards in other countries?

U.S. Participation in International Agreement on the Victims of Crime

Human Rights Watch, *Mixed Results: U.S. Policy and International Standards and the Rights and Interests of Victims of Crime*

(2008)

International Standards on the Rights and Interests of Victims of Crime

Many international human rights instruments address or touch on victims' rights, including legal instruments such as the International Covenant on Civil and Political Rights (ICCPR), legally binding on the US federal and state governments, as well as the Convention on the Elimination of Discrimination against Women (CEDAW), and the Convention on the Rights of the Child (CRC). Other international instruments provide guidance on how best to protect and promote victims' rights and meet their needs in domestic legal systems, most notably the 1985 United Nations (UN) Declaration of Basic Principles of Justice for Victims of Crime and Abuse of Power (the "Basic Principles for Victims") adopted by the UN General Assembly, which details international consensus on best practices in relation to victims of crime. In the analysis that follows, this report largely draws on the Basic Principles for Victims, the most comprehensive international treatment of the subject currently available.

The UN General Assembly and the UN Economic and Social Council have also passed several resolutions that articulate the importance of the rights of women and children who are victims of crime.

Treaty Provisions

Several provisions in the ICCPR, which the US has ratified and thereby bound itself to, are relevant to victims of crime. They include:

> Rights to be protected from harm, which impose obligations on the government to have effective criminal laws that prohibit certain behavior, act as a deterrent to committing offenses, and ensure that those who do commit crimes are brought to justice through effective investigation and, where appropriate, prosecution. For example, Article 6.1 of the treaty requires that the right to life be protected by law; Article 7 imposes an obligation to protect individuals from inhuman treatment, including domestic violence; and Article 17 imposes obligations to protect the person, home, and family from unjust attack;

> Rights to be recognized by and treated equally before the law and a right of non-discrimination (Articles 2, 3, 16, and 26);

> Rights to a remedy and to access to justice, including a fair and public hearing in non-criminal claims (Articles 2 and 14); and

Due process rights that are integral to the criminal system (Articles 9, 10, 14 and 15).

The US has also signed, but not ratified, CEDAW and the CRC. As a signatory, while it is not legally bound to implement the specific provisions of those treaties, the US must not act to defeat their object and purpose.

CEDAW requires that there are measures, including in the criminal justice system, to ensure that women are protected from discrimination, exploitation, and harm. The CRC also requires that particular measures be in place to protect children from various forms of harm caused by criminal acts, and to ensure access to rehabilitative services where necessary. Guiding Instruments

The UN's Basic Principles for Victims was "designed to assist governments and the international community in their efforts to secure justice and assistance for victims of crime and victims of abuse of power." There have been a large number of follow-up conferences and activities that governments have organized on the basis of the Basic Principles for Victims.

For example, the UN Economic and Social Council has monitored the implementation of the Basic Principles for Victims by adopting its own resolutions recommending steps for governments and the United Nations to take in ensuring rights for victims of crime. Stemming from the Economic and Social Council's series of resolutions, which have included calls for continued research and technical assistance, the United Nations secretary general and the United Nations Crime Prevention and Criminal Justice Programme have produced a guide for policymakers on implementing the Basic Principles for Victims, a handbook for victims on use and application of the Basic Principles for Victims, and a toolkit for professionals on assessing police, prosecutorial, and judicial policies and practices relating to victims and witnesses. At least two countries, France and Canada, have implemented the Basic Principles for Victims in domestic legislation.

Governments in Europe have also taken steps to ensure that minimum standards are drawn up to protect the rights of victims of crime and guarantee their access to justice. On March 15, 2001, the European Council, a body of the European Union, issued the European Union Framework Decision on the Standing of Victims in Criminal Proceedings, which is legally binding on the member states of the European Union. The Framework Decision includes provisions similar to most of the Basic Principles for Victims.

Some commentators on the Basic Principles for Victims have noted that "twenty years after its adoption . . . the principles contained in this Declaration have been poorly implemented in national legislation and policies." Nevertheless, there is significant evidence that governments throughout the world, including the United States, have gone a long way to protect the rights of crime victims in their domestic legislation and practices.

International Consensus of Crime Victims' Rights and Interests

Upon the recommendation of the UN Economic and Social Council in 1993, the UN secretary general surveyed governments, of which 44 responded, and produced a report on governmental use of and adherence to the Basic Principles for Victims. The United States did not respond to the survey. The main findings of the secretary general can be summarized in the following chart:

Right of a Crime Victim to Government ("State") Responses

Claim a remedy	Thirty-eight states [Author's note: "state" means "nation"] made it mandatory for victims to be able to claim a remedy in all cases. In four states it was mandatory only in specific cases, and in two states this was subject to the discretion of the government. In 32 states, victims did not have to pay to obtain redress. In nine additional states this policy was adhered to "usually."
Restitution	In all responding states [nations], criminal offenders were bound to provide fair restitution to victims. For almost all states restitution included the return of property, payment for harm or loss suffered, and reimbursement of expenses incurred as a result of victimization.
Information	Half of the states [nations] responded that victims were informed of their right to claim a remedy on a mandatory basis. Two-thirds of the states reported that victims were informed of their role in judicial or administrative proceedings, and were informed of the timing and schedule of the process as well as the final disposition, particularly when victims had requested such information or when a serious violent crime was involved.
Participation	Thirty-three states [nations] always allowed the victims' views to be presented at appropriate stages of the criminal proceedings where their personal interests were affected. More than 80 percent of the responding states noted that victims were able to present their concerns either in person or through an attorney or prosecutor.
Expeditious Procedures	Twenty-eight states indicated that redress occurred in less than one year. In 10 states, the average was two to three years. In three states-Australia, Ghana, and Haiti-obtaining redress might take three years or more.
Privacy and Safety	Sixty percent of responding states [nations] reported that measures were always or usually taken to protect the privacy of victims, as well as of their families and witnesses on their behalf, and to protect them from intimidation and retaliation. More than half of the responding states said that they endeavored to ensure the safety of victims and their families and witnesses.

Compensation   For victims who did not get financial restitution from the offender, and other forms one-third of states [nations] filled this gap by providing financial of Assistance compensation to the victim. In addition, victims received material assistance in 23 states, medical assistance in 33 states, psychological assistance in 21 states and social assistance in 33 states. In almost all states, assistance was provided to the victims to enable them to present their concerns throughout the legal process. The use of victims' aid associations as a mechanism for providing assistance was reported by 11 governments.

G. Sources of Victim Participation Laws

1. Modern State Constitutional Victims' Rights Laws

The following excerpts discuss the state *constitutional* rights of victims. Many states give victims statutory rights instead of, or in addition to, constitutional rights. Since 2005, when the article was written, more states have enacted constitutional rights for victims. These laws may be found at NCVLI.org.

Douglas E. Beloof, *The Third Wave of Victims' Rights: Standing, Remedy and Review*
2005 B.Y.U. L. Rev. 255

State constitutional rights of victims can be classified into broad and specific rights. Broad rights include the victims' rights to fairness, respect, dignity, privacy, freedom from abuse, due process and a right to reasonable protection. Nineteen state constitutions provide for "fairness" and/or "due process" to victims. One or more of the rights to "respect," "dignity" and "freedom from abuse" appear in twenty-one state constitutions. The express right to "privacy" for victims can be found in six constitutions. Nine constitutions provide for victims' right to "reasonable protection."

Victims' specific rights can be parsed into the categories of due process, protection and privacy. Due process rights include rights to be notified, be present and be heard at particular stages of the criminal process. Typically, victims' right to be present is limited to critical stages of the criminal process or stages where a defendant also has a right to be present. Victims have rights to notice of their rights and notice of criminal proceedings. While the most common victims' right is to speak at sentencing, some constitutions provide for the right to speak at pretrial release or bail hearings and to be heard concerning a negotiated plea. Constitutions in certain states give victims a right to confer with the prosecution concerning charging or disposition. Some constitutions grant victims the right to be heard at post-conviction release hearings, such as parole hearings. Rights of protection include notice of pre-trial release, imprisonment and post-sentence release or escape. Victims have rights to speedy trial or prompt disposition. Some provide the right to confer with prosecutors. Victims have the right to attend the trial in many jurisdictions.

When victims are exercising their rights, they are no longer merely witnesses or third parties in the criminal process. Rather, victims are "participants" in the criminal process. Participant means "crime victim with rights of intermittent participation in the criminal [trial] process." Victims are participants because they possess independent rights to participate at certain stages of the criminal process. For example, victims have an independent right to give impact statements at sentencing, typically including the right to give a sentencing recommendation. Victims may address the court at sentencing regardless of whether they are called as witnesses by either party and despite the objection of either party. Thus, victims at sentencing are not *witnesses* called by parties to give victim impact *testimony*, but rather are independent *participants* at sentencing hearings with a right to *present* impact information and sentencing recommendations.

Victims are participants, but not full parties to felony criminal cases. For example, victims do not have the right to independently prosecute felony criminal trials, and their role at trial is generally limited to that of observer and witness. Victims do not have to be full parties to exercise their participatory rights in trial courts. While victims are participants in the criminal process when exercising their rights, victims are full parties for purposes of defending their rights. Thus, victims defending against a rights violation in trial or appellate courts are full parties to the rights litigation, while victims exercising rights in trial court are participants in the criminal process.

A right must be personal to victims before they have standing, remedy and review. This requirement does not really pose a problem to victim standing because state constitutional victims' rights are personal to the victim in every state constitution. The personal nature of these rights is revealed by the plain language of the constitutional provisions, as well as relevant court opinions. The titles of the constitutional sections clearly delineate the rights as "Victims' Rights" or "Rights of Crime Victims." The texts of the amendments also make apparent that the rights are personal to the victim by expressly stating that "victims have the right to" or "victims have the following rights," or similar language. State court opinions confirm that victims' rights are personal to the victim. Victims may waive their own rights.

Note: A substantial majority of state constitutions provide for crime victims' rights. A recent effort, named Marsy's Law for All, has reinvigorated the effort to enact enforceable constitutional rights for crime victims. https://marsyslaw.us/

2. Modern Statutes

An important example of a modern victims' rights statute the federal Crime Victims' Rights Act of 2004. This landmark legislation providing modern victims' rights only in federal prosecutions:

18 U.S.C. § 3771. Crime victims' rights.

(a) Rights of crime victims.—A crime victim has the following rights:

(1) The right to be reasonably protected from the accused.

(2) The right to reasonable, accurate, and timely notice of any public court proceeding, or any parole proceeding, involving the crime or of any release or escape of the accused.

(3) The right not to be excluded from any such public court proceeding, unless the court, after receiving clear and convincing evidence, determines that testimony by the victim would be materially altered if the victim heard other testimony at that proceeding.

(4) The right to be reasonably heard at any public proceeding in the district court involving release, plea, sentencing, or any parole proceeding.

(5) The reasonable right to confer with the attorney for the Government in the case.

(6) The right to full and timely restitution as provided in law.

(7) The right to proceedings free from unreasonable delay.

(8) The right to be treated with fairness and with respect for the victim's dignity and privacy.

(9) The right to be informed in a timely manner of any plea bargain or deferred prosecution agreement.

(10) The right to be informed of the rights under this section and the services described in section 503(c) of the Victims' Rights and Restitution Act of 1990 (42 U.S.C. 10607(c)) and provided contact information for the Office of the Victims' Rights Ombudsman of the Department of Justice.

(b) Rights afforded.—

(1) In general.—In any court proceeding involving an offense against a crime victim, the court shall ensure that the crime victim is afforded the rights described in subsection (a). Before making a determination described in subsection (a)(3), the court shall make every effort to permit the fullest attendance possible by the victim and shall consider reasonable alternatives to the exclusion of the victim from the criminal proceeding. The reasons for any decision denying relief under this chapter shall be clearly stated on the record.

(2) Habeas corpus proceedings.—

(A) In general.—In a Federal habeas corpus proceeding arising out of a State conviction, the court shall ensure that a crime victim is afforded the rights described in paragraphs (3), (4), (7), and (8) of subsection (a).

(B) Enforcement.—

(i) In general. — These rights may be enforced by the crime victim or the crime victim's lawful representative in the manner described in paragraphs (1) and (3) of subsection (d).

(ii) Multiple victims. — In a case involving multiple victims, subsection (d)(2) shall also apply.

(C) Limitation. — This paragraph relates to the duties of a court in relation to the rights of a crime victim in Federal habeas corpus proceedings arising out of a State conviction, and does not give rise to any obligation or requirement applicable to personnel of any agency of the Executive Branch of the Federal Government.

(D) Definition. — For purposes of this paragraph, the term "crime victim" means the person against whom the State offense is committed or, if that person is killed or incapacitated, that person's family member or other lawful representative.

(c) Best efforts to accord rights. —

(1) Government. — Officers and employees of the Department of Justice and other departments and agencies of the United States engaged in the detection, investigation, or prosecution of crime shall make their best efforts to see that crime victims are notified of, and accorded, the rights described in subsection (a).

(2) Advice of attorney. — The prosecutor shall advise the crime victim that the crime victim can seek the advice of an attorney with respect to the rights described in subsection (a).

(3) Notice. — Notice of release otherwise required pursuant to this chapter shall not be given if such notice may endanger the safety of any person.

(d) Enforcement and limitations. —

(1) Rights. — The crime victim or the crime victim's lawful representative, and the attorney for the Government may assert the rights described in subsection (a). A person accused of the crime may not obtain any form of relief under this chapter.

(2) Multiple crime victims. — In a case where the court finds that the number of crime victims makes it impracticable to accord all of the crime victims the rights described in subsection (a), the court shall fashion a reasonable procedure to give effect to this chapter that does not unduly complicate or prolong the proceedings.

(3) Motion for relief and writ of mandamus. — The rights described in subsection (a) shall be asserted in the district court in which a defendant is being prosecuted for the crime or, if no prosecution is underway, in the district court in the district in which the crime occurred. The district court shall take up and decide any motion asserting a victim's right forthwith. If the district

court denies the relief sought, the movant may petition the court of appeals for a writ of mandamus. The court of appeals may issue the writ on the order of a single judge pursuant to circuit rule or the Federal Rules of Appellate Procedure. The court of appeals shall take up and decide such application forthwith within 72 hours after the petition has been filed, unless the litigants, with the approval of the court, have stipulated to a different time period for consideration. In deciding such application, the court of appeals shall apply ordinary standards of appellate review. In no event shall proceedings be stayed or subject to a continuance of more than five days for purposes of enforcing this chapter. If the court of appeals denies the relief sought, the reasons for the denial shall be clearly stated on the record in a written opinion.

(4) Error. — In any appeal in a criminal case, the Government may assert as error the district court's denial of any crime victim's right in the proceeding to which the appeal relates.

(5) Limitation on relief. — In no case shall a failure to afford a right under this chapter provide grounds for a new trial. A victim may make a motion to re-open a plea or sentence only if —

> (A) the victim has asserted the right to be heard before or during the proceeding at issue and such right was denied;

> (B) the victim petitions the court of appeals for a writ of mandamus within 14 days; and

> (C) in the case of a plea, the accused has not pled to the highest offense charged.

> This paragraph does not affect the victim's right to restitution as provided in title 18, United States Code.

(6) No cause of action. — Nothing in this chapter shall be construed to authorize a cause of action for damages or to create, to enlarge, or to imply any duty or obligation to any victim or other person for the breach of which the United States or any of its officers or employees could be held liable in damages. Nothing in this chapter shall be construed to impair the prosecutorial discretion of the Attorney General or any officer under his direction.

(e) Definitions. — For the purposes of this chapter:

(1) Court of appeals. — The term "court of appeals" means —

> (A) the United States court of appeals for the judicial district in which a defendant is being prosecuted; or

> (B) for a prosecution in the Superior Court of the District of Columbia, the District of Columbia Court of Appeals.

(2) Crime victim. —

    (A) In general. — The term "crime victim" means a person directly and proximately harmed as a result of the commission of a Federal offense or an offense in the District of Columbia.

    (B) Minors and certain other victims. — In the case of a crime victim who is under 18 years of age, incompetent, incapacitated, or deceased, the legal guardians of the crime victim or the representatives of the crime victim's estate, family members, or any other persons appointed as suitable by the court, may assume the crime victim's rights under this chapter, but in no event shall the defendant be named as such guardian or representative.

(3) District court; court. — The terms "district court" and "court" include the Superior Court of the District of Columbia.

f. (omitted)

3. Anti-Rape Reform

Anti-rape reform issues are woven into the chapter on victim privacy. Other chapters examine participation rights that apply to cases in general, including sexual assault cases. The central themes in anti-rape reform are preventing secondary victimization in the criminal process and reexamining relevance. The defense often puts the victims' character and veracity on trial. Reforms seek to curtail inappropriate procedures that subject victims to smear tactics and invasions of privacy. A separate, but impartial reform is the change of the mental state requirement for rape from purposeful to reckless. The last reform is covered in criminal law classes.

4. Domestic Violence Reform

Domestic violence law reform has reflected the conflicting perceptions of the domestic violence victims' (and defendant's) circumstances. On the one hand, some urge that a domestic violence victim, like other victims, is a person whose autonomous choices concerning prosecution or non-prosecution should be respected. On the other hand, and partly, perhaps because the victim is incapable of making a truly autonomous choice given ongoing violence, some urge the mandatory prosecution of batterers despite a victim's desire not to prosecute. One's opinion on these matters is often determinative of one's perspective on whether battered women should have victims' rights. The argument goes that a victim is incapable of autonomous choice over whether a case should be prosecuted because they are incapable of autonomously exercising victims' rights. Nevertheless, the authors are unaware of any law specifically denying domestic violence victims access to victims' rights.

In the criminal process, domestic violence law reform has two prongs. The first, is the mandatory nature of the process. Mandatory arrest and mandatory prosecution are commonplace, particularly in urban jurisdictions. Second, is the diversion into treatment for the offender. California, for example, does not permit diversion so prosecutes all provable cases. Domestic violence procedures are examined in a discrete chapter.

5. Third Party Practice

Conventional third-party practice in criminal cases is an important and occasionally overlooked source of crime victim protections. While modern crime victim rights give victims the status of participants—a distinct status from a third party but less than a full party—victims may also take advantage of traditional third party procedures. For example, individuals whose evidentiary privileges or legal confidentiality protections are threatened by subpoena or questioning have standing to move to quash the subpoena or refuse to answer questions. In such proceedings, victims may choose to be represented by their own lawyer. This type of due process is not conventionally thought of as being about victims' rights because enforcement of confidentiality is available to all witnesses, including crime victims. Because sexual assault cases more frequently involve defense efforts to seek private information in order to adversely affect the victims' credibility, these cases commonly involve third party practice.

6. Common Law

There is a rich history of victim participation in the criminal process. A variety of these common law victim accommodations survive. They frequently take the form of judge-made common law or codified common law. As examples, the victim's right to approach a grand jury is examined and at common law a victim had no obligation to speak to the defense before trial or the prosecution until subpoenaed to testify in a proceeding. In Chapter 9 on Trial, the victim's ability to privately prosecute petty offenses is explored.

Moreover, the advent of victims' rights has increasing relevance in modern judicially created criminal procedure. Courts continue to exercise their common law authority to alter procedures, taking into account victims' interests.

One dramatic modern example is the trend that can be seen in what appears to be the end of abatement *ab initio*. [*ab initio* means "from the beginning"]. Abatement occurs when a defendant is convicted at the trial court level, but dies before appeals of the conviction are finalized. The theory is that all injuries resulting from the crime are buried with the offender. Abatement *ab initio* allows a defendant to stand as if he had never been convicted of a crime. The theory may make sense if the state alone suffers injury. The theory unravels when victim injuries are recognized. Denying the victim a conviction results in a secondary victimization because the state erases both official recognition of the crime occurred and the accused's guilt. Moreover, a very real practical result is that victims cannot obtain restitution from a convict (or their estate) where there is no conviction.

An increasing number of courts are using their common law authority to end or limit abatement *ab initio* because of crime victim interests. For this and other areas in which judges are weighing victim interests, *see* Douglas E. Beloof, *Weighing Victims' Interests in Judicially Crafted Criminal Procedure*, 56 Cath. L. Rev. 1135 (2007).

7. Courts' Jurisdiction over Crime Victims

In felony cases, victims are not full parties to the criminal action. Generally, courts have more expansive authority over parties than non-parties. Where courts do not possess jurisdiction, it may not be possible to compel victims to comply with court orders, for example certain discovery orders. For example, does a court have jurisdiction to order a rape victim to submit to a psychiatric or physical exam; can a court order a widow whose husband was killed in a home invasion to open her home to the defense? A victim's claim of absence of jurisdiction may ensure their privacy.

8. Judicial and Prosecutorial Discretion

Finally, while not a victims' right at all, prosecutorial and judicial discretion can be exercised to embrace victim participation. As victims become more familiar participants in the process, judges and prosecutors become more willing to exercise their discretion to be more inclusive of victims. For example, courts have discretion to listen to a wide range of information concerning sentencing, including victim impact statements and victims' sentencing recommendations. Thus, even without a legislated right for victims to speak at sentencing, courts in their discretion may allow it.

In sum, the field of crime victims' law is far broader than modern crime victim's constitutional and statutory rights. Important other sources of crime victim law in criminal procedure include feminist procedural law reforms, preexisting third party procedures, the common law, the courts' limited jurisdiction over crime victims, and the discretion of government actors.

Chapter 2

Defining the "Victim"

Introduction

How the term "victim" is defined is critically important to the operation of victims' rights provisions. This chapter describes legal definitions of the victim, typically set forth in state constitutional amendments and statutes protecting victims' rights. As a practical matter, however, the definition of crime victim is also controlled by cultural and institutional biases that operate within the discretionary authority of actors in the criminal process. Finally, biased actions by prosecutors, jurors, and legislators reflect the powerful influence of the culture in deciding who is "worthy" of victim status.

A. Legal Definitions of "Victim"

The "victim" is generally defined in two distinct ways, either as the person harmed (or potentially harmed) by the criminal act or the particular person harmed. As a result, the legally defined category of "victim" is circumscribed by what acts and accompanying mental states legislative bodies decide are crimes. New types of crimes, such as stalking, create new types of victims. Crimes off the books, such as adultery, eliminate a type of victim.

Consider the following typical definitions of victims.

18 U.S.C. 3771(e)

. . . [C]rime victim means a person directly and proximately harmed as a result of the commission of a federal offense or an offense in the District of Columbia.

Ariz. Const. Art. 2 § 2.1

"Victim" means a person against whom the criminal offense has been committed or, if the person is incapacitated, the person's spouse, parent, child or other lawful representative, except if the person is in custody for an offense as is the accused.

California Const., Art. 1 § 28(e)

"Victim" means a person who suffers direct threatened physical, psychological, or financial harm as a result of the commission of a crime or delinquent act.

Mass. Stat. 258B § 1

"Victim" [means] any natural person who suffers direct or threatened physical, emotional, or financial harm as the result of the commission or attempted commission of a crime or delinquency offense, as demonstrated by the issuance of a complaint or indictment, the family members of such person if the person is a minor, incompetent or deceased. . . .

OR. REV. STAT. § 131.007

. . . except as otherwise specifically provided or unless the context requires otherwise, "victim" means the person or persons who have suffered financial, social, psychological or physical harm as a result of a crime and includes, in the case of a homicide or abuse of corpse in any degree, a member of the immediate family of the decedent and, in the case of a minor victim, the legal guardian of the minor.

Notes

1. Which is the broadest definition? Should there be any limit on the kinds of crimes that confer "victim" status?

2. Should victims' rights be extended to victims of crimes for which the *mens rea* is mere negligence (e.g., negligent homicide) rather than intent or recklessness? Consider the following argument by Professor Dubber in VICTIMS IN THE WAR ON CRIME: THE USE AND ABUSE OF VICTIM'S RIGHTS (2002) against extending victims' rights to such crimes:

> [N]egligent crimes differ from intentional ones in that they do not represent an attempt by one person to subjugate another. They may interfere with a person's autonomy, but not for the greater glory of another. The victim of a negligent crime does not experience herself as being subjugated by another person. She suffers harm, even serious harm, to her ability to exercise her capacity for autonomy but not the indignity of having been treated as the means to another person's self-aggrandizement, taken in its strict sense, that is, as the expansion of the offender's self to engulf the victim as a mere appendage.

> It is this personal assault on her personhood that entitles the crime victim to victims' rights, in particular the right to have the offender punished. The offender's punishment is nothing but the dramatic reaffirmation that autonomy after the offender's criminal attempt to deny that autonomy for the sake of her own. And a crucial aspect of that reaffirmation is putting the offender in her place, among the community of persons, alongside the victim. The victim's personhood therefore is reaffirmed by exposing the offender's attempt to deny it as unsuccessful and in fact, futile. Punishment communicates to the offender, the victim, and the onlooker that the offender has not succeeded, and could never have succeeded, in reducing the victim to a nonperson. The offender at best can treat the victim as a nonperson; she cannot transform him into one.

> This process of autonomy affirmation does not, and cannot, take place in negligent crimes. Since negligent crimes are not crimes in this sense, their

victims are not victims of crime. There are "objects" of negligent crimes, as there are "objects" of torts, only in the general, formal sense is an object as that person who suffers the harm described in the definition of the negligent crime or tort.

3. Does Professor Dubber's argument rest on the idea that crimes of negligence should not be included in the criminal code, an argument rejected in many states? *See generally* Kenneth W. Simons, *Culpability and Retributive Theory: The Problem of Criminal Negligence*, 5 J. Contemporary Issues 365 (1994) (reviewing the competing positions on whether to punish crimes of negligence).

———————

Most jurisdictions extend victims' rights only to natural persons, thereby excluding business and governmental entities from their protection. However, for purposes of restitution, many states include such entities.

Michigan Comp. Laws Ann. § 780.826 (Restitution)

"Victim" means an individual who suffers direct or threatened physical, financial, or emotional harm as a result of the commission of a misdemeanor. Victim also includes a sole proprietorship, partnership, corporation, association, governmental entity, or any other legal entity that suffers direct physical or financial harm as a result of a misdemeanor.

Notes

1. If a victim's rights statute gives a right to restitution to a "person," does the government qualify? The federal restitution statute confers a right to restitution to "a victim," defined as "a person directly and proximately harmed as a result of the commission of an offense of which restitution may be ordered." 18 U.S.C. § 3663A(a)(2) (emphasis added). In *United States v. Ekanem*, 383 F.3d 40 (2d Cir. 2004), the court concluded that this phrase should be construed to authorize restitution in favor of the government, reasoning that, read in context, Congress intended "person" to include government.

2. Do entities deserve to be covered by victims' rights enactments? Professor Dubber argues "apersonal victims have no place in the victims' rights movement or in a system of law constructed from the victim's point of view. Apersonal victims are not victims whose rights can be violated by crime or vindicated by law. Insofar as rights are attached to persons, and to persons only, apersonal entities such as corporations or institution are as incapable of bearing rights as are animals or any other entity without personhood." Markus Dirk Dubber, Victims in the War on Crime: The Use and Abuse of Victims' Rights 216 (2002).

3. For an article discussing the definition of "victim" under Marsy's Law, which is enacted in several state constitutions, *see* Geoffrey Sant, *Victimless Crime Takes on a New Meaning: Does California's Victims' Rights Amendment Eliminate the Right to be Recognized as a Victim?*, 39 Legis. J. 43 (2013).

4. For articles discussing the application of victims' rights in environmental crimes, *see* Ashley Ferguson, *We're Victims Too: The Need for Greater Protection of Environmental Crime Victims under the Crime Victims' Rights Act*, 19 PENN STATE ENV. L. REV. 287 (2011); Andrew Atkins, *A Complicated Environment: The Problem with Extending Victims' Rights to Victims' of Environmental Crimes*, 67 WASH. & LEE 1623 (2010); Judson W. Starr, Brian L. Flack, Alison D. Foley, *A New Intersection between Environmental Crimes and Victims' Rights*, 23 WTR NAT'L RESOURCES & ENV. 41 (2009).

5. For an article exploring victim definitions, *see* Andrew Nash, *Victims by Definition*, 85 WASH. U. L. REV. 1419 (2008).

6. Does the extension of victim's rights to nonpersons have anything to teach us about the rights of nonpersons? *See* Douglas E. Beloof, *Crime Victims' Rights: Critical Concepts for Animal Rights*, 7 ANIMAL L. REV. 19 (2001).

B. Attaining the Legal Status of "Victim"

1. Is the Charging Decision Relevant?

At what point does the person harmed attain the legal status of "victim"? In theory, one way to determine victim status would be through the same formal legal mechanisms that determine whether a suspected criminal is a criminal. For example, a person might achieve "victim" status when the defendant is found guilty, either at the end of a trial or upon entry of a guilty plea. Under this approach, a person would, in a sense, be proven a victim of a defendant beyond a reasonable doubt. It would logically follow from this approach that a victim's participation in the criminal process (apart from testifying as a witness) would begin only after conviction. This approach would necessarily mean that crime victims would have legal rights at only a few points in the process after conviction—for example, during sentencing or parole hearings.

Most victims' rights statutes do not impose such a limiting requirement. Instead, some statutes link formal victim status to the filing of criminal charges, while others clearly apply pre-charge. Creating legally-recognized victim status when charges are filed effectively lowers the standard of proof to probable cause (the standard required for initiating criminal cases) and creates victim status at a time when the defendant is legally presumed to be innocent. At the same time, such a definition ties into the charging decision of the prosecutor.

Who determines whether a person is an "victim," of a crime? The majority of statutes defining "victim" do not speak to this. A rare exception to statutory silence on this point is the Maine statute, which provides: "In this section a person who is certified by the prosecutor to be a victim, shall be considered a victim." ME. REV. STAT. ANN. tit. 5, § 200E. In other states, an alleged victim would simply be the person against whom the offense was alleged to have been committed, presumably as determined by the court in cases of dispute. In Arizona, victim status is extended as soon as the police have determined by "probable cause" that a crime against the victim has occurred. Ariz. 13-44 OR. In most jurisdictions it will be up to the courts to determine who is a victim, and when.

In any scheme for defining rights, the decision of the police and the prosecutor may effectively determine the status of a person as a victim — or non-victim — as shown in the following case.

In re McNulty

597 F.3d 344, 346–53 (6th Cir. 2010)

This petition for a writ of mandamus arises from the proceedings in *United States v. Arctic Glacier Int'l Inc.,* No. 1:09-cr-00149 (S.D. Ohio). In that case, Arctic Glacier International was charged in a criminal information with violating 15 U.S.C. § 1 by participating in "a conspiracy to suppress and eliminate competition by allocating packaged-ice customers in southeastern Michigan and the Detroit, Michigan metropolitan area." Petitioner Martin McNulty seeks a writ of mandamus to enforce his rights as a victim of this conspiracy under the Crime Victims' Rights Act (CVRA), 18 U.S.C. § 3771.

I.

Arctic Glacier International, Inc., the wholly-owned subsidiary of Arctic Glacier, Inc., which is the wholly-owned subsidiary of the Arctic Glacier Income Fund (collectively referred to as "Arctic Glacier"), produces packaged ice and sells packaged ice in Canada and certain regions of the United States. Arctic Glacier has admitted to a felony offense of participating in a conspiracy to allocate customers of packaged ice sold in Southeastern Michigan and the Detroit, Michigan area beginning January 1, 2001 and continuing through at least July 17, 2007. . . . According to the plea agreement that Arctic Glacier has reached with the government, sales of packaged ice affected by the conspiracy totaled $50.7 million.

According to his testimony before the district court, Martin McNulty was an executive for Party Time Ice, which was acquired by Arctic Glacier in December of 2004. . . . After Party Time was acquired by Arctic Glacier, McNulty alleges that he was instructed by Arctic Glacier executive Keith Corbin to participate in the customer allocation conspiracy and that Corbin threatened to arrange a boycott by the industry if McNulty refused to do so. McNulty alleges that he refused to do so and expressed his opposition to the conspiracy. He alleges that Arctic Glacier fired him as a result of his refusal to participate in the conspiracy. . . .

Shortly after his termination in late January 2005, McNulty contacted the government and served as an informant in the subsequent antitrust investigation of Arctic Glacier. He alleges that, later in 2005, after the non-compete clause expired, he began applying to other packaged-ice companies, but that he was unable to find employment with any company. . . . He alleges that, as a result of this "blackball[ing,]" his earnings have been substantially reduced, his house has been foreclosed upon, his credit scores have fallen, he has been unemployed for extended periods of time, and he remains unemployed. . . .

On September 20, 2009, the United States filed a sealed information charging Arctic Glacier with a conspiracy "to allocate packaged-ice customers in southeastern Michigan and the Detroit, Michigan metropolitan area." On October 13, 2009, the United States filed a plea agreement pursuant to Federal Rule of Criminal Procedure 11(c)(1)(C) in which Arctic Glacier agreed to plead guilty to the above charge, the parties agreed to recommend a fine of $9 million, and the government agreed not to seek a restitution order.

The government informed McNulty, who had served as an informant during the assembly of the case, that he could request restitution through the probation officer. As per the probation officer's instructions, McNulty sent a letter and accompanying declaration to the probation officer on January 20, 2010 requesting $6.3 million in restitution and that he be recognized as a victim of Arctic Glacier pursuant to the CVRA. The district court [denied restitution holding] that:

The Court determines the victims of the offense in this case were the customers. . . . Mr. McNulty was an employee of defendant, not a customer. There is no evidence he was directly or proximately harmed by the conspiracy. . . .

On February 24, 2010, McNulty brought this petition for mandamus relief from the district court's February 22, 2010 denial of his request for victim status under the CVRA. . . .

II

A "crime victim" is defined under the CVRA as a person "directly and proximately harmed as a result of the commission of a Federal offense or an offense in the District of Columbia." 18 U.S.C. § 3771(e). Because our Court has not had the opportunity to determine whether a petitioner qualifies as a "victim" pursuant to the CVRA, we look to our sister Circuits for guidance.

"The requirement that the victim be 'directly and proximately harmed' encompasses the traditional 'but for' and proximate cause analyses." *In re Rendon Galvis,* 564 F.3d 170, 175 (2d Cir.2009) (citing *In re Antrobus,* 519 F.3d 1123, 1126 (10th Cir.2008) (Tymkovich, J., concurring) (noting that "direct[ ]" harm encompasses a "but-for" causation notion that is different from proximate harm)). "The necessary inquiry is [ ] fact-specific[.]" *Id.* (citations omitted).

The CVRA "instructs the district court to look at the offense itself only to determine the harmful effects the offense has on parties. Under the plain language of the statute, a party may qualify as a victim, even though it may not have been the target of the crime, as long as it suffers harm as a result of the crime's commission." *In re Stewart,* 552 F.3d 1285, 1289 (11th Cir.2008) (CVRA mandamus petition; circuit court held that mortgage borrowers were CVRA victims of conspiracy to deprive bank of honest services, where defendants were bank officer and co-conspirator whose offense caused borrowers to pay excess fees that defendants pocketed). *See, e.g., United States v.*

Johnson, 440 F.3d 832, 835-39, 849-50 (6th Cir.2006) (victims of four predicate criminal acts in RICO conspiracy conviction were MVRA victims, where district court found trial evidence established by a preponderance of the evidence that defendant was actively involved in all four predicate acts); *United States v. Washington,* 434 F.3d 1265, 1266-70 (11th Cir.2006) (police department and another property owner were MVRA victims as to police car and property damaged during chase of defendant fleeing after bank robbery); *Moore v. United States,* 178 F.3d 994, 1001 (8th Cir.1999) (bank customer was MVRA victim of attempted bank robbery; defendant had stood within six feet of customer and pointed sawed-off gun at him); *but see, e.g., In re Rendon Galvis,* 564 F.3d at 175 (mother was "not a crime victim under the CVRA because the harm to her son was not a direct and proximate result of conspiring to import cocaine into the United States, which is the crime of conviction [t]here.").

Thus, in the instant case, the issue becomes whether McNulty was directly and proximately harmed by criminal conduct in the course of the conspiracy or if the actions taken by defendants in the underlying case which allegedly harmed McNulty were merely ancillary to the conspiracy.

In making this determination, we must (1) look to the offense of conviction, based solely on facts reflected in the jury verdict or admitted by the defendant; and then (2) determine, based on those facts, whether any person or persons were "directly and proximately harmed as a result of the commission of [that] Federal offense." *Atl. States Cast Iron Pipe Co.,* 612 F.Supp.2d at 536 (collecting cases stating that this is the methodology used by courts in making this determination).

Here, the offense of conviction is violation of the Sherman Act, 15 U.S.C. § 1, which states: Every contract, combination in the form of trust or otherwise, or conspiracy, in restraint of trade or commerce among the several States, or with foreign nations, is declared to be illegal. Every person who shall make any contract or engage in any combination or conspiracy hereby declared to be illegal shall be deemed guilty of a felony, and, on conviction thereof, shall be punished by fine not exceeding $100,000,000 if a corporation, or, if any other person, $1,000,000, or by imprisonment not exceeding 10 years, or by both said punishments, in the discretion of the court.

"To sustain a § 1 claim, plaintiffs must prove . . . two essential elements: (1) That defendants entered into a contract, combination or conspiracy; and (2) That such contract, combination or conspiracy amounted to an unreasonable restraint of trade or commerce among the several States." *Cont'l Cablevision of Ohio, Inc. v. Am. Elec. Power Co.,* 715 F.2d 1115, 1118 (6th Cir.1983) (citations omitted).

In the plea agreement and at the sentencing hearing, Arctic Glacier pled guilty to "allocat[ing] packaged-ice customers in southeastern Michigan and the Detroit, Michigan metropolitan area." Thus, purported victims of the conspiracy to violate the Sherman Act must show that they were directly and proximately harmed by the defendants' entry into a conspiracy or by the defendants' actions in unreasonable restraint of interstate commerce.

Here, we agree with the district court's holding that McNulty is not a victim for the purposes of the CVRA. The alleged harm to McNulty stemmed from his firing for refusing to participate in the conspiracy and his "blackballing" from employment with packaged-ice companies until he stopped working with the government in exposing the conspiracy. If proven, these would indeed be harms to McNulty, but they are not criminal in nature, nor is there any evidence that they are normally associated with the crime of antitrust conspiracy. . . .

Additionally, that the harm must be "direct" requires that the harm to the victim be closely related to the conduct inherent to the offense, rather than merely tangentially linked. McNulty's firing is not sufficiently related to the offense of conviction for McNulty to qualify as a victim under the CVRA. While the escape from a bank robbery which damages a vehicle, *Washington,* 434 F.3d at 1266-70, or a gun being pointed at an innocent bystander in the course of a robbery, *Moore,* 178 F.3d at 1001, are direct and proximate harms to innocent bystanders that are not part of the elements of the crime, they are directly related to the crime itself (and are, in many instances, crimes in and of themselves). McNulty's firing and blackballing from the industry, if proved, are ancillary to the actions involved in forming a conspiracy and restraining interstate commerce. . . . Thus, the district court did not abuse its discretion in finding that McNulty was not a victim of the crime pursuant to the CVRA.

Notes

1. What if someone is technically a victim of the defendant's crime(s), but the charges are later dropped as part of a plea bargain? *See Littlefield v. Williams,* 540 S.E.2d 81 (S.C. 2000), in which the defendant, Williams, committed multiple white-collar crimes. The prosecutor decided to drop charges related to two alleged victims, Littlefield and Jeter. The South Carolina Supreme Court held that, while "a person becomes a victim the instant the crime is committed or attempted and he or she suffers a harm," once the criminal proceedings and post-conviction actions are resolved, the victim's rights terminate. *Id.* at 86. The court noted that a victim does have the right to be present and "involved in the criminal process concerning the specific charge related to the victim," but once those charges are resolved, the proceedings no longer involve the victim and therefore the rights no longer exist. *Id.* Should prosecutors have such unilateral power to determine who is a "victim"?

2. The Eighth Circuit in *In re McNulty* suggested that that McNulty might have a civil cause of action against the convicted defendants. Can civil justice provide an effective substitute for criminal justice in a fraud case? What about a homicide case? Cf. THE FAMILY OF RON GOLDMAN, HIS NAME IS RON: OUR SEARCH FOR JUSTICE (1997) (discussing successful civil suit in the wake of O.J. Simpson's acquittal on murder charges).

3. In one of the few victim cases to reach the United States Supreme Court, the Court held that federal district courts were not authorized to award restitution to any victim other than the victim of the offense for which the defendant was actually

convicted. The Court reasoned that the federal law providing that "a defendant convicted of an offense" may be ordered to "make restitution to any victim of such offense" authorized restitution only to victims of the offense of conviction. *Hughey v. United States*, 495 U.S. 411 (1990).

4. While the prosecution's indictment frames the issue of who is a "victim," it is not necessary that the victim be specifically named in an information or indictment or that harming the victim be an element of the offense. For instance, in a case cited by the Eighth Circuit in *In re McNulty*, the Eleventh Circuit rejected a claim from the government that certain borrowers harmed by a fraud by a bank employees could not be victims under the Crime Victim's Rights Act because only the bank (not the borrowers) were identified as victims in the criminal information:

> This argument implicitly and mistakenly assumes that any CVRA victim must be mentioned in the indictment or information. Put differently, it assumes that the identity of any CVRA victim must be an element of the offense itself.
>
> The CVRA, however, does not limit the class of crime victims to those whose identity constitutes an element of the offense or who happen to be identified in the charging document. The statute, rather, instructs the district court to look at the offense itself only to determine the harmful effects the offense has on parties. Under the plain language of the statute, a party may qualify as a victim, even though it may not have been the target of the crime, as long as it suffers harm as a result of the crime's commission.

In re Stewart, 552 F.3d 1285, 1289 (11th Cir. 2008).

5. Victims' rights laws generally define a victim by looking to the elements of the offense to see whom the defendant committed the offense against. But what if the offense does not involve any actions against a victim? In *State v. Houston*, 9 P.3d 188 (Utah App. 2000), the defendant had sex with a young victim. He was charged with forcible sodomy—that is, sodomy without the consent of the victim. At trial, he claimed that he had made a reasonable mistake in believing the victim had consented. The jury apparently credited the defendant's version—or at least found that the prosecution had not proven the elements beyond a reasonable doubt. The jury acquitted the defendant of forcible sodomy, but convicted him of simple sodomy, which remains a crime in Utah. The trial judge then ordered the defendant to pay restitution to the victim—$165 for therapy and medical expenses. The appellate court reversed, concluding that a conviction for simple sodomy did not involve lack of consent or force. Accordingly, on that finding, the victim was a "co-participant" in the crime rather than a victim. Because she could not have recovered anything in a civil suit on the same facts, restitution in a criminal case was inappropriate.

6. Many states have extended victims' rights protections to victims of acts of juvenile offenders, even though such acts are not typically defined as crimes. *See, e.g.*, Md. Code Ann., Crim. Law. § 9-301 ("'Victim' means a person against whom a crime or delinquent act has been committed or attempted.").

2. Tracing Harm to the Victim

Many statutes that define a "victim" entitled to exercise crime victims' rights do so in terms of harm to the victim. For example, the federal Crime Victims' Rights Act defines "victim" as "a person directly and proximately harmed as a result of the commission of a Federal offense. . . ." 18 U.S.C. § 3771(e). How tight does the connection have to be between the defendant's crime and the victim's harm in order to confer victim status? The following cases explore this issue.

United States v. Hunter

2008 WL 53125 (D. Utah 2008)

Dale A. Kimball, District Judge, Memorandum Decision and Order

Background

On February 12, 2007, the Antrobuses' 28-year-old daughter, Vanessa Quinn, was tragically killed by Sulejman Talovic at the Trolley Square Shopping Center in one of Salt Lake's most devastating recent criminal incidents. Talovic used a .38 Smith & Wesson handgun and a 12-gauge shotgun to kill five and seriously injure four innocent shoppers at the mall. Quinn was shot with the .38 Smith & Wesson handgun. Talovic bought the .38 Smith & Wesson handgun from Defendant Hunter in June or July of 2006. Hunter is charged in this action with unlawfully selling the firearm to Talovic because he reasonably believed him to be a minor.

Hunter pled guilty to Count I of the Indictment and Count I of the Superseding Misdemeanor Information. Count I of the Indictment charges Hunter with being an unlawful user or addict of controlled substances in possession of a firearm in violation of 18 U.S.C. § 922(g)(3). Count I of the Superseding Misdemeanor Information charges that Hunter unlawfully sold, delivered, or otherwise transferred a handgun to a person he knew or had reasonable cause to believe was a juvenile in violation of 18 U.S.C. §§ 922(x)(1) and 924(a)(6)(B)(i). Count I of the Indictment has no relevance to the present motion.

Hunter's Statement by Defendant in Advance of Plea of Guilty admits to the following facts in relation to Count I of the Superseding Misdemeanor Information:

I did unlawfully sell, deliver, or otherwise transfer a handgun (a Smith & Wesson .38 Special, Model 36 pistol) to a person I had reasonable cause to believe was a juvenile; all in violation of Title 18, United States Code, Section 922(x)(1). The firearm referenced here and in the Indictment was manufactured outside the State of Utah, and I acknowledge that its presence in Utah indicates that it affected interstate commerce.

Discussion

Motion to Determine Crime Victim Status

The Antrobuses' motion seeks declarations that Vanessa Quinn is a victim of Hunter's offense and that they can assert her rights on her behalf pursuant to the

Crime Victims' Rights Act ("CVRA"), 18 U.S.C. § 3771. As Vanessa Quinn's parents, the Antrobuses undoubtedly qualify to be representatives for their deceased daughter under the provision of the CVRA that allows "family members" to assume the crime victim's rights when the victim is not able to assert her own rights. *Id.* § 3771(e). Therefore, the principal issue raised by the Antrobuses' motion is whether Quinn is a victim of Hunter's crime under the CVRA.

A. CVRA

Unlike other victims' rights acts, the CVRA was passed as a means of making "victims independent participants in the criminal justice process" with standing to assert certain procedural and substantive rights. *Kenna v. United States District Court for the Central Dist. of California*, 435 F.3d 1011, 1013 (9th Cir. 2006); *United States v. Sharp*, 463 F.Supp.2d 556, 560 (E.D. Va. 2006). The CVRA guarantees crime victims eight different rights: (1) the right to be reasonably protected from the accused; (2) the right to notice of any public proceedings; (3) the right to be present during public court hearings; (4) the right to be reasonably heard at court proceedings; (5) the reasonable right to confer with the government's attorney; (6) the right to restitution; (7) the right to proceedings without unreasonable delay; and (8) the right to be treated with fairness and with respect for the victim's dignity and privacy. 18 U.S.C. § 3771(a). In this case, the Antrobuses assert that they have the right to make a victim impact statement at Hunter's sentencing and should be awarded $107,000 in restitution to cover funeral expenses and lost income.

In the CVRA, the term "crime victim" is defined as "a person directly and proximately harmed as a result of the commission of a Federal offense." *Id.* at 3771(e). Thus, a person must be directly harmed as a result of the offense and the harm must be proximate to the crime. During the floor debate of the CVRA, one of the bills primary sponsors noted that the definition of "victim" in the CVRA is an "intentionally broad definition because all victims of crime deserve to have their rights protected, whether or not they are the victim of the count charged." 150 Cong. Rec. S 10910, 10912 (daily ed. Oct. 9, 2004) (statement of Sen. Kyl). But despite this legislative history, at least one court has noted that the full Congress passed the CVRA knowing that the Supreme Court has interpreted similar language in prior victims' rights acts not to refer to uncharged conduct. See *United States v. Turner*, 367 F.Supp.2d 319, 326 (E.D.N.Y. 2005) (recognizing that the House report on the CVRA noted that 18 U.S.C. § 3771(a)(6) "makes no change in the law with respect to victims' ability to get restitution.").

In any event, the court must apply the language of the act itself. Under the CVRA, a victim must be both "directly and proximately" harmed by the offense. The term "proximate" means "lying very near or close" with the additional senses "(1) 'soon forthcoming; imminent'; (2) 'next preceding' <proximate cause>; and (3) 'nearly accurate'; approximate." Bryan A. Garner, MODERN LEGAL USAGE, at 711 (2d ed. 1995). "Proximate cause," of course, is a term of art in the law that while "elusive" emphasizes "the continuity of the sequence that produces an event" and refers to "a cause of which the law will take notice." *Id.* While one commentator "terms proximate cause 'concise gibberish,'" *id.*, Black's Law Dictionary fairly aptly defines it as "[t]hat which, in natural and continuous sequence, unbroken by any efficient intervening cause, produces injury, and without which the result would not have happened." BLACK'S LAW DICTIONARY, at 1225 (6th ed. 1990).

The only other court to examine the extent to which a person may qualify as a victim under the CVRA, looked not only to the language of the CVRA but to cases applying the VWPA and the Mandatory Victims Restitution Act ("MVRA") because all three statutes use the language "directly and proximately harmed." *Sharp*, 463 F. Supp.2d at 561–64. The definitions in these statutes are nearly identical. *See also* Paul G. Cassell, *Recognizing Victims in the Federal Rules of Criminal Procedure: Proposed Amendments in Light of the Crime Victims' Rights Act*, 2005 BYU L. REV. 835, 857 (noting that the CVRA's definition of "victim" comes from the earlier MVRA). . . .

In applying the recognized standards for proximate harm, this court concludes that Vanessa Quinn was not directly and proximately harmed by Hunter's sale of a firearm to a minor. Quinn and the Antrobuses are undoubtedly victims of Sulejman Talovic's crimes. But the nexus between Hunter's act of selling a firearm to a minor and Talovic's deadly rampage through a shopping mall eight months later is too factually and temporally attenuated. The Antrobuses argue that Hunter stated to federal officials that he thought Talovic might use the gun to rob a bank and that such a crime would be a violent crime. This statement, however, is not included in Hunter's Statement by Defendant in Advance of Guilty Plea. Nor do they demonstrate that the statement is anything other than general speculation. Even if Hunter believed that Talovic may commit a crime with the handgun, the nature of that crime was unforeseeable.

The Antrobuses rely on several cases in which the court determined direct and proximate harm existed. But in each of those cases, the harm was a result of the defendants' own actions, not the actions of an intervening actor. Because a determination of proximate harm is necessarily a fact-specific inquiry, the court finds these cases factually distinguishable from the present case. In *United States v. Donaby*, 349 F.3d 1046 (7th Cir. 2003), the court determined that a police department could be considered a victim under the MVRA because damage to a police department's car in a high-speed chase was directly and proximately caused by the defendant's bank robbery. *Id.* at 1053. The court recognized that the high-speed chase was a direct and foreseeable consequence of the robbery. *Id.* at 1055. In Donaby, there is no intervening actor, no temporal separation, and the defendant could foresee the damage as a result of the chase.

Moreover, in contrast to this case, the defendant in Donaby made the decision to engage in the high-speed chase in an attempt to successfully conclude his robbery. He also could have surrendered to police before the damage occurred. In this case, even at the time the gun was sold, Hunter had no knowledge as to Talovic's intentions. And, after the gun was sold, Hunter had no contact with Talovic.

The Antrobuses also rely on *United States v. Checora*, 175 F.3d 782 (10th Cir. 1999), in which the Tenth Circuit determined that a murder victim's children were victims of the murder under the MVRA because his death eliminated the child support payments they received. *Id.* at 795. The court concluded that the children were directly and proximately harmed as a result of their father's death because they lost, among other things, a source of financial support. *Id.* The defendant in Checora, however, committed the murder. There was no intervening actor. If the defendant in the present case was Sulejman Talovic, there is no question that Vanessa Quinn would be victims under the CVRA. Because this case is against Hunter, not Talovic, the court finds Checora factually inapplicable.

The only case to both analyze the definition of "victim" under the CVRA and involve the conduct of an intervening actor is Sharp. In Sharp, a woman sought to make a victim impact statement at the sentencing of a drug dealer who sold drugs to her former boyfriend. 463 F.Supp. at 557. The woman asserted that when her boyfriend consumed the drugs he purchased from the drug dealer, he abused her. *Id.* at 558–59. The court concluded that there was not sufficient evidence to demonstrate that the defendant's wrongful act of distributing marijuana directly and proximately harmed the girlfriend. *Id.* at 567. The court stated that the girlfriend "must show more than a mere possibility that an alleged act (the Defendant's federal crime) caused her boyfriend to physically and emotionally abuse her." *Id.* The court noted that "[i]ndividuals, whether 'high' on drugs or drug-fee, are responsible for their actions. The act of consuming marijuana by [the former] boyfriend, not the furnishing of it to him by the Defendant, was, at most, the proximate cause of [the girlfriend's] sustained injuries." *Id.* The court, therefore, concluded that the "former boyfriend's alleged behavior was an independent, intervening cause which broke the chain of necessary causation." *Id.* at 568.

This court agrees with the analysis of Sharp. The actions of Talovic were an independent, intervening cause which broke the necessary chain of causation. While the court does not want to minimize in any way the harm suffered by those who were killed, injured, or had loved ones killed or injured by Talovic, that harm is not sufficiently connected to Hunter's offense of unlawfully selling a firearm to a minor for this court to consider Hunter's actions to be the direct and proximate cause of the harm. The fact-specific inquiry necessary in this determination does not support a finding that Hunter could foresee Talovic's actions. There are cases that find an adequate connection in instances when a defendant hands a gun to a friend during a fight. But this is not such a case. The sale of the handgun was not in the heat of the moment. Hunter sold the gun to Talovic eight months before the shooting and there is no indication that he spoke to Talovic about his intentions. At most, Hunter surmised that Talovic might use it to rob a bank. This type of speculation does not demonstrate the type of knowledge or foreseeability necessary to finding Hunter's sale of the firearm to a minor to be the proximate cause of Quinn's death. . . .

While Quinn and the Antrobuses are clearly victims of a tragic crime, the court concludes that neither are victims, as that term is defined in the CVRA, of Hunter's offense of selling a firearm to a minor. The court concludes that the Antrobuses cannot demonstrate that Hunter's sale of a firearm to a minor "directly and proximately" caused Quinn's death.

Note

1. As discussed in Chapter 12, *infra*, the Antrobuses filed a petition for a writ of mandamus with the Tenth Circuit, asking the Circuit to overrule the district judge's decision. The Tenth Circuit declined to reverse the ruling. While conceding that the Antrobuses had presented a "difficult case," the Tenth Circuit held that "we cannot say that the district court was clearly wrong in its conclusion." *In re Antrobus*, 519 F.3d 1123, 1125 (10th Cir. 2008). Judge Tymkovich concurred to note:

> The harm must "proximately" result from the crime. That is the more difficult issue, but the record suggests that the following evidence could be developed to show that Talovic's crime was a reasonably foreseeable result of the illegal gun sale. (1) Hunter knew Talovic was a minor and could not legally purchase a gun in the first place; (2) the murder weapon was previously stolen; (3) Hunter heard Talovic's intent to commit bank robbery, a crime of violence where the use of a gun could reasonably result in a shooting; and, finally; (4) the shooting was not so remote in time as to be unforeseeable. I do not think it matters that Talovic committed a crime that is different from what he told Hunter; only that the crime could obviously and likely lead to violence. The language included in the indictment in fact makes clear that the government believed Hunter knew that Talovic "intended to carry or otherwise possess, or discharge or otherwise use the handgun in the commission of a crime of violence." If the intervening cause was foreseeable then proximate cause can be established. Taken together, these facts could establish that Ms. Quinn was a crime victim for purposes of the CVRA. This evidence may well be contained in the government's files. Sadly, the Antrobuses were not allowed a reasonable opportunity to make a better case.

In an effort to obtain ordinary appellate review of their claims, the Antrobuses then returned to the Tenth Circuit by filing an ordinary appeal. The Tenth Circuit, however, concluded that crime victims could not take such appeal from any sentence imposed in the case. *United States v. Hunter*, 548 F.3d 1308 (10th Cir. 2008). The Antrobuses also sought to obtain discovery from the Government to prove their claims. Their efforts, however, were rebuffed in the district court and in the Tenth Circuit. *In re Antrobus*, 563 F.3d 1092 (10th Cir. 2009). For a full recounting to the Antrobuses' saga in the courts, *see* Paul G. Cassell, *Protecting Crime Victims in Federal Appellate Courts: The Need to Broadly Construe the Crime Victims' Rights Act's Mandamus Provision*, 87 Den. U.L. Rev. 599 (2010).

Some crimes involve a potentially large number of victims. For example, a polluter may release a harmful substance into the air or water that harms an entire community. How many members of a community are victims of an environmental crime?

Consider the following ruling in which the government sought to have some of its witnesses who were residents of Libby, Montana, and were harmed by asbestos releases, recognized as "victims" in an environmental prosecution against the W.R. Grace Corporation and its responsible corporate executives.

United States of America v. W.R. Grace et al.

597 F. Supp. 2d 1157 (D. Mont. 2009)

David W. Molloy, District Judge.

At the motions hearing held in this matter on January 22, 2009, the Court granted defendants' motion under Fed. R. Evid. 615, determining lay witnesses would be excluded from the proceedings scheduled to commence on February 19, 2009. The government argues that some of its witnesses are victims of the crimes alleged in the Superseding Indictment, and are therefore entitled to exercise the rights Congress has granted to victims of federal criminal offenses through the enactment of the Crime Victim Rights Act, 18 U.S.C. § 3771 ("the Act"), one of which is the right to not be excluded from court proceedings. The issue before the Court is whether the Court's ruling that witnesses will be excluded from these proceedings conflicts with what the Act requires in this case. None of the persons living in Libby, Montana, who believe they may be a victim of alleged crimes is excluded, only those persons listed as witnesses by the government are subject to the defendants' invocation of Rule 615 Fed. R. Evid.

I

On February 2, 2009, the government filed a Motion to Accord Rights to Victim Witnesses, pursuant to the Act and Fed. R. Crim. P. 60(a)(2) and (b)(1). Under Rule 60(b)(1), "[t]he court must promptly decide any motion asserting a victim's rights[.]" The government asserts that its motion is part of the "best efforts" the Act requires it to make on behalf of crime victims, *see* 18 U.S.C. § 3771(c)(1), and correctly identifies the Court's obligation to "take up and decide any motion asserting a victim's right forthwith[,]" *see* 18 U.S.C. § 3771(d)(3). The motion seeks a declaration that the thirty-four persons named in the attachment to the brief in support of the motion meet the definition of "crime victim" under the Act and are therefore entitled to the rights the Act confers.

Under the Act, a Court may not exclude from a public court proceeding a victim testifying as a witness "unless the court, after receiving clear and convincing evidence, determines that testimony by the victim would be materially altered if the victim heard other testimony at that proceeding." 18 U.S.C. § 3771(a)(3); *see also* Fed. R. Crim P. 60(a)(2). The government argues that the thirty-four persons are witnesses and victims under the Act, and therefore the Court cannot exclude them from the proceedings pursuant to Rule 615 without finding by clear and convincing evidence that their testimony would be materially altered if they heard other testimony.

Shortly after the government filed its motion, on February 11, 2009, government witnesses Melvin and Lerah Parker appeared through counsel on a Motion to Assert Rights Pursuant to the Crime Victims' Rights Act. . . .

III

The Act defines a crime victim as a "person directly and proximately harmed as a result of the commission of a federal offense." 18 U.S.C. §3771(e). The Act necessarily presumes, according to its own terms, that it is applicable where 1) the commission of a federal offense has occurred, and 2) as a result of the commission of that federal offense, identifiable persons have been directly and proximately harmed. I cannot conclude, based on the federal offenses the government alleges in the Superseding Indictment, that any of the thirty-four individuals listed in the government's brief meet the definition of crime victim.

. . .

The government's and the Parkers' briefs bring to light an additional problem with identifying victims of the federal offenses alleged in the Superseding Indictment. The government's brief suggests, and the Parker brief explicitly asserts, that the mere fact that individuals are specifically identified as victims in the Superseding Indictment makes them victims under the Act. *See* Govt. Brief at 4; Parker Brief at 8. Section 3771(e) of Title 18 does not define a crime victim as a person identified in an indictment as a victim of the offense alleged. It defines a crime victim as "a person directly and proximately harmed as a result of the commission of a Federal offense." *Id.*

As already discussed at length, the federal offenses the government alleges prohibits conduct, committed with the requisite intent, that results in imminent danger of death or serious bodily injury to someone other than the offender. The offense is known colloquially as "knowing endangerment." The prohibited result is creating a risk of harm to another person. In other words, it is not necessary that "another person" inhale a "hazardous air pollutant" that has been released "into the ambient air" and experience the particular harm associated with the pollutant. The crime is complete when "another person" is placed in "imminent danger," i.e., when the risk of harm is imminent.

According to the charging statutes' own terms, a victim of the offense is another person exposed to an imminent risk of harm. The Criminal Victim's Rights Act, on the other hand, defines a crime victim as "a person directly and proximately harmed." The government has not addressed this problem. One plausible resolution of the issue here is to say that the federal offenses alleged in the Superseding Indictment have "victims" who have been exposed to an imminent risk of harm, but who have not necessarily been harmed. This interpretation leads to the conclusion that because victims of the federal offenses alleged are not necessarily harmed, they are not necessarily victims under the Act, which are by definition persons directly and proximately harmed.

The Parkers argue that in paragraphs 165 and 166, and in of Count III of the Superseding Indictment, they are specifically identified as victims of knowing endangerment. Parker brief at 9–10. Count III alleges Defendants committed the offense of knowing endangerment "by selling real property . . . to the Parker family." See Superseding Indictment ¶ 185. Paragraphs 165 and 166 allege they did so knowing the property was contaminated and failing to disclose the hazard. Leaving aside the question of how the offense, the actus reus of which is complete upon the introduction into the ambient air of a hazardous air pollutant, could be complete upon the transfer of title to real property, Count III seems to allege that the sale of the property exposed the Parker family to an imminent risk of harm. It does not allege the Parkers were directly and proximately harmed as the result of the commission of the offense of knowing endangerment.

In this criminal case the Court is not in a position to address whether individuals have been harmed as result of hazardous air pollutants in Libby, Montana. The Superseding Indictment does not allege that they have. The government and the Parkers seem to conflate the federal offenses alleged in the Superseding Indictment with a more general perception about the effects on the Libby community of exposure to harmful pollutants. But the government has not charged Defendants with harming members of the Libby community. It has charged the offense of knowing endangerment. See Govt. Brief at 6 ("In this case, the Superseding Indictment charges knowing endangerment under the Clean Air Act . . . and a conspiracy to violate the Clean Air Act (with a knowing endangerment object.")). Because of the nature of the government's theory, this Court cannot conclude there are identifiable "crime victims" as the Act defines the term.

IV

The Court recognizes, as the government emphasizes, that many people believe they have been harmed by Defendants. Those who hold this belief are welcome to attend the trial, which is a public proceeding. It is this Court's duty, however, to ensure a fair and efficient trial on the merits of the government's case. As counsel for the government is well aware, it is customary in this Court for counsel for either side to invoke Rule 615 and for witnesses to be excluded from trial proceedings on this basis. The rule is a procedural protection for either or both parties. It can be invoked when one or the other litigants wants to keep witnesses from hearing each other, or other evidence. When the rule is invoked by either party, "the court shall order witnesses excluded so that they cannot hear the testimony of other witnesses." Rule 615, Fed. R. Evid.

If there were identifiable victims of the federal offenses the government alleges in the Superseding Indictment, the Court would be faced with the apparent conflict between what the Act requires and the purpose of Rule 615. The Court would be required under the Act to allow victim-witnesses in the courtroom unless after a hearing it concluded that clear and convincing showed that testimony by the witness would be materially altered if they heard other testimony at that proceeding. 18 U.S.C. § 3771(a)(3). Because there are no identifiable victims, as the Act defines them, of the federal offenses alleged in the Superseding Indictment, the Court need not engage in this inquiry.

Notes

1. The Parkers and the government filed petitions for a writ of mandamus with the Ninth Circuit, asking that the district court's ruling be overturned. The Parker's petition argued:

> Petitioners Melvin and Lerah Parker are spending today at their home in Libby, Montana, rather than attending the trial of the defendants in the federal courthouse in Missoula, Montana. They have been barred by court order from watching the trial because they are witnesses in the case.
>
> The Parkers are keenly interested in that trial. They wish to learn everything they can about the crimes, about the medical evidence on asbestosis, and, more generally, about whether justice is being done in this criminal prosecution. The Parkers would have a statutory right to attend the trial if they are "crime victims" under the CVRA. CVRA promises all "victims" of federal crimes a series of rights, including a right to attend the trial. 18 U.S.C. § 3771(a)(3). It broadly defines a "crime victim" as "a person directly and proximately harmed as a result of the commission of a Federal offense." 18 U.S.C. § 3771(e). Nonetheless, the district court has refused to recognize the Parkers as victims of the crimes be tried.
>
> The court reasoned that because the charges in this case allege release of hazardous asbestos placing the Parkers in imminent danger of death or serious bodily injury—rather than actually killing or seriously injuring them—they were not "victims" of alleged offenses. The district court's conclusion threatens to strip crime victims of their rights in a whole host of federal criminal proceedings and should be reversed for [two] separate reasons.
>
> First, the Superseding Indictment alleges that the Parkers have been placed in "imminent danger of death or serious bodily injury." Being placed in grave danger is, ipso facto, a harm sufficient to trigger the protections of the CVRA. Any other conclusion would mean that there would be no "victims" of a whole host of federal offenses that involve threat of injury rather than actual physical injury, including not only the most serious environmental crimes but other federal offenses such as attempted murder, drive-by shooting, assault, child endangerment, and mailing of threatening communications. These offenses are not "victimless" crimes because they create fear and other emotional injuries. The Parkers have been harmed by the defendants' crimes because of the obvious psychic harm stemming from being placed in the shadow of imminent death and serious bodily injury. Moreover, in this case the Parkers have suffered very tangible harm from being forced to undertake medical monitoring to detect any asbestosis that might develop. For reasons such as these, this Court has already held that a person who is knowingly exposed to a hazardous substance has been harmed. *United States v. Elias*, 269 F.3d 1003, 1021–22 (9th Cir. 2001).

Second, even if physical injury were a necessary precondition for the Parkers to claim their rights, they have suffered physical injury. Tragically, they both have asbestosis—a clear physical harm that the district court simply ignored in denying them "crime victim" status.

The Ninth Circuit apparently agreed with the Parkers, and with the Government which filed a petition supporting the Parkers. In a terse order, the Ninth Circuit reversed the district court's decision and held that the Parkers and other government witnesses were "victims." *In re Melvin Parker*, No. 09-70529 (9th Cir. Feb. 27, 2009).

2. The problem presented by the large number of victims in the *Grace* prosecution is part of a broader issue: Who should exercise crime victim's rights where multiple people have been harmed, but no one person has suffered particular harm? For example, who is a victim when a defendant traffics in illegal drugs or commits treason hurting the nation's security? Is anyone a victim of these offenses? In a report defending a federal constitutional amendment conferring rights on "a victim of a crime of violence," the Senate Judiciary Committee suggested that no one was a victim of such offenses:

> Because of the formulation used in the amendment ("a victim of a crime of violence") it is presumed that there must be an identifiable victim. Some crimes, such as drug or espionage offenses, do not ordinarily have such an identifiable victim and therefore would not ordinarily be covered by the amendment. However, in some unusual cases, a court or legislature might conclude that these offenses in fact "involved" violence against an identifiable victim. For example, treason or espionage against the United States resulting in death or injury to an American Government official would produce an identifiable victim protected by the Amendment. S. Rep. 106-254: Crime Victims' Rights Constitutional Amendment at 29–30 (Apr. 4, 2000).

3. In cases involving diverse victims, would it make sense to have a representative of some larger community serve as a stand-in for any particular victim? Several states seem to allow this. *See, e.g.*, GA. CODE ANN. § 17-10-1.2 (allowing sentencing testimony from any witness with personal knowledge of the victim's personal characteristics and the emotional impact of the crime on the victim, the victim's family, or the community); *Commonwealth v. Penrod*, 578 A.2d 486, 492 (Pa. 1990) (allowing sentencing testimony from victims, family members, and friends at the sentencing "regarding the impact of the offense on the victim, the impact on the community generally, and/or the impact on the family members or friends as members of the community"). *See generally* Katie Long, Note, *Community Input at Sentencing: Victim's Right or Victim's Revenge*, 75 BOSTON U.L. REV. 195 (1995).

3. The Defendant as a "Victim"

Victims' rights enactments generally exclude those involved in the crime from their coverage. Typical of these exclusions is Pennsylvania's:

"Victim" shall mean a person against whom a crime has been committed, other than the alleged offender. . . .

———————

Should someone who is not specifically charged as a defendant but is nonetheless possibly involved in the crime be considered a "victim"? Consider the following case:

Knapp v. Martone, a Judge of the Superior Court of the State of Arizona

823 P.2d 685 (Ariz. 1992)

MOELLER, Justice.

STATEMENT OF THE CASE

Petitioner Linda Knapp asks that we accept jurisdiction of this special action and vacate the trial court's order compelling her to submit to a court-ordered deposition requested by her former husband, John Henry Knapp (defendant).[1] Ariz. Const. art. 6, § 5(1) grants us jurisdiction over common law writs, which are now presented as special actions pursuant to Rules 4(a) and 7(a), Ariz. R. P. Spec. Act., 17B Ariz. Rev. Stat. ("A.R.S.").

QUESTION PRESENTED

Is Linda Knapp a "victim" within the meaning of the Arizona Victims' Bill of Rights, Ariz. Const. art. 2, § 2.1?

FACTS AND PROCEDURAL BACKGROUND

In 1973, defendant was charged with two counts of first degree murder of his daughters, aged two and three. Defendant's first trial ended in a mistrial. At his second trial, defendant was convicted of murdering his children and sentenced to death. The convictions and sentences were affirmed on appeal to this court. *State v. Knapp*, 562 P.2d 704 (1977), cert. denied, 435 U.S. 908, (1978). In post-conviction proceedings in 1987, the trial court granted defendant a new trial based on newly discovered scientific evidence. In December 1987, the trial court dismissed the case without prejudice.

In October 1990, the state re-charged defendant with first degree murder. Because of defendant's earlier claims that his confession was given to protect his wife, the state, in the 1990 information, added an alternative allegation charging defendant as an accessory. In oral arguments in the trial court, the state acknowledged that, under

———————

1. In published opinions, we avoid using the victim's real name when the victim's identity is not material to a discussion of the case and when disclosure might further traumatize the victim. In this case we use petitioner's real former married name because the facts of the case make her identity obvious, and because it has already been widely disseminated by the news media for many years.

the accessory theory, the co-conspirator would be Mrs. Knapp. However, the state has never charged her with a crime nor has it named her in an information or indictment. Although the state disclaimed any intent to call Mrs. Knapp as a witness, defendant sought to depose her. He claims she is a potential defense witness, and he is entitled to depose her although he has access to all the transcripts of her earlier interviews and testimony. Mrs. Knapp objected to the proposed deposition, arguing that, as a victim under the Victims' Bill of Rights, Ariz. Const. art. 2, § 2.1, she has the right to refuse to submit to a deposition. The trial court overruled her objection and ordered her to submit to a deposition based on its finding that she was not a victim "within the definition of the Victim Bill of Rights," and that "it could not have been the intent of the draftspersons (of the Victims' Rights Amendment) to exclude a person, such as Ms. Knapp, who was, is, or could be a suspect in the case."

Mrs. Knapp challenged the trial court's ruling in an unsuccessful special action in the court of appeals. She then filed this special action in this court. . . .

DISCUSSION

Petitioner argues that, as the mother of the two children alleged to have been murdered, she is a "victim" under the Victims' Bill of Rights and may therefore properly refuse defendant's request to depose her. . . . The Victims' Bill of Rights defines "victim" as:

> a person against whom the criminal offense has been committed or, if the person is killed or incapacitated, the person's spouse, parent, child or other lawful representative, except if the person is in custody for an offense or is the accused. Ariz. Const. art. 2, § 2.1(C) (emphasis added).

As mother of the children involved, Mrs. Knapp is a "victim" under the constitutional definition. The only victims excluded from the protection of the Victims' Bill of Rights are those "in custody for an offense" or those who are "the accused." Mrs. Knapp is not "in custody for an offense" nor is she "the accused" in any commonly accepted usage of the term. While the Victims' Bill of Rights itself does not define "accused," the Victims' Rights Implementation Act, A.R.S. § 13-4401(1), which became effective December 31, 1991, defines an "accused" as "a person who has been arrested for committing a criminal offense and who is held for an initial appearance or other proceeding before trial." Mrs. Knapp is therefore not an accused under the constitutional provision, nor will she be one under the prospective statutory provision.

Although the dissent would affirm the trial court's order compelling Mrs. Knapp to submit to a deposition on the theory that she is "the accused" or "an accused," the trial court did not consider her to be an "accused." Instead, the trial court held that Mrs. Knapp was not a "victim" at all on the theory that the drafters of the constitutional amendment did not intend to include as a victim a person "who was, is, or could be a suspect" in a case. Although petitioner at one time may have been a suspect in this case and has received a grant of immunity in exchange for her testimony, she has never been charged with or held for any offense.

This is the first published opinion of this court involving application of the recently-enacted Victims' Bill of Rights. It is important to emphasize that Arizona courts must follow and apply the plain language of this new amendment to our constitution. If trial courts are permitted to make ad hoc exceptions to the constitutional rule based upon the perceived exigencies of each case, the harm the Victims' Bill of Rights was designed to ameliorate will, instead, be increased. Permitting such ad hoc exceptions will encourage defendants or others to assert that the person designated as the victim should, instead, be considered a suspect. These assertions will lead to hearings, such as the one held in this case, to determine whether the rights expressly granted to victims by the Victims' Bill of Rights should be overridden. Such proceedings can only increase the harassment of victims that the Victims' Bill of Rights was designed to decrease.

DISPOSITION

Petitioner is a victim as defined in the Victims' Bill of Rights. As such, she has a constitutional right to refuse defendant's request for a deposition. . . .

FELDMAN, Vice Chief Justice, dissenting.

The court holds that the mother of the two children is a "victim" entitled to invoke the protection of the victims' bill of rights and thus refuse pretrial interview or deposition. *See Ariz. Const.* art. 2, § 2.1. I dissent from this conclusion because the record shows what the majority neglects to mention: the state has alleged that this mother is an unindicted co-conspirator and principal in the murder of her own children.[1]

Of course, the constitutional amendment was never intended to give the rights of a victim to a person whom the state alleges to be a murderer. Although this court usually considers the obvious intent behind the words of the constitution, in this case it chooses to look no further than what it describes as "plain language." Even the plain language, however, does not support such a reversal of the basic purpose of the victims' bill of rights.

The constitutional amendment excludes "the accused" from the definition of "victim." ARIZ. CONST. art. 2, § 2.1(C). Citing no authority, the majority concludes that one whom the state alleges to be a principal in the murder is not an "accused" in the "ordinary meaning" of the word. According to the dictionary, however, an accused is "one charged with an offense; esp: the defendant in a criminal case." WEBSTER'S THIRD NEW INTERNATIONAL DICTIONARY, at 14 (1976).[2] Thus, the

---

1. Mr. Knapp was charged both with first degree murder and as an accessory to murder. The state has "acknowledged that the co-conspirator would be the defendant's ex-wife, [Mrs.] Knapp." Minute Entry of Judge Martone, August 22, 1991.

2. The first definition of the verb "accuse" is "to charge unequivocally with a specified or implied wrong or fault often in a condemnatory or indignant manner <the courtiers accused their queen> <the planes were accused of spreading cholera, typhus, and bubonic plague . . . >." WEBSTER'S THIRD NEW INTERNATIONAL DICTIONARY, at 14 (1976). This indeed is the "ordinary meaning"

dictionary definition of "accused" includes, but is not limited to, the defendant in a criminal case. The drafters of the constitutional provision did not use the word "defendant" but, instead, chose the broader term "accused." As in this case, one may be "accused" and never arrested or prosecuted as a defendant. . . .

The majority argues that we should not permit "trial courts . . . to make ad hoc exceptions" or "encourage defendants or others to assert that the person designated as the victim should, instead, be considered to be a suspect." I agree, but this exceptional case presents neither danger. Mrs. Knapp has not been accused by any ad hoc suggestion of the defendant. She is an "accused" because the state's pleadings accuse her of being a principal in the murder. . . .

The victims' bill of rights was adopted to address the hardships suffered by victims, not to help alleged criminals whenever the strategic ends of the prosecutor are served. Today's decision does just that. Mr. Knapp is now the defendant and Mrs. Knapp has been given immunity in return for her testimony. The majority holds, therefore, that Mrs. Knapp enjoys all the rights of a "victim." If, however, the state had chosen a different strategy, making Mrs. Knapp the defendant and naming Mr. Knapp as the unindicted co-conspirator and principal, it could have used his testimony to try to convict Mrs. Knapp. In the majority's view, Mrs. Knapp would then be the "accused" and Mr. Knapp a "victim" entitled as surviving father to all the benefits of the victims' bill of rights.

Surely those who worked for the victims' bill of rights had something better in mind than making a victim's status wholly contingent on the prosecutor's strategy. The constitutional amendment was never intended to serve or protect those accused by the state of being principals in the crime. The words of the provision do not force us to defy common sense, and we should not. I therefore dissent.

———————

Notes

1. Do you agree with the majority that Mrs. Knapp is a "victim" under the Arizona statutes? To what extent should the charging document (the information) govern this issue as opposed to the prosecution's theory of the case or the facts of what really happened?

2. John Knapp's third trial ended in a mistrial with the jury hung 7–5 for conviction. Finally, the prosecutor concluded that the evidence was insufficient as the case was 19 years old and there had been losses of key witnesses and evidence. Knapp then plead no contest to second degree murder and was sentenced to time served. Interestingly, despite his plea of no contest, some opponents of the death penalty now include him on a list of "innocent" persons who have been released from death row. *See, e.g.,* http://archive.aclu.org/issues/death/17exonerated.html. For an investigation

———————

of the word. It is only the second meaning listed — "to charge with an offense judicially or by a public process" — that pertains to the judicial process, and even that definition is met in this case.

of the case, *see* Roger Parloff, Triple Jeopardy: A Story of the Law at Its Best — and Worst (1996). Does the fact that this capital case was so closely contested justify favoring the defendant and giving him the chance to interview Mrs. Knapp despite the victims' rights enactment?

3. Where it is a clear that a person has been a co-participant in criminal activity, that person is often times excluded from "victim" status if seeking restitution for injuries suffered. For example, in *In re Tyrell A.*, 112 A.3d 468 (Md. App. 2015), two high school students engaged in a fistfight. After one of the students was convicted of affray, the trial judge ordered him to pay restitution to the other student for medical expenses in treating a broken nose. The Maryland Court of Appeals reversed, holding that "[i]t strikes us as unlikely that the General Assembly intended such an arrangement. Absent clear legislative intent to do so, we will not give a statute an unreasonable interpretation. We therefore hold that [applicable statute] does not authorize trial courts generally to order restitution in favor of a person who is a voluntary and willing participant in the crime or delinquent activity that caused his or her injury, absent exceptional circumstances." 112 A.3d at 485.

4. Generally speaking, a person who merely witnesses a crime is not a victim of the crime and not entitled to victim protection. *See Champlin v. Sargeant*, 965 P.2d 763 (Ariz. 1998). But in a case decided after *Knapp*, the Arizona Court of Appeals held that a witness of the defendant's indecent exposure was a "victim" under the Arizona victim's rights statute. The court reasoned that indecent exposure is an offense that requires that another person be present and that the other person "would be offended or alarmed by the act." *Norgord v. State ex rel. Berning*, 33 P.3d 1166 (Ariz. App. 2001). Although the witness was apparently not mentioned in the charging document, the witness was the person that the prosecution was going to allege would be alarmed by the act.

4. A Representative for the Victim

In some cases, the victim of a crime will be in no position to represent her own interests in a criminal proceeding. For example, a victim may be a minor child, incapacitated, or simply too afraid to assert in her interests. In such circumstances, courts may have authority to appoint a representative of the victim.

18 U.S.C. § 3771(e)

For the purposes of this chapter, the term "crime victim" means a person directly and proximately harmed as a result of the commission of a Federal offense or an offense in the District of Columbia. In the case of a crime victim who is under 18 years of age, incompetent, incapacitated, or deceased, the legal guardians of the crime victim or the representatives of the crime victim's estate, family members, or any other persons appointed as suitable by the court, may assume the crime victim's rights under this chapter, but in no event shall the defendant be named as such guardian or representative

In homicide cases, the dead victim obviously is unavailable to assert rights personally. But should family members be recognized as "victims" as well? Most victims' rights enactments include surviving family members within their protections. Some states do this by authorizing family members to appear as "representatives" of the victim. *See, e.g.,* FLA. CONST., art. I, § 16(b) ("Victims of crime or their lawful representatives, including the next of kin of homicide victims, are entitled to . . . [various rights]"). Other states explicitly incorporate family members as "the victim" in homicide cases. Georgia's statute is perhaps the most elaborate:

"Victim" means:

(A) A person against whom a crime has been perpetrated; or

(B) In the event of the death of the crime victim, the following relations if the relation is not either in custody for an offense or the defendant:

(i) The spouse;

(ii) An adult child if division (i) does not apply;

(iii) A parent if divisions (i) and (ii) do not apply;

(iv) A sibling if divisions (i) through (iii) do not apply; or

(v) A grandparent if divisions (i) through (iv) do not apply; or

GA. CODE ANN. § 17-17-3(11).

Do these statutory enumerations prevent others from being considered victims? In homicide cases, should victims be limited to family members?

Beck v. Commonwealth

484 S.E.2d 898 (Va. 1997), cert denied, 522 U.S. 1018

[The defendant was convicted of capital murder. He appealed, challenging the trial court's admission at sentencing of "impact" evidence from not only the victim's family members, but also her co-workers and friends.]

. . .

A. Constitutional Admissibility

We have previously decided that "victim impact testimony is relevant to punishment in a capital murder prosecution in Virginia." *Weeks v. Commonwealth*, 450 S.E.2d 379, 389–90 (Va. 1994). There, we relied on the statement in *Payne v. Tennessee*, 501 U.S. 808 (1991), that "[a] State may legitimately conclude that evidence about the victim and about the impact of the murder on the victim's family is relevant to the . . . decision as to whether or not the death penalty shall be imposed." 501 U.S. at 827.

Citing the foregoing language in Payne, Beck maintains that Payne limits the source of victim impact evidence to family members. We disagree. No such limitation is either express or implied by this language. To the contrary, the Court was describing the nature, not the source, of victim impact evidence. Indeed, it has been expressly recognized that the impact of the loss of the victim of a murder may extend beyond the victim's family members to the victim's friends and community. *Id.* at 830 (O'Connor, J., concurring). Human experience and common knowledge support this recognition of the unique worth of the individual. Thus, there is no merit to Beck's assertion that victim impact evidence is constitutionally limited to that received from the victim's family members.

We hold that the admissibility of victim impact evidence during the sentencing phase of a capital murder trial is limited only by the relevance of such evidence to show the impact of the defendant's actions. While statements from the immediate family members of the deceased will normally be the best source of such evidence, the Eighth Amendment does not restrict the trial court from looking to statements of others well acquainted with the victim. Such evidence provides the sentencing authority with an understanding of the individualized circumstances present in the life of the victim and the specific harm caused by the crime in question. *Id.* at 825. So long as its prejudicial effect does not outweigh its probative value, such evidence is beneficial to the determination of an individualized sentence as is required by the Eighth Amendment. *Id.; see also Wesley v. State*, 916 P.2d 793, 804 (Nev. 1996) (victim impact evidence from neighbors, co-workers and others did not violate defendant's Eighth Amendment rights).

B. Statutory Admissibility

Beck asserts that even if constitutionally permissible, the criminal procedure provisions within Title 19.2 of the Virginia Code limit victim impact evidence in a capital murder case to that received from the victim's family members. In support of this position, Beck relies upon Code §§ 19.2-11.01, 19.2-264.5 and 19.2-299.1. Beck asserts that, when read in concert, these three statutes provide only for gathering and presentation of evidence from those persons designated as "victims" under the Crime Victim and Witness Rights Act (the Act). Code § 19.2-11.01 to -11.4. We disagree.

Pertinent to our resolution of this issue, the code prescribes:

§ 19.2-11.01. Crime victim and witness rights.

A. In recognition of the Commonwealth's concern for the victims and witnesses of crime, it is the purpose of this chapter to ensure that the full impact of crime is brought to the attention of the courts of the Commonwealth;

. . .

a. Victims shall be given the opportunity, pursuant to § 19.2-299.1, to prepare a written victim impact statement prior to sentencing of a defendant and may provide information to any individual or agency charged with investigating the social history of a person or preparing a victim impact statement under the provisions of §§ 16.1-273 and 53.1-155 or any other applicable law.

. . .

B. For purposes of this chapter, "victim" means . . . a spouse, parent or legal guardian of such a person who . . . was the victim of a homicide.

. . .

§ 19.2-299.1. When Victim Impact Statement required; contents; uses.

The presentence report prepared pursuant to § 19.2-299 shall, with the consent of the victim, as defined in § 19.2-11.01, in all cases involving offenses other than capital murder, include a Victim Impact Statement. Victim Impact Statements in all cases involving capital murder shall be prepared and submitted in accordance with the provisions of § 19.2-264.5. . . .

Beck asserts that by limiting the definition of "victim" in the Act to the "spouse, parent or legal guardian" of the deceased, the legislature implicitly intended to limit the admissibility of victim impact evidence to that provided by such persons for the reports described in Code §§ 19.2-264.5 and 19.2-299.1. There is no merit to this assertion.

While the Act provides for the right of victims, as defined therein, to prepare a written impact statement, nothing within the Act limits the nature of victim impact evidence to such statements alone. Similarly, the reference to the Act in Code § 19.2-299.1 merely defines the person or persons whose consent the Commonwealth must obtain in order to include the victim impact statement in the sentencing report. . . .

The clear import of the Act is to preserve the right of victims of crimes to have the impact of those crimes upon their lives considered as part of the sentencing process, if that is their wish, and to protect their privacy thereafter. The requirement in Code § 19.2-299.1 of obtaining victim consent to include the statement of the victim in the pre-sentence report is further recognition of the right of victims to maintain their privacy if they so desire. By exempting the Commonwealth from having to seek such consent when presenting victim impact evidence during capital murder trials, the legislature has recognized expressly that the impact of such crimes is of such magnitude as to require the consideration of victim impact evidence even at the risk of intruding upon the sensibilities of those closest to the victim.

Nothing in Code § 19.2-299.1 expressly or implicitly limits the sources on which the Commonwealth may draw in its preparation of the victim impact portion of the presentence report. Rather, the report is to contain whatever information the trial court "may require related to the impact of the offense upon the victim."

Accordingly, we hold that the statutes do not limit evidence of victim impact to that received from the victim's family members. Rather, the circumstances of the individual case will dictate what evidence will be necessary and relevant, and from what sources it may be drawn. In a capital murder trial, as in any other criminal proceeding, the determination of the admissibility of relevant evidence is within the sound discretion of the trial court subject to the test of abuse of that discretion.

C. Admissibility and Consideration of Evidence Received

We now turn to the victim impact evidence actually received by the trial court during the sentencing phase of Beck's trial. . . .

As noted above, the determination of admissibility of relevant evidence is within the sound discretion of the trial court. . . .

In reviewing an exercise of discretion, we do not substitute our judgment for that of the trial court. Rather, we consider only whether the record fairly supports the trial court's action. We find that none of the declarants of the victim impact evidence received by the trial court was so far removed from the victims as to have nothing of value to impart to the court about the impact of these crimes. Thus, the determination that this evidence was relevant and probative of the issue under consideration was clearly within the trial court's discretion. Similarly, our review of the content of the victim impact evidence reveals no statement concerning the impact of the crimes so inherently prejudicial that its admission would constitute an abuse of discretion. Accordingly, to whatever extent that the trial court chose to consider the evidence it received, we cannot say that doing so constituted an abuse of its discretion.

Notes

1. The *Payne* case, which explores whether it is appropriate to receive victim impact testimony, is explored at length in Chapter 10.

2. *Beck* holds that victim impact testimony from non-family members is allowed so long as the declarant is not "so far removed from the victims as to have nothing of value to impart to the court." This holding is criticized by Professor Markus Dubber:

In other words, the only reason that the entire community of upstanding men and women of Virginia wouldn't be permitted to testify as a victim impact witnesses in every capital sentencing hearing in that state is that, after a while, their testimony might become somewhat duplicative, and not that each and every one of them wouldn't qualify for victim impact victimhood. It's thus a basic principle of the law of evidence—itself based on the need to move things along at trial and not to confuse the jury—that stands between a mass procession of victim impact witnesses at every murder trial, not any limitation on the concept of the victim.

Markus Kirk Dubber, Victims in the War on Crime: The Use and Abuse of Victims' Rights, 215 (2002). Do you agree with Professor Dubber? Or is *Beck's* broad definition of "victim" justified by the far-reaching consequences of a murder?

3. In the absence of such specific statutory authorization of the type found in Virginia, do close family members of homicide victims suffer sufficient direct harm to be recognized as victims in their own right? *See United States v. Bedonie*, 317 F. Supp.2d 1285, 1301 (D. Utah 2004) (raising this issue with regard to an indigent mother who lost financial support when her son was killed but finding it unnecessary to reach a definitive conclusion).

4. While surviving family members are generally defined as victims when a death occurs from a homicide, a death resulting indirectly from a suicide caused by a crime does not confer victim status on family members. *See State v. Superior Court*, 922 P.2d 927, 928 (Ariz. App. 1996) (the parents of a sexual assault victim who later committed suicide not crime victims; the death must be "immediately caused" by the criminal act).

5. How many victim representatives can a court appoint? In an Illinois case involving the murder of woman, the court found that it was error to receive a victim impact statement from the victim's parents as well as two of her children. The court concluded that the Illinois statutes authorized only a single victim's representative. *People v. Richardson*, 751 N.E.2d 1104 (Ill. 2001).

6. In homicide cases, how should family representatives of the victim be appointed when the state does not formally recognize the "family" at hand? For example, in a case involving the death of an intimate partner in a same sex relationship, is the surviving partner the appropriate representative even though not legally a "family" member? *Cf.* Utah Code Ann. §77-38-9(2) (giving court discretion to appoint a representative "upon request from the victim's spouse, parent, child, or close friend").

7. In situations involving child victims, Wisconsin's victims' rights statute specifies that "a parent, guardian, or legal custodian, is also a victim." Wis. Stat. §950.02(4)(a)(1). At the same time, however, Wisconsin's statute provides that a "victim" does not include "the person charged with or alleged to have committed the crime." *Id.*

---

5. Limiting the "Victim" to Violent Crimes

A few victims' rights amendments and statutes limit the definition of "victim" to victims of crimes of violence. For example, the New Mexico Victims' Rights Amendment is restricted to "victims of arson resulting in bodily injury, aggravated arson, aggravated assault, aggravated battery, dangerous use of explosives, negligent use of a deadly weapon, murder, voluntary manslaughter, involuntary manslaughter, kidnaping, criminal sexual penetration, criminal sexual contact of a minor, homicide by vehicle, great bodily injury by vehicle or abandonment or abuse of a child or that victim's representative. . . ." N.M. Const. art. II, §24. Similarly, before the recent enactment of the Crime Victims' Rights Act (18 U.S.C. 3771) federal law allowed only victims of "a crime of violence or sexual abuse" to allocute at sentencing. Fed. R. Crim. Pro. 32(i)(4)(B). The pending Victims' Rights Amendment to the United States constitution (discussed in Chapter 12) extends its rights only to a "victim of a crime of violence." The supporters of the constitutional amendment justified this limitation as a political compromise necessary to pass the amendment. *See* S. Rep. 106-254, Crime Victims' Rights Constitutional Amendment, 106th Cong., 2d Sess. 45 (2000).

Does it make sense to distinguish between victims of violent offenses and victims of other offenses on grounds that violent offenses are different in kind from other offenses? Consider the objections to this approach in the context of allocution (that is, making a statement at sentencing):

Jayne W. Barnard, *Allocution for Victims of Economic Crimes*
77 Notre Dame L. Rev. 39 (2001)

Since 1994, the Federal Rules of Criminal Procedure have required federal courts to entertain in-court victim impact testimony as part of the sentencing process. However, this testimony (also known as victim allocution) is required only in cases in which the defendant is guilty of a crime involving violence or sexual abuse.

This Article argues that this limitation on the ability of victims of non-violent crimes to have access to the courts for purposes of allocution is unwise and inappropriate. Federal courts should be required to entertain in-court victim impact testimony in cases involving non-violent crimes as well as in cases involving violent crimes. Specifically, in-court victim impact testimony should be required in cases involving economic crimes such as mail fraud, wire fraud, securities fraud, telemarketing fraud, and "identity theft." Victims of other federal felonies, to the extent they are clearly identifiable as victims, should also be entitled to victim allocution.

The background for this proposal is simple. Experience in economic crime cases demonstrates that victims of these types of crimes often feel just as violated, anxious, confused, betrayed, and depressed as do victims of violent crimes. Often they are the kinds of "vulnerable victims" recognized in the U.S. Sentencing Guidelines, yet they have few resources by which to express their vulnerability or to feel they have had a real impact on decisions relating to their victimizer's fate.

Federal prosecutors often invite victims of economic crimes to recount their experiences in writing, in order to lend weight to a request for restitution, an enhancement of the defendant's sentence, or an upward departure from the Sentencing Guidelines. Frequently, federal judges will include specific references to these written declarations in the course of the sentencing process. What I am proposing in this Article involves a greater commitment to victims of non-violent crimes, however — a legislatively-assured opportunity to be heard in open court.

Note

1. While some states limit victims' rights to violent crime, the Federal Crime Victims' Rights Act includes victims of white-collar crime. For example, in the infamous fraud of Bernie Madoff, thousands of victims were harmed. Ultimately, the judge sentencing Madoff allowed a representative sample of victims to provide oral victim impact statements, while all defendants were allowed to provide written statements. *See* Paul G. Cassell & Edna Erez, *Victim Impact Statements and Ancillary Harm: The American Perspective*, 15 Can. Crim. L. Rev. 149, 156-60 (2010).

C. Persons Excluded from the Definition of "Victim" Status: Selected Examples

Because of the narrow way in which "victim" is defined in victims' rights enactments, many persons fall outside their protections. This section offers a few selected examples.

1. Suspects as Excluded Victims

A suspect of a crime is not a victim, even if it turns out he was wrongfully suspected. For example, the bombing at the Olympic Games in Atlanta resulted in the destruction of the reputation of Richard Jewell, the FBI's first suspect. Richard Jewell was innocent and was never charged. While Richard Jewell is certainly a "victim" in common parlance or perhaps even in the context of the civil lawsuit he brought later, he was never a "victim" in the context of criminal procedure. No "victim laws" address his circumstance. Criminal procedure offers few constraints against inept government investigators.

2. Wrongfully Convicted Persons as Excluded Victims

Some persons convicted of crimes—including even capital crimes—have been proven to be innocent. The frequency with which this happens and the implications to be drawn from wrongful convictions are the subject of debate. *Compare* Marvin Zalman, *Qualitatively Estimating the Incidence of Wrongful Convictions*, 48 Crim. L. Bull. 221, 222 (2012) (estimating the wrongful convictions happen frequently), with Paul G. Cassell, *The Guilty and the "Innocent": An Examination of Alleged Cases of Wrongful Conviction from False Confessions*, 22 Harv. J.L. & Pub. Pol'y 523, 535 (1999) (raising questions about some claims of "innocence"). If DNA testing reveals a convict's innocence, the convict is, in common terms, a "victim." However, such a person is not a victim in the eyes of the criminal justice system.

3. Defendants as Excluded Victims: The Question of Self-Defense Laws

The law regarding self-defense provides an interesting method of defining the victim. Once prosecutors charge a defendant with a crime, the person harmed by that crime becomes the victim. If the defendant argues self-defense and is later acquitted, he might be regarded in some sense as a "victim" because the jury has arguably found that he acted lawfully against a threat of unlawful force from the person he harmed. Unless new criminal charges are filed against the person harmed, however, the original defendant will never be defined as a victim.

A great deal of controversy has arisen over the issue of whether to expand the self-defense doctrine in certain areas. For example, commentators have debated whether abused women who kill their spouses should be regarded as criminals or victims. *See, e.g.,* Mary Anne Franks, *Men, Women, and Optimal Violence,* 2016 U. Ill. L. Rev. 929, 933 (2016). You may have encountered some of these debates in your Criminal Law class.

Traditional or expanded definitions of the law of self-defense ultimately may define who the "real" victim is. But once a battered woman is charged with a crime, she will not be regarded as a "victim" under laws protecting victims of crime.

4. Victims Falling Outside the Protection of Criminal Statutes

Other battles over the definition of "victim" take place in the context of defining a substantive crime, as opposed to altering traditional standards of defenses. Thus, while battered women or abused children who kill have been protected by altering the traditional self-defense standard, rape victims have been protected in some jurisdictions by lowering the required level of criminal intent. *See, e.g.,* Deborah Tuerkheimer, *Affirmative Consent,* 13 Ohio State J. Crim. L. 441 (2016).

5. The Fetuses of Drug Abusing Mothers as Victims

Some state prosecutors have filed criminal charges against mothers who consume illegal drugs before giving birth to a child under child endangerment or drug distribution statutes. But generally state courts have held that maternal conduct before the birth of a child is not criminally actionable. *See, e.g., Johnson v. State,* 602 So. 2d 1288 (Fla. 1992). In effect, these courts have concluded that viable fetuses are not crime victims. Such a holding presumably renders the child, if born, ineligible for victim's compensation funds for injury suffered from such conduct during the pregnancy. Whether to criminalize such conduct remains the subject of debate. *See, e.g.,* April L. Cherry, *Shifting Our Focus from Retribution to Social Justice: An Alternative Vision for the Treatment of Pregnant Women Who Harm Their Fetuses,* 28 J.L. & Health 6 (2015).

D. Victim Status and the Presumption of Innocence

A defendant is, of course, presumed to be innocent unless and until found guilty by a jury. Is it proper to refer to a person as a "victim" before a jury has decided the defendant's guilt?

To deal with this issue, some states explicitly include an "alleged victim" within the statutory definition of "victim." Other states implicitly include the alleged victim by granting them certain rights during bail hearings or at other points early in the process. As a result, in most contexts in criminal procedure, the term "the victim" means effectively "the victim as alleged in the indictment."

Is it appropriate to give a person legal rights as a victim before a formal adjudication of guilt? In *State ex rel. Romley v. Dairman*, *supra* (involving the appointment of a guardian to protect a child's interest), the court considered and rejected the defendant's claim that appointment of the guardian would violate his presumption of innocence:

State ex rel. Romley v. Dairman, a Judge of the Superior Court of the State of Arizona

95 P.3d 548 (Ariz. 2004)

BARKER, Judge.

* * *

We do not doubt or question the presumption of innocence to which a defendant is entitled. *See In re Winship*, 397 U.S. 358, 363 (1970) (quoting *Coffin v. United States*, 156 U.S. 432, 453 (1895)) (stating that the presumption of innocence is the "bedrock 'axiomatic and elementary' principle whose 'enforcement lies at the foundation of the administration of our criminal law'"). We are concerned, however, with the reliance on the presumption of innocence applicable to a defendant, in determining whether rights pertaining to a victim are or have been invoked. To the extent that evidence of guilt may be required to rebut the presumption for purposes of appointing a representative, that evidentiary burden is satisfied when charges are filed.

As set forth in A.R.S. § 13-4402(A) (2001), "the rights and duties that are established by this chapter [victims' rights] arise on the arrest or formal charging of the person or persons who are alleged to be responsible for a criminal offense against a victim . . . [and] continue to be enforceable . . . until the final disposition of the charges. . . ." Victims' rights accrue at the time of arrest or formal charge of the alleged incident and take root as the criminal proceedings progress. *See, e.g.*, A.R.S. § 13-4406 (2001) (requiring notification to victim of defendant's initial appearance); A.R.S. § 13-4419 (2001) (granting a victim the right to confer with the prosecuting attorney regarding the defendant's case); A.R.S. § 13-4433 (2001) (delineating the scope of a victim's right to refuse an interview by defendant or anyone representing defendant's interests); A.R.S. § 13-4420 (2001) (granting a victim the right to be present at all proceedings in which the defendant has a right to be present); A.R.S. § 13-4424 (granting a victim the right to make a statement for defendant's presentence report); A.R.S. § 13-4427 (granting a victim the right to be present at defendant's probation modification or revocation proceeding).

Obviously, if victims' rights did not accrue until after a determination of guilt, the provisions for victims' rights prior to trial or a guilty plea would be of little value. Our rules also recognize this by referring to the victim as "a person against whom a criminal offense . . . has allegedly been committed." Ariz. R. Crim. P. 39(A)(1) (emphasis added); *see also* A.R.S. § 13-4421 (2001) ("The victim has the right to be heard at the initial appearance of the person suspected of committing the criminal offense against the victim.") (emphasis added); A.R.S. § 13-4422 (2001) ("The victim has the right to be heard at any proceeding in which the court considers the post-arrest release of the person accused of committing a criminal offense against the victim or the conditions of that release.") (emphasis added).

In the context at issue here, victims' rights neither trump, nor are trumped by, a defendant's presumption of innocence. Each set of rights is independent. A defendant is presumed innocent of all charges and is entitled to all rights and duties owed him or her. A victim, on the other hand, is presumed to have been violated for purposes of obtaining victims' rights and is entitled to those rights as provided under our constitution and laws.

The issue of victims' rights and the presumption of innocence arose in the sexual assault case against Los Angeles Lakers basketball star Kobe Bryant. Mr. Bryant's attorneys argued that it was not appropriate to refer to the alleged victim in that case (whom they referred to as merely the "complaining witness") without any finding a guilt. The court ordered briefing on the issue. The National Crime Victims Law Institute filed an amicus brief on behalf of the victim, arguing that referring to her as a "victim" was entirely appropriate:

The victim in the present case is a "victim" for purposes of Colorado law. She is a "natural person," the crime in question is sexual assault, which is listed in the enumerated crimes in the Act, she is not a co-conspirator, and there is nothing in the Amendment or the Act that makes her rights contingent upon the defense asserted or the conviction of the Defendant. Consequently, she is fully entitled to the rights contained in the Amendment and the Act. Further, it is indisputable that the Legislature has labeled these rights as the "rights of the crime victims" and has named the person who exercises these rights, "victim."[4] Despite this, Defendant requests this Court deny her these rights and order that the participants in this case refrain from calling her a "victim."

The victim is entitled to both her constitutional and statutory rights under the Amendment and the Act and to her constitutional and statutory title of "victim." This legal term of art, "victim," precisely describes her independent and distinct status in the criminal justice system when she is exercising her rights under the Amendment and Act. Other terms such as "complaining witness" and "accuser" do not. To call her something other than "victim" when her rights under the Amendment and the Act are being discussed is inaccurate and a denial of both the status and the rights given to her by the legislature and the people of Colorado.

---

4. See COLO. CONST. art. II, § 16a; COLO. REV. STAT. §§ 24-4.1-302 to -304 (2003).

People v. Bryant, Case No. 03-CR-204 (Dist. Ct. Eagle County, Colo. 2004). Response of Amici Curiae to Order Re Briefing on Use of "Victim" to refer to Complaining Witness.

People v. Bryant

Case No. 03-CR-204 (Dist. Ct. Eagle County, Colo. 2004) Order Re Mr. Bryant's Motion to Preclude References to the Accuser as the "Victim"

This matter comes before the Court on Mr. Bryant's Motion to Preclude References to the Accuser as the "Victim." The Court has reviewed the motion, the responses of the People, alleged victim and Amici Curiae, and Defendant's reply. Argument was heard on May 11, 2004.

The issue presented in Defendant's motion is the proper designation to reference the alleged victim, Defendant and the witnesses with the emphasis being on the trial rather than pretrial proceedings. The issue is not, as advocated by the victim organizations, whether the alleged victim acquires a certain legal status as a victim for all purposes in the criminal justice system or whether the alleged victim is entitled to certain statutory rights. The Amici brief fails to acknowledge the Court's prior Order of April 28, 2004 in which the Court rejected Defendant's blanket contention that the alleged victim was not entitled to assert statutory victim's rights based on the specific definition of victim in C.R.S. § 24-4.1-302(5). The Court has, throughout these proceedings, consistently addressed the alleged victim's assertion of her statutory rights and afforded her those rights as warranted. Although the Amici brief far exceeds the scope of Defendant's motion, the Court will consider the argument to the extent that it is relevant to the specific issues raised in the motion.

This semantic debate centers on Defendant's assertion that the use of "victim" improperly negates the presumption of innocence. Defendant cites numerous cases which generally hold that during a trial by jury reference to a complaining witness in a sexual assault matter as a "victim" is erroneous where the defense is based on consent and the credibility of the complaining witness is in issue. Under such circumstances, it remains in dispute whether a crime has actually been committed and therefore the use of the term "victim" creates a bias in that it assumes the commission of a crime prior to any such determination by a jury and is accordingly inconsistent with the presumption of innocence. See *Jackson v. State*, 600 A.2d 21 (Del. 1991); *Allen v. State*, 644 A.2d 982 (Del. 1994); *Veteto v. State*, 8 S.W.3d 805 (Tex. Ct. App. 2000); *Mason v. State*, 692 A.2d 413 (Del. 1996); *Talkington v. State*, 682 S.W.2d 674 (Tex. Ct. App. 1985); *State v. Wright*, No. 02CA008179, 2003 WL 21509033 (Ohio Ct. App. 2003). Although these cases are from other jurisdictions and are not binding precedent, the Court finds the reasoning in these cases to be sound. None of the opponents have been able to effectively rebut the legal principles established in these cases. The People's citation to *Dunton v. People*, 898 P.2d 571 (Colo. 1995) is misplaced in that the Colorado Supreme Court's reference to victim in that case was made after conviction at which point it was logical to do so. The citation to *Bellamy v. State*,

594 So.2d 337 (Fla. Dist. Ct. App. 1992) in the Amici brief is also misplaced in that it concerned the application of a victim's rights statute and the presence of the alleged victim in the courtroom. In declining to find a constitutional violation, the court noted that "[t]he jury was not made aware that his accuser was declared a 'victim' and could remain in the courtroom" which implies a violation had the jury been so informed. *Bellamy*, 594 So.2d at 338.

The current opponents' reliance on the definition of "victim" in C.R.S. § 18-3-401(7) which includes as a "victim" the "person alleging to have been subjected to a criminal sexual assault" is equally unpersuasive. There are additional definitions of "victim" within the Colorado Revised Statutes. *See also* C.R.S. § 18-8-702(1) (victim protection); C.R.S. § 24-4.1-102(10) (crime victim compensation) and C.R.S. § 24-4.1-302(5) (victim's rights). The definitions vary depending on the context and each is limited in application to the particular statutory scheme in which it is found. None of these definitions establish a legal right to be referred to as a "victim" during trial nor is the specific statutory definition of C.R.S. § 18-3-401(7) generally known or expected to be known. The common understanding of the term "victim" certainly implies that a person has been the subject of a particular wrong or crime and its use under these circumstances could improperly suggest that a crime had been committed such that the presumption of innocence might be jeopardized.

The Court therefore concludes that use of the term "victim" at trial would be inappropriate under the alleged facts and defenses in this case. Finally, the Court rejects the suggestion by the opponents that a refusal to permit reference to "victim" at trial in any way jeopardizes any statutory victim's rights or victim compensation rights. Such rights have been and will continue to be evaluated based on the language and legal precedent pertinent to those particular statutes.

Defendant has set forth four specific requests in his motion as follows.

1. "That between now and the end of trial, when the Court is not referring to the accuser in this case by her proper name, the Court refer to her as the 'complaining witness.'" In response, the People and the alleged victim request that the Court refer to the alleged victim as "victim." Defendant clarified in reply that "[i]t is the defense's view that the prosecution and the accuser's attorney are entitled to continue to refer to the accuser as the 'victim' at any time before jury selection commences." All requests are denied. The Court will continue in its use of "alleged victim."

2. "That at trial, the Court order that all prosecuting attorneys and prosecution witnesses are precluded from referring to the accuser as the 'victim.'" In response, the People request that all defense attorneys, witnesses and Defendant refer to the alleged victim as "victim" or by her proper name. Defendant's request is granted. The alleged victim shall not be referred to as "victim" at trial by the People or the witnesses. The People shall so advise the witnesses.

3. "That at trial, the Court, the parties, and all witnesses refer to all persons — including both Mr. Bryant and his accuser — by their individual names." In response, the People request that witnesses be referred to by name and that Defendant may

also be referred to as such. Defendant's request is granted in part and the People's request is granted. At trial, the alleged victim and all other persons shall be referred to by name, except that Defendant may also be referred to as such, since it is an accurate reflection of his legal status. Witnesses shall be so advised by the People and counsel.

4. "That no jury instructions or special interrogatories issued in this case refer to the accuser as the victim, and instead, that they conform to the style of the pattern instructions promulgated by the Colorado Supreme Court, which refer to a 'person.'" In response, the People request that all jury instructions or special interrogatories "refer to the victim as such, where appropriate." Defendant's request is granted. The jury instructions or special interrogatories shall refer to the alleged victim as "person" in accordance with the Colorado Supreme Court pattern instructions.

Notes

1. In *State v. Cortes*, 851 A.2d 1230 (Conn. App. 2004), the court held that the trial court's reference to a complaining witness as "the victim" during its jury charge denied the defendant his right to a fair trial where the case involved a dispute over whether sexual relations were consensual, the defendant objected to the term at the time, and the trial court gave no curative instruction. The appellate court explained:

Accordingly, we agree with the defendant that the court's instructions deprived him of his right to a fair trial. The court's use of the term "victim" in reference to the complainant, under the particular circumstances of this case, may have invaded the fact-finding function of the jury concerning the issue of whether a crime had been committed and, therefore, constitutes reversible error.

2. Could the concerns expressed by the trial judge in the *Bryant* case and the Connecticut Court of Appeals in *Cortes* be handled by a cautionary jury instruction? At the start of a criminal trial, the judge will customarily instruct the jury that the indictment filed against a defendant is not proof of guilt. Suppose that this instruction was expanded to include the following:

Ladies and Gentlemen, you are also instructed that during the trial you will hear the complaining witness in this matter referred to as "the victim." That reference is simply a convenient shorthand and is not to be taken as any evidence or proof of guilt. Whether the defendant is guilty in this case, by proof beyond a reasonable doubt, is a matter for you and you alone.

3. In *State v. Robinson*, 838 A.2d 243 (Conn. App. 2004), the court concluded that a trial judge's repeated references to the complainant as a "victim" did not violate a defendant's rights to a fair trial. Although the court specifically indicated it was not condoning the use of the term "victim," at the same time it held that "any impermissible effect of the use of that term was ameliorated by the court's twice stated instruction to the jurors that it was up to them to decide if the complaining witness was a victim and that any use by the court of that word was inadvertent. Furthermore, the court provided both preliminary and final instructions accurately

describing the defendant's presumption of innocence, further negating any potential harm caused by the court's use of the word victim."

E. Bias and More or Less "Worthy" Victims

1. Prosecutorial Bias in Charging Decisions

Prosecutors generally have extremely broad discretion in deciding whether to charge or not to charge suspects. This discretion creates ample room for cultural bias to creep into charging decisions. Review the scenarios in the following article. Identify any bias. Assuming that, as prosecutor, your overriding goal was to make unbiased charging decisions, in which scenarios would you file charges?

Elizabeth Anne Stanko, *The Impact of Victim Assessment on Prosecutors' Screening Decisions: The Case of the New York County District Attorney's Office*
16 Law & Soc'y Rev. 225 (1981)

Prosecutors, armed with the power to charge a suspect with a criminal offense, allocate their limited resources to those cases which, they believe, constitute the most "trouble" for society. Not surprisingly, what is defined as trouble corresponds with the organizational goal of achieving a high conviction record.

Earlier studies have examined prosecutors' use of legal and social criteria for handling serious criminal offenses. The seriousness of a crime and its evidentiary strength influence the prosecutability of particular cases. Defendant characteristics, such as the existence of a prior criminal record, are also important components of prosecutorial strategy. Some attention has also been given to the victim and the impact of victim characteristics on prosecutorial decision making.

Myers and Hagan, in finding that "the troubles of older, white, male, and employed victims" are considered more worthy of public processing, suggest that certain types of victims affect the allocation of prosecutorial resources. Stereotypes about victims assist them in the sorting (Swigert and Farrell, 1976) of serious cases (those deserving full prosecution) from less serious ones.

This paper explores prosecutors' use of victim stereotypes during the screening and charging stage of serious felony prosecutions....

II. THE RESEARCH SETTING AND ITS ORGANIZATIONAL CONTEXT

The setting of this study [in 1975] is a bureau within the New York County (Manhattan) prosecutor's office that is devoted solely to the screening of felony arrests. This particular office screens a high volume of cases 365 days a year. Focusing only upon serious offenses, assistant prosecutors assigned to this bureau review all the arrest circumstances, assess the evidence against the arrested individual, interview the complainant, and draw an affidavit summarizing the case against the defendant.

* * *

In 1975, a newly elected District Attorney began restructuring the process of prosecution. One of his priorities was to establish an early case assessment bureau (ECAB), whose primary purpose was to review all incoming felony arrests, to weed out those cases that would not lead to convictions, and to forward only solid, convictable cases to the supreme court bureau.

* * *

III. THE VICTIM AS AN ORGANIZATIONAL CONSIDERATION FOR SOLID CASES

How do prosecutors actually make screening decisions? As noted earlier, New York County prosecutors utilize a convictability standard against which each felony case is assessed (Alschuler, 1968). Similar to what Mather (1979) describes as a "dead bang" serious case, screening prosecutors refer to their sure cases as solid cases.[5]

* * *

If a case has strong evidence and an apparently guilty defendant, but is nonetheless not persuasive to a jury, then the outcome is not likely to be successful. In crimes against persons, especially, the victim is both witness to and object of the offense. In these types of crimes, then, the case's persuasiveness to a jury is integrally linked to the victim's credibility. In short, the credibility of the victim becomes an organizational problem for screening prosecutors: whether the victim's story is sufficiently believable to assure a "solid" case.

Victim credibility is less important in cases slated for disposition in the lower courts, since most of these cases will be resolved through plea bargaining. But if those cases forwarded to the supreme court go to trial, then the victim or complaining witness is likely to be subjected to severe cross examination ("impeaching the witness") by defense attorneys. Prosecutors must predict how a judge and jury will react to the victim under these circumstances. And they often base these predictions on common-sense evaluation of how judge and jury will assess a victim's life style and moral character, and derivatively their honesty and trustworthiness as witnesses. Moreover, prosecutors are prone to attribute credibility to certain types of individuals, those who fit society's stereotypes of who is credible: older, white, male, employed victims (*cf.* Myers and Hagan, 1979). In Goffman's (1963) sense, this is what constitutes stereotypical credibility. Indeed, prosecutors are no exception to the generalization that organizations are particularly prone to the use of stereotypical thinking (Swigert and Farrell, 1976). Bureaucracies routinely structure the interaction of participants and, as Goffman notes, this structuring is often without "special attention or thought."

The process of selecting "solid" cases, therefore, focuses on identifying problems that reduce the chance of a successful prosecution. Such problems are likely to be

---

5. All other cases were termed "garbage" cases by prosecutors. These were not considered truly "serious" matters.

perceived in a victim's appearance or character, or in the defects or weaknesses of a category of individuals of which the victim is a part. Gender, race, and occupation have important social meanings; power and status are often accorded on these grounds. A pleasant appearance, residence in a good neighborhood, a respectable job or occupation, lack of nervous mannerisms, and an ability to articulate clearly, are decided advantages. Inferences that a victim might be a prostitute or pimp, a homosexual, or an alcoholic, on the other hand, may seriously damage a victim's credibility. All of these factors must be carefully weighed.

The seven case studies which follow illustrate how prosecutors explore the "problems" of victims in otherwise solid cases. In each case, the screening prosecutor (D.A.) discusses the case with the arresting officer (A.O.), another D.A., or the victim (C.W.). These cases are not a random sample of prosecutorial screening activity, but they do illustrate the process of victim assessment in the selection of solid cases.

Example 1: Robbery in the first degree

Three individuals were arrested and charged with robbery in the first degree. The two complainants in the case had not yet arrived at the D.A.'s office. The D.A. began questioning the arresting officer about the case before the complainants arrived. Here, a prior relationship did not seem to be a problem.

D.A. Does the complainant know the defendant?

A.O. No, never seen him before.

However the address of the complainant was not in a neighborhood the D.A. considered an "upstanding" one. Finally, the question was asked:

D.A. What do we know about the complaining witness?

A.O. He's a Columbia University student.

The D.A. told the arresting officer to bring in the complainants as soon as they arrived. Later, the complainants walked in: two white, articulate graduate students.

The D.A. remarked to me after he briefly interviewed them: "Stand-up complainants. I knew they were stand-up. I marked it [to be forwarded to the grand jury] before I saw them."

The use of the term "stand-up victim" appears frequently in prosecutor's talk. It describes the ideal victim for the solid case: one who can stand up before any jury or judge and present him/herself as a credible witness. As noted by Myers and Hagan (1979) and others (Hall, 1975; Miller, 1970; Stanko, 1977), when evidentiary strength is held constant, higher-status victims are likely to increase the prosecutability of a case.

Note the stereotypical imagery. The prosecutor assesses this victim on the basis of what is "known" about the typical Columbia University student. It is assumed that these students are, as a category, "law-abiding citizens with no noticeable character flaws that undermine their credibility." Indeed, if the victim seems categorically credible, the prosecutor may view the criminal incident more seriously than the arresting officer did. For instance, in the following example, prosecutorial attention focuses primarily on the victim, altering the arresting officer's definition of the criminal offense.

Example 2: Robbery in the third degree

The complainant is an elderly woman. The incident involved a purse snatching by a 16-year-old male. The complainant chased the defendant through a park after the purse was taken. The prosecutor admired the complainant as an individual least deserving of harassment. After the complainant reported the incident, she was excused from ECAB; the prosecutor became excited about the potential case: "I'm going to write it up as a robbery one [first degree] with a tree branch [as the dangerous weapon]. I only wrote up one rob[bery] before with a tree branch [as a weapon] and that was because the victim was John F. Kennedy, Jr. These are the cases that try themselves. Any case that has a stand-up complainant should be indicted. You put her on the stand the judge loves her, the jury loves her, dynamite complainant!

Although the arrest charge was robbery in the third degree, the prosecutor changed the affidavit charge to read robbery in the first degree by defining a tree branch as a "dangerous weapon." In such instances (rare but not unheard of), sympathy for the victim and the prosecutor's positive assessment of the victim's credibility, will result in upgrading to a more severe charge. Presumably, if that same tree branch had been wielded against another teenage male, it would have been viewed as less threatening and thus less likely to sustain a first-degree robbery charge.

In the next example, the vulnerability of a victim's life style is explored for its possible detrimental effects on the seriousness (and thus prosecutability) of an offense.

Example 3: Robbery in the first degree

The complainant is a professional man who works for the Better Business Bureau. He entered the Early Case Assessment Bureau with his Sunday New York Times tucked under his arm. His recall of the incident was clear, and he presented his story articulately. After the complainant had received instructions to appear before the grand jury the next morning and had then left the room, the D.A. remarked to the arresting officer:

D.A. Do you think the defendants know the complainant is a homosexual?

A.O. No.

D.A. Would have been a great alibi [for the defendants]. They could claim that they had met and the complainant invited them up for a drink.

Essentially, the prosecutor indicates that, on second thought, he might have accorded this case nonfelony status (and thus deny it a supreme court hearing), because the victim's homosexuality raised questions about his credibility. Being labeled a homosexual, prosecutors recognize, casts doubt upon the victim's credibility, stereotypes about homosexuals, and the kinds of encounters they are alleged to have, can jeopardize the chances of winning the case. Yet in this particular instance, other factors such as the clarity of the victim's recall and his professional status compensated for this vulnerability. The charge was not altered.

As Goffman (1963) notes in his study of social stigma, characterizations such as those associated with homosexuality inherently carry with them suspicion of deviousness or dishonesty, which in turn invites disbelief of accounts reported by such people. Applying some character labels to victims implies a participation in other activities that are not "law-abiding." Similarly, during the screening of another robbery complaint, the prosecutor specifically addressed the problem with victims who were prostitutes. Reducing the charges, the prosecutor stated: "I have to deal with two complainants who will get up on the stand and say they work the streets." One prosecutor described this practice as turning "complainants into defendants."

Anticipating problems with a victim's character is an organizational strategy where prosecutors predict that a witness will be successfully impeached; they must commit their resources accordingly.

Example 4: Robbery in the second degree

A young black complainant was accosted by two males. The defendants stopped the complainant and told him they wanted money. One put his hand on the complainant's chest and told him if he didn't produce "they could 'cap' him." The prosecutor asked the complainant what 'cap' meant. The complainant replied that he didn't know; all he knew was that he didn't want to be hurt and he assumed that whatever capping was, he didn't want to find out. He gave the defendants his money — included was one ten dollar bill torn in half, which was found in the possession of the defendant. The complainant was not harmed. The prosecutor reduced the charges from robbery in the second degree to grand larceny in the third degree, stating that if the grand jury asked what 'cap' meant he couldn't answer and therefore wouldn't be able to prove the threat of force in the robbery charge.

Rather than concern himself initially with the circumstances of the actions of the defendants, here the prosecutor questions the victim's actions and explanations. The prosecutor reduced the seriousness of the original arrest charge by anticipating the reactions of the grand jury. But how is it possible for the prosecutor not to accept the victim's definition of the encounter as threatening, involving sufficient force to compel him to cooperate with his assailants' demands? Perhaps, as Swigert and Farrell note, "institutionalized conceptions of crime and criminality" influenced the prosecutor's view of the victim's actions. He may suspect, for example, that the victim was in the area for other illegal activities such as the purchase of illegal drugs. Whatever the rationale, the prosecutor relying upon stereotypes about the probable actions of victims in this situation, concludes that this particular victim cannot be one who is clearly classified among those who have been threatened during a robbery (certainly the victim would not have given up his money without a threat of force!).

In another similar incident, the prosecutor's first question to the victim was: "What caused you to be in the area when you were robbed?" As in Example 4, the victim is being asked to justify his presence in a location, including his possible motives for being there, and his actions throughout the criminal incident. The prosecutor's mandate to forward only solid cases requires selection of cases with victims whose reactions to a criminal offense somehow fit the assumed reactions of victims in "real" criminal encounters. The prosecutor must anticipate similar reactions from the judge or jury and therefore prepares the case for what "will happen," not according to what happened.

In the next example, the prosecutor questions the case's seriousness because of the assumed relationship between the complainant and the defendant.

* * *

Example 7: Robbery in the first degree

The complainants were a young, white couple. The male was the primary story teller. He stated that he was delivering furniture in the area. His girlfriend accompanied him occasionally on his deliveries and was with him the night of the robbery. As they parked on the street, three individuals approached them, displayed knives, took them inside a building, and robbed them of $80. He had never seen these individuals before. The police arrived on the scene as the defendants were fleeing the building. The young woman was not able to report many of the details of the robbery. She could not estimate the amount of time they were held in the building or the amount of money that was taken from her. However, she was visibly shaken, attractive, and concerned about the case. The D.A. attended to the woman, focusing his attention upon her. He determined that they were an innocent young couple; the case was slated for the grand jury. About two minutes after the case was sent to the typist, the male complainant returned to the D.A. and stated that he was in the area to buy heroin. He did not want his girlfriend to know about the buy. The D.A. recalled the papers and reduced the charge to a misdemeanor.

The above example illustrates the flexibility of the prosecutor's definition of a serious crime. The robbery offense was determined to be legally sufficient and the witness credible. However, after the male complainant described his motives for being in the area, a felony prosecution was no longer tenable. An individual seeking to purchase drugs places himself "at risk," and—at least as a practical matter—the culpability of the defendants is reduced. It is no longer a "solid" case.

IV. CONCLUSION

One essential concern of a critical approach to criminal justice processing is the assumption that the legal system does not apply the law impartially. Social class, sex, race, and life style are factors often taken into account in the application of the law. But the implicit (never explicitly, of course) use of such attributes in the charging process is not—or at least not only—a measure of outright prosecutorial bias. More often, it emerges as the pragmatism of a prosecutor intent on maximizing convictions and using organizational resources efficiently. Convictions are maximized when only solid cases are brought to trial. A "solid" case must be not only legally sufficient, but also based upon a credible complainant or victim. A victim must be credible not only in the eyes of the prosecutor, but also to the judge and jury. Thus an essential element of the charging decision is the determination of perceived victim credibility.

Credibility is not, however, only a matter of the personal characteristics of the victim. It also pertains to the situation, and to the congruence between situation and individual. Moreover, what emerges most clearly from the cases which I have described, and from my study, is the stereotypical quality of all such attributions. Prosecutors assume that judges and juries — particularly the latter — will find certain kinds of victim claims credible and acceptable, others not. It matters less that a victim with a prior record may have been robbed and beaten than that a jury may be dubious about such a claim, or merely unsympathetic to the victim. Prosecutors may rely on such stereotypes because of their own ideologies, but may also be influenced in accepting them by bureaucratic self-interest. A high batting average for convictions is a dominant organization goal in many prosecutors' offices. Doubts are resolved against the victim except in cases involving glamorous legal issues or particularly notorious crimes. The result may be that victims' quest for justice is often determined more by stereotypes than by the actual harm rendered against them by their assailants.

Notes

1. Should prosecution policies mirror cultural bias or confront the bias? On the one hand, prosecutorial resources are scarce. Given overwhelming caseloads that prosecutors face, a decision to prosecute one case implicitly is a decision not to prosecute another. If the case is a "loser," what justification is there for wasting public resources on it? On the other hand, there may be merit in prosecutors sending a message to the community that certain actions will be criminally prosecuted. Consider, for example, the situation of a prosecutor in the deep South in the 1960s deciding whether to prosecute a violent crime committed by Klan members. Should the fact that such prosecutions have historically been unsuccessful dissuade the prosecutor. Cf. ABA Standard for Criminal Justice — Prosecution Function Standards, Standard 3-3.9(e) ("In cases which involve a serious threat to the community, the prosecutor should not be deterred from prosecution by the fact that in the jurisdiction juries have tended to acquit persons accused of the particular kind of criminal act in question.").

2. The prosecutorial culture mentioned by Professor Stanko favors "winning" cases over other values. What other values should arguably replace the value of "winning" in the decision to prosecute?

3. The kind of bias identified by Professor Stanko in her seminal article have been confirmed on much subsequent research. One recent summary of the literature focusing on the treatment of women in criminal processes concluded that bias remains a serious problem:

It is clear that biases and assumptions about women, gender, and sexuality predispose criminal justice personnel to dismiss sexual assault claims made by certain women, regardless of or in combination with race, class, and education. They also predispose these actors to discount both the narratives and the self-determination of women engaged in prostitution when these do not comport with expectations regarding attitudes and behaviors of women who are deemed sexually exploited. The practices that we have uncovered are also important because they have implications for actual and perceived understanding of justice and access to justice. If women hesitate to seek help from the criminal justice system, or if they are dissuaded from presenting themselves in certain ways, the criminal justice system will fail to adequately and fairly address the real problems that make women vulnerable.

Rose Corrigan & Corey S. Shdaimah, *People with Secrets: Contesting, Constructing, and Resisting Women's Claims About Sexualized Victimization*, 65 Cath. U. L. Rev. 429, 485 (2016).

2. Racial Bias in the System: The Example of Jury Bias Against Black Victims

What should courts do when presented with aggregate statistics suggesting that racial bias has crept into the criminal justice system?

McCleskey v. Kemp
481 U.S. 279 (1987)

Justice Powell delivered the opinion of the Court.

This case presents the question whether a complex statistical study that indicates a risk that racial considerations enter into capital sentencing determinations proves that petitioner McCleskey's capital sentence is unconstitutional under the Eighth or Fourteenth Amendment.

McCleskey, a black man, was convicted of two counts of armed robbery and one count of murder in the Superior Court of Fulton County, Georgia, on October 12, 1978. McCleskey's convictions arose out of the robbery of a furniture store and the killing of a white police officer during the course of the robbery. . . .

* * *

The jury recommended that he be sentenced to death on the murder charge and to consecutive life sentences on the armed robbery charges. . . .

On appeal, the Supreme Court of Georgia affirmed the convictions and the sentences. . . .

[McCleskey's Habeas] petition raised 18 claims, one of which was that the Georgia capital sentencing process is administered in a racially discriminatory manner in violation of the Eighth and Fourteenth Amendments to the United States

Constitution. In support of his claim, McCleskey proffered a statistical study performed by Professors David C. Baldus, George Woodworth, and Charles Pulaski (the Baldus study) that purports to show a disparity in the imposition of the death sentence in Georgia based on the race of the murder victim and, to a lesser extent, the race of the defendant. The Baldus study is actually two sophisticated statistical studies that examine over 2,000 murder cases that occurred in Georgia during the 1970s. The raw numbers collected by Professor Baldus indicate that defendants charged with killing white persons received the death penalty in 11% of the cases, but defendants charged with killing blacks received the death penalty in only 1% of the cases. The raw numbers also indicate a reverse racial disparity according to the race of the defendant: 4% of the black defendants received the death penalty, as opposed to 7% of the white defendants.

Baldus also divided the case according to the combination of the race of the defendant and the race of the victim. He found that the death penalty was assessed 22% of the cases involving black defendants and white victims; 8% of the cases involving white defendants and white victims; 1% of the cases involving black defendants and black victims; and 3% of the cases involving white defendants and black victims. . . .

Baldus subjected his data to an extensive analysis, taking account of 230 variables that could have explained the disparities on nonracial grounds. One of his models concludes that, even after taking account of 39 nonracial variables, defendants charged with killing white victims were 4.3 times as likely to receive a death sentence as defendants charged with killing blacks. The Baldus study indicates that black defendants, such as McCleskey, who kill white victims have the greatest likelihood of receiving the death penalty.

* * *

McCleskey's first claim is that the Georgia capital punishment statute violates the Equal Protection Clause of the Fourteenth Amendment.[6] . . . As a black defendant who killed a white victim, McCleskey claims that the Baldus study demonstrates that he was discriminated against because of his race and because of the race of his victim. . . .

To prevail under the Equal Protection Clause, McCleskey must prove that the decision-makers in his case acted with discriminatory purpose. He offers no evidence specific to his own case that would support an inference that racial considerations played a part in his sentence. Instead, he relies solely on the Baldus study. . . . McCleskey's claim that these statistics are sufficient proof of discrimination, without regard

---

6. As did the Court of Appeals, we assume the study is valid statistically without reviewing the factual findings of the District Court. Our assumption that the Baldus study is statistically valid does not include the assumption that the study shows that racial considerations actually enter into any sentencing decisions in Georgia. Even a sophisticated multiple regression analysis such as the Baldus study can only demonstrate a risk that the factor of race entered into some capital sentencing decisions and a necessarily lesser risk that race entered into any particular sentencing decision.

to the facts of a particular case, would extend to all capital cases in Georgia, at least where the victim was white and the defendant is black.

McCleskey challenges decisions at the heart of the State's criminal justice system. . . . Because discretion is essential to the criminal justice process, we would demand exceptionally clear proof before we would infer that the discretion had been abused. . . . Accordingly, we hold that the Baldus study is clearly insufficient to support an inference that any of the decisionmakers in McCleskey's case acted with discriminatory purpose.

* * *

McCleskey also argues that the Baldus study demonstrates that the Georgia capital sentencing system violates the Eighth Amendment. . . .

To evaluate McCleskey's challenge, we must examine exactly what the Baldus study may show. Even Professor Baldus does not contend that his statistics prove that race enters into any capital sentencing decisions or that race was a factor in McCleskey's particular case. . . . There is, of course, some risk of racial prejudice influencing a jury's decision in a criminal case. . . . The question "is at what point that risk becomes constitutionally unacceptable."

McCleskey's argument that the Constitution condemns the discretion allowed decisionmakers in the Georgia capital sentencing system is antithetical to the fundamental role of discretion in our criminal justice system. Discretion in the criminal justice system offers substantial benefits to the criminal defendant. Not only can a jury decline to impose the death sentence, it can decline to convict, or choose to convict of a lesser offense. . . . Similarly, . . . a prosecutor can decline to charge, offer a plea bargain, or decline to seek a death sentence in any particular case. Of course, "the power to be lenient [also] is the power to discriminate," K. Davis, Discretionary Justice 170 (1973), but a capital-punishment system that did not allow for discretionary acts of leniency "would be totally alien to our notions of criminal justice." *Gregg v. Georgia*, 428 U.S., at 200, n.50.

The discrepancy indicated by the Baldus study is "a far cry from the major systemic defects identified in Furman." Where the discretion that is fundamental to our criminal process is involved, we decline to assume that what is unexplained is invidious. In light of the safeguards designed to minimize racial bias in the process, the fundamental value of jury trial in our criminal justice system, and the benefits that discretion provides to criminal defendants, we hold that the Baldus study does not demonstrate a constitutionally significant risk of racial bias affecting the Georgia capital-sentencing process.

Two additional concerns inform our decision in this case. First, McCleskey's claim, taken to its logical conclusion, throws into serious question the principles that underlie our entire criminal justice system. . . . [I]f we accepted McCleskey's claim that racial bias has impermissibly tainted the capital sentencing decision, we could soon be faced with similar claims as to other types of penalty. Moreover, the claim that his sentence rests on the irrelevant factor of race easily could be extended to apply to claims based on unexplained discrepancies that correlate to membership in other minority groups, and even to gender. . . . Also, there is no logical reason that such a claim need be limited to racial or sexual bias. If arbitrary and capricious punishment is the touchstone under the Eighth Amendment, such a claim could—at least in theory—be based upon any arbitrary variable, such as the defendant's facial characteristics, or the physical attractiveness of the defendant or the victim,[7] that some statistical study indicates may be influential in jury decisionmaking. . . . [T]here is no limiting principle to the type of challenge brought by McCleskey. . . .

Second, McCleskey's arguments are best presented to the legislative bodies. . . . Legislatures also are better qualified to weigh and "evaluate the results of statistical studies in terms of their own local conditions and with a flexibility of approach that is not available to the courts," *Gregg v. Georgia, supra.* . . . Despite McCleskey's wide ranging arguments that basically challenge the validity of capital punishment in our multi-racial society, the only question before us is whether in his case the law of Georgia was properly applied. We agree with the District Court and the Court of Appeals for the Eleventh Circuit that this was carefully and correctly done in this case.

Accordingly, we affirm. . . .

Justice Brennan [with whom Justices Marshall, Blackmun, and Stevens join], dissenting. . . . [omitted].

Justice Blackmun [with whom Justices Marshall, Brennan, and Stevens join], dissenting. . . . [omitted].

Justice Stevens, with whom Justice Blackmun joins, dissenting [omitted].

Steven L. Carter, *When Victims Happen to Be Black*
97 Yale L.J. 420 (1988)

The majority's analysis, although adequate to its own point, entirely misses the more fundamental challenge posed to the criminal justice system by the Baldus study for Warren McCleskey is not the relevant victim in the case that bears his name. To understand who the victims are whose plight the jury reinforced and the Court ignored, it is worth pausing to consider the possibility that the decision in *McCleskey v. Kemp* is starker than the Goetz trial just as the decision in *Korematsu v. United States* was starker than the forced resettlement of Japanese-Americans that it approved. A jury may state a community's outrage, a President may act out a community's fear, but the Supreme Court of the United States is supposed to guard constitutional values in the worst of times; a Constitution that cannot be defended from the passion of the mob is not fundamental law. When the Supreme Court places its imprimatur upon

---

7. Some studies indicate that physically attractive defendants receive greater leniency in sentencing than unattractive defendants, and that offenders whose victims are physically attractive receive harsher sentences than defendants with less attractive victims.

a horror, as it did in Korematsu, the horror becomes a constitutional tragedy, not merely a political one.

In one sense to compare Korematsu to McCleskey is to insult the patriotic Americans whom the Court permitted the military to incarcerate. But the difference is lessened if McCleskey is given a closer look. The significant problem with *McCleskey v. Kemp* is not, as its critics contend, that the Court rejected the claim pressed by Warren McCleskey himself. The problem is that the majority wrote in a way that made it possible to evade a more fundamental difficulty raised by the Baldus study—that racialism might be responsible not only for the disproportionate execution of murderers who happen to be black, but for inadequate protection of murder victims who happen to be black.

Mr. McCleskey was to be executed by the state. But most of the thousands of people who die in this country each year by someone's volitional act are killed not by the state but by other individuals. These murderers are, according to the McCleskey majority, subject to the laws of the state and the discretion of the jury. This is bilateral individualism in its purest form: The guilty must be punished! The citizens of the state can provide the possibility of capital punishment. A jury drawn from those citizens can decide whether the punishment is appropriate in particular cases. As the Court explained, "the inherent lack of predictability of jury decisions does not justify their condemnation. On the contrary, it is the jury's function to make the difficult and uniquely human judgments that defy codification and that 'buil[d] discretion, equity, and flexibility into a legal system.'"

Well, of course! The jury brings with it a range of preconceptions, and if racialist categorizations are widespread in society then racialist preconceptions would be among the factors shaping the "discretion, equity, and flexibility" that the McCleskey Court extolled. Justice Powell, who authored the majority opinion, rejected Mr. McCleskey's reliance on the Baldus study in words so carefully chosen that he must at least have suspected the presence of racialist preconceptions. The question, he explained, was not whether there was "some risk of racial prejudice influencing a jury's decision." The question was, rather, "at what point that risk becomes constitutionally unacceptable." Some risk of racial categorization, in other words, is probably inevitable and even constitutionally permissible. But there is no need to acknowledge a constitutionally acceptable risk of racialism among jurors unless racialist preconceptions are widespread. Once one concedes the ubiquitousness of racial categorizations, it is insupportable to pretend that all of them, or perhaps even many of them, are benign.

Justice Powell was equally cautious in choosing the terms in which he rejected the study itself. The study, he wrote, "does not demonstrate a constitutionally significant risk of racial bias affecting the Georgia capital-sentencing process." No racial bias, he concluded; nothing about racial consciousness. A rational generalization, perhaps he meant to say, is not a bias; it is simply one in a complex set of preconceptions that jurors bring with them into the jury box. Preconceptions, according to the

Court, that the jury system is supposed to bring to bear on criminal cases. Even if one accepts the dubious distinction between bias and preconception, the stark facts unearthed by Professor Baldus show the consequence of those preconceptions. A black defendant whose victim is white is twenty-two times more likely to receive the death penalty than is a black defendant whose victim happens to share his race. This might indeed be a problem for the black murderer, but that possibility pales beside what should be obvious: the massive discrimination against black victims.

The discrimination is evident no matter what argument one chooses as justification for capital punishment. One might, for example, justify the death penalty as a deterrent, arguing that its use in particular circumstances will inhibit others who might repeat them. Or one might justify the death penalty as retribution, involving a statement of the society's outrage at the crime for which the penalty is imposed. On either model, the juries that over time punish black people who kill white people far more harshly than black people who kill black people are making statements about the value of black lives. When black people kill white people, something has occurred that must be deterred, something has happened that must be condemned. When black people kill each other, however, deterrence is ignored and retribution is forgotten. When flexible juries use their discretion to impose the ultimate penalty, the lives of victims who happen to be black are simply worth less.

That, in fine, is what the Baldus study teaches, and the lesson is indeed a stark one. Too stark for the majority, and apparently too stark for the dissenters, who only hinted at the possibility that the true victims of the Georgia capital sentencing system are not the black people among those who are sentenced but the black people among those the criminal law is supposed to protect.[8] It is easy to see why the lesson is too stark to be acknowledged, for it suggests once more the difference that racialist categorizations can make in the lives of real people. When the difference is oppressive, it is racist, and the study's bottom line is that racist policy has been made, and continues to be made, as the result of probably unconscious racialist categorizations about the relative values attached to the lives of people of different skin colors.

* * *

Judicial decision is too crude a screen to filter out all leakage from private conscience into public action. Only a change in popular consciousness can do that, and absent that change, the majority's decision was right, but not for the reasons the Justices thought. The problem has nothing to do with the heinousness of Mr. McCleskey's offense or

---

8. Justice Brennan, for example, recited the figures on the race of the victim but concluded, somewhat awkwardly, that the figures documented "the risk that McCleskey's sentence was influenced by racial considerations." 107 S. Ct. at 1785. The conclusion is of course correct; what remained was to remind the reader of just whose race it was that influenced the sentencing juries. Justice Stevens referred to the process revealed by the study as "a racially discriminatory death penalty." *Id.* at 1806. He, too, was essentially correct; but at the same time, he failed to mention that the evidence of discrimination based on the race of victims showed sentencing disparities significantly larger than did the evidence of discrimination based on the race of perpetrators.

with the right of the people of a state to choose the criminal sanction they prefer. The problem is one of fairness to victims, and it is one for which constitutional adjudication using existing doctrinal tools offers no remedy.[9]

The slippery slope does lie ahead, and the McCleskey case, had it gone the other way, would have taken all of us right to the brink. For if the victims or potential victims of crime can challenge statutes said to be executed in ways that protect them inadequately by imposing too small a penalty, there might well be no stopping point; the criminal law and its pretensions of racial neutrality would be out the window—a result that the constituted authority of the society would never abide. No wonder nine Justices tiptoed around the matter: Sometimes the exposure of the pervasiveness of racialism, and of the racist policy it entails, can cost too much. Better to pretend that the jury behavior reflected by the Baldus study is simply "unexplained," to preserve the image of the dispassionate jury, together with the implicit conclusion that the disproportionate sentences are a coincidence.

* * *

But if the Baldus study is to be treated as evidence of no more than coincidence, then the factors that must coincide are these: When black people who have killed white people come before juries for sentencing it just so happens that their offenses are so serious that the state must take their lives; when black people who have killed black people come before juries it just so happens, in case after case, that their offenses turn out not to be as serious. If one can accept all of this as coincidence, as random, as not linked to race, then *McCleskey v Kemp* ought not to be a troubling case.

If on the other hand one finds this chain of coincidences unlikely, a more tragic explanation is available. According to Simone de Beauvoir, in a culture dominated by men, people come in only two varieties—women and human beings. When women insist on their right to be human beings, she explains, they are accused of wanting to be men. All too often, American legal and political culture seems to suggest the grimly analogous principle that there are two varieties of people who are involved in criminal activity, black people and victims. So perhaps when victims happen to be black, the culture rationalizes the seeming contradiction by denying that there has been a crime.

Notes

1. One commentator, a former Assistant U.S. Attorney and a Professor of Law, created a minor tempest by suggesting that black jurors should sit in judgment on black defendants. Paul Butler, *Racially Based Jury Nullification: Black Power in the Criminal Justice System*, 105 YALE L.J. 677 (1995). Would it make any more sense to

---

9. Several of my colleagues independently suggested a legislative remedy: If the criminal law is underenforced against transgressors whose victims are black, then the deterrence theory implies that the penalty for victimizing black people should be greater than the penalty for victimizing others. This of course is reverse discrimination with a vengeance, and would in any case be unavailable if the underenforcement comes in cases in which the maximum penalty is already death.

say that only black jurors could sit in judgment when the victim was black? Would this resolve the McCleskey "problem"? What if the defendant and victim were of different races?

2. What procedures or techniques would you advocate for to eliminate bias against certain victims? Can diverse juries benefit victims as well as defendants?

3. Did the Supreme Court make a mistake in McCleskey by simply "assuming" that the statistics showed disparate outcomes due to race rather than investigating whether they really proved disparate outcomes. The Court gave no weight to the fact that, after extensive evidentiary hearings, the federal district judge who first handled the case concluded that apparent racial disparities shown in Baldus' summary statistics disappeared when more control variables were added into the equations. *McCleskey v. Zant*, 580 F. Supp. 338 (N.D. Ga. 1984). For example, most police officers are white and murder of a police officer is a quintessential capital crime. Unless this fact is controlled for, aggregate statistics may purport to show a "race of the victim" effect that in reality is attributable to the racially-neutral factor that cop killing is more likely to lead to a death penalty. *See* Stanley Rothman & Stephen Power, *Execution by Quota?*, Public Interest, Summer 1994, at 3. For competing views on this subject, compare Bryan Stevenson, Close to Death: Reflections on Race and Capital Punishment in America, in Debating the Death Penalty: Should America Have Capital Punishment 76 (Hugo Bedau & Paul G. Cassell eds. 2004) (race-of-the-victim effect real) with Paul G. Cassell, *In Defense of the Death Penalty*, *id.* at 183 (questioning this view).

4. While the U.S. Supreme Court had the final word in rejecting a race-of-the-victim argument under the United States Constitution, the issue has continued to be litigated under state constitutions. For example, several concurring justices on the Connecticut Supreme Court recently indicated that they would reach a different result on state constitutional grounds:

> Although the standard set forth in *McCleskey* may be appropriate for challenges to noncapital sentencing determinations, we question whether it provides adequate protection when the ultimate punishment of death is involved. The types of subtle biases that influence members of the majority to make decisions favoring their own race may well be inevitable, albeit regrettable. When unconsciously made, they do not inherently impugn the diligent and good faith work of our prosecutors, police, judges, and jurors. Nor do they mean that the outcomes of a criminal justice system, writ large, are manifestly unjust. But both this court and the United States Supreme Court repeatedly have made clear that "[d]eath is different." Because a sentence of death is uniquely irreversible and deprives the condemned of the ability to exercise *any* of his inalienable rights; *see Furman v. Georgia, supra*, 408 U.S. at 290 (Brennan, J., concurring); it ought not be imposed unless we are assured that the selection between a sentence of death or life imprisonment is based solely on objective, morally defensible criteria. The fact that a white prosecutor or a white juror may be more troubled by the death of a

white victim than of a black or Hispanic victim may be psychologically explicable, but it is not morally defensible. It should not be the basis on which we decide who lives and who dies.

State v. Santiago, 318 Conn. 1, 164–65, 122 A.3d 1, 98–99 (Norcutt, J., concurring), *reconsideration denied*, 319 Conn. 912, 124 A.3d 496 (2015).

3. Legislatively Distinguishing Between Victims: The Example of Hate Crimes

Recently legislators have passed statutes that criminalize "hate crimes" — that is, crimes in which the offender selects a victim because of such factors as race, religion, national origin, or sexual orientation. Typical of such statutes is Florida's, which enhances the penalty for any crime "if the commission of such felony or misdemeanor evidences prejudice based on the race, color, ancestry, ethnicity, religion, sexual orientation, national origin, mental or physical disability, or advanced age of the victim." FLA. STAT. ANN. §775.085. The vast majority of states have similar statutes.

These hate crime statutes have proven controversial. In some ways, the debate is the flip-side of the debate in *McCleskey* case, as opponents of hate crime laws argue that these laws make some victims more "worthy" than others. Can hate crime laws be justified? Consider the following competing views.

Kellina M. Craig, *Examining Hate-Motivated Aggression: A Review of the Social Psychological Literature on Hate Crimes, a Distinct Form of Aggression*
7 AGGRESSION & VIOLENT BEHAVIOR 86 (2002)

1.1. Symbolic and Instrumental Functions

Hate crimes represent a unique form of aggression that includes the intent to harm, but also serves symbolic and instrumental functions for perpetrators. This type of conceptualization of hate crimes borrows loosely from Berk (1990) who describes a useful distinction between hate crimes and other person and property offenses. For the present discussion, hate crimes are regarded as serving a symbolic function to the extent that a message, albeit one of hate, is communicated to a community, neighborhood, or group. Here, it is the symbolic status of the victim(s) that motivates the perpetrators. It matters little whether the victim actually identifies himself as a member of a particular socially identifiable group. Instead, in the eyes of their perpetrators, they symbolize a despised social group. Their victimization serves as a visible indicator of the motives of the perpetrators because their hate crimes indicate the perpetrators' bias.

In addition to the symbolic function of hate crimes, there is also an instrumental function. Hate crimes affect the actions of members of victims' and perpetrators' groups. When a hate crime occurs, members of the victim's social group who are aware of the incident often tailor their subsequent actions. According to the testimonies of antigay survivors of hate crimes and the people who know them, avoiding a particular business establishment or street, moving from the neighborhood, or significantly altering one's routine activities may seem to be especially practical options following a hate crime. Thus, hate crimes effectively curtail the behaviors and movement of members of the victim's group. People who are not members of the victim's social group, but who also belong to minority groups, may behave similarly, fearing for their own safety. It is also likely that members of the perpetrator's groups may feel pressured to behave in unusual ways when encountering or interacting with either victims or members of the victim's social group. Hate crimes are instrumental in restricting the behaviors and choices of large numbers of people—in both victims' and perpetrators' groups.

1.2. Presence of Multiple Perpetrators

Another way that hate crimes differ from other aggressive offenses is that hate crimes typically involve multiple perpetrators. Hate crime activity is very much a group activity in which perpetrators operate as a group in order to attack or harm perceived members of a social group. Although the National Crime Victimization Survey (NCVS) reports a tendency for violent crimes to be perpetrated by people acting alone, nearly two-thirds of hate crimes reported to the police involve two or more perpetrators—reflecting a tendency for these crimes to be carried out by multiple perpetrators. Further, a recent analysis of hate crime occurrence in Los Angeles county suggests that the actual number of perpetrators is related to the severity of the crimes, such that the greater the size of the group of perpetrators, the more severe the crimes.

Reasons for the group nature of hate crimes include the likely cowardice of most perpetrators who, in the absence of the group, would otherwise be unable or unwilling to inflict harm on others. For these individuals, there is safety in numbers. Additionally, when operating as a group, hate crime offenders are more likely to experience a diffusion of responsibility, and insensitivity to normal social restraints. That is, with each additional perpetrator in the group, any one perpetrator is apt to feel increasingly less responsible for the aggressive behavior they have carried out. When individuals temporarily act in socially prohibitive ways with diminished capacity for personal control, the outcome of their behaviors is especially likely to be extreme. This state of affairs is called deindividuation and is proposed to account for some instances of mob behavior, rioting, and other short-term dysfunction. Finally, the presence of multiple perpetrators serves to provide support and confirm each perpetrator's bigotry and hatred for the victim's group. Consequently, the group of perpetrators can effectively incite each other toward aggression.

1.3. Victim's Increased Psychological and Emotional Distress

Hate crimes are also regarded as distinct types of aggressive activity because they often inflict greater psychological distress upon their victims than similarly egregious nonbias aggression (e.g., mugging or robbery). Victims of hate crimes often experience long-term posttraumatic stress symptoms. Research by Herek, Gillis, Cogan, and Glunt (1997) supports this. In their study, 147 gays, lesbians, and bisexuals reported on their experiences with heterosexist victimization. The researchers found that those respondents who were victims of hate crimes manifested higher levels of depression, anxiety, anger, and symptoms of posttraumatic stress than those who had not experienced a heterosexist assault. Herek et al. (1997) found that in some cases, victims of hate crimes needed as much as 5 years to overcome their experience, and this was more than twice the time necessary for victims of nonbias crimes.

In general, victims of hate crimes experience extreme emotional distress including feelings of vulnerability, anger, and depression, as well as difficulty in interpersonal relations. Results of a study conducted at the National Institute Against Prejudice and Violence (NIAPV) are especially useful in understanding the impact of hate crime victimization upon its victims. Although a majority of survivors of racist hate crimes that were interviewed did not receive physical injuries, these very same respondents admitted feeling extreme anger and fear following the incident. Further, they listed specific behavioral responses that included both avoidant strategies, such as relocating, as well as potential retaliatory ones, such as purchasing a firearm. Although the behavioral responses of hate crime victims are varied, hate crime victimization generally extracts an extreme psychological and emotional toll from its victims.

1.4. Deteriorating Social Relations

The distinct psychological and emotional effects of hate crimes are not limited to interpersonal dynamics, but may also infect relations between and within larger social groups. Supreme Court Justice Rehnquist, in deciding whether the First Amendment rights of a hate crime perpetrator were violated, noted in his opinion that hate-motivated conduct inflicts harm on society (*Wisconsin v. Mitchell*, 1993). In his brief, the Justice suggested that, in addition to the harm sustained by the immediate victim of the hate crime, hate crimes instill fear beyond the immediate victim. Indeed, fear is felt well beyond the geographic and temporal locale of the incident to affect all members of the victim's social category.

Hate crimes create a climate of suspicion and fear, affecting members of the victim's group, as well as relations between the groups to which the victim and perpetrators belong. According to Weinstein (1992, p. 10), hate crimes " . . . can have a powerful in terrorem effect, particularly for members of minority groups who historically have been, or currently are, victims of racist violence." Hate crimes are based primarily on the victim's perceived membership in a demographic group. Any single incident has threatening implications for all members of that group and reminds them that they could be next.

In his seminal brief, the Justice also speculated about the likelihood for hate crimes to incite community unrest and to provoke retaliation. With respect to the latter, retaliation would seem to be an especially likely outcome following a highly publicized hate crime incident. The norm of reciprocity provides a convenient way of considering such motives. According to this, much of human behavior is governed in a quid pro quo manner. That is, people respond to others in ways and to the degree that resembles that of the other person's initial response. Research suggests that the recipient of a harmful act tends to respond to its provider with a harm that is comparable in both quantity and quality. This possibility was investigated recently in one experimental study, and the findings though mixed, suggest that retaliatory efforts will differ according to the victim's specific social group. Thus, whether retaliation is likely to follow, a hate crime seems to depend largely upon the group in which the victim belongs. In the case of racist hate crime, Garofalo (1991) presents evidence of reciprocity between African American and White perpetrators and victims. There may be a greater willingness for retaliation between these two groups than among other groups.

As for the likelihood of community unrest, few empirical data exists. However, the near twofold increase in hate crimes in New York City following the infamous Howard Beach incident in 1986 in which an African American young man was killed after being chased by a mob of White youths is often cited as evidence of this. Several other authors have noted the capacity of hate violence to spark large-scale urban disturbance. Whether hate crimes provoke community unrest requires systematic empirical investigation, and this represents an important area for inquiry. What seems to be most apparent, following a well-publicized hate crime, is an overall deterioration in the quality of intergroup and interpersonal relations. . . .

In summary, hate crimes, whether violent or nonviolent, differ from alternate crimes in several ways. Unlike nonbias crimes, hate crimes also function as symbolic assaults against victims and members of victims' groups. Victims experience emotional distress well after their initial victimization, and may substantially alter their lifestyle. In some cases, retaliation may be a likely consequence of the initial assault. Finally, hate crimes are usually perpetrated by multiple offenders, and when they occur, diminish the overall quality of intergroup relations.

Heidi M. Hurd & Michael S. Moore, *Punishing Hatred and Prejudice*

56 Stan. L. Rev. 1081 (2004)

Greater Psychological Trauma to the Principal Victims of Hate/Bias Crimes

A . . . common claim made on behalf of sentence enhancements for hate/bias crimes is that such crimes cause greater psychological trauma to their immediate victims than do otherwise-motivated crimes. . . . The claim in each case is that victims of hate/bias crimes experience these traumas at a greater rate than victims of otherwise-motivated crimes, including otherwise-motivated crimes of violence such as robbery and mayhem.

The conclusions drawn from these empirical claims are that hate/bias crime offenders deserve more punishment because they are more blameworthy; that they are more blameworthy because they have done greater wrong; and that they have done greater wrong because they have (typically) caused more harm, namely, the psychological traumatization of victims (in the ways just detailed).

In assessing this argument for hate/bias crime sentencing enhancements, the first question is whether its empirical presuppositions are accurate. All crimes of violence tend to produce psychological trauma in their victims. As one study notes, "[T]he predominant emotional responses of hate violence victims appear similar to those of victims of other types of personal crime." The question is whether hate/bias-motivated crimes of violence produce significantly more trauma than do otherwise-motivated but identical crimes of violence. James Jacobs and Kimberly Potter have recently reviewed some of the leading studies that claim to establish greater trauma for hate/bias crime victims. They conclude that such studies are defective in not comparing the trauma of hate/bias crime victims with the trauma of comparable crime victims. For without comparing ordinary assault victims with hate/bias-motivated assault victims (when the severity of the assaults and the injuries are equivalent), how can one isolate the traumatizing effects of hate and bias?

Sometimes those seeking to justify hate/bias crime legislation via the psychological-trauma argument try to bolster the plausibility of their empirical claim by piggy-backing it on the claim that hate/bias crimes involve heightened violence. With more severe violence, it is of course plausible to anticipate more severe psychic trauma. Yet a complete answer to this argument is provided by the fact that the law governing aggravated assaults adjusts punishments to the relative degree of violence and injury (including psychic trauma) perpetrated by aggressors. Part of what makes aggravated assaults worse than simple assaults is the greater psychic trauma accompanying more severe attacks and more severe physical injuries. That factor has already been taken into account in setting the punishments for the different categories of aggravated assaults, so one would unjustifiably "double count" this factor by adding enhanced penalties to hate/bias-motivated crimes because of the psychic traumas that attend more severe violence.

Despite these reservations about the empirical claim, let us suppose that it is true — that to some extent hate/bias crime victims experience greater trauma (fear, lowered self-esteem, anger, depression, etc.) than do victims of otherwise-motivated but otherwise-comparable crimes. Such a supposition allows us to reach other problems with this argument for sentence enhancements.

One such problem is the proxy problem we encountered before with respect to the claim that hate/bias crimes magnify physical injuries. Just as the hate/bias motive of an actor is not itself a physical injury to a victim, it is not itself a psychic trauma to a victim either. Those who justify hate/bias crime legislation on this basis thus are proposing that the defendant's motive function as a proxy for what really heightens the gravity of the wrong, namely, the victim's psychic trauma.

But hate and bias are particularly bad proxies for a victim's psychic trauma. It is not hatred and bias, as such, that hurt; rather, it is the perception of hatred and bias that hurts. An assault that is in fact motivated by hatred or bias, but which is not perceived by the victim as being so motivated, can hardly be said to cause heightened psychic trauma. (Inversely, of course, an assault that is not motivated by hatred or bias may nevertheless be perceived as being so motivated and so may indeed cause elevated psychic injury.) So if the psychic trauma to victims of hate/bias crimes is thought to be the gravaman of the offense, then the law should not be concerned with the motive of the offender, but rather, with the perception of the defendant's motive by the victim. Then hate/bias-motivated offenders who do not cause the psychic harms that, ex hypothesi, attend the perception of hatred and bias would not be subject to enhanced punishment for a wrong they did not commit; and offenders who are not hateful or biased in their motives, but who know or are reckless with regard to the fact that they will be taken to be hateful or biased, should receive an enhanced sentence, by virtue of the greater wrong that they do in causing such a perception.

However, even if hate/bias crimes were redefined so as to make the victim's perception of hate/bias definitional of the offense, there would still be an unacceptable proxy function operative in hate/bias crime legislation. A victim's perception of hate/bias in his attacker is still not the same thing as the experience of greater psychic trauma. Nor is the one universally accompanied by the other. A victim of a bias-motivated assault who perceives the bias in it may not suffer any greater psychic trauma than the typical victim of an otherwise-motivated assault; additionally, one who suffers terribly in her mind after an assault need not suffer so because she perceived the assault to be biased in its motivation. Perceived bias, in other words, is still over and underinclusive as a proxy for severe psychic trauma.

So if one is truly concerned with adjusting penalties to the psychic traumas experienced by crime victims generally (and to the psychic traumas experienced by victims of hate/bias-motivated crimes in particular), the best thing to do would be to argue for a new form of aggravated assault, one that explicitly adds the element of the victim's extreme emotional distress to the actus reus of the offense. Then when such trauma is caused by an offender's apparent hate or bias, enhanced punishment would be appropriate, but not otherwise.

Vicarious Injuries to Members of the Victim's Larger Community

The psychological traumas suffered by the principal victim of a hate/bias-motivated crime are also said to be suffered by other members of the group(s) that share with the principal victim the characteristic(s) that prompted the defendant to target him or her. . . .

An initial response to claims such as these may be to doubt the relevance of harms to persons other than the crime victim in gauging the degree of wrong done by the offender. After all, it is a serious wrong to murder another, no matter whether the one murdered was a much-loved father of small children or a much-despised old hermit. To say otherwise is to say that the wrongness of a defendant's act turns on how many family members, friends, and caring acquaintances the victim has. Those who find this implication unpalatable might thus be inclined to say that, as a moral matter, how others are affected by someone's misfortune at being a crime victim is not to be considered in assessing the wrongness of the perpetrator's act.

Our view is that such collateral harms are generally relevant to assessing the wrongfulness of an offender's actions and may be taken into account either in the definition of the actus reus of more serious grades of offenses or in the appraisal of victim impact statements at sentencing. When we set severe punishments for assassinations of public officials and assaults upon police officers, we take into account the collateral harms (to persons other than the direct victims of those crimes) caused by such acts. When we allow grandmothers of murder victims to submit victim impact statements at the sentencing of offenders, we are inviting jury consideration of collateral harms in assessing the degree of wrong done by those convicted of murder. Sentence enhancements for hate/bias crimes thus might be based on the collateral harms that those crimes cause.

There are nevertheless serious problems for the collateral-harms defense of sentence enhancements. First, there is the nagging question of empirical fact: Is it really true that members of groups suffer more vicarious psychic injury in response to hate/bias-motivated crimes than in response to otherwise-motivated crimes? The question, again, is not whether such vicarious suffering exists at all; it is, rather, the comparative question of whether it exists to a significantly greater degree within groups targeted by hate/bias crimes than it does within groups related in various ways to crime victims generally. As we saw before, the social science literature on this topic—even for principal victims of bias crimes—is not very reassuring. And if we must make the judgment from the armchair, our bets are with John Donne, who famously intoned that when the bell tolls for any it tolls for all—white, black, Catholic, Jewish, gay, straight, disabled, male, female, etc.

Second, the same proxy problems exist for vicarious psychic-trauma arguments as exist for the direct versions of these arguments. Again, the hateful or biased motivations of an offender are a poor proxy for the vicarious psychic trauma of members of the victim's community. The group's perception of hate/bias would be a better proxy. And even perceived hate/bias is a proxy that is both over and underinclusive. It is also quite unnecessary. If severe collateral trauma is caused by an offender's crime (whatever its motivation), that harm can be taken into account through victim impact statements at sentencing provided by representative members of the community that is harmed. There is no need to enhance the sentences of all offenders who commit crimes out of hatred or bias simply because some of them cause greater, independently provable harms to their victims (including those who are victims vicariously). Those who culpably cause such harms (whatever their motivations) ought to pay for them with greater sentences; those who do not cause such harms ought not to be penalized because others do.

The case for the enhanced sentences of hate/bias-motivated crimes based on secondary psychic trauma is thus even shakier than was the case based on the psychic trauma of principal victims of hate/bias crimes. Neither the factual premises nor the normative inferences implicit in these arguments appear sustainable.

Notes

1. Do you agree with Hurd and Moore that "hate and bias are particularly bad proxies for a victim's psychic trauma"? Of course, all criminal statutes must be drafted with some imprecision. Do statutes that enhance penalties for, e.g., racist assaults really sweep too broadly?

2. Which victims are sufficiently worthy to qualify for the protection of hate crimes? In *In re B.C.*, 680 N.E.2d 1355 (Ill. 1997), the court held that an Illinois hate crimes statute extended to displaying a swastika-adorned figure of a Ku Klux Klan figure standing over the bleeding corpse of an African-American even where no racial minority saw the display. The court concluded that the display might be harmful to "the public at large." Does this unduly extend hate crimes legislation? *See* Lawrence Bradfield Hughes, *Can Anyone Be the Victim of a Hate Crime?*, 23 U. DAYTON L. REV. 591 (1998).

3. The Supreme Court has rejected First Amendment challenges to narrowly drawn hate crimes laws. For example, in *Wisconsin v. Mitchell*, 508 U.S. 476 (1993), the Court held that enhanced penalties against a defendant for selecting his victim based on the victim's race did not punish a defendant's beliefs, but rather targeted the special harms caused by hate crimes. Similarly, in *Virginia v. Black*, 538 U.S. 343 (2003), the Court upheld Virginia's statute forbidding cross-burning "with intent to intimidate." On the other hand, the Supreme Court has made clear that the First Amendment allows speakers to make hateful comments. *See, e.g., Snyder v. Phelps*, 562 U.S. 443 (2011) (affirming decision invalidating jury verdict in favor of father against fundamentalist church stemming from anti-homosexual demonstration near service member's funeral).

4. The precise drafting of hate crimes legislation has proven challenging. In *Botts v. State*, 2004 WL 2378432 (Ga. 2004), the Georgia Supreme Court struck down as unconstitutionally vague a statute enhancing a criminal sentence where the defendant selected his victim "because of bias or prejudice." The court reasoned:

The broad language in OCGA § 17-10-17, by enhancing all offenses where the victim or his property was selected because of any bias or prejudice, encompasses every possible partiality or preference. A rabid sports fan convicted of uttering terroristic threats to a victim selected for wearing a competing team's baseball cap; a campaign worker convicted of trespassing for defacing a political opponent's yard signs; a performance car fanatic convicted of stealing a Ferrari — any "bias or prejudice" for or against the selected victim or property, no matter how obscure, whimsical or unrelated to the victim it may be, but for which proof beyond a reasonable doubt might exist, can serve to enhance a sentence. Absent some qualification on "bias or prejudice," OCGA § 17-10-17 is left "'so vague that persons of common intelligence must necessarily guess at its meaning and differ as to its application.'" *Payne v. State*, 563 S.E.2d 844 (Ga. 2002). Accordingly, we hold that OCGA § 17-10-17 is too vague to justify the imposition of enhanced criminal punishment for its violation.

4. Victims in Trust Relationships and Vulnerable Victims

Should punishment for crimes against especially vulnerable victims or victims in trust relationships be especially harsh?

Elizabeth Rapaport, *The Death Penalty and Gender Discrimination*

25 Law & Soc'y Rev. (1991)

. . .

III. A GENDERED INTERPRETATION OF THE CONCEPTION OF OFFENSE SERIOUSNESS EMBEDDED IN CAPITAL PUNISHMENT LAW

In a series of cases beginning in 1976, the Supreme Court has placed jurisdictions wishing to impose the death penalty under constitutional obligation (1) to guide and limit the discretion of sentencers in order to avoid the arbitrariness in death sentencing that infected the system in the past and (2) to abjure the death sentence altogether for crimes that our society no longer regards as sufficiently reprehensible to merit capital punishment. The Court has interpreted both mandatory death sentencing for a particular crime and death as a penalty for a crime that does not involve a fatality as violating the contemporary U.S. perceptions of the limits of retributive justice. Most states that retain the death penalty, thirty-four out of thirty-seven, have responded to the requirement that discretion be guided by enacting statutes that enumerate the aggravating factors, which, if found to be present, and if not outweighed by mitigating factors, would permit the sentencing authority to impose the death penalty. Analysis reveals that three broad categories of murders are stigmatized as death eligible in the death penalty statutes of this type: (1) predatory murder, (2) murder that hinders or threatens the enforcement of law or other governmental functions, and (3) murder that evinces excessive violence or brutality.

* * *

If we examine the results of this analysis of the statutes with the eye of a feminist critic, we will note that special protection is not given to domestic life or relationships. The worst cases of domestic violence, unlike the worst cases of robbery violence, are not, as such, eligible for capital adjudication. Domestic crimes may nonetheless become capital cases if they are regarded as especially brutal crimes or if they are also pecuniary crimes. But the paradigmatic domestic killing, arising out of hot anger at someone who is capable, as it were by definition, of calling out painful and sudden emotion in his or her killer, is virtually the antithesis of a capital murder. Yet there are features of domestic homicides that could plausibly be regarded as among the most reprehensible crimes: They involve the betrayal of familial trust and responsibility on which not only domestic peace but presumably our civilization depends, as much it depends on honoring the law of mine and thine and respecting the authority of the state. They also have characteristics that could be read as inherent extreme brutality. The victims of family murders are typically especially vulnerable to their killers because of physical weakness and psychological dependency. Often the victims have been the objects of prior and habitual violence by their killers.

Whether or not one endorses or opposes capital punishment on moral or other grounds, and whether or not one would wish to see its domain enlarged for any purpose, there is, from a feminist point of view, an invidious subordination of the interests of women involved in the failure of the statutes to attach our society's most profound condemnation to crimes that destroy the domestic peace. These murders are also far more likely to have women and children as victims than are economic crimes. Our law reveals a disposition to regard killing a stranger for gain as more heinous than killing a spouse or child in anger. This hierarchy of opprobrium both privileges the interests of men over those of women and children and support patriarchal values. In what follows I first elaborate a feminist critique of the hierarchy of opprobrium in the statutes. I then argue that including the worst domestic murders among the most severely stigmatized crimes, despite the apparent counter-intuitiveness of such a proposal, is consistent with the doctrinal structure of our law of homicide and the policies that may be inferred to underlie it.

Notes

1. Does the idea of the death penalty for killing a spouse or an offspring bother you? How about life imprisonment? Can you counter the argument made by Professor Rapaport that killings in a trust relationship are more heinous than stranger to stranger killings?

2. Sentencing enhancements for crimes against "vulnerable victims" are commonplace. For example, the federal sentencing guidelines provide a two-level enhancement for the offense level of any crime "[i]f the defendant knew or should have known that a victim of the offense was a vulnerable victim." U.S. Sentencing Guidelines § 3A1.1. The Commentary to this Guideline further defines a "vulnerable victim" as a person who is "unusually vulnerable due to age, physical or mental condition, or who is otherwise particularly susceptible to the criminal conduct."

3. Oregon has fashioned a specific non-capital homicide statute to facilitate conviction for a serious crime when children are killed:

OR. REV. STAT. § 163.118(1)(C)

Criminal homicide constitutes murder . . . by abuse when a person, recklessly under circumstances manifesting extreme indifference to the value of human life, causes the death of a child under 14 years of age . . . and the person has previously engaged in a practice of assault . . . or causes the death by neglect or maltreatment.

In Oregon all other homicides committed recklessly under circumstances manifesting extreme indifference to the value of human life are classified as Manslaughter in the First Degree, a lesser degree of homicide than Murder by Abuse. Adult victims are not included in the statute. Oregon has also made the murder of a person under the age of 14 years of age a capital offense.

Chapter 3

Investigation

Introduction

This chapter surveys the role of crime victims in investigating crimes and their rights during the investigative process. It begins by discussing the fact that many crimes are never reported to police. It then reviews ways in which victims can try to force an adequate public investigation of a crime. (Issues surrounding grand juries, which might be viewed as part of the investigative process, are deferred to Chapter 4, which examines charging decisions.) The chapter then turns to issues surrounding the private financing of official investigations. The chapter also looks at limits on private investigations of crime, including restrictions on private searches and citizen's arrest, as well as the application of the exclusionary rule to private investigation. The chapter concludes by examining victims' rights during the investigative process.

A. Reporting of Crimes

Many serious crimes are never reported to the police. The reasons for lack of reporting are varied, but have been summarized as including the following situations:

- Victims may consider the crime unimportant and therefore decline to call the police.

- Victims may not trust the police or have little confidence in the ability of the police to solve the crime.

- Victims without property insurance may believe it is useless to report a theft.

- Victims may fear reprisals from an offender's friends or family.

- Some victims may have "dirty hands" through being involved in illegal activities themselves and may not want to get the police involved.

Larry J. Siegel, Criminology: The Core 31 (2017).

The net effect of underreporting of crimes, difficulty in solving crimes, difficulty in convicting offenders, and lack of prison space and reluctance to incarcerate offenders, creates a "national crime funnel," which means, for every reported crime, the chances of an offender going to prison are small. For example, in 2006, while about six million violent crimes were committed, only approximately 113,000 persons went to prison.

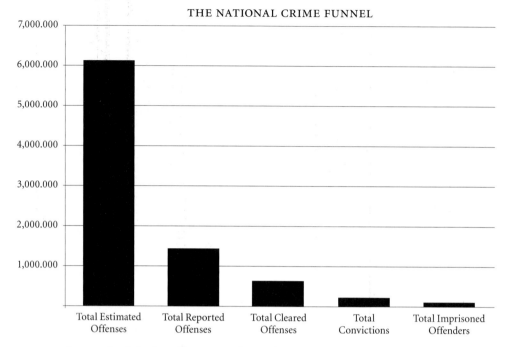

Source: Paul G. Cassell, *Freeing the Guilty Without Protecting the Innocent:
Some Skeptical Observations on Proposed New "Innocence" Procedures,*
56 N.Y. L. REV. 1063, 1079 (2012).

Should more be done to encourage victims to report crimes? One example of legislation designed to encourage crime reporting is what is commonly referred to as the "U visa," which was created by Congress in 2000 to provide a mechanism to encourage undocumented immigrants who had been trafficked, exploited, victimized, or abused to "report these crimes to law enforcement and fully participate in the investigation of the crimes" without fear of removal or deportation. Victims of Trafficking and Violence Prevention Act, Pub. L. 106-386, § 1513(a)(1) (2000). *See generally* Lisa Locher, *"U Visa" Relief for Undocumented Victims of Crime,* 61 BOSTON BAR J. 25 (2017).

B. Victims' Rights During the Investigative Process

1. When Do Victims' Rights Start?

During the investigative process, do crime victims have any rights? Or do victims' rights statutes only come into play later in the process, after charges are filed? Courts that have reached the issue have generally held that victims do have some rights under crime victims' statutes, even before charges are filed. This issue is discussed in the following law review article about application of the federal Crime Victims' Rights Act (CVRA) before the formal filing of criminal charges:

Paul G. Cassell, Nathanael J. Mitchell & Bradley J. Edwards, *Crime Victims' Rights During Criminal Investigations: Applying the Crime Victims' Rights Act Before Criminal Charges Are Filed*

104 J. Crim. L. & Criminology 59 (2014)

An analysis of the CVRA's application before prosecutors have filed charges must begin by assessing the CVRA's purposes because any interpretation of the CVRA that is divorced from the statute's purposes would run the risk of defeating the statute's aims. It is axiomatic that courts should "give faithful meaning to the language Congress adopted in the light of the evident legislative purpose in enacting the law in question." As discussed above, one important goal of the CVRA was to keep crime victims informed about any developments in the criminal justice process. But the need to be informed does not begin with the filing of a formal criminal charge. A crime victim needs to know what is happening before formal charging-during a criminal investigation, for example-just as much as she needs to know what is happening in court. Indeed, she may have a greater need to know, as she may be concerned that the criminal who harmed her is still on the loose, posing a danger to her.

Similarly, concerning the second purpose—facilitating victim participation—without a right to pre-charging involvement, victims may be effectively shut out of the process entirely. The Epstein case provides a useful illustration of why the CVRA must be understood to extend rights to victims prior to indictment. The prosecutors handling the investigation reached an agreement with Epstein that barred federal prosecution of sex offenses committed against dozens of victims, including Jane Doe Number One and Jane Doe Number Two. If CVRA rights did not extend to the negotiations surrounding the agreement, then the victims *never* would have had any ability to participate in the resolution of the case.

A construction of the CVRA that extends rights to victims before charges are filed would be entirely consistent with the CVRA's participatory purpose. If victims have the ability to participate in a precharging plea bargaining process, for example, victims can help ensure that prosecutors do not overlook anything that should be covered in the plea deal. For example, victims might be able to obtain agreement to a "no contact" order or valuable restitution-points that the prosecutor might fail to consider in crafting a plea. Similarly, allowing victims to participate early in the process avoids retraumatizing victims. . . .

Because crime victims lack a right to appointed counsel, many victims have difficulty litigating the scope of their rights. But in a few cases, victims have been able to secure counsel to argue that they have rights in the criminal justice process during the investigation of federal crimes. When those cases have reached the issue of whether the CVRA applies before charges have been filed, courts have uniformly agreed with the victims' position.

Perhaps the leading case to date to assess this question is the Fifth Circuit's decision in *In re Dean*, 527 F3d 391 (5th Cir. 1998) (discussed in Chapter 7, below). There, a wealthy corporate criminal defendant reached a generous plea deal with the Government—a deal that the Government filed for approval with the district court without conferring with the victims. Citing procedural rights under the CVRA, the victims requested that the trial court reject the plea agreement.' The District Court for the Southern District of Texas specifically concluded that victims' CVRA rights could apply during the investigation of the crime: "There are clearly rights under the CVRA that apply before any prosecution is underway." The district court concluded, however, that the Government had not violated the CVRA because it had secured judicial permission to dispense with notification to victims.

The victims sought appellate review in the Fifth Circuit. There, the court concurred with the district court that CVRA rights apply before trial. Unlike the district court, however, it held that the Government had violated the victims' rights:

> The district court acknowledged that "[t]here are clearly rights under the CVRA that apply before any prosecution is underway." Logically, this includes the CVRA's establishment of victims' "reasonable right to confer with the attorney for the Government." At least in the posture of this case (and we do not speculate on the applicability to other situations), the government should have fashioned a reasonable way to inform the victims of the likelihood of criminal charges and to ascertain the victims' views on the possible details of a plea bargain.

The Fifth Circuit then remanded the matter to the district court to determine the appropriate remedy for the violation of the victims' rights.

The Fifth Circuit's decision in *Dean* has been cited favorably in four recent district court decisions, which provides further support for the conclusion that the CVRA applies before charges have been filed. In *United States v. Rubin*, 558 F.Supp. 2d 411 (E.D.N.Y. 2008) victims of a federal securities fraud argued that they had CVRA rights even before prosecutors filed a superseding indictment covering the specific crimes affecting the victims. Citing *Dean*, the District Court for the Eastern District of New York agreed that the rights were expansive and could apply before charges were filed but were subject to the outer limit that the Government has at least "contemplated" charges.

Similarly, in *United States v. Oakum*, No. 3:08cr12, 009 WL 790042 (E.D. Va. 2009), the District Court for the Eastern District of Virginia considered a claim that CVRA rights did not apply until after a defendant had been convicted. In rejecting that argument, the court agreed with the *Dean* court that victims acquire rights even before a prosecution begins.

The District Court for the Northern District of Indiana held to the same effect in *In re Petersen*. No. 2:14-CV-298 RM, 2010 WL 5108692 (N.D. Ind. 2010). There, the court held that a victim's right to be treated with fairness and with respect for [his or her] dignity and privacy "may apply before any prosecution is underway and isn't necessarily tied to a 'court proceeding' or 'case.'" The court, however, found that the "conclusory allegations" in the victims' petition did not "create a plausible claim for relief under the CVRA."

Perhaps the most extensive discussion of this issue has come from the Epstein case discussed earlier. Overruling the Government's argument that the CVRA only applies after the formal filing of charges, *Does v. United States*, 817 F. Supp. 2d 1337 (S.D. Fla. 2011), held that "the statutory language clearly contemplates precharge proceedings." The court in *Does* explained that "[c]ourt proceedings involving the crime are not limited to post-complaint or postindictment proceedings, but can also include initial appearances and bond hearings, both of which can take place before a formal charge." The court also noted that the CVRA's "requirement that officials engaged in 'detection [or] investigation' [of crimes] afford victims the rights enumerated in subsection (a) surely contemplates pre-charge application of the CVRA." Finally, the court in *Does* noted that "[i]f the CVRA's rights may be enforced before a prosecution is underway, then, to avoid a strained reading of the statute, those rights must attach before a complaint or indictment formally charges the defendant with the crime."

2. The Federal Example of Victims' Rights During the Investigative Process

While the U.S. Justice Department has been litigating against victims' rights during the investigative process (as discussed in the previous section), federal investigative agencies have been providing in place victims' rights during the investigative process. The Attorney General has promulgated extensive "guidelines" for federal law enforcement agencies about how crime victims should be treated during federal investigations. For example, federal law enforcement agencies are directed to refer crime victims to appropriate services during the investigation, as this guideline makes clear:

> At the earliest opportunity after detection of a crime at which it may be done without interfering with an investigation, a responsible official shall provide identified victims with information about services available to them. (42 U.S.C. § 10607(b)(2)). The information shall include the name, title, business address, and telephone number of the responsible official to whom services requests should be addressed (42 U.S.C. § 10607(b)(3)), and the types of services available, including, as appropriate—
>
> > 1. The place where the victim may receive emergency medical or social services. (42 U.S.C. § 10607(c)(1)(A)).
> >
> > 2. The availability of any restitution or other relief (including crime victim compensation programs) to which the victim may be entitled under this or any other applicable law and the manner in which such relief may be obtained. (42 U.S.C. § 10607(c)(1)(B)).

> 3. Public and private programs that are available to provide counseling, treatment, and other support to the victim. (42 U.S.C. § 10607(c)(1)(C)).

The responsibility for providing a victim with referrals for services during the investigation lies with the responsible official for the investigative agency. Once an investigation has transferred to the prosecutorial entity or charges are filed, responsible officials from the prosecutorial entity are responsible for ensuring referrals for services are made as appropriate. If a victim has already received referrals for services from the investigative agency, the prosecutorial entity and investigative agency shall employ their best efforts to coordinate any existing and new referrals to ensure consistency, avoid duplication of services, and meet the best interests of the victim and the case. U.S. DEPT. OF JUSTICE, OFFICE FOR VICTIMS OF CRIME, art. IV, § H (2011 ed.).

3. Notice of Rights to Crime Victims During Investigations

As discussed in Chapter 12 below, a number of states have recently adopted "Marsy's Laws" in their state constitutions, providing a bill of rights for crime victims in state constitutions. One common provision in these Marsy's Law provisions is a requirement that crime victims receive notice of their rights. For example, the California Constitution provides a list of 16 rights for crime victims and then, in the last provision, a requirement that victims be "informed of the rights enumerated in paragraphs (1) through (16)." CALIFORNIA CONST., art. I, § 28(b)(17). Similarly, the North Dakota Constitution provides a list of victims' rights, which includes "the right to be informed of these rights, and to be informed that victims can seek the advice of an attorney with respect to their rights. This information shall be made available to the general public and provided to all crime victims in what is referred to as a Marsy's Card." N.D. CONST., art. I, § 25.

To provide notice of rights, law enforcement agencies have standardized forms (or, as in North Dakota, a "Marsy's card") listing victims' rights. The California form advises victims of their 16 rights and then provides a list of victim service providers who can offer further assistance to victims.

C. Obtaining an Adequate Public Investigation

1. Generally

Police and other law enforcement agencies operate with limited resources. Frequently, they lack the time to investigate minor crimes. Investigative resources frequently require agencies to prioritize certain investigations based on such factors as the significance of the crime, the ease of identifying the perpetrator, and the values of the law enforcement bureaucracy.

As a practical matter, in almost all jurisdictions no effective formal criminal procedures exist that allow a crime victim to compel a law enforcement or prosecutorial agency to investigate a crime. These agencies largely have discretion to use their resources as they see fit. Laws of mandamus, equal protection, and civil rights are rarely available to force authorities to investigate. The limitations of these formal mechanisms are explored in Chapter 4 in the analogous context of the charging decision.

Absent criminal procedures, options for a victim frustrated by an inadequate public investigation include: complaining to higher-ups in the agency; getting the attention of another investigative agency; pursuing a private investigation; pursuing a civil suit; obtaining the interest of the media; and contacting political representatives or others who might be able to create pressure for an investigation. Each of these approaches has obvious limits.

If a public investigation is stalled, a victim can complain to a higher-up within the investigating agency. But any relief is highly dependent on the particular circumstances of the case and the agency and, as with any other public bureaucracy, forcing police agencies to take additional steps is often quite difficult. Similarly, obtaining the interest of another investigative agency is very difficult, and it is only an exceptional case that receives this kind of review.

As an alternative to public investigation, a crime victim can always fund their own private investigation. Of course, most crime victims lack the resources and ability to conduct their own investigations. And even for well-funded victims, conducting an effective private investigation typically requires finding someone with experience in detective work. Even skilled private investigators, however, lack many of the tools available to public investigators, such as the ability to obtain search warrants or wiretaps. If the victim succeeds in collecting evidence, the victim can provide the evidence to a public agency for consideration of prosecution. Or the victim can pursue her own civil suit. But civil suits provide nothing other than money damages, and a victim can collect such damages only if the offender has significant financial assets, a situation that is often not the case.

A victim can also turn to the media in an effort to bring wrongdoers to light. The media, however, is usually interested in only "high-profile" injustices, rather than subtle ones, and their interest often may be difficult to obtain or sustain.

The victim may also try to turn to a political representative. But it is unusual for political actors to seriously challenge a decision not to investigate further, and such actors typically lack relevant information about the course of an investigation.

The upshot is that in many, if not most, cases a victim without an adequate public investigation will receive no justice at all.

2. Police Investigation

Because crime victims often have no formal "right" to an adequate public investigation, challenges to the adequate police investigations often rest on other grounds, such as civil rights violations.

Elliot-Park v. Manglona

592 F.3d 1003 (9th Cir. 2010)

KOZINSKI, Chief Judge:

We consider whether law enforcement officers who are accused of failing to investigate a crime or make an arrest due to the race of the victim and that of the perpetrator are entitled to qualified immunity.

Facts

We recite the facts as Ae Ja Park Elliott alleges them in her complaint. Elliott, who is racially and ethnically Korean, was driving south along 16 Highway in Papago, Saipan. Norbert Duenas Babauta, who is racially and ethnically Micronesian, was driving north along the same highway when he sped through a turn, crossed onto oncoming traffic and crashed into Elliott's car. Officer Manglona noticed the accident and approached. When Elliott asked him to call her husband, he shoved her inside her car and told her to shut up and calm down. Manglona then began conducting interviews of the witnesses, drivers and passengers. Officers Macaranas and Langdon arrived shortly thereafter and spoke to both drivers. The officers are all racially and ethnically Micronesian.

The three officers had cause to believe Babauta had been driving under the influence of alcohol: He was teetering and slurring his words, he reeked of alcohol and had bloodshot eyes, his truck bed was littered with empty beer cans and he told Manglona that he had "blacked out" while driving. Despite these obvious signs of intoxication, the officers didn't administer field sobriety or blood alcohol tests, or otherwise investigate whether Babauta had been driving drunk. Nor did the officers charge him with a DUI or any other crime or infraction. Manglona also falsely stated in his accident report that Babauta "had not been drinking."

Dr. Thomas Austin, who examined Elliott and Babauta at the hospital, called DPS to complain after he learned that Babauta hadn't been charged with a DUI. After this complaint, and perhaps some others, the Department of Public Safety (DPS) initiated an investigation, but the three officers conspired with others to obstruct the investigation and prevent prosecution of Babauta. Elliott claims the officers failed to investigate the crime or arrest Babauta because of racial animus against her as a Korean and in favor of Babauta as a Micronesian.

On a motion to dismiss, the district court found that Elliott sufficiently alleged a 42 U.S.C. § 1983 equal protection claim and a 42 U.S.C. § 1985 conspiracy and obstruction of justice claim against the officers. The district court concluded the officers weren't entitled to qualified immunity at the motion to dismiss stage. The officers bring this interlocutory appeal.

Analysis

Unlike prosecutors, who enjoy absolute immunity, police officers are entitled only to qualified immunity in section 1983 cases. *See Malley v. Briggs,* 475 U.S. 335,

341–43, 106 S.Ct. 1092, 89 L.Ed.2d 271 (1986). In a qualified immunity appeal, we normally look first to whether a constitutional violation was alleged and then to whether the defendants have qualified immunity as a matter of law. *See Pearson v. Callahan,* 129 S.Ct. 808, 813, 172 L.Ed.2d 565 (2009). We review the district court's decision de novo. *Newell v. Sauser,* 79 F.3d 115, 117 (9th Cir. 1996).

According to Elliott, the three police officers refused to investigate the incident because Babauta is Micronesian and Elliott is Korean. Elliott also claims that Officer Macaranas fully investigated another drunk driving accident that occurred the same evening where the victim was Micronesian but the driver wasn't. The officers don't dispute that Elliott has pled facts from which a trier of fact could infer racial discrimination.

Instead, the officers argue that individuals don't have a constitutional right to have police arrest others who have victimized them. But Elliott's equal protection claim isn't based on some general constitutional right to have an assailant arrested. Rather, she argues Babauta was given a pass by the police because of the officers' alleged racial bias not only in favor of Babauta as a Micronesian, but also against her as a Korean. And while the officers' discretion in deciding whom to arrest is certainly broad, it cannot be exercised in a racially discriminatory fashion. For example, a police officer can't investigate and arrest blacks but not whites, or Asians but not Hispanics. Police can't discriminate on the basis of the victim's race, either. We recognized as much in *Estate of Macias v. Ihde,* where we held that there is no right to state protection against madmen or criminals, but "[t]here is a constitutional right . . . to have police services administered in a nondiscriminatory manner — a right that is violated when a state actor denies such protection to disfavored persons." 219 F.3d 1018, 1028 (9th Cir. 2000); *see also DeShaney v. Winnebago County Dep't of Soc. Servs.,* 489 U.S. 189, 197 n. 3, 109 S.Ct. 998, 103 L. Ed.2d 249 (1989) ("The State may not, of course, selectively deny its protective services to certain disfavored minorities without violating the Equal Protection Clause.").

The officers concede that the Constitution protects against discriminatory withdrawal of police protection, but they claim that Elliott was not denied this right because they provided her with *some* police services: They called an ambulance and questioned bystanders. According to the officers, only a complete withdrawal of police protective services violates equal protection. But diminished police services, like the seat at the back of the bus, don't satisfy the government's obligation to provide services on a non-discriminatory basis. *See Navarro v. Block,* 72 F.3d 712, 715–17 (9th Cir. 1995) (alleged policy to treat domestic violence 911 calls less urgently could form the basis for an equal protection claim). Certainly the government couldn't constitutionally adopt a policy to spend $20,000 investigating each murder of a white person but only $1,000 investigating each murder of a person of color. Likewise, it doesn't matter that Elliott received some protection; what matters is that she would allegedly have received more if she weren't Korean and Babauta weren't Micronesian.

The officers also suggest that the equal protection clause only protects against selective denial of protective services, and that investigation and arrest aren't protective services unless there is a continuing danger to the victim. But the officers' understanding of protective services is too limited. If police refuse to investigate or arrest people who commit crimes against a particular ethnic group, it's safe to assume that crimes against that group will rise. Would-be criminals will act with a greater impunity if they believe they have a get out of jail free card if they commit crimes against the disfavored group. Babauta may well have been emboldened to drive drunk with empty beer cans rolling around in the back of his truck because he believed that he would suffer no ill consequences should he cause an accident.

In any event, whether investigation and arrest are protective services is immaterial. While the Supreme Court may have written in *DeShaney* that the government couldn't "selectively deny its protective services" to disfavored minorities, 489 U.S. at 197 n. 3, that certainly doesn't imply that the government can selectively deny its non-protective services to disfavored minorities. The government may not racially discriminate in the administration of *any* of its services. *See Palmer v. Thompson,* 403 U.S. 217, 219–223 (1971) (government-funded pools cannot be operated on a racially discriminatory basis); *Hawkins v. Town of Shaw,* 437 F.2d 1286, 1288 (5th Cir. 1971) (municipal services cannot be provided on a racially discriminatory basis).

The dissent agrees that the discriminatory denial of investigative services may violate equal protection. Nevertheless, our colleague questions whether Elliott has an equal protection claim based on the officers' failure to arrest Babauta because arrest decisions are entitled to deference and because Elliott probably suffered little harm. *See id.* at 1011. But even the dissent recognizes that police officers aren't entitled to deference for their decision if it is based on racial animus. *See id.* at 1010–11. And the fact that Elliott may not have been harmed much speaks more to whether she can recover anything beyond nominal damages than to whether she has an equal protection claim. *See also Flores v. Morgan Hill Unified Sch. Dist.,* 324 F.3d 1130, 1135–36 (9th Cir. 2003) (discriminatory failure to investigate *and discipline* student harassment complaints violates equal protection). Certainly, a plaintiff complaining of heart attack symptoms has a claim against a government hospital that turns him away because of his race, even if the symptoms turn out to be caused by heartburn. The officers' alleged discriminatory failure to arrest, as well as investigate, therefore violated equal protection.

Law enforcement officials are entitled to qualified immunity even where their conduct violated a constitutional right unless that right was clearly established at the time of the violation. *Saucier v. Katz,* 533 U.S. 194, 202 (2001). The dispositive inquiry is whether "it would be clear to a reasonable officer that his conduct was unlawful in the situation he confronted." *Id.* Thus, our "task is to determine whether the preexisting law provided the defendants with 'fair warning' that their conduct was unlawful." *Flores,* 324 F.3d at 1136–37 (quoting *Hope v. Pelzer,* 536 U.S. 730, 740 (2002)).

The right to non-discriminatory administration of protective services is clearly established. *See* p. 1006–07 *supra*. Nevertheless, the officers argue that it wasn't clearly established that investigation and arrest are protective services. But the very purpose of section 1983 was to provide a federal right of action against states that refused to enforce their laws when the victim was black. *See Briscoe v. LaHue,* 460 U.S. 325, 338 (1983) ("It is clear from the legislative debates that, in the view of the Act's sponsors, the victims of Klan outrages were deprived of 'equal protection of the laws' if the perpetrators systematically went unpunished."); *Monroe v. Pape,* 365 U.S. 167, 174–180 (1961) ("It is abundantly clear that one reason the legislation was passed was to afford a federal right in federal courts because, by reason of prejudice, passion, neglect, intolerance or otherwise, state laws might not be enforced. . . ."); *Smith v. Ross,* 482 F.2d 33, 37 (6th Cir. 1973) ("Particularly in view of the circumstances surrounding the passage of § 1983, including the concern for protecting Negroes from the widespread non-enforcement of state laws, the remedies provided in § 1983 are most appropriately extended to persons who, because of the unpopularity of their life-styles or the pervasiveness of racist animus in the community, are not protected. . . ." (citation omitted)). It hardly passes the straight-face test to argue at this point in our history that police could reasonably believe they could treat individuals disparately based on their race.

The officers argue that Elliott's equal protection rights weren't clearly established because she can't find a case similar to hers — like a sobriety check and arrest case or a traffic case — where the court found an equal protection violation. But there doesn't need to be a prior case with materially similar facts in order for a right to be clearly established. *Flores,* 324 F.3d at 1136–37 ("In order to find that the law was clearly established, however, we need not find a prior case with identical, or even 'materially similar,' facts." (quoting *Hope,* 536 U.S. at 741)). This is especially true in equal protection cases because the non-discrimination principle is so clear. "The constitutional right to be free from such invidious discrimination is so well established and so essential to the preservation of our constitutional order that all public officials must be charged with knowledge of it." *Flores v. Pierce,* 617 F.2d 1386, 1392 (9th Cir. 1980).

We have recognized the absurdity of requiring equal protection plaintiffs to find a case with materially similar facts. In *Flores v. Morgan Hill Unified School District,* we held that public school administrators who failed to respond to gay students' harassment complaints were not entitled to qualified immunity. 324 F.3d at 1136–38. The administrators argued that "no Supreme Court or Ninth Circuit case had yet established a student's right under the Equal Protection Clause . . . to be protected by school administrators from peer sexual orientation harassment." *Id.* at 1136. But we reasoned that it was "not necessary to find a case applying the [equal protection] principle to a particular category of state officials, such as school administrators," because "[a]s early as 1990, we established the underlying proposition that such conduct violates constitutional rights: state employees who treat individuals differently on the basis of their sexual orientation violate the constitutional guarantee of equal protection." *Id.* at 1137. Thus, "[t]he defendants were officers of the state who had fair warning that they could not accord homosexual and bisexual students less protection." *Id.*

Contrary to the dissent's claim, *see* dissent at 1013, *Flores* isn't limited to the unique characteristics of the school environment. Indeed, *Flores* found that school administrators were on notice that they had to treat gay students the same as straight students based on a case holding that state employees in general can't irrationally discriminate on the basis of sexual orientation. 324 F.3d at 1137. The same holds true here. It's been long established that state employees can't treat individuals differently on the basis of their race. The three officers thus had a more than fair warning that failure to investigate and arrest Babauta because of race violated equal protection.

* * *

The officers admit their appeal of the district court's refusal to dismiss Elliott's section 1985 claim, which alleges that the defendants conspired to deny her equal protection, is tied to the success of their appeal of the section 1983 claim. The district court did not err in failing to dismiss the section 1983 and section 1985 claims.

AFFIRMED.

CALLAHAN, Circuit Judge, concurring and dissenting:

I agree with the first part of the majority opinion: the government may not racially discriminate in the administration of its services. *See* opinion at 1007. I further agree that the right to the non-discriminatory administration of protective services is clearly established. *See* opinion at 1007-08. Nonetheless, I write separately and dissent because I am concerned that the broad language in the majority's opinion fails to recognize the deference courts have given, and should give, police departments in determining when and how to investigate crimes. This underlying theme informs the two specific issues I address. First, I am leery of any suggestion that a person's right to equal protection extends to requiring an arrest of a third person; and second, I do not think that a reasonable officer in the defendants' position was on notice that refusing to give Babauta a sobriety test might constitute a violation of Elliot's right to equal protection of the law. Of course, with the publication of this opinion Ninth Circuit law on this issue will be established.

. . .

The majority's opinion fails to distinguish between investigations and arrests and thus fails to appreciate that the discretionary determination to arrest someone is particularly unsuited to judicial review. The unique nature of the prosecutorial function, which includes the decision to arrest an individual, was recognized by the Supreme Court over thirty years ago in *Imbler v. Pachtman,* 424 U.S. 409 (1976). In *Imbler,* the Supreme Court affirmed the Ninth Circuit's holding that a prosecuting attorney who acted within the scope of his duties in initiating and pursuing a criminal prosecution is entitled to qualified immunity from suit under 42 U.S.C.

§ 1983 "for alleged deprivations of the defendant's constitutional rights." *Id.* at 410. In *Wayte v. United States,* 470 U.S. 598, 607 (1985), the Court reiterated that "the Government retains 'broad discretion' as to whom to prosecute" and that this "broad discretion rests largely on the recognition that the decision to prosecute is particularly ill-suited to judicial review."

The prosecutor's discretion, however, is "subject to constitutional restraints." *United States v. Armstrong,* 517 U.S. 456, 464 (1996) (quoting *United States v. Batchelder,* 442 U.S. 114, 125 (1979)). In *Armstrong,* the Court explained:

> One of these constraints, imposed by the equal protection component of the Due Process Clause of the Fifth Amendment, *Bolling v. Sharpe,* 347 U.S. 497, 500 . . . (1954), is that the decision whether to prosecute may not be based on "an unjustifiable standard such as race, religion, or other arbitrary classification," *Oyler v. Boles,* 368 U.S. 448 (1962). A defendant may demonstrate that the administration of a criminal law is "directed so exclusively against a particular class of persons . . . with a mind so unequal and oppressive" that the system of prosecution amounts to "a practical denial" of equal protection of the law. *Yick Wo v. Hopkins,* 118 U.S. 356, 373 . . . (1886).

> In order to dispel the presumption that a prosecutor has not violated equal protection, a criminal defendant must present "clear evidence to the contrary." [*United States v.*] *Chemical Foundation, . . .* [272 U.S. 1(1926)]. . . . We explained in *Wayte* why courts are "properly hesitant to examine the decision whether to prosecute." 470 U.S., at 608, ... Judicial deference to the decisions of these executive officers rests in part on an assessment of the relative competence of prosecutors and courts. "Such factors as the strength of the case, the prosecution's general deterrence value, the Government's enforcement priorities, and the case's relationship to the Government's overall enforcement plan are not readily susceptible to the kind of analysis the courts are competent to undertake." *Id.* at 607. It also stems from a concern not to unnecessarily impair the performance of a core executive constitutional function. "Examining the basis of a prosecution delays the criminal proceeding, threatens to chill law enforcement by subjecting the prosecutor's motives and decisionmaking to outside inquiry, and may undermine prosecutorial effectiveness by revealing the Government's enforcement policy." *Id.*

517 U.S. at 464–65. The Court went on to reaffirm that "[t]o establish a discriminatory effect in a race case, the claimant must show that similarly situated individuals of a different race were not prosecuted." *Id.* at 465.

These cases, indeed almost all cases concerning selective prosecution, are brought by individuals who are challenging their prosecutions by the government. Here, Elliot's assertion is not that she was selectively prosecuted, but that her constitutional right to equal protection was violated by the officers' failure to investigate and arrest a third party, Babauta. As the decision to arrest and prosecute an individual is entitled to substantial deference from the courts, it follows that the decision not to arrest and prosecute a person is entitled to at least the same degree of deference. This does not suggest that it would be impossible for a plaintiff to allege and show that her right to equal protection was violated by an officer's failure to arrest a third party, but only to clarify that the decision to arrest—as opposed to the officer's duty to investigate—is part of the prosecutorial function and is therefore entitled to greater deference.

3. "Pattern and Practice" Investigation by the U.S. Justice Department

While any single victim may have difficulty challenging the adequacy of a police investigation, a group of victims may have more success in alleging a pattern of under-enforcement. Recently the U.S. Justice Department initiated several investigations into state police agencies, using 42 U.S.C. § 14141, which authorizes the Department to bring suit against police departments engaged in a "pattern or practice" of unconstitutional conduct. The most revolutionary of these investigations was the Department's investigation of rape cases in Missoula, Montana, as described by Professor Deborah Tuerkheimer:

> In the spring of 2013, the Justice Department issued findings in a § 14141 enforcement action that, for the first time, exclusively concentrated on the discriminatory policing of sexual assault. A year earlier, the Justice Department had launched a comprehensive, system-wide investigation into the underenforcement of rape law in Missoula, Montana. At the time, Attorney General Eric Holder cautioned, "The allegations that the University of Montana, the local police department and the County Attorney's Office failed to adequately address sexual assaults are very disturbing."
>
> As the investigation progressed, it became clear that gender bias was indeed undermining the response of the Missoula Police Department ("MPD") to sexual assault. In May 2013, the Justice Department issued a report finding that "deficiencies in MPD's response to sexual assault compromise the effectiveness of sexual assault investigations from the outset, make it more difficult to uncover the truth, and have the effect of depriving female sexual assault victims of basic legal protections." Also in May 2013, the Justice Department entered into a settlement with MPD, which had cooperated with the investigation from the outset.
>
> Two years later, the Justice Department announced that MPD had fully implemented the terms of the agreement and "achieved the overall purpose of the agreement," to improve the police response to sexual assault. The head of the Civil Rights Division, Deputy Attorney General Vanita Gupta, was effusive in her appraisal, suggesting:
>
>> [A]s a result of these reforms, the women of Missoula are safer, more trusting of the criminal justice system, and subject to more fair and respectful treatment by local law enforcement. Missoula's police

department had the courage and leadership to acknowledge that it had a problem and to address it, and as a result, is poised to become a model for communities struggling with these issues around the country.

Missoula is a landmark intervention. It introduces a novel way of catalyzing the enforcement of rape law — a development well worth examining, especially for what it portends. Missoula also represents a significant conceptual breakthrough because it is premised on an understanding of gender-based under-policing as an equal protection violation; one demanding a federal response.

Deborah Tuerkheimer, *Underenforcement As Unequal Protection*, 57 B.C. L. Rev. 1287, 1322–24 (2016).

Notes

1. The Missoula pattern and practice investigation took place during the administration of President Barack Obama. Following the election of President Donald Trump, his Attorney General — Jeff Sessions — released a memorandum titled "Supporting Federal, State, Local and Tribal Law Enforcement" (Mar. 31, 2017) that appeared to suggest a less intrusive approach for the Department's pattern and practice investigations. The memorandum explained that fighting crime was "first and foremost" a task for state, local, and tribal law enforcement and that by "strengthening [the Department's] longstanding and productive relationships with our law enforcement partners, we will improve public safety for all Americans."

2. For a highly readable account of the problems with rape investigations in Missoula, *see* Jon Krakauer, Missoula: Rape and the Justice System in a College Town (2015).

4. Prosecutor Investigation

As with other law enforcement agencies, prosecuting agencies generally have broad discretion about whether to undertake — or direct others to undertake — an investigation of a crime. Issues surrounding ways in which victims can require prosecutors to investigate and prosecute cases are discussed in Chapter 4.

5. Judicial Investigation

Wisconsin has a statutory method by which a citizen can potentially obtain a judicial investigation into an alleged crime. The statute provides as follows:

Wis. Stat. § 968.26 (John Doe proceeding).

If a person complains to a judge that he has reason to believe that a crime has been committed within his jurisdiction, the judge shall examine the complainant under oath and any witnesses produced by him and may, and at the request of the district attorney shall, subpoena and examine other witnesses to ascertain whether a crime has been committed and by whom committed. The extent to which the judge may proceed in such examination is within his discretion. The examination may be adjourned and may be secret. Any witness examined under this section may have counsel present at the examination but such counsel shall not be allowed to examine his client, cross-examine other witnesses or argue before the judge. If it appears probable from the testimony given that a crime has been committed and who committed it, the complaint shall be reduced to writing and signed and verified; and thereupon a warrant shall issue for the arrest of the accused. Subject to §971.23, the record of such proceeding and the testimony taken shall not be open to inspection by anyone except the district attorney unless it is used by the prosecution at the preliminary hearing or the trial of the accused and then only to the extent that it is so used.

State of Wisconsin v. Hazel Washington
266 N.W.2d 597 (Wis. 1978)

[The subject matter of the inquiry was fraud in connection with filing medical assistance claims.]

On December 14, 1976, Hazel Washington, President of Family Outreach Social Services Agency, Inc. (Family Outreach), was served with a subpoena duces tecum signed by Judge Burns. The subpoena required her to produce documents belonging to Family Outreach at a John Doe proceeding presided over by Judge Burns. The John Doe proceeding was being conducted under sec. 968.26, Stats.

Family Outreach provides doctor-prescribed psychotherapeutic services through professional social workers and is compensated primarily through federally financed medical assistance programs. By letters of December 17 and December 20, 1976, Washington informed Judge Burns that she would respectfully decline to produce the documents on the grounds, inter alia, that the subpoena called for the production of documents within the physician-patient privilege and that the subpoena violated Family Outreach's fourth amendment right to be secure from unreasonable searches and seizures. Judge Burns requested that Washington and the State brief and argue the various legal questions raised by Washington.

On January 7, 1977, Judge Burns convened a closed session hearing as part of the John Doe investigation and heard extensive argument by counsel. At the close of the hearing, Judge Burns indicated that he would sign an order requiring Washington to produce the documents in question. On January 18, 1977, Washington was served with Judge Burns' order requiring her to produce the documents on January 21, 1977. The State's brief on appeal and the record indicate that an informal conference was held on January 20, 1977, attended by Judge Burns and counsel for the State and for Washington.

On January 21, 1977, Judge Burns convened another secret session in the John Doe proceedings. Again, counsel argued the legal issues of the subpoena, and then

Washington was called to the stand, advised of her rights against self-incrimination, and asked some preliminary questions which she answered. When asked whether she had brought the documents specified in the subpoena, she declined to produce them, saying she was relying on the "fifth amendment," as well as the legal arguments made by her counsel. The Assistant Attorney General then moved that the John Doe proceedings be adjourned and that a special proceeding be convened in open court pursuant to chapter 295 of the Wisconsin Statutes governing civil contempt. Up until that moment all proceedings had been in closed session, and all "orders" were subject to the secrecy order of the John Doe proceedings. Judge Burns granted the motion and a special proceeding of the court in open session was held, resulting in a court order directing Washington to produce the documents. Washington declined to obey the order, and the court found by a preponderance of the evidence that Washington's refusal constituted contempt of court under chapter 295, Stats. The court ordered that Washington be committed to the Milwaukee county jail for a period of six months or until such time as she complied with the order of the court or until the John Doe proceeding was concluded, whichever came first. Commitment was stayed pending appeal. Appeal was taken from the order of the John Doe judge served on January 18, 1977, and from the order made at the open court hearing on January 21, 1977, both orders requiring Washington to produce the corporate documents, and from the contempt order dated January 25, 1977.

II.

We shall consider first Washington's contention that sec. 968.26, Stats., which gives statutory authority for John Doe proceedings, violates the constitutional requirements concerning separation of powers.

In Washington's view, sec. 968.26, Stats., violates the Wisconsin Constitution by investing in the John Doe judge, a member of the judicial branch of government, an investigatory power which properly can be exercised only by members of the executive branch of government. The investigation of crime is part of the executive's duty to assure faithful execution of the laws. Art. V, sec. 4, Wis. Const. Washington asserts that the function of the John Doe judge merges with that of the prosecutor, a representative of the executive branch, as judge and prosecutor jointly search for evidence of criminal activity.

The rule of a John Doe judge has not been described in detail in the statutes or the cases. The parties in the instant case portray that role in vastly different ways.[5]

---

5. The portrayals appear to be based on counsels' experiences and impressions. Counsel have not attempted to describe the judge conducting the John Doe proceedings in the case at bar. There is very little written material available relating to how John Doe proceedings are conducted. For the complete text of Judge Harvey Neelen's Report After a John Doe Quiz, see *The Milwaukee Journal*, Sunday, January 9, 1949, p.1 (Legislative Reference Library, Madison, Wis.).

Washington's brief and oral argument characterize the John Doe judge as possessing the power to run a criminal investigation "in combination with prosecutors, policemen, and expert analysts." Washington's description of the John Doe process is, in part, as follows:

> . . . Disagreements and unseemly conflicts can and, in Wisconsin, have arisen between judges and District Attorneys or other members of the executive branch concerning the proper outcome of John Doe investigations. When legislators have been targets, judges can and have become embroiled in controversy with the legislative branch over the zeal and methodology of the investigation.
>
> With the very real possibility of conflict developing between the representative of the judicial branch and the representative of the executive branch, a pattern of informal, secret consultation typically develops. Since conflict might jeopardize the investigation, the more usual result is agreement as to the common investigative enterprise. Thus, the judiciary becomes inextricably entwined with the executive and linked with executive functions. Judges become joint participants with prosecutors and policemen in exhaustive, lengthy searches for crime and criminals.
>
> John Doe proceedings as they have evolved in Wisconsin have become tremendous engines of inquiry. They may reach to multiple topics and extend for months or years. They typically operate in complete secrecy. They may utilize the combined resources of many executive branch agencies. The judge running such a proceeding commands an army of aides. . . .

The state portrays the John Doe judge as a neutral detached magistrate whose duty it is to determine on the basis of the evidence presented whether someone will be charged with a crime. . . .

The confusion as to the role of the judge in a John Doe proceeding is more readily understood if one looks at the development of the institution. John Doe proceedings in this state originated in the latter part of the 19th century. The John Doe was developed by the courts of the state pursuant to a statute (in force since 1839) which provided that a magistrate upon complaint made to him that a crime has been committed "shall examine, on oath, the complainant and any witness produced by him." The original statute was not intended to create a primarily investigative proceeding. Rather, it set forth the procedure governing the determination of probable cause for the issuance of warrants generally, a function served after the 1949 revision of the statute. . . .

From a relatively early date, however, the jurisdiction conferred upon magistrates was adapted to serve a broader investigatory purpose. In 1949, the legislature gave the investigatory proceeding developed by the courts a statutory basis separate from proceedings for issuance of warrants generally.

As one might expect from its historical antecedents, while the John Doe permits the investigation of alleged or suspected violations of the law, it serves too to prevent reckless and ill-advised prosecution by requiring that a complaint shall not issue except upon a finding of probable cause.[6]

The State analogizes the function of the John Doe judge to that of the magistrate who determines whether there is probable cause to issue an arrest warrant. This analogy, although incomplete, has merit. . . .

[H]owever, the State ignores a critical difference. . . . The complaint upon which the judge passes judgment must set forth facts which, together with any reasonable inferences therefrom, would lead a reasonable person to conclude that a crime has probably been committed and that the defendant named in the complaint is probably the culpable party. The John Doe complaint, however, need not name a particular accused; nor need it set forth facts sufficient to show that a crime has probably been committed. The John Doe is, at its inception, not so much a procedure for the determination of probable cause as it is an inquest for the discovery of crime in which the judge has significant powers. Under sec. 968.26, Stats., the John Doe judge "may, and at the request of the district attorney shall, subpoena and examine . . . witnesses to ascertain whether a crime has been committed and by whom committed." The statute confers upon the John Doe judge the power to determine the extent of the examination, as well as the power to determine whether the examination will be secret. The John Doe investigation is essentially limited to the subject matter of the complaint upon which the John Doe is commenced. The John Doe judge has no authority to ferret out crime wherever he or she thinks it might exist.

This court has characterized the John Doe as "primarily an investigative device," and has noted that "John Doe is a feeble investigative device indeed, unless both the district attorney and the magistrate are amendable to using their offices in furtherance of the investigation. . . ." *State ex rel. Kurkierewicz v. Cannon*, 42 Wis.2d 368, 376, 377, 166 N.W.2d 255, 259 (1969).

---

6. In *State ex rel. Long* and *Another v. Keyes*, 75 Wis. 288, 294, 295, 44 N.W. 13, 15 (1889), this court discussed the purpose and history of the John Doe proceeding as follows:

> . . . When this (John Doe) statute was first enacted the common-law practice was for the magistrate to issue the warrant on a complaint of mere suspicion, and he was protected in doing so. This was found to be a very unsafe practice. Many arrests were made on groundless suspicion, when the accused were innocent of the crime and there was no testimony whatsoever against them. The law delights as much in the protection of the innocence as in the punishment of the guilty. This statute was made to protect citizens from arrest and imprisonment on frivolous and groundless suspicion. Davis, Crim. Just. 2-12. Mr. Benedict, in his valuable work on Civil Criminal Justice, 804, says: 'Our statute is framed so as to exclude in a great measure the abuses to which such a practice might lead, and undoubtedly was designed to throw the duty of judging, in this respect, entirely upon the magistrate. It should not regard mere allegations of suspicion, but the grounds of the suspicion the facts and circumstances must be laid before him, and these should be sufficient to make it appear that a crime has been actually committed, and that there is probable cause for charging the individual complained of therewith.' (Emphasis supplied.) . . .

By invoking the formal John Doe investigative proceeding, law enforcement officers are able to obtain the benefit of powers not otherwise available to them, i.e., the power to subpoena witnesses, to take testimony under oath, and to compel the testimony of a reluctant witness.[7] Although the judge's subpoena power is important to the prosecution and the judge has broad discretion in conducting the investigation, we reject Washington's characterization of the judge as inevitably the chief investigator or as an arm or tool of the prosecutor's office. We do not view the judge as orchestrating the investigation. The John Doe judge is a judicial officer who serves an essentially judicial function. The judge considers the testimony presented. It is the responsibility of the John Doe judge to utilize his or her training in constitutional and criminal law and in courtroom procedure in determining the need to subpoena witnesses requested by the district attorney,[8] in presiding at the examination of witnesses, and in determining probable cause. It is the judge's responsibility to ensure procedural fairness. *State v. O'Connor*, 77 Wis.2d 261, 284, 252 N.W.2d 671 (1977).

The John Doe judge should act with a view toward issuing a complaint or determining that no crime has occurred. To the extent that the judge exceeds this limitation, there is an abuse of discretion. If the facts show that the judge has extended the proceeding in duration or scope beyond the reasonable intendment of the statute or has otherwise improperly conducted the proceeding and intends to persist, he or she can be restrained by writ of prohibition for abuse of discretion. As the State noted in its brief, the John Doe judge must "conduct himself as a neutral and detached magistrate in determining probable cause which is the basic function of . . . (the) proceeding."

The latitude afforded the John Doe judge under the statute is designed to ensure that the proceeding is conducted in an orderly and expeditious manner. The behavior of the John Doe judge should be such as not to impair his or her ability to make an independent determination of probable cause. Accordingly, communications between the complaint or the prosecutor and the John Doe judge relating to the substance of the proceeding should be made part of the record.

Viewing the role of the John Doe judge as we do, we do not believe that the John Doe statute should fall on the ground that it vests non-judicial powers in the

---

7. In Wisconsin, John Doe proceedings have been more frequently used than grand juries. Commentators note that the John Doe is considered superior to the grand jury because it is less expensive and less cumbersome, yet it affords greater protections to witnesses. Brown, The Wisconsin District Attorney and the Criminal Case 13, 17 (2d ed. 1977); Coffey & Richards, *The Grand Jury in Wisconsin*, 58 Marq. L. Rev. 517, 530 (1974); *State v. Doe*, 78 Wis.2d 161, 164, 254 N.W.2d 210 (1977).

8. We refer throughout the opinion to the participation in the John Doe proceedings by a prosecuting attorney. It is usual but not required that an attorney representing the state's interest in criminal prosecution be involved both in initiating and conducting the proceedings. Sec. 968.26, Stats., does not require the participation of the district attorney nor does it set forth the duties of the district attorney.

judiciary. Although the doctrine of separation of powers is a fundamental principle, it is neither possible nor practicable to categorize all governmental action as exclusively legislative, executive or judicial. The doctrine of separation of powers must be viewed as a general principle to be applied to maintain the balance between the three branches of government, to preserve their respective independence and integrity, and to prevent concentration of unchecked power in the hands of any one branch.

The contemporaneous and practical interpretation of the state constitution supports the conclusion that a John Doe proceeding does not contravene the constitution's mandate of separation of powers. As noted previously, John Doe proceedings in this state date back to at least 1889, forty-one years after the adoption of the Wisconsin Constitution. The John Doe is an institution which has been sanctioned by long usage and general recognition.

We are unwilling to hold that sec. 968.26, Stats., violates the Wisconsin constitution. To the extent that the statute may be viewed as granting both judicial and quasi-executive powers to the John Doe judge, we believe that witnesses and persons accused can be protected by appellate court review of John Doe proceedings and of the court orders which are an outgrowth of those proceedings.

III.

Washington further contends that she was denied due process when the same judge who conducted the John Doe investigation presided at the civil contempt proceedings under chapter 295. Chapter 295 does not on its face apply to John Doe proceedings. Sec. 295.01, Stats., provides that "a court of record may find in contempt any person who disobeys any process or lawful order of the court." (Emphasis added.) A John Doe judge is not the equivalent of a court, and a John Doe proceeding is not a proceeding in a court of record. However, the question before us is not whether a subpoena issued by the John Doe judge is a "profess" or "order" of the court within sec. 295.01, disobedience of which subjects a person to contempt.

As we noted previously, after Washington refused to produce the documents at the January 21, 1977 John Doe proceeding, the Assistant Attorney General moved that the John Doe proceedings be adjourned and that a special proceeding be convened in open court pursuant to ch. 295. Judge Burns granted this motion, and the doors to the courtroom were opened.

The Assistant Attorney General then moved in open court for an order citing Washington for civil contempt. However, Judge Burns stated that he would not consider the question of contempt until he had made "an order as a judge and a court of record that she produce these records." The Assistant District Attorney orally moved that Hazel Washington comply with the subpoena duces tecum which had been served upon her and that she obey the written order of the "John Doe judge" served on her on January 18th. The court by oral order directed Washington to produce the documents pursuant to the motion of the Assistant District Attorney. Washington's attorney then stated that Washington would not produce the documents. The Assistant District Attorney then moved "pursuant to the entire chapter 295 of the

Wisconsin Statutes that Hazel Washington be cited for civil contempt in order to guarantee the production of the documents subpoenaed and ordered to be produced." The court found Washington in contempt under ch. 295.

Thus there is a court order directing Washington to produce the documents (which court order was not obeyed) and a finding of contempt by a court of record. . . .

Note

The Wisconsin Supreme Court upheld John Doe proceedings again in *State v. Unnamed Defendant*, 441 N.W.2d 696 (Wis. 1989), set forth in Chapter 4, below. In that case the court upheld the statute against a separation of powers challenge where the judge was acting alone:

> In this case, the John Doe judge orchestrated the [investigation]. In this case the prosecution was not even consulted.

Wisconsin's procedure is unusual. Is judicial investigation as an alternative to prosecutorial investigation a good idea? Can you envision circumstances in which judicial investigation might be preferable? For example, one criticism of investigations of police brutality is that prosecutors and police depend on each other to perform their duties. Does judicial investigation resolve this problem?

6. Adequate Investigative Techniques

Sometimes the problem is not whether there is an investigation but whether the investigative technique is adequate.

One example of the importance of adequate investigative technique is the emergence of multidisciplinary child abuse teams resulting from both incompetent and impeachable investigative techniques. The core of the problem in child abuse investigations prior to the advent of multidisciplinary teams was the multiple interviews of the child victim. A typical scenario involved the interview of a child by school officials, an interview by protective service workers, an interview by the patrol officer responding, an interview by a detective, interviews by medical personnel, parents, and the prosecutor.

The number of interviews and the unsophisticated nature of interviews posed two central problems. First, multiple interviews were damaging to the child, who was repeatedly required to recount their victimizations. Second, multiple interviews damaged a case for several reasons. First, many people who conducted interviews with children were not trained to do so. A second related issue was that the child's version of events could change depending upon the interviewer's approach to the interview.

Multidisciplinary teams were formed to create an investigatory process that would minimize the impact on the child while maximizing the opportunity to obtain accurate information from the child.

Another area of concern was the lack of medical specialists trained in diagnosing child abuse. One component of multidisciplinary teams are physicians who specialize in this area of medicine. The use of these physicians reduces the risk of misdiagnosis.

The federal statutes mandate the use of multidisciplinary child abuse teams:

18 U.S.C. § 3509(a)(7)(g) provides:

(7) the term "multidisciplinary child abuse team" means a professional unit composed of representatives from health, social service, law enforcement, and legal service agencies to coordinate the assistance needed to handle cases of child abuse:

(g) Use of multidisciplinary child abuse teams.

(1) In general. A multidisciplinary child abuse team shall be used when it is feasible to do so. The court shall work with State and local governments that have established multidisciplinary child abuse teams designed to assist child victims and child witnesses, and the court and the attorney for the Government shall consult with the multidisciplinary child abuse team as appropriate.

(2) Role of multidisciplinary child abuse teams. The role of the multidisciplinary child abuse team shall be to provide for a child services that the members of the team in their professional roles are capable of providing, including:

(A) medical diagnoses and evaluation services, including provision or interpretation of x-rays, laboratory tests, and related services, as needed, and documentation of findings;

(B) telephone consultation services in emergencies and in other situations;

(C) medical evaluations related to abuse or neglect;

(D) psychological and psychiatric diagnoses and evaluation services for the child, parent or parents, guardian or guardians, or other caregivers, or any other individual involved in a child victim or child witness case;

(E) expert medical, psychological, and related professional testimony;

(F) case service coordination and assistance, including the location of services available from public and private agencies in the community; and

(G) training services for judges, litigators, court officers and others that are involved in child victim and child witness cases, in handling child victims and child witnesses.

D. Private Financing of Official Investigations

People v. Eubanks

927 P.2d 310 (Cal. 1996)

WERDEGAR, Justice.

When the victim of an alleged crime contributes financially to the costs of the district attorney's investigation, does the district attorney thereafter suffer from a disabling conflict of interest requiring recusal under Penal Code section 1424? On this question of first impression, we hold such financial assistance to the prosecutor's office may indeed disqualify the district attorney from acting further in a case, if the assistance is of such character and magnitude "as to render it unlikely that defendant will receive fair treatment during all portions of the criminal proceedings." In this case, where a corporation alleged to be the victim of trade secrets theft contributed around $13,000 to the cost of the district attorney's investigation, the superior court did not abuse its discretion in finding the victim's financial assistance created a conflict of interest for the prosecutor. The trial court did err in failing to apply the further test set out in Penal Code section 1424: whether the resulting conflict was so severe as to make fair treatment of the defendants unlikely. We conclude, however, that such a finding would not, on this record, be an abuse of discretion.

In September 1992, defendant Eugene Wang was a vice-president of Borland International, a software developer located in Scotts Valley (Santa Cruz County). Defendant Gordon Eubanks was president and chief executive officer of Symantec, a competitor of Borland. In July of 1992, Wang had expressed dissatisfaction with a Borland management reorganization and threatened to resign. On September 1, 1992, he submitted his resignation. Fearing Wang might have conveyed internal Borland information to outsiders, Borland officers reviewed Wang's electronic mail files. They found several messages to Eubanks containing what they believed was confidential Borland information. Borland contacted the Scotts Valley police, who in turn sought investigative assistance from the district attorney's office.

During the night of September 1, and into the morning of September 2, 1992, Borland officials worked with representatives of the police department and district attorney's office preparing warrant affidavits for searches of defendants' residences and Symantec/headquarters. . . .

Spencer Leyton, a senior Borland executive, indicated Borland's willingness to spend up to $10,000, and possibly more, for experts to assist in the investigation. . . . Borland records show a $25,000 "blanket" purchase order was drawn up and approved by the legal department in November 1992 for "miscellaneous services and fees/Symantec lawsuit." Borland records for the subsequent payments to Klausner, Strawn and others for their work on the criminal investigation bear numerical references to this purchase order.

Klausner and Strawn accompanied representatives of law enforcement agencies who executed the warrant on September 2. Klausner submitted his bill for $1,400 directly to Borland on September 14, 1992. Borland paid it by a check dated January 6, 1993.

Strawn continued to work on the criminal investigation for several weeks, into October 1992, assisting the district attorney's office in retrieving and printing the contents of seized computer disc drives. In late September 1992, knowing Strawn was working on the case, Chief Inspector Johnson discussed with Arthur Danner, the Santa Cruz County District Attorney, whether Borland should be asked to pay Strawn's anticipated bill. Danner made no decision at that time. Johnson testified he then asked Borland executive Leyton whether Borland was "still willing to assist us by carrying the cost of the technicians that were necessary to process this case." Leyton, according to Johnson, answered affirmatively. Some time after that discussion, Johnson again broached the question with Danner, who then approved submitting Strawn's invoices to Borland.

Defendants initially moved to recuse the entire office of the district attorney on the ground that Deputy District Attorney Jonathan Rivers, who had worked on the Eubanks-Wang case, had left the district attorney's office and been retained by Borland to work on Borland's related civil action against Symantec. In the course of a hearing on this issue, defendants learned of the payments by Borland, which were then made a separate ground for requesting recusal.

After hearing the above evidence, the superior court concluded that while Rivers's change of employment did not require recusal of the district attorney's office, the payments did. The court's rationale appears from its comments during argument on the motion (no written statement of reasons was filed). Discounting mere "appearances . . . of impropriety," the court framed the issue as whether the victim's "payment of money for a debt already incurred" by the district attorney creates "an actual conflict" for the prosecutor. The standard to be applied, as the court understood it, was whether "the evidence provides a reasonable possibility that the D.A.'s office may not exercise its discretionary function in an even-handed manner."

The court emphasized Borland's payment of Strawn's bill: "[W]e have a situation here where there was a debt . . . that's already been incurred. That person was going to get paid regardless of who paid it. Borland happens to make the offer and in fact does pay it, and pays other bills as well. Doesn't that put the District Attorney in a position, as human being, to feel a greater obligation for this particular victim than some other fellow or person whom doesn't offer to pay existing debts?" Answering its own rhetorical question, the court found the payment of the district attorney's incurred debt "rather strong evidence of a reasonable possibility that the discretionary function that's fundamental to a District Attorney is compromised and thereby would not necessarily be used in an even-handed manner."

In California, all criminal prosecutions are conducted in the name of the People of the State of California and by their authority. . . . No private citizen, however personally aggrieved, may institute criminal proceedings independently, and the prosecutor's own discretion is not subject to judicial control at the behest of persons other than the accused.

The importance, to the public as well as to individuals suspected or accused of crimes, that these discretionary functions be exercised "with the highest degree of integrity and impartiality, and with the appearance thereof" cannot easily be overstated. The public prosecutor

[I]s the representative not of any ordinary party to a controversy, but of a sovereignty whose obligation to govern impartially is as compelling as its obligation to govern at all; and whose interest, therefore, in a criminal prosecution is not that it shall win a case, but that justice shall be done. As such, he is in a peculiar and very definite sense the servant of the law, the twofold aim of which is that guilt shall not escape or innocence suffer. 'The People' includes the defendant and his family and those who care about him. It also includes the vast majority of citizens who know nothing about a particular case, but who give over to the prosecutor the authority to seek a just result in their name. . . .

While the district attorney does have a duty of zealous advocacy, "both the accused and the public have a legitimate expectation that his zeal . . . will be born of objective and impartial consideration of each individual case." . . . It is a bit easier to say what a disinterested prosecutor is not than what he is. He is not disinterested if he has, or is under the influence of others who have, an axe to grind against the defendant, as distinguished from the appropriate interest that members of society have in bringing a defendant to justice with respect to the crime with which he is charged.

Section 1424, pursuant to which the present motion was made, was enacted in 1980. Only three years earlier, in *People v. Superior Court (Greer),* this court first recognized the judicial power to recuse the district attorney as prosecutor. In *Greer,* we located the source of a court's disqualification power in Code of Civil procedure section 128, subdivision (a)(5), which recognizes a court's power "[t]o control in furtherance of justice, the conduct of its ministerial officers, and of all other persons in any manner connected with a judicial proceeding before it . . ." We further held the separation of powers doctrine did not preclude a trial court from disqualifying a district attorney.

* * *

Section 1424 established both procedural and substantive requirements for a motion to disqualify the district attorney. Substantively, the statute provides the following standard: "The motion shall not be granted unless it is shown by the evidence that a conflict of interest exists such as would render it unlikely that the defendant would receive a fair trial."

We considered and resolved these interpretive questions regarding section 1424 in *People v. Conner.* The distinction between actual and apparent conflict is "less crucial" under the statute, we explained, because of the "additional statutory requirement" that the conflict must "render it unlikely that the defendant would receive a fair trial." We held that a "conflict," for purposes of section 1424, "exists whenever the circumstances of a case evidence a reasonable possibility that the DA's office may not exercise its discretionary function in an evenhanded manner. Thus, there is no need to determine whether a conflict is 'actual' or only gives an 'appearance' of conflict." But however the conflict is characterized, it warrants recusal only if "so grave as to render it unlikely that defendant will receive fair treatment during all portions of the criminal proceedings."

That our analysis focuses on actual likelihood of prejudice, however, should not be taken as suggesting the potential for loss of public confidence in the criminal justice system is either unimportant or unimaginable. To the contrary, the practice of the district attorney here soliciting and accepting the victim's underwriting of significant investigative costs could, especially if replicated on a wide scale, raise an obvious question as to whether the wealth of the victim has an impermissible influence on the administration of justice. A system in which affluent victims, including prosperous corporations, were assured of prompt attention from the district attorney's office, while crimes against the poor went unprosecuted, would neither deserve nor receive the confidence of the public. Even the appearance of such impropriety would be highly destructive of public trust. Under section 1424, however, such apprehensions, alone, are no longer a ground for recusal of the district attorney.

Defendants here have focused on the likelihood of pretrial prejudice, in particular "the very real likelihood that the prosecution would pursue a weak case because it was indebted to Borland." They urge us to uphold the trial court's finding of conflict, which was based upon a perceived reasonable possibility the district attorney, out of a sense of obligation to Borland, would be unwilling to drop the charges or bargain for a lesser plea. Conner established that the potential for such pretrial unfairness is cognizable under section 1424.

Second, section 1424 requires the existence of a "conflict . . . such as would render" a fair trial "unlikely." In *Conner*, we read this language as establishing a two-part test: (i) is there a conflict of interest?; and (ii) is the conflict so severe as to disqualify the district attorney from acting? Thus, while a "conflict" exists whenever there is a "reasonable possibility that the DA's office may not exercise its discretionary function in an evenhanded manner," the conflict is disabling only if it is "so grave as to render it unlikely that defendant will receive fair treatment." As shall be seen in part III.A, post, the trial court here erred by addressing only the first part of the test, existence of a conflict, without deciding whether the conflict was so grave as to make fair treatment unlikely.

The Attorney General fails to persuade us any legal principle restricts the concept of a conflicting interest to a district attorney's personal financial or emotional stake in the prosecution. . . .

Section 1424, on its face, allows recusal on a showing of any conflict of interest that renders fair treatment unlikely, and our decisions interpreting the statute have not further restricted the concept of a conflicting interest. No reason is apparent why a public prosecutor's impartiality could not be impaired by institutional interests, as by personal ones. . . .

Thus, in *Young v. U.S. ex rel. Vuitton et Fils S.A.* (1987), 481 U.S. 787, the high court, pursuant to its supervisory authority, forbade a private law firm from prosecuting a contempt on behalf of the Government, because the first, as a matter of legal ethics, bore the "obligation of undivided loyalty" to its private client, Vuitton, which in turn had a private pecuniary interest in prosecution of the contempt. A public prosecutor must not be in a position of "attempting at once to serve two masters," the People at large and a private person or entity with its own particular interests in the prosecution. Private influence, exercised through control over the prosecutor's personal or institutional concerns, is a conflict of interest, under section 1424, if it creates a reasonable possibility the prosecutor may not act in an evenhanded manner.

In this connection, CDAA draws our attention to statutes establishing industry-financed funding schemes for certain types of fraud prosecutions . . . Without expressing any opinion as to whether these financing schemes may cause a conflict for district attorneys, or as to their desirability from a policy standpoint, we agree with defendants that these statutory schemes are distinguishable in a number of ways from the type of contributions at issue here: the insurers involved in the statutory funding schemes are required by law to contribute to prosecution efforts, unlike Borland, which contributed to the prosecution at the special request of the district attorney's office; the assessments are made industry-wide, rather than on one particular victim corporation, and are spent on investigation and prosecution of automobile and workers' compensation insurance fraud generally, rather than for the particular benefit of any one victim. These factors tend to reduce the likelihood any victim would gain, through financial contributions, influence over the conduct of any particular prosecution.

That the prosecutor may have been able to proceed further or more quickly against defendants with Borland's assistance than without would not, by itself, constitute unfair treatment. As CDAA points out, defendants have "no right to expect that crimes should go unpunished for lack of public funds." . . . For that reason we cannot agree with the suggestion of amicus curiae National Association of Criminal Defense Lawyers that a victim's financial assistance necessarily subjects the defendant to unfair prosecutorial treatment because "[w]hen a private party underwrites the cost of one particular prosecution, that case is not subject to the same economic restraints that limit all other prosecutions." To warrant recusal of the district attorney under section 1424, instead, the evidence must show the prosecutor suffers from a disabling conflict of interest. . . .

Supporting recusal here is the fact the largest payment, that for Strawn's first $9,450 bill, was, as the trial court emphasized, "payment of money for a debt already incurred" by the district attorney. The final decision to obtain payment from Borland was not made until Strawn submitted his first bill. Because Strawn had contracted with the district attorney's office, rather than Borland, Chief Inspector Johnson reasonably believed the district attorney's office would be responsible for

Strawn's bills if Borland did not pay them. Borland paid Strawn's bill, moreover, in response to a direct request from the district attorney's office. While decisions from other jurisdictions have approved of some forms of victim assistance, for example in the form of an attorney hired by a victim or victim's family to assist the public prosecutor, none involved the public prosecutor's request for the victim's assistance to satisfy a monetary debt already incurred. Hence, none assist our analysis here.

The size of the contributions here also tends to show recusal would be within the trial court's discretion. District Attorney Danner testified his office fund for this type of investigation was very limited, and Chief Inspector Johnson apparently regarded the investigatory costs here as large enough to warrant the unusual measure of asking the victim to pay them.

Finally, the trial court's assessment of the strength of the prosecution case supports the decision to recuse. Before hearing the recusal motion, the court held an extensive hearing on the proper means of protecting Borland's asserted trade secrets from disclosure during the criminal proceedings. In the course of that hearing, the court repeatedly stated its firm impression that the subject secrets, which Wang and Eubanks were alleged to have conspired to steal, Wang to have stolen and Eubanks to have received, do not in fact meet the definition of trade secrets for criminal purposes, although they might be trade secrets for purposes of civil remedies. Arguably, a factually weak case is more subject than a strong case to influence by extraneous financial considerations, since in the absence of financial assistance from the victim the prosecutor is more likely to abandon or plea bargain such a case.

Considering the above factors, we cannot say, as a matter of law, that had the trial court addressed the second part of the Conner test the gravity of the identified conflict it would have abused its discretion in finding the conflict so grave as to render fair treatment of the defendants in all stages of the criminal proceedings unlikely. The Court of Appeal therefore erred in holding that, assuming a conflict existed, it was not, as a matter of law, grave enough to justify recusal.

The cause is transferred to the Court of Appeal with directions to vacate its previous judgment and dismiss the appeal as moot.

Notes

1. Private persons may lawfully spend any amount on a private investigation. Nothing prevents the private investigation from being directed by private counsel. In a famous case, Claus von Bulow, a suspect in the death of his wife, heiress Sunny von Bulow, was the target of an investigation that was run by a private attorney representing Sunny von Bulow's children. The private attorney was the former district attorney for Manhattan. *State v. Claus von Bulow*, 475 A.2d 995 (R.I. 1984). The Rhode Island Supreme Court found the defendant's contention that the private investigation was equivalent to an unlawful private prosecution to be without merit. Thus, conducting an investigation and turning the results over to the authorities was permitted. However, government agents may need to obtain a warrant when

expanding the scope of the search beyond the items provided by the private investigator. *Id.*

2. Does the *Eubanks* opinion leave room for a donation of money to assist with future expenses of investigation? If the trial court had ruled the other way, would the ruling be upheld "in the court's discretion"? In a later California case, the California Supreme Court refused to find an abuse of discretion when the trial court refused to find a conflict of interest where a victim-funded investigator had operated for several years within the offices of the Orange County District Attorney. *Hambarian v. Superior Court*, 44 P.3d 102 (Cal. 2002*).*

3. How does a budget-strapped county district attorney afford to prosecute white-collar crime? One answer might be for the victim to retain a private attorney to work with and for the district attorney. *See* Chapter 8, Trial.

4. Would conflict questions arise if the money was given to police, as opposed to the district attorney? Because the opinion is based in statutory conflict standards, and not due process considerations, it is difficult to predict the answer with any certainty.

5. Other courts have been willing to allow industry funding of criminal investigations, provided that prosecutors had complete discretion over whether to file charges. *See, e.g., Commonwealth v. Ellis*, 708 N.E.2d 644 (Mass. 1999). *See generally* Rebecca A. Pinto, Note, *The Public Interest and Private Financing of Criminal Prosecutions*, 77 WASH. U.L.Q. 1343, 1344 (1999) (arguing that private funding could increase egalitarianism in public prosecutions).

What do you think of the private funding scheme set forth in the following article?

Jim Redden, *Hired Gun: Neighborhood Crime Got You Down? Buy Yourself a Prosecutor*

WILLAMETTE WEEK, (Dec. 13, 1990)

Although he is only 24 years old, Corey Dean Tucker is well on his way to becoming a low-level career criminal. In December 1985, Tucker pleaded guilty to second-degree theft and was sentenced to one year's probation. In February 1987, he was given a 30-day jail term for second-degree theft and lying to a police officer. In January 1989, he received five years' probation for possessing illegal drugs. Six months later, he was sentenced to an additional five years' probation for attempting to elude police in a stolen car. Then, on Oct. 11 of this year, Tucker was arrested and cited for breaking into seven cars near the Oregon Convention Center in inner northeast Portland, allegedly ripping out their stereos and grabbing anything loose off their seats.

Despite his previous record, Tucker almost walked away from his recent arrest. None of the seven car owners filed a complaint against him. For that reason, Tucker was released without being formally charged with any crime. But then Wayne

Pearson got involved. Pearson, a deputy Multnomah County district attorney, took a special interest in the case. He personally persuaded the witnesses to testify against Tucker and got him re-cited for the theft. Now a warrant has been issued for Tucker's arrest, and the Portland police are on his trail. "The case had gone to that place where cases go when no one wants to prosecute them," says Pearson, whose boyish good looks belie his 18 years in the District Attorney's Office. "But now we've got a real chance of taking him off the streets for a long time."

Not everyone is pleased with Pearson's involvement in this case, however. That's because Pearson is not just working for the county. The veteran prosecutor is also working for the Holladay District Association, a private group made up primarily of business and property owners in the area where the seven cars were broken into. The association and its supporters are currently paying the county more than $130,000 so that Pearson will work full time on cases in the Holladay District. "This is an example of the landed gentry buying a higher level of law enforcement services than anyone else," claims local defense lawyer John Henry Hingson III. "What are they going to want next, their own judges, their own jails, their own laws? I'm disappointed in this program."

Multnomah County District Attorney Michael Schrunk, who helped initiate the program, denies that there is anything inappropriate about the concept of a private group paying one of his deputy's salaries. "What you have to ask is, 'Are the priorities of the person paying the bill consistent with good public policy?'" reasons Schrunk, "If we could make that district more secure, that's good public policy."

E. Private Investigation

1. The Lawfulness of Use of the Media

Crime victims, unlike prosecutors, are not bound by professional rules of ethics. As a result, victims may interact with the media as they see fit. In the infamous Jon Benet Ramsey case, her father John Ramsey issued a plea for assistance in finding the killer.

The Daily Camera
July 24, 1997

On December 25th, my daughter, JonBenet, was brutally murdered by an intruder who came into our home while we slept. As a parent, there is no greater hurt in life than the loss of a child. I can tell you that to lose our youngest child in such a vile and brutal manner is a hurt beyond what any human being could be expected to endure.

The person who did this crime is an evil person beyond imagination. He must be brought to justice and prevented from stopping the life of another young child who offers so much to the future of our world.

Over the past seven months, I have grown increasingly frustrated as the investigating authorities have limited their investigation into the murder of my daughter, JonBenet Ramsey, to me and members of my family.

We all became aware that we would be investigated as a matter of routine procedure and have refrained from commenting on their work as we had also expected that they would work past us and get on with the investigation into who killed JonBenet.

I am not confident this has happened. Therefore, today I am announcing an escalation in my own efforts to find the murderer of JonBenet. Prominent experts in the fields of criminology, handwriting and language forensics have developed a profile of the probable behavior of JonBenet's killer before and after the crime. Highly qualified handwriting analysis experts have developed a template for our investigators to use in comparing key features of handwriting samples against the note.

Based on tips received from our previous advertisements and other fieldwork, our investigators are looking into solid leads. While we are limited in our work because we do not have access to the forensic information and do not have police powers to search and test, we do have the advantage of knowing that no one in our family is responsible for JonBenet's death and we can evaluate information without prejudice.

We will begin a series of newspaper ads and fliers to alert people to the elements of the behavioral profile and ask them to contact our investigators at (phone number) with information about persons who might fit the profile. If someone has a handwriting sample of a person they believe might fit the profile, our investigators would also like to see that as well.

The profile provided to me suggests the following:

JonBenet's killer may have been suffering from some stress in the weeks and months preceding the crime;

A triggering event, such as a job crisis or crisis in a personal relationship, may have caused this individual to vent anger, perhaps at a female close to him, or perhaps at me personally;

Since the murder, this individual may rabidly read news reports of the investigation, listen to talk radio shows oriented to coverage of the murder;

He possibly has increased his consumption of alcohol or drugs;

He may have even turned to religion;

He may be rigid, nervous and preoccupied in casual conversation;

He may have tried to appear very cooperative with the authorities if he was contacted during the course of the police investigation;

He may have quickly constructed an alibi for his whereabouts the night JonBenet was killed and may have repeated it several times to key individuals around him as if rehearsing them in the answer;

The killer is someone who may have previously been in my home.

We appreciate the help and support we have received from the people of Boulder. Beginning this Sunday, we will begin running ads in the Boulder newspaper and will distribute fliers in appropriate neighborhoods, reminding people of the behavioral profiles and asking for their help in developing more detail about these individuals.

We hope that with the help of one key phone call, this killer can be brought to justice.

Notes

1. At one point, the Ramseys were suspects in the case. DNA testing later cleared them. *New DNA Samples Clear Family in JonBenet Ramsey Case*, USA TODAY, July 8, 2008. The case remains unsolved.

2. The use of the media by victim or offender is lawful. However, the use of the media by prosecutors or defense attorneys may be constrained by ethical guidelines. *See* Comment, Lynn Weisberg, *On a Constitutional Collision Course: Attorney No-Comment Rules and the Right of Access to Information*, 83 J. CRIM. L. & CRIMINOLOGY 644 (1992).

3. Rewards. Posting of rewards for the arrest and conviction of an offender is generally lawful and is essentially an offer governed by contract law. *See* 67 AM. JR. 2D, REWARDS (1985 & Supplement).

2. Private Search by Victim or Other

U.S. CONST. amend. IV

> The right of the people to be secure in their persons, houses, papers, and effects, against unreasonable searches and seizures, shall not be violated, and no Warrants shall issue, but upon probable cause, supported by Oath or affirmation, and particularly describing the place to be searched, and the persons or things to be seized.

In *Burdeau v. McDowell*, 256 U.S. 465 (1921), the defendant's office and safe were broken into. Incriminating documents were retrieved. The acts were clearly illegal but conducted by agents of a private entity. The Court held that the documents were admissible in a federal criminal trial because there was no state action.

————————

Wayne R. Lafave

1 SEARCH AND SEIZURE § 1.8 (3d ed. 1996) (multi-volume treatise)

Although much has happened in the realm of Fourth Amendment jurisprudence since the time of the *Burdeau* decision, the holding . . . seems not to have been disturbed by subsequent developments. While it has occasionally been suggested that *Elkins v. United States*, overturning the so-called "silver platter" doctrine whereby federal authorities were theretofore permitted to receive and use evidence unlawfully acquired by state officers, casts doubt upon the continued vitality of *Burdeau*, that is not the case. *Elkins* never mentioned *Burdeau*, and the reasoning employed in *Elkins* was specifically directed to searches by state officials. Likewise, it can hardly be said that *Mapp v. Ohio* put *Burdeau* in doubt at the state level, for *Mapp* applied the Fourth Amendment to the states via the Fourteenth Amendment, which itself encompasses only state action. And, despite an assertion to the contrary by one court, it is not correct to say that the substantial redefinition of Fourth Amendment coverage in *Katz v. United States* affects the *Burdeau* rule. Notwithstanding the emphasis in *Katz* upon the Amendment's protection of privacy, the Court carefully noted that the Fourth Amendment cannot be translated into a general right of privacy and that the general right is left to the law of the states. It is not surprising, therefore, that the Supreme Court continues to view the *Burdeau* rule as being very much alive.

3. Citizens Arrest

5 Am. Jur. 2d, *Arrest*, Arrest by Private Person
§ 56–58 (1995)

Although the authority of a private person to arrest without a warrant is more limited than that of a police officer, the common law accorded a private person extensive powers to arrest without warrant for felonies and breaches of the peace committed in his or her presence, and on probable cause for past felonies, provided they had actually been committed. The privilege was recognized at common law to facilitate the prompt suppression of a certain kind of offense. In a state where the common law is in force except as modified by statute, and where the statutes make no provision on the subject, a private person's common-law powers to arrest without warrant may still be in effect. Thus, for example, courts have upheld arrests by private citizens made for armed robbery and forgery.

After making an arrest, a private citizen has the duty to bring the person before a magistrate or a peace officer promptly . . .

At common law, a private person can arrest without warrant for felony or breach of the peace committed in his presence. The "in presence" requirement is met if the arrestor observes acts which are in themselves sufficiently indicative of a crime in the course of commission. . . . It is the right and duty of a private person to apprehend one who has committed a felony in his presence, either at the time of its commission or upon immediate pursuit. A private person could also justify the apprehension of another by showing that it was necessary in order to prevent the perpetration of a felony. Where an offense is a felony actually committed in the presence of a private person, such person may, under some statutes, arrest any person he has reasonable ground to believe guilty. Actual knowledge of the commission of the felony is not required to authorize a valid citizen's arrest. All that is required is reasonable grounds to believe that 1) a felony had been committed and 2) that the person arrested was the responsible agent.

In some jurisdictions, a private person may arrest for any misdemeanor committed in his presence. But under the common-law rule, which is codified in some states, such arrests can be made only for a misdemeanor constituting a breach of the peace. But a private person's right to arrest for an affray or breach of the peace exists only while it is continuing, or immediately after it has been committed, or while there is a continuing danger of its renewal, and does not include the right to pursue and arrest for the purpose of insuring the apprehension or future trial of the offender. A private citizen cannot arrest without a warrant for a misdemeanor previously committed unless pursuit for the purpose of arrest is begun immediately.

In some jurisdictions, arrest by a private person for a misdemeanor may be justified only if the person arrested is subsequently found guilty. In any case, it appears that a private person may not arrest for a misdemeanor on suspicion, regardless of how well-founded it may be.

Offense not committed in presence of person making arrest.

Under the common law rule, still in effect in many jurisdictions, a private person may arrest without a warrant in a felony case if the felony has actually been committed and he has reasonable grounds for believing that the person arrested was the one who committed it. The commission in fact of the felony provides the probable cause on which the arrest is based. Under this rule, if no felony has in fact been committed an arrest without warrant by a private person will be illegal, although an officer would have been justified in arresting under the same circumstances.

In some jurisdictions, however, usually by statute, a private person may justify an arrest without warrant, though no felony was actually committed, where he had reasonable grounds for believing that one had been committed and that the person arrested was guilty.

However, one who acts from purely personal motives and in a manner likely to lead to a serious breach of the peace may not be justified merely because he had a legal right to make a citizen's arrest on suspicion of felony.

If a felony has in fact been committed by the person arrested, an arrest without warrant by a private person may be justified whether or not there was time to have obtained a warrant. But it seems that a private person can justify his failure to get a warrant, where he had opportunity to do so, only by showing that the person arrested was actually guilty.

Note

The potential of civil liability is a significant deterrent to citizen's arrest. A victim or witness not precisely conforming to the requirements of the citizen's arrest law is subject to suit for false arrest or false imprisonment by the arrestee.

Chapter 4

Charging

Introduction

This section explores the victim's influence on the prosecutor's charging decision, beginning with the substantial power of prosecutors in the charging decision and criticisms of this centralization of power are examined. The chapter then looks in some detail at informal influence and formal checks on the prosecutor's discretion with a particular emphasis on challenging the prosecutor's decision not to charge. Limitations on the victim's ability to directly bring charges are also reviewed. Finally, the chapter ends by discussing the role of the privately funded prosecutor in grand jury and preliminary hearings; the prosecutor's ability to elect between grand jury and preliminary hearing; the victim's ability to attend grand jury or preliminary hearing; and, the propriety of the presence of a support person for the victim during grand jury and preliminary hearing.

A. The Impact Upon Victims of Different Charging Modes

Public prosecutors charge felonies using one of three methods: grand jury, preliminary hearing, or direct present. For a charge to issue by one of these three procedures there must be probable cause. Grand jury is a group of citizens, varying in size, who hear the prosecutor's evidence. The grand jury operates in secret and the defense does not participate. Preliminary hearings are typically a brief hearing in open court where a judge determines probable cause. The prosecution must provide enough evidence for probable cause. The defense is present, although defense inquiry may properly be restricted to the probable cause evidence presented by the prosecutor. Direct presents on felonies are done in only a few states. The direct present mode of proof varies from submission of victim/witness affidavits to deposition of victims and witnesses. A judge reviews the material submitted.

A victim's interest in privacy may lead them to prefer foregoing attendance at a preliminary hearing in favor of the privacy afforded by grand jury proceedings. In addition, grand jury proceedings do not provide the defendant an opportunity to cross-examine the victim. Therefore, the victim may have a strong preference for a grand jury proceeding, to avoid exposure to cross-examination. In states engaging in direct presents, the impact to victims ranges from little to none where affidavits are submitted, to substantial where victims are cross-examined in deposition.

Professor Paul Cassell has written about the traumatization of victims at preliminary hearings, which applies as well to pre-charge depositions in direct present cases.

Paul Cassell, *Balancing the Scales of Justice: The Case for and the Effects of Utah's Victims' Rights Amendment*

1994 UTAH L. REV. 1373 (1994)

Testifying at preliminary hearings was often traumatic for crime victims in Utah. For example, a daughter who one week earlier had witnessed the murder of her mother and grandmother was required to testify at a preliminary hearing and identify photographs of the bloodied bodies of her loved ones. In another case, an elderly woman's home was burglarized by a man who stole some of her undergarments. The woman was required to testify at the preliminary hearing that those were her undergarments and that, no, the defendant did not have permission to take them. The burglary victim was extremely concerned about being forced to testify, and was more traumatized by her preliminary hearing appearance than by the burglary itself.

Trauma can be especially severe for victims of rape and children who have been sexually abused. These victims are forced to recount the details of horrible crimes against them and must endure cross-examination, while the defendant sits nearby as a threatening presence. For example, a young female victim of sexual assault was so worried about her testimony at a preliminary hearing that she vomited six times the night before and then again in the prosecutor's office. She testified and was cross-examined for two-and-a-half hours, and was extremely upset throughout. Unfortunately, this victim's story is not an isolated incident. Because no jury is present at preliminary hearings to be alienated, defense attorneys often conduct brutal cross-examination designed solely to traumatize victims and discourage them from appearing at trial. Sometimes the trauma even extends over multiple court appearances.

To alleviate some of the trauma that victims experience, the President's Task Force recommended that victims not testify at preliminary hearings. The Task Force stressed that preliminary hearings "should not be a mini-trial, lasting hours, days, or even weeks, in which the victim has to relive his victimization." The Task Force also noted that

> In some cases, the giving of such testimony is simply impossible within the time constraints imposed. Within a few days of the crime, some victims are still hospitalized or have been so traumatized that they are unable to speak about their experience. Because the victim cannot attend the hearing, it does not take place, and the defendant is often free to terrorize others.

The Task Force therefore called for the enactment of legislation to "ensure that hearsay is admissible and sufficient in preliminary hearings, so that victims need not testify in person." Similar recommendations have been made by the U.S. Department of Justice Office for Victims of Crime (in cooperation with the National Association of Attorneys General and the American Bar Association), the Attorney General's Task Force on Family Violence, the American Bar Association's Center on Children and the Law, and other commentators. It should be noted that most cases never go to trial because of plea bargains or other dispositions. As a result, if most victims can be spared from testifying at preliminary hearings, they will be spared from ever testifying.

––––––––––––

In general, in those jurisdictions providing for both preliminary hearing and grand jury charging procedures, state prosecutors are allowed broad discretion in electing between the two charging procedures of grand jury and preliminary hearing. Some states have upheld the election of one procedure over another based merely on the tactical motive of the prosecutor. Selecting preliminary hearing over Grand Jury has been upheld where the prosecutor wanted a clear record of proceedings. *State v. Stewart*, 47 La. An 40, 16 So. 945 (1895); any reason in the exercise of prosecutorial discretion that is not in bad faith has been upheld as the standard. *Lodwick v. Coffey*, 497 S.W.2d 873 (Mo. App. 1973); election due to a greater likelihood of eventual probable cause finding has been upheld, *State v. Maes*, 93 Nev. 49, 559 P.2d 1184 (1977). Other courts have upheld the lawfulness of avoiding preliminary hearing. *State v. Bark*, 82 N.M. 866, 483 P.2d 940, *cert. denied*, 404 U.S. 955, 30 L.Ed 2d 271, 92 S. Ct. 309 (1971 App.). In these states, prosecutor's election of grand jury in lieu of preliminary hearing out of consideration for the victims preference is likely to be allowed.

However, some state courts view as unlawful a tactical motive for electing between the grand jury and preliminary hearing procedures. In these states the question arises whether the use of one procedure over the other to provide a benefit to the victim of crime constitutes an unlawful tactical motive. State courts have answered this question differently.

For example, two continuances of a preliminary hearing which enabled the prosecutor to present the case to the grand jury, thus avoiding preliminary hearing, were not disfavored tactical maneuvering where the reason for the continuance was to avoid the necessity of the defendant's children talking about the killing of their mother. *Smith v. State*, 344 A.2d 251 (Del. Sup. 1975).

To the contrary, the Oregon Supreme Court ruled that a practice of shielding witnesses from examination at a preliminary hearing by taking the case to the grand jury was similar to impermissibly singling out defendants for preliminary hearing or grand jury treatment. In the absence of a statutory *requirement* of preliminary hearing the court stated that each county remained free to choose, as a consistently used procedure, either preliminary hearings or grand juries. *State v. Freeland*, 667 P.2d 509 (Or. Sup. Ct. 1983).

The response of the Multnomah County Prosecutor, whose jurisdiction contains the city of Portland, Oregon, was complete elimination of the use of preliminary hearings in all felony cases. All felony indictments in Portland, Oregon are now obtained by grand jury.

B. Victim Attendance at Grand Jury and Preliminary Hearing

Generally, a victim may appear at a grand jury only in the capacity of a witness. The court in its discretion may authorize attendance beyond this. An exception is where the victim is present via a privately funded attorney who is actively participating in the grand jury process with the permission of the public prosecutor and the court.

A few modern state constitutional amendments appear on their face to permit a victim's presence in grand jury proceedings. *See, e.g.,* IDAHO CONST. art. I, §22(4) ("A crime victim has the following rights: . . . To be present at all criminal justice proceedings."). However, it is not likely that the term "criminal proceedings" in such enactments was included to authorize a victim's general presence in grand juries.

Most state constitution amendments that provide for a victim's appearance at criminal proceedings do so only where a defendant also has the right to be present. For example: "The victim or family member of a victim of crime has a right to be present at any proceeding where the defendant has a right to be present. . . ." OK. CONST. art. 2, §34. Thus, the majority of state constitutional amendments do not provide for a victim's presence at grand jury because the defendant also may not attend the grand jury proceedings.

However, when the formal charging mechanism is preliminary hearing, these state constitutional provisions or their statutory equivalents appear to permit the victim's presence because the criminal defendant also has the right to be present at preliminary hearings. In most circumstances a victim's right to be present during the charging process parallels the right of the criminal defendant. To the extent that both the victim and defendant wish to be present, their interest in a preliminary hearing procedure over a grand jury procedure coincide.

C. Presence of a Support Person for the Victim

1. In Grand Jury Proceedings

Absent a showing of prejudice, it is generally either legally permissible or harmless error for the court to allow a person providing support to the victim/witness into the Grand Jury when the victim is testifying, particularly when the victim is a child. *See, e.g., People v. Verkey,* 185 A.2d 622 (N.Y. 1992) (The mere presence of an unauthorized person before the Grand Jury, however, does not automatically require dismissal of the indictment. There must be some showing that the presence of the unauthorized person created a possibility of prejudice and impaired the integrity of the proceeding.)

The presence of a parent of a minor child in the Grand Jury while the child is testifying has rarely been the basis for reversing an indictment. The better practice is to secure the court's permission beforehand as courts have authority over the admission of support persons into grand jury proceedings.

2. Preliminary Hearings

Some states permit the presence of a support person during all criminal hearings, including preliminary hearing. For example, Kentucky legislation provides:

Ky. Rev Stat. § 421.575
ROLE OF VICTIM ADVOCATES IN COURT PROCEEDINGS

In all court proceedings, a victim advocate, upon the request of the victim shall be allowed to accompany the victim during the proceeding to provide moral and emotional support. The victim advocate shall be allowed to confer orally and in writing with the victim in a reasonable manner. However, the victim advocate shall not provide legal advice or legal counsel to the crime victim. . . .

D. Privately Funded Prosecutors in Grand Jury Proceedings and Preliminary Hearings

1. Grand Jury

Modern cases have relied on the wording of statutes to interpret whether a private prosecutor may appear in the grand jury. For example, under the following New Mexico statute the New Mexico Supreme Court held that the presence and participation of a private prosecutor in the Grand Jury is reversible error:

All taking of testimony will be in private with no persons present other than the grand jury and the persons required or entitled to assist the grand jury including the district attorney, the attorney general and their staffs, interpreters, court reporters and the witnesses. Section 41-5-4 N.M.S.A. 1953 (2d Repl. Vol. 6). State v. Hill, 88 N.M. 216, 539 P.2d 236 (1975).

The *Hartgraves v. State*, 114 P. 343 (Ok. Crim. App. 1911) case reflects the generally accepted view that privately funded attorneys cannot, on their own, present to the grand jury. *Robinson v. State*, 477 N.E.2d 883 (Ind. 1985) reflects the view held in some state jurisdictions that a privately funded attorney may participate in the grand jury if the public prosecution and court approve and where the public prosecutor is present in the Grand Jury.

One of the central questions concerning the appearance of privately funded prosecutors at Grand Jury at the request of the public prosecutor concern the notions of potential prejudice to the accused. In Hartgraves, such prejudice is presumed by the mere presence of a privately funded attorney. In *Robinson*, some actual showing of prejudice must be made by the defendant. Which is the better rule?

One concern about private prosecutors in grand jury is that the grand jury ceases to be a secret proceeding. If the victim is paying for a private prosecutor, would the private prosecutor be able to communicate the content of secret testimony to the victim? This question raises the issue of whether the private prosecutor acting upon request of the victim is an agent of the state or the victim.

The crime victim who initiates a grand jury contact without the public prosecutor [see the previous section] does so as a witness to the crime. Absent statutory authority, the victim may not direct a grand jury proceeding. The private prosecutor is, of course, not a witness to the crime. Because the privately retained prosecutor is neither a public prosecutor nor a witness, they generally may not appear before the grand jury or direct the proceedings absent the permission of the public prosecutor and permission of the court.

2. Privately Funded Prosecuting Attorneys at Preliminary Hearing

A preliminary hearing is a probable cause determination procedure which is utilized either prior to, or as a substitute for, the grand jury hearing. The hearing is held in open court before a judge and the judge makes the probable cause determination. A defendant and his counsel have the right to be present and to make inquiries.

Very few reported cases mention the use of a privately funded attorney at preliminary hearing. Those that do have not ruled upon the propriety of the privately funded attorney participation. *Commonwealth v. Malloy*, 450 A.2d 689, 690; *State v. Woods*, 234 S.E.2d 754 (N.C. App. 1977).

In the minority of jurisdictions which prohibit the use of a privately funded attorney at trial the use of a privately funded attorney at preliminary hearing is probably not going to be permitted.

However, in the majority of jurisdictions which permit privately funded attorneys participation in trial, there are few, if any, compelling reasons to prohibit private attorney participation in preliminary hearings. The presence of a judge at preliminary hearing assures that the private prosecutor will stay within bounds. The defendant and counsel are present and may make objections. The secrecy and privacy values embodied in the Grand Jury process do not usually play a role in preliminary hearings. Finally, the judge is unlikely to be prejudiced by the privately funded attorney's presence.

E. Prosecutorial Discretion

Part of the function of the public prosecutor is to serve as a check on the desire of a victim to prosecute. The prosecutor represents the interests of society. In representing the interests of society in the charging decision, the prosecutor has profoundly broad discretion.

The legitimate discretionary reasons for not prosecuting are legion. Frank Miller, in *Prosecution: The Decision to Charge a Suspect with a Crime* (1959) identified a non-exclusive list of these reasons:

The decision not to prosecute . . . because of the attitude of the victim; the decision not to proceed further because of cost to the system; . . . because of undue harm to the suspect; the existence of alternative procedures; the availability of civil sanctions; the cooperation of the suspect in achieving other law enforcement goals

There have been criticisms and defenses of the mostly unchecked discretion of the prosecutor in making the charging decision.

KENNETH CULP DAVIS, DISCRETIONARY JUSTICE: A PRELIMINARY INQUIRY

(1969)

Confining, Structuring, and Checking the Prosecuting Power

1. *Must the prosecutor's discretionary power be uncontrolled?* Viewed in broad perspective, the American legal system seems to be shot through with many excessive and uncontrolled discretionary powers but the one that stands out above all others is the power to prosecute or not to prosecute. The affirmative power to prosecute is enormous, but the negative power to withhold prosecution may be even greater, because it is less protected against abuse.

The prosecuting power is not limited to those who are called prosecutors; to an extent that varies in different localities the prosecuting power may be exercised by the police, and a goodly portion of it is exercised by regulatory agencies, licensing agencies, and other agencies and officers. The prosecuting power is not limited to the criminal law; it extends as far as law enforcement extends, including initiation of proceedings for license suspension or revocation, and even to enforcement of such provisions as those requiring that rates or charges be reasonable.

Even though the many prosecuting powers at all levels of government obviously vary widely in the extent and manner of confining, structuring, and checking, the major outlines are almost always governed by a single set of universally accepted assumptions. The principal assumptions are that the prosecuting power must of course be discretionary, that statutory provisions as to what enforcement officers "shall" do may be freely violated without disapproval from the public or from other officials, that determinations to prosecute or not to prosecute may be made secretly without any statement of findings or reasons, that such decisions by a top prosecutor of a city or county or state usually need not be reviewable by any other administrative authority, and that decisions to prosecute or not to prosecute are not judicially reviewable for abuse of discretion.

Why these various assumptions are made is not easy to discover; the best short answer seems to be that no one has done any systematic thinking to produce the assumptions, but that the customs about prosecuting, like most other customs, are the product of unplanned evolution. Whatever caused the assumptions to grow as they did, prosecutors usually assert that everybody knows that they are necessary.

But I wonder: Why should a prosecutor say, a county prosecutor have discretionary power to decide not to prosecute even when the evidence of guilt is clear, perhaps partly on the basis of political influence, without ever having to state to anyone what evidence was brought to light by his investigation and without having to explain to anyone why he interprets a statute as he does or why he chooses a particular position on a difficult question of policy? Why should the discretionary power be so unconfined that, of half a dozen potential defendants he can prove guilty, he can select any one for prosecution and let the other five go, making his decision, if he chooses, on the basis of considerations extraneous to justice? If he finds that A and B are equally guilty of felony and equally deserving of prosecution, why should he be permitted to prosecute B for felony but to let A off with a plea of guilty to a misdemeanor, unless he has a rational and legal basis for his choice, stated on an open record? Why should the vital decisions he makes be immune to review by other officials and immune to review by the courts, even though our legal and governmental system elsewhere generally assumes the need for checking human frailties? Why should he have a complete power to decide that one statute duly enacted by the people's representatives shall not be enforced at all, that another statute will be fully enforced, and that a third will be enforced only if, as, and when he thinks that it should be enforced in a particular case? Even if we assume that a prosecutor has to have a power of selective enforcement, why do we not require him to state publicly his general policies and require him to follow those policies in individual cases in order to protect evenhanded justice? Why not subject prosecutors' decisions to a simple and general requirement of open findings, open reasons, and open precedents, except when special reason for confidentiality exists? Why not strive to protect prosecutors' decisions from political or other ulterior influence in the same way we strive to protect judges' decisions?

The unthinking answer to such questions as these is that the prosecutor's function is merely to do the preliminary screening and to present the cases, and that the decisions that count are made on the basis of the trial. But public accusation and trial often leave scars which are not removed by proof of innocence. Mr. Justice Jackson was talking realism when he said, as Attorney General:

> The prosecutor has more control over life, liberty, and reputation than any other person in America. His discretion is tremendous. He can have citizens investigated and, if he is that kind of person, he can have this done to the tune of public statements and veiled or unveiled intimations. Or the prosecutor may choose a more subtle course and simply have a citizen's friends interviewed. . . . He may dismiss the case before trial, in which case the defense never has a chance to be heard. . . . If the prosecutor is obliged to choose his cases, it follows that he can choose his defendants. . . . [A] prosecutor stands a fair chance of finding at least a technical violation of some act on the part of almost anyone. . . . It is in this realm in which the prosecutor picks some person whom he dislikes or desires to embarrass, or selects some group of unpopular persons and then looks for an offense, that the greatest danger of abuse of prosecuting power lies. It is here that law enforcement becomes personal. . . .

Mr. Justice Jackson was discussing what a prosecutor does affirmatively; the damage done by public accusation may be permanent even when innocence is proved in a later proceeding. What a prosecutor does negatively is almost always final and even less protected withholding prosecution, nol pros of a case, acceptance of a plea of guilty to a lesser offense even when such decisions are irrational or improperly motivated and even when the result is unjust discrimination against those who are not similarly favored. The notion that the tribunal that holds the trial corrects abuses of the prosecuting power is obviously without merit.[9]

Nor will the other usual justification for uncontrolled discretionary power of prosecutors stand analysis that the intrinsic nature of the prosecuting function is such that the only workable system is uncontrolled discretion. True, the habit of assuming that *of course* the prosecutor's discretion must be uncontrolled is so deeply embedded that the usual implied response to questions as to whether the prosecuting power can be confined or structured or checked is that the questioner must be totally without understanding. Inability of those who are responsible for administering the system to answer the most elementary questions as to the reasons behind the system is itself a reason to reexamine.

Sarah N. Welling, *Victims in the Criminal Process: A Utilitarian Analysis of Victim Participation in the Charging Decision*

30 Ariz. L. Rev. 85 (1988)

⋆ ⋆ ⋆

IMPLEMENTATION OF VICTIM PARTICIPATION IN THE CHARGING DECISION

Assume a jurisdiction has decided to incorporate victims into the charging decision. Considering the existing law, how should this be done? May existing limits on prosecutorial discretion be used to implement victim participation or must new limits be devised?

1. The Charging Decision is Made by the Prosecutor with Few Limits on Discretion

The charging decision is currently made exclusively by the prosecutor. The prosecutor's initial source of authority is statutes which establish the office of prosecutor and authorize the prosecutor to prosecute all crimes. Some of these statutes explicitly permit the prosecutor to exercise discretion in deciding which cases to prosecute, some statutes are silent on discretion, and some statutes make prosecution mandatory. But, in spite of the mandatory language in this latter type of statute, and in spite of the mandatory language used in criminal codes generally, courts have

---

9. Perhaps nine-tenths of the abuses of the prosecuting power involve failure to prosecute, and courts normally have no occasion to review such cases. Even when an abuse is affirmative, a court is unlikely to review the exercise of the prosecutor's discretionary power. . . .

concluded that it is within the prosecutor's discretion to initiate or decline prosecution and to choose which offense to charge.

The prosecutor's discretion in the charging decision is broad. The few limits which exist on the prosecutor's charging discretion can be divided into those enforced in the courts and those which draw their enforcement from other sources.

a. Limits on Prosecutorial Discretion Imposed by Sources Outside the Courts

There are four limits on the prosecutor's charging decision imposed by forces outside the courts. The first limitation exists in the criminal statutes themselves. Common law crimes are largely extinct. As a result the prosecutor may not charge a crime unless the conduct falls within a criminal statute. This limit is defined by the legislature when the penal code is drafted. However, because legislators draft penal codes in general and often ambiguous language, the initial decision as to what constitutes criminal conduct is effectively left to the prosecutor. Moreover, many criminal statutes overlap, and this overcriminalization gives the prosecutor wider choice at the charging stage.

A second limit on the prosecutor's charging discretion, which is imposed by the legislature, is the level of funding the legislature allocates to prosecutors' offices. This purse string limit has a significant practical impact on charging decisions.

The third limit on the prosecutor's charging discretion, is internal guidelines, a limit which is self-imposed by the executive. These internal guidelines have been adopted recently in response to pressure to limit prosecutorial discretion and to reveal the bases for charging decisions. The efficacy of such self-imposed guidelines in limiting discretion has been questioned, mainly because the guidelines are non-binding.

The fourth limit on the prosecutor's charging discretion is the political pressure to make popular or at least tolerable charging decisions. This pressure is imposed by the general population through its voting right.

Of these four limits, internal guidelines and political pressure on the prosecutor may operate in a given case either to preclude, or to compel, prosecution. In contrast, the requirement of a criminal statute, and the existence of funding limits, would operate only to prohibit a prosecution, never to compel one.

b. Limits on Prosecutorial Discretion Imposed by the Courts

There are four limits on the prosecutor's charging discretion which depend for their enforcement on the courts. The initial limit on the prosecutor's charging discretion is the requirement that there be sufficient evidence to charge a crime. The criminal justice system contemplates that the prosecutor's charging decision is screened at least once for sufficiency of the evidence before trial. If the charging instrument is an indictment, this screening is performed by a grand jury when the indictment is issued or refused; if the charging instrument is an information, the screening is done by the court at a preliminary hearing. This control on charging discretion is reiterated in ethical standards which provide that it is unethical for the prosecutor to institute criminal proceedings in the absence of probable cause. Other recognized charging guidelines echo this requirement that the evidence reach a certain level before charges are filed. Disagreement exists as to the efficacy of this evidence requirement as a limitation on charging discretion.

The second limit on the prosecutor's charging discretion is constitutional. Selective prosecution is well-accepted, but the selection cannot deliberately be based upon "an unjustifiable standard such as race, religion, or other arbitrary classification." Such discriminatory enforcement is unconstitutional as a denial of equal protection. Thus, where laundries operated by Caucasians were granted licenses but laundries operated by Asians were denied licenses on the basis of race, a Chinese launderer's conviction for operating without a license was reversed. This limit is well recognized by the courts, but it is not well used; prosecutors' charging decisions are rarely reversed on this basis.

The third limit imposed on the prosecutor's charging discretion is also constitutional. This limit is often referred to as a ban on "prosecutorial vindictiveness" or "retaliatory prosecution." Specifically, a prosecutor cannot use the charging power to penalize a defendant for exercising constitutional rights; such retaliation violates due process guarantees. Thus, where a prosecutor added six counts to a ten count indictment after the defendant opposed the state's motions for joinder of charges and revocation of bond, the court dismissed the extra six counts.

The fourth limit on charging discretion is the prosecutor's duty to act ethically and in good faith. Courts indulge a presumption that prosecutions are undertaken in good faith, but, if a party can produce evidence of overreaching or bad faith, courts are willing to review the charging decision. The impact of this limit is slight because no decisions are reported wherein the charging decision was reversed on this basis.

Thus, the courts are willing to limit charging discretion only if the prosecution is unconstitutional, unethical or based on insufficient evidence. Courts have occasionally implied the existence of other miscellaneous limits on the prosecutor's charging decision, but the limits discussed above are the only limits established to date. No general cause of action for abuse of discretion exists.

As this review of the law indicates, court-imposed limits upon prosecutorial charging discretion are few, and their practical impact is slight. Moreover, the four limits imposed by the courts operate only to prohibit prosecution; none operates to cause a court to compel prosecution.

F. Victim's Informal Influence in the Decision to Charge

1. Generally

A crime victim has no formal authority to prevent the prosecutor from pursuing a formal charge. The prosecutor, as a representative of the public interest, may proceed over the objection of the victim.

A handful of states have statutes granting the victims the ability to confer with the prosecution concerning the charging decision.

ARIZ. REV. STAT. ANN., tit. 13, § 13-4408 (1996).

[I]f a prosecutor declines to proceed with a prosecution after the final submission of a case by a law enforcement agency at the end of an investigation, the prosecutor shall, before the decision not to proceed is final, notify the victim and provide the victim with the reasons for declining to proceed with the case. The notice shall inform the victim of his right on request to confer with the prosecutor before the decision not to proceed is final. Such notice applies only to violations of a state criminal statute.

Other jurisdictions, like the Federal Crime Victims' Rights provide a general right to confer:

A crime victim has the following rights: . . .

The reasonable right to confer with the attorney for the government in the case. 18 U.S.C. § 3771(a)(5).

Absent a statutory right to consultation, in some types of cases the victims do have informal influence over case initiation.

Generally speaking, a crime victim has more influence in getting a prosecutor not to charge when the offense is minor. Conversely, a victim has more influence in getting the prosecutor to charge when the crime is major. There are exceptions to this generalization:

Rafael Olmeda, *Cooper City Teen Who Shot and Killed Friend Sentenced to Probation in Plea Deal*

SUN SENTINEL, 1/25/2017

Eric Palacios, the Cooper City teenager accused of manslaughter in the accidental shooting death of his closest friend in 2015, struck a deal with prosecutors and was sentenced to at least three years of probation after pleading guilty to firing a weapon in an occupied dwelling.

Palacios, now 16, will spend the next three years delivering the same message he delivered in court Tuesday before Broward Circuit Judge Elijah Williams, said Frank Maister, Palacios' lawyer. "All of these video games, all of these movies, they all normalize guns and they make you feel like playing with a gun is normal, and it isn't," said Maister, paraphrasing his client.

The case against Palacios remained in the juvenile justice system, a decision that was made less than a month after the July 30, 2015 shooting death of Charlie Martin, 14, of Sunrise. Palacios was also 14 at the time.

The boys were fiddling with the gun, which they found in the garage at Palacios' home . . . . It belonged to Palacios' stepfather and was not locked. Martin's older brother, Francisco, was with the other teens, and the Martin family [surviving victims] agreed with the decision to prosecute Palacios as a juvenile.

G. Victims' Formal Influence in the Charging Process

1. Charging Methods

a. Theoretical Models of Charging Methods

Josephine Gittler, *Expanding the Role of the Victim in a Criminal Action: An Overview of Issues and Problems*

11 Pepperdine L. Rev. 117 (1984)

The Private Prosecution and the Victim's Interests

From the perspective of the crime victim's interests, the impact of allowing victim-initiated private prosecutions would be beneficial. If victims were allowed to initiate a criminal action, victims could forestall or override negative prosecutorial charging decisions that would adversely affect their restitutive and retributive interests. A victim may be precluded from obtaining restitution or retribution by the public prosecutor's discretionary decision not to bring a criminal action or to dismiss a criminal action after it has been brought. Likewise, the vindication of a victim's restitutive and retributive interests may be frustrated by the prosecutor's discretionary decisions to charge a single offense where the evidence would warrant charging several offenses or to charge a lesser offense than the evidence warrants because such decisions may narrow the sanctions which may be subsequently imposed on a convicted offender. The availability of a private prosecution would mean that the victim could initiate a criminal action in order to obtain restitution and retribution even when the public prosecutor decides not to charge or not to charge the full range of possible offenses.

The availability of private prosecution could also benefit victims by providing a remedy for prosecutorial charging decisions that are the product of bias against certain classes of victims. A review of the existing literature indicates that factors related to the characteristics of the victim and the nature of the victimization influence prosecutorial charging decisions and that prosecutors are more responsive to requests for prosecution from victims involved in certain types of crimes than in other types of crimes. While the exercise of prosecutorial charging discretion in a manner that reflects bias against certain classes of victims may not be an abuse of discretion or even irrational, it is questionable when the evidence would permit prosecution and the victim has requested prosecution.

Public Prosecution and the Potential Defendant's Interests

. . . From the standpoint of the potential defendant's interests, however, the chief apprehension about private prosecutions brought by victims is that they would reduce the impartiality and fairness of the charging process. This apprehension arises from an image of the victim as an overly vindictive individual and an image of the prosecutor as a disinterested, objective individual-images that do not always correspond to reality. Moreover, it is not necessarily appropriate to apply the same standards and norms to victims' decisions to prosecute and to public prosecutors' decisions to prosecute. Public prosecutors represent the interests of the state and have the responsibility of seeing that justice is done, while victims simply represent their own individual interests. Once the proposition is accepted that victims may have restitutive and retributive interests as arising from the crime deserving of vindication through a criminal prosecution of the offender, differences in the handling of criminal cases deriving from differences in the interests of victims are inevitable. The troublesome aspect of this position is that a victim's desire to prosecute may be related not to restitutive and retributive interests arising from the crime but rather to motives extraneous to these interests . . . .

Private Prosecution, the Interests of the State, and the Public Prosecutor's Charging Discretion

From the perspective of the state's interests, a determination and evaluation of the impact of allowing victims to bring private prosecutions involves a consideration primarily of its impact upon the authority of the public prosecutor who acts as the state's representative in deciding whether to initiate a criminal action. Since the bias for and effect of negative prosecutorial charging decisions with respect to the state's interests vary, the impact of authorizing private prosecutions by victims may vary depending upon the type of decision involved . . . .

Modified Private Prosecution

It must be stressed at this point that private prosecution could be revived in a modified form with various limitations. Private prosecutions by victims need not be authorized in all criminal cases. Its use could be confined to cases involving certain types of offenses which victims are likely to want prosecuted but which public prosecutors are likely to be reluctant to prosecute, being the best candidates for private prosecution.

Private prosecution by victims on a unilateral basis also need not be authorized. Its use could be conditioned on some type of prior approval or authorization. One alternative is to make notification or approval by the public prosecutor a prerequisite for a private prosecution. This alternative would allow a victim to institute a criminal proceeding where the prosecutor had no basic objection to prosecution, but would leave unresolved genuine conflicts between victims and prosecutors as to whether a prosecution should be undertaken.

Another alternative is to make negative prosecutorial charging decisions subject to judicial review when sought by the victim. This alternative has the advantage of providing a judicial evaluation, which is presumably neutral and detached, of the prosecutor's decision not to prosecute or not to prosecute fully contrary to the expressed wishes of the victim. Traditionally, however, the judiciary has been very reluctant to review prosecutorial charging decisions.

Still another alternative . . . is to establish a mechanism whereby the victim could challenge a negative prosecutorial charging decision by directly petitioning a grand jury to initiate a prosecution. Under this approach, if a victim asked the grand jury to initiate a prosecution, the public prosecutor would be forced to articulate his or her reasons for refusing to prosecute, and the grand jury could then assess their validity in light of the victim's desire for prosecution. One of the grand jury's historic functions is to investigate criminal cases and to bring to trial individuals justly accused of a crime. There is also some precedent for and experience with victims presenting a charge of complaint directly to the grand jury. In passing upon a victim's request for the initiation of a criminal prosecution over the objection of the prosecutor, the grand jury would not be able to rely on the investigative assistance of the prosecutor's office as it normally does in a criminal case, but provision could be made for the appointment of special independent prosecutors or investigators to assist the grand jury.

2. Formal Checks on the Prosecutor's Control

Because of the prosecutor's largely unchecked discretion in charging, the question arises, what mechanisms exist to "check" the discretionary power of the prosecutor? A variety of formal mechanisms exist to check the discretionary power of the prosecutor. These are (a) electoral control; (b) Attorney General intervention; (c) judicial review by mandamus; (d) special prosecutors; (e) judicial review of constitutional requirements or pursuant to statutory requirements; and, (f) grand jury review.

a. Electoral Control

In many state jurisdictions, the prosecutor is an elected county or parish official. Some view the ability of the electorate to vote and replace a prosecutor as a sufficient check on prosecutorial charging discretion. For example, the Los Angeles District Attorney was ousted after the botched McMartin Preschool case.

There has been criticism that election mechanisms are not a sufficient "check." First, because individual case decisions will rarely impact on election and, second, because it does not provide a remedy in any particular case.

The United States Attorney General and the United States Attorneys are presidentially appointed, not elected, and are therefore not subject to direct electoral control.

b. Governor Intervention

Generally, a governor has authority to review a local prosecutor's charging decision. In theory, the governor may assign another prosecutor to a prosecution or seek dismissal over the objection of the local prosecutor. In reality, this is rarely done and then in only the most egregious of circumstances. This mechanism is not readily available to the vast majority of victims of crime.

[State's Attorney] Ayala, etc., v. Rick Scott, Governor

224 So.3d 755 (Fla. 2017)

Aramis Donell Ayala, State Attorney for Florida's Ninth Judicial Circuit, petitions this Court for a writ of quo warranto, challenging Governor Rick Scott's authority under section 27.14(1), Florida Statutes (2016), to reassign the prosecution of death-penalty eligible cases in the Ninth Circuit to Brad King, State Attorney for Florida's Fifth Judicial Circuit. We have jurisdiction. *See* article V, § 3(b)(8), FLA. CONST. For the reasons below, we deny Ayala's petition.

BACKGROUND

At a March 15, 2017, press conference, Ayala announced that she "will not be seeking [the] death penalty in the cases handled in [her] office." Several times during the same press conference, Ayala reiterated her intent to implement a blanket "policy" of not seeking the death penalty in any eligible case because, in her view, pursuing death sentences "is not in the best interest of th[e] community or in the best interest of justice," even where an individual case "absolutely deserve[s] [the] death penalty."

In response to Ayala's announcement, Governor Rick Scott issued a series of executive orders reassigning the prosecution of death-penalty eligible cases pending in the Ninth Circuit to King. In support of these orders, the Governor cited his duty as Florida's chief executive officer under article IV, section 1(a), of the Florida Constitution to "take care that the laws be faithfully executed" and his authority under section 27.14(1), Florida Statutes, to assign state attorneys to other circuits "if, for any . . . good and sufficient reason, the Governor determines that the ends of justice would be best served." The reassignment orders do not direct King to pursue the death penalty in any particular case, and in a statement filed in this Court, King has sworn that the Governor made no attempt to influence his decision as to whether the circumstances of any of the reassigned cases warrant pursuing the death penalty.

After unsuccessfully seeking a stay of the reassignment orders in the Ninth Circuit, Ayala filed this petition for a writ of *quo warranto* challenging the Governor's authority to reassign the cases at issue to King. The record reflects that Ayala and her office have abided by the lower courts' denial of her motion and fully cooperated with King.

ANALYSIS

Ayala argues that the Governor exceeded his authority under section 27.14 by reassigning death-penalty eligible cases in the Ninth Circuit to King over her objection because article V, section 17, of the Florida Constitution makes Ayala "the prosecuting officer of all trial courts in [the Ninth] [C]ircuit." While quo warranto is the proper vehicle to challenge the Governor's authority to reassign these cases to King, *see Fla. House of Representatives v. Crist*, 999 So. 2d 601, 607 (Fla. 2008), Ayala is not entitled to relief because the Governor did not exceed his authority on the facts of this case. As Florida's chief executive officer, the

Governor is vested with the "supreme executive power" and is charged with the duty to "take care that the laws be faithfully executed." Art. IV, § 1(a), FLA. CONST. Florida law facilitates the Governor's discharge of this duty, among other ways, through state attorney assignments.

Specifically, section 27.14(1), the constitutionality of which Ayala concedes, provides: If any state attorney is disqualified to represent the state in any investigation, case, or matter pending in the courts of his or her circuit or if, for any other good and sufficient reason, the Governor determines that the ends of justice would be best served, the Governor may, by executive order filed with the Department of State, either order an exchange of circuits or of courts between such state attorney and any other state attorney or order an assignment of any state attorney to discharge the duties of the state attorney with respect to one or more specified investigations, cases, or matters, specified in general in the executive order of the Governor. Any exchange or assignment of any state attorney to a particular circuit shall expire 12 months after the date of issuance, unless an extension is approved by order of the Supreme Court upon application of the Governor showing good and sufficient cause to extend such exchange or assignment. § 27.14(1), FLA. STAT. (2016) (emphasis added).

This Court has previously recognized that the Governor has broad authority to assign state attorneys to other circuits pursuant to section 27.14: It is the duty of the Governor under FLA. CONST. F.S.A., art. IV, § 1(a) in the exercise of his executive power to "take care that the laws be faithfully executed." The exercise of this power and the performance of this duty are clearly essential to the orderly conduct of government and the execution of the laws of this State. An executive order assigning a state attorney is exclusively within the orbit of authority of the Chief Executive when exercised within the bounds of the statute. *See Kirk v. Baker*, 224 So. 2d 311 (Fla. 1969). The Governor is given broad authority to fulfill his duty in taking "care that the laws be faithfully executed," and he should be required to do no more than make a general recitation as to his reasons for assigning a state attorney to another circuit. *Finch v. Fitzpatrick*, 254 So. 2d 203, 204-05 (Fla. 1971); *see also Austin v. State ex rel. Christian*, 310 So. 2d 289, 293 (Fla. 1975) ("The statutes authorizing assignments of state attorneys should be broadly and liberally construed so as to − 5 − complement and implement the duty of the Governor under the Constitution of the State of Florida to 'take care that the laws be faithfully executed.'" (quoting art. IV, § 1(a), FLA. CONST.)). Accordingly, this Court reviews challenges to the Governor's exercise of his "broad discretion in determining 'good and sufficient reason' for assigning a state attorney to another circuit," *Finch*, 254 So. 2d at 205, similar to the way in which it reviews exercises of discretion by the lower courts. *Compare Johns v. State*, 197 So. 791, 796 (Fla. 1940) ("If the Governor should abuse [the assignment] power, by arbitrarily and without any reason whatsoever [for] making such an assignment, it might be that his action could be inquired into by writ of quo warranto . . . ."); with *McFadden v. State*, 177 So. 3d 562, 567 (Fla. 2015) ("Discretion is abused only when the trial court's decision is 'arbitrary, fanciful, or unreasonable.'" (quoting *Gonzalez v. State*, 990 So. 2d 1017, 1033 (Fla. 2008))).

Applying this well-established standard of review to the facts of this case, the executive orders reassigning the death-penalty eligible cases in the Ninth Circuit to King fall well "within the bounds" of the Governor's "broad authority." *Finch*, 254 So. 2d at 204-05. Far from being unreasoned or arbitrary, as required by section 27.14(1), the reassignments are predicated upon "good and sufficient reason," namely Ayala's blanket refusal to pursue the death penalty in any case—6—despite Florida law establishing the death penalty as an appropriate sentence under certain circumstances. *See generally* §921.141, Fla. Stat. (2017). Notwithstanding the Governor's compliance with all of the requirements of section 27.14(1), however, Ayala and her amici urge this Court to invalidate the reassignment orders by viewing this case as a power struggle over prosecutorial discretion. We decline the invitation because by effectively banning the death penalty in the Ninth Circuit—as opposed to making case-specific determinations as to whether the facts of each death-penalty eligible case justify seeking the death penalty—Ayala has exercised no discretion at all. As New York's high court cogently explained, "adopting a 'blanket policy'" against the imposition of the death penalty is "in effect refusing to exercise discretion" and tantamount to a "functional[] veto" of state law authorizing prosecutors to pursue the death penalty in appropriate cases. *Johnson v. Pataki*, 691 N.E.2d 1002, 1007 (N.Y. 1997). Although Johnson applied New York law, the standards to which this Court holds its own judicial officers establish that Ayala's actions have the same impact under Florida law. For example, our trial judges may not "refuse to exercise discretion" or "rely on an inflexible rule for a decision that the law places in the judge's discretion." *Barrow v. State*, 27 So. 3d 211, 218 (Fla. 4th DCA 2010), approved, 91 So. 3d 826 (Fla. 2012). Instead, exercising discretion demands an individualized determination "exercised according to the exigency of the case, – 7 – upon a consideration of the attending circumstances." *Barber v. State*, 5 Fla. 199, 206 (Fla. 1853) (Thompson, J., concurring).

Thus, under Florida law, Ayala's blanket refusal to seek the death penalty in any eligible case, including a case that "absolutely deserve[s] [the] death penalty" does not reflect an exercise of prosecutorial discretion; it embodies, at best, a misunderstanding of Florida law. *Cf. Doe v. State*, 499 So. 2d 13, 14 (Fla. 3d DCA 1986) (holding "the trial court failed to exercise its independent sentencing discretion" in light of its erroneous view of the law); *see also Taylor v. State*, 38 So. 380, 383 (Fla. 1905) (recognizing that "a failure of the state's interests" occurs where "the regular state attorney is unwilling or refuses to act").1 Moreover, while Ayala's blanket prohibition against the death penalty provided the Governor with "good and sufficient reason" to reassign the cases at issue to King, also important to our holding is that the Governor did not attempt to decide which cases are deserving of the death penalty. The Governor's orders do 1. Similarly untenable is Ayala's position that she has the authority to pick and choose (by consenting to reassignment in some cases but objecting in others) when she is the prosecuting officer for the Ninth Circuit. While the Ninth Circuit voters elected Ayala as their state attorney, she holds that position subject to Florida law, including section 27.14, by which the Governor effectuates his constitutional duty to ensure the faithful execution of the law through time-limited state attorney assignments. *See Finch*, 254 So. 2d at 205 ("The purpose of the time limitation in the [assignment] statute is to prevent the Chief Executive from frustrating the will of the voters of a judicial circuit by replacing an elected state attorney with one chosen by the Governor from another circuit."). The Governor did not direct King to seek the death penalty in any of the reassigned cases, and King has sworn that the Governor has not attempted to interfere with his determination as to whether to pursue the death penalty in any case.

Rather, consistent with the Governor's constitutional duty, effectuated pursuant to his statutory assignment authority, the executive orders ensure the faithful execution of Florida law by guaranteeing that the death penalty—while never mandatory—remains an option in the death-penalty eligible cases in the Ninth Circuit, but leaving it up to King, as the assigned state attorney, to determine whether to seek the death penalty on a case-by-case basis. On these facts, the Governor has not abused his broad discretion in reassigning the cases at issue to King. Because the power to prosecute, including whether to seek the death penalty, is a purely executive function, *see State v. Bloom*, 497 So. 2d 2, 3 (Fla. 1986), we also reject Ayala's argument that the executive orders violate the separation of powers doctrine of article II, section 3, of the Florida Constitution by impermissibly encroaching upon the judiciary. *See Fulk v. State*, 417 So. 2d 1121, 1126 (Fla. 5th DCA 1982) ("Although state attorneys, like all attorneys, are officers of the court, the execution of criminal statutes by enforcement, including prosecution, is an executive function of government. The state attorney, when acting as a prosecuting officer under Article V, section 17, of the Florida Constitution and under chapter 27 of the Florida Statutes, is performing an executive function and not a judicial function.") (Cowart, J., concurring specially) (footnote omitted).

CONCLUSION

The executive orders reassigning death-penalty eligible cases in the Ninth Circuit to King do not exceed the Governor's authority on the facts of this case. Therefore, we deny Ayala's petition.

Notes

1. The surviving family members were victims under Florida law. The victims' attorney filed an *amicus curiae* (friend of the court) brief on behalf of the victims.

2. For the same result in a similar dispute, *see In re Application of Johnson v. Pataki*, 229 A.D.2d 242 (N.Y. 1997).

c. Mandamus

Mandamus is a review process of an official's (1) failure to act when lawfully required to act or (2) acting when lawfully prohibited from acting. Mandamus may not be used to challenge discretionary actions or discretionary failures to act. Because prosecutors operate within broad discretionary parameters which allow them to prosecute or not prosecute as a discretionary *policy* matter, mandamus almost always fails as a mechanism for review of prosecutorial charging decisions.

Ascherman v. Bales

78 Cal. Rptr. 445 (Cal. App. 1969)

MOLINARI, P.J.—This is an appeal from a minute order denying plaintiff's motion for a peremptory writ of mandate to compel the District Attorney of Marin County to initiate and prosecute a charge of perjury against Vivian Schandelmeier. The basis of the instant petition is the uncontradicted verified allegation that Schandelmeier gave perjured testimony in an administrative proceeding involving the application of plaintiff, a physician and surgeon licensed to practice in California, for admission to the medical staff of Marin General Hospital.

Although this allegation must be taken as admitted because it was not denied by respondent, we are constrained to hold that there is no merit to petitioner's contention that the failure of the district attorney to prosecute, although requested by plaintiff to do so, was an abuse of discretion which may be remedied by writ of mandate. It is well established that, except where a statute clearly makes prosecution mandatory, a district attorney is vested with discretionary power in the investigation and prosecution of charges and a court cannot control this discretionary power by mandamus.

In the instant case, the charges involved concern matters of investigation and prosecution in which the district attorney is vested with discretionary power. Government Code section 26501 provides that "The district attorney shall institute proceedings before magistrates for the arrest of persons charged with or reasonably suspected of public offenses when he has information that such offenses have been committed. . . ." Although this statute uses the word "shall," the ensuing clause implies that the duty entailed by the statute is discretionary. (*Taliaferro v. Locke, supra,* 182 Cal. App. 2d 752, 757.) Accordingly, it was held in *Locke* that mandamus will not lie to compel the district attorney to prosecute every charge of crime that might be made by an individual desiring the prosecution of third persons. (P. 755.)

In *Boyne, supra,* the Supreme Court observed that where there is a clear case that the district attorney has wilfully, corruptly, or inexcusably refused to perform his duty, the proper remedy is to proceed against him for malfeasance or nonfeasance in office. (100 Cal. At p. 267.)[10]

The order is affirmed.

Sims, J., and Elkington, J., concurred.

---

10. In the present case petitioner alleges upon information and belief that the failure to institute the requested prosecution "was motivated by political considerations and a desire to spare embarrassment to the Directors of the Marin Hospital District. . . ."

Notes

1. One commentator recommends creating a mandamus procedure by which citizens could compel federal prosecutions of civil rights crimes. Note, *Discretion to Prosecute Federal Civil Rights Crimes*, 74 YALE L.J. 1297 (1965).

2. The *Ascherman* court's treatment of mandamus actions brought to compel prosecution is in accord with the view of the federal courts and many state courts.

d. Special Prosecutors

Rarely invoked, the use of special prosecutors arises in cases of conflict, corruption, or due to public outrage at the way a matter is being handled by the existing prosecutors, or when the case is very complex. *See* Taylor, *A Needed Legal Specialty: The Special Prosecution*, 61 JUDICATURE 220 (1977).

Paul Gustafson, *Civil Verdict Will Not End Parents' Quest*

Star-Tribune Newspaper of the Twin Cities,
Mpls.-St. Paul June 22, 1997

Jane Neumann's 1993 death was murder, not suicide, her parents say. Now that a civil verdict has bolstered their claim, they're ready for the next step. They'd like to see their former son-in-law, who they and a jury believe killed Neumann, jailed.

While grateful to the jurors [in the civil wrongful death trial] who found her former son-in-law, Jim Neumann, responsible for his wife's death, Patricia Johnston has already set her sights on new legal challenges.

She and her husband, Charlie, of Afton, are to return to the St. Croix County Courthouse in Hudson, Wis., on Monday. They'll ask a judge to order appointment of a special prosecutor and to change the death certificate of their daughter, Jane Neumann, to say she was the victim of murder, not suicide. They also hope the Wisconsin courts will award them custody of their 4-year-old grandson.

"I don't know what kind of chance we've got," she said after last week's civil verdict against Jim Neumann. "But a focus of ours from the very beginning was Johnny and his welfare."

As much as anything, she said, she is relieved that people now know her vibrant daughter did not kill herself 3 years ago at age 30.

"I don't want to call it a victory," Patricia Johnston said. "This is Jane's story . . . and about seeing her vindicated."

On the day in November 1993 that Johnston buried her daughter, she sought out her son-in-law for answers. She couldn't fathom why Jane, an outgoing young mother, would kill herself at the happiest point in her life, leaving behind an infant son and a devoted husband. "Jim said, 'Because it was the happiest time of her life. She didn't want to grow old. It was the best time to go,'" Johnston recalled. "He had all the answers."

But as Jim Neumann's account changed again and again, the Johnstons became convinced of the unthinkable: that he was responsible for Jane's death at the couple's home outside Hudson.

St. Croix County authorities had quickly concluded that Jane Neumann's death was a suicide. They have stuck by that despite new evidence suggesting the possibility of homicide.

Last week the Johnstons waited in the courtroom after the civil verdicts, hoping authorities would arrest Jim Neumann. It didn't happen.

"You think about that," Charlie Johnston said. "Twelve citizens unanimously voted to say there was a murder and that Jim Neumann was the culprit. Then, a short time after it seems justice is being served, that man is released. To me, it seems like they [St. Croix County authorities] are part of the crime."

Jim Neumann, who denies that he killed Jane, has returned to his home in Washington state. Neither he nor his attorney could be reached.

St. Croix County District Attorney Eric Johnson said Friday that his office will go over evidence and testimony presented at the civil trial and decide whether a further review of Jane Neumann's death is warranted. Johnson also said he may consider asking the Wisconsin attorney general's office to look at the case.

Johnson denies that his office or the St. Croix County Sheriff's Department rushed to judgment or botched the investigation of Jane Neumann's death.

"There were some things that probably should have been done differently, but the general investigation was competent," he said.

Changing stories

Patricia Johnston is a cheerful woman with gracious manners. She is also a writer and a historian who can talk about the mountain of details concerning her daughter's death with critical dispassion, but only to a point.

"Thinking about it as a crime, I can shut my emotions off. But when I think about Jane . . ." she said, stopping in midsentence and looking away as tears welled up in her eyes.

Her daughter's death was overwhelming because it seemed so inexplicable, Johnston said. Then came Jim Neumann's wildly divergent accounts.

He first told authorities that he returned home from work on Nov. 22, 1993, to discover the aftermath of a break-in and his wife dead of a gunshot wound to the face. Within days, however, his story changed. Rather than a break-in, he said, he had discovered a suicide scene. Jane Neumann had killed herself by rigging up a shotgun propped through a hole in a wall and discharging it by tying fishing line around the trigger, he said. He also said he found a suicide note by her body.

To spare the family the pain of suicide, Neumann said, he destroyed the note, threw the shotgun off a highway bridge over the St. Croix River and concocted the story about a break-in.

St. Croix County authorities charged him with obstructing justice and lying to sheriff's deputies. He pleaded guilty in 1994 and paid about $4,500 in fines and court costs.

For example, Jim Neumann told his boss that Jane's suicide note said she was despondent about leaving a job several months before her death. But he told another person that his wife was upset because she believed that her young son was more attached to his day-care provider than to her.

Her parents also couldn't believe that Jane Neumann, who was squeamish around blood and hated guns, and who told her brother only weeks before her death that she was the happiest she had ever been, would buy a shotgun and shoot herself.

St. Croix County authorities still weren't convinced they had a murder on their hands but agreed in march 1995 to ask the Wisconsin Division of Criminal Investigation (DCI) to review the case.

In December 1996 the DCI turned over to District Attorney Johnson the results of its investigation into Neumann's death. Johnson said it concluded that "there was no additional evidence that would support a homicide charge."

However, the Johnstons' attorney Mark Gherty, says he learned that state officials also said in a letter to Johnson that they could not rule out homicide. Johnson said Friday that it is possible that an assistant attorney general said such a thing in a letter, but that he does not remember it.

While awaiting the DCI ruling, the Johnstons filed the civil wrongful-death action against Jim Neumann and mounted their own investigation with help from Patricia Johnston's employer, W. Duncan MacMillan, an heir to the Cargill fortune.

Trial testimony

Patricia Johnston the historian notes that her daughter died on the anniversary of President John Kennedy's assassination, but there was another event in November 1963 with which she draws eerie parallels: the murder case of St. Paul lawyer T. Eugene Thompson.

He was convicted of having his wife murdered, and Johnston recalls that prosecutors suggested in his trial that shortly before her death he got rid of the couple's dog so that it would not alert his wife to the intruder hired to kill her.

Jim Neumann and her daughter also had a dog, Molly. Just weeks before her death, Jim Neumann took it to the local animal shelter, a shelter employee testified during the civil trial.

In records submitted as evidence at the trial, Jim Neumann had listed "death of the owner," as the reason the pet was taken to the shelter.

Jurors also heard his female co-workers and his wife's sisters testify that he propositioned them or sexually harassed them before and after Jane Neumann's death.

Neumann, a computer programmer, also admitted that on the day of his wife's death, he called from work 10 times to a home telephone answering machine that allowed him to monitor sounds in his house.

Also at the trial, Milwaukee County Medical Examiner Jeffrey Jentzen testified that although Neumann may have killed herself, her death was "most probably a homicide."

Jurors also heard expert testimony that the pressure required to pull a shotgun trigger with fishing line would have left marks on Jane Neumann's fingers. No such marks were found.

District Attorney Johnson, however, notes that Ramsey County Medical Examiner Michael McGee, who performed the autopsy, has not changed his mind about ruling Neumann's death a suicide.

On Monday, the Johnstons hope to see the official record changed.

Paul Gustafson, *Special Prosecutor to Be Asked to Review Woman's Death*

June 24, 1997

Authorities ruled Jane Neumann's death a suicide, but last week a civil jury found that her husband, Jim, was responsible.

The Wisconsin attorney general's office will be asked to act as special prosecutor and review the 1993 death of Jane Neumann, of Hudson, Wis., who a civil jury said last week was the victim not of suicide but a killing perpetrated by her husband, Jim Neumann.

St. Croix County District Attorney Eric Johnson said Monday that he will ask the attorney general's office to review the case because he or members of his staff could become witnesses should a review of the case result in criminal charges. He also said that the attorney general's office has greater resources with which to conduct a review.

Johnson announced his decision after a court hearing Monday during which attorney Mark Gherty, representing Jane Neumann's parents, Charlie and Patricia Johnston, of Afton, Minn., asked St. Croix County District Judge Eric Lundell to appoint a special prosecutor.

Before Lundell considered the request, Johnson said in court that he would not oppose the move. After meeting with the Johnstons and Gherty Monday afternoon, he confirmed that he will ask for a special prosecutor.

Lundell also set a preliminary hearing for next Monday on the Johnston's other requests: that their daughter's death certificate be changed to list her manner of death as homicide, not suicide, and that they be given custody of their 4-year-old grandson.

The first child-custody issue that must be decided is who will hear the dispute, a Wisconsin judge or a judge in Washington state, where Jim Neumann lives with his new wife and the boy.

At the time of Jane Neumann's death on Nov. 22, 1993, Jim Neumann told authorities that he returned from work to his home outside Hudson to discover the aftermath of a break-in and his 30-year-old wife dead of a gunshot wound to the face. Within days, however, his story changed. Rather than a break-in, he said, he had discovered that his wife had committed suicide by rigging a shotgun propped through a hole in a wall and firing it by tying fishing line around the trigger.

To spare the family the pain of suicide, Neumann said he destroyed the suicide note, threw the shotgun in the St. Croix River and concocted the break-in story.

Jurors in his wrongful-death trial heard testimony that Neumann told different stories about what the suicide note contained, was propositioning and sexually harassing other women and, just weeks before his wife died, dropped the family dog off at an animal shelter stating as the reason: "death of owner."

Jurors also heard experts testifying for the Johnstons question suicide as the cause of death, and challenge Jim Neumann's story about how he found a shotgun rigged so that his wife could shoot herself.

The Johnstons said after Monday's hearing that they were pleased that Johnson agreed to ask for a special prosecutor.

However, Jim Neumann's parents, George and Ivie, told reporters after Monday's hearing that they maintain their son is innocent. "The jury did not go by the evidence . . . Jim is not a vicious person," his mother said.

Fallout from last week's verdict in the wrongful-death case brought by the Johnstons now also includes a St. Croix County Sheriff's Department review of how it handled the investigation, and of the civil trial testimony of sheriff's investigator Earl Clark.

Clark testified that the district attorney's office ordered the criminal investigation closed shortly after Jane Neumann's death.

Johnson denied Monday that he or anyone in his office ordered a halt to the investigation. He said he was in the courtroom during Clark's testimony in the civil trial and was "shocked" by the investigator's statement.

Johnson and St. Croix County Sheriff Paul Burch said that Clark has told them that his testimony was misunderstood.

Notes

1. Ultimately, a judge ordered a finding on Jane Neumann's death changed from suicide to homicide.

2. In addition to demonstrating circumstances in which crime victims might acquire a special prosecutor, these newspaper articles illustrate the potential use of another mechanism, i.e., a civil lawsuit, in the quest to have charges filed.

3. For a fascinating in-depth account of a similar civil suit—the success of which resulted finally in criminal charges and ultimately a murder conviction, read: ANN RULE, DEAD BY SUNSET: COLIN PERFECT HUSBAND, PERFECT KILLER? (1995).

e. Judicial Review Pursuant to Constitutional or Statutory Provisions

In the federal system and many state jurisdictions judicial review of charging decisions results in the almost inevitable ruling that the prosecutor was properly acting within their discretion in charging or refusing to charge.

In the federal system the only potential checks on prosecutorial discretion, other than direct legislative action, are the equal protection clause of the U.S. Constitution and civil rights statutes. These are explored below.

In many state jurisdictions mechanisms of review of prosecutorial discretion exist in the form of limited judicial review of prosecutorial charging decisions or in judicially authorized grand jury review of prosecutorial charging decisions. These are explored below.

f. Grand Jury Review

In many states victims may seek review of a charging decision by bringing the matter to the attention of the Grand Jury. Some jurisdictions allow direct victim access to the Grand Jury. Others require an exhaustion of other remedies; still others require judicial screening of a victim's request to present a matter to the Grand Jury.

These last two mechanisms, grand jury and judicial review, exist to check the discretionary power of the prosecutor in the charging decision and are the topics to which a later section of this chapter is devoted.

3. The Limitations on Private Prosecution for Contempt

Young v. United States ex rel. Vuitton et Fils S.A. et al.

481 U.S. 787 (1986)

JUSTICE BRENNAN delivered the opinion of the Court with respect to Parts I, II, III-A, and IV, and an opinion with respect to Part III-B, in which JUSTICE MARSHALL, JUSTICE BLACKMUN, and JUSTICE STEVENS join.

Petitioners in these cases were found guilty of criminal contempt by a jury, pursuant to 18 U.S.C. § 401(3), for their violation of the District Court's injunction prohibiting infringement of respondent's trademark. They received sentences ranging from six months to five years. On appeal to the Court of Appeals for the Second Circuit, petitioners urged that the District Court erred in appointing respondent's attorneys, rather than a disinterested attorney, to prosecute the contempt. The Court of Appeals affirmed, 780 F.2d 179 (1985), and we granted certiorari, 477 U.S. 903 (1986). We now reverse, exercising our supervisory power, and hold that counsel for a party that is the beneficiary of a court order may not be appointed to undertake contempt prosecutions for alleged violations of that order.

I

The injunction that petitioners violated in these cases is a result of the settlement of a lawsuit brought in December 1978, in the District Court for the Southern

District of New York, by Louis Vuitton, S.A., a French leather goods manufacturer, against Sol Klayminc, his wife Sylvia, his son Barry (the Klaymincs), and their family-owned businesses, Karen Bags, Inc., Jade Handbag Co., Inc., and Jak Handbag, Inc. Vuitton alleged in its suit that the Klaymincs were manufacturing imitation Vuitton goods for sale and distribution. Vuitton's trademark was found valid in *Vuitton et Fils S.A. v. J. Young Enterprises, Inc.*, 644 F.2d 769 (CA9 1981), and Vuitton and the Klaymincs then entered into a settlement agreement in July 1982. Under this agreement, the Klaymincs agreed to pay Vuitton $100,000 in damages, and consented to the entry of a permanent injunction prohibiting them from, *inter alia*, "manufacturing, producing, distributing, circulating, selling, offering for sale, advertising, promoting or displaying any product bearing any simulation, reproduction, counterfeit, copy, or colorable imitation" of Vuitton's registered trademark. App. to Pet. for Cert. 195-A to 196-A.

[The Court recited the evidence before the trial court indicating that the injunction was being violated.]

On the basis of this evidence, Bainton [attorney for Vuitton] requested, and the District Court signed, an order on April 26 directing petitioners to show cause why they and other parties should not be cited for contempt for either violating or aiding and abetting the violation of the court's July 1982 permanent injunction. App. to Pet. for Cert. 205-A. Petitioners' pretrial motions opposing the order to show cause and the appointment of Bainton and Devlin [attorneys for Vuitton] as special prosecutors were denied, and two of the defendants subsequently entered guilty pleas. Sol Klayminc ultimately was convicted, following a jury trial, of criminal contempt under 18 U.S.C. § 401(3), and the other petitioners were convicted of aiding and abetting that contempt. The trial court denied their post-trial motions.

On appeal to the Court of Appeals for the Second Circuit petitioners argued, *inter alia*, that the appointment of Bainton and Devlin as special prosecutors violated their right to be prosecuted only by an impartial prosecutor. The court rejected their contention, 780 F.2d 179 (1985), citing its decision in *Musidor, B.V. v. Great American Screen*, 658 F.2d 60 (1981), cert. denied, 455 U.S. 944 (1982). It suggested that an interested attorney will often be the only source of information about contempts occurring outside the court's presence, 780 F.2d, at 183, and stated that the supervision of contempt prosecutions by the judge is generally sufficient to prevent the "danger that the special prosecutor will use the threat of prosecution as a bargaining chip in civil negotiations. . . ." *Id.*, at 184. Furthermore, the court stated that the authority to prosecute encompasses the authority to engage in necessary investigative activity such as the "sting" conducted in this case. *Id.*, at 184–185. The Court of Appeals therefore affirmed petitioners' contempt convictions.

II

A

Petitioners first contend that the District Court lacked authority to appoint *any* private attorney to prosecute the contempt action against them, and that, as a result, only the United States Attorney's Office could have permissibly brought such a prosecution. We disagree. While it is true that Federal Rule of Criminal Procedure 42(b) does not provide authorization for the appointment of a private attorney, it is long settled that courts possess inherent authority to initiate contempt proceedings for disobedience to their orders, authority which necessarily encompasses the ability to appoint a private attorney to prosecute the contempt. . . .

The ability to punish disobedience to judicial orders is regarded as essential to ensuring that the Judiciary has a means to vindicate its own authority without complete dependence on other Branches. If a party can make himself a judge of the validity of orders which have been issued, and by his own act of disobedience set them aside, then are the courts impotent, and what the Constitution now fittingly calls 'the judicial power of the United States' would be a mere mockery.

Gompers v. Bucks Stove & Range Co., 221 U.S. 418, 450 (1911). As a result, "there could be no more important duty than to render such a decree as would serve to vindicate the jurisdiction and authority of courts to enforce orders and to punish acts of disobedience." *Ibid.* Courts cannot be at the mercy of another Branch in deciding whether such proceedings should be initiated. The ability to appoint a private attorney to prosecute a contempt action satisfies the need for an independent means of self-protection, without which courts would be "mere boards of arbitration whose judgments and decrees would be only advisory." *Ibid.*

B

Petitioners contend that the ability of courts to initiate contempt prosecutions is limited to the summary punishment of in-court contempts that interfere with the judicial process. They argue that out-of-court contempts, which require prosecution by a party other than the court, are essentially conventional crimes, prosecution of which may be initiated only by the Executive Branch.

The underlying concern that gave rise to the contempt power was not, however, merely the disruption of court proceedings. Rather, it was disobedience to the orders of the Judiciary, regardless of whether such disobedience interfered with the conduct of trial.

The distinction between in-court and out-of-court contempts has been drawn not to define when a court has or has not the authority to initiate prosecution for contempt, but for the purpose of prescribing what procedures must attend the exercise of that authority. As we said in *Bloom v. Illinois*, 391 U.S. 194, 204 (1968), "[b]efore the 19th century was out, a distinction had been carefully drawn between contempts occurring within the view of the court, for which a hearing and formal presentation of evidence were dispensed with, and all other contempts where more normal adversary procedures were required." Thus, for instance, this Court has found that defendants in criminal contempt proceedings must be presumed innocent, proved guilty beyond a reasonable doubt, and accorded the right to refuse to testify against themselves, *Gompers, supra,* at 444; must be advised of charges, have a reasonable opportunity to respond to them, and be permitted the assistance of counsel and the right to call witnesses, *Cooke v. United States*, 267 U.S. 517, 537 (1925); must be given a public trial before an unbiased judge, *In re Oliver*, 333 U.S. 257 (1948); and must be afforded a jury trial for serious contempts, *Bloom, supra*. Congress also has regulated the manner in which courts exercise their power to prosecute contempts, narrowing the class of contempts subject to summary punishment, Act of Mar. 2, 1831, 4 Stat. 487. Furthermore, Rule 42 itself distinguishes between contempt committed in the presence of the court, which may be summarily punished, and all other contempts, which may be punished only upon notice and hearing.[11]

The manner in which the court's prosecution of contempt is exercised therefore may be regulated by Congress, *Michaelson*, 266 U.S., at 65–66, and by this Court through constitutional review, *Bloom, supra*, at 201–208, or supervisory power, *Cheff v. Schnackenberg*, 384 U.S. 373, 384 (1966). However, while the exercise of the contempt power is subject to reasonable regulation, "the attributes which inhere in that power and are inseparable from it can neither be abrogated nor rendered practically inoperative." *Michaelson, supra*, at 66. Thus, while the prosecution of in-court and out-of-court contempts must proceed in a different manner, they both proceed at the instigation of the court.

The fact that we have come to regard criminal contempt as "a crime in the ordinary sense," *Bloom, supra*, at 201, does not mean that any prosecution of contempt must now be considered an execution of the criminal law in which only the Executive Branch may engage. Our insistence on the criminal character of contempt prosecutions has been intended to rebut earlier characterizations of such actions as undeserving of the protections normally provided in criminal proceedings. *See, e.g., In re Debs*, 158 U.S. 564, 596 (1895) (no jury trial in criminal contempt actions because a court in such a case is "only securing to suitors the rights which it had adjudged them entitled to"). That criminal procedure protections are now required in such prosecutions should not obscure the fact that these proceedings are not intended to punish conduct proscribed as harmful by the general criminal laws. Rather, they are designed to serve the limited purpose of vindicating the authority of the court. In punishing contempt, the Judiciary is sanctioning conduct that violates specific duties imposed by the court itself, arising directly from the parties' participation in judicial proceedings.[12]

---

11. These measures, carefully instituted over time on the basis of experience with contempt proceedings, undercut JUSTICE SCALIA's argument that court appointment of contempt prosecutors raises the prospect of "'the most tyrannical licentiousness,'" *post*, at 822 (quoting *Anderson v. Dunn*, 6 Wheat. 204, 228 (1821)), representing a situation in which "judge[s] in effect mak[e] the laws, prosecut[e] their violation, and si[t] in judgment of those prosecutions," *post*, at 822, and in which we "permi[t] a judge to promulgate a rule of behavior, prosecute its violation, and adjudicate whether the violation took place." *Post*, at 824.

12. JUSTICE SCALIA's concurrence suggests that the logic of resting a court's ability to institute a contempt proceeding on the need to vindicate the court's authority would support "an inherent power on the part of Congress to prosecute and punish disobedience of its laws." *Post*, at 821. A court's authority would support "an inherent power on the part of Congress to prosecute and punish disobedience of its laws." *Post*, at 821. A court's authority is inherently limited, however, by the

Petitioners' assertion that the District Court lacked authority to appoint a private attorney to prosecute the contempt action in these cases is thus without merit. While contempt proceedings are sufficiently criminal in nature to warrant the imposition of many procedural protections, their fundamental purpose is to preserve respect for the judicial system itself. As a result, courts have long had, and must continue to have, the authority to appoint private attorneys to initiate such proceedings when the need arises.

C

While a court has the authority to initiate a prosecution for criminal contempt, its exercise of that authority must be restrained by the principle that "only '[t]he least possible power adequate to the end proposed' should be used in contempt cases." *United States v. Wilson*, 4210 U.S. 309, 319 (1975) (quoting *Anderson v. Dunn*, 6 Wheat, at 231). We have suggested, for instance, that, when confronted with a witness who refuses to testify, a trial judge should first consider the feasibility of prompting testimony through the imposition of civil contempt, utilizing criminal sanctions only if the civil remedy is deemed inadequate. *Shillitani v. United States*, 384 U.S. 364, 371, n.9 (1966).

This principle of restraint in contempt counsels caution in the exercise of the power to appoint a private prosecutor. We repeat that the rationale for the appoint authority is necessity. If the Judiciary were completely dependent on the Executive Branch to redress direct affronts to its authority, it would be powerless to protect itself if that Branch declined prosecution. The logic of this rationale is that a court ordinarily should first request the appropriate prosecuting authority to prosecute contempt actions, and should appoint a private prosecutor only if that request is denied. Such a procedure ensures that the court will exercise its inherent power of self-protection only as a last resort.

In practice, courts can reasonably expect that the public prosecutor will accept the responsibility for prosecution. Indeed, the United States Attorney's Manual § 9-39.318 (1984) expressly provides: "In the great majority of cases the dedication of the executive branch to the preservation of respect for judicial authority makes the acceptance by the U.S. Attorney of the court's request to prosecute a mere formality. . . ." Referral will thus enhance the prospect that investigative activity will be conducted by trained prosecutors pursuant to Justice Department Guidelines.

In this case, the District Court did not first refer the case to the United States Attorney's Office before the appointment of Bainton and Devlin as special prosecutors.

---

nature of the judicial power, for the court has jurisdiction in a contempt proceeding only over those particular persons whose legal obligations result from their earlier participation in proceedings before the court. By contrast, the congressional prosecutorial power the concurrence hypothesizes would admit of no such limit; the parties potentially subject to such power would include the entire population. Acknowledging the limited authority of courts to appoint contempt prosecutors thus provides no principle that can be wielded to eradicate fundamental separation-of-powers boundaries.

We need not address the ramifications of that failure, however. Even if a referral had been made, we hold, in the exercise of our supervisory power, that the court erred in appointing as prosecutors counsel for an interested party in the underlying civil litigation.

III

In *Berger v. United States*, 295 U.S. 78, 88 (1935) this Court declared:

> The United States Attorney is the representative not of an ordinary party to a controversy, but of a sovereignty whose obligation to govern impartially is as compelling as its obligation to govern at all; and whose interest, therefore, in a criminal prosecution is not that it shall win a case, but that justice shall be done. As such, he is in a peculiar and very definite sense the servant of the law, the twofold aim of which is that guilt shall not escape nor innocence suffer.

This distinctive role of the prosecutor is expressed in Ethical Consideration (EC) 7-13 of Canon 7 of the American Bar Association (ABA) Model Code of Professional Responsibility (1982): "The responsibility of a public prosecutor differs from that of the usual advocate; his duty is to seek justice, not merely to convict."

Because of this unique responsibility, federal prosecutors are prohibited from representing the Government in any matter in which they, their family, or their business associates have any interest. 18 U.S.C. § 208(a). Furthermore, the Justice Department has applied to its attorneys the ABA Model Code of Professional Responsibility, 28 CFR 45.735-1(b) (1986), which contains numerous provisions relating to conflicts of interest. The concern that representation of other clients may compromise the prosecutor's pursuit of the Government's interest rests on recognition that a prosecutor would owe an ethical duty to those other clients. "Indeed, it is the highest claim on the most noble advocate which causes the problem fidelity, unquestioned, continuing fidelity to the client." *Brotherhood of Locomotive Firemen & Enginemen v. United States*, 411 F.2d 312, 319 (CA5 1969).

Private attorneys appointed to prosecute a criminal contempt action represent the United States, not the party that is the beneficiary of the court order allegedly violated. As we said in *Gompers*, criminal contempt proceedings arising out of civil litigation "are between the public and the defendant, and are not a part of the original cause." 221 U.S., at 445. The prosecutor is appointed solely to pursue the public interest in vindication of the court's authority. A private attorney appointed to prosecute a criminal contempt therefore certainly should be as disinterested as a public prosecutor who undertakes such a prosecution.

If a Justice Department attorney pursued a contempt prosecution for violation of an injunction benefitting any client of that attorney involved in the underlying civil litigation, that attorney would be open to a charge of committing a felony under § 208(a). Furthermore, such conduct would violate the ABA ethical provisions, since the attorney could not discharge the obligation of undivided loyalty to both clients where both have a direct interest.[13] The Government's interest is in dispassionate assessment of the propriety of criminal charges for affronts to the Judiciary. The private party's interest is in obtaining the benefits of the court's order. While these concerns sometimes may be congruent, sometimes they may not. A prosecutor may be tempted to bring a tenuously supported prosecution if such a course promises financial or legal rewards for the private client. Conversely, a prosecutor may be tempted to abandon a meritorious prosecution if a settlement providing benefits to the private client is conditioned on a recommendation against criminal charges.

Regardless of whether the appointment of private counsel in this case resulted in any prosecutorial impropriety (an issue on which we express no opinion), that appointment illustrates the *potential* for private interest to influence the discharge of public duty. Vuitton's California litigation had culminated in a permanent injunction and consent decree in favor of Vuitton against petitioner Young relating to various trademark infringement activities. This decree contained a liquidated damages provision of $750,000 for violation of the injunction. The prospect of such a damages award had the potential to influence whether Young was selected as a target of investigation, whether he might be offered a plea bargain, or whether he might be offered immunity in return for his testimony. In addition, Bainton was the defendant in a defamation action filed by Klayminc arising out of Bainton's involvement in the litigation resulting in the injunction whose violation was at issue in this case. This created the possibility that the investigation of Klayminc might be shaped in part by a desire to obtain information useful in the defense of the defamation suit. Furthermore, Vuitton had various civil claims pending against some of the petitioners. These claims theoretically could have created temptation to use the criminal investigation to gather information of use in those suits, and could have served as bargaining leverage in obtaining pleas in the criminal prosecution. In short, as will generally be the case, the appointment of counsel for an interested party to bring the contempt prosecution in this case at a minimum created *opportunities* for conflicts to arise, and created at least the *appearance* of impropriety.[14]

---

13. *See, e.g.,* EC 5-1, *supra*; EC 5-18 ("A lawyer employed or retained by a corporation or similar entity owes his allegiance to the entity and not to a stockholder, director, officer, employee, representative, or other person connected with the entity. In advising the entity, a lawyer should keep paramount its interests and his professional judgment should not be influenced by the personal desires of any person or organization").

14. The potential for misconduct that is created by the appointment of an interested prosecutor is not outweighed by the fact that counsel for the beneficiary of the court order may often be most familiar with the allegedly contumacious conduct. That familiarity may be put to use in *assisting* a disinterested prosecutor in pursuing the contempt action, but cannot justify permitting counsel for the private party to be in control of the prosecution. Nor does a concern for reimbursement of the prosecutor support such an appointment, as the Court of Appeals for the Second Circuit suggested in *Musidor, B.V. v. Great American Screen*, 658 F.2d 60, 65 (1981). The Solicitor General has represented to the Court that the General Counsel of the Administrative Office for the United States Courts has construed the statutes appropriating funds for the operation of the federal courts to permit reimbursement of legal fees to attorneys appointed as special prosecutors in contempt actions, Brief for United States as *Amicus Curiae* 25–26, and that such payments have been approved

As should be apparent, the fact that the judge makes the initial decision that a contempt prosecution should proceed is not sufficient to quell concern that prosecution by an interested party may be influenced by improper motives. A prosecutor exercises considerable discretion in matters such as the determination of which persons should be targets of investigation, what methods of investigation should be used, what information will be sought as evidence, which persons should be charged with what offenses, which persons should be utilized as witnesses, whether to enter into plea bargains and the terms on which they will be established, and whether any individuals should be granted immunity. These decisions, critical to the conduct of a prosecution, are all made outside the supervision of the court.

The requirement of a disinterested prosecutor is consistent with our recognition that prosecutors may not necessarily be held to as stringent a standard of disinterest as judges. "In an adversary system, [prosecutors] are necessarily permitted to be zealous in their enforcement of the law," *Marshall v. Jerrico, Inc.*, 446 U.S. 238, 248 (1980). We have thus declined to find a conflict of interest in situations where the potential for conflict on the part of a judge might have been intolerable. *See id.*, at 250–252 (fact that sums collected as civil penalties returned to agency to defray administrative costs presented too remote a potential for conflict in agency enforcement efforts). Ordinarily we can only speculate whether other interests are likely to influence an enforcement officer, and it is this speculation that is informed by appreciation of the prosecutor's role. In a case where a prosecutor represents an interested party, however, the ethics of the legal profession *require* that an interest other than the Government's be taken into account. Given this inherent conflict in roles, there is no need to speculate whether the prosecutor will be subject to extraneous influence.[15]

As we said in *Bloom*, "In modern times, procedures in criminal contempt cases have come to mirror those used in ordinary criminal cases." 391 U.S., at 207. The requirement of a disinterested prosecutor is consistent with that trend, since "[a] scheme injecting a personal interests, financial or otherwise, into the enforcement

---

in the past at the hourly rate at which Justice Department attorneys are compensated. *Id.*, at 26, n. 20. Furthermore, the normal practice of first referring the matter to the United States Attorney's Office should minimize the number of instances in which such reimbursement is necessary.

15. An arrangement represents an actual conflict of interest if its potential for misconduct is deemed intolerable. The determination whether there is an actual conflict of interest is therefore distinct from the determination whether that conflict resulted in any actual misconduct.

It is true that prosecutors may on occasion be overzealous and become overly committed to obtaining a conviction. That problem, however, is personal, not structural. As the Court of Appeals for the Sixth Circuit said in disapproving the appointment of an interested contempt prosecutor in *Polo Fashions, Inc. v. Stock Buyers Int'l, Inc.*, 760 F.2d 698, 705 (1985), cert. pending, No. 85-455, such overzealousness

> [D]oes not have its roots in a conflict of interest. When it manifests itself the courts deal with it on a case-by-case basis as an aberration. This is quite different from approving a practice which would permit the appointment of prosecutors whose undivided loyalty is pledged to a party interested only in a conviction.

process may bring irrelevant or impermissible factors into the prosecutorial decision."[16]

The use of this Court's supervisory authority has played a prominent role in ensuring that contempt proceedings are conducted in a manner consistent with basic notions of fairness. *See, e.g., Cheff,* 384 U.S., at 380 (requiring jury trial for imposition of contempt sentences greater than six months); *Yates v. United States,* 356 U.S. 363, 366–367 (1958) (reducing contempt sentence in light of miscalculation of number of offenses committed); *Offutt v. United States,* 348 U.S. 11, 13, 17–18 (1954) (contempt conviction reversed in case in which judge involved in personal conflict with contempter). The exercise of supervisory authority is especially appropriate in the determination of the procedures to be employed by courts to enforce their orders, a subject that directly concerns the functioning of the Judiciary. We rely today on that authority to hold that counsel for a party that is the beneficiary of a court order may not be appointed as prosecutor in a contempt action alleging a violation of that order. . . .

[The Court then held that the harmless error rule should not apply to the facts of the case.]

IV

Between the private life of the citizen and the public glare of criminal accusation stands the prosecutor. That state official has the power to employ the full machinery of the state in scrutinizing any given individual. Even if a defendant is ultimately acquitted, forced immersion in criminal investigation and adjudication is a wrenching disruption of everyday life. For this reason, we must have assurance that those who would wield this power will be guided solely by their sense of public responsibility for the attainment of justice. A prosecutor of a contempt action who represents the private beneficiary of the court order allegedly violated cannot provide such assurance, for such an attorney is required by the very standards of the profession to serve two masters. The appointment of counsel for Vuitton to conduct the contempt prosecution in these cases therefore was improper. Accordingly, the judgment of the Court of Appeals is

Reversed.

JUSTICE BLACKMUN, concurring.

I join JUSTICE BRENNAN's opinion. I would go further, however, and hold that the practice federal or state of appointing an interested party's counsel to prosecute

---

16. *Marshall v. Jerrico, Inc.,* 446 U.S. 238, 249–250 (1980). *See Polo Fashions, Inc., supra* (appointment of interested prosecutor disapproved through exercise of supervisory authority); *Brotherhood of Locomotive Firemen & Enginemen v. United States,* 411 F.2d 312, 319 (CA5 1969) (appointment of interested prosecutor characterized as due process violation). Most States have acknowledged this principle as well. "[W]hen a private attorney is also interested in related civil litigation, the majority of states will not permit him to participate in a criminal prosecution." Note, *Private Prosecutors in Criminal Contempt Actions Under Rule 42(b) of the Federal Rules of Criminal Procedure,* 54 Ford. L. Rev. 1141, 1155 (1986) (footnote omitted).

for criminal contempt is a violation of due process. This constitutional concept, in my view, requires a disinterested prosecutor with the unique responsibility to serve the public, rather than a private client, and to seek justice that is unfettered.

JUSTICE SCALIA, concurring in the judgment.

I agree with the Court that the District Court's appointment of J. Joseph Bainton and Robert P. Devlin as special counsel to prosecute petitioners for contempt of an injunction earlier issued by that court was invalid, and that that action requires reversal of petitioners' convictions. In my view, however, those appointments were defective because of a failing more fundamental than that relied upon by the Court. Prosecution of individuals who disregard court orders (except orders necessary to protect the courts' ability to function) is not an exercise of "[t]he judicial power of the United States," U.S. Const., Art. III, §§ 1, 2. Since that is the only grant of power that has been advanced as authorizing these appointments, they were void. And since we cannot know whether petitioners would have been prosecuted had the matter been referred to a proper prosecuting authority, the convictions are likewise void. . . .

JUSTICE WHITE, dissenting.

I agree with the Court that as a general rule contempt cases such as this should in the first instance be referred to the United States Attorney and that a district court's well-established authority to appoint private counsel to prosecute should be exercised only after that official declines to prosecute. I would also prefer that district courts not appoint the attorney for an interested party to prosecute a contempt case such as this. But as I understand Rule 42, it was intended to embrace the prior practice and to authorize, but not to require, the appointment of attorneys for interested parties. I would leave amendment of the Rule to the rulemaking process. I agree with the Court of Appeals that there was no error, constitutional or otherwise, in the appointments made in this action and that petitioners were not denied due process of law by being tried and convicted of contempt. Because I discern no ground for concluding that petitioners did not receive a fair trial, I would affirm the Court of Appeals.

Notes

1. *Vuitton* serves as one of the key cases for determining the scope of the victim's role in the criminal justice system. However, *Vuitton* did not involve a conventional criminal prosecution but rather a court initiated prosecution justified by the inherent contempt authority of the judiciary. The courts' rulings were not based on issues of constitutionality but rather the court's supervisory authority over court practices. Nevertheless, *Vuitton* has been influential in other lower court cases that have set the permissible scope of victim participation in prosecutions instituted by entities other than the court.

2. In Tennessee, "[a] victim of crime or the family members of a victim of crime may employ private legal counsel to act as co-counsel with the district attorney general or the district attorney general's deputies in trying cases, with the extent of participation of such privately employed counsel being at the discretion of the district

attorney general. . . ." T.C.A. § 8-7-401(a) (2002). The trial court must hold a hearing to determine whether the private legal counsel employed as a special prosecutor is qualified and whether there exists a conflict of interest. T.C.A. § 8-7-401(b)(1) (2002). *State v. Parks*, No. E2010-02557-CCA-R3CD, 2012 WL 525500, at *6 (Tenn. Crim. App. Feb. 17, 2012)

4. Victim Access to the Complaint Filing Process

A "complaint" or "information" in the criminal context describes a procedure before a magistrate. It is an initial accusation against an offender, charging a violation of the criminal law. The complaint is commonly a sufficient instrument for misdemeanor prosecution, but not felony prosecution. The instrument which is sufficient for felony prosecution is obtained via preliminary hearing or grand jury shortly after the filing of complaint.

A magistrate reviews the complaint for probable cause. If probable cause is found a complaint provides the court with initial jurisdiction over a criminal matter, commences an action, allows for initial arraignment and arrest of the accused.

In the absence of a statute restricting who may make a complaint, any competent person, including victims of crime, may file a complaint. This was the rule at common law, and remains true in many state jurisdictions. Some states have no prerequisites to filing a complaint, others require screening by a prosecutor. *E.g.*, Ariz. R. Crim. P. 2.4 (providing that a criminal proceeding may commence by two avenues: (1) "a complaint is made upon oath before a magistrate" and the magistrate finds "probable cause to believe" that defendant committed an offense; or (2) "a complaint is signed by a prosecutor"); Wisc. Stat. Ann. § 968.26(2)(a) ("If a person who is not a district attorney complains to a judge that he or she has reason to believe that a crime has been committed within the judge's jurisdiction, the judge shall refer the complaint to the district attorney.) (Wisc. Stat. Ann. § 968.26(2)(b) ("If a district attorney receives a referral under par. (am), the district attorney shall, within 90 days of receiving the referral, issue charges or refuse to issue charges. If the district attorney refuses to issue charges, the district attorney shall forward to the judge . . . all law enforcement investigative reports on the matter that are in [his or her] custody[,] . . . his or her records and case files on the matter, and a written explanation why he or she refused to issue charges. . . . The judge shall convene a proceeding as described under sub. (3) if he or she determines that a proceeding is necessary to determine if a crime has been committed.") Wisc. Stat. Ann. § 968.26(2)(d) ("In [such] a proceeding . . . the judge may issue a criminal complaint if the judge finds sufficient credible evidence to warrant a prosecution of the complaint.").

Citizens may not make out a complaint in a federal court, unlike many state procedures, where a citizen or victim may file an initial complaint subject to a subsequent probable cause review by the prosecutor and/or magistrate. The federal approach precludes the filing of an information. In *New York v. Muka*, 440 F. Supp. 33, 36 (N.D.N.Y. 1977), a citizen attempted to file a federal information. The District

Court refused the filing holding that, "It is well settled that a private citizen has no right to prosecute a federal crime."

5. Limits on Direct Private Prosecution for Crimes Other Than Contempt

State of New Jersey v. Kinder

701 F. Supp. 486 (D.N.J. 1988)

Nature of the Case

This is a criminal case instituted by a private complainant, Deborah Hadley, who charged defendant William Kinder with simple assault and battery in violation of N.J. Stat. Ann. 2C:12-1a. The Municipal prosecutor is not prosecuting this action. Until after argument of the motion addressed in this opinion, Ms. Hadley represented herself, but at trial she will prosecute the action through her private attorney pursuant to New Jersey Municipal Court Rule 7:4-4(b). This case was removed by defendant from the Municipal Court of New Brunswick, New Jersey, to this court pursuant to 28 U.S.C. § 1442(a). Defendant's motion to dismiss pursuant to Fed. R. Crim. P. 12(b) is presently before the court. Defendant contends, *inter alia*, that the authorization in Rule 7:4-4(b) for the use of a private prosecutor is unconstitutional. Despite certification by this court pursuant to 28 U.S.C. § 2403(b), the New Jersey Attorney General's Office has declined to exercise its right to intervene.

FACTS

Defendant has related the following facts in an affidavit. Ms. Hadley works as a letter carrier in the New Brunswick Section of the United States Post Office in New Brunswick, New Jersey. On June 30, 1988, defendant was the acting supervisor of the North Brunswick Section of that office. It was his responsibility to assure that the letter carriers who serve North Brunswick picked up mail at the post office and delivered it to the residents of North Brunswick.

On June 30, Ms. Hadley was on "partial disability" which restricted her from actually delivering the mail. Instead, she was responsible for casing the mail for delivery. Defendant contends that on numerous occasions on the day in question he observed that Ms. Hadley was not doing her job, but was conducting non-work related conversations with other postal employees. Defendant claims that Ms. Hadley twice refused to obey defendant's order to leave the work floor so that he could reprimand her in private. Ms. Hadley charges that sometime after these refusals defendant committed an assault and battery by pushing her with his body.

A summons was issued to the defendant by the New Jersey Municipal Court on July 7, 1988. The summons and complaint charge defendant with simple assault and battery in violation of N.J. Stat. Ann. 2C:12-1a. The maximum penalty for such an offense is six months in prison and a fine of $1,000. N.J. Stat. Ann. 2C:43-3, 43-8.

On July 29, 1988, defendant removed the Municipal Court action to this court pursuant to 28 U.S.C. § 1442(a). In a letter to defense counsel after the case was removed, the Municipal Prosecutor declined to prosecute stating that his "prosecutorial powers are limited to the Municipal Court, City of New Brunswick" and therefore it is "inappropriate" for him to prosecute matters in any other court. The prosecutor also stated that "Citizen Complaints" like the one involved in this matter "are not prosecuted by the Municipal Prosecutor."

DISCUSSION

A threshold issue to be resolved in this case is whether the New Jersey Municipal Court Rule 7:4-4(b) must be applied, despite the fact that this former Municipal Court action was removed to federal court. It is firmly established that when a criminal case is removed from state to federal court, the federal court must conduct the trial under federal rules of procedure, while applying the criminal law of the state.

New Jersey Municipal Court Rule 7:4-4(b) provides:

> Appearance of Prosecution. Whenever in his judgment the interests of justice so require, or upon the request of the court, the Attorney General, county prosecutor, municipal court prosecutor, or municipal attorney, as the case may be, may appear in any court on behalf of the state, or of the municipality, and conduct the prosecution of any action, but if the Attorney General, county or municipal court prosecutor or municipal attorney does not appear, any attorney may appear on behalf of any complaining witness and prosecute the action on behalf of the state or the municipality (emphasis added).

This Rule contains both procedural and substantive rights, allowing a complaining witness who is the victim of a disorderly persons offense to enforce the criminal law in cases where the state or municipality lacks the resources to do so. The importance of the Rule becomes evident when one realizes that absent its use, disorderly persons offenses would go unprosecuted, harming not only the state's interest in enforcing its laws, but also the victim's (if not society's) interest in obtaining satisfaction for wrongs committed. Beyond the importance of this rule, it is significant that there is no provision of the Federal Rules of Criminal Procedure which conflicts with its provisions. . . .

Having found that Rule 7:4-4(b) is applicable to this case, it is necessary to consider defendant's contention that the Rule violates his constitutional right to due process, including his right to a fair trial. *See, e.g., Strickland v. Washington,* 466 U.S. 668, 685–85 (1984) (discussing the right to a fair trial as an element of the Due Process Clause and the Sixth Amendment). The defense contends that permitting Ms. Hadley's attorney to prosecute defendant would be unconstitutional because there is an impermissible conflict of interest between Ms. Hadley's attorney's role as private counsel and his role as prosecutor in this case. More specifically, defendant argues that there is an inherent conflict which exists when a prosecutor has a pecuniary or other interest in the outcome of a criminal prosecution. Such a conflict was acknowledged in *United States v. Heldt,* 668 F.2d 1238, 1277 (D.C.Cir. 1981), *cert. denied,* 456 U.S. 926 (1982), where the Court stated:

. . . a public prosecutor, as the representative of the sovereign, must 'seek justice to protect the innocent as well as to convict the guilty.' . . .

Our system of justice accords the prosecutor wide discretion in choosing which cases should be prosecuted and which should not. If the prosecutor's personal interest as the defendant in a civil case will be furthered by a successful criminal prosecution, the criminal defendant may be denied the impartial objective exercise of that discretion to which he is entitled.

Id. at 1275–76. The defense in this case contends that this type of conflict renders Ms. Hadley's private attorney incapable of both faithfully representing Ms. Hadley's interests and simultaneously exercising the duties of a prosecutor. Those prosecutorial duties include the duty to disclose evidence favorable to the accused, *see Brady v. Maryland*, 373 U.S. 83 (1963); *State v. Agurs*, 427 U.S. 97 (1976) (discussing the various duties of a criminal prosecutor), and the duties imposed by the New Jersey Rules of Professional Conduct which impose additional disclosure requirements and require that a prosecutor refrain from prosecuting a charge which is not supported by probable cause.

Defendant urges that the holding in *Young v. United States ex rel. Vuitton et Fils S.A.*, 481 U.S. 787 (1987) requires that this court forbid the prosecution of defendant by a private attorney. In *Vuitton*, the Supreme Court reversed the criminal contempt convictions of five defendants who allegedly violated a preliminary injunction prohibiting them from further infringing on a leather-goods manufacturer's trademark. The Court reversed the convictions because defendants were prosecuted by private attorneys who had represented the leather-goods manufacturer in the underlying trademark litigation. *Vuitton*, however, is distinguishable in two important respects from the issue presented here. First, *Vuitton* involved a criminal contempt proceeding in the federal courts which was disposed of not on constitutional grounds, but rather on the Supreme Court's use of its supervisory power. Second, the defendants in *Vuitton* were given sentences ranging up to five years, far exceeding the maximum exposure for a disorderly persons offense which is the subject of the present case.

Despite the fact that *Vuitton* is not controlling here, it is useful in identifying areas of concern which arise when a private attorney is allowed to conduct a criminal prosecution. These concerns are present even in a case like the present one involving a disorderly persons offense. They are not, however, of the same magnitude in such cases. The *Vuitton* Court noted the intolerable ethical tension which resulted when a private litigator, who had "an interest in obtaining the benefits of the court's order," acted as the criminal prosecutor, who is supposed to be "appointed solely to pursue the public interest in vindication of the court's authority." To be sure, this ethical tension is also present in the instant matter, where a private attorney is hired by the complaining witness to prosecute a disorderly persons offense. It cannot be denied that Ms. Hadley's attorney may have an interest, albeit speculative, in fees resulting from a civil suit which may follow this action if the defendant is convicted. Similarly, her attorney has duties owing to her as a paying client which may conflict with the duties of a criminal prosecutor. However, any conflict of interest arising out of the situation presented here does not constitute a violation of due process under the circumstances of this case.[17]

State courts which have invalidated criminal prosecutions by private attorneys have done so in cases involving serious crimes and those involving situations where a public prosecutor has expressly refused to prosecute the defendant.[18] There is, however, a dearth of cases which discuss private prosecutions of disorderly persons charges or other petty offenses. One lower New York court considering this issue noted: "the right of the complainant to prosecute the case by himself or to hire an attorney to assist him has never been doubted." *People v. Wyner*, 207 Misc. 673, 142 N.Y.S.2d 393 (County Court, Westchester County, 1955).

I am mindful that the issue here concerns a widespread practice in the municipal courts of New Jersey and embodied in Rule 7:4-4(b) which allows citizens to enforce the laws of the state in instances where the municipal prosecutor routinely does not prosecute because of a lack of resources. As I noted earlier, it is apparent that the practicalities of the situation are such that absent this practice the sanctions of the disorderly persons statutes would be unavailable in large numbers of cases throughout New Jersey. Moreover, the possible intrusions which the practice under Rule 7:4-4(b) may impose on the liberty interests of an accused is minimal, since the Rule only applies to cases before the Municipal Court which has jurisdiction over a limited number of criminal offenses which are accompanied by jail terms not exceeding six months and fines not exceeding $1,000. N.J. STAT. ANN. . 2A:8-21; 2C:43-3, 43-8. The United States Supreme Court has itself recognized that the full panoply of procedural protections is not required where lesser charges are involved and minimal punishment is authorized. *See, e.g., Duncan v. Louisiana*, 391 U.S. 145, 88 S.Ct. 1444, 20 L.Ed.2d 491 (1968) (right to trial by jury provided in Bill of Rights does not apply to crimes with possible penalties of six months or less, if such crimes otherwise

---

17. Absent a violation of defendant's constitutional rights, there is no basis for invalidating the use of a private prosecutor in this case. Unlike the Court in *Vuitton*, this court may not use its supervisory power to invalidate this practice because it is authorized by state law and is not a product of the federal courts' inherent power.

18. *See, e.g., State v. Harton*, 163 Ga.App. 773, 296 S.E.2d 112 (1982) (prohibiting private prosecution for vehicular homicide absent consent and oversight of the district attorney); *State ex rel. Wild v. Otis*, 257 N.W.2d 361 (Minn. 1977), *appeal dismissed*, 434 U.S. 1003, 98 S.Ct. 707, 54 L.Ed.2d 746 (1978) (where county attorney refused to prosecute and grand jury refused to indict on charges of perjury conspiracy and corruptly influencing a legislator, private citizen could not prosecute and maintain such charges; dicta suggesting this might be permissible with legislative approval and court appointed private attorney as prosecutor); *see also Commonwealth v. Eisemann*, 308 Pa.Super. 16, 453 A.2d 1045 (1982) (Pennsylvania Rules of Civil Procedure require that a person who is not a police officer must get the district attorney's approval to file felony or misdemeanor charges which do not involve a clear and present danger to the community; *People ex rel. Luceno v. Cuozzo*, 97 Misc.2d 871, 412 N.Y.S.2d 748 (City Court, White Plains 1978) ("exercising its discretion," court prohibits private criminal prosecution against police officer where complainant was charged with a criminal offense arising out of same occurrence).

qualify as petty offenses). This rationale would seem to apply with full force in the present situation.

There are several compelling reasons to uphold New Jersey's Municipal Court Rule. The Rule facilitates a kind of peoples' court wherein citizens may bring their disputes and uphold the laws of the community through the uncomplicated procedures of the municipal court. While there is the possibility of frivolous suits and vindictive behavior by some complainants, abuses are checked and deterred by the court's discretion and by the various other remedies available for malicious prosecution. The possibility for prosecutorial abuses under this system is not fantasy, but in the present case there is little chance that the defendant will suffer even the slightest injustice, especially considering the quality of his defense. It is indeed a rare instance where, as here, a defendant charged with a disorderly persons offense has the Office of the United States Attorney and all of its resources at his disposal to defend against the charge.

It is important to emphasize that this is not a case involving an offense arising under federal law subject to prosecution by federal authorities. Nor is this a prosecution for a felony or misdemeanor which can result in a criminal record, a lengthy term and a loss of certain privileges of citizenship. This is not a prosecution for criminal contempt which also involves the possibility of a lengthy jail term in addition to the more concrete conflicts of interest which exist when an attorney prosecutes a person in a criminal matter while simultaneously representing that person's opponent in an underlying civil matter. *See, e.g., Vuitton, supra.* This is also not a case where the public prosecutor has declined to prosecute the defendant after expressly finding that there is no probable cause for such action. In all of those cases, I have no doubt that a private attorney would be precluded by the United States Constitution, the federal courts' supervisory power and/or federal statutes and rules from conducting a criminal prosecution. The instant case, however, is decided in the context of a state disorderly persons charge where the term of imprisonment does not exceed six months.

For the reasons set forth above, defendants' motion to dismiss will be denied.[19]

Notes

1. The *Kinder* case probably reflects the law of due process as it limits direct private prosecution after the *Vuitton* case. *See also Cronan v. Cronan,* 774 A.2d 866 (R.I. 2001).

2. Should the length of sentence be the determining factor in allowing private prosecution?

3. Note the title of the case. It is brought in the name of the sovereign New Jersey, not the name of the private citizen. In *Robertson v. U.S. ex rel. Watson,* 560 U.S.

---

19. After the denial of this motion, but before issuance of this opinion, a trial was held and the defendant William Kinder was found not guilty.

272, 279–80, 130 S. Ct. 2184, 2188–89 (2010), four Justices, dissenting from dismissal of a granted certiorari petition, opined that: ". . . [respondent] argues that '[i]n England and in America at the time of the Founding, prosecutions by victims of crime and their families were the rule, not the exception.'" But such prosecutions, though brought by a private party, were commonly understood as an exercise of sovereign power—the private party acting on behalf of the sovereign, seeking to vindicate a public wrong.

In England, for example, private parties could initiate criminal prosecutions, but the Crown—entrusted with the constitutional responsibility for law enforcement— could enter a *nolle prosequi* to halt the prosecution. *See, e.g., King v. Guerchy,* 1 Black W. 545, 96 Eng. Rep. 315 (K.B.1765); *King v. Fielding,* 2 Burr. 719, 720, 97 Eng. Rep. 531 (K.B. 1759); *see also King v. State,* 43 Fla. 211, 223, 31 So. 254, 257 (1901) (Private prosecutions in England were understood to be "conducted on behalf of the crown by the privately retained counsel of private prosecutors"); P. Devlin, The Criminal Prosecution in England 21 (1958).

Watson's arguments based on American precedent fail largely for the same reason: To say that private parties could (and still can, in some places) exercise some control over criminal prosecutions says nothing to rebut the widely accepted principle that those private parties necessarily acted (and now act) on behalf of the sovereign. *See, e.g., Cronan ex rel. State v. Cronan,* 774 A.2d 866, 877 (R.I. 2001) ("[A]ttorneys conducting private prosecutions stand in the shoes of the state"); *State v. Westbrook,* 279 N.C. 18, 36, 181 S.E.2d 572, 583 (1971) ("The prosecuting attorney, whether the solicitor or privately employed counsel, represents the State"); Sidman, *The Outmoded Concept of Private Prosecution,* 25 Am. U.L. Rev. 754, 774 (1976) ("[T]he privately retained attorney becomes, in effect, a temporary public prosecutor").

6. Challenging the Public Prosecutor's Decision Not to Prosecute

Should a prosecutor's decision not to prosecute remain unchecked by any other procedure? England has recently decided to allow review of a no-prosecution decision. One hundred forty-six suspects were charged after victims sought review of official no-charge decisions. The no-charge decisions were reversed under the victims' right to review scheme implemented in 2013 in England and Wales. These included 80 cases of violence and 27 involving alleged sexual offenses. "It is part of an effort to improve confidence in the justice system." Danny Shaw, *Victims' Right of Review Sees 146 Charged,* BBC News, July 19, 2014 (http://www.bbc.com/news/uk -28377445).

Justice Day of the Wisconsin Supreme Court opined that, "In this period when we see interest in 'victim's rights' coming to the fore, certainly having one's tormentor brought to justice should be near the top of any victim's rights program, second only to the right not to be a victim in the first place." *State of Wisconsin v. Unnamed Defendant*, 441 N.W. 2d 696 (Wis. 1989).

Yet in the United States, famous for checks and balances in other contexts, there are few, if any, effective means of checking prosecutors' decisions not to charge.

In federal court a federal prosecutor's decision not to prosecute is almost absolute. A failure to prosecute will only be reviewed when it violates constitutional standards which govern prosecutorial conduct. In some state jurisdictions a crime victim may seek judicial review of the prosecutor's decision not to prosecute pursuant to statute. Most state jurisdictions allow a victim the access to the grand jury historically permitted at common law. Citizen access to the grand jury varies from state to state. Some states allow citizen access without limitation. Others require an exhaustion of other remedies available to challenge the charging decision before the citizen may approach the grand jury. A list of these remedies is set forth at the beginning of this chapter.

These varied approaches are reflections of differing views on whether the prosecutor's authority not to prosecute should remain substantially unchecked.

If the prosecutor's decision not to prosecute is to be meaningfully reviewed, an issue arises as to whether the judiciary or the grand jury is the best institution to conduct the review.

a. Compelling the Prosecutor to Charge: Victim Standing, Equal Protection and Civil Rights

In the federal system very limited laws exist enabling review of the prosecutor's decision not to charge. Theoretically, a prosecutor's act of not charging a crime would fall outside his discretion if it violated the Equal Protection Clause of the U.S. Constitution or civil rights legislation.

i. Equal Protection Challenges to the Decision Not to Prosecute

U.S. CONST. amend. XIV:

Section 1. . . . "Nor shall any State deprive any person of life, liberty, or property, without due process of law; nor deny to any person within its jurisdiction the equal protection of laws. . . ."

Section 5. "The Congress shall have the power to enforce, by appropriate legislation, the provisions of this article."

In no modern federal case has a victim been able to establish a sufficiently adequate nexus between harm suffered and the need for the remedy of a criminal prosecution to achieve standing to compel a prosecution. Achieving federal judicial review of a prosecutor's decision not to prosecute is extremely difficult, if not impossible, under the federal equal protection clause because of issues of relating to standing and because of the numerous grounds on which prosecutors may lawfully decline to prosecute in their discretion.

Linda R.S. v. Richard D.

410 U.S. 614 (1973)

Mr. Justice Marshall delivered the opinion of the Court.

Appellant, the mother of an illegitimate child, brought this action in United States District Court on behalf of herself, her child, and others similarly situated to enjoin the "discriminatory application" of Art. 602 of the Texas Penal Code. A three-judge court was convened pursuant to 28 U.S.C. § 2281, but that court dismissed the action for want of standing.[20] 335 F. Supp. 804 (N.D. Tex. 1971). We postponed consideration of jurisdiction until argument on the merits, 405 U.S. 1064, and now affirm the judgment below.

Article 602, in relevant part, provides: "any parent who shall wilfully desert, neglect or refuse to provide for the support and maintenance of his or her child or children under eighteen years of age, shall be guilty of a misdemeanor, and upon conviction, shall be punished by confinement in the County Jail for not more than two years." The Texas courts have consistently construed this statute to apply solely to the parents of legitimate children and to impose no duty of support on the parents of illegitimate children. *See Home of the Holy Infancy v. Kaska*, 397 S.W.2d 208, 210 (Tex. 1966); *Beaver v. State*, 96 Tex. Cr. R. 179, 256 S.W. 929 (1923). In her complaint, appellant alleges that one Richard D. is the father of her child, that Richard D. has refused to provide support for the child, and that although appellant made application to the local district attorney for enforcement of Art. 602 against Richard D., the district attorney refused to take action for the express reason that, in his view, the fathers of illegitimate children were not within the scope of Art. 602.[21]

---

20. The District Court also considered an attack on Art. 4.02 of the Texas Family Code, which imposes civil liability upon "spouses" for the support of their minor children. Petitioner argued that the statute violated equal protection because it imposed no civil liability on the parents of illegitimate children. However, the three-judge court held that the challenge to this statute was not properly before it since appellant did not seek an injunction running against any state official as to it. *See* 28 U.S.C. § 2281. The Court, therefore, remanded this portion of the case to a single district judge. 335 F. Supp. 804, 807. The District Court's disposition of petitioner's Art. 4.02 claim is not presently before us. *But see Gomez v. Perez*, 409 U.S. 535 (1973).

21. *See, e.g., State v. Harton*, 163 Ga.App. 773, 296 S.E.2d 112 (1982) (prohibiting private prosecution for vehicular homicide absent consent and oversight of the district attorney); *State ex rel. Wild v. Otis*, 257 N.W.2d 361 (Minn. 1977), *appeal dismissed*, 434 U.S. 1003, 98 S.Ct. 707, 54 L.Ed.2d 746 (1978) (where county attorney refused to prosecute and grand jury refused to indict on charges of perjury conspiracy and corruptly influencing a legislator, private citizen could not prosecute and maintain such charges; dicta suggesting this might be permissible with legislative approval and court appointed private attorney as prosecutor); *see also Commonwealth v. Eisemann*, 308 Pa.Supr. 16, 453 A.2d 1045 (1982) (Pennsylvania Rules of Civil Procedure require that a person who is not a police officer must get the district attorney's approval to file felony or misdemeanor charges which do not involve a clear and present danger to the community); *People ex rel. Luceno v. Cuozzo*, 97 Misc.2d 871, 412 N.Y.S.2d 748 (City Court, White Plains 1978) ("exercising its discretion," court prohibits private criminal prosecution against police officer where complainant was charged with a criminal offense arising out of same occurrence).

Appellant argues that this interpretation of Art. 602 discriminates between legitimate and illegitimate children without rational foundation and therefore violates the Equal Protection Clause of the Fourteenth Amendment. *Cf. Gomez v. Perez*, 409 U.S. 535 (1973); *Weber v. Aetna Casualty & Surety Co.*, 406 U.S. 164 (1972); *Weber v. Aetna Casualty & Surety Co.*, 406 U.S. 164 (1972); *Glona v. American Guarantee & Liability Ins. Co.*, 391 U.S. 73 (1968); *Levy v. Louisiana*, 391 U.S. 68 (1968). *But cf. Labine v. Vincent*, 401 U.S. 532 (1971). Although her complaint is not entirely clear on this point, she apparently seeks an injunction running against the district attorney forbidding him from declining prosecution on the ground that the unsupported child is illegitimate.

Before we can consider the merits of appellant's claim or the propriety of the relief requested, however, appellant must first demonstrate that she is entitled to invoke the judicial process. She must, in other words, show that the facts alleged present the court with a "case or controversy" in the constitutional sense and that she is a proper plaintiff to raise the issues sought to be litigated. The threshold question which must be answered is whether the appellant has "alleged such a personal stake in the outcome of the controversy as to assure that concrete adverseness which sharpens the presentation of issues upon which the court so largely depends for illumination of difficult constitutional questions." *Baker v. Carr*, 369 U.S. 186, 204 (1962).

Recent decisions by this Court have greatly expanded the types of "personal stake[s]" which are capable of conferring standing on a potential plaintiff. But as we pointed out only last Term, "broadening the categories of injury that may be alleged in support of standing is a different matter from abandoning the requirement that the party seeking review must himself have suffered an injury." *Sierra Club v. Morton*, 405 U.S. 727, 738 (1972). Although the law of standing has been greatly changed in the last 10 years, we have steadfastly adhered to the requirement that, at least in the absence of a statute expressly conferring standing,[22] federal plaintiffs must allege some threatened or actual injury resulting from the putatively illegal action before a federal court may assume jurisdiction.[23]

Applying this test to the facts of this case, we hold that, in the unique context of a challenge to a criminal statute, appellant has failed to allege a sufficient nexus between her injury and the government action which she attacks to justify judicial intervention. To be sure, appellant no doubt suffered an injury stemming from the failure of her child's father to contribute support payments. But the bare existence of an abstract injury meets only the first half of the standing requirement. "The party

---

22. It is, of course, true that "Congress may not confer jurisdiction on Art. III federal courts to render advisory opinions," *Sierra Club v. Morton*, 405 U.S. 727, 732 n.3 (1972). But Congress may enact statutes creating legal rights, the invasion of which creates standing, even though no injury would exist without the statute. *See, e.g., Trafficante v. Metropolitan Life Ins. Co.*, 409 U.S. 205, 212 (1972) (White, J., concurring); *Hardin v. Kentucky Utilities Co.*, 390 U.S. 1, 6 (1968).

23. One of the leading commentators on standing has written, "Even though the past law of standing is so cluttered and confused that almost every proposition has some exception, the federal courts have consistently adhered to one major proposition without exception: One who has no interest of his own at stake always lacks standing." K. Davis, Administrative Law Treatise 428–429 (3d ed. 1972).

who invokes [judicial] power must be able to show . . . that he has sustained or is immediately in danger of sustaining some *direct* injury *as the result of* [a statute's] enforcement." *Massachusetts v. Mellon*, 262 U.S. 447, 488 (1923) (emphasis added). *See also Ex parte Lévitt*, 302 U.S. 633, 634 (1937). As this Court made plain in *Flast v. Cohen, supra*, a plaintiff must show "a logical nexus between the status asserted and the claim sought to be adjudicated. . . . Such inquiries into the nexus between the status asserted by the litigant and the claim he presents are essential to assure that he is a proper and appropriate party to invoke federal judicial power." *Id.* at 102.

Here, appellant has made no showing that her failure to secure support payments results from the nonenforcement, as to her child's father, of Art. 602. Although the Texas statute appears to create a continuing duty, it does not follow the civil contempt model whereby the defendant "keeps the keys to the jail in his own pocket" and may be released whenever he complies with his legal obligations. On the contrary, the statute creates a completed offense with a fixed penalty as soon as a parent fails to support his child. Thus, if appellant were granted the requested relief, it would result only in the jailing of the child's father. The prospect that prosecution will, at least in the future, result in payment of support can, at best, be termed only speculative. Certainly the "direct" relationship between the alleged injury and the claim sought to be adjudicated, which previous decisions of this Court suggest is a prerequisite of standing, is absent in this case.

The Court's prior decisions consistently hold that a citizen lacks standing to contest the policies of the prosecuting authority when he himself is neither prosecuted nor threatened with prosecution. *See Younger v. Harris*, 401 U.S. 37, 42 (1971); *Bailey v. Patterson*, 369 U.S. 31, 33 (1962); *Poe v. Ullman*, 367 U.S. 497, 501 (1961). Although these cases arose in a somewhat different context, they demonstrate that, in American jurisprudence at least, a private citizen lacks a judicially cognizable interest in the prosecution or nonprosecution of another. Appellant does have an interest in the support of her child. But given the special status of criminal prosecutions in our system, we hold that appellant has made an insufficient showing of a direct nexus between the vindication of her interest and the enforcement of the State's criminal laws. The District Court was therefore correct in dismissing the action for want of standing,[24] and its judgment must be affirmed.[25]

---

24. We noted last Term that "[t]he requirement that a party seeking review must allege facts showing that he is himself adversely affected does not insulate executive action from judicial review, nor does it prevent any public interests from being protected through the judicial process." *Sierra Club v. Morton*, 405 U.S., at 740. That observation is fully applicable here. As the District Court stated,

> The proper party to challenge the constitutionality of Article 602 would be a parent of a legitimate child who has been prosecuted under the statute. Such a challenge would allege that because the parents of illegitimate children may not be prosecuted, the statute unfairly discriminates against the parents of legitimate children. 335 F. Supp., at 806.

25. Since we dispose of this case on the basis of lack of standing, we intimate no view as to the merits of appellant's claim. But *cf. Gomez v. Perez*, 409 U.S. 535 (1973).

So ordered.

Mr. Justice White, with whom Mr. Justice Douglas joins, dissenting.

Appellant Linda R.S. alleged that she is the mother of an illegitimate child and that she is suing "on behalf of herself, her minor daughter, and on behalf of all other women and minor children who have sought, are seeking, or in the future will seek to obtain support for so-called illegitimate children from said child's father." Appellant sought a declaratory judgment that Art. 602 is unconstitutional and an injunction against its continued enforcement against fathers of legitimate children only. Appellant further sought an order requiring Richard D., the putative father, "to pay a reasonable amount of money for the support of his child."

Obviously, there are serious difficulties with appellant's complaint insofar as it may be construed as seeking to require the official appellees to prosecute Richard D. or others, or to obtain what amounts to a federal child-support order. But those difficulties go to the question of what relief the court may ultimately grant appellant. They do not affect her right to bring this class action. The Court notes, as it must, that the father of a legitimate child, if prosecuted under Art. 602, could properly raise the statute's underinclusiveness as an affirmative defense. *See McLaughlin v. Florida*, 379 U.S. 184 (1964); *Railway Express Agency v. New York*, 336 U.S. 106 (1949). Presumably, that same father would have standing to affirmatively seek to enjoin enforcement of the statute against him. *Cf. Rinaldi v. Yeager*, 384 U.S. 305 (1966); *see also Epperson v. Arkansas*, 393 U.S. 97 (1968). The question then becomes simply: why should only an actual or potential criminal defendant have a recognizable interest in attacking this allegedly discriminatory statute and not appellant and her class? They are not, after all, in the position of members of the public at large who wish merely to force an enlargement of state criminal laws. *Cf. Sierra Club v. Morton*, 405 U.S. 727 (1972). Appellant, her daughter, and the children born out of wedlock whom she is attempting to represent have all allegedly been excluded intentionally from the class of persons protected by a particular criminal law. They do not get the protection of the laws that other women and children get. Under Art. 602, they are rendered nonpersons; a father may ignore them with full knowledge that he will be subjected to no penal sanctions. The Court states that the actual coercive effect of those sanctions on Richard D. or others "can, at best, be termed only speculative." This is a very odd statement. I had always thought our civilization has assumed that the threat of penal sanctions had something more than a "speculative" effect on a person's conduct. This Court has long acted on that assumption in demanding that criminal laws be plainly and explicitly worded so that people will know what they mean and be in a position to conform their conduct to the mandates of law. Certainly Texas does not share the Court's surprisingly novel view. It assumes that criminal sanctions are useful in coercing fathers to fulfill their support obligations to their legitimate children.

Unquestionably, Texas prosecutes fathers of legitimate children on the complaint of the mother asserting nonsupport and refuses to entertain like complaints from a mother of an illegitimate child. I see no basis for saying that the latter mother has no standing to demand that the discrimination be ended, one way or the other.

If a State were to pass a law that made only the murder of a white person a crime, I would think that Negroes as a class would have sufficient interest to seek a declaration that that law invidiously discriminated against them. Appellant and her class have no less interest in challenging their exclusion from what their own State perceives as being the beneficial protections that flow from the existence and enforcement of a criminal child-support law.

I would hold that appellant has standing to maintain this suit and would, accordingly, reverse the judgment and remand the case for further proceedings.

Mr. Justice Blackmun, with whom Mr. Justice Brennan joins, dissenting.

By her complaint, appellant challenged Texas' exemption of fathers of illegitimate children from both civil and criminal liability. Our decision in *Gomez v. Perez*, 409 U.S. 535 (1973), announced after oral argument in this case, has important implications for the Texas law governing a man's civil liability for the support of children he has fathered illegitimately. Although appellant's challenge to the civil statute, as the Court points out, is not procedurally before us, *ante*, at 615 n.1, her brief makes it clear that her basic objection to the Texas system concerns the absence of a duty of paternal support for illegitimate children. The history of the case suggests that appellant sought to utilize the criminal statute as a tool to compel support payments for her child. The decision in *Gomez* may remove the need for appellant to rely on the criminal law if she continues her quest for paternal contribution.

The standing issue now decided by the Court is, in my opinion, a difficult one with constitutional overtones. I see no reason to decide that question in the absence of a live, ongoing controversy.

Note

The *Linda R.S. v. Richard D.* holding was reaffirmed by *per curiam* opinion in *Leeke v. Timmerman*, 454 U.S. 83 (1981). No significant change in the law of victim standing to challenge the charging decision has occurred in federal case law or federal legislation. Footnote 22 of *Linda R.S.* notes that legislation can provide victim standing. This is why modern victims' rights are largely statutory or constitutional.

Douglas E. Beloof, *Weighing Crime Victims' Interests in Judicially Crafted Criminal Procedure*
56 Cath. U. L. Rev. 1135 (2007)

Linda R.S. v. Richard D. provides an example of public prosecutorial discretion historically never ceded to citizens. In *Linda R.S.,* the mother of an illegitimate child alleged an equal protection violation and sought to compel a Texas county prosecutor to bring charges of criminal nonsupport after the prosecutor declined to do so because, "in his view," the statute did not extend to "children born out of wedlock." Holding that Linda R.S. had no standing to use a mandamus action to compel a prosecutor to charge, the Court stated that "in American jurisprudence at least, a private citizen lacks a judicially cognizable interest in the prosecution or nonprosecution of another."

Although the *Linda R.S.* opinion is silent on the procedural point, its holding is consistent with traditional state mandamus limitations—that mandamus could not be used to compel a discretionary act of the public prosecutor. Even in the era of private prosecution, public prosecutors had discretion to direct, or not direct, state resources to prosecution.

Citizens' common law private prosecution rights did not allow citizens to seek a writ of mandamus requiring a public prosecutor to exercise prosecutorial charging discretion.

Instead of compelling the public prosecutor to charge, citizens brought charges independently of the public prosecutor. For example, in the Maryland case of *Brack v. Wells*, decided three decades before *Linda R.S.*, the state's high court ruled that mandamus could not be used to compel a public prosecutor to charge:

> As a general rule, whether the State's Attorney does or does not institute a particular prosecution is a matter which rests in his discretion. Unless that discretion is grossly abused or such duty compelled by statute or there is a clear showing that such duty exists mandamus will not lie.

Further, the *Brack* court stated that mandamus would not lie when there was another remedy available: That other remedy was for the citizen to independently approach the grand jury.

Unquestionably, Linda R.S., as a Texan, could have directly approached a Texas grand jury in an attempt to secure a charge. Written before *Linda R.S.,* the seminal Texas case of *Hott v. Yarbrough* opined: "Equally clear is the right of any one who may consider himself aggrieved by the actual or supposed commission of a crime to call the matter to the attention of the grand jury for investigation and action." The Fifth Circuit Court of Appeals, interpreting Texas case law after *Linda R.S.,* confirmed that Texas citizens had a common law right of direct access to the grand jury: "Under Texas law, the grand jury has the authority to conduct their own investigations, to subpoena evidence and witnesses. . . . and to indict on matters as to which the district attorney has presented no evidence and sought no indictment." The *Linda R.S.* case did not alter Linda R.S.'s personal right to independently approach the Texas grand jury. Nor did it alter the fact that her right to seek grand jury charging was judicially cognizable. Instead, *Linda R.S.* involved a procedurally inappropriate challenge to public prosecutorial discretion because she sought to compel the public prosecutor to bring charges, an approach that failed her as it had failed the Maryland victim in *Brack* and victims in other jurisdictions. It failed her because citizen actions to compel public prosecutors invaded the unceded discretion of the government not to initiate charging procedures.

The *Linda R.S.* case is limited to procedural contexts where state public prosecutors *already* exercise lawful discretion. Put another way, *Linda R.S.* means "that, in American jurisprudence at least, a private citizen lacks a judicially cognizable interest in the prosecution or nonprosecution of another" in procedures where public prosecutorial discretion already exists.

The cases cited in *Linda R.S.* also support the idea that government discretion must already exist before citizens can be said to have "no judicially cognizable interest in the prosecution or non-prosecution of another." The *Younger v. Harris* Court held that no standing existed for persons to join with the criminal defendant as interveners in a civil injunction to halt prosecution when those persons were neither prosecuted nor threatened with prosecution. In *Bailey v. Patterson*, the Court held that plaintiffs had no standing to enjoin prosecution where there was no allegation that plaintiffs were being prosecuted or threatened with prosecution. In both *Younger* and *Bailey*, the uncharged citizen had no standing to challenge the public prosecutor's exercise of already existing lawful discretion to bring charges. Finally, in *Poe v. Ullman*, plaintiffs were denied standing to bring a civil declaratory judgment action to invalidate state criminal statutes because plaintiffs were neither prosecuted nor threatened with prosecution. While *Poe* involved a civil challenge to a criminal statute, rather than a challenge to a prosecution, prosecutorial discretion remains centrally relevant to the decision. In *Poe*, where the prosecution exercised its *already existing* discretion not to seek a charge, plaintiff had no standing to challenge the criminal statute.

The procedural context, internal citations, and the reality of citizens' judicially cognizable interests in grand jury charging in Texas all support the interpretation that the *Linda R.S.* language means that where prosecutors *already exercise* lawful discretion, citizens lack an interest in prosecution or nonprosecution of another that is sufficient to trump that discretion." Thus, *Linda R.S.* did not establish any new area of public prosecutorial discretion, it preserved pre-existing discretion.

Notes

1. Assuming a victim seeking federal charges could establish a sufficient nexus between the harm and the criminal remedy they would be presented with the challenge of showing that the refusal to prosecute was a violation of prosecutorial discretion of constitutional proportions. In *Wayte v. United States*, 105 S. Ct. 1524 (1985), the United States Supreme Court set forth the federal approach:

> In our criminal justice system, the Government retains "broad discretion" as to whom to prosecute. *United States v. Goodwin*, 457 U.S. 368, 380, n.11 (1982); "[S]o long as the prosecutor has probable cause to believe that the accused committed an offense defined by statute, the decision whether or not to prosecute, and what charge to file or bring before a grand jury, generally rests entirely in his discretion." *Bordenkircher v. Hayes*, 434 U.S. 357, 364 (1978). This broad discretion rests largely on the recognition that the decision to prosecute is particularly ill-suited to judicial review. Such factors as the strength of the case, the prosecution's general deterrence

value, the Government's enforcement priorities, and the case's relationship to the Government's overall enforcement plan are not readily susceptible to the kind of analysis the courts are competent to undertake. Judicial supervision in this area, moreover, entails systematic costs of particular concern. Examining the basis of a prosecution delays the criminal proceeding, threatens to chill law enforcement by subjecting the prosecutor's motives and decisionmaking to outside inquiry, and may undermine prosecutorial effectiveness by revealing the Government's enforcement policy. All these are substantial concerns that make the courts properly hesitant to examine the decision whether to prosecute.

As we have noted in a slightly different context, however, although prosecutorial discretion is broad, it is not "'unfettered.' Selectivity in the enforcement of criminal laws is . . . subject to constitutional constraints." *United States v. Batchelder*, 442 U.S. 114, 125 (1979) (footnote omitted). In particular, the decision to prosecute may not be "'deliberately based upon an unjustifiable standard such as race, religion, or other arbitrary classification,'" *Bordenkircher v. Hayes, supra*, 434 U.S., at 364 (1962), including the exercise of protected statutory and constitutional rights, *see United States v. Goodwin, supra*, 457 U.S., at 372.

2. State courts are free to interpret rules of standing differently from federal courts under state constitutional equal protection provisions. Additionally, Congress or state legislatures have the legal authority to convey standing to crime victims by statute. Several states have conveyed standing to victims for judicial review of decisions not to prosecute. This is discussed in a following section of this chapter.

ii. Civil Rights-Based Challenges to the Decision Not to Prosecute

If a prosecutor violated civil rights legislation in electing not to prosecute, the court could theoretically review the decision not to prosecute. However, as in *Linda R.S.*, barriers presented by standing requirements impose significant obstacles to having a case heard on its merits. Even in the context of alleged civil rights violations, federal courts are reluctant to review decisions involving prosecutorial discretion. Following a prison riot that made national news, the state of New York's agents stormed Attica prison. Inmates were killed and assaulted. Efforts to compel investigation and prosecution were met with rulings that they had no standing and the case was dismissed. *Inmates of Attica Correctional Facility v. Nelson A. Rockefeller et al.*, 477 F.2d 375 (2d Cir. 1973).

Notes

1. *See* Donald G. Gifford, *Equal Protection and the Prosecutor's Charging Decision: Enforcing an Ideal*, 9 Geo. Wash. L. Rev. 659 (1981). Making the argument that Linda R.S., the person, should have been granted standing and offering alternative analyses.

2. Congress has the authority to provide a review mechanism of the decision not to prosecute by passing a statute. It has elected not to. Some state legislatures have

passed such statutes. These statutes are examined in the section immediately following.

3. For in-depth description of a case attempting to utilize equal protection and civil rights guarantees to enforce arrest and prosecution of wife batterers, *see* Laurie Woods, 5 Women's Rts. L. Rep. 7 (1978).

_____

b. Compelling the Prosecutor to Charge: Approaches Other Than Equal Protection and Civil Rights Actions

i. Statutory Judicial Review of Prosecutor's Decision Not to Charge followed by Private Citizen Complaint

Several states have enacted statutes providing for judicial review of the prosecutor's decision not to charge.

Pennsylvania has expressly articulated by rule a private complaint process which may result in a complaint being approved by the court, even in certain circumstances where the prosecutor does not approve of the complaint.

Commonwealth v. Benz

565 A.2d 764 (Pa. 1989)

NIX, Chief Justice.

The subject of this discretionary appeal raised by the Commonwealth [32] is the Superior Court's order reversing the lower court's disapproval of a private criminal complaint and directing that such a complaint be authorized pursuant to Pa. R. Crim. P. 133. The fundamental issue presented in this appeal is whether a decision not to prosecute on the ground of lack of evidence to establish a *prima facie* case, made by the office of the district attorney and confirmed by a judge of the court of common pleas, is reviewable by the Superior Court. The Commonwealth's framing of the issue has tended to obfuscate the relatively straight-forward question legitimately raised. Additionally, the Commonwealth has attempted to implicate constitutional principles and principles of law not presently germane to the instant inquiry. For the reasons that follow, we conclude that the Superior Court did have jurisdiction to hear the appeal pursuant to 42 Pa. C.S. § 742. [33] Moreover, that court

_____

32. The caption to this case is misleading because, although the Commonwealth is the appellant, Joseph F. Benz, who is listed as the appellee, is not a party to this case and has not filed a brief. The true appellee in this case is the private complainant, Laverda Hicks, the mother of the decedent.

33. § 742. Appeals from courts of common pleas.

The Superior Court shall have exclusive appellate jurisdiction of all appeals from final orders of the courts of common pleas, regardless of the nature of the controversy or the amount involved, except such classes of appeals as are by any provision of this chapter within the exclusive jurisdiction of the Supreme Court or the Commonwealth Court.

correctly concluded that there was sufficient evidence to establish a *prima facie* case. Therefore, we affirm the order of the Superior Court.

This case arose out of an altercation between Paaron Jones and Officer Joseph E. Benz of the Pittsburgh Police Department. On June 29, 1981, both men were in the West Penn Memorial Hospital to visit patients. While still in the lobby, Officer Benz, who was not in uniform, entered the elevator with packages for his ailing wife. Paaron Jones approached the elevator to speak with another passenger whom he knew. At the time Mr. Jones was on crutches with a broken leg in a cast and smelled of alcohol. He held the elevator door open with one of the crutches and continued to converse with the passenger on the elevator. After some delay of the elevator an argument began between Jones and Benz, resulting in Jones striking Benz with his crutch. After Benz had retrieved his packages and entered a second elevator, Jones again struck Benz, sending him to the floor. While Benz was still on the floor, Jones struck him across the back with a crutch. Realizing that the altercation was getting out of control, Benz pulled out his badge and firearm and identified himself as a police officer. At that time Jones attempted to flee through the front exit and Benz pursued him with his firearm drawn, stating that he was under arrest and he should lie face down on the floor. Instead, a scuffle again resulted. This time, however, Benz had his gun exposed. During the fight the gun discharged and Jones was struck in the head with the bullet. The emergency unit was able to save Jones only for him to live in a vegetative state for four years until July 25, 1985, when he died as a result of the gunshot wound.

After Jones' death an open inquest was conducted by the coroner, and the coroner's jury recommended that Benz be charged with voluntary manslaughter. Nevertheless, the District Attorney of Allegheny County did not file charges. The District Attorney decided that the eye-witness testimony was so disjointed as to make it inconclusive and instead relied on medical evidence of possible powder burns on the victim's head and scientific evidence concerning the retention of the shell of the bullet in the chamber of the gun. That evidence seemed to indicate that the victim was in close proximity to Benz when the gun discharged. That conclusion supported the claims made by Benz that the two men were wrestling over the weapon and that the shot was fired accidentally.

In September of 1985 the District Attorney's office sought review of its decision from the Office of the Attorney General. The District Attorney's office turned over all its files concerning the matter and fully cooperated with the investigation by the Attorney General. In February of 1986 that office concluded that no abuse of prosecutorial discretion had occurred; that a fair investigation had been conducted by that office; and that the filing of criminal charges in this matter would have been inappropriate and unsupported by the available evidence.

On May 21, 1986 Laverda Hicks, the mother of the victim, then sought approval of a private criminal complaint pursuant to Pa. R. Crim. P. 133. That rule states:

(a) When the affiant is not a law enforcement officer and the offense(s) charged include(s) a misdemeanor or felony which does not involve a clear and present danger to any person or to the community, the complaint shall be submitted to an attorney for the Commonwealth, who shall approve or disapprove without unreasonable delay.

(b) If the attorney for the Commonwealth

(1) Approves the complaint, the attorney shall indicate this decision on the complaint form and transmit it to the issuing authority;

(2) Disapproves the complaint, the attorney shall state the reasons on the complaint form and return it to the affiant. Thereafter the affiant may file the complaint with a judge of a Court of Common Pleas for approval or disapproval;

(3) Does not approve or disapprove within a reasonable period of time, the affiant may file the complaint on a separate form with the issuing authority, noting thereon that a complaint is pending before an attorney for the Commonwealth. The issuing authority shall determine whether a reasonable period has elapsed, and, when appropriate, shall defer action to allow the attorney for the Commonwealth an additional period of time to respond.

The District Attorney disapproved the complaint on the grounds that insufficient evidence existed to establish that a crime had been committed. Subsequently, Ms. Hicks sought judicial review of the matter. The court of common pleas accepted the petition but denied approval after a review of the record. It held that the district attorney did not abuse his discretion by not prosecuting Benz. Ms. Hicks appealed to the Superior Court for a review of the final order of the court of common pleas pursuant to 42 Pa. C.S. § 742 and Pa. R.A.P. 1112. The Superior Court reversed the lower court and determined that evidence was available to establish a *prima facie* case.

In this case, the Commonwealth stated as its reason for the decision not to prosecute the lack of evidence sufficient to establish a *prima facie* case.[34] Therefore, a court is required to review the appropriateness of that determination. It has always been the burden of the Commonwealth, if it intends to proceed with prosecution, to establish a *prima facie* case that a crime has been committed and that the accused is the one who committed it. *Commonwealth v. Mullen*, 460 Pa. 336, 333 A.2d 755 (1975); *see also Commonwealth v. Ruza*, 511 Pa. 59, 511 A.2d 808 (1986); *Commonwealth v. Wojdak*, 502 Pa. 359, 466 A.2d 991 (1983). Traditionally, the final determination of sufficiency of the evidence has been a judicial judgment. *Rice v. Shuman*, 513 Pa. 204, 519 A.2d 391 (1986); *Commonwealth v. Shaver*, 501 Pa. 167, 460 A.2d 742 (1983). This is to be distinguished from the prosecutorial discretion not to bring prosecution even

---

34. If the district attorney had stated policy reasons to support the decision not to prosecute, this Court would show the deference accorded to such a discretionary use of the executive powers conferred in that officer. However, because the reason stated was the ultimate determination by the district attorney that no crime had been committed, this Court is authorized to review that determination without the special deference afforded a separate branch of government.

if a prima *facie* case may be established from the evidence available. *See, e.g., Pugach v. Klein*, 193 F. Supp. 630 (S.D.N.Y. 1961).

The evidence in this instance unquestionably established a homicide. It is also unquestioned that the person responsible for the death of Paaron Jones was Officer Benz. Whether the homicide was justifiable or excusable is a matter of defense. *Commonwealth v. Capitolo*, 508 Pa. 372, 498 A.2d 806 (1985); 18 Pa. C.S. § 503. Thus, evidence as to justification or excuse would not negate a determination of a *prima facie* case, but is a matter that is properly raised in defense at trial. *See, e.g., Commonwealth v. Reilly*, 519 Pa. 550, 549 A.2d 503 (1988); *Commonwealth v. Warren*, 475 Pa. 31, 379 A.2d 561 (1977). Therefore, with sufficient evidence to establish a *prima facie* case, the Superior Court correctly reversed the lower court's holding that the district attorney's decision not to prosecute Officer Benz was proper for the reason stated.

The Commonwealth seeks to raise the question of the constitutional principle of separation of powers in this instance by asserting that judicial intervention impermissibly trammelled upon the prosecutorial discretion. The fallacy of this argument is its lack of relevancy. The prosecutor in this instance never purported to predicate his decision not to prosecute upon the exercise of his prosecutorial discretion to make policy. He expressly stated that the decision to decline prosecution resulted from his determination that the evidence would not sustain a *prima facie* case. Thus the issue before both lower courts required an assessment of that legal judgment and not an intrusion upon prosecutorial discretion. Had the district attorney utilized policy discretion to refuse prosecution and had the lower courts reviewed that decision, the question of separation of powers would have been appropriately raised. However, we need not stray from the issues properly presented to decide this case.

In this case, the prosecutorial decision not to prosecute was based upon a legal determination of the sufficiency of the evidence to establish a *prima facie* case. This type of decision is within the purview of the judicial system to review. The Superior Court found that sufficient evidence existed to sustain a *prima facie* case and ordered that the district attorney's office commence prosecution.

LARSEN, Justice, concurring.

I concur in the result only. I write separately to express my vehement disagreement with the majority's interpretation and application of Pa. R. Crim. P. Rule 133.

Rule 133 provides in relevant part:

(a) When the affiant is not a law enforcement officer . . . the complaint shall be submitted to an attorney for the Commonwealth, who shall approve or disapprove without unreasonable delay.

(b) If the attorney for the Commonwealth . . .

(2) Disapproves the complaint, the attorney shall state the reasons on the complaint form and return it to the affiant. Thereafter the affiant may file the complaint with a judge of a Court of Common Pleas *for approval or disapproval*; . . .

(emphasis added).

The rule does *not* state that the common pleas court judge shall act in an appellate capacity when approving or disapproving a private criminal complaint. Nor does the rule state that the court's function in approving or disapproving a private criminal complaint is to assess whether the prosecutor abused his or her discretion in disapproving the complaint. Thus, it does not matter on what basis the prosecutor makes his or her decision for the matter to be "within the purview of the judicial system to review." Maj. op. at 768.[35] Indeed, soon after Rule 133 went into effect, Superior Court correctly noted that the rule "protects the interest of the private complainant by allowing for the submission of the disapproved complaint to a judge of a court of common pleas. The judge's *independent* review of the complaint checks and balances the district attorney's decision and further hedges against possibility of error." *Petition of Piscanio*, 235 Pa. Super. 490, 494–95, 344 A.2d 658, 661 (1975), *allocatur denied* (emphasis added).

The Commonwealth, as appellant in this case, has lost sight of the fact that throughout the history of this Commonwealth and until 1974, private criminal complaints were not subject to review by the district attorney. From time immemorial, the right of the citizen to seek redress in the courts has always been preserved. And it was for the *courts*, through the office of an issuing authority, to determine, before issuing process, whether (1) the complaint was properly completed and executed; (2) the affiant was a responsible person; and (3) there was probable cause for the issuance of process. Pa. R. Crim. P. Rule 106 as adopted Jan. 31, 1970, eff. May 1, 1970.

Clearly, the changes that were made to this procedure were not intended to radically alter the practice of instituting criminal proceedings by private criminal complaint. Rather, the changes were intended to enable the district attorney to merely weed out frivolous cases. If the private complainant is not satisfied with the determination of the district attorney under the present rules of procedure, he or she still has, and *must* have, access to the judiciary. The changes made to our rules of criminal procedure merely concerned *who* was to approve the complaint in the first instance. In fact, with regard to related amendments made to the rules of criminal procedure in 1974, the comment to Rule 134 stated simply that it was now for the district attorney to "evaluate the responsibility of the charge contained in the complaint." Comment to Rule 134 as adopted Sept. 18, 1973, eff. Jan. 1, 1974.

Thus, by preserving the right of a private complainant to obtain the independent approval or disapproval of the complaint by a judge of the court of common pleas, Rule 133 does not contemplate that criminal proceedings initiated by private complaint will be subject to the "policy" and discretion of the district attorney. . . .

PAPADAKOS, Justice, Dissenting.

---

35. The majority seems to be of the opinion that the decision of the prosecutor can only be reviewed by the court where it is based on the merits of the case and not on some nebulous matter of policy.

I dissent. The majority makes the exercise of prosecutorial discretion in refusing to prosecute justiciable. That is error in my opinion. Long ago, this Court recognized that a district attorney's power to approve or disapprove private criminal complaints is consistent with that office's unreviewable authority to initiate or discontinue prosecutions generally. *Commonwealth v. Ragone*, 317 Pa. 113, 176 A. 454 (1935). Pa. R. Crim. P. 133 protects the interests of the private complainant (often times, the victim) by allowing for the submission of a disapproved private complaint to a trial judge whose independent review checks and balances the district attorney's decision and further hedges against possible error. At least, that is the theory behind the adoption of Rule 133 as set out in the A.B.A. Project on Standards for Criminal Justice, *Standards Relating to the Prosecution Function and the Defense Function*, § 3.4 (and the comments thereto) (Approved Draft, 1971), upon which the Rule was based. History, logic and efficiency require that this limitation on a prosecutor's discretion must be read as narrowly as possible lest we make the already overburdened criminal justice system wholly impossible to administer. Read in that light, I am convinced that a trial judge's decision to agree with a district attorney's judgment not to prosecute is unreviewable and, for the reason that, *inter alia*, the private complainant has no standing to appeal. In his dissent in *In re Wood*, 333 Pa.Superior Ct. 597, 482 A.2d 1033 (1984), Judge Del Sole put it this way, correctly in my opinion:

> Pa. R. Crim. P. 133(B) gives a victim-complainant the right to seek approval from the Court of Common Pleas of a private criminal complaint which has been disapproved by the district attorney. However, that rule of court does not make the victim-complainant a party to the action.

> Criminal prosecutions are not to settle private grievances, but are to rectify the injury done to the Commonwealth. The individual who is the victim of a crime only has recourse to a civil action for damages. . . . The Court in [*Commonwealth v.*] *Malloy*[, 304 Pa.Superior Ct. 297, 450 A.2d 689 (1982),] cited with approval the language of the United States Supreme Court in *Linda R.S. v. Richard D. & Texas, et al.*, 410 U.S. 614, 619, 93 S.Ct. 1146, 1149, 35 L.Ed.2d 536 (1973), that " . . . a citizen lacks standing to contest the policies of the prosecuting attorney when he himself is neither prosecuted nor threatened with prosecution . . . (I)n American jurisprudence at least, a private citizen lacks a judicially cognizable interest in the prosecution or nonprosecution of another."

> The state is the party-plaintiff in a criminal prosecution. The victim-complainant is not a party to the proceeding. The victim acts only as a prosecuting witness, even in the case of a private criminal complaint. . . . Therefore, the victim-complainant has no standing to appeal from the disapproval of private criminal complaints. . . .

482 A.2d at 1037. . . . I would expressly disapprove of the majority opinions in *In re Wood* and *Commonwealth v. Muroski, supra*, to the opposite effect, as being unwise and contrary to law.

McDERMOTT, J., joins in this dissenting opinion.

Notes

1. Pennsylvania has gone further than courts in most jurisdictions in upholding review of a prosecutor's decision not to charge. Policy matters are traditionally an area where judges are reluctant to review. The *Benz* court deferred to prosecutorial discretion if the failure to prosecute was based on policy matters. [The numeration of the Rule utilized in *Benz* has changed to Pa. R. Crim. P. Rule 506]. Alternatively, in some states grand juries arguably provide a review mechanism that can charge a crime regardless of a prosecutor's policy reasons for not charging.

2. The *Benz* court's deference to prosecutorial discretion in matters of policy has been criticized as an unnecessarily restrictive view of the separation of powers in light of the tradition of broad judicial discretion, the courts' rule-making authority, and public policy concerns. Beth Brown, Note, *The Constitutional Validity of Pennsylvania Rule of Criminal Procedure 113(b)(2) and the Traditional Role of the Pennsylvania Courts in the Prosecution Function*, 52 U. Pitt. L. Rev. 269. The author points out that prosecutors might easily evade court review by making charging decisions based only on policy. In *In re Private Complaints of Rafferty*, 969 A.2d 578 (2009) the appellate court considered what a policy reason was under the statute: "... [T]he Attorney General denied Appellant's private criminal complaints on the basis the complaints 'lacks prosecutorial merit.' This Court has consistently held that a determination that the case 'lacks prosecutorial merit' is a 'policy determinatiom' subject to the aforementioned standard of review." (omitting cites). Therefore, contrary to Appellant's contention, the trial court did not err in concluding that the Attorney General's decision not to prosecute was 'indeed a policy determination' which would not be disturbed absent an abuse of discretion."

3. The victim in *Benz* was represented by private counsel for obtaining a criminal charge.

4. One state trial court has held that if the grand jury has issued a "not true bill" declining charges, a private citizen's criminal complaint has no effect. This was superseded by the Missouri Court of Appeals, which dismissed the appeal from the trial court ruling, holding that there was no statute providing for citizen complaint in Missouri, so the victim had no standing. *Mollette v. Wilson*, 478 S.W.3d 428 Mo. Ct. App. 2015).

5. The Wisconsin John Doe proceeding, reviewed in the first section of this chapter on investigation, may also be used by the courts to charge. This proceeding survived constitutional scrutiny in *State of Wisconsin v. Unnamed Defendant*, 441 N.W. 2d 696 (Wis. 1989). The concurrences in the case reveal different perspectives on judicial charging:

HEFFERNAN, Chief Justice (concurring).

As the author of the majority opinion, I agree with it and join it; but I cannot but feel a sense of unease over the validation of secs. 968.02(3) and 968.26, Stats., when viewed from a public policy aspect. I therefore write additionally in concurrence.

The criminal law reform undertaken by the Criminal Rules Committee of the Judicial Council had as one of its purposes the elimination of the last vestiges of the pernicious practice of private prosecutions by persons who owe no allegiance to society as a whole. For a general public policy statement, see *State v. Scherr*, 101 N.W.2d 77 (1960) ("It is against public policy and the impartial administration of criminal law for a court to allow attorneys for private persons to appear as prosecutors.") and *State v. Peterson*, 218 N.W. 367 (1928) ("Our scheme contemplates that an impartial man selected by the electors of the county shall prosecute all criminal actions in the county unbiased by desires of complaining witnesses or that of the defendant.").

Both of the statutes validated herein make it possible for persons to trigger the prosecutorial powers of the state in any kind of criminal action where "probable cause" can be established. No consistent prosecutorial policy in respect to the initiation of charges can be maintained under these circumstances. What will be charged can lie within the whim of any complainant. The de facto standard for prosecuting attorneys is, in the experience of this writer, but for the exceptional case, not to invoke the awesome power of the state unless the crime in all likelihood can be proved beyond a reasonable doubt. Our imprimatur upon these statutes may well give a gloss that runs counter to the legislative intent of Wisconsin's criminal law reforms. The writer is not unmindful of the predicament of a victim of a crime who is afforded no relief by a recalcitrant prosecutor. It would appear, however, that this situation might better be alleviated by legislative approval of a limited judicial review of a prosecutor's declination to prosecute. . . .

* * *

I invoke all of the above utterances on the occasion of the overruling of a decision so recently written by the author of this opinion, an opinion that I believe was in the public interest and in accordance with rational prosecutorial policy, but which has not withstood subsequent scrutiny on a constitutional basis.

DAY, Justice (concurring).

I write this concurrence to the majority opinion in response to the concurrence written by its author. That concurrence is critical of both John Doe statutes secs. 968.26 and 968.02(3), Stats., which provide for judicial review where a district attorney refuses to prosecute.

The concurrence refers to the "awesome power of the state" in criminal matters. To the ever increasing army of crime victims, "awesome impotence" of government would appear to be a more accurate description. President Bush has recently requested Congress for a multi-billion dollar program to build more federal prisons, increase law enforcement personnel and "win back the streets" of our large cities where armed thugs terrorize the citizenry. We now have Washington, D.C. winning the title of "Murder Capitol of the World."

An article by Richard B. Abell, Assistant United States Attorney General, in charge of the Office of Justice Programs, appearing in the March 21, 1989 issue of the Wall

Street Journal shows the fact is that the apprehension and imprisonment of criminals for substantial periods of time "works." That is it cuts down the amount of crime and saves society billions of dollars. Building prisons and utilizing them is a good investment. The article points out that a Rand Corporation study shows that in 1983 there were 42.5 million victimizations. In a country of 250 million that is a shocking statistic. "We find a typical offender in the survey is responsible for $430,000 in crime costs. The costs to imprison this offender for one year is $25,000. Thus a year in prison costs $405,000 less than a year of criminal activity. A year of crime is seventeen times more expensive for society than a year in prison." A chart accompanying the Abell article shows a direct correlation between incarceration rates and the crime rate. In 1960 the chance that an offender (in Part I Crimes, i.e., Homicide, forceable rape, robbery, aggravated assault, burglary, larceny, theft, motor vehicle theft) would receive a prison sentence was 6.2 percent per 100 crimes. The number of Part I Crimes was less than 2 percent per 100 population. In 1974 the chances for imprisonment fell to 2.1 percent and the number of crimes rose to 4.8 percent per 100 population.

What all the statistics on monetary crime costs do not reflect is the "misery index," the individual physical and emotional suffering of those crime victims and their families who have been murdered, beaten, robbed and "ripped off" by the criminal element in our midst.

In this period when we see interest in "victim's rights" coming to the fore, certainly having one's tormentor brought to justice should be near the top of any victim's rights program, second only to the right not to be a victim in the first place.

This is not, as the author of the majority opinion in his concurrence sees it, as somehow a tendency in the direction of "the pernicious practice of private prosecutions" nor does it "allow attorneys for private persons to appear as prosecutors." Neither statute allows private counsel to act as prosecutor. Prosecution can only be done by the elected district attorney or special prosecutors appointed by the courts. Nowhere do our statutes permit private attorneys representing victims to prosecute and try criminal defendants.

The John Doe provisions have been frequently used by district attorneys to ferret out the perpetrators of crime where ordinary investigative procedures fail. I believe it would be a mistake to alter a procedure that has served us well since before statehood. Section 968.02(3), Stats., is a clear expression of legislative intent that victims have recourse to the courts when a district attorney refuses to act.

Crime victims should have recourse to the judicial branch when the executive branch fails to respond. This seems to me to be in keeping with constitutional rights. The first amendment to the United States Constitution guarantees the right "to petition the government for a redress of grievances." The Wisconsin Constitution also provides in art. I, sec. 4: "The right of the people peaceably to assemble, to consult for the common good and to petition the government, or any department thereof, shall never be abridged." The statutory provisions here under consideration are a legislative codification of the right to petition the judicial branch for a "redress of grievances" when that is appropriate.

I would retain these statutes.

STEINMETZ, Justice (concurring).

I disagree with the Chief Justice's statement in his concurring opinion that secs. 968.02(3) and 968.26, Stats., may be against good public policy from a historical perspective. These statutes are a part of the public policy of this state and have withstood the test of time, and as Justice Day describes in his concurring opinion, these statutes promoted victims' rights before that term became popular in political circles.

The fear that, "What will be charged can lie within the whim of any complainant" (Chief Justice Heffernan's concurring op. at 702) is an unfounded one. Section 968.02(3), Stats., requires the circuit judge to find that "there is probable cause to believe that the person to be charged has committed an offense after conducting a hearing" and the judge "may" then issue a complaint. Section 968.26 only requires the issuance of a complaint "[i]f it appears probable from the testimony given that a crime has been committed and who committed it. . . ." The validation of these statutes does not, as the concurrence suggests, revive "the pernicious practice of private prosecutions by persons who owe no allegiance to society as a whole."

The John Doe statute particularly assists the district attorneys as well as victims. The district attorney can ask a judge to conduct a John Doe and thereby (1) force victims to testify under oath; (2) ask for witness immunity to develop the investigation; and (3) have an investigation conducted in secret at the judge's discretion to protect the development of the investigation. These are tools of investigation not within the authority of the district attorney.

I agree entirely with the majority decision.

Note

The United States Supreme Court in a 7–1 opinion held that prosecution is not an exclusively executive function. In *Morrison v. Olsen*, 108 S. Ct. 2597 (1988), decided one year after the *Connors* case, the United States Supreme Court reviewed the constitutionality of The Ethics in Government Act. The Act provides for a special prosecutor to investigate and determine if high ranking government officials should be prosecuted. After notification of the alleged violation, the Attorney General has 90 days to decide whether to recommend appointment of a special prosecutor. The Special Division of the Washington D.C. Circuit then appoints the special prosecutor. In upholding this law, the U.S. Supreme Court determined that prosecution is not a core executive function. One author's review of historical materials supports the view that the framers did not intend to make prosecution a core executive function. Stephanie Dangel, Note, *Is Prosecution a Core Executive Function? Morrison v. Olsen and the Framers' Intent*, 99 Yale L.J. 1069 (1990).

ii-a. Common Law Right of Citizen to Approach Grand Jury

Most jurisdictions have not eliminated the citizen's common law right to approach the grand jury seeking investigation and charging. Some states have codified it. Some states allow a citizen to directly approach the grand jury foreperson without any preliminary requirements. Others require exhaustion of remedies.

Notes

1. *Brack v. Wells*, 40 A.2d 319 (Md. 1944) ("It is the opinion of this Court that every citizen has a right to offer to present to the grand jury violations of the criminal law. This does not mean that an individual member of that body may be approached. The citizen should exhaust his remedy before the magistrate and state's attorney as was done in the instant case, and if relief can not be had there, he then has the right to ask not be had there, the grand jury for permission to appear before that body.")

2. For a collection of cases and statutes, see National Crime Victim Law Institute, Fifty states and D.C. Survey of Laws that Authorize or Recognize Private-Citizen Initiated Investigation and/or Prosecution of Criminal Offenses (2015).

3. In Colorado, the prosecution's decision will only be reviewed if it is arbitrary and capricious. *Sandoval v. Farish*, 675 F.2d (Sup. Ct. Colo. 1984). Given prosecutors' broad discretion, does this standard provide any meaningful review?

ii-b. Constitutional Right of Citizen Access to Grand Jury

A majority of courts ruling on the issue have held that citizen access to the grand jury is a common law right which can only be taken away by statute. However, in West Virginia no statute can abrogate a citizen's right to access to the Grand Jury.

State ex rel. Miller v. Smith

285 S.E. 500 (W. Va. 1981)

McGRAW, Justice:

This case comes before us on a writ of prohibition seeking to restrain the respondent, the Prosecuting Attorney of Clay County, from attempting to dissuade or discourage the grand jury from hearing the petitioner or any evidence he might have regarding a complaint which he seeks to lay before it. The petitioner contends that the use of persuasion by the prosecuting attorney to influence the decision of the grand jury whether or not to entertain the petitioner is an exercise of power beyond his jurisdiction. We find merit in this contention and grant a molded writ.

The petitioner claims he was the victim of a malicious wounding perpetuated by two policemen on October 17, 1980. The petitioner prosecuted two criminal warrants against the accused perpetrators of the deed, which were dismissed by C. Velt King, a Clay County Magistrate. Subsequently, the petitioner submitted his evidence of the incident to the prosecuting attorney. According to the prosecuting attorney, his investigation of the incident revealed that late in 1980 the petitioner was stopped by a city patrolman and a deputy sheriff for driving under the influence. The prosecuting attorney contends, that when stopped by the officers, the petitioner resisted arrest, crawled under his car, kicked at the arresting officer and would not come out from under the car. The State admits in its brief that the incident which the petitioner describes as a malicious wounding occurred when the officers used chemical mace on the petitioner. Based upon the results of his investigation, the prosecuting attorney determined not to present the matter before the grand jury attending the March 1981 term of the Circuit Court of Clay County.

Notwithstanding this decision, the petitioner advised the prosecuting attorney that he would be present on the day the grand jury was scheduled to convene, in order to petition the foreman for permission to appear and to submit evidence of the alleged offense. The respondent replied that he would invoke the powers of his office as prosecuting attorney to instruct the Sheriff of Clay County to prevent the petitioner from so petitioning the foreman of the grand jury, or from appearing before that, or any future, grand jury for the purpose of presenting evidence regarding this particular complaint.

Undaunted by the prosecuting attorney's warning, the petitioner and a corroborating witness appeared at the Clay County Courthouse on the day the grand jury was to meet. At that time the issue of his appearance before the grand jury was referred to the Honorable Albert L. Sommerville, Jr., Chief Judge of the Fourteenth Judicial Circuit. However, upon being made aware of the facts and issues involved, Judge Sommerville declined to intervene.

Although maintaining his earlier position, the respondent advised the petitioner that he would inform the grand jury that the petitioner was present and wished to appear before them to submit evidence of an alleged criminal offense. The prosecuting attorney, however, further advised the petitioner that he would also attempt to discourage and dissuade the grand jury from entertaining the petitioner or from hearing any evidence he might have to offer regarding his complaint. Following the respondent's presentation, the grand jury deliberated and voted not to hear evidence from the petitioner.

Subsequently the petitioner sought this writ of prohibition alleging that the actions of the prosecuting attorney with regard to the grand jury constitute an exercise of power beyond his jurisdiction.

This case presents three issues which are before this Court for the first time: (1) does a person have a lawful right to personally complain of a criminal offense to a grand jury, over the objection of the prosecuting attorney; (2) may a prosecuting attorney render unsworn testimony before a grand jury; and (3) does prohibition lie against a prosecuting attorney who attempts to stop a grand jury from hearing independent evidence.

These three issues concern the fundamental nature and purpose of the grand jury in our system of criminal justice. Therefore before addressing the issues raised by the petitioner we shall attempt a brief exposition of the history of the grand jury in order to illustrate the roles of the judge, the prosecutor and the citizen-complainant with regard to the grand jury.

The grand jury is an integral part of our judicial system with ancient origins. It appears to have derived from the Frankish custom of requiring folks to appear before the king with information of immediate concern to the administration of justice in the kingdom. W. Holdsworth, *A History of English Law* 312 (1903). When the Franks were conquered by the Normans the custom survived, and thus was brought to England by William the Conqueror in 1066. The records after the Norman conquest show an increased use of the sworn inquests of neighbors as a part of the system of royal justice. In fact, the great fiscal record, the Domesday Book, was compiled from the verdicts of these inquests. 1 F. Pollock and F. Maitland, *History of English Law*, 144 (2d ed. 1968).

During the reign of Henry II, a judicial device similar to that of our present day petit jury was used for the purpose of civil litigation with respect to land. The Grand Assize, the possessory assizes and the assize ultram each used this procedure to settle questions of ownership and possession of land. During Henry's reign the accusing jury also became a part of the judicial mechanism and developed a protective, in addition to its original investigative, function:

> Henry insisted, first for Normandy in the year 1159, and then for England in the year 1164, that the ecclesiastical courts ought to make use of this institution. Laymen ought not to be put to answer in those courts upon a mere unsworn suggestion of ill fame. Either someone should stand forth and commit himself to a definite accusation, or else the ill fame should be sworn to by twelve lawful men of the neighborhood summoned for that purpose by the sheriff: in other words, the ecclesiastical judge ought not proceed *ex officio* upon private suggestions. 1 F. Pollock and F. Maitland, *supra* at 151.

By the time of the Assize of Clarendon in 1166 the accusing jury had become a rather prominent institution. In every county, twelve men out of every "hundred" (a political subdivision of the shire) were called to appear before the itinerant judge appointed by the king. The judge presented a list of crimes and offenses and asked the jurors whether they knew of anyone in the hundred who had committed the offenses enumerated. The jurors replied on the basis of their personal knowledge, and, based on their replies, the judge made a decision whether the accusations were well founded. *Petition of McNair*, 324 Pa. 48, 187 A. 498 (1936).

By the fifteenth century the grand jury system had become an established institution in the English judicial system and enjoyed a great popularity. This popularity was subsequently shared by the colonials in America. At the time of the American Revolution, the grand jury was perceived by most Americans as a highly esteemed institution, a perception enhanced by the spirit of independence and resistance to imperial government displayed by some of the colonial grand juries. Francis Hopkinson, a pamphleteer of the revolutionary period, reflected the popular attitude when he described the grand jury as "a body of truth and power inferior to none but the legislature itself." R. Younger, *The People's Panel: The Grand Jury in the United States* (1631–1941), 41 (1963). Our founding fathers also shared in this sentiment. Thomas Jefferson, for example, referred to the grand jury as both the "true tribunal of the people" and as the "sacred palladium of liberty." S. Padover, THE COMPLETE JEFFERSON at 128 (1943).

Along with the resistance of the colonial grand juries to the British monarchy, one widely publicized English case enhanced immensely the prestige of the grand jury in America. The case involved Lord Ashley, Earl of Shaftsbury, who was implicated in a plot to assassinate the king and "[bring] this kingdom of England to a commonwealth without a king. . . ." *Earl of Shaftsbury's Case*, 8 St. Tr. 759, 778 (1681). He was charged with high treason by the royal prosecutor, who presented the case to a grand jury in London. The grand jury refused to indict, and the popular Lord Ashley went free. This statement against absolute monarchial power has been cited for years as an example of the grand jury as a barrier against both the despotism of the Crown and prosecution based on "partisan passion or private enmity." *In re Russo*, 53 F.R.D. 564, 568 (C.D. Calif. 1971).

History shows us that although the grand jury developed as a "palladium of liberty," it could on occasion be made the vehicle of abuse. For example, the subsequent episodes of Shaftsbury's story do not portray the grand jury in so complimentary a fashion. When the Royalists rigged the election of two Tory sheriffs, who had the duty of selecting the grand jury, and a Tory Mayor of London was elected, the king was assured that the next grand jury would be more amenable to his designs for the Earl of Shaftsbury. Shaftsbury was forced to flee to Amsterdam, where he died in exile. Lewis, *The Grand Jury: A Critical Evaluation*, 13 Akron L.R. 38 (1979).

In recent years the grand jury has been criticized for the same type of abuses present in the later episodes of Shaftsbury's case, by those who believe it has become a tool of the prosecutor rather than fulfilling its original purpose. *See* Lewis, *The Grand Jury: A Critical Evaluation, supra*; Rodis, *A Lawyer's Guide to Grand Jury Abuse*, 14 CRIM. L. BUL. 123 (1978). The grand jury as we know it today is a lineal descendant of the Thirteenth Century juries employed to screen criminal accusations and present evidence of criminal offenses. 1 W. *Holdsworth, supra* at 321, and is designed to fulfill much the same functions. Its primary responsibilities include the determination of whether there is probable cause to believe a crime has been committed, and the protection of citizens against unfounded criminal accusations. 1 W. *Holdsworth, supra*, at 321, and is designed to fulfill much the same functions. Its primary responsibilities include the determination of whether there is probable cause to believe a crime has been committed, and the protection of citizens against unfounded criminal accusations. *See United States v. Calandra*, 414 U.S. 388 (1974). Thus, historically the grand jury serves a dual function: it is intended to operate both as a sword, investigating cases to bring to trial persons accused on just grounds, and as a shield, protecting citizens against unfounded malicious or frivolous prosecutions.

Federal grand juries have not followed this historical mold as closely as have those of West Virginia. In recent years the function of the federal grand jury has shifted away from that of a shield between the citizenry and the government, towards that of a sword in the hands of the United States Attorney. This shift is a result of the federal grand jury's evolution from that of an independent institution, to one dominated by the United States Attorney. *See* Zwerling, Federal Grand Juries v. Attorney Independence *and the Attorney-Client Privilege*, 27 HASTINGS L.J. 1263, 1268 (1978); Boudin, *The Federal Grand Jury*, 61 GEO. L.J. 1 (1972). Evidence of this shift can be found in the recent development of various immunities afforded to witnesses before federal grand juries. *See, e.g.*, 18 U.S.C. §§ 6002–03 (1976); *Kastigar v. United States*, 406 U.S. 441 (1972).

Such a shift in the function of the federal grand jury corrupts its historically developed fundamental principles. Fortunately, the West Virginia Constitution protects us from such abuse, for under the state constitution it is our sworn duty to support the fundamental principles upon which our legal institutions are founded. W. VA. CONST. art. 3, § 20; art. 4, § 5. Heeding this constitutional directive, we are therefore bound to preserve the dual function of the grand jury as both sword and shield. We cannot permit its degradation into a De Torquemadian engine of persecution.

I.

Our state constitution guarantees that "[t]he courts of this State shall be open, and every person, for an injury done to him, in his person, property or reputation, shall have remedy by due course of law; and justice shall be administered without sale, denial or delay." W. VA. CONST. art. 3, § 17. We stated in *State ex rel. Skinner v. Dostert*, W. Va., 278 S.E.2d 624 (1981):

> As criminal offenses are offenses against the State which must be prosecuted in the name of the State, W. VA. CODE § 62-9-1 (1977 Replacement Vol.); *Moundsville v. Fountain*, 27 W. Va. 182 (1885), the prosecutor, as the officer charged with prosecuting such offenses, has a duty to vindicate the victims and the public's constitutional right of redress for a criminal invasion of rights. The "spirit of law" has long been and it has been long held that "[t]he public has rights as well as the accused, and one of the first of these is that of redressing or punishing their wrongs." *Ex parte Santee*, 2 Va. Cas. (4 Va.) 363 (1823). 278 S.E.2d at 631.

The citizen who alleges that his rights have been criminally invaded is entitled to seek redress through the courts and is so entitled as a matter of constitutional right. Thus, the circuit court must guarantee that the grand jury is open to individual citizens seeking to redress wrongs by laying a complaint before it. *See Annot.*, 156 A.L.R. 330 (1945).

To fulfill its functions of protecting individual citizens and providing them with a forum for bringing complaints within the criminal justice system, the grand jury must be open to the public for the independent presentation of evidence before it. If the grand jury is available only to the prosecuting attorney and all complaints must pass through him, the grand jury can justifiably be described as a prosecutorial tool.

This ancient body, as a fundamental constitutional institution, must not be fettered or restricted to the degree that it is inaccessible to the citizens it was designed to serve and protect. We therefore hold that, by application to the circuit judge, whose duty is to insure access to the grand jury, any person may go to the grand jury to present a complaint to it. This principle of approachability lies in the foundation of the very concept of a grand jury. As with any institution, as it removes itself from the public and becomes inaccessible, it becomes more susceptible to abuse. The grand jury can maintain its accessibility and relevancy only through constant judicial vigilance. If the grand jury is to be a meaningful institution, its integrity must be maintained as an independent body, free from all outside interference and prosecutorial control or direction. This can only be insured by vigilance over the administration of justice, which is the duty of the courts. *See generally State ex rel. Casey v. Wood*, 156 W. Va. 329, 193 S.E.2d 143 (1972).

II.

The petitioner contends that in the course of the prosecuting attorney's attempt to dissuade the grand jury from hearing the petitioner's evidence, the prosecutor improperly rendered unsworn testimony relating to the circumstances surrounding the incident giving rise to the petitioner's complaint. We agree with the petitioner that such a course of action on the part of a prosecutor is clearly improper. . . . A prosecuting attorney can only appear before the grand jury to present by sworn witnesses evidence of alleged criminal offenses, and to render court supervised instructions, . . . ; he is not permitted to influence the grand jury in reaching a decision, nor can he provide unsworn testimonial evidence.

[W]e wish to emphasize that any attempt by a prosecuting attorney to render unsworn testimony before a grand jury cannot be tolerated. Such unsworn testimony, particularly on the part of a prosecuting attorney, seriously threatens the integrity of the grand jury's judicial function and constitutes an ethical violation of standards of acceptable prosecutorial behavior. *See, e.g.,* 1 American Bar Association, *Standards for Criminal Justice* § 8.5 (2d ed. 1980).

* * *

In *State ex rel. City of Huntington v. Lombardo, supra*, we recognized that prohibition will lie when a purely ministerial body attempts to usurp a judicial function. *See also Smoot v. Dingess*, W. Va., 236 S.E.2d 468, 474 (1977) (Miller, J., concurring). Therefore if the actions of the respondent in this case constitute an usurpation of judicial power, prohibition will lie. The actions of the respondent of which the petitioner complains are his attempts to influence the grand jury regarding the independent presentation of evidence by a private citizen. Because we find that such actions on the part of the respondent constitute an usurpation of judicial power, we hold that prohibition is a proper proceeding in this case.

By attempting to influence the grand jury the respondent usurps both the power of the circuit court, and of the grand jury itself. The grand jury is an integral part of the judicial system and enjoys a special relationship with the court by which it is convened. *See State ex rel. Casey v. Wood, supra.* Because of this special relationship the court has a particular responsibility to insure the fairness of grand jury proceedings. When the prosecuting attorney attempts to influence the grand jury not to hear evidence which a citizen wishes to present, he improperly infringes the supervisory function of the circuit court.

Under West Virginia law, once a grand jury is properly selected, the judge appoints a foreman. W. Va. Code § 52-2-5 (1981 Replacement Vol.). After that appointment, the grand jury has an independent existence proscribed only by the court's limited supervisory powers, the grand juror's oath, and the applicable rules of criminal procedure. Once their oath is administered, the grand jurors become officers of the court with the duty to "diligently inquire and true presentment make of all such matters as may be given you in charge or come to your knowledge. . . ." W. Va. Code § 52-2-5. By attempting to dissuade the grand jury from hearing evidence the prosecuting attorney further usurps the judicial powers of the grand jury itself.

The role of the prosecuting attorney in relation to the grand jury is strictly circumscribed. The prosecutor's responsibility is to attend to the criminal business of the State, and when he has information of the violation of any penal law, to present evidence of those offenses to the grand jury. W. Va. Code § 7-4-1. Thus, the jurisdiction of the prosecuting attorney encompasses only the presentation of evidence. If instructions on law or the legal effect of evidence are in order, those instructions must come from the circuit court. *See* W. Va. Code § 52-2-6 (1981 Replacement Vol.). Any advice to the grand jury by the prosecutor is subject to court supervision. An attempt by the prosecuting attorney to discourage or dissuade the grand jury from hearing evidence is therefore outside his jurisdiction, and could rise to the level of obstruction of justice. *See* W. Va. Code § 61-5-17 (1977 Replacement Vol.).

Accordingly, we hold that a prosecuting attorney who attempts to influence the grand jury by means other than the presentation of evidence or the giving of court supervised instruction, exceeds his lawful jurisdiction and usurps the judicial power of the circuit court and of the grand jury. Consequently, prohibition will lie to prevent such usurpation of judicial power.

In summary, an individual citizen-complainant has a constitutional right to appear before a grand jury to present evidence of an alleged offense. A prosecuting attorney may not render unsworn testimonial evidence before the grand jury. Prohibition will lie against a prosecuting attorney who attempts to usurp the judicial function of the circuit court and of the grand jury by attempting to discourage it from hearing the independent presentation of evidence by a citizen complainant.

Molded writ granted.

Notes

1. So far, West Virginia is alone in declaring access to the Grand Jury to be a state constitutional right. In the absence of constitutional protection of access to the grand jury, nothing prevents legislatures from eliminating citizen access to grand jury. Some states have eliminated grand juries altogether in favor of preliminary hearings.

2. Tennessee is among many states that have codified a procedure for a citizen's direct access to the Grand Jury:

TENN. CODE ANN. § 40-12-104

Application to testify by person having knowledge of commission of offense.

(a) Any person having knowledge or proof of the commission of a public offense triable or indictable in the county may testify before the grand jury.

(b) The person having knowledge or proof shall appear before the foreman. The person may also submit the sworn affidavits of others whose testimony the person wishes to have considered.

(c) The person shall designate two (2) grand jurors who shall, with the foreman, comprise a panel to determine whether the knowledge warrants investigation by the grand jury. The panel may consult the district attorney general or the court for guidance in making its determination. The majority decision of the panel shall be final, and shall be promptly communicated to the person along with reasons for the action taken.

(d) Submission of an affidavit which the person knows to be false in any material regard shall be punishable as perjury. An affiant who permits submission of his affidavit, knowing it to be false in any material regard, is guilty of perjury. Any person subsequently testifying before the grand jury as to any material fact known by him to be false is guilty of perjury.

---

ii-c. Victim Access to Grand Jury via Prosecutorial or Judicial Approval

Another approach to victim's access to the Grand Jury is that the right of a private party to present before a grand jury does not exist absent a request from the Grand Jury or prosecutorial or judicial approval. The federal laws provide an example of this.

In re New Haven Grand Jury

604 F. Supp. 453 (D. Conn. 1985)

JOSÉ A. CABRANES, District Judge:

The question presented is whether an individual has a right to communicate with a federal grand jury, absent a request from the grand jury, without the approval of the United States Attorney or a judge. It is a question faced with increasing frequency by courts confronted by a variety of persons who profess to lack confidence in the judgment of prosecutors and judges and who believe themselves to be the most appropriate instruments for the vindication of the interests of justice. I conclude that, as a general proposition, such private prosecutorial initiatives are not permitted by [federal] law. . . .

Introduction

A consideration of applicable law and the full record of these proceedings yields the inescapable conclusion that neither a grand jury target nor a private complainant has a right to communicate.

The capacity in which the correspondent wishes to communicate with the New Haven grand jury is not apparent from his letter to the Clerk, but two general possibilities come to mind. They are: (a) as a *target* or *potential target* of a grand jury investigation or (b) as a *complainant* or *informer*. The United States Attorney reported that the correspondent is a potential target of the New Haven grand jury. *See* Response of the United States Attorney (filed June 6, 1984) ("Response") at 4. At least with respect to the Hartford grand jury, it appears that the correspondent sought to communicate directly, in writing or otherwise, with a federal grand jury without the approval of a prosecutor or judge. There is no constitutional, statutory, or common law right to communicate directly with a federal grand jury without the participation of a prosecutor or judge, and attempts to transmit written communications directly to a grand jury may constitute a crime.

In any event, because this correspondent has a well-documented history of persecuting innocent persons through abuse of legal processes, he may not appear before a federal grand jury in this District until and unless he is invited or ordered by a grand jury to do so and he may not have communications conveyed to a grand jury without the approval of the United States Attorney or the court.

I.

[T]he initiation by a private party of written communications with a grand jury, with the exception of a request for an opportunity to appear, may constitute a crime. *See* 18 U.S.C. § 1504. The statute on jury tampering by written communications is instructive because "[t]he purpose of 18 U.S.C.[] § 1504 was to prevent anyone from attempting to bring pressure upon or [to] intimidate a grand juror by a written communication with that intent." *United States v. Smyth*, 104 F. Supp. 283, 299 (N.D. Cal. 1952). The statute prohibits written communications addressed to the grand jury as a body and intended to be seen by all of the jurors, as well as those addressed to an individual juror. *See Duke v. United States, supra*, 90 F.2d at 841 (target of a grand jury investigation convicted under predecessor statute to 18 U.S.C. § 1504 for transmitting a letter to grand jury foreman with purpose of "get[ting] before the grand jury [his] contentions and unsworn statements").

II.

A complainant or informer has no greater right to appear before a grand jury or to communicate directly with it in writing than does a target or potential target of a grand jury. *See People v. Parker*, 74 N.E.2d 523, 525–526 (Ill. 1947) (*per curiam*) (rejecting First Amendment challenge to a state court criminal contempt conviction for mailing letter to grand jury foreman alleging a conspiracy between a newspaper, prosecutors and politicians) ("*Parker II*"), *aff'd per curiam by equally divided court*, 334 U.S. 816 (1948); *United States v. Kilpatrick*, 16 F. 765, 769, 771 (W.D.N.C. 1883) (there is "no right to communicate private information to a grand jury for the purpose of obtaining a presentment" and it is a crime for "any individual, acting as a volunteer, to approach or communicate with the grand jury in reference to any matter which either is or may come before [it]."); *Charge to Grand Jury*, 30 F. Cas. 992, 994–995 (C.C.D. Cal. 1872) (No. 18,255) (Field, Circuit Justice).

As noted, direct communication with a grand jury may be a crime under 18 U.S.C. § 1504. Describing the frequency of private communications to the grand jury "filled with malignant and scandalous imputations" against judges and others, and the damage to the grand jury system that such communications cause, Justice Field described the then-recently-enacted predecessor to 18 U.S.C. § 1504 as intended to secure the grand jury "from intimidation or personal influence of every kind." *Charge to Grand Jury, supra* 30 F. Cas. at 995. He instructed the grand jury to turn over such communications to the prosecutor for use against the originators. *Id.*

II.

It has been observed that the grand jury functions both as "a sword and a shield of justice." *United States v. Cox*, 342 F.2d 167, 186 (5th Cir.) (Wisdom, J., concurring). *See generally United States v. Calandra*, 414 U.S. 338, 342–346 (1974). As a sword, the function of the grand jury is, in the words of Professor Lester B. Orfield, "to bring to trial persons accused of crime upon just grounds." Orfield, *The Federal Grand Jury*, 22 F.R.D. 343, 394 (1958). As a shield, the grand jury's function is "to protect persons against unfounded or malicious prosecutions by insuring that no criminal proceeding will be undertaken without a disinterested determination of probable guilt." *Id.*

Although Professor Orfield has noted that "[t]he [investigative or] inquisitorial function has been called the more important[,]" *id.*, the grand jury's shield function remains significant. Indeed, it has been said that "[t]he Grand Jury earned its place in the Bill of Rights by its shield, not by its sword." *United States v. Cox, supra*, 342 F.2d at 186 (Wisdom, J., concurring). The grand jury remains a primary security to the innocent against hasty, malicious and oppressive prosecution . . . standing between the accuser and the accused . . . to determine whether a charge is founded upon reason or was dictated by an intimidating power or by malice and personal ill will.

Wood v. Georgia, 370 U.S. 375, 390 (1962). *See* M. Frankel & G. Naftalis, *The Grand Jury* 22, 120 (1977) (stressing protective functions of the grand jury); Wickersham, *The Grand Jury: Weapon Against Crime and Corruption*, 51 A.B.A.J. 1157, 1157–1161 (1965) (same).

A rule that would permit anyone to communicate with a grand jury without the supervision or screening of the prosecutor or the court would compromise, if not utterly subvert, both of the historic functions of the grand jury, for it would facilitate the pursuit of vendettas and the "gratification of private malice." *Charge to Grand Jury, supra*, 30 F. Cas. at 994–995. A rule that would open the grand jury to the public without judicial or prosecutorial intervention is an invitation to anyone interested in trying to persuade a majority of the grand jury, by hook or by crook, to conduct investigations that a prosecutor has determined to be inappropriate or unavailing. The protection of society at large, as well as the preservation of the grand jury as an instrument of justice, requires that the court place limits on direct and unsupervised communications with the grand jury by disgruntled individuals who may have personal axes to grind.

"Runaway grand juries" a potential result or goal of any rule favoring unsupervised access to a grand jury may have a certain romantic allure, but federal law leaves little or no room for that species of romance.

It is true, of course, that a federal grand jury cannot be compelled to follow a course of action desired by either the prosecutor or by the court, and it is the grand jury that determines whether there is probable cause to believe that an offense has been committed. It is equally true, however, that no grand jury, "runaway" or otherwise, is vested with the discretionary power to determine whether a prosecution shall be commenced or maintained. It is well to remember that the commencement of a federal criminal case by submission of evidence to a grand jury is "an executive function within the exclusive prerogative of the Attorney General," *In re Persico*, 522 F.2d 41, 54–55 (2d Cir. 1975); *see also United States v. Chanen*, 549 F.2d 1306, 1312–1313 (9th Cir. 1977); that "in American jurisprudence at least, a private citizen lacks a judicially cognizable interest in the prosecution or nonprosecution of another[,]" *Leeke v. Timmerman*, 454 U.S. 83, 85–86 (1981), *quoting Linda R.S. v. Richard D.*, 410 U.S. 614, 619 (1973); and that "the decision to prosecute is solely within the discretion of the prosecutor," *id.* at 87; *see also United States v. Cox, supra*, 342 F.2d at 171. Accordingly, a rule that would afford the general public unsupervised access to the grand jury is a rule calculated to empower the mischievous and the criminal and injure the innocent.

Any person may bring evidence of wrongdoing by a third party to the attention of the federal prosecutor. If a complainant is frustrated by a prosecutor's decision not to prosecute, it does not follow that the complainant should have unsupervised recourse to the grand jury. Because the powers exercised by a grand jury are great, and because they are exercised largely in secret, they are subject to the supervision of a judge, *Branzburg v. Hayes*, 408 U.S. 665, 688 (1972), "to prevent [wrongs] before [they] occur." *United States v. Calandra, supra*, 414 U.S. at 346, 94 S. Ct. at 619. If a complainant believes that the prosecutor wrongfully has ignored a legitimate and significant report of illicit conduct, he may make an application to the court concerning access to the grand jury. *Charge to Grand Jury, supra*, 30 F. Cas. at 994; *United States v. Kilpatrick, supra*, 16 F. at 769. Private prosecutions vanished from our system of jurisprudence centuries ago, along with trial by battle.[39]

---

39. *See generally United States v. Cox, supra*, 342 F.2d at 186–187 (Wisdom, J., concurring); *Charge to Grand Jury, supra*, 30 F. Cas. at 995, n.3; S. Milsom, *Historical Foundations of the Common Law* 406–410 (2d ed. 1981); *Grand Jury Reform: Hearings on H.R. 94 Before the Sub-comm. on*

The oft-noted principle that "the public . . . has a right to every man's evidence," *see, e.g., United States v. Dionisio*, 410 U.S. 1, 9 (1973), *Branzburg v. Hayes, supra,* 408 U.S. at 688 & n.26, does not suggest, much less compel, a different result. That principle merely states the historically grounded *obligation* of every person, regardless of rank or station, to appear and give evidence before a grand jury in response to a grand jury subpoena. It does not follow from this principle that individuals have a *right* to appear before a grand jury or otherwise to communicate their views or opinions to a grand jury.

In those jurisdictions where evidence of a criminal offense may be presented at the grand jury at the discretion of the court, the question of what discretionary standards the court applies to allow or deny grand jury access becomes significant.

In re Application of Larry A. Wood to Appear Before the Grand Jury Appeal of United States
833 F.2d 113 (8th Cir. 1987)

The United States appeals from an order of the United States District Court for the District of Nebraska, ordering the United States Attorney of that district to present to the grand jury allegations of wrongdoing on the part of an FBI agent and an Assistant United States Attorney lodged by Larry A. Wood, a private citizen and previously acquitted defendant. Alternatively, the court ordered that Wood be permitted to personally appear before the grand jury to present his allegations. We affirm the district court.

After reviewing the facts the court held:

We come then to the second issue and that is, whether, as an enforcement mechanism, the district court erred in holding that if the U.S. Attorney failed to comply with the order to resubmit the matter to the grand jury, the application of Wood to appear before the grand jury would be granted. We think not. The general rule is, of course, that an individual cannot bring accusations before a grand jury unless invited to do so by the prosecutor or the grand jury. A well-recognized exception to this rule is that the court in its supervisory power can authorize an individual to appear before a grand jury if it feels that the circumstances require. Mr. Justice Field announced the rule in his charge to a federal grand jury in 1872:

> You will not allow private prosecutors to intrude themselves into your presence, and present accusations. Generally such parties are actuated by a private enmity, and seek merely the gratification of their personal malice. If they possess any information justifying the accusation of the person against whom

---

Immigration, Citizenship, and International Law of the House Comm. on the Judiciary, 95th Cong., 1st Sess. 58–64 (1977) ("*Hearings*") (statement of Prof. John Scott, Legal Historian, Rutgers University School of Law.

they complain, they should impart it to the district attorney who will seldom fail to act in a proper case. But *if the district attorney should refuse to act, they can make their complaint to a committing magistrate, before whom the matter can be investigated, and if sufficient evidence be produced of the commission of a public offense by the accused, he can be held to bail to answer to the action of the grand jury.*

Charge to Grand Jury, 30 F.Cas. 992 (C.C.D.Cal.1872) (No. 18,255) (emphasis added); *see also In re New Haven Grand Jury*, 604 F.Supp. 453, 457, 460–61, n. 8–11 (D.Conn. 1985). Certainly, this alternative is significantly less intrusive on the powers of the prosecutor than an order requiring the representation to be made. Moreover, the order is not violative of the general rule that the executive branch has exclusive authority and absolute discretion to decide whether to prosecute a case. *See United States v. Nixon,* 418 U.S. 683 (1974). Here, the court order does not require the United States Attorney to prosecute or, for that matter, to re-present the matter to the grand jury. It simply states that, unless he does, Larry Wood may appear before the grand jury and do so. Thereafter, the prosecutor is free to prosecute or not, as his judgment dictates. *Nixon v. Sirica*, 487 F.2d 700 (D.C.Cir. 1973).

———————

Note. Like the federal courts, some states also provide for judicial screening of victim access to the grand jury. *See, e.g., In re Petition of Thomas*, 434 A.2d 503 (Me. 1981).

ii-d. Access to Grand Jury by Citizen Petition

Nebraska and several other states have statutes authorizing the citizenry to *require* the courts to call a grand jury to review a particular case:

NEB. REV. STAT. § 29-1401 (emphasis added): It shall be *mandatory* for such district courts to call a grand jury in each case upon the petition of registered voters of the county of the number of not less than ten percent of the total vote cast for the office of Governor in such county at the most recent general election held therein for such office.

Rather than having judicial control over citizen access to the grand jury, access is controlled by requiring acquiescence of a percentage of the actively voting electorate. Newspaper accounts provide an example of the utilization of the statute.

Sharon Cohen, *A Mother's Mission: Ghost of Death Haunts Search for Daughter*

L.A. TIMES, Sept. 2, 1990

[Madison, Nebraska] Joyce Cutshall is consumed by a battle she can never win. She thinks her daughter is dead, but can't prove it. She suspects she is buried nearby, but can't find her.

She wants to bring her home, but can't do it.

She has made that her mission, taking the law into her own hands to find out what happened to her child. Fearful that Jill's case would sink deeper in police files, the determined mother who had never touched a legal book started a petition drive, forced a grand jury probe, and prompted an arrest.

Three years after Jill's disappearance, Joyce Cutshall believes she is closer than ever to the truth a truth that will bring even greater agony.

"I feel that this last chapter is going to be my absolutely most difficult," she says. "It's a very, very strange feeling to work so hard toward something to know that at the end of it, it's going to bring as much grief and pain as a mother can feel."

This fall, when David Phelps, 26, goes on trial on charges of kidnapping Jill, Cutshall will be there, hoping his words will lead to her daughter's body, knowing that even if she wins, she loses. The prospect is frightening, yet comforting.

"Once I can put Jill to rest in my own mind and have a place that I can go and visit her whenever I'm having a difficult day or feel the need to see her," she says, "that will help me deal with the fact that I won't have a chance to hold her again."

For now, she lives with memories how Jill loved butter. And mementos: pictures of horses and hearts, a note to "the greatest mom in the world," crayon drawings of the sun, flowers and rainbows her symbol for the future and poems.

"The world is a great round ball thing that is made by God," Jill wrote. "It has good things on it and bad things on it. The world is great to me."

On August 13, 1987, 9-year-old Jillian Dee Cutshall vanished from the world she so cherished.

She disappeared in Norfolk, where she was spending the summer with her father, Roger. The Cutshalls divorced in 1985; Jill and her brother, Jeff, lived in Kansas with their mother.

Jill, her mother says, feared staying in her father's apartment house alone; it was seedy, noisy, filled with transients. So when he and his new wife left for work at 6 a.m., she did her chores, then walked to the baby sitter's six blocks away.

That day, she was last seen at 6:30 a.m. on her sitter's stoop, where she normally waited until someone inside awoke.

Jill had been repeatedly warned about strangers. But the blonde, blue-eyed youngster "just loved people," her mother says. "She trusted them. She always found something good in everybody, even if they weren't good."

At first, Joyce Cutshall thought Jill would return in a week, then months. "After the third month," she says, "I emotionally and mentally was telling myself that if we work hard enough, we'll have her back in a year."

A year passed. No Jill.

Hope turned to heartache . . . .

    . . . Last summer, when [police chief] Mizner placed Jill's case on semi-
    active status, Cutshall was outraged.

"If you cannot rely on people that you're supposed to be able to rely on to do the job, I guess the old adage is . . . 'Do it yourself.'" She began.

Cutshall discovered that under Nebraska law, authorities had to convene a grand jury if presented with petitions from at least 10% of county voters participating in the last gubernatorial election.

In December, while others shopped for Christmas gifts, she collected signatures. While the local mall was being decorated, she was setting up a table and banner reading: "Jill Cutshall Needs a Grand Jury."

A dozen volunteers gathered signatures at the mall and braved blizzards to collect more in door-to-door visits. Petitions were presented to authorities on Feb. 20 the day after Jill's birthday "my gift to her," her mother says.

Authorities, she says, certified 1,471 signatures, hundreds more than needed.

Cutshall plays down her doggedness, saying: "I don't have anything extra. The only thing I have is the love for my daughter."

In June, a grand jury indicted Phelps on charges of abduction with intent to commit sexual assault. Last month, he returned to Nebraska from Iowa and pleaded not guilty. He's being held on $100,000 bond.

Notes

1. Phelps was ultimately convicted of the charge. *See Man Guilty: Missing Girl a Mystery*, Chi. Trib., Mar. 21, 1991 at C8.

2. Access to grand jury by the electorate may avoid the roadblock of prosecutorial decisions not to prosecute which are based on policy. It also avoids judicial review and the discomfort courts express with reviewing prosecutorial discretion. What are the negative aspects of grand jury access via citizen petition?

3. The practical procedures for victim access to the grand jury vary considerably. In Texas, a crime victim may directly contact a member of the grand jury to ask for an investigation and the right to testify. *Smith v. Hightower*, 693 F.2d 359, 368 n.21 (5th Cir. 1981). In Maryland, other remedies must be exhausted before the crime victim has direct access to the grand jury. *Brack v. Wells, supra*. The other remedies to be exhausted were seeking public prosecution from the local prosecutor and requesting a complaint from the court. In Colorado, the crime victim first requests prosecution from the district attorney. If confronted with refusal, the crime victim may contact the grand jury. If the grand jury declines, the victim can petition the court to order the grand jury to allow the crime victim to testify before it.

4. There are many detractors of the Grand Jury system. Some states have eliminated Grand Juries altogether. The fundamental criticism is that, in practice, they do not effectively shield the accused from erroneous charges. *See* Andrew D. Leipold, *Why Grand Juries Do Not (and Cannot) Protect the Accused*, 80 Corn. L. Rev. 260 (1993).

5. Victim Access to Indictment Process: Preliminary Hearing.

In jurisdictions where preliminary hearing can substitute for Grand Jury the preliminary hearing procedure has not provided private citizens significant access to the indictment process.

One explanation may be that private citizens are not lawyers and generally might not be permitted to conduct a preliminary hearing. Moreover, the courts, unlike the grand jury, are not traditionally an investigative body. Thus, absent an attorney acting as prosecutor, there is no institutional mechanism in place to perform the functions necessary for the court to determine probable cause.

6. Several commentators have proposed model legislation to codify procedures for the review of decisions not to prosecute. Kenneth L. Wainstein, *Judicially Initiated Prosecution: A Means of Preventing Victimization in the Event of Prosecutorial Inaction*, 76 CALIF. L. REV. 727 (1988); Peter Davis, *The Crime Victim's Right to a Criminal Prosecution: A Proposed Model Statute for the Governance of Private Prosecution*, 38 DEPAUL L. REV. 329 (1989). Other commentators have recommended the abolition of private prosecution. John D. Bessler, *The Public Interest and the Unconstitutionality of Private Prosecutors*, 47 ARK. L. REV. 511 (1994).

––––––––––

Cases of persons victimized by police brutality present difficult issues.

Peter L. Davis, *Rodney King and the Decriminalization of Police Brutality in America: Direct and Judicial Access to the Grand Jury as Remedies for Victims of Police Brutality When the Prosecutor Declines to Prosecute*

53 MD. L. REV. 263 (1994)

There are no accurate, national statistics on the number of police assaults on civilians. However, a Gannett News Service study of one hundred police brutality lawsuits nationwide found "that taxpayers are punished more than the officers responsible for the violence. The 100 cases, involving police departments that lost lawsuits and had to pay victims at least $100,000, cost the nation's taxpayers nearly $92 million. But of 105 officers involved, only five were fired and 19 were promoted." The Christopher Commission concluded that "[p]olice violence is not a local problem"; and shortly after the King episode the heads of police departments from ten major cities around the country "called for a national commission on crime and violence to track instances of police brutality, stating that the problem of excessive force is real and is linked to drugs, strife, and urban decay." And Hubert Williams, formerly Chief of Police of Newark, New Jersey, now President of the Police Foundation, said: "Police use of excessive force is a significant problem in this country, particularly in our inner cities."

This Article begins with the premise that police brutality particularly, but not exclusively, against minorities is *de facto* decriminalized in the United States and has been so for many years. The Article argues that decriminalization has occurred for many reasons, including the influential role of the police in an organized society, the desensitization of the public and the judicial system to the realities of police criminal behavior, the symbiotic relationship of prosecutors and the police, the growth of the legal doctrine of prosecutorial discretion and the corresponding decline of private prosecutions, and the waning independence of the grand jury . . .

Gaining access to a grand jury either directly or through the impaneling judge certainly would limit the prosecutor's total monopoly and increase his or her accountability. Of equal importance, it would be a powerful weapon in the hands of citizens who are now all too often shut out of the criminal courts.[40] The crime victim would have a far better chance of securing a criminal prosecution against his victimizer; the whistleblower would have a far better chance of exposing public and private corruption. Battered women, gays, lesbians, minorities, the homeless society's most marginal and most vulnerable would be given a chance to tell their stories of victimization to those who are not part of the professional law enforcement system.

Most of all, however, giving citizens direct access to the grand jury helps to ameliorate the problem of the symbiotic relationship between police and public prosecutors. When plain, ordinary citizens are able to approach the grand jury or the empaneling judge, it is likely that far more indictments will issue against brutal police officers particularly in the less sensational cases.

Permitting citizens to exercise the right to approach the grand jury directly, and ensuring that fairness results once citizens do appear there, puts tremendous responsibility on the shoulders of the judiciary. "The judiciary may be the last hope for salvaging the grand jury from obsolescence. By vigorous use of its powers and discretion, the judiciary could restore the grand jury to a position of independence and usefulness."[41] Although the courts retain this general and the responsibility for supervising the grand jury, the degree of willingness to protect the independence of the grand jury from prosecutorial domination obviously will vary from judge to judge.

ii-e. Judicial Interpretation of Federal Rule 7(c): The Federal Prosecutor's Veto Power over Federal Grand Jury Indictments

Even under circumstances where a federal judge approves victim access to the federal grand jury, the U.S. Attorney could veto the federal grand jury indictment by refusing to affix her signature to the indictment. In *United States v. Cox*, 231 F.2d 167 (D.C. Miss. 1965), over vigorous dissent, the circuit court held that even if the grand jury returns a true bill, there can be no formal indictment without the U.S. Attorney's signature. The court was interpreting congressional legislation. States are not bound by this legislation which applies only in federal cases.

---

40. "The advantage of citizen participation in an age when people feel increasingly alienated from the legal system should not be lightly discarded." Coffey & Norman, *supra* note 217, at 767.
41. *Id.* at 757 (quoting Johnston, *supra* note 444, at 157).

Notes

1. Is allowing citizen access to grand jury a foundation of liberty as the West Virginia court argues in *Ex rel. Miller v. Smith*? If so, the federal government's elimination of any meaningful review mechanism available to citizens represents a significant consolidation of power residing almost exclusively in the government. Is this good policy?

2. Does allowing citizen access to the grand jury open the door to abuse of the indictment process? If so, does West Virginia's procedure allow for citizen-initiated indictments which may be ill-advised as a matter of policy?

3. Contrary to federal law, a majority of state jurisdictions allow a grand jury to indict in the face of prosecutorial opposition.

Chapter 5

Pretrial Proceedings

Introduction

After the filing of criminal charges, various pretrial matters affecting crime victims can arise. This chapter considers some of the more important issues facing victims after prosecutors file criminal charges against a defendant: obtaining legal representation; securing a speedy trial; avoiding a change of venue to a distant location; securing discovery from the defendant and the state; securing protection from a defendant; avoiding multiple, separate trials; finding an unbiased judge; and objecting to application of the exclusionary rule.

A. Legal Representation

After a prosecutor files criminal cases, the case will move toward a resolution — either through dismissal of the charges, a plea bargain, or a trial. During the pretrial phase, many issues can develop that affect the victim's interests: Can the defendant obtain discovery from the victims? Should the trial be moved to a distant city because of pre-trial publicity?

A victim may desire — and need — legal representation to protect her interests when these issues arise. If she has sufficient means, she can hire her own attorney, who can then file appropriate pleadings on these issues. More typically, however, victims will lack the resources to hire counsel. Just as criminal defendants are disproportionately poor, crime victims come predominantly from those of limited means.

Unlike criminal defendants, however, crime victims have no constitutional right to counsel appointed at state expense. Instead, victims must either represent themselves or try to find legal assistance to pursue their rights. The difficulty in obtaining legal counsel is probably a major reason why victims' rights are chronically underenforced and why there are relatively few reported appellate court opinions on victims' issues. (The problems of enforcing victims' rights are explored at greater length in Chapters 11 and 12.)

In a few cases, courts have appointed counsel for the victim. When a victim of limited means needs legal representation, courts probably have inherent authority to appoint a volunteer attorney to represent the victim. In many jurisdictions, courts have this authority in civil cases. *See* Judy Zelin, *Court Appointment of Attorney to Represent, without Compensation, Indigent in Civil Action*, 52 ALR 4th 1063; *Court*

Appointment of Attorneys in Civil Cases: The Constitutionality of Uncompensated Legal Assistance, 81 COLUM. L. REV. 366 (1981). This authority probably extends to appointing attorneys to represent victims of crime in criminal proceedings. Before the existence of state funds to pay for lawyers for defendants, courts appointed lawyers to represent the accused in criminal cases without compensation.

A notorious case involved the prosecution of a Hispanic police officer in Miami, Florida, for the shooting death of the black driver of a motorcycle who was attempting to avoid a police stop for running a traffic signal. A passenger on the motorcycle was also killed as a result of the crash. Serious civil disturbances erupted in Miami. A Dade County trial judge entered the following order, a separate and unrelated portion of which was reversed on other grounds:

State v. Lozano

Case No. 89-02972 (Cir. Ct. of the 11th Judicial Cir., Dade County, Florida),
opinion reprinted in 616 So.2d 73 (Fla. App. 1993) (Appx. A)

The relatives of the shooting victims have rights in connection with this case. Our Florida Constitution [Art. I, Section 16(b), Fla. Const.] provides:

> Victims of crime or their lawful representatives . . . are entitled to the right to be informed, to be present, and to be heard when relevant, at all crucial stages of criminal proceedings, to the extent that these rights do not interfere with the constitutional rights of the accused.

The relatives of the victims, Clement Lloyd and Allan Blanchard, are entitled to have an attorney participate in this case. The court will appoint a Black attorney for this purpose. . . .

It is therefore Ordered and Adjudged: . . .

The court will appoint an attorney to represent the victims in this proceeding. . . .

Notes

1. While the basis for appointment of counsel was not articulated in *Lozano*, above, it is probable that this was done pursuant to the court's inherent authority. Courts have inherent power to do what is reasonably necessary for the fair administration of justice, including providing counsel for indigent persons.

2. In *State Pub Defender v. Iowa Dist. Ct. for Newbury County,* 2009 WL 1492720 (Iowa Ct. App. 2009), the court held that a statute governing expenditures of public defenders did not authorize legal aid to victim to prepare victim impact statement.

3. The notion of court-appointed attorneys for indigent victims has not been a reform seriously pursued by the victims' rights movement. The absence of a lobby pursuing such a reform may reflect the political problem associated with a notion that carries a significant fiscal impact. Should an indigent victim fund be established in serious crimes where conflict exists?

4. Some statutes specifically authorize appointment of counsel for a victim in special circumstances, particularly in cases involving children. *See* 18 U.S.C. § 3509(h) (authorizing court appointment of a guardian *ad litem* for child victims).

5. Some states have created funding mechanisms for crime victim representation. Arizona imposes a special assessment on all convictions, part of which goes to funding crime victim legal representation. *See* Ariz. Rev. Stat. § 41-1727 (establishing victims' rights enforcement fund). New Jersey's victim compensation program provides modest funding for legal services to crime victims, including rights enforcement. King County, comprising the metropolitan region of Seattle and outlying cities, has recently funded counsel for victims killed by police violence. Seattle Times, January 29, 2018, https://www.seattletimes.com/seattle-news/crime/leveling -of-the-playing-field-families-of-those-killed-by-police-to-get-attorneys-in-king -county-inquests/.

6. Judicial appointment of counsel can also be done on appeal. A federal court "concerned about the lack of representation for the victims and their families . . . appointed pro bono counsel to serve as amicus curiae to protect their interests. . . ." *U.S. v. Kaczynski*, 551 F.3d 1120 (9th Cir. 2008).

————————

While in most states victims struggle to secure legal counsel to protect their rights, a recent innovative effort to provide legal counsel has occurred in the U.S. military. Under intense pressure from Congress, the public, the media, and anti-rape advocates, the military has adopted reforms to improve its response to sexual assault allegations. An important part of these reforms is the establishment of a Special Victim Counsel (SVC) for sexual assault victims. The SVC program helps victims navigate the military's reporting process for sexual assault and any subsequent proceedings, as explained by two commentators:

Margaret Garvin & Douglas E. Beloof, *Crime Victim Agency: Independent Lawyers for Sexual Assault Victims*
13 Ohio St. J. Crim. L. 67 (2015)

Special victims' counsel are available to victims of sex-related offenses regardless of whether they file a restricted report, file an unrestricted report, or chose not to file a report. The primary duty of an SVC is to zealously represent his or her clients' rights and interests, including during the criminal investigation, preliminary hearing, pretrial litigation, plea negotiations, court-martial proceedings, and post-trial phase of a court-martial . . . . Finally, SVCs educate clients on the military justice system, the roles of sexual assault response personnel, and the variety of medical and other non-legal assistance available to them. SVCs are not part of the Victim and Witness Assistance Program (VWAP), but Air Force guidance, for example, notes that the legal services provided through its program are intended to align with and strengthen the VWAP by representing the interests of a client so that he or she can fully participate in the military criminal justice process.

Once the criminal process is engaged, SVCs provide significant legal support to the victim. In the first 11 months of the Air Force SVC program, the workload included 7,966 telephone consultations with clients, 1,328 in-person meetings with clients, 10,381 correspondences on behalf of clients, 11,431 correspondences with clients, 7,904 telephone consultations on behalf of clients, 726 in person meetings on behalf of clients, attendance at 215 client interviews with defense counsel, attendance at 146 client interviews with law enforcement, attendance at 550 client interviews with trial counsel (prosecutors), 193 assertions of clients' privacy rights during discovery, 80 representations of clients for collateral misconduct (where victim may have been engaged in improper conduct at the time of assault), advisement of clients regarding immunity on 113 occasions, assistance with expedited transfer on 73 occasions, filing or answering a motion on 107 occasions, arguing 78 motions, and assisting with 29 Freedom of Information Act requests. In all, SVCs spent 18,919 hours on representation of sexual assault victims during this initial period.

Of related significance are the results of SVC victim satisfaction surveys from the Air Force (the only branch to conduct a survey): 92% were "extremely satisfied" with the advice and support the SVC provided during the Article 32 hearing and court-martial; 98% would recommend that other victims request an SVC; and, finally, 96% indicated their SVC helped them understand the investigation and court-martial processes. In hearings conducted by the military, the Adult Sexual Assault Crimes Panel had the opportunity to hear from military sexual assault victims who were assigned a[n SVC]. Each witness who had been assigned an SVC testified that the SVC was critical to his or her ability to understand the process and participate effectively as witnesses against their accuser. The outcome of an acquittal in some of the cases did not lessen the value the victim placed on the SVC's representation.

Note

Could the SVC program serve as a model for the civilian justice system? Professors Garvin and Beloof believe so, arguing that "[a]s experience in the military justice system amply demonstrates, independent lawyers for sexual assault victims are integral to this vision [of crime victim agency]. Without legal counsel for victims, the justice system will never be able to respond effectively to victims' powerful concerns. Just as the military has begun providing legal counsel for victims in its justice process, our country's civilian processes must also begin to provide legal counsel to sexual assault victims." Margaret Garvin & Douglas E. Beloof, *Crime Victim Agency: Independent Lawyers for Sexual Assault Victims*, 13 Ohio St. J. Crim. L. 67, 88 (2015)

Some states try to resolve the problem of non-representation of victims by giving the prosecution a right to enforce the rights of crime victims.

TEXAS CONSTITUTION, Art. 1, § 30d

The state, through its prosecuting attorney, has the right to enforce the rights of crime victims.

If victims can assert rights, what happens if the victim's position conflicts with the prosecutor's position? Arizona has a court rule requiring prosecutors to refer victims to independent counsel when there is a conflict.

ARIZ. RULE CRIM. PRO. 39

(c) Assistance and Representation

1. The victim shall also have the right to the assistance of the prosecutor in the assertion of the rights enumerated in this rule or otherwise provided for by law. The prosecutor shall have the responsibility to inform the victim, as defined by these rules, of the rights provided by these rules and by law, and to provide the victim with notices and information which the victim is entitled by these rules and by law to receive from the prosecutor.

2. The prosecutor shall have standing in any judicial proceeding, upon the victim's request, to assert any of the rights to which the victim is entitled by this rule or by any other provision of law.

3. In any event of any conflict of interest between the state or any other prosecutorial entity and the wishes of the victim, the prosecutor shall have the responsibility to direct the victim to the appropriate legal referral, legal assistance, or legal aid agency.

4. In asserting any of the rights enumerated in this rule or provided for in any other provision of the law, the victim shall also have the right to engage and be represented by personal counsel of his or her choice.

Notes

1. The Arizona rule envisions referring crime victims to "the appropriate legal referral, legal assistance, or legal aid agency." What if no such agency exists?

2. Does the Arizona rule require disqualification where the prosecutor has previously prosecuted the victim? In *State ex rel Romley v. Superior Court in and for the County of Maricopa*, 891 P.2d 246 (Ariz. App. 1995), the court found no conflict of interest or appearance of impropriety that required a prosecutor's disqualification from a criminal prosecution of various defendants even though the prosecutor had pursued criminal charges against the victim arising out of incident unrelated to defendants. The court held that although the Victims' Bill of Rights imposed duties on prosecutors with respect to victims, the prosecutor did not represent the victim, but, rather, represented state and therefore disqualification was not required.

3. The circumstances in which prosecutors can ethically represent victims are discussed are discussed in Chapter 11.

B. Speedy Trial for Victims

The Sixth Amendment to the Constitution guarantees criminal defendants the right to a speedy trial. The federal government and many states now have parallel statutory or constitutional provisions granting speedy trial rights to victims.

18 U.S.C. § 3771(a)

A crime victim has the following rights: . . .

(7) The right to proceedings free from unreasonable delay. . . .

ARIZ. CONST., art. II, § 2.1

. . . a victim of crime has a right . . .

[t]o a speedy trial or disposition and prompt and final conclusion of the case after the conviction and sentence.

ILLINOIS CONST., art. I, § 8.1(a)

Crime victims . . . shall have the following rights as provided by law:

* * *

The right to timely disposition of the case following the arrest of the accused.

———

Federal law contains a statute giving child victims (or witnesses) the ability to press for a speedy trial and the Crime Victims' Rights Act provides victims with additional rights against delay. These laws are the subject of the following case, which has two opinions and orders.

United States v. Biggs (I)

2017 WL 5599467 (U.S. Dist. Ct. D. Or)

OPINION AND ORDER

Ann Aiken, United States District Judge

Defendant Donald Courtney Biggs moves to continue the date of his jury trial, which had been set for December 4, 2017. He also moves to exclude the time of the continuance under the Speedy Trial Act. The government opposes the motion to continue. For the reasons set forth below, defendant's motion is granted.

In determining whether a continuance should be granted, I consider (1) defendant's diligence in preparing his case; (2) the likelihood the continuance would serve a useful purpose; (3) whether the continuance would inconvenience the parties, the court, or other witnesses; and (4) whether defendant would be prejudiced by the denial of a continuance. United States v. Mejia, 69 F.3d 309, 314 (9th Cir. 1995). I also bear in mind that, under the Crime Victims' Rights Act, victims have "the right to proceedings free from unreasonable delay," 18 U.S.C. § 3771(a)(7).

Defense counsel, Terry Kolkey, was appointed to represent defendant on May 9, 2017. He is the third appointed counsel to represent defendant in this matter.

Beginning in mid–August, Mr. Kolkey and Assistant United States Attorneys Amy Potter and Pamela Paaso engaged in substantial plea negotiations. All parties apparently believed a plea agreement was likely, as they joined in a September 28 motion to continue pretrial filing deadlines so they could focus on continuing negotiations. I granted that motion, keeping the December 4 trial date but continuing the pretrial conference to November 28, with pretrial filings due November 8.1

At the end of October, Ms. Potter and Ms. Paaso made an offer to defendant. That offer had been approved by their direct supervisor, but remained subject to final confirmation by a supervisor higher up the chain of command. The parties proceeded as though that approval would go through, discussing a date for a plea hearing and proposing statements of offense conduct for the plea agreement. On October 30, Mr. Kolkey learned that the supervisor had declined approval of the plea offer and that the case would be proceeding to trial.

Neither the government nor defendant was prepared for this turn of events, as demonstrated by their November 6 joint motion to extend the pretrial filing deadline to November 20. They disagreed, however, on whether to continue the trial date as well; Mr. Kolkey asserted he needed ninety additional days to prepare, while the government insisted the trial should continue as scheduled:

The fact that Mr. Kolkey needs ninety days to prepare for trial does not demonstrate a lack of diligence. After familiarizing himself with the law and facts at issue in this case, Mr. Kolkey reasonably directed his efforts toward plea negotiations. The government maintains that the December 4 trial date always remained on the table and that Mr. Kolkey should have been preparing for trial during plea negotiations. But as a practical matter, that is simply not how criminal lawyers tend to approach cases. Moreover, the government's suggestion that Mr. Kolkey should have been simultaneously preparing for trial and engaging in negotiations is undercut by the fact that the government was not ready with pretrial filings on the previously-scheduled deadline. Importantly, Mr. Kolkey is defendant's third attorney and has only been appointed on this case for six months; the United States Attorney's Office, by contrast, has been involved in the case for more than two years. Based on the facts outlined above, I find that defendant has been diligent in preparing his case, that the continuance serves the useful purpose of ensuring defense counsel is adequately prepared for trial, and that defendant could be prejudiced if I denied the continuance.

The victims' right to have the case resolved in a reasonable timeframe weighs against granting the request for a continuance. In addition, this continuance inconveniences the Court and it undoubtedly also inconveniences the government. But those factors, while important considerations, do not outweigh the defendant's right to due process. A defendant has a right to an attorney who is prepared for trial and it is the rare court-appointed counsel who would have the resources to mount full-scale trial preparation when he reasonably believes the parties have reached a pretrial resolution. To avoid similar last-minute continuances in the future, the United States

Attorney's Office should involve supervisors possessing final approval at an earlier stage in the plea negotiation process.

The parties' joint motion for extension of time to file trial documents (doc. 63) is GRANTED and defendant's motion to continue trial (doc. 66) is GRANTED. Trial is continued eighty-four days and reset for February 26, 2018. Defendant stated at the November 13, 2017 telephonic status conference that he is waiving his rights under the Speedy Trial Act for the period of the continuance. Accordingly and in the interests of justice, the time from December 5, 2017 to March 5, 2018 is excluded under the Speedy Trial Act. I have given due consideration to the victims' rights to a speedy resolution of this matter, but find that a continuance is necessary for the reasons set forth above.

IT IS SO ORDERED.

United States v. Biggs (II)

2018 WL 785864 (U.S. Dist. Ct. Or. 2018)

Ann Aiken, United States District Judge

Defendant Donald Courtney Biggs moves to continue the date of his jury trial, which is set for February 26, 2018. The government opposes the motion to continue. I denied the motion orally following the February 7, 2018, telephonic hearing on the motion. This opinion and order further explains the reasons behind that denial.

In determining whether a continuance should be granted, I consider (1) defendant's diligence in preparing his case; (2) the likelihood the continuance would serve a useful purpose; whether the continuance would inconvenience the parties, the court, or other witnesses; and whether defendant would be prejudiced by the denial of a continuance. *United States v. Mejia*, 69 F.3d 309, 314 (9th Cir. 1995). I also bear in mind that child victims and witnesses have general and special rights to reasonably prompt judicial proceedings under federal law.

I have carefully considered the relevant factors and conclude that a continuance is not warranted. The first factor favors a continuance, as defendant, through defense counsel Terry Kolkey, has been diligent in preparing his case.

Turning to the second factor, the nature of this case and the fact that Mr. Kolkey's trial preparation only began in earnest in November (after the parties' plea agreement fell through) suggest that granting a continuance might serve a useful purpose. However, it appears that a continuance would in fact have limited utility in this case. In his motion, Mr. Kolkey cited three reasons that a continuance was necessary: both he and his expert needed additional time to review the forensic (video) evidence, which until now has been available to him only on-site during limited hours at the Medford Police station; he needed additional time to review documentary evidence and contact witnesses related to out-of-state trips that form the foundation of the interstate travel counts of the indictment, in part because he did not receive the contact information for potential witnesses until February 2, 2018, due to a redaction error; and he needed additional time to review evidence, including 2200 pages of text messages, related to the evidence described in the government's 404(b) notice. In response to the motion and on the record at the telephonic hearing, the government agreed to address those concerns by, among other actions, (1) making the forensic evidence available twenty-four hours a day, seven days a week, both in Medford and in Portland, where the defense expert is located; (2) dismissing the interstate travel charges; and (3) permitting defense counsel to use the government's technology to search the text messages more quickly.

The hearing on the motion convened at 10:30am on February 6. I adjourned the hearing to permit the lawyers to discuss the government's proposed accommodations. When the hearing reconvened at 2:00pm, Mr. Kolkey and the Assistant United States Attorneys explained that they had reached agreements that would substantially narrow the issues to be adjudicated at trial and, consequently, the evidence Mr. Kolkey would have to review and develop before trial. Mr. Kolkey did not withdraw the request for a continuance, but represented to the Court that he believed he could, with diligent preparation, be ready by February 26. In reliance on that representation and in recognition of the government's willingness to take Mr. Kolkey's motion seriously and offer pragmatic solutions, I conclude that any useful purpose served by a continuance would be very limited.

The third factor weighs heavily against a continuance. This case involves minors who the government plans to call as witnesses; the government represents that some of those individuals will graduate from high school this spring, which means that they may no longer live in the area if this case is delayed four to six months, per the request for a continuance. The trial is set to begin more than two and a half years after defendant was indicted in this case. I have already granted one continuance over the government's objection. The government and court staff have rearrangement their schedules and made travel arrangements to be available for a two-week trial. Jury summonses have already issued. In short, a continuance would significantly inconvenience the witnesses, the government, and the Court.

The fourth and most important factor is prejudice to the defendant. I conclude that defendant will not be prejudiced by the denial of the request for a continuance. Although the concerns Mr. Kolkey raised were valid, the government stepped up to meet those concerns; as a result, the scope of disputed issues in this case narrowed considerably, such that Mr. Kolkey stated that he believes he can be ready by February 26. I note that in addition to the accommodations made by the government, the Court has agreed to delay pretrial filing deadlines by two full weeks, with pretrial motions briefing now due to be completed just four days before the pretrial conference. That delay further alleviates the risk of prejudice to defendant by giving Mr. Kolkey more time to review the evidence before filing those motions.

Finally, I note that granting a continuance at this juncture would risk violating the rights of the minor victims and witnesses. Crime victims have "the right to proceedings free from unreasonable delay." 18 U.S.C. § 3771(a)(7). Moreover, because this is a proceeding in which children will be called to give testimony, the government has requested that this case be designated as "of special public importance," pursuant to 18 U.S.C. § 3509(j). Such designation requires the Court to "ensure a speedy trial in order to minimize the length of time the child must endure the stress of involvement with the criminal process." *Id.* I agree with the government that this case is of special public importance and the request for designation is granted. The statutory rights outlined above and the designation of this case as of special importance further weigh against granting a continuance.

Defendant's motion to continue trial (doc. 82) is DENIED. Trial will proceed as scheduled on February 26, 2018.

IT IS SO ORDERED.

Notes

1. The *Biggs* case is a good example of how competing interests are managed by trial courts. For a similar case under the statute providing child victim cases priority in federal court docketing, *see United States v. Broussard*, 767 F. Supp. 1536 (D. Ore. 1991) Issues of scheduling the trial are typically left to the sound discretion of the trial judge. As a result, it is difficult to enforce a right to "speedy" trial, since what is speedy is often in the eye of the beholder. To deal with the problem of the "inherent human tendency to postpone matters," the President's Task Force on Victims of Crime recommended that judges be required to state in writing their reasons for granting any continuance. PRESIDENT'S TASK FORCE ON VICTIMS OF CRIME, FINAL REPORT 75 (1982).

2. In formulating a list of factors a trial court should consider when ruling on a motion for a continuance, the Colorado Supreme Court has included "the victim's position regarding the continuance," noting that this is a "required factor in Colorado if the victims' rights act applies."

People v. Brown, 2014 CO 25, ¶ 24, 322 P.3d 214, 221 (*citing* COLO. REV. STAT. § 24–4.1–303(3), C.R.S. (2013).

3. In *U.S. v. McDaniel*, 411 F.Supp.2d 1323 (D. Utah 2005), the district court denied defendant's motion to replace counsel, because substituting counsel did not certify he would be prepared on the trial date. Lacking such certification, denial of substitution safeguarded the victims right to proceeding free from unreasonable delay under the CVRA.

4. Defendants have a constitutional right to a speedy trial in the Sixth Amendment. To enforce this right in federal cases, the Speedy Trial Act requires that a trial be held within 70 days after the initial appearance of the defendant. The Act contains various exclusions of time—e.g., for consideration of motions, mental examinations of defendants, trials of co-defendants, and the like. *See* 18 U.S.C. §§ 3161 *et seq.* Should a victim's right to a speedy trial be enforced similarly?

5. One commentator has expressed concern over a speedy trial provision for victims contained in the proposed Victims' Rights Amendment to the United States

Constitution (discussed in Chapter 12). The provision would guarantee victims "the right to a final disposition free from unreasonable delay." Contends Professor Mosteller:

> Phrased modestly [this] provision appear[s] to pose little threat to defendants' traditional rights, and if enforced by the courts as limits on defendants' rights, they would be of little concern. However, in the hands of some legislators operating under the popular pressure to act harshly and decisively against criminals, such provisions could pose a real threat to currently understood forms of fairness.

Robert P. Mosteller, *Victims' Rights and the United States Constitution: An Effort to Recast the Battle in Criminal Litigation*, 85 GEORGETOWN L. REV. 691 (1997).

—————

If victims have the right to a speedy *trial*, should they also have the right to a prompt conclusion of other proceedings? Consider the following case, in which a rape victim attempted to obtain a court order forcing a convicted defendant to begin serving his sentence.

Hagen v. Commonwealth

772 N.E.2d 32 (Mass. 2002)

CORDY, J

Debra Hagen appeals from a judgment entered by a single justice of this court denying her petition under G.L. c. 211, § 3. As the victim of a crime, Hagen sought relief from the denial of her motion to revoke the stay of execution of the defendant's sentence in the underlying criminal action which had been entered pending his appeal. Her motion was brought in the Superior Court pursuant to § 3 (*f*) of the "victim's bill of rights," G.L. c. 258B, which provides victims of crime with the "basic and fundamental right [ ] . . . to a prompt disposition of the case in which they are involved." In a memorandum and judgment, the single justice concluded that, "[n]otwithstanding the fact that a stay of execution of the sentence in the underlying criminal action has been in effect since 1988," the victim had no standing to bring a motion to revoke the stay because she is "not a party to the proceedings and she has no judicially-cognizable interest in the prosecution of another." We affirm the judgment of the single justice. We conclude, however, that a victim asserting the right of prompt disposition under the statute should be provided with an opportunity to address the court when that right is jeopardized.

1. *Background.* We review the tortured procedural history in this case. A grand jury returned two indictments charging rape and one indictment charging indecent assault and battery in April, 1987, against James J. Kelly, who was convicted by a jury on all charges in October, 1987. Kelly then collapsed in the courtroom and was taken to a hospital by ambulance. After several delays, Kelly was sentenced in April, 1988, to two concurrent ten-year sentences on the rape convictions and one concurrent

five-year sentence on the indecent assault and battery conviction, to be served at the Massachusetts Correctional Institution at Concord. Execution was stayed pending his release from the hospital.

On April 26, 1988, Kelly filed a motion to stay execution of his sentence pending appeal and a motion for a new trial. The primary ground asserted for a new trial was ineffective assistance of trial counsel. The motion to stay execution of the sentence was allowed in July, 1988, "without prejudice to further consideration of the motion for a stay of execution at the time the motion for a new trial was decided."

In early 1992, Hagen inquired by letter to the court regarding the reason for the delay in the execution of Kelly's sentence. The inquiry was forwarded to the prosecutor who, Hagen maintains, sought her agreement that Kelly be granted a new trial in exchange for his guilty plea and a disposition placing him on probation. Hagen refused, and in May, 1992, Kelly's motion for a new trial was denied.

On May 22, 1992, Kelly filed a notice of appeal from both the judgments of conviction and the denial of the motion for a new trial. The appeal was not processed in the ordinary course: the court reporter did not deliver the one-volume transcript of the hearing on the motion for a new trial to the court clerk until March, 1993; portions of the trial transcript were not delivered to the clerk until September, 1994; and, although the appeal was entered in the Appeals Court in October, 1994, the Appeals Court (after staying the appellate proceedings while the parties attempted to remedy the record deficiencies) vacated the entry of the appeal in April, 1996, as "premature."

During 1996 and early 1997, the parties reportedly sought to reconstruct missing portions of the trial transcript. The record, however, is devoid of any action taken from 1997 through 2000. The Commonwealth represents that this period of inaction on the appeal was discovered during a "routine review" of the prosecution's appellate files in December, 2000. As a result, the Commonwealth filed a motion to revoke the stay of execution of sentence pending appeal in February, 2001.

In May, 2001, Hagen, represented by counsel, filed a motion requesting the court to revoke Kelly's stay of execution of sentence or to issue a warrant directing that Kelly be taken into custody forthwith to begin serving his sentence. Hagen's motion argued that the delay in execution of Kelly's sentence violated her right to a "prompt disposition" under G.L. c. 258B, § 3 (f). The defendant objected to Hagen's motion and her counsel's notice of appearance. A Superior Court judge sustained the defendant's objection "insofar as [Hagen's counsel] seeks to 'appear' for victim and thus confer upon victim 'party' status," but did permit Hagen's counsel to address the court "in connection with victim's thoughts" on the Commonwealth's motion to revoke the stay. The Commonwealth's motion was denied in June, 2001.

Hagen filed a petition in the county court pursuant to G.L. c. 211, § 3, "seek [ing] review of the judge's order . . . [denying her] limited standing to assert the merits of her position and to seek a remedy under [G.L. c.] 258B, § 3 (f) [,] and . . . [review of the judge's order denying] the Commonwealth's revocation motion." The petition requested that the single justice (1) issue an order "directing that the lower court take appropriate steps to cause [Kelly] to begin serving his sentence forthwith"; (2) issue an order "reversing the lower court's order granting a stay of execution in June 2001, which order was issued without explanation or justification"; and (3) "[a]ny other relief deemed appropriate and just." The single justice denied the petition on the ground that Hagen "is not a party to the proceedings and she has no judicially-cognizable interest in the prosecution of another." That denial is now before us.

2. *Discussion.* The discretionary power of review under G.L. c. 211, § 3, is recognized as "extraordinary," and will be available only in "the most exceptional circumstances." *Costarelli v. Commonwealth,* 374 Mass. 677, 679, 373 N.E.2d 1183 (1978). Parties seeking relief under G.L. c. 211, § 3, must demonstrate both violation of their substantive rights and absence of another "adequate or effective avenue of relief." *Victory Distribs., Inc. v. Ayer Div. of the Dist. Court Dep't,* 755 N.E.2d 273 (Mass. 2001). We will not disturb a decision of a single justice on appeal unless there is an abuse of discretion or other clear error of law. *Caggiano v. Commonwealth,* 550 N.E.2d 389 (Mass. 1990). There was no error.

"In 1983, Massachusetts approved a victims' bill of rights, providing crime victims the right to be informed of and participate in criminal prosecutions. *See* G.L. c. 258B, inserted by St. 1983, c. 694, § 2. The statute generally requires the staff of the district attorneys to ensure that victims and witnesses are afforded such rights. *See* G.L. c. 258B, § 3." *Commonwealth v. Bing Sial Liang,* 747 N.E.2d 112 (Mass. 2001). The purpose of § 3, as described by the Legislature in its prefatory language is:

> To provide victims a meaningful role in the criminal justice system, victims and witnesses of crime, or in the event the victim is deceased, the family members of the victim, shall be afforded the following basic and fundamental rights, to the greatest extent possible and subject to appropriation and to available resources, with priority for services to be provided to victims of crimes against the person and crimes where physical injury to a person results. . . .

G.L. c. 258B, § 3.

Hagen contends that the single justice erred in ruling that she had no standing to seek revocation of Kelly's stay of execution. She claims that G.L. c. 258B, § 3 (*f*), confers on her a right to file a motion to revoke the stay of execution because the section requires "a prompt disposition of the case in which [victims] are involved." The deprivation of this right, Hagen maintains, violates her Federal and State constitutional rights to due process.

In enacting G.L. c. 258B, § 3 (*f*), the Legislature clearly intended to confer on victims the right to ensure the prompt trial and, if convicted, the prompt sentencing of the perpetrators of the crimes against them. This intention is apparent from the definition of the term "[d]isposition" set forth in G.L. c. 258B, § 1, as "the sentencing or determination of penalty or punishment to be imposed upon a person convicted of a crime or found delinquent or against whom a finding of sufficient facts for conviction or finding of delinquency is made." We can fairly assume that the Legislature was aware that the appellate process may be time consuming, but that sentences are not normally stayed pending appeal. Implicit in the legislative scheme is the expectation that a sentence lawfully imposed will not be avoided because of some inordinate delay in the processing of the appeal. We conclude that the Legislature sought to assure for victims a prompt disposition within the context of the trial process and do not read § 3 (*f*) to confer on victims the right to secure the prompt disposition of postsentencing proceedings. In the present case, the defendant was tried and sentenced within one year of indictment, and Hagen alleges no delay in that part of the process. The statutory requirement of a "prompt disposition" thus has been satisfied.

Our holding that Hagen lacks standing to file a motion to revoke a postconviction stay of sentence does not imply our approbation of the lengthy delay in the final disposition of this case. The record provides no plausible excuse for a delay of four years in holding the hearing on the defendant's motion for a new trial or a delay of almost nine years between the filing of the notice of appeal and the Commonwealth's motion to revoke the stay of the defendant's sentence pending appeal. If the appeal is not perfected, it is incumbent on the Commonwealth to take some action to resolve the case. The rights of the victim and the public to finality demand more than the Commonwealth has produced here.

Judgment affirmed.

Notes

1. James Kelly claimed to have serious health problems and was even wheeled into court in a wheelchair for one proceeding. But an investigation by the *Boston Herald* a short time later found him well enough to carry out trash from his house, weed his yard, and smoke cigarettes despite heart problems. *See* Jack Sullivan, *Why Is He Free?*, Boston Herald, July 27, 2001.

2. Does it really make sense to give a victim the right to a prompt disposition of a case if the sentencing can be delayed for years afterwards? Consider the following analysis of the Hagen case, penned by noted Harvard Law Professor Laurence Tribe *before* the Massachusetts Supreme Judicial Court held oral argument in the matter:

Laurence H. Tribe, *A Black Hole for Victims' Rights*
Boston Globe, March 29, 2002, at A19

A CASE SET for argument on Monday before the Massachusetts Supreme Judicial Court dramatizes the need to take victims' rights more seriously than we do now—and the fallacy of the argument that victims' rights must come at the expense of defendants' rights or of prosecutorial flexibility.

Over 16 years ago, James Kelly brutally raped Debra Hagen in Leominster. A jury convicted Kelly on two counts of rape and one count of indecent assault and battery, and in April 1988 the trial judge sentenced him to serve two 10-year jail terms and one five-year term, to run concurrently.

Fourteen years have passed; we've lived through recession and boom, two Bush presidencies, the rise of the Internet, and Sept. 11. Through all that time Kelly has yet to serve a single day in jail.

First the court granted him a stay for health reasons. Later in 1988, Kelly filed a new trial motion. The state claims it simply forgot to respond, apparently losing some of the trial transcripts along the way. The case lay dormant until 1992, when Hagen wrote to ask the trial judge for an explanation.

The district attorney's office responded by urging that she be satisfied with a deal that would revoke Kelly's prison sentence and put him on probation. The odds were good that he would receive a new trial, she was told. Kelly was aging rapidly and in poor health. Wouldn't she prefer not to relive the attack by having to take the witness stand? Wouldn't she prefer closure?

In fact, the new trial motion was denied, but the state still did nothing to take Kelly into custody. Hagen — who finally left Massachusetts to avoid crossing paths with her attacker — desperately wanted to put the attack behind her. But consenting to a "get out of jail free" card for a rapist who had served not one day of his sentence provided anything but comfort. And escorting Kelly to prison to begin serving his term while appealing the denial of his new trial motion would have violated none of his rights and imposed no undue burden on the state.

After nine more years of state resistance, Hagen sought relief under the Massachusetts victims' rights statute. One provision said victims "shall be afforded . . . a prompt disposition of the case in which they are involved." But Worcester County District Attorney John Conte calls that nothing more than a suggestive guide and claims that because he represents the people, his word on what constitutes a prompt disposition is final and unreviewable.

In legal jargon, the district attorney's argument is that — despite what the victims' rights statute calls "basic and fundamental rights" — victims lack "standing." They have no power to enforce their rights in the courts. In fact, they have no right to be heard at all. Besides, he adds, the "disposition" in this case occurred more than promptly enough: It was disposed of, as far as he's concerned, when the rapist was sentenced back in 1988.

To put it bluntly, no disinterested reader of the Commonwealth's statutes, which say the victim's rights last "until the final disposition of the charges, including . . . all postconviction . . . [and] appellate proceedings," could possibly find Conte's argument convincing. It's an argument more worthy of Franz Kafka or George Orwell than of a self-respecting law enforcement officer.

One can only hope that the SJC, guided by the light of reason, will let Debra Hagen's voice be heard through her own lawyer, not through her supposed surrogate in the person of the district attorney.

Indeed, this 14-year-long procedural black hole by itself demonstrates a compelling need to empower victims with a meaningful voice in the criminal justice system — through an amendment to the federal Constitution if necessary.

Some questions in this field are doubtless difficult. Exactly what remedy to order for the inexcusable delay in this case remains to be debated. Other questions are painfully simple: "Justice should be denied or delayed to no one," the Magna Charta proclaimed many centuries ago. The SJC should heed those words.

Ours is the Commonwealth that proclaimed, long before our nation's Constitution was written, that its government was one of laws, not men. When its laws assure all citizens that their fundamental rights as victims of crime to a prompt disposition shall be secure, let no man tell them they lack standing to redeem that guarantee. Otherwise, that guarantee will, to quote Justice Jackson, be but "a promise to the ear to be broken to the hope, like a munificent bequest in a pauper's will."

3. On February 4, 2003, his appeals finally exhausted, James Kelly (then 73 years old) was ordered to begin serving his 10-year-sentence. Ms. Hagen's attorney, Wendy Murphy, reported that Hagen was "very emotional" upon learning of the ruling. "She's been dealing with this for 18 years," Murphy said. "This was the day she could close the door. He was a godfatherly figure in her life. He betrayed her trust." *Rapist Ordered to Begin Serving Time*, Boston Globe, Feb. 4, 2003, at B2. Kelly died in prison three months later. *Frail, Elderly Rapist Dies in Prison*, Boston Herald, May 24, 2003.

4. Federal law gives victims the right "to *proceedings* free from unreasonable delay." It includes habeas corpus proceedings. 18 U.S.C. § 3771(a)(7). Utah's speedy trial provision gives victims the right to a prompt *appellate* disposition. *See* Paul Cassell, *Balancing the Scales of Justice: The Case for and the Effects of Utah's Victims' Rights Amendment*, 1994 Utah L. Rev. 1373, 1402 (1994). Would Ms. Hagen's legal arguments have been more successful under federal or Utah law?

5. Delay in post-trial proceedings has been most controversial in death penalty cases. Victim advocates have argued that years and years of delay in carrying out a death sentence caused by repetitive habeas corpus filings is unfair to victims. *See, e.g., Federal Habeas Corpus Reform: Eliminating Prisoners' Abuse of the Judicial Process, Hearing on S. 623 before the Sen. Jud. Comm.*, 104th Cong, 1st Sess. 6 (1995) (statement of Lee Chancellor, Vice President, Citizens for Law and Order) (arguing that habeas reform is necessary in order to "eliminate unnecessary delay and repetitive litigation" and provide "finality of judgment," thereby allowing the families of victims to end their "perpetual agony and pain"). To deal with this issue, the Anti-Terrorism and Effective Death Penalty Act contained limitations on successive federal habeas

corpus filings. Whether these limitations are unfair to prisoners is a matter of debate. *See* Deborah L. Stahlkopf, Note, *A Dark Day for Habeas Corpus: Successive Petitions Under the Anti-Terrorism and Effective Death Penalty Act of 1996*, 40 ARIZ. L. REV. 1115 (1998).

6. A federal district court has held that trial within seven months of charging complied with the CVRA. *U.S. v. Kaufman,* 2005 WL 1868682.

C. Victims' Interests in Venue Decisions

A defendant has a right to have a trial in the area where the crime was alleged to have been committed. For federal crimes, Article III of the Constitution requires that "the Trial of all Crimes, except in Cases of Impeachment shall be by Jury; and such Trial shall be held in the State where the said Crimes shall have been committed. . . ." Of more general application is the Sixth Amendment to the Constitution, which guarantees defendants the right to a trial "by an impartial jury of the State and district wherein the crime shall have been committed. . . ."

Sometimes, however, defendants will argue that pre-trial publicity or bias prevents a trial in the district where the crime was committed and will seek a change of venue. To what extent should courts consider the victim's interest in seeing justice done in their local community when a defendant alleges that his right to a fair trial requires moving the trial? Consider how the federal trial judge weighed these competing interests in the Oklahoma City bombing case.

United States v. McVeigh

918 F. Supp. 1467 (W.D. Oka. 1996)

Memorandum Opinion and Order on Motions for Change of Venue

MATSCH, Chief Judge.*

This criminal proceeding arises from an explosion in Oklahoma City, Oklahoma, on April 19, 1995, at 9:02 a.m. The measurable effects of that event include the deaths of 168 identified men, women and children, injuries to hundreds of other people, the complete destruction of the Alfred P. Murrah Federal Office Building and collateral damage to other buildings, including the United States Courthouse. A damage assessment prepared for the Office of State Finance, The State of Oklahoma, estimated the total incident cost at $651,594,000. The immeasurable effects on the hearts and minds of the people of Oklahoma from the blast and its consequences were thoroughly explored in

---

* Chief Judge Richard P. Matsch, District of Colorado, sitting by designation. [Authors' note: All federal judges in the Western District of Oklahoma had previously recused in the case.]

the hearing on the defendants' motions for a change of venue under Rule 21(a) of the Federal Rules of Criminal Procedure in Oklahoma City on January 30 through February 2, 1996.

Article III of the United States Constitution provides that criminal trials shall be held in the state where such crimes have been committed. The Sixth Amendment of the Constitution provides as follows:

> In all criminal prosecutions, the accused shall enjoy the right to a speedy and public trial, by an impartial jury of the State and district wherein the crime shall have been committed—

The Due Process Clause of the Fifth Amendment of the United States Constitution requires fundamental fairness in the prosecution of federal crimes. The right to an impartial jury in the Sixth Amendment and the fundamental fairness requirement of the Due Process clause will override the place of trial provisions in both Article III and the Sixth Amendment in extraordinary cases. That is the foundation for FED. R. CRIM P. 21(a) providing for a change of venue to protect from prejudice. The rule reads as follows:

> The court upon motion of the defendant shall transfer the proceeding as to that defendant to another district whether or not such district is specified in the defendant's motion if the court is satisfied that there exists in the district where the prosecution is pending so great a prejudice against the defendant that the defendant cannot obtain a fair and impartial trial at any place fixed by law for holding court in that district.

The Notes of Advisory Committee on Rules, published with this rule in 1944, make clear that a change of venue can be granted only on the motion of a defendant since the constitutional requirement for trial in the state and district where the offense was committed under Article III and Amendment VI is a right of the defendant. The filing of the motion waives that right.

The initial question is whether the evidence now before the court shows that there is so great a prejudice against these defendants in the Western District of Oklahoma that they cannot obtain a fair and impartial trial at any place fixed by law for holding court in this district.

Oklahoma City is the principal place for holding court. Judge Alley found that obtaining an impartial jury in Oklahoma City would be "chancy." He designated Lawton, Oklahoma as the place for this trial under the authority of FED. R. CRIM. P. 18 requiring that due regard be given to the convenience of the defendants and the witnesses. The defendants filed objections to that designation. The evidence presented at the hearing on the defendants' Rule 21(a) motion demonstrates that a trial of these charges in Lawton is not practicable. The facilities there are inadequate. It was stipulated that renovations to the courthouse and related facilities would cost at least $1 million dollars. The time needed for construction would delay scheduling the trial.

There is no disagreement among the parties with Judge Alley's concern about a trial in Oklahoma City. The effects of the explosion on that community are so profound and pervasive that no detailed discussion of the evidence is necessary. The motions for change of venue are granted as to the Western District of Oklahoma.

The selection of an alternative venue is within the discretion of the court. The government has suggested transfer to the Northern District of Oklahoma with trial at the restored historic courthouse in Tulsa. Although the defendants argue that they do not have to prove prejudice in that district, the court has considered Tulsa as the presumptive transferee district because of the language of Article III, Sec. 2, cl. 3, and the expressed wishes of many of the victims as revealed in the evidence and the arguments of government counsel.

Although no one has suggested a trial in the Eastern District of Oklahoma, to avoid further controversy the focus of this inquiry is enlarged to consider whether there is so great a prejudice against these defendants in the State of Oklahoma that they cannot obtain a fair and impartial trial anywhere in the state.

Ordinarily, the effects of pre-trial publicity on the pool from which jurors are drawn is determined by a careful and searching voir dire examination. That is the preferred practice in this judicial circuit. *United States v. Pedraza,* 27 F.3d 1515, 1525 (10th Cir.), *cert. denied,* 513 U.S. 941 (1994). Deferment of the venue motions in this case is impracticable and inimical to the public interest in obtaining a just determination of these charges without undue delay. It is apparent that some special precautions and logistical arrangements must be taken in preparation for trial of these charges at any location. The scope and intensity of the public interest necessitates it. The safety of the accused and all trial participants must be considered as well. Moreover, a failed attempt to select a jury would, itself, cause widespread public comment creating additional difficulty in beginning again at another place for trial.

The parties have submitted a large volume of evidence concerning news coverage of the explosion, the rescue effort, the investigations by law enforcement agencies and media sources, the arrests of the defendants, court proceedings and community activities. Extensive print news coverage in Oklahoma City, Tulsa and Lawton has been submitted. Videotapes of local and national telecasts from April 19, 1995, to the date of the motions hearing were admitted and have been reviewed.

As time passed, differences developed in both the volume and focus of the media coverage in Oklahoma compared with local coverage outside of Oklahoma and with national news coverage. These differences were discussed in the testimony of Russell Scott Armstrong, an expert in news media analysis. In the weeks following the explosion, there was less media coverage of the explosion outside of Oklahoma. Developments in the government investigation were reported, but such reports were primarily factual in nature. Oklahoma coverage, in contrast, remained focused on the explosion and its aftermath for a much longer period of time. Television stations conducted their own investigations, interviewing "eyewitnesses" and showing reconstructions and simulations of alleged events. Such "investigative journalism" continued for more than four months after the explosion. Perhaps most significant was the continuing coverage of the victims and their families. The Oklahoma coverage was more personal, providing individual stories of grief and recovery. As late as December 1995, television stations in Oklahoma City and Tulsa were broadcasting special series of individual interviews with family members and people involved in covering the explosion and its aftermath. . . .

The emotional burden of the explosion and its consequences has been intensified by the repeated and heavy emphasis on the innocence of the victims and the impact of their loss on their families. The tragic sense is heightened by the deaths of infants and very young children in the day care center. The horror of that fact has been powerfully portrayed by the symbols of teddy bears and angels displayed everywhere in Oklahoma. They were placed on a Christmas Tree at the State Capitol. The public sympathy for victims is so strong that it has been manifested in the very courthouse where these motions were heard, when on the first day of the hearing a T-shirt was sold bearing the following inscription:

Those Lost Will Never

Leave Our Hearts

Or be Forgotten

April 19, 1995

United States Court

Western District of Oklahoma

The shirt also exhibited the purple ribbon which is a ubiquitous symbol of empathy and unity throughout Oklahoma, even appearing on special license plates.

The intensity of the humanization of the victims in the public mind is in sharp contrast with the prevalent portrayals of the defendants. They have been demonized. The videotape footage and fixed photographs of Timothy McVeigh in Perry have been used regularly in almost all of the television news reports of developments in this case. All of the Oklahoma television markets have been saturated with stories suggesting the defendants are associated with "right wing militia groups." File film shows people in combat fatigues firing military style firearms to illustrate the suggested association. That theme has particularly been emphasized with Terry Nichols and his brother. These films have also been shown in Denver and on national news programs but not with the frequency of the use by broadcast outlets in Oklahoma.

The possible prejudicial impact of this type of publicity is not something measurable by any objective standards. The parties have submitted data from opinion surveys done by qualified experts who have given their opinions about the results and their meaning. The government places heavy reliance on this evidence to support the position that a fair and impartial jury can be selected in the Northern District of Oklahoma for a trial in Tulsa. Such surveys are but crude measures of opinion at the time of the interviews. Human behavior is far less knowable and predictable than chemical reactions or other subjects of study by scientific methodology. There is no laboratory experiment that can come close to duplicating the trial of criminal charges. There are so many variables involved that no two trials can be compared regardless of apparent similarities. That is the very genius of the American jury trial. . . .

Extensive publicity before trial does not, in itself, preclude fairness. In many respects media exposure presents problems not qualitatively different from that experienced in earlier times in small communities where gossip and jurors' personal acquaintances with lawyers, witnesses and even the accused were not uncommon. Properly motivated and carefully instructed jurors can and have exercised the discipline to disregard that kind of prior awareness. Trust in their ability to do so diminishes when the prior exposure is such that it evokes strong emotional responses or such an identification with those directly affected by the conduct at issue that the jurors feel a personal stake in the outcome. That is also true when there is such identification with a community point of view that jurors feel a sense of obligation to reach a result which will find general acceptance in the relevant audience.

The opinion surveys done for this hearing attempted to test the ability of the persons questioned to be fair and impartial jurors. There has been disagreement with some of the questions included in the survey form used by Dr. Donald E. Vinson. The government's response has been that there are no significant differences in the results obtained with those from the defendants' questionnaire. That is the type of dispute of interest in academic circles. What is most important to this court is that the survey forms do not recognize the expanded role of a jury in a death penalty case. The first duty is to determine after hearing all of the evidence in the case, whether the government has proved all of the essential elements of each charge beyond a reasonable doubt. The jury must separate that standard of legal guilt from any opinions concerning probabilities or any notions of moral culpability. The commonly used phrase "presumption of innocence" is not an appropriate or even apt description of the position of an accused in this court. What is more descriptive is whether a juror is ready, willing and able to give a defendant the benefit of a reasonable doubt after careful consideration of all of the evidence admitted at a trial.

If a defendant is found guilty on any of the present charges, the jury will then be required to determine whether death is justified for the offense of conviction after consideration of the mitigating and aggravating factors presented by evidence received at a further hearing.

Because the penalty of death is by its very nature different from all other punishments in that it is final and irrevocable, the issue of prejudice raised by the present motions must include consideration of whether there is a showing of a predilection toward that penalty. Most interesting in this regard is the frequency of the opinions expressed in recent televised interviews of citizens of Oklahoma emphasizing the importance of assuring certainty in a verdict of guilty with an evident implication that upon such a verdict death is the appropriate punishment. It is significant that there is a citizens' movement in Oklahoma to support pending legislation which would sharply limit the reviewability of a death sentence.

Upon all of the evidence presented, this court finds and concludes that there is so great a prejudice against these two defendants in the State of Oklahoma that they cannot obtain a fair and impartial trial at any place fixed by law for holding court in that state. The court also finds and concludes that an appropriate alternative venue is in the District of Colorado.

Denver, Colorado meets all of the criteria that have been cited by past cases as relevant when selecting an alternative venue. *See, e.g., United States v. Tokars,* 839 F.Supp. 1578 (N.D.Ga. 1993); *United States v. Moody,* 762 F.Supp. 1491 (N.D.Ga. 1991). Denver is a large metropolitan community with many community resources. It is readily accessible, being well-served by daily non-stop flights from all relevant cities. The court facilities in Denver are well-suited for accommodating the special needs of this trial. The United States Marshal for the District of Colorado is well equipped to provide adequate security services. A large jury pool is available.

In reaching this ruling, the court is acutely aware of the wishes of the victims of the Oklahoma City explosion to attend this trial and that it will be a hardship for those victims to travel to Denver. The attorneys for the government have earnestly argued that statutory provisions for victims must be considered by the court. The Department of Justice is required to give prescribed care and consideration to those affected by criminal conduct. The United States Attorney for the Western District of Oklahoma has clearly complied with these requirements by providing information and staff assistance and will continue to do so. Assistant United States Attorney K. Lynn Anderson, who heads the Victim Assistant Unit of the United States Attorney's Office, described the Unit's continuing efforts to assist and inform the 2,200 people identified in the Unit's data base. Further, as observed on the record at the hearing, this court has considered the brief filed on behalf of victims as *amicus curiae.* The interests of the victims in being able to attend this trial in Oklahoma are outweighed by the court's obligation to assure that the trial be conducted with fundamental fairness and with due regard for all constitutional requirements.

Upon the foregoing, it is ORDERED that this criminal proceeding is transferred to the United States District Court for the District of Colorado.

Notes

1. Professor Kershen has argued that the trial should have been held in Oklahoma City because that was the community in which the crime occurred. He cites the common law vicinage right to support his argument. Can his argument be squared with the Sixth Amendment, which provides that "[i]n all criminal prosecutions, the accused shall enjoy the right to a speedy and public trial, by an impartial jury of the State and district wherein the crime shall have been

committed. . . ."? For a development of the argument, *see* Drew L. Kershen, *Vicinage*, 29 Okla. L. Rev. 803 (1976).

2. Apart from any Sixth Amendment argument for an individual victim's right to a trial in the local community, can the general public assert such a right? *See* Steven A. Engel, *The Public's Vicinage Right: A Constitutional Argument*, 75 N.Y.U. L. Rev. 1658 (2000) (arguing that the constitutionally-recognized public right of access to a trial implicitly suggests such a right).

3. In *U.S. v. Agri Processors, Inc.*, 2009 WL 221715 (N.D. Iowa Mar. 19, 2009) (slip op), The district court denied a motion to change venue noting that an impartial jury could be seated and "a change of venue might adversely affect the rights of victims to appear at court proceedings."

4. If a change of venue is ordered, should the trial judge consider the race of the victim, as well as the racial composition of the judicial districts involved, in making transfer decisions? Two highly publicized cases involving the prosecution of police officers for using excessive force against minority arrestees have posed this issue. Hispanic police officer William Lozano was prosecuted for manslaughter in connection with the deaths of two African-Americans during a police chase. Four white police officers were prosecuted for the beating of a black motorist, Rodney King. Legal commentary on these cases generally encouraged the idea of considering the race of the defendant *and* the victim in transferring the case. *See, e.g., M. Shanara Gilbert, An Ounce of Prevention: A Constitutional Prescription for Choice of Venue in Racially Sensitive Criminal Cases*, 67 Tul. L. Rev. 1855 (1993); *see also* Laurie Levenson, *Change of Venue and the Rule of the Criminal Jury*, 66 S. Cal. L. Rev. 1533 (1993) (urging consideration of the community's interest in justice without focusing exclusively on racial characteristics).

Would a victim's argument against changing venue to a distant location be strengthened by relying on victims' rights enactments rather than on the vicinage provisions in the Constitution. Relying on the New Jersey Victims' Rights Amendment, a trial judge in New Jersey decided not to change venue to the distant city of Camden in a capital case involving extensive pre-trial publicity. Instead, the trial judge used a "foreign jury"—that is, to use a jury imported from another county that had not been tainted by the publicity. The trial court relied on the hardship to the victim's family in traveling to another city when already coping with their young daughter's death as grounds for this decision. The New Jersey Supreme Court then reviewed the issue, as discussed in the following excerpt.

State v. Timmendequas

737 A.2d 55 (N.J. 1999), *cert. denied*, 534 U.S. 858 (2001)

* * *

Defendant also contends that the trial court improperly considered the impact changing venue to Camden County would have on the victim's family, both financially and emotionally. The Victim's Rights Amendment was approved by New Jersey voters in 1991. That Amendment provides that:

> A victim of a crime shall be treated with fairness, compassion and respect by the criminal justice system. A victim of a crime shall not be denied the right to be present at public judicial proceedings except when . . . the victim is properly sequestered in accordance with the law. . . . A victim of a crime shall be entitled to those rights and remedies as may be provided by the Legislature.

N.J. CONST., art. I, ¶ 22.

Defendant urges the Court to hold that the amendment merely allows victims to attend a trial and no more. Defendant views the Legislature's commitment to victim's rights too narrowly. Over the past decade, both nationwide and in New Jersey, a significant amount of legislation has been passed implementing increased levels of protection for victims of crime. *State of New Jersey in the Interest of J.G., N.S. and J.T.*, 701 A.2d 1260 (N.J. 1997); *State v. Muhammad*, 678 A.2d 164 (N.J. 1996). Specifically, in New Jersey, the Legislature enacted the "Crime Victim's Bill of Rights," N.J.S.A. 52:4B-34 to -38. *Muhammad, supra*, 678 A.2d 164. That amendment marked the culmination of the Legislature's efforts to increase the participation of crime victims in the criminal justice system. *Id.* The purpose of the Victim's Rights Amendment was to "enhance and protect the necessary role of crime victims and witnesses in the criminal justice process. In furtherance of [that goal], the improved treatment of these persons should be assured through the establishment of specific rights." N.J.S.A. 52:4B-35 (1985). One of the enumerated rights guaranteed for victims is "[t]o have inconveniences associated with participation in the criminal justice process minimized to the fullest extent possible." N.J.S.A. 52:4B-36(d).

Giving those words their ordinary meaning, we find that the Crime Victim's Bill of Rights was aimed at preventing the types of hardship argued by the State on behalf of the victim's family. The hardships documented in the Kankas' affidavits are significant. The trip to Camden would add two hours a day to the already substantial period of time spent away from their two young surviving children. The emotional toll of the trial and the financial expense of traveling would greatly add to that burden. Considerations of "fairness" and "respect," *supra*, justify the trial court's decision to balance the very real harms the Kankas would suffer if venue were changed to Camden. We recognize that the trial court also must give due respect to the Constitutional rights of defendant. In reversing the change of venue order, the trial court stated that "[t]he court does not see any diminishment of the defendant's rights . . ." resulting from the decision to empanel a foreign jury.

The court explicitly stated that it was not favoring the rights of the victims over those of defendant. Rather, it was simply taking their concerns into consideration, as it had not done previously. Taking the concerns of the victim's family into account does not constitute error, provided that the constitutional rights of the defendant are not denied or infringed on by that decision. As we find no infringement upon defendant's constitutional rights, we reject this argument.

_____

Notes

1. Defendant Timmendequas was a vicious sexual predator, whose young victim was Megan Kanka — the Megan in "Megan's Law" discussed in Chapter 10 below.

2. The federal rules of criminal procedure now require that the trial court consider the interests of crime victims before granting a defendant's motion to transfer a case. *See United States v. Larsen*, 2014 WL 177411, at *4 (S.D.N.Y. Jan. 16, 2014) ("Rule 21(b), as amended in 2010, expressly 'requires the court to consider the convenience of victims . . . in determining whether to transfer all or part of the proceeding to another district for trial.'").

3. Would a better solution to the change of venue issue be to simply abolish a defendant's right to change venue? *Compare* George P. Fletcher, With Justice for Some: Victims' Rights in Criminal Trials 252 (1995) (calling for abolition of a defendant's right to change venue because it "is, in effect, to accord the defense a whole peremptory challenge against the entire community") *with* Stephen J. Schulhofer, *The Trouble with Trials, The Trouble with Us*, 105 Yale L.J. 825, 843 ("[Fletcher's] analogy [to peremptory challenges] would be apt if either side were permitted to impose a change of venue without giving reasons. In fact, changes of venue are granted only when the prosecution or defense can show that prejudicial publicity will make it extremely difficult to empanel an unbiased jury where the crime occurred.").

_____

D. The Victim's Ability to Obtain Discovery from the Defendant

Victims may have an interest in obtaining discovery from a defendant for various reasons. For example, a victim of fraud may want to learn about where assets were hidden or disposed. A victim of a sexual assault may want to know the HIV status of the defendant. More generally, the victim may just want information about the crime committed against them.

Crime victims generally have no direct way of obtaining discovery from the defendant in the criminal system. *See U.S. v. Sacone*, 2007 WL 451666 (D. Conn. 2007) (CVRA provides no mechanism for a victim to acquire information from a defendant). As a result, victims tend to resort to other devices to obtain discovery. The most common approach is for a victim to file a civil suit and use civil discovery processes.

Two significant practical obstacles stand in the way of obtaining information from criminal defendants through civil suits. The first is the defendant's Fifth Amendment right not to incriminate himself. The defendant asserting a Fifth Amendment right cannot be compelled to answer questions in a civil deposition (although the defendant's failure to answer is admissible evidence in civil case). A second concern is that it is often unwise for a victim to actively pursue a civil claim while the prosecution is pending for several reasons. First, pursuing a civil suit may jeopardize the prosecution of the criminal case by opening the victim up to suggestions she only wants to get money. Second, in filing a civil suit, a victim exposes herself to a civil deposition, a procedure not generally available to the defendant in a criminal action. Third, a separate civil suit may turn out to be largely unnecessary or not cost effective; if the defendant is convicted in a criminal case, the court may order restitution to the victim (as discussed in Chapter 10) without the need for any civil suit. Finally, a criminal conviction may serve as res judicata as to the issue of defendant's liability. By waiting until the criminal case is over, it may be that most civil liability issues are resolved by conviction.

As a result of these practical considerations in the victim's quest for information, the victim generally looks to get information about the defendant from the state, as discussed in the next section.

E. The Victim's Ability to Obtain Discovery from the State

At first blush, it sounds like a simple enough process for the victim to get material from the state. The prosecutor, however, may not want to disclose information to the victim. The prosecutor may be more concerned about winning the criminal case and may conclude that disclosing information will enhance the defense's opportunity to impeach the victim by claiming the victim has conformed her testimony to the reports of others. Apart from a winning a particular case, a prosecutor may have institutional interests to protect. For example, there might be other targets of the investigation which the authorities do not want to reveal or the file may contain information from other agencies provided on a promise of confidentiality.

Despite such concerns, in many cases prosecutors decide to freely provide information to the victim. But when the prosecutor decides to withhold information, the options for a victim are limited. A few states have given victims a right to obtain information about the crime, either by constitutional amendment or by statute:

S.C. CONST., Art. I, § 24

. . . victims of crime have the right to:

. . . have reasonable access after the conclusion of the criminal investigation to all documents relating to the crime against the victim before trial. . . .

OR. REV. STAT. § 135.857 Disclosure to victim; conditions.

In any criminal prosecution arising from an automobile collision in which the defendant is alleged to have been under the influence of alcohol or drugs, the district attorney prosecuting the action shall make available, upon request, to the victim or victims and to their attorney, or to the survivors of the victim or victims and to their attorney, all reports and information disclosed to the defendant pursuant to OR. REV. STAT. 135.805 to 135.873. The reports and information shall be made available at the same time as it is disclosed to the defendant or as soon thereafter as may be practicable after a request is received. The district attorney may impose such conditions as may be reasonable and necessary to prevent the release of the reports and information from interfering with the trial of the defendant. The district attorney may apply to the court for an order requiring any person receiving such reports and information to comply with the conditions of release.

Most states do not have provisions like those in South Carolina or Oregon. In most jurisdictions, criminal laws do not give victims an explicit right to discover from the state. For the victim to obtain information from the state in the face of prosecutorial opposition, the victim must often rely on more general provisions, such as the general right to "fairness" analyzed in the following case.

State ex rel. Hilbig v. McDonald
839 S.W.2d 854 (Tex. 1992)

BIERY, Justice.

This is an original proceeding in which the relator, State of Texas through its Bexar County District Attorney, Steve Hilbig, seeks a writ of mandamus requiring the respondent, Honorable Terry McDonald, judge to set aside his order of May 1, 1992, entitled "Order Granting Production of Statement of Loniel Thomas Bell to the Texas Department of Human Services, entered in cause number 92-CR-1897, The State of Texas v. Loniel Thomas Bell." Pursuant to our order of June 12, 1992, we have conditionally granted the writ.

Bell has been indicted for aggravated sexual assault. On behalf of the alleged child victim and the victim's parents, an attorney filed an application for disclosure of documents from the district attorney's files for use in a civil suit which may be filed. The trial court granted the application in the May 1st order.

The State does not have an adequate remedy by appeal because the order is not one from which the State may appeal. TEX. CODE CRIM. PROC. ANN. art. 44.01 (Vernon Supp. 1992).

The State maintains the trial court did not have authority to issue the order because the victim lacked standing to act, in effect, as a party. *State ex rel. Wade v. Stephens,*

724 S.W.2d 141, 144 (Tex. App. Dallas 1987, orig. proceeding); TEX. CONST. art. I, § 30(e); TEX. CODE CRIM. PROC. ANN. art. 56.02(d) (Vernon Supp. 1992). The State also argues that discovery from the district attorney's file is not one of the rights of a crime victim. TEX. CONST. art. I, § 30(a), (b); TEX CODE CRIM. PROC. art. 56.02(a), (b) (Vernon Supp. 1992).

Respondent counters that the victim was asserting constitutionally mandated rights and was not acting as a party. Respondent asserts the victim was entitled to the statement under the right to be treated with fairness and the right to confer with a representative of the prosecutor's office. TEX. CONST. art. I, § 30(a)(1), (b)(3). Additionally, respondent argues that the victim has standing because under TEX. CODE CRIM. PROC. ANN. art. 21.31 (Vernon 1989) the victim is the only one who can request that the defendant be tested for acquired immune deficiency syndrome (AIDS) or human immunodeficiency virus (HIV) infection.

The victim, as a real party in interest, raises arguments in concert with Judge McDonald. The victim stresses the statement is necessary to determine whether to petition the court to have Bell tested for AIDS or HIV infection and that there is a suggestion in the record that Bell may be HIV positive. Additionally, the victim maintains that disclosure of the statement is required by the Texas Open Records Act. TEX. REV. CIV. STAT. ANN. art. 6252-17a (Vernon Supp. 1992).

Bell, also as a real party in interest, contends that disclosure of his statement may serve as a waiver of his rights pertaining to the statement. He further argues that prejudicial pretrial publicity may result, denying him a fair trial.

In this case of first impression, we conclude that a crime victim does not have a constitutional or statutory right to discover evidence regarding the pending criminal case that is contained within the prosecutor's file.

Initially, we hold that the Texas Open Records Act does not control this matter. This is not an Open Records Act case.

The statute and constitutional amendment do not contain any provision expressly giving crime victims the right to discover evidence within the prosecutor's file.

In looking at the intent of the Legislature and people of the State of Texas we have examined the analyses of the two bills.

Article 56.02 was enacted through House Bill 235 of the 69th Legislature, ch. 588, § 1, of the Texas General Session Laws. The bill analysis of the House Committee on Criminal Jurisprudence, attached as Appendix A, describes the purpose of the bill, which created other statutes in addition to article 56.02: "This bill would provide certain rights to victims of sexual assault and bodily injury crimes and to families of victims who have died as a result of criminal offenses. These rights include the right to be informed, to be heard, and to be Protected." HOUSE COMM. ON CRIMINAL JURISPRUDENCE, BILL ANALYSIS, Tex. H.B. 235, 69th Leg., R.S. (1985).

In the House Study Group analysis of HB 235, attached as Appendix B, the digest portion of the report states in part:

Victims would have the right to receive adequate protection from harm and threats arising from cooperation with prosecution efforts; to have the magistrate consider the safety of the victim or his or her family's safety when setting bail; to be informed of relevant court proceedings, criminal-investigation procedures, and general criminal-justice procedures; to provide information to a probation department conducting a presentencing investigation; to receive information concerning victim restitution, to receive payment of medical expenses incurred as a result of sexual assault; to be referred to available social-service agencies; and to be notified of parole proceedings and be given a chance to provide information to the Board of Pardons and Paroles if a parole hearing is held. . . .

HOUSE STUDY GROUP, BILL ANALYSIS, Tex. H.B. 235, 69th Leg., R.S. (1985).

This bill analysis summarizes the arguments of the bill supporters:

For too long, the victims of crime have been left out of the criminal-justice process. They are often regarded as mere witnesses of the state or simply as troublesome spectators. This attitude gives an increasing number of victims and their families the impression the state is more concerned with the rights of the criminal than with those of the victim.

This bill would help restore society's confidence in the legal system by making victims active participants in the criminal-justice process. Under the bill, victims could . . . provide vital information to criminal-justice officials who determine punishment or parole. Now victims often are not even aware that their assailants have been released and are back on the streets.

This bill would cost very little. Any modest burden this bill would place on criminal-justice officials is fully justified. . . .

The constitutional amendment providing for victim's rights was proposed by House Joint Resolution 19 in the 71st Legislative Session. The House Committee on Criminal Jurisprudence bill analysis, attached as Appendix C, sets out the purpose: "CSHJR 19 constitutionally guarantees crime victims certain rights in crucial stages of the criminal justice process and prevents certain appeals based on a victim's presence in a Proceeding." HOUSE COMM. ON CRIMINAL JURISPRUDENCE, BILL ANALYSIS, H.J.R. 19, 71st Leg., R.S. (1989).

The House Research Organization bill analysis of the constitutional amendment, attached as Appendix D, states in the digest portion:

The rights of crime victims would include fair treatment, respect for their dignity and privacy, and reasonable protection from the accused throughout the criminal justice process. Upon request, the crime victim would be notified of court proceedings, allowed to be present at all related court proceedings, unless the court found that the victim's testimony would be "materially affected." The victim would be allowed to confer with the prosecutor's office, receive restitution and receive information about the accused's conviction, sentence, imprisonment and release. . . .

House Research Organization, Bill Analysis, H.J.R. 19, 71st Leg., R.S. (1989).

The summary of the supporters' position set out in this bill analysis states:

> CSHJR 19 and its implementing legislation, HB 197, would signal to criminals that the Legislature and the citizens of Texas are committed to a criminal justice system that firmly guards the rights of those victimized by crime. At times it has seemed that criminals are given rights greater than those of victims; HR 19 is an attempt to correct that balance.
>
> This proposed constitutional amendment, similar to the one enacted in Michigan, would serve to enlighten the public about the purpose and nature of the criminal justice system. When coupled with the Crime Victims' Bill of Rights that was enacted by the 69th Legislature, this amendment and its implementing legislation would finally address the plight of the innocent. Adoption of this proposal was one of the recommendations of the House Select Committee on Sentencing and Recidivism, which said victims need a set of rights in the law analogous to those accorded criminal defendants.
>
> The rights listed in the proposed amendment may seem basic to those unfamiliar with the system — the right to be present at court hearings involving the offense, for instance — but in reality these rights are not guaranteed under the present system. Victims are now sometimes victimized twice — once by the criminal and again by the criminal justice system.
>
> Spelling out victim's rights in the state Bill of Rights would put them on a par with the rights of defendants. However, the provision would also limit a victim's right to interfere with the right of an accused to a fair trial. *Id.*

We do not believe the Legislature intended crime victims to have a right to discover material within the prosecutor's file in a pending criminal matter. The Legislature intended to do away with the problems associated with victims who have been ignored, shunted aside, and kept in the dark by the criminal justice system. This is what is meant by "fairness." The Legislature intended to give victims access to the prosecutor — not to the prosecutor's file. . . .

As we stated in our order of June 12, 1992, we are confident that Judge McDonald will set aside his order in question in this case. The writ of mandamus will issue only if he does not do so.

————————

Notes

1. Leaving victim access up to the state authorities, as done in *Hilbig*, is the law in most states. Thus, absent specific statutes governing the situation, the state's disclosure of the file to the victim will usually be a matter of police and prosecutorial discretion.

2. A recurring issue of access to information is whether victims should have access to a pre-sentence report (PSR) to help prepare an effective victim impact statement

at sentencing. *See generally* Note, *Victim Participation in the Criminal Justice System: In re Kenna and Victim Access to Presentence Reports*, 2007 UTAH L. REV. 235 (2007). Consider the following argument made in favor of giving victims access to PSRs in all federal cases to help implement the victims right to be heard at sentencing under the Crime Victims' Rights Act by giving them the opportunity to address federal sentencing guidelines issues:

> Congress intended the victim's right to be heard to be construed broadly, as Senator Feinstein stated: "The victim of crime, or their counsel, should be able to provide any information, as well as their opinion, directly to the court concerning the . . . sentencing of the accused." It is hard to see how victims can meaningfully provide "any information" that would have a bearing on the sentence without being informed of the Guidelines calculations that likely will drive the sentence and reviewing the document that underlies those calculations.
>
> An independent basis for victims reviewing presentence reports is within the victim's broad right under the CVRA to be "treated with fairness." This right easily encompasses a right of access to relevant parts of the presentence report. The victim's right to fairness gives victims a free-standing right to due process. As Senator Kyl instructed, "Of course, fairness includes the notion of due process. . . . This provision is intended to direct government agencies and employees, whether they are in the executive or judicial branches, to treat victims of crime with the respect they deserve and to afford them due process." Due process principles dictate that victims have the right to be apprised of Guidelines calculations and related issues. The Supreme Court has explained that "[i]t is . . . fundamental that the right to . . . an opportunity to be heard 'must be granted at a meaningful time and in a meaningful manner.'" It is not "meaningful" for victims to make sentencing recommendations without the benefit of knowing what everyone else in that courtroom knows: the recommended Guidelines range and how that range was derived. Congress plainly intended to pass a law establishing "[f]air play for crime victims, meaningful participation of crime victims in the justice system, [and] protection against a government that would take from a crime victim the dignity of due process." In federal sentencing today, meaningful participation means participation regarding Guidelines issues.

Paul G. Cassell, *Recognizing Victims in the Federal Rules of Criminal Procedure: Proposed Amendments in Light of the Crime Victims' Rights Act*, 2005 BYU L. REV. 835, 894–895 (2005).

3. A number of states have given sexual assault victims the right to obtain information about the defendant's HIV status. For example, in a footnote in the *Hilbig* opinion, the Texas Supreme Court stated: "We note that our disposition of this case does not affect the victim's ability to petition the trial court to have the defendant tested for AIDS or HIV infection pursuant to article 21.31 of the Code of Criminal

Procedure." To facilitate a victim's access to HIV information, a minority of states make HIV testing of accused sex offenders mandatory after charges have been filed but before conviction. Most states make testing mandatory following conviction.

4. In one high-profile case concerning enforcement of victims' rights, crime victims have obtained discovery from the government. In *Does v. United States*, 817 F.Supp.2d 1337 (S.D. Fla. 2011), crime victims alleged that the government had concealed a non-prosecution agreement from them in violation of their "right to confer" under the Crime Victims' Rights Act, 18 U.S.C. § 3771. After allowing the case to move forward, the district court also ruled that limited discovery was available to the victims. The Court explained:

> At the August 12, 2011 hearing on this motion, the United States agreed that this Court, under its inherent authority to manage this case, could impose discovery obligations on each party. Because the Court finds that some factual development is necessary to resolve the remaining issues in this case, it will permit Plaintiffs the opportunity to conduct limited discovery in the form of document requests and requests for admissions from the U.S. Attorney's Office. Either party may request additional discovery if necessary.

817 F.Supp.2d at 1344.

Sometimes victims will seek access to information about juvenile offenders. Traditionally, many juvenile proceedings have been confidential to give the offender a chance to reform without the disability of a permanent, public criminal record. Recently, however, many jurisdictions are lifting the veil of secrecy from juvenile offenders. For instance, in *Matter of Falstaff Brewing Corp. re: Narragansett Brewery Fire*, 637 A.2d 1047 (R.I. 1994), the Falstaff Brewing Company attempted to obtain a juvenile's police records relating to a brewery fire. The Company relied on a Rhode Island statute that allowed victims to obtain information about juvenile proceedings for the purpose of filing a civil suit:

R.I. Gen. Laws § 14-1-66

> Application by victim to obtain name of juvenile. — Upon written motion by the victim of a crime or his attorney, the family court may, in its discretion, and upon good cause shown, divulge the name and address of the juvenile accused of committing the crime solely for the purpose of allowing the victim to commence a civil action against the juvenile and/or his parents to recover for damages sustained as a result of said crime. . . .

The Rhode Island Supreme Court concluded that this statute entitled the Company to access not only to the juvenile's name and address, but also to accompanying police reports. The Court recognized the interests of juveniles in confidentiality, but concluded it was outweighed by the rights of victims:

> In conclusion, we note that this opinion does not disregard the legislative intent to afford juveniles the opportunity to enter adulthood free of the

stigmatization that follows criminal offenders. The notoriety that would attach to publication of juvenile offenses could "follow troubled minors throughout their lives and hamper their educational, social, and employment opportunities" and even backfire by conferring "celebrity status . . . with the resulting public recognition acting as a spur to future delinquent behavior." Paul R. Kafoury, *Children Before the Court*, 17 New Eng. J. on Crim. & Civ. Confinement 55, 56 (Winter 1991). We recognize the purpose of fostering juvenile rehabilitation by hiding "youthful errors and 'bury[ing] them in the graveyard of the forgotten past.'" *Smith v. Daily Mail Publishing Co.*, 443 U.S. 97, 107 (1979) (*quoting In re Gault*, 387 U.S. 1, 24–25 (1967)). But critics of a closed juvenile justice system believe that disclosing identities of minors can deter juvenile crime and foster greater responsibility for conduct. Kafoury, *supra*, at 56. They argue that "[v]iolent juvenile crime and serious property offenses . . . [are] particular targets of firm policies favoring exposure of juvenile offenders. This trend appears to be a reflection of a sweeping societal concern with serious juvenile offenses . . . which . . . justify disclosure of the juvenile's identity." *Id.* at 66. *See State of New Jersey in the Interest of B.C.L.*, 413 A.2d 335, 342–43 (N.J. 1980).

We are of the opinion that the legislative intent to allow victims, pursuant to § 14-1-66, to pursue civil actions against juveniles is clear and cannot be ignored. Where the Family Court, in exercise of its discretion, determines as it did in the case before us that good cause has been shown to warrant release of a juvenile's name to a victim for purposes of seeking restitution, we find that § 14-1-66 also authorizes the review of the juvenile's police record by the victim, though not by the general public, as it pertains to the act alleged to have caused damage to the victim. Falstaff shall limit its use of information in the police record solely for purposes of discovery and prosecution in respect to its civil action.

F. Discovery from the Victim

This topic is covered in Chapter 6 on Victim Privacy.

G. Protection from the Defendant

1. Laws of "Reasonable Protection"

Some states and the federal government give victims a right to "reasonable protection" from the offender during the criminal justice process. Several states have such a provision as part of the state constitution.

18 U.S.C. § 3771(a)(1)

A crime victim has the following rights:

The right to be reasonably protected from the accused.

CONN. CONST. amend. XXIX

In all criminal prosecutions, a victim . . . shall have the following rights: . . .

(3) The right to be reasonably protected from the accused throughout the criminal justice process.

ILL. CONST., art. 1 § 8.1(7).

Crime victims . . . shall have the following rights as protected by law: . . .

the right to be reasonably protected from the accused throughout the criminal justice process.

Other states give victims the right to be free from "harassment and abuse."

COLO. REV. STAT. § 24-4.1-302.5

1. In order to preserve and protect a victim's rights to justice and due process, each victim of a crime shall have the following rights:

(a) The right to be treated with fairness, respect, and dignity, and to be free from intimidation, harassment, or abuse, throughout the criminal justice process. . . .

UTAH CONST., art. I, § 28

To preserve and protect victims' rights to justice and due process, victims of crimes have these rights, as defined by law:

(a) To be treated with fairness, respect, and dignity, and to be free from harassment and abuse throughout the criminal justice process.

––––––––––

The legal significance of these general provisions appears to have been limited to judicial proceedings. The provisions appear to extend rights to individual victims, which might be relied upon, for example, in bail, or parole hearings. Moreover, as a statement of government policy, such provisions may provide a foundation for more specific legal protections.

Mary Margaret Giannini, *Redeeming an Empty Promise: Procedural Justice, The Crime Victims' Rights Act, and the Victim's Right to Be Reasonably Protected from the Accused*
78 TENN. L. REV. 47 (2010)

First, the right needs to be re-written in such a way to emphasize the victim's participatory role in the criminal justice process, rather than promising a specific outcome. Hence, the CVRA's statutory language in section 3771(a)(1) should be amended to read: "A crime victim has . . . the right to have the victim's safety considered in determining the defendant's release from custody." Recall that in concert with the CVRA's current grant to victims that they be reasonably protected from the accused, the statute also grants victims the right to reasonable notice of any public court or parole proceeding involving the crime or any release or escape of the accused, the right not to be excluded from any such proceedings, the right to be reasonably heard at any such proceedings, and the right to confer with the attorney for the government on the case. These are all process-based rights, which, when exercised in the context of a court's release consideration hearing for a defendant, would give meaning to a right which seeks to prevent the defendant from causing the victim further harm. If a victim can confer with the government lawyer on the case, and is on notice of upcoming parole or release hearings, the victim can decide whether to exercise the right to be heard at those proceedings. If so, the victim can share safety concerns with the court, which the court can, in turn, consider in making its release decision.

Curiously enough, earlier statutory formulations regarding the victim's right to be reasonably protected from the accused were phrased in terms that focused far more on the victim's safety and role in the process of determining the defendant's release, than on promising a direct right to protection. Two previously proffered versions of the language which eventually appeared in the CVRA read as follows: victims have the right to have "the safety of the victim considered in determining a [defendant's] release from custody[,]" and the victim has the "right to adjudicative decisions that duly consider the victim's safety." Many state laws parallel this type of language. For example, Alaska grants victims the right to protection through the imposition of appropriate bail or conditions of release by the court, as well as the right to be heard at any proceeding where the accused's release from custody is considered. Similarly, Colorado and Florida grant victims the right to information regarding the steps they can take to protect themselves from harassment or harm from the offender, and Indiana and Maryland indicate that victim safety should be considered in the process of determining whether to release the defendant from custody. Therefore, altering the statutory language of the CVRA so that it focuses on considering the victim's safety, rather than making an outright promise of protection, is not unreasonable or unprecedented. Moreover, such an approach furthers the goal of enhancing the victim's appropriate participation in the criminal process. By framing the victim's protection right in terms of victim participation, rather than a specific outcome such as protection, the victim's ability to enforce the right is also more assured.

2. Criminalizing the Failure to Report Crime

For victims to be protected within the criminal justice system, the crime must come to the attention of state authorities. Should victims be protected by requiring that persons who witness a crime must report the crime to the authorities—i.e., making a bystander to violent crime liable for complicity? Consider the following argument in favor of such liability.

Amos N. Guiora, The Crime of Complicity: The Bystander in the Holocaust (2017)

Circumstances and Physicality

Caution is necessary when proposing bystander complicity be codified as a crime. Overreach is dangerous and counterproductive. Codification must focus on the bystander physically positioned to provide assistance to the victim.

The issue of circumstances and physicality is of great importance. That was very clear in the context of the Amsterdam bicycle accident. That incident clearly illustrates both the scope and limit of the proposed legislation; the two—individually and together—define which bystanders would be required to act and which fall outside its proposed range.

Let us carefully examine two contemporary examples. Both cases are deeply disturbing; they have, justifiably, attracted significant media attention and public commentary. Public attention is due, in part, to the fact both are sexual assaults that occurred on college campuses. Understandably, this is an issue that has garnered significant media coverage, forcing college administrators to directly address student conduct.

Outrage has been expressed regarding particular aspects of both cases. That outrage is shared by this writer.

The perpetrators in both cases have had their crimes adjudicated before a court of law; in both cases, the perpetrator was convicted. However, as reprehensible as the criminal conduct was—and it certainly was—the perpetrators are not the focus.

A summary of the facts reads as follows:

Stanford University

Just after 1 a.m. on January 18, 2015, law enforcement officers responded to a report of an unconscious female in a field near the Kappa Alpha fraternity house, according to a sentencing memo.

They found the victim on the ground, in a fetal position, behind a garbage dumpster. She was breathing but unresponsive. Her dress was pulled up to her waist. Her underwear was on the ground; her hair disheveled and covered with pine needles.

About 25 yards away, two men, passersby, had pinned down and restrained a young man who was later identified as (Brock) Turner. "We found him on top of the girl!" one of the men said. Turner smelled of alcohol as he was handcuffed.

One of the men later told authorities that Turner had been on top of the motionless women.

Hey, she's f___ unconscious!" one of the men yelled. Turner managed to get away briefly, but the man tripped and later tackled him. Turner was held down until deputies arrived.

A witness told investigators that the day of the assault "he saw a female subject lying on the ground behind the dumpster . . . He also noticed a male subject standing over her with a cell phone. He was holding the cell phone. The cell phone had a bright light pointed in the direction of the female, using either a flashlight app in his phone or its built-in flash."

According to the probation document, Turner told deputies that he walked away from the frat house with the victim and they kissed.

They ended up on the ground, where he removed the victim's underwear and digitally penetrated her for about five minutes, Turner told deputies. "He denied taking his pants off and said his penis was never exposed."

Vanderbilt University

On June 22, 2013, a woman met up with Brandon Vandenburg at a popular bar near Vanderbilt University. She could not remember a period of hours between sipping a blue drink Vandenburg gave her at the bar and waking up in his bed, alone and in the worst pain she's felt, at 8 a.m. the next day, she said.

He told her that she had gotten drunk and he had taken care of her, and that she had consented to having sex with him. Three days later the woman discovered the devastating truth.

That was the day the woman went to get a three-hour medical exam known as a rape kit. Detectives convinced her to go after seeing surveillance video of her being carried into Vandenburg's dorm, unconscious.

Vandenburg's cell phone showed Internet searches in that same time period, including "can police recover deleted picture messages." One Officer Gish found the deleted pictures and videos of the rape about a week later.

They showed, according to a trial testimony:

Vandenburg carried her unconscious body into his room at Gillette Hall about 2:30 a.m. June 23, 2013, asking three teammates he ran into for help. They put her on the floor and at least two of them penetrated her with their fingers and one sat on her face, raising his middle finger for a photograph, according to trial testimony.

Vandenburg could not get an erection, so he watched pornography on his laptop.

He tried to wake up his roommate on the top bunk saying, "we have this b—in here" and "we're gonna f—her."

Vandenburg sent videos to four friends and destroyed condoms. The man she trusted giggled and goaded his teammate, "squeeze that s—," referring to a bottle in her anus.

The Complicity and Culpability of the Bystander (aka, How to Succeed in Rape Culture Without Trying)

The two perpetrators, Brock Turner (Stanford) and Brandon Vandenburg (Vanderbilt), are beyond the scope of our inquiry.

Similarly, the public discussion regarding the rape, drinking, "hook up," and "macho-masculine" athletic culture at U.S. colleges is left to others.

Our sole focus is assessing the *complicity and culpability* of the bystander.

To do so requires examining in detail the decisions of the three bystanders — two at Stanford, one at Vanderbilt. As previously noted, *both action and nonaction reflect a conscious, knowing decision.*

The question is whether the decision is punishable.

Stanford

Two individuals riding their bicycles noticed at 1 a.m. a man on top of a woman behind a dumpster on a path on the Stanford campus. Their attention was drawn by her seeming unconsciousness. When they called out to the male, he ran; they gave chase, pinned him down and called law enforcement.

The question before us is whether they would be culpable — in accordance with how I define bystander complicity — for not intervening on her behalf.

Stanford Bystander

The hour was late, the bystanders were riding bicycles and intimacy on college campuses is a reality. This particular location was not known to be a common "coupling" location.

Vanderbilt

The victim was brought by Vandenburg to his dormitory room when she was unconscious; she was repeatedly raped and sodomized. Vandenburg was unable to engage in sexual intercourse because of his drunken condition; however, he encouraged others to rape the victim, recorded the crime, and shared the video with others.

Vanderbilt Bystander

The bystander, a fellow football player, pretended to be asleep on the upper bunk while the victim was raped, sodomized, and otherwise violated for over thirty minutes, by his roommate and others. The bystander, Mack Prioleau, pretended to be asleep as the rape occurred just a few feet away: He testified that he knew exactly what was going on but failed to intervene because the situation "made him uncomfortable." Apparently, when faced with the choice to either have an uncomfortable conversation with his roommate, or enable a violent rape, the bystander chose the latter. At some point later in the night, he left the room and went to another room in the dormitory.

After the rape, the bystander again chose not to help the victim; during his testimony, he admitted to helping cover up the crime by texting another member of the football team, telling him to "keep his mouth shut" about the rape. The next day, the bystander mopped the victim's vomit off the floor. At no point did the bystander call the police, call for an ambulance, or check on the victim's well-being.

The bystander was not the rapist — but his choice of inaction demonstrates a vicious passivity, where doing mothering is the preferred path of least resistance. Mr. Prioleau was not charged with any crime, nor was he suspended from the university.

The Vanderbilt bystander manifests the consequences of nonintervention and demonstrates why it is appropriate and just to impose criminal liability. There is no doubt Mr. Prioleau had every opportunity to act on behalf of the victim; nevertheless, he made the conscious decision not to do so.

The choice not to act was an unequivocal decision Mr. Prioleau made; in deliberately choosing nonaction, he consciously facilitated the perpetrators' conduct and deliberately placed the victim in greater danger.

The fact Tennessee authorities chose not to prosecute him reflects the failure of the legislature to protect victims. What, after all, is at the core of bystander complicity legislation if not an additional, and much needed, mechanism whereby *victims* can be protected.

Based on the bicycle accident, I would suggest the following:

1. Had the two bicyclists not intervened, they would not be liable for the crime of nonintervention. Given the late hour it was difficult to see, they were riding their bicycles which affects ability to perceive events, and the activity the victim and assailant were engaged in was not "out of place" on a college campus, though the specific location was not considered common for "hook ups."

2. The roommate is the "poster child" for the legislation I am recommending: He was well aware of her physical condition, he was fully awake and fully capable of either expressing strong disapproval regarding the rape or alerting the authorities in any number of different ways. He chose to do nothing. For the consequences and harm to the victim, in this particular case, the bystander must bear liability.

A Duty to Aid a Victim or Report a Crime

California and Tennessee, the states where these crimes took place, both lack duty-to-assist laws that might have proved critical in both deterring the vicious passivity represented by the Vanderbilt bystander, and encouraging and protecting the behavior of the bystanders at Stanford. That additional protection would be the requirement imposed on bystanders to intervene.

Few states currently have duty-to-intervene statutes. Two states that do, Minnesota and Wisconsin, illuminate the positive role the legislature can and must play in addressing bystander complicity.

Subdivision 1 of Minnesota Statute 604A.01, reads as follows:

Duty to assist.

> *A person at the scene of an emergency who knows that another person is exposed to or has suffered grave physical harm shall, to the extent that the person can do so without danger or peril to self or others, give reasonable assistance to the exposed person. Reasonable assistance may include obtaining or attempting to obtain aid from law enforcement or medical personnel. A person who violates this subdivision is guilty of a petty misdemeanor.*

Wisconsin Statute 940.34, Duty to aid victim or report crime, includes the following provision:

(1)(a) Whoever violates sub. (2)(a) is guilty of a Class C misdemeanor.

(2)(a) Any person who knows that a crime is being committed and that a victim is exposed to bodily harm shall summon law enforcement officers or other assistance or shall provide assistance to the victim.

Had California or Tennessee adopted and enforced duty-to-act statutes such as these, the bystander in the Vanderbilt case would have been found guilty of an actual crime. This scenario is not as daunting as it might seemingly be on its face. Currently, every state has mandatory child-abuse reporting laws that help protect children by obligating non-offending adults to file a report if they have "reasonable grounds" to believe that a child is being abused or neglected.

In other words, a person is obligated to report with a protective-service agency if there is a suspicion of abuse. Duty-to-intervene laws demand much the same as child-abuse reporting laws, with an even easier standard to follow — intervening is a legal duty when one *knows* firsthand that a person is being brutally victimized.

A recommended statute would read as follows:

Any person at the scene of an emergency who knows that another person is exposed to or has suffered grave physical harm shall, to the extent that the person can do so without danger or peril to self or others, give reasonable assistance to the exposed person. Reasonable assistance may include obtaining or attempting to obtain aid from law enforcement or medical personnel. A person who violates this section shall be fined not more than $500.

The statute might also impose a criminal record. However, limits are necessary in drafting such statutes because it would be self-defeating to recommend unfeasible and impractical legislation.

Notes

1. Professor Guiora proposes that bystanders should have a duty to aid a crime victim. Would it be more appropriate to require a limited duty to report a crime being committed against a crime victim? *See generally* Jack Wenik, *Forcing Bystanders to Get Involved: The Case for Statute Requiring Witnesses to Report Crime*, 94 YALE L.J. 1787 (1985).

2. Responding to a notorious case in which one man raped and killed a young girl inside of a bathroom while another man — a bystander named David Cash — stood idly by, the Nevada legislature passed a statute requiring, with limited exceptions, "a person who knows or has reasonable cause to believe that another person has committed a violent or sexual offense against a child who is 12 years of age or younger" to report that offense to a law enforcement agency as "as soon as reasonably practicable but not later than 24 hours after the person knows or has reasonable cause to believe

that the other person has committed the violent or sexual offense against the child." Nev. Rev. Stat. § 202.822. Failure to comply is a misdemeanor offense.

3. Is a criminal sanction the only sanction available for those, like David Cash, who fail to report a crime? According to press reports, David Cash initially got media attention from the incident, a fact that (he claimed) helped him get dates at the University of California at Berkeley, where he was a student. After a while, however, negative graffiti appeared around campus, his dorm mates shunned him, and the student legislature voted to urge him to withdraw. Relying on these facts, commentator Doug Bandow notes: "Some people demanded that the government find a way to prosecute him. Yet not everything that is immoral should be illegal. The state has a duty to punish those who harm others; it is not, in contrast, well-equipped to make people moral. In a case like this, government shouldn't try to do so." Doug Bandow, *Where the Law Does Not Reach*, Wash. Times, Feb. 17, 2000, at A16.

4. If a statute requires reporting of crimes, should a rape victim's omission of non-reporting be categorized as criminal behavior? Or should such a victim have the ability not to report as part of her individual autonomy?

5. Virtually every state has passed some kind of child protection act. These acts require reporting of suspected incidents of child abuse to the appropriate authorities. Most of these statutes apply only to those directly involved in child care—e.g., teachers, social workers, doctors, and nurses. Failure to report in many cases results in criminal penalties. *See, e.g.*, Cal. Penal Code § 11166; N.Y. Soc. Serv. Law § 413. A significant minority of states have passed statutes that impose a duty of mandatory reporting on any person who has reason to suspect that a child is being neglected or abused. *See, e.g.*, Del. Code Ann. Tit. 16, § 903; N.J. Stat. Ann. § 9:6-8.10.

Is there justification for restricting these statutes to professionals (e.g., teachers and social workers)? Does the special vulnerability of child victims justify restricting these statutes to crimes against children? What about elder abuse?

6. Would criminal sanctions for failing to report a crime actually discourage reporting in some situations? Professor Eugene Volokh argues that sanctions might disincentivize "delayed Samaritans" (those who initially do not report a crime but later change their minds) and "passive Samaritans" (those who do not report a crime until the police seek them out). Eugene Volokh, *Duties to Rescue and the Anticooperative Effects of Law*, 88 Geo. L.J. 105 (1999).

3. Pretrial Release and Future Dangerousness

The federal government and a minority of states have provisions allowing the denial of a defendant's request for pretrial release if the defendant poses a danger to the community or the individual victim. Most state laws continue to reflect the traditional view that the only basis for denying bail in noncapital cases is whether the defendant is likely to flee the court's jurisdiction.

United States v. Salerno

481 U.S. 739 (1987)

CHIEF JUSTICE REHNQUIST delivered the opinion of the Court.

Responding to "the alarming problem of crimes committed by persons on release," Congress formulated the Bail Reform Act of 1984 as the solution to a bail crisis in the federal courts. The Act represents the National Legislature's considered response to numerous perceived deficiencies in the federal bail process. By providing for sweeping changes in both the way federal courts consider bail applications and the circumstances under which bail is granted, Congress hoped to "give the courts adequate authority to make release decisions that give appropriate recognition to the danger a person may pose to others if released." S. Rep. No. 98-225, at 3.

To this end, . . . the Act requires a judicial officer to determine whether an arrestee shall be detained. Section 3142(e) provides that "[i]f, after a hearing pursuant to the provisions of subsection (f), the judicial officer finds that no condition or combination of conditions will reasonably assure the appearance of the person as required and the safety of any other person and the community, he shall order the detention of the person prior to trial." Section 3142(f) provides the arrestee with a number of procedural safeguards. He may request the presence of counsel at the detention hearing, he may testify and present witnesses in his behalf, as well as proffer evidence, and he may cross-examine other witnesses appearing at the hearing. If the judicial officer finds that no conditions of pretrial release can reasonably assure the safety of other persons and the community, he must state his findings of fact in writing, § 3142(i), and support his conclusion with "clear and convincing evidence," § 3142(f).

The judicial officer is not given unbridled discretion in making the detention determination. Congress has specified the considerations relevant to that decision. These factors include the nature and seriousness of the charges, the substantiality of the Government's evidence against the arrestee, the arrestee's background and characteristics, and the nature and seriousness of the danger posed by the suspect's release. Should a judicial officer order detention, the detainee is entitled to expedited appellate review of the detention order.

Respondents Anthony Salerno and Vincent Cafaro were arrested on March 21, 1986, after being charged in a 29-count indictment alleging various Racketeer Influenced and Corrupt Organizations Act (RICO) violations, mail and wire fraud offenses, extortion, and various criminal gambling violations. The RICO counts alleged 35 acts of racketeering activity, including fraud, extortion, gambling, and conspiracy to commit murder. At respondents' arraignment, the Government moved to have Salerno and Cafaro detained pursuant to § 3142(e), on the ground that no condition of release would assure the safety of the community or any person. The District Court held a hearing at which the Government made a detailed proffer of evidence. The Government's case showed that Salerno was the "boss" of the Genovese Crime Family of La Cosa Nostra and that Cafaro was a "captain" in the

Genovese Family. According to the Government's proffer, based in large part on conversations intercepted by a court-ordered wiretap, the two respondents had participated in wide-ranging conspiracies to aid their illegitimate enterprises through violent means. The Government also offered the testimony of two of its trial witnesses, who would assert that Salerno personally participated in two murder conspiracies. Salerno opposed the motion for detention, challenging the credibility of the Government's witnesses. He offered the testimony of several character witnesses as well as a letter from his doctor stating that he was suffering from a serious medical condition. Cafaro presented no evidence at the hearing, but instead characterized the wiretap conversations as merely "tough talk."

The District Court granted the Government's detention motion, concluding that the Government had established by clear and convincing evidence that no condition or combination of conditions of release would ensure the safety of the community or any person:

> The activities of a criminal organization such as the Genovese Family do not cease with the arrest of its principals and their release on even the most stringent of bail conditions. The illegal businesses, in place for many years, require constant attention and protection, or they will fail. Under these circumstances, this court recognizes a strong incentive on the part of its leadership to continue business as usual. When business as usual involves threats, beatings, and murder, the present danger such people pose in the community is self-evident.

631 F. Supp. 1364, 1375 (SDNY 1986).

Respondents appealed, contending that to the extent that the Bail Reform Act permits pretrial detention on the ground that the arrestee is likely to commit future crimes, it is unconstitutional on its face. . . .

II

A facial challenge to a legislative Act is, of course, the most difficult challenge to mount successfully, since the challenger must establish that no set of circumstances exists under which the Act would be valid. The fact that the Bail Reform Act might operate unconstitutionally under some conceivable set of circumstances is insufficient to render it wholly invalid, since we have not recognized an "overbreadth" doctrine outside the limited context of the First Amendment. *Schall v. Martin, supra*, at 269, n.18. We think respondents have failed to shoulder their heavy burden to demonstrate that the Act is "facially" unconstitutional.[38]

Respondents present two grounds for invalidating the Bail Reform Act's provisions permitting pretrial detention on the basis of future dangerousness. First, they

---

38. We intimate no view on the validity of any aspects of the Act that are not relevant to respondents' case. Nor have respondents claimed that the Act is unconstitutional because of the way it was applied to the particular facts of their case.

rely upon the Court of Appeals' conclusion that the Act exceeds the limitations placed upon the Federal Government by the Due Process Clause of the Fifth Amendment. Second, they contend that the Act contravenes the Eighth Amendment's proscription against excessive bail. We treat these contentions in turn.

A

The Due Process Clause of the Fifth Amendment provides that "No person shall . . . be deprived of life, liberty, or property, without due process of law. . . ." This Court has held that the Due Process Clause protects individuals against two types of government action. So-called "substantive due process" prevents the government from engaging in conduct that "shocks the conscience," *Rochin v. California*, 342 U.S. 165, 172 (1952), or interferes with rights "implicit in the concept of ordered liberty," *Palko v. Connecticut*, 302 U.S. 319, 325–326 (1937). When government action depriving a person of life, liberty, or property survives substantive due process scrutiny, it must still be implemented in a fair manner. *Mathews v. Eldridge*, 424 U.S. 319, 335 (1976). This requirement has traditionally been referred to as "procedural" due process.

Respondents first argue that the Act violates substantive due process because the pretrial detention it authorizes constitutes impermissible punishment before trial. *See Bell v. Wolfish*, 441 U.S. 520, 535, and n.16 (1979). The Government, however, has never argued that pretrial detention could be upheld if it were "punishment." The Court of Appeals assumed that pretrial detention under the Bail Reform Act is regulatory, not penal, and we agree that it is.

As an initial matter, the mere fact that a person is detained does not inexorably lead to the conclusion that the government has imposed punishment. *Bell v. Wolfish, supra*, at 537. To determine whether a restriction on liberty constitutes impermissible punishment or permissible regulation, we first look to legislative intent. *Schall v. Martin*, 467 U.S., at 269. Unless Congress expressly intended to impose punitive restrictions, the punitive/regulatory distinction turns on "'whether an alternative purpose to which [the restriction] may rationally be connected is assignable for it, and whether it appears excessive in relation to the alternative purpose assigned [to it].'" *Id.*, quoting *Kennedy v. Mendoza-Martinez*, 372 U.S. 144, 168–169 (1963).

We conclude that the detention imposed by the Act falls on the regulatory side of the dichotomy. The legislative history of the Bail Reform Act clearly indicates that Congress did not formulate the pretrial detention provisions as punishment for dangerous individuals. Congress instead perceived pretrial detention as a potential solution to a pressing societal problem. There is no doubt that preventing danger to the community is a legitimate regulatory goal.

Nor are the incidents of pretrial detention excessive in relation to the regulatory goal Congress sought to achieve. The Bail Reform Act carefully limits the circumstances under which detention may be sought to the most serious of crimes. *See* 18 U.S.C. § 3142(f) (detention hearings available if case involves crimes of violence, offenses for which the sentence is life imprisonment or death, serious drug offenses, or certain repeat offenders). The arrestee is entitled to a prompt detention hearing, . . .

and the maximum length of pretrial detention is limited by the stringent time limitations of the Speedy Trial Act. Moreover, the conditions of confinement envisioned by the Act "appear to reflect the regulatory purposes relied upon by the" Government. . . . [T]he statute at issue here requires that detainees be housed in a "facility separate, to the extent practicable, from persons awaiting or serving sentences or being held in custody pending appeal." We conclude, therefore, that the pretrial detention contemplated by the Bail Reform Act is regulatory in nature, and does not constitute punishment before trial in violation of the Due Process Clause.

The Court of Appeals nevertheless concluded that "the Due Process Clause prohibits pretrial detention on the ground of danger to the community as a regulatory measure, without regard to the duration of the detention." Respondents characterize the Due Process Clause as erecting an impenetrable "wall" in this area that "no governmental interest rational, important, compelling or otherwise may surmount."

We do not think the Clause lays down any such categorical imperative. We have repeatedly held that the Government's regulatory interest in community safety can, in appropriate circumstances, outweigh an individual's liberty interest. For example, in times of war or insurrection, when society's interest is at its peak, the Government may detain individuals whom the Government believes to be dangerous. *See Luedecke v. Watkins*, 335 U.S. 160 (1948) (approving unreviewable executive power to detain enemy aliens in time of war); *Moyer v. Peabody*, 212 U.S. 78, 84–85 (1909) (rejecting due process claim of individual jailed without probable cause by Governor in time of insurrection). Even outside the exigencies of war, we have found that sufficiently compelling governmental interests can justify detention of dangerous persons. Thus, we have found no absolute constitutional barrier to detention of potentially dangerous resident aliens pending deportation proceedings. We have also held that the government may detain mentally unstable individuals who present a danger to the public, *Addington v. Texas*, 441 U.S. 418 (1979), and dangerous defendants who become incompetent to stand trial, *Jackson v. Indiana*, 406 U.S. 715, 731–739 (1972); *Greenwood v. United States*, 350 U.S. 366 (1956). We have approved of post-arrest regulatory detention of juveniles when they present a continuing danger to the community. Even competent adults may face substantial liberty restrictions as a result of the operation of our criminal justice system. If the police suspect an individual of a crime, they may arrest and hold him until a neutral magistrate determines whether probable cause exists. *Gerstein v. Pugh*, 420 U.S. 103 (1975). Finally, respondents concede and the Court of Appeals noted that an arrestee may be incarcerated until trial if he presents a risk of flight, . . . or a danger to witnesses.

Respondents characterize all of these cases as exceptions to the "general rule" of substantive due process that the government may not detain a person prior to a judgment of guilty in a criminal trial. Such a "general rule" may freely be conceded, but we think that these cases show a sufficient number of exceptions to the rule that the congressional action challenged here can hardly be characterized as totally novel. Given the well-established authority of the government, in special circumstances, to restrain individuals' liberty prior to or even without criminal trial and conviction, we think that the present statute providing for pretrial detention on the basis of dangerousness must be evaluated in precisely the same manner that we evaluated the laws in the cases discussed above.

The government's interest in preventing crime by arrestees is both legitimate and compelling. In *Schall,* we recognized the strength of the State's interest in preventing juvenile crime. This general concern with crime prevention is no less compelling when the suspects are adults. Indeed, "[t]he harm suffered by the victim of a crime is not dependent upon the age of the perpetrator." *Schall v. Martin,* 467 U.S., at 264–265. The Bail Reform Act of 1984 responds to an even more particularized governmental interest than the interest we sustained in *Schall.* The statute we upheld in *Schall* permitted pretrial detention of any juvenile arrested on any charge after a showing that the individual might commit some undefined further crimes. The Bail Reform Act, in contrast, narrowly focuses on a particularly acute problem in which the Government interests are overwhelming. The Act operates only on individuals who have been arrested for a specific category of extremely serious offenses. Congress specifically found that these individuals are far more likely to be responsible for dangerous acts in the community after arrest. Nor is the Act by any means a scattershot attempt to incapacitate those who are merely suspected of these serious crimes. The Government must first of all demonstrate probable cause to believe that the charged crime has been committed by the arrestee, but that is not enough. In a full-blown adversary hearing, the Government must convince a neutral decisionmaker by clear and convincing evidence that no conditions of release can reasonably assure the safety of the community or any person. While the Government's general interest in preventing crime is compelling, even this interest is heightened when the Government musters convincing proof that the arrestee, already indicted or held to answer for a serious crime, presents a demonstrable danger to the community. Under these narrow circumstances, society's interest in crime prevention is at its greatest.

On the other side of the scale, of course, is the individual's strong interest in liberty. We do not minimize the importance and fundamental nature of this right. But, as our cases hold, this right may, in circumstances where the government's interest is sufficiently weighty, be subordinated to the greater needs of society. We think that Congress' careful delineation of the circumstances under which detention will be permitted satisfies this standard. When the Government proves by clear and convincing evidence that an arrestee presents an identified and articulable threat to an individual or the community, we believe that, consistent with the Due Process Clause, a court may disable the arrestee from executing that threat. Under these circumstances, we cannot categorically state that pretrial detention "offends some principle of justice so rooted in the traditions and conscience of our people as to be ranked as fundamental." *Snyder v. Massachusetts,* 291 U.S. 97, 105 (1934).

B

Respondents also contend that the Bail Reform Act violates the Excessive Bail Clause of the Eighth Amendment. We think that the Act survives a challenge founded upon the Eighth Amendment.

The Eighth Amendment addresses pretrial release by providing merely that "[e] xcessive bail shall not be required." This Clause, of course, says nothing about whether bail shall be available at all. Respondents nevertheless contend that this Clause grants them a right to bail calculated solely upon considerations of flight. They rely on *Stack v. Boyle*, 342 U.S. 1, 5 (1951), in which the Court stated that "[b]ail set at a figure higher than an amount reasonably calculated [to ensure the defendant's presence at trial] is 'excessive' under the Eighth Amendment." In respondents' view, since the Bail Reform Act allows a court essentially to set bail at an infinite amount for reasons not related to the risk of flight, it violates the Excessive Bail Clause. Respondents concede that the right to bail they have discovered in the Eighth Amendment is not absolute. A court may, for example, refuse bail in capital cases. And, as the Court of Appeals noted and respondents admit, a court may refuse bail when the defendant presents a threat to the judicial process by intimidating witnesses. Respondents characterize these exceptions as consistent with what they claim to be the sole purpose of bail to ensure the integrity of the judicial process.

While we agree that a primary function of bail is to safeguard the courts' role in adjudicating the guilt or innocence of defendants, we reject the proposition that the Eighth Amendment categorically prohibits the government from pursuing other admittedly compelling interests through regulation of pretrial release. The above-quoted dictum in *Stack v. Boyle* is far too slender a reed on which to rest this argument. The Court in *Stack* had no occasion to consider whether the Excessive Bail Clause requires courts to admit all defendants to bail, because the statute before the Court in that case in fact allowed the defendants to be bailed. Thus, the Court had to determine only whether bail, admittedly available in that case, was excessive if set at a sum greater than that necessary to ensure the arrestees' presence at trial.

The holding of *Stack* is illuminated by the Court's holding just four months later in *Carlson v. Landon*, 342 U.S. 524 (1952). In that case, remarkably similar to the present action, the detainees had been arrested and held without bail pending a determination of deportability. The Attorney General refused to release the individuals, "on the ground that there was reasonable cause to believe that [their] release would be prejudicial to the public interest and *would endanger the welfare and safety of the United States.*" *Id.* at 539 (emphasis added). The detainees brought the same challenge that respondents bring to us today: the Eighth Amendment required them to be admitted to bail. The Court squarely rejected this proposition:

> The bail clause was lifted with slight changes from the English Bill of Rights Act. In England that clause has never been thought to accord a right to bail in all cases, but merely to provide that bail shall not be excessive in those cases where it is proper to grant bail. When this clause was carried over into our Bill of Rights, nothing was said that indicated any different concept. The Eighth Amendment has not prevented Congress from defining the classes of cases in which bail shall be allowed in this country. Thus, in criminal cases bail is not compulsory where the punishment may be death. Indeed, the very language of the Amendment fails to say all arrests must be bailable.

Id., at 545–546 (footnotes omitted).

Carlson v. Landon was a civil case, and we need not decide today whether the Excessive Bail Clause speaks at all to Congress' power to define the classes of criminal arrestees who shall be admitted to bail. For even if we were to conclude that the Eighth Amendment imposes some substantive limitations on the National Legislature's powers in this area, we would still hold that the Bail Reform Act is valid. Nothing in the text of the Bail Clause limits permissible government considerations solely to questions of flight. The only arguable substantive limitation of the Bail Clause is that the government's proposed conditions of release or detention not be "excessive" in light of the perceived evil. Of course, to determine whether the government's response is excessive, we must compare that response against the interest the government seeks to protect by means of that response. Thus, when the government has admitted that its only interest is in preventing flight, bail must be set by a court at a sum designed to ensure that goal, and no more. *Stack v. Boyle, supra.* We believe that when Congress has mandated detention on the basis of a compelling interest other than prevention of flight, as it has here, the Eighth Amendment does not require release on bail.

III

In our society liberty is the norm, and detention prior to trial or without trial is the carefully limited exception. We hold that the provisions for pretrial detention in the Bail Reform Act of 1984 fall within that carefully limited exception. The Act authorizes the detention prior to trial of arrestees charged with serious felonies who are found after an adversary hearing to pose a threat to the safety of individuals or to the community which no condition of release can dispel. The numerous procedural safeguards detailed above must attend this adversary hearing. We are unwilling to say that this congressional determination, based as it is upon that primary concern of every government a concern for the safety and indeed the lives of its citizens on its face violates either the Due Process Clause of the Fifth Amendment or the Excessive Bail Clause of the Eighth Amendment.

The judgment of the Court of Appeals is therefore

Reversed.

Justice Marshall, with whom Justice Brennan joins, dissenting.

This case brings before the Court for the first time a statute in which Congress declares that a person innocent of any crime may be jailed indefinitely, pending the trial of allegations which are legally presumed to be untrue, if the Government shows to the satisfaction of a judge that the accused is likely to commit crimes, unrelated to the pending charges, at any time in the future. Such statutes, consistent with the usages of tyranny and the excesses of what bitter experience teaches us to call the police state, have long been thought incompatible with the fundamental human rights protected by our Constitution. Today a majority of this Court holds otherwise. Its decision disregards basic principles of justice established centuries ago and enshrined beyond the reach of governmental interference in the Bill of Rights. . . .

* * *

The essence of this case may be found, ironically enough, in a provision of the Act to which the majority does not refer. Title 18 U.S.C. § 3142(j) provides that "[n]othing in this section shall be construed as modifying or limiting the presumption of innocence." But the very pith and purpose of this statute is an abhorrent limitation of the presumption of innocence. The majority's untenable conclusion that the present Act is constitutional arises from a specious denial of the role of the Bail Clause and the Due Process Clause in protecting the invaluable guarantee afforded by the presumption of innocence.

* * *

The statute now before us declares that persons who have been indicted may be detained if a judicial officer finds clear and convincing evidence that they pose a danger to individuals or to the community. The statute does not authorize the Government to imprison anyone it has evidence is dangerous; indictment is necessary. But let us suppose that a defendant is indicted and the Government shows by clear and convincing evidence that he is dangerous and should be detained pending a trial, at which trial the defendant is acquitted. May the Government continue to hold the defendant in detention based upon its showing that he is dangerous? The answer cannot be yes, for that would allow the Government to imprison someone for uncommitted crimes based upon "proof" not beyond a reasonable doubt. The result must therefore be that once the indictment has failed, detention cannot continue. But our fundamental principles of justice declare that the defendant is as innocent on the day before his trial as he is on the morning after his acquittal. Under this statute an untried indictment somehow acts to permit a detention, based on other charges, which after an acquittal would be unconstitutional. The conclusion is inescapable that the indictment has been turned into evidence, if not that the defendant is guilty of the crime charged, then that left to his own devices he will soon be guilty of something else. "'If it suffices to accuse, what will become of the innocent?'" *Coffin v. United States, supra*, at 455 (quoting Ammianus Marcellinus, Rerum Gestarum Libri Qui Supersunt, L. XVIII, c. 1, A.D. 359).

To be sure, an indictment is not without legal consequences. It establishes that there is probable cause to believe that an offense was committed, and that the defendant committed it. Upon probable cause a warrant for the defendant's arrest may issue; a period of administrative detention may occur before the evidence of probable cause is presented to a neutral magistrate. Once a defendant has been committed for trial he may be detained in custody if the magistrate finds that no conditions of release will prevent him from becoming a fugitive. But in this connection the charging instrument is evidence of nothing more than the fact that there will be a trial, and

> [R]elease before trial is conditioned upon the accused's giving adequate assurance that he will stand trial and submit to sentence if found guilty. Like the ancient practice of securing the oaths of responsible persons to stand as

sureties for the accused, the modern practice of requiring a bail bond or the deposit of a sum of money subject to forfeiture serves as additional assurance of the presence of an accused.

Stack v. Boyle, 342 U.S. 1, 4–5 (1951) (citation omitted).

The finding of probable cause conveys power to try, and the power to try imports of necessity the power to assure that the processes of justice will not be evaded or obstructed. "Pretrial detention to prevent future crimes against society at large, however, is not justified by any concern for holding a trial on the charges for which a defendant has been arrested." 794 F.2d 64, 73 (CA2 1986) (quoting *United States v. Melendez-Carrion*, 790 F.2d 984, 1002 (CA2 1986) (opinion of Newman, J.)). The detention purportedly authorized by this statute bears no relation to the Government's power to try charges supported by a finding of probable cause, and thus the interests it serves are outside the scope of interests which may be considered in weighing the excessiveness of bail under the Eighth Amendment. . . .

IV

. . . "It is a fair summary of history to say that the safeguards of liberty have frequently been forged in controversies involving not very nice people." *United States v. Rabinowitz*, 339 U.S. 56, 69 (1950) (Frankfurter, J., dissenting). Honoring the presumption of innocence is often difficult; sometimes we must pay substantial social costs as a result of our commitment to the values we espouse. But at the end of the day the presumption of innocence protects the innocent; the shortcuts we take with those whom we believe to be guilty injure only those wrongfully accused and, ultimately, ourselves.

Throughout the world today there are men, women, and children interned indefinitely, awaiting trials which may never come or which may be a mockery of the word, because their governments believe them to be "dangerous." Our Constitution, whose construction began two centuries ago, can shelter us forever from the evils of such unchecked power. Over 200 years it has slowly, through our efforts, grown more durable, more expansive, and more just. But it cannot protect us if we lack the courage, and the self-restraint, to protect ourselves. Today a majority of the Court applies itself to an ominous exercise in demolition. Theirs is truly a decision which will go forth without authority, and come back without respect.

Notes

1. The Arizona Supreme Court has interpreted *Salerno* as blocking the state from simply detaining all defendants charged with sex offenses against minors. While such defendants could be detained pretrial, individualized findings of dangerousness are required. *Simpson v. Miller*, 387 P.3d 1270 (2017).

2. Some states *require* the prosecutor to move to revoke bail if the victim is threatened or intimidated. *See, e.g.,* INDIANA CODE § 33-14-10-6; OR. REV. STAT. § 135.970.

3. Note that pretrial detention due to potential future dangerousness does not necessarily hinge on potential harm to a particular identified victim. Pretrial detention protects against potential victimization of anyone in the community.

4. Problem: Suppose defendant Joe is arrested for domestic violence. He has a history of assaulting his wife Mary. He has been arrested several times for domestic violence, but never convicted. Assuming a pretrial detention law identical to the federal statute, would you as a judge hold Joe pending trial? What if a defendant, Sam, was a career burglar? A drug dealer?

5. A number of states and the federal government have given victims the right to be heard at bail hearings. *See, e.g.,* 18 U.S.C. § 3771 ("Rights of crime victims. — A crime victim has the following rights: (1) The right to be reasonably protected from the accused. . . ."), ARIZONA CONST. ART. II Section 2.1. (A) ("To preserve and protect victims' rights to justice and due process, a victim of crime has a right: To be treated with fairness, respect, and dignity, and to be free from intimidation, harassment, or abuse, throughout the criminal justice process."); AK. CONST., art. II, § 24 (victims have the right "to be heard . . . at any proceeding where the accused's release from custody is considered"); S.C. CONST., art. I, § 24(A)(5) (victims have the right to "be heard at any proceeding involving a post-arrest release decision"); WASH CONST., art. II, § 35 (victims have the right "to make a statement . . . at any proceeding where the defendant's release is considered").

Do victims deserve the right to be heard at bail hearings? The Senate Judiciary Committee recently recommended that the U.S. Constitution be amended to guarantee all victims the right to be heard at bail hearings. (This Victims' Rights Amendment is discussed in Chapter 11.) The Committee Report on the amendment justified a right to be heard at bail hearings as follows:

Senate Report No. 108-191

By the Senate Judiciary Committee (Nov. 7, 2003)

Victim participation in bail hearings can also serve valuable functions, particularly in alerting courts to the dangers that defendants might present if released unconditionally. Without victim participation, courts may not be fully informed about the consequences of releasing a defendant. "It is difficult for a judge to evaluate the danger that a defendant presents to the community if the judge hears only from the defendant's counsel, who will present him in the best possible light, and from a prosecutor who does not know of the basis for the victim's fear. . . . The person best able to inform the court of [threatening] statements that may have been made by the defendant and the threat he poses is often the person he victimized." PRESIDENT'S TASK FORCE ON VICTIMS OF CRIME, FINAL REPORT 65 (1982).

The Committee heard chilling testimony about the consequences of failing to provide victims with this opportunity from Katherine Prescott, the President of Mothers Against Drunk Driving (MADD):

> I sat with a victim of domestic violence in court one day and she was terrified. She told me she knew her ex-husband was going to kill her. The lawyers and the judge went into chambers and had some discussions and they came

out and continued the case. The victim never had the opportunity to speak to the judge, so he didn't know how frightened she was. He might have tried to put some restrictions on the defendant if he had known more about her situation, but it was handled in chambers out of the presence of the victim.

That night, as she was going to her car after her shift was over at the hospital where she was a registered nurse, she was murdered by her ex-husband, leaving four young children, and then he took his own life—four children left orphans. I will always believe that if the judge could have heard her and seen her as I did, maybe he could have done something to prevent her death.

Note

If the victim has the right to be heard at a bail hearing, how does the victim know whether to try to invoke that right? In Arizona, the prosecutor must notify the victim if he decided not to move to revoke the bond of a defendant who has made threats against the victim. ARIZ. REV. STAT. § 13-4432.

4. Programs of Protection

Victims can be protected by witness relocation programs, as discussed in the following article.

Peter Finn and Kerry Murphy Healey, *Relocating Intimidated Witnesses: An Underutilized Protection Approach*

30 PROSECUTOR 24 (1996)

Introduction

Many police investigators and prosecutors have become increasingly disturbed by their inability to investigate and prosecute cases successfully because key witnesses refuse to provide critical evidence or are unwilling to testify due to fear that the defendant or his family and friends will retaliate. The problem is particularly acute, and apparently increasing, in the case of gang- and drug-related crimes. Refusal by witnesses to cooperate with investigations and prosecutions should be a major concern—it undermines the functioning of the justice system while at the same time erodes confidence in government's ability to protect its citizens.

A number of law enforcement agencies and prosecutorial offices across the country have already taken steps to prevent witness intimidation. These efforts include increased attention to traditional approaches to witness security, such as regularly requesting high bail for known intimidators, aggressively prosecuting reported intimidation, closely managing key witnesses and expanding victim and witness assistance services. However, these traditional approaches to addressing witness intimidation tend to have limited effectiveness. As a result, a number of jurisdictions have increasingly begun to use or to expand their use of more innovative approaches, such as providing relocation services to threatened witnesses.

Witness relocation should be a critical component of all serious witness security efforts. Indeed, many police investigators and prosecutors consider secure relocation to be the single most reliable protection for witnesses. However, lack of funds and personnel and problems related to managing relocated witnesses, make it difficult for most jurisdictions to use relocation as often as they would like. This article examines methods a number of prosecution offices have used successfully to relocate witnesses. Information in the article is based on telephone interviews with 32 criminal justice professionals from 20 urban jurisdictions; telephone interviews with four to six criminal justice system professionals in each of four other jurisdictions—Las Vegas, Los Angeles, Minneapolis and Philadelphia; on-site interviews with over 50 practitioners in Baltimore, Des Moines, New York City, Oakland, San Francisco and Washington, D.C.; and conversations with several officials at the U.S. Department of Housing and Urban Development.

There are three levels of witness relocation: emergency relocation, which is needed immediately and typically lasts only a few days; short-term or temporary relocation, which normally lasts for a few months to up to a year (or until the conclusion of the trial); and permanent relocation.

H. Joinder and Severance

1. Joinder of Trials: Generally

In most jurisdictions, the inconvenience to a crime victim is one of many factors weighed in determining whether two or more defendants charged with the same crime are to be tried separately or together. The victim has several interests in a single trial—e.g., minimizing disruption in employment and family life and avoiding secondary trauma by having to provide testimony at only one trial. Usually trial courts have discretion to consider such factors, along with all other relevant factors, in deciding whether to hold a single or multiple trials. Oregon has gone further and has codified a requirement that victim interests be considered before multiple defendants can obtain severed trials:

OR. REV. STAT. § 136.060(1)

Jointly charged defendants shall be tried jointly unless the court concludes before trial that it is clearly inappropriate to do so and orders that a defendant be tried separately. In reaching its conclusion the court shall strongly consider the victim's interest in a joint trial.

Three Defendants Face Joint Trial in Double Killing

THE OREGONIAN, Sept. 16, 1997, at B7

Three young Multnomah County [Oregon] men accused of murdering two target shooters for thrills last year will be tried together, a judge ruled Monday. The ruling, by Multnomah County Circuit Judge James Ellis, will spare the victims' families further emotional turmoil, said Bill Williams, deputy district attorney.

"The emotional aspect of reliving the death of their loved ones three times is too much to ask," Williams said.

[The victims], both of Northeast Portland, died from multiple gunshot wounds Oct. 2 while they shot at targets at an old gravel pit on Larch Mountain, inside Mount Hood National Forest 30 miles east of Portland. . . .

"We're extremely grateful for today's decision," said Dunwoody's widow, . . . "looking at the evidence one time is necessary. But three times is, in a way, abuse. . . ."

---

2. Dual Juries to Allow a Single Trial

If two defendants are joined together for trial, it is possible that evidence admissible against one defendant may not be admissible against another. This problem arises most frequently in situations where one defendant has confessed to police after his arrest that both he and his co-defendant committed the crime. The confession is admissible against the confessing defendant, but is not admissible against the co-defendant; it would be hearsay and its admission would deprive the co-defendant of the right to confront the defendant about the truth of that confession. This is known as a "*Bruton* problem"—named after the Supreme Court decision identifying the issue. *See Bruton v. United States*, 391 U.S. 123 (1968).

In such circumstances, the prosecution may have to ask the court to sever the trial of the two defendants, potentially forcing the victim(s) and their families to endure two separate trials. An alternative is for the court to empanel two separate or "dual" juries. The dual juries hear most evidence together, with one jury or the other being excused during testimony that relates only to a single defendant. Is this procedure permissible?

State v. Kman

2017 WL 937575 (Del. Super. Ct. 2017)

Before the Court is the State's Motion to Sever the murder trials of codefendants Michael Kman and Ryan Shover. The State moves for severance of the trials on grounds that the State expects to elicit testimony from alleged co-conspirators that Kman confessed to the charged crimes and implicated Shover. All parties and the Court agree that, under *Bruton v. United States*, the State would be constitutionally barred by the Sixth Amendment from producing such testimony in a joint trial of the two defendants. The State therefore has moved to sever the trial in order to present the co-conspirators' evidence at Kman's trial.

The State also wishes to try the defendants simultaneously, but before two separate juries.

. . .

In the context of *Bruton* issues in federal cases, one authority has commented on the propriety of the dual jury practice:

> Applying this *Bruton* rule, trial courts have generally granted severances under [Federal Rule of Civil Procedure] 14, where confessions or other admissions can be admitted against only one defendant. A few courts, however, have experimented with other procedures in an attempt to satisfy *Bruton* while avoiding the time and expense of separate trials for codefendants. Among such procedures are the use of bifurcated trials, in which a verdict is returned on one defendant before the jury hears the admission of the codefendant, and multiple jury trials, in which different juries return verdicts on different defendants and hear only the evidence admissible against the particular defendant whose case they are considering.

Annotation, *Propriety of Use of Multiple Juries at Joint Trial of Multiple Defendants in Federal Criminal Case*, 72 A.L.R. Fed. 875, § 1 (2011); *see also Annual Review of Criminal Procedure*, 41 Geo. L.J. Ann. Rev. Crim. Proc. 331–32 (2012) (providing that "[a]s an alternative to severance, some courts have utilized separate juries in trials with multiple defendants.").

In a law review note analyzing the use of dual juries, Kaitlin Canty reviewed the use of dual juries in United States federal and state courts. Kaitlin A. Canty, Note, *To Each His Own Jury: Dual Juries in Joint Trials*, 43 Conn. L. Rev. 321, 324 n.14 (2010). In her thirty-five page law review note, Canty extensively sets forth a detailed overview of state and federal courts' use of the multiple jury procedure, a thorough analysis of the costs and benefits of the procedure, and recommended guidelines for implementing the procedure. This Court has relied (as have other authorities) on Canty's law review note for guidance this decision.

"Although used primarily in connection with the problem of codefendant statements, multiple juries have also been utilized in order to minimize prejudice at a joint trial of codefendants who assert antagonistic defenses, for purposes of judicial economy, and to spare the victim the ordeal of testifying at multiple trials." Fern L. Kletter, Annotation, *Propriety of Use of Multiple Juries at Joint Trial of Multiple Defendants in State Criminal Prosecution*, 41 A.L.R. 6th 295, § 2. In Wayne R. LaFave's treatise, *Criminal Procedure*, the practice is described as another "remed[y] for a *Bruton*-type confession." 5 Wayne R. LaFave et al., Criminal Procedure, § 17.2(b) (4th ed. 2016). That treatise cites *People v. Harris*, in which the California Supreme Court observed, "[i]n every federal and state decision called to our attention by the parties, the court has upheld against constitutional attack the dual jury procedure as used in the case before it." *People v. Harris*, 767 P.2d 619, 634 (Cal.

1989). Additionally, Canty observed that "the vast majority of [appellate] courts have upheld convictions [resulting from multiple jury trials], even while criticizing the practice." Canty, *supra*, at 324 n.14. . . .

However, the general practice of holding dual jury trials has not been endorsed by all jurisdictions. In *People v. Ricardo B.*, the New York Court of Appeals advised its lower courts that the use of multiple juries is "the exception, not the rule. . . . The first order of business of the criminal courts . . . is justice, not economy or convenience and the use of multiple juries can only magnify the problems inherent in joint trials because of the need to insulate the juries from inadmissible evidence or argument." 535 N.E.2d 1336, 1339 (N.Y. 1989). Although the New York Court of Appeals issued this warning to the lower New York courts, it did recognize that "multiple juries have obvious attractions, particularly in cases involving *Bruton* problems or antagonistic defenses." *Id.*

. . .

In this case, as many of the witnesses that would testify at separate trials of Kman and Shover would be the same, it is logical to have them to testify at only one joint trial with two juries. The only issue that would possibly warrant complete severance, the *Bruton* issue, is dispatched of by use of a dual jury procedure. Otherwise, the evidence presented at separate trials of the defendants will largely overlap. As previously stated, the procedure will mitigate any unfair prejudice that could be posed by any antagonistic defenses at trial. Additionally, considerable judicial economy will be achieved by implementing the dual jury procedure in this case. Accordingly, as proper guidelines will be followed to ensure the defendants a fair trial, the use of a dual jury trial in this case is appropriate.

Notes

1. Most appellate courts have approved the use of dual juries, although federal courts have been more enthusiastic about the procedure than state courts.

2. In *Hedlund v. Superior Court in and for Maricopa County*, 832 P.2d 219 (Ariz. App. 1992), the court held that Arizona's Victims' Bill of Rights did not give victims any substantive right to have dual juries empaneled. The court explained that while the Bill of Rights "does afford victims the right to a speedy trial or disposition, it does not make any reference to the procedures by which this right is to be enforced."

I. Victims and Judicial Bias

During pre-trial proceedings, issues may arise about whether judges are biased in favor of or against victims. Generally, judges are subject to disqualification for bias, as provided in statute or court rule. For example, the federal statute on disqualification provides: "Any justice, judge, or magistrate of the United States shall disqualify himself in any proceeding in which his impartiality might reasonably be questioned." 28 U.S.C. § 455. Motions for recusal are typically addressed to the discretion of the trial judge. Reversals on appeal for failure to recuse are rare.

When a victim sends a letter to a judge asking for "justice" and the judge reads the letter, does this create grounds for recusal?

People v. Michael M.

475 N.Y.S.2d 774 (N.Y. Co. Ct. 1984)

RAYMOND HARRINGTON, Judge

"The Courtroom is the focal point of the entire criminal justice system. . . . Particularly for the victim, the judge is the personification of justice." (*President's Task Force Report on Victims of Crime*, December, 1983, p. 73.)

Certainly the trial judge should ideally be perceived as "the personification of justice" by *everyone* involved in the system, including the defendant. More particularly, however, victim's rights in the criminal justice system are now being asserted more forcefully than ever before. Certainly these rights have long languished, overwhelmed by other considerations.

Victims' rights should be recognized, asserted and protected by the judiciary without doing harm to fundamental rights of defendants. The Court, ever mindful of balancing those rights, is asked to disqualify itself from presiding over this matter because prior to a resolution of this case, the victim's family and friends have written to this trial judge demanding "justice." Is a defendant's right to a fair trial compromised by the trial judge being aware of the outrage of the alleged victim's friends and family? Are communications by the victim's family to the trial judge prior to verdict or plea an appropriate manner for the victim to exercise *his right* to participate in plea and sentence negotiations? Should these communications be encouraged or discouraged?

In this case the defendant, sixteen years old, is indicted for the crime of Sodomy in the First Degree. It is alleged that he anally sodomized a twenty-two month old infant. By the nature of these charges, it is understandable that those closest to this incident have responded with intense feelings. The parents and grandparents of the alleged infant victim have reacted with anger, outrage, and a cry for just retribution. The friends of the defendant have reverted to bewilderment, mystified that their "student," parishioner or "friend" as the case may be, might be responsible for these charges. Nevertheless, they remain supportive of the defendant.

The intensity of emotions generated by these particular charges has found an outlet in many letters to the Court. The infant's family, in particular, has written several letters to the Court. Actually five letters have been received by the Court from the family of the infant and friends of his parents, addressed to the Honorable Abbey Boklan and referred to this Court by that honorable Judge when the case was assigned to this Judge. Counsel for the defendant was advised of the existence of these letters at the first conference before this Court, and they were and are available for either counsel's inspection and/or copying. Thereafter, sixteen letters were received by the Court from many distinguished members of the community on behalf of the defendant. Teachers, priests and basketball coaches have all spoken highly of the defendant and his family. These letters are also available for either counsel's inspection.

Having said this by way of introduction, the issue before this Court is defendant's application that the Court recuse itself in the instant matter. The grounds for this particular request are . . . that the Court has become prejudiced against the defendant by virtue of a "deluge" of letters to the Court by the victim's family and friends. . . .

In the first instance, what the defendant has characterized as a "deluge" of letters is not fittingly so described. Without commenting on the relevancy, poignancy and literary quality of any of the letters received by the Court, the defendant has certainly "won the battle" on any quantifiable basis.

On the other hand, this Court perceives little or no distinction between the manner in which this case has proceeded, including the submission of letters, and a myriad of other cases that have come before this trial judge. Indeed, many more notorious cases before this and other Courts have resulted in larger and more vociferous outcries from the victims and, indeed, the entire community.

On the most personal level, this Court, having examined its conscience, states categorically and without reservation that it harbors no prejudice against this defendant by reason of the letters, plea discussions or any other facts now known to this trial judge. Accordingly, the application then turns on whether the Court must, as a matter of law, recuse itself because of some apparent prejudice to the defendant or an appearance of impropriety created by virtue of the letters and/or plea discussions.

Recently the National Conference of the Judiciary on the Rights of Victims of Crime issued a *Statement of Recommended Judicial Practices* [published by the National Institute of Justice, U.S. Department of Justice (April 1984).] (*See* NYLJ, May 1, 1984, pp. 1 and 36.) This manifesto was the product of a conference of judges of courts of general jurisdiction of all our states at the American Bar Association's National Judicial College. Those recommendations state, in part, that " . . . victims shall be allowed to participate and, where appropriate, to give input through the prosecutor . . . 'concerning' . . . plea and sentence negotiations." (*Cf. Fair Treatment Standards for Crime Victims, supra.*) Furthermore "victim impact statements prior to sentencing should be encouraged and considered." 1 CPL 390.30[3] as amd. by Laws of 1982, ch. 612, eff. Nov. 1, 1982.) On the other hand, the Canons of Judicial Conduct require that " . . . A judge should . . . except as authorized by law, neither initiate nor consider *ex parte* or other communications concerning a pending . . . proceeding." (*Code of Judicial Conduct*, Canon 3, Standards [A][4], *Judiciary Law.*) The ethical standards of the prosecutor and defense counsel also prohibit *ex parte* communications with the Court. (ABA Standards, The Prosecution Function, § 2.8[c]; *Code of Professional Responsibility,* EC 7-35, *Judiciary Law.*)

The better practice is that the prosecutor and defense counsel should try to funnel through their offices all communications to the Court concerning pending matters, and to submit the same on notice to their adversary. The Court is mindful that citizens have their own constitutional rights to communicate with the Courts as their elected public officials, whether on behalf of the defendant or the alleged victim. Counsel cannot reasonably be expected to control every exercise of freedom of speech by individual citizens, whether they be friends of the victim or the defendant, or are just concerned members of the public.

A Judge should not consider *ex parte* communications; but, written documents provided to the Court, whether supplied by either side or unsolicited, can be considered by the Court where they are openly disclosed to the parties. This Court concludes, therefore, that all of these letters are not *ex parte* communications under these circumstances. The Court is satisfied that they can be considered in plea and sentence negotiations.

Moreover, this Court believes that a victim's communications to the Court, when done in the foregoing manner, *at any stage* of a criminal proceeding should be encouraged and considered by the judiciary. It is important in all criminal cases for the Court to know that there are "victims," and to appreciate their concerns about plea bargaining and sentencing. In most instances, victims can and should communicate to the Court through the prosecutor, but they should not be limited to that form of communication and participation in the system. Indeed, if the crime victim cannot vent his frustrations to the trial judge, that "personification" of justice, it undermines all of our efforts to ensure that justice is done under law. This is particularly so in the most heinous of crimes, where the system tries to channel the victim's desire for revenge into a civilized form. By all means, this the judiciary must encourage.

* * *

Conclusion

Again, having examined its own conscience, this Court states categorically and without reservation that it harbors no prejudice against this defendant and sees no reason in law or in conscience why it cannot preside over a fair trial for this defendant. The motion is therefore denied.

Notes

1. About one-third of the states allow the parties to exercise a "peremptory" challenge against the judge—that is, to remove the judge without assigning a particular reason merely by filing a notice of challenge. These statutes give the parties in a criminal case the right to challenge the judge. Victims do not have the right to peremptorily challenge a judge.

2. The fact that judge may have been the victim of a crime does not ordinarily provide grounds for recusal. For example, Chief Justice Earl Warren's father was murdered before he joined the Supreme Court, but Warren did not recuse from murder cases.

3. Defense attorneys argued that Judge Michael Luttig of the Fourth Circuit should recuse in death penalty cases because his father was murdered and his killer sentenced to death. (The circumstances surrounding this case are discussed in Chapter 10.) Judge Luttig responded:

> Because of the time that has elapsed since my dad's murder; the dissimilarity of the circumstances surrounding my dad's and Leanne Whitlock's murders; and the lack of any overlap in the legal issues presented in the appeals of the two cases, I do not believe that it can reasonably be maintained either that I cannot impartially sit in judgment of this appeal or that my impartiality can fairly be questioned. Nor, any more than recusal from discrimination cases should be required by judges who themselves, or whose families, have been subjected to invidious racial or sexual discrimination, do I believe that my recusal is required from this and all other murder cases for the reason alone that my dad was the victim of a murder.
>
> The purpose of [the disqualification statute] is not to require recusal from the courts of all who have experienced the fullness of life—good and bad; and certainly its purpose is not to enable forum shopping by parties to litigation. Rather, its purpose is only to ensure that the matters before the courts are decided by a judiciary that is impartial both in fact and in appearance. I do not believe that this indisputably important purpose is, in any way, compromised or disserved by my participation in this case. As I have earlier stated in open court, capital defendants are entitled to fair and impartial consideration of their claims by me when I am randomly selected to serve on the panel hearing their cases. Neither before nor after my dad's murder have they received less.
>
> *Strickler v. Pruett*, 149 F.3d 1170 (table), 1998 WL 340420 (4th Cir. 1998) (unpublished).

4. In a federal case, the defendant complained that a trial judge entered an order requiring that the attorney representing the alleged victims of the crime be added to the service list for filings in the case. The defendant argued that he received this order "without forewarning or explanation" and that this is a "bizarre practice" demonstrating judicial bias. In rejecting these arguments, the court explained:

> This action was taken pursuant to the clear provisions of the Crime Victims' Rights Act, 18 U.S.C. § 3771. This statute had previously been called to the court's attention by the United States in a motion requesting that the government be relieved from its statutory victim notification requirements. After studying this statute, the court denied the government's motion to depart from the stringent victim notification requirements

therein, (Doc. # 50), and promptly entered the order requiring notice to Ms. Ford. The court rejects the argument that following the provisions of this statute—to which, as noted, it has required the government's strict adherence as well—constitutes a "bizarre practice" or otherwise indicates that the court harbors personal bias against defendant Cunningham.

United States v. Gallion, No. CRIMA 07-39 WOB, 2008 WL 1904669, at *6 (E.D. Ky. Apr. 29, 2008)

5. If the prosecution believes that a judge is biased against it, it may pursue recusal in the same fashion as a defendant. It is not as clear, however, that the victim may pursue such remedies on her own. For a rare example of a victim filing a motion seeking recusal of a judge, *see* Nesreen Khashan, *Another Motion Seeks Judge's Removal: "Gratuitous Favoritism" Alleged in Weitzel Case*, OGDEN STANDARD-EXAMINER, Sept. 28, 2001. Ultimately the recusal issues in this case were resolved when recusal was ordered based on the *prosecution's* motion. *See* Stephen Hunt, *Weitzel Judge Ousted*, SALT LAKE TRIB., Nov. 17, 2001.

6. Most reported court decisions involving allegations of judicial bias during sentencing are based on the judge's exposure to "victim impact" evidence or harsh comments toward a defendant at sentencing. Generally allegations of bias at this stages have been rejected, as illustrated in the following ruling from the Utah Supreme Court rejecting a challenge to a judge who had expressed anger towards a father who had sexually abused his daughter:

> Certainly, we expect our judges to "be patient, dignified, and courteous to litigants, jurors, witnesses, lawyers, and others with whom the judge deals in an official capacity." But that does not mean that due process or our Code of Judicial Conduct are violated whenever a defendant's criminal conduct and subsequent excuses inspire anger in a judge. Perhaps there is a judge who could remain emotionally neutral when faced with a father who sexually abused his daughter, tended to blame her for the abuse, and then tried to rationalize it by stating that he thought it would have been a good experience for her. But no law requires it. Thus, Mr. Munguia's due process rights were not violated by Judge Kouris, and he did not need to recuse himself.

State v. Munguia, 2011 UT 5, ¶ 19, 253 P.3d 1082, 1089–90.

J. Victims and the Exclusionary Rule

As discussed at length in criminal procedure courses, evidence that the state has illegally seized is often suppressed from a criminal trial. This is known as the "exclusionary rule." The purpose of the exclusionary rule is to deter police misconduct by excluding the fruits of illegal searches.

Whatever effect the exclusionary rule may have on the police, is it fair to victims?

William T. Pizzi, *The Need to Overrule* Mapp v. Ohio

82 U. Colo. L. Rev. 679 (2011)

Section I—Changing Conceptions of Criminal Cases

Criminal cases were conceptualized rather simply in 1961. On one side was the defendant and on the other side was "the State." In a two-sided world, it is easy to enforce rules between the parties—if one side errs, we punish that side to the benefit of the "other side." But the world of criminal trials is no longer two-sided. Starting in the 1970s, a powerful victims movement emerged in the United States (as well as abroad) based on the premise that the criminal justice equation at that time failed to take into account the stake that victims, or the family of victims, have in the criminal case. Victims are not "the State," have nothing to do with the police, but at the same time they have a stake in the outcome of the criminal case.

In the United States, understanding how to accommodate the interest of victims in our criminal justice system has not been easy, given our conceptualization of trials as being two-sided. But over the last thirty years, every state has passed either statutes or constitutional amendments insisting that victims be kept informed of the progress of the case, be notified of important court hearings, and be consulted about possible plea bargains. Although the system has stopped short of giving victims participatory rights at trial, victims today often have been given the right to be heard on the issue of sentencing or, at least, to submit in writing a statement of the impact of the crime on their life.

This has not been an easy solution as there is considerable question about the relevance of this information to the issue of punishment. This tension over the relevance of victim impact evidence at sentencing is reflected in the Supreme Court's amazing flip-flop on the issue, ruling in 1987 and 1989 that victim impact evidence in capital cases was inadmissible as violative of the Eighth Amendment and then deciding, in 1991, in *Payne v. Tennessee* that victim impact evidence was perfectly admissible and relevant to a jury's sentencing decision in a capital case.

Allowing victims to offer impact statements at sentencing is controversial. But even if one disagrees with that development in the law, there can be no doubt that the system that existed in 1961 has changed and victims are seen today to have a legitimate interest in the criminal process. One indication of this shift is the fact that certain of the federal rules of criminal procedure have been amended recently to conform to provisions of the Crime Victims' Rights Act of 2004. Among the changes are provisions that require notice to victims of court proceedings; that give victims a right to be heard not just at sentencing, but also on bail and plea decisions; and that make it much more difficult for defendants to sequester victims—as compared to other witnesses—prior to their testifying at trial.

Many countries that have trial systems not based on the adversary model have gone much farther than the United States and give victims, usually victims of serious crimes, a right to participate in criminal trials, sometimes on a rather equal basis with the defense.

Recently, the International Criminal Court, as well, adopted procedures granting a right to victims of genocide and crimes against humanity to participate in trials of these horrific crimes. The International Criminal Court is designed for cases that, even with adequate resources, present enormous logistical difficulties to which victim participation will add another layer of complexity. But the recognition that victims of horrific crimes should have a right to some level of participation—a right not granted victims at previous international criminal tribunals—suggests how much the treatment of victims has changed over the last few decades and how it continues to evolve.

Against the emergence of laws throughout the United States and internationally recognizing that victims have the right to have their interests articulated and considered on many issues in the criminal process, it has become clearer that the two-sided adversary process in the United States and other common law countries is a conceptual structure for testing evidence, not the reflection of a metaphysical reality. Criminal cases are often multi-sided and in a game that is no longer zero-sum, a macho exclusionary rule that demands that reliable evidence be suppressed without consideration of the seriousness of the crime balanced against the nature of the violation becomes very difficult to defend.

In short, the legal landscape has changed dramatically since *Mapp* was decided. In 1961, there was no National Organization for Victim Assistance, an organization that was not founded until 1975, and today often files amicus briefs in courts in support of better treatment for victims of crime in the criminal justice system. Nor in 1961 was there a separate office set up in the Justice Department—the Office for Victims of Crime—that is directed to improving the way victims are treated in the system.

Mapp was a very strange case procedurally as the Court had granted certiorari to decide if Dolly Mapp's possession of "obscene" films found during the search was protected by the First Amendment. The Fourth Amendment issue was never pressed by Mapp's counsel either in their brief or in oral argument.

Obviously, the Court felt confident enough to decide *Mapp* without a full set of briefs directed to the Fourth Amendment issue. One can be certain today that there would be strong opposition to a Fourth Amendment exclusionary rule from victims' rights organizations and, at a minimum, the Court would have to speak to the impact of exclusion on victims in its opinion.

Although defenders of the exclusionary rule are likely to insist that *Mapp* would and should be decided the same way if it were argued today, this seems extremely unlikely for another reason: other common law countries that have adopted exclusionary rules over the last few decades have not opted for exclusionary rules based on deterrence.

Consider, for example, Canada, which adopted its Charter of Rights and Freedoms in 1982. Section 8 of the Charter guarantees "everyone . . . the right to be secure from unreasonable search or seizure." The Charter also contains an exclusionary provision set out in section 24(2) that states that evidence found by a court to have been obtained in violation of a right in the Charter "shall be excluded if it is established that, having regard to all the circumstances, the admission of it in the proceedings would bring the administration of justice into disrepute."

The leading case interpreting section 24(2) remains the Canadian Supreme Court's decision in 1987, *Collins v. The Queen*, where the Court instructed that courts should balance a number of factors in deciding whether the admission of evidence obtained in violation of a Charter right should be suppressed, including (1) the type of evidence obtained; (2) the nature of the right violated; (3) the seriousness of the violation; (4) the culpability of the officer; (5) the urgency of the action taken; (6) the seriousness of the offense; (7) the importance of the evidence to the case; and (8) the availability of other remedies. In reaching this conclusion, the Court emphasized that "[section] 24(2) is not a remedy for police misconduct" but rather is intended to protect the administration of justice from being tarnished by the admission of improperly seized evidence.

Similarly, New Zealand and England base their exclusionary rules, not on deterrence, but on the effect on the judicial process of the admission of evidence that has been improperly seized. Like, Canada, they balance a range of factors to see if exclusion is an appropriate and proportional remedy including the extent of the breach, the good faith or not of the officer involved, the seriousness of the crime, the importance of the evidence, and the reliability and probative value of the evidence.

When one considers the emergence of victims' rights here and abroad as well as the range of other options from other national systems that would be available were the Court deciding *Mapp* today as an initial matter, one suspects the Court would take a different path.

Lynne N. Henderson, *The Wrongs of Victim's Rights*
37 Stanford L. Rev. 937 (1985)

* * *

Perhaps the most cynical manipulation of victim's rights is the invocation of these "rights" by crime control advocates as a justification for abolition of the fourth amendment's exclusionary rule. The California "Victims' Bill of Rights" attempted to circumvent the exclusionary rule in a section titled "Truth in Evidence," and the President's Task Force recommended abolishing the fourth amendment exclusionary rule altogether.

The exclusionary rule as a mechanism for enforcing the fourth amendment's prohibition on unreasonable searches and seizures has been the subject of endless debate. Liberals see the exclusionary rule as a sometimes troubling, but necessary, means of preventing Gestapo-like police tactics. Conservatives see it as a counterintuitive, counterproductive rule that allows "criminals" to go unpunished. Liberals may overstate the case when they argue that the exclusionary rule is the only thing that stands between the populace and a police state and that any diminution of the rule is a step towards fascism. But the knock on the door at night is just as threatening to existence as the nighttime burglar.

Whether or not the exclusionary rule is the appropriate solution to the problem of individual security against the state, it has had a salutary effect on police practices and has promoted efficiency in investigations. Nevertheless, the present Supreme Court has steadily moved toward abolishing the rule. Doctrinally, the Court has narrowed the rule from a general protection against governmental intrusions to a tool for specific deterrence of particular police misconduct.

The exclusionary rule has a minimal effect in the vast majority of cases: The rule affects only a very small percentage of prosecutions. But opponents of the rule perceive it as interfering with effective and efficient law enforcement. They have never abandoned their efforts to abolish it and now have recharacterized their opposition to the rule as an issue of "victims' rights." Their assertion that "victims' rights" compel the abolition of state and federal exclusionary rules seems post hoc, and the efforts to define a victims' "right" that outweighs the constitutional right to be protected from unreasonable searches and seizures are strained. For example, the President's Task Force asserts:

> It must be remembered that the exclusionary rule is a remedy only, and not a very good one. It thus rewards the criminal and punishes, not the police, but the innocent victim of the crime and society at large for conduct they may not condone and over which they have little or no control.[5]

After enumerating all the perceived "costs" to the criminal process "handcuffing police," suppression of "perfectly good" evidence, court delays, and the lack of any danger to the rights of "law abiding" citizens, the Task Force goes on to state:

> Victims are adversely affected by the rule's operation at every turn. When the police fail to solve the crime because of inaction, the victim suffers. When cases are not charged or are dismissed and the "criminal goes free because the constable blundered," *the victim is denied justice.* When the case is continued interminably or must be retried, the victim is hurt time and time again.

The Task Force uses the symbols of both past and future victims as embodied by society's interest in crime prevention to justify abolition of the exclusionary rule in a confusing way; the Task Force decries the costs to society of allowing the guilty to go unpunished and emphasizes the rule's interference with efficiency in the process. Even the Task Force's claims that area more applicable to past victims are grossly exaggerated, reflecting a hostility to the rule itself, rather than any particular

---

5. President's Task Force on Victims of Crime, Final Report 25 (1982).

solicitude for past victims. For example, the statement that the exclusionary rule causes police inaction simply does not make sense. The suggestion that the exclusionary rule is the major source of continuances, delays, and retrials is not supported by available statistical evidence. In the vast majority of cases involving core crime, the exclusionary rule makes no difference to the result. Indeed, it has become almost a truism in defense circles that, while courts may grant suppression motions in drug cases, they invariably deny them in murder cases. The strongest refutation of the Task Force position, however, is that reversals of convictions on fourth amendment grounds appear to constitute only a tiny fraction of all reversals of criminal convictions by appellate courts.

Undeniably, retrials of serious cases necessitated by an appellate court reversal may be difficult for past victims. But it seems unlikely that the degree of difficulty is necessarily related to the *reason* for the reversal and retrial, or that having to testify again because of a reversal resulting from fifth or sixth amendment violations or instructional errors is less "traumatic." The attitudes of the police or prosecutor towards the grounds for the reversal might, however, exacerbate the situation if the prosecutor emphasizes to the victim the "needlessness" of having to retry the case, or criticizes the appellate court's solicitude towards the guilty "criminal."

A second argument offered by the Task Force in opposition to the exclusionary rule is that it denies the victim justice. This argument appears to assume that a victim has a right to a conviction of the accused or, perhaps, a right to revenge. But the history of the criminal process does not support a finding of such a right. . . .

Notes

1. President Reagan's Task Force on Victims of Crime published an influential report on crime victims in 1982. The report concluded that victims were ignored in the criminal justice system and recommended that victims be given a series of rights throughout the criminal process—including requiring victim impact statements at sentencing, making bail more difficult to obtain for dangerous offenders, and abolishing the exclusionary rule. Many victims' reforms in the last two decades stem from the Task Force Report.

2. If the exclusionary rule were abolished, what might replace it? There have been several bills introduced in Congress to abolish the exclusionary rule and substitute a civil damages remedy. Under this approach, police departments could introduce illegally seized evidence in court (except, perhaps, in cases of bad faith or shocking behavior) but would be subject to damages for violation of rights. This approach would have the advantage of not penalizing victims. It would also provide a remedy not just for guilty criminals (who have something to gain from the suppression of incriminating evidence) but also for innocent persons (who have nothing to hide and therefore gain nothing from the suppression of evidence). For arguments in favor of such a proposal, *see* AKHIL AMAR, THE CONSTITUTION AND CRIMINAL PROCEDURE

(1997); Office of Legal Pol'y, U.S. Department of Justice, Report to the Attorney General on the Search and Seizure Exclusionary Rule (1986), reprinted in 22 U. Mich. J.L. Ref. 573, 591–95 (1989); Dallin H. Oaks, *Studying the Exclusionary Rule in Search and Seizure*, 37 U. Chi. L. Rev. 665 (1970). For arguments against such a proposal on grounds that it leaves Fourth Amendment rights inadequately protected, *see* Carol S. Steiker, *Second Thoughts about First Principles*, 107 Harv. L. Rev. 820 (1994).

3. Professor Henderson refers to the California Victims' Bill of Rights, which contained a "Truth in Evidence" provision: "Except as provided by statute hereafter enacted by a two thirds vote of the membership in each house of the Legislature, relevant evidence shall not be excluded in any criminal proceeding. . . ." The provision did not affect the federal exclusionary rule, but did repeal expansive state exclusionary rules that extended beyond federal requirements. In *In re Lance W.*, 694 P.2d 744 (Cal. 1985), the California Supreme Court upheld the provisions and concluded that it swept away California's "vicarious exclusionary" rule which allowed a defendant to object to evidence illegally seized in violation of the rights of a third person. Florida has enacted a similar provision.

4. Many states have interpreted the search and seizure provisions in their state constitutions in "lockstep" with the federal provisions. Some states—such as California and Florida (before enactment of the Truth in Evidence provisions)—extended their state constitutional protections well beyond federal protections. For an argument that state constitutions were never intended to exclude relevant evidence, *see* Paul G. Cassell, *The Mysterious Creation of Search and Seizure Exclusionary Rules Under State Constitutions: The Utah Example*, 1993 Utah L. Rev. 751. This argument has found favor with at least some justices on the Utah Supreme Court. *See State v. Rowan*, 2017 UT 88, 2017 WL 5992040 (2017) (Lee, J., concurring) (agreeing the state exclusionary rule "imposes societal costs unnecessary to the goal of remedying the effects of the unlawful search" and calling for reconsideration of Utah's exclusionary rule).

5. In *People v. Nestrock*, 735 N.E.2d 1101 (Ill. App. 2000), the police violated a state eavesdropping statute to obtain a tape-recorded conversation between the defendant and her friend. The state argued that the evidence should be nonetheless admissible under the State Victims' Rights Amendment, but the court disagreed:

> The State's final argument on this issue is that this court should engage in a balancing of defendant's rights and the victims' rights when deciding this case. The State cites the Rights of Crime Victims and Witnesses Act (Act) (725 Ill. Comp. Stat. 120/1 *et seq.* (West 1996)) and the crime victims' rights amendment to the Illinois Constitution (Ill. Const. 1970, art. I, § 8.1). Neither the Act nor the amendment lends any support for the approach the State suggests. This court certainly feels sympathy for the victims' grievous loss. However, as the State well knows, courts must base their decisions on the law, not on sympathy. At the risk of stating the obvious, the Act and the amendment do not alter the fundamental principles on which our legal

system is based. Those principles mandate that a conviction based on illegally obtained, inadmissible evidence cannot stand.

6. In the *Nestrock* case in the previous note, the argument for suspending the exclusionary rule rested on only general victims' rights provisions. Would the argument have been stronger in Arizona and South Carolina, where in addition to general provisions the states' constitutional amendments protecting victims' rights specifically provide that victims "have the right to . . . have all rules governing criminal procedure and the admissibility of evidence in all criminal proceedings protect victims' rights and have these rules subject to amendment or repeal by the legislature to ensure protection of these rights. . . ."? *See* ARIZ. CONST., art. II, §2.1(A)(11); S.C. CONST., art. I, §24(12).

7. One of the big issues in the exclusionary rule debate is whether the rule really affects crime rates. A recent study compared states that had the exclusionary rule before the Supreme Court's 1961 decision in *Mapp v. Ohio* with those that did not. Comparing these states, the study found that *Mapp* increased crimes of larceny by 3.9 percent, auto theft by 4.4 percent, burglary by 6.3 percent, robbery by 7.7 percent, and assault by 18 percent. Even larger impacts occurred in suburban cities—where the imposition of the exclusionary rule increased violent crimes by 27 percent and property crimes by 20 percent. Raymond A. Atkins & Paul H. Rubin, *Effects of Criminal Procedure on Crime Rates: Mapping Out the Consequences of the Exclusionary Rule*, 46 J.L. & ECON. 157 (2003). The study concluded: "These increases in crime rates are a weighty cost attached to each of the Supreme Court's decisions to change criminal procedure. Society may decide the benefits of our new protections are worth these costs, but an informed debate requires that these costs be known and considered."

Chapter 6

Crime Victim Privacy

Introduction

The Supreme Court "has recognized that a right of personal privacy, or a guarantee of certain areas or zones of privacy does exist under the Constitution . . . . [and is] founded in the Fourteenth Amendment's concepts of personal liberty and restrictions upon state action." *Roe v. Wade*, 410 U.S. 113, 152–53 (1973). Some states have constitutionalized a general right to privacy. *See, e.g.,* CAL. CONST. art. I, § 1 (providing that all people have certain inalienable rights "[a]mong these are . . . pursuing and obtaining safety, happiness, and privacy"), while some other states' constitutions and statutes recognize victims' privacy rights specifically. *See, e.g.,* TEX. CONST. art. I, § 30 (providing that crime victims have "the right to be treated with fairness and with respect for the victim's dignity and privacy throughout the criminal justice process). In addition to these constitutional provisions, there are myriad statutes and rules that afford crime victims privacy rights.

These laws present many practical questions that need resolution during criminal proceedings, such as: what is sufficiently "private" to warrant protection? Can a victim's identity, locating information, sexual history, treatment, or educational records be kept private during criminal procedure? If so, from whom can they be kept private? Can the information be protected if the defendant believes that that the very information that a victim hopes to keep private is necessary to prepare a defense? What if the media claims a First Amendment right to know the information? These are just a handful of the questions with which courts must grapple and which will be discussed in this chapter.

A. Protecting Victim Privacy by Protecting Identity

1. Protecting Identity

People v. Ramirez

55 Cal. App. 4th 47 (1997)

Reardon, J.

Appellant Luciano Ramirez was convicted of assault with intent to commit rape, attempted rape, sexual battery, and failing to register as a sex offender. Two prior felony convictions alleged as strikes and as serious priors were found true.

Appellant challenges, on constitutional grounds, the validity of section 293.5, a statute that allows under certain circumstances the alleged victim of a sex offense to be identified as "Jane Doe" rather than by her true name. We uphold the validity of section 293.5, reject appellant's remaining contentions, and affirm.

I. Facts

In June 1995, Jane Doe, a 25-year-old married flight attendant, was a resident of Seattle, but based in San Francisco. She shared a "commuter apartment" with other female flight attendants, including Wanda Craig, in Burlingame's North Park Apartments.

[The court then describes the circumstances of the sexual assault which are not relevant to the legal ruling.]

. . .

II. Discussion

A. Appellant's Challenge to the Validity of Section 293.5 Lacks Merit

Appellant challenges the validity of section 293.5 on four grounds: (1) that the identification of the victim as "Jane Doe" interfered with counsel's "ability to make intelligent challenges of the prospective jurors"; (2) that the victim "was less vulnerable to cross-examination" because of her identification as "Jane Doe"; (3) that the victim's privacy interest does not outweigh the appellant's right "to have the jury hear the witness's true name"; and (4) that the instruction mandated by subdivision (b) of section 293.5, that "the alleged victim is being so identified only for the purpose of protecting . . . her privacy," lessens the prosecution's burden of proof resulting in a denial of due process.

1. The Statute

Section 293.5 provides in relevant part that: "(a) [T]he court, at the request of the alleged victim, may order the identity of the alleged victim in all records and during all proceedings to be either Jane Doe or John Doe, if the court finds that such an order is reasonably necessary to protect the privacy of the person and will not unduly prejudice the prosecution or the defense. (b) If the court orders the alleged victim to be identified as Jane Doe or John Doe pursuant to subdivision (a) and if there is a jury trial, the court shall instruct the jury, at the beginning and at the end of the trial, that the alleged victim is being so identified only for the purpose of protecting his or her privacy pursuant to this section."

2. Background

Following a series of United States Supreme Court decisions barring government from punishing publication of truthful information lawfully obtained, including a rape victim's identity [cites omitted], and heeding the high court's admonition that "[i]f there are privacy interests to be protected in judicial proceedings, the States must respond by means which avoid public documentation or other exposure of private information," our Legislature, in 1992, unanimously passed Senate Bill No. 296. . . .

The section is intended to protect the privacy of victims of sex offenses, to encourage such victims to report the offenses so that rapists may be apprehended and prosecuted, and to protect these victims from harassment, threats, or physical harm by their assailants and others.

There can be little dispute that the state's interest in protecting the privacy of sex offense victims is extremely strong and fully justified. "No crime is more horribly invasive or more brutally intimate than rape." (Marcus & McMahon, *Limiting Disclosure of Rape Victims' Identities* (1991) 64 So.Cal.L.Rev. 1020, 1030.) Justice White described the crime as the "ultimate violation of self," short of homicide. (The Florida Star v. B.J.F., supra, 491 U.S. at p. 542 [109 S.Ct. at p. 2614] (dis. opn. of White, J.).) The effects of rape, however, do not end with the crime itself. "At the same time a victim is suffering from the severe emotional and physical traumas brought on by the rape, she is also being scrutinized and judged by her community. There is no other crime in which the victim risks being blamed and in so insidious a way . . . ." (Marcus & McMahon, supra, at p. 1030.)

In addition to the protection of the victim's privacy, the state has a strong interest in ensuring that sex offenses are duly and promptly reported. If has been stated that "rape remains the most underreported crime within the criminal justice system" (Marcus & McMahon, *Limiting Disclosure of Rape Victims' Identities*, supra, 64 So.Cal.L.Rev. at pp. 1049–1050, fn. omitted), and studies indicate "that rape victims allege they would be far more willing and likely to come forward, report the crime, and assist the authorities as necessary, if statutorily enforced anonymity were available or dependable" (Berlin, Revealing the Constitutional Infirmities of the "Crime Victims Protection Act," Florida's New Privacy Statute for Sexual Assault Victims (1995) 23 Fla. St. U. L.Rev. 513, 520).

Finally, with respect to the need to protect the victim from harassment, threats, or physical harm from her assailant or others, one need only look to the facts of The Florida Star v. B.J.F., supra, 491 U.S. at page 528 [109 S.Ct. at page 2606], where the victim's mother, after disclosure of the victim's name, received "several threatening phone calls from a man who stated that he would rape B.J.F. again" and that as a result of these threats the victim was required "to change her phone number and residence, to seek police protection, and to obtain mental health counseling." (Ibid.)

3. Standard of Review

It is well settled that all "presumptions and intendments favor the validity of a statute and mere doubt does not afford sufficient reason for a judicial declaration of invalidity. Statutes must be upheld unless their unconstitutionality clearly, positively and unmistakably appears. [Citations omitted]" (It is equally well settled that the person attacking the statute bears the burden of demonstrating its invalidity . . . and that "[o]ne who seeks to raise a constitutional question must show that his or her rights are affected injuriously by the law which he or she attacks and that he or she is actually aggrieved by its operation." . . .

4. Jury Selection

In giving the names of witnesses to the prospective jurors, the court identified the victim as "Jane Doe," explaining that "Miss Doe is so identified only for the purposes of protecting her rights to privacy under the Penal Code, Section 293.5." Because her true name was not given, prospective jurors, appellant contends, could not comply with the court's directive "if you know any of those individuals, please let us know . . . ." The fact that the victim testified in person at trial and was seen by the sworn jurors, none of whom notified the court or counsel that he or she recognized the victim, does not deter appellant. He argues that a juror may have known the victim by name but not in person and that he was entitled to explore the nature and scope of that assumed knowledge. In nonlegal jargon, we think this is a stretch.

In order to establish prejudice on the basis that the statute, as applied, prevented the examination of prospective jurors concerning knowledge of the victim, appellant would have to show, at a minimum, that some juror who actually served on the jury returning the verdict had such knowledge. . . . This he has not done. Secondly, even if appellant were only required to establish the possibility of such an occurrence, his speculation in this regard is not supported by reality. Short of the status of celebrity or public figure, which is not an issue here, knowledge about an individual is generally acquired through some form of personal contact. Given the trial court's admonition, it is unreasonable to conclude that a juror, recognizing the victim in court, would suppress that information and not inform the court. Even if we were to indulge appellant in his claim that a juror may have known the victim only by name, we fail to see where this argument leads. If the juror only knows the victim by name and is not given the name, there is no way that the juror could relate, whatever information he or she had, to this victim. In short, if the sole source of identification is the true name of the victim and that name is never provided, the juror would not know the victim and would view the testimony of the victim like any other unknown witness in the case.

Finally, the jury was specifically instructed to decide the case based on "the evidence received in the trial and not from any other source." (CALJIC No. 1.00.) In the complete absence of any evidence to the contrary, we must presume that the jury followed this instruction.

In sum, appellant has failed to demonstrate that the identification of the victim as "Jane Doe" resulted in the denial of his right to a fair and impartial jury.

5. Confrontation

Appellant next contends that allowing the victim to testify as "Jane Doe," as authorized by section 293.5, violated his right to confront and cross-examine the witness. He relies primarily on Smith v. Illinois (1968) 390 U.S. 129, a case where the accused was prevented from learning the true name and address of the principal witness against him. Appellant candidly concedes that here, unlike the situation in Smith, the defense was provided with complete discovery, including the true name and address of the victim. This is a significant distinction that does make a difference.

In terms of confrontation and cross-examination, the only limitation imposed on appellant was to prevent reference to the victim by her true name in front of the jury. Such a limitation has been specifically upheld against a similar challenge where, as here, the defense was provided with the true name of the witness. (See *Clark v. Ricketts* 958 F.2d 851 (9th Cir. 1991).) In distinguishing *Smith v. Illinois*, supra, 390 U.S. 129, the court in Clark stated, "[T]here is no absolute right of an accused to have a jury hear a witness's true name . . . ." . . . We agree with the rule and rationale of Clark and also reject the challenge herein.

Alternatively, appellant argues that if preventing disclosure of the victim's name to the jury may be justified in some situations, no justification can be found where the interest to be protected is merely "the privacy" of the victim of a sex offense. We reject this contention for a number of reasons.

"Privacy" is not an insignificant interest-it is described in our state Constitution as one of our "inalienable rights." In the context of the victim of a sex offense, our Legislature, through the enactment of section 293.5, has likewise determined that the privacy interest of such a victim is significant. Appellant does not quarrel with this premise nor with the conclusion that many victims are reluctant to report sex offenses "because of fear they will be publicly identified and humiliated." . . . Appellant does not dispute the purpose of the legislation, heretofore discussed, nor does he challenge the statute's probable success in accomplishing the stated purpose. He argues, solely, that the state's interest in encouraging the reporting of sex offenses and the prosecution of sex offenders is insufficient to outweigh his right to confront the victim by name in court.

The right of the accused to confront and cross-examine the accuser is an express constitutional right. (U.S. Const., Amend. VI; *Pointer v. Texas* (1965) 380 U.S. 400 [85 S.Ct. 1065, 13 L.Ed.2d 923].) "However, even a criminal defendant's express constitutional right to cross-examination and confrontation is not absolute." (In re Elizabeth T. 9 Cal.App.4th 636, 640 [12 Cal.Rptr.2d 10] (1992).) As stated by our high court in *Maryland v. Craig* 497 U.S. 836 [110 S.Ct. 3157, 111 L.Ed.2d 666] (1990): "'Of course, the right to confront and to cross-examine is not absolute and may, in appropriate cases, bow to accommodate other legitimate interests in the criminal trial process.'" (Id. at p. 849 [110 S.Ct. at p. 3165] [compelling state interest in protecting child victims of sex crimes from further trauma may outweigh right to confrontation], quoting *Chambers v. Mississippi* 410 U.S. 284, 285 [93 S.Ct. 1038, 1041, 35 L.Ed.2d 297] (1973).) What constitutes an appropriate case requires a balancing of the state's interest on the one hand and the nature of the defendant's right and degree of limitation on the other. . . .

The statute under attack specifically provides for such a balancing test by requiring that identification of the victim as "Jane Doe" only take place "if the court finds that such an order is reasonably necessary to protect the privacy of the person and will not unduly prejudice the prosecution or the defense." The record reflects that the trial court conducted the required balancing test.

Providing for a balancing test that weighs the privacy interest of the victim of a sex offense and the resulting state interest in facilitating the reporting of sex offenses against the minimal intrusion on an accused's nonabsolute right of confrontation is not, in our view, constitutionally infirm, nor did its application in the instant case violate appellant's confrontation and cross-examination rights.

6. Statutorily Mandated Instruction

Finally, appellant challenges the portion of the statute that requires the trial judge to instruct the jury "that the alleged victim is being so identified [as Jane Doe or John Doe] only for the purpose of protecting his or her privacy pursuant to this section." (§ 293.5, subd. (b).) The jury was so instructed in this case. Appellant contends that the instruction creates the inference that the trial court believes the "alleged victim is an actual victim," thereby lightening the prosecution's burden of proof resulting in a denial of due process. He suggests that the jury should have been cautioned against drawing any inference concerning appellant's guilt from the use of a fictitious name by the alleged victim. We reject this contention.

Because it "must be presumed that the jurors followed the instructions of the trial court," (*People v. Beach* 147 Cal.App.3d 612, 624 [195 Cal.Rptr. 381](1983)) we must conclude, based on the instructions as a whole, that no improper inference could be drawn from the trial court's explanation of the use of the name "Jane Doe" by the "alleged victim." (§ 293.5, subd. (b).)2

. . . .

Judgment affirmed.

Poché, Acting P. J., and Hanlon, J., concurred.

Notes

1. In *Ramirez* a pseudonym (i.e., "Jane Doe") was used to protect victim privacy as opposed to simply using the victim's initials. From a privacy perspective, what are the pros and cons of each method of protecting identity? Even with the use of a pseudonym, how well protected was the victim's identity in the case in light of the fact that her roommate's name was used, and other identifying details (e.g., marital status, career, location) were discussed in the opinion? Are the potentially identifying facts that were included necessary for the court's decision?

2. The statute at issue in the case is specific to victims of sexual violence. Two sexual violence experts have stated, "[f]or most sexual assault victims, privacy is like oxygen; it is a pervasive, consistent need at every step of recovery." Ilene Seidman & Susan Vickers, *The Second Wave: An Agenda for the Next Thirty Years of Rape Law Reform*, 38 SUFFOLK U. L. REV. 467, 473 (2005). What do you think of the policy decision to distinguish privacy protections by crime type?

3. Sometimes victim privacy concerns are raised in civil litigation and the media objects to a victim's use of a pseudonym. For instance, in the civil case of *Plaintiff B. v.*

Francis, 631 F.3d 1310 (11th Cir. 2011), four victim-plaintiffs sued Joseph Francis and companies owned or controlled by him for damages arising from defendants' depiction of the plaintiffs, while minors, in sexually explicit situations in the *Girls Gone Wild* films. Plaintiffs filed a motion to appear anonymously at trial. Intervenor-Appellee Florida Freedom Newspapers argued the motion should be denied, and defendants joined. The district court denied the plaintiffs' motion, finding that the presumption of openness outweighed plaintiffs' desire to proceed anonymously because plaintiffs did not show that they would be forced to disclose information of the "utmost intimacy" and because the court was not convinced of the harm that would befall the plaintiffs if their identities were known. On appeal, the court noted the presumption of openness is not absolute, and that a party may proceed anonymously if there is a substantial privacy right at issue, and that such a right is at issue if the party would be required to disclose information of the "utmost intimacy." The appellate court found that the trial court failed to take into account the degree of intimacy the plaintiffs' testimony, and the evidence of harm that they faced if they were forced to reveal their identities, including trauma of having their names on searchable online databases where anyone entering their names would find information about their appearance in these videos. In light of this, the appellate court remanded for further consideration regarding the privacy interests of some of the plaintiffs, and directed the district court to enter an order granting the motion to remain anonymous for others.

4. Often prosecutors and victims seek to protect victim and witness privacy by sealing documents. Courts have recognized that filing documents under seal may be an inadequate protection for victim privacy. *See, e.g., United States v. Darcy*, No. 1:09CR12, 2009 WL 1470495 (W.D.N.C. May 26, 2009) (order) (in a case involving a minor victim, striking the government's motion to seal its Motion for Relief under the Crime Victims' Rights Act (CVRA), 18 U.S.C. § 3771, in light of the fact that any seal in the case would automatically be lifted at the conclusion of the criminal proceeding under the local rules of criminal procedure; and directing the government to file a corrected Motion for Relief with "Jane Doe #1" substituted for the name of the victim). What considerations do you think should guide when to use each type of privacy protection (e.g., sealing documents, redacting, pseudonyms)?

———————

In *Ramirez*, discussed above, privacy was explicitly provided for by statute, and the request for such privacy was initiated by the prosecution and the victim; sometimes courts address the issue of identity privacy *sua sponte* (on the court's own initiative).

State v. Zimmerman

2010 WL 4550716 (N.M. Ct. App. 2010)

Robles, J.

Gerald Zimmerman (Defendant) appeals his conviction for criminal sexual penetration (CSP) [of his stepdaughter] in the first degree. The judgment and sentence was filed on July 24, 2007. Defendant timely filed a notice of appeal on August 20, 2007. As discussed in this Opinion, we affirm Defendant's conviction.

. . .

II. Discussion

As an initial matter, we express a point of concern. The names of the two children in this case were used in briefing to this Court. Although we are not aware of a specific rule that prevents the parties from using children's names in adult proceedings, we nonetheless express our concern about publically identifying minors who are or may have been victims of assault. N.M. Const. art. II, § 24(A) (applying victims' rights to cases involving criminal sexual penetration, criminal sexual contact of a minor, and child abuse); *State v. Fry*, 2006–NMSC–001, ¶ 3 n. 1, 138 N.M. 700, 126 P.3d 516 (filed 2005) ("We do not refer to the victim by name out of respect for her dignity and privacy."). The New Mexico Constitution guarantees "respect for the victim's dignity and privacy throughout the criminal justice process." N.M. Const. art. II, § 24(A)(1). Attorneys in this state should refrain from alluding to matters that are not reasonably relevant to the case at bar or that are unnecessary for fair representation and may embarrass a third party. *See* Rule 16–304(E) NMRA; Rule 16–404(A) NMRA. We strongly suggest that in briefs to this Court, counsel use a minor child's initials or other appropriate abbreviation whenever capable of doing so.

Notes

1. In acting *sua sponte*, the court relied on the New Mexico constitutional guarantee of "respect for the victim's dignity and privacy throughout the criminal justice process." Do you think the court could have acted *sua sponte* without such a provision?

2. In this case the victims were children. Do you think that children have unique privacy considerations?

3. Is it proper for a court to act *sua sponte* on a victim's right? What if the court errs in understanding how the victim would choose to exercise that right (e.g., a victim wants to be known by his/her/their name but the court encourages a pseudonym)?

4. Victims' names are permanently available to anyone once they are in a published court opinion. With the existence of the Internet and more courts making opinions readily available online, should victims be able to redact their names from these opinions after publication using Jane or John Doe as substitutes?

5. Some victim advocacy groups, such as the Voices and Faces Project (http://www.voicesandfaces.org/index.html), are actively working to dismantle the legacy of shame victims feel in the aftermath of sexual violence by bringing the names, faces, and stories of survivors of sexual violence and trafficking to the attention of the public. What do you think of efforts calling on victims to name themselves publicly?

6. Victim privacy can also be implicated in public records requests made under the Freedom of Information Act (FOIA) or equivalent state laws. These requests can occur before, during or after a criminal prosecution and may seek documents ranging from 9-1-1 recordings to law enforcement body-worn camera footage to victim information held by state agencies. *See, e.g., Banks v. Dep't of Justice*, 757 F. Supp. 2d 13 (D.D.C. 2010) (granting summary judgment for the Federal Bureau of Prisons after concluding that it properly redacted sensitive victim-related information because the victims named in the records had a substantial privacy interest in the personal information contained in the records, and because no overriding public interest existed).

—————

2. Protecting Locating Information

Some victims are concerned that disclosure of their personal information may make them vulnerable to future victimization. For example, a victim of domestic violence may seek to escape an abusive partner by moving to new address; or a stalking victim may try to disrupt a perpetrator's contact by changing a telephone number. These efforts are for naught if the victim's new address or telephone number is readily accessible in court records or during court proceedings.

To address these concerns, several states have passed statutes barring disclosure of information that could be used to locate a victim.

Tex. Crim. Proc. Code Ann. § 56.09

As far as reasonably practical, the address of the victim may not be a part of the court file except as necessary to identify the place of the crime. The phone number of the victim may not be a part of the court file.

Utah Code Ann. § 77-38-6(1)

The victim of a crime has the right, at any court proceeding, including any juvenile court proceeding, not to testify regarding the victim's address, telephone number, place of employment, or other locating information unless the victim specifically consents or the court orders disclosure on finding that a compelling need exists to disclose the information. A court proceeding on whether to order disclosure shall be in camera.

Note

The Utah statute contains an exception allowing disclosure of the victim's address in cases of "compelling need." Might there be rare cases where the Constitution requires that a defendant have access to an address to prepare his defense? *See* Nora V. Demleitner, *Witness Protection in Criminal Cases: Anonymity, Disguise or Other Options?*, 46 Am. J. Comp. L. 641, 663 (1998) (advancing this argument).

—————

In contrast to the above-discussed statutory exclusions of information from disclosure, some statutory schemes seem to require disclosure of locating information. When faced with requirements such as these, prosecutors and victims may argue that victims' rights together with the general right to privacy, should prevent disclosure of certain locating or identifying information.

State v. Mullen

503 S.W.3d 330 (Mo. Ct. App. 2016)

Lawrence E. Mooney, Presiding J.

The Circuit Attorney filed petitions for writs of mandamus, disputing the trial court's denial of her motions for protective order in fourteen underlying criminal cases. We issued preliminary orders and ordered the cases consolidated, briefed, and orally argued. Today, we quash the preliminary orders in part and make them permanent in part. We agree with the trial court's conclusions that Missouri Supreme Court Rule 25.03 is constitutional and that the Circuit Attorney failed to prove that good cause existed for protective orders. But we disagree with the trial court's interpretation of the scope of disclosure required by Rule 25.03. Therefore, the trial court should deny the Circuit Attorney's motions that she not be required to disclose the last known addresses of witnesses. But the trial court should grant the Circuit Attorney's motions that the scope of discovery under Rule 25.03 does not require her to divulge the phone numbers, dates of birth, and social-security numbers of witnesses.

Factual and Procedural Background

The defendants in the fourteen underlying criminal cases each requested that the Circuit Attorney provide discovery under Missouri Supreme Court Rule 25.03. That Rule requires that the Circuit Attorney provide discovery to defendants upon request, including the names and last known addresses of all persons the Circuit Attorney intends to call as witnesses.

The Circuit Attorney moved for a protective order in each case pursuant to Missouri Supreme Court Rule 25.11, which authorizes the trial court, on motion and for good cause shown, to order that specified disclosures be denied. The Circuit Attorney in her motions sought to withhold the phone numbers, dates of birth, social-security numbers, and last known addresses of victims and witnesses contained in the police reports. She offered to produce victims and witnesses to defense counsel at her office, for a deposition or interview, in lieu of providing the information.

The Circuit Attorney has a long-standing practice, dating back some ten years, of deleting this information from police reports, even deleting the last known addresses, before providing the reports to defense counsel. The Circuit Attorney established this practice based on her own conclusion that Rule 25.03 was unconstitutional in light of an amendment to the Missouri Constitution adopted in 1992. That amendment provides that crime victims have a right to "reasonable protection" from a defendant.

In the last ten years, the Circuit Attorney never sought the trial court's permission to deviate from the mandates of the Missouri Supreme Court Rules and never sought a declaration that Rule 25.03 was unconstitutional. She seeks protective orders now, apparently for the first time, after protests from defense counsel.

The fourteen motions filed by the Circuit Attorney were identical, with the exception of the list of pending charges for each defendant. The Circuit Attorney lodged alternative arguments and requests for court action. She first challenged the constitutionality of Rule 25.03, contending that to the extent the Rule required disclosure of the last known address and any other personal identifying information, the Rule violated the victims' and witnesses' constitutional right to privacy. She thus sought the trial court's declaration that Rule 25.03 was unconstitutional as applied to crime victims and witnesses. Alternatively, the Circuit Attorney sought protective orders allowing her to redact the victims' and witnesses' last known addresses and other personal identifying information from the police reports. In arguing that good cause existed for granting her motions, she alleged generally that victims and witnesses were subject to threats, intimidation, potential identity theft, and other cybercrimes. She further generally averred that this had a chilling effect on her ability to prosecute defendants. However, the Circuit Attorney never alleged that any victim or witness in any of the underlying criminal cases had been subject to threats, intimidation, or any untoward consequence. In the event the court rejected this argument, the Circuit Attorney alternatively argued that she could redact all personal identifying information other than the last known addresses of victims and witnesses because the rule on its face only required disclosure of last known addresses.

Judge Michael K. Mullen called the Circuit Attorney's motions for hearing. The court addressed each of the fourteen cases individually. However, the Circuit Attorney never adduced any specific evidence that any victim or witness in any of the cases had been subject to threats, intimidation, or any untoward consequence. Instead, she reargued the general, non-specific allegations contained in her motions.

The trial court denied the Circuit Attorney's motions, concluding that Rule 25.03 is constitutional. The court further held that the Circuit Attorney failed to show good cause for protective orders under Rule 25.11. The court ordered the Circuit Attorney "to comply with Rule 25.03 and provide defendant with last known addresses of all endorsed witnesses and an unredacted police report." An unredacted police report would include phone numbers, dates of birth, and social-security numbers of victims and witnesses.

The Circuit Attorney now seeks writs of mandamus. She asks that we order the trial court to hold Rule 25.03 unconstitutional to the extent it requires disclosure of personal information of crime victims and witnesses. Alternatively, the Circuit Attorney asks that we order the trial court to issue protective orders in the underlying cases.

. . .

Constitutional Challenge

The trial court concluded that Rule 25.03 did not violate the Missouri Constitution. Constitutional interpretation is a question of law that we review *de novo*. *State v. Jackson*, 384 S.W.3d 208, 211 (Mo. 2012).

Rule 25.03, at the center of this ongoing dispute, reads in pertinent part:

(A) Except as otherwise provided in these Rules as to protective orders, the state shall, upon written request of defendant's counsel, disclose to defendant's counsel such part or all of the following material and information within its possession or control designated in said request:

(1) The names and last known addresses of persons whom the state intends to call as witnesses at any hearing or at the trial, together with their written or recorded statements, and existing memoranda, reporting or summarizing part or all of their oral statements. . . .

The Circuit Attorney must provide the information upon written request of defense counsel, without the necessity of a court order. The Missouri Supreme Court adopted this Rule in June of 1979. The Rule became effective on January 1, 1980, some thirty-six years ago.

In 1992, the citizens of Missouri amended the Missouri Constitution to establish certain rights of crime victims. Mo. Const. Art. I, Sec. 32. Thus, the Missouri Constitution recognizes that crime victims have:

the right to reasonable protection from the defendant or any person acting on behalf of the defendant.

Mo. Const. Art. I, Sec. 32 (1)(6).

The Circuit Attorney argues that in light of this constitutional provision, Rule 25.03 is unconstitutional as applied to crime victims and witnesses. We acknowledge the constitutional protections afforded crime victims, and we understand their importance. We sympathize with the plights of victims and witnesses, and are grateful for their participation in the criminal-justice system. We take seriously the retribution that victims and witnesses may face. But we reject the Circuit Attorney's constitutional challenge. Importantly, the Rule opens with cautionary language providing that Rule 25.03 does not even apply if the Circuit Attorney, or any prosecutor, shows good cause for issuance of a protective order under Rule 25.11. Thus, far from trampling the rights of victims, Rule 25.03 specifically limits mandatory disclosure if a protective order is warranted.

Missouri amended its constitution to secure crime victims' rights nearly a quarter of a century ago. The Circuit Attorney generally complains that the Rule contains inadequate safeguards to protect the privacy rights of victims and witnesses. If this is true, other avenues exist and have existed, to address this issue. Whether the Rule should be revised is an issue better addressed through these other avenues. Indeed, counsel represented at oral argument that a reexamination of the Rule is currently underway by a committee of the Missouri Supreme Court.

We reject the Circuit Attorney's challenge to the constitutionality of Rule 25.03.

Good Cause for Protective Order

The Circuit Attorney alternatively contends that good cause exists to issue a protective order under Rule 25.11, allowing her to redact information from police reports before turning those reports over to the defense. A trial court has broad discretion in administering rules of discovery. *State ex rel. Tuller v. Crawford*, 211 S.W.3d 676, 678 (Mo. App. S.D. 2007). This Court will not disturb the trial court's ruling absent an abuse of that discretion. *Id.*

Rule 25.11, the rule governing protective orders in the criminal setting, provides that "[t]he court may at any time, on motion and for good cause shown, order [s] pecified disclosures be denied, regulated, restricted, or deferred, or make such other order as it deems appropriate. . . ." Rule 25.11(A).

For purposes of assessing the trial court's good-cause ruling only, we assume that all the information sought to be withheld falls within the ambit of Rule 25.03's mandatory disclosure requirement. We will later address that precise issue.

In her motions for protective orders, the Circuit Attorney argued that the trial court must restrict information about victims and witnesses to ensure their safety, protection, and peace of mind, and to prevent identity theft. But the Circuit Attorney failed to allege any specific facts in support of her conclusions. Indeed, other than a listing of the involved charges in the case, the identical motions are completely devoid of any facts whatsoever. The Circuit Attorney's argument at the hearing was likewise lacking in substance. There, she relied heavily, if not entirely, on that fact that she had filed criminal charges. We agree with the trial court that the mere filing of criminal charges does not create good cause for a protective order under Rule 25.11.

A trial court has the discretion to determine whether good cause exists, but a court must have evidence presented to it before the court can exercise its discretion. *State v. Rushing*, 232 S.W.3d 656, 661–62 (Mo. App. S.D. 2007). When a protective order is not supported by an evidentiary showing of good cause, an order would be both unauthorized and arbitrary. *Id.* at 661–62. The Circuit Attorney failed to provide this evidentiary showing. The trial court did not abuse its discretion in denying the Rule 25.11 motions for failure of the Circuit Attorney to show good cause.

Scope of Disclosure

Though we find no fault in the trial court's conclusion that the Circuit Attorney failed to demonstrate good cause for protective orders, we do conclude that the trial court erred in the scope of disclosure ordered. Again, the trial court ordered the Circuit Attorney "to comply with Rule 25.03 and provide defendant with last known addresses of all endorsed witnesses and an unredacted police report."

Resolution of the dispute here requires interpretation of Rule 25.03. We are to interpret Missouri Supreme Court Rules in the same fashion as statutes, and statutory interpretation is a question of law, which this Court reviews *de novo. Ressler v. Clay County*, 375 S.W.3d 132, 136 (Mo. App. W.D. 2012).

According to the Rule, the State is required to disclose:

> The last known addresses of persons whom the state intends to call as witnesses at any hearing or at the trial, together with their written or recorded statements, and existing memoranda, reporting or summarizing part or all of their oral statements. . . .

We interpret Missouri Supreme Court Rules by applying principles similar to those used for interpreting state statutes. *State ex rel. Vee–Jay Contracting Co. v. Neill*, 89 S.W.3d 470, 471–72 (Mo. banc 2002). In interpreting a rule, this Court is to ascertain the intent of our Supreme Court, by considering the plain and ordinary meaning of the words in the rule. *Id* at 472.

Rule 25.03 explicitly requires the State to disclose last known addresses. The Circuit Attorney's practice of routinely withholding this information is in direct contravention of the mandates of the Rule.[6] This practice should stop immediately.[7]

What then, of other personal identifying information, such as the phone numbers, dates of birth, and social-security numbers that may be included in the police reports? These items are not expressly mentioned in Rule 25.03, although they all existed in 1979 when the Missouri Supreme Court adopted the Rule. If the Missouri Supreme Court intended for this additional identifying information to be routinely disclosed, the Court could have expressly listed the items, as it did with addresses. The Missouri Supreme Court did not. It is a well-established rule of statutory construction that when a statute—here a rule—enumerates the subjects or things on which it is to operate, it is to be construed as excluding from its effect all those not expressly mentioned. *Rupert v. State*, 250 S.W.3d 442, 448–449 (Mo. App. E.D. 2008); *Greenbriar Hills Country Club v. Dir. of Revenue*, 935 S.W.2d 36, 38 (Mo. banc 1996).

Defense counsel contend that identifying information is a statement of a witness, and as such must be disclosed. We are not persuaded.

If the word "statement," as used in Rule 25.03, encompasses all personal identifying information, then it was unnecessary for the Missouri Supreme Court to specifically include the phrase "last known addresses." We presume every word, sentence, or clause in the rule has effect, and that the Missouri Supreme Court did not insert idle verbiage or superfluous language. . . . Defense counsels' interpretation would render part of the Rule superfluous.

---

6. If the Circuit Attorney believes and can demonstrate with specific evidence in an individual case that good cause exists to withhold an address, she may move the trial court for a protective order under Rule 25.11.

7. We reject the Circuit Attorney's contention that she can comply with her discovery obligations by producing a victim or witness for a deposition or interview, in lieu of providing the requested information. This does not suffice. This is not what the Missouri Supreme Court Rule mandates. Further, victims and witnesses do not belong to the prosecution. State v Berstein, 372 S.W.2d 57, 61 (Mo. 1963).

Webster's Dictionary defines "statement" as: "1. Act of stating, reciting, or presenting, orally or on paper; as, the statement of a case. 2. That which is stated; an embodiment in words of facts or opinions; a narrative; recital; report; account." Webster's New International Dictionary 2461 (2d ed. 1950).

Rule 25.03 exists to provide the defendant with an appropriate opportunity to avoid surprise and to prepare his or her case in advance of trial. *Henderson*, 410–760/64; *State v. Smith*, 491 S.W.3d 286, 298 (Mo. App. E.D. 2016). A "statement," as that term is used in Rule 25.03, is a "narrative, recital, report or account." It is information that "tells the story" of the incident. Personal identifying information does not purport to recite, narrate, report, or account the incident. Accordingly, the Circuit Attorney may redact phone numbers, dates of birth, and social-security numbers from the police reports. Any such redaction by the Circuit Attorney must be made obvious, so that the defense counsel knows that information has been withheld. Our ruling today does not leave defendants without recourse. Should defendants find that they need additional personal identifying information for any witness, they may petition the trial court for disclosure of the information, upon a showing of good cause, under Missouri Supreme Court Rule 25.04.

Conclusion

Our preliminary order in mandamus is made permanent in part and quashed in part. The trial court shall order the Circuit Attorney to disclose the last known addressees of witnesses, but the Circuit Attorney may redact the witnesses' phone numbers, dates of birth, and social-security numbers. We trust that henceforth routine discovery will be provided routinely. Put simply, the parties shall follow the Missouri Supreme Court Rules.

Notes

1. In *Mullen*, the Circuit Attorney had a long-standing practice of deleting information from police reports before providing the reports to defense counsel. If a prosecutor holds the opposite view, i.e., that all of the information sought is proper and necessarily disclosable, how likely is it that a victim's privacy will be protected in a case?

2. The arguments in *Mullen* were presented under the umbrella of a victims' right to reasonable protection, rather than privacy.

3. Because a defense attorney may, as a matter of due process, ask a victim if they will speak with the defense pretrial, absolutely barring of the asking by defense counsel is likely unconstitutional. Appellate courts have, however, generally upheld trial courts that have barred an inquiry by defense counsel into the home addresses of victims. *See, e.g., Winkle v. State*, 488 S.W.2d 798 (Tex. Ct. Crim. App. 1972) (absent showing of particularized need, no basis for forcing rape victim to testify regarding her current address and place of employment); *McGrath v. Vinzant*, 528 F.2d 681 (1st Cir. 1976) (weighing defendant's need against risk to victim in affirming ban on question about rape victim's new home address); *Holmes v. States*, 557 So.2d 933 (Fla.

App. 1990) (questions about address properly barred based on showing of actual threat to victim/witness).

4. As more courts move case files online, the risks of inadvertent disclosure and broad dissemination of victims' private information increases. Some argue that in light of this categorical exclusions of victim information from online court files are appropriate, others argue against such an approach. *See* David S. Ardia, *Privacy and Court Records: Online Access and the Loss of Practical Obscurity*, 2017 U. Ill. L. Rev. 1385 (2017).

5. As more law enforcement officers wear bodyworn cameras the likelihood of private information being caught on film increases. In 2016 the International Association of Chiefs of Police (IACP hosted a multi-day, multidisciplinary, national forum on creating effective victim-centered body-worn camera policies and programs for law enforcement. The resulting report documenting deliberations issued in January 2017 and can be found on the IACP website ww.iacp.org and at this specific url: http://www.theiacp.org/portals/0/documents/pdfs/DeliberationsfromtheIACP NationalForumonBWCsandVAW.pdf

---

B. Protecting Victim Privacy During Attempted Pretrial Discovery

1. Limits on the Defendant's Ability to Interview the Victim

At common law, a defendant had no right to force a victim (or witness) to submit to a pretrial interview. But a defendant did have the right to *attempt* to interview a victim, that is, to ask a victim if she will consent to an interview. Prosecutors are not permitted to interfere with the defendant's access to victims. Victims are generally free to refuse to speak with the defense.

Some states have codified the victim's common law ability to refuse an interview.

Mass. Gen. Laws 258B § 3 Rights afforded victims, witnesses or family members.

. . . [V]ictims and witnesses of crime . . . shall be afforded the following basic and fundamental rights . . . :

to be informed of the right to submit to or decline an interview by defense counsel or anyone acting on the defendant's behalf, except when responding to lawful process, and if the victim or witness decides to submit to an interview the right to impose reasonable conditions on the conduct of the interview.

Some states provide for notice to the victim of the ability to refuse to be interviewed before trial. In some jurisdictions, notice is provided by the defense; in others, by the prosecution.

Ariz. Rev. Stat. § 13-4433(B)

The defendant, the defendant's attorney or other person acting on behalf of the defendant shall only initiate contact with the victim through the prosecutor's office. The prosecutor's office shall promptly inform the victim of the defendant's request for an interview and shall advise the victim of the victim's right to refuse the interview.

Or. Rev. Stat. § 135.970(2)

If contacted by the defense, the victim must be clearly informed by the defendant's attorney either in person or in writing, of the identity and capacity of the person contacting them, that the victim does not have to talk to the defendant's attorney or other agents of the defendant unless the victim wishes, and that the victim may have a district attorney present during any interview.

Some states have enacted additional restrictions on pretrial interviews. For instance, Alaska passed provisions including requiring disclosure of interview recording (despite the fact that generally one-party consent recording is permissible in the state); defense interviewer's identity and association with the defendant; the permissibility of having a prosecuting attorney present during the interview; written consent for such an interview in the case of a sexual assault victim, prior consent to recording. Despite the lack of a common law right to interview victims, courts have weighed these restrictions against defendants' rights and struck some provisions. *See State v. Murtagh*, 169 P.3d 602 (2007) (holding certain restrictions on pretrial interviewing unconstitutional and noting that "[t]here are potential tensions between the requirements of due process and the constitutionally based rights of victims and witnesses. No single formula is available for resolving these tensions. But one method that should be helpful is to require that statutes asserting the rights of victims and witnesses conflict to the least degree reasonably possible with the rights of defendants. Another method is to require that where possible such statutes apply to both the prosecution and the defense so that they do not unduly advantage either side.")

When a victim refuses to be interviewed, the defense may introduce this fact as showing bias or hostility. If this occurs, it may be appropriate for the judge to instruct the jury that the victim has a right to refuse to be interviewed. *See State v. Riggs*, 942 P.2d 1159 (Ariz. 1997).

2. Limits on a Defendant's Ability to Depose a Victim

Usually a defendant can depose a victim (or a witness) in a criminal case only for the purpose of perpetuating testimony. For example, when a victim is dying or will otherwise be unavailable for trial, the defendant will likely be able to obtain a court order permitting a deposition to preserve the testimony. *See* FED. R. CRIM. PROC. 15 (authorizing pre-trial deposition "to preserve testimony for trial" in "exceptional circumstances and in the interest of justice").

Arizona has gone much further. In Arizona, the defendant could take a victim's deposition where the victim's testimony was necessary to prepare an adequate defense, the victim was not a witness at a preliminary hearing, and the victim did not cooperate in granting a personal interview. *See State v. Draper*, 784 P.2d 259 (Ariz. 1989). In 1990, the Victims' Bill of Rights added to the Arizona Constitution nullified Arizona's deposition statute:

ARIZONA CONST., Art. 2, §2.1 Victim's Bill of Rights:

> (A) To preserve and protect victim's rights to justice and due process, a victim of crime has a right:

> * * *

> (5) to refuse an interview, deposition or other discovery request by the defendant, the defendant's attorney or other person citing on behalf of the defendant.

Does a defendant have superior federal constitutional rights to victims' rights to refuse interviews and depositions?

State ex rel. Romley v. Hutt, Judge of the Superior Court of the State of Arizona

987 P.2d 218 (Ariz. App. 1999)

THOMPSON, Judge.

This special action arises out of a request by Real Party in Interest Robin Treen (defendant) to interview victim James Hickey (Hickey). The trial court ordered the interview, and the state challenges the order as violative of the Victims' Bill of Rights. . . . For the following reasons, we accept jurisdiction and grant relief.

. . .

DISCUSSION

In 1990, the people of Arizona amended their constitution to include a Victims' Bill of Rights, which states:

> (A) To preserve and protect victims' rights to justice and due process, a victim of crime has a right:

> * * *

> (5) To refuse an interview, deposition, or other discovery request by the defendant, the defendant's attorney, or other person acting on behalf of the defendant.

Ariz. Const., Art. 2, § 2.1(A)(5).

Arizona's appellate courts have considered the victim's right to decline a defense interview "absolute." *See State v. Roscoe,* 912 P.2d 1297, 1303 (Ariz. 1996). However, in some cases some victims' rights may be required to give way to a defendant's federal constitutional rights. *See State ex rel. Romley v. Superior Court,* 836 P.2d 445, 453–54 (Ariz. App. 1992) (disclosure of victim's medical records ordered). Defendant argues that she should be allowed to inquire of [the victim] Hickey as to the reasons for his refusal to be interviewed, asserting that "[a] witness's refusal to grant a pretrial interview is often relevant to the witness's credibility." But our supreme court has said that the refusal of a crime victim to grant an interview does not necessarily indicate bias. *See State v. Riggs,* 942 P.2d 1159, 1166 (Ariz. 1997). Defendant further claims that her federal Sixth Amendment right to confront witnesses outweighs the victim's state constitutional rights. However, confrontation rights under the Sixth Amendment do not normally afford criminal defendants a right to pretrial discovery. *See Pennsylvania v. Ritchie,* 480 U.S. 39, 52–53 (1987) (plurality decision). The right to confront witnesses at trial "does not include the power to require the pretrial disclosure of any and all information that might be useful in contradicting unfavorable testimony." *Id.* at 53. Defendant also invokes *State ex rel. Dean v. City Court of City of Tucson,* 844 P.2d 1165 (Ariz. App. 1992), for the notion that there is no violation of victims' rights when a victim is compelled before trial to disclose information in a court hearing. The *Dean* opinion, however, which involved compulsory process at a probable cause hearing, does not support the trial court's order for a pretrial discovery interview. *See id.* at 1166. Indeed, *Dean* specifically disallowed the use of a preliminary hearing as a discovery device. *See id.* at 1167 (citing *State v. Bojorquez,* 535 P.2d 6 (Ariz. 1975) for the proposition that "pretrial hearings are not to be used for purposes of discovery"). Defendant in these proceedings has sought to explain why she should be allowed pretrial inquiry of the victim regarding bias, interest or hostility. We reject these arguments. But defendant has not even attempted to support the further reaches of the trial judge's ruling. The judge determined that:

> The facts of this case are . . . so entwined the victim with the defendant in terms of the agreement and any breach of that agreement that becomes the essence of the offense that to not conduct a pretrial interview of the witness effectively denies the defendant the ability to prepare for trial and thus to effectively prepare a defense at trial.

The trial court accordingly ordered a victim interview in which defendant would be allowed to explore not just whether the refusal of an interview demonstrated bias, interest or hostility, but also allegations that Treen breached an agreement with Hickey, and that the Treens lacked permission to use his car. In short, the trial court ordered a victim interview to explore the state's case, and did not even purport to limit the interview to questions of bias, interest or hostility.

The trial court's determination that key elements of the charge, and the defense to the charge, will likely involve information provided by Hickey does not justify breach of Hickey's constitutional right to decline to be interviewed. Certainly, Hickey is a key witness, and it would be useful to defendant to talk to him before trial, but our constitution precludes this, and no superior constitutional right of defendant's compels it. Indeed, the trial court's conclusions regarding the facts of this case would be broadly applicable in a great many criminal cases involving victims. Victims are often important, crucial, and even critical witnesses. It is no doubt a sound practice for lawyers to interview witnesses before trial. But to compel victim interviews based on the kind of generic considerations presented here would nullify a significant constitutional protection afforded crime victims. The victim's right to refuse a defense interview protects the victim's privacy and allows him to minimize contact with the defendant, if he so chooses. In order to uphold the determination of the people of this state that such protections be available to crime victims, we must reverse the trial court's order of a compelled victim interview in this case.

Notes

1. Does the fact that defendants can argue that their federal constitutional rights trump the state constitutional rights of victims warrant placing victims rights' in the federal constitution to avoid confusion and uncertainty that might undercut victims' rights? This issue is explored in Chapter 12 on the Future of Victims' Rights.

2. Where a deposition is granted, the victim is entitled in some jurisdictions to have a support person present at deposition. For instance, in Florida, FLA. STAT. § 960.001(g) provides: "At the request of the victim, the victim advocate designated by state attorney's office, sheriff's office, or municipal police department, or one representative from a not-for-profit victim services organization, including, but not limited to, rape crisis centers, domestic violence advocacy groups, and alcohol abuse or substance abuse groups shall be permitted to attend and be present during any deposition of the victim."

3. For a discussion of victims' rights as they intersect with the state's ability to compel information from them, see Chapter 4 on Charging.

---

3. Limits on a Defendant's Examination of a Victim's Physical Property

In some cases, defense counsel may wish to examine the victim's physical property to prepare for trial. For example, defense counsel may want to visit the "scene of the crime" to understand trial testimony—even where that scene is the victim's home. Courts have reached conflicting results on how to handle such requests.

People in the Interest of E.G.

368 P.3d 946 (Colo. 2016)

Chief Justice Rice delivered the Opinion of the Court.

In this case we must decide whether a trial court has the authority to grant a defendant's discovery motion seeking access to the private residence of a third party. The defendant, E.G., was convicted of two counts of sexual assault on a child as part of a pattern of sexual abuse. Before trial, he filed a motion requesting court-ordered access to his grandmother's basement—the scene of the crime. The trial court concluded that it had no authority to order such access and denied the motion.

The court of appeals disagreed with the trial court's reasoning, though not its result. *People in the Interest of E.G.*, 371 P.3d 693 (2015). It held that a trial court does indeed have authority to order defense access to a third-party residence. *Id.* It nevertheless affirmed the denial of the motion for access because it concluded that E.G. had "failed to demonstrate" that inspection of the crime scene was "necessary to present his defense." We granted the People's petition for certiorari to determine under what circumstances—if any—a trial court has authority to grant a defendant access to a private residence. We conclude that the trial court lacked authority to order such access and therefore affirm on alternate grounds.

I. Facts and Procedural History

E.G. was charged as an aggravated juvenile offender, and a jury found him guilty of two counts of sex assault on a child as part of a pattern of abuse. . . . The victims were twelve-year-old twin brothers who disclosed to their father that their older cousin, E.G., had repeatedly raped them several years earlier in the basement of their mutual grandmother's house.

Prior to trial, E.G. moved the court to order the victims' grandmother "to allow Defense Counsel and [her investigator] to have access to the residence" so that counsel could "view and photograph the crime scene." As grounds for his motion, E.G. cited authority from other jurisdictions suggesting that such access was necessary under principles of fundamental fairness and due process of law. The court denied the motion, reasoning that it could not "order a private entity to open up their private residence." The court explained that it had not seen "any Colorado law, statutory or case law that indicate[d]" that the court had any authority to order the requested access. The trial went forward, and E.G. was convicted.

On appeal, E.G. challenged the denial of his motion for access to the home, and the court of appeals held that the trial court erred when it held that it did not have the authority to order defense access to the private property of a non-party. *E.G.* According to the court of appeals, the trial court's authority stemmed from the defendant's "constitutional right to present evidence on his behalf and to confront adverse witnesses" and the right to "compel material evidence from private third parties." To obtain such access, the court explained, a defendant "must demonstrate that the evidence is relevant, material, and necessary to his defense, and the court must balance the defendant's proffered justification with the rights and legitimate interests of the non-party." After creating this test, the court of appeals subsequently concluded that E.G. failed to satisfy it. Thus, the court of appeals affirmed the trial court's denial of the motion for access on alternate grounds. We granted the People's petition for certiorari.

II. Standard of Review

Generally speaking, appellate courts will review a trial court's discovery order in a criminal case for abuse of discretion. *See* Crim. P. 16(I)(d)(1); *People ex rel. Shinn v. Dist. Ct.*, 172 Colo. 23, 469 P.2d 732, 733–34 (1970). However, a trial court abuses its discretion if it exceeds the bounds of its legal authority. *See Spahmer v. Gullette*, 113 P.3d 158, 164 (Colo. 2005). Thus, the precise question we are faced with today—whether a trial court has the authority to order a third party to open her home to the defendant—presents a legal question that we will review de novo. *See Stackhouse v. People*, 2015 CO 48, ¶ 4, —— P.3d ——.

III. Analysis

Defendant argues that the trial court erred when it denied his motion for investigatory access to a non-party's private home. The threshold question we must answer—and a question we address in conjunction with a related case, also issued today, *In re People v. Chavez*, CO 20, 368 P.3d 943 (2016)—is whether a trial court has any authority to issue such an order in the first place. We analyze the potential sources of authority and conclude that nothing authorized the trial court to grant the defendant's request for access to a private home. Because we hold that the trial court's original ruling was correct—it did not have authority to order the access—we now affirm the court of appeals on alternate grounds.

A. The Right to be Free From Unreasonable Intrusion Into One's Home

The Fourth Amendment to the United States Constitution provides that "the right of the people to be secure in their persons, houses, papers, and effects, against unreasonable searches and seizures, shall not be violated." The Colorado Constitution contains a nearly identical provision. See Colo. Const. art. II, § 7 ("The people shall be secure in their persons, papers, homes and effects, from unreasonable searches and seizures. . . ."). "The clearest right is to be free from unreasonable governmental intrusion into one's home." *People v. O'Hearn*, 931 P.2d 1168, 1172–73 (Colo. 1997). A court order forcing an individual to open her private home to strangers is certainly government intrusion.

Under these circumstances, (1) the deprivation would be "caused by the exercise of some right or privilege created by the State" (namely, a court order) and (2) E.G., the "party charged with the deprivation," would qualify as a state actor "because he [would have] acted together with or . . . obtained significant aid from state officials"—in this case, the district court judge. *Lugar v. Edmondson Oil Co., Inc.*, 457 U.S. 922, 937, 102 S.Ct. 2744, 73 L.Ed.2d 482 (1982); cf. *Walter v. United States*, 447 U.S. 649, 662, 100 S.Ct. 2395, 65 L.Ed.2d 410 (1980) (Blackmun, J., dissenting) ("[T]he Fourth Amendment proscribes only governmental action, and does not apply to a search or seizure, even an unreasonable one, effected by a private individual not acting as an agent of the Government or with the participation or knowledge of any government official."); *Burdeau v. McDowell*, 256 U.S. 465, 475, 41 S.Ct. 574, 65 L. Ed. 1048 (1921) (holding that there was no Fourth Amendment violation where "no official of the . . . government had anything to do with the wrongful seizure").

Accordingly, E.G.'s grandmother had a constitutional right to be free from an unreasonable search of her home conducted by the defense.

Against this backdrop, we must analyze whether E.G.'s own constitutional rights granted him the ability to obtain access to the home. Thus, this case directly confronts the tension between the constitutional rights of an innocent third party who had the misfortune of seeing her home become the scene of a crime and the constitutional rights of the criminal defendant charged with that crime.

B. Development of Criminal Discovery

"The right of discovery in criminal cases is not recognized at common law." *Walker v. People*, 126 Colo. 135, 162, 248 P.2d 287, 302 (1952); *see* also Michael Moore, Criminal Discovery, 19 Hastings L.J. 865, 865 (1968) ("It is an often-cited proposition that at common law the defendant in a criminal trial had no right to discover any of the prosecution's case against him."). Early American courts, with some exceptions, adopted the common-law doctrine that they lacked the power, absent authorizing legislation, to order the prosecutor to provide discovery to a defendant. *Moore*, supra, at 866. In the ensuing years, however, many courts left the common-law doctrine behind. *See id.* at 867–69 (explaining that in almost all states, criminal discovery is in the discretion of the trial judge). The twentieth century saw many changes to the law of criminal pretrial disclosure. In 1963, the seminal case of *Brady v. Maryland* established a constitutional right to the disclosure of exculpatory information in the prosecutor's possession. 373 U.S. 83, 83 S.Ct. 1194, 10 L.Ed.2d 215 (1963). Around the same time, states and legislatures began to expand criminal discovery rights through statute and through the rules of criminal procedure. See, e.g., Crim. P. 16; Utah R. Crim. P. 16.

Despite, or perhaps as a result of, the wide expansion of discovery rights through statutes and court rules, Colorado remains one of the few states that has never deviated from the traditional doctrine holding that courts lack power to grant discovery outside of those statutes or rules. *See Walker*, 248 P.2d at 302. In *Walker*, a defendant had requested and was denied pretrial access to certain physical evidence specimens upon which he wished to conduct "chemical experiments." Id. This court rejected his assignment of error, explaining that the trial court properly denied his request because it had no authority to do otherwise: "[T]he doctrine of discovery is . . . a complete and utter stranger to criminal procedure, unless introduced by appropriate legislation." *Id.*

Because Colorado law establishes that a trial court has no freestanding authority to grant criminal discovery beyond what is authorized by the Constitution, the rules, or by statute, we must scrutinize those sources to determine whether the trial court had the ability to grant E.G. access to his grandmother's private home.

C. Rule 16 of the Colorado Rules of Criminal Procedure

Crim. P. 16 ensures that a defendant has access to material and information in the government's possession or control, but it does not address a defendant's ability to access material and information held by private third parties. It thus cannot provide a source of authority for a court to order access to a private third party's home.

In *Brady v. Maryland*, 373 U.S. 83, 87, 83 S.Ct. 1194, 10 L.Ed.2d 215 (1963), the Supreme Court first recognized that "the suppression by the prosecution of evidence favorable to an accused upon request violates due process where the evidence is material either to guilt or to punishment." See also *United States v. Bagley*, 473 U.S. 667, 682, 105 S.Ct. 3375, 87 L.Ed.2d 481 (1985) (holding that regardless of whether the defense makes a request, constitutional error results from government suppression of favorable evidence). Crim. P. 16 prevents the prosecution from committing such a violation. Under Crim. P. 16(I)(a)(2), the prosecutor is required to "disclose to the defense any material or information within his or her possession or control which tends to negate the guilt of the accused as to the offense charged or would tend to reduce the punishment therefor." The rule also goes further and lists many other types of material and information "within the possession or control of the prosecuting attorney" (or "other governmental personnel") that the prosecutor must "make available" to the defense. Crim. P. 16(I)(a)(1). However nothing in Crim. P. 16(I)(1)(a)-(c) grants the trial court authority to order access to a private home that is not subject to the court's jurisdiction. Neither the prosecutor nor any other government personnel was in possession of E.G.'s grandmother's house. Therefore, Crim. P. 16(I)(1)(a)-(c) did not provide the court with authority to order access to the home.

16 Crim. P. 16(I)(d)(1) provides generally that "the court in its discretion may, upon motion, require disclosure to the defense of relevant material and information not covered by Parts I(a), (b) and (c), upon a showing by the defense that the request is reasonable." But to "require disclosure," the court must have authority over the thing disclosed—and the court has no authority to order "disclosure" of a nonparty's home. And of course, the rule's language requiring "disclosure" of "material or information" does not easily seem to apply to a request for access to a home. In any event, as we explained in *People v. District Court*, "Crim. P. 16(I)(d)(1) is not intended to afford an accused an additional opportunity to pursue material which could not be discovered under Crim. P. 16(I)(a)(1) or (a)(2)." 790 P.2d 332, 338 (Colo.1990). Thus, Crim. P. 16(I)(d)(1) does not provide broad power to the courts to grant criminal defendants access to a non-party's private property. Having established that Crim. P. 16 does not apply to third parties, we turn to the second primary component of a criminal defendant's discovery rights: Crim. P. 17 and the right to compulsory process.

D. The Compulsory Process Clause of the Sixth Amendment and the Rule 17 Subpoena Power

Rule 17 of the Colorado Rules of Criminal Procedure provides criminal defendants with a means to vindicate their constitutional rights to compulsory process. *People v. Spykstra*, 234 P.3d 662, 671 (Colo.2010). E.G. argues that the Sixth Amendment's compulsory process clause underlies the trial court's authority to issue an order granting a defendant access to the home of a private third party—and the court of appeals suggested the same, below. The Sixth Amendment right to compulsory process is a trial right to compel witnesses to testify and to bring tangible evidence to court with them; it does not provide a trial court with the authority to order a non-party to allow access to her private home.

The Sixth Amendment provides that "[i]n all criminal prosecutions, the accused shall enjoy the right . . . to have compulsory process for obtaining witnesses in his favor." U.S. Const. amend VI. The court of appeals cited *Washington v. Texas*, 388 U.S. 14, 19, 87 S.Ct. 1920, 18 L.Ed.2d 1019 (1967), for the proposition that, as a part of the constitutional right to present evidence and confront witnesses, a defendant has "the right to compel material evidence from private third parties." It went on to conclude that therefore, under Washington, "a defendant's right to inspect an alleged crime scene clearly implicates concepts of fundamental fairness and due process." Here, the court of appeals went too far.

In *Washington*, the Supreme Court applied the Compulsory Process Clause of the Sixth Amendment to the states and held that "[a]n accused . . . has the right to present his own witnesses to establish a defense" because "[t]his right is a fundamental element of due process of law." 388 U.S. at 19, 87 S.Ct. 1920. However, *Washington* does not support the notion that the Compulsory Process Clause provides a tool by which a defendant can obtain investigatory access to private property. In fact, "[a]part from serving to secure witnesses and evidence for in-court presentation, the Compulsory Process Clause . . . has never been found by the Court to guarantee access to evidence more generally." *People v. Baltazar*, 241 P.3d 941, 944 (Colo.2010) (citations omitted).

In Colorado, Crim. P. 17 provides a defendant with the tools of compulsory process. Crim. P. 17 provides that "in every criminal case" the defendant has the "right to compel the attendance of witnesses and the production of tangible evidence by service upon them of a subpoena to appear for examination as a witness." The rule provides that a defendant may issue a subpoena commanding a witness "to attend and give testimony" and that he "may also command the person . . . to produce . . . books, papers, documents, photographs, or other objects." Crim. P. 17(a), (c). Thus, under Crim. P. 17, a defendant may obtain limited access, through the subpoena power of the court, to tangible, material evidence and witness testimony. See Spykstra, 234 P.3d at 669. This court has long emphasized that pretrial subpoenas under Crim. P. 17(c) have a "limited scope" and may not be used as an investigatory tool. Id.; see also Crim. P. 17(c) (providing that "the court on motion made promptly may quash or modify the subpoena if compliance would be unreasonable or oppressive").

Moreover, this case does not involve a rule 17(c) subpoena. And even if it did, no such subpoena could issue under rule 17(c) for access to a private home. Crim. P. 17(c) applies explicitly to the production, in court, of "books, papers, documents, photographs, or other objects."

Contrary to E.G.'s argument, we have never upheld a general right of criminal defendants to discovery under the Compulsory Process Clause. In *Spykstra*, we held that "compulsory process and due process may require pretrial access to evidence which may be material to the defense." 234 P.3d at 671. But the *Spykstra* court concluded that the subpoena authority under Crim. P. 17(c) provides the defense with all of the access to material possessed by third persons that the Constitution requires. Id. ("Crim. P. 17(c) strikes the balance between a defendant's right to exculpatory evidence with the competing interests of a witness to protect personal information. . . ."); see also *United States v. Pollard (In re Martin Marietta Corp.)*, 856 F.2d 619, 621 (4th Cir. 1988) ("Rule 17(c) implements the Sixth Amendment guarantee that an accused have compulsory process to secure evidence in his favor."). Accordingly, Crim. P. 17 does not provide authority by which a trial court can order defense access to a private home of a non-party that is not in the possession or control of the government.

E. The Due Process Clause

We now turn to the Due Process Clause. As we have explained, it is well established that "[t]here is no general constitutional right to discovery in a criminal case, and *Brady* did not create one." *Weatherford v. Bursey*, 429 U.S. 545, 559, 97 S.Ct. 837, 51 L. Ed.2d 30 (1977); accord *Spykstra*, 234 P.3d at 670; see also Brady, 373 U.S. at 87, 83 S. Ct. 1194; *United States v. Beasley*, 576 F.2d 626, 630 (5th Cir. 1978) ("Brady is not a discovery rule, but a rule of fairness and minimum prosecutorial obligation."). In *Brady*, the Court held that a defendant has a right to obtain material, exculpatory evidence from the prosecution, which "if suppressed, would deprive the defendant of a fair trial." *Bagley*, 473 U.S. at 675, 105 S.Ct. 3375 (citing *Brady*, 373 U.S. at 87, 83 S.Ct. 1194). But Brady and its progeny did not give defense counsel the "right to conduct his own search of the State's files." *Pennsylvania v. Ritchie*, 480 U.S. 39, 59, 107 S.Ct. 989, 94 L.Ed.2d 40 (1987); see also *United States v. Agurs*, 427 U.S. 97, 109, 111, 96 S.Ct. 2392, 49 L.Ed.2d 342 (1976) (stating that "the Constitution surely does not demand" that a prosecutor turn over "everything that might influence a jury . . . as a matter of routine practice"). Nor did those cases expand a defendant's discovery rights to anything beyond favorable, material evidence in the possession of the government.

In *Baltazar*, we rejected the idea that due process requires that defendants receive expanded discovery rights. 241 P.3d at 944. We explained that the U.S. Supreme Court "has found, at most," that a defendant has "an entitlement of access to evidence and witnesses that would be both constitutionally material and favorable to the accused." Id. Similarly, in Bagley, the Court explained that a prosecutor is required "only to disclose evidence favorable to the accused that, if suppressed, would deprive the defendant of a fair trial." 473 U.S. at 675, 105 S.Ct. 3375 (footnote omitted); see also *Brady*, 373 U.S. at 87, 83 S.Ct. 1194 ("[S]uppression by the prosecution of evidence favorable to an accused upon request violates due process where the evidence is material either to guilt or punishment. . . ."). These cases stand for the proposition that a defendant has a right of "access" only to favorable evidence that is in the government's possession or control. *Bagley*, 473 U.S. at 675, 105 S.Ct. 3375; *Brady*, 373 U.S. at 87, 83 S.Ct. 1194; *Baltazar*, 241 P.3d at 944.

The Due Process Clause does not provide a defendant with a right to use court-provided "investigative tool[s]." *Baltazar*, 241 P.3d at 943–44 (explaining that a defendant has no right to use Crim. P. 17 subpoenas as an investigative tool because there is "no general constitutional right to discovery in a criminal case"). There is no broad constitutional right of a defendant to access the court's powers to conduct his own investigation. "The United States Supreme Court has implied as much both by the limitations it has imputed to Rule 17(c) and by its due process, access-to-evidence jurisprudence." *Id.* at 944. Accordingly, due process does not provide a mooring upon which we may hitch E.G.'s proposed discovery right.

. . .

F. The Confrontation Clause

We note finally that this case does not present a Confrontation Clause issue. Under the Sixth Amendment, a criminal defendant has the right "to be confronted with the witnesses against him." See generally *Crawford v. Washington*, 541 U.S. 36, 42, 124 S. Ct. 1354, 158 L.Ed.2d 177 (2004). However, "the right to confrontation is a trial right; it is not 'a constitutionally compelled rule of pretrial discovery.'" *Spykstra*, 234 P.3d at 670 (quoting *Ritchie*, 480 U.S. at 52, 107 S.Ct. 989 (plurality opinion)). For this reason, the court of appeals' reliance on *Chambers v. Mississippi*, 410 U.S. 284, 294, 93 S. Ct. 1038, 35 L.Ed.2d 297 (1973), was misplaced. See E.G., (citing Chambers for the proposition that "a defendant's right to inspect an alleged crime scene clearly implicates concepts of fundamental fairness and due process"). In *Chambers*, the defendant had been prevented from cross-examining a witness at trial. 410 U.S. at 291, 93 S.Ct. 1038. The Court held that this was error because the right to cross-examine a witness is "implicit in the constitutional right of confrontation." *Id.* at 295, 93 S.Ct. 1038.

In this case, E.G. was not denied the right to cross-examine an adverse witness at trial. Moreover, it is well established that "the Confrontation Clause does not guarantee 'access to every possible source of information relevant to cross-examination.'" *Spykstra*, 234 P.3d at 670–71 (quoting *Dill v. People*, 927 P.2d 1315, 1322 (Colo.1996)). "The ability to question adverse witnesses . . . does not include the power to require the pretrial disclosure of any and all information that might be useful in contradicting unfavorable testimony." Ritchie, 480 U.S. at 53, 107 S.Ct. 989. Because the access sought by E.G. was unrelated to the trial right to confront witnesses, the Confrontation Clause does not apply here.

IV. Conclusion

In sum, neither a criminal defendant, nor anyone else, including the prosecuting attorney, has a constitutional right to force a third party to open her private home for an investigation. *Weatherford*, 429 U.S. at 559, 97 S.Ct. 837; Spykstra, 234 P.3d at 670. Under the Constitution and our Rules of Criminal Procedure, a defendant is entitled to receive exculpatory evidence in the possession of the prosecutor and other government entities; he must have the opportunity to view and challenge the prosecutor's evidence and confront the witnesses against him; and he may obtain evidence and compel his own witnesses to testify pursuant to Crim. P. 17. But a defendant may not use the power of the court to transgress the constitutional rights of private citizens in order to build his defense.

Under the circumstances presented here, neither the United States Constitution, the Colorado Rules of Criminal Procedure, nor any statute provides the trial court with authority[6] to grant E.G. access to his grandmother's private home without her consent. *See State ex rel. Beach v. Norblad*, 308 Or. 429, 781 P.2d 349, 350 (1989) (holding that "Mrs. Beach is not a party to the criminal case. Absent party status, counsel has not identified any other basis (and we know of none) under which the defendant trial judge could at this stage of the proceedings issue such an order to Mrs. Beach. She is under no obligation to obey an order that the defendant trial judge lacked authority to issue." (citation omitted)). In the absence of a due process right—or any other right—to access a third-party home, the trial court had no authority to issue such an order and E.G.'s motion was properly denied.

Accordingly, we hold that the trial court indeed lacked the authority to grant defense counsel access to the private home of a third party. Because the court of appeals upheld the trial court's denial of the motion for access, we hereby affirm its judgment on alternate grounds.

JUSTICE GABRIEL, concurring in the judgment.

In my view, in an appropriate case, a defendant's due process right to a fair trial requires that he or she be given the right to access a crime scene that is under a third party's control. I further believe that in such a case, the trial court is empowered to order access to the crime scene through its inherent right to enforce its jurisdiction. In this case, however, I do not believe that E.G. has established what I believe should be the requisite showing to obtain access to a crime scene under a third party's control. Accordingly, I generally agree with the court of appeals division's thoughtful analysis in this case, and I would affirm its judgment on the same grounds. I therefore respectfully concur in this court's judgment only.

In my view, in an appropriate case, a defendant's due process right to a fair trial requires that he or she be given the right to access a crime scene that is under a third party's control. I further believe that in such a case, the trial court is empowered to order access to the crime scene through its inherent right to enforce its jurisdiction. In this case, however, I do not believe that E.G. has established what I believe should be the requisite showing to obtain access to a crime scene under a third party's control. Accordingly, I generally agree with the court of appeals division's thoughtful analysis in this case, and I would affirm its judgment on the same grounds. I therefore respectfully concur in this court's judgment only.

---

6. We note that, were the crime scene to be in the possession or control of the prosecutor or another government entity, our analysis of the issues would likely be very different.

I. Facts and Procedural History

The majority has set forth most of the pertinent facts. I would add, however, that although E.G.'s grandmother had allowed the state unfettered access to the crime scene in her home and had initially agreed to give E.G.'s representatives access, she ultimately changed her mind and refused to allow E.G.'s counsel and counsel's investigator access to the home to view and photograph the crime scene.

In my view, this kind of unequal access to the evidence in a case is pertinent to an analysis of whether a defendant was afforded his or her due process right to a fair trial.

II. Analysis

Although I agree with much of the majority's analysis, I part company with my colleagues regarding their discussions of a defendant's due process rights and of a trial court's authority to allow a defendant access to a crime scene that is under a third party's control. I address these issues in turn.

A. Due Process Right to Access a Crime Scene

The Due Process Clauses of the United States and Colorado constitutions guarantee every criminal defendant the right to a fair trial. *Morrison v. People*, 19 P.3d 668, 672 (Colo.2000); see also U.S. Const. amends. V, VI, XIV (setting forth the rights to due process and the rights of an accused in a criminal prosecution); Colo. Const. art. II, §§ 16, 25 (same). In particular, "[t]he right of an accused in a criminal trial to due process is, in essence, the right to a fair opportunity to defend against the State's accusations." *Chambers v. Mississippi*, 410 U.S. 284, 294, 93 S.Ct. 1038, 35 L.Ed.2d 297 (1973).

In light of the foregoing principles, this court has recognized that due process may require pretrial access to evidence that may be material to a defendant's defense. See *People v. Spykstra*, 234 P.3d 662, 671 (Colo.2010); see also *Commonwealth v. Matis*, 446 Mass. 632, 915 N.E.2d 212, 213 (2006) (noting a criminal defendant's unquestioned right under the Sixth Amendment and the Massachusetts Declaration of Rights to obtain relevant evidence bearing on his or her guilt or innocence or that otherwise helps his or her defense). . . .

In recognizing this right of access to material evidence, our prior decisions have been in accord with the decisions of other jurisdictions that have, subject to certain limitations, allowed a defendant access to a crime scene that is under a third party's control.

For example, in *Henshaw v. Commonwealth*, 19 Va.App. 338, 451 S.E.2d 415, 419 (1994), the Virginia Court of Appeals relied on the due process rights set forth in the Virginia Constitution to hold that in an appropriate case, a criminal defendant has the right "to view, photograph, and take measurements of the crime scene."

Similarly, in *Matis*, 915 N.E.2d at 213, the Massachusetts Supreme Judicial Court opined that the trial court had the authority to order access to a crime scene in a private residence, subject to certain conditions.

And most recently, the New Jersey Supreme Court held that a trial court correctly concluded that upon a proper showing, a defendant was entitled to inspect a crime scene in the alleged victim's home. See State in Int. of A.B., 219 N.J. 542, 99 A.3d 782, 793 (2014). In reaching this conclusion, the court observed that New Jersey courts do not countenance "trial by surprise." Id. at 789. The court further opined, "Visiting the scene of the crime can be critical in preparing a defense." Id. at 790; see also State v. Brown, 306 N.C. 151, 293 S.E.2d 569, 578 (1982) (concluding in a case in which police had control of the crime scene, which was an apartment, that it was a denial of fundamental fairness and due process for the defendant to be denied the limited inspection of the crime scene that he had requested, particularly given that the state had been given access to the scene and had relied heavily on information gained therefrom in prosecuting the defendant).

Those courts that have recognized a defendant's due process right to access a crime scene that is under a third party's control, however, have further opined that such access is not unlimited. Rather, a court must consider the third party's significant privacy interest in his or her home. See, e.g., Bullen v. Superior Court, 204 Cal.App.3d 22, 251 Cal.Rptr. 32, 33 (1988) (recognizing a homeowner's "fundamental right to privacy free from judicially mandated intrusion into her home"); Matis, 915 N.E.2d at 215 (recognizing the "legitimate privacy interests" involved); A.B., 99 A.3d at 785 (recognizing the right of a purported victim and her family to privacy); Henshaw, 451 S.E.2d at 420 (noting the private citizen's constitutional right to privacy); see also Chard, 808 P.2d at 355–56 (noting the significant interests of a child sexual abuse victim who is ordered to submit to an involuntary physical examination).

Thus, the Massachusetts Supreme Judicial Court has concluded that before a court will allow a defendant access to a crime scene in a private residence, the owner of the residence and the prosecution must be given both notice of the defendant's motion for pretrial access and the opportunity to be heard. See Matis, 915 N.E.2d at 214–15.

Likewise, jurisdictions that have recognized a defendant's right of access to a crime scene that is under a third party's control have required courts considering a request for access to balance the defendant's need for such access against the homeowner's privacy interests. See, e.g., Bullen, 251 Cal.Rptr. at 34 (requiring a defendant to demonstrate sufficient plausible justification and good cause for the intrusion and concluding that the defendant's "conclusional" showing in the case before it was inadequate); Matis, 915 N.E.2d at 215 (noting that a court order allowing access to a crime scene in a private residence "must be carefully tailored to protect the legitimate privacy interests involved"); A.B., 99 A.3d at 785 ("The right of the accused to a fair trial, and the right of a purported victim and her family to privacy must be balanced."); Henshaw, 451 S.E.2d at 419–20 (requiring a weighing of the defendant's due process rights against the homeowner's privacy interests).

For example, in Henshaw, 451 S.E.2d at 419–20, the court held that due process gave the defendant a right of access to a crime scene, provided first that the defendant established a substantial basis for claiming that the proposed inspection and observation would produce evidence that was relevant and material to the defense or that would allow the defendant meaningfully to defend against the pending charges. If the defendant made such a showing, then he or she would be entitled to access the crime scene, subject to such reasonable limitations and restrictions as the court deemed necessary, unless the private citizen's constitutional right to privacy outweighed the defendant's right to view or inspect the premises. Id. at 420. A homeowner's mere desire that the defendant or his or her representatives not be allowed access, however, would not alone be sufficient to overcome a showing of need by the defendant. Id.

In my view, the test articulated by the Henshaw court strikes the correct balance between the defendant's due process rights and the homeowner's privacy rights.

Accordingly, I would conclude that E.G. had a due process right to access the crime scene in this case, subject to three conditions. First, E.G. had to give notice to E.G.'s grandmother and to the People of his request for access, and both the grandmother and the People had to be given an opportunity to be heard with respect to E.G.'s request. Second, E.G. had to establish (1) a substantial basis for believing that the proposed inspection and observation would produce evidence that was relevant and material to his defense or that would allow him meaningfully to defend against the pending charges and (2) that his right of access was not outweighed by the grandmother's and victims' constitutional rights to privacy. Third, any right of access would be subject to such reasonable limitations and restrictions as the trial court may deem necessary, including time limits for the inspection, restrictions as to where within the premises the defense team may investigate, and limits as to who may participate in the inspection (e.g., defense counsel and an expert or investigator but not the defendant himself or herself).

I am not persuaded otherwise by the majority's implication that allowing a defendant access to a crime scene that is under a third party's control amounts to a per se unreasonable search within the meaning of the Fourth Amendment and is thus precluded in every case, regardless of the circumstances. I have seen no case concluding that in circumstances like those present here, a third party's privacy right automatically trumps a defendant's due process right to access a crime scene that is under the third party's control. Nor has the majority cited such a case.

Moreover, I cannot agree to a rule that would sweep so broadly as to preclude, in every case, access to a crime scene that is under a third party's control, regardless of the extent to which the parties have had disparate access to the evidence and the prosecution has taken advantage of such unequal access. In my view, in an appropriate case, as for example when the government is given unrestricted access and relies extensively at trial on evidence derived therefrom, due process and fundamental fairness require that the defendant also be given access. See Brown, 293 S.E.2d at 578 (concluding that it was a denial of fundamental fairness and due process for the defendant to be denied the limited inspection of the premises of the crime scene that he had requested, particularly when the state had been given access to the scene and had relied heavily on information gained therefrom in prosecuting the defendant).

Nor am I persuaded by the majority's suggestions that a defendant's due process rights are (1) limited to the right to access only material and favorable evidence in the government's possession or control and (2) adequately protected by the fact that the prosecution is required to disclose material, exculpatory information in its possession. See maj. op. at ¶¶ 23–25. In inspecting a crime scene, the state and a defendant generally have opposite goals. The state is attempting to solve a crime and obtain a conviction. The defendant, in contrast, is trying to uncover evidence that will help him or her avoid being convicted of a crime. That is simply the nature of our adversary system, and to allow one party access to substantial evidence while denying the other party corresponding access undermines the proper functioning of that system.

For these reasons, I would conclude that in an appropriate case, a defendant has a due process right to access a crime scene that is under a third party's control.

B. Courts' Authority to Order Access to a Crime Scene

The question thus becomes whether a trial court has the authority to order such access. Unlike the majority, I believe that it does.

In Pena v. District Court, 681 P.2d 953, 956 (Colo.1984) (quoting Jim R. Carrigan, Inherent Powers and Finance, 7 Trial 22 (Nov.-Dec. 1971)), we stated:

The inherent powers which courts possess consist of: "[A]ll powers reasonably required to enable a court to perform efficiently its judicial functions, to protect its dignity, independence, and integrity, and to make its lawful actions effective. These powers are inherent in the sense that they exist because the court exists; the court is, therefore it has the powers reasonably required to act as an efficient court."

See also § 13–1–115, C.R.S. (2015) ("The courts have power to issue all writs necessary and proper to the complete exercise of the power conferred on them by the constitution and laws of this state.").

Applying similar principles on facts analogous to those present here, the New Jersey Supreme Court recently observed that courts have the inherent power to order discovery when justice so requires. A.B., 99 A.3d at 789. The court further stated, "We must be mindful that the purpose of pretrial discovery is to ensure a fair trial. A criminal trial where the defendant does not have 'access to the raw materials integral to the building of an effective defense' is fundamentally unfair." Id. (quoting Ake v. Oklahoma, 470 U.S. 68, 77, 105 S.Ct. 1087, 84 L.Ed.2d 53 (1985)). And as noted above, the court recognized that visiting a crime scene can be "critical" in preparing a defense. Id.

I am persuaded by this reasoning and would thus recognize a trial court's inherent authority to allow access to a crime scene that is under a third party's control, if the defendant satisfies the burden set forth above. Indeed, it would be difficult to square a contrary conclusion with our longstanding case law authorizing a trial court to permit the jury in a criminal case to view a crime scene. See People v. Favors, 192 Colo. 136, 556 P.2d 72, 75–76 (1976); cf. C.R.C.P. 47(k) (authorizing the trial court in a civil case to order that a jury be permitted to examine "any property or place," if the court determines that it is proper for the jury to do so). If the court is authorized to allow jurors to access a crime scene, surely the court has the authority to allow the defense team to do so.

C. Application

Having concluded that E.G. has a due process right to access a crime scene that is under a third party's control, pending the proper showing, and that the court has the authority to order such access, on the conditions set forth above, the question remains whether E.G. has satisfied his above-defined burden here. Like the division below, see People in Int. of E.G., 2015 COA 18, ¶¶ 19–21, 371 P.3d 693, I conclude that he has not.

Specifically, E.G. did not establish a substantial basis for believing that the proposed inspection and observation would produce evidence that was relevant and material to his defense or that would allow him meaningfully to defend against the pending charges. He did not explain why the evidence sought was necessary to his defense. Nor did he explain why viewing and photographing the crime scene was necessary to his defense. To the contrary, E.G.'s request was general and conclusory.

Nor am I persuaded by E.G.'s argument that had he been given access to the crime scene, he could have explored sound dynamics in the house, examined the specific layout of the rooms in relation to the basement, and potentially impeached witnesses' testimony at trial using that evidence. Beside the fact that this argument is in large measure speculative, as the division observed, E.G. did not present these justifications to the trial court, and an appellate court will not consider such arguments for the first time on appeal. Id. at ¶ 20.

In these circumstances, I cannot say that E.G. has made a showing of need for access sufficient to outweigh the grandmother's and victims' constitutional rights to privacy.

III. Conclusion

For these reasons, I would affirm the division's decision on the grounds on which it relied. Accordingly, I respectfully concur in the judgment only.

———————

Notes

1. Do you agree with the reasoning in the majority or the concurrence in *E.G.*? What are the implications for defendants and for victims if the trial court has no authority to order access to a private home?

2. Courts in some jurisdictions have found a right of access for defendants in state constitutional provisions, but also find that courts can employ restrictions to ensure a balance between personal privacy, due process, and the effective assistance of counsel. *See, e.g., State v. Tetu*, 139 Hawai'i 207 (2016) (finding that "defendant's right to due process under article I, section 5 and the right to effective assistance of counsel under article I, section 14 of the Hawai'i Constitution independently provide a

defendant with the right to access a crime scene. When the crime scene is located on private property, the court should impose time, place, and manner restrictions to protect the privacy interests of those who may be affected by the intrusion.") Is allowing access with restrictions the proper balance of rights?

———————

4. Limits on Defendant's Ability to Conduct a Psychological Examination of the Victim

In some cases, particularly sexual assault cases, a defendant may seek a court order directing a victim to be psychologically examined. How should courts handle such motions?

State v. Eddy
321 P.3d 12 (Kan. 2014)

The opinion of the court was delivered by Johnson, J.:

Rasmus R. Eddy directly appeals his jury convictions for multiple counts of serious sex offenses perpetrated against A.E., his 4-year-old granddaughter. Eddy raises two arguments on appeal: (1) The State presented insufficient evidence to prove that he committed rape by the alternative means of penetrating the victim with an object, and (2) the district court erroneously denied his request to have a psychological evaluation performed on the victim. This court has direct jurisdiction pursuant to K.S.A. 22–3601(b) (1), prior to its 2011 amendments. We affirm.

FACTUAL AND PROCEDURAL OVERVIEW

The incidents underlying the charges against Eddy occurred in the spring of 2009, while A.E. was staying at Eddy's house for a few days at Eddy's request. The child related to her mother and other relatives that she had seen naked adults on Eddy's computer; that Eddy had touched her in the vaginal area with his finger; and that Eddy had licked her vagina. Eddy admitted to the police that he had allowed the child to view pornography on his computer. He explained the touching by saying that he had rubbed baby oil on a sore that was located on the inside of the child's labia. Eddy explained the licking by describing how the child, while naked, playfully climbed over his head a number of times, causing his face to contact her vaginal area. He also said that the child insisted that he kiss her "owie," i.e., her labial sore, and that he had pretended to do so by placing his hand over her vagina and kissing the inside of her thigh or the back of his own hand. Eddy also told the police that the child had grabbed his penis unexpectedly on two occasions during her visit.

. . .

The jury acquitted Eddy on one of the aggravated criminal sodomy charges, Count VIII, but convicted him on all of the other counts.

. . .

PSYCHOLOGICAL EVALUATION OF THE VICTIM

For his other issue, Eddy contends that the district court erred in denying his request to have A.E. undergo a psychological evaluation to determine the admissibility of her testimony. He argues that an examination was warranted because: (1) A.E. was an impressionable 4–year–old girl who was subject to her mother's control for a full month before giving a statement to law enforcement officers, and (2) A.E.'s allegations were uncorroborated. We do not find Eddy's proffered reasons to evaluate A.E. to be compelling.

Standard of Review

This court applies an abuse of discretion standard when reviewing a district court's decision on a motion for a psychological evaluation of a complaining witness. State v. Stafford, 296 Kan. 25, 39, 290 P.3d 562 (2012).

"Judicial discretion is abused if judicial action (1) is arbitrary, fanciful, or unreasonable, i.e., if no reasonable person would have taken the view adopted by the trial court; (2) is based on an error of law, i.e., if the discretion is guided by an erroneous legal conclusion; or (3) is based on an error of fact, i.e., if substantial competent evidence does not support a factual finding on which a prerequisite conclusion of law or the exercise of discretion is based." State v. Ward, 292 Kan. 541, 550, 256 P.3d 801 (2011), cert. denied——U.S.——, 132 S.Ct. 1594, 182 L.Ed.2d 205 (2012) (citing State v. Gonzalez, 290 Kan. 747, 755–56, 234 P.3d 1 [2010]).

The party asserting an abuse of discretion has the burden of persuasion. State v. Woodward, 288 Kan. 297, 299, 202 P.3d 15 (2009).

Analysis

Appellate courts are typically loathe to find an abuse of discretion when a district court refuses to order a psychological examination of a young sex abuse victim, unless the circumstances are extraordinary. "In general, a defendant is entitled to a psychological examination of a complaining witness in a sex crime if **compelling** circumstances justify such an examination." (Emphasis added.) Stafford, 296 Kan. at 40, 290 P.3d 562.

To assess the existence of compelling circumstances, a court should examine the totality of the circumstances, and, at least since our decision in State v. Gregg, 226 Kan. 481, 602 P.2d 85 (1979), courts have applied certain factors. Recently, we considered the following nonexclusive list of factors: (1) whether there is corroborating evidence of the complaining witness' version of the facts, (2) whether the complaining witness demonstrates mental instability, (3) whether the complaining witness demonstrates a lack of veracity, (4) whether the complaining witness has made similar charges against others that were proven to be false, (5) whether the defendant's motion for an evaluation appears to be a fishing expedition, and (6) whether the complaining witness provides an unusual response when questioned about his or her understanding of what it means to tell the truth. State v. Berriozabal, 291 Kan. 568, 581, 243 P.3d 352 (2010).

With respect to the first factor, Eddy contends that there was no evidence to corroborate A.E.'s allegations. Granted, the State did not present any physical or medical evidence to corroborate the charges. But Eddy's own statements, both to law enforcement officers and at trial, provided plenty of corroboration for A.E.'s description of events. He admitted touching the inside of A.E.'s labia; he admitted contact between his mouth and A.E.'s genitalia; and he admitted showing the child pornography on his computer. Indeed, some of the convictions were based solely upon Eddy's own statements, such as the counts related to A.E. touching or seeing Eddy's penis, because the child never told anyone that she saw or touched her grandpa's penis. While Eddy put his own spin on why the alleged acts occurred, he nevertheless corroborated that they did occur. A psychological examination of the victim would have added nothing to the question of the defendant's specific intent.

With respect to the remaining factors, Eddy did not present any evidence that A.E. displayed any mental instability, demonstrated any lack of veracity, made any similar charges against others that were proven to be false, or indicated an inability to understand what it means to tell the truth. To the contrary, the motion for an evaluation in this case appears to be a prime example of a fishing expedition.

Eddy tries to suggest that A.E.'s mother was involved in "heated custody proceedings" with A.E.'s father, which provided the incentive for the mother to plant permanent false memories in A.E.'s mind in order to frame A.E.'s grandfather for sex abuse, and that the 4-week delay in obtaining A.E.'s law enforcement interview provided mother with the opportunity to effect her scheme. There are a number of disconnects in that line of reasoning.

First, the record does not support the heated custody dispute claim. Rather, there was some testimony that A.E.'s mother and father were quarreling because mother wanted father to take A.E. for awhile, but he was financially unable to do so. Moreover, Eddy does not explain why framing him for sex abuse would have provided A.E.'s mother with any advantage in her alleged dispute with her ex-husband.

Most importantly, however, on May 1, 2009, A.E. told the same thing to her mother, her grandmother, her great aunt, and the sexual assault nurse examiner. Then, 4 weeks later, on May 28, 2009, she repeated the same allegations to the law enforcement officer. The only inconsistency to which Eddy can point is that in the later interview, A.E. used the term "nasty" for the first time. Again, Eddy fails to explain the significance of that distinction. Even if A.E.'s mother planted the notion that the sex abuse was "nasty," it does not render suspect the child's consistent statements of what Eddy did to her. Certainly, it is not a compelling circumstance that would justify a psychological examination.

In sum, Eddy fails to establish any valid reason that would support a finding of compelling circumstances to warrant a psychological examination of the sex abuse victim in this case. As such, the district court's denial of the evaluation motion cannot be deemed an abuse of discretion. The ruling is affirmed.

Affirmed.

———————

Notes

1. In *Eddy* it is recognized that the decision concerning a psychological exam is within the discretion of the trial court; this approach is the law in most jurisdictions. *See, e.g., In re Michael H.*, 602 S.E.2d 729, 2002 WL 32641211 (S.C. 2004) (concluding, over strong dissent, that trial judges should have discretion to order psychological examination where the defendant can show a compelling need for such an examination). Courts have articulated different factors to consider in exercising this discretion, including (1) the nature of the examination requested and the intrusiveness inherent in that examination; (2) the victim's age; (3) the resulting physical and/or emotional effects of the examination on the victim; (4) the probative value of the examination to the issue before the court; (5) the remoteness in time of the examination to the alleged criminal act; and (6) the evidence already available for the defendant's use. *See State v. Delaney*, 417 S.E.2d 903 (W. Va. 1992); *see also Koerschner v. State*, 13 P.3d 451 (Nev. 2000) (listing similar factors). Trial courts have only rarely issued such orders.

2. A minority of jurisdictions hold that the court has no authority to issue such an order. *See, e.g., State v. Hiatt*, 733 P.2d 1373, 1376–77 (Or. 1987) (no psychological exam allowed absent statutory authorization); *accord, State v. Gabrielson*, 464 N.W.2d 434 (Iowa 1990); *State ex rel. Holmes v. Lanford*, 764 S.W.2d 593, 594 (Tex. Ct. App. 1989). For example, in *State v. Looney*, 240 S.E.2d 612 (N.C. 1978), the North Carolina Supreme Court held that to require victims to undergo such evaluations would be "a drastic invasion of the witness' own right of privacy" and "in and of itself, humiliating and potentially damaging to the reputation of the victim." The same court later affirmed this rule, explaining that "the possible benefits to an innocent defendant, flowing from such a court ordered examination of the witness, are outweighed by the resulting invasion of the witness' right to privacy and the danger to the public interest from discouraging victims of crime to report such offenses." *State v. Horn*, 446 S.E.2d 52 (N.C. 1994).

3. Some jurisdictions have passed statutes that explicitly bar psychological examination orders in sexual violence cases solely for the purpose of assessing credibility. *See, e.g.,* Cal. Penal Code § 1112; 725 Ill. Comp. Stat. 5/115-71.

———————

5. Limits on Defendant's Ability to Physically Examine a Victim

Defendants have not only sought psychological examinations of crime victims, but also physical examinations. Courts have taken different approaches to evaluating these requests. A majority hold that a trial court has discretion to order such an examination, but should do so only when "compelling circumstances" or something similar exist. A minority hold trial courts have no authority to order such examinations. The merits of these competing positions are discussed in the following case.

People v. Lopez
800 N.E.2d 1211 (Ill. 2003)

Justice KILBRIDE delivered the opinion of the court:

In this case we decide whether a trial court can order the physical examination of an alleged sex offense victim. Defendant was charged with aggravated criminal sexual abuse under section 12-16(c)(1)(i) of the Criminal Code of 1961 (Criminal Code) (720 ILCS 5/12-16(c)(1)(i) (West 1998)). He sought a gynecological examination of the alleged victim, B.B., who was three years old at the time. The circuit court of Du Page County granted defendant's request, and B.B.'s family refused to comply. As a sanction, the court granted defendant's motion *in limine* to prohibit the State from introducing any medical expert evidence of its own. We hold that a trial court cannot order the physical examination of a complaining witness in a sex offense case. We further hold that, when a trial court rules on the admission of evidence in a sex offense case where a defendant has requested the physical examination of a complaining witness and the witness refuses to submit to the examination, the court must balance the due process rights of the defendant against the privacy rights of the alleged victim, by deciding what medical evidence, if any, the State is allowed to introduce.

I. BACKGROUND

At the behest of B.B.'s family, Dr. E. Anderson examined B.B., who was 20 months old at the time, and concluded that she was a victim of sexual abuse. This conclusion was based in part on Dr. Anderson's finding that her labial origin "show[ed] a small false passage, suggestive of partial tearing" and also on the presence of scar tissue surrounding the vagina. Dr. Anderson reported that he was unable to inspect B.B.'s hymen adequately because B.B. complained of discomfort and "with[drew] from the situation." Dr. Anderson explained that, while he could not "100%" rule out a developmental anomaly, he felt that B.B.'s condition was the result of a traumatic injury. He further commented that:

> Certainly, visualization of the hymen would provide additional useful info[rmation] for a definitive [diagnosis], although the synechia is suggestive of previous scarring and raw edges coming together, suggestive of trauma. . . . Due to the swelling of the tissues, I should note that it was difficult to decide whether the tissue adhesion was with the labia minora or with the actual [vaginal] wall, although it would appear to be most likely labial.

Dr. M. Flannery also examined B.B. She prepared 17 colposcopic photographs of B.B.'s vaginal region. Based on her examination, Dr. Flannery concluded that B.B.'s condition was "suspicious for trauma most likely consistent with digital penetration." Dr. Flannery's findings, in part, noted: "Thin hymenal rim with partial obliteration of the rim posteriorly. Edges of the hymen are thickened. Notched areas at approximately the two o'clock and ten o'clock positions. Widened elongated hymen."

Following B.B.'s medical examinations, defendant was indicted for aggravated criminal sexual abuse under section 12-16(c)(1)(i) of the Criminal Code (720 ILCS 5/12-16(c)(1)(i) (West 1998)). Approximately three months after the medical examinations, the State presented defendant with the reports of Dr. Anderson and Dr. Flannery. On defendant's request, the State later provided defendant with copies of the photographs taken by Dr. Flannery.

Approximately 13 months after the examinations, when B.B. was about three years old, defendant filed a motion to produce B.B. for an independent gynecological examination. Attached to defendant's motion to produce was the affidavit of his medical expert, Dr. R. Slupnik. Dr. Slupnik stated that she had reviewed the medical records and the photographs of B.B. According to Dr. Slupnik, she was "unable to arrive at a conclusion" about Dr. Flannery's finding of a "partial obliteration of the [hymenal] rim posteriorly." Dr. Slupnik opined:

> Partial obliteration of the hymen is not conclusively seen on the photographs submitted to me. Some clarification of the area of the hymen at 6 or 7 o'clock could be obtained by various other exam techniques, including a change of position. A repeat examination of the alleged victim would resolve whether there is partial obliteration posteriorly. The examination would be conducted with the patient in supine (lying on her back) position, with the knees apart (so-called 'frog-leg' position) as well as in the prone position ('knee chest'). One ounce of sterile water would be used to rinse the hymen of any mucus or other debris and to facilitate its depiction. The exam would take approximately 5 minutes. Other than Q-tips, no other instruments would be used during the exam. Further, 'findings' which were allegedly present during Dr. Flannery's exam 14 months ago should still be present now, if they are specific for sexual abuse. A female hymen does not re-grow, re-generate, or re-attach if truly traumatized by blunt force penetrating trauma. Findings that are specific for sexual abuse will be permanent.

A hearing was held on the motion to produce B.B. for an independent gynecological examination. At the hearing, the State contended that an examination as proposed by Dr. Slupnik would last longer than five minutes and also denied that the evidence of trauma seen by Dr. Flannery would still be present. The State complained that defendant waited too long to file his motion to produce B.B. The State further clarified that Dr. Flannery did not suggest that there was medical evidence conclusive of "digital penetration," but simply that the condition of B.B.'s genitalia was "suspicious for trauma most likely consistent with digital penetration."

Defendant argued that the chief reason Dr. Slupnik wished to examine B.B. independently was that she did not believe the photographs conclusively showed a partial obliteration of the hymen. In response to the State's reference to defendant's delay in requesting the independent physical examination, defendant suggested that the trial court's congested docket was, in part, responsible for the delay.

Following the hearing, the trial court granted defendant's motion for an examination of B.B. by Dr. Slupnik. The trial court record is silent as to the rationale behind this decision. The lone comment on the issue is the court's observation during argument that Dr. Flannery would not be permitted to testify at trial regarding her conclusions because Dr. Flannery could not "even testify as to a speculation." The trial court later denied the State's motion to reconsider without hearing argument from the parties.

B.B.'s family refused to produce her for the examination. As a result, defendant moved to dismiss the indictment. Defendant contended that Dr. Slupnik's examination "could clearly exonerate" him and that his "due process right to a fundamentally fair trial will be destroyed without the opportunity to obtain the potentially exonerating evidence that could come along only from an independent examination of [B.B.]."

In response, the State sought an evidentiary hearing to determine the appropriate sanction to be levied for the failure to produce B.B. so that the parties could present the testimony of their experts. [The State tried three more times to get the judge to hold an evidentiary hearing] . . .

The State [argued] . . . that the court's previous balancing of the respective interests was inadequate in that the court had not taken into account all of the evidence that the State intended or attempted to present. The State noted that Dr. Slupnik's sole disagreement with Dr. Anderson and Dr. Flannery concerned the finding that B.B.'s genital area showed a partial posterior obliteration of the hymen. The State again suggested that an evidentiary hearing should be conducted to determine whether a finding of a partial posterior obliteration of B.B.'s hymen is necessary to a conclusion that her genital area had been traumatized. The State further asserted that the real concern with another physical examination was its potential psychological impact given its nature and that it would be the third examination for B.B.

Following the hearing on defendant's motion *in limine,* the court denied the State's request for an evidentiary hearing and granted defendant's motion. The court, in relevant part, found that:

> [T]he body of the young child is effectively still the physical evidence in this case. . . . The proposed defense examination of the 'evidence' would be more than potentially useful. In light of the incomplete or inconclusive findings of the State's two experts and as it could determine whether or not 'findings' specific for sexual abuse are present, that exam could determine whether the alleged victim is a victim indeed (leaving as the only practical issue the identity of the perpetrator of the abuse). There is a clear need for the exam.

The trial court recognized that both defendant's due process rights and the alleged victim's rights were at issue. Nevertheless, the court found that under *People v. Newberry*, 652 N.E.2d 288 (Ill. 1995), and *People v. Wheeler*, 602 N.E.2d 826 (Ill. 1992), cross-examination of the State's experts was insufficient to protect defendant's rights because an expert who has personally examined a victim is in a better position to render an opinion than a nonexamining expert.

As a result of these findings, the court ordered that the expert testimony and reports of Dr. Anderson and Dr. Flannery be excluded from evidence. In addition, the trial court precluded the State from introducing the evidence of nonexamining experts.

II. ANALYSIS

A. Physical Examination

In *People v. Glover*, 273 N.E.2d 367 (Ill. 1971), the defendant, charged with deviate sexual assault, sought both a psychiatric examination of the complaining witness to investigate her alleged history of "'emotional instability and immaturity'" and an ophthamological examination "to determine her ability to see and identify the defendant" because it was dark at the time of the alleged assault. *Glover*, 273 N.E.2d 367. The trial court denied the motion to compel the examinations. On appeal, this court stated that "[t]here is no question of [an Illinois court's] jurisdiction to order an examination of the complaining witness in a case involving a sex violation." *Glover*, 273 N.E.2d 367, citing *People ex rel. Noren v. Dempsey*, 139 N.E.2d 780 (Ill. 1957). Nevertheless, we affirmed the trial court's denial of the motions for the examinations and held that: (1) requests for such examinations must be premised upon a compelling reason demonstrated by the defendant; and (2) the decision to order an independent examination is subject to the discretion of the trial court. *Glover*, 273 N.E.2d 367.

It is well settled that prior precedent should be overturned "only on the showing of good cause," only where there is "'special justification'" for the departure, or only where the reasons for departure are "compelling." *People v. Tisdel*, 775 N.E.2d 921 (Ill. 2002)

For the reasons that follow, we find that such compelling justification exists in this case. We, therefore, overrule *Glover* and hold that a trial court may not order the physical examination of a complaining witness in a sex offense case.

1. *Criminal Versus Civil Proceedings*

Noren, the sole case cited in *Glover* for the proposition that a trial court can compel the physical examination of a complaining witness, involved a negligence action for personal injuries suffered by a plaintiff in an automobile accident. The defendant sought a physical examination of the plaintiff to determine the extent of the plaintiff's injuries in order to prepare for trial. . . . Thus, it is apparent that *Noren* was concerned solely with civil cases, involving a plaintiff's physical condition.

Alleged victims in criminal cases, unlike plaintiffs in civil cases, are not parties to the action, nor are they under control of the State. The appellate court in *People v. Visgar*, 457 N.E.2d 1343 (Ill. App. 1983), noted *Glover's* shortcoming of relying on a civil case. Nevertheless, due to the apparent unequivocal nature of our holding in *Glover* and given that *Glover* was again cited with approval in *People v. Rossi*, 284 N.E.2d 275 (Ill. 1972), and in a handful of appellate court cases (*see, e.g., People v. Davis*, 422 N.E.2d 989 (Ill. App. 1981); *People v. Dentley*, 334 N.E.2d 774 (Ill. App. 1975)), the *Visgar* court relied on it to justify the continued power of a trial court to compel the physical examination of a complaining witness in a sex offense case.

The defendant in *Visgar*, charged with the lewd fondling of a child, sought a physical examination to determine "whether [the complaining witness'] hymen was intact." *Visgar*, 457 N.E.2d 1343. Reasoning that there was no allegation that the complaining witness was injured or that her vagina had been penetrated, the trial court found that an examination "would not be necessary for any purpose." *Visgar*, 457 N.E.2d 1343. Thus, unlike the case at hand, the appellate court in *Visgar* was not faced with the decision of affirming a trial court's decision to order the physical examination of a complaining witness.

2. Other Jurisdictions

Here, the appellate court turned to the other jurisdictions that utilize the "compelling need" test because neither *Glover* nor *Visgar* provided any guidance on how to implement the test. See, *e.g., People v. Chard*, 808 P.2d 351 (Colo. 1991); *Bartlett v. Hamwi*, 626 So. 2d 1040 (Fla.App. 1993); *State v. D.R.H.*, 604 A.2d 89 (N.J. 1992); *State v. Garrett*, 384 N.W.2d 617 (Minn. App. 1986); *State v. Ramos*, 553 A.2d 1059 (R.I. 1989); *State v. Barone*, 852 S.W.2d 216 (Tenn. 1993); *State v. Delaney*, 417 S.E.2d 903 (W.Va. 1992). In *Chard*, for example, the Colorado Supreme Court considered a defendant's request for involuntary, independent psychological and physical examinations of a child who was an alleged victim of a sex offense. Relying on prior case law relating to involuntary psychological examinations, the court expressly adopted the "compelling need" test for involuntary physical examinations. *Chard*, 808 P.2d at 353. *Chard* listed the factors to be considered in determining whether a "compelling need" is present. Those factors are: (1) the complainant's age; (2) the remoteness in time of the alleged criminal incident to the proposed examination; (3) the degree of intrusiveness and humiliation associated with the procedure; (4) the potentially debilitating physical effects of such an examination; and (5) any other relevant considerations. *Chard*, 808 P.2d at 355, citing *Ramos*, 553 A.2d at 1062. In assessing those factors, the trial court must "balance the possible emotional trauma, embarrassment or intimidation to the complainant against the likelihood of the examination producing material, as distinguished from speculative, evidence." *Chard*, 808 P.2d at 356.

Like *Chard*, the other jurisdictions that have adopted the "compelling need" test for involuntary physical examinations have relied, at least in part, on the court's authority to order a psychological examination. *See D.R.H.*, 604 A.2d at 93 (noting, where defendant sought only a physical examination, the inherent power of the judiciary to order a witness to submit to a psychiatric or psychological examination); *Ramos,* 553 A.2d at 1062 (noting, where defendant sought only a physical examination, that a number of courts have held that a trial court has discretionary power to order a witness in a criminal trial to submit to a psychiatric examination); *Barone,* 852 S.W.2d at 221 (noting, where defendant sought only a physical examination, the trial judge has the inherent power to compel a psychiatric or psychological examination of the victim). In the other jurisdictions that hold a trial court may not order an unwilling witness to submit to a physical examination (see, *e.g., State v. Hewett,* 376 S.E.2d 467, 472 (N.C. App. 1989); *State ex rel. Wade v. Stephens,* 724 S.W.2d 141, 143–44 (Tex. Ct. App. 1987)), the courts likewise have no discretionary authority to order a complaining witness to submit to a mental examination (*State v. Clontz,* 286 S.E.2d 793, 796 (N.C. 1982); *State ex rel. Holmes v. Lanford,* 764 S.W.2d 593, 594 (Tex. Ct. App. 1989)).

Similarly, in Illinois, a court has no authority to "order [the] mental examination of [a] sex victim." 725 ILCS 5/115-7.1 (West 1998). When our decision in *Glover* was issued, section 115-7.1 was not yet in existence. *See* 725 ILCS 5/115-7.1 (West 1998) (added by Pub. Act 83-289, §1, eff. January 1, 1984). Accordingly, the legislature's decision to prohibit trial courts from ordering the mental examination of complaining witnesses provides further support for our decision to likewise proscribe trial courts from ordering physical examinations.

3. Wheeler *and Physical Examinations*

Section 115-7.1 of the Code of Criminal Procedure of 1963 (Ill. Rev. Stat. 1989, ch. 38, par. 115-7.1, now codified as 725 ILCS 5/115-7.1 (West 1998)) was at issue in *People v. Wheeler,* 602 N.E.2d 826 (Ill. 1992), relied on by the trial court in this case. In *Wheeler,* the defendant was charged with aggravated sexual assault. Before trial, he had learned that the State intended to introduce expert testimony that the alleged victim suffered from rape trauma syndrome. According to section 115-7.2 of the Code (Ill. Rev. Stat. 1989, ch. 38, par. 115-7.2, now codified as 725 ILCS 5/115-7.2 (West 1998)), such testimony was admissible. The defendant moved the trial court to order the alleged victim to submit to a psychological examination by his own expert, but section 115-7.1 precluded such an order. At trial, the State called its expert, who had personally examined the alleged victim. The defendant appealed his conviction, arguing that sections 115-7.1 and 115-7.2, as applied, denied him due process of law. The appellate court disagreed and affirmed. *People v. Wheeler,* 575 N.E.2d 1326 (Ill. App. 1991). We granted the defendant's subsequent leave to appeal and reversed. *Wheeler,* 602 N.E.2d 826.

Initially, we noted that a defendant's right to due process is the right to a fundamentally fair trial, including the right to present witnesses in his own behalf. *Wheeler,* 602 N.E.2d 826, citing *Chambers v. Mississippi,* 410 U.S. 284, 294 (1973). We then described the legislative intent of the relevant sections of the Code of Criminal Procedure:

> Section 115-7.1 was intended to protect sex-offense victims from the embarrassment of psychological examinations regarding the victim's

competency and credibility as a witness. The protection afforded by section 115-7.1 was necessary because, until recently, sex-offense victims were subjected to increased scrutiny by the courts. The rationale for this higher scrutiny was grounded on the often quoted maxim that rape "is an accusation easily made, hard to be proved and still harder to be defended by one ever so innocent."

People v. Freeman (Ill. 1910), 91 N.E. 708, quoting 3 S. GREENLEAF, EVIDENCE § 212 (15th ed. 1892). Wheeler, 602 N.E.2d 826.

We then recounted the unwarranted suspicion that victims of sexual assaults faced in criminal trials, as exemplified by passages found in *Wigmore on Evidence* (3A J. WIGMORE, EVIDENCE § 924a, at 737 (Chadbourn rev. ed. 1970)). These passages recommended mandatory psychiatric evaluation for all complaining witnesses in sex offense cases to ascertain the victims' "'probable credibility'" and "'to determine whether the victim suffers from some mental or moral delusion or tendency . . . causing distortion of the imagination in sex cases.'" *Wheeler,* 602 N.E.2d 826, quoting 3A J. WIGMORE, EVIDENCE § 924a, at 747 (Chadbourn rev. ed. 1970), quoting ABA COMMITTEE ON THE IMPROVEMENT OF THE LAW OF EVIDENCE(1938).

Next, we acknowledged that while Illinois wisely chose not to adopt the extreme position presented in *Wigmore*, our courts still retained the discretionary authority to order victims of sex offenses to undergo psychological examinations when supported by compelling reasons. *Wheeler,* 602 N.E.2d 826, citing *Glover,* 273 N.E.2d 367. Recognizing that our courts did not have a similar power with respect to victims of nonsexual offenses, we noted that in cases of sexual assault a victim's competency and credibility was subject to attack based *only* on the nature of the offense. To eliminate this disparity, as well as the potential for embarrassment and intimidation of victims of sex offenses by defense counsel through the use of psychological evaluations focusing on the victims' competency and credibility, the legislature enacted section 115-7.1. *Wheeler,* 602 N.E.2d 826.

We then distinguished section 115-7.2 from section 115-7.1 because it did not relate to the victim's competency and credibility. Rather, section 115-7.2 permitted the admission of expert testimony concerning the presence of rape trauma syndrome, a subcategory of post-traumatic stress syndrome. *Wheeler,* 602 N.E.2d 826. "Unlike psychological evidence regarding the victim's competency and credibility as a witness, evidence of rape trauma syndrome is substantive evidence that a sexual assault occurred" by showing that the complainant suffers from symptoms common among most sexual assault victims. *Wheeler,* 602 N.E.2d 826.

After recognizing the value of a personal examination to a testifying expert, we stated that, although the defendant was free to call a nonexamining expert, the State's ability to call an examining expert gave it "a clear advantage" in its effort to prove that the alleged victim suffered from rape trauma syndrome. *Wheeler,* 602 N.E.2d 826. Thus, we held that, under those circumstances, the defendant's trial was "fundamentally unfair." *Wheeler,* 602 N.E.2d 826.

This court further concluded that, unless the complainant consented to an examination by the defendant's expert, the State was precluded from admitting an examining expert's testimony that the victim had post-traumatic stress syndrome. *Wheeler,* 602 N.E.2d 826. Even if the victim consented to the examination, we required the defense expert to be qualified by the court and that the examination "*be strictly limited to whether the victim has symptoms consistent with 'any recognized and accepted form of post-traumatic stress syndrome.'* (Emphasis added.) . . ." *Wheeler,* 602 N.E.2d 826, quoting ILL. REV. STAT. 1989, ch. 38, par. 115-7.2, now codified as 725 ILCS 5/115-7.2 (West 1998).

We also emphasized the need to protect victims' privacy in cases of sexual assault, as well as the concomitant right to refuse an examination for any reason. Nonetheless, we acknowledged the need for the victim's right to be free of intrusion to be balanced against the defendant's constitutional right to a fair trial. We concluded that if a victim refuses to undergo an examination, the State is precluded from introducing evidence of rape trauma syndrome from an examining expert. The State could, however, still introduce rape trauma evidence through the testimony of nonexamining experts. *Wheeler,* 602 N.E.2d 826. This decision protected the victim's rights by leaving the victim with the ultimate decision on whether to submit to an examination. It also ended the unacceptable and intolerable defense tactic of using psychological examinations as tools to harass, intimidate, and embarrass sexual assault victims. *Wheeler,* 602 N.E.2d 826.

The same fundamental considerations and rights are at issue in cases where a defendant seeks an order to compel a physical examination. Victims of sexual assault should no more be subjected to physical examinations by experts proffered by the defense than they should be required to submit to psychological evaluations. The effects of both types of examinations can be intolerably harassing and intimidating and can cause further harm to the victim. We believe that this court struck the proper balance between a victim's right to be free of intrusions and a defendant's right to a fair trial, and that the *Wheeler* holding should be applicable in cases where defendants seek either psychological or physical examinations of victims in sexual offense cases.

B. Discovery Sanction

By our holding that the trial court could not order the physical examination of B.B., we have rendered the issue of the discovery sanction moot . . . .

III. CONCLUSION

For these reasons, we hold that a trial court cannot order a complaining witness in a sex offense case to submit to physical examination. To ensure a defendant's constitutional rights to a fair trial is not compromised by the inability to obtain an independent physical examination, trial courts should exercise vigilance when rendering decisions on what evidence the State is allowed to produce. The appellate court decision is affirmed in part and vacated in part, and the cause is remanded to the circuit court for further proceedings consistent with this opinion.

Appellate court judgment affirmed in part and vacated in part; cause remanded.

Justice FREEMAN, specially concurring:

I join in the result reached by the majority because I believe defendant failed to demonstrate a compelling need for an independent physical examination of the victim. I cannot join the balance of the majority opinion, however, because the majority eschews the compelling need test and holds that a trial court has no jurisdiction to order the physical examination of a victim of a sex offense. While I recognize that, in so holding, the majority attempts to protect victims of sex offenses, I believe the majority needlessly hampers the State in its prosecution of such crimes and unwittingly places the victims of sex offenses in situations where they will feel compelled to comply with the very requests for physical examinations the majority seeks to deny.

* * *

Notes

1. In future cases in Illinois, what evidence should trial courts exclude when a victim refuses to submit to a physical examination by the defense? *Lopez* seems to suggest the question turns on whether the state has some kind of "advantage" in the process. If so, did the state have such an advantage where photographs were taken during the examination and were equally available to the defense?

2. In states that allow the defense to obtain a physical examination of the victim under certain circumstances, the question remains what factors should be considered in making that determination. One commentator has identified and described several distinct Due Process tests each used by an appellate court from different jurisdictions. These tests are: (1) the material assistance approach—whether the examination could lead to evidence of "material assistance" to the defense, as held in, *e.g.*, *Turner v. Commonwealth*, 767 S.W.2d 557 (Ky. 1989); (2) the exculpatory evidence approach—whether the evidence likely to be obtained during an examination would bar conviction, has held in, *e.g.*, *People v. Nokes*, 228 Cal.Rptr. 119 (Cal. App. 1986); and (3) the compelling need approach—whether a compelling need exists for the examination, as discussed in *Lopez*. Under the compelling need approach, the author identifies two distinct tests: (a) an *ad hoc* balancing approach and (b) a factor specific balancing approach, which requires the defendant to show that the initial physical examination was conducted improperly. Note, *A Fourth Amendment Approach to Compulsory Physical Examinations of Sex Offense Victims*, 57 U. CHI. L. REV. 873 (1990).

3. When a court orders a victim to submit to a physical examination, the victim's Fourth Amendment right to be free from unreasonable searches and seizures is implicated. *See Pelster v. Walker*, 185 F.Supp.2d 1185 (D.Or. 2001) (in a case in which a victim opposed their physical examination "the Fourth Amendment applies equally and identically to all persons. Any search or seizure must be reasonable and any

warrant must be based on probable cause. No court has recognized a different standard based on an individual's status as a victim, suspect, or defendant.").

4. The Arizona Court of Appeals has refused to allow fingerprinting of the victim at the request of the defense. The court explained that such an order would violate the victim's "rights to justice and due process" enshrined in Arizona's Victims Bill of Rights. *Romley v. Schneider*, 45 P.3d 685 (Ariz. App. 2002).

5. Occasionally, defendants will attempt to obtain an order for a second autopsy to be conducted by a pathologist retained by the defendant. These motions are typically denied. *See, e.g., Payne v. State*, 291 S.E.2d 266 (Georgia 1982) (no abuse of judicial discretion in denying defense motion for second autopsy where the victim's remains are no longer within the state's control); *State v. Delgros*, 662 N.E.2d 858 (Ohio Ct. App. 1995). *But cf. Rey v. State*, 897 S.W.2d 333 (Tex. Ct. Crim. App. 1995) (capital defendant entitled to appointment of his own pathologist where mechanism of death in dispute).

C. Ex Parte Subpoenas for Victims' Confidential Records

United States v. McClure

2009 WL 937502 (E.D. Cal. 2009)

WILLIAM B. SHUBB, District Judge.

I. *Factual and Procedural Background*

Defendant Ronald Anthony McClure, Jr., is charged in two indictments with violations of 18 U.S.C. § 922(g) (felon in possession of a firearm and ammunition), *id.* § 1201(a)(1) (kidnaping), *id.* § 1513(b)(2) (retaliating against a witness), and *id.* § 15191(a)(1) (sex trafficking of children by force, fraud, or coercion). Plaintiff United States of America ("Government") now moves to preclude defendant from obtaining any *ex parte* early return subpoenas issued under Federal Rule of Criminal Procedure 17(c).

II. *Discussion*

Federal Rule of Criminal Procedure 17(c) provides:

> A subpoena may order the witness to produce any books, papers, documents, data, or other objects the subpoena designates. The court may direct the witness to produce the designated items in court before trial or before they are to be offered in evidence. When the items arrive, the court may permit the parties and their attorneys to inspect all or part of them.

Fed.R.Crim.P. 17(c)(1).

In order to obtain a Rule 17(c) subpoena before trial, the proponent must make a showing that the evidence sought is relevant, admissible, and specific. *United States v. Nixon,* 418 U.S. 683, 700, 94 S.Ct. 3090, 41 L.Ed.2d 1039 (1974). In addition, even if the proponent makes this showing, a court must also consider "whether the materials are 'otherwise procurable reasonably in advance of trial by exercise of due diligence,' whether the proponent can 'properly prepare for trial without such production and inspection in advance of trial,' and whether 'the failure to obtain such inspection may tend unreasonably to delay the trial.'" *United States v. Reyes,* 239 F.R.D. 591, 598 (N.D.Cal. 2006) (quoting *Nixon,* 418 U.S. at 699, 702); *see United States v. Eden,* 659 F.2d 1376, 1381 (9th Cir. 1981).

The Government points out that "there appears to be a trend started by defense counsel in child sex trafficking cases to seek, *ex parte,* the early return of Rule 17(c) subpoenas." (Mot. Preclude 2.) These subpoenas typically request records held by juvenile courts and Child Protective Services that pertain to certain government witnesses. (*Id.*) The Government contends that these subpoenas often fail to meet the requirements of *Nixon* and, more generally, are unwarranted intrusions into the private and confidential files of minors. (*See id.* at 2, 6–10, 27.) Furthermore, because defendants often obtain these subpoenas *ex parte,* the Government has been unable to oppose their issuance in an adversarial setting. (*Id.* at 2–3, 27–28.)

Following Judge Karlton's opinion in *United States v. Tomison,* the judges in this district have generally permitted Rule 17(c) subpoenas to be obtained *ex parte* when a party "makes a showing of the need for confidentiality." 969 F.Supp. 587, 591 n. 8 (E.D.Cal. 1997); *see United States v. Wells,* No. 04-69, 2005 WL 3822883, at *3 (E.D.Cal. Dec. 20, 2005) (England, J.). The judges in the Northern District of California appear to follow a similar practice. *See United States v. Johnson,* No. 94-48, 2008 WL 62281, at *2 (N.D.Cal. Jan. 4, 2008); N.D. Cal. Local R.Crim. P. 17-2(a)(1) ("[A] Rule 17(c) subpoena may be obtained by filing either a noticed motion . . . or, for good cause, an *ex parte* motion without advance notice to the opposing party.").

In *United States v. Sanchez,* No. 05-443, slip. op. at 2 (E.D.Cal. Jan. 22, 2007) the undersigned judge expressed agreement with the holding of *Tomison,* i.e., that requests for subpoenas under Rule 17(c) are generally considered *ex parte,* while rejecting any notion suggested in *Tomison* that Rule 17(c) may be properly used as a discovery device. As stated in this court's previous order in *Sanchez,*

> Rule 17(c) was designed as a method of compelling witnesses with relevant and admissible documentary evidence to bring those documents to the trial or hearing at which they will be offered in evidence. The fact that the rule goes on to permit the court to direct the witnesses to produce the designated items in court before they are actually to be offered into evidence was not meant to convert Rule 17(c) into a discovery device. The discovery tools available to defendants in criminal cases are limited, and are to be found elsewhere in the Federal Rules of Criminal Procedure, not in Rule 17.

United States v. Sanchez, No. 05-443, slip. op. at 3 (E.D.Cal. Jan. 9, 2007).

The Government suggests that *Tomison* and *Sanchez* need to be re-examined in light of recent amendments to Rule 17(c). Specifically, effective December 1, 2008, the following provision was added to Rule 17(c):

> [A] subpoena requiring the production of personal or confidential informa-tion about a victim may be served on a third party only by court order. Before entering the order and unless there are exceptional circumstances, the court must require giving notice to the victim so that the victim can move to quash or modify the subpoena or otherwise object.

Fed.R.Crim.P. 17(c)(3).

Thus, where the subpoena requires the production of personal or confidential information about a victim, Rule 17(c)(3) now requires that the court find "excep-tional circumstances" before allowing the subpoena to be served without giving prior notice to the victim. This does not mean that Rule 17(c) subpoenas may no longer be obtained *ex parte*. It does mean, however, that in addition to the *Nixon* require-ment that the evidence sought be relevant, admissible, and specific, where personal or confidential information about a victim is sought, "exceptional circumstances" must be shown to exist before the court may grant an *ex parte* request for a subpoena under Rule 17(c).

The Advisory Committee's Notes to this provision provide that "[s]uch excep-tional circumstances would include . . . a situation where the defense would be unfairly prejudiced by premature disclosure of a sensitive defense strategy." Fed.R.Crim.P. 17(c)(3) advisory committee's notes (2008 Amendment). The Notes then "leave to the judgment of the court" as to "whether such exceptional circum-stances exist to be decided *ex parte* and authorize service of the third-party sub-poena *without notice to anyone*." *Id.* (emphasis added).

The Government argues that applications for Rule 17(c) subpoenas cannot be issued *ex parte* in this case because "there is no legal structure in place to prevent or deter overreaching," and thus any application should be "subject to adversar[ial] test-ing." (*Id.* at 27:21–23, 2:28–3:1.) *Tomison* and several other cases considered this argument and rejected it. *See Tomison,* 969 F.Supp. at 594 ("[T]here is no reason to suppose that the government's participation is required to ensure that the court per-forms its duty in determining that the requisites for issuing the subpoena have been demonstrated."); *United States v. Beckford,* 964 F.Supp. 1010, 1028 (E.D.Va. 1997) ("The Government's concern that an *ex parte* procedure will cause subpoenas *duces tecum* to be issued without a showing of relevance, admissibility, and specificity is unfounded." (citing *United States v. Reyes,* 162 F.R.D. 468, 471 (S.D.N.Y. 1995)); *United States v. Jenkins,* 895 F.Supp. 1389, 1393–94 (D.Haw. 1995) ("Reviewing applications for subpoenas *duces tecum,* a court needs no assistance in applying the *Nixon* stan-dard."); *see also Bowman Dairy Co. v. United States,* 341 U.S. 214, 220, 71 S.Ct. 675, 95 L.Ed. 879 (1951) ("The burden is on the court to see that the subpoena is good in its entirety and it is not upon the person who faces punishment to cull the good from the bad."); *United States v. Eden,* 659 F.2d 1376, 1381 (9th Cir. 1981) (providing that determinations of relevance, admissibility, and specificity "are of course committed to the sound discretion of the trial court").

Although these authorities run counter to the Government's position, recent experience appears to justify the Government's concerns. Specifically, the Government has provided several Rule 17(c) subpoenas issued in this district that seem to fall short of *Nixon* 's requirements. (*See* Mot. Preclude Exs. 6–7 (requiring a custodian of juvenile records to produce "certified copies of any and all information" pertaining to a victim in a child sex trafficking case); *id.* Ex. 14 (requiring a custodian of records at Child Protective Services to produce "[a]ll documents pertaining to referrals" in a family court file, "including but not limited to . . . referral reports, 'screener narratives,' and investigative reports").)

As the Supreme Court and Ninth Circuit have long instructed, "Rule 17(c) was not intended to provide an additional means of discovery. Its chief innovation was to expedite the trial by providing a time and place before trial for the inspection of the subpoenaed materials." *Bowman,* 341 U.S. at 220; *see United States v. MacKey,* 647 F.2d 898, 901 (9th Cir. 1981) ("[A] Rule 17(c) subpoena is not intended to serve as a discovery tool . . . or to allow a blind fishing expedition seeking unknown evidence." (citing *Bowman,* 341 U.S. at 220; *United States v. Brown,* 479 F.Supp. 1247, 1251 n. 7 (D.Md. 1979)).

Consistent with this view, the undersigned shares the Government's concern that many of the subpoenas in its possession appear to authorize "fishing expeditions." *See United States v. Sanchez,* No. 05-443, slip. op. at 4 (E.D.Cal. Jan. 9, 2007) ("Whenever a subpoena calls for 'all records regarding' a particular subject, 'including but not limited to' the described documents [,] it signals a fishing expedition."). This concern is heightened by Rule 17(c)(3)'s command that except in exceptional circumstances victims receive notice when a party seeks production of their personal or confidential information "so that the victim can move to quash or modify the subpoena." Fed.R.Crim.P. 17(c)(3).

Despite these concerns, however, the court cannot grant the sweeping remedy requested by the Government, namely, a categorical bar against *ex parte* subpoenas *duces tecum* in this case. Caselaw, the Advisory Committee's Notes, and the text of the Rule 17(c) itself indicate that the court must make an individualized, case-by-case determination as to whether the proponent of a Rule 17(c) subpoena has made a sufficient "showing of the need for confidentiality." *Tomison,* 969 F.Supp. 587, 591 n. 8 (E.D.Cal. 1997); *see, e.g., United States v. Daniels,* 95 F.Supp.2d 1160, 1163 (D.Kan. 2000) ("A determination of whether an *ex parte* application [under Rule 17(c)] is necessary must be evaluated on a case by case basis."); *Reyes,* 162 F.R.D. at 470 ("Under Rule 17(c), the Court exercises its discretion on a case-by-case basis to determine whether subpoenaed material should be deposited with the Court and whether this material should be disclosed to the adverse party.").

Therefore, to satisfy itself that the requirements of Rule 17(c)(3) and *Nixon* are met in this proceeding, the court will order that any *ex parte* application for early return subpoenas *duces tecum* in this case be made directly to the undersigned [judge]. If an *ex parte* application seeks the "production of personal or confidential information about a victim," the proponent must make a sufficient showing of "exceptional circumstances" to preclude notice to the victim or the Government. Fed.R.Crim.P. 17(c)(3). If the proponent fails to do so, the court will deny the application without prejudice to its filing as a noticed motion. In both *ex parte* and noticed proceedings, moreover, an early return subpoena *duces tecum* will only issue where the proponent satisfies the *Nixon* standards of relevance, admissibility, and specificity.

IT IS THEREFORE ORDERED that the Government's motion to preclude defendant from obtaining *ex parte* Rule 17(c) subpoenas be, and the same hereby is, DENIED; and

IT IS FURTHER ORDERED that any *ex parte* application for early return subpoenas *duces tecum* in this case be made directly to the undersigned and shall be consistent with this Order.

Notes

1. An improper *ex parte* subpoena of a victim's confidential records not only prevents the prosecution from being able to contest the subpoena, but also the victim whose privacy interest is at stake. Federal Rule of Criminal Procedure Rule 17(c)(3) was first urged by the ABA Victims Committee after passage of the CVRA, and addresses this problem as follows:

> After a complaint, indictment, or information is filed, a subpoena requiring the production of personal or confidential information about a victim may be served on a third party only by a court order. Before entering the order and unless there are exceptional circumstances, the court must require giving notice to the victim so that the victim can move to quash or modify the subpoena or otherwise object.

2. In the vast majority of state statutes, the problem of *ex parte* subpoenas of victims' confidential records has not been addressed.

3. In criminal cases it is common for subpoenas to issue for a wide variety of victim information, including the victim's cell phone, diary, social media content, Google searches, medical, mental health and education records, and more. Some of these items fit easily into confidentiality and privilege categories; general victims' rights provides potential additional bases to resist subpoenas. In *In re Zito*, No. 09-70554 (9th Cir. Feb. 26, 2009) (order). *See generally* Paul G. Cassell, *Treating Crime Victims Fairly: Integrating Victims into the Federal Rules of Criminal Procedure*. 2007 Utah L. Rev. 861, 901–19 (reviewing the issue). In addition, general privacy protections recognized for all persons provide a basis. *See Riley v. California*, 573 U.S. __ (2014) (unanimously holding that the warrantless search and seizure of digital contents of a cell phone during an arrest is unconstitutional).

4. What about personal property that contains a great deal of personal information, such as cell phones and computers? The U.S. Supreme Court has ruled that,

absent an exigency, the government must have a warrant to search a cell phone. The court noted that documents and communications are all stored there and that "[t]he sum of an individual's private life can be reconstructed through a thousand photographs labeled with dates, locations and descriptions. . ." *Riley v. California*, 134 S.Ct. 2473, 2489 (2016).

D. Protecting Victim Privacy through Evidentiary Rules

1. Evidentiary Privileges

In addition to the more commonly recognized privileges such as attorney-client, doctor-patient, and priest-penitent, most states have passed statutes creating evidentiary privileges concerning crime victims' confidential communications to crisis counselors/victim advocates. Most commonly these statutes limit the privilege to statements surrounding incidents of alleged sexual assault or domestic violence or both. In the absence of legislation, a few state courts have exercised their common law authority to extend the common law mental health privileges to include the crime victim-crisis counselor and victim-advocate relationship. Frequently, crisis counselors and victim-advocates are not psychiatrists, psychologists, or clinical social workers and therefore do not fall within other privileges.

Federal Rule of Evidence 501 leaves the issue of privileges to the federal courts. At least one federal trial court [in a civil case] has recognized a federal victim-advocate privilege.

Doe v. Old Dominion University

2018 WL 653797 (E.D. Va. 2018)

OPINION & ORDER

HENRY COKE MORGAN, JR., SENIOR UNITED STATES DISTRICT JUDGE

This matter is before the Court on the following three (3) Motions filed by Defendant Old Dominion University ("Defendant" or "ODU"): (1) Motion to Compel Plaintiff's Production of Written Discovery Answers and Responses, Doc. 43 ("Motion to Compel Plaintiff"); (2) Motion to Compel SurvJustice, Inc.'s Response to Subpoena Duces Tecum, Doc. 48 ("Motion to Compel SurvJustice"); and (3) Motion to Compel Jane Doe's Parents' Response to Subpoena Duces Tecum, Doc. 50 ("Motion to Compel Plaintiff's Parents"). On December 6, 2017, the Court convened a hearing and heard argument on the Motions. The Court RESERVED RULING on the Motions at that time, and ORDERED Plaintiff and Non–Parties SurvJustice and Plaintiff's Parents to produce the withheld documents for an in camera inspection by the Court. See Doc. 76 at 2.

All three (3) Motions to Compel arise from the Parties' disagreement as to whether a victim-advocate privilege applies to the withheld discovery in this case. At the

December 6, 2017 hearing, the Court FOUND that a qualified privilege exists for communications between a sexual assault victim and his or her advocate. The privilege can be overcome if, on review, the Court determines that the potential relevance of the communications outweighs the public policy interest in keeping them confidential. By Order dated December 11, 2017, the Court GRANTED the Motions to Compel IN PART, and attached copies of the emails that were subject to production. Doc. 85 at 1. The Court ORDERED Plaintiff to produce two (2) additional documents for its review, an image file and a Google Document. See id. at 2. Plaintiff produced the image file but was unable to retrieve the relevant version of the Google Document. See Doc. 96.

Having reviewed the image file produced by Plaintiff, the Court hereby GRANTS the Motion to Compel Plaintiff, Doc. 43, and Motion to Compel SurvJustice, Doc. 48, as to one (1) additional email, which is attached to this Order and is hereby SEALED. The Court DENIES the Motions to Compel as to the remaining withheld documents. The Court explains its ruling in further detail below.

. . .

II. LEGAL STANDARDS

. . .

A party may refuse to disclose otherwise discoverable material by asserting a privilege. FED. R. CIV. P. 26(b)(5). In a civil case involving a federal claim, privilege is governed by the federal common law, unless otherwise provided by the U.S. Constitution, a federal statute, or rules prescribed by the Supreme Court of the United States. See FED. R. EVID. 501. "Evidentiary privileges in litigation are not favored." *Herbert v. Lando*, 441 U.S. 153, 175, 99 S.Ct. 1635, 60 L.Ed.2d 115 (1979). A court should only create and apply a privilege if it "promotes sufficiently important interests to outweigh the need for probative evidence." Univ. of Pa. v. E.E.O.C., 493 U.S. 182, 189, 110 S.Ct. 577, 107 L.Ed.2d 571 (1990) (quoting *Trammel v. United States*, 445 U.S. 40, 51, 100 S.Ct. 906, 63 L.Ed.2d 186 (1980)).

III. DISCUSSION

A. Victim–Advocate Privilege

Plaintiff objects to the production requests at issue here on the basis of what she has termed a "victim-advocate privilege." Plaintiff asserts the victim-advocate privilege, "whether by statute or otherwise, including, but not limited to," Section 63.2–104.1 of the Virginia Code. Id. at 1–2. This provision states:

> In order to ensure the safety of adult and child victims of domestic violence, dating violence, sexual assault, or stalking, . . . and their families, programs and individuals providing services to such victims shall protect the confidentiality and privacy of persons receiving services.

Va. Code Ann. § 63.2–104.1(A) (West 2017). Programs and individuals providing such services shall not "[d]isclose any personally identifying information or individual information collected in connection with services requested, utilized, or denied," unless "compelled by statutory or court mandate." Id. § 63.2–104(B)(1) and (C).

1. Defendant's Position

Defendant argues that no such privilege exists, and that the Court should not create one in this case. See Doc. 44 at 11 ("[Defendant] could find no authority from the Fourth Circuit (or elsewhere in the federal civil judiciary) creating or recognizing such a privilege."). Defendant argues that Plaintiff's citation to the Virginia Code is misplaced, because "this Title IX action involves a federal, not a state, claim, and, thus, federal law supplies the rules of decision." Id. Defendant further argues that, even if state law did apply, the provision Plaintiff cited does not create a victim-advocate privilege. Defendant asserts that "the only federal court to address the question of a privilege under Virginia Code § 63.2–104.1 has specifically held that the provision created no privilege." Id. at 12 (citing Eramo v. Rolling Stone, Inc., 314 F.R.D. 205, 212–13 (W.D. Va. 2016)).

Defendant insists that a court should not "create and apply an evidentiary privilege unless it 'promotes sufficiently important interests to outweigh the need for probative evidence.'" Doc. 68 at 3 (quoting *Univ. of Pa.*, 493 U.S. at 189, 110 S.Ct. 577 (quoting *Trammel*, 445 U.S. at 51, 100 S.Ct. 906)). Defendant further asserts that Plaintiff has placed her communications with SurvJustice into issue by "affirmatively fil[ing] as Exhibit 3 to her Amended Complaint a December 15, 2014, communication between herself and one of her victim-advocates." *Id.* Defendant argues that "[b]ecause the plaintiff has voluntarily placed all of these matters in issue, they are relevant and merit a full and fair inquiry on the part of [Defendant]." *Id.* Defendant insists that access to these communications "is essential for its defense against the plaintiff's Title IX allegations[,] the plaintiff's demand for monetary damages and injunctive relief, and the accrual of the plaintiff's Title IX claim for the purposes of [Defendant's] statute of limitations defense." *Id.* at 4.

2. Plaintiff's Position

In opposition, Plaintiff acknowledges that federal law governs the privilege issues in this case, but notes that no constitutional provision, federal statute, or Supreme Court decision provides the necessary guidance here. See Doc. 62 at 4. Accordingly, this Court has the authority "to define a new privilege by interpreting common law principles in light of reason and experience." Id. at 4–5 (citing Fed. R. Evid. 501; *Jaffee v. Redmond*, 518 U.S. 1, 8, 116 S.Ct. 1923, 135 L.Ed.2d 337 (1996)). Given that authority, Plaintiff argues that the Court should recognize a victim-advocate privilege in this case, for the same reasons the Supreme Court recognized a psychotherapist-patient privilege in Jaffee v. Redmond. See *id.* at 5. In *Jaffee*, the Supreme Court articulated four (4) reasons for recognizing the privilege:

> 1. Successful psychotherapy "depends upon an atmosphere of confidence and trust in which the patient is willing to make a frank and complete disclosure of facts, emotions, memories, and fears." *Jaffee*, 518 U.S. at 10, 116 S. Ct. 1923.

2. The privilege "serves the public interest by facilitating the provision of appropriate treatment for individuals suffering the effects of a mental or emotional problem," as "[t]he mental health of our citizenry . . . is a public good of transcendent importance." *Id*. at 11, 116 S.Ct. 1923.

3. "[T]he likely evidentiary benefit that would result from the denial of the privilege is modest. . . . Without a privilege, much of the desirable evidence to which litigants . . . seek access—for example, admissions against interest by a party—is unlikely to come into being. This unspoken 'evidence' will therefore serve no greater truth-seeking function than if it had been spoken and privileged." Id. at 11–12, 116 S.Ct. 1923.

4. "All 50 States and the District of Columbia have enacted into law some form of psychotherapist privilege." Id. at 12, 116 S.Ct. 1923.

First, Plaintiff argues that, like the psychotherapist-patient privilege, the victim-advocate privilege depends on confidentiality. Confidentiality "is essential to ensuring that the sexual assault survivor approaches the advocate in the first place," and it "is needed to ensure that the victim feels safe sharing the details of his or her situation with the advocate so that the advocate can ensure that the victim's rights are being protected." Second, Plaintiff argues that the privilege here would "serve[ ] the public good by promoting public safety." By "increasing the likelihood that gender violence is reported," the privilege would ensure safer communities. Third, Plaintiff argues that, like in Jaffee, the evidentiary benefit in rejecting the privilege would be minimal, because doing so would chill communications between victims and their advocates. "Thus, the exact discovery that ODU seeks would not exist because Ms. Doe would not have felt comfortable engaging in open communications with SurvJustice," if she believed those communications would not be privileged. Finally, Plaintiff argues that "the majority of states and the District of Columbia have enacted statutes that afford some form of confidential protections in the victim-advocate relationship." In this case, Plaintiff "expected that the confidentiality provided by her own state's statute, the state in which she was violently raped, the state in which ODU is located, and the state in which [Plaintiff] exchanged privileged, confidential communications with SurvJustice as she attempted to recover from being assaulted, would protect those communications."

Plaintiff further argues that the *Eramo* case cited by Defendant is inapposite to the facts of this case. In *Eramo*, while the Western District of Virginia "declined to implement a victim-advocate privilege under Va. Code § 63.2–104.1, [it] did not hold that no such privilege exists." Id. at 12. Rather, the court "found that even if the privilege does exist, the third party from whom documents were sought had 'waived such privilege by voluntarily disclosing the contents of her communications with Eramo and UVA to defendants.'" Id. at 12–13 (quoting *Eramo*, 314 F.R.D. at 213).

3. The Court Recognizes a Victim–Advocate Privilege

The Court agrees with Plaintiff that communications between sexual assault victims and their advocates should be privileged. The Supreme Court has held that recognition of a testimonial privilege "may be justified . . . by a 'public good transcending the normally predominant principle of utilizing all rational means for ascertaining truth.'" *Jaffee*, 518 U.S. at 9, 116 S.Ct. 1923 (quoting *Trammel v. United States*, 445 U.S. 40, 50, 100 S.Ct. 906, 63 L.Ed.2d 186 (1980)). This Court FINDS that protecting confidential communications between victims and their advocates "promotes sufficiently important interests to outweigh the need for probative evidence," and thus that a victim-advocate privilege is necessary for the same reasons as the psychotherapist-patient privilege in *Jaffee*. *Id*. at 9–10, (quoting Trammel, 445 U.S. at 51, 100 S.Ct. 906).

First, the privilege is "rooted in the imperative need for confidence and trust." *Id*. at 10, (quoting *Trammel*, 445 U.S. at 51, 100 S.Ct. 906 (1980)). For the victim advocate to be effective, the victim must "make a frank and complete disclosure of facts, emotions, memories, and fears" regarding the assault. *See id*. Only with such a comprehensive understanding can the advocate ensure the victim has access to the information and resources he or she needs in the aftermath of a sexual assault. As with the psychotherapist-patient relationship that was found to be privileged in Jaffee, the success of the victim-advocate relationship is threatened by even "the mere possibility of disclosure." *Id*. at 10. Thus, private interests counsel in favor of keeping victim-advocate communications confidential.

A victim-advocate privilege also serves public ends. The Jaffee Court decided that a psychotherapist-patient privilege is warranted, because "[t]he mental health of our citizenry, no less than its physical health, is a public good of transcendent importance." *Id*. at 11. The attorney-client privilege is required to "promote broader public interests in the observance of law and administration of justice." See id. (quoting *Upjohn Co. v. United States*, 449 U.S. 383, 389, 101 S.Ct. 677, 66 L.Ed.2d 584 (1981)). The victim-advocate privilege furthers each of these interests. Professional mental health services and other accommodations relating to the victim's mental health are among the resources that flow from a successful victim-advocate relationship. And encouraging full and frank disclosure within the victim-advocate relationship promotes "the observance of law and administration of justice," by increasing the likelihood that sexual assaults will be reported, investigated, and prosecuted. Considering how widespread and yet underreported sexual violence apparently is in the United States today, encouraging victim speech is especially important.

On the other side of the equation, denying the victim-advocate privilege offers only minimal, if any, evidentiary benefit. As in the psychotherapist-patient or attorney-client relationship, "confidential conversations between [victims and their advocates] would surely be chilled" if the privilege were denied. 116 S.Ct. 1923. Especially given the advocate's role in helping the victim to recognize and enforce legal rights and remedies, it is unlikely that victims would disclose to their advocate any information that could potentially be used against them in future litigation, if they knew those communications would not be privileged. Cf.*id*. at 12, 116 S.Ct. 1923 ("Without a privilege, much of the desirable evidence to which litigants such as petitioner seek access—for example, admissions against interest by a party—is unlikely to come into being. This unspoken 'evidence' will therefore serve no greater truth-seeking function than if it had been spoken and privileged."), Thus, the amount of evidence that, but for the privilege, would be available for discovery is likely very small.

Finally, forty (40) states and the District of Columbia have enacted some type of protection for victim-advocate communications. See Jaffee, 518 U.S. at 12–13, 116 S. Ct. 1923 ("We have previously observed that the policy decisions of the States bear on the question whether federal courts should recognize a new privilege or amend the coverage of an existing one." (citing Trammel, 445 U.S. at 48–50, 100 S.Ct. 906; United States v. Gillock, 445 U.S. 360, 368 n.8, 100 S.Ct. 1185, 63 L.Ed.2d 454 (1980))). This not only suggests that "'reason and experience' support recognition of the privilege," id. at 13, 116 S.Ct. 1923, but it also highlights the disruptive effect that ignoring the privilege would have on victim-advocate communications across the country. As in Jaffee, "any State's promise of confidentiality would have little value if the patient were aware that the privilege would not be honored in a federal court." Id.

In light of these considerations, the Court FINDS that communications between a sexual assault victim and his or her advocate are privileged, pursuant to Federal Rule of Evidence 501 and the Supreme Court's decision in Jaffee. As most of the state laws indicate, however, the privilege is not absolute. See, e.g., Va. Code Ann. §63.2–104.1(C) (noting that release of victim-advocate communications may be compelled by statutory or court mandate). Accordingly, the Court further FINDS that communications otherwise protected under this privilege may be released, if the Court determines that their theoretical relevance outweighs the public policy in favor of keeping them confidential. It is the Court's duty to review in camera the content of the communications before making this determination.

The Court notes that the analysis required under a qualified evidentiary privilege, the Federal Rules of Civil Procedure, and the Virginia confidentiality statute are essentially the same. For example, although the Court is not bound by the Virginia statute in this case, a Virginia state court considering whether victim-advocate communications will be produced must first make a determination that such communications' probative value outweighs the public and private interests in keeping them confidential. And Rule 26(b)(1) of the Federal Rules of Civil Procedure limits the scope of discovery to matters that are "relevant to any party's claim or defense and proportional to the needs of the case, considering[, among other factors,] the parties' relative access to relevant information, . . . the importance of the discovery in resolving the issues, and whether the burden or expense of the proposed discovery outweighs its likely benefit." Fed. R. Civ. P. 26(b)(1) (emphasis added). Even without finding that the communications between Plaintiff and her advocate are covered by an evidentiary privilege, then, the Court would have to determine whether the theoretical relevance of the withheld emails is proportional to the needs of the case, considering the significant public policy interests discussed above.

. . .

IV. CONCLUSION

For the foregoing reasons, and pursuant to its authority under the Federal Rules of Evidence and applicable Supreme Court precedent, the Court FINDS that communications between a sexual assault victim and his or her advocate are protected by a qualified evidentiary privilege. See Fed. R. Evid. 501; Jaffee, 518 U.S. 1, 116 S.Ct. 1923. The Court has reviewed the withheld documents, and GRANTS Defendant's Motions to Compel, Docs. 43, 48, 50, IN PART, as to the emails attached to its December 11, 2017 Order and to this Order. The Court DENIES the Motions to Compel as to the remaining emails.

Notes

1. The policies generally underlying the law of evidentiary privilege are briefly set forth in McCormick on Evidence (3d Ed. 1982) pp. 171–72.

2. This crisis-counselor/victim advocate privilege has not explicitly been recognized under the Federal Rules of Evidence nor by the U.S. Supreme Court. The U.S. Supreme Court has, however, judicially created the federal psychotherapist-patient privilege pursuant to their authority under FRE 501. *Jaffee v. Redmond*, 518 U.S. 1 (1996). In *Jaffee,* survivors of a man killed by a policewoman brought a civil action in U.S. District Court pursuant to 42 U.S.C. § 1983. In the process they discovered that the policewoman, prior to the shooting, had undergone 50 counseling sessions with a clinical social worker licensed as such by the state of Illinois. The court held that an absolute privilege existed protecting confidential communication between a licensed clinical social worker and the patient: "The balancing component implemented by the Court of Appeals and a few states is rejected, for it would eviscerate the privilege thereby making it impossible for participants to predict whether the confidential conversations will be protected." 116 S. Ct., at 1932.

In *People v. Foggy,* 521 N.E.2d 86 (Ill. 1988), the court analyzed a statute granting an absolute sexual assault counselor-victim privilege. The court neither upheld the absolute privilege nor did it turn it into a qualified privilege. The court opined;

> It is important to note that in this case the defendant's request for an *in camera* inspection of the counseling records was merely general; he did not allege that information may exist in the counseling files that would be subject to disclosure. Moreover, the defendant had access to the array of unprivileged statements made by the complaining witness to other persons following the commission of the offenses, including the nearly contemporaneous statements made by the victim to the store clerk, and also had available the victim's testimony at the preliminary hearing. Because of the strong policy of confidentiality expressed in section 8-802.1 and the absence of any indication by the defendant that the victim's communications with the

counselor would provide a source of impeachment, we do not believe that the privilege was required to be breached in this case. "The vague assertion that the victim may have made statements to her therapist that might possibly differ from the victim's anticipated trial testimony does not provide a sufficient basis to justify ignoring the victim's right to rely upon her statutory privilege." *People v. District Court* (Colo. 1986), 719 P.2d 722, 726.... Under the circumstances present here, to abrogate the privilege in this case would require its abrogation in every case, and that we decline to do.

We note that under the theory proposed by the dissent, in every case a trial judge could become privy to all counseling records of a sexual assault victim, regardless of what was discussed in the counseling sessions and in the absence of any demonstrated need that would justify such an intrusion. The victim in this case was told that the services of the Quad City Counseling Program were both free and confidential, but under the dissent's view that advice would no longer be appropriate — a special admonition would become necessary, to accommodate the very real possibility that a judge later would be examining the records of the counseling sessions. This, we believe, would seriously undermine the valuable, beneficial services of those programs that are within the protection of the statute....

We conclude that the defendant was not denied due process, nor was his confrontation right violated, by the trial judge's refusal in this case to conduct an *in camera* inspection of the victim's counseling records.

. . . .

Justice SIMON, dissenting:

In the not so distant past a rape victim was forced to undergo an adjudicative ordeal equaling the horror of the original assault in order to bring her attacker to justice.... In its zeal to erase the legal indignities suffered by victims of rape in the past, however, I believe the legislature has gone too far. To deem all communications between victim and counselor absolutely privileged impermissibly impinges upon a defendant's constitutional rights to due process of law and confrontation of the witnesses against him. A balance must be struck between the rights of the accuser and the rights of the accused, in which the victim is shielded from needless intrusions into the rape-counseling process, without denying the defendant the right to discover and utilize information tending to exculpate him. Allowing, at a minimum, *in camera* inspection by the trial court of the communications between the rape crisis counselor and the victim would achieve the balance necessary to protect the interests of both parties....

In summary, when the defendant's rights to due process and confrontation are weighed against the State's interest in the absolute confidentiality of the witness' records, it is clear to me that the State's interest must yield. The statute enacted by the legislature, cloaking communications between rape victims and rape counselors in an absolute privilege, is unconstitutional. Numerous other courts have reached similar conclusions. . . .

. . . .

In addition, the concern that *in camera* review of the counseling records would negatively affect the therapeutic relationship between the victim and the counselor is not well founded. Neither the thoughts and feelings of the victim, nor the comments of the counselor, would be exposed as a result of an *in camera* review. The trial court would be looking for, and disclosing to the defendant if necessary, only the facts of the alleged incident as communicated by the victim to the counselor. Such a minimal intrusion should have little, if any, chilling effect on the therapeutic relationship.

Notes

1. Note that in *Foggy* there is a legislated absolute privilege. The court does not expressly overturn the absolute nature of the privilege, but seems open to a qualified privilege. Is an absolute privilege, an automatic *in camera* inspection, or an *in camera* inspection upon a showing by the defendant the best approach? The Supreme Court of Pennsylvania has upheld a truly absolute privilege in the face of a defendant's challenge based upon state and federal due process and confrontation clauses. *Commonwealth v. Wilson*, 529 Pa. 298, 602 A.2d 1290 (1992), *cert. den.*, 504 U.S. 977 (1992).

2. Note that the requirement of a showing by the defendant often may be difficult or impossible for the defendant to meet without knowledge of the records themselves.

3. Once the victim statements to the counselor are in the hands of the prosecutor, they are probably discoverable to the defense. In *Commonwealth v. Miller*, 399 Pa. Super. 180, 582 A.2d 4 (1990), the court held that a report on the victim prepared by the rape crisis center and provided to the prosecution must be provided to the defendant. The failure to turn over the material was a violation of the defendant's right to confrontation and compulsory process. But *see, Commonwealth v. Askew*, 446 Pa. Super. 301, 666 A.2d 1062 (1995), in which a minor victim of sexual assault was not found to waive the privilege where the victim's mother consented to the disclosure by the child's counselor. The privilege was not waived because the counselor was mandated by law to report child abuse. A prosecutor's failure to provide the records is an error subject to the harmless error rule. *Commonwealth v. Davis*, 543 Pa. 628, 674 A.2d 214 (1996).

---

2. Rape Shield

Rape shield statutes and rules of evidence specifically address the admissibility into evidence of a victim's past sexual behavior. The federal version of the rape shield law is embodied in Federal Rule of Evidence 412, which provides:

Rule 412. Sex Offense Cases; Relevance of Alleged Victim's Past Sexual Behavior or Alleged Sexual Predisposition

(a) **Evidence generally inadmissible.** The following evidence is not admissible in any civil or criminal proceeding involving alleged sexual misconduct except as provided in subdivisions (b) and (c):

> (1) Evidence offered to prove that any alleged victim engaged in other sexual behavior.

> (2) Evidence offered to prove any alleged victim's sexual predisposition.

(b) **Exceptions.**

(1) In a criminal case, the following evidence is admissible, if otherwise admissible under these rules:

> (A) evidence of specific instances of sexual behavior by the alleged victim offered to prove that a person other than the accused was the source of semen, injury, or other physical evidence;

> (B) evidence of specific instances of sexual behavior by the alleged victim with respect to the person accused of the sexual misconduct offered by the accused to prove consent or by the prosecution; and

> (C) evidence the exclusion of which would violate the constitutional rights of the defendant.

> (2) In a civil case, evidence offered to prove the sexual behavior or sexual predisposition of nay alleged victim is admissible if it is otherwise admissible under these rules and its probative value substantially outweighs the danger of harm to any victim and of unfair prejudice to any party. Evidence of an alleged victim's reputation is admissible only if it has been placed in controversy by the alleged victim.

(c) **Procedure to determine admissibility.**

(1) A party intending to offer evidence under subdivision (b) must—

> (A) file a written motion at least 14 days before trial specifically describing the evidence and stating the purpose for which it is offered unless the court, for good cause requires a different time for filing or permits filing during trial; and

> (B) serve the motion on all parties and notify the alleged victim or, when appropriate, the alleged victim's guardian or representative.

(2) Before admitting evidence under this rule the court must conduct a hearing in camera and afford the victim and parties a right to attend and be heard. The motion, related papers, and the record of the hearing must be sealed and remain under seal unless the court orders otherwise.

Federal Rule 412 provides that the court must conduct an *in camera* hearing on a rape shield motion. These closed hearings afford victims privacy protections by ensuring that litigation surrounding whether their prior sexual conduct should be admitted into evidence does not itself result in public exposure of their private information. Recently courts have been faced with challenges to holding rape shield proceedings in camera and have had to determine whether and when these proceedings should be open. *Compare State v. McBale*, 305 P.3d 107 (Or. 2013) (rejecting defendant's argument that the rape shield statute's mandatory *in camera* procedure violated the open courts clause of the state constitution and his right to a public trial under the state and federal constitutions) *with Commonwealth v. Jones*, 37 N.E.3d 589 (Mass. 2015) (concluding "that, before a judge may order the court room closed for a rape shield hearing, the judge must make a case-by-case determination in accordance with the four-prong framework articulated by the United States Supreme Court in *Waller*, 467 U.S. at 48, 104 S.Ct. 2210, decided after the enactment of the rape shield law at issue here).

The exceptions articulated in Federal Rule of Evidence 412 are similar to the exceptions in most state rape shield provisions, including the exception for "evidence the exclusion of which would violate the constitutional rights of the defendant." How do courts analyze a defendant's constitutional rights in the face of an assertion that the evidence at issue is protected by rape shield?

Wood v. Alaska
957 F.2d 1544 (9th Cir. 1992)

RYMER, Circuit Judge:

Kenneth Wood was convicted in Alaska state court of raping an adult woman, M.G. In a pre-trial hearing, the trial court issued a protective order excluding any evidence that M.G. had posed for *Penthouse* magazine and acted in X-rated movies and other sexual performances, and that she had shown Wood the Penthouse photographs and discussed her experiences with him. Wood appealed his conviction unsuccessfully in the Alaska state courts, arguing among other things that the exclusion of this evidence violated his Sixth Amendment rights. He then filed this petition for writ of habeas corpus in the district court on the same ground. The district court denied the petition, and Wood appeals.

We hold that excluding the evidence did not violate Wood's Sixth Amendment rights. The facts proffered, that M.G. posed for *Penthouse* and acted in pornographic movies and other sexual performances, are not relevant in themselves. We recognize that the facts that she showed Wood the *Penthouse* photographs and told him about her acting experiences are relevant to a limited degree because they are acts with the defendant that tend to establish the nature of their relationship. We conclude, however, that the trial court did not err in excluding evidence of M.G.'s modeling and acting, as well as evidence of her communicating those experiences to Wood, because the court could reasonably conclude that the prejudicial effect of the evidence outweighs its limited probative value. We therefore affirm.

I

Wood and M.G. met in October 1983. At the time, M.G. was living with her boyfriend, Bob Berube, and Wood was their neighbor. Wood and M.G. became friends, seeing each other frequently over the next six months.

Wood and M.G. dispute the nature of their relationship during those six months. Wood testified that they had a sexual relationship and had intercourse regularly, even though M.G. was still somewhat involved with Berube. He also said that a common occurrence for them was to have an argument and then, after resolving the argument, have sex. He presented several witnesses who testified to their perceptions that Wood and M.G. had a sexual relationship. M.G. testified that, to the contrary, their relationship was platonic. She said that they did not have intercourse, although she did admit that one night when they were both drunk, they did engage in kissing and petting. She also testified that she had an off-and-on relationship with Berube, but that she slept with Berube almost every night even during the times that they were separated. She confided in Wood about some of the problems she and Berube were having.

On April 11, 1984, M.G. was visiting at a friend's house when Wood showed up and wanted to talk to her about their relationship. M.G. did not want to talk to him about it. Wood testified that their sexual relationship had slowed down by that time because M.G. was confused about her feelings toward him and toward Berube. M.G. explained in her testimony that she had been trying to drop Wood out of her life because he wanted more than a platonic relationship and she did not. Wood finally persuaded M.G. to leave the friend's house and go with him to get cigarettes.

While they were in the car, Wood persisted in trying to talk about the relationship, and they began to argue. M.G. asked that he drive her home, and when he refused she tried to jump out of the moving car. Wood struck her several times after she tried to get out of the car. Wood testified that he only slapped her to get her to calm down. M.G. testified that he hit her head against the dashboard, and that he pulled out a gun and threatened to use it on her.

Wood then drove M.G. to another male friend's home where M.G. had been staying. Wood testified that M.G. had calmed down and that they had reconciled their differences at that point. He said that they then went into the friend's apartment and made love and that it was entirely consensual. M.G. testified that he threatened to hurt her if she did not go in the apartment and that he again pulled out the gun. She agreed to go in with him, and he put the gun back under the seat of the car. She testified that he told her to go into the bedroom and take off her clothes and that he would have sex with her "either willingly or forcefully." Once in the bedroom, she said he told her to lie down and be still and he would not hurt her. She complied, and they had intercourse and oral sex. Afterward, Wood left the apartment and M.G. called Berube and reported the incident to the police.

Before trial, the state moved for a protective order under Alaska's rape shield statute to prevent Wood from introducing evidence of M.G.'s prior sexual conduct. Alaska Stat. § 12.45.045(a) requires the court to determine, in an in camera hearing, the admissibility of evidence of previous sexual conduct: If the court finds that evidence offered by the defendant regarding the sexual conduct of the complaining witness is relevant, and that the probative value of the evidence offered is not outweighed by the probability that its admission will create undue prejudice, confusion of the issues, or unwarranted invasion of the privacy of the complaining witness, the court shall make an order stating what evidence may be introduced and the nature of the questions that may be permitted. The defendant may then offer evidence under the order of the court.

At the pre-trial hearing on the motion, Wood testified that several months before the alleged rape, M.G. told him that she had posed for *Penthouse*, acted in pornographic movies, and had been paid to have sex in a room full of mirrors with people taking pictures. He had a copy of the *Penthouse* magazine, and the state conceded that it was M.G. in the photographs, but he did not have copies of any films. Wood testified that M.G. showed him the *Penthouse* photographs, and he testified that he perceived that "in some respects it seemed to be sexual come-on" but that it was not "totally" a come-on. At some time after that, he said, M.G. approached him directly and said she wanted to have sex with him. He testified that about a week after that, they did have intercourse for the first time.

Wood's counsel argued that the evidence of these sexual acts and the fact that M.G. had presented them to Wood was relevant to show that the two had a sexual relationship. After hearing testimony of Wood's witnesses and considering the government's proffer of M.G.'s testimony, the trial court ruled that the evidence would be excluded. It explained: The defendant himself here placed only the most tenuous contact I think between the photographs and the consent issue. If he indeed sincerely believed that she was promiscuous and rather loose, he certainly had his own independent fund of information to conclude that. Perhaps it might be the relative ease with which he and she formed a sexual liaison. Perhaps it's something as yet unspecified in this record that they talked about and what he suspected. That's never been stated as to, you know, what her contact — or conduct with others might have been, and I think that it adds almost nothing to establishing the consent issue, whereas even in today's modern times as the state correctly argues, it's very — it is possible that some people even in today's modern times would have such a negative view of such a person that they would revert to what was the time-honored position which would virtually deny a person with this in her background the protection of the rape law. A bad social result and one that society has clearly gone beyond. The trial court concluded: "So no use will be made of these exhibits [the *Penthouse* photographs]. They will not be introduced. They will not be referred to and both sides will be required to scrupulously instruct their witnesses that these issues are not to be inquired into." It also prevented the introduction of any evidence relating to M.G.'s pornographic acting.

Wood was found guilty at trial of two counts of sexual assault in the first degree. He appealed his conviction to the Alaska Court of Appeals. Among other grounds, he argued that the exclusion of the evidence of M.G.'s past sexual conduct violated his Sixth Amendment rights to confront the witnesses against him and to present a defense. The Court of Appeals affirmed the conviction in a 2–1 decision. *Wood v. State*, 736 P.2d 363 (Alaska Ct. App. 1987). It concluded that the trial court did not abuse its discretion in excluding the evidence because it had limited probative value, and whatever value it had was outweighed by its probable prejudicial effect. In dissent, Judge Singleton opined that Wood should have been permitted to examine M.G. regarding the possibility that she informed the defendant of her "modeling" experience. *Id.* at 367–68 (Singleton, J., dissenting). Wood then appealed to the Alaska Supreme Court. The Supreme Court initially granted review but after receiving formal briefing, vacated its order granting review. Two of the five justices dissented from the denial of review and would have reversed the conviction.

Wood then filed this petition for writ of habeas corpus in the district court under 28 U.S.C. § 2254, again arguing that the trial court's exclusion of the evidence violated his Sixth Amendment rights. The district court denied the petition. It reasoned that Wood did not have a constitutional right to present the evidence based on the record in the pre-trial hearing. It went on to state that he did have such a constitutional right after M.G. testified because the evidence was then relevant to impeach her testimony. The district court denied the petition, however, because Wood made no effort to introduce the evidence after M.G. testified, and his argument therefore related only to the constitutionally sound decision made at the pre-trial hearing to exclude the evidence.

Wood appeals, arguing that he was not obligated to renew his objection to the exclusion of the evidence after M.G. testified. He also argues that this court should accept the district court's conclusion that the exclusion of the evidence violated his Sixth Amendment rights. The state argues that the district court correctly concluded that Wood could not raise an argument based on the relevance of the evidence after M.G. testified because he never presented that argument to the state courts. It also argues that, even if Wood's failure to object did not preclude relief, the exclusion of the evidence was not unconstitutional either before or after M.G. testified.

* * *

III

* * *

Wood argues that excluding the evidence of M.G.'s sexual conduct violated his rights under the Sixth Amendment to confront the witnesses against him and to present a defense. These rights encompass the rights to cross-examination, ... A defendant has no right, however, to present irrelevant evidence. . . . It is within the trial court's discretion to determine which issues are relevant. *See id.*

Even relevant evidence can be excluded in certain circumstances. The right to present relevant testimony "may, in appropriate cases, bow to accommodate other legitimate interests in the criminal trial process." *Chambers v. Mississippi*, 410 U.S. 284, 295 (1973). The Supreme Court has recognized that a state has a legitimate interest in protecting rape victims against unwarranted invasions of privacy and harassment regarding their sexual conduct. Lucas, 500 U.S. at ___, 111 S.Ct. at 1146. Also, "trial judges retain wide latitude insofar as the Confrontation Clause is concerned to impose reasonable limits on . . . cross-examination based on concerns about, among other things, harassment, prejudice, confusion of the issues, the witness' safety, or interrogation that is repetitive or only marginally relevant." *Delaware v. Van Arsdall*, 475 U.S. 673, 679.

In determining whether Wood's Sixth Amendment rights were violated, we make a two-part inquiry. We inquire, first, as to whether the excluded evidence is relevant. If it is not relevant, Wood had no constitutional right to present it. If the evidence is relevant, we ask next whether other legitimate interests outweighed Wood's interest in presenting the evidence. Because trial judges have broad discretion both to determine relevance and to determine whether prejudicial effect or other concerns outweigh the probative value of the evidence, we will find a Sixth Amendment violation only if we conclude that the trial court abused its discretion. . . . A trial court does not abuse its discretion so long as the jury has "sufficient information" upon which to assess the credibility of witnesses. *United States v. Kennedy*, 714 F.2d 968, 973 (9th Cir.1983), *cert. denied*, 465 U.S. 1034 (1984); *see also Van Arsdall*, 475 U.S. at 680 ("We think that a criminal defendant states a violation of the Confrontation Clause by showing that he was prohibited from engaging in otherwise appropriate cross-examination . . . 'to expose to the jury the facts from which jurors . . . could appropriately draw inferences relating to the reliability of the witness.'") (*quoting Davis*, 415 U.S. at 318).

A

Wood argues that the evidence of M.G.'s prior sexual conduct is relevant to show that she had a sexual relationship with Wood, which in turn is relevant to show that she consented to sex on April 11, 1984. The state does not dispute that the issue of whether M.G. had a sexual relationship with Wood prior to the alleged rape is relevant to whether she consented on that night. The state does dispute, however, that the evidence of M.G.'s modeling in *Penthouse* and acting in pornographic movies is relevant to establish that she had a sexual relationship with Wood or that she had consensual intercourse with him on the night in question.

Wood contends that the evidence is directly relevant to show that M.G. would have had a sexual relationship with him because it shows that she is a woman of questionable sexual morals. Other courts [reviewing] this theory of admissibility have consistently rejected it as reflecting outdated views of women and sexuality, and we similarly reject it. . . . The fact that M.G. was willing to pose for *Penthouse* or act in sexual movies and performances says virtually nothing about whether she would have sex with Wood. It only tends to show that she was willing to have sex, not that she was willing to have sex with this particular man at this particular time. Whether M.G. was willing to have sex at all is not an issue in the case because she admitted that she slept with Berube, and she in no way represented that she was adverse to having sex. Because the evidence of M.G.'s prior sexual acts with others does not establish anything that was not already established, it lacks probative value on the question of whether she had a sexual relationship with Wood.

Wood's next argument is that the evidence is relevant to impeach M.G.'s general credibility as a witness. Yet, the fact that she posed in the nude or acted in pornographic performances does not in any way indicate that she is a dishonest person or had a motive to lie in this case.

Wood emphasizes, as did the district court, that the article accompanying the Penthouse photographs indicates that she is not credible because it quotes her as saying, "I love pretending." But the quote simply comes from a discussion of her ambition to be an actress: "[M.G.]'s 'purpose' [in life] is to put her considerable talents, youthful good looks, and other blessings to work as an actress. 'I love pretending. . . . I have a real instinct for the stage.'" That M.G. wants to be an actress has little relevance to whether she was lying on the stand. Moreover, to the extent that her acting ambition does have any relevance to her credibility as a witness, it was not necessary to introduce the *Penthouse* evidence to establish it. Nothing in the combination of the words and the pictures indicates that M.G. is prone to rape fantasies or otherwise especially likely to lie about being raped. Wood could simply have inquired into her love of pretending without referring to the *Penthouse* article.

Thus, evidence of M.G.'s modeling and acting is not relevant in itself to establish either that she and Wood had a sexual relationship or that she is an unreliable witness. That M.G. told Wood about it and showed him sexually explicit photographs of herself, on the other hand, is relevant. Wood testified at the pre-trial hearing that M.G. showed him the Penthouse pictures and discussed her acting and modeling with him. These communications could be interpreted as sexually provocative acts. That M.G. may have communicated in these ways with Wood therefore has some tendency to show that she was not uninterested in a sexual relationship with him, and in turn that the relationship was, as Wood claimed, sexual rather than platonic.

A rape victim's communications and acts with the defendant are fundamentally different from prior sexual conduct with persons other than the defendant. While a rape victim's sexual history with others only goes to show a generalized attitude toward sex that says little if anything about the victim's attitude toward sex with the defendant, the victim's prior acts with the defendant can shed considerable light on her attitude toward having sex with him. For this reason, rape shield laws often have specific exceptions for evidence of prior sexual conduct with the defendant, *see*, e.g., Fed.R.Evid. 412(b), and the Supreme Court has also indicated that prior sexual conduct with the defendant is relevant to the issue of consent, *see Lucas*, 500 U.S. at ___, ___, 111 S.Ct. at 1746–47. Whether or not M.G.'s communications with Wood are considered "sexual conduct," their sexual nature certainly has some bearing on whether she in fact chose to have a sexual relationship with him.

Of course, even if M.G. did have a sexual relationship with Wood, she did not necessarily consent to sex on April 11, 1984. But evidence need not be dispositive to be relevant, and Wood need not demonstrate that the outcome in his case would have been different had the evidence been introduced in order to establish a Sixth Amendment violation. *See Van Arsdall*, 475 U.S. at 679–80. Whether or not Wood and M.G. had a previous sexual relationship is clearly relevant to the ultimate question of consent because it helps establish Wood's defense that they had consensual intercourse that night after a fight as they had in the past. It would also serve to impeach M.G.'s testimony that they had a purely platonic relationship. If the jury disbelieved her on that point, it might also disbelieve her on the question of whether she consented on the night of the alleged rape. Thus, the proposition that they had a sexual relationship is material, and to the extent the evidence of M.G.'s display of nude photographs to Wood and discussions with him about her pornographic acting makes that proposition more likely, it is relevant.

In sum, the evidence of M.G.'s modeling and acting experiences is irrelevant in itself. That she may have talked about them with Wood and shared her photographs with him is relevant, however, because it tends to make more probable Wood's story that they had a sexual relationship.

B

Even though the evidence is relevant, it may properly be excluded if its probative value is outweighed by other legitimate interests. The Supreme Court has held that certain legitimate interests can justify excluding evidence of a prior sexual relationship between a rape victim and a criminal defendant. *Lucas*, 500 U.S. at ___, ___, 111 S.Ct. at 1747–48. The *Lucas* Court stated that the rape shield statute in question (requiring notice of an intention to present evidence of past sexual conduct) "represents a valid legislative determination that rape victims deserve heightened protection against surprise, harassment, and unnecessary invasions of privacy." 500 U.S. at ___, 111 S.Ct. at 1746. These considerations are in addition to the more traditional considerations about prejudice and confusion of the issues that trial courts may always balance against probative value in deciding whether to admit or exclude evidence. *See id.*

Wood argues that the interest in protecting rape victims' privacy does not apply here. He points out that the sexual acts in question were not private at all. M.G. posed in a nationally circulated magazine, and she allegedly acted in movies distributed to the public and permitted herself to be photographed by strangers while having sex.

We agree. This case is different from the typical case in which the intimate details of a rape victim's private life would be subject to scrutiny. The purpose of M.G.'s prior sexual acts was to be publicly observed. The state cannot claim M.G. has a privacy interest in acts that were fully intended to be public. *Cf. Douglass v. Hustler Magazine, Inc.*, 769 F.2d 1128 (7th Cir. 1985) (nude model appearing in Playboy is public figure), *cert. denied*, 475 U.S. 1094 (1986).

Concluding that the interest in M.G.'s privacy is not present here does not end our inquiry, however, because other legitimate interests are implicated as well. The state points out that another purpose of the rape shield statute is to encourage reporting by limiting embarrassing trial inquiry into past sexual conduct. In the traditional case, the rape victim has two incentives not to report: to avoid harassing questions, and to avoid making public acts that were intended to be private. Here, because M.G.'s acts were never intended to be private, only the first incentive applies. *Cf. id.* at 1144 (explaining that emotional injury in having already public pictures presented in different magazine was not that great).

This limited interest in encouraging reporting would not in itself outweigh Wood's interest in presenting relevant evidence. In *Davis*, 415 U.S. 308, the Court held that the state's interest in keeping a witness's juvenile record private did not outweigh the defendant's interest in introducing evidence of the record to show the witness's bias. The Court concluded that "[w]hatever temporary embarrassment might result to [the witness] or his family by disclosure of his juvenile record . . . is outweighed by petitioner's right to probe into the influence of possible bias in the testimony of a crucial . . . witness." *Id.* at 319. Similarly, in this case, we conclude that the embarrassment to M.G. of having her modeling and acting experiences revealed would be so minor in light of the public nature of the acts that it cannot overcome Wood's right to present relevant evidence.

But, unlike *Davis*, the interests in this case go beyond that of protecting the witness. Of significantly more import are the concerns, intrinsic to the truth-finding process itself, that introducing the evidence would confuse the issues and unduly prejudice the jury. Introducing evidence of M.G.'s discussions with Wood would necessarily also introduce evidence of several previous incidents of sex with others, as well as evidence of exhibitionism. Because M.G.'s acting and modeling experiences are not themselves relevant, the jury could be led to base its decision on irrelevant facts.

Moreover, if the jury considers these facts, it could feel hostility for her as an immoral woman, and it could base its decision on that hostility rather than on the actual facts of the case. The proffered evidence in this case is particularly prejudicial because it indicates not only that M.G. had extramarital sex, but also that she posed nude and had sex both for money and for the purpose of making pornography. Because many people consider prostitution and pornography to be particularly offensive, there is a significant possibility that jurors would be influenced by their impression of M.G. as an immoral woman. They could also conclude, contrary to the rape law, that a woman with her sexual past cannot be raped, or that she somehow deserved to be raped after engaging in these sexual activities. In light of these considerations, we conclude that the risk of confusion and prejudice is substantial.

On the other side of the balance, while evidence that M.G. showed Wood sexually provocative pictures of herself and told him about her sexual experiences is probative to some extent of the nature of their relationship, its value is far from substantial. It is not inconsistent with M.G.'s story that she discussed her sexual experiences with Wood; purely platonic friends may discuss their sexual experiences. Showing sexually provocative nude photographs to a platonic friend may be more unusual, but in this case it might only indicate that M.G. wanted to show off her modeling experience. Wood testified at the pre-trial hearing that M.G. seemed proud of the fact that she had posed for Penthouse. Other witnesses testified that she had offered to show them the pictures as well, once in Wood's presence, and one of the witnesses testified that she actually showed him the pictures. This testimony reduces the probative value of M.G.'s showing sexually provocative pictures to Wood because it indicates that M.G. may not have been interested in Wood in particular. Wood was also equivocal about whether her showing him the pictures was a sexual come-on. He answered first that he interpreted it that way, but when asked again whether he thought it was a come-on, he said, "Slightly, I wouldn't say totally, no."

The evidence also diminishes in probative value when viewed in the context of the entire case. Wood was permitted to present direct evidence that he and M.G. had a sexual relationship. To that end, he testified himself that they had sex, and he presented witnesses who testified that M.G. and Wood kissed and hugged and put their arms around each other, that they went into Wood's bedroom often and they once came out of the bedroom partially undressed, that they once slept together in a double-sized sleeping bag, and that M.G. described their relationship as "fucking or fighting." Wood was also able to inquire into other aspects of their relationship that would indicate that they had a close relationship, such as that they spent time together and that M.G. confided in him about problems between her and Berube.

* * *

The evidence that M.G. discussed her sexual experiences and showed him nude pictures is simply one more indication that they had a sexual relationship; it does not add any significantly new dimension to the overall story presented. Unlike in Davis, where the evidence would have explained why the witness might be lying, M.G.'s actions with Wood do not explain anything. She would not have been any more likely to want a sexual relationship with Wood because of what she showed and told; at most, these acts would reflect that M.G. had already developed a sexual interest in Wood. Moreover, that she showed the pictures and told Wood about her past does not establish any motive for M.G. to lie about being raped. All evidence relevant to that point—her relationship with Berube, for example—was admitted. Thus, the proffered evidence is not as critical as in cases where the excluded evidence would establish the bias of a crucial prosecution witness and thereby forcefully undermine the credibility of the witness and the strength of the state's entire case. *See, e.g., Olden v. Kentucky*, 488 U.S. 227 (1988) (finding Sixth Amendment violation when trial court excluded evidence of rape victim's relationship with another man because rape victim was crucial prosecution witness and evidence would have explained why she had motive to lie about being raped).

Because the evidence that M.G. showed Wood her Penthouse photographs and discussed her pornographic acting experiences with him is not highly probative and the risk of confusion and prejudice is substantial, we conclude that the trial court acted within its discretion when it excluded the evidence. . . .

Wood has not stated a violation of his Sixth Amendment rights to present relevant evidence or to confront the witnesses against him, and his petition for a writ of habeas corpus was therefore properly denied.

AFFIRMED.

Notes

1. From almost the moment they were adopted through to the present, there has been much debate regarding the merits of rape shield laws. *Compare* Ann Althouse, *Thelma and Louise and the Law: Do Rape Shield Rules Matter?* 25 Loy. L. Rev. 757 (1992) (discussing both the limitations and promise of rape shield provisions) *with* I. Bennett Capters, *Real Women, Real Rape*, 60 UCLA L. Rev. 826 (2013) (discussing critiques of rape shield laws, asserting that rape shield laws only benefit some — i.e., those "who because of age and race and class can easily pass as chaste and worthy of the law's protections," and challenging the advisability of evidentiary rules specific to rape). Wendy J. Murphy is a former assistant district attorney in Middlesex County, Massachusetts, who practices in Boston, representing crime victims. She lectures at the New England School of Law. She has critiqued the use of rape shield laws as an excuse to interrogate victims about their sexual history. *See* Wendy J. Murphy, *Rape Shield Laws Wrongly Protect Interrogation of Victims*, Daily Journal Newswire, April 2, 2004. In light of these debates and the reality that issues of what is and is not relevant are likely grounded in cultural beliefs — e.g., a view that prior sexual conduct has a bearing on the issue of consent would impact one's assessment of relevancy of prior sexual conduct — what is your assessment of rape shield provisions?

2. A victim who is denied the protection of a federal rape shield protection may seek review of that decision. *See Doe v. United States,* 666 F.2d 43 (4th Cir. 1981) (recognizing a victim's right to appeal a rape shield issue after examining the text, purpose, and legislative history of Rule 412, and finding that while Rule 412 does not explicitly refer to a victim's right to appeal, such a right is implicit as "a necessary corollary" of the rule's explicit protection of victims' privacy interests; in reaching its conclusion the court stated that because "[n]o other party in the evidentiary proceeding shares these interests to the extent that they might be viewed as a champion

of the victim's rights," the congressional intent behind Rule 412 would be "frustrated if rape victims are not allowed to appeal an erroneous evidentiary ruling made at a pretrial hearing conducted pursuant to the rule.")

E. Protecting Victim Privacy by Limiting Access to Judicial Proceedings

1. Closing the Courtroom

To protect victim privacy, some judges have ordered courtrooms closed during sensitive testimony, such as the testimony of minor victims during sexual assault cases. Courtroom closures raise First Amendment concerns.

Globe Newspaper Co. v. Superior Court for the County of Norfolk

457 U.S. 596 (1981)

JUSTICE BRENNAN delivered the opinion of the Court.

Section 16A of Chapter 278 of the Massachusetts General Laws,[42] as construed by the Massachusetts Supreme Judicial Court, requires trial judges, at trials for specified sexual offenses involving a victim under the age of 18, to exclude the press and general public from the courtroom during the testimony of that victim. The question presented is whether the statute thus construed violates the First Amendment as applied to the States through the Fourteenth Amendment.

I

The case began when appellant, Globe Newspaper Co. (Globe), unsuccessfully attempted to gain access to a rape trial conducted in the Superior Court for the County of Norfolk, Commonwealth of Massachusetts. The criminal defendant in that trial had been charged with the forcible rape and forced unnatural rape of three girls who were minors at the time of trial — two 16 years of age and one 17. In April 1979, during hearings on several preliminary motions, the trial judge ordered the courtroom closed. Before the trial began, Globe moved that the court revoke this closure order, hold hearings on any future such orders, and permit appellant to intervene "for the limited purpose of asserting its rights to access to the trial and hearings on related preliminary motions." The trial court denied Globe's motions, relying on Mass. Gen. Laws Ann., ch. 2789, § 16A (West 1981), and ordered the exclusion of the press and general public from the courtroom during the trial. The

---

42. Massachusetts Gen. Laws Ann., ch. 278, § 16A (West 1981), provides in pertinent part: "At the trial of a complaint or indictment for rape, incest, carnal abuse or other crime involving sex, where a minor under eighteen years of age is the person upon, with or against whom the crime is alleged to have been committed, . . . the presiding justice shall exclude the general public from the court room, admitting only such persons as may have a direct interest in the case."

defendant immediately objected to that exclusion order, and the prosecution stated for purposes of the record that the order was issued on the court's "own motion and not at the request of the Commonwealth."

Within hours after the court had issued its exclusion order, Globe sought injunctive relief from a justice of the Supreme Judicial Court of Massachusetts. The next day the justice conducted a hearing, at which the Commonwealth, "on behalf of the victims," waived "whatever rights it [might] have [had] to exclude the press." Nevertheless, Globe's request for relief was denied. Before Globe appealed to the full court, the rape trial proceeded and the defendant was acquitted.

Nine months after the conclusion of the criminal trial, the Supreme Judicial Court issued its judgment, dismissing Globe's appeal. Although the court held that the case was rendered moot by completion of the trial, it nevertheless stated that it would proceed to the merits, because the issues raised by Globe were "significant and troublesome, and . . . 'capable of repetition yet evading review.'" As a statutory matter, the court agreed with Globe that § 16A did not require the exclusion of the press from the entire criminal trial. The provision was designed, the court determined, "to encourage young victims of sexual offenses to come forward; once they have come forward, the statute is designed to preserve their ability to testify by protecting them from undue psychological harm at trial." Relying on these twin purposes, the court concluded that § 16A *required* the closure of sex-offense trials only during the testimony of minor victims; during other portions of such trials, closure was "a matter within the judge's sound discretion." The court did not pass on Globe's contentions that it had a right to attend the entire criminal trial under the First and Sixth Amendments, noting that it would await this Court's decision then pending in *Richmond Newspapers, Inc. v. Virginia*, 488 U.S. 555 (1980).

Globe then appealed to this Court. Following our decision in *Richmond Newspapers*, we vacated the judgment of the Supreme Judicial Court, and remanded the case for further consideration in light of that decision. *Globe Newspaper Co. v. Superior Court*, 449 U.S. 894 (1980).

On remand, the Supreme Judicial Court, adhering to its earlier construction of § 16A, considered whether our decision in *Richmond Newspapers* required the invalidation of the mandatory closure rule of § 16A. 423 N.E.2d 773 (Mass. 1981). In analyzing the First Amendment issue, the court recognized that there is "an unbroken tradition of openness" in criminal trials. But the court discerned "at least one notable exception" to this tradition: "In cases involving sexual assaults, portions of trials have been closed to some segments of the public, even when the victim was an adult." The court also emphasized that § 16A's mandatory closure rule furthered "genuine State interests," which the court had identified in its earlier decision as underlying the statutory provision. These interests, the court stated, "would be defeated if a case-by-case determination were used." While acknowledging that the mandatory closure requirement results in a "temporary diminution" of "the public's knowledge about these trials," the court did not think "that *Richmond Newspapers* require[d] the invalidation of the requirement, given the statute's narrow scope in an area of traditional sensitivity to the needs of victims." The court accordingly dismissed Globe's appeal.

Globe again sought review in this Court. For the reasons that follow, we reverse, and hold that the mandatory closure rule contained in § 16A violates the First Amendment.

II

In this Court, Globe challenges that portion of the trial court's order, approved by the Supreme Judicial Court of Massachusetts, that holds that § 16A requires, under all circumstances, the exclusion of the press and general public during the testimony of a minor victim in a sex-offense trial. . . .

III A

The court's recent decision in *Richmond Newspapers* firmly established for the first time that the press and general public have a constitutional right of access to criminal trials. Although there was no opinion of the Court in that case, seven Justices recognized that this right of access is embodied in the First Amendment, and applied to the States through the Fourteenth Amendment. . . .

Of course, this right of access to criminal trials is not explicitly mentioned in terms in the First Amendment. But we have long eschewed any "narrow, literal conception" of the Amendment's terms, *NAACP v. Button*, 371 U.S. 415, 430 (1963), for the Framers were concerned with broad principles, and wrote against a background of shared values and practices. The First Amendment is thus broad enough to encompass those rights that, while not unambiguously enumerated in the very terms of the Amendment, are nonetheless necessary to the enjoyment of other First Amendment rights. *Richmond Newspapers, Inc. v. Virginia*, 448 U.S., at 579–580, and n.16 (plurality opinion) (citing cases); *id.*, at 587–588, and n.4 (BRENNAN, J., concurring in judgment). Underlying the First Amendment right of access to criminal trials is the common understanding that "a major purpose of that Amendment was to protect the free discussion of governmental affairs," *Mills v. Alabama*, 384 U.S. 214, 218 (1966). By offering such protection, the First Amendment serves to ensure that the individual citizen can effectively participate in and contribute to our republican system of self-government. *See Thornhill v. Alabama*, 310 U.S. 88, 95 (1940); *Richmond Newspapers, Inc. v. Virginia*, 448 U.S., at 587–588 (BRENNAN, J., concurring in judgment). See also *id.*, at 575 (plurality opinion) (the "expressly guaranteed freedoms" of the First Amendment "share a common core purpose of assuring freedom of communication on matters relating to the functioning of government"). Thus to the extent that the First Amendment embraces a right of access to criminal trials, it is to ensure that this constitutionally protected "discussion of governmental affairs" is an informed one.

Two features of the criminal justice system, emphasized in the various opinions in *Richmond Newspapers*, together serve to explain why a right of access to *criminal trials* in particular is properly afforded protection by the First Amendment. First, the criminal trial historically has been open to the press and general public. "[A]t the time when our organic laws were adopted, criminal trials both here and in England had long been presumptively open." *Richmond Newspapers, Inc. v. Virginia, supra*, at 569 (plurality opinion). And since that time, the presumption of openness has remained secure. Indeed, at the time of this Court's decision in *In re Oliver*, 333 U.S. 257 (1948), the presumption was so solidly grounded that the Court was "unable to find a single instance of a criminal trial conducted in camera in any federal, state, or municipal court during the history of this country." *Id.*, at 266 (footnote omitted). This uniform rule of openness has been viewed as significant in constitutional terms not only "because the Constitution carries the gloss of history," but also because "a tradition of accessibility implies the favorable judgment of experience." *Richmond Newspapers, Inc. v. Virginia, supra*, at 589 (BRENNAN, J., concurring in judgment).

Second, the right of access to criminal trials plays a particularly significant role in the functioning of the judicial process and the government as a whole. Public scrutiny of a criminal trial enhances the quality and safeguards the integrity of the fact finding process, with benefits to both the defendant and to society as a whole. Moreover, public access to the criminal trial fosters an appearance of fairness, thereby heightening public respect for the judicial process. And in the broadest terms, public access to criminal trials permits the public to participate in and serve as a check upon the judicial process an essential component in our structure of self-government. In sum, the institutional value of the open criminal trial is recognized in both logic and experience.

B

Although the right of access to criminal trials is of constitutional stature, it is not absolute. See *Richmond Newspapers, Inc. v. Virginia, supra*, at 581, n.18 (plurality opinion); *Nebraska Press Assn. v. Stuart*, 427 U.S., at 570. But the circumstances under which the press and public can be barred from a criminal trial are limited; the State's justification in denying access must be a weighty one. Where, as in the present case, the State attempts to deny the right of access in order to inhibit the disclosure of sensitive information, it must be shown that the denial is necessitated by a compelling governmental interest, and is narrowly tailored to serve that interest. See, *e.g.*, *Brown v. Hartlage*, 456 U.S. 45, 53–54 (1982); *Smith v. Daily Mail Publishing Co.*, 443 U.S. 97, 101–103 (1979); *NAACP v. Button*, 371 U.S., at 438. We now consider the state interests advanced to support Massachusetts' mandatory rule barring press and public access to criminal sex-offense trials during the testimony of minor victims.

IV

The state interests asserted to support § 16A, though articulated in various ways, are reducible to two: the protection of minor victims of sex crimes from further trauma and embarrassment; and the encouragement of such victims to come forward and testify in a truthful and credible manner. We consider these interests in turn.

We agree with appellee that the first interest — safeguarding the physical and psychological well-being of a minor — is a compelling one. But as compelling as that interest is, it does not justify a *mandatory* closure rule, for it is clear that the circumstances of the particular case may affect the significance of the interest. A trial court can determine on a case-by-case basis whether the closure is necessary to protect the welfare of a minor victim. Among the factors to be weighed are the minor victim's age, psychological maturity and understanding, the nature of the crime, the desires of the victim, and the interests of parents and relatives. Section 16A, in contrast, requires closure even if the victim does not seek the exclusion of the press and general public, and would not suffer injury by their presence. In the case before us, for example, the names of the minor victims were already in the public record, and the record indicates that the victims may have been willing to testify despite the presence of the press. If the trial court had been permitted to exercise its discretion, closure might well have been deemed unnecessary. In short, § 16A cannot be viewed as a narrowly tailored means of accommodating the State's asserted interest: that interest could be served just as well by requiring the trial court to determine on a case-by-case basis whether the State's legitimate concern for the well-being of the minor victim necessitates closure. Such an approach ensures that the constitutional right of the press and public to gain access to criminal trials will not be restricted except where necessary to protect the State's interest.

Nor can § 16A be justified on the basis of the Commonwealth's second asserted interest in the encouragement of minor victims of sex crimes to come forward and provide accurate testimony. The Commonwealth has offered no empirical support for the claim that the rule of automatic closure contained in § 16A will lead to an increase in the number of minor sex victims coming forward and cooperating with state authorities. Not only is the claim speculative in empirical terms, but it is also open to serious question as a matter of logic and common sense. Although § 16A bars the press and general public from the courtroom during the testimony of minor sex victims, the press is not denied access to the transcript, court personnel, or any other possible source that could provide an account of the minor victim's testimony. Thus § 16A cannot prevent the press from publicizing the substance of a minor victim's testimony, as well as his or her identity. If the Commonwealth's interest in encouraging minor victims to come forward depends on keeping such matters secret, § 16A hardly advances that interest in an effective manner. And even if § 16A effectively advanced the State's interest, it is doubtful that the interest would be sufficient to overcome the constitutional attack, for that same interest could be relied on to support an array of mandatory closure rules designed to encourage victims to come forward: Surely it cannot be suggested that minor victims of sex crimes are the *only* crime victims who, because of publicity attendant to criminal trials, are reluctant to come forward and testify. The State's argument based on this interest therefore proves too much, and runs contrary to the very foundation of the right of access recognized in *Richmond Newspapers*: namely, "that a presumption of openness inheres in the very nature of a criminal trial under our system of justice." 448 U.S., at 573 (plurality opinion).

V

For the foregoing reasons, we hold that § 16A, as construed by the Massachusetts Supreme Judicial Court, violates the First Amendment to the Constitution.[43] Accordingly, the judgment of the Massachusetts Supreme Judicial Court is

Reversed.

JUSTICE O'CONNOR, concurring in the judgment [omitted].

CHIEF JUSTICE BURGER, with whom JUSTICE REHNQUIST joins, dissenting.

Historically our society has gone to great lengths to protect minors *charged* with crime, particularly by prohibiting the release of the names of offenders, barring the press and public from juvenile proceedings, and sealing the records of those proceedings. Yet today the Court holds unconstitutional a state statute designed to protect not the *accused*, but the minor *victims* of sex crimes. In doing so, it advances a disturbing paradox. Although states are permitted, for example, to mandate the closure of all proceedings in order to protect a 17-year-old charged with rape, they are not permitted to require the closing of part of criminal proceedings in order to protect an innocent child who has been raped or otherwise sexually abused.

The Court has tried to make its holding a narrow one by not disturbing the authority of state legislatures to enact more narrowly drawn statutes giving trial judges the discretion to exclude the public and the press from the courtroom during the minor victim's testimony. *Ante*, at 611, n.27. I also do not read the Court's opinion as foreclosing a state statute which mandates closure except in cases where the victim agrees to testify in open court. But the Court's decision is nevertheless a gross invasion of state authority and a state's duty to protect its citizens—in this case minor victims of crime. I cannot agree with the Court's expansive interpretation of our decision in *Richmond Newspapers, Inc. v. Virginia*, 448 U.S. 555 (1980), or its cavalier rejection of the serious interests supporting Massachusetts' mandatory closure rule. Accordingly, I dissent.

I

The Court seems to read our decision in *Richmond Newspapers, supra*, as spelling out a First Amendment right of access to all aspects of all criminal trials under all circumstances. *Ante*, at 605, n.13. That is plainly incorrect. . . .

Several States have long-standing provisions allowing closure of cases involving sexual assaults against minors.

---

43. We emphasize that our holding is a narrow one: that a rule of mandatory closure respecting the testimony of minor sex victims is constitutionally infirm. In individual cases, and under appropriate circumstances, the First Amendment does not necessarily stand as a bar to the exclusion from the courtroom of the press and general public during the testimony of minor sex-offense victims. But a mandatory rule, requiring no particularized determinations in individual cases, is unconstitutional.

It would misrepresent the historical record to state that there is an "unbroken, uncontradicted history" of open proceedings in cases involving the sexual abuse of minors. *Richmond Newspapers, supra,* at 573. Absent such a history of openness, the positions of the Justices joining reversal in *Richmond Newspapers* give no support to the proposition that closure of the proceedings during the testimony of the minor victim violates the First Amendment.

II

The Court does not assert that the First Amendment right it discerns from *Richmond Newspapers* is absolute; instead, it holds that when a "State attempts to deny the right of access in order to inhibit the disclosure of sensitive information, it must be shown that the denial is necessitated by a compelling governmental interest, and is narrowly tailored to serve that interest." *Ante,* at 606–607. The Court's wooden application of the rigid standard it asserts for this case is inappropriate. The Commonwealth has not denied the public or the media access to information as to what takes place at trial. As the Court acknowledges, Massachusetts does not deny the press and the public access to the trial transcript or to other sources of information about the victim's testimony. Even the victim's identity is part of the public record, although the name of a 16-year-old accused rapist generally would not be a matter of public record. Mass. Gen. Laws Ann., ch. 119, § 60A (West Supp. 1982–1983). The Commonwealth does not deny access to information, and does nothing whatever to inhibit its disclosure. This case is quite unlike others in which we have held unconstitutional state laws which prevent the dissemination of information or the public discussion of ideas.

The purpose of the Commonwealth in enacting § 16A was to give assurance to parents and minors that they would have this moderate and limited protection from the trauma, embarrassment, and humiliation of having to reveal the intimate details of a sexual assault in front of a large group of unfamiliar spectators — and perhaps a television audience — and to lower the barriers to the reporting of such crimes which might come from the victim's dread of public testimony. *Globe Newspaper Co. v. Superior Court,* 401 N.E.2d 360, 372 (Mass. 1980); 423 N.E.2d 773, 779 (Mass. 1981).

Neither the purpose of the law nor its effect is primarily to deny the press or public access to information; the verbatim transcript is made available to the public and the media and may be used without limit. We therefore need only examine whether the restrictions imposed are reasonable and whether the interests of the Commonwealth override the very limited incidental effects of the law on First Amendment rights. See *Richmond Newspapers,* 448 U.S., at 580–581 (plurality opinion); *id.,* at 600 (Stewart, J., concurring in judgment); *Pell v. Procunier,* 417 U.S. 817 (1974); *Saxbe v. Washington Post Co.,* 417 U.S. 843 (1974); *Cox v. New Hampshire,* 312 U.S. 569 (1941). Our obligation in this case is to balance the competing interests: the interests of the media for instant access, against the interest of the State in protecting child rape victims from the trauma of public testimony. In more than half the states, public testimony will include television coverage.

III

For me, it seems beyond doubt, considering the minimal impact of the law on First Amendment rights and the overriding weight of the Commonwealth's interest in protecting child rape victims, that the Massachusetts law is not unconstitutional. The Court acknowledges that the press and the public have prompt and full access to all of the victim's testimony. Their additional interest in actually being present during the testimony is minimal. While denying it the power to protect children, the Court admits that the Commonwealth's interest in protecting the victimized child is a compelling interest. *Ante*, at 607. This meets the test of *Richmond Newspapers, supra.*

The law need not be precisely tailored so long as the state's interest overrides the law's impact on First Amendment rights and the restrictions imposed further that interest. Certainly this law, which excludes the press and public only during the actual testimony of the child victim of a sex crime, rationally serves the Commonwealth's overriding interest in protecting the child from the severe — possibly permanent — psychological damages. It is not disputed that such injury is a reality.

The law also seems a rational response to the undisputed problem of the underreporting of rapes and other sexual offenses. The Court rejects the Commonwealth's argument that § 16A is justified by its interest in encouraging minors to report sex crimes, finding the claim "speculative in empirical terms [and] open to serious question as a matter of logic and common sense." *Ante*, at 609–610. There is no basis whatever for this cavalier disregard of the reality of human experience. It makes no sense to criticize the Commonwealth for its failure to offer empirical data in support of its rule; only by allowing state experimentation may such empirical evidence be produced. "It is one of the happy incidents of the federal system that a single courageous State may, if its citizens choose, serve as a laboratory; and try novel social and economic experiments without risk to the rest of the country." *New State Ice Co. v. Liebmann*, 285 U.S. 262, 311 (1932) (Brandeis, J., dissenting).

The Court also concludes that the Commonwealth's assertion that the law might reduce underreporting of sexual offenses fails "as a matter of logic and common sense." This conclusion is based on a misperception of the Commonwealth's argument and an overly narrow view of the protection the statute seeks to afford young victims. The Court apparently believes that the statute does not prevent any significant trauma, embarrassment, or humiliation on the part of the victim simply because the press is not prevented from discovering and publicizing both the identity of the victim and the substance of the victim's testimony. *Ante*, at 609–610. Section 16A is intended not to preserve confidentiality, but to prevent the risk of severe psychological damage caused by having to relate the details of the crime in front of a crowd which inevitably will include voyeuristic strangers.[44] In most states, that crowd may

---

44. As one commentator put it: "Especially in cases involving minors, the courts stress the serious embarrassment and shame of the victim who is forced to testify to sexual acts or whose intimate life is revealed in detail before a crowd of the idly curious." Berger, *Man's Trial, Woman's Tribulation: Rape Cases in the Courtroom*, 77 Colum. L. Rev. 1, 88 (1977). The victim's interest in avoiding the

be expanded to include a live television audience, with reruns on the evening news. That ordeal cold be difficult for an adult; to a child, the experience can be devastating and leave permanent scars.

The Commonwealth's interests are clearly furthered by the mandatory nature of the closure statute. Certainly if the law were discretionary, most judges would exercise that discretion soundly and would avoid unnecessary harm to the child, but victims and their families are entitled to assurance of such protection. The legislature did not act irrationally in deciding not to leave the closure determination to the idiosyncracies of individual judges subject to the pressures available to the media. The victim might very well experience considerable distress prior to the court appearance, wondering, in the absence of such statutory protection, whether public testimony will be required. The mere possibility of public testimony may cause parents and children to decide not to report these heinous crimes. If, as psychologists report, the courtroom experience in such cases is almost as traumatic as the crime itself, a state certainly should be able to take whatever reasonable steps it believes are necessary to reduce that trauma. Furthermore, we cannot expect victims and their parents to be aware of all of the nuances of state law; a person who sees newspaper, or perhaps even television, reports of a minor victim's testimony may very well be deterred from reporting a crime on the belief that public testimony will be required. It is within the power of the state to provide for mandatory closure to alleviate such understandable fears and encourage the reporting of such crimes.

JUSTICE STEVENS, dissenting [omitted].

Notes

1. The dissent is disturbed because victims appear to have lesser enforceable "privacy" interests than the accused. Should "privacy" interests of victims and defendants be the same? Switching to the context of adult court, should defendants have a right to conceal their identity?

2. The GLOBE newspaper sought disclosure of an extortion victim's name, which was in the record as a pseudonym. Because the government had not disclosed the victim's name, the court denied the motion. The court noted that once the victim testified, the Globe could refile its motion. At such future time the court observed that it could still seal the documents if the interests favoring nondisclosure outweighed the public's right of access. *See, e.g., MLW,* 2009 U.S. D. Ct., Lexis 3345 (D. Mass. Jan. 20, 2009).

3. *Globe Newspaper* held that a mandatory requirement of closure of a courtroom any time testimony of a minor child was involved was constitutionally overbroad. It left open the possibility that "particularized determinations in individual cases"

---

humiliation of testifying in open court is thus quite separate from any interest in preventing the public from learning of the crime. It is ironic that the Court emphasizes the failure of the Commonwealth to seal the trial transcript and bar disclosure of the victim's identity. The Court implies that a state law more severely encroaching upon the interests of the press and public would be upheld.

might allow closure. What sorts of determinations might satisfy this requirement and when must they be made?

4. Closing a courtroom to protect victim privacy may have little effect if trial participants—prosecutors, defense attorneys, and the like—are free to disclose the proceedings. To solve this problem, some courts have imposed "gag orders" on trial participants barring discussion with the media. While such orders raise constitutional problems, courts have tended to uphold them if they are directed at trial participants rather than the media. *See, e.g., KPNX Broadcasting Co. v. Arizona Superior Court*, 459 U.S. 1302 (1982).

5. In the face of a record with insufficient findings justifying closure, courts have remanded for further consideration of the issue rather than ordering a new trial, and at least one court has upheld a closure where a court *sua sponte* closed the courtroom to the public for the duration of the child-victim's testimony and only after trial conducted a post-trial hearing to supplement the record with facts and reasons for the closure. *State v. Slota*, 862 N.W.2d 113 (S.D. 2015). Do you think these are adequate remedies? Considering the reverse, what options or remedies are available to a victim if the court declines to close the courtroom?

2. Limiting Media Technology in the Courtroom

Whether criminal proceedings should be televised or subject to other media technology presents a conflict between competing interests. On the one hand are interests in a public trial and promoting freedom of the press. On the other are the defendant's interest in a fair trial and the victim's interest in either privacy or in having the matter broadcast.

Most state courts grant the trial judge discretion to permit or deny television coverage of any particular trial. The federal rules prohibit television coverage, but the issue of permissibility of which methods of media coverage are left to the trial court's discretion. In exercising this discretion trial courts factor the interests of victims, defendants, the media, the public, and the jury.

———

U.S. v. Kaufman

2005 WL 2648070 (D. Kan. 2005)

MEMORANDUM AND ORDER

BELOT, J.

This case comes before the court on a Motion to Intervene and to Oppose Exclusion of Sketch Artists filed by Media General Operations, Inc., d/b/a KWCH–TV CHANNEL 12, a Wichita television station. (Doc. 275.)

. . .

I. FACTS

Defendants are charged in a thirty-four count second superseding indictment with, among other things, Medicare fraud, civil rights violations, and subjecting victims to involuntary servitude, all in violation of various provisions of Title 18 of the United States Code. (Doc. 121.) The case has garnered more than trivial interest in the local media. Unfortunately, this case involves allegations of sexual misconduct by defendants toward their mentally ill patients. Some of this conduct is recorded in graphic detail on video tapes. In light of the congressional mandate to protect the privacy and dignity of victims under the Crime Victims' Rights Act, 18 U.S.C. § 3771, the court has already directed that these videos be displayed on a screen that is visible to the jury, the court, and the parties, but not to people seated in the gallery. No objection has been made to this procedure by the parties or by the media. Other than that, and despite the graphic detail which already has come out and which is certain to come out through further witness testimony, the court has not otherwise closed the proceedings to the public. Both the media and the general public have the opportunity to attend the proceedings and describe what they witness to anyone who will listen.

When Channel 12 filed its motion seeking a ruling on whether sketch artists would be allowed in the courtroom (Doc. 275), the court questioned the parties, none of whom desired to have a sketch artist in the courtroom. On October 14, 2005, in open court, the court questioned the members of the jury regarding their feelings about being drawn by a sketch artist. No juror indicated any desire to have his or her likeness drawn and displayed on television. In anticipation of the court's inquiry to the jury, Channel 12 filed a document in which it stipulated that if sketch artists were permitted to conduct their operations in the courtroom, they would not sketch victims or jurors. (Doc. 287.) At the end of this inquiry, the court offered Channel 12 the opportunity to offer any additional evidence or argument that it wished. Channel 12 briefly reiterated its prior arguments.

II. ANALYSIS

The general principle that the public and the press have a First Amendment right of access to criminal proceedings is well established. See *United States v. McVeigh*, 119 F.3d 806, 811 (10th Cir.1997) (citing *Globe Newspaper Co. v. Superior Court*, 457 U.S. 596, 102 S.Ct. 2613, 73 L.Ed.2d 248 (1982); *Richmond Newspapers, Inc. v. Virginia*, 448 U.S. 555, 558–81, 100 S.Ct. 2814, 2818–30, 65 L.Ed.2d 973 (1980) (plurality opinion)). Nevertheless, "[a]lthough the right of access to criminal trials is of constitutional stature, it is not absolute." *Globe Newspaper*, 457 U.S. at 606, 102 S.Ct. at 2620. Any restrictions must be "necessitated by a compelling governmental interest, and . . . narrowly tailored to serve that interest." *Id.* at 607, 102 S.Ct. at 2620.

Here, the trial has been completely open to the press and the public with the exception that sexually-graphic videos of mentally ill victims are shown in a manner so that they are not viewable by individuals in the gallery. This restriction was necessary to protect the victims' "right to be treated with fairness and with respect for the victim[s'] dignity and privacy." 18 U.S.C. § 3771(a)(8). Other than this restriction, no limitation has been placed on the public's right to be present and hear the extensive, graphic testimony about the content of those videos. Accordingly, the threshold issue here is the much narrower question of if, and to what extent, the First Amendment grants sketch artists the right to attend and sketch the proceedings in a criminal trial.

As an initial matter, "representatives of the press and general public must be given an opportunity to be heard on the question of their exclusion." *Globe Newspaper*, 457 U.S. at 609 n. 25, 102 S.Ct. at 2621 (internal quotations omitted). For the reasons set forth in its previous order (Doc. 278), the court was unaware of Channel 12's interest until it filed its Motion to Intervene. Therein, Channel 12 requested a hearing. Since a hearing would necessarily interrupt the underlying criminal trial, the court directed Channel 12 to file an offer of proof regarding any matters it intended to prove at the hearing. (Doc. 278.) Channel 12 filed an offer of proof in the form of an affidavit from one of its managers. (Doc. 281.) Unfortunately, that offer of proof only encompassed events related to communications between Channel 12 and the United States Attorney's Public Affairs Officer as it pertained to having sketch artists in the courtroom. Channel 12 offered no explanation regarding what its artist intended to sketch, which raised the court's concern that Channel 12 intended to sketch and show likenesses of protected witnesses and jurors. Nevertheless, the court still afforded Channel 12 an opportunity to be heard in open court on October 12, 2005. Hence, the court finds that Channel 12 has received its notice and opportunity to be heard. There is no purpose in conducting further hearings on this matter and Channel 12 has not requested one.

The court finds that sketch artists have no First Amendment right to attend and sketch the proceedings in a criminal trial. This is because the First Amendment interests vindicated by their activities are *de minimis*. In finding that the press holds a general First Amendment right of access to criminal trials, the Supreme Court focused on the important role of the media in keeping the public informed regarding the proper and effective functioning of their government, particularly in the area of criminal judicial proceedings. *Globe Newspaper*, 457 U.S. at 604–06, 102 S.Ct. at 2618–20. There can be no doubt that allowing the press to report on the trial is critical to keeping the public informed. Most citizens lack the time and opportunity to attend a criminal trial, particularly one of this extended duration. Their ability to stay abreast of the proceedings through newspapers, television, and other media outlets is thus essential to give practical meaning to the First Amendment right of access.

However, unlike the written or spoken word, sketches of courtroom proceedings do little, if anything, to inform the public about the course of the trial. It conveys nothing about the allegations, the testimony, or other non-testimonial evidence received in the case. Likewise, the sketches give no sense of whether the case is being handled in a fair, legitimate manner, or whether there is some problem with corruption, misconduct, or other irregularity that might indicate a failure in our system of justice. In fact, the one device that would provide visual images that could fulfill some of these important functions is a video camera. Yet, the Supreme Court has made clear that there is no constitutional right to have video cameras in the courtroom. *Estes v. Texas*, 381 U.S. 532, 85 S.Ct. 1628, 14 L.Ed.2d 543 (1965). In fact, Federal Rule of Criminal Procedure 53 expressly forbids photographing and broadcasting criminal proceedings. See also *United States v. Kerley*, 753 F.2d 617, 622 (7th Cir.1985) (Rule 53 does not violate the First Amendment); *United States v. Hastings*, 695 F.2d 1278, 1283–84 (11th Cir.1983) (same). Likewise, still cameras lack a constitutionally protected right of access to the courtroom. Indeed, the court can add little to the Eighth Circuit's recent summary of the law in this area:

> While Richmond mandates that criminal trials be open to the public, no court has ruled that videotaping or cameras are required to satisfy this right of access. Instead, courts have universally found that restrictions on videotaping and cameras do not implicate the First Amendment guarantee of public access. *See Whiteland Woods v. Township of West Whiteland*, 193 F.3d 177, 184 (3rd Cir.1999) (holding that public has no right to videotape Planning Commission meetings that were required to be public); *United States v. Kerley*, 753 F.2d 617, 621 (7th Cir.1985) (holding that the public has no right to videotape trial even when the defendant wishes it to be videotaped); *Westmoreland v. Columbia Broadcasting System, Inc.*, 752 F.2d 16, 23 (2d Cir.1984) ("There is a long leap, however, between a public right under the First Amendment to attend trials and a public right under the First Amendment to see a given trial televised."), cert. denied, 472 U.S. 1017, 105 S.Ct. 3478, 87 L.Ed.2d 614 (1985); *United States v. Hastings*, 695 F.2d 1278, 1284 (11th Cir.), cert. denied, 461 U.S. 931, 103 S.Ct. 2094, 77 L.Ed.2d 303 (1983) (holding that the press had no right to videotape criminal trials); cf. *Nixon v. Warner Communications Inc.*, 435 U.S. 589, 609, 98 S.Ct. 1306, 55 L.Ed.2d 570 (1978) (holding that no First Amendment right existed to publish or copy exhibits displayed in court); *United States v. McDougal*, 103 F.3d 651, 659 (8th Cir.1996), cert. denied, 522 U.S. 809, 118 S.Ct. 49, 139 L.Ed.2d 15 (1997) (holding that First Amendment right of access does not extend to videotaped deposition testimony of then-President Clinton). As the Second Circuit has observed, "the First Amendment right of access is limited to physical presence at trials." *United States v. Yonkers Bd. of Educ.*, 747 F.2d 111, 113 (2d Cir.1984).

> *Rice v. Kempker*, 374 F.3d 675, 678–79 (8th Cir.2004). Given that cameras and recording devices would tend to provide the public with a far better picture (no pun intended) of what transpired in the courtroom, and yet the Constitution does not mandate their admission, there can be little doubt that the First Amendment does not give sketch artists the right to sketch criminal trials.

The court now considers the restrictions proposed by Channel 12: that it will not sketch and televise likenesses of victims or jurors. Even in the absence of Channel 12's proposal, the court finds that 18 U.S.C. § 3771(a)(8) requires that sketch artists' activities in the courtroom be restricted under the circumstances of this case. First, there is a compelling government interest in protecting the dignity, as well as the physical and psychological well-being, of mentally-ill alleged crime victims who have been potentially exploited through extensive video recording of themselves engaged in bizarre sexual behavior under the tutelage of their social worker. *See Globe Newspaper*, 457 U.S. at 607–08, 102 S.Ct. at 2620–21 (finding that "safeguarding the physical and psychological well-being of a minor" in the context of a sex-crimes case was a compelling interest).

Next, the court finds that Channel 12's proposal is a narrowly tailored remedy that will protect this interest. Dr. Walt Menninger, whose name is well known to anyone having the remotest knowledge of psychiatry and mental illness, testified that schizophrenia is the "cancer of mental illness." Another highly respected witness, Dr. Bonnie Buchele, testified that many schizophrenics are fearful of everything. Most, if not all, of the witnesses entitled to protection under 18 U.S.C. § 3771 suffer from forms of schizophrenia. The court has already viewed the testimony of two mentally ill witness and observed the distress that these individuals exhibited trying to concentrate on the questions and formulate answers. If that distress was compounded with concerns that the witness' picture was going to be shown on television as one of those "victims" who appeared in the graphic videos, the victim undoubtedly would not only face considerable additional distress and loss of dignity, but the individual might not even be able to testify, thereby damaging the truth-seeking function of a criminal trial. *See Estes*, 381 U.S. at 544–50, 85 S.Ct. at 1634–36.

In addition, there are presently before the court three motions to quash subpoenas of mentally-ill witnesses based on, among other things, their inability to withstand the stress of testifying in open court. These motions contain statements and opinions from mental health professionals indicating that the mental health of these individuals may degenerate considerably if they are forced to testify. The court will have to give a great deal of consideration to balancing the health and welfare interests of these potential witnesses against the rights of the defendants who have subpoenaed them. The calculus would become even more difficult, and the potential harm to the victim-witnesses even greater, should these individuals be forced to face the additional stress of having a sketch artist working in the courtroom during their testimony. While the court has not yet ruled on these motions to quash subpoenas, the court finds that, absent Channel 12's proposed remedy, giving sketch artists unfettered leave to sketch in the courtroom could make it more difficult for the court to allow defendants to call these witnesses, thereby encroaching on defendants' Sixth Amendment compulsory process right.

Aside from the victims, the jurors have also gone on the record as being opposed to having their likenesses sketched. The court has authority to proscribe sketching jurors. See, e.g., *KPNX Broad. Co. v. Arizona*, 459 U.S. 1302, 1307–08, 103 S.Ct. 584,

587, 74 L.Ed.2d 498 (1982) (Rehnquist, Circuit Justice) ("I think that in all probability the trial judge's order would be more defensible on federal constitutional grounds if he had flatly banned courtroom sketching of the jurors, and if he had extended the ban to those who sketch for the print media as well as to those who sketch for television.")

In conclusion, the court finds:

1. Channel 12 has no First Amendment right to have sketch artists in the courtroom.

2. Title 18 U.S.C. § 3771 proscribes all forms of identification of the victims in this case, including, but not limited to, sketching for purposes of television.

3. Identification of jurors by sketching can be, and will be, prohibited.

4. Channel 12 will be permitted to have one sketch artist attend the trial. The artist shall not sketch jurors or victims. Channel 12 must identify, through communication with counsel for the parties, when a victim will appear as a witness. During each victim's appearance, no sketching materials of any kind will be visible in the courtroom.

5. This order applies only to Channel 12. No other sketch artists will be permitted in the courthouse or in the courtroom for the duration of the trial.

6. This order applies only to this trial. If must not be interpreted by Channel 12 or any other news provider as this court's general permission to allow sketch artists in the courtroom.

IT IS SO ORDERED.

Note

Do you think trial courts should have discretion to allow or disallow cameras or other media technology? For a discussion of the considerations, *see* Wendy Murphy, *Cameras in the Courtroom: Serving the Public's Right to Know or Boosting the Media Profits?* THE CRIME VICTIMS REPORT 33 (July 1999).

F. Constitutional Limitations on Protecting Victim Privacy

The First Amendment restricts the ability of the state to bar publication or broadcast of victim names that were legally obtained.

The Florida Star v. B.J.F.
491 U.S. 524 (1989)

Justice MARSHALL delivered the opinion of the Court.

Florida Stat. § 804.03 (1987) makes it unlawful to "print, publish, or broadcast . . . in any instrument of mass communication" the name of the victim of a sexual offense.[39] Pursuant to this statute, appellant The Florida Star was found civilly liable for publishing the name of a rape victim which it had obtained from a publicly released police report. The issue presented here is whether this result comports with the First Amendment. We hold that it does not.

I

The Florida Star is a weekly newspaper which serves the community of Jacksonville, Florida, and which has an average circulation of approximately 18,000 copies. A regular feature of the newspaper is its "Police Reports" section. That section, typically two to three pages in length, contains brief articles describing local criminal incidents under police investigation.

On October 20, 1983, appellee B.J.F.[40] reported to the Duval County, Florida, Sheriff's Department (Department) that she had been robbed and sexually assaulted by an unknown assailant. The Department prepared a report on the incident which identified B.J.F. by her full name. The Department then placed the report in its pressroom. The Department does not restrict access either to the pressroom or to the reports made available therein.

A Florida Star reporter-trainee sent to the pressroom copied the police report verbatim, including B.J.F.'s full name, on a blank duplicate of the Department's forms. A Florida Star reporter then prepared a one-paragraph article about the crime, derived entirely from the trainee's copy of the police report. The article included B.J.F.'s full name. It appeared in the "Robberies" subsection of the "Police Reports" section on October 29, 1983, one of 54 police blotter stories in that day's edition. The article read:

> [B.J.F.] reported on Thursday, October 20, she was crossing Brentwood Park, which is in the 500 block of Golfair Boulevard, en route to her bus stop, when an unknown black man ran up behind the lady and placed a knife to her neck and told her not to yell. The suspect then undressed the lady and had sexual intercourse with her before fleeing the scene with her 60 cents, Timex watch and gold necklace. Patrol efforts have been suspended concerning this incident because of a lack of evidence.

In printing B.J.F.'s full name, The Florida Star violated its internal policy of not publishing the names of sexual offense victims.

---

39. The statute provides in its entirety:
"Unlawful to publish or broadcast information identifying sexual offense victim. No person shall print, publish, or broadcast, or cause or allow to be printed, published, or broadcast, in any instrument of mass communication the name, address, or other identifying fact or information of the victim of any sexual offense within this chapter. An offense under this section shall constitute a misdemeanor of the second degree, punishable as provided in § 775.082, § 775.083, or § 775.084." Fla. Stat. § 794.03 (1987).

40. In filing this lawsuit, appellee used her full name in the caption of the case. On appeal, the Florida District Court of Appeal *sua sponte* revised the caption, stating that it would refer to the appellee by her initials, "in order to preserve [her] privacy interests." 499 So. 2d 883, 883, n. (1986). Respecting those interests, we, too, refer to appellee by her initials, both in the caption and in our discussion.

On September 26, 1984, B.J.F. filed suit in the Circuit Court of Duval County against the Department and The Florida Star, alleging that these parties negligently violated § 794.03. See n. 1, *supra*. Before trial, the Department settled with B.J.F. for $2,500. The Florida Star moved to dismiss, claiming, *inter alia*, that imposing civil sanctions on the newspaper pursuant to § 794.03 violated the First Amendment. The trial judge rejected the motion.

At the ensuing daylong trial, B.J.F. testified that she had suffered emotional distress from the publication of her name. She stated that she had heard about the article from fellow workers and acquaintances; that her mother had received several threatening phone calls from a man who stated that he would rape B.J.F. again; and that these events had forced B.J.F. to change her phone number and residence, to seek police protection, and to obtain mental health counseling. In defense, The Florida Star put forth evidence indicating that the newspaper had learned B.J.F.'s name from the incident report released by the Department, and that the newspaper's violation of its internal rule against publishing the names of sexual offense victims was inadvertent.

At the close of B.J.F.'s case, and again at the close of its defense, The Florida Star moved for a directed verdict. On both occasions, the trial judge denied these motions. He ruled from the bench that § 794.03 was constitutional because it reflected a proper balance between the First Amendment and privacy rights, as it applied only to a narrow set of "rather sensitive . . . criminal offenses." At the close of the newspaper's defense, the judge granted B.J.F.'s motion for a directed verdict on the issue of negligence, finding the newspaper *per se* negligent based upon its violation of § 794.03. This ruling left the jury to consider only the questions of causation and damages. The judge instructed the jury that it could award B.J.F. punitive damages if it found that the newspaper had "acted with reckless indifference to the rights of others." The jury awarded B.J.F. $75,000 in compensatory damages and $25,000 in punitive damages. Against the actual damages award, the judge set off B.J.F.'s settlement with the Department.

The Florida Star appealed to this Court. We noted probable jurisdiction, and now reverse.

II

The tension between the right which the First Amendment accords to a free press, on the one hand, and the protections which various statutes and common-law doctrines accord to personal privacy against the publication of truthful information, on the other, is a subject we have addressed several times in recent years. Our decisions in cases involving government attempts to sanction the accurate dissemination of information as invasive of privacy, have not, however, exhaustively considered this conflict. On the contrary, although our decisions have without exception upheld the press' right to publish, we have emphasized each time that we were resolving this conflict only as it arose in a discrete factual context.

The parties to this case frame their contentions in light of a trilogy of cases which have presented, in different contexts, the conflict between truthful reporting and state-protected privacy interests. In *Cox Broadcasting Corp. v. Cohn*, 420 U.S. 469 (1975), we found unconstitutional a civil damages award entered against a television station for broadcasting the name of a rape-murder victim which the station had obtained from courthouse records. In *Oklahoma Publishing Co. v. Oklahoma County District Court*, 430 U.S. 308 (1977), we found unconstitutional a state court's pretrial order enjoining the media from publishing the name or photograph of an 11-year-old boy in connection with a juvenile proceeding involving that child which reporters had attended. Finally, in *Smith v. Daily Mail Publishing Co.*, 443 U.S. 97 (1979), we found unconstitutional the indictment of two newspapers for violating a state statute forbidding newspapers to publish, without written approval of the juvenile court, the name of any youth charged as a juvenile offender. The papers had learned about a shooting by monitoring a police band radio frequency and had obtained the name of the alleged juvenile assailant from witnesses, the police, and a local prosecutor.

Appellant takes the position that this case is indistinguishable from *Cox Broadcasting*. Alternatively, it urges that our decisions in the above trilogy, and in other cases in which we have held that the right of the press to publish truth overcame asserted interests other than personal privacy, can be distilled to yield a broader First Amendment principle that the press may never be punished, civilly or criminally, for publishing the truth. Appellee counters that the privacy trilogy is inapposite, because in each case the private information already appeared on a "public record," and because the privacy interests at stake were far less profound than in the present case. In the alternative, appellee urges that *Cox Broadcasting* be overruled and replaced with a categorical rule that publication of the name of a rape victim never enjoys constitutional protection.

We conclude that imposing damages on appellant for publishing B.J.F.'s name violates the First Amendment, although not for either of the reasons appellant urges. Despite the strong resemblance this case bears to *Cox Broadcasting*, that case cannot fairly be read as controlling here. The name of the rape victim in that case was obtained from courthouse records that were open to public inspection, a fact which Justice WHITE's opinion for the Court repeatedly noted. Significantly, one of the reasons we gave in *Cox Broadcasting* for invalidating the challenged damages award was the important role the press plays in subjecting trials to public scrutiny and thereby helping guarantee their fairness. That role is not directly compromised where, as here, the information in question comes from a police report prepared and disseminated at a time at which not only had no adversarial criminal proceedings begun, but no suspect had been identified.

Nor need we accept appellant's invitation to hold broadly that truthful publication may never be punished consistent with the First Amendment. Our cases have carefully eschewed reaching this ultimate question, mindful that the future may bring scenarios which prudence counsels our not resolving anticipatorily. . . . Indeed, in *Cox Broadcasting*, we pointedly refused to answer even the less sweeping question "whether truthful publications may ever be subjected to civil or criminal liability" for invading "an area of privacy" defined by the State. Respecting the fact that press freedom and privacy rights are both "plainly rooted in the traditions and significant concerns of our society," we instead focused on the less sweeping issue "whether the State may impose sanctions on the accurate publication of the name of a rape victim obtained from public records—more specifically, from judicial records which are maintained in connection with a public prosecution and which themselves are open to public inspection." We continue to believe that the sensitivity and significance of the interests presented in clashes between First Amendment and privacy rights counsel relying on limited principles that sweep no more broadly than the appropriate context of the instant case.

In our view, this case is appropriately analyzed with reference to such a limited First Amendment principle. It is the one, in fact, which we articulated in *Daily Mail* in our synthesis of prior cases involving attempts to punish truthful publication: "[I]f a newspaper lawfully obtains truthful information about a matter of public significance then state officials may not constitutionally punish publication of the information, absent a need to further a state interest of the highest order." According the press the ample protection provided by that principle is supported by at least three separate considerations, in addition to, of course, the overarching "'public interest, secured by the Constitution, in the dissemination of truth.'" *Cox Broadcasting, supra*, 420 U.S., at 491, quoting *Garrison, supra*, 379 U.S., at 73 (footnote omitted). The cases on which the *Daily Mail* synthesis relied demonstrate these considerations.

First, because the *Daily Mail* formulation only protects the publication of information which a newspaper has "lawfully obtain[ed]," the government retains ample means of safeguarding significant interests upon which publication may impinge, including protecting a rape victim's anonymity. To the extent sensitive information rests in private hands, the government may under some circumstances forbid its nonconsensual acquisition, thereby bringing outside of the *Daily Mail* principle the publication of any information so acquired. To the extent sensitive information is in the government's custody, it has even greater power to forestall or mitigate the injury caused by its release. The government may classify certain information, establish and enforce procedures ensuring its redacted release, and extend a damages remedy against the government or its officials where the government's mishandling of sensitive information leads to its dissemination. Where information is entrusted to the government, a less drastic means than punishing truthful publication almost always exists for guarding against the dissemination of private facts. *See, e.g., Landmark Communications, supra*, 435 U.S., at 845, ("[M]uch of the risk [from disclosure of sensitive information regarding judicial disciplinary proceedings] can be eliminated through careful internal procedures to protect the confidentiality of Commission proceedings"); *Oklahoma Publishing*, 430 U.S., at 311, (noting trial judge's failure to avail himself of the opportunity, provided by a state statute, to close juvenile hearing to the public, including members of the press, who later broadcast juvenile defendant's name); *Cox Broadcasting, supra*, 420 U.S., at 496 ("If there are privacy interests to be protected in judicial proceedings, the States must respond by means which avoid public documentation or other exposure of private information").

A second consideration undergirding the *Daily Mail* principle is the fact that punishing the press for its dissemination of information which is already publicly available is relatively unlikely to advance the interests in the service of which the State seeks to act. It is not, of course, always the case that information lawfully acquired by the press is known, or accessible, to others. But where the government has made certain information publicly available, it is highly anomalous to sanction persons other than the source of its release. We noted this anomaly in *Cox Broadcasting*: "By placing the information in the public domain on official court records, the State must be presumed to have concluded that the public interest was thereby being served." The *Daily Mail* formulation reflects the fact that it is a limited set of cases indeed where, despite the accessibility of the public to certain information, a meaningful public interest is served by restricting its further release by other entities, like the press. As *Daily Mail* observed in its summary of *Oklahoma Publishing*, "once the truthful information was 'publicly revealed' or 'in the public domain' the court could not constitutionally restrain its dissemination."

A third and final consideration is the "timidity and self-censorship" which may result from allowing the media to be punished for publishing certain truthful information. *Cox Broadcasting* noted this concern with over-deterrence in the context of information made public through official court records, but the fear of excessive media self-suppression is applicable as well to other information released, without qualification, by the government. A contrary rule, depriving protection to those who rely on the government's implied representations of the lawfulness of dissemination, would force upon the media the onerous obligation of sifting through government press releases, reports, and pronouncements to prune out material arguably unlawful for publication. This situation could inhere even where the newspaper's sole object was to reproduce, with no substantial change, the government's rendition of the event in question.

Applied to the instant case, the *Daily Mail* principle clearly commands reversal. The first inquiry is whether the newspaper "lawfully obtain[ed] truthful information about a matter of public significance." It is undisputed that the news article describing the assault on B.J.F. was accurate. In addition, appellant lawfully obtained B.J.F.'s name. Appellee's argument to the contrary is based on the fact that under Florida law, police reports which reveal the identity of the victim of a sexual offense are not among the matters of "public record" which the public, by law, is entitled to inspect. But the fact that state officials are not required to disclose such reports does not make it unlawful for a newspaper to receive them when furnished by the government. Nor does the fact that the Department apparently failed to fulfill its obligation under §794.03 not to "cause or allow to be . . . published" the name of a sexual offense victim make the newspaper's ensuing receipt of this information unlawful. Even assuming the Constitution permitted a State to proscribe *receipt* of information, Florida has not taken this step. It is clear, furthermore, that the news article concerned "a matter of public significance," in the sense in which the *Daily Mail* synthesis of prior cases used that term. that is, the article generally, as opposed to the specific identity contained within it, involved a matter of paramount public import: the commission, and investigation, of a violent crime which had been reported to authorities. *See Cox Broadcasting, supra* (article identifying victim of rape-murder); *Oklahoma Publishing Co. v. Oklahoma County District Court*, 430 U.S. 308 (1977) (article identifying juvenile alleged to have committed murder); *Daily Mail, supra* (same); *cf. Landmark Communications, Inc. v. Virginia*, 435 U.S. 829 (1978) (article identifying judges whose conduct was being investigated).

The second inquiry is whether imposing liability on appellant pursuant to §794.03 serves "a need to further a state interest of the highest order." *Daily Mail*, 443 U.S., at 103. Appellee argues that a rule punishing publication furthers three closely related interests: the privacy of victims of sexual offenses; the physical safety of such victims, who may be targeted for retaliation if their names become known to their assailants; and the goal of encouraging victims of such crimes to report these offenses without fear of exposure.

At a time in which we are daily reminded of the tragic reality of rape, it is undeniable that these are highly significant interests, a fact underscored by the Florida Legislature's explicit attempt to protect these interests by enacting a criminal statute prohibiting much dissemination of victim identities. We accordingly do not rule out the possibility that, in a proper case, imposing civil sanctions for publication of the name of a rape victim might be so overwhelmingly necessary to advance these interests as to satisfy the *Daily Mail* standard. For three independent reasons, however, imposing liability for publication under the circumstances of this case is too precipitous a means of advancing these interests to convince us that there is a "need" within the meaning of the *Daily Mail* formulation for Florida to take this extreme step. *Cf. Landmark Communications, supra* (invalidating penalty on publication despite State's expressed interest in nondissemination, reflected in statute prohibiting unauthorized divulging of names of judges under investigation).

First is the manner in which appellant obtained the identifying information in question. As we have noted, where the government itself provides information to the media, it is most appropriate to assume that the government had, but failed to utilize, far more limited means of guarding against dissemination than the extreme step of punishing truthful speech. That assumption is richly borne out in this case. B.J.F.'s identity would never have come to light were it not for the erroneous, if inadvertent, inclusion by the Department of her full name in an incident report made available in a pressroom open to the public. Florida's policy against disclosure of rape victims' identities, reflected in §794.03, was undercut by the Department's failure to abide by this policy. Where, as here, the government has failed to police itself in disseminating information, it is clear under *Cox Broadcasting, Oklahoma Publishing*, and *Landmark Communications* that the imposition of damages against the press for its subsequent publication can hardly be said to be a narrowly tailored means of safeguarding anonymity. Once the government has placed such information in the public domain, "reliance must rest upon the judgment of those who decide what to publish or broadcast," *Cox Broadcasting*, 420 U.S., at 496, and hopes for restitution must rest upon the willingness of the government to compensate victims for their loss of privacy and to protect them from the other consequences of its mishandling of the information which these victims provided in confidence.

That appellant gained access to the information in question through a government news release makes it especially likely that, if liability were to be imposed, self-censorship would result. Reliance on a news release is a paradigmatically "routine newspaper reporting techniqu[e]." *Daily Mail, supra*, at 103. The government's issuance of such a release, without qualification, can only convey to recipients that the government considered dissemination lawful, and indeed expected the recipients to disseminate the information further. Had appellant merely reproduced the news release prepared and released by the Department, imposing civil damages would surely violate the First Amendment. The fact that appellant converted the police report into a news story by adding the linguistic connecting tissue necessary to transform the report's facts into full sentences cannot change this result.

A second problem with Florida's imposition of liability for publication is the broad sweep of the negligence *per se* standard applied under the civil cause of action implied from § 794.03. Unlike claims based on the common law tort of invasion of privacy, civil actions based on § 794.03 require no case-by-case findings that the disclosure of a fact about a person's private life was one that a reasonable person would find highly offensive. On the contrary, under the *per se* theory of negligence adopted by the courts below, liability follows automatically from publication. This is so regardless of whether the identity of the victim is already known throughout the community; whether the victim has voluntarily called public attention to the offense; or whether the identity of the victim has otherwise become a reasonable subject of public concern because, perhaps, questions have arisen whether the victim fabricated an assault by a particular person. Nor is there a scienter requirement of any kind under § 794.03, engendering the perverse result that truthful publications challenged pursuant to this cause of action are less protected by the First Amendment than even the least protected defamatory falsehoods: those involving purely private figures, where liability is evaluated under a standard, usually applied by a jury, of ordinary negligence. We have previously noted the impermissibility of categorical prohibitions upon media access where important First Amendment interests are at stake. *See Globe Newspaper Co. v. Superior Court of Norfolk County*, 457 U.S. 596, 608 (1982) (invalidating state statute providing for the categorical exclusion of the public from trials of sexual offenses involving juvenile victims). More individualized adjudication is no less indispensable where the State, seeking to safeguard the anonymity of crime victims, sets its face against publication of their names.

Third, and finally, the facial underinclusiveness of § 794.03 raises serious doubts about whether Florida is, in fact, serving, with this statute, the significant interests which appellee invokes in support of affirmance. Section 794.03 prohibits the publication of identifying information only if this information appears in an "instrument of mass communication," a term the statute does not define. Section 794.03 does not prohibit the spread by other means of the identities of victims of sexual offenses. An individual who maliciously spreads word of the identity of a rape victim is thus not covered, despite the fact that the communication of such information to persons who live near, or work with, the victim may have consequences as devastating as the exposure of her name to large numbers of strangers. *See* Tr. of Oral Arg. 49–50 (appellee acknowledges that § 794.03 would not apply to "the backyard gossip who tells 50 people that don't have to know").

When a State attempts the extraordinary measure of punishing truthful publication in the name of privacy, it must demonstrate its commitment to advancing this interest by applying its prohibition even-handedly, to the smalltime disseminator as well as the media giant. Where important First Amendment interests are at stake, the mass scope of disclosure is not an acceptable surrogate for injury. A ban on disclosures effected by "instrument[s] of mass communication" simply cannot be defended on the ground that partial prohibitions may effect partial relief. *See Daily Mail*, 443 U.S., at 104–105 (statute is insufficiently tailored to interest in protecting anonymity where it restricted only newspapers, not the electronic media or other forms of publication, from identifying juvenile defendants). Without more careful and inclusive precautions against alternative forms of dissemination, we cannot conclude that Florida's selective ban on publication by the mass media satisfactorily accomplishes its stated purpose.

III

Our holding today is limited. We do not hold that truthful publication is automatically constitutionally protected, or that there is no zone of personal privacy within which the State may protect the individual from intrusion by the press, or even that a State may never punish publication of the name of a victim of a sexual offense. We hold only that where a newspaper publishes truthful information which it has lawfully obtained, punishment may lawfully be imposed, if at all, only when narrowly tailored to a state interest of the highest order, and that no such interest is satisfactorily served by imposing liability under § 794.03 to appellant under the facts of this case. The decision below is therefore

Reversed.

Justice SCALIA, concurring [omitted]

Justice WHITE, with whom THE CHIEF JUSTICE and Justice O'CONNOR join, dissenting.

"Short of homicide, [rape] is the 'ultimate violation of self.'" *Coker v. Georgia*, 433 U.S. 584, 597 (1977) (opinion of WHITE, J.). For B.J.F., however, the violation she suffered at a rapist's knife-point marked only the beginning of her ordeal. A week later, while her assailant was still at large, an account of this assault identifying by name B.J.F. as the victim was published by The Florida Star. As a result, B.J.F. received harassing phone calls, required mental health counseling, was forced to move from her home, and was even threatened with being raped again. Yet today, the Court holds that a jury award of $75,000 to compensate B.J.F. for the harm she suffered due to the Star's negligence is at odds with the First Amendment. I do not accept this result. . . .

III

At issue in this case is whether there is any information about people, which though true may not be published in the press. By holding that only "a state interest of the highest order" permits the State to penalize the publication of truthful information, and by holding that protecting a rape victim's right to privacy is not among those state interests of the highest order, the Court accepts appellant's invitation to obliterate one of the most noteworthy legal inventions of the 20th century: the tort of the publication of private facts. Even if the Court's opinion does not say as much today, such obliteration will follow inevitably from the Court's conclusion here. If the First Amendment prohibits wholly private persons (such as B.J.F.) from recovering for the publication of the fact that she was raped, I doubt that there remain any "private facts" which persons may assume will not be published in the newspapers or broadcast on television.

Of course, the right to privacy is not absolute. Even the article widely relied upon in cases vindicating privacy rights, Warren & Brandeis, *The Right to Privacy*, 4 Harv. L. Rev. 193 (1890), recognized that this right inevitably conflicts with the public's right to know about matters of general concern and that sometimes, the latter must trump the former. *Id.* at 214–215. Resolving this conflict is a difficult matter, and I fault the Court not for attempting to strike an appropriate balance between the two, but rather, fault it for according too little weight to B.J.F.'s side of equation, and too much on the other.

I would strike the balance rather differently. Writing for the Ninth Circuit, Judge Merrill put this view eloquently:

> Does the spirit of the Bill of Rights require that individuals be free to pry into the unnewsworthy private affairs of their fellowmen? In our view it does not. In our view, fairly defined areas of privacy must have the protection of law if the quality of life is to continue to be reasonably acceptable. The public's right to know is, then, subject to reasonable limitations so far as concerns the private facts of its individual members. *Virgil v. Time, Inc.*, 527 F.2d 1122, 1128 (1975), *cert. denied*, 425 U.S. 998 (1976).

Ironically, this Court, too, had occasion to consider this same balance just a few weeks ago, in *United States Department of Justice v. Reporters Committee for Freedom of Press*, 489 U.S. 749 (1989). There, we were faced with a press request, under the Freedom of Information Act, for a "rap sheet" on a person accused of bribing a Congressman — presumably, a person whose privacy rights would be far less than B.J.F.'s. Yet this Court rejected the media's request for disclosure of the "rap sheet," saying:

The privacy interest in maintaining the practical obscurity of rap-sheet information will always be high. When the subject of such a rap sheet is a private citizen and when the information is in the Government's control as a compilation, rather than as a record of 'what the government is up to,' the privacy interest . . . is . . . at its apex while the . . . public interest in disclosure is at its nadir. *Id.*, at 780.

The Court went on to conclude that disclosure of rap sheets "categorical[ly]" constitutes an "unwarranted" invasion of privacy. *Ibid.* The same surely must be true—indeed, much more so—for the disclosure of a rape victim's name.

I do not suggest that the Court's decision today is a radical departure from a previously charted course. The Court's ruling has been foreshadowed. In *Time, Inc. v. Hill*, 385 U.S. 374, 383–384, n.7 (1967), we observed that—after a brief period early in this century where Brandeis' view was ascendant—the trend in "modern" jurisprudence has been to eclipse an individual's right to maintain private any truthful information that the press wished to publish. More recently, in *Cox Broadcasting*, 420 U.S. at 491, we acknowledged the possibility that the First Amendment may prevent a State from ever subjecting the publication of truthful but private information to civil liability. Today, we hit the bottom of the slippery slope.

I would find a place to draw the line higher on the hillside: a spot high enough to protect B.J.F.'s desire for privacy and peace-of-mind in the wake of a horrible personal tragedy. There is no public interest in publishing the names, addresses, and phone numbers of persons who are the victims of crime—and no public interest in immunizing the press from liability in the rare cases where a State's efforts to protect a victim's privacy have failed. Consequently, I respectfully dissent.

Notes

1. *The Florida Star* violated its own internal guidelines in publishing B.J.F.'s name. Most major news organizations follow similar policies. The rationales generally offered for such polices are:

- Rape is different from any other crime. Society often blames the victims. Studies show that rape victims suffer from the stigma of being "damaged" by the experience.

- Rape victims are less likely to report the crime if they know their names will appear in the newspaper. Rape is already the most underreported crime in the country.

- Because rape victims are treated with such insensitivity by society, they deserve a level of privacy not afforded other crime victims.

See Kelly McBride, *Rethinking Rape Coverage: Should Anonymity be Absolute?*, The Quill, Oct. 1, 2002.

2. If the Florida statute at issue in *Florida Star* could not survive First Amendment scrutiny, could the statute be revised? In 1995, the Florida Legislature passed the

Crime Victims Protection Act, codified at Fla. Stat. §92.56, which restricts disclosure of the identity of victims of sexual assault:

(1) All court records, including testimony from witnesses, that reveal the photograph, name, or address of the victim of an alleged offense described in chapter 794 or chapter 800, or act of child abuse, aggravated child abuse, or sexual performance by a child as described in chapter 827, are confidential and exempt from the provisions of §24(a), Art. I of the State Constitution and may not be made public if, upon a showing to the trial court with jurisdiction over the alleged offense, the state or the victim demonstrates that:

(a) The identity of the victim is not already known in the community;

(b) The victim has not voluntarily called public attention to the offense;

(c) The identity of the victim has not otherwise become a reasonable subject of public concern;

(d) The disclosure of the victim's identity would be offensive to a reasonable person; and

(e) The disclosure of the victim's identity would:

1. Endanger the victim because the assailant has not been apprehended and is not otherwise known to the victim;

2. Endanger the victim because of the likelihood of retaliation, harassment, or intimidation;

3. Cause severe emotional or mental harm to the victim;

4. Make the victim unwilling to testify as a witness; or

5. Be inappropriate for other good cause shown.

Anyone disclosing the name in violation of the statute is in contempt of court.

Does the statute comply with the Supreme Court's dictates? One commentator argues that this statute is unconstitutionally overbroad (for example, it applies to a variety of crimes other than rape) but could be tightened up to comply with constitutional requirements. *See* Kunoor Chopra, *Peeping Press v. Private Persecution: A Resolution of the Conflict Between Freedom of the Press and Freedom from the Press*, 19 Loy. L.A. Ent. L.J. 253 (1999).

———

If the court accidentally fails to preserve confidentiality of private materials, can it order the press not to disclose those materials?

People v. Bryant

94 P.3d 624 (Colo. 2004)

Justice HOBBS delivered the opinion of the court.

Pursuant to C.A.R. 21, we accepted jurisdiction in this original proceeding to review an order by the District Court for Eagle County in a criminal prosecution against Kobe B. Bryant for allegedly sexually assaulting a woman.

In accordance with section 18-3-407(2), 6 C.R.S. (2003), ("rape shield statute") the District Court, on June 21 and 22, 2004, held *in camera* proceedings regarding the "relevancy and materiality of evidence of specific instances of the victim's[41] . . . prior or subsequent sexual conduct, or opinion evidence of the victim's . . . sexual conduct." § 18-3-407(2)(a).

On June 24, 2004, the court reporter mistakenly sent the transcripts of the *in camera* proceedings by electronic transmission to seven media entities ("Recipients") via an electronic mailing list for subscribers to public proceeding transcripts in the case, instead of using only the electronic mailing list for persons authorized to receive transcripts of *in camera* proceedings. There is no dispute that this was an error, and no dispute that the Recipients would otherwise not have received the transcripts.

The District Court's October 31, 2003, order previously entered in this case prohibits court personnel from disclosing to any unauthorized person information that is not part of the court's public records. . . .

Upon discovering the transmission mistake, the court reporter immediately notified the District Court, which promptly issued its June 24th order to the Recipients:

> It has come to the Court's attention that the *in camera* portions of the hearings in this matter on the 21st and 22nd were erroneously distributed. These transcripts are not for public dissemination. Anyone who has received these transcripts is ordered to delete and destroy any copies and not reveal any contents thereof, or be subject to contempt of Court.

So Ordered this 24th day of June 2004.

Four days later, the Recipients filed their original proceeding petition, asking that we exercise jurisdiction to review the District Court's order and set it aside as an unconstitutional prior restraint against publication, in violation of the First Amendment to the United States Constitution and article II, section 10 of the Colorado Constitution. Keeping the District Court's order in effect for purposes of our accelerated review, we have received answer briefs from the Colorado Attorney General on behalf of the District Court and from the District Attorney for Eagle County. The Recipients filed their reply brief. We now enter our decision.

We determine that the District Court's order is a prior restraint against publishing the contents of the transcripts. We also determine that, narrowly tailored, the prior restraint is constitutional under both the United States and the Colorado Constitutions. The state has an interest of the highest order in this case in providing a confidential evidentiary proceeding under the rape shield statute, because such hearings protect victims' privacy, encourage victims to report sexual assault, and further the prosecution and deterrence of sexual assault.

---

41. In this opinion, we use the term "victim" as it is used under the rape shield statute. It implies nothing with respect to the veracity of the charges.

II. First Amendment Prior Restraint Law

The First Amendment limits the choices the government may make in its efforts to regulate or prohibit speech, but it does not bar all government attempts to regulate speech, and it does not absolutely prohibit prior restraints against publication. *Neb. Press Ass'n v. Stuart,* 427 U.S. 539, 570 (1976).

The term "prior restraint" describes "administrative and judicial orders *forbidding* certain communications when issued in advance of the time that such communications are to occur." *Alexander v. United States,* 509 U.S. 544, 550 (1993). Prior restraint of publication is an extraordinary remedy attended by a heavy presumption against its constitutional validity. *N.Y. Times Co. v. United States,* 403 U.S. 713, 714 (1971). "The thread running through [the prior restraint cases] is that prior restraints on speech and publication are the most serious and the least tolerable infringement on First Amendment rights." *Neb. Press,* 427 U.S. at 559, 96 S.Ct. 2791.

To justify a prior restraint, the state must have an interest of the "highest order" it seeks to protect. *Fla. Star v. B.J.F.,* 491 U.S. 524, 533 (1989). The restraint must be the narrowest available to protect that interest; and the restraint must be necessary to protect against an evil that is great and certain, would result from the reportage, and cannot be mitigated by less intrusive measures. *CBS, Inc.,* 510 U.S. at 1317.

Nevertheless, the Supreme Court has recognized that protecting the privacy of rape victims is a highly significant state interest, requiring courts to consider both the First Amendment and the compelling privacy interests in the particular factual context of the case in reaching their decisions. *Fla. Star,* 491 U.S. at 530, 537. "We continue to believe that the sensitivity and significance of the interests presented in clashes between First Amendment and privacy rights counsel relying on limited principles that sweep no more broadly than the appropriate context of the instant case." *Id.* at 533.

We therefore turn to Colorado's rape shield statute, which serves purposes the Supreme Court identified in *Florida Star* as being of the highest order.

III. Colorado's Rape Shield Statute

Rape is among the most intimate and personally-devastating invasions a person may experience in his or her lifetime. It typically produces emotionally-destructive reverberations for the victim and the victim's family long after its occurrence. It can destroy the ability of a person to enjoy his or her sexuality with another.

The price of making a sexual assault victim's testimony available to courts of law historically exposed the victim to detailed questioning about his or her sexual relationships with others on the theory that a person who consented to a sexual relationship in the past was more likely to have consented in the case at hand. This tactic of "putting the victim on trial" attempts to characterize the accuser as a person who consented to the alleged unlawful sexual conduct. *See People v. McKenna,* 585 P.2d 275, 277–78 (Colo. 1978). Due to the likelihood or possibility that this defense will be invoked, exposing the victim's most intimate life history to public view, victims often are deterred from reporting the crime, or having reported it, from following through in the role of complaining witness. *Id.* at 278.

At the time the Colorado General Assembly enacted the rape shield statute, many sexual assaults were never reported because victims of rape were often ashamed, humiliated, or terrified about the specter of their most private hurt being publicly revealed. Therefore, the offenses could not be prosecuted under the state's criminal laws. In 1975, the FBI reported that forcible sexual assault was one of the most under-reported crimes, with the estimated actual rate of occurrence ranging from 80% to 350% more than the number reported. M. Ireland, *Reform Rape Legislation: A New Standard of Sexual Responsibility,* 49 U. Colo. L. Rev. 185, 186 n. 4 (1978) (citing Fed. Bureau of Investigation, Uniform Crime Reports 22–24, 37, 42 (1975)). "Rape crisis centers tend[ed] to support . . . that at least 90 percent of actual rapes [were] never reported." N. Gager & C. Schurr, Sexual Assault: Confronting Rape in America 91 (1976).

The FBI acknowledged in its Uniform Crime Reports that law enforcement administrators recognize that their sexual assault statistics are low because "fear and/or embarrassment on the part of victims" deter them from reporting the crime. N. Gager & C. Schurr, *supra,* at 1 (citing excerpt from a Uniform Crime Report from 1968–1973). One of the main reasons why so few sexual assaults were reported was fear of court harassment and embarrassing publicity. *Id.* at 93; National Institute of Law Enforcement and Criminal Justice, U.S. Dept. of Justice, Forcible Rape 21 (March 1978) ("National Institute") ("The victim who fears that her past sexual activities may be exposed in public is less likely to report her rape and pursue prosecution."). In addition, many victims have reported that "involvement with the criminal justice system has been almost as bad as the sexual assault itself." National Institute, *supra,* at 34.

Because a defendant may seek to inject irrelevant details about the victim's personal sexual conduct into the case, the Colorado General Assembly has enacted a carefully-crafted judicial mechanism that allows the prosecution and defense — in private, that is, "*in camera*" — to explore and argue about the relevancy and materiality of evidence tendered to the trial judge for admission at the public trial of the case. *McKenna,* 585 P.2d at 279; *People v. Harris,* 43 P.3d 221, 226 (Colo. 2002); *see* § 18-3-407, 6 C.R.S. (2003).

This statute deems the prior or subsequent sexual conduct of any victim to be presumptively irrelevant to the criminal trial. *See People v. Murphy,* 919 P.2d 191, 195, 197 (Colo. 1996). It sets forth a detailed procedure by which a defendant may request that a court make an exception to this general rule. According to this procedure, the defendant must submit a written motion stating that the defendant "has an offer of proof of the relevancy and materiality of evidence of specific instances of the victim's . . . sexual conduct." § 18-3-407(2)(a). The motion must be accompanied by an "affidavit in which the offer of proof shall be stated." § 18-3-407(2)(b).

If the court finds the offer of proof sufficient, it must hold an *in camera* hearing to determine whether the prior sexual conduct is "relevant to a material issue to the case." During the *in camera* hearing, the parties may call witnesses, including the victim. To the extent that the court deems the sexual conduct relevant to the case, this evidence will be admissible at the public trial. *McKenna,* 585 P.2d at 276. However, the statute contemplates that contents of the *in camera* hearing and any transcripts thereof will remain confidential and under seal in the future, with the possible exception of use at the trial to impeach a witness' credibility or for some other admissible purpose.

IV. Application to This Case

We determine that the District Court's order is a prior restraint because it prohibits specific entities possessing the *in camera* June 21 and June 22, 2004, transcripts from revealing the contents. *See Alexander v. United States,* 509 U.S. 544, 550 (1993).

We also determine that, narrowly tailored, the prior restraint is constitutional. The state has an interest of the highest order in this case in providing a confidential evidentiary proceeding under the rape shield statute, because such hearings protect victims' privacy, encourage victims to report sexual assault, and further the prosecution and deterrence of sexual assault.

We further determine that a narrowly tailored order can be fashioned in this case, and it is necessary to protect against an evil that is great and certain and would result from the reportage.

1. The District Court's Order Is a Prior Restraint on Publication of Lawfully Obtained Information

The Recipients contend that the District Courts order forbidding publication of the information contained in the *in camera* transcripts constitutes a prior restraint. In this respect, we agree with Recipients, and they are entitled to the heavy presumption against the constitutionality of a prior restraint. An accidental leak of privileged information does not necessarily entitle a court to punish or impose a secrecy order upon the media. *See, e.g., Landmark Communications, Inc. v. Virginia,* 435 U.S. 829 (1978).

We also agree with Recipients that their acquisition of the transcripts was not illegal. Absent the prior court order, the statute, and the subsequent court order, Recipients would be free to publish the contents. *See, e.g., Bartnicki v. Vopper,* 532 U.S. 514, 528 (2001), for the proposition that a court must focus on the document's character and the consequences of public disclosure rather than the origin of the documents).

2. Facts and Context of This Case

The Supreme Court's precedent requires us to base our review on the specific facts and context of this case. Here, we ground our decision on uncontested facts derived from the following parts of the record: (1) the briefs filed with us; (2) the Colorado Courts' webpage entries; and (3) the sealed *in camera* transcripts that we rely upon but do not publish in this opinion. Additionally, we take notice of matters of common knowledge in this jurisdiction.

The pre-trial proceedings in this case are constantly monitored and reported by the press. Such media-intense activity has befallen a small mountain courthouse and has prompted a sizeable commitment of Colorado judicial resources. Among these is the constant updating of the Colorado Courts' webpage to provide the press and the public with contemporaneous and archive-accessible electronic documents and scheduling dates for pre-trial and trial activities.

The electronic technology being utilized helps to facilitate for Coloradans and the world a high-degree of access to the public proceedings in this case. Yet, while most aspects of the judicial role in proceedings are highly visible and responsive to the media's First Amendment-protected right to report news to the public, the District Court closed the *in camera* rape shield hearings held on June 21 and June 22, 2004, following public announcement on June 17 and June 18 of their closure.

The District Court placed into effect reasonable procedures, in advance, to prevent the media from attending and reporting these proceedings. By a standing order entered in the case dated October 31, 2003, the District Court prohibited the parties, attorneys, and court personnel—including the court reporter—from publicly revealing the hearing contents. The District Court allowed only authorized persons, including witnesses, to attend the *in camera* hearings. To make the *in camera* evidence and arguments accessible to the court and the parties, so that the District Court could make its rape shield statute determinations, the court reporter transcribed the *in camera* proceedings, marking every page of the *in camera* transcripts with highly visible lettering: "* * IN CAMERA PROCEEDINGS * *." The court reporter then transmitted the contents of the *in camera* proceedings mistakenly by utilizing the wrong e-mail list.

Recipients, the few media entities on whose computer screens the electronic document appeared, obtained a private transmission placed under seal by the District Court. The District Court did not intend to make these transcripts publicly available, nor did the court reporter. The private and protected nature of these transcripts was manifest to the Recipients from the bold notation on each page and the District Court's prior orders and actions.

Recipients were in a position to receive this transmission from the court reporter only because the District Court's accommodation allowed them to contract for the court reporter's electronic delivery to them of public court proceedings in the case as soon as they were available.

When the court reporter realized the transmission mistake, she notified the District Court Judge who had presided over the *in camera* proceedings. The District Court Judge then ordered the Recipients not to reveal the contents of those transcripts and to destroy them. Such order preceded any publication of the transcripts. The *in camera* transcripts continue to remain under seal. Recipients were and are amply apprised of this.

The District Court's order pertains only to the contents of these transcripts. The District Court took the only remaining action available to uphold the protections afforded by the rape shield statute, which embraces all of the state interests at stake in this case. It ordered the Recipients not to reveal the contents of the transcribed *in camera* proceedings. Were the District Court to allow publication of the mistakenly transmitted transcripts, it would abrogate all of its duties under the rape shield statute, and its own prior orders.

3. Prior Restraint Necessary; Harm Great and Certain

Recipients do not dispute the constitutionality of excluding the public and press from the *in camera* hearings, nor do they challenge the requirement that the parties, witnesses, and court personnel must maintain the secrecy of the proceedings. Rather, the Recipients argue in this case that at the moment the transcript arrived at their computers, they lawfully acquired the information and were entitled to publish it. . . .

A. *Florida Star* and Other Applicable Cases

We reason from Supreme Court case examples that reject the argued basis for sanctions or prior restraint. These include the posited-but-rejected justifications of: removing incentives for parties to intercept private conversations, *Bartnicki v. Vopper*, 532 U.S. 514, 529 (2001); minimizing the harm to persons whose conversations have been illegally intercepted, *Id.*; protecting anonymity of juvenile offenders and encouraging their rehabilitation, *Smith v. Daily Mail Publ'g Co.*, 443 U.S. 97, 104 (1979); and protecting the reputation of state judges and maintaining the institutional integrity of the court system, *Landmark Communications, Inc. v. Virginia*, 435 U.S. 829, 833 (1978).

In many of these cases, the Court pointed to the strength of the interest asserted but held that it did not satisfy the high standard required by First Amendment law, or was not supported by empirical evidence. Nevertheless, the facts and context of this case justify the District Court's prior restraint against revealing the contents of the *in camera* transcripts.

In *Michigan v. Lucas*, 500 U.S. 145 (1991), the United States Supreme Court acknowledged the widespread adoption of rape shield statutes, and noted that the purpose behind them is "to protect victims of rape from being exposed at trial to harassing or irrelevant questions concerning their past sexual behavior." *Id.* at 146. . . .

Likewise, in *Florida Star v. B.J.F.*, 491 U.S. 524 (1989), the Supreme Court acknowledged the compelling interest of protecting a sexual assault victim's privacy. . . .

While the Court acknowledged that the privacy interests involved were highly significant, it held that imposing damages on the newspaper for publishing the victim's name violated the First Amendment. The Court left open the possibility that "in a proper case, imposing civil sanctions for publication of the name of a rape victim might be so overwhelmingly necessary to advance these interests as to satisfy the *Daily Mail* standard."

In the case before us, the state's interest in protecting the victim's privacy is even stronger than in *Florida Star*. The Defendant Bryant is an internationally-recognized professional basketball player. The press has been covering every minute detail of this case, and most of this coverage has been published or broadcast nationwide. In addition, the reported news is typically posted on the Internet, and thus available to computer users world-wide. The *in camera* transcribed proceedings of June 21 and 22 address the prior and subsequent sexual conduct of the victim apart from her encounter with Defendant Bryant. A victim's sexual conduct is even more private than a victim's identity, which the Court held was of utmost importance in *Florida Star*.

Moreover, in contrast to *Florida Star,* the contents of the *in camera* transcribed proceedings were not publicly available, there was no burden on the press to determine whether it should risk publication and sanctions in light of the District Court's prior restraint order, and the specter of the press having to impose self-censorship was not an issue, as the transcripts were clearly marked private by the "In Camera" notation. In addition, this case is distinguishable from *Near, Landmark,* and *New York Times* because the contents of these transcripts do not implicate suppression of public policy debate or criticism of public officials. To the contrary, the testimony concerns conduct that is intensely private and personal.

B. Our Determinations Regarding the Harms in This Case

Under the circumstances and context of this case, any details of the victim's sexual conduct reported from the *in camera* transcripts will be instantaneously available world-wide and will irretrievably affect the victim and her reputation. She is entitled to rely on the protective provisions of the rape shield statute, which the state affords her in her capacity as complaining witness in a sexual assault prosecution. This includes the District Court's prohibition against the further release of the contents of the transcribed *in camera* proceedings.

Recipients have presented to us an affidavit attaching many press articles containing information about the victim's purported sexual activity before and after her encounter with Defendant Bryant. In addition, the probable cause order made public in this case contains hearsay references to DNA testing, the victim's clothing, and evidence that the victim had engaged in sexual activity with other persons. The argument is that the victim's privacy is already hugely compromised and publication of the *in camera* proceedings will not result in graver infringement on the victim's privacy.

We have reviewed the transcripts of these hearings and disagree. The applicable United States Supreme Court standard of review does not require us to disclose what is in the *in camera* proceedings versus what is already in the public domain. Doing this would contravene the rape shield statute by revealing what is in the transcripts and destroying the confidentiality of that information, before the trial court determines whether the information is relevant and material.

Rather, the applicable standard of review requires us to determine whether publication of these transcripts would cause great and certain harm to a state interest of the highest order. We conclude that it would.

First, the evidence and the opinion testimony presented at these *in camera* proceedings were taken under oath in a court of law. Reporting these court proceedings will add a level of official legitimacy and detail to the information that does not attend press reports — the ring of authenticity, the stamp of authority. . . .

We do not accept the proposition that the greater the press attention to a case the less important it becomes to keep *in camera* rape shield transcripts from being published. If the contents of these transcripts are reported, the world will have access to graphic detail of sworn evidence and opinion testimony about the victim's sexual conduct that the public trial of the case may not reveal, because the District Court may determine it to be irrelevant and immaterial under the rape shield statute. The very damage that the rape shield statute is designed to prevent — confirming through *in camera* court proceedings the details of this victim's sexual conduct that are not relevant or material — would thereby occur.

Second, the state's interests of the highest order in this case not only involve the victim's privacy interest, but also the reporting and prosecution of this and other sexual assault cases. Revealing the *in camera* rape shield evidence will not only destroy the utility of this very important legal mechanism in this case, but will demonstrate to other sexual assault victims that they cannot rely on the rape shield statute to prevent public airing of sexual conduct testimony the law deems inadmissible. This would directly undercut the reporting and prosecution of sexual assault cases, in contravention of the General Assembly's legislative purposes.

Third, it is absolutely essential to our analysis that these transcripts are still private. Reportage of their contents would make all matters contained therein public. The court reporter's mistake handed to only a few media entities contains material that was plainly marked and intended to be kept private. The very purpose of such a marking is to make authorized readers aware that the information contained therein is restricted to use only in and for the proceedings in which the evidence and argument thereon was taken. In this case, the confidentiality markings served to notify the non-authorized readers, Recipients, that this document remained under seal. Reportage of these transcripts would greatly and certainly magnify the harm of the mistaken transmission, to the immediate detriment of the victim and the state.

Taken together, the harms in making these *in camera* judicial proceedings public would be great, certain, and devastating to the victim and to the state. These harms justify the remedy we fashion in this case. "For even though the broad sweep of the First Amendment seems to prohibit all restraints on free expression, this Court has observed that freedom of speech . . . does not comprehend the right to speak on any subject at any time." *Seattle Times, Co. v. Rhinehart*, 467 U.S. 20, 31 (1984) (citations and quotations omitted).

If the District Court cannot prevent the release of the contents of the *in camera* transcripts while it expeditiously proceeds to make its relevancy and materiality determinations, as contemplated in the rape shield statute, the state will be unable to implement its interest of the highest order in providing a confidential evidentiary proceeding under the rape shield statute, because such hearings protect victims' privacy, encourage victims to report sexual assault, and further the prosecution and deterrence of sexual assault.

Accordingly, upon reviewing *de novo* the record in this case, including the *in camera* transcripts, we determine that indeed the District Court's order is a prior restraint against publication, which is presumptively unconstitutional under the First Amendment. However, given the circumstances of this case, the state's interest in keeping the *in camera* proceedings confidential is sufficiently weighty to overcome the presumption in favor of dissemination at this time. We also determine that this prior restraint is necessary to protect against an evil that is great and certain and would result from the reportage. . . .

V. Order and Judgment

Accordingly, we uphold the prohibition against revealing the contents of the transcribed *in camera* proceedings of June 21 and 22, 2004, and affirm the District Court's order to that extent.

Justice BENDER, dissenting.

The only objective that could be accomplished by the district court's order is to protect the confidentiality of this *in camera* hearing. That duty was our responsibility, which we unfortunately failed to carry out. Having failed, we, the judiciary—the government—cannot now order the media to perform the role that we were obligated, but failed, to do—to protect the privacy interests of the alleged victim. Nonetheless, the majority approves the court's power to prevent the dissemination of speech which the court deems dangerous or offensive. In doing so, the majority authorizes the court, rather than the media, to determine what can or cannot be published concerning truthful information regarding a matter of public importance. The power the majority authorizes is the power of the government to censor the media, which is precisely the power the First Amendment forbids. The appropriate standard for deciding the validity of the prior restraint in this case was best articulated by Justice Potter Stewart who said: "Though government may deny access to information and punish its theft, government may not prohibit or punish the publication of that information once it falls into the hands of the press, unless the need for secrecy is manifestly overwhelming." *Landmark Communications, Inc. v. Virginia*, 435 U.S. 829, 849 (1978) (Stewart, J., concurring). That need is not present here.

Notes

1. The victim in the Kobe Bryant case ultimately declined to assist in the criminal prosecution, citing lack of confidence in the criminal justice system. The prosecutor dropped the charges. The victim then filed a civil suit against Kobe Bryant. A

federal judge rejected her request to remain anonymous in that suit, concluding that the public's interest in open court proceedings outweighed her desire to shield her identity. Erin Gartner, *Judge Says Bryant's Accuser Must be Identified in Civil Lawsuit*, AP Newswire, Oct. 7, 2004. Ultimately the civil case was settled. The settlement terms were not disclosed.

2. Some news organizations have a policy that even if the name of a sexual assault or child victim is lawfully obtained, they will not print it in relation to a criminal case, but they will print the name of the victim if the victim pursues a civil case. Does the different treatment of the type of proceeding make sense? Does the different treatment of types of victimization make sense?

Chapter 7

Plea Bargains and Other Pretrial Dispositions

Introduction

This chapter explores the victim's role in dispositions of cases by methods other than trial. The victim's participation in plea bargain procedures and outright dismissal is examined. Attention is also given to non-criminal dispositions of pretrial intervention, deferred sentencing diversion, civil compromise, and mediation.

Once criminal charges are filed they are resolved by trial or, in the vast majority of cases, plea bargain. Other, less utilized dispositions include: dismissal of the criminal charge, either outright or pursuant to a variety of procedures, including civil compromise, mediation and diversion, or deferred sentencing. This chapter explores the role and significance of the crime victim in pretrial disposition.

A. Dismissal Outright

1. Pretrial Dismissal Outright—Victim's Inability at Common Law to Dismiss Charges

Commonwealth v. Cundiff

147 S.W. 767 (Ky. 1912)

Appeal from Circuit Court, Wolfe County, Kentucky

Leonard Cundiff was indicted for an offense, and from an order directing that the indictment be filed away the Commonwealth appeals.

* * *

Lassing, J. At the September term, 1911, of the Wolfe circuit court, the grand jury returned an indictment against Leonard Cundiff, charging him with the crime of having carnal sexual intercourse with a female under 16 years of age. . . . On the 26th day of January . . . the accused filed the affidavit of Anna Cundiff [the victim], in which she states, in substance, that she is the daughter of Willie and Laura Cundiff; that she is 16 years of age and resides with her parents; that she was delivered of a child on August 25, 1911; that the accused is the father of her child; that he is her cousin; that they lived near each other and were associated with each other a great deal; that, when the matter complained of in the indictment occurred, she and the accused were young, and did not realize the enormity of their crime; that she has, by reason thereof, suffered great humiliation and remorse, and is in a weakened physical condition, and she does not believe that she can stand the strain on her health and mind, should she be compelled to appear in open court and testify, and asked to have the charge against the accused dismissed. The accused also, at the same time, filed the affidavit of Willie and Laura Cundiff, the father and mother of the girl, in which they asked that the prosecution be dismissed. Upon the filing of these affidavits, the court, upon its own motion, over the objection of the attorney for the commonwealth, ordered the indictment filed away and directed the money, which had been placed in the hands of the jury commissioner by the accused, be returned to him and the accused discharged. Feeling that the court was without authority to file the indictment away, over his objection, the commonwealth attorney prayed, and has prosecuted, this appeal.

The sole question is: May the court on its own motion, by filing the indictment away, prevent the prosecution of one charged with a crime? For the purposes of this case, it may be conceded that the motive actuating the court was good. His sympathy for this unfortunate girl and the feelings of her father and mother no doubt induced him to take the step which he did. But in matters of this kind courts must be governed in their action, not by sympathy, but by the rules of procedure made and adopted for their guidance. We know of no authority anywhere given to the court to control or direct the dismissal of the prosecution where the indictment upon which it is based is good. Section 118, Kentucky Statutes, provides: "It shall be the duty of the commonwealth's attorney to attend to each circuit holden in his district, and prosecute all violations of the criminal and penal laws therein, and discharge all other duties assigned him by law."

Under the authority of this statute, he is given practical control of all criminal prosecutions. He is the chosen representative of the state. If for any reason he sees fit, he can dismiss an indictment, provided he proceeds according to section 123, Kentucky Statutes, which provides:

> Before the court shall permit any commonwealth's or county attorney to dismiss any indictment or enter a nolle prosequi in any case, such attorney shall file a statement, in writing, setting forth the reasons for such dismissal or such failure to prosecute which statement shall be signed by the commonwealth's or county attorney, as the case may be, and spread upon the order book of the court, and an order entered in accordance therewith.

This provision of the statute makes plain: First, that where an indictment, for any cause, is to be dismissed or filed away, it can only be done upon motion of the commonwealth's attorney, or the county attorney who may be acting for him; and, second, that it cannot be done by even the commonwealth's or county attorney, except the reasons therefor be reduced to writing, and the court, upon having considered the reasons upon which the discontinuance of the prosecution is sought, gives his consent that it may be done. A prosecution by indictment is a litigation in which the state is plaintiff or complainant, and is represented by the commonwealth's attorney. The judge does not represent the state any more than he does the defendant in the prosecution. His right to control the prosecution goes only to the extent of determining whether or not the indictment is good on demurrer. If he holds it to be a good indictment, he is without power to direct its dismissal. Nor does the fact that the injured party, or those who would naturally be aggrieved because of the wrongs complained of in the indictment, want the prosecution dismissed, change the situation. The prosecution is not for their benefit, but for the public good. While the party who has suffered the immediate wrong at the hands of the accused may be of material aid to the commonwealth in imposing upon the accused the punishment which his offense merits, she is without power to direct or control the prosecution, much less to have the court discontinue it.

The action of the court in filing away the indictment had the effect to continue indefinitely the case, and for all practical purposes defeat the commonwealth in its effort to bring to justice one charged with the commission of a serious crime, and this at a time when the representative of the commonwealth was demanding that he be given an opportunity to proceed with the prosecution. To uphold such a ruling would be to put it in the power of a court to defeat the ends of justice at any time where it was shown that the injured party did not desire the case prosecuted. If such a rule obtained, where one had committed a crime, it would only be necessary for him to procure the consent of the injured party or of the relatives of the injured party, that the prosecution should be dismissed. Thus, a premium would be placed upon crime; for, not only would the original crime go unpunished, but the action of the court would be frequently brought about by the practice of corrupt or improper methods in procuring from the prosecuting witness, or her relatives, the desired request that the prosecution be terminated or discontinued. The mere statement of the condition which such a course of practice might produce is sufficient to condemn it. In filing away the indictment the trial judge erred.

The case is reversed and remanded, with directions that the indictment be placed upon the docket, a bench warrant issue for the defendant, and the trial proceed as though the order filing it away had not been entered.

Notes

1. While a victim may not formally obtain a dismissal, a victim may employ informal influences to try to get the state to move to dismiss charges, such as failing to appear for trial. *See People v. Williams*, 625 N.W.2d 132 (Mich. Ct. App. 2001) (reversing trial court dismissal of a domestic violence prosecution, over prosecutor's objection, merely because the victim failed to appear at trial).

2. As discussed in the next section of this chapter, many state courts now do have the authority to dismiss a case in the interest of justice on the court's own motion. However, victims still do not have any legal *control* over the decision to dismiss.

3. Assuming you were a prosecutor with authority to dismiss, would you dismiss the charges against Cundiff?

4. More modern cases reach similar results to *Cundiff*, concluding that the decision to dismiss charges must be left to the prosecution, not the courts. *See, e.g., Commonwealth v. Everett*, 39 N.E.3d 775 (Mass. App. 2015) (while "[a]t one time, judges did enjoy a limited authority to dismiss criminal complaints over the Commonwealth's objection in 'the interests of public justice,' such judicial power no longer exists"); *People v. Morrow*, 524 N.W.2d 324 (Mich. Ct. App. 1995) ("under the facts of this case, we find that the trial court exceeded its authority when it dismissed the information against defendant at the pretrial stage of the proceedings because the decision whether to dismiss a case or proceed to trial is within the prosecutor's sole discretion.").

2. Victim's Rights to Confer with Prosecutor and Address the Court on Motion to Dismiss

A minority of the states have statutory provisions for the prosecutor to consult with the victim regarding a contemplated dismissal. For example:

> ARIZ. REV. STAT. § 8-290.09. Victim conference with prosecuting attorney
>
> A. *On request* of the victim, the prosecuting attorney *shall confer* with the victim about the disposition of a delinquent offense, including the victim's views about a decision not to proceed with prosecution, *dismissal*, withdrawal of a request for transfer, plea or disposition negotiations and, if a petition has been filed, preadjudication diversion programs. . . .
>
> C. The right of the victim to confer with the prosecuting attorney does not include the authority to direct the prosecution of the case.

South Carolina has a law designed to provide the court with the victim's view on the propriety of dismissal:

> The state victim/witness program shall work with the solicitors of this state, the Attorney General's office, and relevant professional organizations to develop guidelines for solicitors to follow in the handling of victims, to include. . . . Providing information on the views of victims of violent crime on . . . dismissals . . .

Many states have provisions concerning victim's attendance at "critical stages." However, this may or may not give a victim the ability to object to dismissal. In *Gansz v. People*, 888 P.2d 256 (1995), the Colorado Supreme Court held that this language did not give the victim in Colorado the right to be heard by the court on a motion to dismiss.

3. The "Interests of Society" Limitation on the Prosecutor's Ability to Dismiss

If a formal charge has been brought, a prosecutor may later wish to dismiss the charge. At common law the prosecutor had the power to dismiss a case without judicial review. The prosecutor's dismissal of a case was called a *nolle prosequi*. The original purpose of this power was to dismiss cases where the private prosecution was oppressive, and to terminate private prosecutions where the private prosecutors were simultaneously pursuing a civil claim.

In a minority of states the common law authority of the prosecutor to dismiss remains unchecked. In federal court and in a majority of state courts, dismissal may be granted only with the court's approval.

> In some jurisdictions, prosecutors still possess, as at common law, the absolute power to enter a nolle prosequi. In most jurisdictions, however, the decision to dismiss a pending prosecution can no longer be made by the prosecutor alone; the nolle prosequi as known to the common law has been abolished. The manner in which and the limitations under which the dismissal power may be exercised vary: The prosecutor may file a dismissal of an indictment or information only with the "consent of the court," "leave of court," or "permission of the court"; a prosecution may be dismissed by the court on motion of the prosecutor; a prosecution may be dismissed by the court on its own motion; or a prosecution may be dismissed by the court either on its own motion or upon the application of the prosecutor. Moreover, many jurisdictions require that the reasons for the dismissal be set forth in the order. . . .

1 WHARTON'S CRIMINAL LAW § 61 (15 ed. 2017).

———————

The courts may reject a prosecutor's dismissal motion for various reasons, including when dismissal is contrary to the public interest. The public interest category includes victim considerations, as suggested in the following widely cited case:

United States v. Cowan

524 F.2d 504 (5th Cir. 1975)

MURRAH, Circuit Judge:

The first sentence of Rule 48(a) Fed. R. Crim. P. provides that "The Attorney General or the United States attorney may by leave of court file a dismissal of an indictment, information or complaint and the prosecution shall thereupon terminate." In our case the trial judge denied the United States Attorney's motion under Rule 48(a) to dismiss pending criminal proceedings and upon formal declination of the government to proceed, appointed private, special prosecutors to continue the prosecution of the case. The government took a timely appeal from the order appointing the special prosecutors under 28 U.S.C. § 1291 and, in the alternative, sought a writ of mandamus to require dismissal. It is conceded that the order appointing special prosecutors is final and appealable under § 1291. Inasmuch as the order appointing the special prosecutors is necessarily based upon the power of the court under Rule 48(a) to deny the motion to dismiss, the meaning and scope of that Rule are at issue, and we need not, therefore, consider the propriety of an extraordinary writ of mandamus.

Traditionally and at common law, public prosecutions were within the exclusive control of the district attorney with the absolute power to enter a nolle prosequi at any time before the jury is impanelled "except in cases where otherwise provided in some act of Congress." Confiscation Cases, 74 U.S. 457, 20 Wall. 92, 22 L.Ed. 320. *See also United States v. Brokaw*, 60 F. Supp. 100 (S.D. Ill. 1945). "The Federal Rules of Criminal Procedure have the force and effect of law. Just as a statute . . ." *Dupoint v. United States*, 388 F.2d 39, 44 (5th Cir. 1967). The precise question is the extent to which the phrase "by leave of court" in Rule 48(a) limits or conditions the common law power of the Attorney General acting through his subordinates to dismiss an indictment without leave of court. The question is presented on these pertinent facts.

In February of 1974, a federal grand jury in the Northern District of Texas returned a seven-count indictment against Jake Jacobsen. Six of the counts charged Jacobsen and Roy Cowan with the fraudulent misapplication of funds of a federally insured savings and loan association in San Angelo, Texas. A seventh count charged Jacobsen alone with knowingly making a false statement under oath to the grand jury. . . .

Meanwhile and in May of the same year, the Watergate Special Prosecution Force (*see* 28 C.F.R. 0.37 and 0.38) and Jacobsen's Washington counsel negotiated an agreement whereunder Jacobsen agreed to plead guilty to a one-count charge to be filed in the District of Columbia alleging violation of 18 U.S.C. § 201(f) (bribing a public official) and make a full and truthful disclosure of all relevant information and documents within Jacobsen's knowledge and possession concerning matters then under investigation by the Watergate Special Prosecution Force, and if required, be a witness on any charges arising out of any such investigation. The Special Prosecution Force agreed not to press any potential charges against Jacobsen in the District of Columbia arising out of the relevant investigation. It was also a part of the plea agreement that the government would dismiss the Texas indictment.

Apparently Jacobsen appeared before a grand jury in the District of Columbia in May giving testimony incriminating himself and others. In any event, in July the grand jury returned an indictment in the District of Columbia charging Jacobsen in one count with violation of 18 U.S.C. § 201(f) and as an unindicted co-conspirator in a conspiracy count against former Secretary of the Treasury John Connally. In August, Jacobsen entered a guilty plea to the bribery count (18 U.S.C. § 201(f)). The plea was accepted and the sentence postponed. . . .

In accordance with the plea agreement, the United States Attorney for the Northern District of Texas moved under Rule 48(a) to dismiss the indictment set for trial

in September. . . . The motion to dismiss recited that the Office of the Special Prosecutor and the Attorney General believed that Jacobsen's testimony was necessary to
the investigation and prosecution of the indictment in the District of Columbia; that
if it did not enter into the plea agreement, the testimony of Jacobsen in that case, or
any other case in which his testimony is relevant, would be lost; that the motion to
dismiss the Texas charges was made in good faith, in accordance with the plea agreement and not for purposes of harassment; and that the interest of justice will be best
served by disposing of the charges against Jacobsen in this manner. . . .

In an exhaustive opinion, the trial court asserted its discretionary power under
Rule 48(a) to grant or deny the motion for leave to dismiss the Texas indictment
against Jacobsen. Upon denial of the motion to dismiss, the United States Attorney
filed its notice of intention not to prosecute. Whereupon, the court, asserting its
inherent power to protect the public interest in these extraordinary circumstances,
appointed private special prosecutors "with full authority to control the course of
investigation and litigation related to the offenses charged in the indictment and to
handle all aspects of the case to the same extent as the United States Attorney in any
criminal prosecution."

The Attorney General stakes his claim to absolute power to dismiss the proceedings even without "leave of court" squarely upon the Doctrine of Separation of Powers as derived from the provisions of the Constitution establishing three separate, but
co-equal branches of government, each supreme in its own sphere; and more particularly upon Article II, Section 3 which provides in material part that the President
"shall take Care that the Laws be faithfully executed" and upon 28 U.S.C. §§ 516, 519,
empowering the Attorney General as surrogate of the President to conduct or supervise all litigation in which the government is a party. The court-appointed prosecutors counter that the Doctrine of Separation of Powers implied in the Constitution
does not cast the three branches of our government into water-tight compart-
ments; that room is left for some commingling of responsibilities in the orderly
administration of governmental affairs; that by the promulgation of Rule 48(a) as
part of the Rules of Criminal Procedure, Congress intended to vest in the courts a
shared responsibility for the dismissal of prosecutions once lodged in the court; and
that the power to grant leave to dismiss a criminal prosecution carries with it the
correlative power to exercise a discretion to deny leave to dismiss and, if necessary,
to effectuate such denial by the appointment of private prosecutors.

To sustain the asserted absolute power to dismiss the proceedings without "leave
of court," the Attorney General relies heavily on *United States v. Cox*, 342 F.2d 167
(5th Cir. 1965) and its progeny.

* * *

The holding in *Cox* is doubtless the law on its facts, and nothing we say here is
intended to derogate from it. But ours is not a *Cox* case. *Cox* involved a challenge to
the power of the court to direct the commencement of a prosecution, under Rule
7(c). We are concerned with the power of the court to supervise the termination of

a prosecution in being, under Rule 48(a). While the dicta in all the opinions in the *Cox* case provide a formidable preface to our inquiry, this dicta is inconclusive here because that court was not called upon to distinguish between the power to initiate and the power to terminate prosecutions.

The question is squarely presented here for the first time as a controversy between the Executive and Judicial Branches of government involving opposing asserted powers under the Rule. We now come face to face with the controversy, and it becomes "'the province and duty of the judicial department to say what the law is.'" . . .

In situations like these history has its claims, and we think it is appropriate to review it. Before the adoption of 48(a), more than thirty states had, by statute or judicial decision, modified the common law to give courts a responsible role in the dismissal of a pending criminal proceeding by requiring an "order" or "leave" or "consent" of court. The state case law interpreting this change is sparse, but what there is of it consistently affirms the power and duty of the court to exercise discretion to grant or withhold leave to dismiss pending criminal prosecutions in "the public interest." The American Law Institute's Model Code of Criminal Procedure, drafted in the decade before the Rule, codified the state statutory law, clearly articulating a judicial discretion of significant scope:

> The court either on the application of the prosecuting attorney or on its own motion may in its discretion for good cause order that a prosecution by indictment or information be dismissed. The order for dismissal shall be entered [of record] on the minutes with the reasons therefor.

> No prosecution by indictment or information shall be dismissed, discontinued or abandoned except as provided in this chapter. § 295 Official Draft with Commentary (June 15, 1930).

Upon the adoption of the Federal Enabling Act, a distinguished committee commissioned by the Supreme Court submitted a number of drafts for the criticism of the bench and bar. *See* Orfield, Criminal Procedure under the Federal Rules § 48:17, pp. 336–337 (1967). The Advisory Committee submitted a preliminary draft to the Supreme Court including as a predecessor to Rule 48(a) the following: "The Attorney General or the United States Attorney may file a dismissal of the indictment or information with a statement of the reasons therefor and the prosecution shall thereupon terminate." *Id.* at p. 338. Professor Orfield, a member of the original Advisory Committee and the author of a treatise on the criminal rules, tells us that in the Supreme Court's response to the Committee's draft, "[t]he court pointed out that the proposed Rule [now 48(a)] gave the Attorney General or the United States Attorney unqualified authority to nolle prosse a case without consent of the court," and inquired "Is this now the law, and should it be the law, any more than that the Government can confess error on appeal in a criminal case without consent of the court? Cit[ing] *Young v. United States*, 315 U.S. 257–259 [62 S. Ct. 510, 86 L.Ed. 832] (1942)." *Id.*

In the Young case the government confessed error on appeal but the Supreme Court took the case to examine independently the confessed error. In the opinion the court stated, "The public interest that a result be reached which promotes well-ordered society is foremost in every criminal proceeding. The interest is entrusted to our consideration and protection as well as that of the enforcing officers." 315 U.S. at 259, 62 S. Ct. at 511.

In a resubmitted draft, the Committee made no changes in this Rule despite the Reporter's suggestion that the Committee reconsider it "in the light of the suggestion of the Supreme Court and its statement in *Young v. United States*," and § 295 of the American Law Institute Code of Criminal Procedure and the law of thirty states, requiring the consent of the court. Orfield, Criminal Procedure Under the Federal Rules, § 48:17, p. 339. The Supreme Court deleted the phrase "with a statement of the reasons therefor," and, in lieu thereof, inserted the phrase "by leave of court." *Id.* at 48:19, p. 343. As thus amended, 48(a) was submitted to Congress and adopted. It seems manifest that the Supreme Court intended to make a significant change in the common law rule by vesting in the courts the power and the duty to exercise a discretion for the protection of the public interest. The early case law interpreting the Rule supports this theory.

* * *

This brings us pointedly to an accommodation of the intended scope of the Rule and the sweep of the Constitution. Chief Justice Burger (then Judge of the District of Columbia Circuit) put our problem in proper perspective when he observed:

> Few subjects are less adapted to judicial review than the exercise by the Executive of his discretion in deciding when and whether to institute criminal proceedings, or what precise charge shall be made, or whether to dismiss a proceeding once brought. *Newman v. United States, supra* at 480.

* * *

Surely, we should approach our task with the humility which characterizes the proper exercise of all power.

It seems to us that the history of the Rule belies the notion that its only scope and purpose is the protection of the defendant. The Supreme Court's deliberate insertion of the phrase "by leave of court," the phrase itself denoting judicial choice, must be taken in the context of the Court's contemporaneous *Young* decision and the state modifications of the common law as codified by the American Law Institute. Viewed in this light, we think it manifestly clear that the Supreme Court intended to clothe the federal courts with a discretion broad enough to protect the public interest in the fair administration of criminal justice. It is against this background that we consider the overpowering effect of the Doctrine of Separation of Powers. . . .

* * *

We think the rule should and can be construed to preserve the essential judicial function of protecting the public interest in the evenhanded administration of criminal justice without encroaching on the primary duty of the Executive to take care that the laws are faithfully executed. The resulting balance of power is precisely what the Framers intended. As Judge Wisdom put it, quoting Montesquieu, "'To prevent the abuse of power, it is necessary that by the very disposition of things, power should be a check to power' . . . [thus] the framers wove a web of checks and balances designed to prevent abuse of power" and "were too sophisticated to believe that the three branches of government were absolutely separate, air-tight departments." *United States v. Cox, supra* at 190. From this, it seems altogether proper to say that the phrase "by leave of court" in Rule 48(a) was intended to modify and condition the absolute power of the Executive, consistently with the Framer's concept of Separation of Powers, by erecting a check on the abuse of Executive prerogatives. But this is not to say that the Rule was intended to confer on the Judiciary the power and authority to usurp or interfere with the good faith exercise of the Executive power to take care that the laws are faithfully executed. The rule was not promulgated to shift absolute power from the Executive to the Judicial Branch. Rather, it was intended as a power to check power. The Executive remains the absolute judge of whether a prosecution should be initiated and the first and presumptively the best judge of whether a pending prosecution should be terminated. The exercise of its discretion with respect to the termination of pending prosecutions should not be judicially disturbed unless clearly contrary to manifest public interest. In this way, the essential function of each branch is synchronized to achieve a balance that serves both practical and constitutional values.

Judging this case by these standards in the light of the Rule's history and constitutional context, we are convinced that the trial court exceeded the authority committed to it under the Rule.

Judge Hill was "unable to perceive how the best interest of justice could be served by dismissing serious charges with a potential penalty of thirty-five years imprisonment and a $70,000 fine in exchange for a guilty plea in an unrelated case carrying a maximum penalty of two years and a $10,000 fine." He also referred to the fact that "the investigatory material developed by [Texas] state and federal agencies was turned over to the federal officials with the understanding that the federal government would initiate and pursue appropriate prosecution"; that the government's "bare assertion" of reasons for dismissal was unaccompanied by factual evidence. In these circumstances, he concluded, "the interest of justice would not be served by a dismissal of this case." The brief of the court-appointed prosecutors seems to impugn the good faith of the government by suggesting that the motion to continue the trial, filed jointly by the prosecution and both defendants in June 1974, was calculated to facilitate the surreptitious performance of the plea agreement negotiated one month earlier between Jacobsen and the Watergate Special Prosecution Force, and thus dispense with the trial of the Texas case.

We think this appraisal of the whole matter misapprehends the relative roles of the Executive and the Judiciary under 48(a). The considerations which prompted Judge Hill to overrule the motion to dismiss are . . . legally insufficient to overcome the presumption of the government's good faith and establish its betrayal of the public interest. We do not think the plea negotiations between the two prosecutorial arms of the government and counsel for both defendants were improper, even though not disclosed to the sentencing judges until consummation. It is not suggested that the facts recited in the joint motion for continuance were untrue, or that they were inadequate grounds for a continuance. In this situation, we can hardly say that the motion was a sham or a deception. It was not incumbent upon the government to inform the sentencing judges of the plea negotiations until after they had been consummated. The result of these negotiations was finally placed before both sentencing courts in the form of plea agreements, which themselves have a legitimate and desirable function in the effective administration of criminal justice. . . . Nor was it clearly contrary to the public interest for the government to accept in these plea agreements a reduction in the maximum possible sentence of Cowan and Jacobsen, when, as stated in the government's motion, it served to further an investigation by an especially created and wholly autonomous arm of the Executive. We cannot agree with Judge Hill's view that this motion lacked specificity of evidentiary proof. The representations in the motion and the supporting memorandum were not merely conclusory; they specified the investigation being pursued in the District of Columbia and the necessity of obtaining Jacobsen's cooperation under the plea agreement calling for dismissal of the Texas charges. We are convinced that this is legally sufficient to justify leave of court to dismiss the Texas charges against Jacobsen in consideration of his guilty plea in the District of Columbia.

In sum, it was within the province of the two prosecutorial arms of the government to weigh the relative importance of two separate prosecutions in two separate districts and dispose of them as practical considerations seemed to dictate. Nothing in this record overcomes the presumption that they did so in good faith for substantial reasons sufficiently articulated in the motion to dismiss. . . .

Having concluded that the trial court exceeded the bounds of its discretion under Rule 48(a) in denying the government's motion to dismiss, we have no cause to consider the propriety of its order effectuating that denial by appointing special prosecutors. The case is reversed and remanded with directions to sustain the motion to dismiss.

Notes

1. How much weight should a court give to the victim in determining whether to grant a motion to dismiss? Is the interest of the victim part of the public interest? A rare case in which a district court denied a motion to dismiss based on victim-related concerns is *United States v. Biddings*, 416 F. Supp. 673 (D. Ill. 1976). There, the trial judge explicitly distinguished *Cowan*, explaining:

> The case at bar presents a more compelling situation for denying dismissal than in *Cowan*. The two victims of the Federal offense have not recanted and believe that the defendant Darrell Biddings is the individual who kidnaped them, drove their automobile for several miles, and finally shot them as they were fleeing. They have no reason to be prejudiced against this defendant or to favor Larry Edwards. Also, the victims of the holdup in the restaurant which immediately preceded the kidnaping and theft of the second automobile are generally in agreement that Biddings and not Edwards committed

this offense, yet the Illinois authorities have indicated to the United States Attorney that they will not prosecute for the holdup. Thus the court is presented with a situation where several serious crimes have been committed by one or more individuals, one of whom has been convicted on positive and corroborated eye-witness identifications, and whose alibi defense has been rejected by a jury. Juxtaposed to these circumstances is the accusation, by two girls who are friendly with the defendant Biddings, of a man who is now serving two life terms in the Indiana penitentiary.

We believe that it would delegate to the prosecutor the right to decide between conflicting evidence and make a mockery of the grand jury system and of the law of identification if this indictment is abandoned under these circumstances. *See United States v. Telfaire*, 152 U.S.App. D.C. 146, 469 F.2d 552, 558 (1972); *United States v. Hodges*, 515 F.2d 650 (7th Cir. 1975). The manifest public interest, represented by several unrecanting victims, requires a trial to vindicate them or the defendant, as alternatively requested by his attorney.

At the time of original trial we commented that the only offenses for which Biddings was indicted were the kidnapping and the interstate transportation of a stolen vehicle. The proof of the robbery of the restaurant was ancillary to this charge and was merely to fortify kidnapping the government's belief that the same person committed both offenses. This may very well have been the case, but on the other hand the indictment can be tried without any testimony from the witnesses at the restaurant robbery. This is not to say that the defendant will not bring this out, but if he does so, he will then be confronted with several additional unimpeached eyewitnesses who presumably will identify him as the culprit.

The motions to dismiss are denied.

2. A court may refuse to dismiss a case pursuant to Rule 48(a) where the prosecutor's motion to dismiss is motivated by considerations clearly contrary to the public interest. *See Rinaldi v. United States*, 434 U.S. 22 (1977). Examples of motivations that could support a finding of bad faith include "the prosecutor's acceptance of a bribe, personal dislike of the victim, and dissatisfaction with the jury impaneled." *Rice v. Rivera*, 617 F.3d 802, 811 (4th Cir. 2010).

———————

To what extent should the government be required to explain its motion to dismiss, particularly where a victim's interests are involved?

United States v. Heaton

458 F. Supp. 2d 1271 (D. Utah 2006)

CASSELL, District Judge.

On January 4, 2006, the United States charged defendant Aaron Anthony Heaton with the Class C felony of using a means of interstate commerce to entice an individual under the age of 18 to engage in unlawful sexual activity. On October 6, 2006, the government filed a motion for leave to dismiss that charge without prejudice pursuant to Rule 48(a) of the Federal Rules of Criminal Procedure. The motion is only one sentence long — this one sentence both makes the motion and avers only that the dismissal is "in the interest of justice."

It may well be that dismissal of this charge is appropriate. Rule 48(a), however, provides that dismissal must be "with leave of court." The purpose of this leave-of-court requirement is to allow the court to review the grounds for the dismissal. Usually, of course, the court will approve a government motion to dismiss, as "a court is generally required to grant a prosecutor's Rule 48(a) motion to dismiss unless dismissal is clearly contrary to manifest public interest." But even though the standard is a deferential one, the court must make its own independent determination that dismissal is warranted. A mere conclusory statement from the government that dismissal is appropriate does not allow the court to satisfy its obligations.

There is a particular need to examine the reasons for dismissal in this case to ensure that the crime victim's rights are fully protected. The indictment alleges a sexual offense against a young victim. Under the Crime Victims' Rights Act (CVRA), this victim has the broad right "to be treated with fairness and with respect for [her] dignity and privacy."

This victim's right to fairness extends to the court's decision regarding whether to dismiss an indictment even though no public proceeding will be held on the issue. Although some of the other rights in the Crime Victims' Rights Act (such as the right to be heard and the right to not be excluded) are limited to "public proceedings," the right to fairness is not so restricted. Under the conventional rules of statutory construction, where the legislature has used a limiting term in one part of a statute but left it out of others, the court should not imply the term where it has been excluded. Therefore, the crime victims' right to be treated with fairness and dignity applies not only to public court proceedings but more broadly to all aspects of the criminal justice system — including the court's decision whether to grant the government's motion to dismiss.

This interpretation of the Act is fully consistent with the legislative history. Congress plainly intended to give victims broad rights to fair treatment. As Senator Kyl, one of the chief sponsors of the Crime Victims' Rights Act explained,

> The broad rights articulated in this section are meant to be rights themselves and are not intended to just be aspirational. One of these rights is the right to be treated with fairness. Of course, fairness includes the notion of due process. . . . This provision is intended to direct government agencies and employees, whether they are in executive or judicial branches, to treat victims of crime with the respect they deserve and to afford them due process.

When the government files a motion to dismiss criminal charges that involve a specific victim, the only way to protect the victim's right to be treated fairly and with respect for her dignity is to consider the victim's views on the dismissal. It is hard to begin to understand how a victim would be treated with fairness if the court acted precipitously to approve dismissal of a case without even troubling to consider the victim's views. To treat a person with "fairness" is generally understood as treating them "justly" and "equitably". A victim is not treated justly and equitably if her views are not even before the court. Likewise, to grant the motion without knowing what the victim thought would be a plain affront to the victim's dignity. Indeed, even the pre-CVRA case law recognized a dismissal to be "clearly contrary to the public interest" if the prosecutor appeared to be motivated to dismiss by animus toward the victim. *In re Richards,* 213 F.3d at 787; *see also United States v. Hamm,* 659 F.2d 624, 629–30 (5th Cir. 1981). The court cannot make a fully informed decision about whether the prosecutor is acting out of animus to a victim without having the victim's views on the subject.

To be sure, the CVRA also provides that it shall not be construed "to impair the prosecutorial discretion of the Attorney General. . . ." 18 U.S.C. § 3771(d)(6). But executive discretion is not impaired when, after a prosecutor has determined to file a motion to dismiss, the court considers a victim's views in aid of *its* determination whether to grant such a motion.

For all these reasons, before granting any motion by the government under Rule 48(a) to dismiss charges involving a specific victim, the court must have the victim's views on the motion. The CVRA provides a convenient mechanism for this to happen. The Act guarantees victims the "reasonable right to confer with the attorney for the Government in the case." This right is not limited to particular proceedings—it is "intended to be expansive," and thus applies broadly to "any critical stage or disposition of the case." Therefore, in passing on any government motion under Rule 48(a) in any victim-related case, the court will expect to see the prosecutor recount that the victim has been consulted on the dismissal and what the victim's views were on the matter.

Accordingly, in this case, so that the court can discharge its obligations under Rule 48(a), the government is directed to provide a basis for its motion within 14 days of the date of this order. This pleading shall also recount the victim's views on the dismissal. If appropriate, this pleading can be filed under seal.

Note

By requiring the prosecutor to represent to the court that the victim had been consulted, this district court judge took an expansive view of the Crime Victim's Rights Act. Was the judge reading too much into the CVRA? *Cf. United States v. Holland,* 380 F. Supp. 2d 1264, 1279 (N.D. Ala. 2005) (mem.) (calling the CVRA "the new, mushy, 'feel good statute'").

4. Outright Pretrial Dismissal on the Motion of the Court or Defendant

Unlike Federal Rule 48, which does not allow for dismissal in the interests of justice on the court's own motion, many states allow a judge to dismiss a case in the interests of justice on the court's own motion over the objection of the prosecuting attorney. How should such motions be decided when a victim's issues are implicated?

State v. Busch
669 N.E.2d 1125 (Ohio 1996)

PFEIFER, Justice.

We hold that a trial court has the discretion to *sua sponte* dismiss a criminal case over the objection of the prosecution where the complaining witness does not wish for the case to proceed.

We need look no further than Crim.R. 48(B) for authority for trial judges to dismiss criminal actions *sua sponte*. The rule reads:

> "*Dismissal by the court.* If the court over objection of the state dismisses an indictment, information, or complaint, it shall state on the record its findings of fact and reasons for the dismissal."

Crim.R. 48(B) recognizes by implication that trial judges may *sua sponte* dismiss a criminal action over the objection of the prosecution, since the rule sets forth the trial court's procedure for doing so. The rule does not limit the reasons for which a trial judge might dismiss a case, and we are convinced that a judge may dismiss a case pursuant to Crim.R. 48(B) if a dismissal serves the interests of justice.

Trial judges are at the front lines of the administration of justice in our judicial system, dealing with the realities and practicalities of managing a caseload and responding to the rights and interests of the prosecution, the accused, and victims. A court has the "inherent power to regulate the practice before it and protect the integrity of its proceedings." *Royal Indemn. Co. v. J.C. Penney Co.* (1986), 27 Ohio St.3d 31, 33–34, 27 OBR 447, 449, 501 N.E.2d 617, 620. Trial courts deserve the discretion to be able to craft a solution that works in a given case. Certainly a court's resources in a domestic violence case are better used by encouraging a couple to receive counseling and ultimately issuing a dismissal than by going forward with a trial and impaneling a jury in a case where the only witness refuses to testify.

We do not suggest that in every domestic violence case where the victim refuses to testify a trial judge has the unfettered power to dismiss the case. The seriousness of the injuries, the presence of independent witnesses, the status of counseling efforts, whether the complainant's refusal to testify is coerced, and whether the defendant is a first-time offender are all factors a trial judge should consider, and factors that a reviewing court may consider in determining whether the trial court abused its discretion.

In this case, the trial judge did not abuse his discretion in dismissing the charges. Although Cordiano's injuries were relatively serious, Busch had not physically abused her before or after the incidents at issue. The record is devoid of evidence other than Cordiano's testimony that might prove a case against Busch. The trial court methodically over a period of at least a month determined that Cordiano was not being coerced and truly did not wish to testify. The court had her August 5, 1994 affidavit to that effect. She so testified under oath in a pretrial, on two other occasions when the trial was continued, and finally on the day when the charges were dismissed. The trial judge made sure the couple was in counseling, that Cordiano wanted to see the charges dropped, and that she was not being coerced. The trial court knew that Cordiano had spoken with prosecutors and a representative of the prosecutor's witness assistance program. Cordiano also testified that she did not fear a flare-up in Busch's behavior.

An abuse of discretion implies that the trial court's attitude, as evidenced by its decision, was unreasonable, arbitrary, or unconscionable. *State v. Jenkins* (1984), 15 Ohio St.3d 164, 222, 15 OBR 311, 361, 473 N.E.2d 264, 313. The trial court in this case handled the case well. It was not until Cordiano had testified on several occasions that the trial court finally dismissed the charges. Until that point, the court used a possible dismissal as an incentive for the couple to continue in counseling.

In this case, the trial court used its judicial power to do its best with a matter which no longer seemed to fit the court system. Trial judges have the discretion to determine when the court has ceased to be useful in a given case. The trial judge made a permissible determination here.

Accordingly, we reverse the judgment of the court of appeals.

Judgment reversed.

MOYER, C.J., and RESNICK and FRANCIS E. SWEENEY, Sr., JJ., concur.

STRATTON, Justice, concurring.

While I agree that the facts in this case justify the trial court's decision to dismiss on the basis of the court's discretion, that discretion should be cautiously exercised in domestic violence cases, in particular, when the motion is predicated on the victims' unwillingness to testify against their abusers.

In cases of domestic abuse, victims of battering often try to escape from their abusive partners, only to return once the immediate shock of the attack has receded or when the abusers "repent" and promise to change their behavior. All too frequently, these tragedies play out in the courts, as battered victims initially agree to testify against their abusers, only to drop the charges once the victims have convinced themselves that the abusive behavior was a passing aberration. Often, the victims have no income, nowhere to go, young children to consider, and may truly love their partners and believe that the future holds hope. Sometimes, if victims continue to press charges, they are further threatened by their abusers and drop the charges out of fear. Both police and trial courts are frequently frustrated by dealing initially with a distraught and injured victim who shows up weeks later to abruptly drop all charges.

In this case, the trial court exercised careful discretion, continued the case several times to be sure the pattern did not recur and that counseling continued, gave the victim time to think, and carefully questioned her motives in dropping the charges. Therefore, the judge did not abuse his discretion in dismissing the charges.

However, there may clearly be times that the prosecution should be permitted to move forward despite the victims' objections, especially when a pattern of abuse continues and all the pressures previously mentioned weaken the victims' resolve to pursue their abusers, or if the victims fear even greater retaliation if the case is pursued by the victims themselves. Society would never tolerate such assaults against total strangers. Such conduct should not be excusable or somehow less egregious because one is in a marriage or partnership. In these circumstances, the court must provide the forum to call abusers to account for their actions.

COOK, Justice, dissenting.

Because a criminal case is a controversy between the defendant and the state, a court errs in dismissing a criminal complaint over the objection of the state, solely to accommodate the wishes of a complaining witness.

Cordiano's lack of interest in and opposition to the prosecution of Busch are of no moment. The state of Ohio is the complaining party in this case. Cordiano is, at most, a potential witness for the real party. Although the majority suggests that the prosecution in this case could not proceed without Cordiano's testimony, we do not know that from the record on appeal. The trial judge made no such finding. Moreover, there is no apparent reason why Cordiano could not be compelled to testify against her boyfriend.

The majority construes Crim.R. 48(B) to permit dismissal of a criminal case whenever the "dismissal serves the interests of justice." The "interests of justice" in the criminal law discipline are punishment and deterrence of criminal behavior. This may well be different from the sociological or theological "interests of justice" that appear to have motivated the trial court here and in turn the majority of this court. *See Dayton v. Thomas* (App.1980), 17 O.O.3d 255, 256–257. "Courts do not assume the authority of enforcing the precepts of mere morality, nor is it their function to declare the law of social ethics." *Id.,* 17 O.O.3d at 256, citing *State v. Baxter* (1914), 89 Ohio St. 269, 283, 104 N.E. 331, 335. The time to consider facts that occurred outside the crime is in sentencing. *Thomas, supra,* 17 O.O.3d at 257.

The majority concludes that since Crim.R. 48(B) does not limit the reasons that a trial judge might dismiss a case, it thereby grants broad discretion bounded only by serving the "interests of justice." I respectfully disagree. Crim.R. 48(B) is procedural, not substantive. "[T]he rule does not alter the pre-rule Ohio practice concerning the court's inherent power to dismiss." *State v. Sutton* (1979), 64 Ohio App.2d 105, 108, 18 O.O.3d 83, 85, 411 N.E.2d 818, 821. In fact, the rule requires the court to specify the reason for dismissal so that it may be reviewed for its validity.

A survey of recent cases confirms that courts have properly exercised inherent power to dismiss cases over the objection of the state for (1) want of prosecution, (2) regulation of the practice before the court, such as dismissal for prosecutorial misconduct, and (3) preservation of the defendant's statutory and constitutional rights, including speedy trial and double jeopardy issues. *See, e.g., State v. Hancock* (1990), 67 Ohio App.3d 328, 586 N.E.2d 1192; *Sutton, supra; State v. Long* (May 8, 1979), Jefferson App. No. 1290, unreported.

The case found to be in conflict with the instant case, *Cleveland v. Hall* (Mar. 10, 1983), Cuyahoga App. No. 45179, unreported, 1983 WL 5829, states that it is improper for a trial court to dismiss the complaint just because the complaining witness changes her mind. In *Dayton v. Thomas, supra,* the appellate court similarly found that "[w]hen the trial judge sustained defense counsel's motion for dismissal simply because the prosecuting witness did not wish to proceed, he deprived the State of Ohio [of] its right to a fair trial." *Id.,* 17 O.O.3d at 257.

The "inherent powers" rationale of the majority fails to bolster its position. To dismiss a complaint is not, as the majority states, within the purview of "'regulat[ing] the practice before [a court] and protect[ing] the integrity of its proceedings.'" As the court in *Thomas* posited, "inherent powers" has not been applied independently of the judicial process—that is, as a factor not connected with determining or expediting the determination of judicial controversies. *Id.* Courts do not have inherent power to reject the judicial process as a means of determining controversies, over the objection of a party to a case. *Id.*

I therefore respectfully dissent. I would affirm and hold that a trial court lacks authority to dismiss charges solely to assuage the complaining witness.

Notes

1. In a later case in Ohio, applying *Busch,* the Ohio Court of Appeals reversed a trial court's dismissal of a domestic violence case:

> In the present case, the municipal court dismissed the domestic violence charge pending against Heard without considering several of the above-mentioned factors [for *Busch*]. While the court heard from Heard's husband about the events that took place on the evening of February 16, 2016, the court did not hear from T.A., the victim of the alleged crime, from Sergeant Cravens, the complainant and investigator of the alleged crime, or the state, the prosecutors of the crime.[1] As this court recently recognized, "a Crim.R. 48(B) 'interests of justice' dismissal necessarily involves a consideration of the safety and well-being of the child victims." *Murray,* 2016-Ohio-7364, 2016 WL 6069067 at ¶ 15. Where the domestic violence offense involves a child-victim, the court should receive input from the child as to the events that transpired and led to the charges and should consider the safety and well-being of the child. Here, there is nothing in the record to suggest that the municipal court gave any consideration to the child-victim's perspective of the events, to whether the child-victim had been exposed to such harm in the past, to the risk the child-victim faced to further exposure of such harm, or to whether Heard had participated in counseling or some

other form of therapeutic intervention to mitigate any continued risk of harm to T.A. or others living in her home. As the municipal court did not receive any input from the victim, the complainant, or the state and further failed to consider the factors set forth in *Busch*, we find that the municipal court abused its discretion in dismissing Heard's domestic violence charge based upon the specific facts of this case.

State v. Heard, 80 N.E.3d 1062, 1064–65 (Ohio Ct. App. 2017).

2. Applying *Busch*, another Ohio Court of Appeals ruling reversed the dismissal of a child endangerment charge, explaining that an "interests of justice" dismissal necessarily involves a consideration of the safety and well-being of the child victims. A trial judge should consider the "degree of danger the defendant's conduct presented to the child victims, the risk to the child victims of further exposure to danger, and whether the defendant has engaged in efforts to mitigate any continued risk to the safety of the child victims." *State v. Murray*, 2016-Ohio-7364, ¶ 15 (Ohio Ct. App. 2016).

3. No jurisdiction allows a victim to formally make a motion for dismissal. Because victims do not have standing to move for dismissal, they must convince a formal party to move to dismiss.

4. Standing issues aside, are there policy reasons why a victim should or should not be allowed to make a motion for dismissal in furtherance of justice?

5. Should judges have no discretion to dismiss domestic violence cases?

———————

B. Victim Participation in Plea Bargains

1. Background

In 1976, it was noted that it was unusual for victims to be informed of or consulted about plea bargains. William F. McDonald, *Towards a Bicentennial Revolution in Criminal Justice: The Return of the Victim*, 13 AMER. CRIM. L. REV. 649, 663 (1976). In 1982, Professor Abraham Goldstein suggested that victims be allowed to consult with prosecutors and have standing to address the court concerning plea bargains. He cited a lone New Mexico statute allowing victims to be heard in court on restitution matters concerning victim input in other jurisdictions. He stated,

> There is no bar to a victim presenting his views on these [restitution] matters to the prosecutor, provided he is given a fair opportunity to do so. But if the prosecutor decides not to listen, the question arises as to whether the victim should have the right to participate in the restitution hearing itself on the issue of damages.

Abraham Goldstein, *Defining the Role of the Victim in Criminal Prosecution*, 52 MISSISSIPPI L.J. 515, 552 (1982).

In 1987, Professor Sarah Welling identified seven state statutes as explicitly or implicitly granting the victim a right to participate in the plea bargaining process. The participation was either by conferring with the prosecutor (four states) or being heard by the court prior to acceptance of the plea (three states). Sarah Welling, *Victim Participation in Plea Bargains*, 65 WASH. U.L.Q. 301 (1987).

As time has marched on, victim involvement in plea bargaining has clearly become a common feature of American criminal justice. *See generally* Dana Pugach & Michal Tamir, *Nudging the Criminal Justice System into Listening to Crime Victims in Plea Agreements*, 28 HASTINGS WOMEN'S L.J. 45 (2017). According to one tabulation, 12 states have constitutional provisions providing a general right for victims to confer or consult with the prosecution and four states include a specific right of consultation before any disposition, all of which could include consultation regarding plea bargains. PEGGY M. TOBOLOWSKY ET AL., CRIME VICTIM RIGHTS AND REMEDIES 84 (3d ed. 2016). One state includes a specific right of consultation regarding plea negotiations for certain offenses, while eight states provide a constitutional right to be heard at important stages of the criminal justice process, which should include plea hearings. *Id.* at 84-85. Beyond constitutional provisions, about 40 states either specifically authorize or require prosecutors to consult with crime victims regarding plea negotiations or agreements, or provide a general crime victim right to confer with the prosecution (which could include plea negotiations), or both. *Id.* at 85. The upshot is that the vast majority of states have constitutional or statutory provisions that require or allow victim participation in plea bargaining. And the federal system, too, in the Crime Victims' Rights Act (CVRA), gives victims a specific right to be heard on plea bargains, as well as a general right to confer with prosecutors.

In every jurisdiction victims have the right to address the court at sentencing. The right to speak at sentencing likely gives victims the ability to address the court concerning a plea bargain. In *People v. Stringham*, 253 Cal. Rptr. 484, 206 (Cal. App. 1988), the defendant argued that a victims' right to address the court at sentencing did not include the ability to address the plea bargain. The court, ruling under statutory victims' rights dismissed the argument, opining that:

> If, as occurred here, a defendant obviates the necessity of a trial by entering a plea of guilty, matters will proceed directly to the sentencing hearing. If the victim or next of kin is dissatisfied with the plea and wishes to protest, the earliest opportunity to do so will be at that hearing. The sentencing hearing will commence with the court making the inquiry demanded by section 1200. Having no inkling of the victim's or next of kin's disgruntlement, the defendant will answer that there is no legal cause why judgment should not be pronounced. Only thereafter will the victim or next of kin have an opportunity to make the statement expressly authorized by section 1191.1. To accept defendant's argument that the court is at that point divested of its power to reject the plea bargain would consign the statement to utter ineffectuality: the court would have to listen to the statement and then ignore it, powerless to do anything based upon the statement protesting such a fait

accompli. This situation might only be aggravated if the bargain included a specified sentence, for then the victim or next of kin would not even have the satisfaction of arguing for a more severe punishment.

Plea agreements consist of two components. First, the charges to be pleaded to, and second, the sentence that is to be recommended. The laws just mentioned provide a victim with the ability to provide input toward *both* components of the plea bargain: the appropriate charge and the appropriate sentence. Even in the small minority of states not providing for a victim to confer with prosecutors or address the court, these states almost invariably have laws providing for victim input at sentencing. These laws allow the victim to communicate their view concerning the appropriate sentence for the defendant. It may be that laws allowing for victim input at sentencing implicitly include a victim's ability to be heard concerning the plea bargain. *See, e.g., People v. Stringham*, 206 Cal. App. 184, 253 Cal. Rptr. 484 (1988) (holding that a plea bargain that has been accepted by one judge be rejected by another judge following the commencement of sentencing proceedings at which a murder victim's next of kin appears and denounces the negotiated disposition).

States that have no laws specifically addressing the victim's role in plea bargains still permit victim participation in the plea bargain decision-making process to the extent permitted by the prosecutor. In states that have laws specifically providing for a prosecutor to consult with a victim, the statutes providing for prosecutor consultation with victims range from advisory to mandatory. The Michigan statute is representative of mandatory consultation requirements:

MICH. COMP. LAWS. 780.756 § 6.(3):

(3) Before finalizing any negotiation that may result in a dismissal, plea or sentence bargain, or pretrial diversion, the prosecuting attorney shall offer the victim the opportunity to consult with the prosecuting attorney to obtain the views of the victim about the disposition of the prosecution for the crime, including the victim's views about dismissal, plea or sentence negotiations, and pretrial diversion programs.

Still other states have codified the common law permissive approach:

MCKINNEY'S CONS. LAW N.Y. § 642. Criteria for fair treatment standards

Such fair treatment standards shall provide that:

1. The victim of a violent felony offense, a felony involving physical injury to the victim, a felony involving property loss or damage in excess of two hundred fifty dollars, a felony involving attempted or threatened physical injury or property loss or damage in excess of two hundred fifty dollars or a felony involving larceny against the person should be consulted by the district attorney in order to obtain the views of the victim regarding disposition of the criminal case by dismissal, plea of guilty or trial. In such a case in which the victim is a minor child, or in the case of a homicide, the district attorney should consult for such purpose with the family of the victim.

Several states require certification to the court that the prosecution has conferred with, or made reasonable efforts to confer with, the victim concerning the offer. Absent such certification, the plea cannot be accepted by the court.

2. Rationales Underlying Victim Participation in Plea Bargaining

There is significant public distrust of the plea bargain process. Participation of the victim in the process and agreement by the victim in the plea agreement serves to moderate societal distrust and provide credibility to a public skeptical of the plea agreement process.

The victim's interests in participating in the plea bargaining process are many. The fact that they are consulted and listened to provides them with respect and an acknowledgment that they are the harmed individual. This in turn may contribute to the psychological healing of the victim. The victim may have financial interests in the form of restitution or compensatory fine which need to be discussed with the prosecutor. Consultation with the prosecutor promotes the education of the victim about customary sentences for the particular crime or about particular circumstances of the defendant which may lead to a better understanding of the reasons behind the plea agreement. The victim may have a particular view of what crime and sentence are appropriate under the circumstances. Consultation with the victim may aid the prosecutor in formulating a just plea bargain. Similarly, because judges act in the public interest when they decide to accept or reject a plea bargain, the victim is an additional source of information for the court.

Sarah N. Welling, *Victim Participation in Plea Bargains*
65 Wash. U. L.Q. 301 (1987)

The Prosecution's Interest

No legitimate interests of the prosecutor would be significantly slighted by victim participation in plea bargains. The prosecutor's responsibility is to seek justice on behalf of society. Exposing the prosecutor and/or court to information from the victim should only enhance the prosecutor's ability to meet this goal. As a practical matter, though, the prosecutor may have goals other than achieving justice for society. Specifically, one goal might be the quick summary disposition of a large volume of cases. Victim participation might hinder this goal in two ways. First, prosecutors may fear that victim participation would disrupt the plea bargain hearing and render it confrontational. But empirical evidence indicates that victim participation at plea bargain hearings is not disruptive or confrontational, nor does it slow the process. Second, prosecutors might argue that victim participation will impair quick summary disposition. Prosecutors would reason that victim participation might render plea bargains more risky for and therefore less attractive to defendants. Consequently, fewer defendants would plead guilty and the system would founder under the increased demand for trials. Thus the prosecutor and even society would be disserved by victim participation.

There are several responses to this point. First, the argument assumes that victim participation renders plea bargains less attractive to the defendant. Victim participation may increase the risk to the defendant that the judge will reject the bargain, but the resolution of the case will still be fast and certain if the plea bargain is accepted. Thus plea bargains may be more risky to the defendant as a result of victim participation, but they will still retain other attractive qualities. At any rate, in one study the empirical evidence indicated that victim participation did not decrease the number of plea bargains entered and did not disrupt speedy disposition. Second, the evidence conflicts on whether reducing plea bargaining creates a corresponding decrease in the number of guilty pleas. Third, as a policy matter, the need of administrative efficiency should not determine the structure of our criminal justice system. Rather, the search for justice should determine the system's structure.

The Defendant's Interests

None of the defendant's rights is impaired by victim participation at plea bargain hearings. The victim's participation at the plea bargain hearing would not implicate the defendant's constitutional right to confront and cross-examine witnesses for two reasons. First, a guilty plea constitutes a waiver of this right. Second, the Supreme Court has held that a defendant has no confrontation or cross-examination rights at sentencing hearings. By analogy, the defendant should be denied these rights at plea bargain hearings as well.

As with prosecutors, the defendant may have interests as a practical matter outside of the exercise of particular rights. Specifically, the defendant's interest is in getting the court to accept the plea bargain. Victim participation might increase the risk to the defendant that the court would reject the plea bargain. Although acceptance of the plea bargain may be a practical interest of the defendant, the defendant has no right to have the court assess the plea bargain on less than the total amount of available information. Another interest of the defendant will be to minimize the sentence, and participation of the victim may be inimical to this interest. Again, though, the defendant has no legitimate right to be sentenced based only on partial information.

3. The Permissible Scope of Victim Participation in Plea Bargain

Once victims are allowed to participate in the plea bargain process, the question remains: to what extent may the victim participate? The victims may communicate their views to the prosecutor. The prosecutor may consider the views of the victim in determining what plea bargain to offer or whether to offer a plea bargain at all.

The ultimate decision to extend a plea offer to a defendant is made by the prosecutor, not the crime victim. Currently, the crime victim has no statutory authority in any jurisdiction to "veto" a plea offer which the prosecutor has decided to extend to the defendant.

A significant issue, addressed in the following cases, is whether a prosecutor may extend a tentative offer to a defendant contingent upon the victim's approval of the offer. In other words, is it lawful for the prosecutor to grant an individual victim, for all practical purposes, veto power over the plea agreement?

McKenzie v. Risley
842 F.2d 1525 (9th Cir. 1988)

On Sunday, December 22, 1974, approximately two and one-half weeks before McKenzie's trial [Montana State court capital murder trial] was scheduled to begin, the prosecution and defense counsel reached a tentative agreement permitting McKenzie to plead guilty to two of the charged offenses in exchange for receiving a fifty-year sentence. On the following day, counsel for McKenzie and the state met with the trial judge who reluctantly approved the proposal and set December 30 as the date to receive the plea. On the evening of December 23, the attorneys met again and defense counsel left the meeting believing that a final binding agreement had been reached. The prosecutors, on the other hand, had the impression that the plea agreement was contingent on obtaining the approval of the victim's family. That contingency was not satisfied and on December 28 the prosecution advised defense counsel that there would be no deal. The defendant later offered on the record to plead guilty as contemplated by the plea agreement, but the state objected and accordingly, no guilty plea was entered.

McKenzie contends that the principle of *United States v. Jackson*, 390 U.S. 570 (1968), applied by this court in *United States v. Stockwell*, 472 F.2d 1186 (9th Cir.), *cert. denied*, 411 U.S. 948 (1973), renders unconstitutional the imposition of a sentence of death on a defendant who would have received a prison sentence had he pled guilty. We are unpersuaded.

Jackson struck down the death penalty portion of the Federal Kidnaping Act, 18 U.S.C. § 1201(a). That statute, as construed by the Supreme Court, gave the jury discretion to sentence to death any defendant convicted of violating its provisions, but provided for a maximum sentence of life imprisonment in the event a defendant pled guilty or waived his right to a jury trial. The Court held that this statute created an unconstitutional burden on a defendant's "Fifth Amendment right not to plead guilty and . . . Sixth Amendment right to demand a jury trial," *id.* (footnote omitted), and therefore was unconstitutional because it unfairly coerced guilty pleas and jury waivers. *Id.* at 583.

McKenzie's situation is precisely the converse. He would have us hold constitutionally infirm a process that discouraged a guilty plea and jury waiver and encourage him to exercise his constitutional rights. Defendants have no constitutional right to plead guilty to lesser crimes than those charged, *see Mabry v. Johnson*, 467 U.S. 504, 507–08 & n. 5 (1984), or to avoid trial. Therefore, none of McKenzie's constitutional rights were burdened when the state refused to go through with the proposed plea agreement. Moreover, the statutory scheme under which McKenzie was convicted did not provide for differing treatment for those who pled guilty and those who exercised their right to a jury trial. In either case, the full range of sentencing options was available to the sentencing judge. *Jackson* simply does not apply.

* * *

In his final brief on rehearing, appellant argues that the trial court violated the principle of *Booth v. Maryland*, 107 S. Ct. 2529 (1987), by permitting the wishes of the victim's family "to control Duncan McKenzie's fate." Second Supplemental Brief of Appellant on Rehearing *En Banc* at 18. Although there is no evidence that the trial judge improperly considered the impact of the crime on the victim's family in making his sentence determination, McKenzie contends that merely letting the family influence the decision to bring him to trial introduced an impermissible element of arbitrariness.

The Montana state district court, like trial courts elsewhere, had no power to control the prosecutor's decision whether to plea bargain. To the extent the victim's family's wishes were given any consideration, it was in the decision to take the case to trial, not in sentencing. We see no impropriety in that.

———————

State of Oregon v. McDonnell

794 P.2d 780 (Or. 1990)

UNIS, J.

This is an automatic and direct review of a judgment of conviction of aggravated murder and sentence of death. ORS 163.150(1)(g).

Defendant was charged with the aggravated murder of Joey Deah Bouwsema Keever, whose death resulted from multiple knife wounds. Prior to trial, the Douglas County District Attorney informed defendant that he was willing to enter into a plea agreement with defendant if the victim's parents agreed. Under the proposed plea agreement, defendant would plead guilty to aggravated murder and the district attorney would not present any evidence to the jury to support a sentence of death during the penalty phase of the trial. As a consequence, defendant would receive a life sentence. *See* ORS 163.150 (*amended by* Or. Laws 1989, ch. 720, § 2). The proposed plea agreement was acceptable to defendant. It was not, however, acceptable to the victim's parents. The district attorney, therefore, decided to proceed to trial and seek a death penalty.

Defendant then moved the trial court for an order requiring the district attorney to enter into the plea agreement. . . .

* * *

[T]he record does not reveal what, if any, plea agreement the district attorney would have approved had he not conditioned his acceptance on the victim's parents' concurrence in the plea agreement. The trial court denied defendant's motion. A jury trial followed. Defendant was found guilty of aggravated murder and was sentenced to death.

* * *

The state concedes that the district attorney cannot let victims or their families play the decisive role in plea negotiations by deferring to their judgment whether a plea agreement is appropriate. The state further concedes that the district attorney's refusal to enter into the proposed plea agreement unless he had the victim's parents' concurrence was error. The state based its concession, however, under the statutes that govern a district attorney's authority to enter into a plea agreement, rather than under any constitutional provision.

* * *

The state characterizes the error which it concedes occurred in this case as having been caused by the district attorney impermissibly delegating the decision to enter into a plea agreement to the victim's parents. The state is correct that, based on the limited record before us, the district attorney improperly delegated the decision whether to enter into plea negotiations to the victim's parents. Unfortunately, the record is too limited to permit us to determine the extent of that delegation.

[T]he only evidence in this case concerning the proposed plea agreement consisted of the stipulation of the parties. Defendant objected to the trial court considering any evidence other than the parties' stipulation in ruling on his motion to require the district attorney to enter into the plea agreement. The stipulation of the parties only states that "if the parents of the alleged victim would agree to such a resolution of this case, [the district attorney] would accept a plea to the offense of aggravated murder and would decline to present any evidence to the jury during the penalty phase of the trial." The record does not show what other considerations, if any, the district attorney used in assessing the proposed plea agreement. The stipulation does not indicate, for example, whether the district attorney decided to enter into the plea agreement based on appropriate criteria but conditioned his acceptance on the victim's parents' concurrence or if the district attorney entirely delegated that decision to the victim's parents.

Only one fact is clear: the victim's parents' wishes were the controlling factor in the district attorney's decision. . . . If a district attorney decides to engage in plea negotiations, he or she must be guided by the statutory criteria and other relevant considerations involving the public's interest in an effective administration of criminal justice. The district attorney cannot delegate to others this responsibility for carrying out public policy.

This is not to say that crime victims and their families have no part in plea agreements. They potentially play an important role in the plea negotiation process. District attorneys legitimately may consult with them. *Cf. In re Collins*, 308 Or. 66, 73 n.12, 775 P.2d 312 (1989). The victim's financial interests are at stake with respect to any agreement a prosecutor may consider regarding restitution. Victims are important sources of information about the circumstances of the offense, and sometimes about the accused as well. *See generally* Welling, *Victim Participation in Plea Bargains*, 65 WASH. U. L.Q. 301 (1987); Gifford, *Meaningful Reform of Plea Bargaining: The Control of Prosecutorial Discretion*, 1983 U. ILL. L. REV. 37, 90. That is equally true in murder cases, where a victim's family may be able to provide information or insights about the victim or the defendant which assist in the district attorney's understanding of the crime or are in other ways relevant to the decision whether to negotiate a plea. The American bar Association in 1980 recommended that the "prosecuting attorney should make every effort to remain advised of the attitudes and sentiments of victims and law enforcement officials before reaching a plea agreement." As the ABA commentary explains:

> The victim is all too often the forgotten person in the plea negotiation process. In some jurisdictions, the victim may not even be informed of the disposition of the case which was based upon the violation of his or her rights as a citizen. Victims who are shut out of the disposition process in this manner may develop a cynical attitude toward the criminal justice system and may become reluctant to cooperate with law enforcement officers in the future. In order to prevent these feelings, it is important that the prosecutor make every effort to contact the victim to listen to the victim's views, and to explain the plea negotiation process to the victim.
>
> * * *
>
> Of course, the prosecutor is not bound to act in accordance with the suggestions or feelings of victims. . . . The duty of the prosecutor is to act in the best interests of society at large, and numerous factors normally must be considered in addition to the views of victims. . . .

It is one thing, however, for a district attorney to consult with a victim or a victim's family for purposes of gaining information that may bear on factors relevant to an assessment of whether a plea agreement will serve the public's interest in "the effective administration of criminal justice." ORS 135.405(1). It is another to permit the victims or their families to control the plea agreement decision.

Given our conclusion that, based on the limited record in this case, the district attorney committed error, we next address the appropriate remedy. Defendant contends that the district attorney should be directed to accept the plea agreement.

Where a district attorney's exercise of judgment or discretion not to enter into a plea agreement is set aside because it rested wholly on improper considerations, the remedy is for the district attorney to make a new decision based solely on proper criteria and upon the facts that existed when the plea agreement was contemplated. This result follows unless the record demonstrates what that decision would be. Here, as indicated above, the record in this case does not establish what the then district attorney's independent decision was or would have been. We, therefore, vacate the judgment and remand the case to the trial court for an evidentiary hearing to determine how the prosecutor would have exercised his judgment and discretion on the basis of proper criteria and the facts that existed at the time he declined to enter into the plea agreement. If, after hearing the evidence, the trial court finds that the district attorney would have reached the same decision to proceed with the prosecution of the accused on proper grounds, then the judgment of conviction and sentence of death shall be reinstated and an appeal therefrom may proceed. If, however, the trial court finds that the prosecutor would have accepted the negotiated plea, then, as the state concedes, the defendant shall be permitted to enter a plea of guilty to the crime of aggravated murder and the trial court shall sentence him to life imprisonment. If after an evidentiary hearing defendant is permitted by the trial court to enter a plea of guilty to the crime of aggravated murder and does not do so, the judgment should be reinstated and an appeal therefrom may proceed.

The judgment of the Douglas County Circuit Court is vacated, and the case is remanded to that court with instructions.

Notes

1. The few courts that have ruled on the issue of prosecutors granting victims a "veto" over the plea bargain split along the lines of the *McDonnell* and *McKenzie* cases. The broader question of whether victims should, as a matter of policy, have "veto" power is discussed below.

2. Can it ever be in the interest of society to allow the victim to determine whether a plea bargain is appropriate? If so, is the prosecutor acting in the interests of society when she allows the victim to "veto" the deal? What is the interest of society in preventing a victim from having the authority to veto a plea bargain?

3. In the *McDonnell* case, above, the Oregon Attorney General conceded "that the district attorney cannot let the victims play the decisive role in plea negotiations." Are the state's interests different and distinct from the victim's interest?

4. The *McDonnell* and *McKenzie* cases explore victim involvement *before* a prosecutor extends a plea. Of course, if a prosecutor extends a plea and the defendant accepts, reliance interests may arguably exist on the part of the defendant that, in some jurisdictions, would make it difficult to unwind the plea. *See State v. Means*, 926 A.2d 328, 335 (N.J. 2007) (holding that a unilateral mistake made by the prosecutor in failing to consult with a victim did not, standing alone, constitute sufficient reasons to invalidate a plea agreement).

4. The Court's Role in Accepting or Rejecting a Plea Agreement

A trial court judge generally has the discretion to accept or reject a plea bargain. If the court rejects the plea bargain, the case is typically resolved by trial.

The federal trial courts' role in accepting or rejecting a plea bargain is defined by Federal Rule of Criminal Procedure 11. The federal courts have broad discretion to accept or reject plea agreements.

United States v. Bean

564 F.2d 700 (5th Cir. 1977)

AINSWORTH, Circuit Judge:

On this appeal, defendant Bean raises [the] two contention[s]: (1) that the district court abused its discretion in refusing to accept a plea bargain entered into by the prosecutor, the defendant and his attorney; . . .

Bean was charged on October 22, 1976 with theft of property whose value exceeded $100 in violation of 18 U.S.C. § 661 and with burglary of a habitation in violation of V.T.C.A., Penal Code § 30.02. . . .

On November 30 a rearraignment was held at the defendant's request. At this time the court was informed that a plea bargain had been reached between the government prosecutor, the defendant and his counsel. Bean would plead guilty to the theft count and cooperate with the prosecutor in investigating others involved in the burglary. In return the prosecutor would move for a dismissal of the second count — the burglary count. Judge Spears indicated that he was reluctant to accept the plea because the offense of entering a home at night where people were sleeping was a much more serious offense than the theft of an automobile. The theft count carried a maximum sentence of five years whereas the burglary count carried a sentence of between five and ninety-nine years. Bean was allowed to plead guilty to the first count with the understanding that if the plea bargain was ultimately rejected by the court he would be permitted to withdraw his plea. After further consideration Judge Spears notified the parties that he would not accept the plea bargain. On December 12, 1976, Bean was permitted to withdraw his guilty plea.

Defendant's attorney then filed a motion objecting to the denial of the plea bargain. The district court denied the motion, stating that the bargain was "contrary to the manifest public interest." . . .

Bean was tried by a jury and convicted on both counts. The trial judge sentenced Bean to serve five years on Count 1 and ten years on Count 2 with the sentences to run concurrently. . . .

An analysis of the propriety of refusing a plea bargain begins with Rule 11 of the Federal Rules of Criminal Procedure. As enacted in 1966, this Rule attempted to codify existing practices concerning the entry of a plea at arraignment. As plea bargaining became more common in response to the growing caseloads of the courts, the 1974 amendments to the Rule gave explicit recognition to the practice. Rule 11(e) provides a mechanism for sanctioning discussions between the defendant and the prosecutor and for presenting the agreement in open court for approval by the judge.

While Rule 11(e) provided guidelines for plea bargaining procedure, the Rule does not contravene a judge's discretion to reject such a plea. The Rule itself states that "the court may accept or reject the agreement. . . ." Fed.R.Crim.P. 11(e)(2). Indeed, the judge must refuse the plea in the absence of a factual basis for the plea. *See* Fed.R.Crim.P. 11(f). The drafters of the Rule intended for the judge to retain discretion in accepting plea bargains. The Notes of the Committee on the Judiciary, House Report No. 94-247, state: "The procedure is not mandatory; a court is free not to permit the parties to present plea agreements to it." 18 U.S.C.A., Federal Rules of Criminal Procedure; Rules 10 to 17.1, at 17. . . .

The plea agreement procedure does not attempt to define criteria for the acceptance or rejection of a plea agreement. Such a decision is left to the discretion of the individual judge. *Id.* at 26. Those cases that have previously considered courts' refusals to accept plea bargains have found that the judge has discretion in accepting pleas. . . .

While appellate courts have reviewed the refusals of plea bargains, little attention has been given to the formulation of a standard for the district court's exercise of discretion. . . .

In considering plea bargains, courts may be governed by the same broad standards that apply in sentencing. The trial court's control over the length of sentence is analogous to that in plea bargains since in plea bargaining the defendant is ultimately concerned with the duration of imprisonment. Even when the agreement relates to the dismissal of some of the charges, the primary effect is to limit the punishment which the court may impose. *See* Alschuler, *The Trial Judge's Role in Plea Bargaining, Part I*, 76 COLUM. L. REV. 1059, 1074 (1976). Consistently, this circuit, as well as other circuits, has permitted the decision of the trial court as to sentencing to prevail except in extreme circumstances. A sentencing court exercises broad discretion which is not subject to appellate review "except when arbitrary or capricious action amounting to a gross abuse of discretion is involved." *United States v. Weiner*, 5 Cir., 1969, 418 F.2d 849. *United States v. Gamboa*, 5 Cir., 1976, 543 F.2d 545, 546. *See also United States v. Bernstein*, 5 Cir., 1977, 546 F.2d 109, 110 (district judge's sentence upheld in the absence of "gross or outrageous abuse of sentencing"). Such abuse of discretion has usually been found when the sentencing decision jeopardizes a constitutional right, such as the right to an appeal or to a jury trial, or contains an error of statutory procedure. *See* U. CIN. L. REV. 195, 197–98 (1972).

As Rule 11 provides for plea bargains including the dismissal of charges as well as recommendations of length of sentences, another possible analogy is found in Federal Rule of Criminal Procedure 48(a), which pertains to the dismissal of indictments by the Attorney General or the United States Attorney. Traditionally, prosecutors were able to dismiss indictments at any time. *See United States v. Cowan*, 5 Cir., 1975, 524 F.2d 504, 505. While Rule 48(a) requires leave of court to grant a dismissal, appellate review of these refusals has been more stringent than review of sentencing. However, since the counts dismissed pursuant to plea bargains often carry heavier penalties than the counts for which a guilty plea is entered, a plea bargain to dismiss charges is an indirect effort to limit the sentencing power of the judge. *See* Alschuler, *supra* at 1074, 1136–37. Because the judge's discretion over the duration of imprisonment is being limited, the standard for review of refusal of plea bargains should be closer to the standards for review of sentencing than for review of a dismissal which does not involve a plea bargain under Rule 48(a).

Without deciding what unusual circumstances may result in the refusal of a plea bargain being an abuse of discretion, we find that Judge Spears' action in this case was well within the scope of his discretion. A decision that a plea bargain will result in the defendant's receiving too light a sentence under the circumstances of the case is a sound reason for a judge's refusing to accept the agreement. The amendment to Rule 11 does not compel a judge to impose an inappropriate sentence. *See* Hoffman, *supra* at 17. Rule 11(e)(2) explicitly states that the court "may defer its decision as to the acceptance or rejection (of the plea bargain) until there has been an opportunity to consider the presentence report." If the court did not have discretion to refuse a plea bargain because the agreement is against the public interest in giving the defendant unduly favorable terms, this provision would be largely unnecessary. Further, as we have said, the length of sentence has almost always been a matter within the discretion of the district court.

In this case, Judge Spears was faced with a man who was charged with burglarizing at night a home on Fort Sam Houston in Texas, while Lieutenant Colonel Robert W. Oppenlander, his wife, two daughters and one son were asleep inside. In addition, the presentence report indicated that Bean had previously been committed to four years in the Texas Department of Corrections for state charges of burglary and theft of a business at nighttime. Bean had also served twenty days for unlawfully carrying a weapon in San Antonio. Given this information Judge Spears was reluctant to accept a plea bargain that would allow Bean to plead guilty to only the theft of an automobile.

Thus the district judge found that the plea bargain did not provide for imposition of a sentence commensurate with the offense and the dangerous character of the offender. Although the plea bargain was cast in the form of a dismissal of the burglary count, the effect was to limit Bean's maximum sentence to five years instead of the possible maximum of ninety-nine years or life for burglary. Hence, the district judge properly exercised reasonable discretion in rejecting the plea bargain in order to impose an appropriate sentence for the defendant. . . .

Having considered all of the defendant's contentions and finding them without merit, the judgment of conviction is

AFFIRMED.

Notes

1. A majority of state courts, like the federal courts, also allow the trial judge broad discretion in rejecting a plea bargain. Most states require the court to articulate the reasons for the rejection on the record for purposes of appellate review.

2. In those jurisdictions where a victim may communicate their views on the plea bargain to the judge, a victim's disagreement with a prosecutor over a plea bargain may continue in the formal forum of the courtroom. There the victim may urge the court to reject the agreement. A judge has the inherent authority to reject a negotiated plea based upon a victim's denunciation of the plea bargain at sentencing.

3. Federal Rule of Criminal Procedure 48 prohibits judicial participation in plea bargaining. As a result, in rejecting a plea bargain, a federal trial court judge may have to "walk a fine line." *See United States v. Scott*, 877 F.3d 42 (1st Cir. 2017). Accordingly, if a trial judge believes that a proposed plea is insufficiently attentive to a crime victim's interests, the preferred course of action would be for the trial judge to simply explain that fact to the parties, not indicate some minimum level of punishment or restitution that would be appropriate. *Id.* at 48.

4. While the federal rules prohibit judicial involvement in plea bargaining, state approaches vary widely. Roughly half the states permit judicial participation in plea bargaining; the other half do not allow it. In jurisdictions where judges may not participate in plea bargaining, it *may* be that the court may not make judicial acceptance of the plea bargain contingent on the victim's acceptance. In Minnesota, a trial judge's preliminary demand that parents of the victim consent to the plea agreement before the trial judge would accept the plea bargain was held to be an invalid condition by one appellate court. In dicta, the appellate court held that the trial court would be impermissibly participating in the plea negotiation. *State v. Nelson*, 257 N.W.2d 356, 358 (Minn. 1977).

Abraham S. Goldstein, *Converging Criminal Justice Systems: Guilty Pleas and the Public Interest*
49 SMU L. Rev. 575 (1996)

* * *

A Public Trial for Especially Public Matters?

Are there circumstances when the trial court should refuse to permit a guilty plea and should, instead, insist on a public trial? The issue has taken on increasing importance because ever more cases are testing and straining public confidence in our processes of justice. Women's groups complain that pleas to lesser offenses are accepted too casually in rape cases and that wife-battering cases are not prosecuted at all. Minority groups insistently demand that allegations of police brutality be fully aired and readily voice their suspicions that disparate standards are being applied under the cover of prosecutorial discretion. Most people are convinced that white collar offenders get away with the proverbial "slap on the wrist" through the use of plea bargaining. In such highly charged contexts, should the parties be permitted to deny the public of the educative and the deterrent role that attaches to a contested and visible public trial?

It is obvious that, in many such cases, the public has a greater than ordinary interest in knowing the full facts of the case. The same is true when a crime involves a sensational public figure (either as defendant or victim). In such cases, "rumors and suspicions that there is 'more than meets the eye' abound . . . the sparse information contained in the charge and the monosyllabic guilty plea" offers too little information to ally those suspicions. Indeed, in cases like the killing of Martin Luther King or President Kennedy, or the more recent police beating of Rodney King or the killing of Yankel Rosenbaum, "more is at stake than one-to-one justice between State and accused or accused and victim. . . . Anything short of complete disclosure in such cases inflames public cynicism about our system of justice to a dangerous point." . . .

The public interest in a public trial, though rarely articulated, is implicit in the position taken everywhere that judges have virtually complete discretion to refuse a guilty plea. In exercising that discretion, judges should take into account the risk of public misunderstanding and cynicism about guilty pleas. I do not mean to suggest that a guilty plea can never satisfy the public's need for information and that all cases must go to public trial. The plea does, after all, produce a formal judgment of conviction based upon a charge of a crime, which usually recites the essential facts constituting the elements of crime. But guilty pleas, especially when reached after negotiations, too often appear to the public as the product of collusion or corruption. Some process is needed to reassure the public that due process is being rendered. If the trial judge determines that the public interest requires a public airing of the facts culminating in a criminal charge, he should do one of two things: (1) he should reject the plea and insist on the prosecution putting its witnesses on record, with the defendant either challenging those witnesses or acquiescing in what they have said; or (2) if he decides to accept a guilty plea, he should follow the English practice and require a presentation, in open court, of the testimony of the principal witnesses and such stipulations of fact as make a contested trial inappropriate.

5. Rejecting a Plea for Failure to Consult with the Victims

Should a trial judge reject a plea bargain reached by the prosecutor and the defense when the victim has not been consulted?

United States v. Stevens

239 F. Supp. 3d 417 (D. Conn. 2017)

Jeffrey Alker Meyer, United States District Judge.

This case involves the prosecution of a young man who distributed heroin that was lethally laced with fentanyl. The victim overdosed and died. The Government entered into a plea agreement with terms that were highly favorable to the defendant without first consulting about the agreement with the victim's surviving family. I will reject the plea agreement on the ground that the Government has not respected the rights and interests of the victim's family.

Background

On the night of June 3, 2016, defendant Christopher Stevens arranged by text message to distribute heroin to a man in East Lyme, Connecticut. Shortly after 1:00 a.m., local police responded to a report of a car parked with its engine running just a short distance from the man's home. Inside the car police found the man and his 3–year-old son. The man was dead in the driver's seat from an overdose of heroin that had been laced with fentanyl. His 3–year-old child was fortunately unharmed.

Law enforcement authorities later tracked the defendant down through the text messages found on the victim's phone. The defendant was arrested in July 2016, and he appeared before me more than six months later for the purpose of waiving indictment and entering a plea of guilty to a charge of distribution of heroin, in violation of 21 U.S.C. § 841(a)(1) and § 841(b)(1)(C).

At the guilty plea hearing there were no members of the victim's family present. When I inquired if the family had received notice and if they had any objection to the terms of the plea, the prosecutor seemed uncertain, explaining that he had recently assumed responsibility for this case from another prosecutor but that he believed the victim's family had received notification about the plea hearing from the victim-witness coordinator at the U.S. Attorney's Office.

I asked the prosecutor: "Are they [the family] okay with the essential terms of the plea agreement, as far as you know? Any objections or concerns?" The prosecutor replied:

> Not that I'm aware of, Your Honor. Nothing has been brought to my attention, at least at this juncture. Again, unfortunately, I did not necessarily speak, but again, our victim liaison people in our officer did not apprise me of any issues.

I asked the prosecutor whether he had personally spoken with the victim's family, and he stated that he was "kind of new to this case" and that "I personally have not spoken with the family, but through our office victim liaison as well as with the [DEA] agent, the family is apprised of the nature of proceedings and that today was scheduled for the change of plea."

Although I proceeded with the plea hearing, I made clear that I would not accept the plea of guilty until learning more about what the victim's family's views were with respect to this plea. I entered an order requesting the prosecution to "file a statement describing how it has complied with its obligations under 18 U.S.C. § 3771 [the Crime Victims' Rights Act] and whether the victim's family and/or estate concurs with the proposed terms of the plea agreement." Doc. # 46.

The Government soon filed a statement recounting that the parties had "reached and finalized a plea agreement" at some point during the week of January 9, 2017, that the Government contacted the Clerk's office on January 13, 2017, to request assignment of the case to a judge, and that the Court thereafter scheduled the plea hearing for January 18, 2017. Doc. # 47 at 1.

The Government's statement went on to describe the following concerning contacts with the mother of the victim — and most significantly disclosing for the first time that the victim's family did not agree with the terms of the plea:

> Due to the short period of time elapsing from this assignment and the scheduled date which included an overlap with the Martin Luther King holiday, the Victim Witness Coordinator for the United States Attorney's Office, who had previously been in contact with the mother of the victim in this case during the post-arrest pendency of this matter, immediately contacted the mother by telephone to advise her that a plea proceeding had been scheduled. The Coordinator advised the mother of the date and time of the hearing and offered to meet with her to discuss the expected proceedings. *When the mother was advised that the expected plea was to a charge of distribution of heroin, the mother expressed dissatisfaction that the death of her son was not charged.* She further advised the Coordinator that she did not expect to attend the scheduled plea hearing, but that she might consider attending and speaking at the sentencing hearing.

Doc. # 47 at 2 (emphasis added).

According to the Government's statement, the coordinator later contacted the victim's mother after the plea hearing to advise her of the sentencing date and offered to meet with her. The victim's mother declined to meet, stating that "the renewal of this case signified by the entry of the plea was extremely painful to her" but that "she might decide to meet at a later date." *Id.* . . .

Discussion

Victims of crime have long had an uncertain role in the criminal justice process. Some centuries ago, victims *were* the criminal justice process — if a victim was criminally wronged, it fell upon the victim to mount a private prosecution for punishment and restitution. Times changed. By the Enlightenment era, crimes were conceptually re-conceived as public wrongs to be subject to public prosecution. Victims could not necessarily be trusted to prosecute public wrongs, and victims were relegated to pursuing civil tort remedies while trusting that the state would do justice for the criminal wrongs they suffered. Over the years, as the state acquired a monopoly over a professionalized public prosecution process, victims were increasingly marginalized without a clearly defined role.[1]

By the 1980s, the pendulum began to swing back again in favor of victims, particularly as victims organized and reasserted themselves through a victims' rights movement. This in turn led to a groundswell of reforms at both the state and federal levels to confer formal protections or "rights" for victims.[2]

---

1. *See generally* DOUGLAS E. BELOOF, PAUL G. CASSELL & STEVEN J. TWIST, VICTIMS IN CRIMINAL PROCEDURE 3–11 (Carolina Acad. Press 2005).

2. *See* Paul G. Cassell, *The Victims' Rights Amendment: A Sympathetic, Clause-by-Clause Analysis*, 5 PHOENIX L. REV. 301, 303–09 (2012) (describing movement and history of statutory reforms).

In 2004, Congress consolidated and strengthened prior reform laws by means of enacting the Crime Victims' Rights Act (CVRA), 18 U.S.C. § 3771. The CVRA stemmed from a concern in part that "prosecutors and law enforcement officers too often ignored or too easily dismissed the legitimate interests of crime victims." *United States v. Turner*, 367 F.Supp.2d 319, 322 (E.D.N.Y. 2005). The legislative history of the CVRA confirms that "[v]ictims of crime often do not feel their voices are heard or that their concerns are adequately addressed in the judicial process," and that "[m]any express frustration with a judicial system that affords many rights to the accused while giving few to the victim." H.R. Rep. 108–77 at 3, 2005 U.S.C.C.A.N. 2274, 2276 (Sept. 30, 2004).

In order to recognize the interests of victims in the criminal justice process, the CVRA enumerates ten basic "rights" for the victim of a federal crime:

(1) The right to be reasonably protected from the accused.

(2) The right to reasonable, accurate, and timely notice of any public court proceeding, or any parole proceeding, involving the crime or of any release or escape of the accused.

(3) The right not to be excluded from any such public court proceeding, unless the court, after receiving clear and convincing evidence, determines that testimony by the victim would be materially altered if the victim heard other testimony at that proceeding.

(4) The right to be reasonably heard at any public proceeding in the district court involving release, plea, sentencing, or any parole proceeding.

(5) The reasonable right to confer with the attorney for the Government in the case.

(6) The right to full and timely restitution as provided in law.

(7) The right to proceedings free from unreasonable delay.

(8) The right to be treated with fairness and with respect for the victim's dignity and privacy.

(9) The right to be informed in a timely manner of any plea bargain or deferred prosecution agreement.

(10) The right to be informed of the rights under this section and the services [provided by law].

18 U.S.C. § 3771(a).

Importantly, the CVRA imposes no less than an *affirmative* obligation on judges to ensure that the victim's rights are respected: "In any court proceeding involving an offense against a crime victim, the court shall ensure that the crime victim is afforded the rights" as listed above. 18 U.S.C. § 3771(b). For the many guilty pleas and sentencings that are scheduled before me, I inquire of the Government at the outset of the proceedings whether and how it has respected the rights and interests of the victims.

An additional way that a court may respect the rights of victims is by declining to accept a guilty plea if the Government has chosen not to honor those rights in the first instance. A district court has broad discretion to reject a plea agreement in the interests of the "sound administration of justice." *See United States v. Severino*, 800 F.2d 42, 46 (2d Cir. 1986). The sound administration of justice requires not only respect for the rights and interests of criminal defendants but also respect for the rights and interests of crime victims.

That brings me to this case. As I understand the Government's submission, the prosecution did not consult with the victim's mother or family about the anticipated terms of the plea agreement before entering into the agreement with the defendant. The victim's mother learned about the plea agreement only after the fact from a victim-witness coordinator at the U.S. Attorney's Office. The victim's mother was upset that the Government decided to pursue a charge of heroin distribution but without including a charge for the death of her son.

I was told at the plea hearing that the victim's family had not objected to the plea, when in fact the victim's mother did object in her conversation with the victim witness coordinator. Did the coordinator fail to tell the prosecutor? Or did she tell the prosecutor, and this did not register with the prosecutor at the time of the plea hearing? I do not know. Either scenario suggests something less than the full attention to the views and concerns of a victim's family that the family deserved.

In any event, just as the victim's mother surmised, the Government could indeed have charged the defendant with a more serious crime of distributing narcotics that resulted in someone's death. *See* 21 U.S.C. §841(b)(1)(C); *Burrage v. United States*, 571 U.S.—, 134 S. Ct. 881, 187 (2014). Rather than charge the most serious readily provable offense, the Government agreed after negotiations with defense counsel to file a far less serious charge for simple distribution of a small amount of heroin—a charge that by its elements takes no account of the fact that the distribution of narcotics in this case resulted in the death of a victim.

Now the Government may have strong reasons for electing not to pursue the most serious of charges. For one thing, the more serious charge carries a mandatory minimum 20-year prison sentence. A reasonable prosecutor could well conclude that such a severe sentence is not warranted in the absence of evidence that the defendant intended or wanted to kill the victim, or for any other mitigating reason.

But that is not the issue at this point. The question for now is did the Government have a good or defensible reason for not speaking with the victim's family about its intentions *prior* to sealing a plea deal with the defendant? I do not think so.

For many years the United States Attorney's Office in Connecticut has had a victim-witness coordinator. The professionals who have served in that role are very dedicated and caring people who strive to do their job well. But they are not the prosecutor. They are not the decisionmaker.

The CVRA does not contemplate that prosecutors will outsource all "victim" communications to coordinators or other administrative personnel. To the contrary, among the rights guaranteed to victims by the CVRA is the "reasonable right to confer with the attorney for the Government in the case." 18 U.S.C. § 3771(a)(5).

Just what does this right to confer mean? Surely it must mean more than that a prosecutor need only answer phone calls or emails if a traumatized victim has the verve to initiate a conversation with the prosecutor about the case. Instead, the right to confer with the prosecutor should be read in light of one of the CVRA's primary purposes: to give victims a meaningful voice in the prosecution process. In my view, the CVRA's right to confer with the prosecutor requires at the least that a prosecutor take reasonable steps to consult with a victim before making a prosecution decision that a prosecutor should reasonably know will compromise the wishes and interests of the victim.

Other courts agree. The Fifth Circuit has concluded that "in passing the [CVRA], Congress made the policy decision—which we are bound to enforce—that the victims have a right to inform the plea negotiation process by conferring with prosecutors before a plea agreement is reached." *In re Dean*, 527 F.3d 391, 395 (5th Cir. 2008) (*per curiam*); *see also Jordan v. Dep't of Justice*, 173 F.Supp.3d 44, 51 (S.D.N.Y. 2016) (describing scope of the reasonable-right-to-confer-with-prosecutor under the CVRA); *Doe v. United States*, 950 F.Supp.2d 1262, 1267 (S.D. Fla. 2013) ("the court concludes that the 'reasonable right to confer . . . in the case' guaranteed by the CVRA at § 3771(a)(5) is properly read to extend to the pre-charge stage of criminal investigations and proceedings, certainly where—as here—the relevant prosecuting authority has formally accepted a case for prosecution").

The Department of Justice also agrees. Its guidelines instruct prosecutors to consult with victims if feasible *before* they seal plea deals with criminal defendants. "Prosecutors should make reasonable efforts to notify identified victims of, and consider victims' views about, prospective plea negotiations. Prosecutors should make these reasonable efforts with a goal of providing victims with a meaningful opportunity to offer their views before a plea agreement is formally reached." U.S. Department of Justice, *Attorney General Guidelines for Victim and Witness Assistance* 41 (2012), *available at* https://www.justice.gov/sites/default/files/olp/docs/ag_guidelines2012 .pdf; *see also* ABA Standards of Criminal Justice, Pleas of Guilty, Standard 14–3.1(e)— Responsibilities of the Prosecuting Attorney ("The prosecuting attorney should make every effort to remain advised of the attitudes and sentiments of victims and law enforcement officials before reaching a plea agreement."); Elliot Smith, *Comment: Is There A Pre–Charge Conferral Right in the CVRA?*, 2010 U. Chi. Legal F. 407 (2010) (arguing that the CVRA requires the prosecutor to consult with the victim prior to a plea agreement and regardless whether charges have already been filed).

There are many reasons why victims should have a voice before the prosecutor offers a plea agreement to a criminal defendant. "The fact that they are consulted and listened to provides them with respect and an acknowledgement that they are the harmed individual," and "this in turn may contribute to the psychological healing of the victim." Douglas E. Beloof, Paul G. Cassell & Steven J. Twist, Victims in Criminal Procedure 478 (Carolina Acad. Press 2005). In addition, as a practical matter, "the victim may have financial interests in the form of restitution . . . which needs to be discussed with the prosecutor" in order to be accounted for in a plea agreement. *Id.*

The victim's personal views may (or should) be important to the prosecutor in deciding what is a just resolution of the case by means of a guilty plea. This is not to say that the victim is the prosecutor's principal or "client," much less to say that the prosecutor must agree with or adopt the victim's views. After all, we have our system of public prosecution in large part because we long ago realized the shortcoming of private prosecutions: that "private justice is either too ineffective, or, conversely, *too* effective — it gives rise to feuds and leads to wholesale bloodshed," and "public prosecution is supposed to do away with private vengeance." Lawrence M. Friedman, A History of American Law 217–18 (3d ed. 2005). Although the victim has no veto over the prosecutor's choices, the choices that a prosecutor makes will be better informed if the prosecutor learns and tries to understand the perspective of the person most deeply affected by a crime.

Often enough, victims may urge the prosecutor to deal severely with defendants who have hurt them. Some victims, however, may urge leniency for reasons of mercy, compassion, or forgiveness. Whatever the views that a victim may have, the integrity of a criminal prosecution is stronger if the prosecutor learns about these views if possible before making major decisions in a case.

Prosecutors may also have important information for victims to know. Victims are not criminal justice professionals. They may automatically expect the prosecutor to "throw the book" at the defendant and seek the maximum sentence allowed by law. A prosecutor who speaks with the victim may moderate these expectations by explaining what is the customary sentence for the crime in question as well as explaining any mitigating facts that the prosecutor may have learned about the defendant and that the victim may not know.

If a dialogue between the prosecutor and a victim takes place (if at all) only after a plea agreement has been reached, the public will understandably have less confidence that a plea bargain is a just and fair resolution. And the victim will understandably have less confidence that his or her feelings and views have been heard and respected. *See* Michael M. O'Hear, *Plea Bargaining and Victims: From Consultation to Guidelines*, 91 Marq. L. Rev. 323, 326–31 (2007) (summarizing "procedural justice" benefits that accrue when prosecutors consult with victims in connection with the plea bargaining process); *see also* Bennett L. Gershman, *Prosecutorial Ethics and Victims' Rights: The Prosecutor's Duty of Neutrality*, 9 Lewis & Clark L. Rev. 559, 572–76 (2005) (discussing ethical concerns that may arise if prosecutors do not exercise judgment independent of victims).

All that said, I do not understand the CVRA to impose a categorical requirement that in every case a prosecutor personally contact and consult with every victim prior to entering into a plea agreement. There may be instances of urgency or investigative secrecy when it is not practically feasible or advisable for a prosecutor to consult with the victim in advance. And the need for pre-plea consultation diminishes if the prosecutor pursues a plea agreement that does not compromise the expected views and interests of the victim — for example, if the plea agreement involves a charge to the most serious readily provable offense and fully protects the victim's right to restitution.

But that is not what happened here. A mother has lost her son forever. And the prosecution agreed to settle for a lesser charge without first consulting with the mother. Even when she was consulted, she learned of the terms of the plea deal only after the fact as a *fait accompli* from an administrative coordinator at the U.S. Attorney's Office. The mother's and the family's rights and interests were not appropriately honored and respected.

A 3-year-old boy now has no father. Who will care for him financially? The plea agreement here potentially shortchanges the victim's family's right to restitution, contrary to the explicit right of victims under the CVRA to full and timely restitution. *See* 18 U.S.C. § 3771(a)(6). The plea agreement provides in part for restitution including the payment of funeral expenses but without mentioning the potential for payment of future lost income. Doc. # 42 at 2, 9. Future lost income is a proper component of restitution for cases in which a victim's death has resulted. *See United States v. Messina*, 806 F.3d 55, 67–71 (2d Cir. 2015).

So why was there nothing in the plea agreement and nothing said at the guilty plea hearing about potential restitution for the victim's lost future income? I do not know. What I do know is that the prosecution did not consult with the family in the first instance to learn about the financial hardships that may result from the victim's death and to discuss the possible scope of a restitution order and how a restitution order could help meet the future financial needs of a fatherless 3-year-old boy. The Government acted contrary to the obvious interests of the victim's family and contrary to the Court's local rules which provide in part that "[t]he attorney for the government shall state on the record at any change of plea or sentencing proceeding the government's understanding of the amount of possible restitution based upon consultation with, *inter alia*, the victim." D. Conn. L. Crim. R. 32(m).

Victims do not know the ins-and-outs of the restitution statutes. Prosecutors should. The Government's pre-plea consultation with a victim's family should include advising the family of a possible restitution claim, to ascertain whether the family wishes the Government to pursue such restitution at sentencing, and to make clear to a defendant at the time of a plea agreement what the possible and likely scope of restitution may be.

Is it too much to ask of prosecutors that they personally consult with crime victims? I do not think so. After all, most crimes charged by federal prosecutors are regulatory violations that do not have identified victims. *See* U.S. Sentencing Commission, 2015 Sourcebook of Federal Sentencing Statistics, Figure A—Offenders in Each

Primary Offense Category, *available at* http://www.ussc.gov/research/sourcebook–2015. For the fraction of federal criminal prosecutions that have identified victims, there is no good reason to suppose that prosecutors cannot consult with those victims before they conclude plea agreements. That is especially true if a prosecutor is thinking of offering a defendant a plea agreement that falls short of what a victim might reasonably expect the prosecutor to pursue on the victim's behalf.

A prosecutor in another case once appeared before me for the sentencing of a bank robbery case. That prosecutor had written a sentencing memorandum invoking the terrified feeling that the bank tellers felt when the defendant waved around a firearm and demanded money. But no tellers or victims were in court. And no victim impact statements had been submitted. The prosecutor did not know why the victims were not there and why they had not been heard from. When I asked the prosecutor if he or she had personally spoken with the terrified victims, the prosecutor said no. The prosecutor claimed not to be aware that prosecutors should personally communicate with victims.

If a prosecutor walks into a courtroom and realizes that he or she has never personally spoken or corresponded with the crime's victim, then that should be a sign that the victim's interests have probably not been fully served and respected. That should be a sign that other interests have likely eclipsed the interests of the real people who have been harmed and whose only real recourse is the prosecutor who has slighted or overlooked them. Prosecutors are busy. But it is hard to imagine what priorities should rank higher in a prosecutor's workday than to make sure that each victim of a crime is appropriately and lawfully respected.

Conclusion

The Government did not respect the rights and interests of the victim's family before entering into the plea agreement in this case. Because the sound administration of justice does not support acceptance of a plea agreement when the Government does not respect the rights of crime victims, the Court rejects the parties' plea agreement.

If the parties wish to renew guilty plea proceedings, they may schedule a new plea hearing and submit a new plea agreement. If the parties do so, the Government is requested to file a memorandum with the new proposed plea agreement addressing whether it has now fully consulted with the victim's family prior to committing to an agreement (or whether it has been impossible to do so) and whether the agreement otherwise appropriately protects the restitution interests of the victim's family.

Notes

1. Most courts have extremely busy dockets and virtually automatic acceptance of pleas reached by the prosecution and the defense is the rule. What factors led the judge in the *Stevens* case to take a hard look at this particular plea?

2. The following scenarios explore the difficulties surrounding victim participation in plea bargaining.

A. Tom, a nine-year-old boy, has disclosed to his mother, Jane, that his father, John, has sexually abused him. Jane reports the crime to the police and John is arrested and formally charged.

Jane has no readily marketable job skills, while John earns a very good living. Prison for John means poverty for Jane and Tom, the child victim. Probation would allow John to work and live outside the home while supporting Jane and Tom.

Jane wants John to get a probationary sentence to keep him out of prison.

What is the appropriate sentence? What sentence is in the best interest of society? What sentence is in the best interest of the child? Suppose John had a previous conviction for sexually abusing a child. Would this change your view of an appropriate sentence?

B. An indicted securities dealer has defrauded hundreds of investors. His attorney proposes that if he returns some of the illegally obtained money to the victims that prison time will be reduced from five to two years.

What is the appropriate response? What if the victims agree with the proposal in order to get their money back? What if the government would benefit by receiving a large fine and costs of prosecution, but the victims would get no restitution?

3. A victim's plea for the maximum term is not an impermissible breach of the state's plea bargain promise to remain silent on sentencing. *Sharp v. State*, 908 S.W.2d 752 (Mo. Ct. App. 1995).

4. The federal Crime Victims' Rights Act has provided a basis for unsealing plea bargains to reveal the names of the convicted. *See U.S. v. Crompton Corp.*, 399 F. Supp. 2d 1047 (N.D. Cal. 2005) (in light of the CVRA, redacting names in a plea agreement "is untenable and would only serve to conceal from the true victims of the crime, the public at large, the fairness and transparency of the sentencing").

––––––––––

Stevens mentions a local rule requiring prosecutors to provide information to the court about the victim's need for restitution. Would it make sense to require prosecutors to more broadly inform the trial court about the victim's views on a plea bargain when presenting it to the trial court for review, perhaps by way of documentation of the victim's views? Consider the following argument along these lines:

Dana Pugach & Michal Tamir, *Nudging the Criminal Justice System into Listening to Crime Victims in Plea Agreements*
28 Hastings Women's L.J. 45 (2017)

An example of the importance of involving victims in plea agreements, have recently been given in a Utah child abuse case. A judge refused to accept a plea where the victims' parents had not been allocated the right to confer with the prosecutor and a very lenient plea had been struck behind their back. Judge Randall Skanchy rejected the agreement after the mothers of the three children voiced their objections to the deal and described the injuries their children had suffered. One of the mothers voiced frustration with the prosecutors and praised the judge's decision: "I think he actually listened to us," she said, "we haven't gotten questions answered from day one, we've just been passed off." Another mother said that in light of the injury to her daughter and the others, she did not believe the plea deal was strong enough, but she would have supported a plea deal with sufficient consequences and an admission of guilt.

This story demonstrates the core issues analyzed in this article. Despite the existence of statutory victims' rights, and the importance of victims' involvement in pleas for the victims, for the Criminal Justice System and for society—victims are still not always perceived as rightful participants. The mothers' complaints exemplify the secondary victimization caused by their exclusion from the process. The judge's acceptance of their reservations and the resulting rejection of the plea demonstrates the value of information and the results of the lack of it. The rejection of the plea emphasizes that defendants do not have a legitimate right in the lower sentence offered by a plea, when it is an unduly favorable bargain, resting on partial information. Perhaps most importantly though, the mother's heartfelt statement shows that victims do not necessarily oppose plea agreements. They only want to take part in the process and voice their concerns.

As a solution, we turn to nudge theory, which has almost never been used in criminal law, but is particularly advantageous for the discussed issue. Nudge theory involves choice architecture and claims that a certain degree of paternalism should be acceptable even to those who most embrace freedom of choice. Thus, a nudge is any aspect of choice architecture that alters people's behavior in a predictable way without forbidding any options or abolishing their discretion. Choice architecture can help to induce greater deliberation by actors and is especially important for changing routine behaviors. We argue that deliberation can facilitate a critical thought by the prosecutors and the judges, and can alter their perspectives on how plea bargains should be performed, from the initial negotiations to the court.

For that reason, we suggested the development of a nudge toolbox that will nudge the prosecutor to approach the victim, inform her, and give her a meaningful opportunity to express her view prior to sealing the plea. The main rules we suggested ensure that the process is fully documented and that a decision is made only following the presentation of this document. The rules do not alter the prosecutor's discretion but structures its administration. Recording all contact with the victim will necessitate a significant degree of attention and consideration, and will diminish the tendency to resort to the default option of sealing quick agreements. The judge too operates in circumstances, where she is likely to resort to the default option of a swift approval of agreements. These circumstances include the case load and the need to deliver decisions in due time. Being presented with structured information regarding the victim's view will lead the judge to a more deliberate decision, without limiting her discretion.

This apparently simple and minor change, has a potential to make major contribution towards the implementation of the broadly defined CVRA rights and to the inclusion of victims in plea agreements. Furthermore, it will answer some of the strongest critiques of plea bargains by making the process more transparent. This will not necessarily lead to fewer plea agreements, but it will hopefully lead to more balanced ones, reflecting all the relevant interests. The prosecution and the defendant will have an interest in reaching an agreement that will not be rejected by the court. Thus, victim input may contribute to what may be seen as a fairer conclusion of the plea agreement.

6. Plea Bargaining and the Victim's Right to Confer with the Prosecutor

In re Dean

527 F.3d 391 (5th Cir. 2008)

PER CURIAM:

In the related criminal proceeding, twelve of the victims asked the district court to reject the plea agreement, alleging violations of the Crime Victims' Rights Act ("CVRA"), 18 U.S.C. § 3771. The district court denied the request. *See United States v. BP Prods. N. Am. Inc.,* No. H-07-434, 2008 WL 501321, 2008 U.S. Dist. LEXIS 12893 (S.D.Tex. Feb. 21, 2008). The victims petition for writ of mandamus with the prayer that "[t]he decision of the district court should be reversed and the case remanded with instructions that the plea agreement [not be] accepted and the parties are permitted to proceed as they determine — so long as it is in a way that respects crime victims' rights." We find a statutory violation but, for reasons we explain, we deny relief.

I.

[a]n explosion at a refinery operated by the criminal defendant, BP Products North America Inc. ("BP"), killed fifteen and injured more than 170. Extensive civil litigation ensued.

The Department of Justice investigated the possibility of federal criminal violations. Before bringing any charges, the government, on October 18, 2007, filed a sealed *ex parte* motion for "an order outlining the procedures to be followed under the [CVRA]." The government announced that a plea agreement was expected to be signed in about a week and that because of the number of victims, "consulting the victims prior to reaching a plea agreement would not be practicable" and that notifying the victims would result in media coverage that "could impair the plea negotiation process and may prejudice the case in the event that no plea is reached."

As explained in the district court's order, the government, in its sealed *ex parte* motion, made specific recommendations for how the court should fashion a "reasonable procedure" under the CVRA's multiple crime victim exception. The district court responded with impressive speed, issuing on that same day a sealed order finding that notification to victims in advance of the public announcement of a plea agreement was impracticable because of the "large number of victims" and because, on account of the extensive media coverage, "any public notification of a potential criminal disposition resulting from the government's investigation [of the] explosion would prejudice [BP] and could impair the plea negotiation process and may prejudice the case in the event that no plea is reached." The *ex parte* order prohibited the government from notifying victims of a potential plea agreement until one had been executed; it directed that once an agreement had been signed, the government "shall provide reasonable notice to all identifiable victims and afford the victims the rights set forth [in the CVRA] prior to actual entry of the guilty plea. . . ."

The government filed the criminal information under seal on October 22. Two days later, the government and BP signed the plea agreement. The next day, the information was unsealed, and the plea agreement was announced. The government mailed three notices to the victims, in November and January, advising of scheduled proceedings and of their right to be heard. On November 20 and 23, various victims moved to appear and asked that the plea agreement be rejected or at least that the court handling the criminal matter require a presentence report.

After two district judges had declared themselves recused, the matter was permanently assigned, as a criminal matter, to the judge who entered the February 21 order that is the subject of this mandamus petition. Some victims appeared through counsel at a status conference on November 28 and presented their opposition to the plea agreement; 134 of them filed victim impact statements.

BP pleaded guilty at a hearing on February 4. All victims who wished to be heard, personally or through counsel, were permitted to speak. The attorneys reiterated the victims' request that the court reject the plea agreement on the basis of the CVRA violations alone; the district court reserved decision on the victims' other challenges to the plea agreement. As the district court describes it, "the victims focused on three challenges: the fine was too low; the probation conditions were too lenient; and certain CVRA requirements had been violated."

On February 21, the district court entered the above-cited order, denying the victims' request that the court reject the plea agreement. Feeling aggrieved by the order, the victims filed the instant mandamus petition on February 28. Also on that date, a panel of this court, in compliance with the requirement of 18 U.S.C. § 3771(d)(3) that we act within seventy-two hours, entered an order granting the mandamus petition in part: It directed the district court to take no further action to effect the plea agreement, pending further order and awaiting additional briefing.

* * *

B.

[2] With due respect for the district court's diligent efforts to do justice, we conclude that, under the specific facts and circumstances of this case, it was contrary to

the provisions of the CVRA for the court to permit and employ the *ex parte* proceedings that have taken place-proceedings that have no precedent, as far as we can determine. To obtain the order, the government filed only a brief *ex parte* statement, apparently with a proposed order. The fact of the *ex parte* motion and order was compounded by the intentional delay of three months before the victims were notified that the *ex parte* proceeding had occurred.

The district court acknowledged that "[t]here are clearly rights under the CVRA that apply before any prosecution is underway." Logically, this includes the CVRA's establishment of victims' "reasonable right to confer with the attorney for the Government." 18 U.S.C. § 3771(a)(5). At least in the posture of this case (and we do not speculate on the applicability to other situations), the government should have fashioned a reasonable way to inform the victims of the likelihood of criminal charges and to ascertain the victims' views on the possible details of a plea bargain.

The district court's reasons for its *ex parte* order do not pass muster. The first consideration is the number of victims. The government and the district court relied on the provision of the CVRA that states that "[i]n a case where the court finds that the number of crime victims makes it impracticable to accord all of the crime victims the rights described in subsection (a), the court shall fashion a reasonable procedure to give effect to this chapter that does not unduly complicate or prolong the proceedings." 18 U.S.C. § 3771(d)(2). Here, however, where there were fewer than two hundred victims, all of whom could be easily reached, it is not reasonable to say that notification and inclusion were "impracticable." There was never a claim that notification itself would have been too cumbersome, time-consuming, or expensive or that not all victims could be identified and located; the government itself suggested a procedure whereby the victims would be given prompt notice of their rights under the CVRA after the plea agreement was signed.

The real rub for the government and the district court was that, as the district judge who handled the *ex parte* proceeding as a miscellaneous matter reasoned, "'[d]ue to extensive media coverage of the . . . explosion . . . , any public notification of a potential criminal disposition resulting from the government's investigation . . . would prejudice BP . . . and could impair the plea negotiation process and may prejudice the case in the event that no plea is reached.'" In making that observation, the court missed the purpose of the CVRA's right to confer. In passing the Act, Congress made the policy decision—which we are bound to enforce—that the victims have a right to inform the plea negotiation process by conferring with prosecutors before a plea agreement is reached. That is not an infringement, as the district court believed, on the government's independent prosecutorial discretion; instead, it is only a requirement that the government confer in some reasonable way with the victims before ultimately exercising its broad discretion.

It is true that communication between the victims and the government could, in the district court's words, "impair the plea negotiation process," if, by using the word "impair," the court meant that the views of the victims might possibly influence or affect the result of that process. It is also true (and we cannot know whether the court considered) that resourceful input from victims and their attorneys could facilitate the reaching of an agreement. The point is that it does not matter: The Act gives the right to confer. The number of victims here did not render notice to, or conferring with, the victims to be impracticable, so the victims should have been notified of the ongoing plea discussions and should have been allowed to communicate meaningfully with the government, personally or through counsel, before a deal was struck.

Note

Professor O'Hear argues that meaningful consultation with both the defendant and the victim concerning plea bargains should be embedded in prosecutorial guidelines. Michael M. O'Hear, *Plea Bargaining and Victims from Consultation to Guidelines*, 91 Marq. L. Rev. 323 (2007).

7. Should Victims Have a "Veto" Over Plea Bargains?

Professor George Fletcher has proposed expanding the victim's role in plea bargains to make the victim a *party* for purposes of having an absolute *veto* power over a plea bargain. Consider his arguments in favor of this proposal (which does not appear to be formally the law of any state) and the following responses:

George Fletcher, With Justice for Some: Protecting Victims' Rights in Criminal Trials
(1995)

Under the current state of the law, the victim has the greatest power at the stage where he or she least deserves and needs it at sentencing. As a structural matter, the system can tolerate victim input at the time of sentencing, for at that stage everything is admissible. Everyone in town has a say about what should be done with a convicted felon. The victim too might as well fuel the public's lust for vengeance or promote the virtue of forgiveness. It would be a mistake, however, to privilege this input from the victim and treat it as critical to a proper level of punishment.

Punishment responds to the wrong the offender commits, but not to the particular wrong as measured by victims willing to testify. Killing a homeless beggar is as great a wrong as depriving a family of a loved one. Or at least that is what we have always assumed about homicide. It hardly makes sense to think of life as sacred if its value is a function of how much others love or need the person killed. That the victim is a human being is sufficient to determine the evil of killing. Thus the suffering of the survivors hardly seems the right basis for determining, say, whether the death penalty is justified.

The power that could make a difference in the life of victims lies not at the end of the process but at the beginning. In contrast to England, the United States [in federal prosecutions] no longer permits private prosecutions. The police and the public prosecutor [federal] gain control over the case and from the outset regard it as their own. They dispose of it at will. The American Bar Association proposes that prosecutors confer and hear the victim out "to the extent practicable," but that does not go far enough. At the stage of plea-bargaining, the victim should be regarded *as a party* whose consent should be necessary to short-circuit the trial process. Recognizing this power of the victim would unquestionably compromise the options of prosecutors, and for that reason they would likely oppose it. But bringing the victim into the limelight would bring new legitimacy to the occasionally shady practice of plea-bargaining.

Bringing the victim in from the cold might reorient plea-bargaining in a direction that many German reformers have urged. German scholars would like to see the criminal process serve the goal of reconciliation between offender and victim. If the victim must sign off on every plea bargain, prosecutors would have an incentive to create a mood between victims and offenders that would facilitate understanding between them. Under these circumstances, the victim would have a less urgent need for vindication at a public trial; there would be no reason to object to the offender's pleading guilty to a lesser charge. By gaining control over the wrong that has occurred to him, the victim would have greater hope of reestablishing his position as a person secure in his rights, and from this position of strength he could approach the offender with a less compelling need for vengeance.

Note

A victim's veto over pleas has also been proposed in Karen L. Kennard, *The Victim's Veto: A Way to Increase Victim Impact on Criminal Case Dispositions*, 77 Cal. L. Rev. 417, 453 (1989), which argues that a veto would give crime victims an effective voice in the outcome of their criminal cases and increase victim satisfaction with the criminal justice system.

Lynne Henderson, *Whose Justice, Which Victims? Book Review of With Justice for Some: Victim's Rights in Criminal Trials*
94 Mich. L. Rev. 1596 (1996)

Fletcher's veto appears to be a one-way veto. A victim can force a trial, but not a plea bargain, presumably because what victims really want is a trial (even though they may have to settle for a finding of attribution but not guilt). The absolute veto, unlike many current laws that promote victim consultation or participation in plea bargain decisions, would "empower" victims. He argues that victims' participation in the plea bargain process would allow them to be heard and taken seriously certainly a goal of victim-participation laws generally because prosecutors will pay attention only if victims have veto power (pp. 191–92, 248). He advocates this position even though he notes prosecutors might oppose it because it "compromises the[ir] options," presumably options unworthy of respect (p.248). Fletcher also claims that veto power over plea bargains would further encourage "victim-offender reconciliation" and diminish the victim's "urgent need for vindication at a public trial" (p.248). The proposal's unarticulated assumptions about the nature of crime victims, what they want, and what is good for them are mystifying in light of the known complexities of victim responses to crime. The presumption that victims have an urgent need for vindication is bizarre. They may want a conviction, or revenge, or they may not, and with no urgency at all. They may need time to heal before a trial, which may be a far more pressing concern; they may want to avoid a trial altogether. Moreover, Fletcher ignores the potential for coercion of defendants and victims, as well as the fact that a veto alone does not greatly increase victim participation in the process. Prosecutors could simply submit proposals to victims without consulting with them. Finally, the proposal for veto power over plea bargains places the state's penal resources in the hands of individuals, again making criminal convictions more a matter of private, rather than public, law.

———————

Professor Stephen Schulhofer, a strenuous supporter of the abolition of plea bargains, has also reviewed Fletcher's proposal for a victim veto.

Stephen J. Schulhofer, *The Trouble with Trials; The Trouble with Us*

105 Yale L.J. 825 (1995)

Fletcher [has] a recommendation to give victims a veto over any proposed plea agreement. If no terms acceptable to the victim could be negotiated, the prosecution would have to take the case to trial. As is, "victims' rights" legislation in many jurisdictions requires the prosecutor to consult the victim before finalizing a plea bargain; Fletcher's proposal would take this development one step further by making the victim's consent essential.

It is easy to picture the howls of protest that Fletcher's proposal will evoke from seasoned practitioners and "practical" people of all sorts: Constrain the prosecutor's discretion over plea bargaining? Increase the probability that cases may have to be tried? Unthinkable or so they will say. I do not share these concerns. Prosecutors negotiating guilty pleas have too few incentives to respect fully the victim's and the public's interests in an adequate penalty for the offender. Defense attorneys' interests often diverge from those of their clients; as a result, they may encourage settlement even when a trial would be in their clients' interests. More checks on the exercise of prosecutorial discretion and more trials would be all to the good. But the problem for Fletcher's proposal is in the principle that lies at its core. Why should a person who would be instantly disqualified from serving on the defendant's jury be granted a veto over the terms of a disposition by plea? If the plea bargaining system is to be retained at all, why should victims have control over decisions that we want to further public, not private, purposes?

As structured, moreover, Fletcher's proposal would only marginally affect the trial rate or the kinds of bargains struck in cases that settle. And the proposal would not bring victims into the process in any genuinely satisfying way. These failures result from the ease with which a victim's veto could be evaded. Fletcher's proposal requires victim consent only for a *bargain*, not for an unbargained (or "open") plea. Indeed, extending the victim veto power to include open pleas would be difficult to justify. But this qualification renders Fletcher's safeguard porous. Prosecutors could conduct pre-charge or pre-indictment negotiations over charges to which the defendant would enter an open plea. A bargain could then be struck whether the victim liked it or not, or defendants could enter open pleas and hope for leniency from the judge. In order to keep guilty pleas flowing, a system of tacit concessions would undoubtedly develop.

Either way, a system of plea bargaining would remain in place, and as before there would be no need for victim consent. . . .

C. Dismissal Pursuant to Pretrial Intervention, Diversion and Deferred Sentence Programs

Diversion and deferred sentencing procedures exist in many states. The procedures allow a person arrested to ultimately obtain a dismissal in their case if they comply with certain conditions. *See, e.g.,* Cory R. Lepage & Jeff. D. May, *The Anchorage, Alaska Municipal Pretrial Diversion Program: An Initial Assessment*, 34 ALASKA L. REV. 1 (2017). These procedures are commonly available for crimes surrounding alcohol and drug problems.

Diversion or pretrial diversion programs may be set forth by statute or by policies adopted by prosecuting agencies and courts. The Oregon Statute for Diversion for Driving Under the Influence of Intoxicants provides an example of a thoroughly developed diversion statute which focuses on a particular offense — drunk driving:

ORS 813.200

813.170 Plea agreement prohibited . . . a person charged with the offense of driving under the influence of intoxicants shall not be allowed to forfeit bail or plead "guilty" or "no contest" to any other offense in exchange for a dismissal of the offense charged. No district attorney or city attorney shall make any motion and no judge shall enter any order in derogation of this section. This section does not prohibit diversion. . . .

DIVERSION

813.200. Notice of availability of diversion; petition; form; contents. . . .

. . .

(4) In addition to any other information required by the Supreme Court to be contained in a petition for a driving while under the influence of intoxicants diversion agreement, the petition shall include:

(a) A waiver by the defendant of the right to speedy trial or sentencing in any subsequent action upon the charge;

(b) An agreement by the defendant to complete at an agency or organization designated by the city or state court a diagnostic assessment to determine the possible existence and degree of an alcohol or drug abuse problem;

(c) An agreement by the defendant to complete, at defendant's own expense based on defendant's ability to pay, the program of treatment indicated as necessary by the diagnostic assessment;

(d) An agreement by the defendant to not use intoxicants in conjunction with the defendant's operation of a motor vehicle and to comply fully with the laws of this state designed to discourage the use of intoxicants in conjunction with motor vehicle operation;

(e) A notice to the defendant that the diversion agreement will be considered to be violated if the court receives notice that the defendant at any time during the diversion period committed the offense of driving while under the influence of intoxicants or committed a violation of ORS 811.170;

. . .

(g) A waiver by the defendant of any former jeopardy rights . . . in any subsequent action upon the charge or any other offenses based upon the same criminal episode;

* * *

813.215. Eligibility for diversion. A defendant is eligible for diversion if:

(1) The defendant had no charge of driving while under the influence of intoxicants . . . pending on the date of commission of the present offense and within 10 years before the date of the commission of the present offense the defendant has not been convicted of or forfeited bail or security for such an offense;

(2) The defendant was not participating in a driving while under the influence of intoxicants diversion program or in any similar alcohol or drug rehabilitation program in this state or in any other jurisdiction on the date of commission of the present offense and within 10 years before the date of commission of the present offense the defendant has not participated in any such program;

(3) The defendant had no charge of murder, manslaughter, criminally negligent homicide or assault that resulted from the operation of a motor vehicle pending in this state or in any other jurisdiction on the date of commission of the present offense and within 10 years before the date of commission of the present offense the defendant has not been convicted of any such charge;

(4) The present driving while under the influence of intoxicants offense did not involve an accident resulting in death or physical injury, . . . to any person other than the defendant;

* * *

813.250. Motion to dismiss charge on completion of diversion; admissibility of statements. (1) At any time after the conclusion of the period of a driving while under the influence of intoxicants diversion agreement described in ORS 813.230, a defendant who has fully complied with and performed the conditions of the diversion agreement may apply by motion to the court wherein the diversion agreement was entered for an order dismissing the charge with prejudice.

———————

A minority of the states have given victims a statutory right to confer with prosecutors concerning prosecution alternatives. For example, OHIO REV. CODE ANN. § 2930.06 provides:

The prosecutor in a case, to the extent practicable, shall confer with the victim in the case before pretrial diversion is granted to the defendant in the case. . . .

Not all diversion and deferred sentencing programs are directed at curing drug and alcohol problems. Some laws seek to provide relief from the criminal laws to worthy defendants. Under these laws, victims may or may not play a meaningful role in the decision to divert or defer charges.

State v. Ridgway

504 A.2d 1241 (N.J. Super. 1985)

HAINES, A.J.S.C.

Thomas P. Ridgway has been indicted under *N.J.S.A.* 2C:11-5, the death by auto statute [establishing liability for driving (with the mental state of recklessness) resulting in death]. His application for admission to the pretrial intervention program (PTI) has been denied. That denial, having been appealed, is addressed by this opinion. It holds that the denial was arbitrary, amounting to a patent and gross abuse of discretion, requiring reversal.

Ridgway is 19 years old, the divorced father of one child. He is gainfully employed as an "on-demand" painter with no physical, psychological or drug addiction problems and no criminal record. The accident did not involve alcohol or other drugs.

This is defendant's second PTI appeal. His application was first rejected by the PTI director . . .

The rejection was appealed. The appellate record revealed the failure of the director and the prosecutor (sometimes referred to collectively as "the State") to consider defendant as an individual; his background, character, and prospects, except for his motor vehicle record, were barely mentioned. Consideration of the individual is a central requirement of the PTI program. *State v. Sutton*, 80 N.J. 110, 119, 402 A.2d 230 (1979). While the prosecutor referred to rehabilitation, a PTI goal, he did so only in conclusory terms. Defendant's motor vehicle record, a central theme supporting the rejection, had not been analyzed by either the director or the prosecutor. In fact, it did not appear to be a record upon which the denial of a PTI application could be based. The State's decision was therefore reached after consideration of an apparently irrelevant factor and without consideration of required factors. It was a manifest abuse of discretion, *State v. Bender*, 80 N.J. 84, 402 A.2d 217 (1979), requiring a remand with direction for a reexamination of the application.

* * *

The director then rejected the application again. He based the rejection upon a consideration of all PTI statutory criteria and *R*.3:28 Guidelines ("*GL*"). His reasons (paraphrased) for denying the application were:

1. The nature of the offense, including the factual background, does not favor admission.

2. The family of the complainant is opposed.

3. Since the defendant denies having any personal problems, there are no PTI services to offer him.

4. If driver training is indicated, it is a matter for the Motor Vehicle Department which is not subject to a PTI order.

5. The interest of the victim and society in prosecution outweighs the interest of the defendant in admission. Deterrence is in the interest of society and is to be obtained through prosecution.

6. There is no social problem to be exacerbated by prosecution.

7. The need to prosecute outweighs the need for admission.

8. The harm to society, if prosecution is abandoned, outweighs any benefit to society which diversion could provide.

9. " . . . there is no need to rehabilitate, because you tell us this was an accident caused by mechanical failure and nothing more."

10. This is not a victimless crime.

He made the following favorable findings:

1. There is no record of antisocial behavior.

2. The driving record is satisfactory.

3. Defendant's actions were not assaultive in the sense that the term is normally used.

4. There is no history of violence.

5. No organized crime is involved.

The prosecutor again supported the denial of admission, incorporating his prior reasons, but agreeing that defendant's driving record is not a basis for denial. He added:

1. Defendant claims he is not guilty and therefore does not recognize his responsibility. PTI would be ineffective.

2. Driver training would not be appropriate.

He noted the following favorable factors:

1. There is no evidence of alcohol or drug abuse.

2. The defendant has no record.

The State's Reasons or Lack of Reasons.

Thomas P. Ridgway appears to be an ideal candidate for PTI admission. He is young. He has family responsibilities. He is employed. He has no criminal record. He has no psychological problems and is not involved with drugs. His accident did not involve alcohol or any other drug. These circumstances invite a careful appraisal of defendant as an individual and an equally careful articulation of reasons for the rejection of his application.

Consideration of the individual is a necessity with respect to the PTI program. In *State v. Sutton, supra*, the Court said:

> Prosecutorial decisions and PTI matters are primarily individualistic in nature. In making any determination, the Prosecutor must assess a particular applicant's "amenability" and potential "responsiveness to rehabilitation" assessments which are dependent upon such factors as a defendant's age, past criminal record, education, family ties, standing in the community, and employment performance. Also relevant are "subjective" evaluations, such as the Prosecutor's assessment of a particular defendant's sincerity, the motive underlying the commission of the crime, and the degree of local public anxiety attaching to certain forms of misconduct. [80 N.J. at 109, 402 A.2d 230]

* * *

These individual criteria were ignored by both prosecutor and director in the present case.

The matter has been remanded once because there was no consideration of the individual. Once is enough. There has been no negative assessment of defendant as an individual, and the facts would not warrant such an assessment. It must be assumed, therefore, that his individual characteristics support admission. The significance of this assumption cannot be overlooked.

* * *

In the present case, the reasons given are insufficient. They are either conclusory or too vague to support the prosecutorial position. As a consequence, that position is arbitrary.

It is to be recognized that the PTI standards to be applied by the director and the prosecutor are not precise. This is a circumstance dictated by the subject matter which the statute and Guidelines address. They deal with human behavior: motivation, desire, character traits, probabilities of controlling criminal behavior, needs of victims and society, exacerbation of social problems as a result of prosecution and the balancing of supervisory treatment against the public need for prosecution. Society normally leaves such standards to the consideration of social science experts and philosophers. This is not to suggest that they are inappropriate or unenforceable, only that difficulties are to be expected when they are applied in a setting which provides scant facts and little time for mature reflection. Indeed, in the case of the prosecutor, the information is second-hand, limited to facts supplied by the director and the investigation of the crime. He has no access to defendant, personally.

The standards must be applied conscientiously and articulately. The decision to prosecute or not to prosecute turns upon their correct application. It is a decision of vital significance to a person charged with crime. The obligation of the director and the prosecutor, therefore, is to so state their reasons for a PTI denial as to make it clear that they satisfy the standards. That requirement has not been met here.

This conclusion can be demonstrated only by an analysis of the reasons given here. Since nothing in the enabling material distinguishes the weight to be given to the prosecutor's decisions from the weight to be given the director's, and since they agree on the PTI rejection, there is no reason in this case to make any different analysis of their separately stated reasons. Those reasons will be considered as though spoken with a single voice. They are set forth below with the analysis which reflects their inadequacies.

(1) *The nature of the offense.*

Like all other criteria addressed by the State (used hereinafter to refer to both prosecutor and director), this is a required consideration pursuant to *N.J.S.A.* 2C:43-12(e); *GL3*(i). There is some question as to whether the nature of the crime, standing alone, may be sufficient to support the prosecutorial denial. . . .

GL3(i) answers the question, avoiding the problem of vagueness otherwise infecting the words "the nature of the offense." It cites both *Leonardis* opinions and recognizes that "there must be a balance struck between a defendant's amenability to correction, responsiveness to rehabilitation and the nature of the offense." The guideline then continues by defining the "nature" of those offenses, which standing alone, may be a basis for denial of a PTI application. They are described as first and second degree crimes and certain drug offenses. The guideline does not refer to death by auto which is a fourth degree offense. *N.J.S.A.* 2C:11-5 (Now third degree by later statutory amendment). This explains *Leonardis II* which permits a PTI denial to be based solely upon the nature of the offense "where appropriate." It is appropriate when a first or second degree offense is involved or when certain drug offenses are involved, not otherwise.

This translation solidifies the language of the criteria which would otherwise be illusory. What is the "nature" of an offense? Does it involve the extent of the injury to person or property, the harm to society or the shock to the sensibilities? How are these to be measured? One offense, for example, may be more harmful than another to a particular student of social problems, a particular director, a particular prosecutor or a particular segment of society. Unless the word "nature" is narrowed by the above reading of *GL3*(i), it cannot be enforced.

In the present case, the State considered the fact that defendant was not charged with a "victimless" crime when he assessed the "nature of the offense." One of the purposes of PTI, and the apparent source of the State's reason, is to permit "the least burdensome form of prosecution possible for defendants charged with "victimless" offenses." *N.J.S.A.* 2C:43-12; GL 1(c). This purpose is not offered as a definition of "the nature of the offense," and "victimless" is not defined. This court's interpretation of the language of the standard denies the validity of the State's reason. Its "nature of the offense" was not otherwise explained except by a statement that: "The crime we are dealing with here involves the death of a 16-year old boy." These approaches are inadequate even if GL3(i) does not apply. They do not advise defendant as to why the "nature" of his offense prevents his admission to PTI while the "nature" of other offenses (such as welfare fraud, a frequent subject of favorable PTI treatment, though clearly damaging to character and society) does not.

(2) *The facts of the case.*

Defendant has said that a brake failure caused the accident. The State challenges his veracity by noting that a State police examination found no mechanical problems with either the brake or the air horn, which allegedly was not sounded prior to the accident. This point-counterpoint presents problems. The State is required to consider the facts of the case. It assumes guilt for PTI purposes. It properly relies upon the fact that death resulted from a motor vehicle accident and upon any other uncontradicted facts. It walks on thin ice, however, when it begins to examine factual controversy.

The State here accepts the information provided by a police examination as conclusive. It ignores the fact that defendant may be able to refute the police testimony at trial. His assertions may be proven correct. The nature, adequacy and expert nature of the investigation have not been delineated, and there has been no opportunity for cross-examination. The State may assume guilt when defendant claims innocence; it may not become involved in deciding other factual disputes when considering a PTI admission. Were its obligation otherwise, the State would be obliged to conduct a trial before reaching any PTI conclusion. That is not an approach to be used in a PTI proceeding. Consequently, the State's reliance in the present case upon its version of disputed facts was improper.

(3) *The family is opposed to PTI admission.*

This is a factor which must be considered. The position of the family, a victim in the true sense of the word, is understandable. Nevertheless, families in these situations naturally take positions based only upon their own losses, their own feelings. They have little access, if any, to facts about defendants. Their opposition is not likely to be based upon PTI considerations. It may be based upon revenge, or upon the very opposite, some undisclosed interest in the welfare of society. It is opposition which is not explained and which defendant cannot meet. It cannot have been intended by the Legislature to be a conclusive consideration.

(4) *PTI is inappropriate because defendant does not have any personal problems.*

One of the purposes of PTI is "[t]o provide defendants with opportunities to avoid ordinary prosecution by receiving early rehabilitative services, when such services can reasonably be expected to deter future criminal behavior by defendant, and when there is an apparent causal connection between the offense charged and the rehabilitative need, without which cause both the alleged offense and the need to prosecute might not have occurred." *GL*1(a); *N.J.S.A.* 2C: 43-12a(1). Since Thomas P. Ridgway has not been involved with alcohol or other drugs and has not exhibited any personal problems requiring specific treatment, the State concluded that PTI is not appropriate. The position, if sound, would limit PTI admission to those needing treatment for the purpose of correcting personal problems, such as drug abuse. It would deny admission to those persons without such problems, persons who, logically, are less likely to be involved in future criminal behavior because they have fewer, if any, problems to be resolved. It is hard to believe that the Legislature or the Supreme Court intended this distinction to be made.

Furthermore, the purpose of rehabilitation through treatment is only one of the purposes of PTI. Two others, both appropriate here, are:

> To provide an alternative to prosecution for defendants who might be harmed by the imposition of criminal sanctions as presently administered, when such an alternative can be expected to serve as sufficient sanction to deter criminal conduct. [GL1(d)]

> To relieve over-burdened criminal calendars in order to focus expenditure of criminal resources on matters involving serious criminality and severe correctional problems. [GL1(e)]

Here there is no showing of any severe correctional problem and, or, any, "serious criminality." It is also a PTI purpose "to deter future criminal or disorderly behavior by a defendant/participant in pretrial intervention." *GL*1(e). It is obvious that this purpose is more likely to be served by diverting a defendant who has no personal problems than it is by diverting one who has such problems. Thus, the State has improperly considered one purpose of PTI to the exclusion of three others (out of a total of five purposes), more appropriate for consideration in the present case. In addition, since it failed to consider defendant as an individual, its conclusion that the probationary arrangement always present in a PTI admission will not be helpful to defendant in deterring future conduct or in providing rehabilitation has no basis in fact.

(5) *Relationship of the crime to a situation conducive to change through participation in supervisory treatment.*

Defendant suggests that supervisory treatment driver training may be an appropriate means through which to satisfy this standard. The State takes the position that such training is within the control of the Division of Motor Vehicles. This is not necessarily so. The PTI Program makes creative use of a broad range of treatments and conditions. It requires counseling, restitution, community service and other appropriate responses, sometimes through private resources. There is no reason that it could not require defendant to undertake driving instruction with or without the cooperation of the Division of Motor Vehicles. In fact, there appears to be little reason for Ridgway to undertake driver training. He offers the suggestion for the purpose of countering the State's argument that PTI is not appropriate because it has no services to offer him. The suggestion is unnecessary. The State cannot single out one purpose of PTI to the exclusion of all others.

(6) *The needs and interests of the victim and society.*

The State's position is that society requires prosecution in order to maintain confidence in the enforcement of our motor vehicle rules, thereby insuring its belief that members of the public will not be endangered by motor vehicle operators who do not obey the law. The State reaches this conclusion, without considering the needs and interests of the victim, perhaps, because the fact of the family's opposition has been addressed.

The State clothes this reason in conclusory terms. Logic certainly insists that enforcement of our motor vehicle laws, criminal and otherwise, is a necessity, if they are to have any validity. But this can be said about every criminal offense. Death by auto is not peculiar in that respect. If this is a valid reason for denying a PTI application, it is one that can be used with every application. The intent of the statutes is to the contrary: "*Any* defendant charged with crime is eligible for enrollment in a PTI Program. . . ." *GL3*(i). It is clear that the State has not provided any valid reason showing that the needs of society require prosecution or that the instant offense is to be treated differently than any other.

(7) *The need to prosecute outweighs the value of PTI.*

The State, in addressing this criterion, merely parrots the rules. It presents no added facts supporting the supposed need to prosecute and none reflecting the value of pretrial intervention to either defendant or society. It is a test which the State has not satisfied.

(8) *Whether the harm to society caused by abandoning prosecution outweighs the benefit to society of a PTI admission.*

The State takes the position that harm outweighs benefit. It presents no new reasons for reaching this conclusion. Nothing in the record shows what harm will be done to society by abandoning prosecution; nothing shows the benefits which society will reap through the use of diversion. It is a criterion which cannot be considered; it is not supported by reasons.

(9) *Failure to admit guilt.*

> This is not among the statutorily mandated criteria. Refusal to admit guilt may be considered in connection with defendant's potential for rehabilitation, but PTI admission may not be denied on the ground of refusal to admit guilt. *State v. Maddocks*, 80 N.J. 98, 108, 402 A.2d 224 (1979); *State v. Smith*,

92 N.J. 143, 455 A.2d 1117 (1983). The State's rejection letters ignore this distinction. The prosecutor's letter, for example, states: "While an admission of guilt is not required by the *Guidelines*, acceptance of responsibility for his actions in this case is essential. Without recognition of responsibility, the defendant is demonstrating an attitude that renders PTI ineffective." These are conclusory statements. They are based upon the factual dispute concerning mechanical failure. Admission of guilt is not essential to an acceptance of responsibility. One who kills another, as in war or in any other setting, may accept a great deal of responsibility without admitting participation in a criminal happening. Furthermore, the State's position, stripped to its essentials, is that PTI admission may be denied because guilt has been denied. This is contrary to law.

Summary

This analysis leaves the State with only one acceptable reason for rejecting defendant's application: the objection of the victim's family. The reasons supporting admission weigh heavily in the other direction. He is only 19 years of age, has no record, has family responsibilities, is employed and meets three of the five purposes of pretrial intervention, namely:

1. He is a defendant who may be harmed by the imposition of criminal sanctions as presently administered. The PTI alternative can be expected to serve as a sufficient sanction to deter future criminal conduct.

2. Admission will relieve an overburdened criminal calendar, permitting the expenditure of criminal justice resources on matters involving serious criminality and severe correctional problems not present here.

3. Admission will deter future criminal or disorderly behavior by the defendant.

These positive factors were not addressed by the State. It gave no consideration to the individual. Its reasons for rejection are not only inadequate but arbitrary.

Conclusion

A reversal of the State's rejection of defendant's PTI application is *permissible* only if it is shown to be a patent and gross abuse of discretion. The rule is set forth in *State v. Bender*, 80 N.J. 84, 402 A.2d 217 (1979):

> Ordinarily, an abuse of discretion will be manifest if defendant can show that a prosecutorial veto (a) was not premised upon the consideration of all relevant factors, (b) was based upon a consideration of irrelevant or inappropriate factors, or (c) amounted to a clear error in judgment. In order for such an abuse of discretion to rise to the level of "patent and gross" it must further be shown that the prosecutorial error complained of will clearly subvert goals of Pretrial Intervention. [*Id.* at 93, 402 A.2d 217]

State v. Maguire, 168 N.J.Super. 109, 401 A.2d 1106 (App. Div. 1979), noted that the "patent and gross" standard is extremely difficult to define and apply. It construed the term to mean: "When the result reached has gone so wide of the mark sought to be accomplished by PTI that fundamental fairness and justice require court intervention." *Id.* at 115, n. 1, 401 A.2d 1106.

In the present case, the State failed to consider the individual after two opportunities to do so. This is a significant and elementary failure. Nearly all of the reasons upon which the rejection was based were irrelevant or inappropriate because they were misconceived or were not supported by adequate reasons. The factors favoring admission to the program were given little or no attention. These circumstances, considered together, amount to a clear error in judgment. The prosecutorial veto therefore amounted to a patent and gross abuse of discretion. The rejection is reversed. Defendant is admitted to the PTI program.

State v. Houston

900 S.W.2d 712 (Tenn. Cr. App. 1995)

HAYES, Judge.

This is an appeal pursuant to Rule Nine of the Tennessee Rules of Appellate Procedure from the judgment of the Criminal Court for Hamilton County affirming the district attorney general's denial of pre-trial diversion.

After reviewing the record, we affirm the trial court's judgment.

The appellant seeks to divert the offense of assault, Tenn. Code Ann. § 39-13-101, a Class A misdemeanor. The appellant was originally charged with aggravated assault. After a preliminary hearing, the case was bound over to the Grand Jury of Hamilton County on that charge. After hearing testimony from both the victim and the appellant, the grand jury returned an indictment for misdemeanor assault.

The appellant is currently a captain with the Chattanooga Police Department. He has served with the Department for twenty-five years. At the time of the offense, the appellant had been assigned to the Chattanooga City Court. His duties included the scheduling and coordinating of police officers for court appearances.

The victim is a twenty-eight year employee of the City of Chattanooga. He currently serves as the Court Administrator for the City Court Clerk's Office. His duties include the scheduling of cases on the court's docket.

On August 26, 1992, the appellant and the victim had a heated argument in the area immediately outside the courtrooms located in the Chattanooga City Court building. The appellant became angry when the victim refused to discuss an administrative problem. During the argument, the appellant called the victim a "bastard" several times in a loud voice. The victim attempted to walk away from the argument on more than one occasion, but the appellant followed, yelling at the victim to come back and "stand up like a man." During the final encounter, the appellant "got up into [the victim's] face" and said "I'm calling you a bastard. What are you going to do about it?" The victim responded by cursing at the appellant. The appellant then struck the victim in the face, breaking his jaw and two of his teeth. The victim immediately underwent four hours of surgery to repair the damage. The surgery involved the implantation of a steel plate to repair the victim's jaw bone. As a result of the incident, the victim has incurred more than $14,000 in medical expenses, and had been unable to return to work as of the date of the preliminary hearing in this case.

After his indictment, the appellant moved for pretrial diversion. To support his request, the appellant forwarded to the district attorney the transcript of the preliminary hearing, the appellant's pretrial diversion investigation, letters of good character from associates, the appellant's personnel file from the Chattanooga Police Department, and an incident report filed by the officer responding to the victim's complaint.

On July 15, 1993, the district attorney denied the appellant's request for pretrial diversion. The district attorney acknowledged the appellant's excellent work record and social history, but denied diversion based on the following grounds:

(1) The defendant is a police officer of the rank of captain as such he functions under a public trust and is held to a higher standard than the ordinary citizen as his actions reflect on law enforcement and our [system] of justice;

(2) The victim was an official of the court performing his duties as such at the time of the attack;

(3) Given the crime with which the defendant is charged the victim's injuries are particularly great;

(4) The defendant was armed at the time of the confrontation with a deadly weapon; and

(5) The victim attempted to retreat and was pursued by [the appellant].

The appellant filed a petition for a writ of certiorari in the Criminal Court for Hamilton County, seeking to overturn the district attorney's denial of diversion. On July 16 and August 5, 1993, the trial court held a hearing to determine whether the denial constituted an abuse of discretion. After considering the evidence, the trial court affirmed the district attorney's decision. Houston now appeals that ruling.

The decision to grant pretrial diversion rests within the district attorney's discretion. TENN. CODE. ANN. §40-15-105(b)(3) (Supp. 1994). The district attorney's decision is presumptively correct and shall be reversed only when the appellant establishes that there has been a patent or gross abuse of prosecutorial discretion. *State v. Hammersley*, 650 S.W.2d 352, 356 (Tenn. 1983). In order to establish abuse of discretion, "the record must show an absence of any substantial evidence to support" the district attorney's refusal to grant pretrial diversion. *Id.*

When deciding whether to grant pretrial diversion, the district attorney should consider the following factors: (1) the circumstances of the offense; (2) the defendant's criminal record, social history and present condition, including mental and physical conditions if appropriate; (3) the deterrent effect of punishment on other criminal activity; (4) the defendant's amenability to correction; and (5) the likelihood that pretrial diversion will serve the ends of justice and the best interests of both the public and the defendant. *State v. Washington*, 866 S.W.2d 950, 951 (Tenn. 1993). This court may not substitute its judgment for the district attorney's when reviewing a denial of pretrial diversion. *State v. Watkins*, 607 S.W.2d 486, 488 (Tenn. Crim.App. 1980), *perm. to appeal denied*, (Tenn. 1980). Our role is limited to determining whether any substantial evidence exists to support that decision within the framework of these factors.

In the present case, the district attorney clearly considered all applicable *Washington* factors. The district attorney conceded that the appellant has an excellent work and social history, and no prior criminal record. He concluded, however, that other factors opposing diversion outweighed the appellant's favorable personal history. The five reasons given for denial fit into the following two *Washington* categories: the circumstances of the offense; and the likelihood that pretrial diversion will serve the ends of justice and the best interests of both the public and the defendant.

The circumstances of the offense strongly support denial of pretrial diversion. As the district attorney pointed out, the victim's injuries were particularly great. Moreover, the appellant committed the offense during the middle of working hours in the Chattanooga City Court building, and the victim was a court official performing his duties at the time of the attack. The trial court rejected the appellant's contention that this incident was simply an argument between "two friends." The court in fact found that "there was some intent to do . . . harm or injury" to the victim. In an appeal of this nature, the trial court's findings of facts are binding on us unless the evidence preponderates against such findings. *State v. Helms*, 720 S.W.2d 474, 476 (Tenn. Crim.App. 1986), *perm. to appeal denied*, (Tenn. 1986).

The ends of justice and the best interests of the public also favor denial of pretrial diversion. As the trial court stated:

> [T]here needs to be respect for the law, and it would be hard to enforce that respect for the law and see that there is respect for the law when the very people who are enforcing the law are violating the law themselves in front of everybody else.

While the appellant's personal history does demonstrate his amenability to rehabilitation, the district attorney must consider other factors when deciding whether to grant pre-trial diversion. *State v. Carr*, 861 S.W.2d 850, 855 (Tenn. Crim.App. 1993). We have held on several occasions, that in an appropriate case, the circumstances of the offense and the need for deterrence may outweigh all other relevant factors and justify a denial of pretrial diversion. *Id.; see also State v. Helms*, 720 S.W.2d 474 (Tenn. Crim.App. 1986), *perm. to appeal denied*, (Tenn. 1986). We conclude that the circumstances of this offense, the need to serve the ends of justice, and to protect the interests of the public outweigh all factors in favor of diversion. We therefore conclude, as did the trial court, that the district attorney's denial of diversion did not constitute an abuse of discretion.

The judgment of the trial court is affirmed.

SCOTT and WHITE, JJ., concur.

Notes

1. The police captain in *State v. Houston*, was denied diversion. Ridgeway, the defendant charged with death by auto, was granted diversion. The resulting harm to the victim was greater in the *Ridgeway* case. Did the harm to the victims, the status of the victims or the victims' wishes have any significant influence on the outcome in either case? How much weight, if any, should be given to the harm to the victim or to the victim's opinion in making the diversion decision?

Note that Oregon's drunk driving diversion statute, set forth earlier in this chapter, precludes diversion when there was harm to another person.

2. In *Houston*, eligibility for diversion was an issue determined within the court's discretion. In *Ridgeway*, eligibility for diversion was a matter of prosecutorial discretion. Which approach is better? Which official is in a better position to weigh the proper significance of victim input concerning a diversion decision?

D. Restorative Justice

1. Background on Restorative Justice

The traditional criminal justice processes have often been described as "retributive." Would crime victims fare better if the criminal justice system focused more on "restorative justice"?

Dena M. Gromet et al., *A Victim-Centered Approach to Justice? Victim Satisfaction Effects on Third-Party Punishments*

36 Law & Hum. Behav. 375 (2012)

Retributive justice has been described broadly as an area of inquiry that addresses the punishment of offenders and the reaffirming of societal boundaries and values. Retribution aims to make the offender suffer for his wrongs and to symbolically reinforce the values of the group. The infliction of punitive measures on wrongdoers is motivated by the moral outrage that people feel in response to transgressions that violate group norms, values, and laws. In practice, retributive justice is achieved through court procedures, in which a judge unilaterally imposes a sentencing decision. Retributive outcomes usually involve the imposition of punitive sanctions, such as prison sentences.

In contrast, restorative justice uses a bilateral process in which those who have been affected by the offense are brought together to determine how to best repair the harms that the offense has caused. The focus of restorative justice is on restoration of all the actors affected by the injustice: the offender, the victim, and the community, sometimes including supporters of the offender and/or the victim, as well as unaffiliated community members. Restorative justice attempts to separate the bad act (the offense) from the offender, which is known as reintegrative shaming. This process allows for the condemning of the bad act without condemning the actor himself, which provides an avenue for restoring the offender as a law-abiding member of the community. For the victims, restorative justice aims to provide material and psychological restoration to the victims, with the goal of restoring them to where they were before the offense occurred. For the community, restorative justice seeks to repair any harm that has been caused to the community (both actual and symbolic), as well as to help build relationships between the offender and community members to aid in the offender's reintegration into society.

These restorative goals are typically achieved through procedures that involve a face-to-face meeting of the victim, the offender, and supporters for both sides, as well as community members acting as representatives of community interests. With the assistance of a trained facilitator, they jointly determine the harms that the offense has caused, and what must be done to repair those harms.

2. Is Restorative Justice Separate from Criminality and Guilt?

The starting point of a restorative justice procedure remains a criminal offense:

> Before a restorative justice procedure can be initiated, offenders must admit their guilt. Then, during the facilitated meeting, offenders explain what they did and why they did it. Victims then have a chance to explain how the crime harmed them, and the offenders have an opportunity to apologize for the harm they caused. Together, the conference participants work out an agreement for what the offenders must do to repair the harm caused by the offense. These agreements usually involve an apology, monetary compensation, and some type of reparative services aimed at helping the victim and/or the community (for a broader overview of restorative conferencing procedures.

> Thus, one of the fundamental differences between restorative and retributive responses to wrongdoing is the explicit focus on attempting to address victim concerns. Restorative justice practices provide a forum in which victims can express their concerns, giving them the opportunity to play a direct role in the justice proceedings and outcomes. Offering victims direct involvement in the justice-restoration process should lead to greater levels of victim satisfaction and feelings of fairness. In contrast, the practices of retribution typically employed in Western systems of criminal

justice focus primarily on making offenders suffer for the wrongs they have committed. This approach tends to neglect the importance of addressing the harms caused to crime victims or providing them with a voice in the justice process. Indeed, one of the explicit criticisms of traditional court procedures is that they typically ignore the needs of victims, "robbing them" of their rights. However, the infliction of retribution on offenders could provide a symbolic affirmation of victims in the context of their social groups. . . .

Given the emphasis that restorative justice places on victims (and the relative neglect of concrete victim concerns by retributive justice), it is not surprising that restorative justice is known as a particularly victim-oriented response to injustice. Indeed, some advocates of restorative justice have argued that justice responses need only achieve what is necessary for the victim and offender to reconcile, although others have argued for the importance of additional retribution. Empirically, the evidence demonstrates that restorative processes are better at producing victim satisfaction than retributive ones. Crime victims report being more satisfied with the justice process, feeling more fairly treated, and having less negative emotions after participation in restorative, as compared with traditional retributive justice procedures.

Dena M. Gromet et al., *A Victim-Centered Approach to Justice? Victim Satisfaction Effects on Third-Party Punishments*, 36 Law & Hum. Behav. 375, 2012.

3. Civil Compromise

While "restorative justice" may appear to be a recent innovation, similar models have long been recognized in traditional criminal justice processes. For example, where specifically authorized by statute, a criminal charge may be civilly compromised by agreement between the victim and defendant. A civil compromise is a settlement between the victim and the defendant. These settlements are typically monetary in nature, but may involve other terms, such as counseling or community service. Once a civil compromise is accepted by the court, the criminal charges are dismissed. Absent a civil compromise statute, there is no common law authority for the civil compromise settlement procedure. The federal law does not provide a general civil compromise statute. Several states have enacted civil compromise statutes.

Civil compromise statutes permit compromise only in minor criminal offenses. In some jurisdictions the distinction between minor and major offenses hinges on whether the crime is a misdemeanor or a felony. In other jurisdictions a minor offense is defined as one punishable by fine, without jail time as a possible consequence.

The first civil compromise statute was passed in New York in 1813:

The policy underlying compromise statutes was explained by the New York Commissioners on Practice and Pleading as follows:

There are many cases which are technically public offenses, but which are in reality rather of a private than a public nature, and where the public interests are better promoted by checking [money] than by encouraging criminal prosecutions. Of this class are libels, and simple assaults and batteries. . . .

[C]ases of this nature, have by the policy of our statutes, always been considered fit subjects of compromise; a policy which has been carried by the courts still further than the terms of the statute.

Cited in *People v. Mooltan*, 182 Cal. Rptr., at 766 (1982) (brackets added).

Generally, a trial court's approval of the civil compromise is required. A court's refusal to dismiss a case pursuant to civil compromise statute is within the court's discretion. The additional approval of the prosecutor is statutorily required in some, but not all, jurisdictions. Oregon's civil compromise statute is representative:

ORS 135.703 Crimes subject to being compromised; exceptions. (1) When a defendant is charged with a crime punishable as a misdemeanor for which the person injured by the act constituting the crime has a remedy by a civil action, the crime may be compromised, as provided in ORS 135.705, except when it was committed:

(a) By or upon a peace officer while in the execution of the duties of office:

(b) Riotously;

(c) With an intent to commit a crime punishable only as a felony; or

(d) By one family or household member upon another family or household member, as defined in ORS 107.705, or by a person upon an elderly person as defined in ORS 124.005 and the crime was:

(A) Assault in the fourth degree under ORS 163.160;

(B) Assault in the third degree under ORS 163.165;

(C) Menacing under ORS 163.190;

(D) Recklessly endangering another person under ORS 163.195; or

(E) Harassment under ORS 166.065.

* * *

135.705 Satisfaction of injured person; dismissal of charges. (1) If the person injured acknowledges in writing, at any time before trial on an accusatory instrument for the crime, that the person has received satisfaction for the injury, the court may, in its discretion, . . . order the accusatory instrument dismissed. . . .

In cases involving civil compromise procedure, separation of powers challenges have been raised under state constitutions to challenge the statutory exclusion of or the statutory participation of the prosecutor in the court's decision to dismiss.

In *State v. Nelles*, 713 P.2d 806 (Alaska App. 1986), the prosecutor appealed from the dismissal of a case by the trial court pursuant to a civil compromise. Defendant had allegedly assaulted his girlfriend. The prosecutor alleged that "the district court's order of dismissal, [over the objection of the prosecution], amounts to 'a usurpation of the executive power residing in the states attorney's office to bring charges and determine their disposition.'" The court stated:

> In the present case there was no judicial interference with the prosecution's initial decision to charge Nelles. Judge Crutchfield did subsequently exercise his discretion to dismiss the case. Yet this dismissal was expressly authorized by the legislature. . . . There is no suggestion in the civil compromise statutes that the courts power to dismiss is conditioned upon agreement of the prosecutor. See Annot. 42 ALR 3d 315, 319. . . . , *see also Ho v. Barneys Club, Inc.*, 28 Cal. 3d 603, 170 (1970) (in explaining the civil compromise statute, the court stated that the prosecutor has no role in the dismissal of civil compromise). The state has cited no case purporting to hold that prosecutorial consent is necessary as a matter of constitutional law, and we are aware of none. 713 P.2d at 810. [Brackets added.]

The Alaska civil compromise statute was amended as a result of the *Nelles* case to exclude civil compromise in the case of domestic violence. *See Municipality of Anchorage v. Sandes*, 902 P.2d 347 (Alaska App. 1995). The civil compromise has become disfavored in domestic violence cases and several compromise statutes specifically exclude domestic violence cases.

In an Arizona case a statutory scheme requiring consent of the prosecutor as a condition precedent to a civil compromise was challenged as an unconstitutional invasion of the powers of the *judiciary*. In rejecting the attack the court stated: "The executive branch has broad discretion in the enforcement of criminal laws and in deciding what charges, if any, will be filed against a defendant . . . that function carries with it the discretion to proceed or not to proceed once an action has been commenced unless the legislature has restricted that authority. . . ." *State v. Larson*, 764 P.2d 749, 751 (Ariz. 1988).

The benefits and problems of civil compromise based dismissals are similar to those found in dismissals pursuant to mediation settlements. These are discussed in the following section.

4. Victim-Offender Mediation

The mediation of minor criminal charges is another resolution procedure that is available in some jurisdictions. The result of a successful mediation process is the absence of a charge or dismissal of the defendant's charge. While not widespread, the mediation process offers potential advantages and disadvantages for victims compared to traditional criminal justice approaches. Mediation in criminal cases is explored in the following excerpts:

Gabriel Hallevy, *Therapeutic Victim-Offender Mediation Within the Criminal Justice Process—Sharpening the Evaluation of Personal Potential for Rehabilitation While Righting Wrongs Under the Alternative Dispute Resolution Philosophy*

16 HARV. NEGOT. L. REV. 65 (2011)

Victim-offender mediation is part of the wider concept of restorative justice. Restorative justice assumes that a deeper connection exists between the victim of the offense, the offender, and the community than is assumed by the formal criminal justice system. The victim and the offender are members of the community, and they have to resume their lives within that community. With this in mind, the concept of restorative justice emphasizes the social interactions among the victim, the offender, and the broader community. These social interactions include emotional, economic, and cultural aspects, among others.

Restorative justice takes into account the needs of the community as well as the victim, since both are damaged by criminal acts. These aspects of restorative justice made it an important paradigm for righting wrongs through the criminal justice process, as the justice attained is sometimes more complete than traditional punitive measures. Victim-offender mediation plays a major role in this therapeutic function of restorative justice.

Through victim-offender mediation, all parties involved may agree upon an appropriate response to the offense, which they feel is just and fair. They are not restricted by formal legal requirements, and the response may be creative, innovative, and unknown to the formal criminal justice process. For instance, the offender may undertake to assist the victim in activities of daily life that are difficult for the victim, to accompany the victim to the authorities, or to compensate the victim by labor or other means. A friendly understanding or rapport between the parties may enable solutions that a court could not have imposed.

Even though victim-offender mediation theory regards the commission of the offense as a trigger for conflict, it differs from other solutions in its suggestion of a broad and multidimensional social response to crime. The legal definition of the offense is not particularly important during the mediation. Instead, the mediation emphasizes righting wrongs. No social response can restore the situation to its status quo ante, but analyzing the harm caused by the crime and attempting to heal the injuries can go some distance toward righting the wrongs. Mediation between victims and offenders, with the involvement of the community, has great potential for achieving these aims.

Victim-offender mediation does not function merely as an alternative to the formal criminal justice process. In fact, it may be integrated into the formal process at any stage in which it could be useful. This article proposes the use of the victim-offender mediation process as an indicator of an offender's personal rehabilitation potential, which could take place before the offender is sentenced. But victim-offender mediation may take place much sooner (e.g., soon after the offense was committed, possibly even before the offender is indicted) or much later (e.g., concurrent with serving the sentence, during appeal processes). The most effective time it would seem for victim-offender mediation is before sentencing, so that the sentence would include the social response to the offense.

The victim-offender mediation process is a voluntary process; no party is forced to participate. Required enforcement of such a process would be counterproductive, since the most important part of the process is the open, honest communication between the victim and the offender, with no fear of consequences. In most legal systems, anything said during the meeting is confidential and inadmissible as evidence in court. However, victim-offender mediation is not exactly an ADR process, since it does not replace the criminal trial in court. It may affect the results of that trial, but does not replace it.

The personal and open communication between the parties creates a dynamic which encourages emotional, cognitive, and behavioral changes in both parties. These changes relate to each party personally, to the crime committed, and between the parties. These changes are crucial for the parties to reach a mutual voluntary decision regarding the most appropriate social response under the specific circumstances. For the offender, these changes are part of the realization of his personal rehabilitation potential via the mediation process. In most cases, these changes in the offender are visible to the participants in the process, and the depth of those changes is often impressive.

However, the mediation process may affect participants differently, as they have different needs and expectations during that process. Each participant plays a different role during the mediation, though the general purpose of the process is shared—restorative justice for all parties. The different roles played by the participants during the mediation process and the distinct contributions each makes in furtherance of the restorative justice goal shall be discussed below.

The Role of the Victim

It might be mistakenly thought that the role of the victim during victim-offender mediation is passive, considering the victim's similar role during the commission of the offense. In fact, the victim is an active partner in the process. Although during the criminal trial, the victim is not a counterpart of the defendant, instead playing the more passive role of a witness who does not participate in the decision making of the formal criminal process, the victim plays a major role during the mediation process. The process allows the victim to give a voice to his feelings, wishes, injuries, fears, and needs. For the victim, the immediate purpose is to enable him to recover from the consequences of the crime committed against him.

Different victims react differently to crimes committed against them. For some, it causes a minor change in their daily routine, but for others, the change is permanent and accompanied by fears or phobias. The feelings that the victim brings to the mediation process are generally feelings of helplessness, fear, shame, anger, frustration, and sadness. The victim's first step is to share those feelings with the community and with the offender who caused these feelings to arise with his criminal behavior. The offender's attitude in reacting to these feelings is critical. An offender who is empathetic toward these feelings requires a different rehabilitation program from an offender who is apathetic and alienated. The offender's reactions, therefore, convey valuable information to officials charged with assessing his personal rehabilitation potential.

In order to create restorative justice, the victim has to share not just his feelings, but also his needs with the other participants. Although different victims have different needs, some are more common. These include the need to restore (or sometimes create) self-confidence, the need to resume a daily routine, and the need to overcome anxiety aroused by the offense.

The way the victim conveys these feelings and needs affects the offender's capacity for change. In this way, the victim, in fact, plays a key role in the offender's rehabilitation process and also affects the outcome of the rehabilitation potential evaluation. Because of this, some have indicated that the victim possesses the key to the rehabilitation of the offender. The offender's dependence on the victim at that point is often significant for both offender and victim, since the offender may experience some of the helplessness the victim had felt as a result of the offense. For the victim, this may constitute retributive justice, while the offender may begin to understand the victim's feelings and empathize with those feelings, through experiencing them himself.

Jennifer Gerarda Brown, *The Use of Mediation to Resolve Criminal Cases: A Procedural Critique*
43 EMORY L.J. 1247 (1994)

In the ancient days of Western legal systems, criminal offenders could settle with victims and their families to avoid prosecution. For some criminal offenders in the United States, privatized criminal law survives: Victim-Offender Mediation ("VOM") allows offenders to avoid public prosecution or punishment by mediating criminal cases with their victims. An offender may be given the opportunity to participate in VOM at various stages in the criminal justice process. VOM may even divert cases from the criminal justice system, with little or no involvement by state officials unless the mediation fails to resolve the case. Today, more than 100 VOM programs exist in the United States. In 1993, U.S. programs disposed of 16,500 cases involving 12,931 victims and 14,059 offenders.

Offenders participate in VOM in order to reduce their expected punishment. An offender who participates may be rewarded by dismissal of charges or reduction of penalties. An offender who refuses to participate or fails to reach an agreement with the victim, on the other hand, returns to the criminal justice system for possible prosecution or sentencing. The outcome of the mediation can influence judges, parole boards, and prosecutors as they decide how to charge or punish the offender. And the outcome of the mediation turns in large part upon the victim's satisfaction.

Thus, VOM transforms the criminal justice paradigm by placing victims at the center, rather than on the periphery, of the criminal process. In effect, VOM transfers the power to resolve all or part of a criminal case from the state to a private party—the victim. As a result, VOM represents a return to an earlier model of criminal justice. In VOM, as in ancient criminal practice, the victim controls the offender's fate.

[P]lacing such control in the hands of the victim is inconsistent with the character and purpose of the criminal law as it has evolved since ancient times. As currently structured, VOM's relationship to the criminal justice system disserves the interests of victims, offenders, and the state.

VOM disserves the interests of victims by stressing forgiveness and reconciliation before victims have the vindication of a public finding that the offender is guilty. In addition, VOM suppresses victims' outrage and loss by assuming that these negative feelings can be expressed and resolved in the course of a few hours spent meeting with the offender.

VOM disserves offenders in three ways: by using selection criteria that are not clearly related to the goals of the program; by eliminating procedural protections such as the right to counsel or rules of evidence; and by using the leverage of pending criminal process to gain advantages for the victim, a private party. If offenders believe that they will be worse off in the ordinary criminal justice system should they fail to reach a mediated agreement satisfactory to their victims, the offenders may have an unduly strong incentive to mediate and reach agreement, no matter what the psychological or monetary cost.

VOM characterizes many crimes as private disputes that fracture relationships between individuals; the state's interest in these disputes is minimal. The structure of VOM often belies this assumption, however, because the mediation occurs before a backdrop of state involvement and coercion. Victims of crime negotiate not only with their own individual bargaining strength, but also with the threat of enhanced state punishment should the parties fail to reach agreement. The victim appropriates some of the state's leverage over the offender because both the victim and the offender know that the offender is more likely to be prosecuted or incarcerated if the victim is not satisfied with the negotiation.

VOM disserves the interests of the state because it devalues the substantive and procedural norms observed in public processes. Despite proponents' claims that VOM can resolve criminal cases according to the substantive standards of the "community" in which the crime occurred, such a community rarely exists in the United States today apart from the state itself. When centralized rules of criminal law are rejected in the name of a "community" that may not even exist, any standard may fill the vacuum to resolve individual cases. Success is measured by the victim's satisfaction with the outcome rather than consistency with substantive legal rules. VOM programs ignore procedural norms because the end (the parties' ability to reach agreement) often justifies the means (lack of counsel for the offender, coercion prior to and during the mediation).

* * *

By proposing a separation between mediation and the criminal justice system, they intentionally seek to eliminate one of the stated goals of most VOM programs: to serve as an alternative to incarceration. Allowing offenders to buy their way out of prison with monetary and nonmonetary compensation to victims unacceptably confounds the private goals of mediation and the public goals of criminal law. If a jurisdiction is serious about creating alternatives to incarceration, then the state, rather than crime victims or private administrators of VOM programs, ought to decide whether offenders are entitled to such alternatives. And the state should place these alternatives in the hands of private parties only after they have fully accounted for the "process dangers" of such a change.

Notes

1. Gabriel Hallevy, the author of the first article above, believes that victim-offender mediation empowers victims. But Jennifer Brown, the author of the last article, is concerned that victim-offender mediation disserves the interests of victims by stressing forgiveness and reconciliation over other possible interests. Who has the better argument? Are there ways of structuring victim-offender mediation to navigate these concerns?

2. Some programs for criminal mediation do not explicitly provide for victim participation, but often victims are involved at the request of prosecutors. *See* Maureen E. Laflin, *Criminal Mediation Has Taken Root in Idaho's Courts*, 56 ADVOCATE 37 (2013).

3. Should victims who believe in restorative justice be able to choose to participate in a restorative process of civil compromise or mediation, rather than a process based on retribution? What difference would there be in your opinion if the crime were serious? If it was a second offense? If it was a crime between family members?

4. An extreme form of victim-offender mediation is a face-to-face confrontation between the victim (or, in a homicide case, the victim's family) and the offender. These victim-offender reconciliation programs are discussed at the end of Chapter 10, below.

Chapter 8

Domestic Violence

Introduction

Many, but not all, domestic violence victims are or become uncooperative in the prosecution of the batterer. The reasons for non-cooperation include: The victims' safety, the safety of their children, economic dependence, and learned helplessness. Moreover, domestic assaults and rapes were not, in the culture of law enforcement and, perhaps much of society, considered criminal. Spousal rape, for example, was not a crime until states began criminalizing it in the 1970s. Assault of another person has always been a crime. While technically including domestic violence, the crime of assault against batterers was rarely pursued.

Prosecution of domestic violence reflects a change in cultural understanding of what constitutes a "crime." It has similarly changed our understanding of who is a crime "victim." Women do not have to give up their personhood when they elect to have a partner. It also presents unique challenges for criminal procedure.

A. Criminal Procedure

1. Historical Background

Today domestic violence is a crime in all 50 states. Things have not always been this way.

State v. Black

60 N.C. 262 (Win. 1864)

The defendant was indicted for an assault on Tamsey Black, his wife. The evidence showed that the defendant and his wife lived separate from one other. The defendant was passing by the house of one Koonce, where his wife then resided, when she called to him in an angry manner and asked him, if he had patched Sal Daly's bonnet, (Sal Daly being a woman of ill-fame.) She then went into the house, and defendant followed her and asked her what she wanted, when she repeated her question about the bonnet. Angry words then passed between them. He accused her of connection with a negro man, and she called him a hog thief, whereupon the defendant seized her by her hair, and pulled her down upon the floor, and held her there for some time. He gave her no blows, but she stated [at] the trial, that her head was considerably hurt, and that her throat was injured, and continued sore for several months, but that he did not choke her, nor attempt to do so. At the trial she was entirely recovered. After she got up from the floor, she continued her abuse of him. . . .

Pearson, C.J. A husband is responsible for the acts of his wife, and he is required to govern his household, and for that purpose, the law permits him to use towards his wife such a degree of force, as is necessary to control an unruly temper, and make her behave herself; and unless some permanent injury be inflicted, or there be an excess of violence, or such a degree of cruelty as shows that it is inflicted to gratify his own bad passions, the law will not invade the domestic forum, or go behind the curtain. It prefers to leave the parties to themselves, as the best mode of inducing them to make the matter up and live together as man and wife should.

Certainly, the exposure of a scene like that set out in this case, can do no good. In respect to the parties, a public exhibition in the Court House of such quarrels and fights between man and wife, widens the breach, makes a reconciliation almost impossible, and encourages insubordination; and in respect to the public, it has a pernicious tendency: so . . . such matters are excluded from the Courts, unless there is a permanent injury or excessive violence or cruelty indicating malignity and vindictiveness.

In this case the wife commenced the quarrel. The husband, in a passion provoked by excessive abuse, pulled her upon the floor by the hair, but restrained himself, did not strike a blow, and she admits he did not choke her, and she continued to abuse him after she got up. Upon this state of facts the jury ought to have been charged in favor of the defendant. . . .

It was insisted by Mr. Winston [counsel for the state] that, admitting such to be the law when the husband and wife lived together, it did not apply when, as in this case, they were living apart. That may be so when there is a divorce "from bed and board," because the law then recognizes and allows the separation, but it can take no notice of a private agreement to live separate. . . .

Note

Today, domestic violence is prosecuted as assault. Some jurisdictions have enacted assault statutes particular to domestic violence. Many urban prosecutors' offices now have domestic violence prosecution departments. What has prompted this change is a shift in cultural perspectives about women and the relationship between couples and the state. Domestic violence is no longer "a family matter." Prosecutorial approaches are roughly divided into two categories: (1) diversion or mediation for first-time offenders, and (2) strictly criminal prosecution.

The court's notion that a husband could take action against his wife without criminal sanction unless there was "excessive violence" was sometimes understood to mean that a husband could beat his wife with a switch no larger than his thumb — the so-called "rule of thumb." *See generally,* Henry Ansgar Kelly, *Rule of Thumb and the Folklore of the Husband's Stick,* 44 J. LEGAL ED. 341 (1994) (citing historical authorities that legitimize corporal punishment of wives and others that condemn the practice).

2. The Statistics

Sharon Cammack & Patric Pujo, *Domestic Violence: A National Epidemic*

HOUSTON LAWYER, Oct. 2004, at 42

The Victims of Domestic Violence

The national statistics for domestic violence occurrences are staggering. On a daily average, more than three women are murdered by their husbands or boyfriends. In 1999, intimate partners committed 1,642 murders; of these, 74 percent of the victims were women. In 2000, an intimate partner killed 1,247 women and 440 men. In 2001, intimate partner violence by current or former spouses, boyfriends or girlfriends occurred nearly 700,000 times. Subsequent years reflect similar numbers. Eighty-five percent of these victims are women. These statistics represent only reported incidents and do not include recurring incidents or multiple victimizations. One in five women is victimized repeatedly. The net result of this violence is that over 140,000 of the 700,000 annual victims are subjected to repeated attacks. In addition, national estimates for 2000 revealed 503,485 women were stalked by an intimate partner.

Despite the overwhelming nature of these statistics, the national figures show a slight decline in domestic violence over the last 10 years. In 1993, men were the victims in approximately 162,870 violent crimes involving a domestic partner. By 2001, this figure fell to an estimated 103,220 crimes. Intimate partner violence against women also declined from 1993 to 2001. In 1993, women were victimized in approximately 1.1 million non-fatal violent crimes. By 2001, this figure declined to a still shocking 588,490 incidents of intimate partner violence. . . .

Domestic violence is not isolated to the poor or uneducated of our society. It is not confined to any ethnic or religious group. And it is not directed only against a wife by her husband. Domestic violence occurs in any type of intimate relationship: married, divorced, separated, heterosexual, gay, lesbian, transgendered, and even in dating relationships. Domestic violence does not discriminate. While the majority of its victims are adult women, domestic violence targets men, the elderly, and teenagers.

———————

National Coalition Against Domestic Violence, Domestic Violence Fact Sheet (2015):

WHAT IS DOMESTIC VIOLENCE? Domestic violence is the willful intimidation, physical assault, battery, sexual assault, and/or other abusive behavior as part of a systematic pattern of power and control perpetrated by one intimate partner against another. It includes physical violence, sexual violence, threats, and emotional/psychological abuse. The frequency and severity of domestic violence varies dramatically.

DID YOU KNOW?

- In the United States, an average of 20 people are physically abused by intimate partners every minute. This equates to more than 10 million abuse victims annually.

- 1 in 3 women and 1 in 4 men have been physically abused by an intimate partner.

- 1 in 5 women and 1 in 7 men have been severely physically abused by an intimate partner.

- 1 in 7 women and 1 in 18 men have been stalked. Stalking causes the target to fear she/he or someone close to her/him will be harmed or killed

- On a typical day, domestic violence hotlines nationwide receive approximately 20,800 calls.

- The presence of a gun in a domestic violence situation increases the risk of homicide by 500%.

- Intimate partner violence accounts for 15% of all violent crime.

- Intimate partner violence is most common among women between the ages of 18-24.

- 19% of intimate partner violence involves a weapon.

WHY IT MATTERS Domestic violence is prevalent in every community, and affects all people regardless of age, socio-economic status, sexual orientation, gender, race, religion, or nationality. Physical violence is often accompanied by emotionally abusive and controlling behavior as part of a much larger, systematic pattern of dominance and control. Domestic violence can result in physical injury, psychological trauma, and even death. The devastating consequences of domestic violence can cross generations and last a lifetime.

SEXUAL ASSAULT

- 1 in 5 women and 1 in 59 men in the United States is raped during his/her lifetime.

- 9.4% of women in the United States have been raped by an intimate partner.

STALKING

- 19.3 million women and 5.1 million men in the United States have been stalked.

- 66.2% of female stalking victims reported stalking by a current or former intimate partner.

HOMICIDE

- 1 in 3 female murder victims and 1 in 20 male murder victims are killed by intimate partners.
- A study of intimate partner homicides found 20% of victims were family members or friends of the abused partner, neighbors, persons who intervened, law enforcement responders, or bystanders.
- 72% of all murder-suicides are perpetrated by intimate partners.
- 94% of murder-suicide victims are female.

PHYSICAL/MENTAL EFFECTS

- Victims of intimate partner violence are at increased risk of contracting HIV or other STI's due to forced intercourse and/or prolonged exposure to stress.
- Intimate partner victimization is correlated with a higher rate of depression and suicidal behavior.
- Only 34% of people who are injured by intimate partners receive medical care for their injuries.

ECONOMIC EFFECTS

- Victims of intimate partner violence lose a total of 8,000,000 million days of paid work each year, the equivalent of 32,000 full-time jobs.
- Intimate partner violence is estimated to cost the US economy between $5.8 billion and $12.6 billion annually, up to 0.125% of the national gross domestic product.
- Between 21-60% of victims of intimate partner violence lose their jobs due to reasons stemming from the abuse.
- Between 2003 and 2008, 142 women were murdered in their workplace by former or current intimate partners. This amounts to 22% of workplace homicides among women.

3. The Reluctant Criminal Justice Response

While domestic violence has been a crime in this country for at least the last several decades, the criminal justice response (both by police and prosecutors) has varied. A study published in 1983 presents the status of domestic violence cases in the criminal justice system at that time, noting the reluctance with which police, prosecutors, judges (and even victims) pursued domestic violence cases in the criminal justice system.

Maureen McLeod, *Victim Noncooperation in the Prosecution of Domestic Violence*

21 Criminology 395 (1983)

POLICE NONCOOPERATION

The law enforcement response to domestic violence is often perceived as inadequate or inappropriate. Martin (1979) notes that police may utilize a call screening process to prioritize their calls or to selectively fail to respond to particular classes of calls such as complaints of spousal assaults. When police do acknowledge a spousal assault, the law enforcement response may fall short of the victim's expectations. Paterson (1979) observes that the nature of the police response may fall within one of several categories that denigrate the legitimacy of the victim's complaint. For example, the police may empathize with the offender's situation, refuse to search for an offender not present at the scene, or discourage the victim from making a citizen's arrest.

This informal posture may be adopted because of the absence of explicit guidelines, official departmental policy, personal safety concerns, or personal biases. In jurisdictions with no explicit procedural guidelines for domestic violence intervention, individual officers are free to exercise broad discretion in structuring their responses to these situations. In one small New Hampshire town, for example, police initiated a discretionary $12 filing fee for assault charges, that was levied in cases of spousal assaults but rarely in instances of nonfamilial assaults.

An informal response to domestic violence may be official departmental policy. The following techniques for dispute resolution, taken from a training bulletin released by the Oakland (California) Police Department in June 1975, reflect current departmental positions in several jurisdictions.

> The police role in a dispute situation is more often that of a mediator and peacemaker than enforcer of the law. In dispute situations, officers are often caught between an obligation to enforce the law on one hand and, on the other, the possibility that police action such as arrest will only aggravate the dispute or create a serious danger for the arresting officer due to possible efforts to resist arrest. . . . Normally, officers should adhere to the policy that arrests shall be avoided except as necessary to (1) protect life and property and (2) preserve the peace.

Concern for personal safety is an influential factor in determining the frequency and intensity of the law enforcement response to domestic violence. FBI statistics are commonly cited to support the contention that the greatest proportion of police injuries are incurred while responding to domestic violence calls. In fiscal year 1980, 32.9% of all assaults and 11.5% of all homicides of police officers resulted during a "disturbance call." Previous interpretations of this statistic have been challenged. As defined by the Uniform Crime Reporting Program, a "disturbance call" includes not only domestic violence but also bar fights, disorderly conduct, and reports of a "man with gun." Margarita's (1980) study of assaults and homicides of New York police officers further questions the contention that domestic violence calls are potentially the most life-threatening police encounters.

Individual officers' biases and perceptions of spousal assaults perhaps play the major role in shaping law enforcement's response to domestic violence. Many officers view the incident as a private matter falling outside the realm of legal intervention. Others have expressed the belief that arrest is sometimes inappropriate because the victim may provoke the offender and thus be deserving of his violent outburst. A study conducted by the Police Executive Research Forum (PERF) of the responses of police officers to domestic violence found that 19% of the officers surveyed indicated that they would avoid arrest whenever possible. When asked to identify factors influencing their decision not to arrest in domestic violence situations, the reason cited most often was the officer's belief that victims refuse to press charges, followed by the belief that the victims tend to drop formalized charges.

Because of these beliefs and because in fact many spouse abuse cases are never formally adjudicated due to victim noncooperation, a frequently observed mode of police response focuses on the informal resolution of spousal conflicts. The designation of these incidents as disputes or disturbances — not as assaultive actions — supports the officers' contention that spouse abuse is not criminal violence but merely a temporary state of familial disequilibrium that requires remedial rather than disruptive intervention. Thus, the police officer perceives his role to be one of mediator.

Statutory enactments serve as another delimiter of the law enforcement response to spousal assaults. A recent survey of domestic violence legislation revealed that 16 states allow for a misdemeanor arrest if the officer has probable cause to believe that an assault has occurred. In all other jurisdictions a misdemeanor arrest is authorized only if the offense was committed in the officer's presence.

PROSECUTORIAL NONCOOPERATION

While police nonresponse and nonarrest policies and practices are formidable barriers to the criminal prosecution of spouse abuse cases, they are not the only obstacles to be overcome. The reluctance of prosecutors to file formal charges in domestic violence situations has been documented. This inaction may stem from a prosecutor's belief that initiating such proceedings is a misappropriation of time and resources because a vast majority of victims decline to actively pursue prosecution at this point. A second factor influencing the exercise of prosecutorial discretion is individual beliefs about the nature and causation of spousal violence. A prosecutor may recommend that a case be *nolle prossed*, be prosecuted as a misdemeanor rather than as a felony, or be handled through social service or civil channels because of personal beliefs that the victims have provoked violence or that both parties share responsibility for the violent outburst.

In some jurisdictions quasi-judicial remedies are utilized in resolving the conflict. Field and Field (1973) have described such a process in Washington, D.C. The prosecutor conducts an informal hearing during which the defendant is threatened with arrest and/or the possibility of divorce proceedings.

A similar procedure was observed more than a decade ago in Detroit. Parties to a domestic assault were requested by the responding officer to appear the following morning in a designated courtroom. The mock judicial proceedings that ensued were allegedly conducted by a police officer who introduced himself as a member of the judiciary. If the injuries were serious the case would be referred to the prosecutor for further consideration. In the majority of cases, however, the hearing officer would inform the offender that he was subject to a peace bond, a fictional disposition. The imposition of this "sentence" was not recorded on any official document nor were its conditions enforced. Nevertheless, it was argued that this procedure served as a successful deterrent to further abuses.

JUDICIAL NONCOOPERATION

For cases in which criminal proceedings are initiated, the judge may opt to dismiss the charges at the preliminary hearing. If the offender enters a guilty plea or is found guilty by a jury, the judge may suspend the sentence, place the offender on probation, or levy the minimum sentence allowed by law. Several states have designated specific penalties that may be imposed upon conviction for spousal assault. The variation in these penalties suggests legislative dissension as to the seriousness of spouse abuse. For example, the schedule of allowable incarcerative terms ranges from a maximum of one month in Massachusetts to a maximum of up to five years for a second offense in Ohio. The fine structure covers an equally broad expanse, ranging from a maximum fine of $100 in Massachusetts to a possible maximum of $10,000 in Wisconsin.

VICTIM NONCOOPERATION

A report published by PERF proposes a number of measures designed to alter the nature of police intervention in domestic violence situations. PERF argues that spouse abuse can no longer be considered a private family matter outside the jurisdiction of law enforcement authorities. Emphasis is placed on the need for more comprehensive arrest policies and increased awareness of the needs and fears of the battered or threatened victim. The report recommends that police departments adopt explicit policies that clearly delineate these objectives and provide meaningful guidelines for their implementation. In a similar fashion, prosecutors' offices have become increasingly sensitized to the complexity of the domestic violence situation and the often conflicting demands of victim needs and resources.

Although long overdue, these measures will be meaningless if the victim refuses to cooperate in the prosecution. Victim noncooperation can be operationalized in several manners—failure to call the police, failure to cooperate at the time of the police intervention, failure to sign the formal complaint, failure to appear at the district attorney's office to formally document the charges, and failure to appear at the scheduled court hearing.

Although it is useful to examine the phenomenon of victim noncooperation at each of these decision points, very little is known about the initial decision *not* to notify law enforcement officials. Estimates of the rate of nonreporting of spouse abuse are as disparate as are the estimates of the incidence of spouse abuse. A recent study of the level and nature of violence among intimates (spouse, relatives, friends, neighbors, classmates, co-workers, etc.) suggests that 55% of intimate violence is never reported to the police. This figure is markedly conservative in relation to other estimates. Walker (1979) contends that less than 10% of seriously injured women report abuse to the police and that this figure drops further in the case of women who escape serious injury. A similar estimate was derived by the Kentucky Commission on Women (Schulman, 1980). Its survey of 1,793 women resulted in the acknowledgment of 881 violent incidents, only 10% of which were reported to the authorities. The highest estimate of nonreporting has been reported by Steinmetz (1977). From a sample of 56 Delaware families, she estimates that 269 of every 270 incidents of wife beating go unreported—a nonreporting rate of 99.6%.

Several psychological and situational explanations have been advanced to account for victim noncooperation throughout the prosecution process. Research findings have suggested that approximately 71% of those unreported victimizations were not reported to the police because of the victim's definition of the incident as a private or personal matter.

Other explanations focus on the formidable economic consequences of prosecution for the victim and her family, the socialization of women to expect and to accept violence, the inconvenience of prosecution, and the fear of reprisal. . . .

Notes

1. At the time this article was written (1983), did police, prosecutors, and judges really view domestic violence victims as "victims" worthy of protection through the criminal justice system?

2. A victim of domestic violence has access to the same criminal procedure victim participation and protection laws as a victim of any other crime. Thus, a domestic violence victim is restrained by law in the same way as other victims. One restraint is that domestic violence victims, like all victims of other crimes, have no authority to dismiss the criminal case. As discussed in Chapter 3, victims of minor crimes may have informal influence with prosecutors not to bring charges. However, domestic violence is not a minor crime. This means domestic violence victims do not typically exercise successful informal influence over police and prosecutors to drop the charges.

3. Domestic violence criminal law and procedure reforms are credited to the efforts of women's anti-domestic violence organizations. The victims' rights movement has not played a significant role.

4. Samantha Swindler, *Victim Questions Why Judge Cut Off Statement*, THE OREGONIAN, A2, Feb. 25, 2018, recounts a courtroom scene where the judge taking the

plea of a batterer told the victim before she was done with her statement "I don't want to hear it." When the District Attorney tried to intercede, the judge said, "I know what you think." After sentencing, the D.A. asked the judge to let the victim finish her statement, to which the judge replied, I think [the victim] has said enough." A lawyer for the victim will seek a resentencing hearing under Oregon's enforceable victims' rights statute. (See Chapter 11 on Remedies and Review)

4. Specific Criminal Procedural Reforms

Because of the initial reluctance of criminal justice agencies to aggressively pursue domestic violence cases, advocates for victims of domestic violence (particularly grass roots women's service organizations and both national and local women's organizations) have made a tremendous effort to change the view of the dominant culture concerning domestic violence and to improve the legal system's response to domestic violence. To change the belief system or bias of a culture is a profoundly difficult task. Generally, the change has not required rewriting statutes criminalizing assault (these statutes facially prohibit all types of assault) but rather getting the system to enforce these existing laws against domestic violence perpetrators.

Interestingly, many advocates for domestic violence victims have generally urged law enforcement and prosecution approaches that leave victims without any significant influence over the process. For example, these advocates have urged a system of "mandatory arrest" in which police are required to arrest and book all perpetrators of domestic violence. Similarly, these advocates have urged prosecutors to follow "no drop" policies—that is, a policy of not dropping criminal charges even when the victims refuses to cooperate with the prosecution or recants her initial claim of abuse. These approaches of minimizing victim autonomy and participation stand in seeming contrast to the mainstream of the victims' rights movement, which has sought to significantly expand victim participation in the process. For example, several chapters in this book explore a victim's ability to pursue criminal charges (Chapter 4 on Charging) or to dismiss charges (Chapter 7 on Pretrial Disposition)—areas in which victims' advocates have generally sought to place victims in the middle of the process.

Is there a different dynamic to domestic violence prosecutions that justifies treating victims differently? Advocates for domestic violence victims often argue that women who are victims of domestic violence may have the absence of free will due to, for example, the psychological state of learned helplessness, the repetitive and cyclical nature of domestic violence, and threats toward children in the home. These factors, some advocates argue, distinguish domestic violence from, say, an armed robbery or burglary. Moreover, regardless of the victim's wishes, proponents of mandatory arrest and no-drop polices stress that domestic violence is a "public harm" in which the state should be involved.

The following sections explore these issues by examining the debate over mandatory arrest and no-drop policies. Are these policies "pro-victim"? In any event, are these polices good for society?

a. Mandatory Arrest Policies

Mandatory arrest polices frequently eliminate a police officer's discretion and require the officer to make an arrest where there is probable cause to believe domestic abuse has occurred. An example is Oregon's mandatory arrest law:

OR. REV. STAT. § 133.055 (emphasis added)

(2)(a) [W]hen a peace officer is at the scene of a domestic disturbance and has probable cause to believe that an assault has occurred between spouses, former spouses or adult persons related by blood or marriage or persons of opposite sex residing together or who formerly resided together, or to believe that one such person has placed the other in fear of imminent serious physical injury, the officer *shall arrest* and take into custody the alleged assailant or potential assailant.

(b) When the peace officer makes an arrest under paragraph (a) of this subsection, the peace officer is not required to arrest both persons.

(c) When a peace officer makes an arrest under paragraph (a) of this subsection, the peace officer shall make every effort to determine who is the assailant or potential assailant by considering, among other factors:

(A) The comparative extent of the injuries inflicted or the seriousness of threats creating a fear of physical injury;

(B) If reasonably ascertainable, the history of domestic violence between the persons involved;

(C) Whether any alleged crime was committed in self-defense; and

(D) The potential for future assaults.

(3) Whenever any peace officer has reason to believe that a family or household member has been abused or that an elderly person has been abused, that officer shall use all reasonable means to prevent further abuse, including advising each person of the availability of a shelter or other services in the community and giving each person immediate notice of the legal rights and remedies available. The notice shall consist of handing each person a copy of the following statement:

IF YOU ARE THE VICTIM OF DOMESTIC VIOLENCE, you can ask the district attorney to file a criminal complaint. You also have the right to go to the circuit court and file a petition requesting any of the following orders for relief: (a) An order restraining your attacker from abusing you; (b) an order directing your attacker to leave your household; (c) an order preventing your attacker from entering your residence, school, business or place of employment; (d) an order awarding you or the other parent custody of or visitation with a minor child or children; (e) an order restraining your attacker from molesting or interfering with minor children in your custody; (f) an order directing the party not granted custody to pay support of minor children, or for support of the other party if that party has a legal obligation to do so.

Notes

1. According to one tabulation, more than half the states have mandatory arrest laws of various forms. Deborah Epstein, *Procedural Justice: Tempering the State's Response to Domestic Violence*, 43 Wm. & Mary L. Rev. 1843, 1855 n.42 (2002). Twenty-one states require arrest when there is probable cause to believe violation of an order occurred. *See, e.g.,* Cal. Penal Code §836(d). An additional 13 states (including Oregon, as noted above) mandate arrest when there is a finding of domestic violence, regardless of whether a protective order is violated. *See, e.g.,* Mass. Gen. Laws Ann. ch. 209A, §6.

2. One impetus for states and police departments to adopt mandatory arrest policies is to avoid the prospect of a civil suit for providing inadequate protection. The case of *Thurman v. City of Torrington*, 595 F. Supp. 1521 (D. Conn. 1984), is often cited as a spark to such laws. In *Thurman*, Tracy Thurman called police several times seeking protection from her estranged and abusive husband, but police offered little help. Shortly after these calls, she was attacked and received stab wounds to the neck and chest, which left her paralyzed and caused permanent disfigurement. She filed a lawsuit against the city and several police officers, ultimately obtaining a $2.3 million verdict for failure to provide adequate protection and for violation of her right to equal protection. *See* Vito Nicholas Ciraco, Note, *Fighting Domestic Violence With Mandatory Arrest: Are We Winning? An Analysis in New Jersey*, 22 Women's Rts. L. Rep. 169 (2001). *See generally* Lauren L. McFarlane, *Domestic Violence Victims v. Municipalities: Who Pays When the Police Will Not Respond?*, 41 Case W. Res. L. Rev. 929 (1991).

3. Oregon's mandatory arrest statute tries to prevent one form of police noncooperation: simply arresting both the perpetrator and the victim for "mutual combat" or mutual abuse. Rather than permitting an arrest-them-all approach, Oregon's statute requires police to determine who is the primary aggressor.

————————

Is mandatory arrest a superior approach to allowing police officers to exercise the broad discretion they traditionally enjoy in the field? Consider the following competing views:

Joan Zorza, *Mandatory Arrest for Domestic Violence: Why It May Prove the Best Step in Curbing Repeat Abuse*
10 Criminal Justice 2 (1995)

Traditional Police Response Criticized

For many years, most battered women and their advocates were disappointed by how the police traditionally responded when a woman was beaten. Police were taught that domestic violence was a private matter, ill-suited to public intervention. As a result, police often either ignored domestic violence calls, or purposely delayed responding for several hours. When they did respond, they often sided with the abusive man. At best, they removed the abusive man from the home on the theory that all he needed was to cool off. But most police avoided arresting the abuser whenever possible, often warning the victim that arrest would only result in making her situation worse because her abuser would probably lose his job or be forced to pay badly needed money for bail or court costs. The few arrests that police made were usually done to vindicate an attack on the policy, or because the abuser was wanted for some other crime.

Faced with such little assistance, it is no wonder that battered women learned that calling the police was futile. One 1970s study of 109 severely battered women found that they reported less than 2 percent of the assaults that they suffered from their lover to the police.

In recent years, the criminal justice system has questioned what approach the police should use to respond to calls from women who claim they are the victims of battering. With society's recognition that domestic violence is a serious crime with serious consequences to the victim as well as any children in the home, the criminal justice system has been far more inclined to hold in disfavor the old policy of treating domestic violence as merely a private dispute between the two individuals. Furthermore, many myths that helped to support the old police rationale for not arresting the abuser have been discredited. For example, police were taught that domestic violence calls were particularly dangerous, which was often cited in part to justify not treating these cases like other crimes. However, domestic violence calls, which account for 30 percent of all police calls in the United States, account for only 5.7 percent of police deaths, making responding to them one of the least dangerous of all police activities.

Similarly, the myth that any battered woman can safely leave her abuser whenever she wants, ignores the reality that violence escalates and becomes most severe when the victim leaves or attempts to leave.

Another myth still used to justify not treating domestic violence like any other crime is that battered women, unlike other crime victims, seldom follow through on criminal charges against their abusers. Yet battered women, who are frequently threatened and often beaten by their abusers while the criminal cases are pending, are no more likely to try to drop charges than any other victims of violent crimes who are threatened or harmed by the perpetrator of the crime.

Experiments Show Arrest Deters Best

As the controversy has grown about how police should respond in domestic violence cases, domestic violence offenses have been singled out to determine whether arrest is the most effective deterrent. Although feminists have observed that it is primarily when women and children are the victims that studies (and/or therapy) are advocated instead of criminal sanctions, the idea of experiments to test this theory, once raised, took on immediate appeal. Indeed, the very first scientifically controlled experiment from early 1981 to mid-1982 to test the effectiveness of arrest took place in Minneapolis, Minnesota, where a comparison was made of recidivism rates for misdemeanor domestic violence cases among three types of police response: those abusers the police arrested, those they removed from the household, and those situations in which the police acted only as mediators.

Lawrence W. Sherman and Richard A. Berk, who conducted the experiment, demonstrated that six months after the initial police response, 10 percent of those arrested, 24 percent of those removed from the scene, and 19 percent of those who simply received advice had repeated their violence. The figures were based on official records. Interviews with the victims also confirmed that arresting the abusers put the victims at considerably lower risk of repeat victimization: only 19 percent of arrested abusers—compared to 33 percent of those removed and 37 percent of those advised—had repeated their violence.

Lawrence Sherman made headlines in 1983 when he announced to the press that his police experiment proved that arrest better deterred men who beat their partners than did any other police response. His claims were bolstered by the results of a second police study conducted by Richard A. Berk and Phyllis Newton involving 783 wife-battering incidents in California during a 28-month interval.

Most battered women's advocates were pleased with the results of the two experiments, having long been frustrated by police inaction in abuse cases. But, they also knew that in addition to protecting the abuse victim, arresting the batterer sent a clear message to the victim, her children, and the rest of society that it was a crime to beat a woman and that society would no longer tolerate it. They hoped that treating domestic violence as a crime would force society to stop blaming the victim, and instead hold the abuser accountable for his abuse. Accordingly, most advocates have urged tougher police arrest laws for domestic assaults.

In 1977, Oregon enacted Chapter 845, the first statute in the country that required police to arrest abusers in cases of misdemeanor domestic violence offenses based on probable cause. By mid-1983, when the Minneapolis police experiment results were released, 33 states *allowed* police to arrest perpetrators of misdemeanor domestic violence incidents upon probable cause, and six states *required* police to make arrests in at least some domestic violence assaults. Today, every state allows police to make an arrest based upon the probable cause that a domestic violence offense has occurred, and more than half of the states and the District of Columbia have laws requiring police to arrest on probable cause for at least some domestic violence crimes.

Developments in the Law: Legal Responses to Domestic Violence
106 Harv. L. Rev. 1498 (1993)

. . . mandatory arrest may backfire and lead to increased violence if it angers the batterer further. Five recent studies designed to replicate the Minneapolis study have questioned the wisdom of mandating arrest. Two of them confirmed the deterrent effect of arrest found in Minneapolis, but in three others, arrest correlated with an *increase* in subsequent violence. Although these studies were intended to be replications, generalization across and comparison between them is difficult because their experimental designs actually varied considerably. One consistent finding across all six studies that may explain the inconsistent results, however, was a robust correlation between the deterrent effect of arrest and the employment status of the batterer: arrest correlated with increased violence when the batters were unemployed, but it correlated with decreased subsequent abuse by employed batterers. Another possible reason for the diverse findings may lie in differential prosecution or conviction rates. For example, in the Milwaukee study, only five percent of those arrested were prosecuted and only one percent were eventually convicted. The study's conclusion that arrest correlated with a subsequent increase in violence thus might suggest not that mandatory arrest is ineffective, but that the stakes need to be higher and prosecution more vigorous in order to achieve a substantial deterrent effect.

Dennis P. Saccuzzo, *How Should the Police Respond to Domestic Violence: A Therapeutic Jurisprudence Analysis of Mandatory Arrest*

39 Santa Clara L. Rev. 765 (1999)

Let's assume that mandatory arrest of domestic violence offenders actually does little to deter recidivism and can, in some cases, even have negative effects such as increasing violence. What valid or rational reason would there be for such policy?

Five Reasons in Favor of Mandatory Arrest

Assuming no deterrence effect, Evan Stark[1] provides five important reasons to support mandatory arrest for batterers. First, mandatory arrest serves to control police behavior. As Stark noted, "the absence of a standard for police practice increased women's sense of powerlessness and thus posed a major obstacle to their empowerment." Thus, mandatory arrest serves to empower women.

Second, mandatory arrest provides protection from immediate violence. When the police stop short of arrest, a battered woman remains vulnerable to further abuse and violence. Mandatory arrest not only removes this immediate threat, but also gives the battered person time to consider her options and, if necessary, take evasive action.

A third factor to consider in support of mandatory arrest is its generally deterring effect. Statistical studies have focused on the role of specific deterrence, that is, deterring future violence in the arrested batterer. What these studies fail to address is how a policy of mandatory arrest might deter would be batterers in the general population. Thus, the general-specific deterrence distinction reveals the limits of statistical studies of specific deterrence.

---

1. Evan Stark, *Mandatory Arrest of Batterers: A Reply to Its Critics*, in Do Arrest and Restraining Orders Work? 115–49 (Eve S. Buzawa & Carl G. Buzawa eds., 1996).

A fourth reason for mandatory arrest can be found in the message it conveys to society. As Stark notes, "Making battering the only crime in which police discretion is removed acknowledges a special social interest in redressing the legacy of discriminatory treatment of women by law enforcement." Thus, mandatory arrest communicates to the society at large as well as to the batterer and battered person that battering is a serious crime that will not be tolerated.

Finally, mandatory arrest serves a "redistributive" function in that police resources are redistributed to women on a more equal basis. The message is that the police are a resource and that battered women have just as much right to that resource as any other segment of society.

Notes

1. Should victims have a voice in the decision about whether to arrest their abuser? Similar issues are discussed in Chapter 5, which explores whether victims should have a voice in the decision about whether to file criminal charges generally?

2. The empirical evidence on whether mandatory arrest laws are successful is conflicting. As Joan Zorza noted, the initial study done in Minneapolis was a resounding success: mandatory arrest was an effective deterrent. But follow-up studies suggested the mandatory arrest might increase subsequent violence. The architect of the Minneapolis study made a 180-degree conversion. Once a strong supporter of mandatory arrest, empirical researcher Lawrence Sherman, now advocates its abandonment based on the new empirical data. Evan Stark, *Mandatory Arrest of Batters: A Reply to its Critics*, in Do ARRESTS AND RESTRAINING ORDERS WORK? 115, 125–26 (Eve S. Buzawa & Carl G. Buzawa eds. 1996).

3. Is it realistic to speak of victims of domestic violence as having a choice to make while their abuser is still in their home?

4. Do mandatory arrest policies suffer from the problem that "one size can't fit all"? *See* Barbara Fedders, *Lobbying for Mandatory-Arrest Policies: Race, Class, and the Politics of the Battered Women's Movement*, 23 N.Y.U. REV. L. & SOC. CHANGE 281 (1997) (arguing "[a]dvocating a uniform set of remedies for all women inappropriately simplifies the problem, to the detriment of those women whose experiences put them at the margins of the [battered women's] movement's theory and organizing practices").

5. Even if mandatory arrest laws are problematic, would their repeal now send the wrong message? Professor Stark argues even if mandatory arrest laws do not reduce recidivism (the empirical measure of "success" in the various studies), they nonetheless have the positive "indirect function of setting a standard of zero tolerance for battering that other institutions can emulate." Stark, *supra* note 2, at 129.

6. Is mandatory arrest really "mandatory." In an opinion that shocked the anti-domestic violence community, the United States Supreme Court addressed this issue.

Castle Rock v. Gonzales

545 U.S. 748 (2005)

Justice SCALIA delivered the opinion of the Court.

We decide in this case whether an individual who has obtained a state-law restraining order has a constitutionally protected property interest in having the police enforce the restraining order when they have probable cause to believe it has been violated.

I

The horrible facts of this case are contained in the complaint that respondent Jessica Gonzales filed in Federal District Court. (Because the case comes to us on appeal from a dismissal of the complaint, we assume its allegations are true.) Respondent alleges that petitioner, the town of Castle Rock, Colorado, violated the Due Process Clause of the Fourteenth Amendment to the United States Constitution when its police officers, acting pursuant to official policy or custom, failed to respond properly to her repeated reports that her estranged husband was violating the terms of a restraining order.

The restraining order had been issued by a state trial court several weeks earlier in conjunction with respondent's divorce proceedings. The original form order, issued on May 21, 1999, and served on respondent's husband on June 4, 1999, commanded him not to "molest or disturb the peace of [respondent] or of any child," and to remain at least 100 yards from the family home at all times. The bottom of the preprinted form noted that the reverse side contained "IMPORTANT NOTICES FOR RESTRAINED PARTIES AND LAW ENFORCEMENT OFFICIALS." The preprinted text on the back of the form included the following "WARNING":

"A KNOWING VIOLATION OF A RESTRAINING ORDER IS A CRIME.... A VIOLATION WILL ALSO CONSTITUTE CONTEMPT OF COURT. YOU MAY BE ARRESTED WITHOUT NOTICE IF A LAW ENFORCEMENT OFFICER HAS PROBABLE CAUSE TO BELIEVE THAT YOU HAVE KNOWINGLY VIOLATED THIS ORDER."

The preprinted text on the back of the form also included a "NOTICE TO LAW ENFORCEMENT OFFICIALS," which read in part:

"YOU SHALL USE EVERY REASONABLE MEANS TO ENFORCE THIS RESTRAINING ORDER. YOU SHALL ARREST, OR, IF AN ARREST WOULD BE IMPRACTICAL UNDER THE CIRCUMSTANCES, SEEK A WARRANT FOR THE ARREST OF THE RESTRAINED PERSON WHEN YOU HAVE INFORMATION AMOUNTING TO PROBABLE CAUSE THAT THE RESTRAINED PERSON HAS VIOLATED OR ATTEMPTED TO VIOLATE ANY PROVISION OF THIS ORDER AND THE RESTRAINED PERSON HAS BEEN PROPERLY SERVED WITH A COPY OF THIS ORDER OR HAS RECEIVED ACTUAL NOTICE OF THE EXISTENCE OF THIS ORDER."

On June 4, 1999, the state trial court modified the terms of the restraining order and made it permanent. The modified order gave respondent's husband the right to spend time with his three daughters (ages 10, 9, and 7) on alternate weekends, for two weeks during the summer, and, "'upon reasonable notice,'" for a midweek dinner visit "'arranged by the parties'"; the modified order also allowed him to visit the home to collect the children for such "parenting time."

According to the complaint, at about 5 or 5:30 p.m. on Tuesday, June 22, 1999, respondent's husband took the three daughters while they were playing outside the family home. No advance arrangements had been made for him to see the daughters that evening. When respondent noticed the children were missing, she suspected her husband had taken them. At about 7:30 p.m., she called the Castle Rock Police Department, which dispatched two officers. The complaint continues: "When [the officers] arrived . . . , she showed them a copy of the TRO and requested that it be enforced and the three children be returned to her immediately. [The officers] stated that there was nothing they could do about the TRO and suggested that [respondent] call the Police Department again if the three children did not return home by 10:00 p.m."

At approximately 8:30 p.m., respondent talked to her husband on his cellular telephone. He told her "he had the three children [at an] amusement park in Denver." She called the police again and asked them to "have someone check for" her husband or his vehicle at the amusement park and "put out an [all points bulletin]" for her husband, but the officer with whom she spoke "refused to do so," again telling her to "wait until 10:00 p.m. and see if" her husband returned the girls.

At approximately 10:10 p.m., respondent called the police and said her children were still missing, but she was now told to wait until midnight. She called at midnight and told the dispatcher her children were still missing. She went to her husband's apartment and, finding nobody there, called the police at 12:10 a.m.; she was told to wait for an officer to arrive. When none came, she went to the police station at 12:50 a.m. and submitted an incident report. The officer who took the report "made no reasonable effort to enforce the TRO or locate the three children. Instead, he went to dinner."

At approximately 3:20 a.m., respondent's husband arrived at the police station and opened fire with a semiautomatic handgun he had purchased earlier that evening. Police shot back, killing him. Inside the cab of his pickup truck, they found the bodies of all three daughters, whom he had already murdered.

On the basis of the foregoing factual allegations, respondent brought an action under Rev. Stat. § 1979, 42 U.S.C. § 1983, claiming that the town violated the Due Process Clause because its police department had "an official policy or custom of failing to respond properly to complaints of restraining order violations" and "tolerate[d] the non-enforcement of restraining orders by its police officers." The complaint also alleged that the town's actions "were taken either willfully, recklessly or with such gross negligence as to indicate wanton disregard and deliberate indifference to" respondent's civil rights.

Before answering the complaint, the defendants filed a motion to dismiss under Federal Rule of Civil Procedure 12(b)(6). The District Court granted the motion, concluding that, whether construed as making a substantive due process or procedural due process claim, respondent's complaint failed to state a claim upon which relief could be granted.

A panel of the Court of Appeals affirmed the rejection of a substantive due process claim, but found that respondent had alleged a cognizable procedural due process claim. On rehearing en banc, a divided court reached the same disposition, concluding that respondent had a "protected property interest in the enforcement of the terms of her restraining order" and that the town had deprived her of due process because "the police never 'heard' nor seriously entertained her request to enforce and protect her interests in the restraining order."

* * *

The critical language in the restraining order came not from any part of the order itself (which was signed by the state-court trial judge and directed to the restrained party, respondent's husband), but from the preprinted notice to law-enforcement personnel that appeared on the back of the order. See *supra*, at 2801. That notice effectively restated the statutory provision describing "peace officers' duties" related to the crime of violation of a restraining order. At the time of the conduct at issue in this case, that provision read as follows:

* * *

"(b) *A peace officer shall arrest, or, if an arrest would be impractical under the circumstances, seek a warrant for the arrest of a restrained person* when the peace officer has information amounting to probable cause that:

* * *

The Court of Appeals concluded that this statutory provision—especially taken in conjunction with a statement from its legislative history, and with another statute restricting criminal and civil liability for officers making arrests—established the Colorado Legislature's clear intent "to alter the fact that the police were not enforcing domestic abuse restraining orders," and thus its intent "that the recipient of a domestic abuse restraining order have an entitlement to its enforcement." Any other result, it said, "would render domestic abuse restraining orders utterly valueless."

———

The Court of Appeals quoted one lawmaker's description of how the bill "'would really attack the domestic violence problems'":

"'[T]he entire criminal justice system must act in a consistent manner, which does not now occur. The police must make probable cause arrests. The prosecutors must prosecute every case. Judges must apply appropriate sentences, and probation officers must monitor their

> probationers closely. And the offender needs to be sentenced to offender-specific therapy.
>
> "'[T]he entire system must send the same message . . . [that] violence is criminal. And so we hope that House Bill 1253 starts us down this road.'" 366 F.3d, at 1107 (quoting Tr. of Colorado House Judiciary Hearings on House Bill 1253, Feb. 15, 1994; emphasis deleted).

———

This last statement is sheer hyperbole. Whether or not respondent had a right to enforce the restraining order, it rendered certain otherwise lawful conduct by her husband both criminal and in contempt of court. See §§ 18-6-803.5(2)(a), (7). The creation of grounds on which he could be arrested, criminally prosecuted, and held in contempt was hardly "valueless"—even if the prospect of those sanctions ultimately failed to prevent him from committing three murders and a suicide.

We do not believe that these provisions of Colorado law truly made enforcement of restraining orders *mandatory*. A well established tradition of police discretion has long coexisted with apparently mandatory arrest statutes.

> "In each and every state there are long-standing statutes that, by their terms, seem to preclude nonenforcement by the police. . . . However, for a number of reasons, including their legislative history, insufficient resources, and sheer physical impossibility, it has been recognized that such statutes cannot be interpreted literally. . . . [T]hey clearly do not mean that a police officer may not lawfully decline to . . . make an arrest. As to third parties in these states, the full-enforcement statutes simply have no effect, and their significance is further diminished." 1 ABA Standards for Criminal Justice 1-4.5, commentary, pp. 1–124 to 1-125 (2d ed. 1980) (footnotes omitted).

The deep-rooted nature of law-enforcement discretion, even in the presence of seemingly mandatory legislative commands, is illustrated by *Chicago v. Morales* (1999), which involved an ordinance that said a police officer "'shall order'" persons to disperse in certain circumstances, 47, 1849. This Court rejected out of hand the possibility that "the mandatory language of the ordinance . . . afford[ed] the police *no* discretion." 62, n. 32 1849. It is, the Court proclaimed, simply "common sense that **all** police officers must use some discretion in deciding when and where to enforce city ordinances." (emphasis added).

Against that backdrop, a true mandate of police action would require some stronger indication from the Colorado Legislature than "shall use every reasonable means to enforce a restraining order" (or even "shall arrest . . . or . . . seek a warrant"), §§ 18-6-803.5(3)(a), (b). That language is not perceptibly more mandatory than the Colorado statute which has long told municipal chiefs of police that they "shall pursue and arrest any person fleeing from justice in any part of the state" and that they "shall apprehend any person in the act of committing any offense . . . and, forthwith and without any warrant, bring such person before a . . . competent authority for examination and trial." Colo.Rev.Stat. § 31-4-112 (Lexis 2004). It is hard to imagine that a Colorado peace officer would not have some discretion to determine that—despite probable cause to believe a restraining order has been violated—the circumstances of the violation or the competing duties of that officer or his agency counsel decisively against enforcement in a particular instance. The practical necessity for discretion is particularly apparent in a case such as this one, where the suspected violator is not actually present and his whereabouts are unknown. *Cf. Donaldson v. Seattle*, 65 Wash.App. 661, 671–672, 831 P.2d 1098, 1104 (1992) ("There is a vast difference between a mandatory duty to arrest [a violator who is on the scene] and a mandatory duty to conduct a follow up investigation [to locate an absent violator]. . . . A mandatory duty to investigate . . . would be completely open-ended as to priority, duration and intensity").

The dissent correctly points out that, in the specific context of domestic violence, mandatory-arrest statutes have been found in some States to be more mandatory than traditional mandatory-arrest statutes. *Post,* at 2816–2819 (opinion of STEVENS, J.). The Colorado statute mandating arrest for a domestic-violence offense is different from but related to the one at issue here, and it includes similar though not identical phrasing. *See* Colo.Rev.Stat. § 18-6-803.6(1) (Lexis 1999) ("When a peace officer determines that there is probable cause to believe that a crime or offense involving domestic violence . . . has been committed, the officer shall, without undue delay, arrest the person suspected of its commission . . ."). Even in the domestic-violence context, however, it is unclear how the mandatory-arrest paradigm applies to cases in which the offender is not present to be arrested. As the dissent explains, *post,* at 2817, and n. 8, much of the impetus for mandatory-arrest statutes and policies derived from the idea that it is better for police officers to arrest the aggressor in a domestic-violence incident than to attempt to mediate the dispute or merely to ask the offender to leave the scene. Those other options are only available, of course, when the offender is present at the scene. *See* Hanna, *No Right to Choose: Mandated Victim Participation in Domestic Violence Prosecutions,* 109 HARV. L.REV. 1849, 1860 (1996) ("[T]he clear trend in police practice is to arrest the batterer *at the scene* . . ." (emphasis added)).

As one of the cases cited by the dissent, *post,* at 2818–2819, recognized, "there will be situations when no arrest is possible, *such as when the alleged abuser is not in the home." Donaldson,* 65 Wash.App., at 674, 831 P.2d, at 1105 (emphasis added). That case held that Washington's mandatory-arrest statute required an arrest only in "cases where the offender is on the scene," and that it "d[id] not create an on-going mandatory duty to conduct an investigation" to locate the offender. *Id.,* at 675, 831 P.2d, at 1105. Colorado's restraining-order statute appears to contemplate a similar distinction, providing that when arrest is "impractical"—which was likely the case when the whereabouts of respondent's husband were unknown—the officers' statutory duty is to "seek a warrant" rather than "arrest." § 18-6-803.5(3)(b).

---

b. "No Drop" Prosecution Policies

Even if a domestic violence perpetrator is arrested, prosecution frequently is unsuccessful. One of the particular problems that arises is that before trial victims frequently recant their earlier statement regarding abuse. The scope of this problem is outlined in the following article:

Douglas E. Beloof & Joel Shapiro, *Let the Truth Be Told: Proposed Hearsay Exceptions to Admit Domestic Violence Victims' Out of Court Statements as Substantive Evidence*
11 COLUM. J. GENDER & L. 1 (2002)

Non-cooperation by recantation or failure to appear at trial is an epidemic in domestic violence cases. Persons qualified to give expert testimony at trial on domestic violence, including psychologists, counselors, police detectives, directors of battered women's shelters, and victim advocates, consistently testify that, in their experience, it is commonplace for domestic violence victims to recant or minimize initial reports of abuse. The head of the Family Violence Division of the Los Angeles District Attorney's Office estimates that ninety percent of domestic violence victims recant. A psychologist specializing in the treatment of battered women has estimated the non-cooperation rate to be eighty percent. Similarly, one judge reports that in as many as eighty percent of domestic violence prosecutions the victim refuses to cooperate at trial. Increasingly, courts have taken judicial notice of the unreliability of the domestic violence victim's recantations. Thus, recantation is the norm rather than the exception, in domestic violence cases. This is hardly surprising. Batterers put hydraulic pressures on domestic violence victims to recant, drop the case, or fail to appear at trial.

The reasons that victims do not cooperate are closely related to the victim's need for physical and emotional survival and the safety of her children. "Many domestic violence professionals are becoming convinced . . . that the primary reason women stay with the batterer is out of fear." Victims have good reason to be afraid. Many women stay in battering relationships because when they have tried to leave they have been beaten. Leaving a batterer is a very risky undertaking. Victims have reason to fear financial ruin. The leading cause of homelessness among women and children is domestic violence. Studies reveal that domestic violence has led to the circumstances of between thirty-five and fifty percent of all homeless women and children. In addition to the toll homelessness takes on women and children, it "places an enormous financial and physical strain on our social services system."

Given that victims will frequently be uncooperative with the prosecution of domestic violence cases, many prosecutor's office have adopted "no drop" policies. These policies limit the discretion of prosecutors to dismiss or "drop" criminal charges for domestic violence. Without such a policy, a prosecutor would be free to dismiss domestic violence charges on grounds of a victim's non-cooperation. Under such a policy, the prosecutor must pursue the charges. The prosecutor must attempt to prove the case despite victim non-cooperation, by using such things as 9-1-1 tapes, photographs taken at the scene, police officer testimony, and even by compelling the victim to testify despite her unwillingness to do so.

Should crime victims be forced to cooperate in the prosecution of their abusers? Consider the following competing arguments in favor of and against "no drop" policies:

Cheryl Hanna, *No Right to Choose: Mandated Victim Participation in Domestic Violence Prosecutions*
109 Harv. L. Rev. 1849 (1996)

The Dilemmas Posed by No-Drop Policies

Although advocates [for victims of domestic violence] have lobbied for better prosecutorial response, they remain ambivalent about the use of state power, such as subpoenas, in prosecution strategy. Just how far the state should go in forcing women to participate before dismissing charges remains an issue of intense debate.

Pro-prosecution advocates argue that aggressive policies take the burden off the victim by removing her as the "plaintiff." They contend that the batterer has less incentive to try to control or intimidate his victim once he realizes that she no longer controls the process. They also argue that because domestic violence is a public crime, the state has a responsibility to intervene aggressively. For these advocates, this response communicates and follows through on the message that the state will not tolerate violence of any sort. These arguments are rooted in the feminist principle that, when the state refuses to intervene under the rationale that domestic violence is a private family matter, the state not only condones but, in fact, promotes such violence.

However, many advocates for battered women argue that the use of state power, such as subpoenas, has the unintended effect of punishing or "revictimizing" the victim for the actions of the abuser by forcing the victim into a process over which she has no control. . . .

Reactions by battered women's advocates to a 1983 Alaska case illustrate this debate. After Maudie Wall filed an abuse complaint against her husband, she changed her mind and decided that she did not want to testify. Under the Anchorage no-drop policy, Mrs. Wall was jailed overnight for her refusal to cooperate. She was released when her husband agreed to accept a probation and counseling. The prosecutor reasoned:

> [W]hen the police get called and a complaint is filed, it is no longer a private matter. . . . Our only alternative was to drop the case and thereby show defense attorneys and defendants we will not stick to our guns, and the long-range consequences for our [no-drop] policy would be disastrous.

Many in the domestic violence advocacy community condemned the decision of the Anchorage Assistant Municipal Prosecutor. For example, Lisa Lehrman, an advocate and attorney for battered women, commented that "someone who is the victim of a violent crime ultimately should not be forced to testify, despite a no-drop policy. These situations are just too complicated." Like Ms. Lehrman, many in the domestic violence advocacy community argued that forcing Ms. Wall to participate and jailing her for refusing to do so went a step too far, regardless of the long-term consequences for the legitimacy of the no-drop program. . . .

[A]nne Coughlin argues, law and society excuse women for criminal misconduct "on the ground that they cannot be expected to, and, indeed, should not, resist the influence exerted by their [intimate partners]." Society excuses women who respond with violence because it views them as less rational. Thus, women are rewarded for acting irrationally. Men, however, are expected to resist outside pressures to commit crimes, and society vests in them the "authority to govern both themselves and their irresponsible wives." Although the battered women's syndrome defense is intended to achieve justice in individual cases, we have to acknowledge its unintended consequences: reinforcing the societal hierarchy and institutionalizing the belief that women are incapable of rational self-control. We must repeatedly reexamine whether, given legal and social progress, this defense still discourages violence and promotes gender equality.

We should acknowledge, however, that mandated participation will have costs. By removing the choice to pursue the prosecution, the state may inadvertently force some women to relinquish individual responsibility for their lives. Like the battered women's syndrome defense, mandated participation can reinforce the notion that battered woman are incapable of making rational decisions. It further heightens the danger that women will somehow be blamed for their reluctance to respond actively to the battering by freely participating in the prosecution process.

At this point in history, however, the long-term benefits of mandated participation outweigh the short-term costs—costs that can be greatly diminished if we examine the issue in a pragmatic context. In particular, we need to examine the influence that mandated participation has on the effectiveness of the criminal justice system as well as the impact of such a policy on individual women. Although any criminal response to battering creates a double bind, the better, albeit not perfect, solution is mandated participation. . . .

Feminists overwhelmingly criticized the prosecutor who jailed Maudie Wall overnight, claiming that the state had gone too far. Much of that criticism is misplaced. First, Ms. Wall's overnight stay in jail may have been the first time that she recognized the seriousness of the abuse against her. Second, her inaction had consequences for the state. Resources had been expended in the case against the abuser. If such cases are dismissed, "wasting" resources on cases never pursued, already tight prosecutors' budgets could come under further attack. Third, if Mr. Wall knew that he could get away with his abusive behavior, he would have been much more likely to batter his wife again. Ms. Wall's long-term situation would be worse, not better.

In most cases, such extreme sanctions will probably not be necessary. Once the existence of a mandated participation policy is common knowledge, women will be much more likely to cooperate. Batterers will be less likely to intimidate women throughout the process and defense attorneys will be much more willing to enter into plea agreements if they know that the state is serious about pursuing its domestic violence cases.

When cases are dismissed because the prosecutor fails to mandate participation, police officers and other criminal justice personnel may question the legitimacy of the trial preparation process. Tremendous progress has been made in instituting preferred and mandatory arrest policies, and officers are increasingly being trained to respond to domestic violence as a serious crime. When police do make an appropriate arrest, only to see the case dismissed at trial because the victim did not want to proceed, their decreased confidence in the value of arrest can undermine their diligence when policing domestic violence. Furthermore, if police and prosecutors understand that the victim cannot prevent the case from being prosecuted, they will be more likely to take greater care in their investigations. . . .

The San Diego experience illustrates that mandated participation can be an effective prosecutorial strategy. San Diego found that abusers became more violent when they learned that the case would not be prosecuted if the victims refused to cooperate. The city then instituted an official policy enabling prosecutors to request arrest warrants for victims who are subpoenaed and fail to appear in court. Once a case is investigated, the specialized domestic violence prosecutor decides whether the case merits a bench warrant or whether it can proceed without the victim's testimony. In cases in which the victim's testimony is essential, the prosecutor may request a continuance and a bench warrant for her. In some cases, the prosecutor may ask the judge to hold the warrant while the victim is notified of the pending risk of arrest.

In the first six years after this policy went into effect, the San Diego Police executed only eight arrest warrants and jailed only two victims overnight. Because the prosecutor is willing to mandate victim participation when appropriate, the city can now convict more batterers without being overly punitive toward reluctant victims. Since the program's inception, domestic homicides have decreased from thirty in 1985 to seven in 1994, and the city's re-arrest and re-prosecution rates have also dropped. Thus, from a pragmatic perspective, the goals of criminal prosecution are well served under a mandated participation model.

Concerns About Revictimization

As discussed earlier, one of the reasons why feminist theory may counsel against mandated participation is the fear of "revictimizing the victim." Because preserving autonomy in individual cases is less burdensome for the prosecutor than going against the victim's wishes, a decision to drop the case often rests on the rationale that mandated participation would only harm the victim further. Yet a properly designed mandated participation program can directly address "revictimization."

This danger is often exaggerated. Revictimization arguments implicitly equate forced participation in a criminal case with beating and abuse. This analogy fails to account for the distinction between the illegal act of battery and the legal options open to the state to pursue prosecution. It also trivializes and obscures the actual physical harm inflicted by battering.

Abused women can be required to cooperate with the state and can be compelled to testify, except in those few jurisdictions where they can claim marital privilege. Yet police and prosecutors do not always use the legal options available to them. Failing to appear after being subpoenaed, recanting prior testimony on the stand, committing perjury, and providing false or misleading information during interviews with officers of the law all have legal sanctions. It is certainly desirable to counsel, support, and inform the victim in an effort to encourage cooperation. However, when those attempts fail, using state powers to compel participation is often a better alternative than dismissing the case outright. . . .

Linda G. Mills, *Killing Her Softly: Intimate Abuse and the Violence of State Intervention*
113 HARV. L. REV. 550 (1999)

Though the research suggests that mandatory interventions may not be the safest state response for all battered women, these policies have some benefits. The gains from these categorical strategies are essentially twofold. First, we send a message to men who batter their partners that their battering has consequences. This message is intended to have a deterrent effect, and indeed, some of the arrest studies demonstrate that it probably does. Second, we gain a standard by which we can hold officers, prosecutors, and physicians accountable for not intervening in domestic violence cases. These two gains are significant and reflect important policy goals.

On the other hand, we lose a great deal from mandatory arrest and prosecution policies. First, these policies may result in high rates of retaliatory violence, especially against African-American battered women and battered women involved with men who are unemployed or otherwise without community ties. Second, these policies reinforce the negative dynamics of rejection, degradation, terrorization, isolation, missocialization, exploitation, emotional unresponsiveness, and confinement intrinsic to the battering relationship. State perpetuation of these dynamics systematically denies the battered woman the emotional support she needs to heal. Although we can never precisely measure the effects of this state violence, studies of emotional trauma's impact on its victims suggest that this form of abuse would have long-term and devastating effects.

Rather than employ one-dimensional responses in every case, we need to enhance the clinical ability of law enforcement personnel, prosecutors, and other professionals, including doctors, who are in a position to help battered women. These professionals need to learn skills that draw on the rich clinical literature and that address the trauma of each specific victim. In addition, state actors should develop cooperative relationships with clinicians who understand the complexities of relating to trauma victims and who are trained to distinguish the survivor who will benefit from self-assertion from the victim who, because of severe mental illness, is incapable of hearing her own voice. Allocating precious resources to developing multidisciplinary responses that are committed to a Survivor-Centered Approach will provide the long-term results we all hope to achieve.

In sum, when the strategies born of broad feminist goals conflict with the interests of individual battered women, we must rethink the strategies. I suggest that prosecution and arrest be used in domestic violence cases only when women desire them or are otherwise incapable of deciding what is in their best interest. Instituting programs that strip law enforcement personnel, prosecutors, and physicians of their discretion is not an appropriate or effective response to domestic violence. Instead, we need to develop systems that respond to each battered woman on an individual basis and that help her determine what intervention strategy is best for her.

Clinical responses should not be viewed as a threat to the feminist project, but rather as an avenue to heal the divides—public versus private, state versus victim—that separate those who legislate and implement change from those who experience its repercussions. That some women in the feminist legal community have adopted a strategy that is, albeit unwittingly, designed to ignore battered women's individual narratives is self-defeating. That some women persist in supporting these mandatory interventions once their emotional abuse and paternalistic underpinnings have been revealed is disingenuous. Feminists should reflect on the abusive character of the state power they have unleashed upon the women they seek to protect. My argument is that when they fail to do so, feminists add to, rather than alleviate, the survivor's trauma.

Notes

1. Are no drop polices generally good for victims? Are they generally good for society?

2. Outside of the domestic violence context, prosecutors generally do not follow "no-drop" procedures and mandated participation for simple assault. What justification is there for this dissimilar treatment of the two types of assaults? To what extent is the justification based on beliefs about the nature of the victims in each context?

3. Even if "no drop" policies often produce successful outcomes, what is the justification for denying prosecutor's discretion to determine whether a case should be prosecuted or dismissed? *See* Nichole Miras Mordini, Note, *Mandatory State Interventions for Domestic Abuse Cases: An Examination of the Effects on Victim Safety and Autonomy*, 52 DRAKE L. REV. 295 (2004) ("Domestic violence affects different women in different ways and a 'one-size-fits-all' policy for the prosecution of these cases will not serve the needs of the battered woman or the community.").

4. In some jurisdictions, domestic violence prosecutions are typically resolved by an agreement between the prosecutor and the defendant to divert the matter to a counseling program. If the defendant successfully completes the program, the charges will be dismissed. For discussion of the pros and cons of such programs, *see* Leonore M.J. Simon, *A Therapeutic Jurisprudence Approach to Domestic Violence Cases*, 1 PSYCHOL. PUB. POLICY & L. 43 (1995). Does it make sense for prosecutors

to drop criminal charges when a defendant agrees to undergo counseling in a domestic violence case when they would not follow such an approach to other crimes? In California there is no such diversion available; cases are prosecuted to conviction, acquittal, or dismissal. Should the purpose of state intervention be to treat or punish the violent offender?

5. Do advocates for domestic violence, particularly legal advocates, overstate the ability of the law to solve problems? *See* Leigh Goodmark, *Law is the Answer? Do We Know That for Sure?: Questioning the Efficacy of Legal Interventions for Battered Women*, 23 St. Louis U. Pub. L. Rev. 7 (2004) (urging lawyers to think beyond the legal system when responding to domestic violence).

6. The extreme difficulty of changing societal attitudes may be demonstrated by the example of jury attitudes towards alcohol. Mothers Against Drunk Driving has waged an ongoing campaign to change public attitudes towards drinking and driving, yet a study comparing jury leniency in 1958 with 1993 concludes that little has changed in juror attitudes. Rebecca S. Bromley, *Jury Leniency in Drunk Driving Cases, Has It Changed?*, 20 Law & Psych. Rev. 27 (1996).

7. Why do rape victims have greater influence over continued prosecution than domestic violence victims?

5. Domestic Violence Shelters

Developments in the Law: Legal Responses to Domestic Violence
106 Harv. L. Rev. 1498 (1983)

Shelters and Support Services for Battered Women

A shelter is often the battered woman's first encounter with the legal system after she flees her assailant. Shelters are peculiarly necessary for domestic violence victims; unlike most other victims of violent crime, the domestic violence victim faces the prospect of a domicile occupied by the assailant. Shelters for battered women provide immediate safety and support, and are thus indispensable to a successful response to domestic violence.

Shelters are part of a larger array of services that includes hotlines, "drop-in centers," support groups, counseling, advocacy, and miscellaneous financial and social services. Some of these services usher the victim into the shelter; once at the shelter, the woman may gain access to further resources and information, as well as the traditional legal devices. In examining shelters and related services, important differences among jurisdictions include the types of intervention provided, the source and amount of funding, and the manner of delivery of the services, as well as the integration of shelters with other means of intervention. Shelters are typically underfunded, understaffed, and unable to respond fully to the needs of battered women. Other means of intervention must therefore supplement shelters.

Many jurisdictions provide for crisis intervention — immediate physical refuge from a violent situation — as well as farther-reaching counseling, information, and advocacy services. A given jurisdiction may provide other tangible physical services, such as child care, housing access, job referral, food and clothing, transportation, and case monitoring. In this manner, depending on the resources of the particular jurisdiction, shelters may act as a point of access to the larger support system. . . .

Even if shelters are provided, they are not always available to all potential users because of lack of knowledge or other barriers to access. Some states have attempted to address this problem. A survey of state legislation reveals efforts to increase accessibility of shelters and services to victims, to promote victim awareness of resources, to facilitate police involvement in referral, and to address confidentiality concerns.

States have tried in various ways to solve the problem of victims' ignorance of available facilities and services. State agencies, police, and hospital staff often act to channel women into the support system. For example, a Chicago program links police with a support group that provides contact, legal information, and aid to victims. Statutes may require that police transport victims to a shelter and provide notice of rights and services. In many areas, hotlines provide the initial contact that brings the woman into the support system, although several jurisdictions pursue around-the-clock accessibility through various other means.

Refuge in a shelter may lead victims to pursue traditional legal means of intervention, namely protection orders and criminal prosecution. Some jurisdictions integrate shelters with these other devices through police referral. For example, special police reports or filings may inform prosecutors of victim entrance into shelters. At the shelters, provision of counseling or victim advocacy may be coordinated with legal services, thus facilitating criminal prosecution, the pursuit of a protection order, or other alternatives. States may also provide formal court advocacy projects for victims along with shelters and related services. Thus, shelters play an important role in heightening victim awareness of services and resources, and facilitating the victim's access to legal and related support systems.

Commentators have assessed the efficacy of shelters with various criteria, including termination of abusive relationships, recurrence of violence, and "self-reported measures of effectiveness." These empirical studies have proven inconclusive as to the overall effectiveness of shelter and service intervention, but suggest that women who receive such intervention still remain "at risk," though the shelters do help to reduce violent episodes. This finding suggests that shelters, to go beyond temporarily preventing immediate violent contact, must be integrated with other traditional mechanisms if they are to respond effectively to woman battering. The efforts at integration mentioned above facilitate this effective response.

Notes

1. How do victims of domestic violence learn about battered women's shelters? Washington requires all police officers responding to a report of domestic violence to

advise victims of their legal rights, including information about domestic violence shelters in the immediate area and a statewide 24-hour toll-free hotline. WASH. REV. CODE § 10.99.030.

2. Children abused in the home are the subjects of state child protective service agencies. These agencies are often grossly underfunded. A shortage of adequate foster homes is always a problem. Civil and criminal protective orders are generally available to protect the child from the abusive adult. The processes of reintegrating families or terminating the rights of parents are civil in nature. If the abuser is prosecuted, a guardian ad litem or representative may be appointed by the court to assert the child's rights.

B. Orders of Protection

1. Criminal Protection Orders

Cristopher R. Frank, Comment, *Criminal Protection Orders in Domestic Violence Cases: Getting Rid of Rats with Snakes*
50 U. MIAMI L. REV. 919 (1996)

. . . II. Criminal Protection Orders *A. Criminal Protection Orders Generally*

A criminal protection order ("CPO") is often where there has been an arrest in a case involving domestic violence. For those jurisdictions that have specifically legislated to empower criminal courts to issue such orders, judges will make the CPO a condition of the bail offered to a domestic violence defendant. The conditions contained within the CPO itself, by which the defendant must abide, may be numerous, and the discretion accorded to judges in deciding when to issue a CPO and which conditions to include will vary by jurisdiction.

The CPO is distinguished from the civil protection order, which is a civil remedy afforded to individuals, usually women, through a specific petitioning process. A civil protection order is appropriate where no arrest has been made in connection with an alleged incident of domestic violence, yet the victim voluntarily seeks assistance from the courts. Civil protection orders often impose upon an alleged batterer many of the same conditions imposed upon a criminal defendant and have generally withstood constitutional challenges. In a criminal action, where a CPO would be issued, the state is a party and there is an impliedly higher standard of proof.

The comparison between criminal and civil orders of protection is inevitable. An obvious and facially persuasive argument used by those courts and commentators opposed to the systematic issuance of criminal orders of protection is that relief is already universally available to alleged victims via the petitioning process in the civil arena. Even so, the distinction between the two types of orders is sometimes blurred or confused. Indeed, a violation of a civil protection order will often be prosecuted as a criminal contempt charge.

B. Holding Defendants Prior to Release

Many commentators feel that the unique nature of the crime of domestic violence, where the parties are not strangers, warrants extreme measures concerning temporary denial of bail to defendants charged in domestic violence cases, and some courts and legislatures have responded to this argument. For instance, in North Carolina, where a judicial officer determines if the immediate release of a domestic violence defendant will be dangerous to either the alleged victim or another person, the officer "may retain the defendant in custody for a reasonable period of time while determining the conditions of pretrial release." Other statutes are not as open ended. In Utah, a person arrested for a domestic violence offense may not be released prior to "the close of the next *court* day following the arrest," unless the release is conditioned upon either a court order or written pledge barring the defendant from any contact with the alleged victim. A provision in the same act requires an alleged victim to waive in writing any court required "stay-away order," or else a defendant is automatically barred from returning to his home.

Many advocates of domestic violence law reform praise such legislation as necessary for combating domestic violence crimes. They contend that domestic violence often involves unbridled emotion in the form of rage, and for that reason a mandatory "cooling off" period is needed to insure against recurring violence upon release. This assumes that all situations resulting in an arrest involve such rage, and such an assumption precludes an examination of the factual conditions of each arrest. This approach is facially inconsistent with the constitutional requirements of bail determination, which compel courts to make a case by case determination of whether a reasonable foundation exists for denying or revoking bail. Legislation designed to protect against recurring domestic violence through initial denial of bail must be true to this constitutional mandate.

III. Issuance of Criminal Protection Orders

A. The Power and Discretion of Courts

The power of the criminal courts to make determinations concerning bail is well grounded in both legislative and judicial history. Questions arise, however, when the judiciary creates conditions to pretrial release that are imposed through both civil and criminal protection orders. While the specific functions of the governmental branches are difficult to point out, and in some cases overlap, separation of powers concerns are often raised where an undue amount of judicial discretion has been granted by state legislatures. The concern in regard to protective orders, both criminal and civil, is that the judiciary takes on a quasi-legislative role in defining what otherwise lawful conduct becomes criminal if engaged in by a domestic violence respondent/defendant. In response to this valid concern, legislatures can and should specifically define the options available to a judicial officer in fashioning reasonable conditions of release, and appellate courts can ensure that lower court determinations are both constitutionally sound and within the scope of judicial powers.

Laws empowering courts to condition release of a domestic violence defendant on the issuance of a CPO vary widely as to the discretion allowed to those courts in determining the conditions. Minnesota, for example, allows for a judge to impose any conditions of release, while Alaska, and many other states, set out a specific list of conditions from which a judge may choose. Where a broad license is provided to the court to fashion any condition for release the statute may be in violation of either the state or federal constitutions. Therefore, legislatures must ensure that particular conditions are set out for judicial application. . . .

D. The Standard of Order Issuance

A defendant's general right to bail (except in the most serious cases) is derived from the Eighth Amendment and is codified in most state constitutions. However, a general presumption of release without condition, or release upon the least onerous condition or conditions available to the court, applicable to criminal defendants generally, has not survived the changes in domestic violence law.

A CPO may be issued under current state statutes, for example, when reasonably necessary to protect the alleged victim, when release without condition would be inimical to public safety, when the safety and protection of the petitioner may be impaired, and where there is possible danger or intimidation to the alleged victim or another. Conversely, some statutes enabling courts to issue CPOs for domestic violence offenses are silent as to the standard of issuance a court should apply, apparently leaving such a determination to the established judicial rules concerning bail. Those states that do not set out a standard of issuance leave open the possibility that such orders will be issued as a matter of course, with no inquiry by the court as to the basis of the CPO.

The relatively low threshold for issuance of a CPO can be contrasted with the standard for issuance of an ex parte civil protection order which may require an "immediate and present danger of abuse." Of course, in a criminal context probable cause will exist to presume that abusive conduct has occurred, and thus, a lower threshold for issuing a protective order may be warranted. Courts should nevertheless apply a cognizable standard even in the criminal arena, since in practical terms the resulting deprivations to the criminal defendant and the civil respondent are the same.

E. Evidentiary Standard for Criminal Protection Orders

Courts have differed as to what standard of proof to apply in cases where a CPO is sought. However, what is clear is that the traditional evidentiary standard of proof for criminal proceedings beyond a reasonable doubt is not to be employed. "Reasonable factual support" for the issuance of a protective order prior to trial, as applied by a New York court in *People v. Forman*, amounts to a preponderance of the evidence standard usually employed in a civil context. The determination as to what standard to apply generally has been left to the courts by the legislatures who have passed domestic violence criminal protection legislation.

The *Forman* court touched on, but refused to decide, whether a higher standard of proof might be constitutionally compelled. "[T]he court does not determine in this case whether a finding of a danger of intimidation or injury to complainant need only have reasonable factual support in the record . . . or, whether a higher evidentiary standard is required under the Fourteenth Amendment to support defendant's continued exclusion from his home." Courts have not, on the whole, taken this question seriously, but the issue deserves greater attention as the universe of judicial options for the victims of domestic violence, both civil and criminal, expands to address the problem. . . .

IV. Conditions of Criminal Protection Orders

The conditions specifically allowed by state statutes that permit courts to issue CPOs are varied. The most common is a condition prohibiting further acts of abuse by the alleged batterer against the alleged victim. Such a condition is uncontroversial and seemingly innocuous as a prerequisite for release. More serious questions are raised by the issuance of a CPO that requires a defendant to stay away from the home of the alleged victim. Where the parties are not currently cohabitating, such a condition is less burdensome upon a defendant than where the issuance of the CPO results in the exclusion of the defendant from property he would otherwise be lawfully allowed to possess and enjoy.

Other possible conditions of pretrial release for a defendant in a domestic violence case may involve staying away from the school, business, or workplace of the alleged victim, or may preclude the defendant from any contact with the alleged victim whatsoever. Mutual orders of protection exist where a court conditions the release of a defendant on the parties' having no contact with each other. While at one time popular in both civil and criminal proceedings, these mutual orders have become generally discouraged and are now rarely used.

The defendant also may be ordered to refrain from molesting, removing, or using the personal property identified in the CPO, even where the court fails to inquire into who possesses the right to use or holds title to that property. A final condition that may be included in a CPO states the terms under which a defendant may visit his or her child. Where the possible permissible conditions to be included in a CPO are set out by statute, the discretion of the court is minimized and concerns of creating a "mini-criminal code" are mitigated. Where a court can fashion any sort of condition to a CPO, the potential for over-burdening the rights of a presumably innocent defendant are increased.

V. Procedural Requirements

A. Criminal Protection Order Hearings

There are a number of procedural requirements that must be met when a criminal defendant is deprived of a constitutionally identified right or liberty interest. Foremost among these is the right to a hearing concerning the deprivation. In those jurisdictions that have legislated to allow the issuance of criminal protective orders, the approaches to the hearing issue have been varied. North Carolina and Utah, for example, have enacted statutes that are silent on the subject of holding a hearing to determine the propriety of issuing a restrictive CPO, presumably leaving the question to their respective judicial systems. Conversely, Ohio's law specifically requires that a hearing concerning whether or not to issue the CPO occur within twenty-four hours of the filing of a motion that requests its issuance.

Where no legislative guidance is provided concerning whether to have a hearing, or in what form that hearing should take place, courts have nonetheless found that hearings are constitutionally compelled. In *People v. Derisi*, a New York court found a domestic violence defendant was entitled to a hearing on his continued exclusion from his home and personal possessions following the issuance of a CPO. While the statute under which the CPO had been issued did not expressly mandate that a hearing be held, the court found that other provisions of the state code compelled the issuing court to allow for a hearing when the defendant challenged the CPO.

The right to be heard in cases where a CPO has been or will be issued is important, yet it is certainly distinct from the right to an evidentiary hearing on the need for such an order. In *People v. Forman*, another New York court, passing on the same statute at issue in *Derisi*, held that not only was a hearing necessary but that a "defendant, by counsel was entitled to present facts and law in opposition to the [CPO] application." The New York statute, in fact, requires that "[s]ufficient facts must be present to enable the court to make a determination 'on the basis of the available information.'"

When courts construe vague or incomplete legislation to require an evidentiary showing on the part of the prosecution seeking a CPO, and allow a defendant to present a case in opposition of that order, fundamental notions of due process are upheld.

In practice, however, many courts empowered to issue CPOs as a condition of pretrial release may be disregarding the requirement of a hearing. Where a statute is silent as to the necessity and right of a hearing, and where CPOs are continually issued absent a meaningful judicial inquiry, the integrity of the justice system is compromised. Jurisdictions must draft appropriate legislation to ensure that where deprivations of liberty interests of domestic violence defendants take place, the primary procedural safeguard of a hearing is offered and conducted in a meaningful manner.

B. Other Procedural Concerns

Apart from the requirement of a hearing, defendants in domestic violence cases should enjoy the same protections and procedural safeguards afforded to all criminal defendants charged with similar crimes. Where a CPO is issued, for example, a defendant is entitled to a clear and definite statement as to the conditions of that order, as well as notice as to its issuance. Any legislature empowering criminal courts to issue CPOs should make such requirements explicit in a statute, because a violation of a CPO implicates the future liberty interests of a defendant and an unclear or unarticulated order increases the likelihood of a violation and subsequent arrest or prosecution for criminal contempt.

Utah's Cohabitant Abuse Procedures Act, for example, requires that where a defendant is arrested for domestic violence, the arresting officer must provide both the alleged victim and batterer with a written notice of the automatic requirements of the CPO statute, which includes a mandatory no contact provision. While the judge or magistrate must thereafter issue written findings and determinations following the defendant's nonwaivable first appearance, the statute does not require that the defendant be provided with a copy of any court order ultimately issued. By failing to require that a copy be presented to the defendant, the statute leaves such notification to the discretion of the court issuing the order. An amended Minnesota statute requires that the defendant be served with a copy of the CPO, but also specifically states that failure to do so does not invalidate the conditions of the order.

Such provisions work to deny a defendant the adequate notice necessary to ensure compliance with a CPO and implicate serious due process concerns. Legislation and court proceedings allowing for both civil and criminal protection orders should, therefore, include a clear statement of the conditions being imposed upon a defendant which should be presented to the defendant prior to release. The duration of the CPO should likewise be made clear to the defendant upon release.

Legislation that allows for the issuance of CPOs should also state specifically that such an issuance is not admissible as evidence of guilt in the eventual trial for the crime charged. The vast majority of state statutes relating to CPOs, however, contain no such procedural safeguard. One notable exception is Ohio's statute which ensures that a temporary CPO issued as a condition of pretrial release "[s]hall not be construed as a finding that the alleged offender committed the alleged offense, and shall not be introduced as evidence of the commission of the offense at the trial of the alleged offender on the complaint upon which the order is based." Including such a provision in CPO legislation is essential to maintaining fairness in judicial systems that so often issue such orders automatically in all domestic violence cases.

C. Interests and Rights of Defendants at Issue

No examination of the issues surrounding criminal protective orders is complete without an analysis of the defendant's rights and interests in cases where a CPO is issued. Victim advocates are often anxious to minimize, or even deny, the domestic violence defendant's rights. They may fear that recognition of the principle that the basic protections guaranteed to all criminal defendants should apply equally to those charged with domestic violence, would compromise and curtail the progress made in combating the problem. A recognition of the interests in question and the applicability of the constitutionally mandated protections to these cases does not necessarily lead to this result, and should nonetheless operate outside of these collateral concerns.

The Fifth and Fourteenth Amendments to the U.S. Constitution prohibit the federal government and any state from arbitrarily depriving any person, including the criminal defendant, of property, or liberty. The interest at risk of deprivation via the process in question must be considered by the court poised to impose the deprivation. The United States Supreme Court, in *Mathews v. Eldridge*, considered this question after a worker was denied a hearing before the termination of his federal disability benefits. Under the Due Process Clause of the Fifth Amendment, the Court set out a test that came to apply to the states as well, and that has been employed by courts in examining deprivation of property rights in domestic violence cases. The Court enumerated four factors to consider in determining whether a deprivation imposed by a state comports with the guarantees of due process. The first factor is the private interest that will be affected by the state's action. Unless the interest at issue meets the threshold requirement of being constitutionally protected, however, procedural concerns such as a meaningful hearing are not implicated. The other factors include the risk of erroneous deprivation, the probable value of additional safeguards, and the interest of the state government at issue. When acting to deprive a domestic violence defendant of a liberty or property interest, therefore, a court considering issuance of a CPO must first identify and consider the interest in order for the deprivation to be constitutional.

What a court may define as a properly held property interest has been broadened, and sometimes limited over time. It is beyond dispute, however, that an individual has a property interest in the enjoyment of his personally owned or leased property. Courts that have passed on the constitutionality of civil protective orders have consistently held that depriving someone of the use and possession of his home directly implicates a constitutionally recognized property right.

The U.S. Constitution requires that the property interest be weighed against the state's interest. A tension develops between the state's legitimate police power in protecting state citizens and the individual's right to possess and enjoy personal property. Identifying that the tension exists is the first step in fashioning an appropriate order. Courts, by dispensing with procedural protections designed to facilitate the informed consideration of the rights at stake in a particular case, often fail to make factual inquiries into the living status of the parties to a domestic violence case, or fail to inquire into the property interests the defendant and alleged victim hold in a particular home. When this occurs the proper balance between the rights and duties at issue can not be found.

Not surprisingly, however, most statutes allowing for CPOs do not require that courts make such an inquiry. The exception is the Illinois CPO statute. This enactment sets out, as one of the remedies to be afforded in a CPO, a grant of exclusive possession and use of a residence to an individual that the court has preliminarily found to have been abused. Such a grant is made only where the alleged victim has a right to occupy the residence or household, which is defined in the same section, and where both the alleged victim and defendant have a right to occupancy, only after balancing the hardships to each, with the presumption of greater hardship to the petitioner/alleged victim.

The Illinois law, which applies in both criminal and civil settings, goes a long way to ensure a judicial inquiry into the property interests involved takes place before the criminal defendant/civil respondent is excluded from his residence. Jurisdictions that do not provide for such an inquiry risk creating a system where courts issuing CPOs fail to consider the property rights of the parties to a domestic violence case, in obvious violation of constitutional protections.

A defendant's interest in his property is by no means the sole interest at issue when a court considers a CPO. For example, the reputation of the defendant, as well as the custody and visitation rights of the defendant with regard to his children, are other general liberty interests that a court issuing a CPO must consider. As in the case of property deprivations, however, very few jurisdictions require that courts consider these interests when issuing the orders that burden them. Where legislation does not require meaningful review and balancing based on the facts of an individual case, judges may be all too willing to ignore these safeguards. Leaving to the discretion of a court what import, if any, to place upon an interest held by the domestic violence defendant cheapens the same interests held by the entire community. A legislature is uniquely positioned to make a statement in favor of preserving the presumption of innocence and procedural protections for all citizens, in the same way it may make a powerful statement concerning the protection of all citizens from abuse in domestic settings. By setting out in the language of a statute, all the interests that a court must consider in fashioning the best conditions for pretrial release in domestic violence cases, lawmakers can ensure that a reasoned decision, insulated from the political pressures of the day, and particularly suited for the parties involved, is a just and best result.

Notes

1. Many states provide that upon release of a defendant the court shall order him to have no-contact with the victim. These no contact provisions apply to victims of all crimes, not just domestic violence. Some statutes mandate the courts to require no contact with the victim. Other statutes leave the no-contact order in the discretion of the court.

Colo. Rev. Stat. § 18-1-1001. Restraining order against defendant.

(1) There is hereby created a mandatory restraining order against any person charged with a violation of any of the provisions of this title, which order shall remain in effect from the time that the person is advised of his rights at arraignment or the person's first appearance before the court and informed of such order until final disposition of the action or until further order of the court. Such order shall restrain the person charged from harassing, molesting, intimidating, retaliating against, or tampering with any witness to or victim of the acts charged.

(2) At the time of arraignment or the person's first appearance before the court, the court shall inform the defendant of the restraining order effective pursuant to this section and shall inform the defendant that a violation of such order is punishable by contempt.

(3) The provisions of the restraining order issued pursuant to this section may be continued by the court after sentencing if the court deems such action reasonable and necessary. In addition, nothing in this section shall preclude the defendant from applying to the court at any time for modification or dismissal of such order or the district attorney from applying to the court at any time for further orders, additional provisions under the restraining order, or modification or dismissal of the same.

2. In a few states prosecutors are instructed to obtain the victim's input regarding pretrial release. For example, Florida law provides:

FLA. STAT. § 960.001.

(g) *Consultation with victim or guardian or family of victim.* In addition to being notified of the provisions of § 921.143, the victim of a felony involving physical or emotional injury or trauma or, in a case in which the victim is a minor child or in a homicide, the guardian or family of the victim shall be consulted by the state attorney in order to obtain the views of the victim or family about the disposition of any criminal or juvenile case brought as a result of such crime, including the views of the victim or family about:

1. The release of the accused pending judicial proceedings; . . . .

2. Civil Protective Orders

The criminal protective order discussed in the previous section depends upon the state filing a criminal case. If the state elects not to file criminal charges, the victim cannot obtain a *criminal* protective order. A victim, however, is always free to seek her own *civil* protective order, obtained from the civil courts. Victims most commonly seek civil protective orders in domestic violence cases. Courts will issue protective orders on a showing of reasonable fear of imminent physical harm. The following case is typical of the kinds of orders sought and the legal issues that arise.

Chapman v. Chapman

2004 WL 1047577 (Ohio App. 2004)

WOLFF, J.

Thomas L. Chapman ("Thomas") appeals from a judgment of the Montgomery County Court of Common Pleas, Domestic Relations Division, which granted the petition of his former wife, Catherine R. Chapman ("Catherine"), for a civil protection order.

The Chapmans have four children, two of which are currently minors. The record suggests that both parents resided together with their minor children, Kelsey and Elizabeth, until September 24, 2001.

On May 29, 2002, Catherine sought a civil protection order against Thomas. On June 4, 2002, a hearing was held before a magistrate. During the hearing, Catherine and Thomas testified regarding several incidents during which Thomas allegedly had threatened her. Catherine testified that in April 2000, Thomas had thrown a set of keys at her; the keys bounced off the floor and hit her in the face near her eye. She stated that she had bled and had a "black and blue mark" for a few days. Thomas testified that the key incident "never happened." He stated that the family was vacationing in Annapolis, Maryland, and that Catherine became belligerent when they were checking out of the motel room. When they got in the car, Catherine had no marks on her face. He also testified that perhaps she was referring to an incident several months before. At that time, he was "getting the keys down from the pass-through from the beginning of the hallway into the kitchen, and they fell off the shelf—and glanced off of her face on the way down." On July 4, 2000, Thomas allegedly picked up Catherine, shoved her against a desk and threw her against a wall. Catherine stated that she had a broken shoulder at the time. Thomas testified that Catherine had kicked down the door to Kelsey's room, grabbed her by the hair, dragged her into his bedroom, and beat her. Thomas testified that he had pulled Catherine off of Kelsey, who was twelve years old at the time. He stated that Catherine left the house after the incident, and he questioned whether her shoulder was broken.

Catherine testified that on April 3, 2002, when she was traveling out-of-state on a spring break vacation, Thomas had left threatening telephone messages, asking where the children were.

On April 12, 2002, Catherine had picked up their daughter, Elizabeth, from Thomas' home while he was not there and had taken her to Girl Scout camp. She testified that Thomas came to the camp with a police officer and "started yelling and screaming and ranting at [her]," saying that he needed to "teach [her] what the laws were and how to respect the laws, and he was going to force me to obey the laws, and he would do whatever it took to destroy me." She testified that his gestures and movements were "very intimidating." She further indicated that Thomas had scared several of the girl scouts, causing them to cry. Thomas testified that prior to April 2002, Catherine had taken the children on weekends when he was supposed to have custody of them. He stated that on April 12, 2002, he went to pick up Elizabeth from Girl Scout camp, because Catherine had taken her "illegally." Thomas forcibly took his daughter from the camp. He denied that he had made any threatening gestures to Catherine.

Thomas further testified that Catherine's visitation with Kelsey ended at 8:00 a.m. on Monday mornings, at which time Catherine was required to take Kelsey to school, to a day care provider or to his home. On Monday, May 6, 2002, Kelsey had called her father, informing him that she was sick and that she wanted to stay with her mother. Thomas testified that he told his former wife that she had to return Kelsey to him. After consulting with her attorney, Catherine decided that she would keep her daughter with her rather than have Thomas' mother, who had been ill and was unable to care for Kelsey, watch Kelsey. Both parties testified that Thomas had appeared at Catherine's apartment with a police officer to retrieve Kelsey. Catherine testified that "[h]e was extremely agitated" and that he was "raising his arms and gesturing and * * * getting closer to me and moving back." She stated that she was fearful of some sort of physical harm by him, because "he has done it in the past where's gotten upset and it has come into physical confrontation." Thomas stated that he would not allow Kelsey to stay with her mother when she was sick on Monday, May 6, 2002, because Catherine had over-medicated their children in the past and she is abusive to Kelsey specifically. Thomas also indicated that he would have been home with Kelsey, as he works from his home. He denied threatening Catherine on May 6, 2002.

In addition, Catherine testified that Thomas owns many high-powered weapons, an AK47 automatic weapon, a high-powered rifle and several handguns. In response to whether he had any weapons, Thomas testified that he does not own an AK47, and that since the divorce case began, he took all of his weapons to his father's home. Catherine further indicated that Thomas had threatened to destroy her physically and financially, including during the confrontations on April 12, 2002, and May 6, 2002. Catherine testified that police officers witnessed these statements, but that they had told her that there was nothing they could do to stop him from verbally harassing her without an order. It is undisputed that Catherine had filed a prior petition for a protection order based on the incidents in 2000. Catherine testified that she dismissed that petition based on an agreement with Thomas. . .

On June 26, 2002, the magistrate issued a permanent civil protection order, based on the events in 2000 and 2002. The magistrate, alluding to a "subjective standard," granted the order based on Catherine's perception that Thomas' actions represented a threat to her. Thomas filed objections to the magistrate's decision. He argued that the magistrate erred in failing to take into account "objective" testimony which contradicted Catherine's perception of events.

On November 19, 2002, the trial court overruled the objections, finding that the magistrate had competent, credible evidence to support the issuance of the order. The court noted that the magistrate had the best opportunity to evaluate the credibility and demeanor of the witnesses and that Chris Chapman's testimony was considered by the magistrate but apparently deemed insufficient by the magistrate to negate Catherine's "subjective evidence."

Thomas appeals the trial court's judgment, arguing that the judgment is against the manifest weight of the evidence.

In his appeal, Thomas asserts that the evidence before the trial court does not support the issuance of a civil protection order. He argues that the incidents in 2000 were remote in time and should not be considered. He further argues that the events on April 12, 2002, and May 6, 2002, do not indicate that Catherine was reasonably placed in fear of imminent physical harm. He states that the fact that he brought a police officer with him suggests that he did not intend to harm his ex-wife. Thomas contends that the trial court should have employed a "reasonableness" standard as to whether his former wife was placed in fear of physical harm.

A petition for a domestic violence civil protection order shall be granted if a person places a family or household member in fear of imminent physical harm by the threat of force. R.C. 3113.31(A)(1)(b). The petitioner must show by a preponderance of the evidence that conditions exist which justify the issuance of such an order.

We have noted that "[f]ear always has a subjective element to it." *Kreuzer v. Kreuzer*, Greene App. No. 2001-CA-49, *2002-Ohio-105*, citing *Eichenberger v. Eichenberger* (1992), 82 Ohio App.3d 809, 815, 613 N.E.2d 678. In *Reynolds v. Reynolds* (Jan. 26, 2001), Montgomery App. No. 18436, we stated that "the standard for reviewing [the petitioner's] fear is subjective, that is, whether her fear was reasonable under the particular circumstances of her particular situation, which must be established by a preponderance of the evidence." Notwithstanding our use of the word "subjective," it is clear from the entire sentence that we intended to say that the standard for reviewing a petitioner's fear is—at least in part—an objective one. The word "reasonable" connotes an objective test. In other words, a petitioner's irrational or unsubstantiated fear is insufficient to warrant the issuance of a protective order. "If an unsubstantiated concern for safety were enough to justify the issuance of protective orders, there would be no need for hearings on these matter." Rather, "[t]hreats of violence constitute domestic violence if the fear resulting from those threats is reasonable." *Kreuzer v. Kreuzer,* Greene App. No. 2001-CA-49, *2002-Ohio-105.*

In *Kreuzer,* we affirmed the trial court's issuance of a civil protection order, stating: "We have read the transcript of the hearing and it fully supports the court's finding that Stacy was in a state of fright, because of fear of imminent harm by the appellant[;] the court found that Stacy's fear was reasonable because of her knowledge and even past subjection to Mr. Kreuzer's bizarre, threatening, and menacing acts over a period of many years since his divorce from Stacy's mother." Thus, a petitioner for a civil protection order must demonstrate both that she was in fear (subjective) and that such fear was reasonable under the circumstances (objective). "[T]he reasonableness of a petitioner's fear should be measured with reference to her history with respondent. . . " *Parrish v. Parrish* (2002), 95 Ohio St.3d 1201, 1208, *2002-Ohio-1623,* 765 N.E.2d 359 (Lundberg Stratton, J., dissenting), citing *Eichenberger,* supra.

———————

Upon review of the transcript, we conclude that the issuance of the civil protection order was neither an abuse of discretion nor against the manifest weight of the evidence. The magistrate and the trial court apparently chose to believe Catherine's testimony that Thomas' actions put her in fear of physical harm. Because the trier of fact sees and hears the witnesses and is particularly competent to decide "whether, and to what extent, to credit the testimony of particular witnesses," we must afford substantial deference to its determinations of credibility. As to whether that fear was reasonable, the court was left with the conflicting evidence of Catherine and Thomas. There were no witnesses, other than the parties, who testified as to what actually occurred on April 2000; July 4, 2000; April 12, 2002; and May 6, 2002. Although their adult son testified that he had never seen Thomas threaten or assault Catherine and that his mother would become verbally abusive, he did not witness any of the events at issue. Accordingly, the magistrate and the trial court could have reasonably found that Chris's testimony was not sufficient "objective evidence" to support his father's version of events.

The magistrate and the trial court also could have reasonably credited Catherine's rendition of events and her testimony that Thomas's verbal attacks have become increasingly more violent during the past two months, including threats to kill her. Moreover, although Thomas disputed Catherine's contention that he owned an AK47, he did not contest her statement that he owned a high-powered rifle and several handguns. His testimony that he had placed them under "lock and key" at his father's residence does not refute Catherine's suggestion that he has access to weapons to carry out his alleged threat. In addition, the presence of a police officer does not necessarily support Thomas' version of events, particularly in light of Catherine's testimony that police officers had told her they could not stop Thomas' abusive behavior without a protective order. Accordingly, although both the magistrate and the trial court could have chosen to credit Thomas' accounts of the confrontations, they had credible, competent evidence to support the issuance of the civil protection order. The trial court's judgment was neither an abuse of discretion nor against the manifest weight of the evidence.

Thomas Chapman's assignment of error is overruled.

The judgment of the trial court will be affirmed.

Margaret Martin Barry, *Protective Order Enforcement: Another Pirouette*

6 HASTINGS WOMEN'S L.J. 339 (1995)

III. The Survivor as Prosecutor

Survivors of domestic violence are at a significant psychological, social, economic, and procedural disadvantage in seeking to enforce protection orders. Many battered women fear threats of reprisal, the loss of their children, shame, and a lack of financial support. They often blame themselves for the violence and try to minimize the extent of it. They also try to rationalize the violence by focusing on the pressures or problems facing their batterers, such as his job or lack of one, his status in the community, and his relationships with the rest of his family. This is a particular problem for African-American women, who must seek help from a system that has thrived on mistreating them and shackling their men and boys.

Thus burdened, women who have successfully obtained a protective order must figure out how to persuade the court to enforce it when violated. Most survivors and batterers enter the protective order stage pro se. States that specify a burden of proof generally require survivors to demonstrate, by a preponderance of the evidence, that the person accused in the petition caused the harm alleged. In most jurisdictions, courts tend to be open to providing an injunction against future harm and to creating other temporary remedies, such as custody and support, that allow the survivor to function in the short term with a modicum of independence from the abuser. The remedial nature of the statutes encourage courts to issue protective orders. Nonetheless, many survivors approach the court with fear of both the abuser and the institution, and they are often confused by the process. Many expect the order obtained to provide a greater shield than it does, believing that the court will automatically mete out punishment upon violation. They see obtaining the protective order as the end of their advocacy, unaware that the order is not self-enforcing and that they must initiate its enforcement.

* * *

IV. Protective Order Enforcement Options

A. *Misdemeanor*

In those jurisdictions in which violation of a protective order is itself a crime, the government prosecutor is responsible for seeking enforcement. Thirty states and the District of Columbia have made the violation of protective orders a misdemeanor. The 1994 Violence Against Women Act makes interstate violation of a protective order a federal crime. This trend toward criminalization is a statement about the seriousness of the orders and the situations they reflect. It formally places enforcement in the criminal context for procedural purposes and relieves the survivor of the onus of conducting the prosecution. In practice, however, this enforcement authority has not been pursued, and the survivor is still expected to take responsibility for enforcement. [C]riminal prosecution does not protect [a victim] from defense counsel, nor does it assure her a determinative voice in enforcement. Since the charge that the perpetrator faces is directly related to the survivor's effort to get protection, retaliation becomes more likely.

Neither the prosecutors nor the courts are accustomed to considering the victims of crimes in more than an abstract way, at least until the sentencing phase of a case where the victim impact statement may have some bearing upon the length of the incarceration. Misdemeanor prosecution of protective order violations challenges the criminal justice system to consider the safety of the survivor and the domestic responsibilities of the defendant in fashioning the appropriate punishments. It is a challenge that courts are increasingly called upon to meet.

Enforcement of the protective order should be cumulative to prosecution of the underlying crime. This underscores the weight the order must be given while demonstrating that domestic violence crimes are not a separate category of lesser offenses. In pursuing both manners of enforcement, complaints must be fashioned so as to avoid double jeopardy challenges. The Supreme Court held in *United States v. Dixon* that such challenges can be avoided so long as the contempt and criminal offenses each contain an element that is not contained in the other. Care should be taken to assure that actions by the batterer that lead to prosecution for violation of the protective order and prosecution for violation of criminal statutes avoid the double jeopardy issue. A survivor proceeding pro se to enforce the protective order is usually unaware of the double jeopardy issue or unable to communicate with the prosecutor on this matter. If state prosecution of protective order contempt citations is not pursued or if counsel is not provided to the survivor, the result may be that the batterer is insulated from penalties under the criminal statutes, which are often more severe.

* * *

If sentencing involves batterer's counseling, the counselors must be trained in the area of domestic violence, the batterer's attendance must be monitored, and consequences must follow a failure to attend. In this way, criminal sanctions can be imposed in a manner that conveys intolerance of domestic abuse while addressing the

survivor's concerns. This calls for an integration of criminal punishment and rehabilitative goals with domestic relations concerns about family welfare.

Show Cause Orders

Where there is reason to believe that a violation of an order has occurred, a court
has the authority to require a person who may have violated the order to demonstrate
why he or she should not be found in contempt. Courts do this by issuing show cause
orders. If the abuser is found to have violated the protective order, then the statutory
sanctions would apply. Procedurally, this puts the initial burden on the batterer and
sends a clear message that the court has an interest in enforcing its own orders. It also
has the benefit of removing from the survivor the onus of initiating prosecution.
Notification of a violation should come by way of a police or probation report filed
with the court or by way of an affidavit filed by the survivor or other witness. Notification should go directly to the judge who issued the order. As a practical matter, to
go forward on a criminal contempt, the batterer may have the right to have defense
counsel appointed. As discussed in the following section, for this procedure to be
effective, counsel for the survivor should also be appointed by the court.

Judges are often unwilling to issue show cause orders because the initiation of such
action adds to already crowded dockets. Thus, for such an enforcement approach to
be reliable, judges would have to be required to issue these orders, either by statute
or by court rule.

Court-Appointed Counsel for the Survivor

In states where the survivor is responsible for pursuing criminal contempt for the
violation of a protective order, the accused has no right to a public prosecutor. There
is neither authority supporting the right to a public prosecutor, nor to court-appointed
counsel, for one seeking to enforce the order. The court may have the authority to
appoint counsel for the survivor, but it is not required to do so. [T]his can leave the
survivor with the overwhelming task of having to battle both her abuser and his
counsel on her own.

Federal funding, comparable to that provided to guarantee defendant's access to
counsel under the Criminal Justice Act, would provide states with the ability to
appoint counsel to represent survivors in enforcing protective orders. Under this
scheme, lawyers trained in domestic violence law would be chosen from a list kept
by the court for appointments. While protecting the rights of the accused in a criminal action is essential, it is no less essential to protect the survivor, who asks the court
to enforce its order.

Since there is currently no federal funding of this type, and with local law and
budget constraints limiting the court's ability to pay fees to counsel, pro bono counsel should, at a minimum, be appointed from a court-maintained list of attorneys
trained in the area of domestic violence to represent the survivor who is seeking to
enforce her protective order. The court or the bar should provide training in this area
for these attorneys. In any event, thrusting the burden of enforcement of civil

protection orders upon the survivor, without assuring that she will be represented, is both unrealistic and ineffective. . . .

Notes

1. Civil protective orders are not limited to domestic violence. For example, protective orders are also issued to rape and stalking victims.

2. Upon service of the civil protective order, the person against whom the order has been entered has an opportunity to contest the propriety of the order itself. This opportunity consists of a hearing where the victim offers evidence in support of continuation of the order and the person who is the subject of the order offers evidence in support of vacating the order. No right to counsel attaches to either party at these civil proceedings, and the parties frequently represent themselves.

3. A number of law schools provide clinical opportunities for their students to help victims of domestic violence obtain protective orders. *See, e.g.,* Stephen Andrew Schmidt, *Pro Bono Work for the Law Student: Working with the Protective Order Pro Bono Project*, RES GESTAE, May 2004.

Chapter 9

Trial

Introduction

This chapter explores victims' rights during the trial. The chapter first examines the jury selection process, focusing on questions to prospective jurors regarding bias in favor of or against victims. Then it turns to the question of whether victims should be able to attend trials as an exception to the general rule keeping potential witnesses outside of the courtroom. The next section discusses whether a victim can have a support person available during the trial. The following section explores the role of an attorney for the victim in the trial. The penultimate section provides a comparative perspective on the victim's involvement in trial, offering examples from various countries in which victims are much more heavily integrated into the trial process. The final section discusses several important evidentiary issues involving victims at trial.

A. Victims and Juries

1. The Victim's Right to a Jury Trial

Defendants have a constitutional right to a jury trial, protected in the Sixth Amendment. Should victims have the parallel right to demand a jury trial? In 1996, Oregon voters approved an initiative adding a victim's bill of rights to the state constitution. The amendment to the constitution gave victims the right to a jury trial:

OR. CONST., art. I, § 42

> To ensure crime victims a meaningful role in the criminal . . . justice system, to accord them due dignity and respect, and to ensure that persons who violate laws for the punishment of crime are apprehended, convicted and punished, the following rights are hereby granted to victims in all prosecutions for crimes: . . .

> The right, in a criminal prosecution, to a public trial without delay by a jury selected from registered voters and composed of persons who have not been convicted of a felony or served a felony sentence within the last 15 years. . . .

In 1998, the Oregon Supreme Court struck down the entire Oregon victims' rights amendment for violating a state rule that constitutional ballot initiatives must contain only one subject. *See Armatta v. Kitzhaber*, 959 P.2d 49 (Oregon 1998).

If effective, the Oregon provision would have had interesting implications. In many jurisdictions (including Oregon), a defendant may waive a jury trial with the permission of the trial court, even over an objection from the state. Defendants typically seek to waive jury trials where they believe a judge is more likely to be sympathetic to them than a jury, particularly where an individual judge is perceived as lenient.

Federal law and the law of some states require the consent of the *prosecutor* before a defendant can waive a jury trial. A victim seeking a jury trial in these jurisdictions would have to rely on informal influences to persuade the prosecutor to invoke the state's right to a jury trial.

Should the rules be changed to require a court to consider a victim's views before waiving a jury trial? Consider the following argument to that effect:

Paul G. Cassell, *Recognizing Victims in the Federal Rules of Criminal Procedure: Proposed Amendments in Light of the Crime Victims' Rights Act*
2005 B.Y.U. L. Rev. 835 (2005)

In the federal courts the "preferred" trial method is a jury trial. As Justice Blackmun has explained, the public has interests, independent of a criminal defendant, in monitoring judges, police, and prosecutors — and in being educated about "the manner in which criminal justice is administered." Nonetheless, the Supreme Court has concluded that defendants can waive their right to a jury trial. To help protect the general public interest in trial by jury, Rule 23 requires not only prosecutor approval but also judicial approval before proceeding by way of bench trial. This approval requires careful weighing of the competing concerns. The Supreme Court has instructed that

> the duty of the trial court [in considering whether to approve a jury trial waiver] is not to be discharged as a mere matter of rote, but with sound and advised discretion, with an eye to avoid unreasonable or undue departures from that mode of trial or from any of the essential elements thereof, and with a caution increasing in degree as the offenses dealt with increase in gravity.[218] This is a "serious and weighty responsibility."

To discharge that serious and weighty responsibility, the trial court should receive as much information as possible. The victim is often well situated to provide information about how the public will view a non-jury trial. The proposed rule change takes the modest step of requiring the court to hear the victim before approving any non-jury trial, a step that is consistent with the CVRA's command that victims be treated with fairness.

Importantly, this change would not interfere with defendants' rights. The Supreme Court has squarely held that the defendant lacks any constitutional right to unilaterally elect a bench trial. Of course, in some circumstances, despite a victim's objection, a non-jury trial nonetheless will be appropriate. Moreover, in extreme cases, the defendant may have a right to a non-jury trial where pretrial publicity has pervasively tainted the jury pool. Nothing in the proposed rule change would interfere with a court's right to approve a bench trial in such circumstances, so long as the court considers the victim's perspective as part of the approval process.

2. Jury Selection and Victims

a. The Defendant's Right to Fair Trial: Challenging Victim Jurors

During jury selection, a defendant (and the prosecution) can challenge prospective jurors for potential bias. A juror shown to be biased will be excused for cause. Typically a juror is considered biased when there is a reasonable question about the juror's impartiality. Bias is revealed by voir dire — the process of the judge or attorneys asking prospective jurors questions before trial. In addition to excusals for cause, each side is typically given a certain number of peremptory challenges — that is, challenges that can be lodged against prospective jurors without the need to give a reason.

One question that has arisen in jury selection is whether a juror's past victimization is sufficiently similar to the crime being tried to create the potential for bias and thus the need for an excusal for cause.

———————

Knox v. State

29 A.3d 217 (Del. 2011)

Police arrested Dechanta Knox on August 5, 2008 and charged her with three counts of issuing a bad check greater than $1,000. After a jury convicted Knox of all offenses, the trial judge learned that Juror No. 8 was a victim in a pending criminal trial being prosecuted by the same Deputy Attorney General. Without examining the juror in court, the trial judge denied Knox's motion for a new trial. When a juror serving on a criminal trial is an alleged victim of a crime and is contemporaneously represented by the Attorney General's office in the prosecution of the alleged perpetrator of the crime against the juror "victim," a mere inquiry by deposition into whether the jury knew the prosecutor or anyone in his office insufficiently probes the ability of that "juror/victim" to render a fair and objective verdict as a matter of law. Therefore, we reverse and remand.

. . .

Customarily we would review a trial judge's determination that a juror can fairly and objectively render a verdict for abuse of discretion. Trial judges have discretion to make credibility determinations, but "the exercise of this discretion is limited by the essential demands of fairness." When the trial judge fails to conduct a sufficient inquiry into juror bias, the appellate court may be required to evaluate independently the fairness and impartiality of the juror. In this case, judicial inquiry for juror bias was limited to a deposition taken outside the presence of the trial judge. Therefore, the trial judge eschewed the opportunity to evaluate the juror's demeanor and credibility, a crucial element in the determination of impartiality. To our knowledge, a decision to inquire into juror bias solely by deposition is without precedent and should not happen again. In effect, the unique circumstances of this case suggest that our inquiry here can be analogized to summary judgment scrutiny, and therefore we review the trial judge's determination of the juror's objectivity *de novo*.

Knox argues that Juror No. 8's bias originated from his experience as an alleged robbery victim. When a victim seeks justice for the crimes committed against him, the victim's interests align with the Attorney General's interests. The victim has a personal appreciation for the role of prosecutors in bringing justice to criminals. The Department of Justice's focus on pursuing cases for "victims" through "victims' services" reinforces the identification of "victims" with the Attorney General. It would be irrational to ignore the influence of the pending joint endeavor on the juror's objectivity in the *Knox* trial. Even in factually unrelated cases, the victim's experience with the Department of Justice, whether good or bad, previous or ongoing, will affect the victim's perspective. In these situations, courts must be wary of the victim's ability to be fair and impartial in the role of a juror.

Other courts have expressed concern regarding a victim's bias in favor of the prosecution while serving on a jury. This case bears a striking similarity to the situation analyzed in *Mobley v. Florida*, 559 So.2d 1201, 1202 (Fla.Dist.Ct.App.1990). In *Mobley,* a juror denied that he had been a victim of a crime during *voir dire* but later remembered and notified the judge during trial. On appeal, the Florida District Court of Appeal held that defense counsel's motion to strike the juror from the panel and substitute an alternate should have been granted. Although the opinion did not explicitly discuss why having been a victim biased the juror, we can readily infer that the appellate court found sufficient bias to reverse the trial judge's denial of defense counsel's motion to strike the juror.

On the other hand, [this case] can be distinguished from cases where a juror was merely a potential witness for the prosecution. In *Commonwealth v. Frye*, 909 A.2d 853 (Pa.Super.Ct.2006) a juror was scheduled to testify as Pennsylvania's sole eyewitness in a different criminal case scheduled to begin the next day. The defendant claimed that a situational relationship between the juror and the prosecutor's office could be inferred from appearing as a prosecution witness, but the court held that the defendant did not present particularized evidence of juror bias. Unlike a witness who is indifferent to the resolution of a case and has no formal relationship with the prosecution, a victim is emotionally invested in the outcome and personally dependent on the attorney general to bring the person the victim perceives to be the wrongdoer to justice. Therefore, Knox presents a case where the question of a juror's objectivity poses a serious issue.

An added layer of complexity involves Juror No. 8's status as a victim in a *pending* criminal case. Because the victim inevitably forms an impression, either positive or negative, about the attorney general's handling of his case, that awareness clouds the victim's judgment as a fair and impartial juror. This problem intensifies when the

Deputy Attorney General is the same in both cases. As a victim of a robbery in a pending case, Juror No. 8 was conscious that the Attorney General's Office would represent him and present evidence intended to convict a perpetrator in another case. The fact that Juror No. 8's case would go to trial only 14 days after Knox suggests an inference that the pending trial would be at the forefront of the juror's mind.

In violent crime cases, trial judges commonly ask venire members whether they or a family member have ever been a victim of a violent crime. The logic supporting this practice is based on a belief that the victims would be unable to separate their personal experiences with violent crime when adjudicating the current case. A victim in a pending robbery trial may have a similar tendency when adjudicating a case about writing bad checks. Both crimes involve the intent to permanently deprive another of property. Although one is theft by force and the other is theft by deception, they both constitute *malum prohibitum.* Furthermore, this policy rests not only on the similarity of the crimes but also on the victim's personal experience with the criminal justice system and the prosecution. Whether the victim believes that justice would be performed or that the defendant might escape punishment in his case, can impact the victim's ability to serve as an impartial juror in a contemporaneous proceeding.

This case is unique because the trial judge neither uncovered Juror No. 8's status during *voir dire* nor conducted a post trial, in court hearing to ask the juror whether he was impartial despite his connection with the Attorney General's Office. If the trial judge had made those determinations, those findings would have been given deference. With no questions on the record directed to Juror No. 8's ability to be impartial despite his experience, we find that Juror No. 8, a victim in a pending criminal trial, lacked the capacity to render a fair and impartial verdict in the Knox trial.

State v. Dotson

234 So.3d 34, 2017 WL 4681942 (La. 2017)

During *voir dire*, the trial court was questioning prospective juror number 9 ("K.C."), who indicated she was an attorney, when the following exchange took place:

[Court:] Have you or a close friend or relative been a crime victim?

[K.C.:] Yes, sir.

[Court:] Could you tell us a little bit about that?

[K.C.:] My mother was raped and murdered.

[Court:] Would that event have any bearing on your ability to be a fair and impartial juror in today's case?

[K.C.:] *Yes, it might.*

. . .

When defense counsel later challenged K.C. for cause, the following exchange took place:

The Court: . . . . Panelist Number 9.

[State]: Acceptable.

[Defense]: Challenge for cause, Your Honor.

The Court: Cause based on what?

[Defense]: Her mother was murdered and raped.

The Court: That's not cause.

[Defense]: She said that would—

The Court: No, she didn't.

. . .

Defendant's challenge for cause as to K.C. was related to the following facts: (1) K.C.'s mother was raped and murdered; and (2) K.C. testified that her mother's ordeal might affect her impartiality in this case.

"[T]he fact that a juror may have painful memories associated with the subject of a criminal trial is not listed as a basis for a challenge for cause under La.C.Cr.P. art. 797." *State v. Magee*, 13-1018, p. 12 (La.App. 5 Cir. 9/24/14), 150 So.3d 446, 454, writ denied, 14-2209 (La. 10/2/15), 178 So.3d 581. That a prospective juror personally has been the victim of a crime will not necessarily preclude that prospective juror from serving on a jury. *State v. Dorsey*, 10-0216, p. 3 (La. 9/7/11), 74 So.3d 603, 631. A prospective juror's relationship to a person who was the victim of a crime likewise does not disqualify a prospective juror from serving. See id.; *State v. Nix*, 327 So.2d 301, 326 (La. 1975) (a prospective juror's relationship to a murder victim—his brother-in-law—was insufficient to establish cause for excusing the venireman).

The law does not require that a jury be composed of individuals who have not personally been a crime victim or who do not have close friends or relatives who have been crime victims. It requires that jurors be fair and unbiased. *Juniors*, 03–2425 at 11, 915 So.2d at 306. Therefore, the prospective juror's past experience as, or relationship to, a victim of a crime similar to that for which the defendant is being tried must be examined in conjunction with other evidence in the record of the *voir dire* proceeding that bears on the prospective juror's ability to be fair and impartial and to apply the law as instructed by the trial court. See *Dorsey*, 10–0216 at 38–39, 74 So.3d at 631; *Nix*, 327 So.2d at 326. Accordingly, the trial court did not abuse its discretion in refusing to find that K.C.'s relationship with her mother, who was raped and murdered, automatically rendered K.C. unable to be impartial in these cases. Although the record establishes a mother/daughter relationship, and this court is sensitive to the impact of crime on a family member, we are constrained by the record which reflects no follow-up questions were posed to in fact establish this prospective juror could not be fair and impartial in these cases.

Upon the trial judge's recognition that K.C.'s relationship with a rape victim was alone insufficient to disqualify K.C., defense counsel referenced K.C.'s response to the trial judge's question regarding her ability to be impartial due to her mother's ordeal. Defense counsel interpreted K.C.'s response as "yes," that is, K.C. could not be impartial in the instant cases against defendant. However, as the trial judge again correctly observed, K.C. did not declare that her mother's rape and murder would affect her ability to be impartial, as her affirmative response was immediately qualified by an expression of uncertainty—"it might." . . . Based on the qualification of K.C.'s affirmative response, this court cannot say that the trial court erred or abused its discretion in finding that K.C. at no point declared that she could not be impartial in these cases; nor from this lone response can "bias, prejudice, or the inability to render judgment according to law . . . be reasonably implied," as found by the appellate court. Furthermore, K.C.'s conditional response neither required that K.C. be rehabilitated, nor relieved defendant (who sought to exclude K.C. for cause) of his burden of demonstrating, through questioning, that K.C. lacked impartiality. See *State v. Taylor*, 99-1311, p. 8 (La. 1/17/01), 781 So.2d 1205, 1214 ("The party seeking to exclude the [prospective] juror has the burden to demonstrate, through questioning, that the [prospective] juror lacks impartiality.").

Guidry, J., dissents and assigns reasons.

I respectfully dissent from the majority's decision today. In this case, the potential juror expressed during *voir dire* an undoubtedly equivocal response that she "might" be impartial or biased against this defendant, charged with two counts of aggravated rape, because her mother had been raped and murdered. In the face of this clear expression of possible bias, there was no follow-up questioning by the trial court, the state, or the defense as to whether the juror would be willing and able to decide the case impartially according to the law and evidence. The trial court, when the prospective juror was later challenged for cause, did not allow a full discussion of the juror's response regarding her possible bias, and more troublingly, insisted the potential juror had not said anything that would bring into question her inability to be impartial, when in fact she did. . . .

While deference is certainly owed to the trial court's determination, where due, I find in this case the trial court abused its discretion, because, upon review of the prospective juror's *voir dire* examination as a whole, her bias, prejudice, or the inability to render judgment according to the law may be reasonably implied.

Note

Issues surrounding juror bias are generally left to the sound discretion of the trial judge. Reversals, such as in the *Knox* case, are quite rare.

The cases above involve situations where the record made clear that someone was the victim of a crime. Should the trial court be required to ask prospective jurors if they have been crime victims?

Pearson v. State

437 Md. 350, 86 A.3d 1232 (Md. 2014)

On request, a trial court must ask a *voir dire* question if and only if the *voir dire* question is "reasonably likely to reveal [specific] cause for disqualification[.]" *Moore v. State*, 412 Md. 635, 663, 989 A.2d 1150, 1166 (2010) (citation omitted). There are two categories of specific cause for disqualification: (1) a statute disqualifies a prospective juror; or (2) a "collateral matter [is] reasonably liable to have undue influence over" a prospective juror. *Washington*, 425 Md. at 313, 40 A.3d at 1021 (citation omitted). The latter category is comprised of "biases directly related to the crime, the witnesses, or the defendant[.]" *Id.* at 313, 40 A.3d at 1021 (citation omitted).

On request, a trial court must ask during *voir dire* whether any prospective juror has had an experience, "status, association, or affiliation[,]" *State v. Thomas*, 369 Md. 202, 211, 798 A.2d 566, 571 (2002) (citation omitted), if and only if the experience, status, association, or affiliation has "a *demonstrably strong correlation* [with] a mental state that gives rise to [specific] cause for disqualification." *Curtin v. State*, 393 Md. 593, 607, 903 A.2d 922, 931 (2006) (emphasis in original) (citation omitted). For example, in *Yopps v. State*, 234 Md. 216, 221, 198 A.2d 264, 267 (1964), a burglary case, this Court held that the trial court did not abuse its discretion in declining to ask during *voir dire* whether any prospective juror or anyone in any prospective juror's family had ever been the victim of a burglary. This Court stated that the proposed *voir dire* question "did not relate to a [specific] cause [for] disqualification[.]" *Yopps*, 234 Md. at 221, 198 A.2d at 267.

Similarly, in *Perry v. State*, 344 Md. 204, 217–19, 686 A.2d 274, 280–81 (1996), a murder case, this Court held that the trial court did not abuse its discretion in declining to ask during *voir dire* whether any prospective juror, anyone in any prospective juror's family, or any prospective juror's "close personal friend" had ever been "a juror, witness, victim or defendant" in "any criminal proceeding." Instead, the trial court asked during *voir dire* whether any prospective juror, anyone in any prospective juror's family, or any prospective juror's "close personal friend" had ever been "a juror, witness, victim or defendant" in "any criminal homicide or aggravated assault proceeding [.]" *Perry*, 344 Md. at 217–18, 686 A.2d at 280. This Court stated:

> A [prospective] juror's having had prior experience as a juror, witness, victim or defendant in a criminal proceeding of any kind, or in one involving a crime of violence, is not per se disqualifying. It is even less tenable to argue that a [prospective] juror is disqualified simply because of the experience of a member of the prospective juror's family or on the part of a close personal friend.

Id. at 218, 686 A.2d at 281 (citing *Yopps*, 234 Md. at 221, 198 A.2d at 267) (emphasis added). This Court also stated:

> A trial court's process of determining whether a proposed inquiry is *reasonably* likely to reveal disqualifying partiality or bias includes *weighing the expenditure of time and resources in the pursuit of the reason for the response*

to a proposed voir dire question against the likelihood that pursuing the reason for the response will reveal bias or partiality. Here, the charges against [the defendant] were murder and conspiracy to commit murder. . . . Without abusing its discretion, the [trial] court could conclude under the circumstances here that there was not a reasonable likelihood of uncovering a disqualification based on some [prospective juror]'s connection, even as a victim, to some other class of crime.

Perry, 344 Md. at 220, 686 A.2d at 282 (some emphasis added).

Here, consistent with existing case law, for three reasons, we conclude that a trial court need not ask during *voir dire* whether any prospective juror has ever been the victim of a crime.

First, a prospective juror's experience as the victim of a crime lacks "a *demonstrably strong correlation* [with] a mental state that gives rise to [specific] cause for disqualification." *Curtin,* 393 Md. at 607, 903 A.2d at 931 (emphasis in original) (citation omitted). *See Perry,* 344 Md. at 218, 686 A.2d at 281 (A prospective "juror's having had prior experience as a . . . victim . . . in a criminal proceeding of any kind . . . is not *per se* disqualifying."); *Yopps,* 234 Md. at 221, 198 A.2d at 267 (In a burglary case, this Court held that the trial court did not abuse its discretion in declining to ask during *voir dire* whether any prospective juror or anyone in any prospective juror's family had ever been the victim of a burglary.). Thus, the "victim" *voir dire* question (as well as the inevitable follow up questions) "merely [allow the defendant to] 'fish[ ]' for information to assist in the exercise of peremptory challenges[.]" *Washington,* 425 Md. at 315, 40 A.3d at 1022 (citations omitted).

Second, the "victim" *voir dire* question may consume an enormous amount of time. *See Perry,* 344 Md. at 219, 686 A.2d at 281 (The trial court noted that the "victim" *voir dire* question "provokes [ ] a huge response which would require follow-up questions galore, and we would have to sit here and listen to each incident that the prospective juror has experienced over [his or her] lifetime[.]"). Many (if not most) prospective jurors have been the victims of some kind of crime. Additionally (as Pearson concedes), the " victim" *voir dire* question necessitates that the trial court ask at least two "follow-up" questions of every single prospective juror who responds affirmatively. In deciding whether to ask a proposed *voir dire* question, a trial court should "weigh[ ] the *expenditure of time and resources* in the pursuit of the reason for the response to [the] proposed *voir dire* question against the likelihood that pursuing the reason for the response will reveal bias or partiality." *Perry,* 344 Md. at 220, 686 A.2d at 282 (emphasis added).

Third, this Court has already held that, on request, a trial court must ask during *voir dire* whether any prospective juror has "strong feelings about" the crime with which the defendant is charged. *State v. Shim,* 418 Md. 37, 54, 12 A.3d 671, 681 (2011). The "strong feelings" *voir dire* question makes the "victim" *voir dire* question unnecessary by revealing the specific cause for disqualification at which the "victim" *voir dire* question is aimed.

———————

Notes

1. One federal court has found reversible error where the trial court failed to ask the following voir dire question at the request of a defendant charged with bank robbery: "Have you or any member of your family ever been the victim of a robbery or other crime?" *United States v. Poole*, 450 F.2d 1082 (3rd Cir. 1972). The court cited several reasons for the reversal. First, the information was relevant to bias. Second, the question was contained in the Bench Book for U.S. District Judges and was a recommended question for use on voir dire.

2. *Pearson* involved the issue of whether a trial judge is required to ask a question about victimization to prospective jurors. But what if the judge has asked such a question and the juror fails to provide the requested information? In *Dunaway v. State*, 198 So. 3d 567 (Ala. 2014), the Court held that a juror's nondisclosure during voir dire that her cousin had been the victim of a shooting prejudiced a capital defendant because it likely caused defense counsel to forgo a for-cause or peremptory challenge to the juror he otherwise would have made.

---

b. Voir Dire: Jurors' Potential Bias against the Victim

A somewhat different issue is posed when jurors are potentially biased against the victim. There is no constitutional requirement that judges allow voir dire on bias against victims. A court may decline in its discretion to allow voir dire on bias against a victim. *See Van Arsdall v. State*, 486 A.2d 1 (Del. 1984) (denying a *defendant's* request to voir dire on the race of the victim); *Commonwealth v. Lawrence*, 536 N.E.2d 571 (Mass. 1989) (same).

In some cases, judges have allowed voir dire about possible jury bias against a victim. Do such questions effectively bias the jury against the defendant?

Dunkin v. State

818 P.2d 1159 (Alaska 1991)

COATS, Judge.

Michael T. Dunkin was convicted, following a jury trial, of murder in the first degree, an unclassified felony with a maximum sentence of ninety-nine years of imprisonment. AS 11.41.100(a)(1). Superior Court Judge Beverly W. Cutler sentenced Dunkin to eighty-five years of imprisonment, recommending that Dunkin be ineligible for parole until he had served fifty years of his sentence. Dunkin appeals his conviction and sentence. We affirm.

Dunkin was convicted of murdering Julius Marshall, a black male employed as an auto mechanic, by shooting him three times in the head and neck at close range. At trial, the state's theory was that Dunkin shot Marshall in an unprovoked attack for racial reasons.

The killing occurred in Palmer on May 26, 1985. Dunkin, who was twenty-two years old, drove to Palmer from Anchorage with his brother James Stevens and

Stevens' friend William Skinner to watch the races. They drove in Dunkin's green jeep. The jeep had a removable top with the words "Boofer hunter" on it; the top was not on the jeep at the time.[1] They spent the afternoon watching the races and drinking beer.

After the races, the three men went four-wheeling in the Knik River area. After about an hour, the jeep got stuck in the river and stalled. Dunkin got a ride to a store where he called for a tow truck. The towing business Dunkin contacted was the Roadrunner Autobody Shop, operated by Julius Marshall.

Dunkin returned to the Knik River and waited for the tow truck. Some time later, Dunkin saw Marshall's truck on the other side of the river pulling another truck out of the water. Dunkin was angry that Marshall was assisting someone else first, and went to Marshall to complain. When Marshall finished pulling out the first vehicle, he came across the river to Dunkin's jeep.

It took Marshall approximately half an hour to pull the jeep out of the river bed. A group of people gathered to watch Marshall at work. Dunkin talked to one of the spectators, Timothy Dunahee, about how much he thought the job would cost. Dunkin told Dunahee he had $150. When Dunahee said he didn't think that would be enough, Dunkin stated that it didn't matter because he was "going to waste the old spook." Dunahee heard Dunkin refer to Marshall as a "boofer," a "nigger" and a "spook." While Dunkin was talking to Dunahee he had a loaded gun strapped around his waist.

Marshall got the jeep unstuck, but it still would not start and it had a flat tire. Dunkin offered to pay Marshall $150 if he would start the jeep; Marshall towed the jeep to his shop on the Palmer-Wasilla highway.

While Marshall was working on the jeep, Dunkin told him that his name was "Tom" and that he worked at Spenard Auto Supply. Neither of these two assertions was true. When Skinner asked Stevens why Dunkin was lying, Stevens said that Dunkin was going to beat up Marshall.

Marshall decided to push start the jeep. Dunkin, Stevens, and Skinner sat in the jeep, while Marshall pushed the jeep with his tow truck. After the jeep started, Dunkin got out of the jeep to pay Marshall.

Skinner saw Dunkin standing next to the tow truck and talking to Marshall. Skinner watched Dunkin pull out the gun and point it at Marshall; Marshall "crunched back" and then smiled as if he thought it was a joke. Dunkin smiled and pulled the trigger three times, firing shots into Marshall's head and neck. Marshall died as the result of these gunshot wounds.

Dunkin drove off in the jeep. As they drove away, Dunkin told Skinner not to worry because "[i]t's just a nigger. It's just a boofer."

---

1. "Boofer" is a derogatory term for a black person.

One of Marshall's neighbors found his body and contacted the troopers. Other neighbors told the troopers that they had heard shots and had seen three people in a green jeep speeding away from Marshall's shop after the shots were fired. . . .

Dunkin . . . suggests that certain statements which the prosecutor made to the jury constituted plain error. During jury voir dire, the prosecutor asked five prospective jurors whether, if race were an issue in the case, the juror could give the victim, Marshall, a fair trial. The final time the prosecutor asked this question, he stated, "Do you promise me that you would give Julius Marshall, a black man, a fair trial, as well as the defendant, a fair trial?" At this point, defense counsel asked to approach the bench; Judge Cutler sustained the defense objection to this question. Following this conference, the prosecutor rephrased the question to "Do you feel that you can give the state as well as the defendant a fair trial in this case knowing that Julius Marshall is a black man?" Dunkin did not ask the court to take any further action. Later in the trial, at the end of his closing argument, the prosecutor stated that "Julius Marshall has a right that justice be done." Dunkin did not object to this statement.

On appeal, Dunkin contends that the prosecutor's admonitions to give Marshall a fair trial were seriously prejudicial. He contends the statement the prosecutor made in closing argument was a call to the jury to avenge the death of Marshall.

Dunkin did not request a curative instruction during voir dire, nor did he object to the prosecutor's statement during closing argument. Therefore, in reviewing these issues this court must apply the plain error standard of review. Alaska Criminal Rule 47(b). In order to establish plain error, Dunkin must prove that the error is:

> (1) so obvious that it must have been apparent to a competent judge and a competent lawyer even without an objection and (2) so substantially prejudicial that failing to correct it on appeal would perpetuate a miscarriage of justice. *Potts v. State*, 712 P.2d 385, 390 (Alaska App. 1985).

Dunkin points out that Marshall was not on trial and argues that the statements which the prosecutor made would tend to inflame the jurors' emotions because of the evidence that this was a racially motivated killing. However, the state could properly inquire of the jurors whether they would be racially prejudiced against Marshall. The trial court promptly responded to Dunkin's objections, and Dunkin never requested that the trial judge take further action. We do not believe there was sufficient danger of prejudice from the prosecutor's questions and statements that the trial court was required to take further action on its own without objection. We do not find plain error. . . .

The conviction and sentence are AFFIRMED.

Notes

1. As noted above, the judge in *Dunkin* could have refused to allow *voir dire* on the race issue and been within her discretion. Should laws be enacted granting the state (and defendant) the right to *voir dire* on victim characteristics?

2. Victims and the state have no "right" to a fair trial absent laws conferring such a right. Many state constitutional provisions require that the victim be "treated with fairness and respect." It is unclear whether such language could be read broadly enough to create a right to a fair trial generally.

3. The fact that a potential juror has been charged with a crime is a sufficiently racially-neutral reason for the prosecution to use a peremptory challenge against a minority juror even if minorities are charged with crimes at higher rates than other persons. *Martinez v. State*, 664 So.2d 103 (Fla. App. 1996).

The denial of a defendants' *voir dire* on victim impact evidence does not deprive the defendant of his right to a fair and impartial jury. *Gentry v. Sinclair*, 609 F. Supp. 2d 1179 (W.D. Wash. 2009).

———————

One concern about peremptory challenges is that a defendant (who typically receives more such challenges than the prosecution) may deploy them to remove all members of the jury who are of the same background as the victim. The defense may not directly discriminate on the basis of race in using peremptory challenges. *See Georgia v. McCollum*, 505 U.S. 42 (1992) (Equal Protection Clause forbids defense counsel from using challenges to discriminate based on race). But beyond that, the defense is free is seek a jury that does not contain any members who are similar to the victim.

Should we create rules to ensure more representative juries?

George Fletcher, *With Justice for Some: Protecting Victims' Rights in Criminal Trials*
(1995)

There is no more disputed question today than our assumptions guiding jury selection. In the last eight years, the Supreme Court has developed a partial set of principles on permissible discrimination in the use of peremptory challenges; a new patchwork of rules governs when prosecutors and defense counsel can exclude candidates for the jury without giving reasons. Neither side may remove African-Americans without providing a race-neutral reason; neither side may exclude men or women without a satisfactory gender-neutral reason. Yet the new policy against discrimination is not likely to protect gays, immigrants, Jews, Asians, Catholics, the young, or the old. Blacks and women are singled out for special treatment, and no one quite knows why.

The Supreme Court may preach as it may, but we cannot banish cultural stereotypes from our thinking. Nor can the public. The only way we can ameliorate the dissonance that arose in cases like Harvy Milk, Rodney King, and Yankel Rosenbaum is to encourage the kind of diversity in jury selection that presupposes rough-and-ready judgments about cultural and class differences. For the sake of justice and for community acceptance of the verdict, it would surely have been better to have gay representation on Milk's jury, blacks involved in judging King's complaint, and some Jews hearing the evidence on the slaying of Rosenbaum. Yet there is no way to write a rule of law that would demand victim representation on the jury. It would be impossible to know which subcultures merited representation (orthodox Jews, Hasidic, Lubavitch?). And who counted as a qualified "representative." The most we can demand is a policy that increases the chances of a diversified jury that, as President Bill Clinton described his cabinet, "looks like America."

The great advantage of victim representation on the jury is not the resulting spin on the outcome but rather the inhibitory effect on the deliberations. With a gay, black, or Jew sitting in the jury room, the jurors are not likely to make comments that subtly reflect shared biases about these subcultures. The way to achieve this diversity is not to impose arbitrary rules on lawyers about when and why they can use their peremptory challenges. The Supreme Court's current policy represents a quest for fictitious homogeneity. It would be better to reduce the number of peremptories on each side sharply, say, to three or fewer, and to let lawyers use them as they see fit.

This is a modification of Justice Marshall's proposal in 1986 to abolish peremptories altogether. He would have been prepared to rule that the mere existence of prosecutorial peremptories was unconstitutional, and he would have "allow[ed] the States to eliminate the defendant's peremptories as well." It would be difficult, however, to reach the conclusion that the Constitution permitted three and only three peremptories on each side. This is a change in the law that will depend on the initiative of state legislatures. . . .

B. Victims in the Courtroom

1. The Victim's Right to Attend the Trial

a. Witness Exclusion Rules and Victims

Traditionally witnesses are excluded from court proceedings. The rationale for this rule is avoiding the risk that one witness observing another witness might end up simply parroting back testimony previously given. Excluding witnesses also increases the effectiveness of cross-examination; a witness who is excluded from the courtroom will not be able to conform his testimony to the testimony of others.

This "rule on witnesses" is enshrined in Rule 615 of the Federal Rules of Evidence. It states the general rule of exclusion and, as traditionally formulated, contains three exceptions:

> At the request of a party the court shall order witnesses excluded so that they cannot hear the testimony of other witnesses, and it may make the order of its own motion. This rule does not authorize exclusion of (1) a party who is a natural person, or (2) an officer or employee of a party which is not a natural person designated as its representative by its attorney, or (3) a person

whose presence is shown by a party to be essential to the presentation of the party's cause.[2]

In criminal trials, a defendant—even a defendant who testifies as a witness—will not be excluded from the trial. He is a "party" who is a "natural person." Similarly, the prosecution will typically be allowed to have a police officer (its case agent) attend the trial, because the presence of an officer is "essential to the presentation" of the prosecution's cause.

Should victims be excluded from criminal trials as potential witnesses? Before the adoption of Rule 615 (and the consequent adoption of similar rules in state evidence codes), victims attended trials in the discretion of the court. After the adoption of Rule 615, victims were generally excluded from the courtroom when they were witnesses. Courts reasoned that victims did not fall within any of the three listed exceptions. Indeed, some defense attorneys even deployed the rule to exclude as potential "witnesses" all victims and victim family members, even when their testimony was not genuinely needed in a case.

Crime victims' advocates have criticized the practice of leaving victims outside the courtroom. They have argued that the exclusion creates an imbalance between the defendant and the victim and leads to secondary victimization of victims who are literally left to wonder if justice is being done. In response to such concerns, most states and the federal government have passed laws granting victims some sort of exemption from witness exclusion rules, as discussed in the next section.

b. Specific Protections of the Victim's Right to Attend the Trial

Some jurisdictions have passed *unqualified* rights for victims to attend trials:

18 U.S.C. § 3771(A) (CVRA)

A crime victim has the following rights: . . .

The right not to be excluded from any . . . public court proceeding, unless the court, after receiving clear and convincing evidence, determines that testimony by the victim would be materially altered if the victim heard other testimony at that proceeding.

Alaska Const., art. I, § 24

Crime victims . . . shall have the following rights:

. . . the right to . . . be allowed to be present at all criminal or juvenile proceedings where the accused has the right to be present. . . .

Arkansas Rule Evid. 616

Notwithstanding any provision to the contrary, in any criminal prosecution, the victim of a crime, and in the event that the victim of a crime is a

---

2. The federal rule has since been amended to add a fourth exception for "a person authorized by statute to be present," as discussed below.

minor child under eighteen years of age, that minor victim's parents, guardian, custodian or other person with custody of the alleged minor victim shall have the right to be present during any hearing, deposition, or trial of the offense.

Most jurisdictions have adopted a *qualified* right for the victim to attend trial. The qualifications are phrased in various ways, focusing on the possible adverse effects on criminal defendants:

KANS. CONST., art. 15, § 15

Victims of crime . . . shall be entitled to certain basic rights, including the right . . . to be present at public hearings, as defined by law, of the criminal justice process, . . . to the extent that these rights do not interfere with the constitutional or statutory rights of the accused.

LA. EVID. art. 615

This article does not authorize exclusion of any of the following: . . .

(4) The victim of the offense, upon motion of the prosecution; however, if a victim is to be exempted from the exclusion order, the court shall require that the victim give his testimony before the exemption is effective and the court shall at the time prohibit the prosecution from recalling the victim as a witness in the state's prosecution in chief and rebuttal. The court shall also enter such other order as may appear reasonably necessary to preserve decorum and insure a fair trial. . . .

MICH. COMP. LAWS§ 780.761 (1998)

The victim has the right to be present throughout the entire trial of the defendant, unless the victim is going to be called as a witness. If the victim is going to be called as a witness, the court may, for good cause shown, order the victim to be sequestered until the victim first testifies. The victim shall not be sequestered after he or she first testifies.

———

Do these constitutional and statutory rights for victims to attend trials infringe a defendant's rights?

In re Mikhel v. D. Ct.

453 F.3d 1137 (9th Cir. 2006)

PER CURIAM.

OPINION

The United States petitions for a writ of mandamus ordering the district court to permit certain crime victims to observe in its entirety the murder trial in which they will testify, pursuant to the Crime Victims' Rights Act ("CVRA"), 18 U.S.C. § 3771. For the reasons explained below, we grant the United States' petition in part.

Defendants are charged, in pertinent part, with kidnaping for ransom and then murdering five people who lived in the Los Angeles area. On May 16, 2006, the United States filed an unopposed motion in limine to permit the family members of the murder victims—including those who were to testify—to witness the defendants' trial in its entirety. The district court denied the motion and held that

> During the guilt or penalty phase of the trial any victim or relative of victim may observe the trial. Now, if that person is going to testify in the guilt phase of the trial, that witness will be excluded until called as a witness. After testifying, that witness may remain. During the penalty phase, the same procedure will be followed.

The court explained that its ruling served to prevent collusive witness testimony and to ensure proper courtroom decorum. The United States petitioned this court for a writ of mandamus.

In recognition of the substantial deference afforded trial courts in these matters, our rules have traditionally provided that non-party witnesses cannot listen to the trial testimony of other witnesses. FED. R. EVID. 615. Rule 615, however, recognizes an exception for "a person authorized by statute to be present." *Id.* And, it turns out, Congress created just such an exception for crime victims when it enacted the CVRA and gave crime victims "[t]he right not to be excluded from any . . . public court proceeding," 18 U.S.C. § 3771(a)(3). A crime victim, however, does not have an absolute right to witness a trial at the expense of the defendant's rights. A district court may exclude a victim-witness from the courtroom if the court finds by "clear and convincing evidence . . . that testimony by the victim would be materially altered if the victim heard other testimony at that proceeding." *Id.* That said, even where a victim-witness may be properly excluded pursuant to § 3771(a)(3), "the court shall make every effort to permit the fullest attendance possible by the victim and shall consider reasonable alternatives to the exclusion of the victim from the criminal proceeding." 18 U.S.C. § 3771(b).

In this case, the district court excluded the victim-witnesses without determining whether their testimony would be "materially altered" were they allowed to witness the entire trial. Nor does it appear that the district court considered whether there were "reasonable alternatives" that would enable the victim-witness to attend the trial pursuant to § 3771(b).

While the district court's summary exclusion of the victim-witnesses may have been proper under Rule 615 prior to the enactment of the CVRA, *see generally United States v. West,* 607 F.2d 300 (9th Cir. 1979), the CVRA abrogated Rule 615, at least with respect to crime victims. A mere *possibility* that a victim-witness may alter his or her testimony as a result of hearing others testify is therefore insufficient to justify excluding him or her from trial. Rather, a district court must find by clear and convincing evidence that it is *highly likely,* not merely *possible,* that the victim-witness will alter his or her testimony. *See United States v. Johnson,* 362 F.Supp.2d 1043, 1056 (N.D. Iowa 2006) (permitting victim-witnesses to testify when "each of these witnesses appears likely to testify during the 'merits phase' only as to discrete factual events surrounding the disappearance of the murder victims and to identify certain clothing and other items recovered during various searches, which are not matters susceptible to 'material alteration' from hearing the testimony of other witnesses").

Thus, we grant the United States' petition in part and instruct the district court to consider whether clear and convincing evidence proves that the victim-witnesses' testimony will be "materially altered" if they are allowed to attend the trial in its entirety. We decline to order the district court to allow the courtroom presence of the victim-witnesses, or to provide any other specific instructions. Rather, we simply remand the issue for reconsideration by the district court in light of this opinion and the requirements of CVRA. We do not reach the merits of any other issue.

––––––––––

Martinez v. State

664 So.2d 1034 (Fla. App. 1996)

[Defendant Martinez was convicted of attempted manslaughter with a firearm. He appealed, arguing that his right to a fair trial was violated when the victim was allowed to attend the opening argument in the case.]

Victims of crime . . . are entitled to the right to be informed, to be present, and to be heard when relevant, at all crucial stages of criminal proceedings, to the extent that these rights do not interfere with the constitutional rights of the accused.

In *Gore v. State*, 599 So.2d 978, 986 (Fla. 1992), our supreme court held that the victim's rights under the Constitution "must yield to the defendant's right to a fair trial." In the present case the trial court, because of the constitutional provision, announced that the victim/witness would be allowed in the courtroom unless the defendant could establish prejudice. We are not prepared to say that the court was wrong in putting the burden of showing prejudice on the defendant, since the analysis has to have a starting point. We do, however, interpret *Gore* as meaning that any doubts should be resolved in favor of the defendant receiving a fair trial.

In the present case the defendant argued to the trial court that the victim/witness, who testified first, should not have been permitted in the courtroom during opening statement because he could have been affected by defense counsel's explanation of the defendant's version of the incident. The trial court rejected that argument, stating that it was insufficient to overcome the victim's constitutional right to be in the courtroom. We disagree. Where, as here, the facts were hotly disputed, the defendant's right to a fair trial outweighed the victim's right to be in the courtroom.

The exclusion of this victim during opening statement, which was all he would have missed since he testified first, would have been a small price to pay to insure that the defendant got a fair trial.

We have concluded, however, that the error was harmless, after reviewing defense counsel's opening statement outlining defendant's version of the events leading up to the shooting, and the testimony of the victim, who categorically denied all of the facts which defendant alleged justified the shooting.

Affirmed.

Notes

1. *Martinez* stands virtually alone in suggesting constitutional problems with victims in the courtroom. Is the rationale of the *Martinez* court vaporous? The court asserts that excluding the victim from opening arguments was necessary to protect a defendant's right to a "fair trial." But the court goes on to find that the victim's presence was harmless error, apparently because it did not make any difference in the defendant's conviction. If the victim's presence does not harm the defendant, why would the defendant have a right to exclude the victim? The question of the basis for a defendant's right to exclude a victim is explored further in the next section.

2. Why would a victim want to attend a trial? Several different and complementary rationales are usually offered: (1) the victim may gain important psychological benefits and perhaps a sense of closure from watching the trial; (2) the victim may have questions answered about why and how the crime was committed; (3) excluding victims may produce "secondary victimization" (a concept described in Chapter 1) by producing feelings of helplessness or unfairness; (4) the victim may be able to improve the truth-finding process by alerting the prosecution to misrepresentations in the testimony of other witnesses; and (5) as a matter of equality, victims should be treated equally with defendants.

3. Victims may have particular interests in not being excluded from sexual assault trials. If the rule applies to such victims, it can lead to secondary victimization: "The defendant is entitled to hear everyone's testimony so as to rebut it later. The [rape] survivor is a witness and is allowed in the courtroom only while she is testifying. Many survivors remarked that this was when they first realized that it was not their trial, that the attacker's rights were the ones being protected, and that they had no control over what happened to their bodies. The structure of the system often results in a second rape." Lee Madigan & Nancy C. Gamble, The Second Rape: Society's Continued Betrayal of the Victim 97 (1989).

4. Some statutes require that a victim be excluded where her testimony would be "materially affected" by watching the trial. How can the trial court determine, in advance of the trial, whether a victim's testimony will be so affected?

5. Federal Rule of Evidence 615 now contains a fourth exception to the witness exclusion rule—for "a person authorized by statute to be present." This provision was added in 1998 as a response to the exclusion of crime victims from court proceedings in the Oklahoma City bombing case. Well before the bombing, Congress had adopted a statute—42 U.S.C. § 10606(b)—guaranteeing victims the right to

attend trials unless their testimony would be "materially affected" from observing the proceedings. During pre-trial proceedings in the bombing case, however, victims of the bombing who were potential witnesses at the sentencing phase were excluded without regard to this provision. The trial judge concluded that Rule 615 essentially superseded the statute. Litigation on behalf of the victims was unsuccessful in protecting the victims' rights (as discussed in Chapter 11, *United States v. McVeigh*). A year later, Rule 615 was amended to make clear that the statutory protection of victims' rights was not trumped by Rule 615. *See* Fed. R. Evid. 615, Advisory Comm. Notes. *See generally* Paul G. Cassell, *Barbarians at the Gates? A Reply to the Critics of the Victims' Rights Amendment*, 1999 Utah L. Rev. 479, 515–22 (recounting victims' unsuccessful efforts to enforce their rights under § 10606(b)).

6. Disruptive *defendants* can be excluded from trials altogether. Courts conclude that they have forfeited any right to attend the trial. *See Illinois v. Allen*, 397 U.S. 337 (1970). Presumably trial courts have at least the same discretion to exclude disruptive victims. *See People v. Ramer*, 21 Cal. Rptr.2d 480 (Ct. App. 1980) (unpublished opinion).

7. A victim's right to attend the trial extends to the right to attend jury selection proceedings. *See State v. Gonzales*, 892 P.2d 838, 848 (Ariz. 1995).

Some cases have many victims. The CVRA makes provisions for multiple victims as explored in the following case.

United States v. Okun

2009 WL 790042 (E.D. Va. 2009)

MEMORANDUM OPINION

ROBERT E. PAYNE, Senior District Judge.

This matter is before the Court on the Government's Motion *In Limine* to Permit Victim-Witnesses to Attend the Entirety of the Trial. Through this motion, the United States seeks to permit testifying witnesses who are also alleged victims ("victim/witnesses") to attend the entirety of the trial under the auspices of the Crime Victims' Rights Act ("CVRA"), 18 U.S.C. § 3771 *et seq*. The Defendant opposes this motion, alleging that the United States has not yet established that these individuals are victims who qualify for rights under the CVRA and that the number of potential victim/witnesses makes allowing all of them to attend the entirety of the trial impractical. For the reasons set forth below, the United States' motion was granted.

I. FACTS

The United States charges the Defendant, Edward H. Okun, in a twenty-seven count Superseding Indictment ("SSI") *inter alia*, mail fraud, wire fraud, money laundering, and various counts of conspiracy. These charges arise from Okun's connection with the 1031 Tax Group ("1031TG"), Okun Holdings, and a number of other qualified intermediary ("QI") companies. Okun was the sole shareholder and owner of these corporations, each of which had its own employees and officers. However, according to the United States, the companies were run pursuant to Okun's instructions and for his financial benefit.

The United States has indicated that it intends to call some of the victims, *i.e.,* the exchangers, at trial as witnesses. The Defendant alleges that approximately eight of the 577 alleged victims will be called at trial, and, at oral argument, the United States confirmed that to be the case.

Evidently, at least some of these victim/witnesses seek to claim the rights afforded to them by the Crime Victims' Rights Act ("CVRA"), 18 U.S.C. § 3771 *et seq.,* to attend the entirety of the trial. The United States is filing this motion on behalf of those victims, as permitted by 18 U.S.C. § 3771(c)(1). The Defendant objects to the attendance of these witnesses, alleging that they are not victims within the meaning of the statute and that it would be impractical to allow all victims to attend the trial.

II. DISCUSSION

The CVRA was designed to protect victims' rights and ensure them access to the criminal justice process. *United States v. Moussaoui,* 483 F.3d 220, 234 (4th Cir. 2007). "The [CVRA] guarantees victims notice of any proceedings, the right to attend those proceedings, the right to confer with the prosecutor, and the right to be reasonably heard at any public proceeding in the district court involving release, plea, sentencing, or parole proceeding." *Id.* . . .

Okun's first argument is that the victim/witnesses do not qualify as victims under the CVRA because, essentially, the United States has not yet proven the underlying criminal conduct. The CVRA defines a victim as "a person directly and proximately harmed as a result of the commission of a Federal offense." 18 U.S.C. § 3771(e). Assuming that the allegations in the SSI are true, therefore, the exchangers would certainly qualify as victims for purposes of the CVRA. Their position as unsecured creditors in the ongoing, related bankruptcy case tends to support the theory that they were directly and proximately harmed by Okun's failure to repay their exchange funds.

Victims have been permitted to exercise CVRA rights before a determination of the defendant's guilt. *See, e.g., United States v. Edwards,* 526 F.3d 747, 757–58 (11th Cir. 2008); *In re Mikhel,* 453 F.3d 1137, 1138–39 (9th Cir. 2006) (per curiam); *see also United States v. Rubin,* 558 F.Supp.2d 211, 418 (E.D.N.Y. 2008) (anyone the government identifies as harmed by the defendant's conduct is a victim). Furthermore, the Fifth Circuit has noted that victims acquire rights under the CVRA even before prosecution. *See In re Dean,* 527 F.3d 391, 394 (5th Cir. 2008). This view is supported by the statutory language, which gives the victims rights before the accepting of plea agreements and, therefore, before adjudication of guilt. *See* 18 U.S.C. § 3771(a)(4). Okun's argument that the United States needs to demonstrate Okun's guilt before the victims gain rights under the CVRA is simply incorrect and essentially would eviscerate the rights given under the CVRA to victims in any pre-conviction proceeding.

Federal Rule of Evidence 615 provides that:

> At the request of a party the court shall order witnesses excluded so that they cannot hear the testimony of other witnesses, and it may make the order of its own motion. This rule does not authorize exclusion of . . . (4) a person authorized by statute to be present.

Generally, therefore, Okun could have the victim/witnesses excluded from the trial before their testimony. However, subsection (4) of Rule 615 carves out an exception to that general rule for persons authorized to be present by statute. The CVRA provides just such an authorization for victims of the crime being tried. *See* 18 U.S.C. § 3771(a)(3); *see also Edwards,* 526 F.3d at 757–58 (18 U.S.C. § 3771(a)(3) is a statutory authorization covered by Rule 615(4); *Mikhel,* 453 F.3d at 1138–39 (holding same); *United States v. Johnson,* 362 F.Supp.2d 1043, 1056 (N.D. Iowa 2005) (holding same).

Under the terms of the CVRA, victims may only be excluded from a court proceeding if "the court, after receiving clear and convincing evidence, determines that the testimony by the victim would be materially altered if the victim heard other testimony at the proceeding." 18 U.S.C. § 3771(a)(3). If the court makes such a determination, it must set forth the reasons for that determination on the record with particularity. *Id.* at (b)(1). Okun has provided no evidence demonstrating that attendance at the trial would have a material effect on the victim/witnesses testimony, nor is any apparent from the record. Therefore, exclusion of the victim/witnesses is inappropriate under 18 U.S.C. § 3771(a)(3). *See Mikhel,* 453 F.3d at 1140 (exclusion only appropriate if clear and convincing evidence is present).

Okun also argues that, due to the number of victims, permitting all victims to attend the trial is impractical, and the Court should therefore fashion an alternate procedure to allow them to exercise their CVRA rights. *See* 18 U.S.C. § 3771(d)(2). As an initial matter, it is important that whatever alternate procedure is enacted vindicates the CVRA rights of the victims. *See Dean,* 527 F.3d at 394–95. Furthermore, any procedure fashioned by the court must demonstrate "respect for the victim's dignity and privacy." 18 U.S.C. § 3771(a)(8). Courts have upheld reasonable alternate procedures under 18 U.S.C. § 3771(d)(2) when they both vindicate the victims' rights and take into account considerations of judicial economy. *See In re W.R. Huff Asset Mgmt. Co.,* 409 F.3d 555, 562–63 (2d Cir.2005); *Rubin,* 558 F.Supp.2d 211 at 222.

Therefore, *assuming that the Court had some notice that an unmanageable number of victims intended to attend the trial,* an appropriate alternate procedure might be to, e.g., arrange for a closed-circuit television broadcast of the trial, arrange for a webcast of the trial, or arrange for an audio broadcast of the trial. It would not be, as Okun suggests, to exclude victim/witnesses based on the large number of victims. This suggestion treats victims as a fungible commodity with class rights instead of individuals with personal rights; this reading of the statute is squarely at odds with the need to "respect [ ] the victim[s'] dignity and privacy." 18 U.S.C. § 3771(a) (8). Furthermore, there has been no showing, at this point, that an unmanageable number of victims intend to attend the trial. Therefore, application of 18 U.S.C. §3771(d)(2) is premature.

III. CONCLUSION

For the reasons set forth above, it is hereby ORDERED that the GOVERNMENT'S MOTION *IN LIMINE* TO PERMIT VICTIM-WITNESSES TO ATTEND THE ENTIRETY OF THE TRIAL (Docket Number 193) is granted.

It is so ORDERED.

Notes

1. The Eleventh Circuit has held that a defendant's argument that the victim should have been excluded "fails for one simple reason: A criminal defendant has no constitutional right to exclude witnesses from the courtroom." *U.S. v. Edwards*, 526 F.3d 747 (11th Cir. 2008).

2. In *Harris v. State*, 979 So. 2d 721 (Miss. Ct. App. 2008), a defendant was found guilty of two counts of aggravated assault for using an automobile to cause injury to his former girlfriend and her young daughter. On appeal, he argued that the trial court erred when it allowed the prosecution to "display" the child victim, who lost a leg as a result of the assault at issue, to the jury during her mother's testimony. The appellate court rejected the claim based on the right of crime victims, under the state constitution and statutes, to be present and heard during criminal proceedings and the requirement that the state prove serious bodily injury as one of the elements of aggravated assault.

----

c. Does a Victim's Right to Attend Trials Infringe a Defendant's Rights?: A Debate

Congress has entertained proposals to adopt a federal constitutional amendment protecting the rights of crime victims. These proposals would give victims an unqualified right "not to be excluded" from public court proceedings. The proposed amendment is discussed at greater length in Chapter 12, but here it is appropriate to consider whether victims should have an unqualified federal constitutional right to attend trials or whether this would unfairly detract from defendants' rights.

Robert P. Mosteller, *Victims' Rights and the United States Constitution: An Effort to Recast the Battle in Criminal Litigation*
85 GEO. L. REV. 1691 (1997)

* * *

The right of victims to be present at public proceedings is a new constitutional concept that would afford victims and their families special constitutional status with respect to the right to attend public judicial proceedings. However, this preference for victims need not be constitutionalized if it does not interfere with the ability of the general public to be present as well. A constitutional provision is required only if it is intended to overcome some right currently protecting defendants or if the drafters of the Amendment have decided to write into the Constitution a universal solution to what I contend is a sometimes substantial and properly debatable procedural issue.

The Amendment's purpose of altering existing defendants' rights is revealed by the apparently more significant right "not to be excluded from public proceedings." Indeed, the phrase "not to be excluded" suggests an intention to make the right to be present absolute. Presumably courts would not ultimately interpret the right in absolute terms because such interpretations are inconsistent with our legal tradition. Nevertheless, the effect of this right is different from—and therefore not just an alternate formulation of—a right to be present, and the intention to overcome the obstacles defendants may currently raise to bar victims' presence is unmistakable.

Many victims have a special interest in witnessing public proceedings involving criminal cases that directly touched their lives. Therefore, victims' rights to attend such proceedings should be guaranteed unless their presence threatens accuracy and fairness in adjudicating the guilt or innocence of the defendant. In most situations, ensuring that victims are able to attend creates no substantial threat to accuracy and fairness, and thus, the right "not to be excluded" both is redundant with a right to be present and would have no adverse effects. In other cases, whether the constitutional right is phrased as a general guarantee of presence or an absolute right not to be excluded is not the most debatable point; rather, the questionable proposition is whether either formulation of the right should be adopted as a federal constitutional mandate. In a final set of circumstances, basic fairness may be threatened by the victims' presence. Here, a largely insurmountable right "not to be excluded" would not be redundant with a more general guarantee of presence, and may well prove to be a pernicious formulation.

Three types of fact patterns illustrate when the decision to formulate the guarantee as a constitutional right and specifically as a right "not to be excluded" becomes significant. These are: (1) cases in which the victim is either not a fact witness or is such a witness but will offer testimony that is unlikely to be influenced by the testimony of others; (2) cases in which the victim is a fact witness whose testimony might logically be influenced by hearing the testimony of others; and (3) cases in which the victim or her family acts emotionally or disruptively in front of the jury. The proposed Amendment treats all three situations in the same fashion: it guarantees victims the right "not to be excluded." In the second and third situations, woodenly guaranteeing this right is, I contend, quite problematic.

Victims and their families rightfully complain when they are excluded by defense attorneys who sometimes use the disingenuous argument that the defense may want to call them as witnesses. However, a nonconstitutional rule of evidence, enacted in several states, eliminates the potential for this abuse in the first class of cases described above. For instance, Rule 615 of the Utah Rules of Evidence excepts "an adult victim in a criminal trial" from those who may be excluded from the courtroom to prevent them from hearing the testimony of other witnesses. Professor Paul Cassell, a strong supporter of victims' rights, has praised this rule as being effective in allowing victims to be present at trial unless the defendant demonstrates that such presence would violate her constitutional rights, which Cassell states "seems unlikely in all but the most extreme circumstances." Certainly, under the first class of cases described above, prohibiting the exclusion of victims does not threaten any recognized constitutional right of defendants.

In the second class of cases described above, a victim's right not to be excluded applied nationally is not a clearly preferable policy. A crime with multiple victims who are also eyewitnesses, such as an armed robbery, presents the problem in archetypal form. In such cases, a substantial danger exists that the testimony of some victim-witnesses will be influenced by their presence in the courtroom during the testimony of others concerning the same set of facts. Should each of those witnesses be permitted to be present during the testimony of the others under a right "not to be excluded" because she is also a victim?

The Rodney King case, with a slight modification of the actual facts, provides an even more poignant example. The police initially claimed that King was resisting arrest, which could constitute a crime of violence under the Amendment. Had a civilian bystander operating a video camera not observed the encounter, King, rather than those who beat him, may well have been prosecuted, and based on the prosecutor's charging decision, the officers who beat him would have been labeled as victims. Under the Victims' Rights Amendment, Sergeant Stacey Koon, Officer Laurence Powell, and all those designated as victims could not be excluded from the courtroom while others testified presumably about King's alleged criminal acts and the officers' reasonable and necessary reactions. Their opportunity to tailor testimony would be obvious. By contrast, the passengers in King's car and any other witnesses testifying for King could still be excluded from the courtroom so that their testimony would not be tainted.

I question whether either the multiple-eyewitness hypothetical or the Rodney King fact pattern would constitute "extreme circumstances," using Professor Cassell's terminology, in which a blanket rule prohibiting exclusion of victims from any public judicial proceeding would violate a defendant's constitutional right—in this case, the right to effective cross-examination under the Sixth Amendment. Nevertheless, whether victims should be guaranteed the right not to be excluded is, in my judgment, a debatable point that should not be answered categorically by a constitutional amendment. Through statutes and court rules, states interested in giving victims this right have taken two other positions in addition to establishing the blanket right noted above. Some states grant the victim the right to be present after she testifies and direct that such testimony be taken as early as possible. Others give the trial judge discretion, but also recognize a need to treat victims with special care. Although these two alternatives have what some supporters of the proposed

Amendment consider the disadvantage of allowing judicial discretion, I contend that such flexibility is appropriate given the competing values involved. The basis for a categorical, constitutional answer that victims should never be excluded is hardly clear enough to overcome state law judgments about police preferences that relate to criminal procedure.

* * *

The third class of cases described above provides the greatest challenge to the validity of the right "not to be excluded"—cases in which the victim or her family acts in an excessively emotional manner in front of the jury or convey their opinions about the proceedings to that jury. Such cases constitute only a small fraction of those in which victims attend trials, and some readers might assume that protecting such conduct is outside the intent of the Amendment. Yet, some protection for the emotional impact of victims' presence *is* the intent of the drafters, as demonstrated by the statement of Senators Kyl and Feinstein: "Another argument is that the presence of victims' families could inflame the jury, making it sympathetic to the prosecution. Yet no one argues that defendants' families should be kept out of court."

Victims and their families may, whether purposefully or unintentionally, alter the outcome of a criminal case by exhibiting their emotions or interjecting their opinions—or both—during public judicial proceedings. Moreover, such displays may be highlighted by legislatively authorized practices, such as placing victims at counsel table with the prosecutor. The wording of the right "not to be excluded" gives no indication that disruption, excessive display of emotion, or other misconduct would override the right. Moreover, as suggested by the statement of Senators Kyl and Feinstein, defendants' due process rights might no longer constitute a basis for exclusion because the victim's right not to be excluded was added to allow victims to bring an emotional component to criminal proceedings and to counterbalance perceived advantages of the defendant in that regard.

One may argue that the rights of defendants and victims should be equal, as one state has established through legislation. The effect of such a provision would be to give victims the same right—absent sufficiently disruptive misbehavior that would override the right—as defendants to remain in the courtroom. However, given the breadth of possible definitions of "victim," which might include not only those individuals directly victimized by crime but also family members, and given the different values protected by victims' and defendants' rights to be present. I question whether such equality is appropriate. Moreover, by making the right of victims to be present very difficult, if not impossible, to forfeit, the Amendment may encourage emotional displays by victims. Injecting further emotion into the jury trial process is an illegitimate goal and is certainly not the appropriate purpose of an amendment to the Constitution. Thus, at a minimum, this provision should be qualified to permit the exclusion of victims whose conduct poses a substantial threat to the fairness of jury trials.

———————

Douglas E. Beloof & Paul G. Cassell, *The Crime Victim's Right to Attend the Trial: The Reascendant National Consensus*

9 Lewis & Clark L. Rev. 481 (2005)

Given that both historical tradition and contemporary practice favor admitting victims to trials, it would be surprising to find the Constitution somehow forbade victim attendance. And, indeed, no language in the Fifth and Sixth Amendments supports the far-reaching argument that it is positively unconstitutional for a state to allow a victim to remain in the courtroom during a criminal trial. Instead, there are three provisions that support, if anything, the opposite view that a victim of a crime can remain in the courtroom: the Sixth Amendment's guarantee of a "public" trial, not a private one; the Sixth Amendment's guarantee of a right to "confront" witnesses, not to exclude them; and the Fifth and Fourteenth Amendment's guarantee of "due process of law," which construed in light of historical and contemporary standards suggests victims can attend trials.

1. The Right to a Public Trial

The effort to discover a federal constitutional right to exclude crime victims founders on the very amendment often cited for support. The Sixth Amendment guarantees a defendant the right to a "public trial." These words suggest that the admission of persons to a trial—not their exclusion—is the constitutionally-protected value.

Nor do these words contain any implicit right to closure. As the Supreme Court's leading opinion on this provision explains, "While the Sixth Amendment guarantees to a defendant in a criminal case the right to a public trial, it does not guarantee the right to compel a private trial. 'The ability to waive a constitutional right does not ordinarily carry with it the right to insist upon the opposite of that right.'" In short, "[t]he right to an open public trial is a shared right of the accused and the public, the common concern being the assurance of fairness."

The application of the public trial right has obvious implications for victims of crime. As the Supreme Court has explained, "public proceedings vindicate the concerns of the victims and the community in knowing that offenders are being brought to account for their criminal conduct . . . ." "Public judicial proceedings have an important educative role . . . . The victim of the crime, the family of the victim, [and] others who have suffered similarly . . . have an interest in observing the course of a prosecution." Victims' concern about the course of a criminal prosecution stem from the fact that society has withdrawn "both from the victim and the vigilante the enforcement of criminal laws, but [it] cannot erase from people's consciousness the fundamental, natural yearning to see justice done—or even the urge for retribution."

Of course, the right to a public trial can be overcome by competing interests. Indeed, crime victims are often beneficiaries of narrowly-drawn court closure orders. And the Sixth Amendment does not, by itself, confer rights on anyone other than the defendant. But the limited claim here is not that the Sixth Amendment requires

Congress and the states to admit crime victims — only that it permits them to do so. Since the Sixth Amendment suggests, if anything, the victim has a right to demand to be admitted to a trial, surely the opposite reading is completely untenable.

2. The Right to Confront Witnesses

The only other language in the Constitution that appears to have direct application to the claim that defendants can exclude crime victims suggests — once again — the opposite conclusion. The Sixth Amendment guarantees that in all criminal prosecutions that "the accused shall enjoy the right . . . to be confronted with the witnesses against him." The provision guarantees, "[s]imply as a matter of English," that the defendant has "a right to meet face to face all those who appear and give evidence at trial." In interpreting the right to confront, the Supreme Court has recited a passage from Shakespeare concerning a face-to-face meeting between the defendant and victim: "Shakespeare was thus describing the root meaning of confrontation when he had Richard the Second say: 'Then call them to our presence — face to face, and frowning brow to brow, ourselves will hear the accuser and the accused freely speak . . . .'" The suggestion that the victim should have been excluded from the courtroom, at least while not testifying, hardly finds support in this vision of confrontation.

Naturally, the right to confront witnesses is not absolute. Crime victims are often the beneficiaries of this fact. But, again, the point here is a limited one: specifically that the Constitution surely cannot be read as forbidding the presence of a victim at trial when the only relevant language suggests that, at least at some point in most cases, the victim's presence is required.

Confrontation contains a second component: the right to cross-examine opposing witnesses. Plainly that component of confrontation is satisfied even when victims remain in the courtroom for trial. Defendants sometimes suggest that their right of confrontation is somehow infringed because their cross-examination of the victim conceivably might have been more effective if she had not heard other witnesses testify. Even if such proof could be made, that would not establish a constitutional violation. The Court has repeatedly held that "[t]he Confrontation Clause guarantees only an opportunity for effective cross-examination, not cross-examination that is effective in whatever way, and to whatever extent, the defense might wish." Thus, in *United States v. Owens,* the Supreme Court held that the right of confrontation was not denied by testimony from a witness who could no longer remember why he had accused the defendant. The Court explained, "The weapons available to impugn the witness' statement when memory loss is asserted will of course not always achieve success, but successful cross-examination is not the constitutional guarantee."

3. The Due Process Clause

Because the only specific provisions of the Bill of Rights with an arguable connection to this issue suggest a defendant may not eject a victim from trial, the only remaining source of such a right would be the general provision guaranteeing that no person shall be deprived of "life, liberty, or property, without due process of law." Yet the Supreme Court has been clear that if "a constitutional claim is covered by a specific constitutional provision . . . , the claim must be analyzed under the standard appropriate to that specific provision, not under the rubric of substantive due process." As just explained, the provisions of the Constitution that seem to bear most specifically on crime victim attendance suggest, if anything, that victims should be allowed in the courtroom, so the due process argument is a virtual non-starter.

Moreover, to ascertain the meaning of this general phrase, one could look either to historical understanding or contemporary societal norms. Under either approach, the Due Process Clause provides no support for a defendant's right to exclude a victim from a trial.

We explored the historical principles surrounding victims attending trial at length earlier. Suffice it to say here that, when the Constitution was drafted, a tradition of private prosecution was well-established. As private prosecutors, victims would not have been excluded from trial. Thus, understood in historical context, it is impossible to argue that due process considerations require that crime victims be excluded from trial. . . .

Given that a party—a witness with a "stake in the outcome of the trial"—has historically not been subject to exclusion, the fallacy of the argument for excluding victims becomes clear. If the victim in a criminal case brought a civil suit against the defendant for the same conduct, she would be a party with a "stake in the trial" and the defendant could not exclude her from the trial. For example, if a woman is raped, she could pursue a civil suit against her attacker even while a criminal trial is pending on the same facts. In that civil suit, she would have a right to attend the trial. If she can remain in the courtroom during that civil trial, then the Due Process Clause cannot require a different result in a criminal trial regarding the same facts. Put another way, it would be strange reading of this Clause to say that while due process probably requires the victim's presence in a civil action for a crime, it positively prohibits her presence in a criminal case for the same conduct. For all these reasons, no historical argument can be made for concluding that the Due Process Clause requires that a victim be excluded from a criminal trial.

While the historical understanding of the Due Process Clause is enough to dispose of the claim that there is a constitutional right to exclude victims, the same conclusion is reached if one looks to contemporary practices. In particular, over the last two decades, Congress and legislatures across the country have acted to insure that a crime victim can remain in the courtroom during a criminal trial. These actions stem from "an outpouring of popular concern for what has come to be known as 'victims' rights' . . . ." In light of these facts, it is hard to see how there is a contemporary understanding that crime victims must be excluded from trials.

———————

Note

Professor Mosteller argues that the Constitution may require exclusion of the victim from the courtroom as a witness in some situations. Professors Beloof and Cassell argue otherwise. Would an intermediate solution be for the courts to require that the victim testify first in a criminal case, thereby avoiding the possibility that the victim's testimony might be tainted by other witnesses? *See* Beloof & Cassell, 9 Lewis & Clark L. Rev. at 540 (noting that Professor Wigmore had proposed this approach to the problem of parties (and thus victims) testifying in a criminal trial.

---

2. A Victim's Right to Sit at Counsel Table

Longstanding practice in federal and state courts allows the prosecutor to have a representative of the investigating law enforcement agency sit at counsel table during trial. This "case agent" is present in order to assist the prosecutor. The presence of the agent is commonly permitted even when witnesses are otherwise ordered excluded from the trial. The appropriateness of the agent's presence is in the sound discretion of the trial court. *See U.S. v. Charles,* 456 F.3d 249 (1st Cir. 2006); allowing a case agent who is also a victim of the assault to sit at counsel table.

No modern federal case is reported on the propriety of allowing a *victim* who is not also a case agent to sit at counsel table. A majority of state courts which have ruled on the issue permit the practice in the discretion of the court. In some states the prosecutor must represent that the victim's presence at counsel table will assist them in the prosecution. In these states the competing considerations are the benefit of assistance which the prosecution receives versus the potential prejudice to the defendant of juror sympathy provoked by the presence of the victim at counsel table.

Alabama has codified the victim's ability to sit at counsel table, regardless of whether the victim will assist the prosecutor.

Ala. Code § 15-14-53

The victim of a criminal offense shall be entitled to be present in any court exercising any jurisdiction over such offense and therein to be seated at counsel table of any prosecutor prosecuting such offense.

Does allowing the victim to sit at counsel table interfere with the defendant's rights?

Crowe v. State

485 So.2d 351 (Ala. Cr. App. 1984), *rev'd on other grounds,* 485 So.2d 373 (Ala. 1986)

TYSON, Judge.

Coy Patrick Crowe was indicted for the capital murder of one James Taylor, whom he shot with a pistol. Mr. Crowe, the appellant herein, was indicted pursuant to

§ 13A-5-40(a)(5), Code of Alabama 1975, for murder of a deputy sheriff while such deputy was on duty.

The jury returned a verdict of "guilty of capital murder as charged in the indictment," and, after a separate sentencing-phase hearing, the jury recommended that the appellant "be punished by life imprisonment." The trial court, after its separate sentencing hearing and determination of the aggravating and mitigating circumstances, ordered that the advisory verdict of the jury was not the proper sentence in this cause, and sentenced the appellant to death by electrocution.

Jerry Taylor testified that he was the brother of James Taylor, the deceased. He stated that the deceased's wife was the woman sitting at the prosecutor's table. He stated that he saw his brother on July 7, 1982, lying on the ground beside a marked patrol car. He stated that James Taylor was dead. He further stated that James Taylor was a Winston County Sheriff's Deputy and was in uniform when he observed him lying on the ground.

* * *

Appellant argues that allowing the victim's widow to sit at the counsel table with the prosecutor violated his constitutional rights. A review of the record indicates that the victim's widow conducted herself in an exemplary manner during the trial. At one point during the trial she did begin to cry and the appellant renewed his objection to her sitting at the counsel table. It should be noted that at the time Mrs. Taylor began to cry, the pathologist who performed the autopsy on her husband was describing in graphic detail the findings of the autopsy. An in-chamber hearing was held in which the trial judge refused to remove her from the counsel table. Appellant's counsel then requested a short recess in order for her to compose herself and this request was granted. The record does not indicate any further incidences of this nature.

Alabama Code § 15-14-53 (1975), provides that "[t]he victim of a criminal offense shall be entitled to be present in any court exercising any jurisdiction over such offense and therein to be seated at the counsel table of any prosecutor prosecuting such offense or other attorney representing the government or other persons in whose name such prosecution is brought."

Alabama Code § 15-14-56(a) (1975), provides that "[w]henever a victim is unable to attend such trial or hearing or any portion thereof by reason of death; . . . or other inability, the victim, the victim's guardian or the victim's family may select a representative who shall be entitled to exercise any right granted to the victim, pursuant to the provisions of this article."

It is clear that Mrs. Taylor had a right to be seated at the prosecutor's table. In view of this right and the fact that the record indicates no prejudice from the trial court's allowing her to be present, we must agree with the trial court on this matter. No constitutional rights of the appellant were abridged because of this one incident.

Notes

1. The Alabama statute permits a victim's presence at counsel table regardless of the prosecutors need for the victim's assistance. In Alabama a victim's presence at counsel table is limited only by a showing of prejudice to the defendant of constitutional proportions. In the *Crowe* case, the appellate court did not find an isolated incident of crying by the widow to rise to the level of constitutional prejudice. Presumably, at some point displays of grief or other emotion might rise to the level of unconstitutional prejudice.

2. In allowing a victim to sit at counsel table, a California appellate court noted that a disruptive victim may be removed just as a disruptive defendant may be removed from the court. *People v. Ramer*, 21 Cal. Rptr. 2d 480 (Ct. App. 1993) (unpublished opinion). The court concluded that a statute giving the victim a right "to be present and seated at all criminal proceedings where the defendant, the prosecuting attorney, and the general public are entitled to be present," CAL. PENAL CODE § 1102.6, gave the trial court discretion to make appropriate seating arrangements, including allowing the victim to sit at counsel table.

3. General provisions allowing victims to be present during trial do not necessarily mean the victim may sit at counsel table. In *Hall v. State*, 579 So.2d 329 (Fla. App.), *rev. denied*, 587 So. 2d 1329 (Fla. 1991), the court specifically held that a Florida state constitutional provision granting victims the right to be present during trial did not confer a right to sit at counsel table or be introduced to the jury.

4. Alabama codifies the ability of the court to remove the victim under certain circumstances:

ALA. CODE § 15-14-54

A victim of a criminal offense shall not be excluded from court or counsel table during the trial or hearing or any portion thereof conducted by any court which in any way pertains to such offense, provided, however, a judge may remove a victim from the trial or hearing or any portion therefore for the same causes and in same manner as the rules of court or law provides for the exclusion or removal of the defendant.

5. Alabama's neighbor, Louisiana, prohibits victims from sitting at counsel table:

LA. EVID., Art. 615.

... The court shall also enter such other order as may appear reasonably necessary to preserve decorum and insure a fair trial provided that the victim shall not be allowed to sit at counsel table.

6. Minnesota allows domestic abuse advocates to sit at counsel table. MINN. STAT. § 518B.

---

3. A Proposed Victim's Right to Participate in the Trial

During a trial, a victim is not entitled to make any sort of statement to the jury or, indeed, to participate in any way. Instead, the victim can only address the jury if the prosecution (or, less likely, the defense) calls her as a witness and asks her questions. While many victims' rights statutes grant victims a right "to be heard," none of these enactments gives victims the right to be heard at trial. Instead, these enactments give victims the right to be heard at other points in the process—bail hearings, plea bargain hearings, sentencings, and parole hearings.

Should victims have the right to make a statement during the trial?

George Fletcher, *With Justice for Some: Protecting Victims' Rights in Criminal Trials*

(1995)

Once we recognize the critical importance of criminal trials in reintegrating the victim into society, we cannot tolerate the occasional alienation of the victim from the adversarial criminal trial. Prosecutors represent the people or the public at large, and therefore they feel justified in downplaying the importance of the person or family (of a deceased) that has suffered most. A startling example of this indifference is Rodney King's silence during the Simi Valley trial. The man whose beating defined the charges watched the trial from his living room. Prosecutor Terry White refused to call him, for fear of damaging the supposedly incontrovertible proof provided by the videotape. When King finally testified at the federal trial, we could grasp the human dimension of the drama. He turned out not to have the menacing demeanor that everyone expected. He provided new evidence (they called me "niggah"); he explained his desire to escape the beating to offset the allegation that he was charging Officer Powell. Without King on the stand, the trial would have lacked important information. Without the victim's voice, the trial could hardly claim to bring about a vindication of the victim as a full-status citizen.

In every homicide case, we encounter an analogous problem. The people most affected by the death, the next of kin, are silent at trial. Because he was not a witness, Norman Rosenbaum, Yankel's brother, could only watch the trial patiently from the audience. He could criticize the process, attack the verdict, but he could not participate in rendering justice. This need not be our reality. Continental European trials permit the victim or the victim's family to appear as a party to the proceeding. We resist this innovation because we assume that the prosecution and the defense have a monopoly as the official parties in dispute. Yet it would hardly do violence to the adversary system to permit some modification of the strict bipolar model.

It might be desirable, in principle, to permit the victim to make an unsworn statement at the outset of the trial. The accused can appear as a lawyer, so why should the victim not be able to appear as a co-prosecutor? There are, however, important disanalogies between the victim and the defendant. The accused understandably seeks to avoid conviction and therefore, as his own lawyer, might say anything to further his case. When the victim speaks, however, he or she appears not in the semitheatrical role of lawyer, not as a player in the drama, but as a real person seemingly speaking the truth. We do not allow the prosecution or the defense to depart from their roles and speak, as it were, in their true voice. Greg Garrison could not tell the Tyson jury that he personally believed that Tyson was guilty. Similarly, it would be at odds with the rules of the game to let the victim deliver a statement without being sworn as a witness and facing cross-examination.

The better approach would be to permit the victim or the next of kin, either in person or through a lawyer, to appear in the trial to ask questions of the witnesses. It is not clear how many victims would do this rather than entrust the case to the prosecutor. The privilege would probably be exercised in rare cases, only where the prosecutor fails to gain the victim's confidence. In the atypical case where the victim wants to intervene, it would be better to allow the third voice at trial rather than freeze out the party for whom the proceedings may carry greater positive meaning than for anyone else.

---

4. The Victim's Display of Emotion during the Trial

What should the trial court do if the victim displays emotion while testifying at trial?

State v. Schaffer
354 S.W.2d 829 (Mo. 1962)

George Schaffer was found guilty by a jury of the offense of rape, and he appeals from the judgment sentencing him to imprisonment for a term of ninety-nine years as fixed by the trial judge under the Habitual Criminal Act § 556.280. . . .

On Thursday, April 21, 1960, about 3 or 3:30 p.m., Patricia's mother sent her to a neighborhood cleaning establishment (located just across the street from defendant's home) to pick up her father's pants. The pants were not ready, and she "started back home." Traveling the usual and normal route homeward would cause her to pass in front of 1521 North Jefferson. While walking along the sidewalk adjacent to those premises, she was grabbed from behind by defendant, and dragged into his house where, to use her language, she "got socked in the stomach and almost choked."

There is no dispute as to the following particular facts (both prosecutrix and defendant having testified to them): That prosecutrix remained in defendant's house or living quarters (comprised of four rooms—"all in line, one room after the other") until about 8 or 8:30 o'clock the next morning; that defendant "shaved" the public hair from the region of her groin (actually he used hair clippers with which he did barbering), and that they spent some part of the night in bed together, both in the nude. . . .

The next and final assignment [of error] . . . challenges a discretionary ruling. The charge is that the court should have declared a mistrial in each of several instances because of prosecutrix giving testimony while in a highly emotional state, "sobbing hysterically, tearfully crying, and unable to testify without interrupting herself by her aforesaid sobbing and crying." We find two instances where defendant moved for a mistrial, once on the ground that the prosecutrix was "sniveling," and another (one page later in the transcript) that she was "crying and sniveling on the stand" and "on the verge of hysteria." In the first instance, the court commented and ruled, "The witness is conducting herself very properly in the court's opinion, the objection is overruled." In the second, the court stated that in its opinion the witness was not hysterical, but "conducting herself here fairly well—she is conducting herself properly, while she is stumbling a little bit, but that is the ordinary thing that happens in rape cases—that is the way girls in rape cases do—they do it all the time. Your objection is overruled." There is nothing in the record to indicate the situation was otherwise than as stated by the court, and no prejudice appears therefrom. No evidence was heard on the motion for a new trial, and the grounds thereof directed to this particular matter, being mere conclusions, do not prove themselves. Defendant's contention is disallowed.

We have examined those portions of the record where on Rule 28.02, V.A.M.R. requires that judgment be rendered whether error is assigned or not, and find the same sufficient. The judgment is, accordingly, affirmed.

_____

Note

Trial judges are generally given broad discretion in handling emotional displays in the courtroom. Appellate courts rarely reverse on such grounds. *See, e.g., State v. Boone*, 820 P.2d 930 (Utah Ct. App. 1991) (alleged crying by victim during closing argument did not deny defendant a fair trial).

_____

Why do we attempt to ban emotion from the courtroom? Can emotion be truly separated from rationality by formal court processes? These questions are a subject of interest for some scholars.

Susan Bandes, *Empathy, Narrative and Victim Impact Statements*
63 U. Chi. L. Rev. 361 (1996)

The scholarship on the role of emotion in law does not seek to establish that there are no significant differences between reason and emotion. Rather, it persuasively demonstrates that the mainstream notion of the rule of law greatly overstates both the demarcation between the two and the possibility of keeping reasoning processes free of emotional variables. Emotion and cognition, to the extent they are separable, act in concert to shape our perceptions and reactions. But more than that, much of the scholarship posits that it is not only impossible but also undesirable to factor emotion out of the reasoning process: by this account, emotion leads to truer perception and, ultimately, to better (more accurate, more moral, more just) decisions.

The law perpetuates the illusion of emotionless lawyering and judging by portraying certain "hard" emotions or emotional stances as objective and inevitable. Yet even a legal process devoid of such "soft" emotions as compassion or empathy is not emotionless; it is simply driven by other passions. As Martha Minow and Elizabeth Spelman point out, "logic . . . [itself] serve[s] human purposes . . . drawing on passions . . . for order, predictability, and security. . . ." Justice Brennan aptly describes as emotional the judge's "visceral temptation to help prosecute the criminal." Nevertheless, the passion for predictability, the zeal to prosecute, and mechanisms, such as distancing, repressing, and isolating one's feelings from one's thought processes, are the emotional stances that have always driven mainstream legal thought; as a result, they avoid the stigma of "emotionalism." That derogatory term is reserved for the marginalized "soft emotions:" compassion, empathy, caring, mercy.

If we accept that emotion cannot be factored out of the reasoning process, we resolve the debate about whether emotion belongs in the law-emotional content is inevitable. Legal reasoning, although often portrayed as rational, does not-indeed, can not-transcend passion or emotion. Instead, it is driven by a different set of emotional variables, albeit an ancient set so ingrained in the law that its contingent nature has become invisible.

The characterization of some emotional variables, stances, or mechanisms as "emotional" and others as "reasonable" is an assertion of power — a camouflaged decision to marginalize the former and privilege the latter. Much of the importance of the scholarship on emotion lies in exposing this assertion of power and challenging the notion of a neutral, emotionless baseline.

Notes

1. How concerned should judges be with emotional displays by the victim (or the defendant)? Every lawyer who has tried criminal cases knows that an emotional moment can have great impact upon a jury. Even if emotion cannot be neatly separated from the content of testimony, is the *effort* to do so good policy?

2. Jurors determine who is telling the truth during the trial by observing the demeanor of the witnesses, including the presence or absence of emotion during their testimony. If so, doesn't an admonition to a victim not to convey emotion harm the jury's ability to determine the truth of the matter? Should trial courts advise the jury about what the victim has been instructed?

C. A Support Person for the Victim in the Courtroom

Many states permit a victim advocate, friend, or relative of the victim to accompany the victim while they attend the trial or testify in court.

CAL. PENAL CODE § 868.5 (West)

(a) Notwithstanding any other law, a prosecuting witness in a case involving a violation or attempted violation of [specified sex offenses] . . . shall be entitled, for support, to the attendance of up to two persons of his or her own choosing, one of whom may be a witness, at the preliminary hearing and at the trial, or at a juvenile court proceeding, during the testimony of the prosecuting witness. Only one of those support persons may accompany the witness to the witness stand, although the other may remain in the courtroom during the witness' testimony.

(b) If the person or persons so chosen are also witnesses, the prosecution shall present evidence that the person's attendance is both desired by the prosecuting witness for support and will be helpful to the prosecuting witness. Upon that showing, the court shall grant the request unless information presented by the defendant or noticed by the court establishes that the support person's attendance during the testimony of the prosecuting witness would pose a substantial risk of influencing or affecting the content of that testimony. In the case of a juvenile court proceeding, the judge shall inform the support person or persons that juvenile court proceedings are confidential and may not be discussed with anyone not in attendance at the proceedings. In all cases, the judge shall admonish the support person or persons to not prompt, sway, or influence the witness in any way. Nothing in this section shall preclude a court from exercising its discretion to remove a person from the courtroom whom it believes is prompting, swaying, or influencing the witness.

(c) The testimony of the person or persons so chosen who are also witnesses shall be presented before the testimony of the prosecuting witness. The prosecuting witness shall be excluded from the courtroom during that testimony.

―――――――――

Can the presence of a support person (or support animal) violate the rights of the defendant?

People v. Spence
212 Cal. App. 4th 478, 151 Cal. Rptr. 3d 374 (2012)

Before D. [an 11-year-old girl] testified [about being sexually assaulted by Spence, a 25-year-old man], the court advised the jury that she would be accompanied to the witness stand by an advocate from the district attorney's office, as well as a therapy dog that would be sitting at her feet (over defense objection that this was excessive; e.g., Spence argued in limine, "a furry friend in the court will cast the witness in even a more sympathetic light"). On appeal, Spence argues these procedures or support system interfered with his due process rights to a fair trial and confrontation of witnesses, by serving to conclusively label D. as a victim who required the support not only of a "victim advocate," but also a therapy dog, to go to the witness stand, and before any verdict was reached. . . .

At the outset of trial, the trial court considered a defense request to preclude the prosecutor from referring to D. as the "victim." The court denied the motion but stated, "my antenna is up, and if I think either side is, you know, trying to suggest that the victim is a proved victim without being proved that she is truly a victim, I'd be happy to reconsider."

This issue next arose when the prosecutor stated that D. had requested the presence of a therapy dog while she was testifying, and sought permission to have the therapy dog and a victim advocate from her office, Ms. Figueroa, accompany D. to the witness stand. The reason for the request was that Spence's family was going to be present and there were concerns that D. might have an emotional meltdown and refuse to testify, since it could be a terrifying situation for her. Defense counsel responded that there would be only a limited number of Spence's family members present, and in any case, it would be agreeable to keep the victim advocate and therapy dog nearby to be available to D., such as in a jury room. However, he objected that it would be "overkill" to allow her to have such a support system with her on the witness stand.

Before empaneling the jury, the court granted these requests by the prosecutor on the grounds that as a witness, D. was "on the young side," and even adult victims may prefer to have advocates in the courtroom, and it was reasonably probable that testifying might be an intimidating situation for D. With respect to the use of the therapy dog, the court referred to the discretion granted to it under Evidence Code section 765 to control court proceedings in the search for truth, and commented that there would be no prejudice in allowing the therapy dog to be present in the courtroom. The court said it was comparable to D. holding a "cute teddy bear in her hands" to provide her comfort. The court explained to counsel that this particular therapy dog had been in the same courtroom before, "and she's almost unnoticeable once everybody takes their seat on the stand. She's very well-behaved and does nothing but simply sit there. And so if that does make it easier for [D.] to testify, I am going to allow it." However, if any issues or improper behavior by the therapy dog occurred, it would be removed from the courtroom. The record does not show any such problems arose.

When D. was called to the witness stand, the court informed the jury she would be entering through the back door rather than the front entrance to the courtroom. The People noted for the record that D. was "accompanied by a victim advocate named Norie Figueroa from our office and a canine therapy dog." . . .

In addition to the general discretionary standards set forth in Evidence Code section 765, for control of a courtroom, the provisions of section 868.5, subdivision (a) apply to a prosecuting witness in a case involving a violation of section 288 or similar sex offense. The witness "shall be entitled, for support, to the attendance of *up to two persons of his or her own choosing,* one of whom may be a witness, at the preliminary hearing and at the trial, . . . during the testimony of the prosecuting witness. Only one of those support persons may accompany the witness to the witness stand, although the other may remain in the courtroom during the witness' testimony. . . ." (§ 868.5, subd. (a); italics added.)

Under section 868.5, subdivision (b), whether or not the support person also serves as a prosecuting witness, "[i]n all cases, the judge shall admonish the support person or persons to not prompt, sway, or influence the witness in any way. Nothing in this section shall preclude a court from exercising its discretion to remove a person from the courtroom whom it believes is prompting, swaying, or influencing the witness."

It is established that a support person's mere presence with a witness on the stand, pursuant to section 868.5, does not infringe upon a defendant's due process and confrontation clause rights, unless the support person improperly interferes with the witness's testimony, so as to adversely influence the jury's ability to assess the testimony. (*People v. Myles* (2012) 139 Cal.Rptr.3d 786, 274 P.3d 413 (*Myles*); *People v. Patten* (1992) 12 Cal.Rptr.2d 284.)

In *People v. Adams* (1993) 23 Cal.Rptr.2d 512 (*Adams*), the court relied on confrontation clause cases, *Coy v. Iowa* (1988) 487 U.S. 1012, and *Maryland v. Craig* (1990) 497 U.S. 836, to conclude that insufficient findings of necessity had been made in the case before it to allow a witness to also serve as the victim's chosen support person. The court acknowledged that section 868.5 "does not articulate the requirement of a case-specific finding of need," but found that the circumstances of that case would have justified such findings, although the lack of them was harmless error. (*Adams, supra,* at pp. 443–444, 23 Cal.Rptr.2d 512.)

In *People v. Johns* (1997), 65 Cal.Rptr.2d 434 (*Johns*), the court rejected claims by the defendant and appellant that the trial court erred in permitting the mother of an 11-year-old sex offense victim to sit with him on the witness stand as his support person, pursuant to section 868.5. The defendant claimed his due process right to confront witnesses had been interfered with, or there would be undue distraction. (*Ibid.*) The court in *Johns* disagreed with any suggestion in *Adams, supra,* 23 Cal. Rptr.2d 512 that further express findings of necessity had been required to justify the presence of a nonwitness support person. The court acknowledged that in the *Adams* case, other factors had justified a higher level of scrutiny there, such as the "issue of intertwining the credibility of that witness [(also a support person)] and the victim in the eyes of the jury, which was not present here. In addition, there was an allegation in *Adams* that the support person, who was the victim's father, had abused the victim, which could have motivated the latter to report the crimes as she did. Thus, there was more of a danger that his presence with her on the stand could influence her testimony, which was not present here."

Analysis: Therapy Dog

To evaluate Spence's arguments the court erred (1) when it allowed both the therapy dog and victim advocate to accompany the child to the witness stand, because section 868.5 permits only one support person or entity to do so, or (2) that no specific enough findings were made here, we look to the statutory language in section 868.5, as well as Evidence Code section 765, to provide the measure of the sufficiency of the express or implied findings made by the court, in the exercise of its overall discretionary power to oversee the court proceedings. . . . In relevant definitions, section 868.5, subdivision (a), provides that a specified witness "shall be entitled, for support, to the attendance of *up to two persons of his or her own choosing,* one of whom may be a witness, at the preliminary hearing and at the trial, . . . during the testimony of the prosecuting witness. Only one of those support persons may accompany the witness to the witness stand, although the other may remain in the courtroom during the witness' testimony. . . ." (Italics added.)

In Evidence Code section 175, a general definition of the term "person" is set forth, as including "a natural person, firm, association, organization, partnership, business trust, corporation, limited liability company, or public entity." The same type of language is found in section 311, setting forth definitions regarding crimes against the person involving sexual assault, and crimes against public decency and good morals; in particular, regarding obscene matter offenses, the term "person" under section 311, subdivision (c) means "any individual, partnership, firm, association, corporation, limited liability company, or other legal entity." (See also § 313, subd. (c), [same language].)

From these definitions, it is easy to conclude that therapy dogs are not "persons" within the meaning of section 868.5, setting limitations on the number of "persons" who may accompany a witness to the witness stand. Moreover, since subdivision (b) of section 868.5 refers to the court's duty to give admonitions under section 868.5 that the advocate must not sway or influence the witness, we cannot imagine that the Legislature intended that a therapy dog be so admonished, nor could any dog be sworn as a witness in this context, so as to invoke the limitation on the number of support persons who may accompany a testifying witness to the stand. In any case, the trial court took care to ensure that the therapy dog would be mainly unnoticeable once everybody took their seats, and that corrective action would be taken if there was a problem, which there was not.

Thus, the circumstances of this case with respect to the use of the therapy dog simply do not fall within the coverage of section 868.5, setting limitations on the number of "persons" who may accompany a witness to the stand. The court appropriately exercised its discretion under Evidence Code section 765, subdivision (b), to set reasonable controls upon the mode of interrogation of the child witness, by providing a therapy dog in this exercise of "special care to protect [the witness] from undue harassment or embarrassment. . . ."

Analysis: Support Person and Support System

To the extent Spence is alternatively claiming that the presence of the human support person, Ms. Figueroa, caused him prejudice at trial, we reject his claim. The prosecutor's office brought in its staff person victim advocate, who was not a witness,

which was allowed by section 868.5, subdivision (a). There was no additional requirement under section 868.5, subdivision (b) that there be a showing of "helpfulness" to
justify the presence of that particular support person, who was not a witness. (See
Johns, supra, 65 Cal.Rptr.2d 434.)

Although it would have been the better practice for the trial court to expressly
make standard admonitions under section 868.5 that this support person should not
do anything to sway or influence the witness, the court could logically have assumed
that it was not necessary to do so, because the nonwitness victim advocate from the
district attorney's office was presumably familiar with courtroom decorum rules. The
record does not show any problems occurred about her behavior or any undue influence on D.'s testimony.

It would also have been appropriate for the trial court, as referenced in *Myles, supra,*
139 Cal.Rptr.3d 786, 274 P.3d 413, to inform the jurors that the witness "was entitled
by law to be attended by a support person during her testimony," and to admonish
them that "the support person was 'not the witness.'" (139 Cal.Rptr.3d 786.) In any
case, since the trial court in this case gave the standard instruction that the jury must
base its decision solely on the evidence received at trial, without being swayed by sympathy or prejudice, it does not appear that any claim of prejudice from the support
person's presence is available on this record. (*Ibid.*)

Under all the circumstances, we cannot say that the hazards identified in *Patten,*
supra, from the presence of a support person (or even a support dog) were present:
"(1) the potential of influencing the jury with a subconscious message that the victim
is traumatized and therefore it is more likely the sexual assault occurred, and (2) the
concern that the presence of a person supporting the witness may add credibility to
the witness's testimony—i.e., the support person is vouching for the credibility of
the witness." (*Johns, supra,* 65 Cal.Rptr.2d 434.)

Moreover, to the extent that the presence of the victim advocate or the support
dog could have been said to create any disruption or distraction, thus violating
confrontation clause protections, the court in *Adams* said: "'[D]istraction and disruption in the courtroom are not absolutes, but are to be measured objectively in
the context of the circumstances presented.' [Citation.]" (*Adams, supra,* 23 Cal.
Rptr.2d 512.) The trial court was aware that D., who as a witness was "on the young
side," had been tearful and upset when interviewed about her injuries by Dr. Viv-
anco and nurse Sager, and the prosecutor had concerns she would have an emotional
meltdown on the stand. D. was interested in having the support dog present in court,
as well as the support person, and the court's implied findings of necessity were
justified.

Even assuming more specific or express findings of necessity would have been
proper to justify having more than one support entity present upon the witness stand,
in light of the general policies or statutory limitations in section 868.5, we are satisfied
that any error in this respect was harmless. There was sufficient other evidence,
beyond the testimony of D., to justify the jury's findings, including testimony of other

witnesses to whom she reported she was molested, and there was physical and forensic evidence in support of her story. There were admissions from Spence, including his dictated and copied letters of apology. No discernible prejudice arose from the support system used here.

The judgment is affirmed.

_____

Notes

1. In the absence of a detailed statute like California's, most courts treat the issue of a support person as one committed to the sound discretion of the trial judge. *See, e.g., Czech v. State*, 945 A.2d 1088 (2008) (establishing factors that trial courts should consider in determining whether a "substantial need" exists for special accommodation for a witness, such as a support person; finding error, but harmless error, when mother allowed to sit behind child during testimony); *Ohio v. Johnson*, 528 N.E.2d 567 (Ohio App. 1986) (child allowed to sit on lap of relative). In allowing support, the trial court must take care not to implicitly endorse the truthfulness of the child's testimony. *See State v. R.W.*, 491 A.2d 1304 (N.J. Super. 1985) (rewarding the child-witness with ice cream and lollipops in the presence of the jury for giving real as opposed to pretend testimony was prejudicial error).

2. The use of support animals for victims is a fairly recent phenomenon. At least five states have approved the approach, providing appropriate circumstances exist. *See State v. Millis*, 391 P.3d 1225, 1234 (Ct. App. 2017) (collecting authorities). *But cf.* Abigayle L. Grimm, *An Examination of Why Permitting Therapy Dogs to Assist Child-Victims When Testifying During Criminal Trials Should Not Be Permitted*, 16 J. Gender, Race & Just. 263, 264 (2013) (arguing for other approaches to the issue).

3. Often the debate in cases such as *Spence* is what showing the prosecution should be required to make to establish the need for a special accommodation. *Compare* Matthew Kaiser, *Sit . . . Stay . . . Now Beg for Me: A Look at the Courthouse Dogs Program and the Legal Standard Pennsylvania Should Use to Determine Whether A Dog Can Accompany A Child on the Witness Stand*, 60 Vill. L. Rev. 343, 373 (2015) (arguing for a balancing of interests standard where a defendant must prove prejudice to such an approach) *with* Angela Nascondiglio, *The Cost of Comfort: Protecting a Criminal Defendant's Constitutional Rights When Child Witnesses Request Comfort Accommodations*, 61 N.Y.L. Sch. L. Rev. 395, 397 (2017) (such approaches should be allowed only on a showing of "compelling necessity").

4. Special accommodations for victims can, with the permission of the trial judge, take varying forms. *See, e.g., People v. Brandon*, 52 Cal. Rptr. 3d 427 (Cal. Ct. App. 2006) (partial publication) (in light of victim's fear of defendant, it was not a violation of the defendant's right of confrontation or due process to allow a victim to testify while wearing sunglasses and scarf).

_____

D. Spectator Support for Victims During Trials

Carey v. Musladin

549 U.S. 70 (2006)

Justice Thomas delivered the opinion of the Court.

This Court has recognized that certain courtroom practices are so inherently prejudicial that they deprive the defendant of a fair trial. *Estelle v. Williams,* 425 U.S. 501, 503-506 (1976); *Holbrook v. Flynn,* 475 U.S. 560, 568 (1986). In this case, a state court held that buttons displaying the victim's image worn by the victim's family during respondent's trial did not deny respondent his right to a fair trial. We must decide whether that holding was contrary to or an unreasonable application of clearly established federal law, as determined by this Court. 28 U.S.C. § 2254(d)(1). We hold that it was not.

I

On May 13, 1994, respondent Mathew Musladin shot and killed Tom Studer outside the home of Musladin's estranged wife, Pamela. At trial, Musladin admitted that he killed Studer but argued that he did so in self-defense. A California jury rejected Musladin's self-defense argument and convicted him of first-degree murder and three related offenses.

During Musladin's trial, several members of Studer's family sat in the front row of the spectators' gallery. On at least some of the trial's 14 days, some members of Studer's family wore buttons with a photo of Studer on them. Prior to opening statements, Musladin's counsel moved the court to order the Studer family not to wear the buttons during the trial. The court denied the motion, stating that it saw "no possible prejudice to the defendant."

Musladin appealed his conviction to the California Court of Appeal in 1997. He argued that the buttons deprived him of his Fourteenth Amendment and Sixth Amendment rights. At the outset of its analysis, the Court of Appeal stated that Musladin had to show actual or inherent prejudice to succeed on his claim and cited *Holbrook v. Flynn,* 475 U.S. 560, 570 (1986), as providing the test for inherent prejudice. The Court of Appeal, quoting part of *Flynn's* test, made clear that it "consider[ed] the wearing of photographs of victims in a courtroom to be an 'impermissible factor coming into play,' the practice of which should be discouraged." Nevertheless, the court concluded, again quoting *Flynn, supra,* at 571, that the buttons had not "branded defendant 'with an unmistakable mark of guilt' in the eyes of the jurors" because "[t]he simple photograph of Tom Studer was unlikely to have been taken as a sign of anything other than the normal grief occasioned by the loss of [a] family member."

At the conclusion of the state appellate process, Musladin filed an application for writ of habeas corpus in Federal District Court pursuant to § 2254. The District Court denied habeas relief but granted a certificate of appealability on the buttons issue.

The Court of Appeals for the Ninth Circuit reversed and remanded for issuance of the writ, finding that under § 2254 the state court's decision "was contrary to, or involved an unreasonable application of, clearly established Federal law, as determined by the Supreme Court of the United States." § 2254(d)(1). We granted certiorari and now vacate.

II

. . .

The effect on a defendant's fair-trial rights of the spectator conduct to which Musladin objects is an open question in our jurisprudence. This Court has never addressed a claim that such private-actor courtroom conduct was so inherently prejudicial that it deprived a defendant of a fair trial. And although the Court articulated the test for inherent prejudice that applies to state conduct in *Williams* and *Flynn*, we have never applied that test to spectators' conduct.

Reflecting the lack of guidance from this Court, lower courts have diverged widely in their treatment of defendants' spectator-conduct claims. Some courts have applied *Williams* and *Flynn* to spectators' conduct. *Norris v. Risley,* 918 F.2d, at 830-831 (applying *Williams* and *Flynn* to hold spectators' buttons worn during a trial deprived the defendant of a fair trial); *In re Woods,* 114 P.3d 607, 616-617 (Wash. 2005) (applying *Flynn* but concluding that ribbons worn by spectators did not prejudice the defendant). Other courts have declined to extend *Williams* and *Flynn* to spectators' conduct. *Billings v. Polk,* 441 F.3d 238, 246-247 (C.A.4 2006) ("These precedents do not clearly establish that a defendant's right to a fair jury trial is violated whenever an article of clothing worn at trial arguably conveys a message about the matter before the jury"); *Davis v. State,* 223 S.W.3d 466, 474-475 (Tex.App.2006) ("Appellant does not cite any authority holding the display of this type of item by spectators creates inherent prejudice"). Other courts have distinguished *Flynn* on the facts. *Pachl v. Zenon,* 929 P.2d 1088, 1093–1094, n. 1 (Or. App. 1996) (in banc). And still other courts have ruled on spectator-conduct claims without relying on, discussing, or distinguishing *Williams* or *Flynn. Buckner v. State,* 714 So.2d 384, 388-389 (Fla.1998) *(per curiam); State v. Speed,* 961 P.2d 13, 29-30 (Kan. 1998); *Nguyen v. State,* 977 S.W.2d 450, 457 (Tex.App.1998).

Given the lack of holdings from this Court regarding the potentially prejudicial effect of spectators' courtroom conduct of the kind involved here, it cannot be said that the state court "unreasonabl[y] appli[ed] clearly established Federal law." § 2254(d)(1). No holding of this Court required the California Court of Appeal to apply the test of *Williams* and *Flynn* to the spectators' conduct here. Therefore, the state court's decision was not contrary to or an unreasonable application of clearly established federal law.

Notes

1. In *Carey,* the United States Supreme Court considered a collateral attack on a state court judgment affirming a conviction. Accordingly, it applied an extremely

deferential standard of review of the trial court's decision to allow spectators to wear buttons, leaving open the possibility that on direct review it might have reached a different result.

2. How should a trial court rule if the defendant's families and supporters want to wear buttons as a show of support for the accused?

3. Do buttons and other symbols related to the victims unfairly divert the jurors' attention away from the guilt-innocence determination that they have to make, as one commentator has argued?

> Given that the American criminal justice system otherwise goes to great lengths to avoid jury bias, jurors should ultimately make decisions based on the evidence at trial and not the sympathetic nature of the victim or the spectator's loss. For example, the voir dire process and rules against the admission of the defendant's previous crimes are meant to filter out potential bias and prevent the jury from acting on an irrational basis. It would be unjust to circumvent these goals by allowing prejudicial spectator demonstrations. Furthermore, because the display itself adds an element of distraction, may prime the jury, and may create an availability heuristic, employing a balancing test that allows certain or limited spectator demonstrations misses the point. T-shirts, buttons, or urns—no matter how many exist—have the ability to take the focus away from the trial and bias the jury. Therefore, only a complete ban on spectator demonstrations can secure a defendant's right to a fair trial.

Sierra Elizabeth, *The Newest Spectator Sport: Why Extending Victims' Rights to the Spectators' Gallery Erodes the Presumption of Innocence*, 58 DUKE L.J. 275, 304–08 (2008).

Long v. State

151 So. 3d 498 (Fla. Dist. Ct. App. 2014)

Brian Scott Long appeals his convictions of two counts of lewd and lascivious molestation and one count of sexual battery by a person in familial or custodial authority. Because men wearing jackets embroidered with "Bikers Against Child Abuse" were in the presence of jurors prior to the commencement of the trial, we conclude that inherent prejudice has been established and that there was an unacceptable risk that impermissible factors affected the jury. Accordingly, Long's convictions are reversed, the sentences vacated, and the cause remanded for a new trial.

Long was charged with multiple counts of lewd and lascivious molestation and sexual battery of his former step-daughter. . . . He argues that a new trial is required because several persons selected to serve on the jury came into close proximity with men wearing leather jackets emblazoned with the phrase: "Bikers Against Child Abuse." These men were observed sitting in a hallway with the jury on the morning trial was scheduled to commence. Prior to the start of trial, defense counsel brought the jury's encounter with "burly" bikers to the attention of the trial court. Defense counsel asserted that a mistrial was in order, and as authority for such, cited *Shootes v. State*, 20 So.3d 434 (Fla. 1st DCA 2009). The prosecutor advised the trial court that these men had befriended the victim and appeared at trial in order to show support for her. The prosecutor added that she instructed the group not to wear their "paraphernalia" in the courtroom.

The trial court interviewed four of the jurors exposed to the bikers. Each juror stated that there was no conversation with the bikers, and each answered affirmatively when asked if he or she could remain impartial despite seeing the bikers. Yet, one juror was dismissed because her answer as to whether she could be impartial was deemed equivocal by the trial court. Another, Mr. Adams, was asked whether the bikers would cause him to "favor the State against the defendant in any way," and the juror replied:

> No. I would be disappointed if they were in the parking lot when we were going home. But other than that—
>
> Court: Why is that, sir?
>
> Juror: I am being honest. I don't think that will happen. I don't think it will have any bearing on the case whatsoever, you know, other than what the facts are presented in here.

After the interviews and after excusing a juror, the trial court was confident that the remaining jurors would be impartial. The bikers were instructed by the trial court, outside of the presence of the jury, not to wear their "insignia" in the court room. They were also instructed not to congregate around the jurors during breaks. A mistrial was thus denied.

The jury returned a guilty verdict on all of the charges pending. The defense moved for a new trial on several grounds, including the ground that the trial court erred in denying Long's motion for a mistrial in view of the prejudice caused by the presence of the "Bikers Against Child Abuse" group . . .

On appeal, Long argues that actual or inherent prejudice resulted from the presence of the bikers at the trial. We agree that an unacceptable risk was created that the verdict reached was, at least in part, a result of the pre-trial encounter with the insignia-laden bikers. Although the trial court appropriately questioned the jurors, at that point in the proceedings, by which time the jury members had been selected but not sworn, the trial court should have selected a new jury panel. That error was aggravated by the continued presence of the bikers in the courtroom in close proximity of the jury.

This court explained in *Shootes v. State* that "[t]he presence of courtroom observers wearing uniforms, insignia, buttons, or other indicia of support for the accused, the prosecution, or the victim of the crime does not automatically constitute denial of the accused's right to a fair trial." 20 So.3d 434, 438 (Fla. 1st DCA 2009); *see also*

Holbrook v. Flynn, 475 U.S. 560 (1986); *Carey v. Musladin,* 549 U.S. 70 (2006). However, there are situations where the atmosphere in the courtroom might infringe on the defendant's right to a fair trial. When such a claim is raised, a case-by-case approach is required to allow courts to consider the "totality of the circumstances." *Shootes,* 20 So.3d at 438 (quoting *Sheppard v. Maxwell,* 384 U.S. 333, 352 (1966)).

As we further explained in *Shootes,* a defendant claiming he was denied a fair trial must show "either actual or inherent prejudice." *Id.; see also Woods,* 923 F.2d at 1457. Actual prejudice requires some indication or articulation by a juror or jurors that they were conscious of some prejudicial effect. *See Pozo v. State,* 963 So.2d 831 (Fla. 4th DCA 2007). Inherent prejudice, on the other hand, requires a showing by the defendant that there was an unacceptable risk of impermissible factors coming into play. *Holbrook,* 475 U.S. at 570; *Woods,* 923 F.2d at 1457.

Inherent prejudice has been shown here. By displaying their insignia, the bikers intended to do more than be present as support for the victim. After all, the victim already knew the bikers. Thus, they could have provided support to her by merely being present without wearing any distinguishing clothing. Instead, in apparent contravention of the prosecutor's instruction, the bikers chose to appear, as the morning trial was set to commence, in clothing which was intended "to communicate a message to the jury." *Woods,* 923 F.2d at 1459. That message was the appellant was a sexual abuser and that sexual abuse was to be condemned by a guilty verdict. As the trial court stated below, the bikers engaged in "reckless advocacy"—advocacy of a certain outcome to be reached by the jury regardless of what the State proved at trial.

The dissent argues that the case before us, which involves the conduct of private spectators, should be treated differently than a case where prejudice against the accused is the result of state-sponsored activity. We fail to see a merit in that distinction for the issue before us is whether there was a risk that Long was denied the right to a trial "by a panel of impartial, 'indifferent' jurors . . . [whose] verdict [was] based upon the evidence developed at the trial" and not upon outside pressures. *Irvin,* 366 U.S. at 722. It matters not whether the impartiality of the jury was adversely affected by a state agent or a private citizen, for the result is the same: a denial of a fair trial.

It is true, as the State emphasizes on appeal, that the jurors who were in close proximity to the bikers prior to trial and who remained on the panel each stated they would not be influenced by the bikers. However, such disavowals of impartiality are only proof that actual prejudice did not occur. It is by no means certain that the jury was not intimidated and thus not improperly influenced by the bikers.

A final point bears mentioning. In denying the motion for a new trial, the trial court indicated that it did not believe it had the authority to exclude "anybody from coming into the courtroom." This view is incorrect. Safeguards may be adopted to ensure that "the administration of justice at all stages is free from outside control and influence" without running afoul of the constitution. *Cox,* 379 U.S. at 562. Indeed, the due process clause of the federal constitution obliges the judiciary to guard against the possibility that "the atmosphere in and around the courtroom might [become] so hostile as to interfere with the trial process, even though . . . all the forms of trial conformed to the requirements of law." *Estes*, 381 U.S. at 561 (1965) (Warren, C.J., concurring); *see also Mills v. Singletary*, 63 F.3d 999 (11th Cir.1995).

Note

Cases regarding spectator conduct supporting a victim require close attention to the facts. On different facts from *Long*, different courts have reached different results. Trial courts tend to be affirmed in these rulings. *See, e.g., Smith v. Dunn*, No. 2:13-CV-00557-RDP, 2017 WL 1150618 (N.D. Ala. 2017) (finding no prejudice from where the victim's family and friends were present in the courtroom, including the victim's brother, a Birmingham police officer in uniform; the victim's family, along with the jury, was given a transcript of police informant Latonya Roshell's testimony, which, according to the defendant, gave the jury the impression that the victim's family's rights were superior to the defendant's rights; and the trial court interrupted the reading of the jury instructions at sentencing because a spectator was crying); *United States v. Taylor*, No. 2:01 CR 73, 2013 WL 2145599 (N.D. Ind. 2013) (no unfairness in trial where approximately 20 firefighters in firefighter apparel sat in the gallery section of the courtroom during closing arguments in case involving murder of father of firefighter); *Smith v. Farley*, 59 F.3d 659, 664 (7th Cir. 1995) (finding no prejudice to defendant accused of murdering police officer from presence of police officers in the gallery; trial court affirmed after reasoning "if you kill a policeman and are put on trial for the crime, you must expect the courtroom audience to include policemen.").

E. Participation of Counsel for the Victim during Trial

The participation of privately funded attorneys in criminal trials was permitted at common law. The advantages and disadvantages of allowing privately funded attorneys to participate at trial were first articulated in two cases reaching opposite conclusions written more than 100 years ago. The arguments for and against permitting the participation of privately funded attorneys have changed little since then.

Meister v. People
31 Mich. 99 (1875)

CAMPBELL, J.:

The respondents below were all tried and convicted of the offense of burning certain insured property, in the city of Saginaw, on the 22d day of June, 1873, with intent to defraud certain insurance companies named in the information. There was no evidence to convict Leizer Meister or William Meister with the burning, as principals present at the fact. The case proceeded throughout on the claim that Rosa Meister, the wife, and Bertha Meister, the sister of William Meister, who occupied the premises, set the property on fire in the absence of the others; and that William and his father Leizer, who lived at some distance off, procured the burning.

At the opening of the trial an objection was made that counsel had been retained by private prosecutors, and at their expense, to aid in conducting the prosecution. Defendants offered to show this fact, and asked to have one of the assisting counsel sworn, who declined to be sworn, and the court refused to require him; and the prosecuting attorney stating the gentlemen referred to were acting at his request, the court permitted them to assist, and overruled the objection. This question has never been presented to the court before. Under the English practice, prosecution by private parties has been the rule rather than the exception, and there is no public prosecutor who has general charge of criminal business. The necessity of such an officer has been urged repeatedly by many of the ablest jurists; and the chief reason suggested has been the abuse of criminal proceedings for private ends, and the subordination of public justice to private control.

In this country we have usually had in every state some officer, or class of officers, appointed for the express purpose of managing criminal business; but the extent and nature of their powers and duties have not been uniform. Sometimes the officers have been permanent, and sometimes counsel have been appointed by the courts to act for the term; and the duties have often been left under vague regulations. Under our territorial statutes, and until the Revised Statutes of 1838, the legislation was not very specific. But by the Revised Statutes of 1838 a regulation was introduced, that was borrowed from the laws of Massachusetts, and that has been preserved ever since. The prosecuting attorney of each county is required to prosecute all criminal cases in the courts of his county, and may be required also to appear for the same purpose before any magistrate, except in certain municipal courts. And he is expressly debarred from receiving any fee or reward from any private person for any services within his official business, and from being retained, except for the public, in any civil action depending on the same state of facts on which a criminal prosecution shall depend. — C.L. §§ 529, 530, 534.

The courts may appoint counsel to act in his place when he is absent or unable to perform his duties, or where the office is vacant; but no other power of appointment is given. Any recognition of other counsel, if valid, can only be by the request of the prosecuting attorney. He cannot abdicate his duties, and the court cannot divide or relieve them, or give to other counsel any authority whatever, independent of his responsibility. — *U.S. v. Morris*, 1 Paine, 209; *Hite v. State*, 9 Yerg., 198; *Com. v. Knapp*, 10 Pick., 477; *Com. v. Williams*, 2 Cush. R., 582.

The question, therefore, seems to narrow itself to the inquiry whether or not the persons allowed to act at the request or by the assent of the prosecuting attorney are subject to any restrictions applicable to him, or whether they may act without reference to their relations to private parties.

It has been quite common in this state for prosecuting attorneys to be aided by counsel, and probably in some cases they have had the help of those retained by private prosecutors. As no objections have been taken in these cases, and no attention has been called to the statute, it cannot be said there has been any practical construction of the statute; and we are obliged to consider the case as one requiring the law to be enforced according to its fair meaning.

The mere appointment of public prosecutors is not inconsistent with private prosecutions, either separately or under official supervision. When the crown officers intervene at common law, they must, as we suppose, have control of the proceedings. The proposals in England to establish a new system do not aim at entirely destroying the right of private prosecution. See *Edinburgh Review, No. 22, Art. 2, on Criminal Procedure in England and Scotland*. But so long as the present system exists, it appears to make it not only the right, but the duty, of individuals to complain of felonious crimes; and the disability against bringing private actions before prosecuting for felonies was imposed to encourage such complaints, and to ensure private diligence in bringing offenders to justice. The premiums offered to informers stand on a similar footing.

The policy of allowing *qui tam* actions has not been encouraged in this state, and criminal penalties have been devoted to public purposes. Neither is the felonious character of an injury held to prevent an action before, any more than after a criminal prosecution. And one of the reasons given for this is the establishment of public prosecutors. — *Hyatt v. Adams*, 16 Mich., 180.

It is impossible to account for the change in our statutes requiring the exclusive control of criminal procedure to be in the hands of public officers who are forbidden to receive pay or in anyway become enlisted in the interests of private parties, unless we assume the law to have been designed to secure impartiality from all persons connected with criminal trials. The law never has prevented, and does not now prevent, private complaints before magistrates, who have a discretion in regard to calling in the prosecuting attorney. In the ordinary course of things the case for the prosecution is brought out on that examination, and justice requires that it should be, where a defendant does not waive examination. But when the charge is presented on which the respondent is to be tried at the circuit (where he must be tried for all statutory and common-law felonies, except petit larceny), the law requires the public prosecutor to assume and retain exclusive charge of the cause, until the case is ended by acquittal or conviction. The chief dangers which the statute intends to guard against must be those attendant on the trial, inasmuch as the preliminary proceedings usually determine the nature and extent of the accusation, and those may be under the charge of private parties. And we must conclude that the legislature do not consider it proper to allow the course of the prosecuting officer during the trial to be exposed to the influence of the interests or passions of private prosecutors. His position is one involving a duty of impartiality not altogether unlike that of the judge himself. We have had occasion heretofore to refer to this duty in these officers of justice. Their position is a trying one, but the duty nevertheless exists, and the law has done much to remove hindrances to its performance, and in no case more plainly than by the prohibition in question here, and that against allowing a circuit judge to act as counsel in his own court, before another judge, as was done in *Bashford v. People*, 24 Mich., 245. See for illustrations *Wellar v. People*, 30 Mich., 16; *Wagner v. People*, 30 Mich., 384; *Hurd v. People*, 25 Mich., 416.

The courts of Massachusetts have passed upon their statute several times. It was first brought to their attention in the case of *Commonwealth v. Knapp*, 10 Pick. R., 477, where it appeared that Mr. Webster had aided without objection in the trial of the principal felon whose accessories were on trial, and that reliance had been had on his aid in the case at bar, and that he was acting without any pecuniary inducement. The court, under these circumstances, holding it had a right to allow the prosecuting officer to obtain help in a proper case, considered it admissible in that instance, but reserved their opinion as to any different circumstances, and laid stress upon the absence of any interest in Mr. Webster beyond "a disinterested regard for the public good." In *Commonwealth v. Williams*, 2 Cush., 582, a similar course was sustained, but the court said it could only be allowed for stringent reasons, and referred again to the absence of any pecuniary compensation from any private individual. They said that such counsel is not under ordinary circumstances to be permitted, yet, when sanctioned by the court under the limitations suggested, it would not furnish sufficient ground for setting aside the verdict. In *Commonwealth v. Gibbs*, 4 Gray, 146, a conviction was set aside because the court had, in the absence of the district attorney, appointed counsel to act in his place, who had been retained by private parties in civil litigation of the same matter. In *Commonwealth v. King*, 8 Gray, 501, a gentleman was allowed to act as counsel who had acted in aid of the prosecution on the preliminary examination, and had also sat upon a commission of inquest concerning the fire which was the occasion of the prosecution. The court held this peculiar familiarity with the facts would make his help valuable; and no suggestion was made by anyone that he was not disinterested, as no interested person, it must be supposed, would have been allowed to sit on the commission.

The supreme court of Maine, in *State v. Bartlett*, 55 Maine, 200, allowed Ge. Shepley to act with the prosecuting attorney, though under retainer from the insurance company at whose instance the case was prosecuted; and disposed of the Massachusetts cases by saying that in the only one where the conviction was set aside, the counsel complained of was in effect acting district attorney, and so within the words of the statute, which they held should only apply to that officer.

The Massachusetts court, in both of the earlier cases, made the absence of compensation a prominent feature; and in all the cases, spoke of the employment of associates as exceptional, and not generally allowable. They do not bear out the Maine decision in their reasoning. And that can only stand on its own reasoning, upon the assumption that the control of the prosecuting attorney will destroy any influence or mischief which might result from the private interests of his colleagues.

But a theory which holds them as anything but his deputies, or assistants in office, would render it difficult to reconcile their appearance with the law, which compels him to conduct the prosecution. Such counsel, in the courts of the United States, are required to take the oath of office, and are made expressly public officers. The experience of trials shows that any other position is fallacious. When counsel are introduced into a cause, and aid in the trial or argument, it is little short of absurd to suppose they can be prevented from having their own way. It would be unseemly and unprofitable for one counsel, during a trial, to interfere with his associate's questions or argument; and competent auxiliaries would not be engaged on terms which would subject them to open slights. We must look at things as they exist; and everyone knows that if a prosecuting attorney allows the counsel of private parties to intervene, it must usually be for the reason that they will save him labor, and assume the burden of the prosecution. The mischief which the law aims to avoid is, prosecution by interested parties; and if such is the policy of the law, it ought to be carried out. It does not assume that there is anything dishonorable in such employment, but it does assume that it is not proper to entrust the administration of criminal justice to anyone who will be tempted to use it for private ends, and it assumes that a retainer from private parties tends to this.

The great scandals which have occurred from the abuse of criminal process to further purposes of gain or vindictiveness, have often demanded notice; and no better remedy has been suggested than the policy of our statute. It does not prevent anyone from hunting up proofs, or furnishing every facility to the officers of the law. But it will be very inefficient, if it is possible to allow those who have a direct pecuniary interest in convicting a prisoner, to take an active part in his trial. Until the legislature sees fit to restore the common-law rule, and leave cases to private prosecution, it must be assumed that they regard it as unsafe, and opposed to even-handed justice.

As the liability of the insurance companies on their policies would be avoided by proof that the property was burned by the assured, the case is one within the statute; and counsel in the interest of the insurers should not have been allowed to appear.

State v. Kent

62 N.W. 631 (N.D. 1895)

CORLISS, J. The plaintiff in error was convicted of the crime of murder. The jury, under the statute, decided that he should suffer death. Comp. Laws, § 6449. Having been sentenced to be hung, he obtained a writ of error, and the whole case is now before us for review.

* * *

We now approach a very interesting question. The state's attorney was assisted on the trial by Mr. Nye, a citizen of Minnesota, and a member of the bar of that state. He was retained by the brothers of the murdered woman to assist in the prosecution. He stated to the trial judge that while he had been paid nothing by his clients, and had

had no talk with them on the subject of fees, he presumed that they would compensate him for his services in the case. He was not employed by the county of Morton, in which the crime was committed, or by the state's attorney of that county, to assist in the prosecution; but the latter stated in open court that he desired to have Mr. Nye assist him, for the reason that he (the state's attorney) was unable, because of physical ailments, to stand the labor and strain of the case, without aid. Mr. Nye was allowed, despite the objection of the counsel for the accused, to assist in the trial of the case, taking a very active part therein. Counsel for the accused insists that this was prejudicial error. There are two grounds on which he assails the action of the trial judge in permitting Mr. Nye to participate in the trial: First, that he was employed by private persons, and not by the public; second, that he was neither a resident nor a member of the bar of this state. We will discuss these two points in the order in which they are stated.

In England, criminal prosecutions were as a rule carried on by individuals interested in the punishment of the accused, and not by the public. The private prosecutor employed his own counsel, had the indictment framed and the case laid before the grand jury, and took charge of the trial before the petit jury. 1 Chit. Cr. Law, 9, 825. This system does not prevail in this state. Here, in each county, there is a public prosecutor, called the "state's attorney" for that county. It is his duty to prosecute all criminal offenses triable in that county. He is paid a salary for that purpose out of the public funds. He is not allowed to receive any fee or reward from or on behalf of any prosecutor or other individual for services in any prosecution or business to which it is his official duty to attend, nor be concerned as attorney or counsel for either party, other than for the state or the county, in any civil action depending on the same state of facts upon which any criminal prosecution commenced, but undetermined, shall depend. Sections 427, 433, Comp. Laws. We do not think that this change in policy indicates a purpose to exclude the counsel for interested persons from all participation in the prosecution. Such counsel cannot initiate the proceedings, or conduct them. The control of criminal prosecution has been taken from private hands, and transferred to public functionaries chosen for that express purpose. But there is nothing in the statute to justify the conclusion that counsel employed by interested persons may not assist the public prosecutor, in case he and the trial judge deem this course proper.

The fact that the state's attorney who controls criminal cases is not allowed to receive any compensation from private prosecutors for the prosecution of a criminal case does not warrant the conclusion that no counsel paid by private persons shall be permitted to assist in the trial of such a case. It is one thing to have the prosecution entirely in the hands of one who may be influenced, because of a retainer, by the strong desire of his client to secure a conviction; but it is an entirely different thing to allow such an interested counsel to aid in the prosecution one who stands affected by no other motive than that of securing the punishment of guilt, and who has absolute control over the case. The law has removed criminal prosecutions from the control of private interests, but it has not excluded such interests from all participation therein. If no error is committed on the trial, we fail to see how an accused can be prejudiced by the fact that those personally interested have employed private counsel to aid the public prosecutor. Certainly, he should not be heard to complain of the zeal of the private counsel, if such counsel has not allowed his zeal to hurry him into error. The best mode of reaching the truth is by the strenuous contentions of opposing counsel, each animated by the conviction that the cause he has espoused is just. The public have some interests at stake in a criminal prosecution. May all the zeal be displayed on one side, and none be tolerated on the other? The public interests demand that a prosecution should be conducted with energy and skill. While the prosecuting officer should see that no unfair advantage is taken of the accused, yet he is not a judicial officer. Those who are required to exercise judicial functions in the case are the judge and the jury. The public prosecutor is necessarily a partisan in the case. If he were compelled to proceed with the same circumspection as the judge and the jury, there would be an end to the conviction of criminals. Zeal in the prosecution of criminal cases is therefore to be commended, and not condemned. It is the zeal of counsel in the court room, alone, of which the accused can complain. No decision can be found which questions the right of the prosecuting officer to consult with, and receive all manner of aid, even during the trial, from counsel for private parties, outside of the court room. And if such zeal in the court room, on the trial, does not result in error, what conceivable difference can it make whether such assistant was employed by the public, or by private persons? May not cross-examination of witnesses be conducted, and arguments to court and jury be made, by one who is as much convinced of the guilt of the accused as his counsel is persuaded of his innocence? The manner of conducting the case in the court room cannot work legal prejudice to the accused, without resulting in error for which the conviction will be set aside. It is therefore of no legal importance what inspires the zeal of the attorney who assists in the trial. Whatever is done to the injury of the prisoner by private counsel, for which he can have no redress, is done out of court; for instance, by concealing or fabricating evidence. At just this point, where the zeal of counsel employed by private parties may be deadly to the accused, no kind of safeguard is or can be thrown around him.

The prosecuting officer may consult with, and be entirely governed by the advice of, such private counsel; and yet the accused has no remedy, if the private counsel does not participate in the trial. If he does so participate, his zeal works no more prejudice to the accused than the zeal of any other equally able counsel who may be employed by the public. The cases all agree that an assistant hired by the public may engage in the trial without giving the prisoner any legal cause for complaint. Of course, the latter may think he is prejudiced because of being compelled to confront an exceptionally able and experienced prosecutor, but this furnishes no legal ground for overthrowing the conviction. The question can be placed in a clear light by the following statement of it: Can a defendant in a criminal case, who is obliged to submit to the zeal of an assistant prosecutor employed by the public, insist that the zeal of an assistant counsel employed by interested parties shall not be displayed against him, although it results in no error on the part of the prosecution in the management of the case? We think there is only one answer to this question, and that is against the right of the accused to complain in either case, so long as no error has been committed by the assistant on the trial. The rule is different, however, in Michigan and Massachusetts, under statutes very similar to ours. *Meister v. People*, 31 Mich. 99; *Sneed v. People*, 38 Mich. 251; *People v. Hurst*, 41 Mich. 328, 1 N.W. 1027; *People v. Bemis* (Mich.) 16 N.W. 794; *Com. v. Gibbs*, 4 Gray, 146. The reasoning of Judge Campbell in *Meister v. People*, while very plausible, does not convince us that there should be interpolated into the statute an implied prohibition against counsel employed by interested parties assisting in the prosecution. We are unable to discover in the statute any other policy than that of transferring the control of criminal prosecutions from private to public hands. We think that the control of the public prosecutor over the proceedings is a sufficient guaranty that the accused will not be made the innocent victim of overzealous prosecution by private persons. While aware that Judge Campbell has made out a strong case in support of his view, we cannot discover in the legislation of this state the evidence of a policy hostile to the quite general practice of allowing the prosecuting officer to be assisted by counsel retained by those having a personal interest in the prosecution distinct from that of the general public. In support of our ruling on this point, we cite the following cases: *State v. Helm* (Iowa), 61 N.W. 246; *Keyes v. State* (Ind. Sup.), 23 N.E. 1097; *Polin v. State* (Neb.), 16 N.W. 899; *State v. Bartlett*, 55 Me. 220; *State v Fitzgerald*, 49 Iowa, 260; *State v. Wilson*; 24 Kan. 189; *Burkhard v. State*, 18 Tex. App. 599–618; *Gardner v. State*, 55 N.J. Law, 17, 26 Atl. 30; *Benningfield v. Com.* (Ky.), 17 S.W. 271; *People v. Tidwell* (Utah), 12 Pac. 61; 1 Bish. Cr. Proc. § 281; Whart. Cr. Pl. & Prac. § 555. The decision of the Wisconsin supreme court in *Biemel v. State,* 37 N.W. 249, sustaining the Michigan and Massachusetts doctrine, appears to be based upon legislation in that state authorizing the trial judge to appoint an assistant whenever he thinks the public interests require it, and providing that such assistant shall be paid out of the public funds. The case of *Lawrence v. State* (Wis.), 7 N.W. 343, is distinguished in the *Blemel* Case on the ground that it was decided before the new statute was passed, giving the trial judge power to appoint an assistant to be paid out of the public treasury. The *Lawrence* Case is more in harmony with, than opposed to, our views. We hold that it was not error to permit Mr. Nye to assist in the prosecution, at the request of the state's attorney, because of his having been employed by the brothers of the murdered woman.

Notes

1. While *Meister* and *Kent* were both decided in the nineteenth century, a number of states permit the participation of private prosecutors at trial with the consent of and with control over critical decisions in the hands of the public prosecutor. *See* Michael Edmund O'Neill, *Private Vengeance and the Public Good*, 12 U. PA. J. CONST. L. 659, 689 (2010) (reporting that Alabama, Georgia, Indiana, New Jersey, New York,

Ohio, Pennsylvania, Tennessee, Vermont, Virginia, West Virginia, and Wisconsin each allow private counsel to participate in a criminal prosecution in some way). In some jurisdictions, the consent of the court is also required. A few states permit the participation without the requirement of prosecutorial consent. For example, Alabama courts allow a privately funded prosecutor to participate without consent of the prosecutor. However, the attorney must obtain permission of the court. *See Hall v. State*, 411 So. 2d 831 (Ala. Crim. App. 1982).

2. Only a handful of courts have forbidden the participation of privately funded attorneys since the decision in *Meister* in 1875. Robert M. Ireland, *Privately Funded Prosecutor of Crime in the Nineteenth Century United States*, 39 Am. J. Legal Hist. 43 (1995). Some of these courts relied on their evolving standards of due process as the rationale for excluding privately funded attorneys from trial. A credible argument can be made that in the modern era due process is no longer evolving to exclude the victim.

3. A jury may not be entitled to know who a privately funded prosecutor represents. *State v. Miller*, 208 S.W.2d 194 (Mo. 1948) (finding no prejudice to defendant where privately funded attorney did not disclose who he represented).

4. Because the victim's attorneys are privately funded, only those victims with means will generally have the benefit of an attorney. Should counsel be appointed to represent indigent victims? Given fiscal realities of governments is this likely to become a reality?

5. Simultaneous representation by privately funded counsel in both civil and criminal matters concerning the same acts of the defendant is viewed in most jurisdictions as an impermissible conflict of interest. For discussion of this issue, recall *Young v. United States ex rel. Vuitton et Fils S.A.*, in Chapter 5, above.

The federal government and many states provide for appointment of a guardian ad litem in certain cases involving children. *See, e.g.,* 18 U.S.C. § 3509(h) ("The court may appoint a guardian ad litem for a child who was a victim of, or a witness to, a crime involving abuse or exploitation to protect the best interests of the child."). Generally, the guardian acts only as an advisor to the child. One court has even found that it was error for the guardian to participate in a trial.

State v. Harrison

24 P.3d 936 (Utah 2001)

[The trial court appointed a guardian ad litem to represent a 17-year-old victim, A.G., in a forcible sexual assault case. The guardian participated in the trial.]

* * *

Permitting the guardian ad litem to question witnesses and make objections was also error. Because a guardian ad litem does not represent an interested party in a criminal trial, the guardian ad litem is not permitted to further the interests of either the State or the defendant in a criminal case. Victims' rights legislation entitles victims to, among other things, be notified of criminal or juvenile justice proceedings, and be present and heard at important hearings. *See, e.g.,* UTAH CODE ANN. § 77-37-3; UTAH CODE ANN. §§ 77-38-3 & -4. However, the right to be notified and present at trial does not include the right to be heard during the guilt phase of the proceedings. *See id.* § 77-38-2(5); § 77-38-3; § 77-38-4(1) & (2) (stating that "[the Rights of Crime Victims Act] shall not confer any right to the victim of a crime to be heard: (a) at any criminal trial . . . unless called as a witness"). In this case, however, the guardian ad litem insisted that he had the right, on behalf of A.G., to object to questions asked by defense counsel, and on more than one occasion, to ask follow-up questions to those of the prosecutor. To the contrary, the guardian ad litem's participation may not include objecting to questions and questioning witnesses in a criminal trial. The role of the guardian ad litem is not to act as an advocate either for the State's position or for the defendant's position in a criminal trial.

Nothing in the statutes under which a guardian ad litem may be appointed by the district court authorizes the guardian ad litem to sit at counsel table with the prosecutor in the criminal action, to object to questions or proceedings during trial, or to question or call witnesses. As the trial court here correctly concluded, there is also no authority for granting the guardian ad litem's request to make opening and closing statements to the jury in the criminal case. The role of the guardian ad litem in the criminal context involving a child victim is as limited as that enjoyed by the child's parent or other legal guardian.

Note

If the guardian was under the control of the public prosecutor and was a lawyer, most jurisdictions would likely permit the guardian's participation.

In cases where a private prosecutor is allowed to participate at the trial, must the public prosecutor remain in effective control of the prosecution?

East v. Scott

55 F.3d 996 (5th Cir. 1995)

Wayne East, a Texas Death Row inmate, appeals the district court's dismissal of his § 2254 habeas corpus petition. . . .

I.

In August 1982, a Taylor County, Texas jury convicted Wayne East of capital murder and sentenced him to die for the murder of Mary Eula Sears. Sears was killed during a burglary of her home. The linchpin of the state's evidence against East was the testimony of his accomplice, Dee Martin. Martin testified that after she and East broke into Sears' house, East bound Sears and repeatedly stabbed her when she refused to remain quiet. The Texas Court of Criminal Appeals subsequently affirmed East's conviction and sentence on direct appeal and the U.S. Supreme Court denied certiorari.

East filed his first state habeas petition in May 1986 and the state trial court stayed East's June 1986 execution date. The trial court granted East's request for an evidentiary hearing, but denied his request for discovery. After the evidentiary hearing, the trial court entered findings of fact and recommended that East's application be denied. The Texas Court of Criminal Appeals subsequently denied East's habeas application without a written order. . . .

II.

East argues that the district court erred in denying his habeas petition in the following respects: (1) in dismissing his petition without allowing him the opportunity for discovery or an evidentiary hearing to resolve his claim that the participation of a private attorney in his prosecution violated the Due Process Clause. . . .

East first contends that the district court should have permitted discovery and held an evidentiary hearing to resolve his claim that the involvement of a private prosecutor in his prosecution denied him due process. Prior to East's trial, the victim's family retained Russell Ormesher, a former Dallas County prosecutor, to assist the Taylor County district attorney in East's capital murder prosecution. East maintains that Mr. Ormesher essentially controlled all the critical trial strategy and prosecutorial decisions, and that Ormesher's role in the prosecution thus violated the Due Process Clause.

The opportunity for an evidentiary hearing in a federal habeas corpus proceeding is mandatory only where there is a factual dispute which, if resolved in the petitioner's favor, would entitle the petitioner to relief and the petitioner has not received a full and fair evidentiary hearing in state court. . . . East's entitlement to an evidentiary hearing on this claim thus turns on whether his claim raises a question of fact which, if decided in his favor, would entitle him to relief. To resolve this issue, we must first examine the case law governing the participation of privately-retained attorneys in criminal prosecutions.

Powers v. Hauck,[3] was the first decision by this court to expressly address whether the participation of a private prosecutor in a criminal prosecution violates the Due Process Clause. In *Powers*, a habeas petitioner convicted of capital murder alleged that the victim's family hired a private attorney to assist in his prosecution. The court adopted the district court's holding that "the mere participation of a special prosecutor alone is not sufficient grounds to show denial of due process, without some additional showing of a violation of the rules relating to prosecuting attorneys." *Id.* The court concluded that the private prosecutor's involvement did not violate due process because the elected district attorney retained control and management of the prosecution and the private prosecutor never acted without the district attorney's consent or supervision. *Id.*

---

3. 399 F.2d 322, 325 (5th Cir. 1968).

In *Woods v. Linahan*, 648 F.2d 973, 976 (5th Cir. 1981), the court similarly held that the participation of a privately-retained attorney in a murder prosecution did not offend due process even though the attorney exercised independent control over the prosecution during its pre-trial stages. The private prosecutor in *Woods* conducted the pre-trial investigation, interviewed witnesses, filed and argued pre-trial motions, and made pre-trial strategy decisions without the supervision or control of the district attorney. According to the court, the private prosecutor's pretrial activity "border[ed] on a constitutional violation" because "these activities were not carried out under the direction, control, or knowledge of the district attorney." *Id.* at 976–977.

However, the court concluded that there was no due process violation in *Woods* because the district attorney assumed control of the prosecution once the trial started. After the trial started, the district attorney assumed control over trial strategy decisions, gave the state's opening and closing arguments, and examined all the witnesses. While the private prosecutor assisted the district attorney during the trial, he never acted without the district attorney's consent or supervision. Thus, as in *Powers*, the *Woods* court held that the private prosecutor's actions did not offend due process because he did not control important phases of the prosecution.[4]

In *Person v. Miller*, 854 F.2d 656, 664 (4th Cir. 1988), *cert. denied*, 489 U.S. 1011 (1989), the Fourth Circuit followed similar reasoning in concluding that a private prosecutor must effectively control a prosecution to violate the accused's due process rights. The court reasoned that, for purposes of due process, it is important to determine whether a private prosecutor controlled crucial prosecutorial decisions, such as "whether to prosecute, what targets of prosecution to select, what investigative powers to utilize, what sanctions to seek, plea bargains to strike, or immunities to grant." *Id.* According to the court, it is control over these critical prosecutorial decisions which determine the fairness of particular prosecutions that is the important consideration; operational conduct of the trial is actually of subordinate concern, except as it may actually impact upon the more fundamental prosecutorial decisions. *Id.* The court reasoned that, while the quantitative division of trial work has some relevance to determining control, the ultimate question must be whether the private prosecutor controlled these crucial prosecutorial decisions. *Id.* at 663.

We agree with the Fourth Circuit's characterization of the proper framework for resolving East's claim. We therefore turn to East's pleadings to determine whether

---

4. East argues that the Supreme Court's decision in *Young v. United States ex rel. Vuitton et Fils S.A.*, 481 U.S. 787 (1987) creates a strict blanket prohibition against the participation of private prosecutors and, therefore, impliedly overrules *Woods* and *Powers*. We disagree that *Young* alters the analysis set out in *Woods* and *Powers*. *Young* merely held that the counsel for a party in the position to gain from a criminal contempt proceeding cannot be appointed by the court to prosecute the party charged with contempt. In contrast to *Woods* and *Powers*, the private prosecutor in *Young* acted as the government's sole representative throughout the trial. Moreover, *Young* was decided under the Court's supervisory power over federal courts, not as a matter of federal constitutional law.

he alleges specific facts suggesting that Mr. Ormesher effectively controlled critical prosecutorial decisions throughout East's prosecution. East makes the following factual allegations regarding Mr. Ormesher's role:

- Ormesher controlled all the significant trial strategy decisions for the prosecution, including the decision to offer a plea bargain to Dee Dee Martin, the prosecution's key witness linking East to Sear's murder,

- Ormesher conducted an independent pre-trial investigation and maintained a separate case file,

- Ormesher interviewed all the state's key witnesses independent of the supervision or control of the Taylor County district attorney,

- Ormesher played a key role during the trial. According to East, Ormesher made the prosecution's opening and closing arguments and participated in the direct examination of the prosecution's most important witnesses,

- Ormesher was a "seasoned" veteran of capital murder prosecutions, while the district attorney prosecuting the case had little experience.

Applying the framework developed in *Powers*, *Woods*, and *Person*, we conclude that these factual allegations raise the inference that Ormesher effectively controlled East's prosecution and, consequently, are facially sufficient to establish a *prima facie* due process claim.

We now turn to East's contention that the district court erred in denying his discovery motion and in failing to hold an evidentiary hearing. Rule 6 of the Federal Rules Governing § 2254 Cases expressly provides for discovery in habeas proceedings if the petitioner shows "good cause" for discovery. According to the commentary to Rule 6,

> [W]here specific allegations before the court show reason to believe that the petitioner may, if the facts are fully developed, be able to demonstrate that he is confined illegally and is therefore entitled to relief, it is the duty of the court to provide the necessary facilities and procedures for an adequate inquiry.

While the district court generally has discretion to grant or deny discovery requests under Rule 6, a court's blanket denial of discovery is an abuse of discretion if discovery is "indispensable to a fair, rounded, development of the material facts." *Coleman v. Zant*, 708 F.2d 541, 547 (11th Cir. 1983) (quoting *Townsend*, 372 U.S. at 322).

Given the nature of East's allegations, we agree that East has shown good cause for discovery under Rule 6. While the state court record reveals the extent to which Ormesher questioned witnesses and participated in the trial, the record is silent as to whether Ormesher effectively controlled critical prosecutorial decisions. Indeed, the Taylor County district attorney, the district attorney's staff, and Mr. Ormesher are likely the only witnesses who can shed any light on this issue. The record indicates that East has not, however, been able to obtain access to these witnesses or their files. The district court denied East's request to depose these witnesses and examine their files. Because access to these witnesses and their files is necessary to fully develop the facts needed to consider East's claim, we conclude that the district court abused its discretion in denying East's discovery requests.

Notes

1. On remand, the trial court concluded that there was no evidence to indicate that the private prosecutor was in charge of the prosecution. *See East v. Johnson*, 123 F.3d 235 (5th Cir. 1997). Other cases have similarly found that public prosecutors remained in control of the prosecution when private prosecutors assisted. *See, e.g., Jordan v. State*, 786 So. 2d 987, 1011–12 (Miss. 2001) (rejecting due process challenge to private lawyer's appointment as special prosecutor, where "either the District Attorney himself or one of his assistants were present with [the attorney] during most of the pre-trial hearings and at trial"); *State v. Nichols*, 481 S.E.2d 118, 122–23 (S.C. 1997) (not unconstitutional for prosecutor to be assisted by three private attorneys hired by victim's family where prosecutor "maintained control of the case"); *State v. Bennett*, 798 S.W.2d 783, 786 (Tenn. Ct. App. 1990) (statute allowing victim to hire private counsel to assist prosecutor constitutional where extent of participation is to be determined by prosecutor); *Riner v. Commonwealth*, 601 S.E.2d 555, 569 (Va. 2004) (requirement that public prosecutor "remain in continuous control of the case" satisfied; not necessary that private attorney "handle only innocuous witnesses and evidentiary matters"). *But see United States v. Smith*, 936 F.2d 581 (9th Cir. unpublished 1991) (reversing conviction obtained by private prosecutors where public prosecutor's role in the case was "*de minimis*").

2. Generally, the laws governing the conduct of the privately funded prosecutor are the same as the laws governing the public prosecutor. *See Cantrell v. Commonwealth*, 329 S.E.2d 22, 25 (Va. 1985) ("[I]n our view . . . [the privately funded prosecutor] is absolutely prohibited from taking any position, making any argument, offering any evidence, or advocating any cause which would be forbidden to a public prosecutor.").

3. Does the participation of private prosecutors in public prosecutions have the potential to unfairly distort incentives? *See generally* Margaret H. Lemos, *Privatizing Public Litigation*, 104 Geo. L.J. 515 (2016) (raising general questions about public litigation being "privatized" to private actors).

F. The Victim's Right to Return of Personal Property

Crime victims often lose valuable property to a criminal, only to lose it again during the criminal justice process. For example, a criminal may steal property from the victim, and then the police may apprehend the criminal—and seize the property as evidence. In the subsequent criminal trial, the prosecution may want to use the property as evidence.

Some states have given victims a right to have their property returned, although how broadly those rights should be interpreted remains unclear. For example, California's "Marsy's Law" provides that a victim has a right "to the prompt return of property when no longer needed as evidence." CAL. CONST., art. I. § 28(a)(14). This right seems to be helpful, but does not provide any clear guidance on when the victims has the right, because it is not clear when property is no longer needed as evidence.

Some states have attempted to resolve this problem by providing alternative ways for the evidence to be introduced. For example, an Arizona statute provides:

> A. On request of the victim and after consultation with the prosecuting attorney, the law enforcement agency responsible for investigating the criminal offense shall return to the victim any property belonging to the victim that was taken during the course of the investigation or shall inform the victim of the reasons why the property will not be returned. The law enforcement agency shall make reasonable efforts to return the property to the victim as soon as possible.

> B. If the victim's property has been admitted as evidence during a trial or hearing, the court may order its release to the victim if a photograph can be substituted. If evidence is released pursuant to this subsection, the defendant's attorney or investigator may inspect and independently photograph the evidence before it is released.

ARIZ. REV. STAT. ANN. § 13-4429.

G. Victim Participation in Trials: A Comparative Perspective

In other countries, victims participate in trial more extensively than is allowed in this country. Consider the following comparative perspectives.

Matti Joutsen, *Listening to the Victim: The Victim's Role in European Criminal Systems*
34 WAYNE L. REV. 95 (1995)

Each of the [European] models of victim prosecution assume that the victim wishes to initiate prosecution or to challenge the prosecutor's decision not to prosecute. The [European] victim may participate in the prosecution in other ways. One important means of participation is by serving as a subsidiary or supporting prosecutor. Such a role allows the victim to propose or submit evidence, to provide input regarding the examination of witnesses, and to be heard in court regarding the penal claim. This form of participation is significant for two reasons. First, participation as a subsidiary prosecutor permits a victim to express his concerns and views to the court. Second, since the public prosecutor is primarily responsible for preparing and presenting the case, the victim is relieved of the prosecutorial burden.

The sparse empirical evidence suggests that considerable use is made of the subsidiary prosecutor even in the Federal Republic of Germany, where other modes of victim participation are rarely used. The role of subsidiary prosecutor also formally exists in Austria, Norway, Yugoslavia, and Sweden.

In Poland, the victim may act as subsidiary prosecutor if it is in the best interest of justice. If his participation hampers the proceedings, the court will deprive the victim of this status. In 1976, the Polish Supreme Court clarified the victim's status in Poland, indicating that refusal to allow the victim the role of subsidiary prosecutor should be the exception.

In the other Socialist countries, the victim is generally permitted and at times encouraged to take an active role in the proceedings. At a minimum, the victim is permitted to review the prosecution's case file. The victim may make suggestions regarding the evidence and the examination of witnesses. The victim generally has the right to address the court, primarily by making comments at the conclusion of the trial. . . .

R.P. Peerenboom, *The Victim in Chinese Criminal Theory and Practice: A Historical Survey*
7 J. CHINESE LAW 105 (1993)

* * *

The enactment of a criminal procedure law in 1980 granted formal rights to the [Chinese] victim. Today the victim has the right to bring a supplementary civil suit, and in certain instances the right of private prosecution. In addition, article 87 of the Criminal Procedure Law provides that where the victim is unable to bring complaint because of coercion or intimidation, the people's procuratorate or close relatives of the victim may initiate action.

Other procedural rights include the right to identify suspects, cross-examine the defendant and witnesses (with the approval of the judge), and make a statement after the state has presented its case and before defense responds. The victim may appeal a procuratorate's decision not to prosecute and a court of first instance's verdict with respect to the victim's supplementary civil suit. The victim and his family (and indeed any citizen) "may present petitions regarding judgments or orders that have already become legally effective . . . but the execution of such judgments or orders cannot be suspended."

Despite the array of procedural rights, the victim is not as well off as one might expect. In practice, victims often do not take advantage of the right to bring supplementary civil or privately prosecuted suits. One reason may be the aforementioned lack of a state-funded compensation system. Prosecutors, moreover, are often hostile to such suits. Some fear that the criminal process may become bogged down in lengthy private disputes while serious offenses against the state are neglected. Others believe that a defendant who is subject to punishment has already paid his dues to society. To require compensation for the victim is to over punish. Either the punishment must be reduced or the compensation forgone. Traditional fear of the legal system may also explain the reluctance of victims to pursue their legal rights. Many may feel the best way to resolve the conflict is through informal means. Indeed, even if they do seek legal redress, victims may find themselves forced into mediation. Article 127 states that "A people's court may conduct mediation in a case of private prosecution; before the judgment is announced, a private prosecutor may arrange a settlement on his own with the defendant or may withdraw his private prosecution."

Even the rights provided are not as expansive as some would like. Though victims do have the right to appeal certain decisions, they are not technically a "party" to a publicly prosecuted law and hence cannot appeal the court's decision as to the guilt or sentence of the defendant. Some have argued that the victim ought to be considered a party, or at least given the right to appeal. Similarly, though victims have the right to speak at trial, they must first attain permission from the judge. Perhaps for most victims a greater constraint on speaking than the need to attain the judge's permission is the lack of legal sophistication. Unsure of the law and wary of the formal legal process, many victims simply choose to remain silent. . . .

William T. Pizzi and Walter Perron, *Crime Victims in German Courtrooms: A Comparative Perspective on American Problems*
32 Stan. L. Rev. 37 (1996)

* * *

II. The Right of the Victim to Participate as Secondary Accuser at Criminal Trials in Germany A. The Nebenklage Procedure in Perspective

The German Nebenklage procedure permits victims to participate through counsel at trial on nearly equal footing with the state's attorney and the defense. Since the purpose of this Article is to provide perspective on current efforts of the victims' rights movement in the United States to secure a right to participate and to be heard at critical stages of the criminal process, one might ask why the authors did not begin with an examination of the Nebenklage procedure. There are several reasons for which the authors believe that discussion of the Nebenklage procedure should follow a more general and thorough discussion of the treatment of victims at German criminal trials.

In the first place, the Nebenklage procedure has to be understood as only one difference, among several, in the way victims are treated in the German criminal justice system. Second, the Nebenklage procedure is limited in its availability. It is not a general right of victims to participate in all criminal trials, but rather is available only in the case of serious crimes that have a very personal impact on the victim (or the victim's family), including murder, assault, kidnaping, and sexual assault. Third, even where the Nebenklage procedure is available, victims do not frequently choose to participate in criminal trials as Nebenklager, with the exception of sexual assault victims whose participation as Nebenklager is much more common.

Finally, the Nebenklage procedure can only be understood against the background of a trial system that is structured very differently from that of the American adversarial tradition, as was explained in Part I. Where a criminal trial is conceived of as a battle between the prosecution and the defense in front of a neutral judge, and where the victim will often be the prosecution's "key witness," it is harder from a structural perspective to understand how the victim's independent interests fit into what will usually be a pitched, two-sided battle. By contrast, in German criminal trials, where the judges are obligated to examine all the relevant evidence in the case, and where judges play the central role in both the production and examination of witnesses, no such structural problem exists. Evidence is not divided into "the prosecution's case" to be followed by "the defense case," and the examination of a witness in a German trial is not broken down into a direct examination to be followed by a cross-examination as it is in American trials. In short, the nonadversarial structure of civil law trials makes it easier to accommodate questions from the victim as Nebenklager without seeming to create an imbalance at trial. Given this background, it is not surprising that a willingness to grant victims a right to intervene and participate at various stages of the criminal process is common today among countries that share the civil law tradition.

B. The Nebenklage Procedure Today

Although the Nebenklage procedure has been a part of German criminal procedure since 1877, a major reform of the Nebenklage procedure took place in 1986. It had become clear by the early 1980s that the procedure needed reform, and there was considerable discussion and debate at that time over possible changes. Part of the impetus for reform came from the unsatisfactory way in which the Nebenklage procedure was working in practice. For example, the category of crimes that permitted victim participation seemed at the same time to be too broad and too narrow. It was broad in that it allowed injured traffic accident victims to intervene as Nebenklager, which they frequently did. In such cases, victim participation was driven by the desires of the insurance companies, rather than the wishes of the victims, because the Nebenklage procedure permitted insurance companies to obtain discovery about the accident more efficiently and without the costs that would be involved if the insurance company had to use the civil process to obtain such information. The use of the Nebenklage procedure to further the private interests of insurance companies was certainly not the objective of the procedure, and it was generally recognized that the Code needed reform to prevent this.

At the same time, the category of crimes for which victims were permitted to participate as secondary accusers at trial was too narrow in that sexual assault was not specifically included. Sexual assault victims had been able to use the Nebenklage procedure on the theory that sexual assault involved an assault (which was a listed crime) and also had the sort of personal impact on the victim that justified the use of the procedure. Nonetheless, women's groups argued that the Nebenklage procedure needed to be improved to give victims of sexual assault greater rights to participate at trail; without these rights, such victims arguably were being victimized a second time by the system. Opposition to broadening the Nebenklage procedure came primarily from the defense bar, which argued that adding a secondary accuser, who would stress the victim's point of view at trial, would strengthen the position of the state's attorney in a dispute over procedure or evidence, making it more difficult for the defense attorney to prevail in such confrontations.

The upshot of the debate was a number of important changes to the Nebenklage procedure. First, in order to stop abuse of the Nebenklage procedure by insurance companies interested only in obtaining discovery for civil purposes, assault victims must now allege serious physical injury, or some other damage to themselves or their reputation, in order to join the trial as Nebenklager. A second important change was the addition of sexual assault to the list of Nebenklage-eligible crimes. This means that sexual assault victims no longer have to justify their participation indirectly using the theory that sexual assaults involve assaults, but now can participate based on the sexual assault itself. Because sexual assault is the category of crime in which victims overwhelmingly elect to participate in the trial, the decision to list sexual assault specifically among the crimes in the Nebenklage statute was an important recognition of the special problems that rape victims face in court.

The third change was to broaden the Nebenklage procedure to permit a lawyer representing the victim to participate at pretrial proceedings as well as at trial. This extension has given the victim's lawyer the opportunity to examine the investigative file in advance of trial and to suggest further factual investigations to the state's attorney if the file appears incomplete from the victim's point of view. Psychologically, it has placed the victim's attorney on a more even footing with both the state's attorney and the defense attorney throughout the criminal process.

A fourth major change in the Nebenklage procedure has made it easier for indigent victims to receive legal advice by providing for the payment of their legal fees, including those for pretrial consultation between the victim and an attorney. Such fees will be paid even if the victim ultimately decides not to participate at trial as Nebenklager. This encourages victims to explore their legal options by assuring them that their indigence will not stand in the way of obtaining legal representation. In fact, the extension of legal fees to cover a victim's pretrial consultations with counsel gives an indigent victim some advantages over even an indigent defendant: because the defendant will be responsible for the victim's legal fees should she be convicted, the defendant's financial burden could be considerably greater than the victim's.

This last reform might seem to threaten the German system with a heavy financial burden. However, the provision of legal counsel to indigent victims so that they can participate at trial as Nebenklager is not as costly as it may appear for two reasons. The primary reason is that, as explained earlier, most victims do not choose to participate in the process as Nebenklager, with the important exception of those who have been victims of sexual assault. A second reason is that legal fees for Nebenklager are not nearly as high as they would be in the United States. Because professional judges have the main burden of preparing the case for trial in the German system, pretrial preparation on the part of lawyers is much more limited than it would be for a similar case in the United States. It is not the function of the victim's lawyer (or the defense lawyer or even the state's attorney) to seek out witnesses and to interview such witnesses prior to trial; indeed, the system prefers that lawyers not conduct such interviews. If the victim (or the defendant) tells her lawyer that a certain witness can corroborate her story, the attorney's function is to bring the name of that witness to the attention of the state's attorney, who will then see that the witness is interviewed by the police and that the interview is made a part of the file. Thus, pretrial preparation by the victim's attorney usually entails a careful review of the file and a discussion of its contents with the victim to make sure that it is complete from her point of view; not much more is required in the way of preparation for trial.

_____

Notes

1. Can the lessons from these other countries be adapted and imported into the United States? Or are the criminal justice systems in these other countries so different that the lessons are not instructive? *See* Michael K. Browne, *International Victims' Rights Law: What Can be Gleaned from the Victims' Empowerment Procedures in Germany as the United States Prepared to Consider the Adoption of a "Victim's Rights Amendment" to its Constitution?*, 27 Hamline L. Rev. 15 (2004) (arguing lessons can be instructive on victim's issues); William T. Pizzi, *Victims' Rights: Rethinking Our Adversary System*, 1999 Utah L. Rev. 349 (same); *cf.* Erik Luna, *A Place for Comparative Criminal Procedure*, 42 Brandeis L.J. 277 (2004) (looking to other countries for lessons on defendants' rights); Craig M. Bradley, The Failure of the Criminal Procedure Revolution (1993) (same). *See generally* Markus Dirk Dubber & Bernd Schunemann, *Symposium: Victims and the Criminal Law: American and German Perspectives*, 3 Buff. Crim. L. Rev. 1 (1999) (discussing how criminal law can more fully and legitimately incorporate victims).

2. Should private prosecutions by victims be allowed in human rights trials? *See* Veronica Michel & Kathryn Sikkink, *Human Rights Prosecutions and the Participation Rights of Victims in Latin America*, 47 Law & Soc'y Rev. 873 (2013) (arguing in three Latin American countries private prosecution is the key causal mechanism that allows societal actors to fight in domestic courts for individual criminal accountability for human rights violations).

_____

H. Selected Evidentiary Issues at Trial

Of course, during a trial issues may arise that directly affect the victims. In the earlier chapter on Victim Privacy, for example, we explored "rape shield rules" limiting the admissibility of evidence of a victim's prior sexual history. In this section, we touch on several evidentiary issues directly affecting victims that are not deeply explored in conventional evidence courses, specifically: (1) evidence that personalizes the victim; (2) special rules to accommodate child victims; and (3) the "forfeiture by wrongdoing" doctrine.

1. Evidence that Personalizes the Victim

Information about the history, circumstances, or family of a victim is circumscribed by the rule of evidence that requires information presented to the jury to be "relevant." *See, e.g.,* Federal Rules of Evidence 401 and 402. Application of this basic rule to information about a victim can prove challenging.

For example, in a homicide case, is it relevant for the prosecution to present an "in-life" victim photograph or a "spark of life" photograph? Courts are divided on this issue.

State v. Morrow

834 N.W.2d 715 (Minn. 2013)

Appellant Aaron Morrow appeals his convictions that arise out of an incident in which he repeatedly fired a semiautomatic AK–47 rifle at Joseph Rivera and two of Rivera's friends. A Ramsey County grand jury indicted him with nine counts, including one count of first-degree premeditated murder and two counts of attempted first-degree premeditated murder. Following a jury trial, Morrow was found guilty as charged.

. . .

Morrow's third claim is that the district court erred in admitting spark of life evidence in the form of a photograph of Rivera as a child. We review a district court's decision to admit photographic evidence for an abuse of discretion. *State v. Day,* 619 N.W.2d 745, 751–52 (Minn.2000).

Although "it is true that the quality or personal details of the victim's life are not strictly relevant to the issue of who murdered the victim, it would seem to tie unduly the hands of the prosecutor to prohibit any mention of the victim's life." *State v. Graham,* 371 N.W.2d 204, 207 (Minn.1985). Because "[t]he victim was not just bones and sinews covered with flesh, but was imbued with the spark of life[,] [t]he prosecution has some leeway to show that spark and present the victim as a human being." *Id.* The State may present spark of life evidence so long as it is not an attempt to invoke undue sympathy or inflame the passions of the jury. *Id.* We have previously held that the district court did not err in allowing spark of life evidence that

included testimony by the victim's brother about the victim's "childhood, his education, his career, and his family" and "a photograph of [the victim] with his wife and
two children at a Christmas party, and . . . a portrait of [the victim] in his police uniform." *State v. Evans,* 756 N.W.2d 854, 878 (Minn.2008). Similarly, we have affirmed
the admission of spark of life photographs "where the photographs were used to provide background information about the family and to personalize [the victim] and
where the number of photographs used for these purposes was small." *State v. Scales,*
518 N.W.2d 587, 593 (Minn.1994).

At trial, the State sought to admit a photograph of Rivera and D.C. taken during
their childhood. Morrow objected, arguing that the photograph was inappropriate
spark of life evidence that should be excluded. The district court allowed the State to
use the photograph, but cautioned the State to rely on the photograph in a manner
that was not calculated to create sympathy for Rivera.

On appeal, Morrow argues that the district court erred in admitting the photograph because it was used to invoke undue sympathy for Rivera and inflame the
passions of the jury. Morrow also suggests that the spark of life photograph prejudiced his claim of self-defense and defense of others by depicting Rivera and D.C. as
young children, because they were grown men at the time of the shooting. The State
contends that the photograph was admissible spark of life evidence.

As in *Evans* and *Scales,* we conclude that the district court did not err in admitting the childhood photograph of Rivera and D.C. The photograph was shown
while D.C. was testifying as to his childhood friendship with Rivera and was briefly
discussed. The State did not rely on the photograph or discuss Rivera's life in the
course of opening or closing statements, and there is nothing in the record to otherwise suggest that the State used the photograph to invoke undue sympathy or
inflame the jury's passions. Rather, the photo was mentioned at the beginning of
the trial when the State briefly outlined Rivera's life and gave background about his
relationship with others involved in the shooting, and was well within the bounds
of the spark of life doctrine. Finally, Morrow's argument that the photo was prejudicial because it undermined his claim of self-defense and defense of others lacks
merit. As noted, the picture was briefly presented, and given that the jury saw D.C.
testify, saw pictures of Rivera's body, and heard testimony about Rivera's stature, it
is unreasonable to conclude that the jury considered the childhood photograph
when evaluating Morrow's justification defenses. For all of these reasons, we hold
that the district court did not err in admitting the spark of life photograph of Rivera
and D.C.

People v. McClelland

350 P.3d 976 (Colo. App. 2015)

Photographs are admissible if they depict relevant facts and are not unnecessarily
inflammatory so as to incite the jury to unfair prejudice against the defendant. *See*

People v. Moreland, 193 Colo. 237, 243, 567 P.2d 355, 360 (1977); *Hampton v. People,* 171 Colo. 153, 166, 465 P.2d 394, 401 (1970).

Several Colorado appellate courts have held that "in life" photographs of homicide victims are admissible. *See People v. Loscutoff,* 661 P.2d 274, 277 (Colo. 1983) (no abuse of discretion in admitting photographs of a murder victim and her young son, taken several months before the murder); *People v. Clary,* 950 P.2d 654, 658 (Colo. App. 1997) (no abuse of discretion in admitting enlarged school photograph of victim); *People v. T.R.,* 860 P.2d 559, 562 (Colo. App. 1993) (no abuse of discretion in admitting photographs of victim and her husband taken eight months before the victim was killed).

However, our courts have not adopted a per se rule allowing "in life" photographs of homicide victims; rather, each decision applied CRE 403's balancing test to determine whether the probative value of the "in life" photographs was substantially outweighed by the risk of unfair prejudice to the defendant.

Alternatively, various other jurisdictions have held that "in life" photographs of homicide victims were inadmissible because of their minimal probative value and the danger that their introduction is merely a means of "engendering sympathy for the victim with the intent of creating an atmosphere of prejudice against the defendant." *Commonwealth v. Rivers,* 537 Pa. 394, 407, 644 A.2d 710, 716 (1994); *see Wilks v. State,* 49 P.3d 975, 983 (Wyo. 2002) ("Admission of homicide victims' 'in life' photographs is discouraged and should be permitted under only very limited circumstances where their relevancy outweighs the potential to inflame the jury."); *see also United States v. Pettigrew,* 468 F.3d 626, 638 (10th Cir. 2006) ("The proffering of a photograph of the deceased victim, while living and posed with her family, as opposed to a photo depicting only the decedent, 'needlessly pushes the prosecutorial envelope, and could, if coupled with errors not present here, jeopardize a conviction.'") (quoting *United States v. Jones,* 24 Fed.Appx. 968, 975 (10th Cir. 2001); *Valdez v. State,* 900 P.2d 363, 381 (Okla. Crim. App. 1995) ("In life" photos inadmissible if they have no probative value.), *superseded by statute as stated in Coddington v. State,* 142 P.3d 437 (Okla. Crim. App. 2006).

These cases establish that "in life" photographs of homicide victims are not per se inadmissible; rather, their admissibility must be determined on a case by case basis. The parties have not identified, nor have we found, any Colorado appellate cases addressing the admissibility of "in life" photographs of a homicide victim where, as here, the defendant claims he acted in self-defense.

The People introduced the photographs of B.B. to establish that he was alive prior to the shooting. Evidence that B.B. was once alive was of consequence to the charges of murder and reckless manslaughter because both crimes require proof that the defendant "caused the death of a person." Therefore, we conclude that the three "in life" photographs were relevant.

Turning to the CRE 403 balancing, we first address the probative value of the three "in life" photographs. "[E]vidence offered to prove undisputed facts has marginal probative value." *Yusem*, 210 P.3d at 468; *see also Masters*, 58 P.3d at 1001; *Vialpando*, 727 P.2d at 1096. Neither B.B.'s identity as the victim, nor whether he was alive at the time of the shooting was disputed. These facts were established by eyewitness testimony, and neither was important to the central issue at trial—whether McClelland's use of force was reasonable.

In short, the "in life" photographs were evidence of an undisputed fact.

We next address the danger of unfair prejudice. The central issue in the case was the reasonableness of McClelland's use of deadly force. This required the jury to evaluate B.B.'s conduct during the confrontation with the McClellands, including his physical appearance and demeanor immediately prior to the shooting.

The three "in life" photographs portrayed a different image of B.B. than that presented by the eyewitness testimony, on which the prosecution unfairly capitalized during its opening and closing arguments. The testimony established that B.B. was yelling and intoxicated immediately prior to the shooting.

Conversely, the three "in life" photographs of B.B. depicted a man smiling in the company of his immediate family members. One depicted B.B. with his son on his son's wedding day. In another, he was flanked by his father and son at a car show.

Further, the People's continual reference to the "in life" photographs and emphasis on B.B.'s family heightened the likelihood that the jury's decision was based on sympathy. The People's opening statement started with a reference to one of the photographs:

> This is [B.B.]. He was somebody's father. Somebody's son. Somebody's brother. Recently he would have become a grandfather. He was a fan of NAS-CAR, Dale Earnhardt in particular. He was a mechanic. His father, Del, would describe him as an exceptional mechanic. [B.B.] was 50 years old when he was needlessly and brutally murdered by the defendant, Logan McClelland.

> In their initial closing argument, the People reiterated that, "[B.B.] was somebody's father. Somebody's son. [Somebody's] brother. Somebody's friend." Similarly, in rebuttal closing argument, the People stated, "[B.B.] is not a ticking time bomb. He is a human being. He's somebody's father. Somebody's brother. Somebody's friend."

We conclude that the admission of the three "in life" photographs unfairly prejudiced McClelland under the circumstances presented here. McClelland asserted he was acting in defense of himself and his father, and B.B.'s demeanor immediately prior to the shooting was a crucial issue at trial. The only visual depiction of B.B. the jury saw portrayed a different image than that presented by the eyewitness testimony. *See People v. Sepeda*, 196 Colo. 13, 22, 581 P.2d 723, 730 (1978) ("As has been said, one picture is worth a thousand words. . . .").

Because the three "in life" photographs had almost no probative value, and because the prosecutor sought to elicit the jury's sympathy based on those photographs during opening statement, trial testimony, and closing arguments, we conclude that the admission of the three "in life" photographs unfairly prejudiced McClelland.

Therefore, we further conclude that the trial court erred when it admitted three "in life" photographs of B.B. However, the prosecution is not necessarily prohibited from introducing "in life" photographs of B.B. on retrial. Rather, on retrial, the court should reconsider whether to allow "in life" photographs in light of the above discussion, and if so, how many, and whether to limit the prosecution's comments about them so as to avoid the risk of unfair prejudice.

Notes

1. Several states have disagreed with *McClelland* and created an absolute right for admission of an "in life" photograph during a homicide case. *See, e.g.,* OR. REV. STAT. ANN. § 41.415 ("In a prosecution for any criminal homicide, a photograph of the victim while alive shall be admissible evidence when offered by the district attorney to show the general appearance and condition of the victim while alive."); TENN. CODE ANN. § 40-38-103 ("In a prosecution for any criminal homicide, an appropriate photograph of the victim while alive shall be admissible evidence when offered by the district attorney general to show the general appearance and condition of the victim while alive."). *See* Paul G. Cassell, *Balancing the Scales of Justice: The Case for and Effects of Utah's Victims' Rights Amendments*, 1994 UTAH L. REV. 1373, 1407 (arguing for such statutes).

2. Many other cases take a more generous view of the circumstances in which "in life" photographs are relevant in a homicide prosecution. *See, e.g., State v. Yates*, 161 Wash. 2d 714, 771, 168 P.3d 359, 390 (2007) (affirming admission of in life photographs because they were relevant to the State's proof of a "common scheme or plan" and assisted the jury in assimilating the evidence); *Taylor v. State*, 304 Ga. App. 573, 576, 696 S.E.2d 498, 502 (2010) ("in life" photographs were admissible for comparison with photographs of the victim after death to prove the identity of the victim).

3. The issue of "in life" photographs is simply an example of a larger issue of whether a prosecutor should be allowed to personalize a victim. For example, in *Lewis v. State*, 24 So. 3d 480 (Ala. Ct. Crim. App. 2006), the prosecutor in a murder case argued in his opening statement that he expected the victim's mother, Sarah Kaye, to testify that her son had purchased a bracelet for his daughter and that a birthday card he had picked out for her was found at his residence. The Court found no error, explain that "Although [t]he comments did personalize the victim, . . . they were brief enough that we cannot conclude that they injected prejudicial or irrelevant material into the sentencing decision."

4. Similar issues about the relevance of a victim's background can arise during closing arguments in a prosecution. For example, *People v. McLean*, 276 N.E.2d 72 (Ill. App. Ct. 1971), reversed a conviction because the prosecutor informed the jury of the existence of the decedent's family. In his closing argument, the State's Attorney stated:

Now ladies and gentlemen, we understand that you have a very solemn duty to perform. We understand without doubt that you are going to be sympathetic because this is a youthful person, no question about it, but we ask you, ought you not also to be sympathetic for the deceased who was also a young person? Ought you not be sympathetic for the family of Loran Overturf, who had a right to have this son live a normal and full and healthy life? This boy was also young. He was also unarmed at the time that he was shot down by this punk.

The Court reversed because these facts were not material to the question of guilt or innocence.

5. If prejudicial evidence about a victim is admitted, admonitory instructions by the trial judge are normally adequate to remedy any error. Thus, a prosecutor's remark in closing argument that the victim's children and wife had a right to the love of the victim was held to be improper, but did not warrant reversal in the face of other evidence of guilt and a trial court's admonition to the jury to disregard the statement. *People v. Thanas*, 486 N.E.2d 1312 (1985), app. den., 490 N.E.2d 701 (1985).

6. In sentencing proceedings, personalization of the victim is generally permitted. *See* Chapter 10 on Sentencing *infra*.

————————

2. Accommodation of Child Witnesses

Testimony by child witnesses presents special problems, particularly in cases involving sexual abuse. In recent years, many states have tried to facilitate the prosecution of child abuse cases by allowing the prosecution to use hearsay statements recounting statements by child victims rather than requiring the victims to testify themselves, as explained in the following article:

Tanya Asim Cooper, *Sacrificing the Child to Convict the Defendant: Secondary Traumatization of Child Witnesses by Prosecutors, Their Inherent Conflict of Interest, and the Need for Child Witness Counsel*
9 Cardozo Pub. L. Pol'y & Ethics J. 239 (2011)

Today, children have broad and specific rights recognized by law to address their needs as victims and witnesses, including rights of protection, privacy, and participation in the criminal justice system; and the provision for and recognition of these rights by the legislature and judiciary signifies a discernible shift in the law. Congress, federal courts, the Supreme Court, and at least thirty-three states now deem child witness interests important in the administration of criminal justice.

In the 1980s, as awareness of child abuse grew, the Supreme Court recognized the vulnerable and unique role child witnesses play in criminal prosecutions, as well as their need for privacy and protection. For example, in the landmark case Pennsylvania

v. Ritchie, 480 U.S. 39 (1987), the Supreme Court held that while the accused is entitled to ask the trial court to review child protective services' files for information material to the preparation of the defense (and for use in cross-examination), he State has a compelling interest in maintaining the confidentiality of its child protection records.

Throughout the 1980s, the Supreme Court struggled to balance the rights of the accused with the government's interest in protecting the child witness from direct confrontation. In Kentucky v. Stincer, 482 U.S. 730 (1987), the Supreme Court found that the criminal defendant had no Sixth Amendment right to confront witnesses against him at a pretrial competency hearing. The Court held that the defendant's exclusion from the pretrial competency hearing of the seven- and eight-year-old girls whom he allegedly sexually abused did not violate his Sixth Amendment right to be confronted by the witnesses against him, especially where his counsel was present at the pretrial hearing, and where at trial, the girls were cross-examined in his presence.

However, just the next year, in *Coy v. Iowa*, the Supreme Court held that the use of screens to separate the testifying child witnesses from the accused at trial violated the Sixth Amendment right to confrontation. In *Coy*, the child witnesses were two thirteen-year-old girls who had been sexually assaulted by a man they could not identify while camping in their backyard. An Iowa statute allowed the trial judge to place a specially-designed screen between the criminal defendant and the children during their testimony. The screen allowed the defendant to dimly see the witnesses but it obstructed their view of him entirely. The defendant objected that the procedure violated his Sixth Amendment and due process rights and made him appear guilty. The Supreme Court agreed. Iowa's enabling statute presumed trauma to the testifying children, but without requiring any individualized findings that the children actually needed special protection, that presumption of trauma was not enough to overcome the defendant's right of confrontation.

Two significant cases that changed the legal landscape for child witnesses were argued and decided on the same day by the Supreme Court in 1990. In *Idaho v. Wright*, the Supreme Court held that admitting the hearsay statements of a child sexual abuse victim to an examining physician under Idaho's residual hearsay exception violated the defendant's Sixth Amendment right to confrontation. In *Wright*, after two sisters, ages 5½ and 2½, disclosed that they were sexually molested by the older girl's father, they were subsequently interviewed by a pediatrician about the abuse. During the younger sister's examination, when questioned about her own abuse, she volunteered information about her sister's abuse to the pediatrician. At trial, the younger girl, who had since turned three years old, was deemed "incapable of communicating with the jury." Instead, the pediatrician testified to what she told him, which the trial court admitted under the residual hearsay exception. The Court found that Idaho had not met its burden of proving that the younger girl's statement "bore sufficient indicia of reliability to withstand scrutiny under the [Confrontation] Clause" because Idaho's residual hearsay exception was not firmly rooted, and because the doctor used leading and suggestive questions and the interview was not recorded, the three-year-old's statement lacked particularized guarantees of trustworthiness.

The next significant decision to impact the law on child witnesses was *Maryland v. Craig*, in which the Court upheld Maryland's statute allowing child witnesses to testify via one-way closed circuit television, without seeing the defendant, because Maryland's statute required that the trial court make an individualized finding and "determine that testimony by the child victim in the courtroom will result in the child suffering serious emotional distress such that the child cannot reasonably communicate." The child witnesses in *Craig* included a six-year-old girl and other young children who were sexually abused while attending Craig's kindergarten class. In support of its motion for the testimonial accommodation, Maryland offered expert testimony that the children would have difficulty testifying in Craig's presence.

Although the defendant objected that the procedure violated her constitutional right to confrontation, the Court held that the right to confrontation is not an absolute, but a trial right, noting that "the Confrontation Clause reflects a preference for face-to-face confrontation at trial 'that must occasionally give way to considerations of public policy and the necessities of the case.'" The *Craig* Court approved the use of closed-circuit television because the Maryland statute preserved the other elements of the Confrontation Clause: the child witnesses were found competent to testify, testified under oath, the defendant had the contemporaneous opportunity to cross-examine them, and all could view the child witnesses' demeanor.

Maryland's interest, moreover, "in protecting child witnesses from the trauma of testifying in a child abuse case is sufficiently important to justify" procedures that depart from face-to-face confrontation with the defendant. "We have of course recognized that a State's interest in 'the protection of minor victims of sex crimes from further trauma and embarrassment' is a 'compelling' one." The Craig court articulated three findings a trial court must make to justify such a special procedure: 1) "[t]he trial court must hear evidence and determine whether use of the one-way closed circuit television procedure is necessary to protect the welfare of the particular child witness who seeks to testify"; 2) "[t]he trial court must also find that the child witness would be traumatized, not by the courtroom generally, but by the presence of the defendant"; and 3) "the trial court must find that the emotional distress suffered by the child witness in the presence of the defendant is more than de minimis, i.e., more than 'mere nervousness or excitement or some reluctance to testify[.]'" In *Craig*, the Supreme Court concluded that "where face-to-face confrontation causes significant emotional distress in a child witness, there is evidence that such confrontation would in fact disserve the Confrontation Clause's truth-seeking goal."

"In direct response to *Craig*," as part of the Crime Control Act of 1990, Congress enacted the Victims of Child Abuse Act of 1990 (VCAA). In this statute, Congress enabled child victims and witnesses with rights in federal court to request protection from directly confronting the defendant with an order "that the child's testimony be taken in a room outside the courtroom and be televised by two-way closed circuit television." However, a court may order the child witness's testimony to be taken by closed-circuit television only after making "a case-specific finding that a child witness would suffer substantial fear or trauma and be unable to testify or communicate reasonably because of the physical presence of the defendant." The VCAA also protects the privacy of the child witnesses' names and information from unfettered disclosure, and ensures children's views are heard without delay. Federal courts have upheld the constitutionality of the statute's provisions for children's protection, privacy, and participation.

Two years after *Craig*, in *White v. Illinois*, the Supreme Court held that the four-year-old, sexually-abused girl's out-of-court statements were admissible as exceptions to the hearsay rule, without requiring the trial court to find the child witness unavailable to testify. The prosecution attempted to have the child witness testify twice: "she apparently experienced emotional difficulty on being brought to the courtroom and in each instance left without testifying." But the trial court made no finding that the child witness was unavailable to testify. The Court declined to impose an "unavailability rule" and found "it clear that the out-of-court statements admitted in this case had substantial probative value, value that could not be duplicated simply by the [child witness] later testifying in court." The Court specifically declined to find a "necessity" requirement applied here, as it had required in *Coy* and *Craig*, because those cases involved in-court procedures that are constitutionally required once a child witness testifies, rather than requirements the Confrontation Clause imposes for the admission of out-of-court declarations.

In 2005, fifteen years after Congress enacted the VCAA, the Crime Victims' Rights Act (CVRA) was passed, affording crime victims many participation rights, including: the right to timely and accurate notice of public court proceedings; the right not to be excluded from public court proceedings; the right to be heard at public court proceedings involving release, plea, sentencing, and parole proceedings; the right to full and timely restitution; the right to proceedings free from unreasonable delay; the right to confer with the prosecutor; and the right to be treated with fairness and respect. In enacting the CVRA, Congress granted victims, and therefore child victim witnesses, the right to be protected from the accused.

In 2009, the American Bar Association adopted several policies "to address the concerns and needs of young children who have to appear in court . . . . Justice requires that, to the extent possible, judges and prosecutors advise victims of their rights and confirm that the victims have understood the rights." The ABA developed a list of ten rights for child witnesses and their guardians:

> 1. You have the right to know what is happening in the court case that came about from the report you made.
>
> 2. You have the right to be in court whenever the judge and the prosecutor are there to discuss the case, before a trial starts.
>
> 3. You have the right to request to speak to the judge anytime the judge makes a major decision in the case.
>
> 4. If you lost money or something valuable was stolen from you or damaged as a result of the crime, you have the right to ask the court to make the defendant pay you back for what you have lost.

5. If your property was stolen and has been recovered you have a right to get your property back as soon as possible.

6. If you are scared or feel threatened, you have the right to ask the judge to provide reasonable protection before, during, and after the trial.

7. There are services and people you can talk to outside of the courtroom about what you are feeling.

8. If you would like to talk to someone privately without your parents or legal guardian knowing, you may ask the judge to appoint a guardian or attorney to represent you.

9. You have the right to ask the judge to allow your parents, your guardian, or another adult whom you trust to be present with you during your testimony.

10. Whether or not there is a trial, you have the right to know if the defendant is sent to jail or prison and, if so, when the defendant is expected to be released.

As a result of the actions of the Supreme Court, Congress, the states, and policymakers, child witnesses' rights have evolved considerably. Probably the most recognized right that children in criminal litigation possess today is the right to protection as testifying witnesses from directly confronting the accused, notwithstanding the express dictates of the Sixth Amendment.[133] Recognizing that child witnesses need protection from direct confrontation, and that this need is clear and compelling, the Supreme Court has legitimized the testimonial experiences of victimized children. With VCAA and CVRA, Congress has codified children's rights to protection, privacy, and participation, which lower courts have upheld.

Note

Should special accommodations for child victims be addressed specifically by statute or court rule? Or should the issue simply be left to the sound discretion of the trial court under general rules giving trial judges ability to manage their cases?

---

3. Forfeiture by Wrongdoing

In recent years, the Supreme Court has taken a restrictive view of admitting hearsay in criminal cases. In particular, in *Crawford v. Washington*, 541 U.S. 36 (2004), the Court drew a firm line against the admissibility of out-of-court "testimony" statements in most circumstances in criminal cases. The general application of *Crawford* is often discussed in evidence classes.

Of particular interest for purposes of crime victims' issues is how *Crawford* might affect the prosecution of domestic violence and battery cases. For example, in

Giles v. California, 554 U.S. 353 (2008), the Court considered an argument that a defendant has "forfeited" his right to exclude out-of-court statements made by a murder victim to police responding to an earlier domestic violence call. Relying heavily on the lack of a historically recognized exception to confrontation rights in such circumstances, the Supreme Court ruled that a defendant does not forfeit his confrontation rights under *Crawford* unless, when he murders the victim, the evidence shows he also intended to silence her as a witness.

The case prompted an interesting exchange about whether domestic violence cases present special challenges that should be recognized in the doctrine.

Giles v. California
554 U.S. 353 (2008)

Justice Scalia for the Court:

. . .

The dissent closes by pointing out that a forfeiture rule which ignores *Crawford* would be particularly helpful to women in abusive relationships — or at least particularly helpful in punishing their abusers. Not as helpful as the dissent suggests, since only *testimonial* statements are excluded by the Confrontation Clause. Statements to friends and neighbors about abuse and intimidation and statements to physicians in the course of receiving treatment would be excluded, if at all, only by hearsay rules, which are free to adopt the dissent's version of forfeiture by wrongdoing. In any event, we are puzzled by the dissent's decision to devote its peroration to domestic-abuse cases. Is the suggestion that we should have one Confrontation Clause (the one the Framers adopted and *Crawford* described) for all other crimes, but a special, improvised, Confrontation Clause for those crimes that are frequently directed against women? Domestic violence is an intolerable offense that legislatures may choose to combat through many means — from increasing criminal penalties to adding resources for investigation and prosecution to funding awareness and prevention campaigns. But for that serious crime, as for others, abridging the constitutional rights of criminal defendants is not in the State's arsenal.

The domestic-violence context is, however, relevant for a separate reason. Acts of domestic violence often are intended to dissuade a victim from resorting to outside help, and include conduct designed to prevent testimony to police officers or cooperation in criminal prosecutions. Where such an abusive relationship culminates in murder, the evidence may support a finding that the crime expressed the intent to isolate the victim and to stop her from reporting abuse to the authorities or cooperating with a criminal prosecution — rendering her prior statements admissible under the forfeiture doctrine. Earlier abuse, or threats of abuse, intended to dissuade the victim from resorting to outside help would be highly relevant to this inquiry, as would evidence of ongoing criminal proceedings at which the victim would have been expected to testify.

Justice Souter, concurring part:

. . .

The rule of forfeiture is implicated primarily where domestic abuse is at issue. In such a case, a murder victim may have previously given a testimonial statement, say, to the police, about an abuser's attacks; and introduction of that statement may be at issue in a later trial for the abuser's subsequent murder of the victim. This is not an uncommon occurrence. Each year, domestic violence results in more than 1,500 deaths and more than 2 million injuries; it accounts for a substantial portion of all homicides; it typically involves a history of repeated violence; and it is difficult to prove in court because the victim is generally reluctant or unable to testify. See Bureau of Justice Statistics, Homicide Trends in the U.S. 1976–2005, online at http://www .ojp.usdoj.gov/bjs/homicide/tables/relationshiptab.htm (as visited June 23, 2008, and available in Clerk of Court's case file); Dept. of Health and Human Services, Centers for Disease Control and Prevention, National Center for Injury Prevention and Control, Costs of Intimate Partner Violence Against Women in the United States (2003); N. Websdale, Understanding Domestic Homicide (1999); Lininger, Prosecuting Batterers after *Crawford*, 91 Va. L. Rev. 747, 751, 768–769 (2005).

Regardless of a defendant's purpose, threats, further violence, and ultimately murder can stop victims from testifying. See *id.*, at 769 (citing finding that batterers threaten retaliatory violence in as many as half of all cases, and 30 percent of batterers assault their victims again during the prosecution). A *constitutional* evidentiary requirement that insists upon a showing of purpose (rather than simply intent or probabilistic knowledge) may permit the domestic partner who made the threats, caused the violence, or even murdered the victim to avoid conviction for earlier crimes by taking advantage of later ones.

In *Davis*, we recognized that "domestic violence" cases are "notoriously susceptible to intimidation or coercion of the victim to ensure that she does not testify at trial." 547 U.S., at 832–833. We noted the concern that "[w]hen this occurs, the Confrontation Clause gives the criminal a windfall." *Id.*, at 833. And we replied to that concern by stating that "one who obtains the absence of a witness by wrongdoing forfeits the constitutional right to confrontation." *Ibid.* To the extent that it insists upon an additional showing of purpose, the Court breaks the promise implicit in those words and, in doing so, grants the defendant not fair treatment, but a windfall. I can find no history, no underlying purpose, no administrative consideration, and no constitutional principle that requires this result.

---

4. Word Bans

In some cases, judges have banned witness from using certain words during their testimony. For example, in one case that created concern among anti-rape advocates, a judge prohibited the prosecutrix in a rape case from using the word "rape." Here are the facts are recounted in a law review article examining the issue:s.

Randah Atassi, *Silencing Tory Bowen: The Legal Implications of Word Bans in Rape Trials*
43 J. Marshall L. Rev. 215 (2009)

The scholarship on the role of emotion in law does not seek to establish that there are no significant differences between

In October 2004 following a Halloween party, Tory Bowen left a downtown Lincoln, Nebraska, bar with Pamir Safi — who later allegedly sexually assaulted her. Bowen has no memory of leaving the bar, and the next thing she remembers is regaining consciousness with Safi already on top of her. Safi was charged with first-degree sexual assault, and the case went to trial. Following a motion by defense counsel, Judge Jeffrey Cheuvront entered an order to exclude the use of such words as "rape" and "victim" but allowed Bowen to use words like "sex" or "intercourse," despite the prosecution's attempt to get those words banned as well. The judge later modified the ruling to allow the use of "sexual assault." Bowen said being forced to use the word "sex" to describe her experience was like being assaulted all over again. The first case ended in a mistrial because the jury could not reach a unanimous verdict.

Following the trial, free speech and feminist activists took up Bowen's cause. The second trial ended with Judge Cheuvront declaring a mistrial because protesters had interfered with jury selection, and the case was not pursued a third time. Bowen filed a lawsuit in federal court, which was dismissed, challenging Cheuvront's actions on the grounds that they violated her constitutional rights. She said she would appeal the decision to the Supreme Court if necessary, and she did just that, but the Supreme Court denied certiorari.

The reasoning behind the judge's decision to allow the word ban was that the word "rape" in a victim's testimony might be unfairly prejudicial to the defendant, who is presumed innocent until proven guilty. Another justification was that use of the word "rape" would allow the witness to testify to a legal conclusion. Judge Cheuvront cited a state law that allowed him to ban words that might be unfairly prejudicial to the defendant.

Note

Is it appropriate for a trial judge to instruct witnesses, including victims, what words they can use during a trial? Would it be better to just leave the subject of word choice up to cross-examination by opposing counsel?

Chapter 10

Sentencing and Parole

Introduction

This chapter discusses victims' participation at sentencing and parole hearings and related issues surrounding criminal sentencing. The chapter begins with a discussion of victim impact statements, first describing those statements, reviewing constitutional limitations on those statements, and debating the wisdom of those statements. The chapter then reviews the law on whether a victim impact statement may go beyond describing the impact of the crime to include a victim's opinion as to what specific sentence is appropriate. After a quick review of victim impact statements at parole hearings, the chapter turns to other aspects of sentencing: restitution for victims' losses from a crime and limitations on a defendant's ability to profit from a crime. The chapter ends with a consideration of restorative proceedings— such as victim-offender face-to-face confrontation.

A. Victim Impact Statements

1. Legal Authority for Victim Impact Statements

At sentencing, virtually all states and the federal government allow a victim to present information bearing on the appropriate sentence in the form of a "victim impact statement" (or "VIS"). A victim can present such a statement in writing to a probation officer preparing a pre-sentence report for a judge or in open court to the sentencing judge (and to the defendant).

ILLINOIS CONST., art. I, § 8.1

Crime victims, as defined by law, shall have the following rights as provided by law:

. . . (5) The right to be heard at any post-arraignment court proceeding in which a right of the victim is at issue and any court proceeding involving a post-arraignment release decision, plea, or sentencing.

NEBRASKA CONST., art. I, § 28

(1) A victim of a crime, as shall be defined by law, or his or her guardian or representative shall have . . . the right to be informed of, be present at, and make an oral or written statement at sentencing, parole, pardon, commutation, and conditional release proceedings.

18 U.S.C. Sec 3771

(a) Rights of Crime Victims. A crime victim has the following rights:

. . . (4) The right to be reasonably heard at any public proceeding in the district court involving release, plea, sentencing, or any parole proceeding.

2. An Example

What does a victim impact statement look like? An illustration of a powerful statement comes from the sentencing of two men, Donald Coleman and Cedric Coleman, convicted of the federal offense of carjacking. The Colemans murdered John Luttig and injured his wife Bobbie Luttig while stealing their car from their garage. At sentencing, John Luttig's son—Michael Luttig—gave the following powerful statement in court asking for the maximum possible sentence for carjacking: life in prison.

Statement of Michael Luttig

Reprinted in TEXAS LAWYER, Mar. 20, 1995, at 4

May it please the court. It is one of life's ironies that I appear before the court for the reason that I do. But I do so to represent my dad—who is not here—and his wife, and daughters. His family, my family.

More than anything else, I do this to honor him, because if the roles were reversed, he would be standing here today, of this I am certain.

I also owe this to the other victims of violent crime who either stand silently by, or who speak and are not heard.

I owe it to the public.

I owe it, as well, to Donald and Cedric Coleman, who may not yet understand the magnitude of the losses they inflicted on the night of April 19.

Words seem trite in describing what follows when your husband is murdered in your presence, when your father is stripped from your life the horror, the agony, the emptiness, the despair, the chaos, the confusion, the sense—perhaps temporary, but perhaps not—that ones life no longer has any purpose, the doubt, the hopelessness. There are no words that can possibly describe it, and all it entails.

But being the victim of a violent crime such as this is the least of these things. Exactly these things in my family's case; the equivalent of these things in the countless other cases.

While it is happening and in the seconds and the minutes thereafter . . .

. . . it's the sheer horror of half-clothed people with guns storming up your drive-way toward you in the dark of night, when you are totally defenseless.

. . . it's what must be the terrifying realization that you are first about to be, and then actually being, murdered.

. . . it's crawling on the floor of your own garage in the grease and filth, pretend-ing you're dead, so that you won't be shot through the head by the person who just murdered your husband.

. . . it's realizing your husband has been gunned down in your driveway on your return from the final class you needed to complete your education—an education that had been the goal of both of you since the day you were married.

. . . it's knowing that the reason that your husband was with you—indeed, the rea-son that you were in the car that night at all—is that his Christmas gift to you the previous year was the promise you could take the class and that he would take you to and from, so that nothing would happen to you.

. . . it's mercilessly punishing yourself over whether you could have done some-thing, anything at all, to have stopped the killing.

Moments later, across a continent . . .

. . . it's being frightened out of your mind in the middle of the night by a frantic banging on your door—calling the police, then canceling the call—and then answer-ing the door. Your body goes limp as you see one of your best friends standing in the doorway. No words need even be spoken. For you know that the worst in life has hap-pened. Then he tells you: "Your Mom just called. Father was just murdered in the driveway of your home."

. . . it's realizing that, at that very moment, the man who you have worshiped all your life is lying on his back in your driveway with two bullets through his head.

Across the globe . . .

. . . it's your husband taking the emergency international call, putting down the receiver, fumbling for the words, as he starts to deliver the news. "This is the hardest thing I will ever have to tell you," he begins.

Then, it is the calls home, or at least to what used to be home, first one, then the other. In eerie stunned calmness, you hear your mother utter the feared confir-mation: "Yes, your dad was just murdered. You better come home." Now you believe.

Within hours . . .

. . . it's arriving home to television cameras in your front yard, to see your house cordoned off by police lines; police conducting ballistics and forensics tests, and studying the place in the driveway where your father had finally fallen dead—all as if it were a set from a television production.

. . . it's going down to the store where your dad had always shopped for clothes, to buy a shirt, a tie that will match his suit, and a package of three sets of underwear (you can only buy them in sets of three) so your dad will look nice when he is buried.

. . . it's being called by the funeral home and told that it recommends that the casket be closed and that perhaps your mom, sister, and wife should not see the body — and you know why, without even asking.

In the days that follow . . .

. . . it's living in a hotel in your own hometown, blocks away from where you have lived your whole life, because you just can't bear to go back.

. . . it's packing up the family home, item by item, memory by memory, as if all of the lives that were there only hours before are no more.

. . . it's reading the letters from you, your sister, and your wife, that your dad secreted away in his most private places, unbeknownst to you. Realizing that the ones he invariably saved were the ones that just said "thanks" or "I love you." And really understanding for the first time that that truly was all that he ever needed to hear or to receive in return, just as he always told you.

In the weeks thereafter . . .

. . . it's living in absolute terror, not knowing who had murdered your husband and tried to murder you, but realizing that often such people come back to complete the deed, and wondering if they would return this time.

. . . it's never spending another night in your own home because the pain is too great and the memories too fresh.

. . . it's all day every day, and all night, racking your brain to the point of literal exhaustion over who possibly could have done this. It's questioningly looking in the corners of every relationship, to the point that, at times, you are almost ashamed of yourself. Yet you have no choice but to continue, because, as they say, it could be anyone.

Then they are finally found, and . . .

. . . it's collapsing on the kitchen floor when you are told — not from relief, but from the ultimate despair in learning that your husband was indeed killed for nothing but a car, and in an act so random as to defy comprehension.

. . . it's watching your mother collapse on the floor when she hears this news and knowing that she will not just have to relive the fateful night in her own mind, now she will have to relive it in public courtrooms, over and over again, for months on end.

In the months that follow. . . .

. . . it's putting the family home up for sale and being told that everyone thinks it is beautiful, but they just don't think they could live there, because a murder took place in the driveway.

... it's the humiliation of being told by the credit card companies, after they closed your husband's accounts because of his death, that they are unable to extend your credit because you are not currently employed.

... it's receiving an anonymous letter that begins, "I just learned of the brutal carjacking and murder of your father," and that ends by saying, "I only wish your mother had been raped and murdered too.'

... it's the crushing anxiety of awaiting the trauma and uncertainties of public trials.

The day arrives, and ...

... it's listening, for the first time, to the tape of your mother's 9-1-1 call to report that her husband, your father, had been murdered. Hearing the terror in her voice, catching yourself before you pass out from the shock of knowing that, through the tape, you are present at the very moment it all happened.

... it's hearing the autopsy report on how the bullets entered your father's skull, penetrated and exited his brain, and went through his shoulder and arm.

... it's looking at the photographs of your dad lying in the driveway in a pool of blood, as they are projected on a large screen before your friends and family, and before what might as well be the whole world.

As the trauma of the trial subsides,

... it's getting down on your hands and knees and straightening your dad's new grave marker and packing the fresh dirt around it, so that it will be perfect, as he always insisted that things be for you.

... it's sitting across from each other at Thanksgiving dinner, each knowing that there is but one thing on the other's mind, yet pretending otherwise for their sake.

... it's wishing for the first time in your life that Christmas would never arrive.

... it's sitting beside your father's grave into the night in 30-degree weather, so that he won't be alone on the first Christmas.

... it's hearing your two-year-old daughter ask for "Pawpaw" and seeing your wife choke back the tears and tell her, "He's gone now, he's in heaven."

In the larger sense ...

... it's feeling your body get rigid every time that you drive into a garage.

... it's being nervous every time you walk to your car, even in the open daylight.

... it's being scared to answer any phone call or any knock at the door at night (or for that matter during the day) because another messenger may be calling.

Finally, it's the long term effects ...

... it's the inexplicable sense of embarrassment when you tell someone that your husband or your father was murdered—almost a sense of guilt over injecting ugliness into their lives.

. . . it's going out to dinner alone, knowing that you will be going out alone the rest of your life.

. . . it's that feeling—wrong, but inevitable—that you will always be the fifth wheel. . .

Of course, for my mother, my sister, my wife and I, the sun will come up again. But it will never come up again for the real victim of this crime. Not only will he never see what he worked a lifetime for, and was finally within reach of obtaining that would be tragedy enough. But, even worse, he died knowing that the only thing that ever could have ruined his life had come to pass—that his wife and his family might have to suffer the kind of pain that is now ours—and he was helpless to prevent it even as he saw its inevitability.

We live by law in this country so that, ideally, no one will ever have to know what it is like to be a victim of such violent crime. If I had any wish, any wish in the world, it would be that no one ever again would have to go through what my mother and father experienced on the night of April 19, what my family has endured since and must carry with us the rest of our lives.

Crimes such as that committed against my family are intolerable in any society that calls itself not only free, but civilized. The law recognizes as much, and it provides for punishment that will ensure at least that others will not suffer again at the same hands, even if it does not prevent recurrence at the hands of others.

On behalf of my dad, and on behalf of my mother and family, I respectfully request that these who committed this brutal crime receive the full punishment the law provides. There were no passive bystanders among the gang that executed my dad.

Thank you, Your Honor.

Notes

1. Following Michael Luttig's emotional impact statement, Senior U.S. District Judge William Steger said he could not go any higher under the federal sentencing guidelines and imposed a 43-year sentence on Donald Coleman and a 40 year sentence on Cedric Coleman. In subsequent state murder proceedings, the Coleman's both testified against the triggerman in the killing—Napolean Beazley—and received life sentences. Beazley, a juvenile at the time of murder, received a death sentence and was executed in 2002.

2. While Michael Luttig spoke as John Luttig's son, he was also a federal judge on the U.S. Court of Appeals for the Fourth Circuit. In a later criminal case before the Fourth Circuit, a capital defendant argued that Judge Luttig should be disqualified from sitting on capital murder cases.

3. Michael Luttig was an articulate and trained lawyer. Most victims of crime are not trained in the law. Several states explicitly allow private counsel to represent victims at sentencing hearings. *E.g.*, Nev. Rev. Stat. § 176.015(3). These provisions

provide a basis for counsel's appearance separate and distinct from the ability of counsel for the victim to appear with the permission of the prosecutor and the court.

---

3. Constitutional Limits on Victim Impact Statements

At sentencing, evidence of *personal characteristics* of the victim is generally allowed. A second type of impact evidence is evidence of the *nature and extent* of harm resulting from the crime. Impact testimony as to harm is also generally admissible. A third type of potential impact evidence is the victim's *opinion* as to what is a proper sentence. Does the Constitution impose any limits on such victim impact statements? At different times, the Supreme Court has offered conflicting answers to this question.

Booth v. Maryland
482 U.S. 496 (1987)

JUSTICE POWELL delivered the opinion of the Court.

The question presented is whether the Constitution prohibits a jury from considering a "victim impact statement" during the sentencing phase of a capital murder trial.

I

In 1983, Irvin Bronstein, 78, and his wife Rose, 75, were robbed and murdered in their West Baltimore home. The murderers, John Booth and Willie Reid, entered the victims' home for the apparent purpose of stealing money to buy heroin. Booth, a neighbor of the Bronsteins, knew that the elderly couple could identify him. The victims were bound and gagged, and then stabbed repeatedly in the chest with a kitchen knife. The bodies were discovered two days later by the Bronsteins' son.

A jury found Booth guilty of two counts of first-degree murder, two counts of robbery, and conspiracy to commit robbery. The prosecution requested the death penalty, and Booth elected to have his sentence determined by the jury instead of the judge. Before the sentencing phase began, the State Division of Parole and Probation (DPP) compiled a presentence report that described Booth's background, education and employment history, and criminal record. Under a Maryland statute, the presentence report in all felony cases also must include a victim impact statement (VIS), describing the effect of the crime on the victim and his family. Specifically, the report shall:

(i) Identify the victim of the offense;

(ii) Itemize any economic loss suffered by the victim as a result of the offense;

(iii) Identify any physical injury suffered by the victim as a result of the offense along with its seriousness and permanence;

(iv) Describe any change in the victim's personal welfare or familial relationships as a result of the offense;

(v) Identify any request for psychological services initiated by the victim or the victim's family as a result of the offense; and

(vi) Contain any other information related to the impact of the offense upon the victim or the victim's family that the trial court requires.

Although the VIS is compiled by the DPP, the information is supplied by the victim or the victim's family. The VIS may be read to the jury during the sentencing phase, or the family members may be called to testify as to the information.

The VIS in Booth's case was based on interviews with the Bronsteins' son, daughter, son-in-law, and granddaughter. Many of their comments emphasized the victims' outstanding personal qualities, and noted how deeply the Bronsteins would be missed.[3] Other parts of the VIS described the emotional and personal problems the family members have faced as a result of the crimes. The son, for example, said that he suffers from lack of sleep and depression, and is "fearful for the first time in his life." He said that in his opinion, his parents were "butchered like animals." The daughter said she also suffers from lack of sleep, and that since the murders she has become withdrawn and distrustful. She stated that she can no longer watch violent movies or look at kitchen knives without being reminded of the murders. The daughter concluded that she could not forgive the murderer, and that such a person could "[n]ever be rehabilitated." Finally, the granddaughter described how the deaths had ruined the wedding of another close family member, that took place a few days after the bodies were discovered. Both the ceremony and the reception were sad affairs, and instead of leaving for her honeymoon, the bride attended the victims' funeral. The VIS also noted that the granddaughter had received counseling for several months after the incident, but eventually had stopped because she concluded that "no one could help her."

The DPP official who conducted the interviews concluded the VIS by writing:

It became increasingly apparent to the writer as she talked to the family members that the murder of Mr. and Mrs. Bronstein is still such a shocking, painful, and

---

3. The VIS stated:

[T]he victims' son reports that his parents had been married for fifty-three years and enjoyed a very close relationship, spending each day together. He states that his father had worked hard all his life and had been retired for eight years. He describes his mother as a woman who was young at heart and never seemed like an old lady. She taught herself to play bridge when she was in her seventies. The victims' son relates that his parents were "amazing people who attended the senior citizens' center and made many devout friends." "As described by their family members, the Bronsteins were loving parents and grandparents whose family was most important to them. Their funeral was the largest in the history of the Levinson Funeral Home and the family received over one thousand sympathy cards, some from total strangers."

devastating memory to them that it permeates every aspect of their daily lives. It is doubtful that they will ever be able to fully recover from this tragedy and not be haunted by the memory of the brutal manner in which their loved ones were murdered and taken from them.

Defense counsel moved to suppress the VIS on the ground that this information was both irrelevant and unduly inflammatory, and that therefore its use in a capital case violated the Eighth Amendment of the Federal Constitution. The Maryland trial court denied the motion, ruling that the jury was entitled to consider "any and all evidence which would bear on the [sentencing decision]." Booth's lawyer then requested that the prosecutor simply read the VIS to the jury rather than call the family members to testify before the jury. Defense counsel was concerned that the use of live witnesses would increase the inflammatory effect of the information. The prosecutor agreed to this arrangement. . . .

We granted certiorari to decide whether the Eighth Amendment prohibits a capital sentencing jury from considering victim impact evidence. . . .

II

[W]e have said that a jury must make an "*individualized* determination" of whether the defendant in question should be executed, based on "the character of the individual and the circumstances of the crime." And while this Court has never said that the defendant's record, characteristics, and the circumstances of the crime are the *only* permissible sentencing considerations, a state statute that requires consideration of other factors must be scrutinized to ensure that the evidence has some bearing on the defendant's "personal responsibility and moral guilt." To do otherwise would create the risk that a death sentence will be based on considerations that are "constitutionally impermissible or totally irrelevant to the sentencing process."

The VIS in this case provided the jury with two types of information. First, it described the personal characteristics of the victims and the emotional impact of the crimes on the family. Second, it set forth the family members' opinions and characterizations of the crimes and the defendant. For the reasons stated below, we find that this information is irrelevant to a capital sentencing decision, and that its admission creates a constitutionally unacceptable risk that the jury may impose the death penalty in an arbitrary and capricious manner.

A

The greater part of the VIS is devoted to a description of the emotional trauma suffered by the family and the personal characteristics of the victims. The State claims that this evidence should be considered a "circumstance" of the crime because it reveals the full extent of the harm caused by Booth's actions. . . .

While the full range of foreseeable consequences of a defendant's actions may be relevant in other criminal and civil contexts, we cannot agree that it is relevant in the unique circumstances of a capital sentencing hearing. In such a case, it is the function of the sentencing jury to "express the conscience of the community on the ultimate question of life or death." ... The focus of a VIS, however, is not on the defendant, but on the character and reputation of the victim and the effect on his family. These factors may be wholly unrelated to the blameworthiness of a particular defendant. As our cases have shown, the defendant often will not know the victim, and therefore will have no knowledge about the existence or characteristics of the victim's family. Moreover, defendants rarely select their victims based on whether the murder will have an effect on anyone other than the person murdered. ...

It is true that in certain cases some of the information contained in a VIS will have been known to the defendant before he committed the offense. As we have recognized, a defendant's degree of knowledge of the probable consequences of his actions may increase his moral culpability in a constitutionally significant manner. We nevertheless find that because of the nature of the information contained in a VIS, it creates an impermissible risk that the capital sentencing decision will be made in an arbitrary manner.

As evidenced by the full text of the VIS in this case, see Appendix to this opinion, the family members were articulate and persuasive in expressing their grief and the extent of their loss. But in some cases the victim will not leave behind a family, or the family members may be less articulate in describing their feelings even though their sense of loss is equally severe. ...

Nor is there any justification for permitting such a decision to turn on the perception that the victim was a sterling member of the community rather than someone of questionable character.[4] This type of information does not provide a "principled way to distinguish [cases] in which the death penalty was imposed, from the many cases in which it was not."

We also note that it would be difficult—if not impossible—to provide a fair opportunity to rebut such evidence without shifting the focus of the sentencing hearing away from the defendant. A threshold problem is that victim impact information is not easily susceptible to rebuttal. Presumably the defendant would have the right to cross-examine the declarants, but he rarely would be able to show that the family members have exaggerated the degree of sleeplessness, depression, or emotional trauma suffered. ... The prospect of a "mini-trial" on the victim's character is more than simply unappealing; it could well distract the sentencing jury from its constitutionally required task—determining whether the death penalty is appropriate in light of the background and record of the accused and the particular circumstances of the crime. We thus reject the contention that the presence or absence of emotional distress of the victim's family, or the victim's personal characteristics, are proper sentencing considerations in a capital case.

---

4. We are troubled by the implication that defendants whose victims were assets to the community are more deserving of punishment than those whose victims are perceived to be less worthy. Of course, our system of justice does not tolerate such distinctions. *Cf. Furman v. Georgia*, 92 S. Ct. 2726, 2728 (1972) (Douglas J., concurring).

B

The second type of information presented to the jury in the VIS was the family members' opinions and characterizations of the crimes. The Bronsteins' son, for example, stated that his parents were "butchered like animals," and that he "doesn't think anyone should be able to do something like that and get away with it." The VIS also noted that the Bronstein's daughter:

> [C]ould never forgive anyone for killing [her parents] that way. She can't believe that anybody could do that to someone. The victims' daughter states that animals wouldn't do this. [The perpetrators] didn't have to kill because there was no one to stop them from looting. . . . The murders show the viciousness of the killers' anger. She doesn't feel that the people who did this could ever be rehabilitated and she doesn't want them to be able to do this again or put another family through this.

One can understand the grief and anger of the family caused by the brutal murders in this case, and there is no doubt that jurors generally are aware of these feelings. But the formal presentation of this information by the State can serve no other purpose than to inflame the jury and divert it from deciding the case on the relevant evidence concerning the crime and the defendant. As we have noted, any decision to impose the death sentence must "be, and appear to be, based on reason rather than caprice or emotion." The admission of these emotionally charged opinions as to what conclusions the jury should draw from the evidence clearly is inconsistent with the reasoned decisionmaking we require in capital cases.[5]

III

We conclude that the introduction of a VIS at the sentencing phase of a capital murder trial violates the Eighth Amendment, and therefore the Maryland statute is invalid to the extent it requires consideration of this information.[6] The decision of the Maryland Court of Appeals is vacated to the extent that it affirmed the capital sentence. The case is remanded for further proceedings not inconsistent with this opinion.

It is so ordered.

JUSTICE WHITE, with whom THE CHIEF JUSTICE, JUSTICE O'CONNOR, and JUSTICE SCALIA join, dissenting. (Omitted.)

JUSTICE SCALIA, with whom THE CHIEF JUSTICE, JUSTICE WHITE AND JUSTICE O'CONNOR join, dissenting. (Omitted.)

————————

————————

5. The same problem is presented by the VIS summary written by the DPP, that might be viewed by the jury as representing the views of the State. As noted, the writer concluded that the crimes had a "shocking, painful, and devast[at]ing effect on the family," and that "[i]t is doubtful that they will ever be able to fully recover."

6. We imply no opinion as to the use of these statements in noncapital cases.

Payne v. Tennessee

501 U.S. 808 (1991)

CHIEF JUSTICE REHNQUIST delivered the opinion of the court.

In this case we reconsider our holdings in *Booth v. Maryland* and *South Carolina v. Gathers*, that the Eighth Amendment bars the admission of victim impact evidence during the penalty phase of a capital trial.

The petitioner, Pervis Tyrone Payne, was convicted by a jury on two counts of first-degree murder and one count of assault with intent to commit murder in the first degree. He was sentenced to death for each of the murders, and to 30 years in prison for the assault.

The victims of Payne's offenses were 28-year-old Charisse Christopher, her 2-year-old daughter Lacie, and her 3-year-old son Nicholas. The three lived together in an apartment in Millington, Tennessee, across the hall from Payne's girlfriend, Bobbie Thomas. . . .

Payne passed the morning and early afternoon injecting cocaine and drinking beer. Later, he drove around the town with a friend in the friend's car, each of them taking turns reading a pornographic magazine. Sometime around 3 p.m., Payne returned to the apartment complex, entered the Christophers' apartment, and began making sexual advances towards Charisse. Charisse resisted and Payne became violent. . . .

When the first police officer arrived at the scene, he immediately encountered Payne who was leaving the apartment building, so covered with blood that he appeared to be "'sweating blood.'" The officer confronted Payne, who responded, "'I'm the complainant.'" When the officer asked, "'What's going on up there?'" Payne struck the officer with the overnight bag, dropped his tennis shoes, and fled.

Inside the apartment, the police encountered a horrifying scene. Blood covered the walls and floor throughout the unit. Charisse and her children were lying on the floor in the kitchen. Nicholas, despite several wounds inflicted by a butcher knife that completely penetrated through his body from front to back, was still breathing. . . .

Charisse's body was found on the kitchen floor on her back, her legs fully extended. She had sustained 42 direct knife wounds and 42 defensive wounds on her arms and hands. The wounds were caused by 41 separate thrusts of a butcher knife. None of the 84 wounds inflicted by Payne were individually fatal; rather, the cause of death was most likely bleeding from all of the wounds.

Lacie's body was on the kitchen floor near her mother. She had suffered stab wounds to the chest, abdomen, back, and head. The murder weapon, a butcher knife, was found at her feet. Payne's baseball cap was snapped on her arm near her elbow. Three cans of malt liquor bearing Payne's fingerprints were found on a table near her body, and a fourth empty one was on the landing outside the apartment door.

Payne was apprehended later that day hiding in the attic of the home of a former girlfriend. As he descended the stairs of the attic, he stated to the arresting officers, "Man, I ain't killed no woman.". . .

During the sentencing phase of the trial, Payne presented the testimony of four witnesses: his mother and father, Bobbie Thomas, and Dr. John T. Huston, a clinical psychologist specializing in criminal court evaluation work. Bobbie Thomas testified that she met Payne at church, during a time when she was being abused by her husband. She stated that Payne was a very caring person, and that he devoted much time and attention to her three children, who were being affected by her marital difficulties. She said that the children had come to love him very much and would miss him, and that he "behaved just like a father that loved his kids." She asserted that he did not drink, nor did he use drugs, and that it was generally inconsistent with Payne's character to have committed these crimes.

Dr. Huston testified that based on Payne's low score on an IQ test, Payne was "mentally handicapped." Huston also said that Payne was neither psychotic nor schizophrenic, and that Payne was the most polite prisoner he had ever met. Payne's parents testified that their son had no prior criminal record and had never been arrested. They also stated that Payne had no history of alcohol or drug abuse, he worked with his father as a painter, he was good with children, and that he was a good son.

The State presented the testimony of Charisse's mother, Mary Zvolanck. When asked how Nicholas had been affected by the murders of his mother and sister, she responded:

> He cries for his mom. He doesn't seem to understand why she doesn't come home. And he cries for his sister Lacie. He comes to me many times during the week and asks me, Grandmama, do you miss my Lacie. And I tell him yes. He says, I'm worried about my Lacie.

In arguing for the death penalty during closing argument, the prosecutor commented on the continuing effects of Nicholas' experience, stating:

> But we do know that Nicholas was alive. And Nicholas was in the same room. Nicholas was still conscious. His eyes were open. He responded to paramedics. He was able to follow their directions. He was able to hold his intestines in as he was carried to the ambulance. So he knew what happened to his mother and baby sister.
>
> * * *
>
> Somewhere down the road Nicholas is going to grow up, hopefully. He's going to want to know what happened. And he is going to know what happened to his baby sister and his mother. He is going to want to know what type of justice was done. He is going to want to know what happened. With your verdict, you will provide the answer.

In the rebuttal to Payne's closing argument, the prosecutor stated:

You saw the video this morning. You saw what Nicholas Christopher will carry in his mind forever. When you talk about cruel, when you talk about atrocious, and when you talk about heinous, that picture will always come into your mind, probably throughout the rest of your lives. . . .

. . . No one will ever know about Lacie Jo because she never had the chance to grow up. Her life was taken from her at the age of two years old. So, no there won't be a high school principal to talk about Lacie Jo Christopher, and there won't be anybody to take her to her high school prom. And there won't be anybody there—there won't be her mother there or Nicholas' mother there to kiss him at night. His mother will never kiss him good night or pat him as he goes off to bed, or hold him and sing him a lullaby.

* * *

[Petitioner's attorney] wants you to think about a good reputation, people who love the defendant and things about him. He doesn't want you to think about the people who love Charisse Christopher, her mother and daddy who loved her. The people who loved little Lacie Jo, the grandparents who are still here. The brother who mourns for her every single day and wants to know where his best little playmate is. He doesn't have anybody to watch cartoons with him, a little one. These are things that go into why it is especially cruel, heinous, and atrocious, the burden that that child will carry forever.

The jury sentenced Payne to death on each of the murder counts. . . .

We granted certiorari to reconsider our holdings in *Booth* and *Gathers* that the Eighth Amendment prohibits a capital sentencing jury from considering "victim impact" evidence relating to the personal characteristics of the victim and the emotional impact of the crimes on the victim's family. . . .

Booth and *Gathers* were based on two premises: that evidence relating to a particular victim or to the harm that a capital defendant causes a victim's family do not in general reflect on the defendant's "blameworthiness," and that only evidence relating to "blameworthiness" is relevant to the capital sentencing decision. However, the assessment of harm caused by the defendant as a result of the crime charged has understandably been an important concern of the criminal law, both in determining the elements of the offense and in determining the appropriate punishment. Thus, two equally blameworthy criminal defendants may be guilty of different offenses solely because their acts cause differing amounts of harm. "If a bank robber aims his gun at a guard, pulls the trigger, and kills his target, he may be put to death. If the gun unexpectedly misfires, he may not. His moral guilt in both cases is identical, but his responsibility in the former is greater."

* * *

Whatever the prevailing sentencing philosophy, the sentencing authority has always been free to consider a wide range of relevant material. In the federal system, we observed that "a judge may appropriately conduct an inquiry broad in scope, largely unlimited as to the kind of information he may consider, or the source from which it may come." Even in the context of capital sentencing, prior to *Booth* the joint opinion of Justices Stewart, Powell, and Stevens in *Gregg v. Georgia*, had rejected petitioner's attack on the Georgia statute because of the "wide scope of evidence and argument allowed at presentence hearings."

Thus we have, as the Court observed in *Booth*, required that the capital defendant be treated as a "'uniquely individual human bein[g],'" (quoting *Woodson v. North Carolina*). But it was never held or even suggested in any of our cases preceding *Booth* that the defendant, entitled as he was to individualized consideration, was to receive that consideration wholly apart from the crime which he had committed. . . . This misreading of precedent in *Booth* has, we think, unfairly weighted the scales in a capital trial; while virtually no limits are placed on the relevant mitigating evidence a capital defendant may introduce concerning his own circumstances, the State is barred from either offering "a glimpse of the life" which a defendant "chose to extinguish," or demonstrating the loss to the victim's family and to society which have resulted from the defendant's homicide.

Payne echoes the concern voiced in Booth's case that the admission of victim impact evidence permits a jury to find that defendants whose victims were assets to their community are more deserving of punishment than those whose victims are perceived to be less worthy. As a general matter, however, victim impact evidence is not offered to encourage comparative judgments of this kind—for instance, that the killer of a hardworking, devoted parent deserves the death penalty, but that the murderer of a reprobate does not. It is designed to show instead *each* victim's "uniqueness as an individual human being," whatever the jury might think the loss to the community resulting from his death might be. The facts of *Gathers* are an excellent illustration of this: the evidence showed that the victim was an out of work, mentally handicapped individual, perhaps not, in the eyes of most, a significant contributor to society, but nonetheless a murdered human being. . . .

[T]he States remain free, in capital cases, as well as others, to devise new procedures and new remedies to meet felt needs. Victim impact evidence is simply another form or method of informing the sentencing authority about the specific harm caused by the crime in question, evidence of a general type long considered by sentencing authorities. We think the *Booth* Court was wrong in stating that this kind of evidence leads to the arbitrary imposition of the death penalty. In the majority of cases, and in this case, victim impact evidence serves entirely legitimate purposes. In the event that evidence is introduced that is so unduly prejudicial that it renders the trial fundamentally unfair, the Due Process Clause of the Fourteenth Amendment provides a mechanism for relief. See *Darden v. Wainwright*. Courts have always taken into consideration the harm done by the defendant in imposing sentence, and the evidence adduced in this case was illustrative of the harm caused by Payne's double murder.

We are now of the view that a State may properly conclude that for the jury to assess meaningfully the defendant's moral culpability and blameworthiness, it should have before it at the sentencing phase evidence of the specific harm caused by the defendant. "[T]he State has a legitimate interest in counteracting the mitigating evidence which the defendant is entitled to put in, by reminding the sentencer that just as the murderer should be considered as an individual, so too the victim is an individual whose death represents a unique loss to society and in particular to his family." By turning the victim into a "faceless stranger at the penalty phase of a capital trial," *Booth* deprives the State of the full moral force of its evidence and may prevent the jury from having before it all the information necessary to determine the proper punishment for a first-degree murder.

The present case is an example of the potential for such unfairness. The capital sentencing jury heard testimony from Payne's girlfriend that they met at church, that he was affectionate, caring, kind to her children, that he was not an abuser of drugs or alcohol, and that it was inconsistent with his character to have committed the murders. Payne's parents testified that he was a good son, and a clinical psychologist testified that Payne was an extremely polite prisoner and suffered from a low IQ. None of this testimony was related to the circumstances of Payne's brutal crimes. In contrast, the only evidence of the impact of Payne's offense during the sentencing phase was Nicholas' grandmother's description in response to a single question that the child misses his mother and baby sister. Payne argues that the Eighth Amendment commands that the jury's death sentence must be set aside because the jury heard this testimony. But the testimony illustrated quite poignantly some of the harm that Payne's killing had caused; there is nothing unfair about allowing the jury to bear in mind that harm at the same time as it considers the mitigating evidence introduced by the defendant. . . .

Under the aegis of the Eighth Amendment, we have given the broadest latitude to the defendant to introduce relevant mitigating evidence reflecting on his individual personality, and the defendant's attorney may argue that evidence to the jury. Petitioner's attorney in this case did just that. For the reasons discussed above, we now reject the view expressed in *Gathers* that a State may not permit the prosecutor to similarly argue to the jury the human cost of the crime of which the defendant stands convicted. We reaffirm the view expressed by Justice Cardozo in *Snyder v. Massachusetts*, "justice, though due to the accused, is due to the accuser also. The concept of fairness must not be strained till it is narrowed to a filament. We are to keep the balance true."

JUSTICE SCALIA, with whom JUSTICE O'CONNOR and JUSTICE KENNEDY join as to Part II, concurring.

. . . If there was ever a case that defied reason, it was *Booth v. Maryland*, imposing a constitutional rule that had absolutely no basis in constitutional text, in historical practice, or in logic. Justice MARSHALL has also explained that "'[t]he jurist concerned with public confidence in, and acceptance of the judicial system might well consider that, however admirable its resolute adherence to the law as it was, a decision contrary to the public sense of justice as it is, operates, so far as it is known, to diminish respect for the courts and for law itself.'" *Flood v. Kuhn*, 407 U.S. 258, 293, n. 4 (1972) (dissenting opinion) (quoting Szanton, *Stare Decisis; A Dissenting View*, 10

HASTINGS L. J. 394, 397 (1959) (internal quotation marks omitted). *Booth's* stunning *ipse dixit*, that a crime's unanticipated consequences must be deemed "irrelevant" to the sentence, 482 U.S. at 503, conflicts with a public sense of justice keen enough that it has found voice in a nationwide "victims' rights" movement.

JUSTICE SOUTER, with whom JUSTICE KENNEDY joins, concurring.

I join the Court's opinion addressing two categories of facts excluded from consideration at capital sentencing proceedings by *Booth v. Maryland*, information revealing the individuality of the victim and the impact of the crime on the victim's survivors.[7] As to these two categories, I believe *Booth* and *Gathers* were wrongly decided. . . .

. . . Murder has foreseeable consequences. When it happens, it is always to distinct individuals, and after it happens other victims are left behind. Every defendant knows, if endowed with the mental competence for criminal responsibility, that the life he will take by his homicidal behavior is that of a unique person, like himself, and that the person to be killed probably has close associates, "survivors," who will suffer harms and deprivations from the victim's death. Just as defendants know that they are not faceless human ciphers, they know that their victims are not valueless fungibles, and just as defendants appreciate the web of relationships and dependencies in which they live, they know that their victims are not human islands, but individuals with parents or children, spouses or friends or dependents. Thus, when a defendant chooses to kill, or to raise the risk of a victim's death, this choice necessarily relates to a whole human being and threatens an association of others, who may be distinctly hurt. The fact that the defendant may not know the details of a victim's life and characteristics, or the exact identities and needs of those who may survive, should not in any way obscure the further facts that death is always to a "unique" individual, and harm to some group of survivors is a consequence of a successful homicidal act so foreseeable as to be virtually inevitable. . . .

I do not, however, rest my decision to overrule wholly on the constitutional error that I see in the cases in question. I must rely as well on my further view that *Booth* sets an unworkable standard of constitutional relevance that threatens, on its own terms, to produce such arbitrary consequences and uncertainty of application as virtually to guarantee a result far diminished from the case's promise of appropriately individualized sentencing for capital defendants. . . .

A hypothetical case will illustrate these facts and raise what I view as the serious practical problems with application of the *Booth* standard. Assume that a minister, unidentified as such and wearing no clerical collar, walks down a street to his church office on a brief errand, while his wife and adolescent daughter wait for him in a parked car. He is robbed and killed by a stranger, and his survivors witness his death.

---

7. This case presents no challenge to the Court's holding in *Booth v. Maryland* that a sentencing authority should not receive a third category of information concerning a victim's family members' characterization of and opinions about the crime, the defendant, and the appropriate sentence.

What are the circumstances of the crime that can be considered at the sentencing phase under *Booth*? The defendant did not know his victim was a minister, or that he had a wife and child, let alone that they were watching. Under *Booth*, these facts were irrelevant to his decision to kill, and they should be barred from consideration at sentencing. Yet evidence of them will surely be admitted at the guilt phase of the trial. The widow will testify to what she saw, and in so doing she will not be asked to pretend that she was a mere bystander. She could not succeed at that if she tried. The daughter may well testify too. The jury will not be kept from knowing that the victim was a minister, with a wife and child, on an errand to his church. This is so not only because the widow will not try to deceive the jury about her relationship, but also because the usual standards of trial relevance afford factfinders enough information about surrounding circumstances to let them make sense of the narrowly material facts of the crime itself. No one claims that jurors in a capital case should be deprived of such common contextual evidence, even though the defendant knew nothing about the errand, the victim's occupation or his family. And yet, if these facts are not kept from the jury at the guilt stage, they will be in the jurors' minds at the sentencing stage.

Booth thus raises a dilemma with very practical consequences. If we were to require the rules of guilt-phase evidence to be changed to guarantee the full effect of *Booth's* promise to exclude consideration of specific facts unknown to the defendant and thus supposedly without significance in morally evaluating his decision to kill, we would seriously reduce the comprehensibility of most trials by depriving jurors of those details of context that allow them to understand what is being described. . . .

In the preceding hypothetical, *Booth* would require that all evidence about the victim's family, including its very existence, be excluded from sentencing consideration because the defendant did not know of it when he killed the victim. Yet, if the victim's daughter had screamed "Daddy, look out," as the defendant approached the victim with drawn gun, then the evidence of at least the daughter's survivorship would be admissible even under a strict reading of *Booth*, because the defendant, prior to killing, had been made aware of the daughter's existence, which therefore became relevant in evaluating the defendant's decision to kill. Resting a decision about the admission of impact evidence on such a fortuity is arbitrary.

JUSTICE MARSHALL, with whom JUSTICE BLACKMUN joins, dissenting. (Omitted.)

JUSTICE STEVENS, with whom JUSTICE BLACKMUN joins, dissenting. (Omitted.)

> [In addition to disagreeing with the majority on substantive analysis, the dissents protested the change in law as having a negative impact on the doctrine of *stare decisis*. The dissents pointed out that the new decision came about from a change in the make-up of the court.]

Notes

1. Justice Rehnquist's choice of language, that VIS "is designed to show instead *each* victim's 'uniqueness' as an individual human being" is significant. Evidence of a person's "uniqueness as an individual human being" was previously used by the court as a description of the type of evidence a defendant could introduce in the hope of defeating the death penalty. The language in *Payne* appears to allow for a similar scope of evidence as to the victim.

2. The Supreme Court's decision in *Payne* allowing victim impact statement is the current state of *federal* constitutional law on victim impact statements. While most states follow *Payne*, they are free to impose different restrictions on the admissibility of impact statements. *See Bivens v. State*, 642 N.E.2d 928 (Ind. 1994) (victim impact evidence admissible in capital cases only where relevant to the death penalty statute's aggravating and mitigating circumstances). *See generally,* Joan T. Buckley, *Victim Impact Evidence in Capital Sentencing Hearings — Post-*Payne v. Tennessee, 79 A.L.R.5th 33 (2000).

3. The Constitution's requirements of due process may impose other constraints on victim impact testimony. For example, in *Buschauer v. State*, 804 P.2d 1046 (Nev. 1990), the court held that where a victim impact statement alleged specific prior criminal acts of the defendant, due process required that the statement be made under oath, with an opportunity for cross-examination, and with reasonable notice to the defendant of the prior acts alleged. Similarly, in *State v. Blackmon*, 908 P.2d 10 (Ariz. App. 1995), the court held that Arizona's Victims' Bill of Rights, giving victims the right to be heard at sentencing, did not abolish the rule that defendants have a due process right to cross-examine victims who testify at presentence hearings. While the victim remains subject to cross-examination when offering "evidence" in the aggravation or penalty phase of a capital sentencing, the Arizona Legislature subsequently passed laws clarifying the victim's role. A.R.S. 13-4426.01 "In any proceeding in which the victim has the right to be heard pursuant to article II, section 2.1, Constitution of Arizona, or this chapter, the victim's right to be heard is exercised not as a witness, the victim's statement is not subject to disclosure to the state or the defendant or submission to the court and the victim is not subject to cross-examination. The state and the defense shall be afforded the opportunity to explain, support or deny the victim's statement." Still others have made the subject one to be handled by the trial judge. *See, e.g.,* N.Y. Crim Proc. L. § 380.50 (allowing the defendant to submit questions for the victim to the judge, but allowing the court, in its discretion, to decline to put any or all of the questions to the victims).

4. Trial judges have the ability to manage the way in which victim impact testimony is presented. For example, judges can give cautionary instructions to jurors about how to assess such testimony and prevent emotional outbursts while the testimony is presented. Do these additional safeguards support the conclusion that victim impact testimony is consistent with constitutional requirements? *See* Douglas E. Beloof, *Constitutional Implications of Crime Victims as Participants*, 88 Cornell L. Rev. 282

(2003) (arguing judicial management of impact testimony ameliorates any lingering constitutional concerns).

5. Some commentators take the position that a *judge's* decision may be prejudiced by victim input at sentencing. Andrew Blu, *Impact of Crimes Shakes Sentencing*, Nat'l L.J. 6–26 (1995) p. A-1; Lynn Henderson, *The Wrongs of Victim Rights*, 37 Stan. L. Rev. 937, 999–1001 (1985).

6. A federal district court has held that there is no constitutional requirement that the defendant be given the opportunity to cross-examine the victim about their impact statement. *Smith v. Schriro*, 2009 WL1457015 (D. Ariz. Mar. 21 2009) (order) ("The *Crawford* decision deals with trial rights. Following the sound reasoning of the above-listed circuit courts, the Court concludes that the right to confrontation is not a sentencing right. Accordingly, Petitioner's Sixth Amendment challenge to the sentencing court's consideration of victim impact statements lacks merit.")

An Air Force Court has reached the same conclusion:

> If a crime victim exercises the right to be reasonably heard, he or she is called by the court-martial (not the prosecution), and the crime victim is not considered a witness for the purposes of Article 42(b) UCMJ, 10 U.S.C. § 842(b). R.C.M. 1001A does not contain the word evidence at all. When R.C.M. 1001A was implemented, R.C.M. 1001 was also modified. R.C.M. 1001(a) states the ordinary sequence of presenting presentencing matters. The revised R.C.M. 1001(a) language explicitly distinguishes between evidence and other matters. Reading the plain language of the rules, we hold that unsworn victim impact statements offered pursuant to R.C.M. 1001A are not evidence. See also United States v. Provost, 32 M.J. 98, 99 (C.M.A. 1991) (if an accused elects to make an unsworn statement, he is not offering evidence). Both R.C.M. 1001(c)(2)(C) and R.C.M. 1001A(e) allow facts in an unsworn statement to be contradicted or rebutted. This does not change the character of the right to speak. *United States v. Hamilton*, 2017 WL 6886141 (A.F.Ct Crim. App.)

7. Under a state statutory right to speak at sentencing a California court held that the right included the ability to address the court concerning the plea bargain. *People v. Stringham*, 253 Cal. Rptr. 484 (Cal. App. 1988). This topic is explored in greater depth in the plea section of Chapter 5 on Pretrial Proceedings.

―――――――

4. The Wisdom of Victim Impact Statements

Even if victim impact statements are constitutionally permissible, do they constitute sound social policy? Consider the following competing views on the desirability of allowing victim impact statements in capital cases.

Susan Bandes, *Empathy, Narrative, and Victim Impact Statements*

63 U. Chi. L. Rev. 361 (1996)

* * *

B. The Defendant

Victim impact statements evoke not merely sympathy, pity, and compassion for the victim, but also a complex set of emotions directed toward the defendant, including hatred, fear, racial animus, vindictiveness, undifferentiated vengeance, and the desire to purge collective anger. These emotional reactions have a crucial common thread: they all deflect the jury from its duty to consider the individual defendant and his moral culpability.

1. Undifferentiated vengeance.

Booth held victim impact statements inadmissible, noting that the jury's decision to sentence the defendant to death must rest on the character of the individual defendant and the circumstances of the crime, and not on extraneous factors such as the character of the victim. *Payne* rejected this rationale, holding that the defendant is not entitled to receive individualized consideration wholly apart from the crime which he ha(s) committed.

The rationale adopted by the *Payne* majority obfuscates the real issue. Of course, in many respects the harm caused by a criminal act is relevant to determining the defendant's level of responsibility, at both the guilt and sentencing phases. To take an easy example, murder and attempted murder are defined and punished differently, even though the act and the intent may be identical in each case, and the only difference may be the fortuity of whether the victim survived or died. But certain other fortuities ought to be irrelevant. Again taking an easy example, the law ought not to condone punishment of a defendant that varies according to the social class or the race of his victim. Such ugly disparities are undeniably part of the realist landscape, but *Payne* completely avoided the question of whether the legal system, by permitting victim impact statements, should encourage them.

The usual justifications advanced for the death penalty are retribution and deterrence. The justifications for admitting victim impact statements, however, arguably satisfy a different, less savory, set of objectives. Justice Scalia's dissenting argument in *Booth*, which ultimately prevailed in *Payne*, was that punishment should be keyed not to the defendant's moral guilt, but to the total harm caused by his actions, whether direct or tangential, intended or unintended, foreseeable or unforeseeable. Steven Gey suggests that this rationale for victim impact statements is far more radical than garden-variety retribution. Gey argues that, under Scalia's view, the sentencing body at a capital trial could "use the unanticipated and unknown consequences of a particular defendant's actions as an aggravating factor" in sentencing the defendant, solely "because society has an abstract need to ameliorate its 'public sense of injustice' at criminal harms generally."

As Gey points out, the idea of venting collective outrage diverges sharply from traditional retributive theory, which does not use punishment merely as a means to promote some other good. Martha Nussbaum makes a similar point. She argues that a characteristic of primitive forms of justice is a lack of concern for the particulars of retribution — such as the existence of mitigating circumstances or even whether the person who pays for the wrong was the one who committed it. She sees victim impact statements as a vehicle for venting society's crude passion for revenge.

2. The right emotions in the wrong contexts.

Victim impact statements illustrate concretely the ambiguous nature of the term empathy, the dangers of arbitrariness and prejudice inherent in encouraging empathy without sufficient structural safeguards, and the undesirability of empathy unaccompanied by critical reflection. Victim impact statements convey information; is Paul Gewirtz correct to suggest that more information is better? Assuming the empathy elicited by the statements is good, why not encourage it by exposing the decision maker to more voices? There are several problems with this reasoning and its underlying assumptions.

First, not everyone is equipped to hear every voice. We feel empathy most easily toward those who are like us. As for people from backgrounds—ethnic, religious, racial, economic—unlike our own, however, there is a pervasive risk that our ability to empathize will be inhibited by ingrained, preconscious assumptions about them. We all have limited perspectives and a limited ability to empathize with those who do not share our life experiences and values.

When the unusual case comes along in which the members of a capital jury are able to see the defendant as one of their own, we take notice. Consider the recent decision of the jury in Susan Smith's trial for drowning her two sons. The jury was drawn from the close-knit community of Union, South Carolina, where Smith and her extended family had lived for a considerable time. The jurors declined to sentence Smith to death, citing sympathy for her difficult life, sympathy for her family, which would lose yet another member if she were executed, and their own need to live in the community with the Smith family. Juror Roy Palmer said that had he voted for death, "he still would have had to pass by Smith's family members in the streets and supermarket aisles of this small town. 'I might have wanted to hang my head,' said Palmer." Most felt outrage and contempt toward Susan Smith, but the jurors saw her as an individual, a human being, someone like them in important ways. Ultimately they felt compassion for her and could not vote to kill her.

More often, for the jury to empathetically connect with the defendant during the sentencing phase of a capital trial is an extremely difficult task. Not only has the defendant been convicted of a heinous crime—a fact that by itself sets him very much apart from the jury's experience—but he may be from a radically different socioeconomic milieu as well. Thus, the jury has difficulty making an empathetic connection without the help of judicial rules and structures that both encourage that connection and place in perspective the more natural, instinctive connection that most jurors feel with the victim. No matter how well intentioned the members of the jury might be, to the extent their feelings toward the defendant are preconscious, widely shared, and therefore, effectively invisible, they will be unable to critique or to distance themselves from those feelings without the help of rules that limit their discretion.

The feeling of identification with the victim of a crime often comes naturally. In fact, some psychological literature identifies fear of being in the same position of suffering as an important component of empathy. Whether this ought to qualify as putting oneself in another's shoes or simply as a prereflective and self-referential reflex is an interesting semantic question. Indeed, some scientists argue this kind of empathy is of a lesser, instinctual variety: These researchers argue that a version of empathy developed with the evolution of mammals, which care for their young over a protracted period and thus require a mechanism for identifying need in others—the young—and responding appropriately. These scientists define empathy as including some seemingly fraternal behaviors that have a nearly automatic feel to them. If you see a person bump a shin into a fire hydrant, for example, you very likely will wince with vicarious pain. Such knee-jerk reactions suggest to some that empathy is an evolutionarily ancient response, its neural and physiological mechanisms in place long before the advent of Homosapiens or even primates.

Even if one chooses to call this reflexive identification empathy, it lacks a crucial component of understanding critical distance. Contrary to Justice Stevens's assertion in his dissent in *Payne*, the problem with victim impact statements is not that they evoke emotion rather than reason. Rather, it is that they evoke unreasoned, unreflective emotion that cannot be placed in any usable perspective. In evidentiary terms, victim impact statements are prejudicial and inflammatory. They overwhelm the jury with feelings of outrage toward the defendant and identification with the victim. Finally, victim impact statements diminish a jury's ability to process other relevant evidence, such as evidence in mitigation. This point identifies the fatal flaw in Gewirtz's "more is better" argument. The admission of a victim impact statement does not simply expand the jury's empathetic horizons by making the victim more human. Instead, it interferes with and indeed may completely block the jury's ability to empathize with the defendant or comprehend his humanity.

———————

Paul G. Cassell, *Barbarians at the Gates? A Reply to the Critics of the Victims' Rights Amendment*
1999 Utah L. Rev. 479

Professor Bandes acknowledges the power of hearing from victims' families. Indeed, in a commendable willingness to present victim statements with all their force, she begins her article by quoting from the victim impact statement at issue in *Payne v. Tennessee*, a statement from Mary Zvolanek about her daughter's and granddaughter's deaths and their effect on her three-year-old grandson:

He cries for his mom. He doesn't seem to understand why she doesn't come home. And he cries for his sister Lacie. He comes to me many times during the week and asks me, Grandmama, do you miss my Lacie. And I tell him yes. He says, I'm worried about my Lacie.

Bandes quite accurately observes that the statement is "heartbreaking" and "(o)n paper, it is nearly unbearable to read." She goes on to argue that such statements are "prejudicial and inflammatory" and "overwhelm the jury with feelings of outrage." In my judgment, Bandes fails here to distinguish sufficiently between prejudice and unfair prejudice from a victim's statement.

It is a commonplace of evidence law that a litigant is not entitled to exclude harmful evidence, but only unfairly harmful evidence. Bandes appears to believe that a sentence imposed following a victim impact statement rests on unjustified prejudice; alternatively, one might conclude simply that the sentence rests on a fuller understanding of all of the murder's harmful ramifications. Why is it "heartbreaking" and "nearly unbearable to read" about what it is like for a three-year-old to witness the murder of his mother and his two-year-old sister? The answer, judging from why my heart broke as I read the passage, is that we can no longer treat the crime as some abstract event. In other words, we begin to realize the nearly unbearable heartbreak — that is, the actual and total harm — that the murderer inflicted. Such a realization undoubtedly will hamper a defendant's efforts to escape a capital sentence. But given that loss is a proper consideration for the jury, the statement is not unfairly detrimental to the defendant. Indeed, to conceal such evidence from the jury may leave them with a distorted, minimized view of the impact of the crime. Victim impact statements are thus easily justified because they provide the jury with a full picture of the murder's consequences.

Bandes also contends that impact statements "may completely block" the ability of the jury to consider mitigation evidence. It is hard to assess this essentially empirical assertion, because Bandes does not present direct empirical support. Clearly many juries decline to return death sentences even when presented with powerful victim impact testimony, with Terry Nichols's life sentence for conspiring to set the Oklahoma City bomb a prominent example. Indeed, one recent empirical study of decisions from jurors who actually served in capital cases found that facts about adult victims "made little difference" in death penalty decisions.[8] . . .

The empirical evidence in noncapital cases also finds little effect on sentence severity. For example, a study in California found that "(t)he right to allocution at sentencing has had little net effect . . . on sentences in general." A study in New York similarly reported "no support for those who argue against (victim impact) statements on the grounds that their use places defendants in jeopardy." A careful scholar recently reviewed comprehensively all of the available evidence in this country and

---

8. Stephen P. Garvey, *Aggravation and Mitigation in Capital Cases: What Do Jurors Think?*, 98 COLUM. L. REV. 1538, 1556 (1998).

elsewhere, and concluded that "sentence severity has not increased following the passage of (victim impact) legislation."[9] It is thus unclear why we should credit Bandes's assertion that victim impact statements seriously hamper the defense of capital defendants.

Even if such an impact on capital sentences were proven, it would be susceptible to the reasonable interpretation that victim testimony did not "block" jury understanding, but rather presented enhanced information about the full horror of the murder or put in context mitigating evidence of the defendant. Professor David Friedman has suggested this conclusion, observing that "(i)f the legal rules present the defendant as a living, breathing human being with loving parents weeping on the witness stand, while presenting the victim as a shadowy abstraction, the result will be to overstate, in the minds of the jury, the cost of capital punishment relative to the benefit." Correcting this misimpression is not distorting the decision-making process, but eliminating a distortion that would otherwise occur. This interpretation meshes with empirical studies in noncapital cases suggesting that, if a victim impact statement makes a difference in punishment, the description of the harm sustained by the victims is the crucial factor. The studies thus indicate that the general tendency of victim impact evidence is to enhance sentence accuracy and proportionality rather than increase sentence punitiveness.

Finally, Bandes and other critics argue that victim impact statements result in unequal justice. Justice Powell made this claim in his since-overturned decision in *Booth v. Maryland*, arguing that "in some cases the victim will not leave behind a family, or the family members may be less articulate in describing their feelings even though their sense of loss is equally severe." This kind of difference, however, is hardly unique to victim impact evidence. To provide one obvious example, current rulings from the Court invite defense mitigation evidence from a defendant's family and friends, despite the fact that some defendants may have more or less articulate acquaintances. In *Payne*, for example, the defendant's parents testified that he was "a good son" and his girlfriend testified that he "was affectionate, caring, and kind to her children." In another case, a defendant introduced evidence of having won a dance choreography award while in prison. Surely this kind of testimony, no less than victim impact statements, can vary in persuasiveness in ways not directly connected to a defendant's culpability; yet, it is routinely allowed. One obvious reason is that if varying persuasiveness were grounds for an inequality attack, then it is hard to see how the criminal justice system could survive at all. Justice White's powerful dissenting argument in Booth went unanswered, and remains unanswerable: "No two prosecutors have exactly the same ability to present their arguments to the jury; no two witnesses have exactly the same ability to communicate the facts; but there is no requirement . . . (that) the evidence and argument be reduced to the lowest common denominator."

---

9. Edna Erez, *Who's Afraid of the Big Bad Victim? Victim Impact Statements as Victim Empowerment and Enhancement of Justice*, 1999 Crim. L. Rev. 545.

Given that our current system allows almost unlimited mitigation evidence on the part of the defendant, an argument for equal justice requires, if anything, that victim statements be allowed. Equality demands fairness not only between cases, but also within cases. Victims and the public generally perceive great unfairness in a sentencing system with "one side muted." The Tennessee Supreme Court stated the point bluntly in its decision in *Payne*, explaining that

> It is an affront to the civilized members of the human race to say that at sentencing in a capital case, a parade of witnesses may praise the background, character and good deeds of Defendant . . . without limitation as to relevancy, but nothing may be said that bears upon the character of, or the harm imposed, upon the victims.

With simplicity but haunting eloquence, a father whose ten-year-old daughter, Staci, was murdered, made the same point. Before the sentencing phase began, Marvin Weinstein asked the prosecutor for the opportunity to speak to the jury because the defendant's mother would have the chance to do so. The prosecutor replied that Florida law did not permit this. Here was Weinstein's response to the prosecutor:

> What? I'm not getting a chance to talk to the jury? He's not a defendant anymore. He's a murderer! A convicted murderer! The jury's made its decision. . . . His mother's had her chance all through the trial to sit there and let the jury see her cry for him while I was barred. . . . Now she's getting another chance? Now she's going to sit there in that witness chair and cry for her son, that murderer, that murderer who killed my little girl! Who will cry for Staci? Tell me that, who will cry for Staci?

* * *

These arguments sufficiently dispose of the critics' main contentions. Nonetheless, it is important to underscore that the critics generally fail to grapple with one of the strongest justifications for admitting victim impact statements: avoiding additional trauma to the victim. For all the fairness reasons just explained, gross disparity between defendants' and victims' rights to allocute at sentencing creates the risk of serious psychological injury to the victim. As Professor Douglas Beloof has nicely explained, a justice system that fails to recognize a victim's right to participate threatens "secondary harm"—that is, harm inflicted by the operation of government processes beyond that already caused by the perpetrator. This trauma stems from the fact that the victim perceives that the "system's resources are almost entirely devoted to the criminal, and little remains for those who have sustained harm at the criminal's hands." As two noted experts on the psychological effects of crime have concluded, failure to offer victims a chance to participate in criminal proceedings can "result in increased feelings of inequity on the part of the victims, with a corresponding increase in crime-related psychological harm." On the other hand, there is mounting evidence that "having a voice may improve victims' mental condition and welfare." For some victims, making a statement helps restore balance between themselves and the offenders. Others may consider it part of a just process or may want "to communicate the impact of the offense to the offender." This multiplicity of reasons explains why victims and surviving family members want so desperately to participate in sentencing hearings, even though their participation may not necessarily change the outcome.

———————

Notes

1. In a reply to Professor Cassell, Professor Bandes argued that "[r]ather than help to heal victims, victim impact statements may actually disempower, dehumanize, and silence them, as well as encourage irrelevant or invidious distinctions about the comparative worth of different victims, based on the social position, articulateness, and race of the victims and their families." Susan Bandes, *A Reply to Paul Cassell: What We Know About Victim Impact Statements*, 1999 Utah L. Rev. 545.

2. Do you have a full understanding of the harm that a crime inflicts on a victim? Reading first-hand accounts from crime victims may shed light on this question. Marvin Weinstein's story (mentioned in the Cassell excerpt) is published in Milton J. Shapiro with Marvin Weinstein, Who Will Cry for Staci? The True Story of a Grieving Father's Quest for Justice (1995). Other good accounts from about the crime victim's perspective include: Marsha Kight, Forever Changed: Remembering Oklahoma City, April 19, 1995 (1998); The Family of Ron Goldman, His Name Is Ron: Our Search for Justice (1997); Nancy Lamb and Children of Oklahoma City, One April Morning: Children Remember the Oklahoma City Bombing (1996); Alice R. Kaminsky, The Victim's Song (1985); Gary Kinder, Victim: The Other Side of Murder (1980); George Lardner Jr., The Stalking of Kristin: A Father Investigates the Murder of His Daughter(1995); Dorris D. Porch & Rebecca Easley, Murder In Memphis: The True Story of a Family's Quest for Justice (1997); Mike Reynolds & Bill Jones, Three Strikes And You're Out . . . A Promise to Kimber: The Chronicle of America's Toughest Anti-Crime Law (1996); Deborah Spungen, And I Don't Want to Live This Life (1983).

3. Some critics of the victim's rights movement believe that the victim's rights movement does nothing more than spread hatred of criminals. For example, Professor Lynne Henderson describes John Walsh (star of *America's Most Wanted*) as "preaching [a] gospel of rage and revenge." Lynne Henderson, *Revisiting Victim's Rights*, 1999 Utah L. Rev. 383. Is this an accurate description of Walsh's efforts? Walsh himself has explained his crusade as making sure that his murdered son Adam "didn't die in vain." John Walsh, Tears of Rage: From Grieving Father to Crusader for Justice: The Untold Story of the Adam Walsh Case (1997).

4. How would the critics reply to Judge Aquilina in Lansing, Michigan, who presided over the prosecution and sentencing of Dr. Lawrence G. Nassar, a prominent doctor for USA Gymnastics who pleaded guilty to multiple sex crimes? The judge

allowed nearly 140 girls and women, including several prominent Olympic athletes, to give victim impact statements against Dr. Nassar. N.Y. TIMES, January 23, 2018, at 1: "Judge Aquilina's vow to let every victim speak has also unexpectedly turned the hearing into a cathartic forum that has emboldened dozens of women who had remained silent to come forward with accounts of abuse by Dr. Nassar. . . . And, in an extraordinary session streamed live on the Internet over several days, she has opened her courtroom to any victim who wishes to speak, for however long she wishes to speak. That goes for their coaches and parents, too . . . 'Leave your pain here,' Judge Aquilina told one young woman, 'and go out and do your magnificent things.'"

5. The victim impact statement is typically limited to victims of the charged crime. One court has held it to be error, to allow victims of uncharged offenses to give an impact statement because their impact testimony was irrelevant. *See Commonwealth v. Smithton*, 631 A.2d 1053 (Pa. Super. Ct. 1993). Consider the preceding note. Is the impact testimony of victims who weren't formally named in the indictments constitutionally irrelevant?

5. The Admissibility of a Victim's Sentencing Recommendation in Capital Cases

The United States Supreme Court shed light on the reach of Payne's "overruling" and specifically addresses the victim "sentencing opinion" issue. The defendant was convicted in the Oklahoma District Court, McClain County, of three counts of first-degree murder and one count of first-degree arson, and was sentenced to death, for his killing of a mother and her two children. Three of the victims' relatives recommended a sentence to the jury. All three recommended death, and the jury agreed. Defendant appealed. The Oklahoma Court of Criminal Appeals, 360 P.3d 1203, affirmed. Upon granting certiorari, the United States Supreme Court held that at capital [death] sentencing, the admission of a victim's family members' sentence recommendation violates the Eighth Amendment. *Bosse v. Oklahoma*, 137 S. Ct. 1 (2016).

Does it make sense in capital cases to bar statements from the family members of a victim about their opinion on the appropriate sentence? Consider the following criticism of this approach.

Markus Dirk Dubber, *Victims in the War on Crime: The Use and Abuse of Victims' Rights*

(2002)

Perhaps nothing illustrates the irrelevance of victims for their own sake more poignantly than the suppression of *mitigating* victim evidence in capital cases, regardless of whether it stems from a derivative victim or even, and most remarkably, from the victim herself. Surviving relatives are prevented from expressing their opposition to capital punishment in general, or to the imposition of capital punishment in the particular case. One might think that this evidence is considered inappropriate because it doesn't, or, perhaps, cannot possibly, reflect the direct victim's interests. Why, after all, should antideath penalty advocates who happened to have a loved one murdered be permitted to push their political agenda at the expense of their silenced relative?

But that can't be it. The mitigating voice of the direct victim, after all, is silenced, as well. Evidence of the direct victim's opposition to capital punishment in generally is categorically excluded. (Evidence of a homicide victim's opposition to capital punishment in the particular case is hard to come by, for obvious reasons.)

Courts throughout the nation agree that mitigating victim impact evidence, whether from derivative or from direct victims, must be kept out of capital sentencing hearings at all costs. This evidence, they announced categorically, is "unrelated to the defendant's culpability—it has nothing to do with the defendant's character or record or the circumstances of the crime—and thus is irrelevant to sentencing." It's merely "opinion" evidence. It relieves the sentencers of their job entirely, rather than providing assistance.

Unfortunately, courts have not been nearly as categorical in their condemnation of *aggravating* "opinion" evidence. Where they have not admitted opinion evidence outright, courts have bent over backward to interpret aggravating victim impact evidence as anything but an opinion regarding the "victim's" preferred sentence. Testimony by an indirect homicide victim that details the direct victim's excruciating suffering during and after the homicide . . . and is present by the prosecutor in support of her call for capital punishment can leave no doubt in the sentencer's mind regarding the witness's opinion about the appropriate sentence. . . . Courts fail to see "opinion" evidence even in cases where surviving relatives use their victim impact evidence to refer to the defendant as a "piece of trash," or ask the sentencing jury to "Show no mercy," and to "[r]enew our faith in the criminal justice system and bring a phase of closure to this ongoing nightmare that fills our lives."

––––––––––––

Can crime victims implicitly communicate sentencing recommendations in capital cases? Consider the actions of the victim's daughter in the following case:

Tom Jicha (TV/Radio Writer), *The Risk of Forgiveness on 48 Hours, Mercy Raises Troubling Questions*

Sun Sentinel (Oct. 2, 1997)

A news program about a life being saved is generally uplifting and the person doing the saving comes off as a heroic figure. This is not necessarily the case with tonight's *48 Hours*. It depends on the viewer's attitude toward the death penalty.

The life preserved is that of a convicted killer, James Bernard Campbell. His champion is the daughter of the minister Campbell murdered. The woman, Hallandale resident SueZann Bosler, also was grievously wounded in the same attack.

On Dec. 22, 1986, the 20-year-old Campbell, intent on robbery, knocked on the door of the Rev. Billy Bosler's parsonage in the Carol City section of north Dade County. As the clergyman opened the door, Campbell struck. Bosler was stabbed about two dozen times. Campbell then went after SueZann, stabbing her five times. One of his thrusts fractured her skull. *48 Hours* correspondent Susan Spencer displays pictures of SueZann's shaven head in the hospital. She has so many grotesquely huge stitches, her skull looks like a baseball.

The savagery of the attack is further illustrated by grisly pictures of the blood-drenched crime scene, which is revisited by SueZann and Spencer. SueZann's frantic 911 call, made just before she collapsed, is replayed.

Campbell was caught, tried and sentenced to death. The jury took only 80 minutes. The prosecutor argued that Campbell's case is the reason the death penalty was created. SueZann's emotional recollections of the horrific experience, parts of which are shown on tape, are believed to have played a key role in the trial.

However, Campbell's death sentence was overturned because of an error by the judge. A resentencing trial produced the same sentence, death by electrocution. This, too, was overturned because of overzealousness on the part of the prosecutor.

By the third sentencing trial, this past June, SueZann Bosler had a change of heart. She had become affiliated with Murder Victims Families for Reconciliation, an organization opposed to the death penalty. Bosler says she has forgiven Campbell and she has become an advocate for sparing his life.

Her efforts faced an obstacle, however. Florida law allows crime victims to testify about the impact of the crime but not to express an opinion on what they feel is the appropriate punishment.

48 Hours shows the Kafkaesque turnabout in the third sentencing trial, in which the judge warns Bosler that if she says on the stand that Campbell should be spared, he will send her to jail for contempt.

Bosler complies with the letter of this edict while circumventing the spirit. She describes the crime in an emotionless, matter-of-fact tone. She refers to Campbell as a gentlemen. Perhaps most significantly, she manages to get her feelings across when the prosecutor asks about her job. The beautician says she has several, including working for the abolition of the death penalty.

How much this weighed on the jury is a matter of conjecture, but the outcome is different this time. The recommendation, to which the judge adhered, is life without possibility of parole for 25 years.

Theoretically, Campbell, who shows no sign of remorse — he refuses to even acknowledge Bosler — could be free before he is 50. If he is able to rehabilitate himself, SueZann Bosler could be seen as an angel of mercy.

Should he kill again in prison, or worse, manage to gain parole and resume a life of violent crime in our community, this might not be the last time SueZann Bosler is featured on a TV news magazine.

In light of the opportunities open to victims like Bosler to implicitly communicate sentencing recommendations, does it make any sense to bar such recommendations. Consider the following:

Douglas E. Beloof, *Constitutional Implications of Crime Victims as Participants*
88 Cornell L. Rev. 282 (2003)

The Supreme Court, attuned to the concept of victim harm originating in the criminal act, the potential for further harm from the criminal process, and the inclusion of victim participation in the states' criminal proceedings, has shown increasing respect for the legitimate interests of crime victims. In *Morris v. Slappy*, the Court recognized that a criminal defendant's rights should not be applied in a manner that unnecessarily harms the crime victim. This unnecessary harm occurs when courts silence victims' sentencing recommendations. For example, victims who want to recommend that death is not appropriate are forced into an agonizing choice among bad options. The first bad option is participating in the sentencing hearing by providing the first two types of victim impact — the deceased's characteristics and the particularized harm to the survivors. According to *Payne*, this option respects the murdered person as a "uniquely individual human being." However, providing victim impact information without giving a participant sentencing recommendation essentially endorses the State's effort to obtain the death penalty.

As a poor second option, the victim can simply refuse to participate in a sentencing hearing in which death is sought. Such refusal is problematic because it tacitly aids the quest for death. The jury is likely to perceive the victim's silence as acquiescence in the public prosecutor's pursuit of capital punishment. Moreover, this option strips victims of the ability to exercise their responsibility to the deceased, because waiving participation means that victims cannot even communicate factual harm to the sentencing authority. A procedure which inherently encourages one type of victim (who would recommend no death) to waive the right to participate in sentencing but not another (who would recommend death) is far from ideal.

A third unsatisfactory option is for the participants to convey victim harm and characteristics in a way that covertly communicates the victim's recommendation for or against death. The news documentary program *48 Hours* provided a vivid example of this option. The defendant in a homicide brutally attacked the victim and her father, a preacher, in the preacher's parsonage. He stabbed the preacher two dozen times and stabbed the daughter, who survived, five times, fracturing her skull. The defendant's death sentencing hearings took place three times because of error unrelated to victim impact evidence. In the first two hearings, the jury sentenced the defendant to death. Between the second and third sentencing hearings, however, the daughter decided to oppose a death sentence. Because Florida law prohibited crime victims from giving their opinion regarding the appropriate punishment, the judge threatened the daughter with contempt if she expressed her recommendation. Therefore, in order to convey her recommendation that the death penalty was inappropriate, the daughter complie[d] with the letter of this edict while circumventing the spirit. She describe[d] the crime in an emotionless, matter-of-fact tone. She refer[ed] to [the murderer] as a "gentleman." Perhaps most significantly, she manage[d] to get her feelings across when the prosecutor ask[ed] about her job. [The daughter] sa[id] she ha[d] several, including working for the abolition of the death penalty.

It is doubtful that the daughter actually thought or felt that the murderer was a gentleman, or that the brutal attack on herself and her murdered father evoked no emotion. Rather, the daughter manipulated her testimony to convey her recommendation that the defendant not receive the death penalty.

The ability of a victim to recommend the propriety of life over death by presenting her victim impact statement with an emotionally flat affect reveals the absurdity of a procedural prohibition on participant sentencing recommendations. A victim can simply suppress the richness of factually-relevant victim impact to achieve the goal of communicating her feelings about the impropriety of the death sentence. In an emotional (if not strictly factual) sense, the procedural exclusion of participant sentencing recommendations encourages the victim to lie. It is a safe assumption that it is easier for those victims seeking the death penalty to implicitly convey their recommendations because they do not need to suppress any emotion. Therefore, the constitutional exclusion of victim sentencing recommendations would merely screen out those victims who are less capable of communicating their sentencing recommendations obliquely.

---

6. Victim Impact Evidence in Non-Capital Cases

Outside of the controversial context of capital cases, victim impact statements are clearly constitutionally permitted and allowed by state constitutional amendment or state statute. In the context of non-capital cases, the few courts ruling on the question have held that where the law so provides, a victim can express an opinion regarding the defendant's sentence in non-capital cases. *See, e.g., Randall v. State*, 846 P.2d 278 (Nev. 1993); *State v. Mattesan*, 851 P.2d 336 (Idaho 1993).

Commonwealth v. Shawn A. McGonagle

SJC-12292, (Mass. January 18, 2018)

LOWY, J. General Laws c. 258B, § 3 (p), permits "victims . . . to be heard through an oral and written victim impact statement at sentencing . . . about the effects of the crime on the victim and as to a recommended sentence. "We transferred this case here on our own motion to answer two questions: first, whether the United States Supreme Court's recent decision in Bosse v. Oklahoma, 137 S. Ct. 1 (2016) (per curiam), precludes a sentencing judge from considering victim impact statements "as to a recommended sentence" under the Eighth Amendment to the United States Constitution and art. 26 of the Massachusetts Declaration of Rights; and second, whether the sentencing recommendation provision violates the defendant's constitutional guarantee of due process. We conclude that a sentencing judge's consideration of victim impact statements "as to a recommended sentence" is constitutional because the concerns underpinning the Supreme Court's treatment of victim impact statements before a jury during the sentencing phase of a capital murder trial differ from those at issue here. We further conclude that a victim's right to recommend a sentence pursuant to G. L. c. 258B, § 3 (p), satisfies the requirements of due process. We therefore answer both questions in the negative and affirm.

Background and prior proceedings.

Following a trial in the District Court, a jury convicted the defendant, Shawn McGonagle, of assault and battery, G. L. c. 265, § 13A. At the defendant's sentencing hearing, the Commonwealth requested that the defendant be sentenced to two and one-half years in a house of correction, the maximum possible sentence under the statute, to be served from and after his release on an unrelated one-year sentence for violating an abuse prevention order. Immediately after the Commonwealth's recommendation, the victim gave an impact statement, during which he told the judge, "I would like . . . for [the defendant] to get the maximum [sentence], and not concurrent." The defendant then requested a sentence of nine months in a house of correction to be served concurrently with his unrelated sentence.

The judge sentenced the defendant to eighteen months in a house of correction to be served concurrently with the sentence he was then serving. This was a lesser term of imprisonment than the maximum possible sentence or the sentences recommended by both the Commonwealth and the victim. The judge did not explicitly reference the victim's statement, but explained that in deciding the appropriate sentence, he placed great weight on the victim's injuries and the defendant's criminal record.

Discussion.

The defendant does not challenge G. L. c. 258B, § 3 (p), in its entirety, but instead only challenges the portion of the statute that permits victims to provide an impact statement "as to a recommended sentence." The defendant relies on Booth v.

Maryland, 482 U.S. 496 (1987); Payne v. Tennessee, 501 U.S. 808 (1991); and Bosse, 137 S. Ct. 1, to support his claim that a victim's recommendation as to a particular sentence violates the proscription against cruel and unusual punishments under the Eighth Amendment, and its "cruel or unusual punishments" counterpart under art. 26. The defendant further contends that allowing a victim to recommend a particular sentence violates due process.

Eighth Amendment and art. 26.

In Booth, the United States Supreme Court held that the introduction of certain types of victim impact statements to a jury "at the sentencing phase of a capital murder trial violates the Eighth Amendment." Specifically, the Court identified two prohibited categories of victim impact statements:

(1) those providing accounts of the emotional impact of the crime and descriptions of the victims' personal attributes; and (2) those addressing the victims' family members' opinions about the crime and the defendant, and recommendations as to the defendant's sentence. Id. at 502. Four years later, however, the Court in Payne held that "the Eighth Amendment erects no per se bar" to the admission of the first category of victim impact statements identified in Booth if the State authorizes their admission. The Court declined to reconsider the Eighth Amendment's prohibition on the second category of victim impact statements concerning "opinions about the crime, the defendant, and the appropriate sentence."

After the defendant was sentenced in this case, the Supreme Court decided Bosse, which clarified its holdings in Booth and Payne. The Court stated that Payne held "that Booth was wrong to conclude that the Eighth Amendment required . . . a ban" on the first category of victim impact statements. Id. The Court then emphasized that Payne was expressly limited to the first category of statements regarding "the personal characteristics of the victim and the emotional impact of the crimes on the victim's family." Id., quoting Payne, 501 U.S. at 817. Thus, Booth's prohibition as to the second category of victim impact statements concerning "characterizations and opinions [from a victim's family] about the crime, the defendant, and the appropriate sentence" remained intact. Bosse, supra.

While the prohibition on the second category of victim impact statements announced in Booth and reaffirmed in Bosse remains binding precedent in capital murder trials, that prohibition has no application here for two reasons. First, this is not a capital murder case. The Supreme Court in Booth, expressly relied on the unique character of the death penalty, a "punishment different from all other sanctions," in rendering its decision (citation omitted). Second, the victim impact statement in this case was made to a judge who imposed the defendant's sentence, not to a jury. While a jury in a capital murder trial may be unable to separate relevant evidence from that which is unduly prejudicial, we trust that judges, when weighing such statements as part of the sentencing determination, will render decisions guided by the best practices for individualized evidence–based sentencing, according to law and logic, not emotion. Cf. Fautenberry v. Mitchell, 515 F.3d 614, 639

(6th Cir.), cert. denied, 555 U.S. 951 (2008) (concerns in Booth "are severely diminished—if not entirely obviated—when the sentencer is a judge or a three- judge panel, rather than a lay jury").

We conclude that the Supreme Court's holding in Booth does not apply to non-capital proceedings and, therefore, it does not prohibit the statement at issue here. The dangerous uses to which a jury in a capital murder trial may put a victim's recommendation as to a particular sentence are not present at a noncapital sentencing proceeding before a neutral, impartial judge.

Due process.

(2) Having concluded that the United States Supreme Court's holding in Booth, supra, under the Eighth Amendment is limited to capital murder trials, we consider whether the sentencing recommendation provision nonetheless violates due process. Where, as here, the statute does not affect a fundamental right or target a suspect class, we apply the rational basis test. Goodridge v. Department of Pub. Health, 440 Mass. 309, 330 (2003). "[R]ational basis analysis requires that statutes 'bear[] a real and substantial relation to the public health, safety, morals, or some other phase of the general welfare'" (citation omitted). Id. We note that "[t]he Legislature is presumed to have acted rationally and reasonably." Commonwealth v. Leis, 355 Mass. 189, 192 (1969).

The Legislature enacted G. L. c. 258B, § 3, as part of an initiative to "provide victims a meaningful role in the criminal justice system . . . to the greatest extent possible." Section 3 "was intended to change the 'traditional view' of victims from virtually silent observers to active participants in the criminal justice process." Hagen v. Commonwealth, 437 Mass. 374, 380–381 (2002). Consistent with this purpose, G. L. c. 258B, § 3 (p), permits "victims . . . to be heard through an oral and written victim impact statement at sentencing . . . against the defendant about the effects of the crime on the victim and as to a recommended sentence." Absent this legislative authorization, crime victims would not have an opportunity to voice the impact of the crime at sentencing, even though the criminal conduct has a direct impact on them. See Hagen, supra at 380. Crime victims are unrepresented at trial. The prosecutor is not their advocate; the prosecutor advocates for the Commonwealth. While victim impact statements give crime victims a voice at sentencing, a victim's ability to state the impact of a defendant's criminal conduct by recommending a particular sentence provides all victims the language to express that impact, regardless of their ability eloquently or precisely to verbalize the impact of the crime.

In addition to providing all crime victims a voice at sentencing, the sentencing recommendation provision of G. L. c. 258B, § 3 (p), assists judges in fashioning just and appropriate criminal sentences. "[T]o impose a just sentence, a judge requires not only sound judgment but also information concerning the crimes of which the defendant stands convicted, the defendant's criminal and personal history, and the impact of the crimes on the victims." Commonwealth v. Rodriguez, 461 Mass. 256, 259 (2012).

A victim may use the opportunity to recommend a particular sentence to the judge to urge imposition of a lengthy sentence or to request mercy. While the decision to impose sentence rests exclusively with the judge, a victim's recommendation, whether it be for a lenient sentence in the hvant consideration in determining the appropriate sentence to impose. Since the statute provides a mechanism for victims to participate in the sentencing process in a way that enhances judges' understanding of the impact of the crime, we reject the defendant's argument that the sentencing recommendation provision of G. L. c. 258B, § 3 (p), lacks a rational basis.

"Few, perhaps no, judicial responsibilities are more difficult than sentencing. The task is usually undertaken by trial judges who seek with diligence and professionalism to take account of the human existence of the offender and the just demands of a wronged society." Rodriguez, 461 Mass. at 259, quoting Graham v. Florida, 560 U.S. 48, 77 (2010). The concerns underlying the Supreme Court's holdings in Booth and Bosse, that sentencing decisions not be made based on emotion, apply in nearly every sentencing decision. They raise an important caution. When a crime victim recommends a particular sentence tope of redemption or for a maximum sentence commensurate with harm, is a releo a judge, that judge must dispassionately consider that recommendation, cognizant that the sentencing decision is the judge's and the judge's alone. We expect judges to make sentencing decisions devoid of emotion, prejudice, and the relative status of a particular crime victim.

Conclusion.

We all stand equal before the bar of justice, and it is neither cruel nor unusual or irrational, nor is it violative of a defendant's due process guarantees, for a judge to listen with intensity to the perspective of a crime victim. We affirm.

Notes

1. Does the fact that some crime victims make victim impact statements while others decline to make such statements exacerbate the concern that such statements lead to unequal justice? Is this a consequence of recognizing victim agency, including agency on whether to exercise rights in the criminal justice system?

2. If the prosecution has promised as part of a plea agreement to recommend a specific sentence, can the prosecution present victim impact testimony in which the victims call for a longer sentence? See State v. Clark, 566 A.2d 1346 (Vt. 1989) (state did not violate plea agreement in assisting victims to present their own recommendation).

3. Most courts ruling on the issue have held that defendants are entitled to victim impact statements as part of the right to discovery. Failure to provide the defense with notice of a victim impact statement might be reversible error when the trial judge relies on the statement to impose a longer sentence. See State v. Dake,

545 N.W.2d 895 (Iowa 1996) (reversing for resentencing where trial judge used victim impact statement without giving statutorily-required notice to the defendant). Some states, however, provide that the defendant is not entitled to a victim impact statement unless it contains exculpatory material, as determined by the judge in an *in camera* review. *See Johnson v. State*, 919 S.W.2d 473 (Tex. Ct. App. 1996).

4. While a victim's right to make an impact statement cannot simply be delegated to a relative or friend, the courts generally have discretionary power to hear and consider other witnesses as appropriate. *See People v. Zikorus*, 197 Cal.Rptr. 509 (Cal. App. 1983) (upholding trial court's decision to hear testimony of a victim's mother).

5. Some judges have imposed sentences on defendants that focus on the victims, often at the request of victims. For example, former Texas Judge Ted Poe has ordered a man convicted of involuntary manslaughter of his friend to carry a picture of the victim in his wallet, place flowers on victim's grave, and write letters to the victim's family during his sentence. An Arkansas judge required a convicted murderer to send $1 to an account set up in the victim's memory on the 19th of each month (the date of the murder). And still another judge allowed victims of a theft to enter the criminal's home and take whatever they wanted. *See* Barbara Clare Morton, *Bringing Skeletons out of the Closet and into the Light—"Scarlet Letter" Sentencing Can Meet the Goals of Probation in Modern America Because it Deprives Offenders of Privacy*, 35 Suffolk U.L. Rev. 97 (2001).

6. Crime victims' rights to notice and to be heard are procedural, and thus do not violate *expost facto* laws. *People v. Huber,* 227 Cal. Rptr. (Cal. App. 1986); *Myers v. Ridge,* 712 A.2d 791 (Pa. Comm. Ct. 1998).

7. Professor Logan argues against permitting the pathos of victims to infuse legal processes and decision making in cases involving the mass killing of innocents. Wayne A. Logan, *Confronting Evil: Victims' Rights in an Age of Terror*, 96 Geo. L.J. 721 (2008).

---

7. Constraints on Victim Impact Testimony under Sentencing Guidelines and Mandatory Minimum Sentence Schemes

Sentencing guideline schemes remove complete sentencing discretion from the court. Guidelines typically provide for a sentence within a permissible range. Aggravating factors operate towards imposition of a sentence at the high end of the range. Mitigating factors operate towards imposition of a sentence at the low end of the range.

As illustrated in the Luttig case at the beginning of this chapter, sentencing guidelines can prevent a judge from imposing a sentence that the victim believes is appropriate. At the same time, sentencing guidelines can provide for consideration of effects on a victim. For example, the federal sentencing guidelines provide for sentencing enhancements in various cases based on the kind of a victim or the effects on the victims. The Guidelines provide additional punishment—calculated by increasing the "level" of an offense—in the following circumstances:

§ 3A1.1. Vulnerable Victim

If the defendant knew or should have known that a victim of the offense was unusually vulnerable due to age, physical or mental condition, or that a victim was otherwise particularly susceptible to the criminal conduct, increase by 2 levels.

§ 3A1.3. Restraint of Victim

If a victim was physically restrained in the course of the offense, increase by 2 levels.

§ 3A1.3. Physical Injury (Policy Statement)

If significant physical injury resulted, the court may increase the sentence above the authorized guideline range. The extent of the increase ordinarily should depend on the extent of the injury, the degree to which it may prove permanent, and the extent to which the injury was intended or knowingly risked. When the victim suffers a major, permanent disability and when such injury was intentionally inflicted, a substantial departure may be appropriate. If the injury is less serious or if the defendant (though criminally negligent) did not knowingly create the risk of harm, a less substantial departure would be indicated. In general, the same considerations apply as in § 5K2.1.

§ 5K2.3. Extreme Psychological Injury (Policy Statement)

If a victim or victims suffered psychological injury much more serious than that normally resulting from commission of the offense, the court may increase the sentence above the authorized guideline range. The extent of the increase ordinarily should depend on the severity of the psychological injury and the extent to which the injury was intended or knowingly risked.

Normally, psychological injury would be sufficiently severe to warrant application of this adjustment only when there is a substantial impairment of the intellectual, psychological, emotional, or behavioral functioning of a victim, when the impairment is likely to be of an extended or continuous duration, and when the impairment manifests itself by physical or psychological symptoms or by changes in behavior patterns. The court should consider the extent to which such harm was likely, given the nature of the defendant's conduct.

§ 5K2.4. Abduction or Unlawful Restraint (Policy Statement)

If a person was abducted, taken hostage, or unlawfully restrained to facilitate commission of the offense or to facilitate the escape from the scene of the crime, the court may increase the sentence above the authorized guideline range.

§ 5K2.5. Property Damage or Loss (Policy Statement)

If the offense caused property damage or loss not taken into account within the guidelines, the court may increase the sentence above the authorized guidelines range. The extent of the increase ordinarily should depend on the extent to which the harm was intended or knowingly risked and on the extent to which the harm to property is more serious than other harm caused or risked by the conduct relevant to the offense of conviction.

§ 5K2.8. Extreme Conduct (Policy Statement)

If the defendant's conduct was unusually heinous; cruel, brutal, or degrading to the victim, the court may increase the sentence above the guideline range to reflect the nature of the conduct. Examples of extreme conduct include torture of a victim, gratuitous infliction of injury, or prolonging of pain or humiliation.

§ 5K2.10. Victim's Conduct (Policy Statement)

If the victim's wrongful conduct contributed significantly to provoking the offense behavior, the court may reduce the sentence below the guideline range to reflect the nature and circumstances of the offense. In deciding the extent of a sentence reduction, the court should consider:

(a) the size and strength of the victim, or other relevant physical characteristics, in comparison with those of the defendant;

(b) the persistence of the victim's conduct and any efforts by the defendant to prevent confrontation;

(c) the danger reasonably perceived by the defendant, including the victim's reputation for violence;

(d) the danger actually presented to the defendant by the victim; and

(e) any other relevant conduct by the victim that substantially contributed to the danger presented.

———————

Note. The victim's right to be heard at sentencing has implications for the court's deciding whether to permit a defendant's request to be sentenced *in absentia* when the victim wants the defendant to hear the victim's impact statement. In *State v. Tedesco*, 214 N.J. 177 (2013), the court opined:

We find no support in the court rule or elsewhere for defendant's position and hold that trial judges have discretion to decide whether to accept a defendant's waiver. In an attempt to justify a waiver, a defendant must advance specific reasons that demonstrate special circumstances. Judges, in turn, must consider various concerns including the interests of the public, the defendant, the victims, and the State.

In this case, we find that defendant's reasons for wanting to be absent from sentencing are not special or persuasive. Balanced against them are factors that favor his presence: the seriousness of the offense, the victim's interest in having defendant present as she addresses the court, and concerns about public accountability, deterrence, and the administration and integrity of the justice system.

In light of those interests, we conclude that the trial court did not abuse its discretion when it ordered defendant to appear at sentencing. We therefore affirm the judgment of the Appellate Division, which upheld the trial court's order, and remand for a sentencing hearing at which defendant shall appear.

Whether or not the content of a victim's impact statement can be considered as an aggravating or mitigating factor is an issue often not explicitly addressed by statutory sentencing guidelines schemes. This lack of clarity has left the issue up to the courts.

Kansas v. Heath

901 P.2d 29 (Kan. Ct. App. 1995)

BARRY A BENNINGTON, District Judge, Assigned:

The district court granted a downward dispositional departure in sentencing defendant Danny L. Heath. The State appeals. We find no reversible error and affirm the trial court.

Heath drove a car involved in an accident in which passenger Kord Cole, a co-worker and friend, died. Heath's blood alcohol level was .151 percent. Heath pled no contest to charges of involuntary manslaughter, a severity level 5 person felony, in violation of K.S.A. 1993 Supp. 21-3404.

Heath filed a timely motion for departure, which the court heard at the sentencing hearing. At sentencing, Heath agreed to his criminal history classification being level "D." His criminal history consisted of: (1) residential burglary, a person felony juvenile adjudication, dated 12-7-78; (2) felony theft, a nonperson felony juvenile adjudication, dated 12-7-78; (3) three misdemeanor convictions for possession of marijuana, dated 9-11-80, 3-23-83, and 6-5-89; and (4) driving while his license was suspended, a nonperson misdemeanor, dated 11-14-90.

The court determined Heath's crime severity level and criminal history classification placed him in the 5-D box on the sentencing grid providing for presumptive imprisonment and a presumptive term of 50–55 months. The trial court, after hearing arguments of counsel and evidence on the issue of departure, imposed a dispositional departure sentence, giving Heath 50 months in prison but placing him on probation under the supervision of community corrects for a duration of 60 months. In the journal entry, the court stated the mitigating factors used as the basis for departure . . .

Second, the trial court considered the fact that the victim's father testified Heath should not be incarcerated. The victim's father stated at the trial, "[T]here's no need that boy going to jail. He quit drinking. The accident's over. As far as I'm concerned, why, he's got a family to take care of."

Third, the trial court considered the fact the victim's mother testified defendant did not intentionally kill her son. In the "Victim Statement" filed by the victim's mother, she stated, "Danny didn't mean to kill Kord but he is responsible.". . .

Testimony of victim's parents as mitigating factor.

The State submits that the statements made by the victim's parents at the departure hearing and in the "Victim Statement" are not a substantial and compelling reason for departure, nor should they be recognized as a mitigating factor in sentencing, while Heath argues that the guidelines embrace victim participation at a departure hearing and it is proper for a trial court to consider the victim's statements and testimony. We hold testimony or evidence from the victims or their families may provide a substantial and compelling reason for departure.

The role of the victim in the criminal justice system has substantially increased in the past few years. The Kansas Constitution, in Article 15, § 15 provides that victims of crime have a right "to be heard at sentencing or at any other time deemed appropriate by the court." K.S.A. 1993 Supp. 21-4718(a)(1) provides that with regard to a sentence departure hearing, "[t]he victim of a crime or the victim's family shall be notified of the right to be present at the hearing." This statute further requires that "[t]he court shall review the victim impact statement."

K.S.A. 1993 Supp. 21-4716(c) provides:

In determining aggravating or mitigating circumstances, the court shall consider:

(1) Any evidence received during the proceeding;

(2) the presentence report;

(3) written briefs and oral arguments of either the state or counsel for the defendant; and

(4) any other evidence relevant to such aggravating or mitigating circumstances that the court finds trustworthy and reliable.

Based upon these constitutional and statutory mandates, we hold the trial court may consider the statements of crime victims or their families as evidence of either aggravating or mitigating circumstances.

The facts of this case give the statements of the victim's parents reliability and trustworthiness. Heath worked with the victim for two years preceding the accident. On the day of the accident, the two were working together on a construction site in Wichita. They made a daily commute together from Hutchinson to Wichita to get to work. In addition to their working relationship, Heath and the victim were also social friends. After leaving work on the day of the accident, they went to a tavern adjacent to the work area and had a couple of beers. After driving 25 to 35 miles back to Hutchinson, Heath swerved to miss an object—a piece of a tire—in the roadway, causing the car to slide off the road into a utility pole.

Other events in this case also demonstrate the support the victim's family showed for Heath. The day Heath was released from the hospital, the victim's parents came to his residence, at which time he promised them he would never drink alcoholic beverages again. The victim's sister also visited Heath after he was released from the hospital and showed her support by sitting beside Heath's wife at the preliminary hearing. Last, before entering the courtroom on the day of the departure hearing, the victim's mother came up to Heath, hugged him, and told him he needed to take care of his family.

Finally, Heath also showed remorse for what he had done. He continuously recognized his responsibility in causing the death of his close friend, Kord Cole. Heath's parents and his brother had died prior to the accident, so he testified he knew the pain and the hurt the victim's family were going through and he was sorry he caused it. Further, Heath testified he had not consumed alcohol since the accident, and he assured the court he could realistically live up to his pledge of abstinence from alcohol.

We find the statements of the victim's family constitute substantial competent evidence supporting the trial court's reasons justifying departure. We also find the statements of the victim's family constitute substantial and compelling reasons for departure as a matter of law.

[Among other reasons, the courts departure from the guidelines was supported by] the victim's family had strong feelings concerning nonimprisonment. We find the court's statements concerning the sentencing guidelines constitute neither a proper basis for departure nor a sufficient reason for reversal. The first two reasons given for the departure are substantial and compelling reasons, although the third is not.

Affirmed.

Notes

1. Mandatory minimum sentences, as opposed to sentencing guidelines, generally result in a victim's input into sentencing having no practical effect. For example, Oregon imposes a mandatory minimum for manslaughter in the second degree. If the *Heath* case were in Oregon, the victim's family in *Heath* would have no ability to mitigate the sentence. In Oregon, the victim's family would have to use informal influence to try to get the prosecutor to reduce the charge to one not carrying a mandatory minimum.

2. Are mandatory minimums in the interest of victim? Assuming, arguendo, that victim input at sentencing is important, do mandatory minimums hurt a victim's autonomous ability to contribute to a just determination of punishment?

3. Some jurisdictions have enacted "presumptive" sentencing structures in which each offense is classified and for each class the Legislature designates a presumptive

term that can be mitigated or aggravated based on defined circumstances. *See, e.g.,* Ariz. Rev. Stat. 13-701 et seq. In such systems, even if the sentence to prison is mandatory (in the case of violent or repeat offenders) there remains a range of sentence terms that the victim may influence.

4. Some view mandatory sentences as the only way to hold the government accountable for the safety of the community. Under this view, the loss of victim influence in sentencing is a necessary evil to keep in place significant sanctions against the tide of budgetary pressure to reduce sentences. Doesn't this undercut arguments for individual victim involvement in other procedural contexts, for example, the charging decision?

5. Mandatory minimum sentences also remove the significance of differences between victims when offenders are convicted of the same type of crime involving different victims in unrelated acts. However, bias against "unworthy" victims may be manifested still in the charging decision or in the plea bargain decision. The prosecutor's control over what crime a person is charged with or what plea bargain is offered is generally not affected by mandatory minimums.

6. For discussion of the pros and cons of mandatory minimum sentences, see Markus Dirk Dubber, *Recidivists Statutes as Arational Punishment*, 43 Buff. L. Rev. 689 (1995); Michael M. Baylson, *Mandatory Minimum Sentences: A Federal Prosecutor's Viewpoint*, 40 Fed. B. News & J., 167 (Mar. 1993); Stephen J. Schulhofer, *Rethinking Mandatory Minimums,* 28 Wake Forest L. Rev. 199 (1993); Orrin G. Hatch, *The Role of Congress in Sentencing: The United States Sentencing Commission, Mandatory Minimum Sentences, and the Search for a Certain and Effective Sentencing System*, 28 Wake Forest L. Rev. 185 (1993); Paul G. Cassell, *Too Severe? A Defense of the Federal Sentencing Guidelines (and a Critique of Federal Mandatory Minimums)*, 56 Stan. L. Rev. 1017 (2004).

8. Community Impact Statements

Should the concept of a victim impact statement be extended beyond individuals to affected communities?

Katie Long, Note, *Community Input at Sentencing: Victim's Right or Victim's Revenge?*
75 B.U. L. Rev. 195 (1995)

Flowing from their heightened interest in the criminal justice system, community groups have found ways to make their voices heard in the sentencing of criminal defendants. Community input has assumed a variety of different forms varying by state, jurisdiction, and case.

The most recent, and perhaps most significant, route for community input has been victim-impact statements. Such statements are designed to illuminate for the sentencing body the specific effects of a crime on its victims. The use of victim-impact statements is commonplace in our criminal justice system. Most jurisdictions now afford victims the opportunity to address the sentencing authority either in person or in writing, and many require the sentencing authority to consider the information provided when determining the appropriate punishment. Propelled by the nation's growing sympathy toward victims, courts have become increasingly flexible as to who, or what, constitutes a victim and how much information a victim can offer. Some judges have permitted community members to make oral or written presentations, implicitly relying on the assumption that the represented community itself is a "victim of the crime." . . .

Arguably, the impact of *Payne* reaches beyond direct victim-impact statements. By permitting the grandmother's testimony, the Court facilitated admission of sentencing evidence from more remote victims. In their opinions, both Justices Rehnquist and O'Connor suggested that a victim's community may be injured by a crime, and that evidence of such harm may be admissible at sentencing. As Justice O'Connor wrote, "A State may decide that the jury, before determining whether a convicted murderer should receive the death penalty, should know the full extent of the harm caused by the crime, including its impact on the victim's family *and community*."

Some courts have adopted this expansive interpretation of the *Payne* decision. One court agreed that the Eighth Amendment is not an absolute bar to community-impact evidence, while other courts are beginning to hear input at sentencing from victims who fall outside the traditional categories of direct victim or survivor. Some courts are willing to admit second-hand, or even third-hand, information.

At the legislative level, many states have codified the result in *Payne* by writing community input into their sentencing laws. These statutes legitimize community sentiment as relevant to the sentencing decision. Sentencing authorities can explore a crime's broader impact, including its effect on individuals other than the direct victim before calculating a sentence. For example, a Pennsylvania court heard a plea from a member of Mothers Against Drunk Driving ("MADD") when sentencing a drunk driver. The court admitted this testimony under a state statute allowing evidence in any form, provided "it relates to the impact on the life of the victim and on the community." In Georgia, legislators recently altered their death penalty statute to provide expressly for community input at the punishment phase of murder trials.

Another method communities use to influence sentencing involves the discretion of judicial sentencing authorities. Federal and state courts traditionally possess considerable latitude in choosing the content and source of information permitted at the sentencing stage of a case. Judges invoke this discretion in admitting community testimony and information in pre-sentence reports. In recent illustrative cases, courts received testimony from co-workers about the effect of the assault of a police officer on department morale, and accepted letters from students and teachers about tension following a shooting near their school. In addition to traditional material gathered from the defendant, the defendant's family, neighbors, employers, and the victim about an offense, pre-sentence reports now typically include an "assessment of community attitudes" towards the offender and the crime, "the kind of community reaction to be expected if the offender were to be placed on probation," and letters from the community.

In sum, the *Payne* ruling solidified and accelerated the expansion of what courts accept as harm-related evidence at sentencing. Relying on a broad interpretation of the opinion, courts have widened the scope of permissible sources and admissible content to allow community input.

––––––––––––

Notes

1. After describing community impact on sentencing, Katie Long goes on to criticize community involvement: "The community already has substantial influence in the criminal justice system. Enlarging its role at sentencing only further tips the scales in favor of vigilante justice and against the criminal defendant. Expanding citizen power in an unchecked and haphazard fashion poses the danger of mob mentality, saving the most damning testimony for the weakest members of society. Punishment may turn on the level of fear or anxiety at the moment." 75 B.U. L. Rev. at 229. Do you agree with this critique?

2. Law professor Paul Robinson has argued that individual crime victims should not have any personal say in the punishment of their own victimizers because they are too close to the case to make objective determinations. On the other hand, he concludes that crime victims' organizations might appropriately receive such a say because the organization sees the full range of cases and thus can realistically and dispassionately assess how any given case compares to the full range of other cases. Paul H. Robinson, *Should the Victims' Rights Movement Have Influence Over Criminal Law Formulation and Adjudication?*, 33 McGeorge L. Rev. 749 (2002). Could community impact organizations fulfill the role of dispassionate assessor that Robinson envisions?

9. Judicial Empathy Toward Victims at Sentencing

United States v. Minard

856 F.3d 555 (8th Cir. 2017)

Before WOLLMAN, LOKEN, and RILEY, Circuit Judges.

Opinion

LOKEN, Circuit Judge.

A Knoxville, Iowa citizen reported an encounter with a suspicious person who knocked on his door, then struck a vehicle while driving away. A dispatched Marion County Deputy located and approached the reported vehicle parked on a dead-end road. The vehicle's armed driver was Nathan Minard, and the vehicle was full of firearms and other items taken in recent local burglaries. Minard was charged and pleaded guilty to being a felon in possession of a firearm in violation of 18 U.S.C.

§ 922(g). The Presentence Investigation Report calculated an advisory guidelines range of 120 to 150 months in prison; the statutory maximum sentence was 10 years.

At sentencing, Ryan McCarthy, one of Minard's burglary victims, addressed the court, explaining the impact the burglary of their residence had on McCarthy, his wife, and their two young children. "My wife, you know, she'll hear something after I've left for work in the morning, you know, she's never going to get by what's happened to us because of his irresponsible actions." When McCarthy completed his statement, the district court stated: "I understand exactly what you're saying. It happened to me, too, when my kids were little, so I know exactly what you're talking about." The prosecutor then stated the government's sentencing position, asking the court to impose the statutory maximum of 120 months, based on Minard's extensive criminal history and the events leading to his arrest in a vehicle full of stolen items and firearms. The district court discussed in detail its consideration of the 18 U.S.C. § 3553(a) sentencing factors and imposed a 120-month sentence.

Minard filed a timely motion under Rule 35 of the Federal Rules of Criminal Procedure, alleging that the district court's statement to the crime victim at sentencing "might have caused the Court to lack impartiality resulting in a harsher sentence," and seeking "re-sentencing to occur before a different Judicial Officer." The district court denied the motion without a hearing, explaining that its statement to the victim "had nothing to do with the sentence imposed. . . . [It was] an expression of empathy, nothing more." Minard appeals, arguing the district court erred in denying his Rule 35 motion because the statement reflected a bias or partiality which required the judge to recuse, sua sponte, pursuant to 28 U.S.C. § 455(a). We conclude this contention is without merit for multiple reasons and therefore affirm.

First, as Minard did not object or move for recusal at sentencing, the issue was not timely raised and our review is for plain error. . . .

Second, "a judge is presumed to be impartial and the party seeking disqualification bears the substantial burden of proving otherwise." United States v. Ali, 799 F.3d 1008, 1017 (8th Cir. 2015) (quotation omitted). Opinions based on facts or events occurring in a judicial proceeding "do not constitute a basis for a bias or partiality motion unless they display a deep-seated favoritism or antagonism that would make fair judgment impossible." Liteky v. United States, 510 U.S. 540, 555, 114 S.Ct. 1147, 127 L.Ed.2d 474 (1994). Here, the district court's spontaneous expression of empathy for a crime victim's impact statement reflected no deep-seated antagonism, and its statement of reasons for imposing a 120-month sentence reflected thorough and proper consideration of the statutory sentencing factors.

Finally, Congress has given crime victims the statutory rights "to be reasonably heard at any public proceeding in the district court involving . . . sentencing," and "to be treated with fairness and with respect for the victim's dignity and privacy." 18 U.S.C. § 3771(a)(4) and (8). Rather than reflect bias or antagonism to Minard, the district court's single statement—directed to the crime victim at the end of the victim's stressful appearance—furthered the congressional policy of encouraging crime victim participation in the criminal justice process.

The judgment of the district court is affirmed.

B. Victim Statements at Parole and Parole Proceedings

A majority of states allow victim input at parole hearings. Generally victim impact statements in parole hearings are handled in much the same way as they are handled in court hearings. At least one federal Court of Appeals, however, has held that in parole hearings defendants are *not* entitled to access to victim impact statements (also described as "protest letters"—that is, letters protesting parole of a defendant). In *Johnson v. Rodriguez*, 110 F.3d 299 (5th Cir. 1997), the court focused on the fact that a convict has no constitutionally cognizable interest in parole to deny a convict's request to see parole letters.

To help organize protest letters, some crime victims groups rely on the internet. For example, Parents of Murdered Children (POMC), a leading crime victims group, operates its "Parole Block Program" on its website, www.pomc.com. The website describes the programs as striving "to give survivors a sense of control, as well as a positive outlet for the anger, frustration and disillusionment with the criminal justice system. PBP allows them to participate in the parole process by attempting to keep murderers behind bars for their minimum sentence, thus protecting society from potential repeat offenders." At the request of survivors, POMC will write and circulate petitions to stop the parole/early release of their loved one's murderer. The petitions are sent to people across the United States. PBP does not lobby for longer sentences, but asks only that the sentences imposed by the courts be served in full. In one case, the program apparently generated approximately 100,000 signatures from across the United States. According to POMC, "since it began, the Parole Block Program has been extremely successful at preventing the early release/parole of those convicted of homicide. POMC has protested the early release/parole of more than 800 murderers since the inception of the program in 1990. More than one murderer a week is kept behind bars as a direct result of the program."

Here is an example of the kind of petition that can be found on POMC's website:

PETITION Received: June, 2004

West Virginia State Parole Board 112 California Ave Building 4, Room 307 Charleston, WV 25305 Parole Hearing: September, 2004

RE: William Samuel Scythes ID#: 17782

On September 18, 1991, William Scythes brutally murdered his wife Sandra Jane Scythes. While Sandra was asleep, Mr. Scythes tied her up and strangled her. After the strangulation, Mr. Scythes deposited Sandra's body in the nearby woods. Two days later Mr. Scythes turned himself in to the authorities.

William Scythes was convicted of first-degree murder and sentenced to life in prison with mercy. He will have served just 14 years when he is considered for parole.

We, the undersigned, STRONGLY OPPOSE the parole of William Samuel Scythes. Justice demands that he serve the full prison term given to him at the time he was sentenced for this heinous crime.

———

Some states have provisions for victim input in pardon proceedings. Such a provision may have added significance in the context of the pardon process that has surfaced where battered women who have killed their mates seek pardons. *See* Thomas Hardy & Rick Pearson, *Edgar Still Stands by Clemencies. Governor Brushes Off Attacks on His Motive*, CHIC. TRIB. May 17, 1994, at 1; and Greg Lucas, Teresa Moore, *Wilson Grants Clemency to 2 Battered Women/Petitions Denied for 14 Other Female Prisoners*, S.F. CHRONICLE, May 29, 1993, at A1.

C. Restitution

In virtually all states, the court imposing a criminal sentence can order that a defendant make restitution to the victim. In some states, victims even have a constitutional right to restitution.

ILLINOIS CONST., art. I, § 8.1

Crime victims, as defined by law, shall have the following rights as provided by law:

* * *

(10) The right to restitution.

S.C. CONST., art. I, § 24

. . . victims of crime have the right to:

* * *

(9) receive prompt and full restitution from the person or persons convicted of the criminal conduct that caused the victim's loss or injury including both adult and juvenile offenders . . .

* * *

18 U.S.C.A. § 2259

§ 2259. Mandatory restitution

(a) In general.—Notwithstanding section 3663 or 3663A, and in addition to any other civil or criminal penalty authorized by law, the court shall order restitution for any offense under this chapter.

(b) Scope and nature of order. —

(1) Directions. — The order of restitution under this section shall direct the defendant to pay the victim (through the appropriate court mechanism) the full amount of the victim's losses as determined by the court pursuant to paragraph (2).

(2) Enforcement. — An order of restitution under this section shall be issued and enforced in accordance with section 3664 in the same manner as an order under section 3663A.

Integrating restitution awards into the criminal justice system has posed a bit of a theoretical challenge. How are restitution awards to be calculated and from which offender, if there are multiple offenders? In some cases, the answers are straightforward, while in others they are quite complex.

State v. Huset

2017 WL 6333865 (Ariz.)

In Arizona, victims have a constitutional right "[t]o receive prompt restitution from the person or persons convicted of the criminal conduct that caused the victim's loss or injury." Ariz. Const. art. 2, §2.1(A)(8). The person convicted of the offense must pay the victim "the full amount of the economic loss as determined by the court and in the manner as determined by the court." A.R.S. §13–603(C). "A loss is recoverable as restitution if it meets three requirements: (1) the loss must be economic, (2) the loss must be one that the victim would not have incurred but for the criminal conduct, and (3) the criminal conduct must directly cause the economic loss." Lewis, 222 Ariz. at 324, (quoting State v. Madrid, 207 Ariz. 296, 298, ¶ 5 (App. 2004)).

(a) Wages

"Economic loss" includes "lost earnings and other losses that would not have been incurred but for the offense." A.R.S. §13–105(16). Lost earnings encompass "not only wages lost due to an injury caused by the criminal conduct, and wages lost because of a trial appearance made mandatory by subpoena, but also [wages lost due to] the victim's voluntary attendance" at court hearings. State v. Lindsley, 191 Ariz. 195, 198 (App. 1997). A restitution award must, however, be based on "proof and not speculation." State v. Iniguez, 169 Ariz. 533, 538 (App. 1991). Economic loss does not include "damages for pain and suffering, punitive damages or consequential damages." A.R.S. §13–105(16).

The victim in this case is a realtor who earns her money through commission on home sales, not through hourly wages. She testified that her presence at trial limited her ability to attend to her business, which includes making phone calls to obtain business. Although she could not say with certainty whether she had lost any business or opportunities to sell homes as a direct result of appearing in court, the court awarded her lost wages by dividing her annual income down to an hourly wage and then multiplying the hourly wage by "an eight-hour workday times six days."

Restitution is designed to ensure that victims receive prompt economic compensation for actual losses. See State v. Guilliams, 208 Ariz. 48, 52 (App. 2004). Here, no evidence was presented showing whether the hearings the victim attended lasted eight full hours per day. Thus, we cannot determine whether the victim actually lost eight hours of work each day, or whether she was unable to work at all during those days. As a result, we vacate the award and remand to the trial court so it can conduct a new restitution hearing and grant an award consistent with the time the victim actually lost as a result of the hearings.

(b) The glass table

The court also awarded the realtor $1,500 for a damaged glass table. Huset argues that "[t]he trial court abused its discretion by ordering Mr. Huset pay $1,500 for the glass table because the economic loss was less than $500."

"Arizona's statutory scheme requiring restitution in criminal cases is based on the principle that the offender should make reparations to the victim by restoring the victim to his [or her] economic status quo that existed before the crime occurred." In re William L., 211 Ariz. 236, 239, (App. 2005). "[I]n assessing restitution for a loss of personal property, the measure of the victim's full economic loss is the fair market value of the property at the time of the loss." State v. Ellis, 172 Ariz. 549, 550 (App. 1992). "Evidence of fair market value may include, among other things, whether the property was new when purchased, the original purchase price, how much time the owner has had the use of the property and the condition of the property" at the time of loss. Id. at 551. We give courts "wide discretion in setting restitution based on the facts of each case." State v. Dixon, 216 Ariz. 18, 21, (App. 2007).

The victim testified that she purchased the table for $500 from a friend, but she bought it from a friend who needed to sell it quickly. When she conducted a Google search to determine a price for a replacement table, she discovered that the price of a replacement table of similar quality was $1,500. The court did not, however, consider whether the table should or could be repaired instead of replaced. Thus, on remand, the court should consider whether the repair cost would be less than the replacement cost and, if so, it should order an award consistent with that cost.

CONCLUSION

We affirm Huset's convictions, vacate the restitution award, and remand this case for a new restitution hearing.

Paroline v. United States

134 S. Ct. 1710 (2014)

Justice KENNEDY delivered the opinion of the Court.

This case presents the question of how to determine the amount of restitution a possessor of child pornography must pay to the victim whose childhood abuse appears in the pornographic materials possessed. The relevant statutory provisions are set forth at 18 U.S.C. § 2259. Enacted as a component of the Violence Against

Women Act of 1994, §2259 requires district courts to award restitution for certain federal criminal offenses, including child-pornography possession.

Petitioner Doyle Randall Paroline pleaded guilty to such an offense. He admitted to possessing between 150 and 300 images of child pornography, which included two that depicted the sexual exploitation of a young girl, now a young woman, who goes by the pseudonym "Amy" for this litigation. The question is what causal relationship must be established between the defendant's conduct and a victim's losses for purposes of determining the right to, and the amount of, restitution under §2259.

I

One person whose story illustrates the devastating harm caused by child pornography is the respondent victim in this case. When she was eight and nine years old, she was sexually abused by her uncle in order to produce child pornography. Her uncle was prosecuted, required to pay about $6,000 in restitution, and sentenced to a lengthy prison term. The victim underwent an initial course of therapy beginning in 1998 and continuing into 1999. By the end of this period, her therapist's notes reported that she was "'back to normal'"; her involvement in dance and other age-appropriate activities, and the support of her family, justified an optimistic assessment. App. 70–71. Her functioning appeared to decline in her teenage years, however; and a major blow to her recovery came when, at the age of 17, she learned that images of her abuse were being trafficked on the Internet. Id., at 71. The digital images were available nationwide and no doubt worldwide. Though the exact scale of the trade in her images is unknown, the possessors to date easily number in the thousands. The knowledge that her images were circulated far and wide renewed the victim's trauma and made it difficult for her to recover from her abuse. As she explained in a victim impact statement submitted to the District Court in this case:

"Every day of my life I live in constant fear that someone will see my pictures and recognize me and that I will be humiliated all over again. It hurts me to know someone is looking at them—at me—when I was just a little girl being abused for the camera. I did not choose to be there, but now I am there forever in pictures that people are using to do sick things. I want it all erased. I want it all stopped. But I am powerless to stop it just like I was powerless to stop my uncle. . . . My life and my feelings are worse now because the crime has never really stopped and will never really stop. . . . It's like I am being abused over and over and over again." The victim says in her statement that her fear and trauma make it difficult for her to trust others or to feel that she has control over what happens to her.

The full extent of this victim's suffering is hard to grasp. Her abuser took away her childhood, her self-conception of her innocence, and her freedom from the kind of nightmares and memories that most others will never know. These crimes were compounded by the distribution of images of her abuser's horrific acts, which meant the wrongs inflicted upon her were in effect repeated; for she knew her humiliation and hurt were and would be renewed into the future as an ever-increasing number of wrongdoers witnessed the crimes committed against her.

Petitioner Paroline is one of the individuals who possessed this victim's images. In 2009, he pleaded guilty in federal court to one count of possession of material involving the sexual exploitation of children in violation of 18 U.S.C. § 2252. Paroline admitted to knowing possession of between 150 and 300 images of child pornography, two of which depicted the respondent victim. Ibid. The victim sought restitution under § 2259, asking for close to $3.4 million, consisting of nearly $3 million in lost income and about $500,000 in future treatment and counseling costs. She also sought attorney's fees and costs. The parties submitted competing expert reports. They stipulated that the victim did not know who Paroline was and that none of her claimed losses flowed from any specific knowledge about him or his offense conduct.

After briefing and hearings, the District Court declined to award restitution. The District Court observed that "everyone involved with child pornography—from the abusers and producers to the end-users and possessors—contribute[s] to [the victim's] ongoing harm." Id., at 792. But it concluded that the Government had the burden of proving the amount of the victim's losses "directly produced by Paroline that would not have occurred without his possession of her images." The District Court found that, under this standard, the Government had failed to meet its burden of proving what losses, if any, were proximately caused by Paroline's offense. It thus held that "an award of restitution is not appropriate in this case." . . .

Paroline sought review here. Certiorari was granted to resolve a conflict in the Courts of Appeals over the proper causation inquiry for purposes of determining the entitlement to and amount of restitution under § 2259. For the reasons set forth, the decision of the Court of Appeals is vacated.

II

Title 18 U.S.C. § 2259(a) provides that a district court "shall order restitution for any offense" under Chapter 110 of Title 18, which covers a number of offenses involving the sexual exploitation of children and child pornography in particular. Paroline was convicted of knowingly possessing child pornography . . .

Section 2259 states a broad restitutionary purpose: It requires district courts to order defendants "to pay the victim . . . the full amount of the victim's losses as determined by the court," and expressly states that "[t]he issuance of a restitution order under this section is mandatory," § 2259(b)(4)(A). Section 2259(b)(2) provides that "[a]n order of restitution under this section shall be issued and enforced in accordance with section 3664," which in turn provides in relevant part that "[t]he burden of demonstrating the amount of the loss sustained by a victim as a result of the offense shall be on the attorney for the Government,"

The threshold question the Court faces is whether § 2259 limits restitution to those losses proximately caused by the defendant's offense conduct. The Fifth Circuit held that it does not, contrary to the holdings of other Courts of Appeals to have addressed the question.

As a general matter, to say one event proximately caused another is a way of making two separate but related assertions. First, it means the former event caused the latter. This is known as actual cause or cause in fact. The concept of actual cause "is not a metaphysical one but an ordinary, matter-of-fact inquiry into the existence . . . of a causal relation as laypeople would view it." [The Court Determined that the Statute Requires Proximate Cause]

Every event has many causes, however, see ibid., and only some of them are proximate, as the law uses that term. So to say that one event was a proximate cause of another means that it was not just any cause, but one with a sufficient connection to the result. The idea of proximate cause, as distinct from actual cause or cause in fact, defies easy summary. It is "a flexible concept" that generally "refers to the basic requirement that . . . there must be 'some direct relation between the injury asserted and the injurious conduct alleged,'" The concept of proximate causation is applicable in both criminal and tort law, and the analysis is parallel in many instances. Proximate cause is often explicated in terms of foreseeability or the scope of the risk created by the predicate conduct. A requirement of proximate cause thus serves, inter alia, to preclude liability in situations where the causal link between conduct and result is so attenuated that the consequence is more aptly described as mere fortuity. . . .

Here, however, the interpretive task is easier, for the requirement of proximate cause is in the statute's text. The statute enumerates six categories of covered losses. . . .

The victim argues that because the "proximate result" language appears only in the final, catchall category of losses set forth at § 2259(b)(3)(F), the statute has no proximate-cause requirement for losses falling within the prior enumerated categories. . . .

Reading the statute to impose a general proximate-cause limitation accords with common sense. As noted above, proximate cause forecloses liability in situations where the causal link between conduct and result is so attenuated that the so-called consequence is more akin to mere fortuity. . . .

III

There remains the difficult question of how to apply the statute's causation requirements in this case. The problem stems from the somewhat atypical causal process underlying the losses the victim claims here. It is perhaps simple enough for the victim to prove the aggregate losses, including the costs of psychiatric treatment and lost income, that stem from the ongoing traffic in her images as a whole. . . . These losses may be called, for convenience's sake, a victim's "general losses." The difficulty is in determining the "full amount" of those general losses, if any, that are the proximate result of the offense conduct of a particular defendant who is one of thousands who have possessed and will in the future possess the victim's images but who has no other connection to the victim.

In determining the amount of general losses a defendant must pay under § 2259 the ultimate question is how much of these losses were the "proximate result" of that individual's offense. *But the most difficult aspect of this inquiry concerns the threshold requirement of causation in fact.* (Emphasis added by casebook authors). To be sure, the requirement of proximate causation, as distinct from mere causation in fact, would prevent holding any possessor liable for losses caused in only a remote sense. But the victim's costs of treatment and lost income resulting from the trauma of knowing that images of her abuse are being viewed over and over are direct and foreseeable results of child-pornography crimes, including possession, assuming the prerequisite of factual causation is satisfied. The primary problem, then, is the proper standard of causation in fact.

A

The traditional way to prove that one event was a factual cause of another is to show that the latter would not have occurred "but for" the former. This approach is a familiar part of our legal tradition, and no party disputes that a showing of but-for causation would satisfy § 2259's factual-causation requirement. Sometimes that showing could be made with little difficulty. For example, but-for causation could be shown with ease in many cases involving producers of child pornography; parents who permit their children to be used for child-pornography production; individuals who sell children for such purposes; or the initial distributor of the pornographic images of a child.

In this case, however, a showing of but-for causation cannot be made. The District Court found that the Government failed to prove specific losses caused by Paroline in a but-for sense and recognized that it would be "incredibly difficult" to do so in a case like this. That finding has a solid foundation in the record, and it is all but unchallenged in this Court. From the victim's perspective, Paroline was just one of thousands of anonymous possessors. To be sure, the victim's precise degree of trauma likely bears a relation to the total number of offenders; it would probably be less if only 10 rather than thousands had seen her images. But it is not possible to prove that her losses would be less (and by how much) but for one possessor's individual role in the large, loosely connected network through which her images circulate. Even without Paroline's offense, thousands would have viewed and would in the future view the victim's images, so it cannot be shown that her trauma and attendant losses would have been any different but for Paroline's offense. That is especially so given the parties' stipulation that the victim had no knowledge of Paroline

Recognizing that losses cannot be substantiated under a but-for approach where the defendant is an anonymous possessor of images in wide circulation on the Internet, the victim and the Government urge the Court to read § 2259 to require a less restrictive causation standard, at least in this and similar child-pornography cases. They are correct to note that courts have departed from the but-for standard where circumstances warrant, especially where the combined conduct of multiple wrongdoers produces a bad outcome. See Burrage, 571 U.S., at — —, 134 S.Ct., at 890 (acknowledging "the undoubted reality that courts have not always required strict but-for causality, even where criminal liability is at issue").

The victim and the Government look to the literature on criminal and tort law for alternatives to the but-for test. The Court has noted that the "most common" exception to the but-for causation requirement is applied where "multiple sufficient causes independently . . . produce a result." This exception is an ill fit here, as all parties seem to recognize. Paroline's possession of two images of the victim was surely not sufficient to cause her entire losses from the ongoing trade in her images. Nor is there a practical way to isolate some subset of the victim's general losses that Paroline's conduct alone would have been sufficient to cause.

Understandably, the victim and the Government thus concentrate on a handful of less demanding causation tests endorsed by authorities on tort law. One prominent treatise suggests that "[w]hen the conduct of two or more actors is so related to an event that their combined conduct, viewed as a whole, is a but-for cause of the event, and application of the but-for rule to them individually would absolve all of them, the conduct of each is a cause in fact of the event." Prosser and Keeton § 41, at 268. The Restatement adopts a similar exception for "[m]ultiple sufficient causal sets." . . . The Government argues that these authorities "provide ample support for an 'aggregate' causation theory," and that such a theory would best effectuate congressional intent in cases like this. The victim says much the same.

These alternative causal tests are a kind of legal fiction or construct. If the conduct of a wrongdoer is neither necessary nor sufficient to produce an outcome, that conduct cannot in a strict sense be said to have caused the outcome. Nonetheless, tort law teaches that alternative and less demanding causal standards are necessary in certain circumstances to vindicate the law's purposes. It would be anomalous to turn away a person harmed by the combined acts of many wrongdoers simply because none of those wrongdoers alone caused the harm. And it would be nonsensical to adopt a rule whereby individuals hurt by the combined wrongful acts of many (and thus in many instances hurt more badly than otherwise) would have no redress, whereas individuals hurt by the acts of one person alone would have a remedy. Those are the principles that underlie the various aggregate causation tests the victim and the Government cite, and they are sound principles.

These alternative causal standards, though salutary when applied in a judicious manner, also can be taken too far. That is illustrated by the victim's suggested approach to applying § 2259 in cases like this. The victim says that under the strict logic of these alternative causal tests, each possessor of her images is a part of a causal set sufficient to produce her ongoing trauma, so each possessor should be treated as a cause in fact of all the trauma and all the attendant losses incurred as a result of the entire ongoing traffic in her images. And she argues that if this premise is accepted the further requirement of proximate causation poses no barrier, for she seeks restitution only for those losses that are the direct and foreseeable result of child-pornography offenses. Because the statute requires restitution for the "full amount of the victim's losses," including "any . . . losses suffered by the victim as a proximate result of the offense," § 2259(b), she argues that restitution is required for the entire aggregately caused amount.

The striking outcome of this reasoning—that each possessor of the victim's images would bear the consequences of the acts of the many thousands who possessed those images — illustrates why the Court has been reluctant to adopt aggregate causation logic in an incautious manner, especially in interpreting criminal statutes where there is no language expressly suggesting Congress intended that approach. See Burrage, 571 U.S., at — —, 134 S.Ct., at 890–891. Even if one were to refer just to the law of torts, it would be a major step to say there is a sufficient causal link between the injury and the wrong so that all the victim's general losses were "suffered . . . as a proximate result of [Paroline's] offense."

And there is special reason not to do so in the context of criminal restitution. Aside from the manifest procedural differences between criminal sentencing and civil tort lawsuits, restitution serves purposes that differ from (though they overlap with) the purposes of tort law. See, e.g., Kelly v. Robinson, 479 U.S. 36, 49, n. 10, 107 S.Ct. 353, 93 L.Ed.2d 216 (1986) (noting that restitution is, inter alia, "an effective rehabilitative penalty"). Legal fictions developed in the law of torts cannot be imported into criminal restitution and applied to their utmost limits without due consideration of these differences.

. . . [A]dopting the victim's approach would make an individual possessor liable for the combined consequences of the acts of not just 2, 5, or even 100 independently acting offenders; but instead, a number that may reach into the tens of thousands.

It is unclear whether it could ever be sensible to embrace the fiction that this victim's entire losses were the "proximate result," §2259(b)(3)(F), of a single possessor's offense. Paroline's contribution to the causal process underlying the victim's losses was very minor, both compared to the combined acts of all other relevant offenders, and in comparison to the contributions of other individual offenders, particularly distributors (who may have caused hundreds or thousands of further viewings) and the initial producer of the child pornography. Congress gave no indication that it intended its statute to be applied in the expansive manner the victim suggests, a manner contrary to the bedrock principle that restitution should reflect the consequences of the defendant's own conduct, see Hughey, 495 U.S., at 416, 110 S.Ct. 1979, not the conduct of thousands of geographically and temporally distant offenders acting independently, and with whom the defendant had no contact.

The victim argues that holding each possessor liable for her entire losses would be fair and practical, in part because offenders may seek contribution from one another. If that were so, it might mitigate to some degree the concerns her approach presents. But there is scant authority for her contention that offenders convicted in different proceedings in different jurisdictions and ordered to pay restitution to the same victim may seek contribution from one another. There is no general federal right to contribution. . . .

The Fifth Circuit's interpretation of the requirements of §2259 was incorrect. The District Court likewise erred in requiring a strict showing of but-for causation. The judgment of the Court of Appeals is vacated, and the case is remanded for further proceedings consistent with this opinion.

It is so ordered.

Chief Justice ROBERTS, with whom Justice SCALIA and Justice THOMAS join, dissenting.

I certainly agree with the Court that Amy deserves restitution, and that Congress—by making restitution mandatory for victims of child pornography—meant that she have it. Unfortunately, the restitution statute that Congress wrote for child pornography offenses makes it impossible to award that relief to Amy in this case. Instead of tailoring the statute to the unique harms caused by child pornography, Congress borrowed a generic restitution standard that makes restitution contingent on the Government's ability to prove, "by the preponderance of the evidence," "the amount of the loss sustained by a victim as a result of" the defendant's crime. 18 U.S.C. § 3664(e). When it comes to Paroline's crime—possession of two of Amy's images—it is not possible to do anything more than pick an arbitrary number for that "amount." And arbitrary is not good enough for the criminal law.

The Court attempts to design a more coherent restitution system, focusing on "the defendant's relative role in the causal process that underlies the victim's general losses." But this inquiry, sensible as it may be, is not the one Congress adopted. After undertaking the inquiry that Congress did require, the District Court in this case concluded that the Government could not meet its statutory burden of proof. Before this Court, the Government all but concedes the point. See Brief for United States 25 ("it is practically impossible to know whether [Amy's] losses would have been slightly lower if one were to subtract one defendant, or ten, or fifty"). I must regretfully dissent.

. . . .

The problem stems from the nature of Amy's injury. As explained, section 3664 is a general statute designed to provide restitution for more common crimes, such as fraud and assault. The section 3664(e) standard will work just fine for most crime victims, because it will usually not be difficult to identify the harm caused by the defendant's offense. The dispute will usually just be over the amount of the victim's loss—for example, the value of lost assets or the cost of a night in the hospital.

Amy has a qualitatively different injury. Her loss, while undoubtedly genuine, is a result of the collective actions of a huge number of people—beginning with her uncle who abused her and put her images on the Internet, to the distributors who make those images more widely available, to the possessors such as Paroline who view her images. The harm to Amy was produced over time, gradually, by tens of thousands of persons acting independently from one another. She suffers in particular from her knowledge that her images are being viewed online by an unknown number of people, and from her fear that any person she meets might recognize her from having witnessed her abuse. But Amy does not know who Paroline is. Nothing in the record comes close to establishing that Amy would have suffered less if Paroline had not possessed her images, let alone how much less. Amy's injury is indivisible, which means that Paroline's particular share of her losses is unknowable. And yet it is proof of Paroline's particular share that the statute requires.

By simply importing the generic restitution statute without accounting for the diffuse harm suffered by victims of child pornography, Congress set up a restitution system sure to fail in cases like this one. Perhaps a case with different facts, say, a single distributor and only a handful of possessors, would be susceptible of the proof the statute requires. But when tens of thousands of copies (or more) of Amy's images have changed hands all across the world for more than a decade, a demand for the Government to prove "the amount of the loss sustained by a victim as a result of *the* offense" — the offense before the court in any particular case — is a demand for the impossible. § 3664(e) (emphasis added). When Congress conditioned restitution on the Government's meeting that burden of proof, it effectively precluded restitution in most cases involving possession or distribution of child pornography. . . .

Justice SOTOMAYOR, dissenting.

This Court has long recognized the grave "physiological, emotional, and mental" injuries suffered by victims of child pornography. The traffic in images depicting a child's sexual abuse, we have observed, "'poses an even greater threat to the child victim than does sexual abuse or prostitution'" because the victim must "'go through life knowing that the recording is circulating within the mass distribution system for child pornography.'" As we emphasized in a later case, the images cause "continuing harm by haunting the chil[d] in years to come."

Congress enacted 18 U.S.C. § 2259 against this backdrop. The statute imposes a "mandatory" duty on courts to order restitution to victims of federal offenses involving the sexual abuse of children, including the possession of child pornography. § 2259(b)(4). And it commands that for any such offense, a court "shall direct the defendant to pay the victim . . . the full amount of the victim's losses."

The Court interprets this statute to require restitution in a "circumscribed" amount less than the "entirety of the victim's . . . losses," a total it instructs courts to estimate based on the defendant's "relative role" in the victim's harm. That amount, the Court holds, should be neither "nominal" nor "severe."

I appreciate the Court's effort to achieve what it perceives to be a just result. It declines to require restitution for a victim's full losses, a result that might seem incongruent to an individual possessor's partial role in a harm in which countless others have participated. And it rejects the position advanced by Paroline and the dissenting opinion of THE CHIEF JUSTICE, which would result in no restitution in cases like this for the perverse reason that a child has been victimized by too many.

The Court's approach, however, cannot be reconciled with the law that Congress enacted. Congress mandated restitution for the "full amount of the victim's losses," § 2259(b)(1), and did so within the framework of settled tort law principles that treat defendants like Paroline jointly and severally liable for the indivisible consequences of their intentional, concerted conduct. And to the extent an award for the full amount of a victim's losses may lead to fears of unfair treatment for particular defendants, Congress provided a mechanism to accommodate those concerns: Courts are to order "partial payments" on a periodic schedule if the defendant's financial circumstances or other "interest [s] of justice" so require. I would accordingly affirm the Fifth Circuit's holding that the District Court "must enter a restitution order reflecting the 'full amount of [Amy's] losses,' and instruct the court to consider a periodic payment schedule on remand.

. . . .

Note: The United States Senate has twice passed legislation to address the restitution conundrum in child pornography cases. Most recently in early 2018. The House has yet to act.

—————

Whatever the theoretical understanding of restitution, implementing restitution awards depends on the statutory authorization and accompanying limitations regarding such awards. A reported case from a federal trial court illustrates questions about when restitution is required for the victim and how much restitution can be ordered.

United States v. Bedonie
United States v. Serawop
317 F. Supp. 2d 1285 (D. Utah 2004)

CASSELL, J.

Factual and Procedural Background

[In *United States v. Bedonie*, defendant Levangela Bedonie pled guilty to involuntary manslaughter within the Navajo Nation for the drunk driving death of victim Brian Johnson. In *United States v. Serawop*, defendant Redd Rock Serawop was found guilty following a jury trial of manslaughter within Indian Country. The victim was his three-month old daughter: Beyonce Serawop.]

* * *

I. The Court Must Order Restitution for the Violent Crimes Committed by Defendants Bedonie and Serawop.

A. The Mandatory Victim Restitution Act Applies to Bedonie's and Serawop's Crimes of Violence.

The court must order both defendants Bedonie and Serawop to pay full restitution if their cases are governed by the Mandatory Victims Restitution Act of 1996[13] rather than its predecessor, the Victim and Witness Protection Act of 1982 (VWPA).[14] The "MVRA's primary purpose is to force offenders to 'pay full restitution to the

—————

13. Pub. L. 104-132, Title II, § 201, 110 Stat. 1214, 1227–1236, *codified as* 18 U.S.C. §§ 3663A, 3664.

14. Pub. L. 97-291, § 4, 96 Stat. 1248, 1249–53, *codified as* 18 U.S.C. §§ 3663, 3664.

identifiable victims of their crimes.'"[15] The Act firmly directs that "[n]otwithstanding any other provision of law, when sentencing a defendant convicted of [certain offenses] . . . the court *shall* order . . . that the defendant make restitution to the victim of the offense or, if the victim is deceased, to the victim's estate."[16] . . . [Eds. — The court concluded the defendants had committed crimes of violence.]

II. Bedonie and Serawop Must Pay Restitution for the Lost Income of their Victims.

A. The Deceased — Mr. Johnson and Beyonce Serawop — Are Entitled to Restitution as "Victims" of the Homicide Offenses Against Them.

Having concluded the court must award full restitution, the issue then arises as to who is the "victim" entitled to restitution. It seems almost self-evident that a person who is murdered is the victim of a homicide offense.[17] But because the issue seems to be contested, it may be useful to explore the issue briefly.

1. Lost Income Is Properly Awardable to Mr. Johnson As the "Victim" of a Homicide.

Mr. Johnson is the victim of defendant Bedonie's crime. The MVRA defines "victim" as:

> [A] person *directly and proximately harmed* as a result of the commission of an offense for which restitution may be ordered including, in the case of an offense that involves as an element a scheme, conspiracy, or pattern of criminal activity, any person directly harmed by the defendant's criminal conduct in the course of the scheme, conspiracy, or pattern. In the case of a victim who is under 18 years of age, incompetent, incapacitated, or *deceased,* the legal guardian of the victim or representative of the victim's estate, another family member, or any other person appointed as suitable by the court, *may assume the victim's rights under this section. . . .*[18]

Under this provision, the person killed in a homicide case is a victim. Obviously, as provided in the first sentence of the definition, someone who is murdered is "directly and proximately harmed" by the offense. The second sentence of the definition does not alter that conclusion. The second sentence lists certain persons who "may *assume* the victim's rights" under the MVRA when a victim is "deceased," including a "representative of the victim's estate." But these persons do not become the victim; they merely represent the victim under the statute.

This distinction is important because defendant Bedonie raises several arguments predicated on the assumption that the victim in her case is Mr. Johnson's *estate* rather than Mr. Johnson himself. To be sure, there may be a close connection between the estate and the victim. But to treat the estate as the victim would contravene the plain

---

15. *United States v. Reano,* 298 F.3d 1208, 1211 (10th Cir. 2002) (quoting S.Rep. No. 104-179, at 12 (1996), *reprinted in* 1996 U.S.C.C.A.N. 924, 925)).

16. 18 U.S.C. § 3663A(a)(1).

18. 18 U.S.C. § 3663A(a)(2) (emphases added).

language of the statute which, as just noted, merely allows a "representative of the estate" to "assume" the victim's rights, not to actually become the victim. Moreover, Bedonie's reading of the statute assumes that in homicide cases the victim will always be the estate. Such a reading would give no effect to another provision, which allows the court to appoint "any other person" found to be "suitable" to assume the victim's rights. In this case, the court will appoint Ms. Johnson—the victim's mother who allocuted eloquently at the sentencing hearing—as the suitable person to represent Mr. Johnson. That appointment is not conditioned on any connection between Ms. Johnson and the victim's estate. Indeed, the court could make such an appointment under the statute if Mr. Johnson had been only incapacitated rather than killed. . . .

For all these reasons, Mr. Johnson is the victim in Ms. Bedonie's case. [Eds.—The court, accordingly, found no need to reach the issue of whether Ms. Johnson, the victim's mother, was also a "victim" of the offense. The court also concluded, for the same reasons, that Beyonce Serawop was the victim of defendant Serawop's offense.]

B. The MVRA Requires a Lost Income Award in Homicide Cases.

Having concluded that the MVRA requires the court to order the defendants to pay full restitution and that Mr. Johnson and Beyonce Serawop are the victims of the defendants' offenses, the court must next determine what is embraced by the concept of "full" restitution. The court concludes that it is required to enter an order of restitution covering the lost income of the Mr. Johnson and Beyonce Serawop. Indeed, the MVRA requires such an award in all cases in which the violent death of a victim has led to lost income.

The relevant provisions of the MVRA read:

The order of restitution shall require that such defendant—

* * *

(2) in the case of an offense resulting in *bodily injury* to a victim—

(A) pay an amount equal to the cost of necessary medical and related professional services and devices relating to physical, psychiatric, and psychological care, including non-medical care and treatment rendered in accordance with a method of healing recognized by the law of the place of treatment;

(B) pay an amount equal to the cost of necessary physical and occupational therapy and rehabilitation; and

(C) *reimburse the victim for income lost by such victim as a result of such offense*;

(3) in the case of an offense resulting in *bodily injury that results in the death* of the victim, pay an amount equal to the cost of necessary funeral and related services; and

(4) in any case, reimburse the victim for lost income and necessary child care, transportation, and other expenses incurred during participation in

the investigation or prosecution of the offense or attendance at proceedings related to the offense.[19]

Defendant Serawop argues that these provisions do not envision lost income awards in homicide cases. His reading starts with subsection (b)(2)(C), which provides that "in the case of an offense resulting in *bodily injury to a victim*" the court shall order restitution to "reimburse the victim for income lost by such victim as a result of such offense." On the other hand, subsection (b)(3) provides that "in the case of an offense resulting in *bodily injury that results in the death of the victim*" the court shall order restitution in "an amount equal to the cost of necessary funeral and related services." Because subsection (b)(3) explicitly requires the court to order restitution to cover the cost of necessary funeral and related services in criminal cases involving a death, defendant Serawop concludes that the more general lost income provisions of subsection (b)(2) are not applicable in homicide cases.

Defendant Serawop's position contradicts logic, the purposes of the MVRA, and the plain language of the statute. To find the MVRA's lost income provisions inapplicable in homicide cases would defy logic and would lead to the perverse result that murderers would usually pay markedly less restitution than criminals who only assault and injure their victims. Under such a reading, the murderer would pay only funeral expenses, while the assaulter would pay for lost income, a potentially much larger sum. Such a result would contradict a core purpose of restitution, which is to "ensure that the offender realizes the damage caused by the offense and pays the debt owed to the victim as well as to society."[20]

Moreover, reading the statute to block lost income awards in homicide cases would conflict with the clear intention of the MVRA: to force offenders to "'pay full restitution to the identifiable victims of their crimes.'"[21] Income is plainly one of the things lost by victims when they are murdered. Indeed, the legislative history reveals clear congressional concern about the failure of federal courts to order restitution in homicide cases. In opening the hearings on the bill that became the MVRA, Senator Hatch critically observed that judges ordered restitution in "only 20.2% of federal criminal cases during fiscal year 1994 . . . [including only] 27.9% of all murders." [22]

Such a conclusion would also flout the plain language of the MVRA. The statute expressly directs judges to require a convicted defendant to pay restitution for income lost "in the case of an offense resulting in bodily injury to a victim."[23] An offense that results in death would plainly be an offense resulting in bodily injury. Death is

---

19. 18 U.S.C. § 3663A(b).

20. *Reano*, 298 F.3d at 1212.

22. *Mandatory Victim Restitution: Hearing on S.173 Before the Senate Committee on the Judiciary*, November 8, 1995 (Statement of Senator Orrin Hatch), *available at* 1995 WL 11869323.

23. 18 U.S.C. § 3663A(b)(2).

simply the most serious form of bodily injury and in no way eliminates the appropriateness of a restitution award. . . .

C. The MVRA Requires an Award for Both Past and Future Lost Income.

Defendant Bedonie does not seriously contest that lost income awards are proper in cases involving crimes of violence. Instead, her main contention is that the court cannot order restitution for *future* lost income of a crime victim. Her argument rests on the MVRA's language allowing a court to order a defendant to "*reimburse* the victim for *income lost* by such victim as a result of such offense."[24] She contends that the "income lost" does "not logically apply to income which the victim may lose in the future, especially in light of the use of the word 'reimburse,' which implies payment only for expenses already incurred."

While creative, defendant Bedonie's argument is unsound. She seems to draw a distinction between *past* and *future* income. Yet, at the conceptual level, there is "no difference of principle between past and future earnings, so far as the purposes of criminal punishment are concerned."[25] Moreover, "lost income" is a phrase frequently used in court opinions around the country in tort cases. Plaintiffs frequently recover "lost income" damages, which include future lost income. Congress presumably was aware of this background when it legislated and, accordingly, the words it chose should be construed in this light. . . .

If any doubt remained on the issue, Congress has resolved it by using a phrase that is very much forward looking. Congress has directed mandatory restitution for "income lost by such victim *as a result of* such offense."[26] Income losses that "result" from an offense are necessarily losses that occur at some future time. It could hardly be otherwise, as crimes do not harm victims retroactively but instead from that time forward.

Defendant Bedonie apparently concedes that Congress has directed courts to award lost income from the time of the crime through sentencing. Any other position would be nonsensical, as it would effectively read the lost income restitution provision out of the statute. But the net result of this concession is that Bedonie must awkwardly interpret the MVRA as permitting lost income awards only from the crime through sentencing, but not thereafter. This curious interpretation would produce significant variance in restitution awards in otherwise identical cases based on such happenstance as the length of time to investigate the case, the diligence with which it is prosecuted, and rapidity with which the court holds the restitution hearing. The possibility of variance would be particularly pronounced in homicide cases, where there is no statute of limitation and where investigation and prosecution can take considerable time. In this case, for example, Bedonie apparently concedes that the court could order restitution for lost income for two years—from the date

---

24. 18 U.S.C. § 3663A(b)(2)(C) (emphasis added).
25. *United States v. Fountain*, 768 F.2d 790, 801 (7th Cir. 1985).
26. 18 U.S.C. § 3663A(a)(2)(C) (emphasis added).

of the homicide (April 19, 2002) through the date of this order. Making restitution awards turn on such fortuitous factors hardly seems to square with the congressional intent to make criminals "'pay full restitution to the identifiable victims of their crimes.'"[27] Accordingly, the court finds that the plain language of the MVRA requires awards of all lost income resulting from the offense at the time of sentencing, both losses that have occurred in the past and that will occur in the future. . . .

III. Defendant Bedonie Should Pay Lost Income Restitution of $446,665 and Defendant Serawop Should Pay Lost Income Restitution of $325,751.

Having determined that lost income (including future income) is awardable as restitution, the next issue then becomes whether the record evidence regarding Mr. Johnson and Beyonce Serawop provide sufficient evidence to support such an award. Of course, the kind of evidence that is available on restitution issues will never be ironclad. As the Tenth Circuit has reminded trial courts, "'[t]he determination of an appropriate restitution is by nature an inexact science.'"[28]. . . .

A. Expert Testimony on the Amount of Lost Income

To assist the court in estimating income that the victims lost, the court appointed a leading expert—Dr. Paul Randle—to evaluate the subject. . . .

1. Dr. Randle's Expect Testimony is Admissible.

The court first finds that Dr. Randle is a well qualified expert in the area of lost income calculations. . . .

2. Lost Income Projections for Mr. Johnson.

Turning first to Mr. Johnson, Dr. Randle made several different income projections. His first scenario assumed that Mr. Johnson would have been employed at his level of education (high school) at age 21 and for the balance of his expected worklife (about 37 years). Dr. Randle further assumed that Mr. Johnson would have earned 58% of the average earnings of a high school graduate in the United States—58% being the average ratio of wages for male Native Americans to wages for white males. Dr. Randle further assumed that Mr. Johnson's wages would have grown at the average rate of wage growth for all U.S. workers over the past 25 years (4.28%). He then reported the wage loss projections in constant 2002 dollars and discounted to present value using a 25-year average return on government treasury bills. This methodology produced a present value of Mr. Johnson's probable wage loss of $433,562, which Dr. Randle viewed as the lower bound for lost income.

Dr. Randle's second scenario used all of the same assumptions except that Mr. Johnson would have achieved one or more years of post-secondary education (as

---

27. *Reano*, 298 F.3d 1212 (quoting S.Rep. No. 104-179, at 12 (1996), *reprinted in* 1996 U.S.C.C.A.N. 924, 925)).

28. *United States v. Williams*, 292 F.3d 681, 688 (10th Cir. 2002) (quoting *United States v. Teehee*, 893 F.2d 271, 274 (10th Cir. 1990)).

he had planned) and then entered the workforce at age 23. This produced a present value of probable wage loss of $495,598.

When the court received Dr. Randle's report, it was concerned about possible constitutional and other problems in relying on race and sex assumptions. So that all possible options would be available for discussion, the court directed Dr. Randle to recalculate lost income without regard to race or sex. Dr. Randle then produced a new report using normal wages for all American workers as the basis for projecting Mr. Johnson's lost income. This produced a lost income calculation of $744,442 (assuming only high school education) or $850,959 (assuming one or more years of post-secondary education).

The court later asked for one last calculation from Dr. Randle. The court received the letter from Mr. Johnson's high school art teacher reporting he earned about $1500 per year from art sales during high school. The court then asked Dr. Randle to assume Mr. Johnson was no more successful than he had been in high school and to use the $1500 figure to project lost income of his expected working lifetime. On that highly conservative assumption, Dr. Randle projected lost income of $40,907.

Based on the testimony of Dr. Randle, the court finds that the range of lost income for Mr. Johnson is between $40,907 and $850,959.

3. Lost Income Projections for Beyonce Serawop.

To project lost income for Beyonce Serawop, Dr. Randle proceeded in a similar fashion.

* * *

B. Race and Sex Adjustments.

The next issue that arises is whether the court should use race- and sex-neutral statistics to calculate the lost income of the victims. Recent legal commentary have raised substantial questions about use of race and sex adjustments. . . .

[The court then discussed cases raising questions about such adjustments.] Reasoning from these cases, some commentators have suggested that use of race and sex in economic calculations is positively unconstitutional. . . . This constitutional argument is worth serious attention. Nonetheless, it is novel. A time honored-principle of constitutional adjudication requires "that court avoid reaching constitutional questions in advance of the necessity of deciding them."[29] Here, there is a narrower ground for rejecting race and sex distinctions. In framing restitution awards, the court certainly operates within a zone of discretion, because the process is not an "exact science."[30] As a matter of fairness, the court should exercise its discretion in favor of victims of violent crime and against the possible perpetuation of inappropriate stereotypes. This is particularly true in this case, where the defendants have deprived their victims of the chance to excel in life beyond predicted statistical

---

29. *Lyng v. Northwest Indian Cemetery Protective Ass'n*, 485 U.S. 439, 445 (1988).
30. *United States v. Williams*, 292 F.3d 681, 688 (10th Cir. 2002).

averages. In fairness to the victims, therefore, the court should not use race- and sex-neutral data in calculating losses. . . .

C. Calculating the Lost Income Awards.

1. The Lost Income of Mr. Johnson.

In light of the foregoing principles and expert testimony, the court will now make specific findings regarding the lost income of Mr. Johnson. Initially, the court concludes that Mr. Johnson would have earned considerable income if he had not been killed by defendant Bedonie. While he was not an exceptional student, he was already showing promise as a talented artist during high school. According to a detailed letter from Superintendent Karen Lesher, his Graphics Arts teacher, Mr. Johnson was "an exceptionally talented student and was recognized by the school community as a resource for art designs for school and community posters, mural, programs, t-shirts, and a variety of publications." . . .

During high school, Mr. Johnson was earning approximately $1200 to $1500 annually. As Dr. Randle calculated, assuming that Mr. Johnson would have done nothing more than continued to earn $1500 annually for the rest of his life by selling art work on the side, the present value of his lost earnings would have been no less $40,907. This is a highly conservative figure. . . .

The court concludes that Mr. Johnson would have succeeded in his aspirations to attend art school and become a professional artist. His teachers believed that he had the talent to succeed. His mother presented several portraits sketched by Mr. Johnson during her sentencing allocution that were quite impressive. . . .

In light of all this evidence, a conservative calculation of the future lost income is $744,442. This figure is the lowest race-neutral figure reported by Dr. Randle. Apart from the arguments rejected in previous sections, neither side has challenged the reasonableness of this figure as a race-neutral figure for future lost income.

Dr. Randle's figure, however, assumes that Mr. Johnson would have been employed constantly. The evidence in the record shows that Mr. Johnson's actual employment history was irregular. Moreover, Mr. Johnson's chosen field of interest — art — is notorious for irregular hours and work. Accordingly, the court concludes reducing the award by a percentage amount is appropriate to reflect these facts. Dr. Randle testified that percentage reductions are reasonable estimation devices. There is, of course, no specific evidence as to the exact percentage discount that might be appropriate. Nor have the parties offered any specific suggestion on these particular points. The court therefore must make a reasonable estimate. The court finds that the evidence suggests that Mr. Johnson would have been employed 60% of the time and thus Dr. Randle's lost income figure should be discounted by 40%. This produces a lost income figure of $446,665. . . .

In sum, the court concludes that $446,665 is a reasonable and conservative calculation of Mr. Johnson's lost income.

2. The Lost Income of Beyonce Serawop.

The facts regarding Beyonce Serawop's lost income are much more limited. This is not surprising, since when defendant Serawop killed the three-month-old baby, he deprived her of the chance to grow and succeed in life. Nonetheless, the court can make some findings that are relevant.

The court finds that Beyonce was a generally healthy and happy baby when defendant Serawop killed her. Beyonce resided on the Uintah-Ouray ("Ute") Reservation. Beyonce's mother, who had some difficulties of her own, loved her daughter very much. Beyonce's autopsy also revealed no major health problems.

Defendant Serawop has also argued that one factor relevant to Beyonce's lost income determination was the fact that she resided in a household where *he* was abusive. He argues, for instance, that because of his history of domestic violence, Beyonce was less likely to graduate from high or, more generally, to be successful in life. The court gives no weight to this argument. Defendant Serawop is hardly entitled to creative an abusive family situation and then argue that, because of this abuse, his daughter was less likely to succeed in a life.

Calculation of Beyonce's lost income can begin with the "floor" set by the stipend she received from her Tribe. As Dr. Randle calculated, the present value of these payments would not have been less than $17,118. Her lost income would have been at least this amount.

The court, however, believes that the limited evidence supports the conclusion that Beyonce would have at least gone on to achieve additional earnings along the lines of Dr. Randle's most conservative race- and sex-neutral calculation of $308,633. This figure assumes that she would have been employed with less than a high school education, beginning at age 17, for the balance of her worklife. . . . This is a conservative figure, as it assumes that Beyonce would not have finished high school; of course, she never had the chance to attend high school because of the crime committed by her father. The court, accordingly, finds that a conservative lost income calculation is $308,633, supplemented with the $17,118 stipend she would have received from her Tribe, for total lost income of $325,751. . . .

D. No Need to Offset for Consumption.

The government and defendants Bedonie and Serawop challenge awarding the victims lost income without deducting for consumption. In the parties' view, awarding lost income produces a "windfall" by allowing recovery for income that never would have gone to the victims' estates; instead, it would have been consumed by the victims had they lived. The parties thus urge the court to deduct the victim's expected consumption from their projected income in calculating restitution.

. . . [T]he MVRA does not permit a consumption reduction. While an offset for consumption may make sense in some civil contexts, its application in the criminal context depends on the terms of the criminal restitution statute at issue. Federal courts have no inherent power to award restitution in a criminal case, so their authority to do so is controlled exclusively by the language of the authorizing statute. [31] . . .

This court's restitution decision is governed by the MVRA. While the statute mandates restitution for "income lost"—not "*net* income lost," as the parties restrictively read the statute. Moreover, construing the statute as covering all income is the only way to achieve the aim of Congress to give full restitution to victims. The lost income provision applies both to crimes of violence that leave victims dead and to crimes of violence that leave victims disabled. If the court were to read the lost income provision as authorizing only net income, then disabled victims of violence would be left grossly undercompensated. . . .

[T]he court is not persuaded that awarding gross income produces any kind of excessive restitution. The government's and defendants' arguments are predicated on the assumption that the "victims" of these homicides are the victims' estates, not the people who were killed. The court has previously explained why the decedents themselves—Mr. Johnson and Beyonce Serawop—are the victims. Although the estates may ultimately receive the restitution award, the MVRA directs an award based on the victim's loss, not the estate's loss.

In homicide cases, good reasons support using the victims' full loss as the measure restitution. One of the core purposes of restitution is to "ensure that the offender realizes the damage caused by the offense and pays the debt owed to the victim as well as to society."[32] When a criminal murders someone, the damage caused by the offense to the victim and to society is the full amount that the victim was contributing to society—as reflected in the victim's total earnings—not some truncated amount that subtracts consumption. . . .

A final note is important here. The court is troubled by the parties' description of an award of gross income restitution as producing some kind of a "windfall." To the extent the claim is made about Mrs. Johnson and Ms. Moya, they have lost a son and a daughter from criminal violence inflicted by the defendants. Nothing that this court can order the defendants to pay will come anywhere close to covering their losses, much less create a "windfall." Moreover, unlike some civil settings where the estate is entitled to recovery, here the recovery is for the deceased victims. They will not given an excessive award. The parties ask the court to subtract consumption because the victims would have had living expenses—such as housing, clothing, and meals. But the defendants in this case deprived the victims of the opportunity to enjoy such consumption. Because of the defendants' criminal violence, the victims never got to buy a home, dress in new clothes, or partake in meals with family and friends. In short, the defendants deprived the Mr. Johnson and Beyonce Serawop of the chance to enjoy life. It hardly creates a "windfall" to require the defendants to pay restitution for the consumption that the victims never had the chance to savor.

---

31. *See United States v. Nichols*, 169 F.3d 1255, 1278 (10th Cir. 1999).
32. *Reano*, 298 F.3d at 1212.

Notes

1. Does awarding restitution to the estate of a murder victim or the mother of a murdered child serve the purposes underlying restitution statute? If so, what are those purposes.

2. In October 2004, Congress passed a new statute guaranteeing victims the right to "full and timely restitution as provided in law." During the course of the legislative debate on the law, its primary Senate sponsor stated: "We specifically intend to endorse the expansive definition of restitution given by Judge Cassell in *U.S. v. Bedonie* and *U.S. v. Serawop* in May 2004." 150 Cong. Rec. S10910 (Oct. 9, 2004) (statement of Sen. Kyl).

3. In *United States v. Johnson*, 378 F.3d 230 (2d Cir. 2004), the court concluded that a district court was required to order restitution under the MVRA even where the victim declined to accept the restitution. The court noted that mandatory nature of the MVRA and reasoned that the purpose behind the MVRA was "not only the compensation of victims, but also the punishment of offenders." Because the victim refused the money, the court directed that the defendant pay restitution to the federal crime victims fund.

4. In *United States v. Terry Nichols*, 169 F.3d 1255 (10th Cir. 1999), the court concluded that the then newly-enacted MVRA could be applied retroactively to determine the restitution obligations of Oklahoma City bomber Terry Nichols. The court concluded that restitution was not punitive in nature and therefore not covered by the prohibitions in the Constitution's Ex Post Facto Clause. Interestingly, this argument was not advanced by the government, but only by victims of the bombing who filed an *amicus* brief with the court.

5. Restitution obligations as part of a criminal judgment are generally not dischargeable in bankruptcy. *See Thompson v. Hewitt*, 311 B.R. 415 (E.D. Penn. 2004) (citing 11 U.S.C. § 523(a)(7) (debts which are a fine, penalty, or forfeiture not dischargeable in Chapter 7 bankruptcy and suggesting restitution is penal in nature).

6. Michigan give crime victims a constitutional right to restitution. Mich. Const., art. I, § 24(1). ("[c]rime victims . . . shall have . . . [t]he right to restitution"). The Michigan Supreme Court has held that this provision modified the traditional rules of abatement, which void a defendants' conviction and judgment upon death if death occurs before appeals are exhausted. *People v. Peters*, 537 N.W.2d 160, 164 (Mich. 1995). This result is criticized in Rosanna Cavallaro, *Better Off Dead: Abatement, Innocence, and the Evolving Right of Appeal*, 73 U. Colo. L. Rev. 943 (2002) (without completed appeal, criminal conviction not sufficient reliable to support restitution order).

7. In most states and under federal statutes, a restitution order can be converted into a civil judgment. *See* Jeanne Von Ofenheim, Comment, *Advising the Small Business Owner about Monetary Recovery in Criminal Cases*, 2 J. Small & Emerging Bus. L. 403 (1998).

8. Should victims be taxed on restitution? *See* Linda Trang Note, *The Taxation of Crime Victim Restitution: An Unjust Penalty on the Victim*, 35 Loy. L.A. L. Rev. 1319 (2002) (Because victim restitution functions as compensation, it should be included in the same gross income exclusion afforded to civil damages under § 104(a)(2) of the Internal Revenue Code and thus be nontaxable).

9. California allows for reasonable attorneys' fees for attorneys assisting victims in restitution recovery.

10. Federal courts have discretion to assign restitution either proportionately or jointly and severely. *U.S. v. Moten*, 551 F.3d 763 (8th Cir. 2008).

D. Sentences Barring Profiting from a Crime

1. "Son of Sam" Laws

Many states have passed laws forbidding defendants from profiting from their crimes. For a compilation, see http://www.firstamendmentcenter.org/son-of-sam-statutes-federal-and-state-summary/. New York enacted the first such statute in response to the serial murders committed by David Berkowitz. He became known to the public through his manifestos as the "Son of Sam" killer. When he was apprehended, the rights to his story were apparently worth substantial sums. To prevent him profiting from his crime, the New York Legislature passed a statute to transfer any profits to crime victims. As the author of the statute explained, "It is abhorrent to one's sense of justice and decency that an individual . . . can expect to receive large sums of money for history once he is captured—while five people are dead, and other people were injured as a result of his conduct."

The U.S. Supreme Court considered the constitutionality of this "Son of Sam" law in *Simon & Schuster v. New York Crime Victims Board*, 502 U.S. 105 (1991). While recognizing the legitimacy of the state's goals, the Court concluded that the law violated the First Amendment. Since then, courts have struggled to determine the constitutionality of state laws passed to comply with the dictates of *Simon & Schuster*. Consider the analysis of the Massachusetts Supreme Court, in response to a request for an advisory opinion from the Massachusetts State Senate about a proposed "Son of Sam" law.

Opinion of the Justices to the Senate

764 N.E.2d 343 (Mass. 2002)

To the Honorable the Senate of the Commonwealth of Massachusetts:

The Justices of the Supreme Judicial Court respectfully submit their answer to the question set forth in an order adopted by the Senate on September 17, 2001, and transmitted to the Justices on September 21, 2001. The order indicates that there is pending before the General Court a bill, Senate No. 1939, entitled "An Act relative to profits from crime." A copy of the bill was transmitted with the order. The bill adds

c. 258D to the General Laws, which requires that certain contracts with a person who committed a crime be submitted to the division of victim compensation and assistance within the Department of the Attorney General (division) for its determination whether the proceeds under the contract are substantially related to a crime. If so, the contracting entity must pay over to the division any monies which would otherwise be owed to the person who committed the crime. The funds are then to be deposited into an escrow account and made available to the victims of the crime.

The order indicates that grave doubt exists as to the constitutionality of the bill, if enacted into law, and requests our opinion on this question:

> Does Senate No. 1939, by restricting the ability of criminal offenders to profit from their crimes, violate the right of freedom of speech as provided by the First Amendment to the Constitution of the United States (which the Fourteenth Amendment applies to the Commonwealth) or as provided in Article XVI of the Declaration of Rights of the Commonwealth?

1. Provisions of the bill. Proposed G.L. c. 258D requires any entity (contracting party) contracting with a "defendant" to submit a copy of the contract to the division within thirty days of the agreement if the contracting party knows or reasonably should know that the consideration to be paid to the defendant would constitute "[p]roceeds related to a crime." §§ 1, 2. It defines "[d]efendant" as "a person who is the subject of pending criminal charges or has been convicted of a crime or has voluntarily admitted the commission of a crime," § 1. It defines "[p]roceeds related to a crime" as "any assets, material objects, monies, and property obtained through the use of unique knowledge or notoriety acquired by means and in consequence of the commission of a crime from whatever source received by or owing to a defendant or his representative, whether earned, accrued, or paid before or after the disposition of criminal charges against the defendant." *Id.* Within thirty days of receipt of the contract, the division must determine whether the proceeds under the contract are "substantially related to a crime, rather than relating only tangentially to, or containing only passing references to, a crime," and must notify the contracting party of its determination. §§ 3, 4. If the division determines that the proceeds under the contract are substantially related to a crime, the contracting party has fifteen days in which to pay to the division the monies owed to the defendant under the contract or post a bond covering such amount. § 5. The contracting party may seek reconsideration of the division's determination, and may seek judicial review of the decision in accordance with G.L. c. 30A, § 14. § 6. However, the obligation to make payment to the division (or post a bond) is not stayed pending a decision on reconsideration or pending judicial review. *Id.*

The monies paid over by the contracting party are placed in an escrow account for the benefit of the victims of the defendant's crime. § 5. The division must notify all known victims of the defendant's crime that the defendant has such a contract and must publish a general notice in a newspaper every six months for a year. § 8. Within three years from the date of the last publication, victims may bring a civil action against the defendant, regardless of the earlier expiration of any applicable statute of limitations. § 9. The escrowed funds are used to satisfy any judgment obtained by the victim against the defendant; however, no funds can be transferred until the defendant is convicted of the crime or has voluntarily admitted the commission of the crime. § 11. After all judgments against the defendant are paid, or if no victim files an action within the required three-year period, one-half the remaining escrowed funds are returned to the contracting party. § 13. The other half is deposited into the victim compensation fund maintained under G.L. c. 258C, § 4 (c). § 13.

2. Background of the proposed legislation. Many States have enacted statutes similar to Senate No. 1939 in an attempt to prevent defendants from reaping financial gain from their crimes and to redirect a defendant's funds to the compensation of crime victims. (citations omitted). In 1977, New York enacted the nation's first such statute in response to the lucrative opportunities presented to the serial killer David Berkowitz, popularly known as the "Son of Sam," for the rights to his story. That statute required any entity contracting with a "person convicted of a crime" for the "reenactment of [the] crime, by way of a movie, book, magazine article . . . or from the expression of such accused or convicted person's thoughts, feelings, opinions or emotions regarding such crime" to submit a copy of the contract and pay over any income under that contract to the State's Crime Victims Board. N.Y. Exec. Law § 632-a (1) (McKinney 1982 & Supp. 1991). Several States, including Massachusetts, quickly followed by enacting similar laws. The first such statute in Massachusetts was modeled after the New York statute and followed its language closely. *See* G.L. c. 258A, § 8.

In 1991, the United States Supreme Court struck down the New York statute, declaring it unconstitutionally overbroad. *Simon & Schuster, Inc. v. New York Crime Victims Bd.*, 502 U.S. 105, (1991). Applying a standard of strict scrutiny, the Court found that the statute was not narrowly tailored to serve the State's compelling interests in ensuring that victims are compensated by those who harm them and in preventing criminals from profiting from their crimes. *Id.* at 121–123. Consequently, both New York and Massachusetts repealed their respective statutes. *See* N.Y. Exec. Law § 632-a (McKinney 1982 & Supp. 1991), repealed by L.1992, c. 618, § 10; G.L. c. 258A, § 8, repealed by St.1993, c. 478, § 3.

Senate No. 1939 is an attempt to reenact a similar statute in Massachusetts, addressing the concerns articulated by the United States Supreme Court in *Simon & Schuster, supra.* We are of the opinion that Senate No. 1939 has not successfully addressed those concerns and therefore still violates the First Amendment to the United States Constitution and art. 16 of the Declaration of Rights, as amended by art. 77 of the Amendments to the Massachusetts Constitution.

3. Analysis. We note at the outset that portions of Senate No. 1939 regulate nonexpressive activity, and those portions would not violate or otherwise impinge on the right of freedom of speech in the First Amendment or art. 16.[34] As such, our an-

---

34. Besides contracts for books, articles, television programs, and films, the bill covers a defendant's sale of tangible property where the value has been enhanced by the defendant's notoriety. *See* Kathleen Burge, *Making a Killing: Bill Takes Aim at Sales by Criminals*, Boston Globe, Dec. 11,

alysis of the constitutional infirmities of the bill pertains solely to the bill's proposed regulation of contracts involving expressive activity under the First Amendment.

a. Content-based regulation. Consistent with other courts, we conclude that Senate No. 1939 is a content-based regulation of speech. *See, e.g., Simon & Schuster,* supra at 115, 122 n.*; *Keenan v. Superior Court,* 40 P.3d 718 (Cal. 2002); *Curran v. Price,* 638 A.2d 93 (Md. 1994); *Bouchard v. Price,* 694 A.2d 670, 676 (R.I. 1997). It burdens only expression with a particular content, namely, works that describe, reenact, or otherwise are related to the commission of a crime. Senate No. 1939 is content-based on its face, as it places a financial disincentive on speakers based on a specified content of their speech: speech substantially related to a crime. *See Simon & Schuster,* supra at 115–116, *citing Leathers v. Medlock,* 499 U.S. 439, 448–449 (1991). Indeed, under § 3, the division is required to analyze the content of any expressive work contemplated under a contract to determine whether the contract comes within the purview of the statute. *See Curran v. Price,* 638 A.2d 93. By definition, if the applicability of the bill's requirements can only be determined by reviewing the contents of the proposed expression, the bill is a content-based regulation of speech.

Supporters of the measure correctly note that the views and opinions being expressed about the defendant's criminal activity are irrelevant to the application of Senate No. 1939. Although the bill does not discriminate between particular viewpoints concerning crime, "[t]he First Amendment's hostility to content-based regulation extends not only to restrictions on particular viewpoints, but also to prohibition of public discussion of an entire topic." *Arkansas Writers' Project, Inc. v. Ragland,* 481 U.S. 221, 230 (1987). Here, expressive works are subject to the requirements of Senate No. 1939 based on their topic, i.e., based on the fact that they discuss or relate to a defendant's involvement in some form of criminal activity. The bill must therefore be classified as content-based.

To pass constitutional muster under the First Amendment, a content-based regulation must be "necessary to serve a compelling state interest and . . . narrowly drawn to achieve that end." *Simon & Schuster,* supra at 118, The Supreme Court has identified two compelling State interests that are served by this type of statute: (1) "ensuring that victims of crime are compensated by those who harm them," and (2) "ensuring that criminals do not profit from their crimes." *Simon & Schuster,* supra at 118, 119. We must therefore determine whether Senate No. 1939 is narrowly tailored to advance either of these State interests. We conclude that it is not, finding Senate No. 1939 overbroad in at least the following respects.

As drafted, the proposed law extends to contracts with persons who were never even charged with any crime. A person who has "voluntarily admitted the com-

---

2001, at B4; Rich Klein, *Sold to Highest Bidder: Online "Murderabilia," Criminals' Keepsakes Going for Hundreds,* Boston Globe, Nov. 30, 2000, at B1. The sale of such items does not involve expressive activity, and regulation of those sales does not implicate the First Amendment or art. 16.

mission of a crime" is included in the definition of "defendant." § 1. One of the main problems with the New York statute in *Simon & Schuster*, supra at 121, 112 S. Ct. 501, was the statute's similarly broad definition of "person convicted of a crime." As the Court noted, because the definition included "any author who admits in his work to having committed a crime, whether or not the author was ever actually accused or convicted," the New York statute reached a large pool of potential authors (such as artists, political dissidents and civil rights leaders), and thereby went far beyond what was necessary to serve the State's compelling interest. *Id.* at 121–122, citing N.Y. Exec. Law § 632-a (10)(b). The Court noted that the New York statute would have an adverse chilling effect on the future creation and dissemination of important literary works and would "reach [ ] a wide range of literature that does not enable a criminal to profit from his crime while a victim remains uncompensated." *Id.* at 122, Not surprisingly, other States have limited the scope of such laws to persons convicted of (or at least charged with) a crime. *See, e.g.,* Cal. Civ. Code § 2225(a)(1) (West Supp. 2002) (limited to "any person convicted of a felony, or found not guilty by reason of insanity"); Colo. Rev. Stat. Ann. § 24-4.1-201(1.5)(a) (I) (2001) (convicted persons); Iowa Code Ann. § 910.15(1)(a) (West 1994) ("initially convicted, or found not guilty by reason of insanity"); Md. Code Ann., Crim. Proc. § 11-621(b)(1) (LexisNexis 2001) (persons "charged with or convicted of a crime"); N.Y. Exec. Law § 632-a (2)(a) (McKinney 1996) (same); 42 Pa. Cons. Stat. Ann. § 8312(a) (convicted persons); Tenn. Code Ann. § 29-13-402(3) (accused and convicted persons); Va. Code Ann. § 19.2-368.19 (convicted persons). Thus, by defining "defendant" to include persons who, although not convicted or even formally accused, have "voluntarily admitted" to the commission of a crime, Senate No. 1939 suffers from the same defect that rendered the New York statute "significantly overinclusive" in *Simon & Schuster*, supra at 121.

With respect to all types of criminal defendants, the law also would impose financial burdens and uncertainties that would, in their practical effect, operate to chill a wide range of expression. The proposed law requires that all monies owed to a defendant be held in escrow by the division for at least three years. §§ 5, 9. If claims are filed, the funds are held until the conclusion of those proceedings. Ultimately, the funds are used to satisfy any judgment obtained against the defendant, with the remainder then split between the contracting party and the general victim compensation fund. § 13. Under this system, the defendant's funds are held for a lengthy and uncertain period of time, and one cannot predict how much of the funds (if any) will ultimately be released.

As the Supreme Court noted in *Simon & Schuster*, supra at 116–117, a provision that escrows a defendant's payments under a contract operates as a "financial disincentive" on both the defendant-author and the publisher. Such a provision may deprive the defendant-author of the financial resources needed to initiate a work, as it precludes advances from the publisher to the author by which the author could support himself or herself during the preparation of the expressive work. Similarly, the prospect of having all of his or her income held in escrow for a long period, with at best uncertain prospects as to how much of it (if any) will ever be paid, makes it very unlikely that a defendant-author would ever agree to undertake such a project. "No man but a blockhead ever wrote, except for money." *United States v. National Treasury Employees Union*, 513 U.S. 454, 469 n.14 (1995), quoting J. Boswell, Life of Samuel Johnson LL.D. 302 (R. Hutchins ed.1952). "[T]o deny compensation for certain speech will chill such speech." *Curran v. Price*, 638 A.2d 93 (Md. 1994). Publishers who can offer potential authors only the prospect of a long delay before payment of a completely uncertain amount of money (if any) will have a difficult time convincing defendants to agree to author their stories or to speak with writers who can use their material to create an expressive work. "Publishers compensate authors because compensation provides a significant incentive toward more expression." *United States v. National Treasury Employees Union*, supra at 469. Interfering with publishers' ability to compensate an entire class of authors will likely prevent publishers from preparing and publishing works concerning persons who have, at some point in their lives, engaged in criminal activity. The administrative burdens associated with notifying the division, challenging division determinations, and depositing funds with the division would make publishers less inclined to pursue such works. Although it is impossible to measure the cost of works that would never come to fruition because of the multiple deterrent effects of the bill, "we cannot ignore the risk that it might deprive us of the work of a future Melville or Hawthorne." *Id.* at 470. These burdens extend to works and authors far beyond those necessary to serve the compelling State interests articulated here.

In comparison to the bill's proposed interference with the publishing industry's ability to obtain information from or publish works about any criminal, we note that there are other less cumbersome and more precise methods of compensating victims and preventing notorious criminals from obtaining a financial windfall from their notoriety. Probation conditions, specifically designed to deal with a defendant's future income and obligations, may be imposed. *See Commonwealth v. Power*, 650 N.E.2d 87 (Mass. 1995), *cert. denied*, 516 U.S. 1042 (1996). Victims may, as part of any civil action against a defendant, seek writs of attachment against the defendant's assets or writs of trustee process of amounts owed to the defendant, including (but not limited to) assets or earnings derived from expressive activity. Injunctive relief is also available. *See Eappen v. Woodward*, U.S. Disc. Ct. No. 98-CV-11173 (D. Mass. June 29, 1998). While such methods may impinge on a defendant's expressive activity, they are specifically adapted to the facts and circumstances of each case. The proposed bill, sweeping broadly across the publishing and entertainment industries and interfering with an entire category of speech, is not narrowly tailored.

b. Prior restraint. Beyond our concerns about the bill's overbreadth, we also note that, in its practical effect, it would operate as a prior restraint on speech, while lacking the procedural protections required for any such prior restraint. As discussed above, the delays and uncertainties surrounding compensation for such works will, even when they do not deter such works entirely, at least postpone their production and ultimate release. And, if the division determines that the proceeds are "substantially related to a crime," that determination may operate to halt the production of the work entirely. Any system of prior restraints "comes . . . bearing a heavy presumption against its constitutional validity." *Bantam Books, Inc. v. Sullivan*, 372 U.S. 58, 70 (1963).

In order to pass constitutional muster under the First Amendment, a statute that establishes a system of prior restraints must provide procedures that will offer "adequate safeguards against undue inhibition of protected expression." *Freedman v. Maryland*, 380 U.S. 51, 60, (1965). Senate No. 1939 fails to provide those procedural safeguards.

The Supreme Court has specified three procedural requirements that must be included in any system of prior restraint. First, the State must bear the burden of proving that a particular work falls within the regulatory sweep of the statute. Second, any restraint prior to judicial determination must be brief and only for the purpose of preserving the status quo; thus, the statute "cannot be administered in a manner which would lend an effect of finality to the [State's] determination." Third, there must be a prompt final judicial determination. *Id.* at 59. *See Curran v. Price, supra*, 638 A.2d 93.

Here, the proposed initial review process fails to satisfy these procedural requirements in several respects. Although Senate No. 1939 does not have a "rebuttable presumption" that a work falls within the reach of the statute, as was the case in Maryland's statute, *see Curran v. Price, supra*, 638 A.2d 93, the proposed bill makes the division's determination (or the program director's decision on reconsideration) final unless the contracting party seeks judicial review. *See* §§ 5, 6. Thus, the division does not have the burden of initiating judicial proceedings, and there is no judicial review unless the contracting party appeals. This is in conflict with the Supreme Court's pronouncement that "only a procedure requiring a judicial determination suffices to impose a valid final restraint." *Freedman v. Maryland*, supra at 58.

Furthermore, § 6 of the proposed law provides for judicial review under G.L. c. 30A, § 14, which places the burden of demonstrating error on the party seeking review (here, the contracting party) and which requires the reviewing court to give substantial deference to the agency's decision. . . . Thus, the bill fails to satisfy the requirement that the burden of proof be placed on the State. *Freedman v. Maryland, supra*.

Finally, Senate No. 1939 provides no assurance of prompt judicial determination. It has no requirement that courts hear such appeals in any specific time frame or even that they act "promptly," and therefore the "[r]isk of delay is built into [the proposed statute], as is borne out by experience." *Id.* at 55. . . .

4. Conclusion. Therefore, we find that Senate No. 1939, as drafted, violates the right of freedom of speech in the First Amendment and art. 16. The various provisions of the bill that render it unconstitutional cannot be severed from the statute without undermining the integrity and purpose of the bill.

The answer to the question is, "Yes."

Notes

1. If the law that the Massachusetts Senate envisioned was unconstitutional, what (if any) revisions would make it constitutional? *See* Kathleen Howe, Comment, *Is Free Speech Too High a Price to Pay for Crime? Overcoming the Constitutional Inconsistencies in Son of Sam Laws*, 24 Loyola L.A. Entertain. L. Rev. 341 (2004). *See generally* Gregory Sarno, *Validity, Construction, and Application of "Son of Sam" Laws Regulating or Prohibiting Distribution of Crime-Related Book, Film, or Comparable Revenues to Criminals*, 60 A.L.R. 4th 1210.

2. Perhaps there is another tactic that states might use. Consider *State of Arizona v. Gravano*, 204 Ariz. 106 (2002), rev denied June 30, 2003, where racketeering forfeiture laws were used: "We consider whether the application of Arizona's forfeiture statutes to royalties from a book about the life and crimes of a convicted racketeer violates constitutional free speech guarantees. We further examine whether the royalties have the causal connection with racketeering required for forfeiture. For the reasons discussed below, we conclude that the statutes are constitutional in this setting and that the royalties are subject to forfeiture as proceeds traceable to racketeering. As a result, we affirm the trial court's judgment ordering forfeiture of the royalties."

3. There are many examples of successful attempts to make money from the sale of crime stories by the criminal as this article from the Washington Lawyer makes clear. Ethan Bordman, *How Much Does Crime Pay?* Washington Lawyer (May 2011).

4. In a 2014 case involving a second wife's efforts to keep the proceeds of her husband's estate from the daughter of the husband's first marriage after the husband murdered the first wife, the New York court held:

Next, we reject Marilyn's contention that the defendant's pension is not subject to execution or attachment . . . As Marilyn correctly contends, section 110 (2) of the Retirement and Social Security Law provides that the right of a person to a pension "[s]hall not be subject to execution, garnishment, attachment, or any other process whatsoever" (Retirement and Social Security Law § 110 [2]). In 2001, however, the Legislature amended the Son of Sam law to subject the "[f]unds of a convicted person" to an action for damages by a crime victim, a crime victim's representative, or certain other persons. The phrase "funds of a convicted person" was broadly defined as "all funds and property received from any source."

We conclude, for the reasons stated by our colleagues in the Appellate Division, Third Department (see Matter of New York State Off. of Victim Servs. v Raucci, 97 AD3d 235 [2012], reversed on other grounds 20 NY3d 1049 [2013]), that the defendant's pension is subject to execution under the Son of Sam law. Both the clear statutory language and the legislative history of the 2001 amendments to the Son of Sam law evince the Legislature's intent to permit crime victims to recover assets from convicted persons, including pensions, regardless of the source of the convicted person's funds . As the Third Department concluded, a contrary holding would "directly thwart[ ] the Legislature's stated intent of holding convicted criminals financially accountable regardless of their source of wealth" .

2. "Murderabilia"

Defendants can profit from their crimes in ways other than selling books. For example, in the previous section, the Massachusetts Supreme Court in *Opinion of the Justices to the Senate* mentioned (in footnote 7) "murderabilia"—the sale for profit of items that are valuable only because of their association with notorious murderers. How should society respond to murderabilia? For contrasting views on Murderabilia, *see* Hilary Hanson, *Murderabilia Has Andy Kahan, Victim Advocate, Up in Arms*, HUFF. POST, October 8, 2012.

In its opinion in *Opinion of the Justices to the Senate*, the Massachusetts Supreme Court said that "murderabilia" did not "involve expressive activity, and regulation of those sales does not implicate the First Amendment or art." Is it true that the sale, for example, of a Charles Manson music CD does not implicate the First Amendment? His compact disc—Lie: The Love & Terror Cult—features music he recorded from behind bars and was recently available through Amazon.com for $14.99.

Several states have banned the sale of murderabilia. The most prominent statute is Texas's, which essentially defines as contraband—and therefore forfeitable to the state—"income from the sale of tangible property the value of which is increased by the notoriety gained from the conviction of an offense by the person accused or convicted of the crime." TEX. CRIM. PROC. CODE. ANN. 59.06(k)(2). The argument for constitutionality of this provision is that it applies only to profits gained from the commission of a crime, rather than the expressions of the crime, and that it is content neutral. Will such statutes survive a challenge based on *Simon & Schuster*? *See* Tracey B. Cobb, Comment, *Making a Killing: Evaluating the Constitutionality of the Texas Son of Sam Law*, 39 HOUS. L. REV. 1483 (2003).

Should murderabilia statutes (such as Texas' mentioned in the previous note) apply to property that has become historically significant? For example, should a museum be able to sell memorabilia connected with John Wilkes-Booth, who was convicted of assassinating President Lincoln?

Can the government seize and sell a killer's property to satisfy restitution? The Ninth Circuit permitted this in the seizure and pending sale of the Unabomber possessions. *U.S. v. Kazynski*, 551 F.3d 1120 (9th Cir. 2008).

E. Protection of Future Victims: The Example of Sex Offenders

So far this chapter has considered ways in which the particular victim of a crime can be protected from a particular defendant. Should the courts also consider protecting *future* victims? In a general sense, all criminal penalties consider future victims. After all, we incarcerate criminals, at least in part, so that they will be deterred from committing other crimes and will be incapacitated from committing other crimes while in prison. But increasingly the court system is considering victims in other ways as well—such as civilly committing dangerous sex offenders and requiring sex offenders to register publicly.

1. Commitment of Dangerous Sex Offenders

Kansas v. Hendricks

521 U.S. 346 (1997)

Justice THOMAS delivered the opinion of the Court.

In 1994, Kansas enacted the Sexually Violent Predator Act, which establishes procedures for the civil commitment of persons who, due to a "mental abnormality" or a "personality disorder," are likely to engage in "predatory acts of sexual violence." Kan. Stat. Ann. § 59-29a01 et seq. (1994). The State invoked the Act for the first time to commit Leroy Hendricks, an inmate who had a long history of sexually molesting children, and who was scheduled for release from prison shortly after the Act became law. Hendricks challenged his commitment on, inter alia, "substantive" due process, double jeopardy, and ex post facto grounds. The Kansas Supreme Court invalidated the Act, holding that its pre-commitment condition of a "mental abnormality" did not satisfy what the court perceived to be the "substantive" due process requirement that involuntary civil commitment must be predicated on a finding of "mental illness." . . .

I

A

The Kansas Legislature enacted the Sexually Violent Predator Act (Act) in 1994 to grapple with the problem of managing repeat sexual offenders. Although Kansas already had a statute addressing the involuntary commitment of those defined as "mentally ill," the legislature determined that existing civil commitment procedures were inadequate to confront the risks presented by "sexually violent predators." In the Act's preamble, the legislature explained:

> [A] small but extremely dangerous group of sexually violent predators exist who do not have a mental disease or defect that renders them appropriate for involuntary treatment pursuant to the [general involuntary civil commitment statute]. . . . In contrast to persons appropriate for civil commitment under the [general involuntary civil commitment statute], sexually violent predators generally have anti-social personality features which are unamenable to existing mental illness treatment modalities and those features render them likely to engage in sexually violent behavior. The legislature further finds that sexually violent predators' likelihood of engaging in repeat acts of predatory sexual violence is high. The existing involuntary commitment procedure . . . is inadequate to address the risk these sexually violent predators pose to society. The legislature further finds that the prog-

nosis for rehabilitating sexually violent predators in a prison setting is poor, the treatment needs of this population are very long term and the treatment modalities for this population are very different than the traditional treatment modalities for people appropriate for commitment under the [general involuntary civil commitment statute].

As a result, the Legislature found it necessary to establish "a civil commitment procedure for the long-term care and treatment of the sexually violent predator." The Act defined a "sexually violent predator" as:

"any person who has been convicted of or charged with a sexually violent offense and who suffers from a mental abnormality or personality disorder which makes the person likely to engage in the predatory acts of sexual violence."

A "mental abnormality" was defined, in turn, as a "congenital or acquired condition affecting the emotional or volitional capacity which predisposes the person to commit sexually violent offenses in a degree constituting such person a menace to the health and safety of others."

As originally structured, the Act's civil commitment procedures pertained to: (1) a presently confined person who, like Hendricks, "has been convicted of a sexually violent offense" and is scheduled for release; (2) a person who has been "charged with a sexually violent offense" but has been found incompetent to stand trial; (3) a person who has been found "not guilty by reason of insanity of a sexually violent offense"; and (4) a person found "not guilty" of a sexually violent offense because of a mental disease or defect.

The initial version of the Act, as applied to a currently confined person such as Hendricks, was designed to initiate a specific series of procedures. The custodial agency was required to notify the local prosecutor 60 days before the anticipated release of a person who might have met the Act's criteria. The prosecutor was then obligated, within 45 days, to decide whether to file a petition in state court seeking the person's involuntary commitment. If such a petition were filed, the court was to determine whether "probable cause" existed to support a finding that the person was a "sexually violent predator" and thus eligible for civil commitment. Upon such a determination, transfer of the individual to a secure facility for professional evaluation would occur. After that evaluation, a trial would be held to determine beyond a reasonable doubt whether the individual was a sexually violent predator. If that determination were made, the person would then be transferred to the custody of the Secretary of Social and Rehabilitation Services (Secretary) for "control, care and treatment until such time as the person's mental abnormality or personality disorder has so changed that the person is safe to be at large."

In addition to placing the burden of proof upon the State, the Act afforded the individual a number of other procedural safeguards. In the case of an indigent person, the State was required to provide, at public expense, the assistance of counsel and an examination by mental health care professionals. The individual also received the right to present and cross-examine witnesses, and the opportunity to review documentary evidence presented by the State.

Once an individual was confined, the Act required that "[t]he involuntary detention or commitment . . . shall conform to constitutional requirements for care and treatment." Confined persons were afforded three different avenues of review: First, the committing court was obligated to conduct an annual review to determine whether continued detention was warranted. Second, the Secretary was permitted, at any time, to decide that the confined individual's condition had so changed that release was appropriate, and could then authorize the person to petition for release. Finally, even without the Secretary's permission, the confined person could at any time file a release petition. If the court found that the State could no longer satisfy its burden under the initial commitment standard, the individual would be freed from confinement.

B

In 1984, Hendricks was convicted of taking "indecent liberties" with two 13-year-old boys. After serving nearly 10 years of his sentence, he was slated for release to a halfway house. Shortly before his scheduled release, however, the State filed a petition in state court seeking Hendricks' civil confinement as a sexually violent predator. On August 19, 1994, Hendricks appeared before the court with counsel and moved to dismiss the petition on the grounds that the Act violated various federal constitutional provisions. Although the court reserved ruling on the Act's constitutionality, it concluded that there was probable cause to support a finding that Hendricks was a sexually violent predator, and therefore ordered that he be evaluated at the Larned State Security Hospital.

Hendricks subsequently requested a jury trial to determine whether he qualified as a sexually violent predator. During that trial, Hendricks' own testimony revealed a chilling history of repeated child sexual molestation and abuse, beginning in 1955 when he exposed his genitals to two young girls. At that time, he pleaded guilty to indecent exposure. Then, in 1957, he was convicted of lewdness involving a young girl and received a brief jail sentence. In 1960, he molested two young boys while he worked for a carnival. After serving two years in prison for that offense, he was paroled, only to be rearrested for molesting a 7-year-old girl. Attempts were made to treat him for his sexual deviance, and in 1965 he was considered "safe to be at large," and was discharged from a state psychiatric hospital.

Shortly thereafter, however, Hendricks sexually assaulted another young boy and girl, he performed oral sex on the 8-year-old girl and fondled the 11-year-old boy. He was again imprisoned in 1967, but refused to participate in a sex offender treatment program, and thus remained incarcerated until his parole in 1972. Diagnosed as a pedophile, Hendricks entered into, but then abandoned, a treatment program. He testified that despite having received professional help for his pedophilia, he continued to harbor sexual desires for children. Indeed, soon after his 1972 parole,

Hendricks began to abuse his own stepdaughter and stepson. He forced the children to engage in sexual activity with him over a period of approximately four years. Then, as noted above, Hendricks was convicted of "taking indecent liberties" with two adolescent boys after he attempted to fondle them. As a result of that conviction, he was once again imprisoned, and was serving that sentence when he reached his conditional release date in September 1994.

Hendricks admitted that he had repeatedly abused children whenever he was not confined. He explained that when he "get[s] stressed out," he "can't control the urge" to molest children. Although Hendricks recognized that his behavior harms children, and he hoped he would not sexually molest children again, he stated that the only sure way he could keep from sexually abusing children in the future was "to die." Hendricks readily agreed with the state physician's diagnosis that he suffers from pedophilia and that he is not cured of the condition; indeed, he told the physician that "treatment is bull." . . .

II

A

Kansas argues that the Act's definition of "mental abnormality" satisfies "substantive" due process requirements. We agree. Although freedom from physical restraint "has always been at the core of the liberty protected by the Due Process Clause from arbitrary governmental action," that liberty interest is not absolute. The Court has recognized that an individual's constitutionally protected interest in avoiding physical restraint may be overridden even in the civil context:

> [T]he liberty secured by the Constitution of the United States to every person within its jurisdiction does not import an absolute right in each person to be, at all times and in all circumstances, wholly free from restraint. There are manifold restraints to which every person is necessarily subject for the common good. On any other basis organized society could not exist with safety to its members.

Jacobson v. Massachusetts, 197 U.S. 11, 26 (1905).

Accordingly, States have in certain narrow circumstances provided for the forcible civil detainment of people who are unable to control their behavior and who thereby pose a danger to the public health and safety. *See, e.g.*, 1788 N.Y. Laws, ch. 31 (Feb. 9, 1788) (permitting confinement of the "furiously mad"); *see also* A. Deutsch, The Mentally Ill in America (1949) (tracing history of civil commitment in the 18th and 19th centuries); G. Grob, Mental Institutions in America: Social Policy to 1875 (1973) (discussing colonial and early American civil commitment statutes). We have consistently upheld such involuntary commitment statutes provided the confinement takes place pursuant to proper procedures and evidentiary standards. It thus cannot be said that the involuntary civil confinement of a limited subclass of dangerous persons is contrary to our understanding of ordered liberty.

The challenged Act unambiguously requires a finding of dangerousness either to one's self or to others as a prerequisite to involuntary confinement. Commitment proceedings can be initiated only when a person "has been convicted of or charged with a sexually violent offense," and "suffers from a mental abnormality or personality disorder which makes the person likely to engage in the predatory acts of sexual violence." The statute thus requires proof of more than a mere predisposition to violence; rather, it requires evidence of past sexually violent behavior and a present mental condition that creates a likelihood of such conduct in the future if the person is not incapacitated. As we have recognized, "[p]revious instances of violent behavior are an important indicator of future violent tendencies."

A finding of dangerousness, standing alone, is ordinarily not a sufficient ground upon which to justify indefinite involuntary commitment. We have sustained civil commitment statutes when they have coupled proof of dangerousness with the proof of some additional fact, such as a "mental illness" or "mental abnormality." . . . These added statutory requirements serve to limit involuntary civil confinement to those who suffer from a volitional impairment rendering them dangerous beyond their control. The Kansas Act is plainly of a kind with these other civil commitment statutes: It requires a finding of future dangerousness, and then links that finding to the existence of a "mental abnormality" or "personality disorder" that makes it difficult, if not impossible, for the person to control his dangerous behavior. The pre-commitment requirement of a "mental abnormality" or "personality disorder" is consistent with the requirements of these other statutes that we have upheld in that it narrows the class of persons eligible for confinement to those who are unable to control their dangerousness.

Hendricks nonetheless argues that our earlier cases dictate a finding of "mental illness" as a prerequisite for civil commitment, citing Foucha, and Addington. He then asserts that a "mental abnormality" is not equivalent to a "mental illness" because it is a term coined by the Kansas Legislature, rather than by the psychiatric community. Contrary to Hendricks' assertion, the term "mental illness" is devoid of any talismanic significance. "[P]sychiatrists disagree widely and frequently on what constitutes mental illness." . . .

Indeed, we have never required State legislatures to adopt any particular nomenclature in drafting civil commitment statutes. . . .

To the extent that the civil commitment statutes we have considered set forth criteria relating to an individual's inability to control his dangerousness, the Kansas Act sets forth comparable criteria and Hendricks' condition doubtless satisfies those criteria. The mental health professionals who evaluated Hendricks diagnosed him as suffering from pedophilia, a condition the psychiatric profession itself classifies as a serious mental disorder. . . . Hendricks even conceded that, when he becomes "stressed out," he cannot "control the urge" to molest children. This admitted lack of volitional control, coupled with a prediction of future dangerousness, adequately distinguishes Hendricks from other dangerous persons who are perhaps more properly dealt with exclusively through criminal proceedings. Hendricks' diagnosis as a pedophile, which qualifies as a "mental abnormality" under the Act, thus plainly suffices for due process purposes.

B

We granted Hendricks' cross-petition to determine whether the Act violates the Constitution's double jeopardy prohibition or its ban on ex post facto lawmaking. The thrust of Hendricks' argument is that the Act establishes criminal proceedings; hence confinement under it necessarily constitutes punishment. He contends that where, as here, newly enacted "punishment" is predicated upon past conduct for which he has already been convicted and forced to serve a prison sentence, the Constitution's Double Jeopardy and Ex Post Facto Clauses are violated. We are unpersuaded by Hendricks' argument that Kansas has established criminal proceedings.

The categorization of a particular proceeding as civil or criminal "is first of all a question of statutory construction." We must initially ascertain whether the legislature meant the statute to establish "civil" proceedings. If so, we ordinarily defer to the legislature's stated intent. Here, Kansas' objective to create a civil proceeding is evidenced by its placement of the Sexually Violent Predator Act within the Kansas probate code, instead of the criminal code, as well as its description of the Act as creating a "civil commitment procedure." . . . Nothing on the face of the statute suggests that the legislature sought to create anything other than a civil commitment scheme designed to protect the public from harm.

Although we recognize that a "civil label is not always dispositive," we will reject the legislature's manifest intent only where a party challenging the statute provides "the clearest proof" that "the statutory scheme [is] so punitive either in purpose or effect as to negate [the State's] intention" to deem it "civil." *United States v. Ward*, 448 U.S. 242, 248–249 (1980). In those limited circumstances, we will consider the statute to have established criminal proceedings for constitutional purposes. Hendricks, however, has failed to satisfy this heavy burden.

As a threshold matter, commitment under the Act does not implicate either of the two primary objectives of criminal punishment: retribution or deterrence. The Act's purpose is not retributive because it does not affix culpability for prior criminal conduct. Instead, such conduct is used solely for evidentiary purposes, either to demonstrate that a "mental abnormality" exists or to support a finding of future dangerousness. . . . In addition, the Kansas Act does not make a criminal conviction a prerequisite for commitment; persons absolved of criminal responsibility may nonetheless be subject to confinement under the Act. An absence of the necessary criminal responsibility suggests that the State is not seeking retribution for a past misdeed. Thus, the fact that the Act may be "tied to criminal activity" is "insufficient to render the statut[e] punitive.

Moreover, unlike a criminal statute, no finding of scienter is required to commit an individual who is found to be a sexually violent predator; instead, the commitment determination is made based on a "mental abnormality" or "personality disorder" rather than on one's criminal intent. The existence of a scienter requirement is customarily an important element in distinguishing criminal from civil statutes. The absence of such a requirement here is evidence that confinement under the statute is not intended to be retributive.

Nor can it be said that the legislature intended the Act to function as a deterrent. Those persons committed under the Act are, by definition, suffering from a "mental abnormality" or a "personality disorder" that prevents them from exercising adequate control over their behavior. Such persons are therefore unlikely to be deterred by the threat of confinement. And the conditions surrounding that confinement do not suggest a punitive purpose on the State's part. . . . [I]t is difficult to conclude that persons confined under this Act are being "punished."

Although the civil commitment scheme at issue here does involve an affirmative restraint, "the mere fact that a person is detained does not inexorably lead to the conclusion that the government has imposed punishment." *United States v. Salerno*, 481 U.S. 739, 746 (1987). The State may take measures to restrict the freedom of the dangerously mentally ill. This is a legitimate non-punitive governmental objective and has been historically so regarded. . . .

Hendricks focuses on his confinement's potentially indefinite duration as evidence of the State's punitive intent. That focus, however, is misplaced. Far from any punitive objective, the confinement's duration is instead linked to the stated purposes of the commitment, namely, to hold the person until his mental abnormality no longer causes him to be a threat to others. . . .

Furthermore, commitment under the Act is only *potentially* indefinite. The maximum amount of time an individual can be incapacitated pursuant to a single judicial proceeding is one year. If Kansas seeks to continue the detention beyond that year, a court must once again determine beyond a reasonable doubt that the detainee satisfies the same standards as required for the initial confinement. This requirement again demonstrates that Kansas does not intend an individual committed pursuant to the Act to remain confined any longer than he suffers from a mental abnormality rendering him unable to control his dangerousness.

Hendricks next contends that the State's use of procedural safeguards traditionally found in criminal trials makes the proceedings here criminal rather than civil. . . . The numerous procedural and evidentiary protections afforded here demonstrate that the Kansas Legislature has taken great care to confine only a narrow class of particularly dangerous individuals, and then only after meeting the strictest procedural standards. That Kansas chose to afford such procedural protections does not transform a civil commitment proceeding into a criminal prosecution.

Finally, Hendricks argues that the Act is necessarily punitive because it fails to offer any legitimate "treatment." Without such treatment, Hendricks asserts, confinement under the Act amounts to little more than disguised punishment. Hendricks' argument assumes that treatment for his condition is available, but that the State has failed (or refused) to provide it. The Kansas Supreme Court, however, apparently rejected this assumption. . . .

Absent a treatable mental illness, the Kansas court concluded, Hendricks could not be detained against his will.

Accepting the Kansas court's apparent determination that treatment is not possible for this category of individuals does not obligate us to adopt its legal conclusions. We have already observed that, under the appropriate circumstances and when accompanied by proper procedures, incapacitation may be a legitimate end of the civil law. Accordingly, the Kansas court's determination that the Act's "overriding concern" was the continued "segregation of sexually violent offenders" is consistent with our conclusion that the Act establishes civil proceedings, especially when that concern is coupled with the State's ancillary goal of providing treatment to those offenders, if such is possible. While we have upheld state civil commitment statutes that aim both to incapacitate and to treat, we have never held that the Constitution prevents a State from civilly detaining those for whom no treatment is available, but who nevertheless pose a danger to others. A State could hardly be seen as furthering a "punitive" purpose by involuntarily confining persons afflicted with an untreatable, highly contagious disease. *Accord Compagnie Francaise de Navigation a Vapeur v. Louisiana Bd. of Health*, 186 U.S. 380 (1902) (permitting involuntary quarantine of persons suffering from communicable diseases). Similarly, it would be of little value to require treatment as a precondition for civil confinement of the dangerously insane when no acceptable treatment existed. To conclude otherwise would obligate a State to release certain confined individuals who were both mentally ill and dangerous simply because they could not be successfully treated for their afflictions. . . .

Alternatively, the Kansas Supreme Court's opinion can be read to conclude that Hendricks' condition is treatable, but that treatment was not the State's "overriding concern," and that no treatment was being provided (at least at the time Hendricks was committed). ("It is clear that the primary objective of the Act is to continue incarceration and not to provide treatment.") Even if we accept this determination that the provision of treatment was not the Kansas Legislature's "overriding" or "primary" purpose in passing the Act, this does not rule out the possibility that an ancillary purpose of the Act was to provide treatment, and it does not require us to conclude that the Act is punitive. Indeed, critical language in the Act itself demonstrates that the Secretary of Social and Rehabilitation Services, under whose custody sexually violent predators are committed, has an obligation to provide treatment to individuals like Hendricks. . . .

Where the State has "disavowed any punitive intent"; limited confinement to a small segment of particularly dangerous individuals; provided strict procedural safeguards; directed that confined persons be segregated from the general prison population and afforded the same status as others who have been civilly committed; recommended treatment if such is possible; and permitted immediate release upon a showing that the individual is no longer dangerous or mentally impaired, we cannot say that it acted with punitive intent. We therefore hold that the Act does not establish criminal proceedings and that involuntary confinement pursuant to the Act is not punitive. Our conclusion that the Act is nonpunitive thus removes an essential prerequisite for both Hendricks' double jeopardy and ex post facto claims.

1

The Double Jeopardy Clause provides: "[N]or shall any person be subject for the same offence to be twice put in jeopardy of life or limb." Although generally understood to preclude a second prosecution for the same offense, the Court has also interpreted this prohibition to prevent the State from "punishing twice, or attempting a second time to punish criminally, for the same offense." *Witte v. United States*, 515 U.S. 389, 396 (1995) (emphasis and internal quotation marks omitted). Hendricks argues that, as applied to him, the Act violates double jeopardy principles because his confinement under the Act, imposed after a conviction and a term of incarceration, amounted to both a second prosecution and a second punishment for the same offense. . . .

Because we have determined that the Kansas Act is civil in nature, initiation of its commitment proceedings does not constitute a second prosecution. *Cf. Jones v. United States*, 463 U.S. 354 (1983) (permitting involuntary civil commitment after verdict of not guilty by reason of insanity). Moreover, as commitment under the Act is not tantamount to "punishment," Hendricks' involuntary detention does not violate the Double Jeopardy Clause, even though that confinement may follow a prison term. . . . If an individual otherwise meets the requirements for involuntary civil commitment, the State is under no obligation to release that individual simply because the detention would follow a period of incarceration. . . .

2

Hendricks' ex post facto claim is similarly flawed. The Ex Post Facto Clause, which "'forbids the application of any new punitive measure to a crime already consummated,'" has been interpreted to pertain exclusively to penal statutes. As we have previously determined, the Act does not impose punishment; thus, its application does not raise ex post facto concerns. Moreover, the Act clearly does not have retroactive effect. Rather, the Act permits involuntary confinement based upon a determination that the person currently both suffers from a "mental abnormality" or "personality disorder" and is likely to pose a future danger to the public. To the extent that past behavior is taken into account, it is used, as noted above, solely for evidentiary purposes. Because the Act does not criminalize conduct legal before its enactment, nor deprive Hendricks of any defense that was available to him at the time of his crimes, the Act does not violate the Ex Post Facto Clause.

III

We hold that the Kansas Sexually Violent Predator Act comports with due process requirements and neither runs afoul of double jeopardy principles nor constitutes an exercise in impermissible ex post facto lawmaking. Accordingly, the judgment of the Kansas Supreme Court is reversed.

[Ginsburg's dissent, joined by three other Justices, argued that the scheme should be unconstitutional because no treatment was provided for earlier while Hendricks was in prison.]

Notes

1. Five years after *Hendricks*, the Supreme Court held that the Kansas Sexually Violent Predator Act did not require the state to prove an offender's complete lack of control over his dangerous behavior, but that the federal constitution does not allow civil commitment under the Act without some kind of lack-of-control determination. *See Kansas v. Crane*, 534 U.S. 407 (2002).

2. For a debate about the wisdom of the Kansas statute, compare Stephen R. McAllister, *Some Reflections on the Constitutionality of Sex Offender Commitment Laws*, 50 U. KAN. L. REV. 1011 (2002) (defending the statute on grounds that, without such provisions, "the States' clear incentive would be to enact lengthy and harsh prison sentences for recidivist sex offenders and let them sit in prison for a long time, many for the rest of their lives") with David J. Gottlieb, *Preventive Detention of Sex Offenders*, 50 U. KAN. L. REV. 1031 (2002) (attacking statute on grounds that "our historical traditions and constitutional protections of individual autonomy and liberty insist that the criminal process be the central means of social control of dangerous behavior, with civil commitment standing as a limited exception available for those individuals for whom the criminal process is unlikely to be effective").

3. What comprises the proper definition of "punishment" is a significant issue. It is significant because many scholars view punishment as the essential element distinguishing civil law from criminal law. For discussion of the difficulty of distinguishing the two, *see Symposium*, 1 J. CONTEMP. LEGAL ISSUES (1996); Stephen J. Schulhofer, *Two Systems of Social Protection: Comments on the Civil-Criminal Distinction, with Particular Reference to Sexually Violent Predator Laws*, 7 J. CONTEMP. LEGAL ISSUES 69 (1996).

4. Assuming that the commitment statutes existed in Kansas at the time of Hendricks' arrest, Kansas could clearly have committed him before the criminal trial. This essentially is pretrial detention available through civil commitment. How does civil commitment compare to the pretrial detention scheme reviewed in the *Salerno* case?

5. Consider the following by John Kip Cornwell, *Protection and Treatment: The Permissible Civil Detention of Sexual Predators*, 53 WASH. & LEE L. REV. 1293 (1996):

> It is not "perverse" to subject individuals to civil detention based on a mental abnormality potentially leading to future sexual misconduct when they were previously determined to be sufficiently responsible to deserve criminal punishment for similar activity. Just as the conceptualization of mental illness may differ in clinical and legal contexts, so too does its definition vary from one legal purpose to another. For example, a mental disease or defect insufficient for trial incompetency may well be adequate for the insanity defense. By the same token, exoneration from criminal guilt may legitimately required

deficits in cognitive and volitional capacities beyond what is necessary to vindicate the regulatory interests of civil commitment.

While increasingly common, psychiatric commitment is not the only means of addressing the problem of sexual predation. Constitutional and financial concerns led Iowa, for example, to repeal the sexual predator commitment law, enacted in 1995, before it went into effect. The legislature simultaneously replaced the statute with enhanced sentencing provisions for "sexually predatory offenses." Under the new measures, repeat offenders face escalating mandatory sanctions, ranging from a doubling of the maximum possible sentence to life in prison. In 1995, Georgia and Arkansas also augmented penalties for sex offenders, though not in as dramatic a fashion as Iowa, while Colorado has increased the presumptive sentencing range for various sex offenses.

Additionally, a number of states are considering "chemical castration" as a condition of parole. California has, in fact, recently enacted a law permitting judges to order chemical castration for paroled persons convicted of certain sex offenses against children under the age of thirteen and requiring such judicial action upon conviction for a second similar offense. Alternatively, under a bill currently pending in Alabama, the court could sentence a male to chemical castration and a female to sterilization upon a second conviction for certain sex crimes involving children under the age of sixteen. Pending legislation in Hawaii goes one step further, *mandating* chemical or physical castration for certain persons convicted of sexual assault. While the future of these legislative proposals is unclear, the constitutionality of a court's authority to order castration or sterilization is open to serious question.

Notwithstanding these extreme proposals, those who doubt the sincerity of states' interest in psychiatrically treating sexual predators generally prefer augmenting criminal punishment to civil detention. However, the fact that states enjoy such latitude in defining appropriate punishment introduces the possibility that fear of recidivism, as opposed to moral blameworthiness, will determine the sentence. Where mentally impaired individuals are concerned, these predictions of dangerousness perhaps are better left to the civil law and the detention it prescribes.

Sexual predation is a particularly noxious and fearsome public problem. Though citizens may, under Megan's Laws, receive notice that a released sex offenders about to move in next door, they cannot stop the offender's arrival into the neighborhood. Only mandatory life sentences for all crimes of sexual violence or indefinite civil commitment can keep predators off the streets. [T]he latter option [has been] adopted by an increasing number of states over the last few years.

[C]urrent sexual predator statutes are constitutional in virtually all respects. Although states cannot warehouse sexual predators in the back wards of psychiatric hospitals without violating substantive due process, government officials need not demonstrate an individual's inability to reason in order to justify psychiatric detention. Neither must states prove that the therapeutic intervention provided is more likely than not to cure an individual's pathology. Clinicians must instead achieve an acceptable level of treatment success over a period of years. In determining "acceptability," courts should take account of prior treatment success or lack thereof.

Clearly, psychiatrists play an important role in this process. By the same token, differences in the application of mental illness in the clinical and legal contexts limit the extent to which one conceptual framework can and should borrow from the other. While the medical community is a useful adjunct, only the legislatures are invested with both *parens patriae* and police powers, which operate jointly to define the scope of permissible psychiatric commitment. Subject to the foregoing conditions, there is an "exceedingly persuasive justification" for the inclusion of sexual predators within this definition.

6. In light of the fact that states could adopt harsh mandatory minimum sentencing schemes for sex offenders and other dangerous criminals, do preventive detention statutes at least have the advantage of transparency—that is, openness about their goals? *See* Paul H. Robinson, *Punishing Dangerousness: Cloaking Preventive Detention as Criminal Justice*, 114 Harv. L. Rev. 1429 (2001) (advancing this argument).

7. Civil commitment of dangerous "mentally disordered" convicted criminals is not limited to sexual offenders. *See* John Kip Cornwell, *Confining Mentally Disordered "Super Criminals": A Realignment of Rights in the Nineties*, 33 Houston L. Rev. 651 (1996).

2. Sex Offender Registration and Community Notification: "Megan's Law"

One way of preventing sexual assault is by warning the surrounding community about the presence of sex offenders. Consider the constitutionality of this approach in light of the following case:

Smith v. Doe

538 U.S. 84 (2003)

Justice KENNEDY delivered the opinion of the Court.

The Alaska Sex Offender Registration Act requires convicted sex offenders to register with law enforcement authorities, and much of the information is made public. We must decide whether the registration requirement is a retroactive punishment prohibited by the *Ex Post Facto* Clause.

I

A

The State of Alaska enacted the Alaska Sex Offender Registration Act (Act) on May 12, 1994. 1994 Alaska Sess. Laws ch. 41. Like its counterparts in other States, the Act is termed a "Megan's Law." Megan Kanka was a 7-year-old New Jersey girl who was sexually assaulted and murdered in 1994 by a neighbor who, unknown to the victim's family, had prior convictions for sex offenses against children. The crime gave impetus to laws for mandatory registration of sex offenders and corresponding community notification. In 1994, Congress passed the Jacob Wetterling Crimes Against Children and Sexually Violent Offender Registration Act, title 17, 108 Stat. 2038, as amended, 42 U.S.C. § 14071, which conditions certain federal law enforcement funding on the States' adoption of sex offender registration laws and sets minimum standards for state programs. By 1996, every State, the District of Columbia, and the Federal Government had enacted some variation of Megan's Law.

The Alaska law, which is our concern in this case, contains two components: a registration requirement and a notification system. Both are retroactive. 1994 Alaska Sess. Laws ch. 41, § 12(a). The Act requires any "sex offender or child kidnapper who is physically present in the state" to register, either with the Department of Corrections (if the individual is incarcerated) or with the local law enforcement authorities (if the individual is at liberty). Alaska Stat. §§ 12.63.010(a), (b) (2000). Prompt registration is mandated. If still in prison, a covered sex offender must register within 30 days before release; otherwise he must do so within a working day of his conviction or of entering the State. § 12.63.010(a). The sex offender must provide his name, aliases, identifying features, address, place of employment, date of birth, conviction information, driver's license number, information about vehicles to which he has access, and postconviction treatment history. § 12.63.010(b)(1). He must permit the authorities to photograph and fingerprint him. § 12.63.010(b)(2).

If the offender was convicted of a single, nonaggravated sex crime, he must provide annual verification of the submitted information for 15 years. §§ 12.63.010(d) (1), 12.63.020(a)(2). If he was convicted of an aggravated sex offense or of two or more sex offenses, he must register for life and verify the information quarterly. §§ 12.63.010(d)(2), 12.63.020(a)(1). The offender must notify his local police department if he moves. § 12.63.010(c). A sex offender who knowingly fails to comply with the Act is subject to criminal prosecution. §§ 11.56.835, 11.56.840.

The information is forwarded to the Alaska Department of Public Safety, which maintains a central registry of sex offenders. § 18.65.087(a). Some of the data, such as fingerprints, driver's license number, anticipated change of address, and whether the offender has had medical treatment afterwards, are kept confidential. §§ 12.63.010(b), 18.65.087(b). The following information is made available to the public:

> the sex offender's or child kidnapper's name, aliases, address, photograph, physical description, description [,] license [and] identification numbers of

motor vehicles, place of employment, date of birth, crime for which convicted, date of conviction, place and court of conviction, length and conditions of sentence, and a statement as to whether the offender or kidnapper is in compliance with [the update] requirements . . . or cannot be located." § 18.65.087(b).

The Act does not specify the means by which the registry information must be made public. Alaska has chosen to make most of the nonconfidential information available on the Internet.

B

Respondents John Doe I and John Doe II were convicted of sexual abuse of a minor, an aggravated sex offense. John Doe I pleaded *nolo contendere* after a court determination that he had sexually abused his daughter for two years, when she was between the ages of 9 and 11; John Doe II entered a *nolo contendere* plea to sexual abuse of a 14-year-old child. Both were released from prison in 1990 and completed rehabilitative programs for sex offenders. Although convicted before the passage of the Act, respondents are covered by it. After the initial registration, they are required to submit quarterly verifications and notify the authorities of any changes. Both respondents, along with respondent Jane Doe, wife of John Doe I, brought an action under Rev. Stat. § 1979, 42 U.S.C. § 1983, seeking to declare the Act void as to them under the *Ex Post Facto* Clause of Article I, § 10, cl. 1, of the Constitution and the Due Process Clause of § 1 of the Fourteenth Amendment. The United States District Court for the District of Alaska granted summary judgment for petitioners. In agreement with the District Court, the Court of Appeals for the Ninth Circuit determined the state legislature had intended the Act to be a nonpunitive, civil regulatory scheme; but, in disagreement with the District Court, it held the effects of the Act were punitive despite the legislature's intent. In consequence, it held the Act violates the *Ex Post Facto* Clause. *Doe I v. Otte,* 259 F.3d 979 (C.A.9 2001). We granted certiorari. 534 U.S. 1126.

II

This is the first time we have considered a claim that a sex offender registration and notification law constitutes retroactive punishment forbidden by the *Ex Post Facto* Clause. The framework for our inquiry, however, is well established. We must "ascertain whether the legislature meant the statute to establish 'civil' proceedings." *Kansas v. Hendricks,* 521 U.S. 346, 361 (1997). If the intention of the legislature was to impose punishment, that ends the inquiry. If, however, the intention was to enact a regulatory scheme that is civil and nonpunitive, we must further examine whether the statutory scheme is "'so punitive either in purpose or effect as to negate [the State's] intention' to deem it 'civil.'" *Ibid.* (quoting *United States v. Ward,* 448 U.S. 242, 248–249, (1980)). Because we "ordinarily defer to the legislature's stated intent," *Hendricks, supra,* at 361, "'only the clearest proof' will suffice to override legislative intent and transform what has been denominated a civil remedy into a criminal penalty," *Hudson v. United States,* 522 U.S. 93, 100 (1997) (quoting *Ward, supra,* at 249).

A

Whether a statutory scheme is civil or criminal "is first of all a question of statutory construction." *Hendricks, supra*, at 361 (internal quotation marks omitted); see also *Hudson, supra*, at 99. We consider the statute's text and its structure to determine the legislative objective. *Flemming v. Nestor*, 363 U.S. 603, 617 (1960). A conclusion that the legislature intended to punish would satisfy an *ex post facto* challenge without further inquiry into its effects, so considerable deference must be accorded to the intent as the legislature has stated it.

The courts "must first ask whether the legislature, in establishing the penalizing mechanism, indicated either expressly or impliedly a preference for one label or the other." *Hudson, supra*, at 99, (internal quotation marks omitted). Here, the Alaska Legislature expressed the objective of the law in the statutory text itself. The legislature found that "sex offenders pose a high risk of reoffending," and identified "protecting the public from sex offenders" as the "primary governmental interest" of the law. 1994 Alaska Sess. Laws ch. 41, § 1. The legislature further determined that "release of certain information about sex offenders to public agencies and the general public will assist in protecting the public safety." *Ibid*. As we observed in *Hendricks*, where we examined an *ex post facto* challenge to a postincarceration confinement of sex offenders, an imposition of restrictive measures on sex offenders adjudged to be dangerous is "a legitimate nonpunitive governmental objective and has been historically so regarded." 521 U.S., at 363. In this case, as in *Hendricks*, "[n]othing on the face of the statute suggests that the legislature sought to create anything other than a civil . . . scheme designed to protect the public from harm." *Id.*, at 361.

Respondents seek to cast doubt upon the nonpunitive nature of the law's declared objective by pointing out that the Alaska Constitution lists the need for protecting the public as one of the purposes of criminal administration. Brief for Respondents 23 (citing Alaska Const., Art. I, § 12). As the Court stated in *Flemming v. Nestor*, rejecting an *ex post facto* challenge to a law terminating benefits to deported aliens, where a legislative restriction "is an incident of the State's power to protect the health and safety of its citizens," it will be considered "as evidencing an intent to exercise that regulatory power, and not a purpose to add to the punishment." 363 U.S., at 616, (citing *Hawker v. New York*, 170 U.S. 189 (1898)). The Court repeated this principle in *89 Firearms*, upholding a statute requiring forfeiture of unlicensed firearms against a double jeopardy challenge. The Court observed that, in enacting the provision, Congress "'was concerned with the widespread traffic in firearms and with their general availability to those whose possession thereof was contrary to the public interest.'" 465 U.S., at 364 (quoting *Huddleston v. United States*, 415 U.S. 814, 824 (1974)). This goal was "plainly more remedial than punitive." 465 U.S., at 364. These precedents instruct us that even if the objective of the Act is consistent with the purposes of the Alaska criminal justice system, the State's pursuit of it in a regulatory scheme does not make the objective punitive. . . .

The procedural mechanisms to implement the Act do not alter our conclusion. After the Act's adoption Alaska amended its Rules of Criminal Procedure concerning the acceptance of pleas and the entering of criminal judgments. The rule on pleas now requires the court to "infor[m] the defendant in writing of the requirements of [the Act] and, if it can be determined by the court, the period of registration required." ALASKA RULE CRIM. PROC. 11(c)(4) (2002). . . .

The policy to alert convicted offenders to the civil consequences of their criminal conduct does not render the consequences themselves punitive. When a State sets up a regulatory scheme, it is logical to provide those persons subject to it with clear and unambiguous notice of the requirements and the penalties for noncompliance. The Act requires registration either before the offender's release from confinement or within a day of his conviction (if the offender is not imprisoned). Timely and adequate notice serves to apprize individuals of their responsibilities and to ensure compliance with the regulatory scheme. Notice is important, for the scheme is enforced by criminal penalties. *See* §§ 11.56.835, 11.56.840. Although other methods of notification may be available, it is effective to make it part of the plea colloquy or the judgment of conviction. Invoking the criminal process in aid of a statutory regime does not render the statutory scheme itself punitive.

Our conclusion is strengthened by the fact that, aside from the duty to register, the statute itself mandates no procedures. Instead, it vests the authority to promulgate implementing regulations with the Alaska Department of Public Safety, §§ 12.63.020(b), 18.65.087(d)—an agency charged with enforcement of both criminal *and* civil regulatory laws. *See, e.g.,* § 17.30.100 (enforcement of drug laws); § 18.70.010 (fire protection); § 28.05.011 (motor vehicles and road safety); § 44.41.020 (protection of life and property). The Act itself does not require the procedures adopted to contain any safeguards associated with the criminal process. That leads us to infer that the legislature envisioned the Act's implementation to be civil and administrative. By contemplating "distinctly civil procedures," the legislature "indicate[d] clearly that it intended a civil, not a criminal sanction." *Ursery,* 518 U.S., at 289, (internal quotation marks omitted; alteration in original).

We conclude, as did the District Court and the Court of Appeals, that the intent of the Alaska Legislature was to create a civil, nonpunitive regime.

B

In analyzing the effects of the Act we refer to the seven factors noted in *Kennedy v. Mendoza-Martinez*, 372 U.S. 144, 168–169), as a useful framework. The factors most relevant to our analysis are whether, in its necessary operation, the regulatory scheme: has been regarded in our history and traditions as a punishment; imposes an affirmative disability or restraint; promotes the traditional aims of punishment; has a rational connection to a nonpunitive purpose; or is excessive with respect to this purpose.

A historical survey can be useful because a State that decides to punish an individual is likely to select a means deemed punitive in our tradition, so that the public will recognize it as such. The Court of Appeals observed that the sex offender registration and notification statutes "are of fairly recent origin," 259 F.3d, at 989, which suggests that the statute was not meant as a punitive measure, or, at least, that it did not involve a traditional means of punishing. Respondents argue, however, that the Act—and, in particular, its notification provisions—resemble shaming punishments of the colonial period.

Some colonial punishments indeed were meant to inflict public disgrace. Humiliated offenders were required "to stand in public with signs cataloguing their offenses." Hirsch, *From Pillory to Penitentiary: The Rise of Criminal Incarceration in Early Massachusetts*, 80 MICH. L. REV. 1179, 1226 (1982); *see also* L. FRIEDMAN, CRIME AND PUNISHMENT IN AMERICAN HISTORY 38 (1993). At times the labeling would be permanent: A murderer might be branded with an "M," and a thief with a "T." R. SEMMES, CRIME AND PUNISHMENT IN EARLY MARYLAND 35 (1938); *see also* Massaro, *Shame, Culture, and American Criminal Law*, 89 MICH. L. REV. 1880, 1913 (1991). The aim was to make these offenders suffer "permanent stigmas, which in effect cast the person out of the community." *Ibid.; see also* Friedman, *supra*, at 40; Hirsch, *supra*, at 1228. The most serious offenders were banished, after which they could neither return to their original community nor, reputation tarnished, be admitted easily into a new one. T. BLOMBERG & K. LUCKEN, AMERICAN PENOLOGY: A HISTORY OF CONTROL 30–31 (2000). Respondents contend that Alaska's compulsory registration and notification resemble these historical punishments, for they publicize the crime, associate it with his name, and, with the most serious offenders, do so for life.

Any initial resemblance to early punishments is, however, misleading. Punishments such as whipping, pillory, and branding inflicted physical pain and staged a direct confrontation between the offender and the public. Even punishments that lacked the corporal component, such as public shaming, humiliation, and banishment, involved more than the dissemination of information. They either held the person up before his fellow citizens for face-to-face shaming or expelled him from the community. *See* Earle, *supra*, at 20, 35–36, 51–52; Massaro, *supra*, at 1912–1924; Semmes, *supra*, at 39–40; Blomberg & Lucken, *supra*, at 30–31. By contrast, the stigma of Alaska's Megan's Law results not from public display for ridicule and shaming but from the dissemination of accurate information about a criminal record, most of which is already public. Our system does not treat dissemination of truthful information in furtherance of a legitimate governmental objective as punishment. On the contrary, our criminal law tradition insists on public indictment, public trial, and public imposition of sentence. Transparency is essential to maintaining public respect for the criminal justice system, ensuring its integrity, and protecting the rights of the accused. The publicity may cause adverse consequences for the convicted defendant, running from mild personal embarrassment to social ostracism. In contrast to the colonial shaming punishments, however, the State does not make the publicity and the resulting stigma an integral part of the objective of the regulatory scheme.

The fact that Alaska posts the information on the Internet does not alter our conclusion. It must be acknowledged that notice of a criminal conviction subjects the offender to public shame, the humiliation increasing in proportion to the extent of the publicity. And the geographic reach of the Internet is greater than anything which could have been designed in colonial times. These facts do not render Internet notification punitive. The purpose and the principal effect of notification are to inform the public for its own safety, not to humiliate the offender. Widespread public access is necessary for the efficacy of the scheme, and the attendant humiliation is but a collateral consequence of a valid regulation.

The State's Web site does not provide the public with means to shame the offender by, say, posting comments underneath his record. An individual seeking the information must take the initial step of going to the Department of Public Safety's Web site, proceed to the sex offender registry, and then look up the desired information. The process is more analogous to a visit to an official archive of criminal records than it is to a scheme forcing an offender to appear in public with some visible badge of past criminality. The Internet makes the document search more efficient, cost effective, and convenient for Alaska's citizenry.

We next consider whether the Act subjects respondents to an "affirmative disability or restraint." *Mendoza-Martinez,* 372 U.S., at 168. Here, we inquire how the effects of the Act are felt by those subject to it. If the disability or restraint is minor and indirect, its effects are unlikely to be punitive.

The Act imposes no physical restraint, and so does not resemble the punishment of imprisonment, which is the paradigmatic affirmative disability or restraint. *Hudson,* 522 U.S., at 104. The Act's obligations are less harsh than the sanctions of occupational debarment, which we have held to be nonpunitive. See *ibid.* (forbidding further participation in the banking industry); *De Veau v. Braisted,* 363 U.S. 144 (1960) (forbidding work as a union official), *Hawker v. New York,* 170 U.S. 189 (1898) (revocation of a medical license). The Act does not restrain activities sex offenders may pursue but leaves them free to change jobs or residences. . . .

Although the public availability of the information may have a lasting and painful impact on the convicted sex offender, these consequences flow not from the Act's registration and dissemination provisions, but from the fact of conviction, already a matter of public record. The State makes the facts underlying the offenses and the resulting convictions accessible so members of the public can take the precautions they deem necessary before dealing with the registrant. . . .

The State concedes that the statute might deter future crimes. Respondents seize on this proposition to argue that the law is punitive, because deterrence is one purpose of punishment. Brief for Respondents 37. This proves too much. Any number of governmental programs might deter crime without imposing punishment. "To hold that the mere presence of a deterrent purpose renders such sanctions 'criminal' . . . would severely undermine the Government's ability to engage in effective regulation." *Hudson, supra,* at 105. . . .

The duration of the reporting requirements is not excessive. Empirical research on child molesters, for instance, has shown that, "[c]ontrary to conventional wisdom, most reoffenses do not occur within the first several years after release," but may occur "as late as 20 years following release." U.S. Dept. of Justice, National Institute of Justice, R. Prentky, R. Knight, & A. Lee, Child Sexual Molestation: Research Issues 14 (1997).

The Court of Appeals' reliance on the wide dissemination of the information is also unavailing. The Ninth Circuit highlighted that the information was available "world-wide" and "[b]roadcas[t]" in an indiscriminate manner. 259 F.3d, at 992. As we have explained, however, the notification system is a passive one: An individual must seek access to the information. The Web site warns that the use of displayed information "to commit a criminal act against another person is subject to criminal prosecution." http:// www.dps.state.ak.us/nSorcr/asp/ (as visited Jan. 17, 2003) (available in the Clerk of Court's case file). Given the general mobility of our population, for Alaska to make its registry system available and easily accessible throughout the State was not so excessive a regulatory requirement as to become a punishment. *See* D. Schram & C. Milloy, Community Notification: A Study of Offender Characteristics and Recidivism 13 (1995) (38% of recidivist sex offenses in the State of Washington took place in jurisdictions other than where the previous offense was committed). . . .

Our examination of the Act's effects leads to the determination that respondents cannot show, much less by the clearest proof, that the effects of the law negate Alaska's intention to establish a civil regulatory scheme. The Act is nonpunitive, and its retroactive application does not violate the *Ex Post Facto* Clause.

Notes

1. A section of the Violent Crime Control and Law Enforcement Act of 1994, known as the Jacob Wetterling Crimes Against Children and Sexually Violent Offender Registration Act, requires states to implement registration programs or face a 10 percent cut in federal funds available under the Omnibus Crime Control Act of 1968. This provides a significant impetus for states to require registration of sex offenders.

2. The Supreme Court has held that sex offenders are not entitled to a hearing to determine whether they are currently dangerous before they are included in a publicly disseminated sex offender registry. *Connecticut Dept. of Public Safety v. Doe*, 123 S. Ct 1160 (2003).

3. Does disclosing the addresses of registered sex offenders create a risk of harassment and abuse? *See* Jennifer Bjorhus, *Sexual Predator Flees Home after Fliers Go Up*, The Oregonian, Sept. 20, 1997, at 8. (Man flees his apartment after police tell neighbors he is a sexual predator).

4. The Alaska Sex Offender Registry is available at: http://www.dps.state.ak.us /nSorcr/asp. As noted in *Smith*, it does not include sex offenders' addresses. Some states have gone further. For example, the Utah sex offender registry, found at http://corrections.utah.gov/asp-bin/sexoffendersearchform.asp, lists sex offenders' addresses. Search the web and determine whether your state has an online sex offender registry program. If it does, how does it compare to Alaska's and Utah's? If your state's registry discloses specific addresses, does it violate a defendant's right

of privacy? *Cf. Fredenburg v. City of Fremont,* 14 Cal.Rptr.3d 437 (Cal. App. 2004) (upholding City's "pin map" website because it did not disclose specific addresses and thus did violate privacy interests); *A.A. v. New Jersey,* 341 F.3d 206 (2003) (any interest by sex offender in non-disclosure of address is outweighed by state interest in notifying the public).

5. For discussion of the wisdom of Megan's Laws, *see* Debate, *Megan's Law and the Protection of the Child in the On-Line Age,* 35 Am. Crim. L. Rev. 1319 (1998).

6. Should Megan's Laws apply to juvenile sex offenders? *See* Comment, *Coming of Age in America: The Misapplication of Sex-Offender Registration and Community Notification Laws to Juveniles,* 91 Cal. L. Rev. 163 (2003) (arguing against requiring juvenile offenders to be disclosed).

7. Apart from the requirements of Megan's Law, landlords and other landowners may have a duty to warn prospective tenants of potential dangerous individuals on the premises. *See* Shelley Saxer, *"Am I My Brother's Keeper?": Requiring Landowner Disclosure of the Presence of Sex Offenders and Other Criminal Activity,* 80 Neb. L. Rev. 522 (2001).

F. Victim-Offender Confrontation

Would it be helpful for crime victims to be able (at their election) to meet face-to-face with their victimizers?

Restorativejustice.org reports on the history and outline of these programs:

The first Victim-Offender Reconciliation Program (referred to here as VOM) began as an experiment in Kitchener, Ontario in the early 1970s (Peachey, 1989 at 14-16) when a youth probation officer convinced a judge that two youths convicted of vandalism should meet the victims of their crimes. After the meetings, the judge ordered the two youths to pay restitution to those victims as a condition of probation. Thus, VORP began as a probation-based/post-conviction sentencing alternative inspired by a probation officer's belief that victim-offender meetings could be helpful to both parties.

Implementation

The Kitchener experiment evolved into an organized victim-offender reconciliation program funded by church donations and government grants with the support of various community groups. Following several other Canadian initiatives, the first United States program was launched in Elkhart, Indiana in 1978. From there it has spread throughout the United States and Europe. It has been estimated that 400 VOM programs exist in the U.S. alone, and similar numbers in Europe. While VOM was not initially viewed as a reform of the criminal justice system, those involved in it soon realized that it raised those possibilities and began using the term restorative justice to describe its individualized and relational elements.

Description

In essence, VOMs involve a meeting between the victim and offender facilitated by a trained mediator. With the assistance of the mediator, the victim and offender begin to resolve the conflict and to construct their own approach to achieving justice in the face of their particular crime. Both are given the opportunity to express their feelings and perceptions of the offence (which often dispels misconceptions they may have had of one another before entering mediation). The meetings conclude with an attempt to reach agreement on steps the offender will take to repair the harm suffered by the victim and in other ways to "make things right".

Participation by the victim is voluntary. The offender's participation is usually characterized as voluntary as well, although it should be recognized that offenders may "volunteer" in order to avoid more onerous outcomes that would otherwise be imposed. Unlike binding arbitration, no specific outcome is imposed by the mediator. Instead, the mediator's role is to facilitate interaction between the victim and offender in which each assumes a proactive role in achieving an outcome that is perceived as fair by both. VOMs involve active involvement by the victim and the offender, giving them the opportunity to mutually rectify the harm done to the victim in a process that promotes dialogue between them.

Mediation, then, is a peace-making or conflict-resolution process that deals with violations of criminal laws by addressing the underlying conflict of and resulting injuries to the victim and offender. It emphasizes their right to participate in attempting to achieve justice rather than deferring the matter entirely to state criminal processes.

Elements

A basic case management process in North America and in Europe typically involves four phases: case referral and intake, preparation for mediation, the mediation itself and any follow up necessary (e.g., enforcement of restitution agreement). Often, a case is referred to VOM after a conviction or formal admission of guilt in court; but, some cases are diverted prior to such a disposition in an attempt to avoid prosecution.

The mediator then contacts the victim and offender to make sure that both are appropriate for mediation. In particular, the mediator seeks assurances that both are psychologically capable of making the mediation a constructive experience, that the victim will not be further harmed by the meeting with the offender, and that both understand that participation is voluntary.

The parties then meet to identify the injustice, rectify the harm (to make things right or restore equity), and to establish payment/monitoring schedules. Both parties present their version of the events leading up to and the circumstances surrounding the crime. The victim has a chance to speak about the personal dimensions of victimization and loss, while the offender has a chance to express remorse and to explain circumstances surrounding his/her behaviour. Then the parties agree on the particular nature and extent of the harm caused by the crime in order to identify the acts necessary to repair the injury to the victim. The terms of the agreed reparation (e.g., restitution, in-kind services, etc.) are reduced to writing, along with payment and monitoring schedules.

Evaluation

Studies have concluded that these programs have high client satisfaction rates, victim participation rates, restitution completion rates, and result in reduced fear among victims and reduced criminal behavior by offenders.

Mark S. Umbreit, Ph.D., *Survivors of Homicide Victims Confront Offenders*

THE CRIME VICTIMS REPORT, v. 1, no. 1 (1997)

A doctor in California whose sister was killed by a drunk driver decides to meet face to face with the woman who was responsible for her sister's death. This unusual meeting occurs in prison after many months of preparation of both parties by a highly trained person who specializes in victim offender mediation. She claims that the experience of directly confronting the source of pain in her life, expressing how special a person her sister was, and letting the offender know how deeply he hurt her was helpful. Following this mediation session, she felt more able to let go of her anger and move on with her life. On the offender's part, for the first time, he began to understand the full impact of his behavior on the lives of others.

A school teacher in Illinois asks to meet with the woman in prison who was responsible for her mother's death. The offender was convicted of negligent homicide as a result of drunk driving. Following 11 months of preparation with all involved, including negotiating access to the prison, a mediator with specialized training in advanced victim sensitive mediation brings the parties together in the prison. During this three hour meeting, the school teacher was able to get answers to many lingering questions, to express her pain directly to the responsible person, and to learn more about who the offender was and what was happening in her life. The offender took full responsibility for her actions, expressed remorse and provided important new information to the school teacher. Both left the meeting feeling better able to move on with their lives.

These are only two examples of a small but growing number of victims and survivors of severe drunk driving offenses who, in their own journey of grieving, have found a direct confrontation with the very person who hurt them (with the assistance of a highly trained mediator) to be an important step in their healing.

While not usually a replacement for some form of incarceration, the process of victim offender mediation appears to be effective in some, but clearly not all, cases of such senseless violence. These face to face meetings, in the presence of a trained mediator, are becoming one more option that is available to interested victims in a growing number of communities. A mediated dialogue between a victim and offender is meant to complement, not replace, many other important services and support groups available to crime victims. Choice rather than coercion is the key principle, along with providing a safe setting, extensive preparation over many months, and a highly competent and sensitive mediator with advanced training in this area.

Bringing victims of violent crime together with their offender and a mediator is only done in a relatively small number of cases involving violent crimes.

Violence Victims Convey Hurt and Get Answers

These victims have a rare opportunity to let criminals know how a crime affects them. Many want to tell the perpetrator such things as, "What you did not only hurt me, it brutalized my children and my husband," or "I'm a real person, not just some object or target."

Mediation Addresses Needs System Usually Ignores: Pre-Occupation with Offenders Often Leaves Victims Feeling Twice Victimized

At a time when there seems to be a renewed enthusiasm for a "get tough" approach to crime, why in the world would many thousands [of] victims of property crimes and a much smaller, but growing, number of victims of violence choose to confront their offender and talk with them? Perhaps it's because these victims receive so little help from the criminal justice system and even less support in their personal struggle to regain a sense of power and control in their lives. Perhaps it's because the system is so pre-occupied with the criminal and so confident it knows best what the victim wants, without any of their input, that many, if not most, victims feel twice victimized; first by the offender and then by the criminal justice system itself. Unfortunately, just as the offender treats the victim as an object, so does the criminal justice system. To the extent that the victim is a piece of evidence, they are likely to receive attention. To the extent that the victim has emotional and informational needs, there is likely to be little patience, time, or resources offered by the justice system.

Many Victims Prefer Restorative Rather Than Retributive Justice

Many victims of crime appear to be less interested in the harsh and costly retribution that politicians frequently speak of. A growing body of research is finding that many victims prefer a simpler, more understandable and humane system, a system that focuses on a restorative, rather than retributive, sense of justice which can more effectively address the emotional and material wounds left in the wake of a serious crime.

While certainly not meant for serial killers and other psychotic criminals, allowing such people as the doctor in California and the school teacher in Illinois to confront the person responsible for their loved ones death in a safe and restorative setting merits far more attention from our nation's criminal justice system.

Note

Another type of victim-defendant confrontation is the requirement of attendance at a victim impact panel (VIP) as a condition of sentencing. Most commonly, the VIP is required of drunk drivers. A victim impact panel consists of several victims of drunk drivers who present a program designed to reach the conscience of the offender in an effort to prevent them from drinking and driving again.

Chapter 11

Remedies and Appellate Court Review for Victims' Rights Violations

Introduction

This chapter investigates superior and inferior remedies for victims' rights violations.

First, the superior remedy of voiding procedures is explored. Voiding is the most effective remedy for victims' rights violations because it returns victims to a position in which they can exercise their rights in the criminal case involving their victimization. Also examined are the two significant limits on the voiding remedy—double jeopardy and express limits in victims' rights provisions themselves. The second section of the chapter is devoted to appellate court review. The introduction to appellate court review materials appears at the beginning of that section.

Second, inferior remedies are examined. These are labeled inferior because these remedies fail to leave victims in a position to exercise their rights. Inferior remedies include ethical discipline of judges, prosecutors, and defense attorneys, monetary recovery for rights violations, injunctive and declaratory relief, and administrative review of rights violations.

A. The Problem of Enforcing Victims' Rights

Noncompliance with victims' rights is commonplace. One study suggests that weak victim's rights laws and the absence of enforcement remedies make it easier for racial bias to enter into the application of victims' rights laws.

Comparison of White and Non-White Crime Victim Responses Regarding Victims' Rights
National Victim Center (June 5, 1997)

. . .

Reported Differences in Receipt of Victim's Rights

While more white and non-white victims in strong protection states were notified of the defendant's release on bail, compared with victims in weak protection states, non-white victims in both groups of states were less likely to receive such notice.

Regarding the bail hearing, there were noticeable differences between white and non-white respondents in the strong protection states, where victims were more likely to be given rights, while in the weak protection states, with fewer victims overall being given rights, the difference in responses of white and non-white victims were not statistically significant. Non-white victims in both groups of states were less likely to be notified of the sentencing hearing than were white victims. Without such notice, victims would be unable to exercise their right to be heard at sentencing. It is interesting to note that there was no measurable difference between white and non-white victims who received notice of the trial, where victims are often essentially functioning as witnesses.

In many other areas, the reported differences between white and non-white respondents did not rise to a level of statistical significance, but may nonetheless be instructive. Those included:

> notice of the possibility of a plea bargain (strong protection states, 63.4% white vs. 42.5% non-white; weak protection states, 55.7% white vs. 44.4% non-white);
>
> notice of postponements/continuances (strong protection states, 87.2% white vs. 78.1% non-white; weak protection states, 73.4% white vs. 68.5% non-white); and
>
> opportunity to make impact statement at parole (strong protection states, 79.7% white vs. 40.6% non-white).

As noted previously, nearly all victims were notified of the trial, and there was no measurable difference in the responses of white vs. non-white crime victims. (Strong protection states, 97.2% white vs. 97.5% non-white; weak protection states 90.5% white vs. 92.2% non-white).

Reported Differences in Satisfaction

More non-white victims reported being dissatisfied with certain aspects of their treatment by the criminal justice system. This was especially true in the states with weak protection of crime victims' rights.

The differences in dissatisfaction were most pronounced with regard to the victims' right to be heard. The majority of non-white victims reported being dissatisfied with their ability to be heard regarding plea bargains or the dropping of the case, and to have a say in the sentencing of the offender.

Importance of Victims' Rights

Crime victims were asked to rate the importance of various victims' rights, either as very important, somewhat important, not too important or not at all important. There was very little difference between the percentages of white and non-white respondents who rated various victims' rights as being "very important."

The following percentages of total non-white respondents rated the following victims' rights as "very important":

notice of arrest (98.3%);

notice of earliest possible release date (92.3%);

opportunity to discuss case with prosecutor (90.4%);

notice of defendant's release on bail (89.9%);

opportunity to be heard re: defendant's release on bail (88.1%);

opportunity to make victim impact statement at parole hearing (86.8%);

opportunity to make victim impact statement at sentencing (86.0%);

opportunity to be heard re. plea bargain (83.7%); and

opportunity to be present during release proceedings (82.5%).

Conclusion

The crime victim survey found that crime victims' rights were important to non-white crime victims as well as white victims. The study found that generally, as with white crime victims, non-white victims were more likely to be provided their rights in the states with strong statutory and state constitutional protection of victims' rights. However, the study also found that in many instances non-white victims were less likely to be provided those rights, in states with strong as well as those with weak protection of victims' rights. The study also found that non-white victims were less satisfied with aspects of their treatment by the criminal justice system

---

B. The Superior Remedy of Voiding Procedures

The voiding remedy is a superior remedy because, upon voiding, the victim is able to exercise their right in the re-hearing. The imposition of a plea, sentence, or parole board decision entered in violation of victims' rights are done in an unlawful manner, and therefor may be invalid. The next cases involve the remedy of voiding. Voiding an entire proceeding is typically accompanied by rejection of all evidence gathered in that proceeding. A more limited remedy than voiding the proceeding is voiding the result. Voiding the result, without voiding the original proceeding, may be available to enforce victims' rights in some circumstances. Voiding the result is done after a motion and hearing on reconsideration. This reconsideration of the result is possible in the context of some victims' rights violations because victims have not been granted the right to cross-examine witnesses. Because victims do not lose any right to cross-examination, courts can reconsider decisions without throwing out all the evidence gathered at prior hearings and still be in compliance with victims' right to notice and to be heard. Where reconsideration is available, the main threat to efficiency—a complete redoing of the entire procedure—is unrealized. Of course, a second hearing to accommodate the victims' right is needed. At a reconsideration hearing, victims can present their direct evidence or information through themselves or their witnesses, and the prior ruling or order will be affirmed or voided. The full parties would be present and have the opportunity to participate as well. Courts would reconsider the result in light of victims' information.

1. Voiding Plea Bargains

If a victim is deprived of his right to be heard before the court accepts a plea bargain, can the victim set aside the plea the remedy this violation? Consider the following case.

State v. Casey

82 P.3d 1106 (Utah 2003)

DURRANT, Justice.

The central issue presented in this appeal is whether the district court deprived M.R., a victim of sexual abuse, of his constitutional and statutory right to be heard at defendant's change of plea hearing. At that hearing, defendant pleaded guilty to lewdness involving a child, a class A misdemeanor. He had previously been charged with aggravated sexual abuse of a child, a first degree felony, and had pleaded not guilty. The reduction in the charge was the result of a plea bargain negotiated between defendant and the State. Prior to the change of plea hearing, M.R.'s mother had advised the prosecutor of M.R.'s and her own desire to make a statement to the court. M.R. and his mother both attended this hearing and, during a recess, M.R.'s mother reiterated to the prosecutor that she and M.R. wished to be heard. The prosecutor did not, however, advise the court of this request. In addition, neither M.R. nor his mother petitioned the court directly for an opportunity to speak. Unaware of M.R.'s request to be heard, the court accepted the defendant's guilty plea to the reduced charge and set the matter for sentencing.

Following this change of plea hearing, M.R.'s mother, acting on behalf of M.R., obtained legal assistance and filed two motions to set aside the plea bargain. In response, the State and defendant filed separate motions to strike M.R.'s pleadings. At the sentencing hearing, the district court heard from M.R. and his mother regarding the appropriateness of the plea bargain, and permitted argument from M.R.'s counsel. Thereafter, the court "informally reopen[ed] the plea for the purpose of [accepting M.R.'s and his mother's] testimony." The court then accepted the testimony that it had just heard. Having accepted M.R.'s and his mother's testimony, the court "reaffirm[ed] defendant's] plea at the class A level." The court then denied both of M.R.'s pending motions and sentenced defendant to eight months in jail on the class A misdemeanor charge. Based on these facts, we conclude that M.R. was initially denied his right to be heard at the change of plea hearing in violation of the Utah Constitution and related statutes, but that the court thereafter remedied this violation by reopening the change of plea hearing and receiving testimony from M.R. and his mother, and permitting argument from M.R.'s counsel. We therefore affirm.

BACKGROUND

On November 3, 1999, the Tooele County Attorney's Office charged defendant with aggravated sexual abuse of a child, a first degree felony, in violation of section 76-5-404.1(3) of the Utah Code. Following a preliminary hearing in which both the victim, M.R., and his mother testified, the district court bound defendant over for trial.

A few weeks later the prosecutor handling defendant's case sent M.R.'s mother a letter explaining that defendant had requested a plea bargain. After receiving this letter, M.R.'s mother, according to her affidavit, met with the prosecutor and obtained an assurance that the first degree felony charge would not be reduced due to the strong evidence of guilt compiled against defendant.

Nevertheless, the prosecutor subsequently offered to reduce the first degree felony charge to lewdness involving a child, a class A misdemeanor, in return for a guilty plea. *See* UTAH CODE ANN. § 76-9-702.5 (1999). M.R.'s mother, upon learning of the State's extension of this offer and defendant's acceptance, contacted the prosecutor and expressed a desire to tell the district court how her family, including M.R., felt about the proposed plea. The prosecutor advised her to attend the change of plea hearing scheduled for October 24, 2000.

I. CHANGE OF PLEA HEARING

M.R. and his mother appeared at this change of plea hearing as directed. At a recess during this proceeding, M.R.'s mother approached the prosecutor, objected to the reduced charge, and reiterated M.R.'s, and her own, desire to make a statement. She later testified that she believed the prosecutor was going to inform the district court of her request. Acknowledging that he did not know that M.R. had a right to be heard either directly or through his legal guardian, the prosecutor maintained the following: (1) he did not intentionally deprive M.R. of his right to be heard at defendant's change of plea hearing, (2) he did not tell M.R.'s mother she and M.R. had no right to testify at the plea hearing, and (3) he told M.R.'s mother that she would eventually have an opportunity to address the court in the pre-sentence report and at the sentencing hearing.

Notwithstanding his conversations with M.R.'s mother, the prosecutor did not inform the district court that M.R. and his mother had requested to be heard at the change of plea hearing. M.R. and his mother also failed to bring the issue to the court's attention. The court therefore proceeded with defendant's change of plea hearing unaware of M.R.'s request. Noting the "dramatic" reduction in the charge, the court refused to be limited to the four-month sentence recommended in the stipulated plea agreement. The State and defendant responded to the court's concern by agreeing to delete the stipulated sentence provision. The court then accepted defendant's guilty plea to the class A misdemeanor charge and set the matter for sentencing.

II. SENTENCING HEARING

Subsequently, M.R.'s mother, acting on behalf of M.R., obtained legal assistance and filed two motions with the district court: a motion for a misplea and a motion to reject the plea bargain. In response, the prosecutor and defendant filed separate motions to strike M.R.'s pleadings, claiming that M.R. lacked standing to set aside the plea because he was not a party to the criminal proceeding.

Without ruling on whether M.R. had standing to challenge defendant's guilty plea, the district court held defendant's sentencing hearing on November 27, 2000. At the start of this hearing, M.R.'s counsel moved the court to set aside the accepted plea. The court initially questioned whether M.R. had the right to be heard but then allowed M.R. and his mother to testify regarding the propriety of the plea bargain. Despite its reservations, the court also permitted extensive argument from M.R.'s counsel.

M.R. and his mother testified that the court should have rejected the plea bargain. Specifically, M.R. declared, "I don't think it's right that [defendant] gets that less of a plea agreement because [of] what he's done[.] He's done it to me . . . and . . . he's hurt my whole family." M.R.'s mother testified that "the [c]ourt should reject the plea bargain [because] a misdemeanor sentence d[id] not truly reflect the seriousness of the offenses committed by [defendant] the same way that a felony conviction would." She further averred that she believed the prosecutor was going to inform the court of M.R.'s, and her own, desire to make a statement at defendant's change of plea hearing. She also stated that she did not know she could interrupt the change of plea hearing and address the court directly.

After M.R. and his mother had testified, the district court turned its attention to M.R.'s attorney and inquired whether M.R. was entitled to use counsel to assert his right to be heard. In response to the court's query, M.R.'s counsel argued that the Victims' Rights Amendment of the Utah Constitution placed M.R. on equal footing with defendant and envisioned that M.R. could employ an attorney in exercising his legal rights. M.R.'s counsel then argued that (1) M.R. had the right to be heard before the court's acceptance of defendant's plea, (2) M.R.'s right to be heard had been violated, and (3) the court should grant a misplea and hear from M.R. before accepting any subsequent plea between the State and defendant. The prosecutor and defendant both objected, asserting that M.R. lacked standing to challenge the accepted plea and that the prosecutor had discretion to determine how defendant's case was negotiated.

Following these objections, the district court noted that it had not been previously informed by M.R. or his representative, i.e., his mother, that M.R. desired to be heard at the change of plea hearing. Despite this lack of notification, the court decided to "informally" reopen the plea hearing in order to accept the testimony that it had just heard from M.R. and his mother. Having accepted this testimony, the court "reaffirm[ed defendant's] plea at the class A level." The court then denied both of M.R.'s pending motions, sentenced defendant to eight months in jail on the class A misdemeanor charge, and fined him.

III. CLAIMS ON APPEAL

M.R. immediately appealed to the Utah Court of Appeals, which certified M.R.'s appeal to us, concluding that a "petition for writ of certiorari would likely be . . . granted [because] resolution of the case ha[d] potentially broad-reaching impact." *See* Utah R. App. P. 43(c)(1).

On appeal, M.R., by and through his legal guardian, contends that (1) he had the right to seek appellate review of the district court's adverse rulings on his two motions, (2) he had the right to be heard through counsel with respect to legal issues related to the constitutional and statutory rights afforded him as a victim, (3) he had a constitutional and statutory right to be heard regarding the appropriateness of the plea bargain, (4) he properly invoked his right to be heard at defendant's change of plea hearing by submitting a request to the prosecutor, and (5) the court, through the negligence of the prosecutor, denied him his right to be heard by accepting the plea bargain without hearing from him.

We conclude that M.R. was entitled to appellate review of the district court's rulings related to his right to be heard. We further hold that M.R., as the victim of a crime, had both a constitutional and statutory right to be heard at defendant's change of plea hearing and that he properly invoked this right by informing the prosecutor that he desired to be heard. Finally, we conclude that the court remedied its initial violation of M.R.'s right to be heard at defendant's change of plea hearing by reopening the plea hearing and receiving testimony from M.R. and his mother, and by permitting argument from M.R.'s counsel.

ANALYSIS I. THE VICTIMS' RIGHTS AMENDMENT, THE VICTIMS' RIGHTS ACT, AND THE RIGHTS OF CRIME VICTIMS ACT

In 1987, the Utah Legislature enacted the Victims' Rights Act. *See* Utah Code Ann. §§ 77-37-1 to -5 (1999). This statute included, among other things, a bill of rights for victims, *id.* § 77-37-3, and declared that these rights must be "protected in a manner no less vigorous than protections afforded criminal defendants." *Id.* § 77-37-1. The Utah Legislature then passed the Victims' Rights Amendment, which was ratified by Utah citizens on November 8, 1994, and took effect on January 1, 1995. Utah Const. art. I, § 28 compiler's notes. This constitutional amendment bestowed specific rights upon crime victims and gave the Utah Legislature the power to "enforce and define [its terms] by statute." Acting pursuant to this authority, the Utah Legislature subsequently enacted the Rights of Crime Victims Act. Utah Code Ann. §§ 77-38-1 to -14 (1999 & Supp. 2001). This act elaborated upon the rights afforded crime victims under the Victims' Rights Amendment and defined several terms included in the amendment. *Id.*

IV. M.R. HAD THE RIGHT TO APPEAL ADVERSE RULINGS RELATED TO HIS MOTION FOR A MISPLEA AND HIS MOTION TO REJECT THE PLEA BARGAIN

We first address whether M.R. had the right to appeal the district court's rulings regarding his right to be heard. The Victims' Rights Amendment does not address the question of M.R.'s right to appeal decisions impacting his right to be heard. The Rights of Crime Victims Act is on point, however, and we conclude that M.R. had the right to seek appellate review pursuant to the plain meaning of that statute. *See* Utah Code Ann. §77-38-11(2)(b)(c) (1999).

We resolve this issue under a plain meaning analysis for two reasons. First, subsection 77-38-11(2)(b) explicitly provides that "[a]dverse rulings on ... a motion or request brought by a victim of a crime or a representative of a victim of a crime may be appealed under the rules governing appellate actions, provided that no appeal shall constitute grounds for delaying any criminal ... proceeding." *Id.* §77-38-11(2)(b). Second, subsection 77-38-11(2)(c) of the Utah Code declares that "[a]n appellate court shall review all such properly presented issues, including issues that are capable of repetition but would otherwise evade review." *Id.* §77-38-11(2)(c). In short, these two provisions demonstrate (1) that crime victims possess the right to appeal rulings on motions related to their rights as a victim and (2) that an appellate court must review appeals of such a nature. Accordingly, M.R.'s appeal is properly before us.

V. M.R. POSSESSED A CONSTITUTIONAL AND STATUTORY RIGHT TO BE HEARD UPON REQUEST AT IMPORTANT CRIMINAL JUSTICE HEARINGS

A. DEFENDANT'S CHANGE OF PLEA HEARING CONSTITUTED AN IMPORTANT CRIMINAL JUSTICE HEARING UNDER BOTH THE UTAH CONSTITUTION AND THE UTAH CODE

We next address whether M.R. had the right to be heard at defendant's change of plea hearing. We conclude that he did, upon request, have such a right pursuant to the plain meaning of the Victims' Rights Amendment and subsections 77-38-4(1) and 77-38-2(5)(c) of the Rights of Crime Victims Act.

In pertinent part, the Victims' Rights Amendment states as follows:

(1) To preserve and protect victims' rights to justice and due process, *victims of crimes have [the right]:*

* * *

(b) *Upon request, to be ... heard at important criminal justice hearings related to the victim,* either in person or through a lawful representative, once a criminal information or indictment charging a crime has been publicly filed in court[.]

Utah Const. art. I, §28(1)(b) (emphasis added). Using comparable language, section 77-38-4 of the Rights of Crime Victims Act similarly declares that "[t]he victim of a crime shall have ... the right to be heard at ... important criminal ... justice hearings...." Utah Code Ann. §77-38-4(1) (1999).

Given that both the Utah Constitution and the Utah Code grant crime victims the right to be heard at "important criminal justice hearings," the question that arises is what constitutes an "important criminal justice hearing" under the Victims' Rights

Amendment and the Utah Code. Section 77-38-2 of the Rights of Crime Victims Act answers this question with respect to both the Utah Constitution and the Utah Code; it defines "important criminal justice hearings" involving the disposition of charges in this way:

> For the purposes of this chapter and the Utah Constitution[,][i]mportant criminal justice hearings . . . means the following proceedings in felony criminal cases . . . : any court proceeding involving the disposition of charges against a defendant [except for] unanticipated proceedings to take an admission or a plea of guilty as charged to all charges previously filed or any plea taken at an initial appearance.

UTAH CODE ANN. § 77-38-2(5)(c) (1999). Thus, the plain language of the statute defines "important criminal justice hearings" as any proceeding involving the disposition of felony charges against a defendant, with two notable exceptions: (1) a plea taken at an initial appearance and (2) a proceeding in which a defendant accepts responsibility for all of the charges previously filed. *Id.*

Here, the change of plea hearing conducted by the district court fell within the definition of an important criminal justice hearing because it disposed of a first degree felony charge filed against defendant in return for a guilty plea on a class A misdemeanor. Further, neither exception applied because the hearing was not an initial appearance and the defendant did not accept responsibility for the first degree felony charge previously filed. Accordingly, M.R.'s constitutional and statutory right to be heard upon request at important criminal justice hearings included the right to be heard upon request at defendant's change of plea hearing.

B. M.R. INVOKED HIS RIGHT TO BE HEARD AT DEFENDANT'S CHANGE OF PLEA HEARING BY INFORMING THE PROSECUTOR THAT HE WISHED TO SPEAK

While it is clear that the Utah Constitution and the Utah Code afforded M.R. the right to be heard upon request at defendant's change of plea hearing, *see* Part V(A) *supra*, neither the constitution nor the code mandates how M.R.'s request must be submitted. Relying on the Victims' Rights Act and the Rights of Crime Victims Act, M.R. argues that a request to be heard at a plea hearing suffices if it is submitted either to the district court or to the prosecutor. The State contends that the two statutes require a crime victim to petition the court directly. After examining the relevant constitutional and statutory authority, we are satisfied that a victim's right to be heard at a plea hearing is triggered where a request has been submitted to the prosecutor handling the case.

We begin our analysis with the Victims' Rights Amendment. This constitutional provision merely notes that the right to be heard is activated "upon request." UTAH CONST. art. I, § 28(b). Unlike the previous constitutional language we have analyzed, we find this language ambiguous and undefined. We thus "consider all other relevant factors." *In re Inquiry Concerning a Judge, the Honorable David S. Young,* 1999 UT 6, ¶ 15, 976 P.2d 581. In particular, we seek guidance from the statutes related to the Victims' Rights Amendment (i.e., the Victims' Rights Act and the Rights of Crime Victims Act). *Cf. In re Worthen*, 926 P.2d 853, 867 (Utah 1996).

The Victims' Rights Act states that "[v]ictims . . . have [the] right to be informed and assisted as to their role in the criminal justice process[, and *a]ll criminal justice agencies have the duty to provide this information and assistance.*" UTAH CODE ANN. § 77-37-3(1)(b) (Supp. 2001) (emphasis added). Additionally, the Victims' Rights Act declares that "[v]ictims . . . have a right to clear explanations regarding relevant legal proceedings[, and *a]ll criminal justice agencies have the duty to provide these explanations.*" *Id.* § 77-37-3(1)(c) (Supp. 2001) (emphasis added). Because prosecutors are a component of the criminal justice system and the Victims' Rights Act applies to "all criminal justice agencies," the aforementioned duties necessarily fall upon prosecutors. *Id.* § 77-37-3(1)(b)-(c). Hence, we conclude that prosecutors must "assist" victims in exercising their right to be heard at plea hearings and provide them with "clear explanations regarding [such] proceedings." *Id.*

We further conclude that a prosecutor's obligation to provide "assistance" to the victim should mean, at a minimum, that a victim may submit a request to be heard at a plea hearing to a prosecutor and expect that the request will be forwarded to the court. Likewise, a prosecutor's obligation to provide a "clear explanation" of events occurring at a plea hearing should mean that a victim can rely on a prosecutor's statement indicating he or she will convey a request to be heard to the district court. We therefore hold that a victim may deliver a request to be heard at a plea hearing to a prosecutor and that a prosecutor receiving such a request must convey it to the court.

This conclusion is supported by the text of the Rights of Crime Victims Act because that statute, while explicitly mandating direct requests in some instances, does not require direct requests to be heard at plea hearings. For example, a victim's request to be heard at an accused's initial appearance is predicated expressly upon delivering a "request to the judge hearing the matter." UTAH CODE ANN. § 77-38-4(1) (1999). This same section, however, conveys a broad right to be heard at various legal proceedings—including plea hearings—without mentioning how the request to be heard must be made. *Id.* Had the Utah Legislature intended to require victims to petition the district court directly in order to invoke their right to be heard at plea hearings, it could have inserted the phrase, "upon request to the judge," into that sentence as well. *Cf. State v. Chaney*, 1999 UT App. 309, ¶ 46, 989 P.2d 1091 (concluding that, due to the placement of the word "intentionally," the Utah Legislature intended to modify only one verb rather than the entire sentence). We conclude that by electing not to incorporate this phrase when referring to plea hearings the Legislature implicitly authorized other methods of delivering requests to be heard. Accordingly, the language of the Rights of Crime Victims Act contradicts the State's theory that requests to be heard at a plea hearing must be delivered directly to the district court.

In addition to having a duty to convey requests to be heard under the Victims' Rights Act and the Rights of Crime Victims Act, prosecutors also have a duty to convey requests to be heard as officers of the court. Prosecutors must convey such requests because they are obligated to alert the court when they know that the court lacks relevant information. *Cf. Clingman v. State,* 23 P.3d 27, 29 (Wyo. 2001). This duty, which is incumbent upon all attorneys, is magnified for prosecutors because, as our case law has repeatedly noted, prosecutors have unique responsibilities. *See, e.g., State v. Thomas,* 1999 UT 2, ¶ 24 n. 3, 974 P.2d 269. Specifically, a prosecutor is a minister of justice, *id.,* possessing "duties that rise above those of privately employed attorneys." *State v. Saunders,* 1999 UT 59, ¶ 31, 992 P.2d 951. The prosecutor "is the representative not of an ordinary party to a controversy, but of a sovereignty whose obligation to govern impartially is as compelling as its obligation to govern at all; and whose interest . . . in a criminal prosecution is not that it shall win . . . but that justice shall be done." *State v. Emmett,* 839 P.2d 781, 787 (Utah 1992).

In light of the fact that prosecutors must defend and uphold the State's interest in procuring justice, they have an obligation to ensure that the constitutional rights of crime victims are honored and protected. In fact, the Victims' Rights Act explicitly declares that the rights extended to crime victims "are to be honored and protected by law in a manner no less vigorous than protections afforded criminal defendants." Utah Code Ann. § 77-37-1 (1999). Accordingly, as an officer of the court, a prosecutor must convey a victim's request to be heard at a change of plea hearing.

It is undisputed by the parties to this appeal that M.R.'s mother, acting on behalf of M.R., informed the prosecutor that M.R. wished to be heard at defendant's change of plea hearing. It is also undisputed that the prosecutor did not convey this request to the district court. Consistent with our foregoing analysis, we conclude that the prosecutor failed to satisfy the obligations imposed upon him by the Victims' Rights Act, the Rights of Crime Victims Act, and his position as an officer of the court.

To begin with, as a representative of a criminal justice agency, the prosecutor violated M.R.'s rights under the Victims' Rights Act (1) by failing to "assist" him in exercising his right to be heard and (2) by failing to provide him with a "clear explanation" regarding the events transpiring at defendant's change of plea hearing. Utah Code Ann. § 77-37-3(1)(b)-(c) (1999). The prosecutor violated both of these statutory duties when he implied that he would convey M.R.'s request to be heard to the district court and then failed to do so.

Moreover, given that the prosecutor received M.R.'s request to be heard and subsequently made no effort to alert the district court, the prosecutor's conduct violated the Rights of Crime Victims Act. That statute, by requiring direct requests to the court at initial appearances but not requiring such direct requests at plea hearings, implicitly authorized requests to be heard at plea hearings to be delivered to prosecutors.

Lastly, the prosecutor breached his duty as an officer of the court because he failed to bring relevant information to the court's attention. *See Clingman,* 23 P.3d at 29. Fully aware of M.R.'s desire to speak at defendant's change of plea hearing, the prosecutor did not inform the court that M.R. had invoked his constitutional and statutory right to be heard. We therefore conclude that M.R. properly submitted his request to be heard at defendant's change of plea hearing to the prosecutor.

VI. THE DISTRICT COURT REMEDIED THE VIOLATION
OF M.R.'S RIGHT TO BE HEARD

Based on the prosecutor's failure to relay M.R.'s request to be heard, the district court initially deprived M.R. of his right to speak at the change of plea hearing. At defendant's sentencing hearing, however, the court learned of M.R.'s earlier desire to be heard. The court then permitted M.R. and his mother to take the stand and testify regarding the appropriateness of defendant's plea bargain. The court also permitted extensive argument by M.R.'s counsel. Restricted in no respect by the court, all three individuals claimed that the plea bargain should have been rejected. After hearing this testimony and argument, the court "informally" reopened defendant's change of plea hearing and accepted the testimony that it had just heard from M.R. and his mother. The court then reaffirmed defendant's plea at the Class A level.

By taking these steps, the district court remedied its initial denial of M.R.'s right to be heard. Our conclusion is based on the following rationale. First, we note that the plea was subject to review up until the time of sentencing. *See Ostler,* 2001 UT 68 at ¶ 10, 31 P.3d 528 (noting that "it makes no sense to deprive the district court of the power to review a plea before it enters a judgment of conviction and sentence."). Accordingly, in exercising its power to reopen the plea, the court permitted M.R. to be heard at a time when he could have persuaded the court to reject the proposed plea. Second, the record clearly demonstrates that the court reaffirmed the plea only after having accepted M.R.'s and his mother's testimony, and permitting argument by his counsel.

Thus, although M.R. was entitled to be heard at defendant's change of plea hearing, we conclude that he has enjoyed the fruits of the right he now claims he was denied. Accordingly, we hold that the district court, to its credit, cured the error initially committed at the change of plea hearing and honored M.R.'s right to be heard as soon as it discovered M.R. wished to be heard.

CONCLUSION

We conclude that M.R. (1) had the right to appeal the district court's rulings related to his right to be heard, (2) had the right to be heard upon request at defendant's change of plea hearing, and (3) properly invoked his right to be heard by informing the prosecutor he wished to speak. We further conclude that, although the prosecutor failed to convey M.R.'s request to the court and this failure initially deprived M.R. of his right to be heard at defendant's change of plea hearing, the court subsequently remedied the error. The court did so by reopening the plea hearing, accepting unrestricted testimony and argument, and reaffirming the plea. We therefore affirm the decision below.

WILKINS, Justice, concurring:

I concur in the result reached in the majority opinion. However, I would affirm the trial court's action only because the conflict between two constitutional principles gives us no other choice. At the time the motion was made, however, the trial court could have, and under the mandate of our constitution should have, granted M.R.'s motion for a misplea.

I fully agree with the analysis set forth in the majority opinion leading to the conclusions that M.R. was entitled to appellate review of the district court's adverse rulings, and that, as a victim of crime, he had both a constitutional and statutory right to be heard at defendant's change of plea hearing. I also agree fully that M.R., in informing the prosecutor of his desire to be heard, did everything necessary to properly invoke his right. However, I believe that when the trial court was finally informed of M.R.'s desire to be heard, it was clearly insufficient for the trial court to "informally" reopen the change of plea hearing and "consider" M.R.'s concerns before summarily reaffirming the "accepted" plea. Doing so merely compounded the error invited by the prosecution in failing to promptly inform the court of M.R.'s initial request to be heard at the change of plea hearing.

Notes

1. The concurring justice concludes that the trial court should have declared a misplea when the violation of victim's right was called to the court's attention. The majority concludes that the trial court's "informal" reopening of the plea was sufficient. Which position seems correct? Have you ever seen defendant's rights treated "informally"? In other areas, are "informal" remedies sufficient protection for constitutional rights?

2. The *Casey* case received prominent coverage in the local newspaper, with much of the coverage quite sympathetic to the victim's plight. As a result of the negative publicity in this case, the prosecutor in the trial court left his position. The publically-elected county attorney promised new efforts to protect victims' rights. And the trial judge in the matter became the first judge in Utah history to be defeated in a non-partisan retention election (although the defeat was primarily due to other issues). Can publicity (and the threat of publicity) serve as an effective means to enforce victims' rights?

3. Note that the court in *Casey* used initials "M.R." rather than the victim's name. Appellate court opinions that contain the full name of the victim, for example a child victim of sexual assault are permanently published and publically available. For the view that victims' names should not be used in appellate opinions *see* Joel M. Schumm, *No Names Please: The Virtual Victimization of Children, Crime Victims and Other Appellate Court Opinions* 42 Ga. L. Rev. 471 (2008); and, the previous chapter on Privacy.

4. In *Gueits v. Kirkpatrick*, 618 F. Supp.2d 193 (E.D.N.Y. 2009), the court redacted any identifying information regarding the victim, declining to use her name "out of respect for her dignity and privacy," both of which are protected under the CVRA.

2. Voiding Sentences

If a victim is deprived of her right to be heard before the court changes a restitution order, can the victim set aside the order to remedy this violation? Consider the following case.

Kenna v. U.S. Dist. C. for C. Dist. CA.

435 F.3d 1011 (9th Cir. 2006)

KOZINSKI, Circuit Judge.

We consider whether the Crime Victims' Rights Act, 18 U.S.C. § 3771, gives victims the right to allocute at sentencing.

Facts

Moshe and Zvi Leichner, father and son, swindled scores of victims out of almost $100 million. While purporting to make investments in foreign currency, they spent or concealed the funds entrusted to them. Each defendant pleaded guilty to two counts of wire fraud and one count of money laundering. More than sixty of the Leichners' victims submitted written victim impact statements. At Moshe's sentencing, several, including petitioner W. Patrick Kenna, spoke about the effects of the Leichners' crimes-retirement savings lost, businesses bankrupted and lives ruined. The district court sentenced Moshe to 240 months in prison.

Three months later, at Zvi's sentencing, the district court heard from the prosecutor and the defendant, as required by Federal Rule of Criminal Procedure 32(i)(4). But the court denied the victims the opportunity to speak. It explained:

> I listened to the victims the last time. I can say for the record I've rereviewed all the investor victim statements. I have listened at Mr. Leichner's father's sentencing to the victims and, quite frankly, I don't think there's anything that any victim could say that would have any impact whatsoever. I — what can you say when people have lost their life savings and what can you say when the individual who testified last time put his client's [sic] into this investment and millions and millions of dollars and ended up losing his business? There just isn't anything else that could possibly be said.

One victim protested that "[t]here are many things that are going on with the residual and second and third impacts in this case that have unfolded over the last 90 days since we were last in this courtroom." But the district judge told the victims that the prosecutor could bring those developments to his attention, and continued to refuse to let the victims speak. Zvi was sentenced to 135 months in prison.

Kenna filed a timely petition for writ of mandamus pursuant to the Crime Victims' Right Act (CVRA), 18 U.S.C. § 3771(d)(3). He seeks an order vacating Zvi's sentence, and commanding the district court to allow the victims to speak at the resentencing.

Analysis

The criminal justice system has long functioned on the assumption that crime victims should behave like good Victorian children — seen but not heard. The Crime Victims' Rights Act sought to change this by making victims independent participants in the criminal justice process. *See* Scott Campbell, Stephanie Roper, Wendy Preston, Louarna Gillis, and Nila Lynn Crime Victims' Rights Act, Pub. L. No. 108-405,

§§ 101–104, 118 Stat. 2260, 2261–65 (2004) (codified at 18 U.S.C. § 3771). The CVRA guarantees crime victims eight different rights, and unlike the prior crime victims' rights statute, allows both the government and the victims to enforce them. *See* 18 U.S.C. § 3771(a), (d)(1); *United States v. McVeigh,* 106 F.3d 325, 335 (10th Cir. 1997) (per curiam).

Kenna and the district court disagree over the scope of one of the rights guaranteed by the CVRA: "The right to be reasonably heard at any public proceeding in the district court involving release, plea, sentencing, or any parole proceeding." 18 U.S.C. § 3771(a)(4). Kenna contends that his right to be "reasonably heard" means that he is entitled to speak in open court at Zvi's sentencing, if that is how he chooses to express himself. The district court argues that the words "reasonably heard" vest the judge with discretion about how to receive the views of the victims, and that the judge is entitled to limit Kenna to written victim statements or his prior statements at Moshe's sentencing. No court of appeals has considered the scope of this CVRA right, and the two district courts that have closely considered it have reached opposite conclusions. *Compare United States v. Degenhardt,* 405 F.Supp.2d 1341, 1345–49 (D.Utah 2005) (CVRA grants victims a right to speak) *with United States v. Marcello,* 370 F.Supp.2d 745, 748 (N.D.Ill. 2005) (no it doesn't).

Kenna would have us interpret the phrase "reasonably heard" as guaranteeing his right to speak. For support, he points to the dictionary definition of "hear"— "to perceive (sound) by the ear." The American Heritage Dictionary of the English Language (4th ed.2000), available at http://www.bartleby.com/61/69/H0106900 .html. Kenna concedes that the district court may place reasonable constraints on the duration and content of victims' speech, such as avoiding undue delay, repetition or the use of profanity.[FN1] However, in Kenna's view, the district court may not prohibit victims from speaking in court altogether or limit them to making written statements. This is the interpretation adopted by the district court in *Degenhardt.*

> [FN1]. The CVRA itself contains one such nod to judicial economy. In crimes with multiple victims, the CVRA allows district courts to fashion "a reasonable procedure to give effect to [the act] that does not unduly complicate or prolong the proceedings." 18 U.S.C. § 3771(d)(2). Such a procedure may well be appropriate in a case like this one, where there are many victims.

But this isn't the only plausible interpretation of the phrase "reasonably heard." According to the district court, to be "heard" is commonly understood as meaning to bring one's position to the attention of the decisionmaker orally or in writing. *See, e.g., Fernandez v. Leonard,* 963 F.2d 459, 463 (1st Cir.1992) ("Where the parties have had a 'fair opportunity to present relevant facts and argument to the court,' a matter may be '"heard" on the papers' alone."(quoting *Aoude v. Mobil Oil Corp.,* 862 F.2d 890, 894 (1st Cir. 1988))). The district court urges us to follow *Marcello* and hold that the CVRA guarantees victims only a right to make their position known by whatever means the court reasonably determines. *See Marcello,* 370 F.Supp.2d at 748. Even though "heard" has been held to include submission on the papers in some contexts, it does not follow that the CVRA calls for an equally broad construction. It merely shows that the district court's interpretation of the term is also plausible.

The district court also argues that, had Congress meant to give victims a right to speak at sentencing hearings, it could easily have done so by using the word "speak" which clearly connotes only oral communications, not written ones. This is the term used in Federal Rule of Criminal Procedure 32(i)(4)(B), which gives the victims of certain types of crimes the right "to speak or submit any information about the sentence." The district court would have us infer from the fact that Congress used the more ambiguous term "heard" that it meant to give victims of crimes not covered by Rule 32 a more circumscribed right to present their views. However, the term "heard" does not appear in isolation in the CVRA. The full phrase we are construing is "[t]he right to be reasonably heard at any public proceeding in the district court involving . . . sentencing." Virtually all proceedings in district court are public in the sense that the papers and other materials may be viewed by anyone on request to the clerk's office. When Congress used the word "public" in this portion of the CVRA, however, it most likely meant to refer to proceedings in open court—much as the word is used in the common phrase "public hearing." So read, the right to be "heard" at a "public proceeding" becomes synonymous with "speak" and we can draw no negative inference from the congressional choice of one term over the other.

In the end, we find none of these textual arguments dispositive and conclude, as did *Degenhardt,* that both readings of the statute are plausible. The statute is therefore ambiguous as to what it means for crime victims to be heard. To resolve this ambiguity, we turn to the legislative history of the CVRA. *See Toibb v. Radloff,* 501 U.S. 157, 162 (1991) ("[A] court appropriately may refer to a statute's legislative history to resolve statutory ambiguity. . . ."). The Senate considered the CVRA in April 2004, and at that time the primary sponsors of the bill, Senators Jon Kyl and Dianne Feinstein, discussed this very issue:

> It is not the intent of the term "reasonably" in the phrase "to be reasonably heard" to provide any excuse for denying a victim the right to appear in person and directly address the court. Indeed, the very purpose of this section is to allow the victim to appear personally and directly address the court.

150 Cong. Rec. S4268 (daily ed. April 22, 2004) (statement of Sen. Kyl); *see also id.* (statement of Sen. Feinstein) ("That is my understanding as well."). Six months later, the CVRA was attached to a House bill, and Senator Kyl reiterated his understanding of the CVRA language.

> It is important that the "reasonably be heard" language not be an excuse for minimizing the victim's opportunity to be heard. Only if it is not practical for the victim to speak in person or if the victim wishes to be heard by the court in a different fashion should this provision mean anything other than an in-person right to be heard.

150 Cong. Rec. S10911 (daily ed. Oct. 9, 2004) (statement of Sen. Kyl).

Floor statements are not given the same weight as some other types of legislative history, such as committee reports, because they generally represent only the view of the speaker and not necessarily that of the entire body. However, floor statements by the sponsors of the legislation are given considerably more weight than floor statements by other members, *see NLRB v. St. Francis Hosp. of Lynwood,* 601 F.2d 404, 415 n. 12 (9th Cir. 1979), and they are given even more weight where, as here, other legislators did not offer any contrary views. Silence, the maxim goes, connotes assent, *see* Robert Bolt, *A Man for All Seasons* act 2, at 88 (1962), and so we can draw from the fact that no one registered disagreement with Senators Kyl and Feinstein on this point the reasonable inference that the views they expressed reflected a consensus, at least in the Senate.

We also note that the CVRA passed as a compromise measure after a lengthy effort to amend the Constitution to protect victims' rights. The proposed constitutional amendment used language almost identical to that ultimately enacted in the CVRA; it guaranteed victims the right "reasonably to be heard." S.J. Res. 1, 108th Cong. (2003). But the legislative history of the proposed amendment is more substantial than that of the CVRA. The Senate Report on the amendment notes that:

> The victim's right is to "be heard." The right to make an oral statement is conditioned on the victim's presence in the courtroom. . . . [V]ictims should always be given the power to determine the form of the statement. Simply because a decision making body, such as the court . . . has a prior statement of some sort on file does not mean that the victim should not again be offered the opportunity to make a further statement. . . . The Committee does not intend that the right to be heard be limited to "written" statements, because the victim may wish to communicate in other appropriate ways.

S.Rep. No. 108-191, at 38 (2003). The statements of the sponsors of the CVRA and the committee report for the proposed constitutional amendment disclose a clear congressional intent to give crime victims the right to speak at proceedings covered by the CVRA.

Our interpretation advances the purposes of the CVRA. The statute was enacted to make crime victims full participants in the criminal justice system. Prosecutors and defendants already have the right to speak at sentencing, *see* Fed.R.Crim.P. 32(i)(4)(A); our interpretation puts crime victims on the same footing. Our interpretation also serves to effectuate other statutory aims: (1) To ensure that the district court doesn't discount the impact of the crime on the victims; (2) to force the defendant to confront the human cost of his crime; and (3) to allow the victim "to regain a sense of dignity and respect rather than feeling powerless and ashamed." Jayne W. Barnard, *Allocution for Victims of Economic Crimes,* 77 Notre Dame L. Rev. 39, 41 (2001). Limiting victims to written impact statements, while allowing the prosecutor and the defendant the opportunity to address the court, would treat victims as secondary participants in the sentencing process. The CVRA clearly meant to make victims full participants.

Nor was Kenna's statutory right vindicated because he had the opportunity to speak at Moshe's sentencing three months earlier. The statute gives victims a "right to be reasonably heard at any public proceeding in the district court involving release, plea, sentencing, or any parole proceeding." 18 U.S.C. § 3771(a)(4). This language means that the district court must hear from the victims, if they choose to speak, at more than one criminal sentencing. The court can't deny the defendant allocution because it thinks "[t]here just isn't anything else that could possibly be said." Victims now have an indefeasible right to speak, similar to that of the defendant, and for good reason: The effects of a crime aren't fixed forever once the crime is committed- physical injuries sometimes worsen; victims' feelings change; secondary and tertiary effects such as broken families and lost jobs may not manifest themselves until much time has passed. The district court must consider the effects of the crime on the victims at the time it makes its decision with respect to punishment, not as they were at some point in the past. Moreover, the CVRA gives victims the right to confront every defendant who has wronged them; speaking at a co-defendant's sentencing does not vindicate the right of the victims to look *this* defendant in the eye and let him know the suffering his misconduct has caused.

* * *

As we explained above, the district court here committed an error of law by refusing to allow petitioner to allocute at Zvi's sentencing and we must therefore issue the writ. We turn now to the scope of the remedy. Kenna asks us to vacate Zvi's sentence, and order the district court to resentence him after allowing the victims to speak. The problem is that the CVRA gives district courts, not courts of appeals, the authority to decide a motion to reopen in the first instance. *See* 18 U.S.C. § 3771(d)(5). Moreover, defendant Zvi Leichner is not a party to this mandamus action, and reopening his sentence in a proceeding where he did not participate may well violate his right to due process. It would therefore be imprudent and perhaps unconstitutional for us to vacate Zvi's sentence without giving him an opportunity to respond.

We could delay further our consideration of the petition and order briefing from the defendant, but we think it more advisable to let the district court consider the motion to reopen in the first instance. In ruling on the motion, the district court must avoid upsetting constitutionally protected rights, but it must also be cognizant that the only way to give effect to Kenna's right to speak as guaranteed to him by the CVRA is to vacate the sentence and hold a new sentencing hearing. We note that if the district court chooses not to reopen the sentence, Kenna will have another opportunity to petition this court for mandamus pursuant to the CVRA. Likewise, defendant will be able to contest any change in his sentence through the normal avenue for appeal (assuming he has not waived such rights as part of the plea bargain).

Finally, we recognize that under 18 U.S.C. § 3771(d)(3), we were required to "take up and decide [this] application forthwith within 72 hours after the petition [had] been filed." *Id.* We acknowledge our regrettable failure to consider the petition within the time limits of the statute, and apologize to the petitioner for this inexcusable delay. It may serve as a small comfort for petitioner to know that, largely because of this case, we are in the process of promulgating procedures for expeditious handling of CVRA mandamus petitions to ensure that we comply with the statute's strict time limits in future cases. As victim participation in the criminal justice system becomes more common, we expect CVRA claims to become more frequent, and thus encourage district courts to modify their own procedures so as to give full effect to the CVRA.

Conclusion

We grant the petition for writ of mandamus and hold that the district court erred in refusing to allow Kenna and other victims to speak at Zvi Leichner's sentencing hearing. The district court shall deem timely a motion pursuant to 18 U.S.C. §3771(d)(5) filed by Kenna or any other of Zvi's victims within 14 days of the date of our opinion. If the district court grants the motion, it shall conduct a new sentencing hearing, according Kenna and the other victims the right to speak as described above.

Notes

1. The Federal District Court below voided the sentence and conducted a sentencing hearing in compliance with the circuit court opinion. The victim was allowed to address the court.

2. In *State v. Barrett v. Barrett*, 350 Or. 390 (2011), the Oregon Supreme Court vacated the sentence as illegal where the victim was not notified of the sentence and so was not able to appear at sentencing or make a victim impact statement.

Douglas E. Beloof, *The Third Wave of Victims' Rights: Standing, Remedy, and Review*
2005 B.Y.U. L. Rev. 255

. . . . [I]n refusing to void a plea bargain, the South Carolina Supreme Court in *Ex Parte Littlefield*, engaged in analytical contortions to hold that states victims' rights expire as a matter of law after the defendant is sentenced:

> Once a criminal case is resolved and the defendant is sentenced, the alleged victim loses his status under the Victims' Bill of Rights. The trial court cannot use the Victims' Bill of Rights to re-open a criminal proceeding. Further, even if the solicitor fails to honor the Victims' Bill of Rights during a criminal proceeding, this court cannot issue a writ of mandamus to re-open a criminal proceeding once it is resolved.[6]

Such a harsh opinion, imposing a judicial barrier to review and remedy well beyond double jeopardy or the plain language of the South Carolina Constitution, reveals the judicial commitment to keeping victims' rights illusory. In fact, the Carolina Constitution provides that "A victim's *exercise* of any right granted by this section shall

---

6. *Ex Parte Littlefield*, 540 S.E.2d 81 (S.C. 2000).

not be grounds for dismissing any criminal proceeding or setting aside any conviction or sentence." This constitutional language plainly does not limit voiding of pleas and sentences as a remedy for the *violation* of a victims' right. Plainly the provision means a victim cannot challenge a sentence imposed after the victim had an opportunity to exercise their rights. Faced with this reality, the court created its own road block to remedy through the artifice of eliminating victim status upon disposition. Of course, criminal defendants do not lose their ability to contest rights violations upon sentencing. The court posited no reason, much less a credible reason, in creating this a double standard for victims' rights. A victim should retain victim status— and standing—at least until the litigation concerning a rights violation is final on review. To rule otherwise creates an Alice-in-Wonderland process in which the rights violation itself results in the termination of victims' status as victims' with rights, thus eliminating any hope of redress.

.... Texas prohibit[s] "contesting the disposition of any charge." ... Texas victims cannot contest sentences taken in a lawful manner that complied with victims' rights. This language does not, however, prohibit victims from contesting a *violation* of their rights. In *Sistrunk v. State*, the victim appealed a violation of their right to speak at sentencing. The case should have been readily disposed of as the Texas constitution prohibits appeals for violations of victims' rights. Because appeal was barred for victims' rights violations, the proper review mechanism was writ. For example, the Connecticut supreme court properly dismissed a victim appeal because appeals are prohibited under the Connecticut constitution. But the Texas intermediate appellate court went out of its way to reach constitutional issues to deny the victim standing. The Texas constitution states that a victim cannot "challenge a disposition." In its rush to denying standing, the court failed to differentiate between lawful and unlawful disposition. The constitution does not prevent victims from contesting *a rights violation*. Indeed, the constitution expressly permits it, providing that "a ... victim has standing to enforce the rights enumerated in this section but does not have standing to participate as a party." Read together, a better interpretation of the standing language and the prohibition on challenging a disposition is that victims cannot contest a lawful disposition. Where victims have been granted their rights to speak at sentencing, the compliance renders the sentence lawful, at least relative to the victim. The constitutional proscription makes more sense under this interpretation. In Texas, victims should not be able to challenge conditions of sentence, but may challenge a rights violation and an unlawful disposition that has been rendered unlawful by the denial of victims' rights.

In addition to judicially inserting unlawful sentences into the term "disposition," the *Sistrunk* court also demonstrated its complete misunderstanding of the nature of crime victims' rights. As one of its rationales for refusing to void the sentence, the court opined "if noncompliance with victim impact statements does not provide a ground for the defendant to set aside his sentence, such noncompliance surely provides no ground for the victim to challenge the sentence."[7]

---

7. *State v. Sistrunk*, WL 1614879, at 4 (2004) (unpublished opinion).

The only kind explanation for this dramatically erroneous analysis is that the court was simply unaware that victims' right are personal to the victim, not the defendant.

3. Voiding Parole Decisions

If a victim is deprived of her right to be heard before the court orders parole, can the victim set aside the order to remedy this violation? Consider the following case.

State ex rel Hance v. Arizona Board of Pardons and Paroles

875 P.2d 824 (Ariz. 1993)

The State of Arizona, appearing through the Coconino County Attorney and acting on behalf of a crime victim brought this special action petition requesting that we vacate an Arizona Board of Pardon and Paroles order releasing prisoner Eric Mageary to home arrest. By prior order, we accepted jurisdiction, set aside the Board's order releasing Mageary to home arrest, and directed the Board to conduct a reexamination proceeding in accordance with the Arizona statutes implementing the Victims' Bill of Rights. Our order stated that an opinion would follow. This is the promised opinion.

The central issue is whether the victim of Mageary's crime is entitled to have a Board of Pardons and Paroles order set aside for failure to include her participation in the release proceedings despite the victim's failure to request notification of the proceedings. We hold today that, as a result of the state's failure to notify the victim of her rights under the Victims' Bill of Rights, the victim's failure to request notice is not dispositive and the Board's release order must be vacated.

The facts relevant to this special action begin with Mageary's rape of the victim and his subsequent conviction and sentencing in 1974 to 25 years to life in prison. From 1982, when Mageary first became eligible for parole, to 1989, the Arizona Board of Pardons and Paroles denied Mageary parole each time he became eligible. The Board granted Mageary parole in 1989 but revoked it within a year for a parole violation. The Board continued to deny Mageary parole each time he became eligible from 1989 to 1993.

On May 5, 1993 the Board held the parole hearing that is the subject of this special action. At that hearing, the Board again denied Mageary parole but did grant release to home arrest.

The victim did not receive prior notice of the May 5 hearing. The Board last attempted to contact the victim in June of 1984 when it sent notice of an upcoming parole hearing to her last known address. The letter was returned as undeliverable. Since 1984, neither the Board nor the County Attorney made any attempt to notify the victim of any parole hearings, including the 1993 hearing that resulted in the release order.

Shortly after the 1993 hearing, the Governor of Arizona wrote to the Board chairman requesting that the Board rescind its decision. The Governor based his request on a Board policy that permits a request for rescission based on, among other things, an allegation that the Board made its decision on incomplete information. The Governor asserted that new information—including a letter from the victim—was available and requested a Board hearing to determine if probable cause existed to rescind the Board's decision.

The Board did not hold a probable cause hearing. Instead the Board chairman responded that a "threshold review" of the Governor's request revealed no new information that justified a rescission hearing.

The Coconino County Attorney also requested rescission and a probable cause hearing. His letter included a letter from the victim and asserted that the victim would appear at a probable cause hearing. In addition, the County Attorney supplied a letter from Mageary's former prison counselor arguing against his release to home arrest. The County Attorney requested a hearing to determine if the information supplied probable cause to rescind the Board's ruling. Nothing in the record reveals whether the Board responded to this request.

Within hours of Mageary's scheduled release to home arrest, the Coconino County Attorney brought this petition for special action directly to this Court asking us to set aside the release order and to direct the Board to hold a reexamination hearing pursuant to both its rescission policy and the Arizona statutes implementing the Victims' Bill of Rights.

On July 7, we temporarily stayed the Board from releasing Mageary pending our resolution of the petition. After oral argument we accepted jurisdiction, vacated the Board's order releasing Mageary to home arrest and directed the Board to hold a reexamination hearing.

I.

Before reaching the merits, we considered whether we have subject matter jurisdiction to entertain this type of special action—one brought directly to this court seeking redress against a state agency.

Prior to a recent statutory amendment, we did not have jurisdiction over this type of special action. The Court of Appeals was created by statute. *Morrison v. Superior Court*, 461 P.2d 170, 171 (Ariz. App. 1969); Ariz. Const. art. 6 § 9. Accordingly, our jurisdiction is limited to that which our Legislature grants. *See Goodrich v. Industrial Comm'n*, 463 P.2d 550, 551–52 (Ariz. App. 1970). Before 1990, the Legislature limited our special action jurisdiction to Industrial Commission matters and to special actions in aid of our appellate jurisdiction. *See* former A.R.S. § 12-120.21(A)(2)-(3). This statute did not grant jurisdiction over a special action seeking extraordinary relief against a state agency or official because it is not in aid of our appellate jurisdiction. *See Goodrich*, 463 P.2d at 551–52.

In 1990, however, the Arizona Legislature expanded our special action jurisdiction. It amended section 12-120.21 by adding subsection (A)(4), which gives this court "[j]urisdiction to hear and determine petitions for special actions brought pursuant to the rules of procedure for special actions, *without regard to its appellate jurisdiction.*" A.R.S. § 12-120.21(A)(4) (emphasis added). Thus, we now have special action jurisdiction in cases to which our appellate jurisdiction does not extend.

Some doubt remains about whether the authors of the 1990 amendment intended to extend our jurisdiction to include a petition seeking redress against a state officer. *See generally* 1 ARIZONA APPELLATE HANDBOOK, § 7.3.2 (Jefferson L. Lankford & Paul G. Ulrich eds., 3d ed. 1992). An argument can be made that subsection (A)(4) was not intended to give us original jurisdiction in a special action against a state officer because that meaning renders redundant subsection (A)(2), which gives us original jurisdiction in special actions involving the Industrial Commission, a state agency. Although we asked the petitioner to brief the issue, it did not do so.

We resolve this issue by holding that subsection (A)(4) gives us jurisdiction over this special action. While we generally assume the Legislature intended a meaning other than one resulting in redundancy, *State v. Wise,* 671 P.2d 909, 911 (Ariz. App. 1983), the legislative intent here is clearly reflected by the broad grant of authority in subsection (A)(4). Had the Legislature intended to limit the expansion of our jurisdiction to exclude petitions against state officers, it would have done so without the sweeping language it chose. We give clear statutory language its usual meaning unless an impossible or absurd consequence results. *In re Marriage of Gray,* 695 P.2d 1127, 1129 (Ariz. App. 1985); *Matter of Pima County Juvenile Appeal No. 74802-2,* 790 P.2d 723, 731 (Ariz. App. 1990); *State v. Wagstaff,* 794 P.2d 118, 123 (Ariz. App. 1990). In this instance, the clear language of subsection (A)(4) grants us jurisdiction which is neither an impossible nor an absurd result. The Legislature retained subsection (A)(2) — regarding Industrial Commission special actions — because no change was needed to simply extend our jurisdiction, a change accomplished by (A)(4). Moreover, retaining subsection (A)(2) ensured that no one would infer that the amendment impaired our jurisdiction over Industrial Commission matters. We conclude that we have jurisdiction over this special action.

Having the authority to hear the petition, we had discretion whether to accept it. We accepted jurisdiction to construe previously uninterpreted provisions of the Victims' Bill of Rights, a matter of statewide significance, and because resolution of this case turns on questions of law, not facts. *See S.A. v. Superior Court,* 831 P.2d 1297, 1298 (Ariz. App. 1992) (accepting special action jurisdiction in case concerning Victims' Bill of Rights).

II.

We turn to the merits. The Coconino County Attorney made two alternative arguments in requesting that we set aside the Board's order releasing Mageary to home arrest. He argued first that the Board's own policy mandates a probable cause hearing upon an allegation that the Board made its decision without complete information. Therefore, the argument continues, the Board's chairman was not authorized to summarily refuse to hold a probable cause hearing after the Governor and the

County Attorney requested rescission. As a remedy, the County asked that we order the Board to hold a reexamination hearing.

Our decision today is prompted by neither the Governor's nor the County Attorney's requests for rescission. The Governor is not a party to this special action. The petitioner is the State of Arizona, through the Coconino County Attorney, asserting the rights of the crime victim. *See* A.R.S. § 13-4437(C) (Supp. 1992). The petitioner has established no basis on which it may advance the Governor's claim. The petitioner is not entitled to relief on a claim that the Board refused the Governor's request.

Nor does our decision depend on the County Attorney's request for a rescission hearing. Nothing in the record presented to us by petitioner establishes how or whether the Board responded to the County Attorney's request. Thus neither the Governor's nor the County Attorney's request for rescission provides a basis for relief.

III.

We turn our attention to the County Attorney's second argument that the failure to notify the victim of her constitutional rights under the Victims' Bill of Rights and, in particular, the failure to notify her of the right to appear at the release hearing, entitles her to have the Board's order set aside.

The Victims' Bill of Rights — embodied in the Arizona Constitution — and its implementing legislation give crime victims several affirmative rights, including the right "[t]o be present at and, upon request, to be informed of all criminal proceedings where the defendant has a right to be present," and the right "[t]o be heard at any proceeding involving a post-arrest release decision, a negotiated plea, and sentencing." Ariz. Const. art. 2 § 2.1(A)(3)-(4). The Victims' Bill of Rights also gives victims the right "[t]o be informed of victims' constitutional rights." *Id.* § 2.1(A)(12). The Legislature implemented the Victims' Bill of Rights through the Victims' Rights Implementation Act, A.R.S. sections 13-4401 to -4437 (Supp. 1992). That Act assigned the obligation of informing victims of their rights to different departments of the executive branch depending on the stage of the criminal proceeding. The Legislature, however, did not enact a provision specifically addressing how to inform victims of crimes of their rights when the crimes were committed prior to the effective date of the Victims' Bill of Rights.

The question is whether this victim was entitled to be notified of the release hearing despite her failure to request such notice. Perhaps the clearest explanation of why she was entitled to notice is also the answer to the Board's argument that it need not have notified her.

The Board asserts that it had no duty to notify the victim of this proceeding because the victim did not request notice. The Board is correct that A.R.S. section 13-4414 requires victims to request notice before the Board is obligated to notify them of post-conviction release hearings:

> *If the victim has made a request for post-conviction notice,* the board of pardons and paroles shall, at least fifteen days before the hearing, give to the victim

written notice of the hearing and of the victim's right to be present and be heard at the hearing.

A.R.S. § 13-4414(B) (Supp. 1992) (emphasis added). The Board is also correct that this victim never requested notice.

However, this victim was never informed of her right to request notice. The Victims' Bill of Rights specifically gives victims the right to be informed of their rights under that amendment: "a victim of a crime has a right . . . [t]o be informed of victims' constitutional rights." ARIZ. CONST. art. 2, § 2.1(A)-(A)(12). Those constitutional rights include the right "[t]o be present at and, upon request, to be informed of all criminal proceedings where the defendant has the right to be present" and "[t]o be heard at any proceeding involving a post-arrest release decision. . . ." *Id.* at § 2.1(A)(3)-(4). Thus, the victim had a constitutional right to be *informed* that she was entitled to request notice of, and to participate in, any post-conviction relief proceeding.

The state cannot now use the victim's failure to request notice as a defense against the victim's right to appear at the release proceeding because the state failed to *first* fulfill its constitutional obligation to inform her of that right. The constitutional mandate is clear: victims must be informed of their rights. Armed with this knowledge, victims may choose to exercise these rights. Conversely, an uninformed victim may not exercise her rights because she is unaware of them, or unaware that the right to notice of a release hearing requires that she first file a request for such a notice.

The Victims' Rights Implementation Act also makes clear that the victim's right to be informed imposes a corollary duty on the state to provide the information. This legislation creates specific obligations on state government to inform victims of their rights at various stages of criminal proceedings. *See* statutes cited in n. 13, *supra.* While the statutory provisions do not specifically address how the state is to inform victims of pre-Bill of Rights crimes, the overriding principle is clear: the linchpin of ARIZ. CONST. art. 2, § 2.1(A)(12) is the right of victims to be informed of their constitutional rights, and the state has an affirmative obligation to so inform them.

This victim was never informed of her constitutional right to request notice of and to participate in post-conviction release proceedings. It is this omission that violated her rights and rendered the release proceedings defective.

IV.

We are also unpersuaded by the Board's argument that its efforts to notify the victim of the release hearing were adequate. Even assuming that notice of this hearing would have satisfied the mandate of ARIZ. CONST. art. 2, § 2.1(A)(12) that victims be informed of their "rights" in general, the Board's efforts to provide notice in this case failed to satisfy the requirements of due process.

We realize that actual notice is not always possible, and we do not suggest that the Victims' Bill of Rights insists that victims actually receive notice in every case.

Nevertheless, the Arizona Constitution protects a victim's rights to "due process." ARIZ. CONST. art. 2, § 2.1(A). Due process in this context is not explained by the constitution or by the implementing legislation. However, due process notice requirements in general are well-established. Due process does not require actual receipt of notice:

> Notice is sufficient for due process purposes if it is "reasonably calculated, under all the circumstances, to apprise interested parties of the pendency of the action and afford them an opportunity to present their objections" or claims.

Matter of Gila River, 236, 830 P.2d 442, 448 (Ariz. App. 1992) (quoting *Mullane v. Central Hanover Bank & Trust Co.*, 339 U.S. 306, 318 (1950)). The *Gila River* court stated that "due process required notice by mail to all beneficiaries who could be located through reasonable efforts." *Id.*

The record lacks evidence that the Board made reasonable efforts to locate this victim. The Board admitted that it had made no effort to contact the victim since it sent a letter to her last known address in 1984, a decade after the conviction. A complete lack of effort is not "reasonable efforts" to locate the victim. We do not, however, attempt to define for all future cases the precise degree and kind of efforts required. Determining what are "reasonable efforts" requires a case by case analysis. In this case we are certain that the Board's total lack of effort to contact this victim was not sufficient.

We now address the argument that the Board emphasized at oral argument. It asserted that it satisfied its obligation to notify the victim by sending notice of the upcoming hearings to the County Attorney who, in turn, could have attempted to notify the victim. It was the County Attorney's fault, the Board argued, that this victim did not receive notice.

Notifying the County Attorney of the upcoming release proceeding was not sufficient under the facts of this record. The record fails to show that either the victim or the prosecutor understood that notice to the prosecutor would constitute notice to the victim. The victim did not agree to use the prosecutor as her agent for this purpose; the prosecutor did not agree to relay the information to the victim. Moreover, the Board's file contains letters from the County Attorney showing that for many years he had been unaware of the victim's address.

We also decline to assign blame. The issue is whether the victim received that which the constitution guarantees: reasonable efforts by the state to notify her of her constitutional rights and, in particular, the right to participate in the post-conviction release process. Nor is it our responsibility, as the County Attorney requests, to assign among agencies of the executive branch the duty of notifying victims of their rights. That is an executive or legislative function. We decide today only that the constitution gives victims the right to be notified and that this victim's right to notification was violated. We would needlessly intrude upon the prerogatives of the other branches of government if we were to do more.

We turn now to the remedy for the violation. If a victim does not receive notice of a post-conviction release hearing to which she was entitled, she may have the results of that hearing set aside and have a new hearing ordered. A.R.S. section 13-4436(B) provides:

> [T]he failure to use reasonable efforts to provide notice and a right to be present or be heard pursuant to this chapter at a proceeding that involves a post-conviction release is a ground for the victim to seek to set aside the post-conviction release until the victim is afforded the opportunity to be present and be heard.

Section 13-4436(C) then provides:

> If the victim seeks to have a post-conviction release set aside pursuant to subsection B, the court, board of pardons and paroles or state department of corrections shall afford the victim a reexamination proceeding after the parties are given notice.

The victim, through the Coconino County Attorney, requested that the results of the hearing be set aside and a reexamination hearing be ordered. The statutes clearly provide for the relief we have granted.

In sum, this victim enjoys the rights granted under the Victims' Bill of Rights. Those rights include the right to have the state use reasonable efforts to inform her that she was constitutionally entitled to request notice of and to participate in post-conviction release proceedings. The state did not meet that obligation. Therefore, it may not use this victim's failure to request notice as an excuse for denying her participation in the hearing held on May 5. Because the victim is entitled to and did not receive the notice, she is entitled to have the release order set aside and to have a new hearing ordered under A.R.S. section 13-4436(B) and (C).

Notes

1. Double jeopardy does not attach to parole board actions, since parole is a matter of executive grace rather than a right of the defendant.

2. While there was a specific statute authorizing voiding in *Hance*, courts have the inherent authority to void parole board orders where victims' rights are violated.

4. Express Limits on Remedy in State Constitutions

Douglas E. Beloof, *The Third Wave of Crime Victims' Rights*
2005 B.Y.U. L. Rev. 255 (2005)

In Virginia's constitutional victims' rights there is an express limit on the voiding remedy there is no victim standing to ensure that rights can be exercised in criminal cases because there is no voiding or reconsideration remedy available. The Virginia constitution provides: "[t]his section does not confer upon any person a right to appeal or modify any decision in a criminal proceeding . . . In Virginia, the rights can be violated intentionally by the government without meaningful redress.

Three states prohibit setting aside a "finding of guilty or not guilty." To the extent that federal double jeopardy limits already prohibit voiding a verdict, these state provisions have little practical additional effect on victims' standing . . . . [Two] states prohibit "setting aside the conviction" and three states prohibit setting aside a "plea of guilty." . . . [Two] states prohibit challenging a "criminal judgment." . . . [One] states prohibit setting aside a "sentence." In these eight states, once the judgment is entered neither a conviction or a sentence can be voided because the remedy is foreclosed by the victims' rights provisions themselves. Courts cannot order a plea or sentence undone if there are express limitations on such a remedy in the constitutional rights provisions.

On the other hand, four states with restrictive language do not prevent a victim from contesting a violation of victims' rights. The Arizona constitution provides that "A victim's *exercise* of any right granted by this section shall not be grounds for dismissing any criminal proceeding or setting aside any conviction or sentence." South Carolina has a similar provision. From this language, it is readily apparent that victims in Arizona and South Carolina can seek to void a plea or sentence if they were *denied* the ability to exercise their rights.

Note

Where brackets with numbers of states appear in the above article, there are now fewer states with such restrictions than there were at the time the article was written. For example, Oregon's law was like Virginia's. Oregon has since amended its constitution to allow for a remedy. In *State v. Barrett v. Barrett*, 350 Or. 390 (2011), the Oregon Supreme Court vacated the sentence as illegal, where the victim was not notified by the deputy district attorney of the sentencing hearing, so was not able to appear at sentencing or make a victim impact statement.

5. Double Jeopardy Limits on Voiding

Douglas E. Beloof, *The Third Wave of Crime Victims' Rights*
2005 B.Y.U. L. Rev. 255 (2005)

Crime victims as participants have procedural rights in some pre-trial settings. For example, in some jurisdictions, participants are entitled to the rights to notice and to be heard at pre-trial release hearings and the right to prompt disposition. Double jeopardy presents no bar to voiding and reconsideration of pre-trial hearings or rulings. Thus, for example, the double jeopardy clause does not prohibit reconsideration of a release order where victims' right to receive notice of, or the opportunity to speak at, a release hearing is violated. The trial court can readily remedy the violation by convening a reconsideration hearing at which the victims' information and opinion are presented. The court can then reconsider whether to modify the earlier decision. As another example, if trials are unduly delayed, victims can assert their rights to a prompt disposition pre-trial without running afoul of double jeopardy.

The protection of double jeopardy is strongest at the trial stage. Double jeopardy attaches at trial when the jury is selected and sworn, or, if a court trial, when the first witness is sworn. The victims' right at trial is the right to attend. Should victims fail to get adequate notice of the right or of the trial date, or if the court refuses attendance, double jeopardy will nevertheless attach as trials begin. The verdict, be it conviction or acquittal, cannot be altered, absent limited exceptions. Because the verdict cannot be altered, victims will not be able exercise their constitutional right to attend the trial. Federal double jeopardy prohibits victims from voiding the trial or verdict in the hope of attending a re-trial. However, as the right to attend trial is an ongoing right, the victim could seek expedited review until the trial is over. Nevertheless, because most criminal trials are fairly brief, it is unlikely that even an expedited writ procedure would conclude before the trial was finished.

There are a few exceptions to the double jeopardy limitations on verdict. For example, the defendant may appeal a conviction which, if reversed, typically results in re-trial. If the victim was excluded by court order in the last trial they can seek a writ of prohibition to prevent a similar order from being imposed in the second trial. If the victim is not notified of the new date and misses the trial, again jeopardy has attached and the victim again is without remedy.

Assuming the defendant himself does not eliminate double jeopardy by successfully securing a mistrial in the trial court, or retrial after appeal, the manifest necessity exception to double jeopardy is applicable only during the course of the trial. Manifest necessity exists where prejudice to either the defendant or the state may be found. Standing alone, the denial of a trial attendance right does not necessarily result in prejudice to victims or the state in the crucial sense that the result of the trial is likely to be altered by the victims' absence. It is possible that victims' presence might actually change the outcome of the trial. For example, if they hear something they know to be false in the trial and are able to reveal the truth. If the parties are unaware of the falsehood, victims may be the only ones capable of revealing it. In this context, victims' presence improves the truth finding function of the trial. Nevertheless, as victims have no other rights at trial relative to the truth finding function, presently it is unlikely that manifest necessity can be the basis for voiding a trial when the victims' right to attend is violated.

Victims have the right to speak at plea bargain hearings. This right is expressly provided for or is implicit in the right to speak at sentencing. In a plea bargain, double jeopardy generally attaches when a court unconditionally accepts the plea. Pleas of guilty may be voided in certain circumstances. The procedural manner in which a plea is given is critical to the legality of the plea. A guilty plea is void if the plea is a sham or if a court is without jurisdiction to take the plea. Pleas of guilty are shams when the state is not present or is uninvolved in the disposition. The theme running through these cases is that the defendant should not become his own prosecutor and confess guilt without the state's involvement, thus avoiding proper prosecution. Victims denied their right to oppose the plea could allege that the plea was a sham. It would be a sham if the prosecutor and the defense attorney proceeded in knowing violation of constitutional sentencing procedure.

The second basis for overturning a plea is that courts lack jurisdiction to take a plea when the proceedings lack fundamental prerequisites to validity. The distinction between a sham proceeding and lack of jurisdiction is that the sham proceedings reflect fraud. The similarities between the denial of state participation and victim participation are great. Victims, like the state, have an independent right to notice of, and to address the court at, a plea hearing. This victims' right is not dependent upon the parties. The violation of victims' constitutional right to speak means the plea is given in a constitutionally improper manner. The appropriate remedy is voiding the plea and remanding to the trial court for plea proceedings in accordance with victims' state constitutional rights. Similar to cases in which the state has no notice of defendants' guilty pleas—absent compliance with the victims' right to speak— the plea lacks a fundamental prerequisite to validity and could be voided by the court without running afoul of double jeopardy. Courts have skirted the issue arising at the confluence of mis-plea and double jeopardy. See, *Ford v. State*, 829 So.2d 946 (Ct. App. Fla. 2002). Justice Wilkins concurrence in the Utah Supreme Court case of *Casey v. State*, reviewed above in the remedies section of this chapter, makes clear that vacation of plea through the declaration of a mis-plea may be an appropriate remedy: "At the time the motion was made, however, the trial court could have, and under the mandate of our constitution should have, granted M.R.'s motion for a misplea."

Notes

1. Unlike plea or sentencing, the only exception to double jeopardy during trial is manifest necessity. Because the only right of a victim at trial is to attend, it is improbable that the victims' absence would constitute a manifest necessity to declare a mistrial. Once a verdict by trial is rendered, double jeopardy prevents victims or the state from voiding the result, even for a victims' rights violation.

2. Douglas E. Beloof, *The Third Wave of Victims' Rights: Standing, Remedy, and Review*, 2005 B.Y.U. L. Rev. 255, 315 (2005).

Most state constitutions expressly grant victims the right to speak at sentencing. Double jeopardy does not prohibit voiding a sentence where victim are denied their right to address the court at sentencing. The two exceptions to double jeopardy in the sentencing context include, first, illegal sentences or, second, sentences conducted in an illegal manner. Illegal sentences are those that fail to comply with a statutory requirement of the substantive sentence itself, rather than violating a procedure prerequisite to imposing sentence. For example, a sentence that flies in the face of a statutorily mandated sentence is an illegal sentence. It is illegal because it conflicts with the statutory sentencing requirements. The failure to impose mandatory restitution is an example of an illegal sentence. On the other hand, sentences taken in violation of victims' procedural due process rights are sentences taken in an illegal manner.

Sentences taken in violation of either the defendants' right or the states' statutory authority to speak at sentencing are plainly sentences taken in an illegal manner. Despite the absence of express language granting the right, the United States Supreme Court has held that criminal defendants must be given an opportunity to speak at sentencing. A trial court's "failure to ask the defendant if he had anything to say before sentence" is imposed requires reversal. Absent explicit limitations, taking a sentence in violation of the victims' right to speak is a sentence taken in an illegal manner.

Denial of prosecutors' right to speak at sentencing is denial of a necessary prerequisite to sentencing and double jeopardy does not prevent a re-sentencing. In *United States v. Crawford* the sentencing court stopped the government from attempting to speak and proceeded to sentence without informing government counsel of the right to be heard. The government had a right to speak under the Federal Rules of Criminal Procedure 32(a)(1)(C), which provided: "The attorney for the government shall have an equivalent [to the defendant] opportunity to speak to the court." Because the defendants knew that a sentence taken in an improper manner was unlawful, they also knew that the sentence was subject to reversal and could have no legitimate expectation of finality in the sentence.

Victims' rights to speak at sentencing are similar to defendants' and the government's rights. For example, the Arizona constitution provides that: "To protect and preserve victims' rights to justice and due process, a victim of crime has a right . . . To be heard at any proceeding involving . . . a negotiated plea, and sentencing." Because the state and defendant know that a sentence taken in an improper manner is unlawful, they have no legitimate expectation of finality in sentences where crime victims' constitutional rights are violated. Furthermore, the victims' interest in punishment, discussed above, and the victims' interest in exercising their rights, makes the voiding remedy available and appropriate for violation of their rights.

C. The Inferior Remedies for Victims' Rights Violations

1. Ethical Violations and Victims' Rights

It is something of a misnomer to call ethical discipline a "remedy" for violation of victims' rights. Ethical discipline of lawyers and judges is not actually remedial. The purpose of ethical rules is to regulate professional conduct and not to provide some benefit to the complainant.

a. Judicial Discipline

Like many jurisdictions, the state of California has a Commission on Judicial Performance. The Commission's sanctions for judicial misconduct vary and include private admonishment, public censure and removal from the bench.

The Commission has given private admonishments to judges for not complying with victim laws. As examples:

At a sentencing hearing, a judge refused to allow victim impact statements in contravention of Penal Code sections 679.02 and 1191.l. STATE OF CALIFORNIA: COMMISSION ON JUDICIAL PERFORMANCE, 1995 ANNUAL REPORT, p. 23.

In scheduling a sentencing hearing, a judge did not make an effort to accommodate the parents of a murder victim who had expressed a desire to be present and heard at a sentencing hearing pursuant to Penal Code sections 679.02 and 1191.1. The Commission acknowledged that the judge had encountered difficulties in scheduling the hearing. STATE OF CALIFORNIA: COMMISSION ON JUDICIAL PERFORMANCE, 1996 Annual Report, p. 24.

California's ethical processes have also resulted in public censure for general mistreatment of a victim.

State of California before the Commission on Judicial Qualifications[1]

Nov. 13, 1970 Inquiry Concerning a Judge No. 10

FINDING OF FACT

Respondent has served as a Judge of the Superior Court of the City and County of San Francisco since December 28, 1966, immediately preceded by service as a Judge of the Municipal Court of that city and county since November 16, 1961.

It is true as alleged in Paragraph I of the foregoing Notice that on or about February 24, 1969, in connection with a criminal prosecution entitled *The People of the State of California vs. Kenneth Beasley, William Augustus Morris and Ricky James Jackson*, No. 73817, in the files of the Superior Court for the City and County of San Francisco, Respondent received a young woman named L.C., the victim of the criminal acts [of sexual assault] alleged to have been committed by the defendants in said action, into his court chambers, . . . and during the conversation concerning the disposition of the criminal charges, Respondent referred to Miss C. as a "horse's ass" in a loud, boisterous tone of voice.

It is true that as alleged in Paragraph II of the Notice that on or about March 21, 1969, in connection with a criminal prosecution entitled *The People of the State of California vs. Kenneth Beasley, William Augustus Morris and Ricky James Jackson*, No. 73817, in the files of the Superior Court for the City and County of San Francisco, Respondent subjected Inspector Arthur Christensen to public ridicule and contempt as partially disclosed in the excerpt from a transcript of the proceedings in open court and presided over by Respondent at that time as follows:

(RESPONDENT): I think it's a lousy deal when an inspector has to sit with a client. The district attorney ought to advise the inspector. I think it is ridiculous.

---

1. Author's Note: this is the predecessor commission to the Commission on Judicial Performance referred to in the previous materials.

Inspector Christensen, can I see you a moment? Is there some reason you have to sit here, or don't you have enough work to do?

INSPECTOR CHRISTENSEN: I was instructed to go down with this young lady by the lieutenant of my detail.

(RESPONDENT): Who?

INSPECTOR CHRISTENSEN: Lieutenant Flahaven.

(RESPONDENT): Who gave him the instructions? Bring Lt. Flahaven down here. I never heard of a sentencing procedure where people have to be in court with a policeman holding their hand. Tell the lieutenant I want to talk to him.

MR. NORMAN (the district attorney): Well, your Honor, I don't think that this is a fair remark.

(RESPONDENT): Mr. Norman, I am not going to listen to what is a fair remark in view of what you did to the court a few weeks ago. I don't want to hear that. I want Lt. Flahaven down here. That is the way it is going to be. And I don't want to hear about what a fair remark is. There are lots of things that are not fair.

MR. NORMAN: For the record I don't think it was.

(RESPONDENT): I don't want police inspectors sitting here in court holding some alleged victim's hands, and I am using the term figuratively. And I want Lt. Flahaven down here. I want to know where these instructions came from. There is lots more work for the police to do in the county than sit here in this court. I want to know who gave the instructions, so bring him down here.

It is true that the facts found in the preceding finding of fact Number 5 constitute conduct prejudicial to the administration of justice that brings the judicial office into disrepute.

RESOLVED that upon consideration of the record of the proceedings in the above entitled matter and the Commission having found and hereby concluding that the conduct of the respondent as found in the Findings constitute conduct prejudicial to the administration of justice that brings the judicial office into disrepute, the Commission by virtue of the powers vested in it by Section 18 of Article VI of the California Constitution, hereby recommends to the Supreme Court of California that the respondent, Bernard B. Glickfeld, be censured.

_____

Note

The above censure was upheld by the California Supreme Court. *In re Bernard Glickfeld*, 479 P.2d 638 (Cal. 1971).

_____

Crime victims' rights are frequently provided as state constitutional rights. An intentional violation of a persons' constitutional rights by a lawyer or judge can be the basis of ethical discipline. The following case reveals a failed attempt by a judge to pressure a public prosecutor into intentionally violating a crime victims' right to be heard at the plea hearing.

Disciplinary Counsel v. (Judge) O'Neill

815 N.E.2d 286 (Ohio 2004)

* * *

In February 1999, William Lane was indicted for multiple felonies relating to a bank robbery in Columbus. Because of his habit of committing robberies in nightwear, he had gained notoriety as the "pajama bank robber." At the first pretrial before Judge O'Neill on March 25, 1999 Lane unexpectedly offered to plea to the indictment. Jeffrey Bobbitt (admitted 1982, Franklin County Public Defender, Staff Attorney since 1982) was defense counsel and Sue Ann Reulbach (admitted 1985, Franklin County Prosecutor's Office since 1991, Senior Trial Staff) was the assigned prosecutor. Around 9:30 a.m. counsel approached and informed Judge O'Neill there would be a plea. When Judge O'Neill wanted to proceed to sentencing, Reulbach explained that the victim, a bank teller, requested to be present and to make a statement at sentencing as required under the Ohio Victims Rights Act. Reulbach requested that the matter be continued to that afternoon or the next day to secure the attendance of the victim. Judge O'Neill asked Reulbach why the victim was not subpoenaed that morning. Reulbach explained that the plea was not expected and victims are not usually present at the first pretrial. Reulbach testified that Judge O'Neill denied the request to reschedule and stated, "Absolutely not, we are going to proceed. I'm going to get this case off my docket." (Transcript Vol. III — 154–156) Reulbach called the victim who was at work at the bank but she could not leave her job at that time.

When Judge O'Neill requested that counsel take their places to do the plea and sentencing, Reulbach refused to proceed until she put on the record that she was not able to comply with the victim's rights statute. Reulbach and Bobbitt testified that a back and forth banter ensued between Judge O'Neill and Reulbach. Reulbach requested to make a record on the victim issue and Judge O'Neill refused to go on the record. As this back and forth continues, Bobbitt observed that the court reporter Grego looked like a marionette with her hands going on and off on the stenotype machine as Reulbach requested a record and Judge O'Neill ordered the record not be taken. Reulbach respectfully but insistently refused to proceed with plea and sentencing until the victim's presence was arranged or she made a record on the absence of the victim. Both counsel testified that Judge O'Neill, not the court reporter, determined that no record would be made. None of these conversations appeared in the transcript. (Transcript Vol. III — 182–185, 156–158) (Exhibit 186) Judge O'Neill stated in her Answer to the Amended Complaint at Para. 207 that "Ms. Reulbach could proffer anything at any time with the court reporter. She additionally avers that the court reporter, Sandy Grego, refused Ms. Reulbach an opportunity to proffer." Grego testified that she did not take a record that day because Judge O'Neill "said no" and at that time, "you couldn't make a proffer unless Judge O'Neill agreed." If Reulbach had asked for a proffer, Grego would have had to ask Judge O'Neill for permission. (Transcript Vol. III — 25, 194, 203)

Reulbach left the courtroom and returned with Ron O'Brien, the Franklin County Prosecutor. O'Brien gave Judge O'Neill a copy of the victims' rights statute and requested that Lane's plea be postponed until 3:00 p.m. when the victim could be present. Judge O'Neill agreed to postpone the plea but offered Bobbitt the opportunity to withdraw Lane's plea based on the morning's events. Bobbitt refused this offer at Lane's insistence and the plea and sentencing take place that afternoon, including testimony from the victim. (Exhibit 186) Judge O'Neill testified that Reulbach was posturing and delaying to allow time for the news media to arrive for the sentencing. (Transcript Vol. V — 193–195). Reulbach denied calling any media, believed they were already in the building that morning and when the plea did take place, no media were present. (Transcript Vol. III — 168–173).

* * *

[For these and other transgressions, the judge was suspended from the practice of law for two years.]

Note

Professor Sarah Welling, a proponent of the victim's participation in plea bargaining has proposed that the best means of victim participation is to allow victims to address the court directly. Furthermore, she believes the appropriate remedy for failure to allow a victim to be heard at a plea bargain hearing should be an ethical complaint:

> If the trial judge denies the victim this right to be heard, the victim must be accorded some remedy. The remedy should not be a cause of action. Granting the victim a cause of action would be unwise for several reasons. A cause of action against the trial judge for damages would certainly enter immunity obstacles. A cause of action not for damages but to set aside the plea bargain after it had been entered would run afoul of the double jeopardy clause. Instead of giving rise to a cause of action, the trial court's denial of the victim's right to be heard should be deemed a violation of the code of judicial conduct, and the victim could file a grievance against the trial judge with the appropriate commission.

Sarah Welling, *Victim Participation in Plea Bargaining*, 65 WASH. U. L.Q. 301, 349 (1987).

Prof. Welling's conclusion that an action "to set aside the plea bargain after it had been entered would run afoul of the double jeopardy clause," would depend on whether jeopardy had attached, which often depends on whether the court simply "receives" the plea for later entry after a pre-sentence investigation has been completed, or instead, "enters" the plea as a final judgment of guilt. *See State v.*

Martinez-Mendoza, 804 N.W.2d 1 (2011) ("Jeopardy attached at the time the trial court accepted defendant's guilty plea *and adjudicated him guilty* in criminal sexual conduct prosecution.") (Emphasis added.) The practice may differ state by state according to their respective Rules of Procedure. Moreover, if the plea is illegal because victims' rights were violated, double jeopardy may not attach.

b. Defense Counsel Discipline

Defense counsel may be disciplined for a direct violation of the victim's rights. Consider this case from Arizona in which defense counsel was suspended from the practice of law for 60 days and ordered to take instruction in victims' rights law.

In the Matter of a Member of the State Bar of Arizona, Michael T. Telep, Jr.

HEARING OFFICER'S REPORT No. 08-2230

PROCEDURAL HISTORY

The parties filed a Tender of Admissions and Agreement for Discipline by Consent and a Joint Memorandum in Support of Agreement for Discipline by Consent on September 23, 2009. No Complaint was filed. A hearing was held on November 3, 2009.

1. At all times relevant, Respondent was a lawyer licensed to practice law in the state of Arizona having been first admitted to practice in Arizona on May 21, 1988. (Transcript of the Hearing page 4, line 3, TR 4:3)

2. In State v. Santa Cruz, Yuma County Superior Court Case No. S1400CR200701317, Respondent's client was charged with several counts of indecent conduct with a minor. (TR4:6)

3. Respondent subpoenaed the minor's high school records.

4. The subpoenas were issued and served without notice to the minor victim or state. The minor's parents learned of them when the school called them to say they had received the subpoenas. (TR 4:22 through 5:1)

5. The prosecutor filed a motion to quash, arguing among other things that at a hearing 5 months earlier she reminded Respondent and the court that the Victims' Rights and criminal subpoena laws forbade such subpoenas. 3

6. At a September hearing, Respondent told the court that he later would file a motion to obtain the minor's medical records. (TR 7:15–20)

7. On October 9, 2008, the Han. Mark Wayne Reeves conducted a hearing in the case. Near the time of that hearing, Respondent subpoenaed the minor's physician's records.

8. At the October hearing, Respondent told the judge that the subpoena was the motion: "I did file a motion. My subpoena—the subpoena is a motion . . . That is my subpoena, and you granted that subpoena vicariously through the subpoena power. We have that. I filed that motion." (TR 7:24 through 8:7)

9. The subpoena directed the doctor to deliver the records to the judge's courtroom on and at the date and time of the next hearing in the case, November 12, 2008.

10. The subpoena also contained bold print instructing the doctor that if the records were delivered to Respondent's office before the hearing date the doctor would not have to appear personally in court. (TR 8:11 through 9:10)

11. Judge Reeves determined that the subpoena was misleading because it appeared as though the court was requesting the medical records when in fact it was Respondent who sought the records. Respondent testified that the attorney for the victim filed a motion to quash. not the prosecutor. (TR 5:8 through 6:6)

12. Judge Reeves concluded that Respondent's attempt to directly subpoena the minor's medical records violated the Victims' Rights laws and related Criminal Rules of Procedure. (TR 11:21–25)

13. At the October hearing, Judge Reeves also determined that Respondent's attempt to subpoena the school records without a court order violated Arizona's Victims' Rights laws. (TR 12:1–9)

14. At the November 12 hearing Judge Reeves asked Respondent why he had not filed a motion for a court order to obtain the school and medical records.

15. The judge also asked Respondent where the medical records were and told Respondent that if he received the medical records they should be delivered to the court where they would remain sealed pending another hearing regarding their disclosure.

16. Specifically, Judge Reeves asked: "And you are not aware of anything about it further, Mr. Telep?" Respondent answered: "Not at this point, your honor." (TR 12:10)

17. Two days later, Respondent delivered the medical records to the court in a sealed envelope.

18. The court's Judicial Assistant called the doctor's office and learned that the records had been delivered to Respondent's office on October 23, 20 days before the hearing at which Respondent denied any knowledge of the whereabouts of the records. (TR 13:23 through 14:3)

19. The court held a hearing on December 9, 2008, to address Respondent's motions to obtain the school and medical records and an OSC regarding Respondent's candor relating to the medical records.

20. Respondent told Judge Reeves that at the time of the November 12 hearing be did not know that the medical records had been delivered to his office.

21. Respondent also told the judge that he had already subpoenaed and received the minor's middle school records and the minor's mother's school records approximately a year earlier.

22. Respondent told Judge Reeves that he had not looked at the school records because he had simply put them away and had not gotten around to examining them. He denied having looked at the medical records, too.

23. Judge Reeves determined that Respondent violated the Victims' Rights laws and rules (Ariz. Const., Art. II, Sec. 2.1; A.R.S. § 13-4401, et. seq.; Rule 39, Ariz.R.Crim.P), and the criminal law subpoena statute (A.R.S. § 13-407l(D)), by issuing subpoenas for the records without a motion and court order and, in so doing, also violated ERs 3.4(c), 4.4(a) and 8.4(d). (TR 15:4–14)

24. Judge Reeves disqualified Respondent from the case and added that his unethical and improper actions severely prejudiced the defendant. He added that Respondent's actions jeopardized legitimate efforts to obtain the records and may necessitate their preclusion from evidence. Judge Reeves observed that the defendant may be entitled to disclosure of the records and they may also contain exculpatory evidence. Only by the appointment of new counsel could the defendant properly request the records sought without the taint and prejudice that Respondent caused. (TR 18:15–19:4)

CONDITIONAL ADMISSIONS

Respondent conditionally admits that his conduct as set forth above violated Rule 42, Ariz. R. Sup. Ct., specifically ERs 1.3, 3.1, 3.2, 3.3, 3.4(c), 4.1, 4.4(a), 8.4(c) and 8.4(d).

Respondent's admissions are being tendered in exchange for the form of discipline contained in this agreement Respondent violated ER 1.3 (diligence and promptness) by failing to file a motion for the victim's school and medical records. Respondent also failed to realize that the victim's medical records had been in Respondent's office for almost 3 weeks before the November 12, 2008 appearance in Judge Reeves' court. (TR 19:7 through 20:16)

Respondent violated ER 3.1 (meritorious claims and contentions) by arguing to Judge Reeves that a subpoena was the same as a motion. ('IR 22:12–23)

Respondent violated ER 3.2 (expediting litigation) by not using a motion instead of a subpoena to acquire the victim's school and medical records. Respondent's failure to use the appropriate method led to his disqualification as counsel by Judge Reeves. Respondent's client remained in custody while the client's criminal case was delayed. (TR 23:3 through 24:1)

Respondent violated ER 3.3 (candor toward tribunal) by telling the court that he would file a motion, when in fact he knew that he had simply served a subpoena for the records. At the hearing Respondent stated that when he told the court on November 12, 2008 that he knew nothing about the medical records, Respondent was not lying. However, two days after the hearing Respondent delivered the medical records to the court in a sealed envelope. The records had been delivered to Respondent's office pursuant to the subpoena three weeks before November 12, 2008. Respondent admitted at the hearing that he further violated ER 3.3 by not correcting his November 12, 2008 statement that he knew nothing about the records when two days later he found the records in his office and delivered them to court. (TR 15:21 through 18:14)

Respondent violated ER 3.4(c) (knowingly disobeying an obligation under the rules of a tribunal) when he knew that he had issued a subpoena for the records but that the judge was requiring a motion pursuant to the relevant statutes. (TR 24:4–14)

Respondent violated ER 4.1 (truthfulness in statements to others) when in front of others in the court room Respondent told the judge that he had filed a motion for the victim's records and that the motion was the subpoena. The others present would have been the prosecutor and counsel for the victim. (TR 24:15 through 25:6)

Respondent violated ER 4.4(a) (respect for rights of others) when he used methods of obtaining evidence that violated the legal rights of the victim. The proper method for obtaining the school and medical records of the victim was to file a motion with the court. (Arizona Constitution, Article ill, Section 2.1; A.R.S. sec. 13-4401, et seq.; Rule 39, Arizona Rules of Criminal Procedure aod A.R.S. sec.13-4071 (D)) (TR 25:7–12)

Respondent violated ER 8.4(c) (conduct involving dishonesty) by telling the court that he would file a motion for the records and then using a subpoena. Respondent also violated ER 8.4(c) by telling the judge that he did not know anything about the medical records, then discovering the records two days later and bringing them to court, but failing to correct his statement that he did not have the records. (TR 25:13–19)

Respondent violated ER 8.4(d) (conduct prejudicial to the administration of justice) when he failed to use the correct procedure for obtaining the records. His misconduct led to his disqualification for violating the victim's rights. His client who remained in custody was made to wait a longer time for a resolution of his criminal case . . . .

Respondent also violated the Constitutional and Statutory Victims' Rights of a minor crime victim when he issued and served subpoenas for the medical and school records without first filing a motion for authority to do so and without giving notice of his actions to the minor, her parents or the state, in violation of Rule 42, Ariz. R. Sup. Ct., ER 4.4 . . . .

The Duty Violated

On the basis of the foregoing, Respondent violated duties owed to the legal system.

Actual and Potential Injury

As a result of Respondent's conduct, there was actual and potential injury to the client, victim and the court system. Judge Reeves discharged Respondent from representing the client thereby requiring that new counsel represent the client resulting in delay. The victim's rights of privacy were violated. Judge Reeves expressed that the client may have had legitimate grounds to obtain the minor's medical and school records but by obtaining them illegally, Respondent may have tainted the process so much that the records might thereafter not be obtainable.

RECOMMENDATION

The objective of lawyer discipline is not to punish the lawyer, but to protect the public, the profession, and the administration of justice. In re Neville, 147 Ariz. 106, 708 P.2d 1297 (1985). Recognizing it is the prerogative of the Disciplinary Commission and the Supreme Court to determine the appropriate sanction, the Hearing Officer asserts that the objectives of discipline will be met by the imposition of the proposed sanction of a 60-day suspension, probation, and the costs and expenses of these proceedings.

SANCTIONS

The Hearing Officer recommends the following sanctions:

1) Respondent will receive a sixty (60)-day suspension;

2) Respondent will be placed on probation for one year to begin upon reinstatement, the terms of which are as follows:

a. Respondent shall within one year following reinstatement attend a Continuing Legal Education program relating to Victims' Rights;

Honorable Jonathan H. Schwartz

Hearing Officer 6S

Notes

1. The Supreme Court of Arizona followed the recommendation of the Hearing Officer. No. SB-10-0022-D (2010).

2. The ethical limits of a defense attorney's relationship with the victim is explored in *In re Complaint as to the Conduct of Paula J. Lawrence*, 98 P.3d 366 (Or. 2004), a case where a senior lawyer represented both the defendant and the victim in a criminal case of domestic violence. The Oregon Supreme Court opined:

> We think that the objective personal interests of an alleged batterer and the batterer's victim are inherently adverse and, therefore, that there is a "likely" conflict of interest when a lawyer gives advice to both the abuser and the victim. For example, an unrepresented victim who is financially or otherwise dependent on the abuser may think that he or she has few options available other than to have the abuser return to the home to support or help the victim and any children involved. The victim, therefore, may be motivated to recant for reasons other than that the abuse did not happen. Such a scenario could place the victim in a position of having to lie, thereby placing the victim in danger of being charged with perjury or filing a false police report, among other things. In addition, a lawyer who has only the victim's interests in mind well may be able to show the victim that other resources are available to assist him or her and that it would be in his or her and (and any children's) best interest to have the abuser prosecuted . . . .

We next turn to the question whether the accused gave Patricia Battle advice other than the advice to secure counsel. The word "advice" is not defined either in DR 7-104(A)(2) or elsewhere in the disciplinary rules. This court has not discussed or defined the term in this context. Indeed, even familiar authority proves less than helpful. However, this is not a proceeding that requires us to explore the outer boundaries of the types of information that a lawyer might offer an unrepresented person without running afoul of DR 7-104(A)(2). Here, the record shows by clear and convincing evidence that the accused had developed a novel interpretation of a new constitutional provision, Article I, section 42, of the Oregon Constitution (1996); that the accused, through Kelly, informed Patricia Battle (who never before had heard of Article I, section 42 (1996)) that, under her theory, Patricia Battle had a constitutional right to have the charges against her assailant dismissed; that the accused suggested to Patricia Battle, through Kelly, that Patricia Battle pursue a specific course of conduct to accomplish that end; that the accused assisted Kelly in drafting an affidavit for Patricia Battle's signature that explained that Patricia Battle wished to avail herself of her alleged constitutional right; and that the accused prepared Patricia Battle for the hearing before Judge Harris, telling her what to say and how to say it. Based on the foregoing, we conclude that the accused gave Patricia Battle, an unrepresented person, "advice," as that word is used in DR 7-104(A)(2).

c. Prosecutor Discipline

In every state, prosecutors can defend victims' rights in certain contexts. Because defendants may challenge their convictions on review by asserting that the victims' exercise of rights constitutes a violation of the defendants' rights, it is necessary for the state to be able to defend the conviction. Defense of the conviction, in this context, means the state is defending the victims' right. Victims' rights are personal to the victim, so the victim also has the ability to defend their rights independently, assuming standing and review are available.

Arizona law provides: "At the request of the victim the prosecutor may assert any right to which the victim is entitled." A.R.S. Sec. 13-4437(1)(C).

State ex rel. Romley v. Superior Court, County of Maricopa
891 P.2d 246 (Ariz. App. 1995)

JACOBSON, Judge.

The Maricopa County Attorney seeks special action review of the trial court's order directing the County Attorney to withdraw from prosecution of one of two criminal cases. The issue we address is whether the prosecutor in a criminal matter has a conflict of interest that requires withdrawal or disqualification when his office is also prosecuting criminal charges against the victim in a separate and unrelated criminal matter. Because we hold that no conflict of interest arises under these circumstances, we vacate the trial court's order requiring the prosecutor to withdraw.

Factual and Procedural Background

Real parties in interest Jesse Andres Flores and Manual D. Gongora (defendants) were indicted on multiple counts of endangerment and misconduct involving weapons, all dangerous felonies, arising out of a drive-by shooting at J.M. (the victim) and his family members. The victim and the defendants are allegedly members of rival gangs. The victim was previously indicted on multiple counts of attempted murder and aggravated assault, all dangerous felonies, arising out of circumstances that did not involve defendants. The Maricopa County Attorney's Office (prosecutor) is involved in the prosecution of both cases.

On August 19, 1994, defendant Gongora filed a Motion for Determination of Counsel, alleging that the prosecutor had a conflict of interest in the prosecution of this case because the County Attorney was also prosecuting the victim in another case; additionally, defendant alleged that this dual prosecution created "an appearance of impropriety." At the hearing on the motion, defendant Flores joined in the motion. The court ordered "that the State withdraw from one of the two cases in which there is a conflict." The state filed its petition for special action from that order, and this court stayed all further proceedings in the trial court pending this resolution. On October 18, 1994, we entered an order accepting jurisdiction and granting relief, with this opinion to follow.

Special Action Jurisdiction

An order granting a motion to disqualify counsel prior to trial is an interlocutory order for which the state has no adequate remedy by appeal pursuant to A.R.S. § 13-4032. For that reason, and because this case involves an issue of law that is likely to reoccur, special action review is appropriate. *See, e.g., Gomez v. Superior Court,* 717 P.2d 902 (1986); *Turbin v. Superior Court,* 797 P.2d 734 (App. 1990); *see also* Rules 1 and 3, Arizona Rules of Procedure for Special Actions. In the exercise of our discretion, we accept special action jurisdiction.

Standing of Real Parties in Interest

As a preliminary matter, we address the prosecutor's contention that the real parties in interest in this case have no standing to assert a conflict of interest because the person subject to any potential conflict under these facts is the victim, who has not moved to disqualify the prosecutor on that basis.

Generally, only a client or a former client has standing to challenge legal representation on grounds of conflict of interest. *In re Yarn Processing Patent Validity Litigation,* 530 F.2d 83 (5th Cir. 1976). In *Yarn Processing,* the court explained:

> To allow an unauthorized surrogate to champion the rights of the former client would allow that surrogate to use the conflict rules for his own purposes where a genuine conflict might not really exist. It would place in the hands of the unauthorized surrogate powerful presumptions which are

inappropriate in his hands. Courts do not generally examine the motives of a moving party in a disqualification motion. Once the preliminary showing is made by the former client, the motion must be granted regardless of whether the former client gains an advantage at the expense of his adversary. . . . We are reluctant to extend this where the party receiving such an advantage has no right of his own which is invaded. *Id.* at 90 (citation omitted).

Other courts have interpreted the last sentence of *Yarn Processing* to allow an exception to the general rule:

[W]here the rights of a particular party may be compromised by representation in which opposing counsel is engaged, then that party has standing to bring a motion to disqualify, regardless of whether the party is a client or former client of the attorney or firm whose representation the party challenges.

Davis v. Southern Bell Tel. & Tel. Co., 149 F.R.D. 666, 673 (S.D.Fla. 1993); *see also Kessenich v. Commodity Futures Trading Comm'n,* 684 F.2d 88, 94 (D.C.Cir. 1982) (granting motion to disqualify filed by party who was not client or former client and who was unaffected by the challenged representation). Arizona courts have also recognized that a party may challenge representation of his opponent, but only "in extreme circumstances." *Alexander v. Superior Court,* 685 P.2d 1309, 1313 (1984).

In this case, defendants contend that the County Attorney's subsequent criminal prosecution of the victim in this case may cause that victim to "feel it is necessary to please the County Attorney's Office" in this case "in hopes they will show some sort of mercy" in the victim's prosecution. In his response to the petition for special action, defendant Gongora argues, "the standing comes in [defendants'] desire to have a fair trial and the avoidance of having alleged victim witnesses['] testimony tainted by a belief that they are helping a family member and friend." Because defendants have alleged a possible harm to their own cases that could potentially affect their own due process rights to a fair trial, we find that they have standing to raise the disqualification issue in this context. However, we note that Arizona courts "view with suspicion motions by opposing counsel to disqualify a party's attorney based upon conflict of interest or appearance of impropriety. . . ." *Gomez,* 717 P.2d at 905.

Role of a Criminal Prosecutor

Defendants' allegation of a conflict is based on the prohibition against litigating adversely to a former client in a subsequent matter. *See generally* ER 1.9, Rules of Professional Conduct, Rule 42, Rules of the Arizona Supreme Court.[2] In their motion in the trial court, defendants argued:

---

2. ER 1.9 provides:

A lawyer who has formerly represented a client in a matter shall not thereafter:

Since the adoption of the Victims' Rights legislation, the duty of a prosecutor to a victim has increased. The increase is almost that of an attorney client. As a result, the prosecution is compelled to represent the victims' rights in terms of notifying of a plea agreement and issues regarding restitution.

In their responding pleading in this court, defendants argue:

In essence, since the adoption of the Victims['] Bill of Rights by Arizona, the prosecuting agencies have become quasi representatives of alleged victims.

Inherent in defendants' allegation of conflict of interest is the contention that the prosecutor cannot "represent" the victim as his "client" in this case and then, through the prosecutor's office, prosecute that "client" in another case. This premise is based on a faulty interpretation of the prosecutor's role in a criminal case as well as a misunderstanding of the prosecutor's relationship to the victim.

It is true that, since passage of the Victims' Bill of Rights, the statutory duties imposed on prosecutors towards victims have increased. *See generally* A.R.S. §§ 13-4401 to -4438 ("Crime Victims' Rights"); *see also* Ariz. Const. art. 2, § 2.1 ("Victims' Bill of Rights"); Rule 39, Arizona Rules of Criminal Procedure. The prosecutor's office must give the victim notice of certain proceedings and notice of the defendant's status, §§ 13-4408 to -4416, and the victim has a right to confer with the prosecuting attorney regarding the disposition of an offense, § 13-4419. Additionally, the defendant's attorney may initiate contact with the victim only through the prosecutor's office, § 13-4433(B). Furthermore, the prosecutor "has standing at the request of the victim to protect the victim from harassment, intimidation or abuse and, pursuant to that standing, may seek any appropriate protective court order." A.R.S. § 13-4433(C). However, even given these additional rights, victims have no "authority to direct the prosecution of the case," A.R.S. § 13-4419(C), which is normally inherent in an attorney-client relationship. Indeed, in some cases the wishes of the victim may be adverse to those of the prosecution. *See, e.g., S.A. v. Superior Court,* 831 P.2d 1297, 1297–98 (Ariz. App. 1992) (victim attempted to avoid testifying despite subpoena issued at direction of prosecutor).

(a) represent another person in the same or a substantially related matter in which that person's interests are materially adverse to the interests of the former client unless the former client consents after consultation; or

(b) use information relating to the representation to the disadvantage of the former client except as ER 1.6 would permit with respect to a client or when the information has become generally known.

The comment to ER 1.9 states, "The underlying question is whether the lawyer was so involved in the matter that the subsequent representation can be justly regarded as a changing of sides in the matter in question." Additionally, the comment to ER 1.7, which involves the "general rule" regarding conflicts of interest, states that "a lawyer ordinarily may not act as advocate against a person the lawyer represents in some other matter, even if it is wholly unrelated."

Although not specifically stated in a published opinion in this jurisdiction, the rule is well established that a prosecutor does not "represent" the victim in a criminal trial; therefore, the victim is not a "client" of the prosecutor. *See Hawkins v. Auto-Owners (Mut.) Ins. Co.,* 579 N.E.2d 118, 123 (Ind.App. 1991), *vacated in part on other grounds,* 608 N.E.2d 1358 (1993) ("A deputy prosecutor does not represent the victims or witnesses in a criminal proceeding, but rather, is the State's representative"); *Lindsey v. State,* 725 P.2d 649, 660 (Wyo. 1986) (Urbigkit, J., dissenting) ("'The prosecutor does not represent the victim of a crime, the police, or any individual. Instead, the prosecutor represents society as a whole,'" *citing* Commentary, *On Prosecutorial Ethics,* 13 HASTINGS CONST. L.Q. 537–39 (1986); *State v. Eidson,* 701 S.W.2d 549, 554 (Mo.App. 1985) ("The prosecutor represents the State not the victim"); *Rutledge v. State,* 267 S.E.2d 199, 200 (Ga. 1980) (special prosecutor hired by the victim's family to assist district attorney did not represent the victim). The nature of this representation, and the distinct role of the prosecutor in a criminal case, is perhaps best articulated by Justice White in a concurring and dissenting opinion in which he was joined by Justices Harlan and Stewart:

> Law enforcement officers have the obligation to convict the guilty and to make sure they do not convict the innocent. They must be dedicated to making the criminal trial a procedure for the ascertainment of the true facts surrounding the commission of the crime. To this extent, our so-called adversary system is not adversary at all; nor should it be. But defense counsel has no comparable obligation to ascertain or present the truth. Our system assigns him a different mission. He must be and is interested in preventing the conviction of the innocent, but, absent a voluntary plea of guilty, we also insist that he defend his client whether he is innocent or guilty. The State has the obligation to present the evidence. . . .

United States v. Wade, 388 U.S. 218, 256–57 (1967) (White, J., concurring and dissenting). That distinction has also been discussed by other authorities:

> The difference in our roles as advocates derives from the degree of our authority and the disparity of our obligations. Defense counsel's legitimate and necessary goal is to achieve the best possible result for his client. His loyalty is to the individual client alone. *The prosecutor, however, enters a courtroom to speak for the People and not just some of the People. The prosecutor speaks not solely for the victim, or the police, or those who support them, but for all the People. That body of "The People" includes the defendant and his family and those who care about him. It also includes the vast majority of citizens who know nothing about a particular case, but who give over to the prosecutor the authority to seek a just result in their name.*

Lindsey, 725 P.2d at 660, *quoting* Commentary, *On Prosecutorial Ethics,* 13 HASTINGS CONST. L.Q. 537–539 (1986) (emphasis added).

Given this unique role of a prosecutor in a criminal action, we hold that the prosecutor does not "represent" the victim as a "client" in a way that runs afoul of the

Rules of Professional Conduct. The prosecutor has no incentive to induce the victim in this case to "please" the prosecutor in a way that would prejudice defendants' rights to a fair trial. We will not presume that the prosecutor will seek defendants' convictions at all costs, when his duty is to see that justice is done on behalf of both the victim and the defendants. *Berger v. United States,* 295 U.S. 78, 88; *see also* ER 3.8, Comment, Rule 42, Rules of the Arizona Supreme Court ("A prosecutor has the responsibility of a minister of justice and not simply that of an advocate"). Under the circumstances of this case, we hold that no conflict of interest exists to justify the trial court's order requiring the prosecutor to withdraw from representation in one of the two subject criminal actions.

Defendants also allege that this dual involvement of the prosecutor in both matters creates "an appearance of impropriety." Although the Model Rules adopted by our supreme court in Rule 42 no longer contain the former Canon 9 appearance of impropriety prohibition, our supreme court has stated that this standard still "survives as part of conflict of interest" analysis, and "should be enough to cause an attorney to closely scrutinize his conduct." *Gomez,* 717 P.2d at 904. However, appearance of impropriety does not necessarily cause disqualification in every case; rather, "[w]here the conflict is so remote that there is insufficient appearance of wrongdoing, disqualification is not required." *Id.*; *see also Sellers v. Superior Court,* 742 P.2d 292, 300 (Ariz. App. 1987) (appearance of impropriety is "too slender a reed" upon which to rest disqualification of opposing counsel).

We conclude that the facts of this case do not raise an "appearance of impropriety" to any level sufficient to cause disqualification of the Maricopa County Attorney's Office from prosecution of either this case or prosecution of the victim in another case. Because we have also held that the victim is not a "client" of the Maricopa County Attorney's Office, we have also concluded that no conflict of interest has arisen on these facts. Therefore, the trial court abused its discretion in requiring the Maricopa County Attorney's Office to withdraw from prosecution of one of the two criminal cases, and we vacate that order.

For the foregoing reasons, we accept jurisdiction and grant relief. With the filing of this opinion, the stay previously in effect is dissolved.

Notes

1. Prosecutorial misconduct occurs when the constitutional rights of criminal defendants are intentionally violated. By analogy, a finding of prosecutorial misconduct should result if there is an intentional violation of crime victims' state constitutional rights. The relationship of prosecutors to victims may serve as a disincentive to victims. As a practical matter, prosecutors exercise so much control over a case that a victim may prefer not to clash with the prosecutor by filing an ethics complaint. Are there any ways to ameliorate this disincentive?

2. If a victim is unaware of their rights, it is unlikely they will file a complaint. One approach to turning ethical rules into workable incentives might be the process

of certification. For example, in the plea bargain context, if a prosecutor must certify to the court that they consulted with the victim and gave the victim notice of their rights, a false certification to the court would constitute an ethical violation.

3. One practical obstacle to creating ethical rules particular to victims' rights is that ethical codes are regulated not by legislative arenas, where the victims' movement has had notable success, but by the legal profession and the courts.

4. For a closer look at prosecutorial ethics *see* Bennett Gershman, *Prosecutorial Ethics and Victims' Rights: The Prosecutors Duty of Neutrality*, 9 Lewis & Clark L. Rev. 559 (2005).

2. The Inferior Remedy of Money Damages

The victims' rights laws of the vast majority of jurisdictions ban any civil cause of action for money damages against the government or courts for failure to notify the victim of or comply with victim's rights. For example, Ohio Constitution, art.1 § 10a provides:

> This section does not confer upon any person a right to appeal or modify any decision in a criminal proceeding, . . . and does not create any cause of action for compensation or damages against the state, any political subdivision of the state, any officer, employee, or agent of the state or of any political subdivision, or any office of the court.

What effect do these limitations have on a victim's efforts to obtain monetary damages? Consider the following effort by an Ohio victim to pursue a civil rights action for a victims' rights violation:

Pusey v. Youngstown
11 F.3d 652 (6th Cir. 1993)

Plaintiff Ethel L. Pusey appeals the District Court's summary judgment dismissing plaintiff's claims in this 42 U.S.C. § 1983 action against an assistant prosecutor in her personal and official capacities, and against the City of Youngstown for her alleged failure to comply with Ohio's victim impact law. For the reasons stated below, we affirm.

Plaintiff filed an action against defendant Maureen Cronin, a City of Youngstown prosecutor, and the City of Youngstown, alleging that the defendants deprived her of her First Amendment right to free speech and her constitutional right to access to the courts. Plaintiff's claims arise out of Cronin's handling of the prosecution of one Eric Bator for the death of plaintiff's son, Derrell Pusey. Bator was initially charged with involuntary manslaughter.

Ohio Rev. Code § 2937.081 requires the prosecutor assigned to certain charged crimes, including involuntary manslaughter, to provide the victim, or the victim's next of kin, with notice of the date, time and place of the trial pertaining to the particular offense or if the prosecution is resolved without trial, the date, time and place at which a guilty plea will be entered.[3]

Section 2937.081(B) provides,

> [A] prosecutor who is assigned for prosecution a criminal case that includes one or more charges of . . . [involuntary manslaughter] . . . shall notify the victim of each offense or count charged of the date, time, and place of the trial pertaining to the particular offense or count, or if the particular offense or count charged is resolved without trial, the date, time, and place at which the prosecutor will enter a nolle prosequi pertaining to the offense or count, at which a plea of guilty or no contest pertaining to the offense or count will be entered, or at which the final disposition of the offense or count otherwise will be made. The notification required by this division shall be provided in accordance with division (E) of this section. Subdivision E provides that the prosecutor may give notification either by mail or orally. *See* OHIO REV. CODE § 2937.081(E).

On September 27, 1991, at a status conference on the case, Cronin entered a nolle prosequi to the charge under OHIO REV. CODE § 2903.04 (involuntary manslaughter) and charged Bator under section 2903.05 (negligent homicide). Bator pleaded no contest to the reduced charge and the plea was accepted by the municipal court. The court scheduled sentencing for December 13, 1991. Plaintiff was not present at the September 27, 1991, hearing.

Plaintiff and her counsel claim Cronin deprived plaintiff of her constitutional rights by failing to notify her that the charge would be reduced at the September 27, 1991, hearing. Cronin, in her affidavit in support of her motion for summary judgment, states that Cronin met with plaintiff on September 25, 1991, and advised plaintiff that there would be a status conference with the judge on September 27, 1991, at which time the charges might be reduced. Her affidavit also states that she orally advised plaintiff's attorney of the status conference.

Ohio Rev. Code § 2937.081 does not require a prosecutor to provide notice when the crime charged is negligent homicide. Cronin nonetheless notified plaintiff that Bator's sentencing hearing on the negligent homicide charge was set for December 13, 1991. Plaintiff attended and spoke at this hearing but the municipal court refused to

---

3. Under Ohio Revised Code § 2943.041(A), if a person is charged with certain crimes (including involuntary manslaughter, but not including negligent homicide), and that charge is resolved in any way except for trial, the court shall determine whether the victim of the act that was the basis of the charge, or a representative member of the victim's family if the victim died as a result of that act, is present at the hearing or proceeding at which the charge is resolved. If the court determines that . . . a representative member of the victim's family is present . . . [the court] shall inform the . . . representative family member that he is entitled to make a statement relative to the victimization and, if applicable, the sentencing of the offender, and the court, subject to any reasonable terms and conditions it imposes, shall permit the victim or representative family member, if he so desires, personally to make such a statement.

allow her attorney to speak for her or to allow her to read a motion to vacate Bator's no contest plea to the reduced charge. Plaintiff argues that Cronin had a duty as an officer of the court to inform the trial judge that the judge's actions were in violation of plaintiff's statutory and constitutional rights.

As a result of the charge reduction and sentencing hearing, plaintiff filed a 42 U.S.C. § 1983 claim against Cronin and the City. Plaintiff alleged that Cronin's failure to notify her that the charges might be reduced, her failure to inform the judge of his obligations to crime victims at the reduction hearing, and Cronin's failure to advise the judge at sentencing that plaintiff had the right to counsel in connection with her exercise of rights under the Ohio victim impact laws, deprived her of her First Amendment right to free speech and denied her access to the courts. Defendants moved for summary judgment on all claims which the District Court granted. This timely appeal followed.

III

As an initial matter, we note that plaintiff cannot complain about Cronin's actions with regard to the sentencing hearing. At that time, Bator had pled guilty to negligent homicide. Ohio Revised Code § 2937.081(B) does not require that the prosecutor give notice to the victim or the victim's family when the charge involved is negligent homicide. Thus, any claim that her rights were violated with regard to the sentencing hearing is without merit.

Additionally, plaintiff alleges that the prosecutor committed a constitutional tort by failing to advise the judge at the sentencing hearing that plaintiff was entitled to assistance of counsel. There is absolutely no basis in law for plaintiff to claim that the prosecutor has deprived her of her constitutional rights because of a failure on the part of a prosecutor to correct the trial judge. Plaintiff does not point to any constitutional or statutory duty of prosecutors to tell the judge before whom they appear that the judge is wrong in his or her ruling.

Finally, plaintiff claims that the prosecutor violated plaintiff's constitutional rights by failing to inform the judge of his obligations to crime victims at the charge reduction hearing. Again, there is no constitutional or other duty on a prosecutor to correct the trial judge.

IV.

We turn then to plaintiff's claim that Cronin violated plaintiff's constitutional rights by failing to tell her that the charge might be reduced at the September 27, 1991 hearing. Under 42 U.S.C. § 1983, plaintiff must establish that Cronin deprived plaintiff of her federal statutory or constitutional rights under color of state law. *Gomez v. Toledo*, 446 U.S. 635, 640 (1980). The parties do not dispute that Cronin acted under color of state law. *The only question is whether plaintiff was deprived of a federal right.* Plaintiff argues Cronin has deprived her of her constitutional substantive due process rights and her procedural due process rights. These alleged rights include her liberty interest in free access to the courts and her First Amendment right to freedom of expression.

A. Procedural Due Process

"We examine procedural due process questions in two steps: the first asks whether there exists a liberty or property interest which has been interfered with by the State, the second examines whether the procedures attendant upon that deprivation were constitutionally sufficient." *Kentucky Dep't of Corrections v. Thompson,* 490 U.S. 454, 460 (1989) (citations omitted). Liberty interests derive from both the Due Process Clause itself and the laws of the states. *Id.* Plaintiff clearly rests the establishment of her liberty interests on Ohio law. Initially, we must determine whether the Ohio crime victim's statute establishes a federally enforceable procedural right. To determine if state law establishes a protected liberty interest we must closely examine the state's statutes and regulations. To establish a liberty interest, the state law must use "'explicitly mandatory language,' in connection with the establishment of 'specified substantive predicates' to limit discretion" of those to whom the statutory duty applies. *Id.* at 463. "[T]he most common manner in which a State creates a liberty interest is by establishing 'substantive predicates' to govern official decisionmaking, and, further, by *mandating the outcome to be reached upon a finding that the relevant criteria have been met.*" *Id.* at 462, (emphasis added).

Ohio Rev. Code § 2937.081 requires the prosecutor assigned to certain charged crimes, including involuntary manslaughter, to provide the victim, or the victim's next of kin, with notice of the date, time and place of the trial pertaining to the particular offense or if the prosecution is resolved without trial, the date, time and place at which a guilty plea will be entered. This statute extends procedural rights, notice, to crime victims but fails "to protect a substantive interest to which the individual has a legitimate claim of entitlement." *Olim v. Wakinekona,* 461 U.S. 238, 250 (1983). "[A]n expectation of receiving process is not, without more, a liberty interest protected by the Due Process Clause." *Id.* at 250, n. 12. *The Ohio victim impact law does not create a liberty interest here because it only provides that the victim has the right to be notified.* The statute does not specify how the victim's statement must affect the hearing nor does it require a particular outcome based on what the victim has said. Thus, plaintiff has failed to establish that Ohio Rev. Code § 2937.081 creates a constitutionally protected liberty interest.

B. Substantive Due Process

Plaintiff also argues that she suffered a deprivation of her substantive due process rights by Cronin's failure to notify her that the charge might be reduced at the September 27, 1991 hearing. The Sixth Circuit has recognized that substantive due process claims arise in a variety of contexts. Deprivations of substantive due process can be divided into "(1) deprivations of a particular constitutional guarantee and (2) actions that 'shock the conscience.'" *Mansfield Apartment Owners Ass'n v. City of Mansfield,* 988 F.2d 1469, 1474 (6th Cir.1993) (citing *Braley v. City of Pontiac,* 906 F.2d 220, 224–225 (6th Cir.1990)).

Plaintiff argues that Cronin's failure to notify her that the charge might be reduced subjected her to governmental action which "shocks the conscience." However, the

Sixth Circuit has stated that use of the "shock the conscience" test is problematic in areas other than excessive force. *Braley,* 906 F.2d at 226. This case does not concern physical force, and we see nothing shocking in the prosecutor's conduct here.

Plaintiff next argues that even if Cronin's actions did not shock the conscience, her failure to notify was arbitrary and capricious in violation of her liberty and expressive interests. We conclude that plaintiff's failure to notify was neither arbitrary nor capricious.

Finally, plaintiff argues that Cronin's failure to notify plaintiff that the charge might be reduced deprived her of her right to freedom of expression and access to the courts as protected by substantive due process. Plaintiff argues Cronin deprived her of her constitutional rights by failing to notify her because exercise of plaintiff's constitutional rights necessarily hinged on notification of the hearing. Even assuming that an expressive right or right to access to the courts exists in this context, we conclude that Cronin's failure to notify plaintiff did not deprive plaintiff of a particular constitutional guarantee. Cronin's failure to notify plaintiff did not prohibit her from attending the hearing or speaking at the hearing. Thus, we conclude that Cronin's failure to notify plaintiff did not deprive her of any substantive due process rights.

Cronin did not deprive plaintiff of her procedural or substantive due process rights and therefore we affirm the District Court's order granting summary judgment to Cronin and the City. Although our conclusion that plaintiff was not deprived of any federal statutory or constitutional rights requires a dismissal of her section 1983 action, we will nevertheless address alternative bases for denying liability.

V.

Initially, we address plaintiff's argument that Cronin is liable under 42 U.S.C. § 1983 in both her official and personal capacities.

A. Official Capacity

In an official capacity action, the plaintiff seeks damages not from the individual officer, but from the entity for which the officer is an agent. The Supreme Court has concluded that, "an official-capacity suit is, in all respects other than name, to be treated as a suit against the entity." *Kentucky v. Graham,* 473 U.S. 159, 166 (1985).

The District Court granted summary judgment dismissing all claims against Cronin in her official capacity. The District Court concluded that Cronin was a state employee and suits against state officers acting in their official capacities are not cognizable under section 1983. *Will v. Michigan Dept. of State Police,* 491 U.S. 58, 71 (1989). The District Court reasoned that Cronin was a state employee because she is an officer of the municipal court which is an arm of state government. However, both parties concede on appeal that the District Court erred when it concluded that Cronin was a state employee. Rather, as both parties noted on appeal, Cronin is an employee of the City of Youngstown.

While we agree with the parties that Cronin is employed by the City of Youngstown, we nevertheless conclude that plaintiff's suit must fail as Cronin acted on behalf of the state when she was prosecuting state criminal charges and reduced the charge at the September 27, 1991 hearing. City prosecutors are responsible for prosecuting state criminal charges. *See* Ohio Rev. Code §§ 1901.34(C), 309.08. Clearly, state criminal laws and state victim impact laws represent the policy of the state. Thus, a city official pursues her duties as a state agent when enforcing state law or policy. *Cf. Scott v. O'Grady*, 975 F.2d 366 (7th Cir. 1992), *cert. denied*, 508 U.S. 942 (1993); *Echols v. Parker*, 909 F.2d 795 (5th Cir. 1990). Because Cronin acts as a state agent when prosecuting state criminal charges, the suit against Cronin in her official capacity is to be treated as a suit against the state. Again, a suit against a state is not cognizable under 42 U.S.C. § 1983. *Will*, 491 U.S. at 71.[4]

Although the District Court granted summary judgment for Cronin in this official capacity action for other reasons, we affirm the District Court's order because Cronin is entitled to summary judgment on other grounds. *Russ' Kwik Car Wash, Inc. v. Marathon Petroleum Co.*, 772 F.2d 214, 216 (6th Cir. 1985) (per curiam).

B. Personal Capacity

Plaintiff also alleged a section 1983 action against Cronin in her personal capacity. However, an official sued in her personal capacity may assert the common law defenses of absolute and qualified immunity. Indeed, the District Court dismissed the claims against Cronin in her personal capacity, ruling that Cronin was absolutely immune from suit.

As an initial matter, we note that plaintiff appeared to concede at oral argument that Cronin is entitled to absolute immunity. However, we address this issue to make clear that prosecutors are entitled to absolute immunity for a failure to notify victims under a victim impact law.

To determine whether a prosecutor is entitled to absolute or qualified immunity for a particular act, we must examine the "nature of the function performed, not the identity of the actor who performed it." *Forrester v. White*, 484 U.S. 219, 229 (1988). In *Imbler v. Pachtman*, 424 U.S. 409 (1976), the Court held that prosecutors sued in their personal capacity under section 1983 are absolutely immune for their conduct in "initiating a prosecution and in presenting the State's case." *Id.* at 431. The Court reasoned that the prosecutors' "activities were intimately associated with the judicial phase of the criminal process." *Id.* at 430. The Court expressly reserved determination of absolute immunity for a prosecutor when she acts in the role of an administrator or investigative officer rather than that of an advocate. *Id.* at 431. More recently, in *Burns v. Reed*, 500 U.S. 478 (1991), the Court concluded that a

---

4. Plaintiff argues that even if a damages action against Cronin in her official capacity is prohibited by the Eleventh Amendment, prospective relief is not prohibited. *Ex parte Young*, 209 U.S. 123 (1908). Plaintiff therefore seeks relief requiring Cronin to conform with constitutional standards. While the Eleventh Amendment does not bar such a suit, prospective relief is not available because we have concluded that Cronin did not violate any constitutional guarantees. Further, plaintiff has failed to allege that she is likely to be in this situation again.

prosecutor is not entitled to absolute immunity when acting as an administrator or investigator, for example, when a prosecutor gives legal advice to police. *See also Buckley v. Fitzsimmons,* 509 U.S. 259 (1993).

Plaintiff argues that the prosecutor is not entitled to absolute immunity for failing to give notice to her because the duty to notify was an investigative or administrative duty. Sixth Circuit precedent has established that "the critical inquiry is how closely related is the prosecutor's challenged activity to his role as an advocate intimately associated with the judicial phase of the criminal process." *Joseph v. Patterson,* 795 F.2d 549, 554 (6th Cir. 1986), *cert. denied,* 481 U.S. 1023 (1987).

We conclude that the prosecutor's failure to notify plaintiff of the September 27, 1991 hearing, where Bator's charge was reduced and he entered a guilty plea, is within the prosecutor's function as an advocate for the state as it is intimately associated with the judicial phase of the criminal process. The court hearing where the charge was reduced and a guilty plea was entered involved a judicial act. Furthermore, the prosecutor's determination to notify or failure to notify is intimately associated with the hearing and is simply a litigation-related duty. Giving notice to witnesses, victims or defendants is certainly one of those core prosecutorial functions which is protected by absolute immunity.

Thus, the District Court correctly determined that Cronin is entitled to absolute immunity from suit in her personal capacity and we affirm the order dismissing all claims against Cronin in her personal capacity. . . .

VI.

We next address plaintiff's section 1983 claim against the City of Youngstown.

To the extent that plaintiff's claim against the City derives from an allegation of wrongdoing on the part of Cronin, it is barred under *Monell v. Department of Social Servs.,* 436 U.S. 658, 691 (1978). A municipality is not liable under 42 U.S.C. § 1983 for its employees' acts on a respondent superior theory. Additionally, as stated, Cronin was acting on behalf of the state when she prosecuted state criminal charges and therefore her actions in prosecuting the charge, at that point, could not be attributed to the City. Municipal liability arises under section 1983 for unconstitutional policies or customs. *Id.* Plaintiff failed to allege any unconstitutional City policy or custom in her complaint.

Plaintiff did argue in her brief in opposition to the City's motion for summary judgment, that Cronin's failure to notify plaintiff may have been pursuant to an unconstitutional custom of the City. A course of conduct constitutes a custom when "such practices of state officials [are] so permanent and well-settled" as to constitute law. *Monell,* 436 U.S. at 691. The plaintiff suggested no facts to support a custom of failing to notify victims. Cronin's affidavit, which was unrefuted, states that she told plaintiff before the September 27, 1991 hearing that charges against Bator might be reduced. Under these circumstances, we see no reason to permit plaintiff to amend at this time to allege a violation of a custom or policy.

For the reasons stated above, we AFFIRM the District Court's order granting summary judgment for the defendants.

Douglas E. Beloof, *The Third Wave of Victims' Rights: Standing Remedy and Review*

2005 B.Y.U. L. Rev. 255

One potential inferior remedy is to make constitutional torts available to compensate victims for rights violations. Citizens have this monetary damages remedy available in other contexts, for example, when their Fourth Amendment right to privacy is violated by the police. While virtually all states ban money damages for victims' rights violations, constitutions could be amended to allow for this remedy. Nevertheless, there are at least three significant obstacles to the inferior remedy of money damages. First, victims' rights are typically violated by prosecutors and judges who are shielded by sovereign immunity and, therefor, cannot be sued for most types of rights violations. "It is always agreed that an immunity protects . . . judges . . . so long as their acts are 'judicial' in nature and within the very general scope their jurisdiction. It applies in civil rights cases . . .[5] "[T]he judicial immunity has always been extended to prosecuting attorneys . . ." Judges are immune even from malicious acts. Prosecutors may be liable for civil rights violations done maliciously. If judges are completely shielded from liability, and prosecutors potentially exposed only when they are malicious, the monetary remedy is simply unavailable for the vast majority of victims' rights violations. . . .

Even where monetary damages are available, it is unlikely victims would collect sufficient damages to deter government misconduct. Substantial damages are intuitively appropriate when a home is wrongfully invaded and searched, a suspect is beaten, or a person falsely arrested. On the other hand, the violation of, for example, a victims' right to speak at sentencing is far harder to quantify. Moreover, a judge who violated the right could readily testify in the civil trial that exactly the same sentence would have been imposed if the victims' right been honored. This likely would eliminate damages or, at least reduce the damages award to relative insignificance. Even if the measure of damages were not the different sentence, but the lost opportunity to be heard, it is unlikely substantial damages would be awarded for such a loss. In sum, with limited damages comes limited deterrence for rights violations and no meaningful remedy.

Notes

1. In the face of some laws with mandatory state constitutional language directing the prosecution to consult with the victim concerning plea bargaining, and where the laws do not preclude civil remedies, there *may* be a cause of action for money damages

---

5. W. Page Keeton, Prosser and Keaton on Torts (5th ed. 1984) Ch. 25 § 132, p. 1056–69.

against the prosecutor which the victim can pursue. *See Knutson v. County of Maricopa, ex rel. Romley*, 857 P.2d 1299 (Ariz. App. 1993) (denying damages only because the constitutional right had not yet taken effect.)

2. ARIZONA REV. STAT. § 13-4437(1)(B). Standing to invoke rights; recovery of damages A victim has the right to recover damages from a governmental entity responsible for the intentional, knowing or grossly negligent violation of the victim's rights under the victims' bill of rights, article II, section 2.1, Constitution of Arizona, any implementing legislation or court rules. Nothing in this section alters or abrogates any provision for immunity provided for under common law or statute.

3. The creation of state constitutional rights might establish a basis for judicially created remedies. However, as discussed above, many state constitutional provisions expressly prohibit monetary damages.

3. The Inferior Remedies of Injunctions and Declaratory Relief

In certain circumstances, a victim might seek an injunction to enforce victims' rights. Injunctions are difficult to obtain, as shown in the following case about police procedures.

City of Los Angeles v. Lyons
461 U.S. 95 (1983)

Justice WHITE delivered the opinion of the Court.

The issue here is whether respondent Lyons satisfied the prerequisites for seeking injunctive relief in the federal district court.

I

This case began on February 7, 1977, when respondent, Adolph Lyons, filed a complaint for damages, injunction, and declaratory relief in the United States District Court for the Central District of California. The defendants were the City of Los Angeles and four of its police officers. The complaint alleged that on October 6, 1976, at 2 a.m., Lyons was stopped by the defendant officers for a traffic or vehicle code violation and that although Lyons offered no resistance or threat whatsoever, the officers, without provocation or justification, seized Lyons and applied a "chokehold"—either the "bar arm control" hold or the "carotid-artery control" hold or both—rendering him unconscious and causing damage to his larynx. Counts I through IV of the complaint sought damages against the officers and the City. Count V, with which we are principally concerned here, sought a preliminary and permanent injunction against the City barring the use of the control holds. That count alleged that the city's police officers, "pursuant to the authorization, instruction and encouragement of defendant City of Los Angeles, regularly and routinely apply these choke holds in innumerable situations where they are not threatened by the use of any deadly force whatsoever," that numerous persons have been injured as the result of the application of the chokeholds, that Lyons and others similarly situated are threatened with irreparable injury in the form of bodily injury and loss of life, and that Lyons "justifiably fears that any contact he has with Los Angeles police officers may result in his being choked and strangled to death without provocation, justification or other legal excuse." Lyons alleged the threatened impairment of rights protected by the First, Fourth, Eighth and Fourteenth Amendments. Injunctive relief was sought against the use of the control holds "except in situations where the proposed victim of said control reasonably appears to be threatening the immediate use of deadly force." Count VI sought declaratory relief against the City, *i.e.*, a judgment that use of the chokeholds absent the threat of immediate use of deadly force is a *per se* violation of various constitutional rights.

The District Court, by order, granted the City's motion for partial judgment on the pleadings and entered judgment for the City on Count V and VI. The Court of Appeals reversed the judgment for the City on Count V and VI, holding over the City's objection that despite our decisions in *O'Shea v. Littleton,* 414 U.S. 488 (1974), and *Rizzo v. Goode,* 423 U.S. 362 (1976), Lyons had standing to seek relief against the application of the chokeholds. 615 F.2d 1243. The Court of Appeals held that there was a sufficient likelihood that Lyons would again be stopped and subjected to the unlawful use of force to constitute a case or controversy and to warrant the issuance of an injunction, if the injunction was otherwise authorized. We denied certiorari. 449 U.S. 934.

On remand, Lyons applied for a preliminary injunction. Lyons pressed only the Count V claim at this point. The motion was heard on affidavits, depositions and government records. The District Court found that Lyons had been stopped for a traffic infringement and that without provocation or legal justification the officers involved had applied a "department-authorized chokehold which resulted in injuries to the plaintiff." The court further found that the department authorizes the use of the holds in situations where no one is threatened by death or grievous bodily harm, that officers are insufficiently trained, that the use of the holds involves a high risk of injury or death as then employed, and that their continued use in situations where neither death nor serious bodily injury is threatened "is unconscionable in a civilized society." The court concluded that such use violated Lyons' substantive due process rights under the Fourteenth Amendment. A preliminary injunction was entered enjoining "the use of both the carotid-artery and bar arm holds under circumstances which do not threaten death or serious bodily injury." An improved training program and regular reporting and record keeping were also ordered. The Court of Appeals affirmed in a brief *per curiam* opinion stating that the District Court had not abused its discretion in entering a preliminary injunction. 656 F.2d 417 (1981). We granted certiorari, 455 U.S. 937 (1982), and now reverse. . . .

III

It goes without saying that those who seek to invoke the jurisdiction of the federal courts must satisfy the threshold requirement imposed by Article III of the Constitution by alleging an actual case or controversy. . . . Plaintiffs must demonstrate a "personal stake in the outcome" in order to "assure that concrete adverseness which sharpens the presentation of issues" necessary for the proper resolution of constitutional questions. *Baker v. Carr*, 369 U.S. 186 (1962). Abstract injury is not enough. The plaintiff must show that he "has sustained or is immediately in danger of sustaining some direct injury" as the result of the challenged official conduct and the injury or threat of injury must be both "real and immediate," not "conjectural" or "hypothetical. . . ."

In *O'Shea v. Littleton*, 414 U.S. 488 (1974), we dealt with a case brought by a class of plaintiffs claiming that they had been subjected to discriminatory enforcement of the criminal law. Among other things, a county magistrate and judge were accused of discriminatory conduct in various respects, such as sentencing members of plaintiff's class more harshly than other defendants. The Court of Appeals reversed the dismissal of the suit by the District Court, ruling that if the allegations were proved, an appropriate injunction could be entered.

We reversed for failure of the complaint to allege a case or controversy. 414 U.S., at 493. Although it was claimed in that case that particular members of the plaintiff class had actually suffered from the alleged unconstitutional practices, we observed that "[p]ast exposure to illegal conduct does not in itself show a present case or controversy regarding injunctive relief . . . if unaccompanied by any continuing, present adverse effects." *Id.* at 495–496. Past wrongs were evidence bearing on "whether there is a real and immediate threat of repeated injury." *Id.* at 496. But the prospect of future injury rested "on the likelihood that [plaintiffs] will again be arrested for and charged with violations of the criminal law and will again be subjected to bond proceedings, trial, or sentencing before petitioners." *Ibid.* The most that could be said for plaintiffs' standing was "that *if* [plaintiffs] proceed to violate an unchallenged law and *if* they are charged, held to answer, and tried in any proceedings before petitioners, they will be subjected to the discriminatory practices that petitioners are alleged to have followed." *Id.* at 497. We could not find a case or controversy in those circumstances: the threat to the plaintiffs was not "sufficiently real and immediate to show an existing controversy simply because they anticipate violating lawful criminal statutes and being tried for their offenses. . . ." *Id.* at 496. It was to be assumed "that [plaintiffs] will conduct their activities within the law and so avoid prosecution and conviction as well as exposure to the challenged course of conduct said to be followed by petitioners." *Id.* at 497.

We further observed that case or controversy considerations "obviously shade into those determining whether the complaint states a sound basis for equitable relief," 414 U.S., at 499 and went on to hold that even if the complaint presented an existing case or controversy, an adequate basis for equitable relief against petitioners had not been demonstrated: [Plaintiffs] have failed, moreover, to establish the basic requisites of the issuance of equitable relief in these circumstances—the likelihood of substantial and immediate irreparable injury, and the inadequacy of remedies at law. We have already canvassed the necessarily conjectural nature of the threatened injury to which [plaintiffs] are allegedly subjected. And if any of the [plaintiffs] are ever prosecuted and face trial, or if they are illegally sentenced, there are available state and federal procedures which could provide relief from the wrongful conduct alleged.

Another relevant decision for present purposes is *Rizzo v. Goode,* 423 U.S. 362 (1976), a case in which plaintiffs alleged widespread illegal and unconstitutional police conduct aimed at minority citizens and against City residents in general. The Court reiterated the holding in *O'Shea* that past wrongs do not in themselves amount to that real and immediate threat of injury necessary to make out a case or controversy. The claim of injury rested upon "what one or a small, unnamed minority of policemen might do to them in the future because of that unknown policeman's perception" of departmental procedures. 423 U.S., at 372. This hypothesis was "even more attenuated than those allegations of future injury found insufficient in *O'Shea* to warrant [the] invocation of federal jurisdiction." *Ibid.* The Court also held that plaintiffs' showing at trial of a relatively few instances of violations by individual police officers, without any showing of a deliberate policy on behalf of the named defendants, did not provide a basis for equitable relief.

Golden v. Zwickler, 394 U.S. 103 (1969), a case arising in an analogous situation, is directly apposite. Congressman Zwickler sought a declaratory judgment that a New York statute prohibiting anonymous handbills directly pertaining to election campaigns was unconstitutional. Although Zwickler had once been convicted under the statute, he was no longer a Congressman apt to run for reelection. A unanimous Court held that because it was "most unlikely" that Zwickler would again be subject to the statute, no case or controversy of "sufficient immediacy and reality" was present to allow a declaratory judgment. 394 U.S., at 109. Just as Zwickler's assertion that he could be a candidate for Congress again was "hardly a substitute for evidence that this is a prospect of 'immediacy and reality,'" *ibid.,* Lyons' assertion that he may again be subject to an illegal chokehold does not create the actual controversy that must exist for a declaratory judgment to be entered.

We note also our *per curiam* opinion in *Ashcroft v. Mattis,* 431 U.S. 171 (1977). There, the father of a boy who had been killed by the police sought damages and a declaration that the Missouri statute which authorized police officers to use deadly force in apprehending a person who committed a felony was unconstitutional. Plaintiff alleged that he had another son, who "*if* ever arrested or brought under an attempt at arrest on suspicion of a felony, *might* flee or give the appearance of fleeing, and would therefore be *in danger* of being killed by these defendants or other police officers . . ." 431 U.S., at 172–173, n. 2. We ruled that "[s]uch speculation is insufficient to establish the existence of a present, live controversy." *Ibid.*

IV

No extension of *O'Shea* and *Rizzo* is necessary to hold that respondent Lyons has failed to demonstrate a case or controversy with the City that would justify the equitable relief sought. Lyons' standing to seek the injunction requested depended on whether he was likely to suffer future injury from the use of the chokeholds by police officers.

Count V of the complaint alleged the traffic stop and choking incident five months before. That Lyons may have been illegally choked by the police on October 6, 1976, while presumably affording Lyons standing to claim damages against the individual officers and perhaps against the City, does nothing to establish a real and immediate threat that he would again be stopped for a traffic violation, or for any other offense, by an officer or officers who would illegally choke him into unconsciousness without any provocation or resistance on his part. The additional allegation in the complaint that the police in Los Angeles routinely apply chokeholds in situations where they are not threatened by the use of deadly force falls far short of the allegations that would be necessary to establish a case or controversy between these parties.

In order to establish an actual controversy in this case, Lyons would have had not only to allege that he would have another encounter with the police but also to make the incredible assertion either, (1) that *all* police officers in Los Angeles *always* choke any citizen with whom they happen to have an encounter, whether for the purpose of arrest, issuing a citation or for questioning or, (2) that the City ordered or authorized police officers to act in such manner. Although Count V alleged that the City authorized the use of the control holds in situations where deadly force was not threatened, it did not indicate why Lyons might be realistically threatened by police officers who acted within the strictures of the City's policy. If, for example, chokeholds were authorized to be used only to counter resistance to an arrest by a suspect, or to thwart an effort to escape, any future threat to Lyons from the City's policy or from the conduct of police officers would be no more real than the possibility that he would again have an encounter with the police and that either he would illegally resist arrest or detention or the officers would disobey their instructions and again render him unconscious without any provocation.

V.

Lyons fares no better if it be assumed that his pending damages suit affords him Article III standing to seek an injunction as a remedy for the claim arising out of the October 1976 events. The equitable remedy is unavailable absent a showing of irreparable injury, a requirement that cannot be met where there is no showing of any real or immediate threat that the plaintiff will be wronged again—a "likelihood of substantial and immediate irreparable injury." *O'Shea v. Littleton,* 414 U.S., at 502. The speculative nature of Lyons' claim of future injury requires a finding that this prerequisite of equitable relief has not been fulfilled.

Nor will the injury that Lyons allegedly suffered in 1976 go unrecompensed; for that injury, he has an adequate remedy at law. Contrary to the view of the Court of Appeals, it is not at all "difficult" under our holding "to see how anyone can ever challenge police or similar administrative practices." 615 F.2d, at 1250. The legality of the violence to which Lyons claims he was once subjected is at issue in his suit for damages and can be determined there.

Absent a sufficient likelihood that he will again be wronged in a similar way, Lyons is no more entitled to an injunction than any other citizen of Los Angeles; and a federal court may not entertain a claim by any or all citizens who no more than assert that certain practices of law enforcement officers are unconstitutional. . . . This is not to suggest that such undifferentiated claims should not be taken seriously by local authorities. Indeed, the interest of an alert and interested citizen is an essential element of an effective and fair government, whether on the local, state or national level. A federal court, however, is not the proper forum to press such claims unless the requirements for entry and the prerequisites for injunctive relief are satisfied.

As we noted in *O'Shea,* 414 U.S., at 503, withholding injunctive relief does not mean that the "federal law will exercise no deterrent effect in these circumstances." If Lyons has suffered an injury barred by the Federal Constitution, he has a remedy for damages under § 1983. Furthermore, those who deliberately deprive a citizen of his constitutional rights risk conviction under the federal criminal laws. *Ibid.*

Beyond these considerations the state courts need not impose the same standing or remedial requirements that govern federal court proceedings. The individual states may permit their courts to use injunctions to oversee the conduct of law enforcement authorities on a continuing basis. But this is not the role of a federal court absent far more justification than Lyons has proffered in this case.

The judgment of the Court of Appeals is accordingly *Reversed.*

Justice MARSHALL, with whom Justice BRENNAN, Justice BLACKMUN and Justice STEVENS join, dissenting.

The District Court found that the City of Los Angeles authorizes its police officers to apply life-threatening chokeholds to citizens who pose no threat of violence, and that respondent, Adolph Lyons, was subjected to such a chokehold. The Court today holds that a federal court is without power to enjoin the enforcement of the City's policy, no matter how flagrantly unconstitutional it may be. Since no one can show that he will be choked in the future, no one — not even a person who, like Lyons, has almost been choked to death — has standing to challenge the continuation of the policy. The City is free to continue the policy indefinitely as long as it is willing to pay damages for the injuries and deaths that result. I dissent from this unprecedented and unwarranted approach to standing.

There is plainly a "case or controversy" concerning the constitutionality of the City's chokehold policy. The constitutionality of that policy is directly implicated by Lyons' claim for damages against the City. The complaint clearly alleges that the officer who choked Lyons was carrying out an official policy, and a municipality is liable under 42 U.S.C. § 1983 for the conduct of its employees only if they acted pursuant to such a policy. *Monell v. New York City Dept. of Social Services,* 436 U.S. 658, 694 (1978). Lyons therefore has standing to challenge the City's chokehold policy and to obtain whatever relief a court may ultimately deem appropriate. None of our prior decisions suggests that his requests for particular forms of relief raise any additional issues concerning his standing. Standing has always depended on whether a plaintiff has a "personal stake in the outcome of the controversy," *Baker v. Carr,* 369 U.S.

186 (1962), not on the "precise nature of the relief sought." *Jenkins v. McKeithen*, 395 U.S. 411, 423 (1969) (opinion of MARSHALL, J., joined by WARREN, C.J., and BRENNAN, J.)....

Notes

1. In *Lyons*, the District Court had "found that Lyons had been stopped for a traffic infringement and that without provocation or legal justification the officers involved had applied a department-authorized chokehold which resulted in injuries to the plaintiff." Thus, the District Court had necessarily found by a preponderance of the evidence (the burden of proof for civil injunctions) that Lyons was the victim of an assault by police.

2. Under some state laws, injunctions are theoretically available against prosecutors. As a general rule, such injunctions are available only when the prosecutor acts maliciously. Furthermore, to obtain an injunction, a victim would have to demonstrate an ongoing pattern of rights violations. This is a substantial undertaking. Such an effort would require access to the names of large numbers of crime victims to gather sufficient evidence to demonstrate that prosecutors or judges were engaging in an ongoing pattern of rights violations. Even if such an investigation were practically feasible or lawful, such intrusions on the privacy of crime victims runs counter to ensuring the values of dignity and privacy of victims that underlie victims' rights. Outside of the context where there is a pattern, it is difficult, if not impossible, to predict when in the future an individual victim's right will be violated. A crime victim who seeks an injunction can expect the same standards in *Lyons* to apply to them. A victim then would have to prove that the prosecutor, for example, would deny them their same rights in the future. Typically, this would mean predicting another crime. If the victim wanted to be sure the prosecutor did not violate another victims' right as the original case proceeded, the court may well perceive this as too speculative a harm.

3. The same case or controversy considerations that prevented Lyons from obtaining an injunction may come into play to put the declaratory judgment remedy beyond victims' reach. In *Lyons*, the court cites *Golden v. Zwickler*, 394 U.S. 103 (1969), in which the plaintiff brought a motion for declaratory judgment. The *Lyons* court stated: "Zwickler's assertion that he could be a candidate for congress again was hardly a substitute for evidence that this is a prospect of immediacy and reality. ...."

4. Utah has a specific provision allowing for declaratory relief. *See* Utah Code Ann.§ 77-38-11(1). *See generally,* Paul G. Cassell, *Balancing the Scales of Justice: The Case for and the Effects of Utah's Victims' Rights Amendment,* 1994 Utah L. Rev. 1373, 1419 (discussing Utah's declaratory relief).

4. The Inferior Remedy of Administrative Review

Administrative review of victims' rights violations may be institutionalized. Like all inferior remedies, this does nothing to ensure that victims whose rights are violated can actually exercise their rights in the cases involving their victimization. Furthermore, there are severe limits on what administrative bodies can accomplish. It is unlikely that the judicial branch, attorneys' general and county prosecutors will support the creation of a separate agency that exercises actual authority over them. Moreover, separation of powers problems hamper any administrative authority over judges. Finally, any hope that such a body could discipline violators of victims' rights is unrealistic. Because transgressors are lawyers and judges, only state and the federal supreme courts and their authorized processes can lawfully discipline bar members for improper conduct falling within the purview of prosecutorial and judicial ethics.

Left without any real authority over judicial and prosecutorial agencies, administrative bodies could not insist on any systemic improvements to ensure rights compliance. Such an agency may add value to the extent that prosecutors and judges take agency advise to correct systemic problems that institutionalize victims' rights violations. *See* Nat'l Crim. Justice Assoc. 168099, *Victims' Rights Compliance Efforts: Experiences in Three States* (Office for Victims of Crime Report, May 1998) (reviewing administrative compliance programs in Colorado, Minnesota and Wisconsin).

———————

Twelve years after Professor Beloof expressed reservations about the propriety of executive administrative authority over courts, the Wisconsin Supreme Court held that a legislatively created Crime Victims' Rights Board had no power to sanction judges who violate victims' rights because it violated separation of powers. Only the Wisconsin Supreme Court and its authorized processes may discipline judges.

The Wisconsin Supreme Court opined:

> In creating an executive branch entity with authority to pass judgment and impose discipline on a judge's exercise of core judicial powers, the Wisconsin legislature violates the Wisconsin Constitution's structural separation of powers and invades a domain recognized for over two hundred years as the exclusive province of the judiciary. Neither the executive branch nor the legislature may reprimand or otherwise discipline a Wisconsin judge. The Wisconsin Constitution reserves such disciplinary powers for the supreme court alone. Nor may the legislature empower the executive branch to threaten any judicial officer with repercussions for exercising constitutional power vested exclusively in the judiciary.

> "Encroachment on judicial power degrades the judicial independence that serves as a bulwark protecting the people against tyranny. By statutorily authorizing executive action against the judiciary, the legislature unconstitutionally conferred power on an executive board to impair, improperly influence, and regulate the judiciary's exercise of its constitutional duties. Specifically, the legislature transgressed the constitutional boundaries of its powers by authorizing the Crime Victims' Rights Board (the Board) to investigate and adjudicate complaints against judges, issue

reprimands against judges, and seek equitable relief and forfeitures through civil actions against judges. We therefore affirm the decision of the circuit court and hold that Wis. Stat. §§ 950.09(2)(a), (2)(c)–(d) and (3) and 950.11 (2015–16)1 are unconstitutional with respect to judges; accordingly, the Board's actions against Judge William M. Gabler are void.

Gabler v. Crime Victims Rights Board, 376 Wis. 2d 147, 897 N.W.2d 384 (2017).

Notes

1. *See* Bruce Vielmetti, *Wisconsin Supreme Court Slaps Down Crime Victims' Rights Board on Judicial Sanctions*, Milwaukee Journal Sentinel, June 28, 2017.

2. Wisconsin is currently moving toward Marsy's Law, which promotes the superior remedy of rights enforceable in appellate courts.

D. Appellate Court Review

An appellate review relating to a crime victim's right can originate in many different ways, most including defense appeals claiming that a victim's right interfered with a defendant's right. This section focuses on victim-initiated efforts to obtain appellate review of trial court decisions denying them rights in the criminal process.

1. The Need for a Victim to Have "Standing" to Pursue Appellate Review

In the Oklahoma City bombing trial, the district judge ruled that victims who would testify at the sentencing phase could not attend the trial. The victims appealed to the Tenth Circuit, relying on former federal statutes creating crime victims' rights to attend trial.

United States v. McVeigh
106 F.3d 325 (10th Cir. 1997)

In these consolidated proceedings, we address an important question of criminal procedure involving significant interests of the defendants, prosecution, crime victims, and public, which has thus far received virtually no judicial attention: whether a pretrial order prohibiting victim-impact witnesses from attending the criminal prosecution in which they are slated to testify is subject to review at the urging of either the government or the nonparty witnesses themselves. Upon careful consideration of the various constitutional and statutory ramifications, we conclude as a general matter, and hold in this particular case, that it is not, though we do not categorically rule out the possibility of mandamus relief for the government in the event of a patently unauthorized and pernicious use of the sequestration power.

In early pretrial hearings, the district court invoked, originally on its own initiative and, thereafter, at the insistence of defense counsel, the traditional rule authorizing the sequestration of witnesses. *See* Fed.R.Evid. 615 ("At the request of a party the court shall order witnesses excluded so that they cannot hear the testimony of other witnesses, and it may make the order of its own motion."). Later, in response to an extensively briefed and formally argued request for reconsideration, the district court reaffirmed its adherence to Rule 615, prompting the current proceedings for review.

The government and the excluded witnesses filed separate appeals, Nos. 96-1469 and 96-1475, respectively, which defendants moved to dismiss on procedural grounds. The excluded witnesses then filed a petition for a writ of mandamus, No. 96-1484, and the government added an informal request for mandamus consideration, both seeking to secure an alternative avenue of review in the event their appeals were deemed defective. This court consolidated all of the proceedings and granted expedited review. The briefs of the parties and amici[1] have now been filed, putting the case at issue. On de novo consideration of the fundamental threshold questions raised by defendants' motions, *see Wilson v. Glenwood Intermountain Properties, Inc.*, 98 F.3d 590, 593 (10th Cir. 1996) (standing); *Comanche Indian Tribe v. Hovis*, 53 F.3d 298, 302 (10th Cir.) (jurisdiction), *cert. denied*, 116 S.Ct. 306, 133 L.Ed.2d 210 (1995), we dismiss the government's appeal on jurisdictional grounds, deny as inappropriate its request for mandamus review, and dismiss the excluded witnesses' appeal and mandamus petition for lack of standing.

· · ·

II

Defendants have raised numerous challenges to the proceedings for review brought by the sequestered victim-impact witnesses themselves. However, we find it necessary to address only the issue of standing. As "an essential and unchanging part of the case-or-controversy requirement of Article III," *Lujan v. Defenders of Wildlife*, 504 U.S. 555, 560 (1992), constitutional standing "is a threshold issue in every case before a federal court, determining the power of the court to entertain the suit." *Boyle v. Anderson*, 68 F.3d 1093, 1100 (8th Cir. 1995), cert. denied, 116 S.Ct. 1266 (1996); *see Board of Natural Resources v. Brown*, 992 F.2d 937, 945 (9th Cir. 1993). Further, Article III standing is a jurisdictional requisite "at every stage of the proceeding." *Citizens Concerned for Separation of Church & State v. City & County of Denver*, 628 F.2d 1289, 1301 (10th Cir. 1980). Accordingly, the excluded witnesses' failure to satisfy constitutional standing requirements would preclude our consideration of both their appeal and their petition for mandamus relief.[7]

---

1. We grant motions filed by The Criminal Justice Legal Foundation and The National Victims Center, Mothers Against Drunk Driving, The National Victims' Constitutional Amendment Network, Justice for Surviving Victims, Inc., Concerns of Police Survivors, Inc., and Citizens for Law and Order, Inc., to submit amicus curiae briefs in support of the appellants.

7. We do *not* hold that the lack of what is often called "appellate standing" necessarily precludes mandamus review. Standing encompasses "constitutional considerations related to the 'case or

Article III imposes three fundamental requirements for standing in federal court:

> First, the [complainant] must have suffered an injury in fact an invasion of a legally protected interest which is concrete and particularized and actual or imminent. Second, a causal connection must exist between the injury and the conduct complained of; the injury must be fairly traceable to the challenged action. Third, it must be likely that the injury will be redressed by a favorable decision.

Committee to Save the Rio Hondo v. Lucero, 102 F.3d 445, 447 (10th Cir. 1996) (quotations and citations omitted). Our disposition turns on the first.

Legally protected interests derive from various sources, including constitutional guarantees, *see, e.g., Journal Publ'g Co.*, 801 F.2d at 1235, statutory provisions, *see, e.g., Wilson*, 98 F.3d at 595, and common law rights, *see, e.g., W.H.I., Inc.*, 992 F.2d at 1064 (enjoyment of property rights). *See also, e.g., San Diego County Gun Rights Comm. v. Reno*, 98 F.3d 1121, 1126–30 (9th Cir. 1996) (discussing constitutional, statutory, and common law economic interests supporting standing). The victim-impact witnesses rely on two of these sources for their asserted interest in attending the criminal trial from which they have been excluded by the sequestration order. First, they cite the Victims' Rights and Restitution Act (Victims' Rights Act) for the particularized right of crime victims "to be present at all public court proceedings related to the offense." 42 U.S.C. § 10606(b)(4). Second, they argue more generally that the right of public access to criminal proceedings, recognized in *Richmond Newspapers, Inc. v. Virginia*, 448 U.S. 555 (1980) (plurality), and *Globe Newspaper Co. v. Superior Court*, 457 U.S. 596 (1982), provides a constitutional basis for their claim of injury.

A

There are a number of problems with the excluded witnesses' reliance on the Victims' Rights Act.[8] The statute charily pledges only the "best efforts" of certain executive branch personnel to secure the rights listed. *See* § 10606(a) ("Officers and employees

_____

controversy' limitation of Article III and also prudential concerns 'that, apart from Art. III's minimum requirements, serve to limit the role of the courts in resolving public disputes.'" *Kansas Health Care Ass'n v. Kansas Dep't of Social & Rehabilitation Servs.*, 958 F.2d 1018, 1021 (10th Cir. 1992) (quoting *Warth v. Seldin*, 422 U.S. 490, 498–500, 95 S.Ct. 2197, 2205–06, 45 L.Ed.2d 343 (1975)). Article III authority is a prerequisite to judicial review, however sought. In contrast, a prudential concern, such as nonparty status, counseling uniquely or primarily against the propriety of appeal, need not bar a petition for mandamus review. *See, e.g., Journal Publ'g Co. v. Mechem*, 801 F.2d 1233, 1235–36 (10th Cir. 1986) (news organization had Article III standing to seek mandamus review of order barring press access, although, as nonparty, it could not challenge order by appeal); *United States v. Schlette*, 842 F.2d 1574, 1576 (9th Cir. 1988) (same); *In re Washington Post Co.*, 807 F.2d 383, 388 & n. 4 (4th Cir. 1986) (same). We emphasize that our standing analysis turns on constitutional considerations, not the excluded witnesses' nonparty status. Consequently, we need not treat separately the district court's denial of their motion to intervene.

8. In conjunction with the Victims' Rights Act, the excluded witnesses also refer generally to 42 U.S.C. § 10608, which provides for closed circuit televising of certain criminal proceedings. This statute does not materially impact our construction and application of § 10606, or our standing analysis generally.

of . . . departments and agencies of the United States engaged in the detection, investigation, or prosecution of crime shall make their best efforts to see that victims of crime are accorded the rights described in subsection (b) of this section."). The district court judge, a judicial officer not bound in any way by this pledge, could not violate the Act. Indeed, the Act's prescriptions were satisfied once the government made its arguments against sequestration before the district court even ruled.

Further, the specific right to attend criminal proceedings is expressly subject to the following qualification: "unless the court determines that testimony by the victim would be materially affected if the victim heard other testimony at trial." § 10606(b)(4). In essence, the statute acknowledges that the policies behind Rule 615 inherently limit the victim's right to attend criminal proceedings.

Finally, and in any event, Congress explicitly instructed that the Act "does not create a cause of action or defense in favor of any person arising out of the failure to accord to a victim the rights enumerated in subsection (b)." § 10606(c). The excluded witnesses argue this provision relates only to independent enforcement actions and does not bar appeal or mandamus challenges within the criminal proceeding itself, but this facially uncompelling contention is undercut further by a decision of this court in an analogous standing context. In *United States v. Kelley*, 997 F.2d 806, 807–08 (10th Cir. 1993), we joined a line of authority holding that crime victims do not have standing under the Victim and Witness Protection Act (VWPA), 18 U.S.C. § 3663, to appeal unfavorable restitution orders. Significantly, this case law rejects victims' arguments for standing under the VWPA because the history and plain language of the VWPA "do not indicate that Congress, either explicitly or implicitly, intended to provide a private cause of action to victims." *Kelley*, 997 F.2d at 808 (quoting *United States v. Johnson*, 983 F.2d 216, 221 (11th Cir. 1993)). A fortiori, the Victims' Rights Act, which explicitly denies any private cause of action, does not grant standing to seek review of orders relating to matters covered by the Act. *See also Hernandez-Avalos v. INS*, 50 F.3d 842, 844, 848 (10th Cir.) (holding party lacked standing to invoke mandamus to enforce statutory directive in light of express prohibition on private right of action in statute), *cert. denied*,116 S. Ct. 92 (1995).

B

Our analysis of the excluded witnesses' constitutional basis for standing rests on a fundamental distinction regarding the character and locus of the public right of access to criminal proceedings derived from the First Amendment by the Supreme Court in *Richmond Newspapers* and *Globe Newspaper Co.* The witnesses do not assert, nor could they, that an order precluding (only) intended witnesses from attending a criminal proceeding generally open to the public and the press violates the public's right of access. Rather, they posit a personal First Amendment right to attend the proceedings, violated despite the public's undisputed access. In our view, recognition of such an entitlement, arguably affording a constitutional basis for disruptive interlocutory review in every criminal prosecution at the behest of any disappointed would-be trial attendee, would entail an unprecedented expansion/transformation of the public trial-access right unwarranted by the policies cited by the Supreme Court as the rationale for gleaning the right from the First Amendment.[9]

A broad survey of public trial-access case law, and review of the particular authorities relied on by the excluded witnesses here, confirm that pertinent constitutional proscriptions are implicated only when, through orders closing proceedings, sealing documents, gagging participants and/or restricting press coverage, a trial court has deprived the public at large direct or indirect access to the trial process. The witness-sequestration order entered in this case has no such effect; members of the public will attend the trial and the press will report on the proceedings to the public generally. We are not aware of any case in which an analogous order was held to implicate the constitutional right recognized in *Richmond Newspapers* and *Globe Newspaper Co.*

Just as important, this assessment of the case law is entirely consistent with the broad, structural interests prompting the Supreme Court to recognize the public trial-access right despite the lack of explicit textual support in the constitution. Such interests include: informing the public discussion of government affairs, assuring the public perception of fairness, promoting the community-therapeutic effect of criminal justice proceedings, providing a public check on corrupt practices, intimidating potential perjurers, and generally enhancing the performance of all involved in the process. *See Globe Newspaper Co.*, 457 U.S. at 604–05; *United States v. Criden*, 675 F.2d 550, 556 (3rd Cir. 1982) (summarizing "six societal interests" cited in *Richmond Newspapers* plurality and concurring opinions). These interests necessitate and are satisfied by a publicly open trial, regardless of the personal attendance of any particular individual. Indeed, "[t]he value of openness lies in the fact that people not actually attending trials can have confidence that standards of fairness are being observed." *Press-Enterprise Co. v. Superior Court*, 464 U.S. 501, 508 (1984).

Accordingly, we hold that the excluded witnesses lack Article III standing to seek review of the sequestration order entered by the district court. We therefore do not have jurisdiction to reach the merits of either their appeal or their mandamus petition.

Notes

1. The Oklahoma congressional delegation, distressed that the approximately 30 victims who were to testify at the sentencing phase of the *McVeigh* trial would be excluded from the trial phase, quickly sponsored the Victims Rights Clarification Act of 1997 (VRCA), which became law. The VRCA provides:

18 U.S.C. § 3510. Rights of victims to attend and observe trial

(a) Non-capital cases. — Notwithstanding any statute, rule, or other provision of law, a United States district court shall not order any victim of an

---

9. We need not and do not address entirely distinct questions regarding the propriety and redress of trial exclusions implicating other constitutional values, such as equal protection or traditional free speech guarantees.

offense excluded from the trial of a defendant accused of that offense because such victim may, during the sentencing hearing, make a statement or present any information in relation to the sentence.

(b) Capital cases.—Notwithstanding any statute, rule, or other provision of law, a United States district court shall not order any victim of an offense excluded from the trial of a defendant accused of that offense because such victim may, during the sentencing hearing, testify as to the effect of the offense on the victim and the victim's family or as to any other factor for which notice is required under section 3593(a).

The VRCA on its face allowed for the Oklahoma City bombing victims who were to testify at sentencing to attend the trial. It seemed as if the victims had a green light to attend the trial. In fact, it was only a yellow light. The trial court judge elected not to rule on the constitutionality of the VRCA until after the trial phase. *United States v. McVeigh*, 958 F. Supp. 512 (D. Colo. 1997). According to Professor Paul Cassell, who represented some of these victims throughout their effort to attend the trial, the delay on the ruling of constitutionality left the victims in a quandary. If they attended the trial they risked being excluded from testifying at sentencing.

Some victims stayed away from the trial. After the trial phase, the judge ruled that the VRCA was constitutional. Nevertheless, those victims who observed the trial were examined by the court in order to determine whether the testimony they were to offer at sentencing had become tainted by what they heard at the trial. Clearly, despite the new law, the trial judge had determined that he still had authority to prohibit the testimony of these victims if their testimony was tainted.

2. The VRCA is limited in scope to a narrow class of crime victims. These are victims who are to testify at sentencing as "impact" witnesses, but who have no testimony to offer during the trial as witnesses to the crime. This narrow class mostly covers surviving family members of persons who are victims of homicide and terrorism, or both, who also are not witnesses to the crime. The majority of victims of violent crime witness the crime and live to tell about it. These victims can still be excluded from the trial by either the United States Justice Department or the defendant as a matter of right pursuant to FRE 615.

3. The lack of victim "standing" identified by the Tenth Circuit in the *McVeigh* decision can be remedied by a statute specifically conferring standing. And, in 2004, Congress specifically gave crime victims standing in the federal system with the passage of the Crime Victims Rights Act. The CVRA specifically provides that "[t]he crime victim or law representative . . . may assert the rights described [under the Act]." 18 U.S.C. § 3771(d)(1). In discussing the import of this provision, the sponsors of the CVRA stated that "[t]his legislation is meant to correct, not continue, the legacy of the poor treatment of crime victims in the criminal process. This legislation is meant to ensure that cases like the *McVeigh* case, where victims of the Oklahoma City bombing were effectively denied the right to attend the trial, [never occur again] and to avoid federal appeals courts from determining, as the Tenth Circuit

Court of Appeals did, that victims had no standing to seek review of their right to attend the trial under the former victims' law that this bill replaces." 150 Cong. Rec. S4260-01, S4269 (Apr. 22, 2004) (statement of Sen. Feinstein).

2. Victims' Rights as Mandatory and Self-Enabling Rights

Related to the problem of standing discussed by the Tenth Circuit in the *McVeigh* case is the question of whether crime victims' rights should be viewed "mandatory" and therefore fully enforceable in appellate and other courts without the need for victims to rely on other statutes or whether they should be viewed as mere advisory and aspirational targets for government action, needing further statutes to take effect. The drafter's of victims' rights legislation have generally sought to create mandatory rights. But sometimes, the court have taken a different view.

Douglas E. Beloof, *The Third Wave of Crime Victims' Rights*
2005 B.Y.U. L. Rev. 255 (2005)

Implicit in the court's analysis [in the *McVeigh* case] is that courts cannot enforce these rights because they are advisory, rather than mandatory. The consequence of advisory victims' rights is that victims do not have standing in appellate courts. Compared with concrete rights that are enforceable on review, federal statutory victims' rights were illusory.

Fortunately, no state constitutional victims' rights provision contains such advisory language. Nevertheless, contrary to the plain meaning of their constitutions, two state courts have declared that plainly mandatory rights are, instead, advisory rights. In the Kansas case of *State v. Holt*, 874 P.2d 1183 (Kans. 1994), the trial judge refused to delay a judicial probation hearing of a misdemeanant to allow the victim to be heard. Under the Kansas Constitution, victims are entitled to "certain basic rights . . . including the right to be informed of and to be present at public hearings, as defined by law . . . and to be heard at sentencing." Kans. Const., art. XV, § 15. Because victims' rights under the Kansas Constitution apply only to public hearings, the case squarely presented the issue of whether a misdemeanor probation hearing is a "public hearing." Ultimately, the Kansas Supreme Court held that "[t]here is nothing in our . . . law which requires a public hearing" in misdemeanor probation hearings.

Under Kansas' precedent, constitutional questions are only addressed when unavoidable. In Holt, the constitution was not implicated because the hearing was not a "public hearing" and victims have no rights at nonpublic hearings. There was no legitimate reason for the court to extend itself to address other constitutional issues because the constitution was not implicated.

Nevertheless, the Holt court went out of its way to render illusory what are transparently mandatory state constitutional victims' rights. In dicta, the court declared the entire victims' rights amendment to be advisory. In Kansas, victims' rights are set forth in mandatory language. The Kansas Constitution provides that "[v]ictims of crime . . . shall be entitled to certain basic rights." KANS. CONST., art. XV, § 15(a). As discussed above, conventional interpretation is that mandated language means mandatory rights. Furthermore, the conventional interpretation of rights in bills of rights is that they are mandatory, and victims' rights are placed within the Kansas Bill of Rights.

There are other persuasive reasons why Kansas' constitutional rights are mandatory. The constitutional provision takes pains to assert that in the case of conflict between victims' rights and defendants' rights, defendants' rights prevail. *Id.* Absolutely no reason exists to include this language if it was not the clear intent that these were mandatory rights. The constitutional provision also states that the legislature "may" provide for other remedies. KANS. CONST., art. XV, § 15(b). This enforcement provision does not strip the rights of their mandatory nature, but rather allows the legislature, as well as the courts, to establish remedies for adequate enforcement. What is more informing about this language is that the Kansas amendment clearly anticipates rights enforcement. Such enforcement is not possible in an advisory rights scheme.

Additional evidence that these rights are mandatory is found in language limiting the civil liability of the state if rights are violated. The Kansas victims' rights provision reads: "Nothing in this section shall be construed as creating a cause of action for money damages against the state, a county, a municipality, or any of the agencies, instrumentalities, or employees thereof." *Id.* Clearly this provision is to limit state judicial creation of *Bivens* type actions — torts derived from violations of mandatory constitutional rights. It would be pointless to limit Bivens actions for advisory rights, as no mere advisory right could be the basis of such a suit. This is because the government cannot be held liable for acting within lawful discretion that exists when rights are advisory. Moreover, other remedies are expressly precluded in the victims' rights provision of the Kansas Constitution. For example, the constitution prohibits reversal of a guilty finding as a remedy to comply with victims' rights. KANS. CONST., art. XV, § 15(c). Such a restriction is completely unnecessary unless remedial enforcement of mandatory rights was contemplated.

Furthermore, the Holt court implies that because the constitution and the statute share the same language, there is no legally significant distinction between the two: "Although [the victims' rights constitutional amendment] was adopted by the voters in 1992, it appears that the constitutional provision does not provide any greater rights than those already granted by statute." *State v. Holt*, 874 P.2d 1183, 1186 (Kan. 1994).

To imply that a constitutional right is the equivalent of a statute is a fundamental constitutional error. Constitutional, rather than statutory, conventions become determinative of whether the right is mandatory and enabled because "[t]he rules distinguishing mandatory and directory statutes are of little value and are rarely applied in ruling upon the provisions of a constitution." Only by defying important constitutional canons and ignoring a handful of others could the Kansas Supreme Court reach its ill-conceived result — that victims' rights are not mandatory. The unprincipled result in Holt strips Kansas victims of standing despite the over-whelming weight of constitutional canons to the contrary.

––––––––––

Contrary to the view taken by the Kansas Supreme Court in *Holt*, most courts have found that victims' rights are mandatory rights. The rights appear in state bills of rights, are labeled "rights," and the rights are conditioned by the term "shall have the following rights" (or similar language). As such, the rights are not merely advisory rights or aspirational rights. Such rights have the force of state constitutional law if they are enabled. Constitutional provisions are either self-enabling or must be legislatively enabled. Constitutional civil rights, like crime victims' rights are generally self-enabling. If rights are not self-enabling they have no force of law until the legislature enables them. For example, all of a criminal defendants' rights under state constitutions are self-enabling. The following Alaska appellate court opinion produces a result in keeping with the conventions of constitutional interpretation.

Landon v. State

1999 WL 46543 (Alaska App. 1999)

Unpublished opinion before COATS, C.J., MANHEIMER and STEWART, JJ.

MEMORANDUM OPINION AND JUDGMENT

COATS, C.J.

A jury convicted Shelton Landon of violating a domestic violence restraining order and criminal mischief in the third degree, both class A misdemeanors. District Court Judge James N. Wanamaker imposed a total composite sentence of 720 days. Landon contends that Judge Wanamaker erred by denying his pretrial motion to exclude the victim from the courtroom during the testimony of other witnesses and by imposing an excessive sentence. We affirm.

On September 5, 1996, Anchorage Police Officer Michael A. Couturier served a domestic restraining order on Landon providing at length that Landon stay away from A.B. and her residence and not to stalk or harass her. The order was to remain in effect for twenty days, but, at a court proceeding on September 23 at which Landon was telephonically present, this order was extended for another six months. In the early morning of October 11, 1996, Anchorage Police Officer Gerald A. Wesley responded to A.B.'s residence, where he found that seven tires had been slashed on the two vehicles parked at that residence. At trial, Wesley testified that when he arrived at the scene, A.B., who appeared very upset and excited, reported that she had just seen Landon running away from the scene. Wesley also testified that he later found and arrested Landon. Wesley testified that neither A.B. nor any other witness had given him any description of Landon's clothing, but did not testify as to what clothing Landon was wearing when he arrested him.

A.B. testified at trial that she had been in her home watching television when she heard a loud popping sound from outside; ab ran outside, where she heard the sound of air hissing out of her tires, and saw Landon running away from the scene and into his car. A.B. testified that she got a clear look at Landon, making eye contact with him; she also testified that she recognized Landon's car (a distinctive gray Nissan) and the red coat that Landon usually wore.

Before the trial, on December 10, 1996, the state issued a written notice of its intent, in accordance with Article I, Section 24, of the Alaska Constitution Court.[11] to have the victim A.B. present throughout the trial proceedings. Landon filed an opposition to this notice and cited Alaska Evidence Rule 615[12] and various provision of the Alaska and United States Constitutions. Second, Landon argues that his "right to due process conflicts with the Victims' Rights Act. In such cases, due process is the superior right." However, numerous courts have considered this issue and have concluded that a defendant has no constitutional right to exclude witnesses from the courtroom during the testimony of other witnesses. We see no reason not to follow the reasoning of these cases. Therefore, we conclude A.B.'s presence during Landon's trial did not violate his due process rights.

Third, Landon asserts that Judge Wanamaker erred when he relied upon Section 24 of the Alaska Constitution in deciding to allow A.B. to remain in the courtroom during Landon's trial. As noted above, Section 24 provides that "[c]rime victims, as defined by law, shall have the following rights as provided by law: . . . the right . . . to be present at all criminal or juvenile proceedings where the defendant has the right to be present[.]"

Landon points out that, at the time of his trial, the Alaska Legislature had not enacted any legislation to implement Section 24. (Again, as noted above, the

---

11. Article I, Section 24 of the Alaska Constitution, also known as the Victims' Rights Amendment, states, in pertinent part: "Rights of Crime Victims. Crime victims, as defined by law, shall have the following rights as provided by law: . . . the right to obtain information about and be allowed to be present at all criminal or juvenile proceedings where the accused has the right to be present."

12. On December 16, in open court, A.B. personally asserted her constitutional right to be present at Landon's trial. After hearing arguments, Judge Wanamaker issued a written order excluding witnesses from the trial proceedings but specifically excepting Landon himself, Wesley, and A.B. At the conclusion of the evidence at trial, the jury convicted Landon of both charges. On appeal, Landon presents three arguments for his contention that Judge Wanamaker erred when he permitted A.B. to remain in the courtroom throughout the trial. First, Landon asserts that A.B.'s presence during the testimony of other witnesses violated his constitutional right to confrontation. In particular, Landon notes that A.B. heard Wesley testify that no witness had given him a description of Landon or his clothing and then later testified herself that "she recognized the defendant, in part, because of the red coat the defendant was wearing when he allegedly ran from her residence." Landon suggests that A.B. could have shaded or altered her testimony as a result of hearing Wesley's testimony, thereby depriving him of his right to "test A.B.'s memory, ability to perceive and relate, and the factual basis of her statements." Landon, like A.B., was able to remain through the entire trial and hear the testimony of all the witnesses before testifying. Landon was able to cross-examine A.B. fully and was free to point out through questioning and argument that A.B.'s testimony might have been influenced by her opportunity to observe the other witnesses testify. We conclude that A.B.'s presence at trial did not violate Landon's right to confront A.B.

legislature has since enacted AS 12.61.010, Alaska's "Victims' Rights Act." Landon argues that Section 24 is not self-implementing; he further argues that, because the legislature had not yet enacted any implementing legislation, Judge Wanamaker could not properly rely on this constitutional provision when he ruled on Landon's motion to exclude A.B. from the trial.

We disagree with Landon's assertion that Section 24 is not self-implementing. The Alaska Constitution itself provides that, to the extent possible, all "provisions of this constitution shall be construed to be self-executing." Examining Section 24, we conclude that it is possible and thus constitutionally necessary to construe the section as self-executing.

Section 24 declares that crime victims have a series of rights among them, the right to be present at criminal proceedings when the defendant has a right to be present. True, Section 24 allows the legislature to define "crime victim" by "law" that is, by legislation. Further, Section 24 states that crime victims shall have the listed rights "as provided by law" thus, presumably authorizing the legislature to enact procedures to govern crime victims' exercise of the listed rights and perhaps to define the scope of those rights in particular situations. Yet, under the facts of Landon's case, there can be no reasonable dispute that A.B. qualified as the "victim" of Landon's crimes, and no reasonable dispute that Landon (and thus A.B.) had the right to be present during Officer Wesley's testimony. Because the situation presented in Landon's case is one of the "core" situations described in Section 24, we conclude that this constitutional provision provided adequate legal authority for Judge Wanamaker's ruling, even though the legislature had not yet enacted the Victims' Rights Act.

. . .

We AFFIRM the convictions and sentence.

3. Review by Writ

As an alternative to filing an appeal, should crime victims be able to seek appellate review of their claims by filing a petition for a writ of mandamus with an appellate court? A writ of mandamus or writ of prohibition in the context of victim rights is an order to a judge or prosecutor to obey mandatory law by engaging in a duty under law or refraining from exceeding their authority. Should crime victims' rights enactments allow victims to file for writ rather than take an appeal to ensure victims' rights are enforced? Consider the following views on this subject.

Douglas E. Beloof, *The Third Wave of Victims' Rights: Standing Remedy and Review*

2005 B.Y.U. L. Rev. 255

An effective means of securing appellate review, assuming the constitutional victims' rights themselves do not preclude it, is to expressly provide for a means of review in constitutions or enabling statutes. There are some state laws that expressly provide for review mechanisms. Two state constitutions explicitly provide for actions to compel government officials to obey victims' rights. The constitution of South Carolina provides that enforcement of victims' rights is by mandamus. The Nevada constitution provides that an action to compel the government to comply with the right is available. Utah law specifically provides that victims may use mandamus to enforce their rights. Arizona has abolished the old form of writs and in its place created "special actions," which crime victims may bring to enforce their rights. Maryland has the right to appeal from an interlocutory or final order that denies or fails to consider a victims' right. Utah statutes also provide for declaratory judgment actions, mandamus and appeal. Michigan statutes allow a victim to appeal to a circuit court judge the parole board's granting of parole.

By granting victims "standing to enforce the rights . . .", the Texas constitution implicitly provides for some sort of review procedure. Florida and Indiana statutes grant victims "standing." In these eight jurisdictions with express review or standing provisions, review of some sort is expressly available. Absent other restrictions in victims' state constitutional rights, writs are implicitly available. Even in the states which have expressly banned appeals, with the exception of Idaho, writs are available.

The problem in review of victims' rights is not the unavailability of writ review, but rather the discretionary nature of writs. The solution to the review problem is to provide for non-discretionary review of victims' rights violations. When victims were merely third parties defending evidentiary privileges or moving to quash subpoenas, the argument that discretionary review was sufficient was perhaps stronger. Today crime victims are participants with constitutional rights. Unlike third parties, victims have due process rights in the criminal process. Unlike third parties, victims' rights legitimize victims' interest in punishment. Procedures should be established granting victims the right to non-discretionary review of rights violations. It could not credibly be suggested that criminal defendants' constitutional rights are to be reviewed only in the discretion of the court. Crime victims' rights should be similarly respected. . . .

In an amendment to the Crime Victims' Rights Act, Congress expressly gave crime victims the right to pursue mandamus relief and required the courts of appeals to decide those petitions under an appellate standard of review. The CVRA provides:

> Motion for relief and writ of mandamus. — The rights described in subsection (a) shall be asserted in the district court in which a defendant is being prosecuted for the crime or, if no prosecution is underway, in the district court in the district in which the crime occurred. The district court shall take up and decide any motion asserting a victim's right forthwith. If the district court denies the relief sought, the movant may petition the court of appeals for a writ of mandamus. The court of appeals may issue the writ on the order of a single judge pursuant to circuit rule or the Federal Rules of

Appellate Procedure. The court of appeals shall take up and decide such application forthwith within 72 hours after the petition has been filed, unless the litigants, with the approval of the court, have stipulated to a different time period for consideration. In deciding such application, the court of appeals shall apply ordinary standards of appellate review. In no event shall proceedings be stayed or subject to a continuance of more than five days for purposes of enforcing this chapter. If the court of appeals denies the relief sought, the reasons for the denial shall be clearly stated on the record in a written opinion. 18 U.S.C. § 3771(d)(3).

This provision gives crime victims the kind of guaranteed access to the appellate courts Professor Beloof recommends. Before the amendment to the CVRA, federal courts were split on the question of whether a mandamus or appellate standard of review applied. *Compare Kenna v. U.S. Dist. Court for C.D. Cal.* 435 F.3d 1011, 1017 (9th Cir. 2006), with *In re Antrobus*, 519 F.3d 1123, 1124–1125 (10th Cir. 2008).

Notes

1. The cases reviewed earlier in this chapter in the voiding remedy section provide examples of courts that granted writ review absent express authority from the legislature.

2. Some courts have looked to the unavailability of an appeal as a basis for writ review. For example, *Ford v. State*, 829 So. 2d 946 (Fla. App. 2002), granted certiorari review for a violation of the victim's state constitutional right in the absence of any express legislation stating, "Our standard of review on this petition for certiorari is whether petitioner has demonstrated a departure from the essential requirements of law for which there will be no adequate remedy on appeal. *Bared & Co., Inc. v. McGuire*, 670 So. 2d 153 (Fla. 4th DCA 1996). Considering that the state concedes that the petitioner's rights as a victim have been denied as to restitution, and that this is a violation of a constitutional right for which there is no appellate remedy, we agree that the petitioner has demonstrated certiorari jurisdiction."

4. Appellate Review under General Appellate Statutes

Assuming that a victim has "standing" to pursue an appeal, can the victim take advantage of general appellate statutes to pursue an appeal? Or are appeals limited to the parties in the criminal case: the state and the defendant? Consider the following two federal cases that seemingly reach different conclusions to that question.

Doe v. United States
666 F.2d 43 1981 (4th Cir. 1981)

Butzner, Circuit Judge:

These appeals concern the district court's evidentiary ruling in a pre-trial proceeding held pursuant to rule 412 of the Federal Rules of Evidence. The court held that evidence concerning the past sexual behavior and habits of the prosecutrix was admissible in the rape trial of Donald Robert Black. We conclude that we have jurisdiction to hear her appeal, and we affirm in part and reverse in part the order of the district court.

The appellant is the alleged victim and chief government witness in the impending rape trial of Black. Pursuant to rule 412 of the Federal Rules of Evidence, Black made a pre-trial motion to admit evidence and permit cross-examination concerning the victim's past sexual behavior. After a hearing, the district court ruled that Black could introduce the evidence which he proffered.

Several days later, the district court granted Black's motion for the issuance of subpoenas for individuals who were to testify about the victim's sexual history. These included the victim's former landlord, a social worker who had previously investigated the victim, a sexual partner of the victim, and two people who claimed to be aware of the victim's reputation for promiscuity.

Thereafter, the victim instituted a civil action seeking the permanent sealing of the record of the rule 412 proceedings and other relief. During the course of this civil action, the court learned that the rape victim had not received notice of the earlier proceeding as mandated by subsection (c)(1) of rule 412. Consequently, it reopened the rule 412 hearing. The court then reaffirmed its prior ruling in the criminal case and entered summary judgment in favor of the defendants in the civil action. The victim appeals from the orders in both the civil and criminal actions.

Black asserts that this court lacks jurisdiction to entertain the victim's appeal from the district court's order in the rule 412 proceeding. Resolution of this issue requires an examination of the procedural provisions of the rule.

Rule 412 places significant limitations on the admissibility of evidence concerning the past sexual behavior of a rape victim. The rule provides the additional safeguard of a hearing in chambers to determine the admissibility of such evidence. These provisions were adopted "to protect rape victims from the degrading and embarrassing disclosure of intimate details about their private lives." 124 Cong.Rec. at H11945 (1978). To effectuate this purpose, subsections (c)(1) and (2) of the rule require that rape victims receive notice of the evidentiary hearing and a copy of the defendant's motion and offer of proof. Additionally, subsection (c)(2) makes provision for the victim's testimony at the evidentiary hearing.

The text, purpose, and legislative history of rule 412 clearly indicate that Congress enacted the rule for the special benefit of the victims of rape. The rule makes no reference to the right of a victim to appeal an adverse ruling. Nevertheless, this remedy is implicit as a necessary corollary of the rule's explicit protection of the privacy interests Congress sought to safeguard. *Cf. Cort v. Ash*, 422 U.S. 66 (1975). No other party in the evidentiary proceeding shares these interests to the extent that they might be viewed as a champion of the victim's rights. Therefore, the congressional intent embodied in rule 412 will be frustrated if rape victims are not allowed to appeal an erroneous evidentiary ruling made at a pre-trial hearing conducted pursuant to the rule.

Section 1291 of title 28 U.S.C. confers on courts of appeals jurisdiction to review final decisions of the district courts. The Supreme Court has held that this finality requirement should be "given a 'practical rather than a technical construction.'" *Gillespie v. U. S. Steel Corp.*, 379 U.S. 148, 152 (1964). The Court also has instructed that the most important considerations for determining whether an order is final are "the inconvenience and costs of piecemeal review on the one hand and the danger of denying justice by delay on the other." *Dickinson v. Petroleum Corp.*, 338 U.S. 507, 511 (1950).

In this case the balancing of these factors weighs heavily in favor of a conclusion of finality. The inconvenience and costs associated with permitting the victim to appeal are minimal. Certainly, they are no greater than those resulting from government appeals of suppression orders that are authorized by 18 U.S.C. § 3731. Because the rule provides for pre-trial evidentiary hearings, appeals are unlikely to involve significant postponements of criminal trials. Indeed, in this case, we heard the appeal and filed an order resolving the issues without any delay of the criminal trial.

On the other hand, the injustice to rape victims in delaying an appeal until after the conclusion of the criminal trial is manifest. Without the right to immediate appeal, victims aggrieved by the court's order will have no opportunity to protect their privacy from invasions forbidden by the rule. Appeal following the defendant's acquittal or conviction is no remedy, for the harm that the rule seeks to prevent already will have occurred. Consequently, we conclude that with respect to the victim the district court's order meets *Gillespie*'s test of practical finality, and we have jurisdiction to hear this appeal.

United States v. Hunter

548 F.3d 1308 (10th Cir. 2008)

Tacha, Circuit Judge:

I. BACKGROUND

Sometime during the summer of 2006, Mr. Hunter sold a handgun to Mr. Talovic, who at the time was seventeen years old. On February 12, 2007, Mr. Talovic entered the Trolley Square Shopping Center in downtown Salt Lake City, armed with the handgun from Mr. Hunter, a shotgun, and ammunition for both. Firing the weapons, he killed one person outside the mall and four more inside the mall. Ms. Quinn, who had been shot twice with the handgun, was one of these victims. Four other people were seriously wounded. Mr. Talovic's rampage ended when an off-duty police officer shot and killed him.

On May 16, 2007, a federal grand jury indicted Mr. Hunter on two felony counts: being a drug user in possession of a firearm, *see* 18 U.S.C. § 922(g)(3), and unlawfully transferring a firearm to a juvenile when knowing or having reason to know that the juvenile intended to use the firearm in committing a crime. *See* 18 U.S.C.

§ 922(x)(1); *id.* § 924(a)(6)(B)(ii). Pursuant to a plea agreement, Mr. Hunter pleaded guilty to the first count and to a new information that charged him with unlawfully transferring a firearm to a juvenile (without any allegation about knowledge), a misdemeanor. *See* 18 U.S.C. § 922(x)(1); *id.* § 924(a)(6)(B)(i). The government agreed to drop the second count, to recommend that Mr. Hunter receive full credit for acceptance of responsibility, and to recommend that Mr. Hunter be sentenced at the low end of the range set forth by the United States Sentencing Guidelines. The district court accepted the agreement in November 2007 and set sentencing for January 14.

On December 13, the Antrobuses moved under the CVRA for Ms. Quinn to be recognized as a victim of Mr. Hunter's unlawful transfer of a firearm. As the guardians of their deceased daughter, they sought, *inter alia,* the right to make a victim-impact statement and the right to restitution. *See* 18 U.S.C. § 3771(a), (d)(3). . . .

The district court concluded that Ms. Quinn was not a victim of Mr. Hunter's criminal gun sale and therefore denied the Antrobuses' motion. The district court reasoned that the unlawful sale was not the proximate cause of Ms. Quinn's death because it was not foreseeable that Mr. Talovic would use the gun in that manner. . . .

The Antrobuses then applied for a writ of mandamus under the CVRA, *see* 18 U.S.C. § 3771(d)(3), asking this court to declare their daughter a victim of Mr. Hunter's unlawful gun sale. *In re Antrobus,* 519 F.3d 1123, 1123 (10th Cir. 2008). Applying the mandamus standard of review, this court stated the Antrobuses' right to the writ was not "clear and indisputable." *Id.* at 1126. Therefore, we denied the writ. *Id.*

On January 14, 2007, the district court sentenced Mr. Hunter to fifteen months in prison and dismissed Count 2 of the indictment, pursuant to the plea agreement. Neither the government nor Mr. Hunter appealed. The Antrobuses, however, filed a timely notice of appeal. Their brief states that they are appealing "from the conviction and judgment entered by the [d]istrict [c]ourt . . . sentencing Mackenzie Glade Hunter to 15 months in prison, as well as the district court's denial of their motion to recognize Vanessa Quinn as a 'victim' under the Crime Victims' Right[s] Act." The government, supported by Mr. Hunter, moved to dismiss the appeal because the Antrobuses were not parties to the underlying criminal proceeding and therefore had no right to appeal from it.

II. DISCUSSION

A crime victim does not have an express right under the CVRA to appeal the defendant's conviction and sentence based on alleged violations of the statute. Rather, the CVRA provides that if the district court denies a crime victim his rights, the victim may immediately petition the court of appeals for a writ of mandamus. 18 U.S.C. § 3771(d)(3). The court of appeals must grant or deny the writ within seventy-two hours. *Id.* The government, however, may assert the victim's rights in any appeal of the defendant's conviction or sentence. *See id.* § 3771(d)(4) ("In any appeal in a criminal case, the Government may assert as error the district court's denial of any crime victim's right in the proceeding to which the appeal applies."); *see also In re*

Antrobus, 519 F.3d at 1129 ("While the CVRA provides individuals seeking review of a district court's 'victim status' decision with mandamus review, it simultaneously affords the government with the ability to obtain ordinary appellate review of the same decision.").

That the CVRA does not provide for victim appeals is consistent with the well-established precept that "only parties to a lawsuit, or those that properly become parties, may appeal an adverse judgment." *Marino v. Ortiz,* 484 U.S. 301, 304 (1988). According to the government, this is not simply a prudential consideration that delimits the rights of litigants; rather, it is a jurisdictional bar that "inheres" in 28 U.S.C. §1291. Thus, the government argues that we do not have jurisdiction under §1291 and must dismiss the Antrobuses' appeal on that basis.

The government's jurisdictional argument misses the mark. §1291 limits our appellate jurisdiction to "all final decisions of the district courts." It constrains what may be appealed, not who may bring such appeals. *See Bode v. Clark Equip. Co.,* 807 F.2d 879, 880–81 (10th Cir. 1986) ("That appellant is a nonparty does not affect our consideration whether the . . . order is appealable [as a final judgment]. Whether a nonparty may appeal, either from an interlocutory order or from a final judgment, is a separate question."). We therefore disagree with the government's position that we lack jurisdiction under §1291 to consider this appeal. . . .

Our inquiry turns, then, to the issue of whether non parties such as the Antrobuses have the right to appeal following a criminal sentence. The Antrobuses have cited several cases in which courts have heard non-party appeals. We find these cases distinguishable. More important, we are aware of no precedent for allowing a nonparty appeal that would reopen a criminal case following sentencing.

In *Devlin v. Scardelletti,* 536 U.S. 1 (2002), the Supreme Court allowed an unnamed class member to appeal from a class action settlement. 536 U.S. at 8–9. . . . *Devlin,* like many of the cases that the Antrobuses cite, is a civil case. On the issue of non-party appeals, there is an important distinction between civil and criminal cases. Civil cases often implicate the pecuniary rights of non-parties, such as the unnamed class member in *Devlin.*

Criminal trials, on the other hand, place an individual citizen against the United States government. While non-parties may have an interest in aspects of the case, they do not have a tangible interest in the outcome. This distinction is evidenced by our procedural rules. The Federal Rules of Civil Procedure allow non-parties to intervene to assert their rights. . . .

A series of restitution cases, however, stands for the proposition that nonparties have no right to post-judgment appeals in criminal cases. In *United States v. Kelley,* 997 F.2d 806 (10th Cir. 1993), the appellant claimed a right to restitution under the Victim and Witness Protection Act ("VWPA"), 18 U.S.C. §3663, but we followed the Eleventh and Second Circuits in holding that Congress neither explicitly nor implicitly provided in the VWPA a private right of action for victims. *Kelley,* 997 F.2d at 807–08. We concluded that this precluded victims from appealing restitution orders.

Kelley, 997 F.2d at 807–08. Similarly, the Eighth Circuit has denied victims the right to appeal from a criminal sentence and assert a right to restitution under the Mandatory Victims Rights Act ("MVRA"). *See United States v. United Sec. Sav. Bank,* 394 F.3d 564, 567 (8th Cir. 2004).

While the restitution issue is not perfectly analogous, those cases offer a significant parallel to the Antrobuses' case. First, restitution is one form of relief that the Antrobuses could seek if Ms. Quinn were granted victim status, just as the non-party appellants sought under the VWPA and the MVRA. *See* 18 U.S.C. § 3771(a)(6). Second, in each restitution case, a non-party tried to assert a right on appeal following a criminal prosecution. And in each instance, even though the non-party appellant had a pecuniary interest at stake, the court of appeals determined that the party could not bring a direct appeal.

There are, however, instances in which courts have allowed non-party appeals in criminal cases. The Antrobuses rely most heavily on our decision in *Anthony v. United States,* 667 F.2d 870 (10th Cir. 1981), the Fourth Circuit's decision in *Doe v. United States,* 666 F.2d 43 (4th Cir. 1981), and a variety of appeals involving the press.

In *Anthony,* the defendant was convicted of unlawfully wiretapping the telephone of Dr. Vernon Sisney. *Anthony,* 667 F.2d at 872. The defendant moved for a new trial based on newly discovered evidence-specifically, tapes that were the product of the defendant's wiretap on Dr. Sisney's phone. *Id.* Over Dr. Sisney's objection and motion to suppress, the district court ordered the discovery of the tapes. *Id.* at 873. Dr. Sisney appealed. Without specifically addressing the issue of non-party appeals, we concluded that Dr. Sisney had an explicit statutory right under 18 U.S.C. § 2518(10)(a) to object to the discovery and to move to suppress the evidence. *Id.* at 877. We then held that the non-final discovery order fell within the collateral-order exception to the final-judgment rule. *Id.* at 878.

In *Doe,* the defendant was charged with rape. *Doe,* 666 F.2d at 45. In a pre-trial motion, he sought to introduce evidence of the sexual history of the victim, who was the government's central witness. *Id.* The district court granted the motion, and the victim appealed. *Id.* The Fourth Circuit looked to Federal Rule of Evidence 412, which governs the admissibility of rape victims' sexual behavior. *Id.* at 46. Although that Rule does not refer to victims' appellate rights, the court held that an appellate remedy is implicit as a necessary corollary of the Rule's purpose in protecting victims. *Id.* Similar to this court in *Anthony,* the Fourth Circuit exercised jurisdiction over the interlocutory appeal on the basis of the order's practical finality. *Id.*

The Antrobuses also cite cases in which news organizations have appealed rulings denying them access to criminal trials. *See In re Subpoena to Testify Before Grand Jury Directed to Custodian of Records,* 864 F.2d 1559, 1561 (11th Cir. 1989) (allowing news organizations to appeal an order prohibiting counsel and parties from disclosing information about grand jury proceedings). . . .

There is a common thread in those criminal cases in which courts have permitted non-party appeals: the appeals all related to specific trial issues and did not disturb a final judgment. In fact, other than *Antar,* which simply unsealed voir dire transcripts, all of the cited appeals were interlocutory. For instance, the *Anthony* court assessed a discovery order. *Anthony,* 667 F.2d at 877. The *Doe* court assessed the admissibility of evidence at trial. *Doe,* 666 F.2d at 45. The media cases dealt with access during trials.

This distinction is significant. Unlike those cases, a successful appeal by the Antrobuses would produce the extraordinary result of reopening Mr. Hunter's sentence. Before sentencing, the Antrobuses sought to exercise their purported rights under the CVRA on the basis that their daughter was a victim of Mr. Hunter's unlawful sale of the firearm. The district court denied their request, and the Antrobuses properly pursued a writ of mandamus to challenge the district court's interlocutory order. They were denied relief, and Mr. Hunter was sentenced. If we were now to deem Ms. Quinn a victim under the CVRA, the Antrobuses would gain several rights, including the right to restitution and to speak at Mr. Hunter's sentencing hearing. 18 U.S.C. § 3771(a)(4), (6). The right to speak at sentencing could only be vindicated by reopening the sentencing proceeding. To our knowledge, there is no precedent— nor any compelling justification—for allowing a non-party, post-judgment appeal that would reopen a defendant's sentence and affect the defendant's rights. Indeed, the restitution cases cited above counsel against such a practice.

Several provisions of the CVRA further support our conclusion. The CVRA explicitly provides for a single avenue through which individuals may seek appellate review of the district court's application of the statute: mandamus. *See* 18 U.S.C. § 3771(d)(3). Given that the CVRA contains this express remedy, we are reluctant to read additional remedies—including the right to a direct appeal—into it.[8] *See Hartman v. Kickapoo Tribe Gaming Comm'n,* 319 F.3d 1230, 1232–33 (10th Cir. 2003) ("'[W]hen legislation expressly provides a particular remedy or remedies, courts should not expand the coverage of the statute to subsume other remedies.'") (quoting *Nat'l R.R. Passenger Corp. v. Nat'l Assoc. of R.R. Passengers,* 414 U.S. 453, 458 (1974)).

If individuals were allowed to re-open criminal sentences after all issues have been resolved—including any mandamus petitions by victims—then the government's prosecutorial discretion would be limited. A successful appeal by the Antrobuses would require a new sentencing hearing that could lead to a new sentence. *See id.* § 3771(a)(4). The government determined what it believed to be the proper sentence

---

8. The Second and Ninth Circuits have implied that they would agree with our conclusion, that mandamus is the only method by which a crime victim may appeal the denial of relief under the CVRA. In applying a traditional abuse-of-discretion review to the district court's decision—as opposed to the heightened level of review typically employed in mandamus actions—both circuits appeared to indicate that appellate rights are limited to mandamus actions under § 3771(d)(3). *See Kenna v. U.S. Dist. Court,* 435 F.3d 1011, 1017 (9th Cir. 2006); *In re Huff Asset Mgmt. Co., LLC,* 409 F.3d 555, 562–63 (2d Cir. 2005). To hold otherwise would effectively grant victims two opportunities to appeal, both of which would be subject to identical appellate standards of review—a clearly inefficient and illogical scheme.

for Mr. Hunter, and Section 3771(d)(6) shows that Congress did not intend to allow non-party appeals that could disturb that judgment.

In sum, neither our case law nor the CVRA provide for non-parties like the Antrobuses to bring a post-judgment direct appeal in a criminal case. We therefore dismiss this appeal.

———————

Notes

1. Both *Doe* and *Hunter* relate to a broad statute conferring on federal appeals courts jurisdiction to hear "appeals from all final decisions of the district courts of the United States. . . ." 28 U.S.C. § 1291. Is *Doe* correct in allowing a victim to take advantage that general statute? And, if so, is the Tenth Circuit justified in distinguishing *Doe* on grounds that the Antrobuses' appeal would "disturb" a final judgment?

2. The Tenth Circuit cited older restitution cases. In these cases, courts had declined to allow crime victims to appeal an adverse restitution decision on grounds that victims did not have a right to restitution. Even on this point, however, the older cases were divided. *See, e.g., United States v. Kones,* 77 F.3d 66 (3rd Cir. 1996) (allowing crime victim to appeal adverse restitution decision). And have those older cases on which the Tenth Circuit relied been implicitly overruled by modern victims' rights statutes that now give victims such a right? One Court of Appeals seems to think so:

> [But these older cases relied upon the fact] that under the VWPA [Victim-Witness Protection Act], a court did not have to award restitution. Restitution fell within the district court's discretion, which meant that a decision to award restitution, or award arguably insufficient restitution, was not fairly traceable to any statutory violation. Furthermore, one can plausibly claim that a restitution order found insufficient by a victim could not be redressed judicially because, as the case law quoted above emphasized, the VWPA used restitution only as a punitive and rehabilitative tool, not a mechanism to partly recompense victims.

See United States v. Perry, 360 F.3d 519 (6th Cir. 2004) (collecting older cases). *Perry,* 360 F.3d 531. In view of the "pro-victim" structure of modern restitution statutes, *id.* at 524, however, the Sixth Circuit in *Perry* refused to follow those decisions and instead allowed a crime victim to appeal from a district court decision releasing a lien in favor of a victim securing a restitution order. *Id.* at 524–27. The argument in support of the *Perry* approach would seem to be greatly strengthened by the passage of the CVRA, which gives crime victims "[t]he right to full and timely restitution as provided in law." 18 U.S.C. § 3771(a)(6).

3. Could a rape victim in a state prosecution obtain the same kind of appellate review as the victim in *Doe* obtained? One commentator argues that it would be difficult:

> Unlike the federal rape shield law, there is nothing in the rape shield procedures of most jurisdictions that allows for the direct participation of the

victim in the trial level hearing. In effect, victims who cannot participate in trial court hearings are barred from making an adequate record for review. In the event of collusion between the parties to defeat the rape shield, or in the event that the state creates an inadequate record, victims are left without an adequate record on review. Without the ability to create an adequate record, the critical foundation of the interlocutory appeal is missing. The Fourth Circuit's observation [in *Doe*], that "[n]o other party in the evidentiary proceeding shares these interests to the extent that they might be viewed as a champion of victims' rights," applies equally to trial court rape shield hearings. A prerequisite to direct rape victim interlocutory appeal is the direct participation of the victim in the trial level hearing.

Only two states, North Dakota and Utah, clearly provide the same procedural trial level participation to victims as does the federal rule. North Dakota requires notice to the victim and "afford[s] the victim and parties a right to attend and be heard." Utah provides that the court must "afford the alleged victim and the parties a right to attend and be heard." In addition, Louisiana also seems to allow victim participation. Louisiana provides that "the victim has a right to attend the hearing and may be accompanied by counsel." There is some reason to believe that these three states would permit victims' interlocutory appeal because, like the federal rape shield procedure, these states allow for victim participation in the trial level rape shield hearing.

In the forty-seven states not providing for victim participation in the trial level hearing it may be difficult to persuade the courts that victims' interlocutory appeals are implicit in rape shield laws. Douglas E. Beloof, *Enabling Rape Shield Procedures Under Crime Victims' State Constitutional Rights to Privacy*, 38 Suffolk U. L. Rev. 291, 295 (2005).

5. Ripeness and Mootness Problems: The Need for Pre-Trial Rulings on Victims' Rights

A victim seeking appellate review of a denial of her rights by the district court may face additional hurdles stemming from the timing of the review. If she files for appellate review too early, she may be told that her claim is not yet "ripe." If she files for review too late, she may be told that her has been rendered "moot." Consider one commentator's analysis of the issues.

Douglas E. Beloof, *The Third Wave of Crime Victims' Rights*
2005 B.Y.U. L. Rev. 255

Problems of ripeness and mootness plague victims' rights. Constitutional victims' rights provisions that prohibit voiding eliminate the potential for remedy and render the rights violation moot. Typically, appellate courts will not review moot cases. Cases are not ripe when they are not yet ready for adjudication or review. The lack of ripeness limits pre-trial appellate review of rights violations. For example, victims might seek to have a court determine well in advance of trial that the victims can exercise their right to attend the trial. However, courts are presently free to put off this decision until trial. This delay pushes the issue to trial, at which time the ruling cannot likely be challenged because double jeopardy proscriptions render the issue moot. The issue is mooted because the trial may be over before the victim can engage an appellate court to review the violation. This double bind of ripeness and mootness precludes victim standing to enforce violations of victims' rights.

An express restriction on review that promotes mootness is manifested in . . . [one] constitution that deny stays for review of denial of victim's rights. The Maryland Constitution, while allowing for appeal, provides: "[n]othing in this article . . . authorizes a victim of crime to take any action to stay a criminal justice proceeding." A "No stay" provision does not expressly prevent review — but does encourage mootness. As one state supreme court justice observed about the no stay provision in Utah enabling statues, when "juxtaposed with the rights of the criminal defendant to a speedy trial and the necessity to move forward with the criminal process . . . appellate relief for [the victim] is a practical impossibility." . . . . Prosecutors and defendants should be required to bring any objection to victims' exercise of their rights well before trial. Courts should also be mandated to rule on these objections sufficiently before trial for the victim to achieve review. Even victims' rights to attend trial, which if violated are presently un-redressable because of double jeopardy, could be the subject of pre-trial rulings and pre-trial writ review.

A model for such proceedings can be found in rape shield laws. For example, the federal rape shield procedure requires a party "to file a written motion at least 14 days before trial if the party intends to offer evidence of the victim's prior sexual behavior or sexual predisposition." In similar fashion, a party objecting to the victims' exercise of their rights could be required to make their objection well in advance of trial to allow time for review. Such a procedure worked well in the Fourth Circuit Court of Appeals case of *United States v. Doe*. Operating within the procedure that required two weeks advance notice, the court found the pre-trial review process quite workable. . . .

The inconvenience and costs of pre-trial review of victims' constitutional rights violations would also be minimal. Should pretrial hearings be required on objections to victims' rights, as rape shield objections are now, then review is unlikely to involve significant delays of criminal trials. Moreover, the injustice to victims in delaying review on many of their constitutional rights is apparent because review after final judgment is no remedy. States provide constitutional rights that are, borrowing from the language of the *Doe* opinion, "for the special benefit of victims." Requiring pretrial rulings solves mootness problems because a remedy can still be achieved on review. The appellate court can order the trial court to comply with the right before the opportunity is foreclosed. The ripeness problem is also cured by the timing deadlines set forth in statute which implicitly mandate ripeness by forcing trial courts to rule pretrial. Finally, putting the burden on the parties to object pre-trial is appropriate because the victim typically has fewer legal advocacy resources than the parties.

An alternative to a statute such as Professor Beloof suggests is for the victim or prosecutor to seek a motion in limine:

United States v. McCray

2017 WL 6471654 (N.D. Ga.)

* * *

D. Victims Presence in Courtroom During Trial

On September 11, 2017, the Government moved in limine to allow victim "A.B" to remain in the courtroom during trial pursuant to the Crime Victims' Rights Act. The Government argues that a crime victim such as A.B. has a statutory right to attend trial even if she is to testify at that trial. The Government seeks an advance ruling from the Court that A.B. shall be permitted to remain in the courtroom throughout the entire trial and related proceedings, i.e., during the pretrial conference, preliminary instructions to the jury, opening statements, the government's case-in-chief, any defense case, closing arguments, jury charge, and verdict. Defendant "objects to the purported victim being allowed to remain in the courtroom during trial." The Defendant contends that AB could observe the proceeding remotely by video feed and that "[t]his alternative eliminates the prejudicial effect of her presence and the government's blatant attempt to interject the improper factor of sympathy." (Id.).

The Crime Victims' Rights Act provides that the victim of a crime has "[t]he right not to be excluded from any . . . public court proceeding." 18 U.S.C. § 3771(a)(3). "The Act, though, authorizes the court to exclude a victim-witness if it finds by clear and convincing evidence that the witness's testimony 'would be materially altered if the victim heard other testimony at that proceeding.'" United States v. Edwards, 526 F.3d 747, 757–58 (11th Cir. 2008) (citing 18 U.S.C. § 3771(a)(3)).

Here, Defendant makes no argument that A.B.'s testimony would be materially altered if she heard other testimony at trial. The Government argues that it is not likely that A.B.'s testimony would be materially altered because: (1) A.B. is the only victim in this case and thus she will not be influenced by the testimony of any other victims; (2) she has been interviewed by law enforcement previously, including twice on video, and thus any alterations to her testimony would be subject to impeachment with her prior Jencks statements; and (3) virtually all of A.B.'s testimony will be corroborated by other reliable evidence. The Court finds that there is not clear and convincing evidence that A.B.'s testimony would be materially altered if she heard other testimony at trial.

Defendant asserts that allowing A.B. to attend trial would be prejudicial and improperly interject sympathy into the trial. But those arguments are not unique to this Defendant, they do not provide a basis to usurp the Crime Victims' Rights Act, and "[a] criminal defendant has no constitutional right to exclude witnesses from the courtroom." Edwards, 526 F.3d at 758 (citing Mathis v. Wainwright, 351 F.2d 489, 489 (5th Cir. 1965)). Defendant's suggestion that A.B. watch the proceedings by video feed would deny A.B.'s statutory right not to be excluded from the courtroom absence a showing that her testimony would be materially altered by her presence.

The Court grants the Government's Motion. A.B. shall be permitted to remain in the courtroom, but seated only in the second row of the gallery, during the trial as allowed by the Crime Victims' Rights Act, 18 U.S.C. § 3771.

———————

Note. A motion in limine need not be granted pretrial. On the other hand the rape shield statuary procedure must be followed. Which better serves the victims' interests?

Chapter 12

The Future of Victims' Rights

Introduction

In the previous chapters you learned about the difficulties that crime victims have had in enforcing their rights; that is; giving victims standing to assert and remedies for violation of the rights that exist. Section A identifies a variety of issues that will continue to be hot topics in victims' rights. Section B discusses the first two waves of victims' reform and identifies the problems that are being addressed in a third wave. This section reports on a new wave of reform—a third wave, as identified by Professor Beloof. Section C identifies the more recent state constitutional amendments and how they are a part of an overall national strategy to establish enforceable rights. Section D reviews the proposed Victims' Rights Amendment to the United States Constitution and asks whether the Amendment might be the appropriate way to create a national standard of enforceable victim's rights. Section E concludes with some brief predictions about the future of the crime victims' movement.

A. A Non-Exclusive List of Unresolved Victim Law Issues

1. Lawyers for Victims

Presently, the only institutions that provide lawyers for victims of crime are the branches of the military. The office of the Judge Advocate General (JAG) has lawyers who are assigned as Special Victim Counsel to victims of sexual assault. The Marines provide victims of all crimes with a Special Victim Counsel. The military was once in the crosshairs of Congress for failure to address sexual assault in their ranks. With the advent of Special Victim Counsel, lawyers for victims and other significant reforms, perhaps the military has a state-of-the-art response to sexual assault victimization that now surpasses the civilian criminal justice system. Should lawyers be appointed for civilian victims of sexual assault?

New Jersey allows limited funds from its victim compensation program for representation of a crime victim asserting their victim's rights in criminal cases. Should other compensation programs follow suit? Federal programs, such as those created by the Victims of Crime Act and Violence Against Women Act are more open to representation of victims in criminal cases. King County in Washington State, comprising the urban area of Seattle and surrounding cities, has recently announced it will provide victims of police shootings with lawyers in inquest proceedings into the shootings. https://www.thestranger.com/slog/2018/01/29/25761114/king-county -will-start-providing-lawyers-to-families-of-police-shooting-victims.

The National Crime Victim Law Institute (NCVLI) has the National Association of Crime Victim Attorneys (NAVRA), which is comprised of pro bono lawyers around the country who volunteer to represent victims enforcing their rights. A few states have legal clinics for crime victims. Getting such clinics in every state might be the best chance of expanding legal representation for victims. Should your law school start such a clinic?

2. Victim Privacy

The result of the duopoly of state and defendant control over the criminal process has left crime victims' privacy in tatters. As but one example, victims in many states are not informed when their third-party records are subpoenaed, while they are in some states and the federal system. Third-party record holders inconsistently defend the privacy of their clients (victims). And victims, even when they receive notice, often do not know how to defend their privacy. Prosecutors are, as often as not, ill schooled in what records and victim information are actually protected by existing privacy laws governing school records, therapy records, etc. Presently, a prosecutor can agree to a defense subpoena for such records and thus a judge issues the subpoena without any safeguard for the victim.

3. Rape Shield Hearings and Review

In the federal system a rape victim can participate in the trial level rape shield hearing and bring an interlocutory appeal of an adverse ruling. This is not the case in the states. Because no one else in the case represents the interests of the victim as well as the victim, without an opportunity for input at the rape shield hearing or review of an adverse rape shield hearing, the shield has no enforcement teeth.

4. Relevant Discovery from Government to Meaningfully Exercise and Enforce Victims' Rights

Victims may need information from the state. For example, they may need information simply to determine whether they fit within the definition of "victim" under a statute or constitution. As another example, they may need information from a presentence report in order to prepare an informed victim impact statement. Such "discovery" from the state could be provided by statute or court opinions because it is a necessary predicate for the victims' right to be exercised.

5. Other Unresolved Issues

1. Many states have speedy trial rights for victims. Victims have these rights on paper, but how are these to be enforced in overcrowded criminal courts?

2. Pre-charging rights remain a fairly open issue. The law is moving slowly in the direction of rights before charging. But just what rights are appropriate before a charge is brought?

3. Victims may speak at plea bargaining and sentencing. What weight should judges give to victims' objections?

4. How can prosecutors be made to meaningfully confer with crime victims?

5. The boundaries of restitution and collectability of it is an emerging area. Why aren't victims getting lost income in homicide and other crimes? Should the government provide easy mechanisms to attach tax returns and income? Should restitution orders be reducible to a civil judgment in favor of the victim?

These are just some examples of the important issues facing crime victims that may be resolved by your generation.

B. The Third Wave of Enforceable Constitutional Amendments

Scholars who have studied the victims' rights movement divide the reforms the movement has achieved into at least two waves. The first wave — running roughly from early 1970s through perhaps the early 1980s — resulted in various *statutory* protections for crime victim's rights, such as state statutes creating victims' rights to attend trials, victim compensation and restitution, bail reform, rape shield laws, and better protective order enforcement in domestic violence cases. The second wave — starting perhaps with the 1982 Report of the President's Task Force on Victims of Crime and extending through today — resulted in various *constitutional* protections for victims' rights, typically in the form of a bill of rights for crime victims. The forms of state constitutional amendments have varied widely, with many lacking enforceability. Are these rights effective or is a "third wave" of victims' reforms needed?

Douglas E. Beloof, *The Third Wave of Crime Victims' Rights: Standing Remedy and Review*
2005 B.Y.U. L. Rev. 255 (2005)

The crime victims' rights movement worked to enact rights in two waves. The first wave of rights were statutory. Unsatisfied with the response of the legal culture to statutory rights, the crime victims' movement began to work to enact state constitutional rights. The achievements of these victims' rights pioneers are nothing short of astonishing. The second wave resulted in thirty-three state constitutions with victims' rights. In the mid-1900s, before the advent of victims' rights, victims were lawfully exiled from criminal processes and rarely notified of important events. Against an entrenched legal culture that completely excluded victims from the criminal process, these pioneers established critical beachheads for the victims' rights movement. As impressive a feat as securing these beachheads was, the first and second wave of statutory and constitutional victims' rights did not establish real crime victims' rights. It is time to move inland. The third wave of victims standing, remedy and review will transform these illusory rights into real rights. . . .

Crime victims state constitutional rights are illusory. . . . There are three main obstacles in the way of turning victims' illusory rights into real rights: the governments' discretion to deny rights, the lack of a meaningful remedy to enforce the rights, and appellate courts' discretion to deny review. There are three types of discretion that eliminate or curtail victim standing. First, the government has the discretion to ignore constitutional rights that are not mandatory or not enabled. Second, some victims' constitutional rights are cast in discretionary language. With limited exceptions, there is no victim standing to obtain review of these discretionary rights when the government disregards them. Third, broad victims' constitutional rights provisions are vague. The vagueness of these provisions gives courts the discretion not to apply them expansively.

Victims' rights are also illusory where there is no adequate remedy. Without remedy rights are unenforceable. In certain constitutions, meaningful remedies for violations of victims' rights are prohibited or unduly restricted, thus limiting standing. Even in jurisdictions where remedy is otherwise available, problems of mootness or lack of ripeness prevent remedy. Furthermore, some state constitutional victims' rights deny the courts any authority to stay proceedings while a rights violation is on review. The unavailability of stays aggravates the mootness problem.

Finally, victims' rights are illusory unless there is a non-discretionary review mechanism. Where remedy is available, and the violation fits within the scope of the rights, review by writ is expressly or implicitly available under all state constitutional victims' rights provisions. But writ review is discretionary. Because review by writ is discretionary it is improbable that individual victims' rights violations will be routinely reviewed.

Troubling too are appellate court deviations from conventional constitutional analysis resulting in denials of victim standing. In states where victim standing should be affirmed, emerging judicial opinions deny standing. For example, constitutional rights must be mandatory before there can be standing, remedy and review. However, despite plain mandatory language and the placement of rights in the states' respective Bills of Rights, the rights are judicially labeled "directory," thus eliminating potential enforcement. Additionally, constitutional rights must be enabled before there can be standing and remedy. Where strong evidence exists that victims' rights are self-enabled, they are held not to be. Even though the absence of express remedial provisions are not fatal to other types of individual rights, courts have held that the absence of such provisions in victims' constitutional rights is fatal to standing. . . .

Providing for standing, remedy and review will make victims' rights enforceable by victims, bring victims' rights into conformance with the conventional model of individual rights, signal courts to follow conventional constitutional analysis in interpreting victim's rights, and enhance government compliance with the rights. This is best achieved by amending or legislatively enabling state constitutions, and by enacting a federal constitutional victims' rights amendment. . . .

Without standing, the remedy of voiding, and non-discretionary review, crime victims' rights are illusory rights. The most significant problem with illusory rights is that crime victims cannot enforce their rights in a way that ensures they will be able to exercise their rights. Instead, the very governments against whom the rights are meant to be exercised remain free to ignore, and even intentionally violate, victims' rights. Many significant problems stem from victims' rights without standing. Without victim standing to enforce victims' rights, judicial hierarchy is turned upside down, the hierarchy of law is upset, adversity is corrupted, rights enforcement is crippled, victims advocacy in favor of defendants is constrained, and constitutional rights are degraded. Given that victims' rights are routinely exercised at the trial court level, significant dysfunctions arise when victims are denied appellate standing. No state appellate court has ever denied victims trial court level access to exercise their rights. . . .

With real rights, like defendants' rights, appellate courts are the ultimate arbiters of the meaning of constitutional rights. On the other hand, illusory victims' rights—with trial level standing and no appellate court standing—turn judicial hierarchy upside down. In this upside down process, trial courts are the ultimate arbiters of victims' constitutional rights. Each trial court can arrive at unique conclusions about the meaning and scope of victims' rights. Moreover, these trial courts can apply their disparate interpretations of constitutional rights without fear of reversal. The result is different rights for different victims based on which trial judge presides over the case. Such a process is designed to erode the integrity of victims' rights, confidence in the judicial system, and time honored judicial hierarchies of constitutional authority. This would never be tolerated for criminal defendants' rights. It should not be tolerated for victims' rights.

In our hierarchy of laws, statutes are lesser laws than constitutions. To provide victims' standing to enforce statutes, but not constitutional rights, contradicts the hierarchy of laws. Making statutory victim accommodations enforceable while constitutional rights are not is backwards. In a variety of statutory contexts, victims have standing, remedy, and review. First, crime victims have standing to seek review of the denial of a personally held evidentiary privilege. For example, crime victims have evidentiary privileges to keep their crisis counseling records confidential. As personally held privileges, victims can seek appellate court review of a denial of these statutory privileges. Standing has been granted to victims in other contexts as well. Thus, mandamus was allowed where a victim challenged an Oregon trial court's jurisdiction to order defendant's counsel into the victim's home and where a Texas trial court had ordered a psychological evaluation of a child sexual assault victim by defendants expert. In *State ex rel. Miller v. Smith*, the West Virginia Supreme Court issued a writ of prohibition, petitioned for by the crime victim, against the public prosecutor to prevent the public prosecutor from interfering with the victim's access to a state grand jury.

In *Doe v. United States*, the court granted an interlocutory appeal to a rape victim from a district court's pre-trial denial of the protections of the federal rape shield law. In *Doe*, the defendant asserted that the court did not have jurisdiction to appeal. First, the court observed that "[t]he text, purpose, and legislative history of [the rape shield law] clearly indicate that Congress enacted the rule for the special benefit of the victims of rape." The court observed that the rule made no reference to appeal. Regardless, the circuit held that the remedy was "implicit as a necessary corollary of the [rape shield] rule's explicit protection of the privacy interests Congress sought to safeguard." The court found significant the fact that "[n]o other party in the evidentiary proceeding shares these interests to the extent that they might be viewed as a champion of victim's rights." The court found that the congressional intent will be "frustrated" if rape victims "are not allowed to appeal an erroneous evidentiary ruling." . . .

Without victim standing, victims' rights can only be contested on review by parties who have no personal stake in the right. This greatly limits true adversariness in victims' rights cases. Absent standing for victims, the defendant and prosecutor are vested with control over the existence and the scope of the victims' rights' controversy. The parties may not be interested in defending victims' rights or may take a position that denies the rights their full potential. For example, if the parties agree that victims' rights violations do not concern them, the rights issue will die regardless of whether appellate courts would ultimately agree with victims' concerns. Furthermore, there are circumstances in which the state and defendants are both adverse to victims' interests. For example, when the parties come to plea agreements, victims have rights to speak to the trial judge in opposition. The parties may act to prevent or circumscribe victims' exercise of their rights. for example, prosecutors may not provide notice of a right or of a hearing date. Without standing and remedy, victims are powerless to enforce their rights to oppose the plea bargain. Such powerlessness eliminates any potential for true adversity.

Denying victims standing to enforce their rights means that only the state can litigate rights violations. However, the state is far from a consistent advocate for crime victims' rights. First, the state itself may be the violator. Thus, in state after state where the prosecution has violated the victims' rights to be heard at a disposition, prosecutors have taken the position that victims cannot seek to void the plea or sentence. If the state is not the violator, it will typically defend victims' rights against defendants' attempts to reverse convictions because the state has an interest in upholding convictions. In any other context, the state cannot consistently be relied upon to defend victims' rights. States' decisions to defend victims' rights are frequently based on other priorities. In a hypothetical case of first impression, whether the state will choose to defend the right is only predictable when the other priorities of the state are known. Changing priorities may lead the state to take diametrically opposed positions concerning the same victims' rights issue. Thus, the state will support the right if convictions are thereby defended, and oppose victims' rights if judicial denial of the rights is of minimal consequence to the prosecution.

Furthermore, prosecutorial control of victims' rights provides fertile ground for ethical conflicts of interest. It is a mistake to define the state and victims as non-adversaries simply because both are harmed by the criminal act and share an interest in punishment. Adversariness exists when prosecutors violate victims' rights. Moreover, the public prosecutor is obligated to the public interest. When the public interest and victims' rights coincide, perhaps no conflict exists. However, when there is conflict the prosecution cannot reasonably be expected to defend the victims' right. Absent provisions for victim standing when there is a conflict, a rights violation will go unredressed. In recognition of this reality, Arizona law provides that "in any event of any conflict of interest . . . the prosecutor shall have the responsibility to direct the victim to the appropriate legal referral, legal assistance, or legal aid agency." When in conflict, the prosecutor cannot serve two masters, and the victim necessarily becomes the odd man out.

Conflict or not, the state is under no legal obligation to defend victims' rights and can decline to defend simply out of indifference. In the context of defendants' rights, the state could not be such an exclusive gatekeeper over review of rights violations. The state should not have such authority over victims' rights. Instead, victims should be able to enforce their rights independently of the state. This is the only way to obtain enforcement of rights when the state has other priorities, faces a conflict, or is simply disinterested.

Absent victim standing, and with the state in control of rights enforcement, victims' rights are always framed as rights conflicting with defendants' rights even though victims' rights are centrally rights against the government. Without victim standing, only the state can defend victims' rights on review. The state is unlikely to seek review where the victims' right to speak on behalf of the defendant was violated, as the state has little interest in victims speaking on behalf of defendants.

Victims cannot look to defendants to make up for the victims' standing deficit, even if the victim intends to exercise their right for the benefit of the defendant. Defendants do not have standing to contest denials of victims' rights, because victims' rights are not personal to defendants. For example, in the Illinois case of *People v. Richardson*, the defendant was denied review under the victims' rights language of the Illinois constitution because the provisions serve "as a shield to protect the rights of victims not a sword allowing the defendant to appeal." As a result, defendants' can only challenge the granting of victims' rights where it conflicts with defendants' rights. Even if defendants could defend victims' rights, defendants as a whole could not be relied upon to advocate for victims' rights. In many cases, victims speak against defendants' positions. Nevertheless, a victims' rights process that precludes appellate court scrutiny when victims intend to speak for defendants and are denied the right, is fundamentally corrupt. Such corruption vividly demonstrates why the government should never be so exclusively in charge of individual constitutional rights. . . .

Of course, arguments can be made that denying victims standing to defend their rights has its benefits. As examples, denying appellate court standing to victims may be efficient. Absent such standing, trial court denial of victims' rights cannot be challenged by the victim on review. Trial courts are more efficient because there is no chance that a trial level proceeding will be delayed while an appellate court determines whether to correct the rights violation. Moreover, appellate courts benefit because they do not expend resources reviewing victims' rights violations. Furthermore, the prosecutor and defendant benefit by maintaining between them complete control over review of victims' rights. This control increases the parties' influence over the development of victims' rights law in appellate courts. Without victims defending their rights on review, parties who are not victims are the exclusive litigants of the meaning and scope of victims' rights. Moreover, denying victims standing prevents conflicts with defendants' rights. For example, delay on review could potentially conflict with a defendants' speedy trial rights. Furthermore, ordering a re-sentencing would unsettle defendants' interest in certainty and finality. However, these arguments are more appropriately reasons for not constitutionalizing victims' rights in the first place.

Victims' broad constitutional rights, such as the right to "fairness," "dignity" and "privacy" are vague rights. Courts are well within their authority to interpret these rights narrowly. However, these rights provide a tremendous opportunity to serve as foundations upon which legislatures may enact more specific rights for victims. As examples, victims' broad right to privacy could result in statutory procedures that allow victims to be formally notified of, and to move to quash, subpoenas duces tecum that seek victims' records kept by third parties other than the victim. Another idea is for the right of privacy to support participation by rape victims in trial level rape shield hearings and for victims to seek review of adverse rulings. Victims' right to be treated with dignity could be the basis for statutes allowing a support person for the victim in the courtroom. Victims' right to due process could support notice and the right to be heard in contexts not expressly provided for specifically in constitutional rights such as suppression hearings.

In some state constitutions the remedies of voiding and reconsideration have been severely curtailed, particularly with regard to pleas and sentences. Until these provisions are amended to allow the voiding of pleas and sentences which have been taken in violation of victims' rights, victims will be without remedy and standing to obtain review. In enabling legislation, it is advisable to expressly provide for remedy. Providing for remedy is not necessary because courts have the inherent authority to void proceedings and reconsider results where constitutional rights are violated. Nevertheless, unprincipled judicial resistance towards remedying victims' rights violations evidenced in this article argues for express provisions. Voiding and reconsideration should be expressly set forth as remedies in enabling legislation.

An effective means of securing appellate review — assuming the constitution does not preclude it — is to expressly provide for a means of review in constitutions or enabling statutes. There are some state laws that expressly provide for review mechanisms. Two state constitutions explicitly provide for actions to compel government officials to obey victims' rights. The constitution of South Carolina provides that enforcement of victims' rights is by mandamus. The Nevada constitution provides that an action to compel the government to comply with the right is available. Utah law specifically provides that victims may use mandamus to enforce their rights. Arizona has abolished the old form of writs and in its place created "special actions," which crime victims may bring to enforce their rights. Maryland has the right to appeal from an interlocutory or final order that denies or fails to consider a victims' right. Utah statutes also provide for declaratory judgment actions, mandamus and appeal. Michigan statutes allow a victim to appeal to a circuit court judge the parole board's granting of parole.

By granting victims "standing to enforce the rights . . . ," the Texas constitution implicitly provides for some sort of review procedure. Florida and Indiana statutes grant victims "standing." In these eight jurisdictions with express review or standing provisions, review of some sort is expressly available. Absent other restrictions in victims' state constitutional rights, writs are implicitly available. Even in the states which have expressly banned appeals, with the exception of Idaho, writs are available.

The problem in review of victims' rights is not the unavailability of writ review, but rather the discretionary nature of writs. The solution to the review problem is to provide for non-discretionary review of victims' rights violations. When victims were merely third parties defending evidentiary privileges or moving to quash subpoenas, the argument that discretionary review was sufficient was perhaps stronger. Today crime victims are participants with constitutional rights. Unlike third parties, victims have due process rights in the criminal process. Unlike third parties, victims' rights legitimize victims' interest in punishment. Procedures should be established granting victims the right to non-discretionary review of rights violations. It could not credibly be suggested that criminal defendants' constitutional rights are to be reviewed only in the discretion of the court.

Rights in constitutional bills of rights are important enough to be accompanied by standing, the remedy of voiding, and non-discretionary review. The very reason to constitutionalize rights is to enforce the rights against government. The two sound alternatives remaining are to remove illusory victims' rights from constitutions or to make the rights real with standing, remedy, and review. In state after state, the people have already decided in favor of victims' constitutional rights. Victims' rights are the most recent state constitutional rights and have been approved at the polls by overwhelming margins. It is as unlikely that victims' rights will be removed from state constitutions as it is that criminal defendants' rights will be removed. As Professor Tobolowsky has accurately observed, "[t]he relevant inquiry is no longer whether victims should have participatory rights in the criminal justice process . . . [t]he relevant focus . . . is to ensure that these victim participatory rights are appropriate and meaningful in the context of the varied and social interests involved in criminal prosecutions." There is no practical way to proceed but to evolve victims' illusory rights into real rights. . . .

Notes

1. Based on what you have seen in this casebook so far, do you agree that crime victims' rights are often "illusory"? If so, why are they illusory and what changes could be made to transform them?

2. Prosecutors do not represent the victim in criminal cases and, as we have seen, they may have interests that don't coincide with the victim's interests. Given these realities, and the need for lawyers to understand how rights can be enforced, should the government pay for victims' lawyers to enforce rights in criminal cases?

C. The Ongoing Advancement of Enforceable State Victims' Rights Constitutional Amendments

One way of improving enforcement of state crime victims' rights enactments is through strengthened state constitutional protections. Between 1982 and 2004, many state constitutional rights for victims were enacted, largely through grassroots efforts. Some of these were flawed in ways set out above in Professor Beloof's article. In 2008, a second wave of state constitutional efforts began. In California, Dr. Henry T. Nicholas (the co-founder of Broadcom Corp.) backed the enactment of "Marsy's Law," named after his sister Marsalee (Marsy) Nicholas. She was stalked and killed by her ex-boyfriend in 1983. Only a week after her murder, Dr. Nicholas and Marsy's mother walked into a grocery store after visiting Marsy's grave and were confronted by the accused murderer. The family had not been told that he had been released on bail. The family also suffered further indignities during the criminal justice process.

Determined to prevent mistreatment of other victims in the process, Dr. Nicholas supported a comprehensive rewrite of California's flawed state constitutional victims' rights amendment. In November 2008, California voters overwhelming approved Proposition 9, making California's amendment arguably the strongest and most comprehensive in the country. Since then, similar Marsy's Law amendments have been added to other state constitutions. These efforts continue as this casebook goes to press.

The amendments in each of the states are slightly different, but they each contain the same core elements: an enumeration of specific rights, a definition of victim, and an express grant of standing to victims to assert the rights guaranteed with a non-discretionary ability to seek review when a right is denied. This development in the third wave of the victims' rights movement validates Professor Beloof's anticipation of it. Under the banner of Marsy's Law for All, the campaign's stated goal is to amend the United States Constitution.

For a more complete review of developments in the constitutional reform movement, see www.nvcap.org and https://marsyslaw.us/.

D. The Proposed Victims' Rights Amendment to the United States Constitution

The boldest proposal for the third wave of victims' rights reforms is for a Victims' Rights Amendment to the United States Constitution. Such an amendment was introduced in every Congress from 1996 through 2003, and then again introduced in every Congress beginning in 2012.

Amending the Constitution is a dramatic step. Do victims' rights belong in the federal Constitution? Consider the following competing views on various versions of a federal Victims' Rights Amendment that have been proposed since 1996. A debate began in earnest on a version drafted and introduced in the Senate more than 20 years ago. The current draft, set forth earlier in this chapter, is a significantly improved document. Nevertheless, the debate in the materials from the late 1990s is relevant in many ways.

Back in 1997, noted constitutional scholar Laurence Tribe set out criteria for supporting a victims rights constitutional amendment:

Statement of Professor Laurence H. Tribe

Harvard University Law School, *in* A Proposed Constitutional Amendment to Protect Victims of Crime: Hearings Before the Senate Judiciary Committee, 105th Cong., 1st Sess. (1997)

Beginning with the premise that the Constitution should not be amended lightly and should never be amended to achieve short-term, partisan, or purely policy objections, I would argue that a constitutional amendment is appropriate only when the goal involves (1) a needed change in government structure, or (2) a needed recognition of a basic human right, where (a) the right is one that people widely agree deserves serious and permanent respect, (b) the right is one that is insufficiently protected under existing law, (c) the right is one that cannot be adequately protected through purely political action such as state or federal legislation and/or regulation, (d) the right is one whose inclusion in the U.S. Constitution would not distort or endanger basic principles of the separation of powers among the federal branches, or the division of powers between the national and state governments, and (e) the right would be judicially enforceable without creating open-ended or otherwise unacceptable funding obligations.

I believe that S.J. Res. 6 meets these criteria. The rights in question — rights of crime victims not to be victimized yet again through the processes by which government bodies and officials prosecute, punish, and release the accused or convicted offender—are indisputably basic human rights against government, rights that any civilized system of justice would aspire to protect and strive never to violate. To protect these rights of victims does not entail constitutionalizing the rights of private citizens against other private citizens; for it is not the private citizen accused of crime by state or federal authorities who is the source of the violations that victims' rights advocates hope to address with a constitutional amendment in this area. Rather, it is the government authorities themselves, those who pursue (or release) the accused or convicted criminal with insufficient attention to the concerns of the victim, who are sometimes guilty of the kinds of violations that properly drawn amendment would prohibit.

Pursuing and punishing criminals makes little sense unless society does so in a manner that fully respects the rights of their victims to be accorded dignity and respect, to be treated fairly in all relevant proceedings, and to be assured a meaningful opportunity; to observe, and take part in, all such proceedings. These are the very kinds of rights with which our Constitution is typically and properly concerned. Specifically, our Constitution's central concerns involve protecting the rights of individuals to participate in all those government processes that directly and immediately involve those individuals and affect their lives in some focused and particular way. Such rights include the right to vote on an equal basis whenever a matter is put to the electorate for resolution by voting; the right to be heard as a matter of procedural due process when government deprives one of life, liberty, or property; and various rights of the criminally accused to a speedy and public trial, with the assistance of counsel, and with various other participatory safeguards including the right to compulsory process and to confrontation of adverse witnesses. The parallel rights of victims to participate in these proceedings are no less basic, even though they find no parallel recognition in the explicit text of the U.S. Constitution.

I have read the letter from law professors, dated April 4, 1997, attacking the proposed Victim's Rights Constitutional Amendment. Although I share many of the broad views set forth in the letter—including the views that the Constitution should not be amended without a strong need and that the constitutional rights of persons accused of crime should not be sacrificed in order to serve other values—I do not believe the letter makes a convincing case for its ultimate conclusions. The case for the proposed amendment need not rest on some nebulous notion that the playing field must be balanced as between criminal defendants and crime victims. It rests on the twin propositions (1) that victims have important human rights that can and should be guaranteed protection without endangering the genuine rights of those accused or convicted, but (2) that attempts to protect these rights of victims at the state level, or through congressional legislation, have proven insufficient (although helpful) in light of the concern—recurring even if misguided—that taking victims' rights seriously, even when state or federal statutes or state constitutions appear to require doing so, will somehow be unfair to the accused or to others even when no actual constitutional rights of the accused or of anyone else would be violated by respecting the rights of victims in the manner requested. The proposed amendment would, in essence, counteract this problem.

Courts have sometimes recognized that the Constitution's failure to say anything explicit about the right of the victim or the victim's family to observe the trial of the accused should not be construed to deny the existence of such a right—provided, of course, that it can be respected consistent with the fair-trial rights of the accused. In Richmond Newspapers v. Virginia, 448 U.S. 555 (1980), for example, the plurality opinion, written by Chief Justice Burger, noted the way in which protecting the right of the press and the public to attend a criminal trial—even where, as in that case, the accused and the prosecution and the trial judge all preferred a closed proceeding— serves to protect not only random members of the public but those with a more specific interest in observing, and right to observe—namely, the dead victim's close relatives. See 448 U.S. at 571 ("Civilized societies withdraw both from the victim and the vigilante the enforcement of criminal laws, but they cannot erase from people's consciousness the fundamental, natural yearning to see justice done—or even the urge for retribution."). Although the Sixth Amendment right to a public trial was held inapplicable in Richmond Newspapers on the basis that the Sixth Amendment secures that right only to the accused, and although the First Amendment right to free speech was thought by some (see, e.g., 448 U.S. at 604–06 (Rehnquist, J., dissenting)) to have no direct bearing in the absence of anything like government censorship, the plurality took note of the Ninth Amendment, whose reminder that the Constitution's enumeration of explicit rights is not to be deemed exclusive furnished an additional ground for the plurality's conclusion that the Constitution presupposed, even though it nowhere enumerated, a presumptive right of openness and participation in trial proceedings. See 448 U.S. at 579–80 & n.15 ("Madison's efforts, culminating in the Ninth Amendment, served to allay the fears of those who were concerned that expressing certain guarantees could be read as excluding others.").

I discuss Richmond Newspapers in some detail here not just because I argued that case but because it illustrates so forcefully the way in which victims' rights to observe and to participate, subject only to such exclusions and regulations as are genuinely essential to the protection of the rights of the accused, may be trampled upon in the course of law enforcement simply out of a concern with administrative convenience or out of an unthinking assumption that, because the Constitution nowhere refers to the rights of victims in so many words, such rights may and perhaps even should be ignored or at least downgraded. The happy coincidence that the rights of the victims in the Richmond Newspapers case overlapped with the First Amendment rights of the press prevented the victims in that case—the relatives of a hotel manager who had been found stabbed to death—from being altogether ignored on that occasion. But many victims have no such luck, and there appears to be a considerable body of evidence showing that, even where statutory or regulatory or judge-made rules exist to protect the participatory rights of victims, such rights often tend to be honored in the breach, not on the entirely understandable basis of a particularized determination that affording the victim the specific right claimed would demonstrably violate some constitutional right of the accused or convicted offender, but on the very different basis of a barely-considered reflex that protecting a victim's rights would represent either a luxury we cannot afford or a compromise with an ignoble desire for vengeance.

As long as we do so in a manner that respects the separation and division of powers and does not invite judges to interfere with law enforcement resource allocation decisions properly belonging to the political branches, we should not hesitate to make explicit in our Constitution the premise that I believe is implicit in that document but that is unlikely to receive full and effective recognition unless it is brought to the fore and chiseled in constitutional stone—the premise that the processes for enforcing state and federal criminal law must, to the extent possible, be conducted in a manner that respects not only the rights of those accused of having committed a crime but also the rights of those they are accused of having victimized.

The fact that the States and Congress, within their respective jurisdictions, already have ample affirmative authority to enact rules protecting these rights is a reason for not including new enabling or empowering language in a constitutional amendment on this subject, but is not a reason for opposing an amendment altogether. For the problem with rules enacted in the absence of such a constitutional amendment is not that such rules, assuming they are enacted with care, would be struck down as falling outside the affirmative authority of the relevant jurisdiction. The problem, rather, is that such rules are likely, as experience to date sadly shows, to provide too little real protection whenever they come into conflict with bureaucratic habit, traditional indifference, sheer inertia, or any mention of an accused's rights regardless of whether those rights are genuinely threatened.

Of course any new constitutional language in this area must be drafted so that the rights of victims will not become an excuse for running roughshod over the rights of the accused. This amendment has been written so that courts will retain ultimate responsibility for harmonizing, or balancing, the potentially conflicting rights of all participants in any given case. Assuring that this fine-tuning of conflicting rights remains a task for the judiciary is not too difficult. What is difficult, and perhaps impossible, is assuring that, under the existing system of rights and rules, the constitutional rights of victims—rights that the Framers of the Constitution undoubtedly assumed would receive fuller protection than has proven to be the case—will not instead receive short shrift.

To redress this imbalance, and to do so without distorting the Constitution's essential design, it may well be necessary to add a corrective amendment on this subject. Doing so would neither extend the Constitution to a purely policy issue, nor provide special benefits to a particular interest group, nor use the heavy artillery of constitutional amendment where a less radical solution is available. Nor would it put the Constitution to a merely symbolic use, or enlist it for some narrow or partisan purpose. It would instead, help solve a distinct and significant gap in our existing legal system's arrangements for the protection of basic human rights against an important category of governmental abuse.

Note

Professor Tribe's public writings on crime victims' rights are collected at 9 Lewis and Clark Law Rev. 659 (2005).

———————

Letter from Law Professors Regarding the Proposed Victim's Rights Constitutional Amendment

in A Proposed Constitutional Amendment to Protect Victims of Crime: Hearings Before the Senate Judiciary Committee, 105th Cong., 1st Sess. (1997)

Dear Senators Hatch and Leahy, and Representatives Hyde and Conyers,

We are law professors and practitioners who oppose the proposal to add a "Victim's Rights Amendment" to the United States Constitution (S.J. Res. 6). Although we commend and share the desire to help crime victims, amending the Constitution to do so is both unnecessary and dangerous. Indeed, ultimately the amendment is likely to be counter-productive in that it could hinder effective prosecution and put an enormous burden on state and federal law enforcement agencies.

The Constitution has been amended only 27 times in 210 years. Amendments should be added to our basic charter of government only when there is a pressing need that cannot be addressed in any other way. No such necessity exists in order to protect the rights of crime victims. Virtually every right contained in the proposed Victim's Rights Amendment can be safeguarded in federal and state laws.

Many of the rights contained in the Victim's Rights Amendment already are provided for in federal and state laws. For example, restitution for crime victims is required in federal court by the Antiterrorism and Effective Death Penalty Act of 1996 and in state courts by laws in virtually every state. Similarly, the right of victims to attend proceedings can be protected by statute as shown by laws that exist in many states and by the recent federal legislation that mandates that victims be allowed to attend even if they will be testifying during the sentencing phase of the proceedings. Victim impact statements are now a routine part of sentencing proceedings at both the federal and state levels.

Over 25 states have amended their state constitutions to protect victims' rights and most others have done this by statute. There is every reason to believe that the legislative process will continue to be responsive to protecting crime victims so that there is simply no need to amend the Constitution to accomplish this.

There are, however, grave dangers in amending the Constitution in this manner. The framers of the Constitution were aware of the enormous power of the government to deprive a person of liberty or even life in a criminal prosecution. The constitutional protections accorded criminal defendants are among the most precious and essential liberties provided in the Constitution. The Victim's Rights Amendment risks undermining these basic safeguards. For example, the proposed Amendment would give a crime victim the right "[t]o a final disposition of the proceedings relating to the crime free from unreasonable delay." Any victim of a violent crime has standing under the Amendment to intervene and assert a constitutional right for a faster disposition of the matter. This could be used to deny defendants needed time to gather and present evidence essential in order to demonstrate their innocence.

The Amendment also would require "consideration for the safety of the victim in determining any release from custody." Pretrial release statutes already provide for consideration of dangerousness when courts decide whether to release criminal defendants before trial. The proposed Amendment, however, would go much further and allow a victim of a crime to argue that it is *unconstitutional* to release a person from prison even though the sentence had been completely served. The authorization for standing for crime victims, contained in section two of the proposed Amendment, would permit any victim of a violent crime to go to court and make such an argument any time any prisoner was about to be released.

Section three of the proposed Amendment authorizes Congress and the states to enact legislation to enforce the Amendment. This authority could be used to negate the rights of criminal defendants in an effort to protect crime victims. Courts would then face the enormously difficult task of determining the extent to which legislation to implement the new Amendment can undermine the rights of those accused of crimes. Also, the authorization for *states* to enact legislation to implement the Amendment is unique among constitutional amendments. It is unclear whether these constitutionally authorized state laws will be supreme over state constitutions or even over federal laws.

Moreover, the Amendment is likely to be counter-productive because it could hamper effective prosecutions and cripple law enforcement by placing enormous new burdens on state and federal law enforcement agencies. Prosecutions could be hindered by the creation of an absolute right for crime victims to attend and participate in criminal proceedings. In many instances, the testimony of a prosecutorial witness will be compromised if the person has heard the testimony of other witnesses. Yet, the proposed Amendment creates an absolute right for a victim to be present at criminal proceedings even over the prosecution's objections.

The right of crime victims to insist on a speedy resolution could force prosecutors to try cases before they were fully prepared. Prosecutorial efforts also could be hampered by the ability of crime victims to "submit a written statement . . . to determine . . . an acceptance of a negotiated plea or sentence." It is unclear how much weight judges will be required to give to a crime victim's objection to a plea bargain. Over 90 percent of all criminal cases are now resolved by plea bargaining. Even a small increase in the number of cases going to trial would unduly burden prosecutors' offices. Often prosecutors enter into plea agreements based on decisions about allocating scarce prosecutorial resources, or based on concerns about weaknesses in the evidence, or based on strategic choices to gain the cooperation of one defendant to enhance the likelihood of convicting others. Prosecutorial discretion would be seriously compromised if crime victims could effectively obstruct plea agreements or require that prosecutors disclose the weaknesses in their case in order to persuade a court to accept a plea.

The Amendment would impose a tremendous new burden on state and federal law enforcement agencies. These departments would be *constitutionally* required to make reasonable efforts to find and notify crime victims every time a case went to trial, every time a criminal case was resolved, and most significantly, every time a prisoner was released from custody. Additionally, the Amendment can be interpreted as creating a duty for the government to provide attorneys for crime victims. The right of victims "to be heard," contained in section two of the proposed Amendment, might well be seen as requiring counsel in order to be heard effectively. This, too, would create a huge costs for government. How would these obligations be funded? In all likelihood, money would be diverted from other law enforcement efforts.

The Amendment also would create an enormous burden on state and federal courts. The Amendment grants crime victims standing and a right to participate in virtually every phase of trial and post-trial proceedings. The burden this imposes is magnified because the Amendment does not define who is a crime victim. Family members and even friends of those attacked in violent crimes can claim to be injured and invoke a constitutional right to intervene and be heard.

Protecting crime victims by federal and state statutes provides flexibility that is absent in a constitutional amendment. Moreover, amending the Constitution in this way changes basic principles that have been followed throughout American history. Principles of federalism always have allowed states to decide the nature of the protection of victims in state courts. The ability of states to decide for themselves is denied by this Amendment. Also, no longer would protecting the rights of a person accused of crime be a preeminent focus of a criminal trial.

Crime victims deserve protection, but this should be accomplished by statutes, not a constitutional amendment. As law professors and practitioners we urge the rejection of the proposed Victim's Rights Amendment as unnecessary and dangerous.

Sincerely,

Professor Erwin Chemerinsky

University of Southern California Law School

Professor Lynne Henderson

Indiana University, Bloomington

Professor Robert P. Mosteller

Duke University School of Law

[*et al.*]

Statement of Professor Paul Cassell

in A Proposed Constitutional Amendment to Protect Victims of Crime: Hearings Before the Senate Judiciary Committee, 105th Cong., 1st Sess. (1997)

The law professors' 1997 letter is filled with dubious claims.

1. Assertion: "[T]he right of victims to attend proceedings can be protected by statute as shown by . . . the recent federal legislation that mandates that victims be allowed to attend if they will be testifying during the sentencing phase of the proceedings."

Response: In fact, the converse is shown. The rights of the Oklahoma City bombing victims have not been protected by the newly passed federal legislation.

2. Assertion: The victim's right to a final disposition free from unreasonable delay "could be used to deny defendant needed time to gather and present evidence essential in order to demonstrate their innocence."

Response: Interestingly, in the 1996 letter [from professors opposing the Amendment], the Committee was told exactly the opposite — that his right would somehow be used "to force prosecutors to try cases before they have adequate evidence." Neither of these conflicting claims is true. Victims only seek a final resolution of cases free from "unreasonable" delay. The citation-free letter from the law professors fails to provide any evidence that comparable provisions in state constitutions and statutes are creating problems for criminal defendants (or prosecutors, for that matter).

3. Assertion: "Prosecution efforts also could be hampered by the ability of crime victims to submit [statements on plea bargains]."

Response: A victim's right to be heard before plea is already the law in many states, yet the law professors provide no reports of prosecutors being hampered. This is likely because this "hypothetical" problem, while perhaps interesting as a classroom discussion point, has not manifested itself in the real world. For example, it is the unqualified conclusion of the Maricopa County prosecutor — who prosecutes in a large metropolitan area (Phoenix) under one of the most expansive victims' rights amendments in the country (which specifically includes a right of the victim to be heard before a plea is accepted) — that "[c]onstitutional rights for victims will not obstruct prosecutors." Problems do not frequently arise from giving victims a right to be heard because most plea bargains reflect a reasonable resolution of the case. In the unusual instance where plea bargaining authority is being abused, the victim's right to be heard serves as a valuable safety valve. It is also important to remember that even in those cases where the victim's views are heard but not accepted by the judge, the victim may still leave the process more satisfied than if there was no opportunity for victim participation at all.

4. Assertion: The amendment creates enforcement authority that "could be used to negate the right of criminal defendants in an effort to protect crime victims."

Response: Enforcement authority is a rather standard feature of state victims' rights amendments, yet the professors provide no examples of enforcement authority being employed in this fashion. This is no doubt because the right to "enforce" a right for a crime victim does not create a right to "negate" rights for criminal defendants. The weakness [in] the professors' claim is demonstrated by the fact that they choose not to offer any specific illustrations of the hypothesized dangers. It is also interesting that in their 1996 letter, the professors appeared to make the opposite claim: that victims would be left with "few, if any, remedies for violations of . . . [the] rights enumerated."

5. Assertion: "The proposed Amendment . . . would . . . allow a victim of a crime to argue that it is *unconstitutional* to release a person from prison even though the sentence had been completed served."

Response: A victim could possibly, as the law professors carefully put it, "argue" this far-fetched point, but the argument would plainly fail. The right conferred by the proposed Amendment is to have the victim's safety considered at the time a decisionmaker is "determining" a release from custody. If the sentence has already been determined and served, there is nothing further to be considered.

6. Assertion: "The ability of the states to decide for themselves is denied by this Amendment."

Response: This concern for federalism will strike some as equivalent to "confirmation conversion," given that many of the signatories to the letter have lauded, for example, Supreme Court decisions by the Warren Court federalizing a whole host of criminal procedure questions (*e.g.*, the exclusionary rule and *Miranda* warnings). The victims' movement has consistently maintained that it merely seeks equal treatment. If defendant's rights are constitutionalized and applied throughout the country, then victims' rights should be too. It is also important to remember that three-quarters of the states will have to ratify any proposed amendment before it takes effect.

These are some of the more obvious problems with the letter. The careful reader familiar with the proposed Victims' Rights Amendment will no doubt see many more. In its deliberations, Congress should, of course, weigh all points of view and all competing concerns. The right of the law professors, no less than other citizens, to provide information to Congress deserves our full respect. But Congress should not give any special weight to misinformed, inaccurate, or inflammatory criticism — such as that unfortunately found in the "law professors'" letters.

CONCLUSION

The United States Supreme Court has recognized that "in the administration of criminal justice, courts may not ignore the concerns of victims." Yet to crime victims, it has appeared in recent years that courts and others in the criminal justice system have been doing just that. Some level of victim frustration with the system is inevitable. But the examples of victims' problems reported to this Committee, both here and in other testimony, suggest substantial justification for frustration with the current patchwork of protections outside the Constitution.

Something more simply must be done. Congress should approve the Victims' Rights Amendment and send it on its way to the states for ratification. Our criminal justice system already provides ample rights for the accused and the guilty; it can — and should — do the same for the innocent.

The most recent version of the proposed Amendment reads as follows:

House Joint Resolution 45, Introduced on April 16, 2015

Proposing an amendment to the Constitution of the United States to protect the rights of crime victims.

Resolved by the Senate and House of Representatives of the United States of America in Congress assembled (two-thirds of each House concurring therein), That the following article is proposed as an amendment to the Constitution of the United States, which shall be valid to all intents and purposes as part of the Constitution when ratified by the legislatures of three-fourths of the several States:

"Article —

"Section 1. The following rights of a crime victim, being capable of protection without denying the constitutional rights of the accused, shall not be denied or abridged by the United States or any State. The crime victim shall have the rights to reasonable notice of, and shall not be excluded from, public proceedings relating to the offense, to be heard at any release, plea, sentencing, or other proceeding involving any right established by this article, to proceedings free from unreasonable delay, to reasonable notice of the release or escape of the accused, to due consideration of the crime victim's safety, dignity, and privacy, and to restitution. The crime victim or the crime victim's lawful representative has standing to assert and enforce these rights. Nothing in this article provides grounds for a new trial or any claim for damages. Review of the denial of any right established herein, which may include interlocutory relief, shall be subject to the standards of ordinary appellate review.

"Section 2. For purposes of this article, a crime victim includes any person against whom the criminal offense is committed or who is directly and proximately harmed by the commission of an act, which, if committed by a competent adult, would constitute a crime.

"Section 3. This article shall be inoperative unless it has been ratified as an amendment to the Constitution by the legislatures of three-fourths of the several States within 14 years after the date of its submission to the States by the Congress. This article shall take effect on the 180th day after the date of its ratification."

Testimony of Professor Douglas E. Beloof
Before the Subcommittee on the Constitution and Civil Justice
of the United States House of Representatives

April 25, 2013

113th Congress, 1st Session

. . .

This Amendment contains the values that everyone in this room agrees upon—that crime victims should be treated with dignity and respect in the criminal process. However, experience teaches that this can only happen for every victim, in every case, if crime victims have enforceable rights. In order for rights to be honored, victims need recourse to remedy. For, without enforceable rights, victims' rights are merely paper promises. And, this is the cruelest kind of promise, assuring victims they have rights, only for them to discover that they do not.

. . .

I concur with Professor Tribe's framework for determining when rights should be added to the Constitution: Where there is "a needed recognition of a basic human right, where a) the right is one that people widely agree deserves serious and permanent respect b) the right is one that is insufficiently protected under existing law, c) the right is one that cannot be adequately protected through purely political action such as state or federal legislation and/or regulation, d) the right is one whose inclusion in the U.S. Constitution would not distort or endanger basic principles of the separation of powers among the federal branches, or the division of power between the national and state governments, and e) the right would be judicially enforceable without creating open-ended or otherwise acceptable funding obligations." . . .

(A) THE PEOPLE WIDELY AGREE THAT VICTIMS' RIGHTS DESERVE SERIOUS AND PERMANENT RESPECT.

Victims' state constitutional rights exist in more than two-thirds of the states. When referred to the people, these amendments are voted in by overwhelming margins. Passage rates are typically in the 75 to 90 percent range. Douglas E Beloof, The Third Wave of Victims' Rights: Standing, Remedy and Review, 2005 B.Y.U. L. Rev. 255, 341 n. 421 (collecting passage percentages in individual states).

At the federal level, the Crime Victims' Rights Act of 2008, 18 U.S.C. 3771, initially passed in the Senate by a vote of 96 to 1. In the House the bill was somewhat modified and passed by a 393 to 14 margin in the House. The bill then passed the Senate by unanimous consent and the President signed it into law.

Outside of Congress, support for the Amendment is strongly bipartisan. Forty nine governors, 50 state attorney generals and the National District Attorneys Association all support it. These organizations and elected officials come from both parties and hold views on other issues across the political spectrum. The organizations that support the Amendment, for example Mothers Against Drunk Driving and Parents of Murdered Children, are nonpartisan. Presidents Clinton and Bush, as well as their Attorneys General supported an amendment. In my home state of Oregon it was a Democrat Attorney General and a Democrat majority in both Houses that made Oregon state's constitutional victims' rights enforceable. Harvard Professor Laurence Tribe, who represented Al Gore in Bush v. Gore before the Supreme Court, has endorsed and participated in prior drafts, some of his language carries over into the current draft.

Clearly, there is wide agreement that victims' rights deserve serious and permanent respect.

(B) THE RIGHT IS ONE THAT IS INSUFFICIENTLY PROTECTED UNDER EXISTING LAW. AND, C) THE RIGHT IS ONE THAT CANNOT BE ADEQUATELY PROTECTED THROUGH PURELY POLITICAL ACTION SUCH AS STATE OR FEDERAL LEGISLATION.

Fundamentally, the objective of victims' rights is to include victim interests in the culture of the criminal justice system. Experience has shown that to change the inertia of the system, a constitutional amendment is needed. While many laws providing for rights exist, enforcement of the rights varies widely and too frequently they are honored in the breach.

A few case examples, from both the Bush and Obama administrations, under the Crime Victims' Rights Act, prove the point:

(1) In a criminal prosecution of British Petroleum for negligent homicide at an oil plant in Texas that killed 15 workers and injured more than 170 others, the Assistant U.S. Attorneys violated the surviving victims' rights by intentionally concealing a lenient plea agreement from the victims. The Assistant U.S. Attorneys, in secrecy from the victims went to the trial court to obtain an order that the victims would be denied their rights under the Act. The federal court of Appeals ruled that the Assistant U.S. Attorneys had acted illegally and admonished it stating, "the government should have fashioned a reasonable way to inform the victims of the likelihood of criminal charges and to ascertain the victims' views on the possible details of a plea bargain."

Nevertheless, the courts did not remedy the violation.

(2) In the Antrobus case, involving the illegal sale of a handgun that resulted in the murder of 5 people and serious injury of four others in a shopping mall in Utah, the Assistant U.S. Attorneys refused to reveal to the victims the statement made by the killer to the gun seller when the gun was purchased that he intended to commit a robbery. This statement likely would have established the murdered girl's family as victims under the act and allowed them to speak at sentencing. The victims were denied victim status by the courts and not allowed to speak at sentencing. Again, the courts provided no relief.

(3) In the *Jane Does v. United States* case, Assistant U.S. Attorneys took the position that it had no obligation to tell girls who were victims of a sexual assault by billionaire Jeffrey Epstein that it was reaching a secret "non-prosecution" agreement with Epstein as part of a lenient plea arrangement. The U.S. Attorneys remarkably took the position that victims had no right under the CVRA to be treated fairly or to be told that the charges were going to be bargained away — all because the Assistant U.S. Attorneys had made the decision to reach a secret deal with the sex offender before formally filing charges against him. The federal district court hearing the matter curtly dismissed the Department's argument, explaining that "the government's interpretation ignores the additional language throughout the statute that clearly contemplates pre-charge protections . . . ." Either directly or indirectly, two federal circuit courts have also rejected the position, that the assistant U.S. Attorneys can strip crime victims of their rights by the simple expedient of not obtaining a grand jury indictment.

(4) In a case involving victims of mortgage fraud, Assistant U.S. Attorneys took the position that these citizens were not victims under the Crime Victims' Rights Act. The Eleventh Circuit criticized the Assistant U.S. Attorneys, opining that, "Although the [victims'] petition does not seek relief against the Assistant United States Attorney prosecuting the case, we expect that attorney to be mindful of the obligations imposed by" the CVRA.

(5) In the botched "Fast and Furious" operation that led to the slaying of Border Patrol Agent Brian Terry, the Assistant U.S. Attorneys filed pleadings actually arguing that Terry was not a "victim" of illegal guns sales that lead to his murder. The Assistant U.S. Attorneys also refused to provide the Terry family with any discovery about the circumstances surrounding the murder so that they could argue to the court that they deserved rights under the CVRA. Ultimately, the Department reassigned the case from the District of Arizona to another prosecutor, and the Terry family was forced to settle its CVRA case for a promise from the Justice Department that it "recommend" to the Court that the Terry family receive rights under the CVRA as a matter of discretion.

The point of these examples is not to deride the Justice Department. Contrary to these examples, there are many fine federal prosecutors who routinely comply with victims' rights. And, both the Clinton and Bush era Justice Departments supported a crime victims' rights amendment. Rather, these examples reveal how statutory rights can be ignored with impunity. Moreover, these examples reveal that under the CVRA often no remedy is provided by the courts.

On the other hand, defendants' constitutional rights are far less likely to be ignored, simply because the rights are constitutional. Prosecutors universally respect defendants' rights precisely because defendants' rights are constitutional rights safeguarded by the Supreme Court. The same will occur when victims' rights are in the Constitution.

D) THE RIGHT IS ONE WHOSE INCLUSION IN THE U.S. CONSTITUTION WOULD NOT DISTORT OR ENDANGER BASIC PRINCIPLES OF THE SEPARATION OF POWERS AMONG THE FEDERAL BRANCHES, OR THE DIVISION OF POWER BETWEEN THE NATIONAL AND STATE GOVERNMENTS.

Separation of powers is enhanced by the Amendment as the Bill of Rights is historically the place for important rights.

While federalism is an important value, this Amendment poses no threat to it. The Supreme Court dictates the baseline of defendant's rights for all the states. Individual rights in criminal procedure are already federal and have been for decades. There is no hint, even in dicta, that the Supreme Court will ever change this reality. Consistent with this constitutional reality, victims' rights are appropriately placed in the federal constitution because the federal constitution is the baseline of individual rights in criminal procedure.

Thus, the ongoing exclusion of victims' rights from the constitution reduces the importance of victims' rights. Moreover, including victims rights' in the constitution works no new damage to federalist principles. *See* Paul G. Cassell, *Barbarians at the Gates? A Reply to the Critics of the Victims Rights Amendment,* 1999 UTAH L. REV. 479, 531 *et seq.*

Without a constitutional amendment there is no national baseline for victims' rights. For example, in the recent Boston Marathon Bombing case, should the defendant recover to face charges, federal charges will provide victims' rights that are, at least, potentially enforceable.

However, under Massachusetts law, rights remain unenforceable on review in state courts. Such disparate treatment of crime victims, simply because of the venue in which a crime occurred, makes little sense.

E) THE RIGHT WOULD BE JUDICIALLY ENFORCEABLE WITHOUT CREATING OPEN-ENDED OR OTHERWISE ACCEPTABLE FUNDING OBLIGATIONS."

One of the weakest arguments made against victims' rights has been that the administrative sky would fall. Nothing could be further from the truth. There is enough experience with victims' rights now both in the states and under the CVRA to know the sky will not fall in the administration of justice around crime victims' rights. In the ten years since the passage of the CVRA, the sky has remained firmly in the heavens. A review of the case law in that ten year period reveals nothing that could credibly be described as overwhelming the administration of the criminal process. See, 26 ALR Fed 2d 451 (collecting cases under the CVRA).

Quite the contrary. The number of federal appellate and district court opinions on the CVRA in ten years is miniscule. The average number of reported appellate cases in each state is similarly small. *Validity, Construction, and Application of State Constitutional or Statutory Victims' Bill of Rights,* 91 A.L.R.5TH 343 (collecting state cases).

To be sure, it is the trial courts that more frequently accommodate victims' rights. However, there is no empirical evidence from courts, state or federal, that victims' rights have clogged the courts. Finally, states already have victims' rights, either constitutional or statutory, so much of the infrastructure already exists in the states to accommodate a federal constitutional right.

F) NO ACTUAL CONSTITUTIONAL RIGHTS OF THE ACCUSED WOULD BE VIOLATED BY THE AMENDMENT.

In terms of conflicts with defendants' rights, in the ten years of cases under the Crime Victims' Rights Act there has been no federal appellate court case that has found a conflict with the defendants' constitutional rights. In fact, the period of time federal appellate courts have had to find a conflict is far greater than 10 years. Many states had victims' rights as early as 1982. Yet, in all that time, no federal appellate court has held that any state victims' right violates defendants' United States Constitutional rights.

The reason for this is straightforward, the CVRA was written carefully to avoid conflict with defendants' rights. The same is true of state constitutional rights for crime victims. Likewise, the Amendment before you has been carefully drafted to avoid conflict with a defendant's constitutional rights. In this regard the Amendment before you states, "Victims' rights, being capable of protection without violating the rights of the accused, shall not be denied or abridged by the United States or any state." H. J. Res. 40, pg 2 lines 3-4.

Human Rights Watch, a well-respected NGO, has published a report on crime victims' rights in America noting the ability to secure defendants' rights while providing for victims' rights as well:

> "Many people have strong interests in the functioning of the criminal justice system: victims of crime, witnesses, those accused of committing crimes, and society at large, which requires the fair and effective administration of justice. In recent decades, both internationally and inside the United States, there has been a growing demand that greater attention be paid to the interests and rights of victims of crime as well as to ensuring their access to justice.

> Unfortunately, the public debate on this topic too often casts the rights and interests of victims and defendants as a zero-sum game in which safeguards for defendants' rights-such as the presumption of innocence and the right to a fair trial-come at the expense of victims, and improvements in the treatment of victims impinge on defendants' rights. While there can be tensions between the legitimate interests of victims and defendants, a criminal justice system based on human rights standards can safeguard the rights of both while advancing justice and the rule of law." Human Rights Watch, U.S. Policy and International Standards on the Rights and Interests of Crime Victims, 1 (2008).

I agree with this assessment. This amendment does safeguard the rights of both defendants and victims while advancing justice and the rule of law.

Steven J. Twist & Daniel Seiden, The Proposed Victims' Rights Amendment: A Brief Point/Counterpoint

5 Phoenix L. Rev. 341 (2012)

I. INTRODUCTION

A federal constitutional amendment for the rights of crime victims was first proposed by President Ronald Reagan's Task Force on Victims of Crime ("Task Force") in 1982. The Task Force understood the serious implications of proposing an amendment to the U.S. Constitution:

> We do not make this recommendation lightly. The Constitution is the foundation of national freedom, the source of national spirit. But the combined experience brought to this inquiry and everything learned during its progress affirm that an essential change must be undertaken; the fundamental rights of innocent citizens cannot adequately be preserved by any less decisive action. In this we follow Thomas Jefferson, who said: "I am not an advocate for frequent changes in laws and constitutions, but laws and institutions must go hand in hand with the progress of the human mind. As that becomes more developed, more enlightened, as new discoveries are made, new truths discovered and manners and opinions change, with the change of circumstances, institutions must advance also to keep pace with the times."

The proposal to amend the Constitution sprang from an understanding developed by the Task Force over the course of many hearings across the country. Those hearings confirmed that "[t]he innocent victims of crime have been overlooked, their pleas for justice have gone unheeded, and their wounds—personal, emotional, and financial—have gone unattended."

Efforts to seek an amendment to the U.S. Constitution were not immediate; indeed the proposal lay dormant for fourteen years while advocates for victims' rights turned instead to the laboratories of the states. In 1982, no state had either a comprehensive constitutional amendment for victims' rights or comprehensive statutes. Just a decade later, every state had statutes addressing victims' rights and thirty-three states had constitutional amendments.

However, despite the legislative successes of the reform movement, even this robust level of legislative activity brought little real reform to the culture of the criminal justice system in the way it treated victims of crimes.

By the mid-1990s the unjust treatment of victims persisted. The nature of that injustice continued to be both procedural and substantive. In too many cases across America, victims were still not given notice of court proceedings, still not allowed to be present in the courtroom during trial, still not given a voice at critical stages, still not free from unreasonable delay, still not receiving restitution, still not having their safety considered when release decisions were made, and still not treated with respect, dignity, or fairness.

In 1996, Senator Jon Kyl (R-AZ) and Senator Dianne Feinstein (D-CA) introduced Senate Joint Resolution 52, a comprehensive constitutional amendment for victims' rights. From 1996 through 2004, hearings were held in the Senate and House to consider the proposals. While there has always been strong majority support for the amendment, there has also been strong minority opposition. Given the Constitution's command that amendments can only be referred to the States upon a two-thirds vote of both houses, the minority has always been sufficient to stop the passage. The purpose of this article is to set forth in short hand form the major arguments against passage of the Victims' Rights Amendment ("VRA") and to offer responses to those arguments. Perhaps the best articulation of the minority view is found in the views of Senators Leahy, Kennedy, Kohl, Feingold, Schumer, and Durbin (collectively "Minority Senators") found in the 2003 Senate Report.

Essentially, the arguments against passage fall into four categories: first, the U.S. Constitution does not have to be amended to provide rights for crime victims, statutes and state constitutions are adequate, and where the constitution need not be amended it should not be amended; second, the rights proposed will diminish the more important rights of the accused; third, the VRA will infringe on the rights of the States; and fourth, many of the individual rights are problematic. Let us take each of these in turn.

II. POINT AGAINST THE AMENDMENT: RIGHTS FOR VICTIMS DO NOT NEED TO BE INCLUDED IN THE U.S. CONSTITUTION; FEDERAL AND STATE STATUTES AND STATE CONSTITUTIONS ARE ADEQUATE

As the Task Force conceded, proposing an amendment to the U.S. Constitution should not be done lightly. Yet there is something compelling about the notion of basic fairness for crime victims. Even the VRA's most ardent critics usually say they support most of the rights in principle. If there is one thing certain in the victims' rights debate, it is that these words, 'I'm all for victims' rights but . . . ,' are heard repeatedly. But while supporting the rights in principle, opponents in practice end up supporting, if anything, mere statutory fixes that have proven inadequate to the task of vindicating the interests of victims.

As Attorney General Reno testified before the Committee on the Judiciary, "[e]fforts to secure victims' rights through means other than a constitutional amendment have proved less than fully adequate." The Crime Victims' Rights Act ("CVRA"), after almost eight years of being tested in the courts, has proven inadequate to change the culture of our justice system in ways that make it fairer for all Americans.

In many states, statutes have proven inadequate to change the justice system. Despite its successes, Arizona's state constitutional amendment has proven inadequate to fully implement victims' rights. While the state's amendment has improved the treatment of victims, it does not provide the unequivocal command that is needed to completely change old ways. In Arizona, as in other states, the existing rights too often "fail to provide meaningful protection whenever they come into conflict with bureaucratic habit, traditional indifference, sheer inertia or the mere mention of an accused's rights—even when those rights are not genuinely threatened."

A study by the National Institute of Justice found that "even in States where victims' rights were protected strongly by law, many victims were not notified about key hearings and proceedings, many were not given the opportunity to be heard, and few received restitution." The victims most likely to be affected by this continuing haphazard implementation are, perhaps not surprisingly, racial minorities. These problems persist today. In Arizona, most crime victims still are not given notice of initial appearances, despite the fact that for some the chance to see a judge before a release decision is made may be a matter of life or death. This is true even though the right to notice has been a command of the Arizona Constitution for almost twenty-two years.

. . .

III. RIGHTS OF DEFENDANTS

Nothing in the VRA undermines rights of the accused. The rights proposed are clear and straightforward, expressed in language that does not undermine, but rather confirm the constitutional rights of the accused: "The rights of a crime victim to fairness, respect, and dignity, being capable of protection without denying the constitutional rights of the accused, shall not be denied or abridged by the United States or any State."

This language reaffirms the constitutional rights of the accused. And none of the specific rights which follow the first sentence undermine in any way the constitutional rights of the accused.

> The crime victim shall, moreover, have the rights to reasonable notice of, and shall not be excluded from, public proceedings relating to the offense, to be heard at any release, plea, sentencing, or other such proceeding involving any right established by this article, to proceedings free from unreasonable delay, to reasonable notice of the release or escape of the accused, to due consideration of the crime victim's safety, and to restitution. The crime victim or the crime victim's lawful representative has standing to fully assert and enforce these rights in any court.

The right to reasonable notice of public proceedings does not undermine in any way the constitutional rights of the accused. There is no constitutional right for a defendant to prevent a victim, or anyone else, from receiving notice of public court proceedings.

The right to reasonable notice of releases or escapes does not undermine in any way the constitutional rights of the accused. There is no constitutional right for a defendant to prevent a victim from knowing when the defendant has escaped or is released.

The right to not be excluded does not undermine in any way the constitutional rights of the accused. There is no constitutional right for a defendant to exclude a victim from trial, even when the victim is also a witness.

The rights to be heard at release, plea, and sentencing proceedings do not undermine in any way the constitutional rights of the accused. While there remain limits regarding relevancy and due process, there is no constitutional right for a defendant to silence completely a victim who wants to be heard at these proceedings.

The right to due consideration for the victim's safety does not undermine in any way the constitutional rights of the accused. There is no constitutional right for a defendant to prevent a court from considering the victim's safety when decisions are made. Indeed, victim safety is a legitimate and, according to the United States Supreme Court, constitutional consideration when making release decisions.

The right to be free from unreasonable delay does not undermine in any way the constitutional rights of the accused. It is undisputed that the defendant has a right to a fair and speedy trial and the right to counsel which, according to the United States Supreme Court, includes the right to an effective lawyer—one who has had enough time to prepare a defense. These rights do not prevent a victim's interest in avoiding unreasonable delay, meaning delay that is unrelated to the legitimate rights of the accused or the state.

The right to due consideration for the victim's safety does not infringe on any right of an accused or convicted offender. A defendant has no constitutional right to deny to a court the ability to consider victim safety when making release, sentencing, or other decisions or to a victim to assert that interest. Indeed, the safety of the public and victim is one of the fundamental purposes of the justice system.

The right to restitution does not undermine in any way the constitutional rights of the accused. There is no constitutional right for a convicted offender to prevent the law from requiring, nor the court from ordering, restitution for the victim.

The right to standing to enforce these rights does not undermine in any way the constitutional rights of the accused. There is no constitutional right for a defendant to prevent a victim from asserting his or her rights in court.

IV. POINT AGAINST THE AMENDMENT: PASSAGE OF THE VRA WOULD INFRINGE ON THE RIGHTS OF THE STATES AND WOULD LEAD TO FEDERAL COURT SUPERVISION OVER THE STATES

. . .

A. The Amendment Will Not End Constructive Experimentation by the States

The Minority Senators assert, "State experimentation with victims' rights initiatives is relatively new and untested; the laboratory evidence is as yet inconclusive." The record before the Congress refutes this assertion. The experiment with state laws, even strong state laws, has proven inadequate to fully protect the rights of victims. Even so, the amendment does not end constructive experimentation by the States. Setting a floor of national rights does not mean that States may not add to those rights as they see fit. Nor does it mean that implementation of the rights must be in a uniform manner. For example, in one state notice may be provided by courts, in another state by prosecutors, and in a third state by a different manner altogether. States may vary in how they permit special actions to enforce the rights in state court.

In the end, the objection of the Minority Senators rings hollow. It is factually wrong and bespeaks a double standard in the protection of the rights of defendants and victims that does not befit a country that pledges itself to "justice for all."

B. The Amendment Does Not Impose an Unfunded Mandate on the States

The Minority Senators express the concern that "[w]e need more information from the States about how much it costs to implement these programs, and what sort of resources are needed to be successful before we rush to validate a series of rights that could overwhelm the Nation's criminal justice system." The rights proposed are not a program but rather in large part limitations on the state from proceeding with a criminal matter without fairness to the victim. The only right with any fiscal consequence is the right to notice and each state will be able to determine how to provide notice, indeed most already claim to do so today. And these costs are already carried by the Crime Victims Fund established by 42 U.S.C. § 10601.96. Rights to be not excluded, to speak, to have safety considered, or to be free from unreasonable delay do not impose additional costs on the system; they may reduce costs in fact by injecting a degree of discipline into the system that it has not had. There is more than enough money collected from criminal defendants across the country to cover the costs.

C. The Amendment Will Not Lead to Extensive Federal Court Supervision of State Law Enforcement Operations

The fear that state sovereignty will be lost is especially curious in the context of criminal procedure given the supremacy of federal law that already pervades the area.

More importantly, the more fundamental purpose of the Constitution is not to enshrine state sovereignty for itself; state sovereignty was merely another means of securing liberty from encroachments of the federal government on the liberty of the people. The purposes of the Constitution include to "secure the Blessings of Liberty." The federal nature of the government formed under the Constitution, the limitation on the power of the federal government, and the checks and balances among the separate branches are all established to protect individual liberty. When the right to liberty is written directly into the Constitution, as in the case of the VRA, the limitation on the power of the states, in fact, advances liberty. When the courts exercise the power to enforce the rights established by the VRA they will be advancing the cause of liberty and the Constitution.

V. POINT AGAINST THE AMENDMENT: THE INDIVIDUAL RIGHTS
PROVIDED TO VICTIMS BY PASSAGE OF THE VRA WILL BE PROBLEMATIC

A. The VRA Would Not Leave Victims Without Adequate Remedies

The proposed VRA has an explicit grant of standing to victims so that they may pursue remedies independent of the government. It is standing that provides the keys to remedies. Experience under the CVRA has demonstrated that victims can pursue and obtain remedies for violations of rights without any disruption in the fair administration of justice.

B. The Obligation Imposed by the VRA to Provide Notice of Proceedings Would Not Impose Enormous Costs on the System

The Minority Senators fear that the right to reasonable notice will lead to staggering costs. It has not. The costs are far from staggering and testimony before the Senate Judiciary Committee confirmed this early on. On May 12, 1997, Rick Romley, then Maricopa County Attorney, offered the following prepared statement for the Senate Judiciary Committee:

> During the victims' rights debate, detractors argued that such an amendment would be cost prohibitive. They predicted that such rights would bankrupt our criminal justice system. While I agree that there are costs associated with victims' rights services, those costs are minor when balanced with the benefit to our state. The citizens of Arizona voiced their opinion — affording victims' constitutional guarantees to participation is worth the expense.

> My Office provides victims [sic] rights services to over 19,000 victims of felonies perpetrated by adult offenders and over 10,000 victims of juvenile delinquents. Victim Advocates provide victims' rights notification and services to help victims navigate their way through what can be an intimidating process. The costs associated with these services account for no more than 3% of my entire budget. Costs associated with victims' rights services are far less than those associated with ensuring that those accused of crime are afforded their constitutional rights.

> To enhance the ability of criminal justice entities to provide victims' rights services, the Arizona legislature adopted a funding measure to offset these costs. Every offender who has been ordered to pay a fine must pay an additional surcharge, a percentage of which is dedicated to funding victims' rights services. As a result, more than two-thirds of the costs my Office incurs as a result of providing victims' rights services are offset by monies paid by convicted offenders.

Congress enacted the CVRA in 2004. The CVRA provides, inter alia, that crime victims have "[t]he right to reasonable, accurate, and timely notice of any public court proceeding, or any parole proceeding, involving the crime or of any release or escape of the accused." In the seven and one half years since the enactment of this provision of the CVRA, the U.S. Department of Justice has not once complained to Congress that it cannot meet the requirements of providing notice. Notice is routinely provided to victims in federal cases. Notice continues to be provided in large local jurisdictions like Maricopa County, Arizona without complication.

Moreover, with technological advances, the costs continue to reduce. The VRA establishes the right to reasonable notice. This permits the use of alternative means of notice in mass victim cases, rendering cost issues inconsequential.

Despite the fact that the cost argument has been shown to be a red herring, there is a deeper, more significant point to be made about the nature of this argument in opposition because it portrays a telling approach to the entire debate. Would costs stop the opponents of the VRA from defending notice for defendants, or the state? Why should victims be excluded from this basic element of fairness? There is an element of second-class citizenship that underlies the role the opponents want to maintain for crime victims. Defendants and the government are surely entitled to notice, but crime victims are not. Surely, in America we are a great enough, decent enough, and compassionate enough country to extend to victims of crime the same notice we give to defendants and the government. Critics, however, say otherwise.

Critics of the VRA may inexplicably argue that just as the court's interpretation of the Sixth Amendment has [led] to a vast increase of cost to the criminal justice system by requiring publicly funded defenders, the same issue of requiring publicly funded victim's attorneys could happen. However, the Sixth Amendment comparison offered by opponents is flawed; clearly there is no parallel 'right to counsel' expressly written into the proposed amendment.

Additionally, under the VRA no sheriff would be required to transport an inmate victim to court because the right not to be excluded only applies when victims can otherwise present themselves at the courthouse.

C. The VRA Would Not Impair the Ability of Prosecutors to Prosecute;
It Will Not Effectively Obstruct Plea Agreements Nor Require Prosecutors to
Disclose Weaknesses in Their Case to Persuade a Court to Accept a Plea

The National District Attorneys Association was a strong supporter of S.J. Res. 1,110 the amendment considered in 2003 and 2004. In 2004, the Attorneys General of forty-eight states, the Virgin Islands, and Washington, D.C. signed a letter supporting S.J. Res. 1. It is unlikely that these prosecutors would support a constitutional amendment if it would impair their ability to prosecute cases.

History confirms good reason for their lack of concern on this point. In the over two decades since the passage of the Victims Bill of Rights ("VBR") in Arizona the right to be heard at a proceeding involving a plea has not obstructed plea agreements. Indeed, roughly the same percentage of cases is today resolved by plea as was resolved by plea before the VBR was passed. Even in those cases involving a failure to inform the victim of the plea, the subsequent proceedings to assert the right of the victim does not impair the process.

The VBR has not required a disclosure to the defense of weaknesses in the government's cases. Pleas are submitted based on an agreed factual basis, which must establish the elements of the offense to which the defendant pleads guilty. The way victim allocution has worked in real practice has not confirmed the fears of opponents.

No language in the VRA would allow a victim to "compromise prosecutorial discretion and independence" to "effectively dictate policy decisions," to place "unknowing, and unacceptable, restrictions on prosecutors" or to "override the professional judgment of the prosecutor" regarding investigation, timing, disposition, or sentencing. These assertions by the Minority Senators are all the more remarkable given their claim to support comprehensive statutory rights.

The VRA gives victims the right to be heard at a public plea proceeding; it is a right simply to a voice, not a veto, not an override, nor the power to dictate, as the opponents assert. From this simple right, opponents project "dangerous" consequences. In the real world, no such consequences unfold. That a judge has the discretion to reject a plea when he or she determines it not to be in the best interests of justice and that a judge may exercise that discretion after hearing from the victim of the crime, does not undermine in any way the prosecutor's authority, any more than when a defendant speaks at a plea proceeding.

Merely giving victims a voice hardly gives victims the power or the right to "obstruct plea proceedings," as opponents assert. No prosecutor could ever be "forc[ed]," as asserted by the Minority Senators, "to disclose investigative strategies or weaknesses in their case" under the amendment. Fearful concerns to the contrary notwithstanding, the real life experience in Arizona, with more than two decades of history and the actual experience of literally hundreds of thousands of cases, confirms no threat to prosecution. At some point the fears of hypothesis must yield to reality. No hands are tied by extending this simple voice to crime victims.

. . .

Prosecutors do not represent victims in a criminal case as a lawyer represents a client, and the suggestion from the Minority Senators that a conflict between the victim and the prosecutor would require prosecutors "to recuse themselves from the case" is unfounded. Victims do not see collateral civil litigation against prosecutors as a meaningful way to enforce rights in a criminal case for good reason: it would never work.

Nothing in the amendment could possibly be construed to "[force] prosecutors to try cases before they are fully prepared." The right to avoid unreasonable delay carries with it no power to force cases to trial prematurely; indeed, such a result itself would be inherently unreasonable.

D. Giving Victims Rights at the Accusatory Stage of Criminal Proceedings Does Not Undercut the Presumption of Innocence

The Minority Senators asserted that "the proposed amendment would undercut . . . the presumption of innocence." This was a display of rhetorical exuberance that must now embarrass its author. The presumption of innocence remains robust and inviolate in Arizona and other jurisdictions whose victims of crime are afforded participatory rights, albeit inadequately. The presumption of innocence fundamentally places on the government the burden to prove beyond a reasonable doubt each element of the offense charged. It does not require that the defendant remain at large pending the outcome of the trial. It does not mean that the government may not be heard on matters of release, or other issues directly affecting the liberty interests of the defendant. Indeed, as the Minority Senators concede, the Supreme Court has established that no provision of the Constitution prohibits courts from considering the safety of the victim in making pretrial detention decisions. It would be odd indeed to conclude that the Bill of Rights could be read to allow consideration of the victim's safety but silence the very voice which expresses the need for that safety.

The example provided by the Minority Senators of an assault defendant who claims self-defense is unpersuasive. The Minority Senators would continue a system in which the defendant may be present and speak and the government may be present and speak, but where only the victim may do neither.

The Minority Senators show a disappointing disregard for the safety of victims that itself demonstrates the need for the VRA. They write, "[w]hile society certainly has an interest in preserving the safety of the victim, this fact alone cannot be said to overcome a defendant's liberty interest as afforded to him under the due process and excessive bail clauses." Where to begin? First, while the statement displays a somewhat grudging acceptance of society's interest in the safety of the victim, it ignores altogether the victim's interest in the safety of the victim. This is precisely the kind of indifference to the plight of the victim that the amendment addresses. Second, according to the Supreme Court, the "interest in preserving the safety of the victim" does overcome a defendant's liberty interest when pre-trial detention is necessary to protect the victim or the community. The failure of the Minority Senators to recognize the centrality of the need to protect the victim is evidence of the cultural divide that crime victims face and is a compelling argument for the amendment.

E. The Right for a Victim to Not Be Excluded Would Not Interfere with the Accused's Right to a Fair Trial

The Supreme Court has explained that "[t]he victim of the crime, the family of the victim, [and] others who have suffered similarly . . . have an interest in observing the course of a prosecution." Professor Cassell's analysis confirms the conclusion that, if anything, the text of the Constitution provides support for the victim's attendance:

> Instead, there are three provisions that support, if anything, the opposite view that a victim of a crime should remain in the courtroom: the Sixth Amendment's guarantee of a "public" trial, not a private one; the Sixth Amendment's guarantee of a right to "confront" witnesses, not to exclude them; and the Fifth and Fourteenth Amendments' guarantee of "due process of law," which construed in light of historical and contemporary standards suggests victims can attend trials.

The Minority Senators oppose the victim's right to be in the courtroom, speculating that victims will lie to conform their testimony to that of other witnesses. The

Minority Senators assert that "sequestration rules . . . are in effect in every jurisdiction in the country." As applied to crime victims, this statement is untrue. Arizona and other states allow victims to be present throughout trial: in Alabama, crime victims even sit at counsel table. Exceptions are made to the sequestration rule for important reasons, for the defendant, and for the government's chief investigator. No rule excludes parties in civil cases, who are also witnesses, and we surely value truth no less in civil cases.

Moreover, the Minority Senators' concern about victims lying is unproven speculation. And, there is no need to speculate; there are States that have not applied the sequestration rule to victims for decades without evidence of resulting perjury.

Common sense is enough to conclude why the exception does not create the evils predicted by the Minority Senators. First, it is perjury and the victim might go to prison. Second, changing a statement subjects the victim to devastating cross examination because of prior inconsistent statements, all of which would have been recorded and made available to the defendant. Third, it would undermine the victim's true goal, which is to see the guilty punished, not the innocent. While a guilty defendant may have a self-interested motive to lie to escape justice, a victim has no similar self-interested motive to see an innocent person convicted while the guilty offender remains at large.

Perhaps these are the reasons why, in twenty-one years, no tailored testimony has been found in Arizona, nor is there any evidence from the real world of a jury discrediting or discounting a victim's testimony as the Minority Senators speculate. The Minority Senators surely know this experience from Arizona. Where their speculative theory conflicts with hard facts, the Minority Senators seem to choose theory every time.

The VRA protects a victim's right not to be excluded from "public proceedings." It leaves untouched the law that defines when proceedings may be closed. As was stated in the Committee Report:

> Victims' rights under this provision are also limited to "public" proceedings. Some proceedings, such as grand jury investigations, are not open to the public and accordingly would not be open to the victim. Other proceedings, while generally open, may be closed in some circumstances. For example, while plea proceedings are generally open to the public, a court might decide to close a proceeding in which an organized crime underling would plead guilty and agree to testify against his bosses. See 28 C.F.R. 50.9. Another example is provided by certain national security cases in which access to some proceedings can be restricted. See The Classified Information Procedures Act, 18 U.S.C. app. 3. A victim would have no special right to attend. The amendment works no change in the standards for closing hearings, but rather simply recognizes that such nonpublic hearings take place.

The Minority Senators challenge the application of section 50.9, yet their hypothetical of the pleading mob soldier fits squarely within the four corners of the rule.

The rule permits the government to seek closure when, among other standards, there is "[a] substantial likelihood of imminent danger to the safety of parties, witnesses, or other persons; or . . . [a] substantial likelihood that ongoing investigations will be seriously jeopardized." These are the very circumstances the Minority Senators posit.

F. The Right for a Victim to Be Heard Would Not Interfere with the Accused's Right to Due Process

By advocating that the victim's right to be reasonably heard would "risk[] the denial of defendants' due process rights," the Minority Senators defend a system in which the defendant may make a sentencing recommendation to the jury, the defendant's family and friends may do so, the defendant's lawyer may do so, and the prosecutor may do so, but the victim may not. With this argument, the Minority Senators misconstrue the Due Process Clause and display an all-too-common callous disregard toward victims' rights.

As evidence for their position, the Minority Senators cite a singular case, in which the victim in a capital case seeks to make a sentencing recommendation to the jury, emphasizing that sentencing decisions need to be reached "without fear, favor, or sympathy." It seems impossible to ignore the irony of that concern, especially regarding sympathy, considering the Minority Senators appear to accept a system that condones repeated pleas for sympathy for the defendant, but would deny victims the right to make, without undue prejudice, a simple statement as to the victim's desired sentence. This double standard of justice is another reason for the VRA.

. . .

> Proof that victims can properly be heard at these points comes from what appears to be a substantial inconsistency by the dissenting senators. While criticizing the right to be heard in the Amendment, these senators simultaneously sponsored federal legislation to extend to victims in the federal system precisely the same rights. They urged their colleagues to pass their statute in lieu of the Amendment because "our bill provides the very same rights to victims as the proposed constitutional amendment." In defending their bill, they saw no difficulty in giving victims a chance to be heard, a right that already exists in many states.

Another common argument used to support the Minority Senators' assertion is that victims' participation at sentencing, specifically victim impact statements, somehow results in unequal justice for varying defendants. Again, Professor Cassell examined this argument and provided a rebuttal and analysis supported by the courts:

> Justice Powell made this claim in his since-overturned decision in Booth v. Maryland, arguing that "in some cases the victim will not leave behind a family, or the family members may be less articulate in describing their feelings even though their sense of loss is equally severe." This kind of difference, however, is hardly unique to victim impact evidence. To provide

one obvious example, current rulings from the Court invite defense mitigation evidence from a defendant's family and friends, despite the fact the some defendants may have more or less articulate acquaintances. In Payne, for example, the defendant's parents testified that he was "a good son" and his girlfriend testified that he "was affectionate, caring, and kind to her children." In another case, a defendant introduced evidence of having won a dance choreography award while in prison. Surely this kind of testimony, no less than victim impact statements, can vary in persuasiveness in ways not directly connected to a defendant's culpability; yet, it is routinely allowed. One obvious reason is that if varying persuasiveness were grounds for an inequality attack, then it is hard to see how the criminal justice system could survive at all. Justice White's powerful dissenting argument in Booth went unanswered, and remains unanswerable: "No two prosecutors have exactly the same ability to present their arguments to the jury; no two witnesses have exactly the same ability to communicate the facts; but there is no requirement . . . [that] the evidence and argument be reduced to the lowest common denominator."

Given that our current system allows almost unlimited mitigation evidence on the part of the defendant, an argument for equal justice requires, if anything, that victim statements be allowed. Equality demands fairness not only between cases, but also within cases. Victims and the public generally perceive great unfairness in a sentencing system with "one side muted." The Tennessee Supreme Court stated the point bluntly in its decision in Payne, explaining that "[i]t is an affront to the civilized members of the human race to say that at sentencing in a capital case, a parade of witnesses may praise the background, character and good deeds of Defendant . . . without limitation as to relevancy, but nothing may be said that bears upon the character of, or the harm imposed, upon the victims."

Fortunately, the majority of jurisdictions in the United States now admit victim impact statements in all cases. Regardless, in spite of their own votes to the contrary, the Supreme Court ruling to the contrary, and the majority of states creating laws to the contrary, the Minority Senators still believed that the defendant's due process rights could be impacted by allowing victims to be heard. Their disregard for these facts, as well as the evidence of the negative emotional impact on victims who are denied the ability to speak, demonstrates the need to make victims' rights a part of the "sovereign instrument of the whole people." If not, victims in the United States will never enjoy the true balance Justice Cardozo described in his statement: "[J]ustice, though due to the accused, is due to the accuser also. The concept of fairness must not be strained till it is narrowed to a filament. We are to keep the balance true."

G. A Victim's Right to Expedite Trial Proceedings Would Not Undermine the Accused's Sixth Amendment Right

The Minority Senators assert that the language of the VRA, giving victims the right to be free from unreasonable delay, will result in defendants being forced to trial before they are prepared, thus undermining basic Sixth Amendment protections. This is simply unfounded, as any fair reader of the actual proposed text will conclude. The amendment speaks of unreasonable delay, not any delay. It requires due consideration, not submission to the will of the victim. What is it that the Minority Senators can fear from this measured, balanced language, other than any fairness for victims? What the amendment will do, and why it is more than "hortatory" as the Minority Senators simultaneously suggest, is give victims a voice in the matter of trial scheduling and continuances. This voice will simply permit a fuller consideration of all the interests at stake when scheduling decisions are made. Today, victims' interests are routinely ignored in these matters.

Professor Cassell offered in his 1999 prepared statement a rebuttal to this objection:

> Opponents of the Amendment sometimes argue that giving victims a right "to consideration" of their interest "that any trial be free from unreasonable delay" would impinge on a defendant's right to prepare an adequate defense. For example, the dissenting Senators in the Judiciary Committee argued that "the defendant's need for more time could be outweighed by the victim's assertion of his right to have the matter expedited, seriously compromising the defendant's right to effective assistance of counsel and his ability to receive a fair trial." Similarly, Professor Mosteller advances the claim that this right "also affects substantial interests of the defendant and may alter the outcomes of cases."
>
> These arguments fail to adequately consider the precise scope of the victim's right in question. The right the Amendment confers is one to "consideration of the interest of the victim that any trial be free from unreasonable delay."
>
> . . .
>
> As this Committee explained:
>
> The Committee intends for this right to allow victims to have the trial of the accused completed as quickly as is reasonable under all of the circumstances of the case, giving both the prosecution and the defense a reasonable period of time to prepare. The right would not require or permit a judge to proceed to trial if a criminal defendant is not adequately represented by counsel.

E. The Next Generation

In concluding this final chapter of the casebook about victim reforms, it may be appropriate to encourage at least some of our readers to consider working in the crime victims' movement. Many of the law students who take a class in victims' rights are interested in working in the criminal justice system. The great majority of students who end up working in the system will serve as prosecutors and defense attorneys. This is very valuable work and it is to be applauded. Our country's criminal justice system cannot work without the dedicated service of lawyers who represent both the state and the defendant.

At the same time, however, the system will function most effectively only when the interests of crime victims are fully and effectively represented as well. As you know from reading this book, it is rare for crime victims to have legal counsel in the criminal process. Of the victims cases reaching the appellate courts, many of them got there only because of the work of an attorney who represented a crime victim on a pro bono basis or of a public interest litigating organization, like the National Crime Victim Law Institute.

We would encourage you to think about pursuing a career in crime victims work or, at least, providing pro bono legal services to victims. Victims services throughout the country are chronically underfunded and understaffed. In your local community, there is likely a domestic violence shelter or rape crisis center that could desperately use your help. No doubt, too, your district attorney or Attorney General frequently confronts cases in which crime victims could use the services of an attorney. State bar associations and legal services associations also frequently receive requests for assistance from indigent victims who have legal problems in the criminal justice system.

Our nation's criminal justice system will be incomplete if the voices of victims are not heard at appropriate points. We encourage you to consider helping those voices to be heard.

Index